The Law and Policy of the World Trade Organization

This is primarily a textbook for graduate and upper-level undergraduate students of law; however, practising lawyers and policy-makers who are looking for an introduction to WTO law will also find it invaluable. The book covers both the institutional and substantive law of the WTO. While the treatment of the law is quite detailed, the main aim of this textbook is to make clear the basic principles and underlying logic of WTO law and the world trading system. Each section contains questions and assignments, to allow students to assess their understanding and develop useful practical skills. At the end of each chapter, there is a helpful summary as well as an exercise on specific, true-to-life international trade problems.

PETER VAN DEN BOSSCHE is Professor of International Economic Law, Head of the Department of International and European Law and Director of Studies of the Magister Iuris Communis programme at Maastricht University, The Netherlands. He studied law at the University of Antwerp (Lic. jur.), the University of Michigan (LLM) and the European University Institute, Florence (Dr. jur.). From 1997 to 2001, Peter Van den Bossche was Counsellor to the Appellate Body of the WTO, Geneva. In 2001 he served as Acting Director of the Appellate Body Secretariat.

The Law and Policy of the World Trade Organization

Text, Cases and Materials

Peter Van den Bossche

Maastricht University

CAMBRIDGE
UNIVERSITY PRESS

CAMBRIDGE UNIVERSITY PRESS
Cambridge, New York, Melbourne, Madrid, Cape Town, Singapore, São Paulo

CAMBRIDGE UNIVERSITY PRESS
The Edinburgh Building, Cambridge CB2 2RU, UK

Published in the United States of America by Cambridge University Press, New York

www.cambridge.org
Information on this title: www.cambridge.org/9780521529815

First published 2005

Printed in the United Kingdom at the University Press, Cambridge

A catalogue record for this book is available from the British Library

Library of Congress Cataloguing in Publication data

Bossche, Peter van den.
 The law of the World Trade Organization / Peter van den Bossche.
  p. cm.
 Includes bibliographical references and index.
 ISBN 0-521-82290-4 (hardback) – ISBN 0-521-52981-6 (paperback)
 1. World Trade Organization. 2. Foreign trade regulation. 3. Tariff – Law and
 legislation. I. Title.
 K4610.B67 2005
 343′.087–dc22   2004061841

ISBN-13 978-0-521-82290-9 hardback
ISBN-10 0-521-82290-4 hardback
ISBN-13 978-0-521-52981-5 paperback
ISBN-10 0-521-52981-6 paperback

Contents

1 ECONOMIC GLOBALISATION AND THE LAW OF THE WTO   1

2 THE WORLD TRADE ORGANIZATION   76

Figures

Tables

Preface and acknowledgments

Since the entry into force of the *WTO Agreement* in January 1995, international trade law has developed from a technical backwater of international law to one of its most vibrant fields. Before 1995, international trade law was taught at few universities and was only of interest to a relatively small group of legal practitioners. Over the past decade, however, interest in this field of international law has increased dramatically. Students, academics, legal practitioners, advisers of businesses and NGOs, and officials of national governments and international organisations have woken up to its importance. Now, most universities give much attention to trade law in international law courses or offer specialised courses on WTO law.

Concrete plans for this book were first made on the eve of my departure from the WTO and return to academia at the end of 2001. For five years, I had the privilege to serve, during the seminal early days of the WTO and its law, as a senior legal advisor to the Appellate Body of the WTO.

This book is primarily a textbook for graduate and senior undergraduate students of law. However, it was also written with practising lawyers and policy-makers, looking for an introduction to WTO law, in mind. The book covers both the institutional and the substantive law of the WTO. Chapter 1 is an introduction on whether economic globalisation and international trade are a bane or a blessing, on the need for WTO law, and on the main principles and sources of this law. Chapter 2 discusses the WTO as the prime intergovernmental organisation for international trade, and deals with its origins, objectives, functions, membership, institutional structure and decision-making procedures. Chapter 3 concerns the WTO's all-important and unique dispute settlement system and explores the origins, principles, institutions and proceedings of WTO dispute settlement. Chapter 4 discusses the fundamental WTO principles of non-discrimination, the most-favoured-nation treatment obligation and the national treatment obligation as they apply to trade in goods and trade in services. Chapter 5 deals with market access for goods, services and service suppliers and discusses, *inter alia*, the WTO rules on tariff and non-tariff barriers to trade in goods and barriers to trade in services. Chapter 6 concerns the WTO rules on unfair trade and, in particular, the rules on dumping and subsidised trade. Chapter 7 deals with the inevitable conflict between trade liberalisation and other societal values and interests. It discusses the many situations in which WTO law allows Members to deviate from the basic rules and let other societal values and interests prevail over trade liberalisation. The concluding Chapter 8 briefly sets out two major challenges for the future of the WTO, namely, the integration of developing countries in the multilateral trading system and the further expansion of the scope of WTO law. While the treatment of the law is often quite detailed, the prime aim of this textbook is to make clear the basic principles and underlying logic of WTO law and the world trading system.

Special attention was given to the focus, approach and structure of this book. Each section contains questions and assignments, to allow students to assess their understanding and to develop useful practical skills. At the end of each chapter, there is a helpful summary as well as an exercise on specific true-to-life international trade problems encountered by the Kingdom of Richland, a developed-country Member, and the Republic of Newland, a developing-country Member. These exercises are ideally intended to be dealt with in tutorials but are equally suitable for individual study. While challenging, these exercises can be done on the basis of the knowledge acquired in the chapter they conclude. It was a deliberate choice to refer sparingly to the vast academic literature on many of the topics addressed in this book. The focus is clearly on the provisions of the WTO agreements themselves, the case law of panels and the Appellate Body and official policy documents. For advanced courses on WTO law, this book can be usefully supplemented by academic articles from the *Journal of International Economic Law*, the *Journal of World Trade*, the *World Trade Review* and other specialised or general law journals. The reader can find suggestions on recent academic articles and case law, organised according to the chapters of this book at www.egeg.org.

In writing this book I owe much to many. I am particularly indebted to Gabrielle Marceau and Denise Prévost who supported and encouraged me from the beginning and commented on all chapters. I am similarly indebted to Edwin Vermulst and Folkert Graafsma who also read through the whole manuscript and made many useful comments, and to Julie Soloway, who made a very important contribution to the section on dumping and anti-dumping measures. I am grateful to Marco Bronckers, Stephanie Cartier, Bill Davey, Piet Eeckhout, Barbara Eggers, Lothar Ehring, Mary Footer, Susan Hainsworth, Valerie Hughes, Pieter-Jan Kuijper, Bernard Kuiten, Hoe Lim, Jim Mathis, Marielle Matthee, Elisabetta Montaguti, Joost Pauwelyn, Roberto Rios Herrera, Jochem Wiers, Jan Wouters and Werner Zdouc, who all read, and commented on, specific chapters, or contributed otherwise to this book. I would like to pay tribute to John Jackson, my first mentor and guide in the land of international trade. I would also like to acknowledge my profound and lasting debt towards the Members of the original Appellate Body, and, in particular, James Bacchus, Claus-Dieter Ehlermann, Florentino Feliciano and Julio Lacarte, whom I had the privilege to serve for five years and from whom I learned so much. I address a special word of thanks to Debra Steger, the first director of the Appellate Body Secretariat and 'sister-in-arms' during the fascinating but very demanding first years of the Appellate Body. I am grateful to Finola O'Sullivan, publisher at Cambridge University Press, and her staff,

Jane O'Regan, Mary Leighton, Martin Gleeson, Eva Huehne and Jennie Rubio, for their confidence and excellent support. I am equally grateful to the Faculty of Law of Maastricht University, for facilitating the work on this book. My special thanks to Paul Adriaans, Sophie Janssen and Roger Snijder. Finally, this book would never have been finished without the untiring help and capable assistance of, in particular, Adeshola Odusanya, Katalin Fritz and Carol Ní Ghiollarnáth, my research assistants, and also Iveta Alexovièová, Natalya Bayurova, Kasper Hermans, Stelios Katevatis, Sergey Ripinsky, Eva Schöfer, Nikolaos Skoutaris, Damian Smith and Ruta Zarnauskaite, all graduate or undergraduate students at Maastricht University in the period 2002–4. Of course, none of those mentioned above bears any responsibility for any error or omission in this book. In recognition of the support I received from so many colleagues and students in the writing of this book, all royalties go to Maastricht University to set up a scholarship and research fund for students and scholars from developing countries.

Peter Van den Bossche
Maastricht, September 2004

GATT Panel Reports

Appellate Body Reports

Awards of the Arbitrator (Article 21.3(c) of the DSU)

Table of agreements and decisions

1

Economic globalisation and the law of the WTO

Contents

1.1. INTRODUCTION

At the largest-ever gathering of Heads of State and Government, the Millennium Summit of the United Nations in September 2000, the UN General Assembly solemnly declared:

> We will spare no effort to free our fellow men, women, and children from the abject and dehumanizing conditions of extreme poverty, to which more than a billion of them

> are currently subjected. We are committed to making the right to development a reality for everyone and to freeing the entire human race from want.[1]

It was decided to *halve* the proportion of the world's people living in absolute poverty by the year 2015.[2] While data of the World Bank show that the number of people in extreme poverty fell from 1.451 billion in 1981 to 1.101 billion in 2001, the enormity of the task ahead is obvious to all.[3] The income gap between the richest 20 per cent of the world's population and the poorest 20 per cent does not cease to grow. During the 1990s, this gap increased from 60:1 to 86:1.[4] In discussing the greatest challenges that the world faces, Jimmy Carter, the former US President, stated in his Nobel Lecture in December 2002:

> Among all the possible choices, I decided that the most serious and universal problem is the growing chasm between the richest and poorest people on earth. The results of this disparity are root causes of most of the world's unresolved problems, including starvation, illiteracy, environmental degradation, violent conflict, and unnecessary illnesses that range from guinea worm to HIV/Aids.[5]

One of the defining features of today's world is the process of economic globalisation, a process characterised by high levels of international trade and foreign direct investment. This chapter examines this process and notes the broad consensus among economists and policy-makers that economic globalisation in general, and international trade and foreign direct investment in particular, offer an unprecedented *opportunity* to eradicate poverty and hunger worldwide. The World Bank, for instance, estimated that abolishing all trade barriers could increase global income by US$2.8 trillion and lift 320 million people out of poverty by 2015.[6]

However, to ensure that this opportunity is realised, economic globalisation has to be *managed* and *regulated* at the international level. If not, economic globalisation is likely to be a curse, rather than a blessing, to humankind, aggravating economic inequality, social injustice, environmental degradation and cultural dispossession. The law of the World Trade Organization is currently the most ambitious effort to manage and regulate international trade. By way of introduction to this book, this chapter discusses the need for

---

[1] United Nations General Assembly, *UN Millennium Declaration*, Resolution adopted on 8 September 2000, para. 11.

[2] *Ibid.*, para. 19.

[3] See World Bank, *World Development Indicators 2004*, www.worldbank.org/data/wdi2004/index.htm, visited on 30 May 2004. See also S. Bhalla, *Imagine There's No Country* (Institute for International Economics, 2002). Note that the cause of the reduction in poverty is primarily the fast economic growth of Asian countries, in particular China. Between 1981 and 1999, the proportion of people in the East Asian and Pacific regions living on less than US$1 per day fell from 56 per cent to 16 per cent. In China, it fell from 61 per cent to 17 per cent. Note, however, that, in Sub-Saharan Africa, the proportion of people living in absolute poverty rose from 42 per cent to 47 per cent. See also M. Wolf, 'An End to Poverty', *Financial Times*, 4 May 2004.

[4] Note that the income gap between the richest 20 per cent of the world's population and the poorest 20 per cent stood at around 3:1 in 1820, 11:1 in 1913 and 30:1 in 1970. See http://hdr.undp.org/reports/global/1999/en, visited on 1 January 2004.

[5] J. Carter, Nobel Lecture, Oslo, 10 December 2002, www.nobel.se, visited on 13 August 2003.

[6] M. Bacchetta and M. Jansen, *Adjusting to Trade Liberalization: The Role of Policy, Institutions and WTO Disciplines*, WTO Special Studies 7 April 2003, 6. The World Bank's Annual Report for 2004 states, on page 5, that trade talks to reduce agricultural protectionism could produce US$325 billion by 2015, lifting 140 million people out of poverty by that date.

international rules on international trade, and gives an overview of basic rules and disciplines of WTO law. It also discusses the different sources of WTO law and examines the sometimes contentious relationship between WTO law and other international law and national laws.

1.2. ECONOMIC GLOBALISATION AND INTERNATIONAL TRADE

1.2.1. The emergence of the global economy

1.2.1.1. The concept of 'economic globalisation'

'Economic globalisation' has been a popular buzzword for more than a decade now. Politicians, government officials, businesspeople, trade unionists, environmentalists, church leaders, public health experts, third-world activists, economists and lawyers all speak of 'economic globalisation'. The concepts of 'globalisation', and 'economic globalisation' in particular, have been used by many to describe the defining feature of the post-Cold War world in which we live. But what do these terms mean?

Joseph Stiglitz, former Chief Economist of the World Bank and winner of the Nobel Prize for Economics in 2001, described the concept of globalisation, in his 2002 book, *Globalization and Its Discontents*, as:

> the closer integration of the countries and peoples of the world which has been brought about by the enormous reduction of costs of transportation and communication, and the breaking down of artificial barriers to the flow of goods, services, capital, knowledge, and (to a lesser extent) people across borders.[7]

In *The Lexus and the Olive Tree: Understanding Globalisation*, Thomas Friedman defined 'globalisation' as follows:

> it is the inexorable integration of markets, nation-states and technologies to a degree never witnessed before – in a way that is enabling individuals, corporations and nation-states to reach around the world farther, faster, deeper and cheaper than ever before, and in a way that is enabling the world to reach into individuals, corporations and nation-states farther, faster, deeper and cheaper than ever before.[8]

Economic globalisation is a multifaceted phenomenon, which undoubtedly is not yet fully understood. In essence, however, economic globalisation is the gradual integration of national economies into one borderless global economy. It encompasses both (free) international trade and (unrestricted) foreign direct investment. Economic globalisation affects people everywhere and in many aspects of their daily lives. It affects their jobs, their food, their health, their education and their leisure time. It affects the price people pay for gasoline, bananas and cars, and the health services accessible to them.

---

[7] J. Stiglitz, *Globalization and Its Discontents* (Penguin, 2002), 9.
[8] T. Friedman, *The Lexus and the Olive Tree: Understanding Globalisation*, 2nd edition (First Anchor Books, 2000), 9.

While economic globalisation is often presented as a new phenomenon, it deserves to be mentioned that today's global economic integration is not unprecedented. During the fifty years before the First World War, there were also large cross–border flows of goods and capital and, more than now, of people. In that period, globalisation was driven by the lowering of trade barriers and by significant reductions in transport costs resulting from technological innovations such as railways and steamships. If one looks at the ratio of trade to output, Britain and France are only slightly more open to trade today than they were in 1913, while Japan is less open now than it was then.[9] That earlier attempt at globalisation ended, however, with the First World War and was followed by one of the darkest times of humankind.

Furthermore, while the *trend* towards globalisation is clear, the extent of today's global economic integration can be, and frequently is, exaggerated. International trade should normally force high-cost, domestic producers to lower their prices and bring the prices of products and services between different countries closer together. However, large divergences in prices persist. Even within the European Union, price differences from one country to another remain significant for a number of products and services. This is partly due to differences in transport costs, taxes and the efficiency of distribution networks, but it is also due, at least outside the European Union, to the continued existence of important barriers to trade. Furthermore, while goods, services and capital move across borders with greater ease, restrictions on the free movement of workers, i.e. restrictions on economic migration, remain multiple and rigorous.

Questions and Assignments 1.1

How would you define 'economic globalisation'? Does economic globalisation also affect non-economic matters? Give three concrete examples of how *you* are affected by economic globalisation. Is economic globalisation a historically unique and all-pervasive phenomenon?

1.2.1.2. *Forces driving economic globalisation*

It is commonly argued that economic globalisation has been driven by two main forces. The first, technology, makes globalisation feasible; the second, the liberalisation of trade and foreign direct investment, makes it happen.[10] Due to technological innovations resulting in a dramatic fall in transport, communication and computing costs, the natural barriers of time and space that separate national markets have been coming down. Between 1920 and 1990, average ocean freight and port charges for US import and export cargo

---

[9] 'One World?', *The Economist*, 18 October 1997.
[10] See also M. Wolf, 'Global Opportunities', *Financial Times*, 6 May 1997.

fell by almost 70 per cent. Between 1930 and 1990, average air-transport fares per passenger mile fell by 84 per cent.[11] The cost of a three-minute telephone call between New York and London has fallen from US$300 in 1930 to US$1 in 1997 (in 1996 dollars); the cost of computer processing power has been falling by an average of 30 per cent per year in real terms over recent decades.[12] As a result of cheap and efficient communication, companies can locate different parts of their production process in different parts of the world while remaining in close contact. Activities such as writing software or accounting can be carried out anywhere in the world, far away from the customer or consumer. New technological developments are likely to further accelerate the process of economic globalisation. The second driving force of economic globalisation has been the liberalisation of international trade and foreign direct investment. Over the last fifty years, most developed countries have gradually but significantly lowered barriers to foreign trade and allowed free movement of capital. In recent years, the liberalisation of trade and investment has become a worldwide trend, including in developing countries, although liberalisation still proceeds at different speeds in different parts of the world.

Basically along the same lines, but with a different emphasis, Thomas Friedman argued in *The Lexus and the Olive Tree* that what caused globalisation to happen, and what continues to drive the process, are what he calls:

- the democratisation of technology;
- the democratisation of finance; and
- the democratisation of information.

The democratisation of technology refers, in particular, to the way we communicate, and is the result of several technological innovations that came together in the 1980s involving computerisation, telecommunications, miniaturisation, compression technology and digitisation.[13] According to Friedman, this made it possible for hundreds of millions of people around the world to connect and exchange information, news, knowledge and money in ways never before witnessed. Friedman argues:

> What this democratization of technology means is that the potential for wealth creation becomes geographically dispersed, giving all kinds of previously disconnected people the chance to access and apply knowledge.[14]

The democratisation of finance refers to the change in *who* invests and *how* investments are made. As Friedman explains:

> when the system of fixed exchange rates and capital controls came unstuck, developed countries gradually democratized their capital markets, opening them to any foreign traders who wanted to play, and then the developing countries followed suit.

---

[11] R. Porter, 'The Global Trading System in the 21st Century', in R. Porter, P. Sauvé, A. Subramanian and A. Beviglia Zampetti (eds.), *Efficiency, Equity, and Legitimacy: The Multilateral Trading System at the Millennium* (Brookings Institution Press, 2001), 4.

[12] 'One World?', *The Economist*, 18 October 1997.

[13] T. Friedman, *The Lexus and the Olive Tree*, 47.   [14] *Ibid.*, 51.

> Soon all sorts of products were available: Mexican bonds, Lebanese bonds, Turkish bonds, Russian bonds, German bonds, French bonds. You could take your choice, and people did. The more individual investors could move their money in and out of these highly competitive global mutual funds, the more these fund managers would move their money between companies and countries, constantly demanding higher, more sustained returns ... [W]e have gone from a world in which a few bankers held the sovereign debts of a lot of countries, to a world in which a lot of bankers held the sovereign debts of a lot of countries, and finally to a world today in which many individuals, through pension funds and mutual funds, hold the sovereign debts of many countries.[15]

Finally, the democratisation of information refers to the change in how knowledge and information is obtained. Thanks to satellite dishes, cable television and, above all, the Internet, many people have virtually unlimited access to information. As Friedman notes:

> the days when governments could isolate their people from understanding what life was like beyond their borders or even beyond their village are over ... Thanks to the democratization of information, we all increasingly know how each other lives ...
> What makes the Internet so dangerous for police states is that they can't afford not to have it, because they will fall behind economically if they do. But if they have it, it means they simply can't control information the way they once did.[16]

In his book, *Has Globalization Gone Too Far?*, Dani Rodrik of the Kennedy School, Harvard University, highlighted yet another, arguably less positive, dimension of globalisation:

> Globalization is not occurring in a vacuum. It is part of a broader trend that we may call marketization. Receding government, deregulation, and the shrinking of social obligations are the domestic counterparts of the intertwining of national economies. Globalization could not have advanced this far without these complementary forces.[17]

While some politicians and opinion-makers claim otherwise, the process of economic globalisation is not irreversible. History shows that – for better or for worse – most man-made changes in society are irreversible. However, it would be very difficult, and foolhardy, for governments to reverse the current globalisation process. Three reasons come to mind. First, new technology has created distribution channels, especially for services, such as satellite communication and the Internet, that governments, with protectionist intentions, will find very difficult to control. Secondly, liberal international trade policies now have a firm institutional basis in the multilateral trading system of the WTO, discussed in detail in this book. Thirdly, the price to be paid, in terms of economic prosperity, for withdrawing from the global economy would be very high. Autarkies, such as North Korea, do not flourish in today's world.

---

[15] *Ibid.*, 59.   [16] *Ibid.*, 67–8.
[17] D. Rodrik, *Has Globalization Gone Too Far?* (Institute for International Economics, 1997), 85.

Questions and Assignments 1.2

What explains the process of economic globalisation? Could governments reverse the process of economic globalisation?

1.2.1.3. *Facts and figures on world trade and investment*

In 1948, world exports of goods amounted to US$58 billion per year. By 2003, world exports of goods had increased to US$7,294 billion, or more than US$7.3 trillion, per year.[18] This represents an increase in international trade of more than 12,500 per cent. World exports of commercial services, marginal in 1948, amounted in 2002 to US$1,540 billion.[19]

The ratio of global trade in goods and commercial services to world gross domestic product (GDP) is a reliable and much-used measurement of economic globalisation. In 1950, exports of goods and commercial services represented 8 per cent of GDP; in 2002, these exports represented 29 per cent, 0.2 per cent down from 2000, the top year thus far. Between 1990 and 2000, the ratio increased from 19.8 per cent to 29.2 per cent.

It is not only the volume and value of world trade in goods and the ratio of global trade to GDP that have changed significantly over the last fifty years. The share of world trade of various regions of the world also changed over this period. Most remarkable are the decline of the share of North America (the United States, Canada and Mexico) from 27.3 percent in 1948 to 16.6 per cent in 2001, and the increase of the share of Western Europe (primarily the European Union) from 31.5 per cent in 1948 to 41.5 per cent in 2001 (down from 44 percent

Table 1.1 Trends in world exports of goods (1948–2002)[20]

World merchandise exports	1948	1950	1973	1990	2000	2002
Billion current $	58	61	579	3,438	6,250	6,240
Billion constant 1990 $	304	376	1797	3,438	6,726	6,836
Exports per capita, 1990 $	123	149	458	654	1,110	1,110

Table 1.2 Trends in global trade to GDP (1950–2002)[21]

Trade to GDP	1950	1973	1990	2000	2002
Exports of goods and services, to GDP, at constant 1987 prices, %	8.0	14.9	19.8	29.2	29.0
Merchandise trade to GDP, at current prices	7.9	11.8	15.3	19.9	19.4
Merchandise trade to GDP, at constant prices	8.8	13.4	15.3	23.9	23.6

---

[18] See WTO, *International Trade Statistics 2004*, 10, at www.wto.org/res_e/statis_e/its2004_e/
its04_bysubject_e.htm, visited on 25 October 2004.
[19] *Ibid.*   [20] See www.wto.org, visited on 6 September 2003.
[21] See www.wto.org, visited on 6 September 2003.

Table 1.3 Share of world exports of goods by region (1948–2003)[22]

	1948	1963	1973	1983	1993	2001	2003
World	100.0	100.0	100.0	100.0	100.0	100.0	100.0
North America	27.3	19.3	16.9	15.4	16.6	16.6	13.7
Latin America	12.3	7.0	4.7	5.8	4.4	5.8	5.2
Western Europe	31.5	41.4	45.4	38.9	44.0	41.5	43.1
Other European States	6.0	11.0	9.1	9.5	2.9	4.8	5.5
Africa	7.3	5.7	4.8	4.4	2.5	2.4	2.4
Middle East	2.0	3.2	4.1	6.8	3.4	4.0	4.1
Asia	13.6	12.4	14.9	19.1	26.1	25.0	26.1
GATT/WTO Members	60.4	72.8	81.8	76.0	89.5	92.5	94.3

in 1993). Equally remarkable are the steep decline of the shares of both Latin-America and Africa, and the significant increase of Asia's share.

In the 1990s, developing countries, *as a group*, increased their share of world exports of goods from 23.4 per cent to 29.8 per cent. During the same period, developing countries increased their share of world exports of commercial services from 18.2 per cent to 23.3 per cent. The share of developing countries in world trade has thus increased over the last decade.[23] However, as Hoekman and Kostecki noted:

> Global trade flows are dominated by exchanges within and between the three major regions of the global economy (the so-called triad): Europe, North America, and East Asia. Trade flows involving other parts of the globe are relatively small, accounting for some 15 per cent of world trade. ... Intra-EU and intra-North America trade accounts for 52 per cent of industrial trade.[24]

Furthermore, it must be noted that all forty-eight least-developed countries together accounted for only 0.5 per cent of world trade. Their share has actually fallen over time – it stood at 1.7 per cent in 1970. South Asia and Sub-Saharan Africa each represent just over 1 per cent of world trade.[25]

Developing countries have registered particularly rapid increases in their ratios of exports to GDP. Exports now account for more than one-quarter of their combined GDP, a proportion which is higher than that of developed countries.[26] Also, the composition of exports from developing countries has changed in recent years. While many developing countries remain dependent on primary commodities, the share of manufactured goods has been growing. Since the early 1990s, there has been a boom in high-technology exports, with countries such as China, India and Mexico emerging as major suppliers of cutting-edge technologies, as well as labour-intensive goods.[27]

---

[22] Based on WTO Secretariat, *International Trade Statistics 2004*, 30. See http://www.wto.org/english/res_e/statis_e/statis_e.htm, visited on 1 September 2004.

[23] See WTO, *International Trade Statistics 2002*, at www.wto.org, visited on 1 January 2004.

[24] B. Hoekman and M. Kostecki, *The Political Economy of the World Trading System*, 2nd edition (Oxford University Press, 2001), 9.

[25] *Ibid.*

[26] Oxfam, *Rigged Rules and Double Standards: Trade, Globalization and the Fight Against Poverty*, 2002, Summary of Chapter 1, www.maketradefair.org, visited on 11 August 2003.

[27] *Ibid.*

Table 1.4 Foreign direct investment (1982–2003)[28]

Item	Value at current prices (billions of US dollars)				Annual growth rate (%)						
	1982	1990	2000	2003	1986–1990	1991–1995	1996–2000	2000	2001	2002	2003
FDI inflows	59	209	1,271	560	22.9	21.5	39.7	27.7	−41.1	−17.0	−17.6
FDI outflows	28	242	1,150	612	25.6	16.6	35.1	8.7	−39.2	−17.3	2.6
FDI inward stock	796	1,950	6,314	8,245	14.7	9.3	16.9	19.1	7.4	12.7	11.8
FDI outward stock	590	1,748	5,976	8,197	18.1	10.7	17.1	18.5	5.9	13.8	13.7
Employment of foreign affiliates (thousands)	19,232	24,197	45,587	54,170	5.6	3.9	10.8	13.3	−3.2	12.3	8.3

With respect to trade between developing countries, Supachai Panitchpakdi, the WTO Director-General, noted:

> Enhanced South–South activity offers a potentially great source of expanded trade opportunities in the coming decade. Between 1990 and 2001, South–South trade grew faster than world trade with the share of intra-developing country trade in world merchandise exports rising from 6.5% to 10.6%.[29]

Another development in international trade worth noting is the increased trade within companies. The foreign sales of the largest 100 transnational corporations are equivalent in value to one-quarter of world trade; approximately two-thirds of all trade takes place within companies. The increase in trade within companies has been one of the most powerful forces behind the expansion of world trade.

Next to international trade, an important aspect of economic globalisation is foreign direct investment (FDI). Table 1.4 demonstrates that FDI inflows have increased from US$57 billion in 1982 to US$1,271 billion in 2000. This represents an increase of 2,230 per cent. During the second half of the 1990s, the annual growth rate of FDI inflows was, on average, 40.8 per cent. Worldwide employment of personnel in foreign affiliates increased from 17.5 million people in 1982 to 45.6 million people in 2000.[30]

After years of rapid growth, in 2001, however, global FDI inflows dropped by over 40 per cent. In 2002, they fell by another 17 per cent to US$651 billion, or just half the record volume of 2000.[31] In 2003, FDI inflows declined again by 18 per cent to US$560 billion. A rebound is likely in 2004.[32]

---

[28] Based on UNCTAD Secretariat, *World Investment Report 2004: The Shift Towards Services*, 9. Data for 2000 (value at current prices): UNCTAD Secretariat, *World Investment Report 2001: Promoting Linkages*, 10. See http://www.unctad.org/Templates/Page.asp?intItemID=1485&lang=1, visited on 1 September 2004.

[29] Supachai Panitchpakdi, 'The Doha Development Agenda: What's at Stake for Business in the Developing World?', *International Trade Forum*, August 2003. See www.tradeforum.org/news/fullstory.php/aid/557/The_Doha_Development_Agenda:_What%92s_at_Stake_for_Business_in_the_Developing_World_.html, visited on 15 May 2004.

[30] UNCTAD Secretariat, *World Investment Report 2001: Promoting Linkages*, 10.

[31] UNCTAD Secretariat, *World Investment Report 2003: FDI Policies for Development: National and International Perspectives*, 3.

[32] See UNCTAD Secretariat, *World Investment Report 2004: The Shift Towards Services*, 33. Note also that FDI inflows to developing countries rose by 9 per cent from US$158 billion in 2002 to US$172 billion in 2003 (*ibid.*).

The 2003 World Investment Report underlined the growing importance of overseas investment in developing countries. FDI stocks in developing countries represented about one-third of their GDP in 2002, compared with just 13 per cent in 1980. The UNCTAD data also show, however, that foreign investment remains very unequally distributed, with the top ten hosts accounting for two-thirds of total FDI inflows. The forty-nine poorest countries accounted for just 2 per cent of FDI inflow in 2002, a share that has changed little since.[33]

The *Financial Times* reported this telling example of economic globalisation in February 2003:

> Dr Martens, boot-maker to generations of punks, skinheads and factory workers, will this month quietly end centuries of volume shoe manufacturing in Britain by moving its production to a dusty plain in southern China.
>
> ... The Pearl river delta – an area the size of Belgium that winds inland from Hong Kong through a series of tightly packed islands – produces $10 billion worth of exports and attracts $1 billion of foreign investment a month. Already, 30m people work in manufacturing here; every day thousands more pour off trains from farms further north.
>
> ... The catalyst for the delta's explosive export growth is globalisation. China joined the World Trade Organization last year. Increasing competition, falling transport costs and flagging consumer demand are forcing multi-national manufacturing companies to flock to the region with the lowest production costs.
>
> In Dr Martens' case, fierce price competition from rival US brands already produced in China forced the company's hand. 'It was absolutely obvious from the moment I arrived that we had to move to China like everyone else,' says David Suddens, managing director. Dr Martens will outsource production to factories owned by Pou Chen and Golden Chang, Taiwanese companies that moved to the mainland to take advantage of lower labour costs.
>
> Pou Chen's plants, one in Zhuhai and one in Dongguan, employ 110,000 people and churn out 100m pairs of shoes a year for Nike, Adidas, Caterpillar, Timberland, Hush Puppy, Reebok, Puma and others.
>
> ... Dr Martens pays its 1,100 UK workers about $490 a week and has built a stadium for the local football club. Pou Chen pays about Rmn800 ($100) a month, or 36 cents an hour, for up to 69 hours a week and provides dormitories for migrant workers who must obey strict curfews. The light, well ventilated working conditions are far better than many visitors expect. Stung by complaints of exploitation, Nike and other buyers have full-time local offices monitoring most aspects of employee life.
>
> ... Nevertheless, older shoe factories are beginning to find it hard to attract and retain workers tempted by better-paid jobs in other plants. Pou Chen is opening a factory further inland where labour is more plentiful. ... Although labour rates are creeping up, the economies of scale keep supply costs down and attract even more companies to relocate.[34]

In August 2003, the *Financial Times* reported on the globalisation of the trade in services with the following story:

> Clutching her side in pain, the woman with suspected appendicitis who was rushed to a hospital on the outskirts of Philadelphia last week had little time to ponder how dependent her life had become on the relentless forces of globalisation. Within minutes of her arrival at the Crozer-Chester Medical Center, the recommendation on whether

---

[33] UNCTAD Secretariat, *World Investment Report 2003: FDI Policies for Development: National and International Perspectives*, 5–7.
[34] D. Roberts and J. Kynge, 'A New Workshop of the World', *Financial Times*, 4 February 2003.

to operate was being made by a doctor reading her computer-aided tomography (CAT) scan from a computer screen 5,800 miles away in the Middle East.

Jonathan Schlakman, a Harvard-trained radiologist based in Jerusalem, is one of a new breed of skilled professionals proving that geographic distance is no obstacle to outsourcing even the highest paid jobs to overseas locations. The migration of white-collar work has moved up the value chain from call centre operators and back-office clerks to occupations such as equity research, accounting, computer programming and chip design.

The trend – still only a trickle at present – may look to some like a temporary fad pursued by companies seeking to cut costs. For trade unions in the US and Europe, it heralds a fundamental restructuring of rich-world economies, akin to the globalisation of manufacturing in the 1980s and the outsourcing of unskilled service jobs in the 1990s.

At present, only 35 patients' scans are transmitted each day from US emergency rooms to Dr Schlakman's small team of doctors in Israel. But with senior radiologists costing up to $300,000 a year to hire in the US and many emergency cases arriving at night, the use of medical expertise based in a different time zone and earning less than half US rates is almost certain to rise. 'It's much more expensive to use night staff in the US because they need time off the following day,' says Dr Schlakman.[35]

Patients also travel around the world to find good and affordable medical care. An increasing number of foreigners are going to India for heart bypass operations. The average cost, including air fare, is about US$7,000 – roughly one-quarter of what it would be in the UK private sector – and there are no waiting lists. At the Escorts Heart Institute in New Delhi, more than 4,000 heart bypass operations – the highest of any single institute in the world – were performed last year. At 0.8 per cent, Escorts' mortality rate was comparable with international standards.[36]

Questions and Assignments 1.3

Discuss the trends in international trade and foreign direct investment in the last ten years. Do these trends reveal an ever-increasing degree of economic globalisation? Comment on the developing countries' share in world trade in goods and services.

1.2.2. Economic globalisation: a blessing or a curse?

1.2.2.1. Backlash against economic globalisation

Everyone around the world feels the effects of economic globalisation, but these effects are not felt by all in an even or equitable way. In recent years, massive street protests in Seattle, Prague, Montreal, Washington, Geneva, Göteborg, Genoa and Zurich have shown that many people in developed countries are 'dissatisfied' with economic globalisation. Also in developing countries, hostility towards economic globalisation is growing and becoming

---

[35] D. Roberts, E. Luce and K. Merchant, 'Service Industries Go Global', *Financial Times*, 20 August 2003.
[36] *Ibid.*

more vocal. As Fred Bergsten, Director of the Institute for International Economics in Washington DC, noted at the 2000 Annual Meeting of the Trilateral Commission:

> there is a big backlash against globalization. We see it in the financial world. We certainly see it in the trading world as well. It's much more fundamental than pure economics. We know that globalization does increase income and social disparities within countries. We know that globalization does leave some countries and certainly some groups of people behind. We do know that a lot of Europeans don't want to eat genetically modified American foods and that adds to their resistance to globalization. We know that a lot of Americans worry about races to the bottom, labor standards, environmental standards, and other perceived doubts about dealing with the rest of the world. We know that a lot of developing countries are raising doubts about the entire system, and such specifics as whether having agreed to the enshrinement of intellectual property rights is really in their national interest. (They would like to pull it back out of the WTO, having agreed to put it in five or six years ago.) So the list is long of the perceived intrusions of globalization into national sovereignties. There is therefore a backlash against it, which I think we have to take as an extremely serious economic, political, and social matter.[37]

According to opponents of the current economic globalisation process, there is excessive emphasis on the economic interests of transnational corporations. In their opinion, social, cultural and environmental interests and the interests of developing countries are not sufficiently taken into account. Often, they hold economic globalisation responsible for world poverty and hunger, environmental disasters, unemployment and many other wrongs of today's world. To many, global economic integration is a malignant force that is destroying the livelihood of millions of workers and exacerbates inequality, social injustice and environmental degradation.

A 2001 study by the Institute of International Economics in Washington DC concluded that numerous surveys indicated that a significant number of Americans opposed further liberalisation of trade, immigration and foreign direct investment, and that an absolute majority of Americans wanted liberalisation to go more slowly. According to the study, most Americans know the advantages of open markets but tend to view the costs – especially the supposedly negative impact on American jobs and wages – as more important.[38] In Europe, the popular backlash against economic globalisation is probably even more pronounced. In some European countries, in particular France, there is a widespread perception that globalisation is a conspiracy of ruthless Anglo-Saxons.[39] In 1997, economists at the Brookings Institution in Washington DC coined the term 'globaphobia' to describe the 'irrational' fear of economic globalisation that seems to haunt the popular psyche these days in most industrial countries.[40]

---

[37] F. Bergsten, 'The Backlash Against Globalization', Remarks Made to the 2000 Annual Meeting of the Trilateral Commission in Tokyo, http://www.trilateral.org/annmtgs/trialog/trlgtxts/t54/ber.htm, visited on 15 May 2004.

[38] As reported by R. Dale, 'Anti-Globalization Forces Gain Steam: Movement Brings Together Strange Bedfellows from Right and Left', International Herald Tribune, 16 March 2001.

[39] F. Bolkenstein, 'To the Enemies of Globalization', Wall Street Journal, 25 September 2000.

[40] R. Dale, 'Prescribing Fact to Cure "Globaphobia"', International Herald Tribune, 7 October 1997.

In commenting on the arguments of the 'anti-globalists', Philip Stevens of the *Financial Times* observed that, while there are important truths in these arguments, they are often confused and contradictory:

> The anarchists have no need of consistency. But the broader coalition of anti-globalists often seems just as inchoate. Non-governmental organisations (NGOs) want the multinationals tamed. Governments must reclaim the sovereignty lost to unaccountable and unscrupulous business executives. The IMF, the World Trade Organization and the rest are agents of a new imperialism. And yet then we hear the protesters call for new global rules to protect the environment and prevent exploitation of labour. Self-interested trade unions stand with self-proclaimed idealists in demanding that rich nations protect jobs by imposing their own labour standards on poor ones. Somewhere in all this there is a cry for a different set of values. It is often hard to find. But it is there. And it explains why the protesters are winning.[41]

As Stevens correctly observes, the constituency of the 'anti-globalists' in developed countries stretches well beyond the mostly young activists protesting on the streets:

> Many who abhor their tactics share their unease. Globalisation is unsettling, for the comfortable middle classes as much as for the politically disaffected. The threats, real or imagined, to national and local cultures are widely felt. So, too, are the unnerving shifts in the boundaries between governments, business and multilateral institutions. As consumers we are stronger; as citizens, weaker.[42]

Moreover, in leading developing countries such as India and Brazil, large sections of the population also appear fearful of, and hostile towards, further trade liberalisation and economic globalisation. Since the disastrous 1999 session of the Ministerial Conference of the WTO in Seattle, a growing number of developing countries have become ever more critical of the current process of economic globalisation.

UN Secretary General Kofi Annan noted in a speech to the World Economic Forum in Davos on 28 January 2001:

> For far too many people in the world today, greater openness looms as a threat – a threat to their livelihoods, to their ways of life, and to the ability of their governments to serve and protect them. Even when it may be exaggerated or misplaced, 'fear has big eyes,' in the words of the Russian proverb. And, we might add, it has the ear of governments, who feel compelled to respond.[43]

The discussion of globalisation and trade liberalisation is often emotionally charged and, therefore, unfortunately not always productive. Oxfam noted in its 2002 study, *Rigged Rules and Double Standards: Trade, Globalization, and the Fight Against Poverty*, the following:

> Current debates about trade are dominated by ritualistic exchanges between two camps: the 'globaphiles' and the 'globaphobes'. 'Globaphiles' argue that trade is

---

[41] P. Stevens, 'A Poor Case for Globalisation: The World's Leaders Are Failing to Address Legitimate Questions Raised by Protesters About the Effects of Global Capitalism', *Financial Times*, 17 August 2001.
[42] *Ibid.*
[43] From the Address by UN Secretary General Kofi Annan in Davos, Switzerland, on 28 January 2001, to the World Economic Forum, www.unis.unvienna.org/unis/pressrels/2001/sg2772.html, visited on 15 May 2004.

already making globalisation work for the poor. Their prescription for the future is 'more of the same'. 'Globaphobes' turn this world-view on its head. They argue that trade is inherently bad for the poor. Participation in trade, so the argument runs, inevitably leads to more poverty and inequality. The corollary of this view is 'the less trade the better'.

The anti-globalisation movement deserves credit. It has raised profoundly important questions about social justice – and it has forced the failures of globalisation on to the political agenda. However, the war of words between trade optimists and trade pessimists that accompanies virtually every international meeting is counter-productive. Both world views fly in the face of the evidence – and neither offers any hope for the future.[44]

1.2.2.2. Problems of current economic globalisation

Economic globalisation and international trade currently gives rise to problems and tensions in developed as well as developing countries.

Bill Jordan, General Secretary of the International Confederation of Free Trade Unions, wrote in December 2000:

> If you want to belittle a point of view, it is easiest to caricature that point of view as nothing more than a slogan daubed on a placard and paraded through the streets. Too often this has led to misrepresenting the views of labor unions in the face of globalization ... The international labor movement is not against globalization; indeed we would agree that globalization can be a big part of the answer to the problems of the world's poor. But it also is a big part of the problem. In other words, globalization is neither entirely beneficial nor entirely harmful. It is not an unstoppable force of nature, but is shaped by those who set the rules. And while it has the potential to help lift more than 2 billion people out of poverty, it is not doing so now.[45]

War on Want, one of the more thought-provoking NGOs with close links to the international labour movement, summarises its position regarding economic globalisation as follows:

> Jobs are always welcomed by those who live in the developing world. But many of these employees are paid next to nothing, and work in dangerous conditions facing physical and verbal abuse from their employers. Meanwhile, in the developed world, workers are being laid off at an alarming rate and made to feel that they need to compete with workers in the developing world. The globalisation of trade and investment affects labour standards, working conditions, the environment, human health and many other aspects of our lives. Currently, too little attention is being paid to these effects. We need to ensure there are global rules to govern the effects of a global economy.[46]

War on Want is not opposed to globalisation, but wants to see the benefits of globalisation more evenly spread across the world. According to this NGO, economic globalisation primarily benefits transnational corporations (TNCs)

---

[44] Oxfam, *Rigged Rules and Double Standards: Trade, Globalization, and the Fight Against Poverty*, 2002, Summary of Chapter 1, http://www.maketradefair.org/en/index.php?file=03042002153411.htm&cat=3& subcat=3& select=4, visited on 15 May 2004.

[45] B. Jordan, 'Yes to Globalization, But Protect the Poor', *International Herald Tribune*, 21 December 2000.

[46] Excerpts from 'The Global Workplace', a project of War on Want, www.globalworkplace.org/?lid=74, visited on 15 May 2004.

and often spells disaster for industries in developing countries as well as for workers worldwide.

> TNCs can treat the world like their assembly line – manufacturing goods where labour is cheapest, basing operations where taxes are lowest and selling goods where the price is highest. If taxes or labour laws are imposed in one country, they can simply move to another.
>
> ... Reducing restrictions on trade and investment has also caused economic instability. If wages are too high or governments introduce regulations such as a minimum wage, corporations can simply move elsewhere, leaving people with nothing. Increasingly, corporations are finding ways to improve their mobility. For example, many companies don't buy factories anymore; instead, they sign short-term contracts with locally based operators. This means working people are afraid of fighting for better conditions because corporations threaten not to renew their contracts if conditions are improved. Moreover, it means that the corporations can claim that responsibility for wages and conditions has nothing to do with them.
>
> ... Industries in developing economies are often fairly new, and not as resilient as large Western corporations. For these local industries, open competition may spell destruction, and this forces these countries to continue their dependence on the production of raw materials and low-cost goods. On the other hand, developed countries often have something to fear from competition with the developing world: lower wages and worse conditions mean that their own companies might be undercut. World trade rules have been designed to prevent unrestricted imports to the developed world and to protect producers in wealthy countries.[47]

ATTAC, the Association for the Taxation of Financial Transactions for the Aid of Citizens, takes a similar position against 'corporate globalisation', which, it contends, results in:

> the concentration of wealth in the hands of the rich few, growing inequality within and between nations, increasing poverty for the majority of the world's peoples, displacement of farmers and workers especially in third world countries, and unsustainable patterns of production and consumption.[48]

With respect to further liberalisation of trade, ATTAC argues:

> The time has come to acknowledge the crises of the international trading system and its main administering institution, the WTO. It is time to stop ... and turn trade around to serve the interest of all. We need to replace this old, unfair and oppressive trade system with a new, socially just and sustainable trading framework for the 21st Century. We need to protect cultural, biological, economic and social diversity; introduce progressive policies to prioritise local economies and trade; secure internationally recognized economic, cultural, social and labor rights; and reclaim the sovereignty of peoples and national and subnational democratic decision making processes. In order to do this, we need new rules based on the principles of democratic control of resources, ecological sustainability, equity, cooperation and precaution.[49]

Developing countries' governments and third-world activists commonly argue: first, that developing countries are being forced to open their markets too far, too fast; secondly, that rich countries are conspiring to keep their

---

[47] *Ibid.*
[48] Excerpts from ATTAC Quarterly Report, September 2001, *International Trade*, No. 2, Vol. I, www.attac.org, visited on 11 August 2003.
[49] *Ibid.*

markets closed to products from developing countries which compete with their products (agricultural products, textiles and clothing); and, thirdly, that developing countries lack the resources and the information to negotiate effectively, to implement trade agreements and to exploit world trade rules to their advantage. As UN Secretary General Kofi Annan once noted:

> Try to imagine what globalization can possibly mean to the half of humanity that has never made or received a telephone call; or to the people of Sub-Saharan Africa, who have less Internet access than the inhabitants of the borough of Manhattan.[50]

While not sharing the extreme positions of anti-globalists and being careful 'not to make the mistake of attributing to globalization the blemishes of other faces',[51] many observers and scholars recognise the dangers of the economic globalisation process.

In *Globalization and Its Discontents*, Joseph Stiglitz reflected on the bright and dark sides of globalisation as follows:

> Opening up to international trade has helped many countries grow far more quickly than they would otherwise have done. International trade helps economic development when a country's exports drive its economic growth. Export-led growth was the centrepiece of the industrial policy that enriched much of Asia and left millions of people there far better off. Because of globalization many people in the world now live longer than before and their standard of living is far better. People in the West may regard low-paying jobs at Nike as exploitation, but for many people in the developing world, working in a factory is a far better option than staying down on the farm and growing rice.
>
> Globalization has reduced the sense of isolation felt in much of the developing world and has given many people in the developing countries access to knowledge well beyond the reach of even the wealthiest in any country a century ago ... Even when there are negative sides to globalization, there are often benefits. Opening up the Jamaican milk market to US imports in 1992 may have hurt local dairy farmers but it also meant poor children could get milk more cheaply. New foreign firms may hurt protected state-owned enterprises but they can also lead to the introduction of new technologies, access to new markets, and the creation of new industries.[52]

However, Stiglitz continued:

> Those who vilify globalization too often overlook its benefits. But the proponents of globalization have been, if anything, even more unbalanced. To them, globalization (which typically is associated with accepting triumphant capitalism, American style) *is* progress; developing countries must accept it, if they are to grow and to fight poverty effectively. But to many in the developing world, globalization has not brought the promised economic benefits.
>
> A growing divide between the haves and the have-nots has left increasing numbers in the Third World in dire poverty, living on less than a dollar a day. Despite repeated promises of poverty reduction made over the last decade of the twentieth century, the actual number of people living in poverty has actually increased by almost 100 million. This occurred at the same time that total world income actually increased by an average of 2.5 per cent annually.[53]

---

[50] From the Address by UN Secretary General Kofi Annan in Davos, Switzerland, on 28 January 2001 to the World Economic Forum, www.unis.unvienna.org/unis/pressrels/2001/sg2772.html, visited on 13 August 2003.
[51] J. Bhagwati, 'Globalization in Your Face', *Foreign Affairs*, July/August 2000, 137.
[52] J. Stiglitz, *Globalization and Its Discontents* (Penguin, 2002), 4–5.
[53] *Ibid.*, 5.

Elsewhere, Stiglitz wrote about the problems and dangers of current economic globalisation and trade liberalisation:

> We should be frank. Trade liberalization, conducted in the wrong way, too fast, in the absence of adequate safety nets, with insufficient reciprocity and assistance on the part of developed countries, can contribute to an increase in poverty...
>
> Complete openness can expose a country to greater risk from external shocks. Poor countries may find it particularly hard to buffer these shocks and to bear the costs they incur, and they typically have weak safety nets, or none at all, to protect the poor. These shocks, resulting essentially from contagion associated with globalization, integration and interdependence can affect workers and employers in the developed world. It must be said, however, that highly industrialized countries are able to deal with these shocks a lot better through re-employment and through other safety nets ...
>
> In summary, while I recognize that there are costs associated with liberalization, which animate much of the support for restrictive trade practices, I am convinced that the benefits of trade liberalization far outweigh these costs. These do not give us license to ignore the costs. Developed countries have recognized the costs, including the political costs, within their own countries, and have introduced provisions in trade agreements that begin to address them.[54]

Dani Rodrik observed that the international integration of markets for goods, services and capital is pressuring societies to alter their traditional practices. In response, broad segments of these societies are putting up a fight:

> Ask business executives and government officials why these changes are necessary, and you will hear the same mantra repeatedly: 'We need to remain (or become) competitive in a global economy'. The opposition to these changes is no less tangible and sometimes makes for strange bedfellows. Labor unions decrying unfair competition from underage workers overseas and environmentalists are joined by billionaire businessmen Ross Perot and Sir James Goldsmith in railing against the North American Free Trade Agreement (NAFTA) and the World Trade Organization (WTO). In the United States, perhaps the most free-market-oriented of advanced industrial societies, the philosophical foundations of the classic liberal state have come under attack not only from traditional protectionists but also from the new communitarian movement, which emphasizes moral and civic virtue and is inherently suspicious of the expansion of markets ... The process that has come to be called 'globalization' is exposing a deep fault line between groups who have the skills and mobility to flourish in global markets and those who either don't have these advantages or perceive the expansion of unregulated markets as inimical to social stability and deeply held norms.[55]

Rodrik identified and discussed three sources of tension between the global market and social stability in developed countries:

> First, reduced barriers to trade and investment accentuate the asymmetry between groups that can cross international borders (either directly or indirectly, say through outsourcing) and those that cannot. In the first category are owners of capital, highly skilled workers, and many professionals, who are free to take their resources where they are most in demand. Unskilled and semiskilled workers and most middle

---

[54] J. Stiglitz, 'Addressing Developing Country Priorities and Needs in the Millennium Round', in R. Porter and P. Sauvé (eds.), *Seattle, the WTO and the Future of the Multilateral Trading System* (Harvard University Press, 2000), 31–60, at 53–5.

[55] D. Rodrik, *Has Globalization Gone Too Far?* (Institute for International Economics, 1997), 2.

managers belong to the second category ... The fact that 'workers' can be more easily substituted for each other across national boundaries undermines what many conceive to be a post-war social bargain between workers and employers, under which the former would receive a steady increase in wages and benefits in return for labor peace ...

Second, globalization engenders conflicts within and between nations over domestic norms and the social institutions that embody them. As the technology for manufactured goods becomes standardized and diffused internationally, nations with very different sets of values, norms, institutions, and collective preferences begin to compete head on in markets for similar goods. And the spread of globalization creates opportunities for trade between countries at very different levels of development ... Trade becomes contentious when it unleashes forces that undermine the norms implicit in domestic practices ... We cannot understand what is happening in these new areas until we take individual preferences for processes and the social arrangements that embody them seriously. In particular, by doing so we can start to make sense of people's uneasiness about the consequences of international economic integration and avoid the trap of automatically branding all concerned groups as self-interested protectionists ...

Third, globalization has made it exceedingly difficult for governments to provide social insurance – one of their central functions and one that has helped maintain social cohesion and domestic political support for ongoing liberalization throughout the postwar period. In essence, governments have used their fiscal powers to insulate domestic groups from excessive market risks, particularly those having an external origin. In fact, there is a striking correlation between an economy's exposure to foreign trade and the size of its welfare state ... At the present, however, international economic integration is taking place against the background of receding governments and diminished social obligations ... Moreover, the increasing mobility of capital has rendered an important segment of the tax base footloose, leaving governments with the unappetizing option of increasing tax rates disproportionately on labor income. Yet the need for social insurance for the vast majority of the population that remains internationally immobile has not diminished.

... The question therefore is how the tension between globalization and the pressures for socialization of risks can be eased. If the tension is not managed intelligently and creatively, the danger is that the domestic consensus in favor of open markets will ultimately erode to the point where a generalized resurgence of protectionism becomes a serious possibility.[56]

In reply to the question contained in the title of his book, *Has Globalization Gone Too Far?*, Rodrik stated that, in his opinion, this is not the case if 'policymakers act wisely and imaginatively'.[57]

In *The Lexus and the Olive Tree*, Thomas Friedman also saw the need for government action when he noted:

the more I observed the system of globalization at work, the more obvious it was that it had unleashed forest-crushing forces of development and Disney-round-the-clock homogenization, which, if left unchecked, had the potential to destroy the environment and uproot cultures at a pace never before seen in human history.[58]

---

[56] *Ibid.*, 4–6.   [57] *Ibid.*, 9.
[58] T. Friedman, *The Lexus and the Olive Tree: Understanding Globalisation*, 2nd edition (First Anchor Books, 2000), 23.

Questions and Assignments 1.4

What are the main dangers associated with the current process of economic globalisation? Who stands to gain most from the current process of economic globalisation? Who loses?

1.2.3. Trade liberalisation versus protectionism

1.2.3.1. *The case for international trade and trade liberalisation*

Economic globalisation in general and international trade in particular is blamed by many for much that is wrong in today's world: from hunger and child labour to environmental pollution and cultural impoverishment. Is international trade beneficial to anyone other than multinational corporations, the well-educated in developed countries and privileged elites in developing countries? Can economic globalisation in general and international trade in particular benefit all humankind?

Most economists agree that countries can benefit from international trade. In 1776, Adam Smith wrote in his classic book, *The Wealth of Nations*:

> It is the maxim of every prudent master of a family, never to attempt to make at home what it will cost him more to make than to buy. The tailor does not attempt to make his own shoes, but he buys them from the shoemaker. The shoemaker does not attempt to make his own cloths, but employs a tailor. The farmer attempts to make neither the one nor the other, but employs those different artificers. All of them find it for their interest to employ their whole industry in a way in which they have some advantage over their neighbours, and to purchase with a part of its produce, or what is the same thing, with the price of a part of it, whatever else they have occasion for.
>
> What is prudence in the conduct of every private family, can scarce be folly in that of a great kingdom. If a foreign country can supply us with a commodity cheaper than we ourselves can make it, better buy it of them with some part of the produce of our own industry, employed in a way in which we have some advantage. The general industry of the country, ... will not thereby be diminished, no more than the above-mentioned artificers; but only left to find out the way in which it can be employed with the greatest advantage. It is certainly not employed to the greatest advantage, when it is thus directed towards an object which it can buy cheaper than it can make.[59]

Smith's lucid and compelling argument for specialisation and international trade was further built upon by David Ricardo who, in his 1817 book, *The Principles of Political Economy and Taxation*, developed the theory of 'comparative advantage'. This theory is still the predominant explanation for why countries, even the poorest, can and do benefit from international trade.

> What did the classical economist David Ricardo (1772–1823) mean when he coined the term *comparative advantage*? Suppose country A is better than country B at making automobiles, and country B is better than country A at making bread. It is obvious

---

[59] A. Smith, *An Inquiry into the Nature and Causes of the Wealth of Nations* (1776), edited by E. Cannan (University of Chicago Press, 1976), Vol. 1, 478–9.

(the academics would say 'trivial') that both would benefit if A specialized in auto-mobiles, B specialized in bread and they traded their products. That is a case of *absolute* advantage. But what if a country is bad at making everything? Will trade drive all producers out of business? The answer, according to Ricardo, is no. The reason is the principle of comparative advantage, arguably the single most powerful insight in economics. According to the principle of comparative advantage, countries A and B still stand to benefit from trading with each other even if A is better than B at making everything, both automobiles and bread. If A is much more superior at making automobiles and only slightly superior at making bread, then A should still invest resources in what it does best – producing automobiles – and export the product to B. B should still invest in what it does best – making bread – and export that product to A, even if it is not as efficient as A. Both would still benefit from the trade. A country does not have to be best at anything to gain from trade. That is *comparative* advantage. The theory is one of the most widely accepted among economists. It is also one of the most misunderstood among non-economists because it is confused with *absolute* advantage. It is often claimed, for example, that some countries have no comparative advantage in anything. That is virtually impossible. Think about it . . .[60]

The Ricardo model is of course a vast simplification, in that it is built on two products and two countries only and assumes constant costs and constant prices. Many of the complexities of the modern economy are not taken into account in this model. Economists in the twentieth century have endea-voured to refine and build on the classic Ricardo model. While pushing the analysis further, the refined models, such as the Hekscher-Ohlin model, have confirmed the basic conclusions drawn from the Ricardo model con-cerning the theory of comparative advantage and the gains from trade via specialisation.[61]

While the theory of comparative advantage has won approval from most economists ever since the early nineteenth century and continues to win approval,[62] Jagdish Bhagwati observed in *Free Trade Today* that it has only infrequently carried credibility with the populace at large. In search for an explanation, he noted:

Part of the reason has to do with the counterintuitive nature of the argument that free trade leads to greater good. When asked by the mathematician Stanislaw Ulam (the brother of the great historian Adam Ulam) which proposition in the social science was the most counterintuitive yet compelling, Paul Samuelson chose the law of compara-tive advantage: in other words, the underlying argument for free trade. Most people think it intuitively sound that you should do most things that you do better than others, not specialize.[63]

---

[60] WTO Secretariat, *Trading into the Future*, 2nd edition (WTO, 1998), 8–9. See also www.wto.org, visited on 15 May 2004.

[61] Note, however, as Jagdish Bhagwati does, that: 'The case of free trade rests on the extension to an open economy of the case for market-determined allocation of resources. If market prices reflect "true" or social costs, then clearly Adam Smith's invisible hand can be trusted to guide us to efficiency; and free trade can correspondingly be shown to be the optimal way to choose trade (and associated domestic production). But if markets do not work well, or are absent or incomplete, then the invisible hand may point in the wrong direction: free trade cannot then be asserted to be the best policy.' See J. Bhagwati, *Free Trade Today* (Princeton University Press, 2002), 12.

[62] For a dissenting, neo-Marxist view from legal scholars, see M. H. Davis and D. Neacsu, 'Legitimacy, Globally: The Incoherence of Free Trade Practice, Global Economics and Their Governing Principles of Political Economy', *Kansas City Law Review*, 2001, 733–90.

[63] J. Bhagwati, *Free Trade Today* (Princeton University Press, 2002), 5.

Paul Samuelson, Nobel Prize Winner for Economics, wrote that there is essentially only one – but one very powerful – argument for freer trade:

> Free trade promotes a mutually profitable division of labor, greatly enhances the potential real national product for all nations, and makes possible higher standards of living all over the globe.[64]

In *Trading into the Future*, the WTO argued for open international trade as follows:

> The data show a definite statistical link between freer trade and economic growth. Economic theory points to strong reasons for the link. All countries, including the poorest, have assets – human, industrial, natural, financial – which they can employ to produce goods and services for their domestic markets or to compete overseas. Economics tells us that we can benefit when these goods and services are traded. Simply put, the principle of 'comparative advantage' says that countries prosper first by taking advantage of their assets in order to concentrate on what they can produce best, and then by trading these products for products that other countries produce best.
>
> Firms do exactly that quite naturally on the domestic market. But what about the international market? Most firms recognize that the bigger the market the greater their potential – they can expand until they are at their most efficient size, and they can have access to large numbers of customers.
>
> In other words, liberal trade policies – policies that allow the unrestricted flow of goods and services – multiply the rewards that result from producing the best products, with the best design, at the best price.[65]

Supachai Panitchpakdi, WTO Director-General, commented in August 2003:

> The international business community knows from experience that severe impediments to trade hurt economic growth. A growing body of evidence indicates that open, export-oriented countries have succeeded in their development efforts, while heavily protected, inward-looking countries have not. There is a clear positive correlation between openness and income and there is little evidence that countries that have protected infant or so-called 'dynamic sectors' have done better than more open, export-oriented economies . . .
>
> An open economy that specializes in its areas of comparative advantage can make more effective investments and, at the same time, create incentives for additional investment. This generally leads to a faster rate of growth than can be achieved in less open economies.[66]

On the question whether free international trade, or rather freer international trade, leads to greater economic *growth*, Jagdish Bhagwati concluded:

> So those who assert that free trade will also lead necessarily to greater growth *either* are ignorant of the finer nuances of theory and the vast literature to the contrary on the subject at hand *or* are nonetheless basing their argument on a different premise: that is, that the preponderant evidence on the issue (in the postwar period) suggests that freer trade tends to lead to greater growth after all.[67]

---

[64] P. Samuelson, *Economics,* 10th edition (1976), 692.
[65] WTO Secretariat, *Trading into the Future*, 2nd edition (WTO, 1998), 8–9. See also at www.wto.org, visited on 1 July 2003.
[66] Supachai Panitchpakdi, 'The Doha Development Agenda: What's at Stake for Business in the Developing World?', *International Trade Forum*, August 2003, www.tradeforum.org, visited on 12 August 2003.
[67] J. Bhagwati, *Free Trade Today* (Princeton University Press, 2002), 42.

A 2001 study by the World Bank showed that the developing countries that increased their integration into the world economy in the 1980s and 1990s achieved higher growth in incomes, longer life expectancy and better schooling. These countries, home to some three billion people, enjoyed an average 5 per cent growth rate in income per capita in the 1990s compared to 2 per cent in developed countries. Many of these countries, including China and India, have adopted domestic policies and institutions that have enabled people to take advantage of global markets and have thus sharply increased the share of trade in their GDP. These countries have been catching up with the rich ones – their annual growth rates increased from 1 per cent in the 1960s to 5 per cent in the 1990s. Indeed, the World Bank's Annual Report for 2004 states that India provides 77 per cent of South Asia's GDP and that its GDP grew by 6.8 per cent in 2003. The GDPs of Bangladesh, Pakistan and Sri Lanka also grew by approximately 5.5 per cent in 2003. However, not all countries have integrated successfully into the global economy. The World Bank's 2001 report found that some 2 billion people – particularly in Sub-Saharan Africa, the Middle East and the former Soviet Union – live in countries that are being left behind. On average, these economies have contracted, poverty has increased, and education levels have risen less rapidly than in the more globalised countries.[68]

As a 2000 WTO study, *Trade, Income Disparity and Poverty*, on the relationship between international trade and poverty concluded, the evidence seems to indicate that trade liberalisation is *generally* a positive contributor to poverty alleviation. It allows people to exploit their productive potential, assists economic growth, curtails arbitrary policy interventions and helps to insulate against shocks in the domestic economy. The study warned, however, that most trade reforms will create some losers (some even in the long run), and poverty may be exacerbated temporarily, but the appropriate policy response in those cases is to alleviate the hardship and facilitate adjustments rather than abandon the reform process.[69] A 2003 WTO study, *Adjusting to Trade Liberalization*, concluded that adjustment costs are typically smaller, and sometimes much smaller, than the gains from trade.[70] Also, governments can identify individuals and groups that are likely to suffer from the adjustment process, and they can develop policies to alleviate the burden on those adversely affected.[71]

In its 2002 study, *Rigged Rules and Double Standards: Trade, Globalization, and the Fight Against Poverty*, Oxfam stated:

---

[68] P. Collier and D. Dollar, *Globalization, Growth and Poverty: Building an Inclusive World Economy* (World Bank, 2001), http://econ.worldbank.org, visited on 15 May 2004. See also J. Sachs and A. Warner, 'Economic Reform and the Process of Global Integration', *Brookings Papers on Economic Activity*, 1 (1995), 1–95; and A. Krueger, 'Trade Policy and Economic Development: How We Learn', NBER Working Paper Series (Working Paper 5896) (1997).

[69] See D. Ben-David, H. Nordström and A. Winters, *Trade, Income Disparity and Poverty*, Special Studies Series (WTO, 2000), 6.

[70] See M. Bacchetta and M. Jansen, *Adjusting to Trade Liberalization: The Role of Policy, Institutions and WTO Disciplines*, WTO Special Studies, 7 April 2003, 6.

[71] *Ibid.*

> History makes a mockery of the claim that trade cannot work for the poor. Participation in world trade has figured prominently in many of the most successful cases of poverty reduction – and, compared with aid, it has far more potential to benefit the poor.
>
> If developing countries increased their share of world exports by just 5 per cent, this would generate $350 billion – seven times as much as they receive in aid. The $70 billion that Africa would generate through a 1 per cent increase in its share of world exports is approximately five times the amount provided to the region through aid and debt relief.
>
> Apart from the financial benefits, export growth can be a more efficient engine of poverty reduction than aid. Export production can concentrate income directly in the hands of the poor, creating new opportunities for employment and investment in the process.

Experience from East Asia illustrates what is possible when export growth is broadbased. Since the mid-1970s, rapid growth in exports has contributed to a wider process of economic growth which has lifted more than 400 million people out of poverty. In countries such as Vietnam and Uganda, production for export markets has helped to generate unprecedented declines in the levels of rural poverty. Where export growth is based on labour-intensive manufactured goods, as in Bangladesh, it can generate large income gains for women.[72]

International trade not only has the potential for bringing economic benefits, there may also be considerable non-economic gains. International trade increases both the incentives for not making war and the costs of going to war. International trade intensifies cross-border contacts and exchange of ideas, which may contribute to better mutual understanding. In a free trading world, other countries and their people are more readily seen as business partners, less as enemies. On the contrary, a country taking trade restrictive measures directly inflicts economic hardship upon exporting countries. Therefore, trade protectionism is a festering source of conflict. Likewise, international trade can make an important contribution to peaceful and constructive international relations. Just two weeks after the terrorist attacks of 11 September 2001 on the World Trade Center in New York and on the Pentagon in Washington DC, US Trade Representative Robert Zoellick made the following simple but profound statement about the importance of continued openness in trade:

> Let me be clear where I stand: Erecting new barriers and closing old borders will not help the impoverished. It will not feed hundreds of millions struggling for subsistence. It will not liberate the persecuted. It will not improve the environment in developing countries or reverse the spread of AIDS. It will not help the railway orphans I visited in India. It will not improve the livelihoods of the union members I met in Latin America. It will not aid the committed Indonesians I visited who are trying to build a functioning, tolerant democracy in the largest Muslim nation in the world.[73]

---

[72] Oxfam, *Rigged Rules and Double Standards: Trade, Globalization, and the Fight Against Poverty*, 2002, Summary of Chapter 2, http://www.maketradefair.org, visited on 11 August 2003.

[73] As reported by the then WTO Director-General Mike Moore in a speech to the Foreign Affairs Commission of the French Assemblée Nationale in October 2001. http://www.wto.org, visited on 6 February 2004.

However, as Edward Alden wrote in the *Financial Times* in February 2003:

> US trade policy risks isolating the Muslim states that are on the front line in the war on terrorism, according to a study released on Tuesday. The report – from the Washington-based Progressive Policy Institute – warns that the Muslim world has been 'the blank spot on the map of the Bush administration's trade policy'. It adds: 'That policy risks undermining, rather than supporting, the war on terrorism.' The failing economies of many Muslim states have been repeatedly acknowledged by the White House as fertile recruiting grounds for terrorist groups. But critics say the US has done little to tackle the problem, and has been stingy with trade concessions to some of its closest allies in the war on terrorism. Kursheed Kasuri, Pakistan's foreign minister, said last week that 'economics is the key to fighting terrorism', and criticised Washington for failing to offer greater trade concessions. Pakistan had hoped for about $1 billion in additional sales of textiles and clothing to the US to offset the costs of the war on terrorism, but – under pressure from its own textile industry – the US granted just $143m.[74]

Apart from peaceful relations between nations, open international trade may also promote democracy. In *Free Trade Today*, Jagdish Bhagwati observed:

> One could argue this proposition by a syllogism: openness to the benefits of trade brings prosperity that, in turn, creates or expands the middle class that then seeks the end of authoritarianism. This would fit well with the experience in South Korea, for instance. It was also the argument that changed a lot of minds when the issue of China's entry into the WTO came up in the US Congress recently. I guess there is something to it.[75]

It has been reported that international trade and investment have already had a certain impact on the political system in China:

> Not only is the southern boom town of Shenzhen about to be designated a test-bed for the boldest political reform since the 1949 revolution but cities in coastal China are also embarking on experiments to introduce checks and balances to single party rule. Yu Youjun, mayor of Shenzhen, said in an interview that the wishes of multinational corporations were one motive for the city's experiment. Foreign companies, especially those establishing high-technology factories, are mindful of the need to protect intellectual property. For this, they need a fair local government. 'Every multinational company and investor is influenced by the investment environment created by governments', said Mr Yu, whose city was chosen 22 years ago as a laboratory for China's first capitalist reforms and now leads the country in per capita income. The 'hard environment' of roads, railways, ports and telecommunications was important for multinationals, Mr Yu said. But more crucial was the 'soft environment', meaning a government that is 'democratic' and transparent. 'We have made achievements in building our economic structural reform', said Mr Yu. 'Now we need to make reforms to our political system to promote democratic politics.'[76]

1.2.3.2. *Reasons and excuses for protectionist trade policies*

While most economists advise that countries should – in their own interest and that of the world at large – pursue policies aimed at promoting international

---

[74] E. Alden, 'US Trade Policy "Isolates Muslim States"', *Financial Times*, 4 February 2003.
[75] J. Bhagwati, *Free Trade Today* (Princeton University Press, 2002), 43–4.
[76] D. Roberts and J. Kynge, 'The New Workshop of the World', *Financial Times*, 3 February 2003.

trade and exchange goods and services on the basis of their comparative advantage, political decision-makers do not necessarily heed this wise advice. In fact, countries actively intervene in international trade by adopting trade restrictive measures. Why do countries adopt protectionist trade measures? Why do they restrict international trade?

There are numerous and varied reasons why countries take trade restrictive measures. A prime reason for a country to take trade restrictive measures is to protect a domestic industry and employment in that industry from competition arising from imported products or commercial services. As noted in the 2003 WTO study on *Adjusting to Trade Liberalization*:

> In the United States, for instance, 45,000 steelworkers have lost their jobs since 1997 and 30 per cent of the country's steel making capacity has filed for bankruptcy since 1998, while steel imports were on the rise. In Mozambique liberalization of trade in cashew nuts resulted in 8,500 of 10,000 cashew processing workers losing their jobs.[77]

When a domestic industry is in crisis and jobs are lost, the political decision-makers may well 'scramble for shelter'[78] by adopting protectionist measures. This may happen even when the decision-makers are well aware that such measures are by no means the best response to the crisis in the industry concerned. While the import competition would probably benefit most of their constituents (through lower prices, better quality and/or more choice), import competition is likely to hurt a small group of their constituents significantly (through lower salaries or job loss). If this small group is vocal and well organised, as it often is, it will put a great deal of pressure on the elected decision-makers to take protectionist measures for the benefit of the few and to the detriment of the many. In such a situation, protectionism can constitute 'good' politics.[79] The *public choice theory* explains that, when the majority of the voters are unconcerned with the (*per capita* small) losses they suffer, the vote-maximising political decision-makers will ignore the interests of the many, and support the interests of the vocal and well-organised few. However, as discussed above, such measures eventually leave everyone worse off. Joseph Stiglitz, reflecting on his own experience as Chairman of the Council of Economic Advisors in the Clinton Administration, observed in this respect:

> One might have thought that each country would promote liberalization in those sectors where it had most to gain from a societal perspective; and similarly, that it would be most willing to give up protectionism in those sectors where protection was costing the most. But political logic prevails over economic logic: after all, if economic logic dominated, countries would engage in trade liberalization on their own. High levels of protection are usually indicative of strong political forces, and these higher barriers may be the last to give way … The political force behind the resistance to free trade is a simple one: Although the country as a whole may be better off under free trade, some special interests will actually be worse off. And although policy could in

---

[77] M. Bacchetta and M. Jansen, *Adjusting to Trade Liberalization: The Role of Policy, Institutions and WTO Disciplines*, WTO, 7 April 2003, 6.

[78] *The Economist*, 3 October 1998, Survey World Trade, 3.

[79] B. Hoekman and M. Kostecki, *The Political Economy of the World Trading System*, 2nd edition (Oxford University Press, 2001), 22.

> principle rectify this situation (by using redistribution to make everybody better off), in actuality, the required compensations are seldom paid ... We must recognize that because the real costs to particular individuals of trade liberalization are likely to be greater in the developing world, as these countries become more democratic, the trade liberalization agenda may be increasingly difficult.[80]

Another reason for national decision-makers to pursue a protectionist trade policy is *infant industry protection.* The argument for infant industry protection was already made by Alexander Hamilton in 1791, Friedrich List in 1841 and John Stuart Mill in 1848, and has been invoked many times since. In the nineteenth century, the infant manufacturing industries of the United States and Germany were protected against import competition on the basis of this argument. Today, this argument may be of particular relevance to developing countries, which may find that while they have a potential comparative advantage in certain industries, new producers in developing countries cannot (yet) compete with established producers in the industrial countries. By means of a customs duty or other import restriction, temporary protection is then given to the national producers to allow them to become strong enough to compete with well-established producers. The infant industry argument for protectionist measures has definitely some appeal and validity. However, protecting the new producers from import competition does not necessarily remedy the problems that caused the new producers to be uncompetitive. Furthermore, the success of an infant industry policy crucially depends on a correct diagnosis of which industries could over time become competitive. It is often very difficult for governments to identify, in an objective manner and free from pressure from special interest groups, the new industries that merit protection. Moreover, in practice, the protection, which is by nature intended to be temporary, frequently becomes permanent. When it becomes clear that the protected national industry will never 'grow up' and will always be unable to face import competition, it is often politically difficult to remove the protection in place.[81]

When a country is in a position to lower the price it pays for imports by restricting its imports, national decision-makers of that country may also be tempted to adopt trade restrictive measures on the basis of the *optimal tariff* argument. If a country can reduce world demand for a product, by raising the tariff on that product, it may make economic sense to raise the tariff, and thus restrict trade, because this will lead to the cutting of the world price of the product concerned. In this way, a country can tilt the terms of trade in its favour. Alan Deardorff and Robert Stern noted in this respect:

> The idealized assumptions of the classic argument for free trade imply the optimality of free trade only for the world as a whole. For individual countries the optimality of free trade requires the additional assumption that the country is too small to have any

[80] J. Stiglitz, 'Addressing Developing Country Priorities and Needs in the Millennium Round', in R. Porter and P. Sauvé (eds.), *Seattle, the WTO and the Future of the Multilateral Trading System* (Harvard University Press, 2000), 51–3.

[81] A. Deardorff and R. Stern, 'Current Issues in US Trade Policies: An Overview', in R. Stern (ed.), *US Trade Policies in a Changing World Economy* (MIT, 1987), 39–40.

influence, through its policies, over the prices at which it trades. Without that assumption it is well known that free trade is not optimal from a national perspective and instead that there exists an optimal degree of trade intervention, known as the optimal tariff, that works by turning the country's terms of trade in its favor ... This argument is sometimes thought to require that the country in question be large and therefore to apply only to such large industrialized countries as the US. However, the argument applies to some extent to any country that is not insignificantly small. Furthermore the size that is important is not the size of the country as a whole but rather its share of world trade in markets in which it exports and imports.

However, as Deardoff and Stern observed, it is a key feature of the optimal tariff argument that it involves gains by one country at other countries' expense. It is thus referred to as an 'exploitative intervention' policy.

Such policies are typically available to more than one country, each of which can have adverse effects on the others (and even many), and therefore require that strategic issues be considered. Like other forms of exploitative intervention the optimal tariff argument is likely to find countries in the classic position of the Prisoners' Dilemma; that is, each country has available a policy that will benefit itself at the expense of others, but if all countries simultaneously pursue that policy, all are likely to lose.[82]

A relatively new argument for national decision-makers to opt for trade restrictions is the *strategic trade policy* argument. In an industry with economies of scale, a country may, by imposing a tariff or quantitative restriction and thus reserving the domestic market for a domestic firm, allow that firm to cut its costs and undercut foreign competitors in other markets. This may work in an industry where economies of scale are sufficiently large that there is only room for very few profitable companies in the world market. Economists reckon that this might be the case for civil aircraft, semiconductors and cars.[83] The aim of government intervention is to ensure that the domestic rather than a foreign company establishes itself on the world market and thus contributes to the national economic welfare. However, as Paul Krugman noted:

Strategic trade policy aimed at securing excess returns for domestic firms and support for industries that are believed to yield national benefits are both beggar-thy-neighbour policies and raise income at the expense of other countries. A country that attempts to use such policies will probably provoke retaliation. In many (though not all) cases, a trade war between two interventionist governments will leave both countries worse off than if a hands-off approach were adopted by both.[84]

This does not mean that such policies will not be pursued, because, as Krugman also pointed out:

Governments do not necessarily act in the national interest, especially when making detailed microeconomic interventions. Instead, they are influenced by interest group pressures. The kinds of interventions that new trade theory suggests can raise national income will typically raise the welfare of small, fortunate groups by large amounts, while imposing costs on larger, more diffuse groups. The result, as with any

---

[82] *Ibid.*, 37–8.　　[83] Survey World Trade, *The Economist*, 3 October 1998, 6.
[84] P. Krugman, 'Is Free Trade Passé?', *Journal of Economic Perspectives*, 1987, 141.

microeconomic policy, can easily be that excessive or misguided intervention takes place because the beneficiaries have more knowledge and influence than the losers .[85]

Trade restrictive measures, and, in particular, customs duties, have also been and still are imposed to *generate revenue for government*. Taxing trade is an easy method to collect revenue. While taxation of trade for revenue is no longer significant for developed countries, for many developing country governments customs duties remain a significant source of revenue.[86]

Governments also adopt trade restrictive measures for reasons of *national security and self-sufficiency*. The steel industry, as well as farmers, can, for example, be heard to argue that their presence and prosperity is essential to the national security of the country. The basic argument is that a country should be able to rely on its domestic industries and farmers to meet its basic needs for vital material and food, because it will be impossible to rely – in times of crisis and conflict – on imports from other countries. Allan Sykes noted in this respect:

> The likelihood of imports becoming unavailable in wartime must then be carefully considered. For a nation like the United States, serious interruption of seaborne commercial traffic seems unlikely to occur for most goods and commodities in any scenario short of global conventional conflict on the scale of World War II. The probability of such conflict seems small at best in the nuclear age. Further, in the event of an interruption in seaborne traffic, adjacent trading partners may be able to take up much of the slack on many items . . .
>
> Where interruption of necessary imports seems a serious risk, the next issue is whether domestic capacity can be restored with reasonable dispatch. Even if an industry has closed down certain productive facilities that might be needed in wartime, it does not follow that those facilities cannot be reopened or rebuilt quickly enough to satisfy essential needs.
>
> Finally, stockpiling during peacetime may well be a superior alternative to the protection of domestic capacity. Where the item in question is not perishable, a nation might be better off by buying up a supply of vital material at low prices in an open trading system than to burden itself over time with the high prices attendant on protectionism as a hedge against armed conflict. The funds tied up in a stockpile have some opportunity cost to be sure, but this cost can easily be smaller than the costs of excluding efficient foreign suppliers from the domestic market. In the end, therefore, arguments for protectionism from the national security perspective require careful scrutiny and will rarely hold up to it.[87]

Finally, and to an ever more significant extent, governments adopt trade restrictive measures, or measures that have a trade restrictive effect, in pursuit of non-economic societal values such as public morals, public health, consumer safety, a clean environment and cultural identity. Trade in products or services that do not meet specific health, safety or environmental regulations or standards or that may, more generally, threaten a fundamental societal value may be prohibited or significantly limited. Many of such trade restrictive measures are not only legitimate but also necessary. Other such measures, however, are mere fronts for protectionist measures intending to shield

---

[85] *Ibid.*   [86] See below, p. 379.
[87] J. Jackson, W. Davey and A. Sykes, *Legal Problems of International Economic Relations*, 4th edition (Westgroup, 2002), 20–1.

domestic producers from import competition. Protectionism can take on very sophisticated guises.[88]

Questions and Assignments 1.5

Why is it that according to most economists even the poorest countries can, at least in theory, benefit from international trade? Why do governments resort to trade restrictive measures?

1.2.4. Globalisation and trade to the benefit of all?

In presenting the United Nations Millennium Report to the UN General Assembly in April 2000, Secretary General Kofi Annan spoke of addressing the inequities of globalisation as the 'overarching challenge' of our times. In this presentation to the General Assembly, he argued as follows:

> the benefits of globalization are obvious ...: faster growth; higher living standards; and new opportunities, not only for individuals, but also for better understanding between nations, and for common action. One problem is that, at present, these opportunities are far from equally distributed. How can we say that the half of the human race, which has yet to make or receive a telephone call, let alone use a computer, is taking part in globalization? We cannot, without insulting their poverty. A second problem is that, even where the global market does reach, it is not yet underpinned, as national markets are, by rules based on shared social objectives. In the absence of such rules, globalization makes many people feel they are at the mercy of unpredictable forces.
>
> So, Mr President, the overarching challenge of our times is to make globalization mean more than bigger markets. To make a success of this great upheaval, we must learn how to govern better, and – above all – how to govern better together. We need to make our States stronger and more effective at the national level. And we need to get them working together on global issues, all pulling their weight and all having their say.[89]

In the Millennium Declaration adopted by the UN General Assembly on 8 September 2000, the Heads of State and Government of the Members of the United Nations solemnly declared:

> We believe that the central challenge we face today is to ensure that globalization becomes a positive force for all the world's people. For while globalization offers great opportunities, at present its benefits are very unevenly shared, while its costs are unevenly distributed. We recognize that developing countries and countries with economies in transition face special difficulties in responding to this central challenge. Thus, only through broad and sustained efforts to create a shared future, based upon our common humanity in all its diversity, can globalization be made fully inclusive and equitable. These efforts must include policies and measures, at the global level, which correspond to the needs of developing countries and economies in transition and are formulated and implemented with their effective participation.[90]

---

[88] See below, pp. 457–80.
[89] United Nations General Assembly, *UN Millennium Declaration*, Resolution adopted on 8 September 2000, para. 11.
[90] *Ibid.*, para. 5.

Three years later, at the Cancún Session of the WTO Ministerial Conference in September 2003, Kofi Annan noted not without a certain measure of frustration:

> The reality of the international trading system today does not match the rhetoric (of improving the quality of life). Instead of open markets, there are too many barriers that stunt, stifle and starve. Instead of fair competition, there are subsidies by rich countries that tilt the playing field against the poor. And instead of global rules negotiated by all, in the interest of all, and adhered to by all, there is too much closed-door decision-making, too much protection of special interests, and too many broken promises.[91]

In its 2002 study, *Rigged Rules and Double Standards: Trade, Globalization, and the Fight Against Poverty*, Oxfam formulated recommendations and suggestions to make economic globalisation and international trade work for the poor. According to Oxfam, international trade can realise its full potential only if rich and poor countries alike take action to *redistribute opportunities* in favour of the poor. This will require action at the national level, new forms of international cooperation, and a new architecture of global governance at the WTO. With respect to action at the national level, Oxfam observed:

> The challenge of extending opportunity at the national level goes beyond the narrow confines of trade policy. Inequalities in health and education services, and in the ownership of assets, are a formidable barrier to making markets work for poor people. Lacking access to land, marketing infrastructure, and financial resources, the poor are often least equipped to take advantage of market opportunities, and the most vulnerable to competition from imports.
>
> In many countries, extensive corruption and excessive bureaucracy act as a tax on trade – and the tax falls most heavily on the poor.[92]

With respect to international cooperation, Oxfam noted:

> International cooperation must be strengthened in a range of areas. Developing countries need development assistance if they are to integrate into world markets on more favourable terms and to extend opportunities to the poor.
>
> Yet rich countries reduced their aid budgets by $13 billion between 1992 and 2000. Some of the heaviest cuts fell on the poorest countries and in areas – such as agriculture – where well-targeted aid can make a difference to levels of poverty.
>
> Failure to resolve the long-standing debt problems of low-income countries, and to respond effectively to new problems in private capital markets, poses further threats. There is a growing danger that many developing countries will be forced by unsustainable debt to transfer the wealth that is generated by exports to creditors in rich countries.[93]

With respect to a new architecture of global governance at the WTO, Oxfam stated:

> The WTO is one of the youngest international institutions, but it is old before its time. Behind the façade of a 'membership-driven' organisation is a governance system based on a dictatorship of wealth. Rich countries have a disproportionate influence. This is

---

[91] See www.wto.mvs.com/mino3_webcast_e.htm/archives, visited on 31 May 2004.
[92] Oxfam, *Rigged Rules and Double Standards: Trade, Globalization, and the Fight Against Poverty*, 2002, Summary of Chapter 9, http://www.maketradefair.org/en/index.php?file=03042002174753.htm&cat=3&subcat=3&select=12, visited on 15 June 2004.
[93] *Ibid.*

> partly because of a failure of representational democracy. Each WTO country may have one vote, but eleven of its members among the least-developed countries are not even represented at the WTO base in Geneva.
>
> Informal power-relations reinforce inequalities in negotiating capacity at the WTO. Meanwhile, beyond the WTO, powerful TNCs exercise a disproportionate influence over the direction of trade policy. Reforms to trade governance are needed in order to make trade work for the poor at all levels.[94]

Oxfam correctly states that, just as in any national economy, economic integration in the global economy can be a source of shared prosperity and poverty reduction, or a source of increasing inequality and exclusion:

> Managed well, the international trading system can lift millions out of poverty. Managed badly, it will leave whole economies even more marginalised. The same is true at a national level. Good governance can make trade work in the interests of the poor. Bad governance can make it work against them.[95]

According to Oxfam, international trade is at present badly managed, both at the global level and, in many countries, at the national level.[96]

In a reaction to this study, the European Commission took issue with Oxfam's finding that the European Union is the most protectionist of the large trading entities *but* fully supported Oxfam's analysis of how trade could help to fight poverty. Commenting on the report, EU Trade Commissioner Pascal Lamy said:

> The Oxfam report is a substantive and in general well-researched contribution to the debate on the link between trade and development. I fully share the basic philosophy underlying the report: trade has the potential to lift millions out of poverty (and this is borne out by past experience, for instance in East Asia), but the benefits of trade are not automatic – a lot depends on the domestic context.[97]

In a speech to the G-20 Finance Ministers and Central Bank Governors in November 2001, James Wolfensohn, the President of the World Bank, made the following analysis of the challenge of economic globalisation:

> In my view, with the improvements in both technology and policies that we have seen over recent decades, some form of globalization is with us to stay. But the kind of globalization is not yet certain: it can be either a *globalization of development and poverty reduction* – such as we have begun to see in recent decades, although this trend still cannot be taken for granted – or a *globalization of conflict, poverty, disease, and inequality*. What can we do to tip the scales decisively toward the right kind of globalization?[98]

To ensure that economic globalisation and trade liberalisation contribute to economic development, equity and the well-being of all people, the President of the World Bank advocated the following four-point agenda for action: better governance, reduction of trade barriers, more development aid and better international cooperation.

---

[94] *Ibid.*   [95] *Ibid.*   [96] *Ibid.*

[97] European Commission, Memorandum, Brussels, 22 April 2002, www.europa.eu.int, visited on 15 July 2004.

[98] 'Responding to the Challenges of Globalization', Remarks to the G-20 Finance Ministers and Central Bank Governors by James D. Wolfensohn, President, World Bank Group, Ottawa, 17 November 2001, www.worldbank.org, visited on 15 November 2002.

First, developing countries must continue the move toward *better policies, investment climate, and governance*. Despite progress in macroeconomic management and openness, there remain many domestic barriers to integration. Many countries have fallen short in creating an investment climate for productivity, growth, entrepreneurship, and jobs. These domestic barriers include inadequate transport infrastructure, poor governance, bureaucratic harassment of small businesses, a lack of electric power, an unskilled workforce. Even with access to foreign markets, a firm is unlikely to export if the environment hinders entrepreneurship and productive activity. And countries also need to make possible the participation of poor people in growth, through support for targeted education, health, social protection, and their involvement in key decisions that shape their lives. Poor people need much greater voice.

Second, all countries – developed and developing – must *reduce trade barriers* and give developing countries a better chance in world markets. . . . Rich countries must increase market access for the exports of developing countries, through both multilateral negotiations and unilateral action, to increase the payoffs to developing-country policy and institutional reforms. Dismantling trade barriers, as our recent publication *Global Economic Prospects: Making Trade Work for the World's Poor* shows, could increase income in developing countries by an estimated $1.5 trillion over a decade and increase GDP growth in the developing countries by 0.5 per cent per year over the long run. This in turn would lift an additional 300 million people out of poverty by 2015 (even beyond the 600 million that will escape poverty with the growth we are currently anticipating). But to make this happen, the developed countries must be willing to put textiles on the negotiating table in addition to agriculture. We must also press ahead with capacity-building to help developing countries negotiate as equal partners. Outside the WTO framework, the Bank, together with other international financial institutions and agencies, can provide "aid for trade" through stepped-up development assistance. This means supporting both the hard and soft infrastructure inside the border – for example, modern ports as well as an efficient customs service – that makes trade expansion possible.

Third, developed countries must *increase development aid*, but allocate it better and cut down the burden its implementation can impose. Private capital flows to developing countries are falling sharply, from $240 billion in 2000 to an estimated $160 billion this year. This makes it still more important that governments increase official assistance. The evidence from the Bank's research is that well-directed aid, combined with strong reform efforts, can greatly reduce poverty. If we are serious about ensuring a beneficial globalization and meeting multilateral development goals we have all signed up to, we must double ODA [overseas development aid] from its current level of about $50 billion a year.

Fourth, we must *act as a global community* where it really matters. Effective globalization requires institutions of global governance, and multilateral action to confront global problems and provide global public goods. This means confronting terrorism, internationalized crime, and money laundering, as we are doing in response to September 11th. But it also means that as a community, we need to address longer-term needs, by: combating communicable diseases like AIDS and malaria; building an equitable global trading system; promoting financial stability to prevent deep and sudden crises; and safeguarding the natural resources and environment on which so many poor people depend for their livelihoods. As we do all this, we must bring poor countries into the decision-making of this global community . . . If we can act on these four priorities, we will have created the climate to achieve true global integration and reach the multilateral development goals that we have all embraced.[99]

It must be noted, however, that not all share the 'optimism' of Annan, Oxfam and Wolfensohn. In a reaction to what some call the rhetoric of 'globalisation

[99] *Ibid.*

as opportunity', the President of Tanzania, Benjamin Mkapa, said in a statement made at the 2000 Annual Meeting of the World Economic Forum in Davos:

> Globalisation can deliver, just as Tanzania can play in the World Cup and win it.[100]

It is clear that economic openness is a necessary but not a sufficient condition for economic development and prosperity. The simple spread of markets will not eliminate poverty. A global economy and more international trade will not automatically lead to rising prosperity for all countries and for all people. Good governance is undoubtedly as important as international trade. Without functioning State institutions and without a legal system that protects fundamental rights and property and enforces contracts, globalisation will not bring prosperity but, on the contrary, poverty, corruption and exploitation.

Also, former GATT and WTO Director General and EU Commissioner, Peter Sutherland, emphasised that more than free markets are needed to eradicate poverty and inequality:

> There are those who oppose redistribution policies in principle, whether in the domestic or the international context. This is wrong. It is morally wrong, it is pragmatically wrong, and we ought not be ashamed to say so. I have been personally and deeply committed to promoting the market system through my entire career. Yet it is quite obvious to me that the market will never provide all of the answers to the problems of poverty and inequality. The fact is that there are those who will not be able to develop their economies simply because market access has been provided. I do not believe that we in the global community will adequately live up to our responsibility if we have done no more than provide the poorest people and the poorest countries with an opportunity to succeed. We must also provide them with a foundation from which they have a reasonable chance of seizing that opportunity – decent health care, primary education, basic infrastructure.[101]

It is worth noting that there may also be a cultural dimension to the issue of globalisation which may make it harder for certain countries and people to make use of the opportunity globalisation, and international trade, offers for economic development:

> Much of Latin America, for example, abandoned trade protectionism and favoritism for local companies. Between 1985 and 1996, average tariffs fell from 50 per cent to 10 per cent. The results have been modest. What explains the contrasts? Perhaps culture. The gospel of capitalism presumes that human nature is constant. Given the proper incentives – the ability to profit from hard work and risk taking – people will strive. Maybe not. In a recent book, "Culture Matters: How Values Shape Human Progress", scholars from the United States, Africa and Latin America argue that strong social and moral values predispose some peoples for and against economic growth. As a result of history, tradition and religion, some societies cannot easily adopt capitalist attitudes and institutions. Even when they try, they often fail because it is so unnatural. "Competition is central to the success of an enterprise, the politician, the intellectual and the professional", writes Mariano Grondona, an Argentine political scientist and columnist. "In resistant societies, competition is condemned as

---

[100] As reported by J. Harris, 'Globalisation and World's Poor', *Economic and Political Weekly*, 9 June 2001, 2034.

[101] P. Sutherland, 'Beyond the Market, a Different Kind of Equity', *International Herald Tribune*, 20 February 1997.

> a form of aggression." Daniel Etounga-Manguelle of Cameroon contends that Africa
> suffers from a reverence for its history. "In traditional African society, which exalts the
> glorious past of ancestors through tales and fables, nothing is done to prepare for the
> future", he writes. Once stated, culture's impact seems obvious.[102]

However, culture, though deep, is not immutable. Culture is changed by
experience. There are multiple examples of cultures changing over time. One
such example, India, has shifted since the late 1980s from protectionism and
State control towards pro-market policies, thereby raising annual economic
growth to about 6 per cent.[103]

Reflecting on the 'acceptability' of economic globalisation and international
trade in particular in developed countries, Dani Rodrik concluded his book *Has
Globalization Gone Too Far?* as follows:

> The broader challenge for the 21st century is to engineer a new balance between market
> and society, one that will continue to unleash the creative energies of private entre-
> preneurship without eroding the social basis of cooperation. The tensions between
> globalization and social cohesion are real, and they are unlikely to disappear of their
> own accord.[104]

The General Secretary of the International Confederation of Free Trade
Unions, Bill Jordan, wrote in December 2000:

> [G]lobalization is neither entirely beneficial nor entirely harmful. It is not an unstop-
> pable force of nature, but is shaped by those who set the rules ... The labor move-
> ment's position is simply that the rules governing globalization should protect the
> interests of the poor and not just the rich, and that the benefits of increased trade and
> increased global output should be shared by all.[105]

Joseph Stiglitz described, in *Globalization and Its Discontents*, the experience of
the United States during the nineteenth century with the formation of its
national economy and the regulating and supporting role played by the federal
government in that process.[106] According to Stiglitz, the experience of the
United States makes a good parallel for today's globalisation. The contrast
helps illustrate the successes of the past and today's failures:

> Today, with the continuing decline in transportation and communication costs, and the
> reduction of man-made barriers to the flow of goods, services, and capital (though there
> remain serious barriers to the free flow of labor), we have a process of "globalization"
> analogous to the earlier processes in which national economies were formed.
> Unfortunately, we have no world government, accountable to the people in every
> country, to oversee the globalization process in a fashion comparable to the way
> national governments guided the nationalization process. Instead, we have a system
> that might be called *global governance without global government*, one in which a few
> institutions – the World Bank, the IMF, the WTO – and a few players – the finance,
> commerce, and trade ministries, closely linked to certain financial and commercial
> interests – dominate the scene, but in which those affected by their decisions are left

---

[102] R. Samuelson, 'Persistent Poverty Defies the Wisdom on Globalization', *International Herald Tribune*,
21 September 2000.
[103] *Ibid.*
[104] D. Rodrik, *Has Globalization Gone Too Far?* (Institute for International Economics, 1997), 85.
[105] B. Jordan, 'Yes to Globalization, But Protect the Poor', *International Herald Tribune*, 21 December 2000.
[106] J. Stiglitz, *Globalization and Its Discontents* (Penguin, 2002), 21.

almost voiceless. It's time to change some of the rules governing the international economic order, to think once again about how decisions get made at the international level – and in whose interests – and to place less emphasis on ideology and to look more at what works … Globalization can be reshaped, and when it is, when it is properly, fairly run, with all countries having a voice in policies affecting them, there is a possibility that it will help to create a new global economy in which growth is not only more sustainable and less volatile but the fruits of this growth are more equitably shared.[107]

Questions and Assignments 1.6

How can economic globalisation and international trade be made 'a positive force for all the world's people' as mandated in the UN Millennium Declaration? What does Joseph Stiglitz mean when he refers to 'global governance without global government'?

1.3. INTERNATIONAL TRADE AND THE LAW OF THE WTO

As discussed above, economic globalisation and international trade need to be properly managed if they are to be of benefit to all humankind. This section discusses:

- the need for and existence of international rules for international trade; and
- the basic rules and disciplines of WTO law.

1.3.1. International rules for international trade

1.3.1.1. Need for international rules

Former GATT and WTO Director-General, Peter Sutherland, wrote in 1997:

The greatest economic challenge facing the world is the *need to create an international system* that not only maximizes global growth but also achieves a greater measure of equity, a system that both integrates emerging powers and assists currently marginalized countries in their efforts to participate in worldwide economic expansion … The most important means available to secure peace and prosperity into the future is to develop effective multilateral approaches and institutions.[108]

[Emphasis added]

These multilateral approaches and institutions, to which Sutherland referred, embrace many structures and take many forms but, as John Jackson noted:

it is very clear that law and legal norms play the most important part of the institutions which are essential to make markets work. The notion that 'rule of law' (ambiguous as

---

[107] *Ibid.*, 21–2.
[108] P. Sutherland, 'Beyond the Market, a Different Kind of Equity', *International Herald Tribune*, 20 February 1997.

> that phrase is) or a *rule-based or rule-oriented system* of human institutions is essential to a beneficial operation of markets, is a constantly recurring theme in many writings.[109]
>
> [Emphasis added]

Ronald Coase, Nobel Prize Winner for Economics, wrote:

> It is evident that, for their operation, markets … require the establishment of legal rules governing the rights and duties of those carrying out transactions … *To realize all the gains of trade*, … there has to be a legal system and political order.[110]
>
> [Emphasis added]

But what exactly is the role of legal rules and, in particular, international legal rules in international trade? How do international trade rules allow countries to realise the gains of international trade?

There are basically four related reasons why there is a need for international trade rules. First, countries must be restrained from adopting trade-restrictive measures both in their own interest and in that of the world economy. International trade rules *restrain* countries from taking trade-restrictive measures. As noted above, national policy-makers may come under considerable pressure from influential interest groups to adopt trade-restrictive measures in order to protect domestic industries from import competition. Such measures may benefit the specific, short-term interests of the groups advocating them but they very seldom benefit the general economic interests of the country adopting them.[111] As Ernst-Ulrich Petersmann observed:

> Governments know very well … that by "tying their hands to the mast" (like Ulysses when he approached the island of the Sirenes), reciprocal international pre-commitments help them to resist the siren-like temptations from "rent-seeking" interest groups at home.[112]

Countries also realise that, if they take trade-restrictive measures, other countries will do so too. This may lead to an escalation of trade-restrictive measures, a disastrous move for international trade and for global economic welfare. International trade rules help to avoid such escalation.

A second and closely related reason why international trade rules are necessary is the need of traders and investors for a degree of *security and predictability*. International trade rules offer a degree of security and predictability. Traders and investors operating, or intending to operate, in a country that is bound by such legal rules will be able to predict better how that country will act in the future on matters affecting their operations in that country. The predictability and security resulting from international trade rules will encourage

---

[109] J. Jackson, 'Global Economics and Intenational Economic Law', *Journal of International Economic Law*, 1998, 5 (reproduced by permission of Oxford University Press).

[110] R. Coase, *The Firm, the Market and the Law* (reprint of 1960 article), Chapter 5, as quoted by J. Jackson, 'Global Economics and International Economic Law', *Journal of International Economic Law*, 1998, 4.

[111] See above, pp. 25–6. On the optimal tariff argument and the strategic trade policy argument, see above, pp. 26–8.

[112] E. U. Petersmann, *The GATT/WTO Dispute Settlement System: International Law, International Organizations and Dispute Settlement* (Kluwer Law International, 1997), 36–7.

investments and trade and will thus contribute to global economic welfare. As John Jackson wrote:

> At least in the context of economic behaviour ... and particularly when that behaviour is set in circumstances of decentralized decision-making, as in a market economy, rules can have important operational functions. They may provide the only predictability or stability to a potential investment or trade-development situation. Without such predictability or stability, trade or investment flows might be even more risky and therefore more inhibited than otherwise ... To put it another way, the policies which tend to reduce some risks, lower the "risk premium" required by entrepreneurs to enter into international transactions. This should result in a general increase in the efficiency of various economic activities, contributing to greater welfare for everyone.[113]

A third reason why international trade rules are necessary is that national governments alone simply cannot *cope with the challenges presented by economic globalisation*. The protection of important societal values such as public health, a clean environment, consumer safety, cultural identity and minimum labour standards is, as a result of the greatly increased levels of trade in goods and services, no longer a purely national matter but ever more a matter with significant international ramifications. Attempts to ensure the protection of these values at the national level alone are doomed to be ineffective and futile. Worse, domestic regulatory measures regarding, for example, product safety, health, environmental protection and labour conditions may constitute import-ant barriers to trade. These measures are often not directly or expressly related to the regulation of trade but the fact that they differ from country to country acts as a significant constraint on trade. International trade rules serve to ensure that countries only maintain national regulatory measures that are *necessary* for the protection of the key societal values referred to above.[114] Furthermore, international trade rules may introduce a degree of harmonisation of domestic regulatory measures and thus ensure an effective, international protection of these societal values.[115]

A fourth and final reason why international trade rules are necessary is the need to achieve a *greater measure of equity* in international economic relations. As Father Lacordaire already stated in his renowned 1835 Conferences at the Notre Dame in Paris:

> Entre le faible et le fort, entre le riche et le pauvre ... c'est la liberté qui opprime et la loi qui affranchit.[116]

Without international trade rules, binding and enforceable on the rich as well as the poor, and rules recognising the special needs of developing countries, many of these countries would not be able to integrate fully in the world trading system and derive an equitable share of the gains of international trade.

---

[113] J. Jackson, 'Global Economics and International Economic Law ' *Journal of International Economic Law*, 1998, 5–6.
[114] See below, pp. 604–7, 609.　　[115] See below, pp. 460, 463–4.
[116] Translation: 'Between the weak and the powerful, between the rich and the poor ... it is freedom that oppresses and the law that sets free.' Abbé Jean-Baptiste Lacordaire (1802–61) was the greatest French pulpit orator of the nineteenth century.

However, for international legal rules to play these multiple roles, such rules have, of course, to be observed. It is clear that international trade rules are not always adhered to. Yet, while most attention, of both the media and academia, is inevitably paid to instances of breach, it should be stressed that international trade rules are generally well observed. Countries realise that they cannot expect other countries to observe the rules if they do not do so themselves. The desire to be able to depend on other countries' compliance with the rules leads many countries to observe the rules even though this might be politically inconvenient in a given situation.[117]

All countries and their people benefit from the existence of rules on international trade making the trading environment more predictable and stable. However, provided the rules take into account their specific interests and needs, developing countries, with generally limited economic, political and military power, should benefit even more from the existence of rules on international trade. The weaker countries are likely to suffer most where the law of the jungle reigns. They are more likely to thrive in a *rules-based*, rather than a power-based, international trading system.

Questions and Assignments 1.7

Is there a need for international rules on trade? Who benefits from these rules and why?

1.3.1.2. International economic law and WTO law

The legal rules, discussed above, governing trade relations between countries are part of international economic law. International economic law is a very broad field of international law. John Jackson once suggested that 90 per cent of international law work relates in fact to international economic law in some form or another. He also observed that international economic law does not enjoy as much glamour or media attention as work on armed conflicts and human rights do.[118]

International economic law can be defined, broadly, as covering all those international rules pertaining to economic transactions and relations, as well as those pertaining to governmental regulation of economic matters. As such, international economic law includes international rules on trade in goods and services, economic development, intellectual property rights, foreign direct investment, international finance and monetary matters, commodities, food,

---

[117] See L. Henkin, *How Nations Behave*, 2nd edition (1979); R. Fisher, *Improving Compliance with International Law* (1981); and A. Chayes, *The New Sovereignty: Compliance with International Regulatory Agreements* (1995), as referred to in J. Jackson, 'Global Economics and International Economic Law', *Journal of International Economic Law*, 1998, 5.

[118] J. Jackson, 'International Economic Law: Reflections on the "Boilerroom" of International Relations', *American University Journal of International Law and Policy*, 1995, 596.

health, transport, communications, natural resources, private commercial trans-actions, nuclear energy, etc. International rules on international trade in goods and services, i.e. international trade law, constitute the 'hard core' of inter-national economic law.

International trade law consists of, on the one hand, numerous bilateral or regional trade agreements and, on the other hand, multilateral trade agreements. Examples of bilateral and regional trade agreements are manifold. The North American Free Trade Agreement (NAFTA) and the Mercosur Agreement are typical examples of regional trade agreements. The Trade Agreement between the United States and Israel or the Agreement on Trade on Wine between the European Community and Australia are examples of bilateral trade agreements. The number of multilateral trade agreements is more limited. This group includes, for example, the 1983 International Convention on the Harmonised Commodity Description and Coding System (the 'Brussels Convention') and the 1973 International Convention on the Simplification and Harmonization of Customs Procedures, as revised in 2000 (the 'Kyoto Convention'). The most important and broadest of all multilateral trade agreements is the *Marrakesh Agreement Establishing the World Trade Organization*, concluded on 15 April 1994. It is the law of this Agreement – the law of the WTO – which is the subject-matter of this book.

Questions and Assignments 1.8

What is international economic law and what does it cover? How does WTO law relate to international economic law?

1.3.2. Basic rules and principles of WTO law

The law of the WTO is complex and specialised. It deals with a broad spectrum of issues, ranging from tariffs, import quotas and customs formalities to intellectual property rights, food safety regulations and national security measures. However, six groups of *basic rules and principles* can be distinguished:

- the principles of non-discrimination;
- the rules on market access, including rules on transparency;
- the rules on unfair trade;
- the rules on conflicts between trade liberalisation and other societal values and interests;
- the rules on special and differential treatment for developing countries; and
- a number of key institutional and procedural rules relating to decision-making and dispute settlement.

These basic rules and principles of WTO law make up what is commonly referred to as the *multilateral trading system*. Referring to this system, Peter Sutherland and others wrote in 2001:

> The multilateral trading system, with the World Trade Organization (WTO) at its centre, is the most important tool of global economic management and development we possess.[119]

Martin Wolf of the *Financial Times* noted in 2001:

> The multilateral trading system at the beginning of the twenty-first century is the most remarkable achievement in institutionalized global economic cooperation that there has ever been.[120]

The following sections of this chapter briefly review these basic rules and principles constituting the multilateral trading system. They will be discussed in greater detail in subsequent chapters of this book.

1.3.2.1. Principles of non-discrimination

There are two principles of non-discrimination in WTO law: the most-favoured-nation (MFN) treatment obligation and the national treatment obligation.

The *MFN treatment obligation* requires a WTO Member that grants certain favourable treatment to another country to grant that same favourable treatment to all other WTO Members. A WTO Member is not allowed to discriminate *between* its trading partners by, for example, giving the products imported from some countries more favourable treatment with respect to market access than the treatment it accords to the products of other Members.[121] The MFN treatment obligation is the single most important rule in WTO law. Without this rule the multilateral trading system could and would not exist. Chapter 4 examines in detail this rule as it applies to trade in goods and trade in services.[122]

The *national treatment obligation* requires a WTO Member to treat foreign products, services and service suppliers not less favourably than it treats 'like' domestic products, services and service suppliers. Where the national treatment obligation applies, foreign products, for example, should, once they have crossed the border and entered the domestic market, not be subject to less favourable taxation or regulation than 'like' domestic products. Pursuant to the national treatment obligation, a WTO Member is not allowed to discriminate *against* foreign products, services and service suppliers. The national treatment obligation is an important rule in WTO law which has given rise to many trade disputes. For trade in goods, the national treatment obligation has *general* application to all trade.[123] By contrast, for trade in services, the national treatment obligation does not have such general application. The national treatment obligation applies only to the extent a WTO Member has explicitly committed itself to grant 'national treatment' in respect of specific

---

[119] P. Sutherland, J. Sewell and D. Weiner, 'Challenges Facing the WTO and Policies to Address Global Governance', in G. Sampson, *The Role of the World Trade Organization in Global Governance* (United Nations University Press, 2001), 81.

[120] M. Wolf, 'What the World Needs from the Multilateral Trading System', in G. Sampson (ed.), *The Role of the World Trade Organization in Global Governance* (United Nations University Press, 2001), 182.

[121] Article I of the GATT 1994 and Article II of the GATS.   [122] See below, pp. 309–26.

[123] Article III of the GATT 1994.

service sectors.[124] Such commitments to give 'national treatment' are made in a Member's Schedule of Specific Commitments on Services. Chapter 4 of this book discusses in detail the national treatment obligation as it applies to trade in goods and services.[125]

1.3.2.2. Rules on market access

WTO law contains four groups of rules regarding market access:

- rules on *customs duties* (i.e. tariffs);
- rules on *other duties and financial charges*;
- rules on *quantitative restrictions*; and
- rules on *other 'non-tariff barriers'*, such as rules on transparency of trade regulations; technical regulations; standards; sanitary and phytosanitary measures; customs formalities; and government procurement practices.

Under WTO law, the imposition of customs duties is not prohibited and, in fact, WTO Members impose customs duties on many products. However, WTO law calls upon WTO Members to negotiate mutually beneficial reductions of customs duties.[126] These negotiations result in tariff concessions or bindings, set out in a Member's Schedule of Concessions. For those products for which a tariff concession or binding exists, the customs duties may no longer exceed the maximum level of duty agreed to.[127] Chapter 5 examines the rules applicable to customs duties.[128] It also discusses the rules on other duties and financial charges.[129]

While customs duties are, in principle, not prohibited, quantitative restrictions on trade in goods are, as a general rule, forbidden.[130] Unless one of many exceptions applies, WTO Members are not allowed to ban the importation or exportation of goods or to subject them to quotas. With respect to trade in services, quantitative restrictions are, in principle, prohibited in service sectors for which specific market-access commitments have been undertaken.[131] In those sectors, quantitative restrictions can be imposed if such restrictions have been inscribed in a Member's Schedule of Specific Commitments. Chapter 5 examines the rules applicable to quantitative restrictions on trade in goods and services.[132]

Among 'other non-tariff barriers', the lack of transparency of national trade regulations definitely stands out as a major barrier to international trade. Uncertainty and confusion regarding the trade rules applicable in other countries has a chilling effect on trade. Likewise, the arbitrary application of these rules also discourages traders and hampers trade. Transparency and the fair

---

[124] Article XVII of the GATS.   [125] See below, pp. 326–69.
[126] Article XXVIII *bis* of the GATT 1994.   [127] Article II of the GATT 1994.
[128] See below, pp. 377–436.   [129] See below, pp. 436–41.   [130] Article XI of the GATT 1994.
[131] Article XVI of the GATS. In fact, the prohibition of Article XVI of the GATS applies more broadly to 'market access barriers' as defined in Article XVI:2. See below, pp. 482–4.
[132] See below, pp. 441–57.

application of trade regulations are therefore part of the basic rules on market access examined in Chapter 5.[133] Non-tariff barriers to trade, such as technical regulations and standards, sanitary and phytosanitary measures, customs formalities and practices of government procurement are, for many products and in many countries, more important barriers to trade than customs duties or quantitative restrictions.[134] Rules on these and other non-tariff barriers are set out in a number of specific WTO agreements, which are examined in Chapter 5.[135]

1.3.2.3. Rules on unfair trade

WTO law, at present, does not provide for general rules on unfair trade practices, but it does have a number of relatively detailed, highly technical and complex rules that relate to specific forms of 'unfair' trade. These rules deal with dumping and subsidised trade.

Dumping, i.e. bringing a product onto the market of another country at a price less than the normal value of that product is condemned but not prohibited in WTO law. However, when the dumping causes or threatens to cause material injury to the domestic industry of a Member, WTO law allows that Member to impose anti-dumping duties on the dumped products in order to offset the dumping.[136] The rules on the imposition of these anti-dumping duties are examined in Chapter 6.

Subsidies, i.e. a financial contribution by a government or public body that confers a benefit, are subject to an intricate set of rules.[137] Some subsidies, such as export subsidies, are, as a rule, prohibited. Other subsidies are not prohibited but, when they cause adverse effects to the interests of other Members, the subsidising Member should withdraw the subsidy or take appropriate steps to remove the adverse effects. If the subsidising Member fails to do so, counter-measures commensurate with the degree and nature of the adverse effect may be authorised.[138] If a prohibited or other subsidy causes or threatens to cause material injury to the domestic industry of a Member producing a 'like' product, that Member is authorised to impose countervailing duties on the subsidised products to offset the subsidisation. Subsidies relating to agricultural products are subject to different (more lenient) rules.[139] The rules applicable to subsidies and countervailing duties are examined in Chapter 6.

---

[133] See below, pp. 457–80.

[134] Furthermore, note that many quantitative restrictions, and, in particular, many import bans, are now in the form of technical regulations (see e.g. the ban on asbestos and asbestos products in *EC – Asbestos*) or sanitary or phytosanitary measures (see e.g. the ban on hormone-treated meat in *EC – Hormones*).

[135] These specific agreements include the *TBT Agreement* and the *SPS Agreement*. See below, pp. 458–66.

[136] Article VI of the GATT 1994 and the *Anti-Dumping Agreement*.

[137] Articles VI and XVI of the GATT 1994 and the *Agreement on Subsidies and Countervailing Measures* (the '*SCM Agreement*').

[138] Until 1 January 2000, there was a third category of so-called 'non-actionable subsidies' regulated in Articles 8 and 9 of the *SCM Agreement*. However, the WTO Members failed to agree on the extension of the application of these provisions and they therefore lapsed (see Article 31 of the *SCM Agreement*).

[139] Articles 6 to 11 of the *Agreement on Agriculture*.

In addition to the rules on dumping and subsidised trade, also the rules on the protection of intellectual property rights set forth in the *Agreement on Trade-Related Intellectual Property Rights* could be regarded as rules to protect against unfair trade. These rules are briefly discussed later in this chapter, but are not examined in detail in this book.[140]

1.3.2.4. Trade liberalisation versus other societal values and interests

Apart from the basic rules and principles referred to above, WTO law also provides for a number of rules that address the conflict between trade liberalisation and other economic and non-economic societal values and interests. These rules allow WTO Members to take account of economic and non-economic values and interests that compete or conflict with free trade. The non-economic values and interests include the protection of the environment, public health, public morals, national treasures and national security. The relevant rules can be found in, for example, Articles XX and XXI of the GATT 1994 and Articles XIV and XIV *bis* of the GATS. The economic interests include the protection of a domestic industry from serious injury inflicted by an unexpected and sharp surge in imports, the safeguarding of the balance of payments and the pursuit of regional economic integration. These 'exceptions' may be invoked by all WTO Members and allow them, *if* they meet certain specific conditions, to deviate from the basic rules and disciplines. The relevant rules can be found in, for example, Articles XII, XIX and XXIV of the GATT 1994, Articles V, X and XII of the GATS and the *Agreement on Safeguards*. The WTO rules allowing Members to take into account economic or non-economic values and interests that may conflict with free trade are examined in detail in Chapter 7.[141]

1.3.2.5. Special and differential treatment for developing-country Members

Recognising the need for positive efforts designed to ensure that developing-country Members, and especially the least-developed countries among them, are integrated into the multilateral trading system,[142] WTO law includes many provisions granting a degree of special and differential treatment to developing-country Members.[143] These provisions attempt to take the special needs of developing countries into account. In many areas, they provide for fewer obligations or differing rules for developing countries as well as for technical assistance. The rules on the special and differential treatment of developing-country Members are examined in detail throughout this book, particularly in Chapter 7.[144]

---

[140] See below, pp. 51–2.   [141] See below, pp. 596–691.   [142] *WTO Agreement*, Preamble, second paragraph.
[143] For example, Article XVIII and Part IV of the GATT 1994 as well as the Enabling Clause. See below, pp. 668–74, 393–4, 676–83.
[144] See below pp. 676–82.

1.3.2.6. *Institutional and procedural rules*

All basic rules and principles referred to above are substantive rules and principles. However, the multilateral trading system also includes, and depends on, institutional and procedural rules relating to decision-making and dispute settlement. The rules regarding the institutions and procedures for the formulation and implementation of trade rules are discussed in detail in Chapter 2. This chapter deals with the mandate, institutions and membership of the WTO. The rules and procedures regarding the settlement of trade disputes are dealt with in Chapter 3.

Questions and Assignments 1.9

What are the basic rules and principles that make up the multilateral trading system? What is the most fundamental principle of WTO law? Does WTO law take into account the special situation of developing countries? Does WTO law address the conflict between trade liberalisation and other economic and non-economic societal values and interests?

1.4. SOURCES OF WTO LAW

WTO law is, by international law standards, a sprawling and complex body of law. This section reviews the sources of WTO law. Not all sources of WTO law reviewed below are of the same nature or are on the same legal footing. Some sources provide for specific legal rights and obligations for WTO Members that these Members can enforce through WTO dispute settlement.[145] Many other sources, reviewed below, do not in and by themselves provide for specific, enforceable rights and obligations. They are nevertheless sources of WTO law as they 'clarify' or 'define' the law that applies between WTO Members on WTO matters.[146]

The principal source of WTO law is the *Marrakesh Agreement Establishing the World Trade Organization*, concluded on 15 April 1994 and in force since 1 January 1995. Other sources of WTO law include WTO dispute settlement reports, acts of WTO bodies, agreements concluded in the context of the WTO, customary international law, general principles of law, other international agreements, subsequent practice of WTO Members, teachings of the most highly qualified publicists and, finally, the negotiating history.

---

[145] I.e. Members can claim the violation of these rights and obligations before WTO dispute settlement bodies.

[146] Arguably, the respondent Member in a dispute could invoke rules 'generated' by these sources of WTO law in defence of a claim of violation. This is, however, controversial. See below, pp. 63–4.

1.4.1. The Marrakesh Agreement Establishing the World Trade Organization

The *Marrakesh Agreement Establishing the World Trade Organization* (the '*WTO Agreement*') is the most ambitious and far-reaching international trade agreement ever concluded. It consists of a short basic agreement (of sixteen articles) and numerous other agreements and understandings included in the annexes to this basic agreement.

Agreement Establishing The World Trade Organization
ANNEX 1
ANNEX 1A: Multilateral Agreements on Trade in Goods
              General Agreement on Tariffs and Trade 1994
              Agreement on Agriculture
              Agreement on the Application of Sanitary and Phytosanitary
              Measures
              Agreement on Textiles and Clothing
              Agreement on Technical Barriers to Trade
              Agreement on Trade-Related Investment Measures
              Agreement on Implementation of Article VI of the General
              Agreement on Tariffs and Trade 1994
              Agreement on Implementation of Article VII of the General
              Agreement on Tariffs and Trade 1994
              Agreement on Preshipment Inspection
              Agreement on Rules of Origin
              Agreement on Import Licensing Procedures
              Agreement on Subsidies and Countervailing Measures
              Agreement on Safeguards
ANNEX 1B: General Agreement on Trade in Services and Annexes
ANNEX 1C: Agreement on Trade-Related Aspects of Intellectual Property
              Rights
ANNEX 2: Understanding on Rules and Procedures Governing the
              Settlement of Disputes
ANNEX 3: Trade Policy Review Mechanism
ANNEX 4: Plurilateral Trade Agreements
              Agreement on Trade in Civil Aircraft
              Agreement on Government Procurement

On the relationship between the *WTO Agreement* and its Annexes as well as on the binding nature of the Annexes, Article II of the *WTO Agreement* states:

> 2. The agreements and associated legal instruments included in Annexes 1, 2 and 3 (hereinafter referred to as "Multilateral Trade Agreements") are integral parts of this Agreement, binding on all Members.
>
> The official version of the *WTO Agreement* and its Annexes is published by the WTO and Cambridge University Press as *Legal Texts: The Results of the Uruguay*

> *Round of Multilateral Trade Negotiations.* The *Legal Texts* are an indispensable
> instrument for international trade law practitioners and scholars.
>   3. The agreements and associated legal instruments included in Annex 4 (hereinafter
> referred to as "Plurilateral Trade Agreements") are also part of this Agreement for
> those Members that have accepted them, and are binding on those Members. The
> Plurilateral Trade Agreements do not create either obligations or rights for Members
> that have not accepted them.

While the *WTO Agreement* consists of many agreements, the WTO Appellate
Body in one of the first cases before it, *Brazil – Dessicated Coconut*, stressed the
'single undertaking' nature of the *WTO Agreement*.[147] All multilateral WTO
agreements apply equally and are equally binding on all WTO Members. The
provisions of these agreements represent 'an *inseparable package* of rights and
disciplines which have to be considered in conjunction'.[148]

Furthermore, Article XVI:3 of the *WTO Agreement* provides:

> In the event of a conflict between a provision of this Agreement and a provision of any
> of the Multilateral Trade Agreements, the provision of this Agreement shall prevail to
> the extent of the conflict.

Most of the substantive WTO law is found in the agreements contained
in Annex 1. This Annex consists of three parts. Annex 1A contains thirteen
multilateral agreements on trade in goods, Annex 1B contains the *General
Agreement on Trade in Services* (the 'GATS') and Annex 1C the *Agreement on
Trade-Related Aspects of Intellectual Property Rights* (the 'TRIPS Agreement'). The
most important of the thirteen multilateral agreements on trade in goods,
contained in Annex 1A, is the *General Agreement on Tariffs and Trade 1994* (the
'GATT 1994'). The plurilateral agreements in Annex 4 also contain provisions
of substantive law but they are only binding upon those WTO Members that
are a party to these agreements.

Annexes 2 and 3 cover, respectively, the *Understanding on Rules and Procedures
for the Settlement of Disputes* and the *Trade Policy Review Mechanism*, and contain
procedural provisions.

1.4.1.1. *General Agreement on Tariffs and Trade 1994*

The GATT 1994 sets out the basic rules for trade in goods. This agreement is,
however, somewhat unusual in its appearance and structure. Paragraph 1 of
the introductory text of the GATT 1994 states:

> The General Agreement on Tariffs and Trade 1994 ('GATT 1994') shall consist of:
>
> a. the provisions in the General Agreement on Tariffs and Trade, dated 30 October
>   1947, annexed to the Final Act Adopted at the Conclusion of the Second Session of
>   the Preparatory Committee of the United Nations Conference on Trade and
>   Employment (excluding the Protocol of Provisional Application), as rectified,

---

[147] See Appellate Body Report, *Brazil – Dessicated Coconut*, 177.
[148] See e.g. Appellate Body Report, *Argentina – Footwear (EC)*, para. 81.

amended or modified by the terms of legal instruments which have entered into force before the date of entry into force of the WTO Agreement;

b. the provisions of the legal instruments set forth below that have entered into force under the GATT 1947 before the date of entry into force of the WTO Agreement:

   i.   protocols and certifications relating to tariff concessions;

   ii.   protocols of accession (excluding the provisions (*a*) concerning provisional application and withdrawal of provisional application and (*b*) providing that Part II of GATT 1947 shall be applied provisionally to the fullest extent not inconsistent with legislation existing on the date of the Protocol);

   iii. decisions on waivers granted under Article XXV of GATT 1947 and still in force on the date of entry into force of the WTO Agreement;

   iv.   other decisions of the CONTRACTING PARTIES to GATT 1947;

c. the Understandings set forth below:

   i.   Understanding on the Interpretation of Article II:1(b) of the General Agreement on Tariffs and Trade 1994;

   ii.   Understanding on the Interpretation of Article XVII of the General Agreement on Tariffs and Trade 1994;

   iii. Understanding on Balance-of-Payments Provisions of the General Agreement on Tariffs and Trade 1994;

   iv.   Understanding on the Interpretation of Article XXIV of the General Agreement on Tariffs and Trade 1994;

   v.   Understanding in Respect of Waivers of Obligations under the General Agreement on Tariffs and Trade 1994;

   vi.   Understanding on the Interpretation of Article XXVIII of the General Agreement on Tariffs and Trade 1994; and

d. the Marrakesh Protocol to GATT 1994.

The GATT 1994 would obviously have been a less confusing and more user-friendly legal instrument if the negotiators had drafted a *new* text reflecting the basic rules on trade in goods as agreed during the Uruguay Round. The current arrangement obliges one to consult the provisions of the GATT 1947, the provisions of relevant GATT 1947 legal instruments and the Understandings agreed upon during the Uruguay Round in order to know what the GATT 1994 rules on trade in goods are. The negotiators, aware that this arrangement might lead to some confusion, felt the need to state explicitly in Article II:4 of the *WTO Agreement* that:

> The General Agreement on Tariffs and Trade 1994 as specified in Annex 1A (hereinafter referred to as "GATT 1994") is legally distinct from the General Agreement on Tariffs and Trade, dated 30 October 1947 ... (hereinafter referred to as "GATT 1947").

It should be stressed that the GATT 1947 is in fact no longer in force. It was terminated in 1996. It is only to facilitate the necessary reference to the provisions of the GATT 1947 that the official WTO *Legal Texts* include the complete text of the GATT 1947 along with the amendments made to this agreement before the entry into force of the *WTO Agreement*.

The GATT 1994 contains rules on most-favoured-nation treatment (Article I); tariff concessions (Article II); national treatment on internal taxation and regulation (Article III); anti-dumping and countervailing duties (Article VI); valuation for customs purposes (Article VII); customs fees and formalities (Article VIII); marks of origin (Article IX); the publication and administration of trade regulations

(Article X); quantitative restrictions (Article XI); restrictions to safeguard the balance of payments (Article XII); administration of quantitative restrictions (Article XIII); exchange arrangements (Article XV); subsidies (Article XVI); State trading enterprises (Article XVII); governmental assistance to economic development (Article XVIII); safeguard measures (Article XIX); general exceptions (Article XX); security exceptions (Article XXI); dispute settlement (Articles XXII and XXIII); regional economic integration (Article XXIV); modification of tariff schedules (Article XXVIII), tariff negotiations (Article XXVIII *bis*); and trade and development (Articles XXXVI to XXXVIII of Part 4). A number of these provisions have been amended by one of the Understandings listed above. The *Marrakesh Protocol* is an important part of the GATT 1994. This Protocol contains the national Schedules of Concessions of all WTO Members. In these national schedules, the commitments to eliminate or reduce customs duties applicable to trade in goods are recorded. The Protocol is over 25,000 pages long and is a key instrument for traders and trade officials.

The provisions of the GATT 1994 will be discussed in detail in Chapters 3 to 7 of this book.

1.4.1.2. *Other multilateral agreements on trade in goods*

In addition to the GATT 1994, Annex 1A to the *WTO Agreement* contains a number of other multilateral agreements on trade in goods. These agreements include:

- the *Agreement on Agriculture*, which requires the use of tariffs instead of quotas or other quantitative restrictions, imposes minimum market access requirements and provides for specific rules on domestic support and export subsidies in the agricultural sector;
- the *Agreement on the Application of Sanitary and Phytosanitary Measures* (the '*SPS Agreement*'), which regulates the use by WTO Members of measures adopted to ensure food safety and protect the life and health of humans, animals and plants from pests and diseases;
- the *Agreement on Textiles and Clothing*, which provides for the gradual elimination by 2005 of quotas on textiles and clothing;
- the *Agreement on Technical Barriers to Trade* (the '*TBT Agreement*'), which regulates the use by WTO Members of technical regulations and standards and procedures to test conformity with these regulations and standards;
- the *Agreement on Trade-Related Investment Measures* (the '*TRIMS Agreement*'), which provides that Members' regulations dealing with foreign investments must respect the obligations in Article III (national treatment obligation) and Article XI (prohibition on quantitative restrictions) of the GATT 1994;
- the *Agreement on Implementation of Article VI of the General Agreement on Tariffs and Trade 1994* (the '*Antidumping Agreement*'), which provides for detailed rules on the use of anti-dumping duties;
- the *Agreement on Implementation of Article VII of the General Agreement on Tariffs and Trade 1994* (the '*Customs Valuation Agreement*'), which sets out in detail the

rules to be used by national customs authorities for valuing goods for customs purposes;

- the *Agreement on Preshipment Inspection*, which regulates activities relating to the verification of the quality, the quantity, the price and/or the customs classification of goods to be exported;
- the *Agreement on Rules of Origin*, which sets out disciplines to govern the application of rules of origin, both during and after a transition period, and provides for negotiations aimed at the harmonisation of rules of origin;
- the *Agreement on Import Licensing Procedures*, which sets out rules on the use of import licensing procedures;
- the *Agreement on Subsidies and Countervailing Measures* (the '*SCM Agreement*'), which provides for detailed rules on subsidies and the imposition of countervailing duties; and
- the *Agreement on Safeguards*, which provides for detailed rules on the use of safeguard measures and prohibits the use of voluntary export restraints.

All of these agreements will be discussed in more detail in the following chapters.

Most of these multilateral agreements on trade in goods provide for rules that are more detailed, and sometimes possibly in conflict with, the rules contained in the GATT 1994. The Interpretative Note to Annex 1A addresses the relationship between the GATT 1994 and the other multilateral agreements on trade in goods. It states:

> In the event of conflict between a provision of the *General Agreement on Tariffs and Trade 1994* and a provision of another agreement in Annex 1A to the *Agreement Establishing the World Trade Organization* (referred to in the agreements in Annex 1A as the "*WTO Agreement*"), the provision of the other agreement shall prevail to the extent of the conflict.
>
> [Emphasis added]

However, it is only where a provision of the GATT 1994 and a provision of another multilateral agreement on trade in goods are in *conflict* that the provision of the other multilateral agreement on trade in goods will prevail. Provisions are in conflict only where adherence to the one provision will lead to a violation of the other provision and the provisions cannot be read as complementing each other. If there is no conflict, both the GATT 1994 and the relevant other multilateral agreement on trade in goods apply. In *Argentina – Footwear (EC)*, the Appellate Body ruled with regard to the relationship between, and the application of, the safeguard provision of the GATT 1994 (Article XIX) and the *Agreement on Safeguards* that:

> The GATT 1994 and the *Agreement on Safeguards* are *both* Multilateral Agreements on Trade in Goods contained in Annex 1A of the *WTO Agreement*, and, as such, are *both* 'integral parts' of the same treaty, the *WTO Agreement*, that are 'binding on all Members'. Therefore, the provisions of Article XIX of the GATT 1994 *and* the provisions of the *Agreement on Safeguards* are *all* provisions of one treaty, the *WTO Agreement*. They entered into force as part of that treaty at the same time. They apply equally and are equally binding on all WTO Members. And, as these provisions relate

to the same thing, namely the application by Members of safeguard measures, the Panel was correct in saying that 'Article XIX of GATT and the Safeguards Agreement must *a fortiori* be read as representing an *inseparable package* of rights and disciplines which have to be considered in conjunction'.[149]

1.4.1.3. *General Agreement on Trade in Services*

Unlike the GATT 1994, the *General Agreement on Trade in Services* (the 'GATS') is a totally new agreement. It is the first ever multilateral agreement on trade in services. The GATS established a regulatory framework within which WTO Members can undertake and implement commitments for the liberalisation of trade in services.

The GATS covers all measures of Members affecting trade in services.[150] Trade in services is defined in Article I:2 of the GATS as the supply of a service:

- from the territory of one Member into the territory of any other Member (cross-border supply);
- in the territory of one Member to the service consumer of any other Member (consumption abroad);
- by a service supplier of one Member, through a commercial presence in the territory of any other Member (supply through a commercial presence); and
- by a service supplier of one Member, through the presence of natural persons of a Member in the territory of any other Member (supply through the presence of natural persons).

'Services' includes any service in any sector except services supplied in the exercise of governmental authority.[151] The supply of services includes the production, distribution, marketing, sale and delivery of a service.[152] It is clear from the third mode of supply, i.e. supply through a commercial presence, that the GATS also covers measures relating to foreign investment by suppliers of services.

The GATS contains provisions on most-favoured-nation treatment (Article II); transparency (Article III); increasing participation of developing countries (Article IV); economic integration (Article V); domestic regulation (Article VI); recognition (Article VII); emergency safeguard measures (Article X); payments and transfers (Article XI); restrictions to safeguard the balance of payments (Article XII); government procurement (Article XIII); general exceptions (Article XIV); security exceptions (Article XIV *bis*); subsidies (Article XV); market access (Article XVI); national treatment (Article XVII); negotiation and schedules of specific commitments (Articles XIX and XXI); dispute settlement (Articles XXII and XXIII); and institutional issues (Articles XXIV to XXVI). Attached to the GATS are a number of annexes, including the Annex on Article II Exceptions, the Annex on Movement of Natural Persons Supplying Services under the Agreement, and

---

[149] Appellate Body Report, *Argentina – Footwear (EC)*, para. 81.
[150] Article I:1 of the GATS.   [151] Article I:3(b) of the GATS.
[152] Article XXVIII(b) of the GATS.

the Annexes on Financial Services. The Schedules of Specific Commitments of all WTO Members concerning their market access and national treatment commitments are also attached to the GATS and form an integral part thereof.[153]

On the relationship between the GATS and the GATT 1994, and in particular the question of whether they are mutually exclusive agreements, the Appellate Body ruled in *EC – Bananas III*:

> The GATS was not intended to deal with the same subject matter as the GATT 1994. The GATS was intended to deal with a subject matter not covered by the GATT 1994, that is, with trade in services. Thus, the GATS applies to the supply of services. ... Given the respective scope of application of the two agreements, they may or may not overlap, depending on the nature of the measures at issue. Certain measures could be found to fall exclusively within the scope of the GATT 1994, when they affect trade in goods as goods. Certain measures could be found to fall exclusively within the scope of the GATS, when they affect the supply of services as services. There is yet a third category of measures that could be found to fall within the scope of both the GATT 1994 and the GATS. These are measures that involve a service relating to a particular good or a service supplied in conjunction with a particular good. In all such cases in this third category, the measure in question could be scrutinized under both the GATT 1994 and the GATS. However, while the same measure could be scrutinized under both agreements, the specific aspects of that measure examined under each agreement could be different. Under the GATT 1994, the focus is on how the measure affects the goods involved. Under the GATS, the focus is on how the measure affects the supply of the service or the service suppliers involved. Whether a certain measure affecting the supply of a service related to a particular good is scrutinized under the GATT 1994 or the GATS, or both, is a matter that can only be determined on a case-by-case basis.[154]

The GATS is examined in detail in Chapters 4, 5 and 7.[155]

1.4.1.4. Agreement on Trade-Related Aspects of Intellectual Property Rights

The *Agreement on Trade-Related Aspects of Intellectual Property Rights* (the 'TRIPS Agreement') is not an agreement concerning trade or trade measures. However, the value of many goods and services, particularly those traded by developed countries, is largely determined by the idea, the design or the invention they incorporate. If that value is not protected by protecting the intellectual property rights in the idea, the design or the invention, trade in these products will not thrive. For that reason, developed-country members sought and obtained the inclusion in the *WTO Agreement* of an agreement specifying minimum standards of protection of intellectual property rights and requiring the effective enforcement of these rights. The *TRIPS Agreement* covers seven types of intellectual property:

- copyright and related rights (Articles 9–14);
- trademarks (Articles 15–21);

---

[153] Article XX of the GATS. The Final Act also contains an Understanding on Commitments in Financial Services that is not part of the *WTO Agreement* but which was the basis for post-1995 negotiations on the liberalisation of financial services. See below, p. 494.
[154] Appellate Body Report, *EC – Bananas III*, para. 221.
[155] See below, pp. 318–26, 365–9, 480–501, 624–75.

- geographical indications (Articles 22–24);
- industrial designs (Articles 25–26);
- patents (Articles 27–34);
- layout-designs (topographies) of integrated circuits (Articles 35–38); and
- undisclosed information, including trade secrets (Article 39).

With regard to these types of intellectual property, the *TRIPS Agreement* provides for minimum standards of protection. With regard to copyright, for example, Article 12 provides:

> Whenever the term of protection of a work, other than a photographic work or a work of applied art, is calculated on a basis other than the life of a natural person, such term shall be no less than 50 years from the end of the calendar year of authorized publication, or, failing such authorized publication within 50 years from the making of the work, 50 years from the end of the calendar year of making.

Furthermore, the *TRIPS Agreement* requires WTO Members to ensure that enforcement procedures and remedies are available to permit effective action against any act of infringement of the intellectual property rights referred to above, including civil and administrative procedures and remedies, provisional measures and criminal procedures (Articles 41–61). Pursuant to Articles 3 and 4 of the *TRIPS Agreement*, each WTO Member must accord other WTO Members national treatment and most-favoured-nation treatment, subject to a number of exceptions. The *TRIPS Agreement* frequently refers to other intellectual property agreements, such as the Paris *Convention for the Protection of Industrial Property* (1967), the Bern *Convention for the Protection of Literary and Artistic Works* (1971), the Rome *Convention for the Protection of Performers, Producers of Phonograms and Broadcasting Organizations* (1961) and the Washington *Treaty on Intellectual Property in Respect of Integrated Circuits* (1989), making provisions of these agreements applicable to all WTO Members.[156]

The *TRIPS Agreement* is referred to, but not examined in detail, in this book.

1.4.1.5. Understanding on Rules and Procedures for the Settlement of Disputes

The *Understanding on Rules and Procedures for the Settlement of Disputes*, commonly referred to as the *Dispute Settlement Understanding* or DSU, is arguably the single most important achievement of the Uruguay Round negotiations. The WTO dispute settlement system applies to all disputes between WTO Members arising under WTO agreements. In 1997, Renato Ruggiero, then Director-General of the WTO, referred to the dispute settlement system provided for by the DSU as:

> ... in many ways the central pillar of the multilateral trading system and the WTO's most individual contribution to the stability of the global economy.[157]

---

[156] E.g. Article 2.1 of the *TRIPS Agreement* (with regard to the Paris Convention); and Article 9 of the *TRIPS Agreement* (with regard to the Bern Convention).
[157] As reported in WTO, *Trading into the Future*, 2nd edition (WTO, 1999), 38.

Building on almost fifty years of experience with settling trade disputes in the context of the GATT 1947, the DSU provides for a dispute settlement system, characterised by compulsory jurisdiction, short timeframes, an appellate review process and an enforcement mechanism.

The DSU provides for rules on the coverage and scope of the dispute settlement system, its administration, its objectives and its operation (Articles 1–3); on mandatory pre-litigation consultations (Article 4); on good offices, conciliation and mediation (Article 5); on the panel process (Articles 6–16 and 18–20); on the appellate review process (Articles 17–20); on compliance and enforcement (Articles 21–22); on a ban on unilateral action (Article 23); on least-developed-country members (Article 24); on arbitration as an alternative means of dispute settlement (Article 25); on non-violation and situation complaints (Article 26); and on the role of the WTO Secretariat (Article 27). Attached to the DSU are Appendices on the WTO agreements covered by the DSU (Appendix 1), on special or additional rules and procedures on dispute settlement contained in WTO agreements (Appendix 2); on the working procedures of panels (Appendix 3); and on expert review groups (Appendix 4).

The WTO dispute settlement system is discussed in detail in Chapter 3.[158]

1.4.1.6. Trade Policy Review Mechanism

It is very important for WTO Members, their citizens and companies involved in trade to be informed as fully as possible about trade regulations and policies of other WTO Members. To that end, many of the WTO agreements referred to above provide for an obligation on WTO Members to inform or notify the WTO of new trade regulations, measures or policies or changes to existing ones. In addition, however, the WTO conducts regular reviews of individual Members' trade policies. The procedural rules for these reviews are set out in Annex 3 on the *Trade Policy Review Mechanism*. This mechanism is discussed in Chapter 2.[159]

1.4.1.7. Plurilateral agreements

All agreements in Annexes 1 to 3 are binding on all WTO Members. Membership of the WTO is conditional upon the acceptance of these 'multilateral agreements'. Annex 4 contains two agreements, referred to as 'plurilateral agreements', which are only binding on those WTO Members that are a party to these agreements.

The first plurilateral agreement is the *Agreement on Trade in Civil Aircraft*. This is, in fact, an agreement concluded during the 1979 Tokyo Round of trade negotiations. Attempts during the Uruguay Round to negotiate a new agreement failed. The *Agreement on Trade in Civil Aircraft*, which is of particular interest to the United States and the European Communities:

---

[158] See below, pp. 172–306.   [159] See below, pp. 94–7.

- provides for duty-free trade in civil aircraft and parts thereof;
- prohibits quotas and other trade restrictions; and
- addresses the issue of government support to aircraft manufacturers.

Disputes relating to this agreement *cannot* be brought to the WTO dispute settlement system for resolution.

The second plurilateral agreement is the *Agreement on Government Procurement*. Under GATT 1994 and GATS rules, WTO Members are free to discriminate in favour of domestic products, services and service suppliers in the context of government procurement. This is an important exception to the national treatment obligations of Article III of the GATT 1994 and Article XVII of the GATS. Under the terms of the *Agreement on Government Procurement*, the parties have agreed to accord national treatment in respect of government procurement by designated government entities.[160] The agreement also obliges parties to make procurement opportunities public, and requires parties to provide for a procedure allowing unsuccessful bidders to challenge a procurement award. Disputes under the *Agreement on Government Procurement* can be, and have already been, brought to the WTO dispute settlement system for resolution.[161]

When the *WTO Agreement* entered into force on 1 January 1995, Annex 4 held four, and not two, plurilateral agreements. However, the *International Dairy Agreement* and the *International Bovine Meat Agreement* were terminated at the end of 1997.

1.4.1.8. Ministerial Decisions and Declarations

Finally, note the twenty-seven Ministerial Decisions and Declarations, which together with the *WTO Agreement* form the Final Act adopted in Marrakesh in April 1994 at the end of the Uruguay Round negotiations. These Ministerial Decisions and Declarations include, for example, the Decision on Measures in Favour of Least-Developed Countries,[162] the Declaration on the Contribution of the World Trade Organization to Achieving Greater Coherence in Global Economic Policymaking,[163] and the Decision on the Application and Review of the Understanding on Rules and Procedures Governing the Settlement of Disputes.[164] These Ministerial Decisions and Declarations do not generate specific rights and obligations for WTO Members which can be enforced through WTO dispute settlement.

Questions and Assignments 1.10

Look in the *Legal Texts* and skim through all the WTO agreements referred to above. Add tabs to your copy of the *Legal Texts* for easy reference to the various agreements. Explain briefly what each of these agreements deals

---

[160] See below, pp. 477–9.   [161] E.g. Panel Report, *Korea – Procurement*.
[162] See below, p. 107.   [163] See below, p. 97.   [164] See below, p. 289.

with. What is the difference between multilateral and plurilateral agreements? What is the relationship between the GATT 1994 and other multilateral agreements on trade in goods? Which agreement prevails in case of conflict? When does a conflict exist? What is the relationship between the GATT 1994 and the GATS? Can these two agreements be applied to one and the same measure?

1.4.2. Other sources of WTO law

While the *WTO Agreement* with its multiple annexes is undisputedly the principal source of WTO law, it is not the only source of WTO law. This section examines:

- WTO dispute settlement reports;
- acts of WTO bodies;
- agreements concluded in the context of the WTO;
- customary international law;
- general principles of law;
- other international agreements;
- subsequent practice of WTO Members;
- teachings of the most highly qualified publicists; and
- the negotiating history.

All the above may, to varying degrees, clarify or define the law applicable between WTO Members on WTO matters.

1.4.2.1. *WTO dispute settlement reports*

Reports of WTO panels and the Appellate Body are the most important 'other' source of WTO law. In addition, reports of old GATT panels are also a source of WTO law. In principle, adopted panel and Appellate Body reports are only binding on the parties to a particular dispute. However, in *Japan – Alcoholic Beverages II* the Appellate Body held with regard to prior GATT panel reports:

> Adopted panel reports are an important part of the GATT *acquis*. They are often considered by subsequent panels. They create legitimate expectations among WTO Members, and, therefore, should be taken into account where they are relevant to any dispute.[165]

In adopting this approach, the Appellate Body was clearly inspired by the practice of the International Court of Justice. Article 59 of the *Statute of the International Court of Justice* provides that the decisions of the Court have no binding force except between the parties and in respect of the particular case. The Appellate Body noted that:

---

[165] Appellate Body Report, *Japan – Alcoholic Beverages II*, 108. With regard to unadopted GATT panel reports, the Appellate Body agreed with the Panel in *Japan – Alcoholic Beverages II* that they 'have no legal status in the GATT or WTO system' but 'a panel could nevertheless find useful guidance in the reasoning of an unadopted panel report that it considered to be relevant' (Panel Report, *Japan – Alcoholic Beverages II*, 108).

> [t]his has not inhibited the development by that Court (and its predecessor) of a body of case law in which considerable reliance on the value of previous decisions is readily discernible.[166]

This Appellate Body ruling in *Japan – Alcoholic Beverages II* on prior GATT panel reports also applies *mutatis mutandis* to WTO panel reports and, even more so, to Appellate Body reports. In *US – Shrimp (Article 21.5 – Malaysia)*, the Appellate Body held with respect to its reasoning in *Japan – Alcoholic Beverages II*:

> This reasoning applies to adopted Appellate Body Reports as well. Thus, in taking into account the reasoning in an adopted Appellate Body Report – a Report, moreover, that was directly relevant to the Panel's disposition of the issues before it – the Panel did not err. The Panel was correct in using our findings as a tool for its own reasoning.[167]

Adopted reports are not binding precedent for panels or the Appellate Body. However, as David Palmeter and Petros Mavroidis stated:

> Adopted reports have strong persuasive power and may be viewed as a form of nonbinding precedent.[168]

Following precedent makes sense for reasons of fairness and legitimacy, for reasons of efficiency and for reasons of legal clarity and certainty. In practice, Appellate Body rulings play a very important role in WTO law, and prior rulings are generally followed by panels and the Appellate Body itself.

1.4.2.2. *Acts of WTO bodies and agreements concluded in the context of the WTO*

Acts of WTO organs, such as authoritative interpretations and waivers,[169] are clearly also a source of WTO law which give rise to rights and obligations for WTO Members that can be enforced through the dispute settlement system. Other acts of WTO organs, for example the Decision of the Ministerial Conference on Implementation-Related Issues and Concerns[170] or the Decision of the SPS Committee on Equivalence,[171] are definitely sources of WTO law and must be taken into account by panels and the Appellate Body. They are an integral part of WTO law. However, they do not provide for rights and obligations which can be enforced through the dispute settlement system. No claim of violation can be based on these acts.[172]

The same holds true for trade agreements which are concluded by WTO Members in the context of the WTO but which are neither attached to the *WTO Agreement* nor included in the list of covered agreements of Appendix 1 of the DSU.

---

[166] *Ibid.*, footnote 30.
[167] Appellate Body Report, *US – Shrimp (Article 21.5 – Malaysia)*, para. 109.
[168] D. Palmeter and P. Mavroidis, 'The WTO Legal System: Sources of Law', *American Journal of International Law*, 1998, 401.
[169] For a discussion of authoritative interpretations and waivers, see below, pp. 144–6, 115–17.
[170] Ministerial Conference, Decision of 14 November 2001, WT/MIN(01)/17, dated 20 November 2001.
[171] Committee on Sanitary and Phytosanitary Measures, Decision on the Implementation of Article 4 of the *Agreement on the Application of Sanitary and Phytosanitary Measures*, G/SPS/19, dated 26 October 2002 (effective 24 October 2001).
[172] For a discussion on the scope of the jurisdiction of the WTO dispute settlement system, see below, pp. 187–90.

1.4.2.3. *Customary international law*

Article 3.2 of the DSU provides, in relevant part:

> The Members recognize that [the WTO dispute settlement system] serves to preserve the rights and obligations of Members under the covered agreements, and to clarify the existing provisions of those agreements *in accordance with customary rules of inter-pretation of public international law*.
>
> > [Emphasis added]

The DSU thus explicitly refers to customary international law on treaty inter-pretation and makes this law applicable in the context of the WTO. It is debated whether other rules of customary international law are also part of WTO law.[173]

In *Korea – Procurement*, the Panel ruled that customary international law applied:

> ... to the extent that the WTO treaty agreements do not "contract out" from it.[174]

As the Panel Report in *Korea – Procurement* was not appealed, the Appellate Body did not have the opportunity to review this finding.

Customary international law is part of general international law and the rules of general international law are, in principle, binding on all States. Each new State, as well as each new treaty, is automatically born into it. The rules of general international law, including the rules of customary international law, fill the gaps left by treaties. They are not applicable *only* when, and to the extent that, a treaty – *in casu*, the *WTO Agreement* – has 'contracted out' of certain rules of general international law.

As noted by Joost Pauwelyn, the Appellate Body and panels have frequently referred to and applied customary international law. They did so independently of giving meaning to specific words in a given WTO provision.[175] The Appellate Body has made reference to and/or applied customary rules on dispute settle-ment and, in particular, on standing,[176] representation by private counsel,[177] the burden of proof,[178] and the treatment of municipal law.[179] In addition, panels have referred to and/or applied customary rules on State responsibility and, in particular, rules on countermeasures[180] and attribution.[181] The custom-ary rules on State responsibility are often referred to as rules the *WTO Agreement* has contracted out of.[182]

---

[173] This debate is of particular relevance with respect to the available remedies for breach of WTO law. See below, pp. 223–5.

[174] Panel Report, *Korea – Procurement*, para. 7.96.

[175] J. Pauwelyn, *Conflict of Norms in Public International Law: How WTO Law Relates to Other Norms of International Law* (Cambridge University Press, 2003).

[176] See Appellate Body Report, *EC – Bananas III*, para. 133.

[177] *Ibid.*, para. 10.

[178] See Appellate Body Report, *US – Wool Shirts and Blouses*, 358–9.

[179] See Appellate Body Report, *India – Patents (US)*, para. 65.

[180] See Panel Report, *EC – Bananas III (Article 22.6 – EC)*, para. 6.16; and Panel Report, *Brazil – Aircraft (Article 22.6 – Brazil)*, para. 3.44 and footnotes 46 and 48.

[181] See Panel Report, *Canada – Dairy*, para. 7.77 and footnote 427; and Panel Report, *Turkey – Textiles*, para. 9.33.

[182] See below, p. 224.

1.4.2.4. General principles of law

Like customary international law, general principles of law are part of general international law. As noted in the previous section, rules of general international law are, in principle, binding on all States. The rules of general international law, including the general principles of law, fill the gaps left by treaties. They are not applicable *only* when, and to the extent that, a treaty – *in casu*, the *WTO Agreement* – has 'contracted out' of certain rules of general international law.

Both panels and the Appellate Body have referred to and used general principles of law as a basis for their rulings or in support of their reasoning. In *US – Shrimp*, the Appellate Body noted with regard to the principle of good faith:

> The chapeau of Article XX is, in fact, but one expression of the principle of good faith. This principle, at once a general principle of law and a general principle of international law, controls the exercise of rights by states. One application of this general principle, the application widely known as the doctrine of *abus de droit*, prohibits the abusive exercise of a state's rights and enjoins that whenever the assertion of a right "impinges on the field covered by [a] treaty obligation, it must be exercised bona fide, that is to say, reasonably". An abusive exercise by a Member of its own treaty right thus results in a breach of the treaty rights of the other Members and, as well, a violation of the treaty obligation of the Member so acting .[183]

The principle of due process,[184] the principle of proportionality,[185] the principle of judicial economy,[186] the principle of non-retroactivity[187] and the interpretative principle of effectiveness,[188] a corollary of the general rule of interpretation, have also been applied by panels and the Appellate Body in numerous reports. In at least one report, the Appellate Body applied the interpretative principle of *in dubio mitius*.[189]

1.4.2.5. Other international agreements

Other international agreements can also be a source of WTO law. This is definitely the case when these agreements are referred to specifically in a WTO agreement. As mentioned above, the *TRIPS Agreement* refers to a number of other intellectual property agreements, such as the Paris Convention (1967) and the Bern Convention (1971), thus making provisions of these agreements part of WTO law, applicable to all WTO Members and enforceable through WTO dispute settlement. The *SCM Agreement* refers to the *OECD Arrangement on Guidelines for Officially Supported Export Credits*.[190]

---

[183] See Appellate Body Report, *US – Shrimp*, para. 158. See also Appellate Body Report, *US – FSC*, para. 166.
[184] See Appellate Body Report, *US – Shrimp*, para. 182.   [185] *Ibid.*, para. 141.
[186] See Appellate Body Report, *Australia – Salmon*, paras. 219–26.
[187] See Appellate Body Report, *Brazil – Dessicated Coconut*, 179; Appellate Body Report, *EC – Bananas III*, para. 235; and Appellate Body Report, *Canada – Patent Term*, paras. 71–4.
[188] See Appellate Body Report, *US – Gasoline*, 18; and Appellate Body Report, *Korea – Dairy*, para. 81.
[189] See Appellate Body Report, *EC – Hormones*, footnote 154.
[190] Annex I(k) to the *SCM Agreement*. Grants by governments of export credits that meet the requirements of this Arrangement are not considered an export subsidy prohibited under the *SCM Agreement*.

Whether, and, if so, to what extent, other international agreements *not* referred to in a WTO agreement can be a source of WTO law, is a controversial issue. This issue is of particular relevance to multilateral environmental agreements (MEAs) and ILO Conventions on minimum labour standards. It is broadly accepted that these other international agreements may play a significant role in the interpretation of WTO legal provisions. Article 31 of the *Vienna Convention on the Law of Treaties* (the '*Vienna Convention*'), which applies in WTO dispute settlement,[191] states in paragraph 3(c) that, in the interpretation of a treaty provision, the interpreter must take into account together with the context:

> any relevant rules of international law applicable in the relations between the parties.

In *US – Shrimp*, the Appellate Body made extensive use of principles laid down in multilateral environmental agreements such as the United Nations Convention on the Law of the Sea, the Convention on Biological Diversity, and the Convention on the Conservation of Migratory Species of Wild Animals, to *interpret* Article XX of the GATT 1994, although not all parties to this dispute were parties to these agreements.[192] As noted by Meinhard Hilf, the Appellate Body in that case imported from these environmental agreements the principle of co-operation into the chapeau of Article XX of GATT 1994.[193]

However, it is controversial whether these other international agreements can be a source of WTO law in the sense that they provide for rights and obligations for Members that can be invoked in WTO dispute settlement procedures. As discussed below, Joost Pauwelyn has argued in this respect that WTO Members cannot base a claim before a WTO panel on the violation of rights and obligations set out in a non-WTO agreement. However, in his opinion, WTO Members that are also parties to a particular non-WTO agreement can invoke in WTO dispute settlement the rules of that agreement as a defence against a claim of violation of WTO rules. This position is, however, quite controversial. Other WTO scholars do not agree that rules of non-WTO agreements can be invoked before a panel or the Appellate Body as a defence.[194]

1.4.2.6. *Subsequent practice of WTO Members*

Pursuant to Article 31(3)(b) of the *Vienna Convention*, 'subsequent practice' is to be taken into account in the interpretation of the rights and obligations set out in the *WTO Agreement*. Therefore, 'subsequent practice' of the WTO, WTO organs or WTO Members must be considered to be a source of WTO law. In *Japan – Alcoholic Beverages II*, the Appellate Body stated:

> the essence of subsequent practice in interpreting a treaty has been recognized as a "concordant, common and consistent" sequence of acts or pronouncements which is sufficient to establish a discernible pattern implying the agreement of the parties

[191] See below, pp. 206–9.   [192] See below, pp. 610–11.
[193] M. Hilf, 'Power, Rules and Principles in WTO/GATT Law', *Journal of International Economic Law*, 2001, 123 (reproduced by permission of Oxford University Press).
[194] See below, p. 64.

regarding its interpretation. An isolated act is generally not sufficient to establish subsequent practice; it is a sequence of acts establishing the agreement of the parties that is relevant.[195]

1.4.2.7. Teachings of publicists and the negotiating history

Pursuant to Article 38(1) of the *Statute of the International Court of Justice*, the 'teachings of the most highly qualified publicists' are subsidiary means for the determination of rules of international law. WTO panels and the Appellate Body have frequently cited the writings of scholars in support of their reasoning.[196]

Pursuant to Article 32 of the *Vienna Convention*, the negotiating history of an agreement may serve as a supplementary means of interpretation. However, there is no formally recorded negotiating history of the *WTO Agreement* and WTO panels and the Appellate Body give little importance to the personal recollections of negotiators.[197]

Questions and Assignments 1.11

Briefly discuss *all* sources of WTO law. Are panel and Appellate Body reports of relevance only to the parties to a dispute? Have the Appellate Body and panels referred to and applied rules of customary international law and general principles of law? Can multilateral environmental agreements concluded between WTO Members be in any way a source of WTO law? Do decisions of WTO organs provide for legal rights and obligations for Members?

1.5. WTO LAW IN CONTEXT

Earlier in this chapter, WTO law was described as a principal component of international economic law, which itself is an important part of public international law. However, the relationship between WTO law and *international law* deserves to be explored further. Likewise, the relationship between WTO law and *national law* also raises questions that need to be addressed.

1.5.1. WTO law and international law

1.5.1.1. WTO law as an integral part of international law

In many handbooks on international law and in many general courses on this topic, little attention is given to international trade law. International law has traditionally excluded the regulation of international trade from its purview.

[195] See Appellate Body Report, *Japan – Alcoholic Beverages II*, 106–7.
[196] See Appellate Body Report, *US – Wool Shirts and Blouses*, 335 (on burden of proof).
[197] See below, p. 209.

Searching for an explanation for this 'segregation' of international trade law, Donald McRae noted in his 1996 Hague Lecture:

> International trade law and international economic law were not of concern to international lawyers; trade and economic law were not central to the way international lawyers defined their discipline … Particular social traditions may have played some role in this. In some countries the idea of commerce, of buying and selling, or of economic matters generally, was not viewed with favour. The professions of medicine and law were respectable; those engaged in business did not have the same social status. This, no doubt, helped fashion the attitudes of international lawyers to international trade law and international economic law … The field of trade law, and that of economic matters generally, are seen as closely intertwined with the field of economics which is perceived as presenting a barrier to those without formal training in that discipline. In his extremely insightful work, *International Law in a Divided World*, Professor Cassese, who does recognize the significance of international economic relations to the study of international law, and devotes a full chapter to it, nevertheless states that "international economic relations are usually the hunting ground of a few specialists, who often jealously hold for themselves the key to this abstruse admixture of law and economics".[198]

McRae also suggested another, and in his view more fundamental, reason for the fact that international trade law has traditionally been regarded as outside the mainstream of international law:

> [T]he problem of fitting international trade and economic law into a discipline that defined itself in terms of peace and security, in terms of territorial integrity and political independence of States, in terms of sovereignty. The rationale of international trade law has nothing to do with sovereignty. International trade law does not rest on that primary assumption of international law, that the world is composed of sovereign nation States, each surrounded by territorial borders within which it exercises plenary authority. International trade law is founded in the primary value of promoting individual economic exchanges, about the value of specialization and the economic welfare that results from specialization and exchange. Rather than focusing on the independence of States, international trade law highlights the concept of interdependence … This, I suggest, has been the underlying intellectual problem for international lawyers.[199]

However, with regard to the latter reason given by McRae for the isolation of international trade law, Joost Pauwelyn noted that since the end of the First World War, international law consists not only of the international law of 'co-existence' referred to by McRae ('a discipline that defined itself in terms of peace and security … territorial integrity and political independence'), but also includes, to an ever increasing degree, the international law of 'co-operation' (a discipline that 'highlights the concept of interdependence').[200] International trade law, like international environmental law and international human rights law, are part of this international law of co-operation.

---

[198] D. McRae, *The Contribution of International Trade Law to the Development of International Law*, Academy of International Law, *Recueil des Cours*, Vol. 260, 1996, 114–15.

[199] *Ibid.*, 116–17.

[200] J. Pauwelyn, *Conflict of Norms in Public International Law: How WTO Law Relates to Other Norms of International Law* (Cambridge University Press, 2003).

Whatever reasons there may have been in the past for the fact that international trade law was not within the mainstream of international law, economic issues and problems have rapidly moved to the frontlines of international relations and international law in the last decades. In a more recent article, McRae described the work of the WTO as the 'new frontier' of international law. He noted:

> There is ... much that is occurring under the WTO dispute settlement process that is of direct relevance to the general field of international law. Much of public international lawyers' perception of international trade law arises from the intersection of trade law with other branches of international law through the application of GATT Article XX, in particular the overlap between trade and environment. While that area provides a fruitful source for considering the relationship of international trade law and international law, the substantive issues relating to these two fields comprise only part of the contribution that is currently being made to the development of international law through the operation of the WTO dispute settlement process ...
>
> [T]he WTO dispute settlement process should be of concern to all international lawyers. It is not just trade lawyers who should be following the work of the Appellate Body. The decisions of the Appellate Body should be scrutinized and analyzed in the general international law legal literature, not just so that scholars and practitioners can understand what the Appellate Body is doing, but also that the Appellate Body can learn what independent international law scholarship is saying about its work. But for this to happen international lawyers will have to reorient their thinking about the relationship between international law and international trade law. They have to move beyond the easy assumption that the WTO is no more than the continuation of a tradition and look at the 'new frontier' of international law that is rapidly emerging from the work of the WTO.[201]

Pieter-Jan Kuijper wrote in 1994 on the relationship between international law and international trade law as follows:

> The final question whether GATT is or is about to become a self-contained system of international law, cannot yet be answered affirmatively. Certainly in the recent past it has not functioned as such, mainly because of US insistence that in certain situations of blockage of the dispute settlement system the normal remedy of unilateral reprisal could be applied. It is not to be excluded that the other participants in the system over-reacted to these claims and as a consequence created the impression that they supported a fully closed system. The intention to move further towards a self-contained system certainly underlies the WTO Agreement and its Dispute Settlement Understanding, but it remains to be seen how the WTO Members will make it function.[202]

A genuine turning point in the relationship between international law and international trade law was the 1996 Appellate Body Report in *US – Gasoline*. In this report, its very first, the Appellate Body ruled that Article 3.2 of the DSU, which directs panels and the Appellate Body to interpret the WTO agreements according to the 'customary rules of interpretation of public international law', reflects:

---

[201] D. McRae, 'The WTO in International Law: Tradition Continued or New Frontier?', *Journal of International Economic Law*, 2000, 30 and 41 (reproduced by permission of Oxford University Press).

[202] P. J. Kuijper, 'The Law of GATT as a Special Field of International Law: Ignorance, Further Refinement or Self-Contained System of International Law?', *Netherlands Yearbook of International Law*, 1994, 257.

> a measure of recognition that the *General Agreement* is not to be read in clinical isolation from public international law.[203]

The discussion above of the sources of WTO law shows that WTO law is *not* a closed, self-contained system, isolated from the rest of international law. General international law, composed of customary international law and general principles of law, is binding on WTO Members and is, in principle, part of the law applicable between WTO Members. Customary rules and general principles fill the gaps left by the *WTO Agreement*, unless the *WTO Agreement* has clearly 'contracted out' of these rules and principles.[204] Furthermore, WTO law must be interpreted taking into account other norms of international law, as long as these other norms represent the 'common intentions' of all WTO Members.[205]

1.5.1.2. *Conflicts between WTO agreements and other agreements*

It may happen that the rights and obligations of WTO Members under the WTO agreements are in conflict with their rights and obligations under other international agreements. A classic example of such a conflict is the situation in which a multilateral environmental agreement (an 'MEA') obliges the parties to that agreement to impose quantitative restrictions on trade in certain products whereas Article XI of the GATT 1994 prohibits such restrictions.

First, it should be noted that WTO rules should, if possible, be interpreted in such a way that they do not conflict with other rules of international law (i.e. the general principle against conflicting interpretation). As Gabrielle Marceau noted:

> Panels and the Appellate Body have the obligation to interpret the WTO provisions in taking into account all relevant rules of international law applicable to the relations between the WTO Members. One of those rules is the general principle against conflicting interpretation (Article 31.3(c) together with 30 of the Vienna Convention). Therefore, in most cases the proper interpretation of the relevant WTO provisions – themselves often drafted in terms of specific prohibitions leaving open a series of WTO compatible alternative measures – should lead to a reading of the WTO provisions so as to avoid conflict with other treaty provisions.[206]

While there will undoubtedly be instances in which conflicts between WTO rules and non-WTO rules can be avoided through clever interpretation, in many other instances this will not be possible. As already briefly mentioned above, Joost Pauwelyn has an innovative and well-thought-out view on the conflict of WTO rules with non-WTO rules.[207] Pauwelyn's view is controversial but is gradually receiving more support from fellow WTO scholars. Central to Pauwelyn's view is that most WTO obligations are essentially reciprocal in nature. Reciprocal obligations are obligations from which parties to a multilateral treaty may deviate, as

---

[203] Appellate Body Report, *US – Gasoline*, 16.   [204] See above, pp. 57–8.
[205] See above, pp. 57–9.
[206] G. Marceau, 'Conflicts of Norms and Conflicts of Jurisdictions: The Relationship Between the WTO Agreement and MEAs and Other Treaties', *Journal of World Trade*, 2001, 1129.
[207] See above, p. 59.

long as such deviation does not infringe the rights of third parties. Pauwelyn explains his view on the conflict between WTO-rules and non-WTO rules as follows:

> In the event of conflict involving WTO provisions, WTO provisions may not always prevail, including before a WTO panel. The trade obligations in the WTO treaty are of the "reciprocal type". They are not of an "integral nature". Hence, WTO provisions can be deviated from as between a limited number of WTO members only, as long as this deviation does not breach third party rights. Affecting the economic interests of other WTO members does not amount to breaching their WTO rights. Recognizing that WTO obligations are of a reciprocal nature allows for the taking into account of the diversity of needs and interests of different WTO Members. It shows that in most cases of conflict between, for example, human rights and environmental conventions (generally setting out obligations of an "integral type"), on the one hand, and WTO obligations (of the "reciprocal" type), on the other, the WTO provisions will have to give way.[208]

According to Pauwelyn, in case of conflict, rules of MEAs or other international agreements, such as human rights treaties, may thus often prevail over rules of WTO law. However, Pauwelyn added:

> ... the fact that non-WTO norms may ... prevail over the WTO treaty, even as before a WTO panel, does not mean that WTO panels must judicially enforce compliance with these non-WTO rules. Non-WTO rules may be part of the applicable law before a WTO panel, and hence offer, in particular, a valid legal defence against claims of WTO breach. However, they cannot form the basis of legal claims, the jurisdiction of WTO panels being limited to claims under WTO covered agreements only.[209]

This particular view of the relationship between WTO rules and conflicting rules of other international agreements is not shared by all WTO scholars. On the contrary, Gabrielle Marceau has argued that WTO panels confronted with a conflict between a WTO rule and a non-WTO rule may perhaps have alternative courses of action to deal with the conflict, but that:

> any of these alternative courses of action would be possible only to the extent that the conclusions reached by the panels do not constitute an amendment of the WTO, or do not add or diminish the rights and obligations of WTO Members or do not affect the rights of third WTO Members.[210]

As Marceau noted, and as discussed in Chapter 3,[211] it is prohibited for panels and the Appellate Body to 'add to or diminish rights and obligations' of WTO Members, as provided for in the WTO agreements.[212] Should panels or the Appellate Body allow a respondent to invoke a non-WTO rule in defence of a claim of violation of WTO law, would they not, in fact, 'add to or diminish rights and obligations' of WTO Members?

---

[208] J. Pauwelyn, *Conflict of Norms in Public International Law: How WTO Law Relates to Other Norms of International Law* (Cambridge University Press, 2003).
[209] *Ibid.*
[210] G. Marceau, 'Conflicts of Norms and Conflicts of Jurisdictions: The Relationship Between the WTO Agreement and MEAs and Other Treaties', *Journal of World Trade*, 2001, 1130.
[211] See below, pp. 184–5.   [212] Articles 3.2 and 19.2 of the DSU.

Questions and Assignments 1.12

Is WTO law a self-contained system of law or is it an integral part of international law? Do you agree with the analysis of Joost Pauwelyn on the relationship between WTO agreements and MEAs? In your opinion, what should a panel do when confronted with a WTO rule that is in conflict with a provision of a MEA concluded *after* the conclusion of the *WTO Agreement*?

1.5.2. WTO law and national law

There are two aspects of the relationship between WTO law and national law that need to be examined: first, the place of national law in WTO law; and, secondly, the place of WTO law in the domestic legal order.

1.5.2.1. National law in WTO law

With regard to the place of national law in WTO law, Article XVI:4 of the *WTO Agreement* states:

> Each Member shall ensure the conformity of its laws, regulations and administrative procedures with its obligations as provided in the annexed Agreements.

It is a general rule of international law, reflected in Article 27 of the *Vienna Convention*, that:

> A party may not invoke the provisions of its internal law as justification for its failure to perform a treaty.

In *Brazil – Aircraft (Article 21.5 – Canada)*, the Appellate Body had occasion to observe:

> We note Brazil's argument before the Article 21.5 Panel that Brazil has a contractual obligation under domestic law to issue PROEX bonds pursuant to commitments that have already been made, and that Brazil could be liable for damages for breach of contract under Brazilian law if it failed to respect its contractual obligations. In response to a question from us at the oral hearing, however, Brazil conceded that *a WTO Member's domestic law does not excuse that Member from fulfilling its international obligations.*[213]
>
> [Emphasis added]

Note, however, that with regard to measures and actions by regional and local governments and authorities, Article XXIV:12 of the GATT 1994 provides:

> Each Member shall take such reasonable measures as may be available to it to ensure observance of the provisions of this Agreement by the regional and local governments and authorities within its territories.[214]

---

[213] Appellate Body Report, *Brazil – Aircraft (Article 21.5 – Canada)*, para. 46.
[214] See also the *Undertaking on the Interpretation of Article XXIV of the General Agreement on Tariffs and Trade 1994*, para. 13.

It follows that WTO Members are obliged to enforce compliance with the obligations under the GATT 1994 by regional and local governments and authorities *only* to the extent that they – i.e. the Members – dispose of the necessary constitutional powers to do so.[215] Note that Article XXIV:12 has been interpreted narrowly.[216] Furthermore, where it is not possible to secure compliance with the obligations under the GATT 1994, the provisions relating to compensation and suspension of concessions, discussed in Chapter 3, apply.[217]

With respect to the question of how panels and the Appellate Body should handle national law, the Appellate Body held in *India – Patents* that, in public international law, an international tribunal may treat municipal law in several ways. Municipal law may serve as evidence of facts and may provide evidence of State practice. However, municipal law may also constitute evidence of compliance or non-compliance with international obligations. The Appellate Body found support for this position in the ruling of the Permanent Court of International Justice in *Certain German Interests in Polish Upper Silesia*, in which the Court had observed:

> It might be asked whether a difficulty does not arise from the fact that the Court would have to deal with the Polish law of July 14th, 1920. This, however, does not appear to be the case. From the standpoint of International Law and of the Court which is its organ, municipal laws are merely facts which express the will and constitute the activities of States, in the same manner as do legal decisions and administrative measures. The Court is certainly not *called upon to interpret* the Polish law as such; but there is nothing to prevent the Court's giving judgment on *the question whether or not*, in applying that law, *Poland is acting in conformity with its obligations* towards Germany under the Geneva Convention.[218]
>
> [Emphasis added]

In *India – Patents (US)*, the Appellate Body thus concluded:

> It is clear that an examination of the relevant aspects of Indian municipal law … is essential to determining whether India has complied with its obligations under Article 70.8(a). There was simply no way for the Panel to make this determination without engaging in an examination of Indian law. But, as in the *Certain German Interests in Polish Upper Silesia* case … before the Permanent Court of International Justice, in this case, the Panel was not interpreting Indian law "as such"; rather, the Panel was examining Indian law solely for the purpose of determining whether India had met its obligations under the *TRIPS Agreement*.[219]

Many WTO panels have in fact conducted a detailed examination of the domestic law of a Member in assessing the conformity of that domestic law with the relevant WTO obligations. Thomas Cottier and Krista Schefer noted in this respect:

---

[215] T. Cottier and K. Schefer, 'The Relationship Between World Trade Organization Law, National Law and Regional Law', *Journal of International Economic Law*, 1998, 85–6 (reproduced by permission of Oxford University Press).

[216] See GATT Panel Report, *Canada – Provincial Liquor Boards (US)*, BISD 39S/27.

[217] See *Undertaking on the Interpretation of Article XXIV of the General Agreement on Tariffs and Trade 1994*, para. 14, last sentence.

[218] [1926] PCIJ Rep., Series A, No. 7, 19.

[219] Appellate Body Report, *India – Patents (US)*, para. 66.

> Interpretation of national or regional rules by respective authorities should essentially be recognized as questions of fact and be treated with deference. Panels have no authority to construe rules of national or regional law *de novo* and to substitute their reading for what national or regional authorities, whether delegations, administrations or courts, have found to be the proper meaning of the law. Yet, a problem arises if it is apparent that the interpretation of national or regional law is manifestly incompatible with the text and/or context of national or regional rules. How should a panel and the Appellate Body react to this situation? … Panels are called upon to declare whether national or regional rules, *and the way they are applied*, are compatible with those set out in the WTO agreements.[220]
>
> [Emphasis added]

Cottier and Schefer thus pleaded for a degree of deference on the part of panels and the Appellate Body for the interpretation given by national authorities to provisions of their national law. However, Cottier and Schefer also stress that panels and the Appellate Body will not only look at whether these provisions are WTO-consistent, but also at whether the way in which these provisions are in fact applied is WTO-consistent.

1.5.2.2. WTO law in national law

With respect to the role of WTO law in the national legal order, it should first be observed that, where a provision of national law allows different interpretations, this provision should, whenever possible, be interpreted in a manner that avoids any conflict with WTO law. In the United States, the European Union and elsewhere, national courts have adopted this doctrine of *treaty-consistent interpretation*. The European Court of Justice (ECJ) stated in 1996 in *Commission* v. *Germany (International Dairy Arrangement)* with regard to the GATT 1947:

> When the wording of secondary EC legislation is open to more than one interpretation, preference should be given as far as possible to the interpretation which renders the provision consistent with the Treaty … Similarly, the primacy of international agreements concluded by the Community over the provisions of secondary Community legislation means that such provisions must, so far as is possible, be interpreted in a manner consistent with those agreements.[221]

The ECJ confirmed the doctrine of treaty-consistent interpretation of national/ EC law with regard to the *WTO Agreement* in its judgments in *Hermès* (1998) and *Schieving-Nijstad* (2001).[222] In many cases, however, it will not be possible to avoid a conflict between a provision of national law and a WTO law provision through treaty-consistent interpretation.

If a conflict between a provision of national law and a WTO law provision cannot be avoided through treaty-consistent interpretation, the question

---

[220] T. Cottier and K. Schefer, 'The Relationship Between World Trade Organization Law, National Law and Regional Law', *Journal of International Economic Law*, 1998, 86.

[221] Judgment of the Court of 10 September 1996, *Commission of the European Communities* v. *Federal Republic of Germany (International Dairy Arrangement)*, Case C-61/94, [1996] ECR I-3989, para. 52.

[222] See Judgment of the Court of 13 September 2001, *Schieving-Nijstad vof and Others* v. *Robert Groeneveld*, Case C-89/99, [2001] ECR I-5851; and Judgment of the Court of 15 June 1998, *Hermès International and FHT Marketing Choice BV*, Case 53/96, [1998] ECR I-3603.

arises as to whether the provision of WTO law can be invoked before the national court to challenge the legality and validity of the provision of national law. Can a German importer of bananas challenge the EC's import regime for bananas in court on the basis that this regime is inconsistent with, for example, Articles I, XI and XIII of the GATT 1994? Can a US meat exporter of beef challenge the EC import ban on hormone-treated meat on the basis that this ban is inconsistent with the provisions of the *SPS Agreement*? This is the issue of the *direct effect* of provisions of WTO law.[223]

It is clear that were provisions of WTO law to have direct effect and could be invoked to challenge the legality of national measures, this would significantly increase the enforceability and effectiveness of these provisions for it would give Members much less flexibility in respect of compliance.

There is a fierce *academic* debate on whether provisions of WTO law should be granted direct effect. On that debate, Cottier and Schefer wrote:

> Among the scholars writing on the topic of direct effect of international trade agreements, there are three that stand out as the main proponents of the two schools of thought on the issue: Jan Tumlir and Ernst Ulrich Petersmann advocating direct effect and John H. Jackson for the critics of direct effect. A fourth author, Piet Eeckhout, has set out what we call an 'intermediate position' on the issue.[224]

With respect to the arguments of the advocates of the direct effect of WTO rules, Cottier and Schefer noted:

> The late Jan Tumlir, whose main thesis supporting direct effect is followed by Ernst Ulrich Petersmann, looks at the direct effect of trade treaties as a weapon against inherently protectionist tendencies in domestic law systems. Tumlir and Petersmann set forth the idea of 'constitutionalizing' international trade principles, elevating the rights of an individual to trade freely with foreigners to the level of a fundamental right. To prevent the erosion of a state's sovereignty, Tumlir suggests granting individuals the right to invoke treaty provisions in front of their domestic courts. Allowing for standing in this way would be available to those citizens harmed by protectionist national policies put into effect by other national interest groups. Thus, direct effect widely defined 'helps to correct the asymmetries in the political process'. Ernst Ulrich Petersmann has written numerous articles that reinforce the need for using the GATT, and now the WTO, system for what he calls 'constitutional restraints' on protectionist behavior. ... Pleading for keeping the possibility of judicial review open to individuals, Jacques Bourgeois put it quite bluntly: 'Quite simply, what is in the end the use of making law, also international law, designed to protect private parties, if these private parties cannot rely on it?'[225]

For the advocates of direct effect of WTO rules, direct effect is a necessary and effective 'weapon' against national governments which encroach on the right to trade freely with foreigners, a right these advocates of direct effect consider to be a fundamental right.

---

[223] The issue of direct effect, i.e. the issue of direct invocability, is to be distinguished from the issue of direct applicability, i.e. the issue whether a national act of transformation is necessary for an international agreement to become part of national law. On the latter issue, it should be noted that WTO law is directly applicable in the EC legal order. It became part of EC law without any act of transformation.

[224] T. Cottier and K. Schefer, 'The Relationship Between World Trade Organization Law, National Law and Regional Law', *Journal of International Economic Law*, 1998, 93.

[225] *Ibid.*, 93–5.

John Jackson, and with him many others, objects to the direct effect of WTO rules. Central to his position against the direct effect of WTO rules is that direct effect might be dangerous for democracy and that it conflicts with the legitimate wish of legislatures to adapt international treaty language to the domestic legal system. Cottier and Schefer noted:

> John Jackson … basically supports US trade policies of denying direct effect due to the imbalances in the institutional balance of government it would cause domestically … He does … find the idea of granting standing and allowing for an international treaty to be superior to federal legislation (let alone the constitution) to be dangerous to the idea of democracy and democratic representation of individuals … While Jackson acknowledges that governments have an obligation to abide by international commitments they undertake, direct effect is not necessary to ensure this. The stronger reasons for denying direct effect are what Jackson calls "functional arguments". These arguments include the fact that '[s]ome constitutions provide for very little democratic participation in the treaty-making process; for example, by giving no formal role to Parliaments or structuring the government so that control over foreign relations is held by certain elites'. There are also legitimate desires of legislatures to adapt international treaty language to the domestic legal system (such as translating the obligations into the native language, using local terms for legal principles, or further explaining certain provisions). And, some governments may want the opportunity to implement the obligations in a national legislative process because 'the act of transformation sometimes becomes part of a purely *internal* power struggle, and may be used by certain governmental institutions to enhance their powers vis-à-vis other governmental entities' or 'even, perhaps, … the legislature desires to preserve the *option to breach* the treaty in its method of application'. Even such uses of the separate implementation process are legitimate in Professor Jackson's mind because 'some breaches may be "minor" and therefore *preferable to the alternative of refusing to join the treaty altogether*'. Finally, Jackson argues that if treaties are given direct effect automatically, the characteristic of direct effect itself will not necessarily guarantee that the national courts will apply the treaty rules.[226]

An intermediate position in this debate on the direct effect of WTO law has been taken by Piet Eeckhout. Eeckhout opposed direct effect of WTO law but conceded that if a case has been specifically decided by the WTO dispute settlement system, domestic effect should be given to this decision. According to Eeckhout:

> the reasons for not granting direct effect – whether it is the agreement's flexibility, or the division of powers between the legislature and the judiciary, or the respect of appropriate dispute settlement forums – cease to be valid where a violation is established.[227]

In principle, the *WTO Agreement* could have specified what effect its provisions are to have in the domestic legal order of WTO Members. However, it did not do so. Therefore, although each Member must execute fully the commitments which it has undertaken, it is free to determine the legal means appropriate for attaining that end in its domestic legal system.

---

[226] *Ibid.*, 97–8.
[227] P. Eeckhout, 'The Domestic Legal Status of the WTO Agreements: Interconnecting Legal Systems', *Common Market Law Review*, 1997, 53.

At present, all of the major trading nations, the European Union, the United States, Japan, Canada and China, refuse to give 'direct effect' to the provisions of WTO law.[228]

The ECJ addressed the issue of whether it could review the legality of Community law in the light of WTO law in its judgment of 23 November 1999 in *Portugal* v. *Council*. As the ECJ did not want:

- to deprive the European Community of the possibility for temporary non-compliance with WTO law provided for in Article 22 of the DSU (the temporary non-compliance argument),[229] and
- did not want to deprive the legislative or executive organs of the Community of the scope for manoeuvre with respect to compliance enjoyed by their counterparts in the Community's trading partners (the non-reciprocity argument),[230]

it concluded:

> having regard to their nature and structure, the WTO agreements are not in principle among the rules in the light of which the Court is to review the legality of measures adopted by the Community institutions.[231]

In support of the conclusion reached, the ECJ noted that this interpretation corresponded to what was stated in the final recital of the preamble to the Council Decision of 22 December 1994 on the conclusion of the *WTO Agreement*. In this Decision, the Council, conforming with the Commission's proposal, stated:

> [b]y its nature, the Agreement Establishing the World Trade Organization, including the Annexes thereto, is not susceptible to being directly invoked in Community or Member State courts.[232]

In its judgement of 14 December 2000 in *Dior* v. *TUK*, the European Court of Justice confirmed its reasoning in *Portugal* v. *Council* and concluded that private persons cannot invoke WTO law before the courts by virtue of Community law.[233]

However, in its recent judgments of 30 September 2003 in the *Biret* v. *Council* cases, the European Court of Justice leaves the possibility open for an action for damages based on a Community measure that was found to be WTO inconsistent by the WTO Dispute Settlement Body *if* the damage occurred

---

[228] For an overview of whether specific WTO Members give direct effect to WTO law in their domestic legal order, see C. George and S. Orava (eds.), *A WTO Guide for Global Business* (Cameron May, 2002), 398.

[229] Judgment of the Court of 23 November 1999, *Portuguese Republic* v. *Council of the European Union*, Case C-149/96, [1999] ECR I-8395, para. 40. With respect to this possibility for temporary non-compliance with WTO law, see below, pp. 220–3.

[230] *Ibid.*, para. 46.   [231] *Ibid.*, para. 47.

[232] Council Decision 94/800/EC of 22 December 1994 concerning the conclusion on behalf of the European Community, as regards matters within its competence, of the agreements reached in the Uruguay Round multilateral negotiations, OJ 1994, L336, 1.

[233] See Judgment of the Court of 14 December 2000, *Parfums Christian Dior SA* v. *TUK Consultancy BV and Assco Gerüste GmbH* and *Rob van Dijk* v. *Wilhelm Layher GmbH & Co. KG and Layher BV*, Joined Cases C-300/98 and C-392/98, [2000] ECR I-11307, paras. 42–4.

after the end of the reasonable period of time for implementation of the recommendations and rulings of the Dispute Settlement Body.[234]

As an exception to the general rule, the European Court of Justice does, however, grant direct effect to provisions of the *WTO Agreement* when the Community intended to implement a particular obligation assumed in the context of the WTO, *or* where the Community measure refers expressly to the precise provisions of the WTO agreements. In its judgment of 22 June 1989 in *Fediol* v. *Commission* and its judgment of 7 May 1991 in *Nakajima* v. *Council*, the ECJ already gave direct effect to provisions of the GATT 1947 in these circumstances.[235] With respect to provisions of the *WTO Agreement*, the ECJ ruled in its judgment of 9 January 2003 in *Petrotub* v. *Council*:

> where the Community intended to implement a particular obligation assumed in the context of the WTO, or where the Community measure refers expressly to precise provisions of the agreements and understandings contained in the annexes to the WTO Agreement, it is for the Court to review the legality of the Community measure in question in the light of the WTO rules (see, in particular, *Portugal* v *Council*, paragraph 49).[236]

With regard to the domestic law effect of WTO law in the US, the Restatement (Third) of Foreign Relations Law of the United States provides:

> Since generally the United States is obligated to comply with a treaty as soon as it comes into force for the United States, compliance is facilitated and expedited if the treaty is self-executing … Therefore, if the Executive Branch has not requested implementing legislation and Congress has not enacted such legislation, there is a strong presumption that the treaty has been considered self-executing by the political branches, and should be considered self-executing by the courts.[237]

In the United States, trade treaties have historically been granted direct effect in court.[238] As has been the case with a number of other recent trade agreements,[239] the approval of the *WTO Agreement* was, however, made conditional upon the inclusion of a provision in the implementing legislation, explicitly denying direct effect to the Agreement.[240] As David Leebron noted:

> Although Congress specifically approved the agreements, it simultaneously provided "no provision of any of the Uruguay Round Agreements, nor the application of any such provision to any person or circumstances, that is inconsistent with any law of the United States shall have effect". Furthermore, Congress mandated that no person other than the United States "shall have any cause of action or defence under any of

---

[234] See Judgment of the Court of 30 September 2003, *Biret International SA* v. *Council of the European Union*, Case C-93/02 P; and Judgment of the Court of 30 September 2003, *Etablissements Biret et Cie SA* v. *Council of the European Union*, Case C-94/02 P.

[235] See Judgment of the Court of 22 June 1989, *Fédération de l'industrie de l'huilerie de la CEE (Fediol)* v. *Commission of the European Communities*, Case 70/87, [1989] ECR 1781; and Judgment of 7 May 1991, *Nakajima All Precision Co.Ltd* v. *Council of the European Communities*, Case 69/89, [1991] ECR I-2069.

[236] See Judgment of 9 January 2003, *Petrotub SA and Republica SA* v. *Council of the European Communities*, Case C-76/00 P, para. 54.

[237] Restatement (Third) of Foreign Relations Law of the United States, para. 111, Reporters' Notes, reproduced in B. Carter and P. Trimble, *International Law* (Little, Brown and Co., 1991), 151.

[238] See T. Cottier and K. Schefer, 'The Relationship Between World Trade Organization Law, National Law and Regional Law', *Journal of International Economic Law*, 1998, 107.

[239] See e.g. the North American Free Trade Agreement (NAFTA), 17 December 1992.

[240] Uruguay Round Agreements Act of 1994, 19 USC § 3512, Pub. L. No. 104–305 (1996), para. 102(c).

the Uruguay Round Agreements" or challenge "any action or inaction … of the United States, any state, or any political subdivision of a state on the ground that such action or inaction is inconsistent" with one of those agreements. In short, the Uruguay Agreements themselves are unlikely to be directly applied in any proceedings other than a proceeding brought by the United States for the purpose of enforcing obligations under the agreements.[241]

Furthermore, Japan, Canada and China do not, generally speaking, grant direct effect to WTO law. With regard to the situation in China, Xin Zhang noted:

Due to policy and technical considerations (following the practices of other important WTO Members), it is proper to reject the direct invocability of most WTO Agreements except for the TRIPS Agreement, which grants civil rights and obligations to private parties in a direct way. This position is evidenced by the mainstream of Chinese academic views as well as the latest judicial interpretation. Therefore, it is fair to say that China follows the practices of some major Members in rejecting the direct invocability of the WTO Agreement, at least in international trade administrative litigations against the Government.[242]

Questions and Assignments 1.13

Can a WTO Member ever invoke national law as a justification for its failure to comply with WTO obligations? In your opinion, should WTO provisions have direct effect? Does any WTO Member give direct effect to WTO provisions in its internal legal order? Why does the ECJ deny direct effect to provisions of WTO law? Are there any exceptions?

1.6. SUMMARY

One of the defining features of today's world is the process of economic globalisation, with high levels of international trade and foreign direct investment. There is broad consensus among economists and policy-makers that economic globalisation in general and international trade in particular offer an unprecedented *opportunity* to eradicate poverty and hunger. However, to ensure that this opportunity is realised, economic globalisation and international trade have to be *managed* and *regulated* at the international level. If not, economic globalisation and international trade are likely to be a curse, rather than a blessing to humankind, aggravating economic inequality, social injustice, environmental degradation and cultural dispossession. Managing and regulating economic globalisation and international trade so that they benefit all is one of the prime challenges of the twenty-first century.

---

[241] D. Leebron, 'Implementation of the Uruguay Round Results in the United States', in J. Jackson and A. Sykes (eds.), *Implementing the Uruguay Round* (Oxford University Press, 1997), 212.
[242] X. Zhang, 'Domestic Effect of WTO Agreements in China: Trends and Implications', *Journal of World Investment*, 2002, 934.

For countries to realise the gains of international trade and for international trade to benefit all of mankind, international rules on trade are necessary for basically four related reasons:

- to restrain countries from taking trade-restrictive measures;
- to give traders and investors a degree of security and predictability regarding the trade policies of other countries;
- to cope with the challenges presented by economic globalisation with respect to the protection of important societal values such as public health, a clean environment, consumer safety, cultural identity and minimum labour standards; and
- to achieve a greater measure of equity in international economic relations.

WTO law, which is the core of international economic law, provides for such rules on international trade. There are six groups of basic rules and principles of WTO law:

- the principles of non-discrimination;
- the rules on market access, including rules on transparency;
- the rules on unfair trade;
- the rules on conflicts between trade and other societal values and interests;
- the rules on special and differential treatment for developing countries; and
- the rules relating to decision-making and dispute settlement.

The principal source of WTO law is the *WTO Agreement*, in force since 1 January 1995. The *WTO Agreement* is a short agreement (of sixteen articles) establishing the World Trade Organization but with, in its annexes, a significant number of agreements with substantive and/or procedural provisions, such as the GATT 1994, the GATS, the *TRIPS Agreement* and the DSU. However, the *WTO Agreement* is not the only source of WTO law. WTO dispute settlement reports, acts of WTO bodies, agreements concluded in the context of the WTO, customary international law, general principles of law, other international agreements, subsequent practice of WTO Members, teachings of the most highly qualified publicists and the negotiating history may all, to varying degrees, be sources of WTO law. Note that not all these elements of WTO law are of the same nature or on the same legal footing. Some sources, such as the *WTO Agreement* and most of the agreements annexed to it, provide for specific legal rights and obligations for WTO Members that these Members can enforce through WTO dispute settlement. Other sources, such as the WTO dispute settlement reports, general principles of law, customary international law and non-WTO agreements, do not provide for specific, enforceable rights and obligations but nevertheless they do 'clarify' and 'define' the law that applies between WTO Members on WTO matters.

While for many years international trade law was not part of the mainstream of international law, WTO law is now the 'new frontier' of international law. Nobody questions that WTO law is an integral part of public international law. However, the relationship between WTO rules and other, conflicting rules of public international law, such as rules of MEAs, is controversial. A generally accepted view on this relationship is yet to emerge.

With regard to the relationship between WTO law and the national law of WTO Members, note that, while some WTO scholars forcefully plead for the granting of direct effect to WTO law in the domestic legal order of WTO Members, none of the major trading nations grants such effect to WTO law. In most WTO Members, a breach of WTO law obligations cannot be challenged or invoked in national courts.

1.7. EXERCISE: GLOBAPHILES VERSUS GLOBAPHOBES

Last Sunday, more than 50,000 people demonstrated in the streets of Nontes, the capital of Newland, against economic globalisation, free trade and the Government's plan to join the WTO. The Republic of Newland is a developing, lower middle income country, with a population of 30 million people. It has a booming, export-oriented toy manufacturing industry and an up-and-coming steel industry. Many of its other industries, however, are unable to compete with foreign goods or services.

The demonstration was organised by the Newland Coalition for a Better World (NCBW), representing Newland's labour unions and its main environmental, consumer and human rights organisations. When small groups of radicals, led by a moustached farmer, attacked and destroyed a McJohn's restaurant along the route, the police intervened to disperse the demonstrators with tear gas. Three hours of violent clashes between the police and a group of about 500 young demonstrators ensued, leaving several people wounded.

At an emergency cabinet meeting called on Sunday evening, the Prime Minister announced that he will invite the chairman of the NCBW to a public debate on economic globalisation, international trade and the Government's plan to join the WTO. On Monday, the chairman accepted the challenge. The debate is to be broadcast live on Wednesday evening.

You serve on the personal staff of the Prime Minister, and it is your job to prepare him for this important debate by briefing him as fully as possible on all the positive and negative aspects – economic, political and legal – of:

- economic globalisation;
- international trade; and
- WTO membership.

With regard to WTO membership, you expect the Chairman of the NCBW, a professor of constitutional law, to question, *inter alia*, why it would be in the interest of Newland to 'squander its sovereignty' and accept a host of new international obligations. You expect him to argue that the core WTO rules and disciplines are about opening foreign markets for the benefit of multinationals. From articles and speeches of the Chairman of the NCBW, you know that three issues are of particular concern to him, namely:

- whether the *WTO Agreement* encompasses all WTO law;
- whether the *WTO Agreement* will prevail over Newland's Constitution and over other international agreements; and
- whether WTO law will have, or should have, direct effect in Newland's courts.

To prepare the Prime Minister well, you and your colleagues decide to stage a trial debate in which one group, Group A, takes a 'globaphile' position and another group, Group B, a 'globaphobe' position.

2

The World Trade Organization

Contents

2.1. INTRODUCTION

The World Trade Organization was established and became operational on 1 January 1995. It is the youngest of all the major international inter-governmental organisations and yet it is arguably one of the most influential in these times of economic globalisation. As Marco Bronckers stated, it has 'the potential to become a key pillar of global governance'.[1] The WTO is also one of the most controversial international organisations. It has been referred as '*un gouvernement mondial dans l'ombre*'.[2] Guy de Jonquières of the *Financial Times* observed that the emergence of the WTO as a prime target for protests of many kinds reflects:

> ... growing public awareness – but often imperfect understanding – of its role in promoting, and formulating rules for, global economic integration.[3]

Many critics of the WTO claim that the WTO is 'pathologically secretive, conspiratorial and unaccountable to sovereign States and their electorate'.[4] According to Joseph Nye, these detractors may, to some extent, have a case. Nye wrote in November 2000:

> [Anti-globalisation protesters] assert that official transnational institutions like the World Trade Organization, the World Bank and the International Monetary Fund are effectively accountable to no one. How true is their claim? Some defenders point out that the WTO, for example, is a weak organization with a small budget and staff, hardly the stuff of world government by fiat. Moreover, unlike unelected nongovernmental organizations, the WTO, the World Bank and the IMF tend to be highly responsive to national governments, which are the real source of legitimacy ... Even though these organizations are inherently weak, their rules and resources can exert powerful effects. Moreover, the protesters are right that a lack of transparency often weakens accountability ... Increased accountability for the WTO, World Bank and other official transnational organizations will address many of the legitimate

---

[1] M. Bronckers, 'More Power to the WTO', *Journal of International Economic Law*, 2001, 41 (reproduced by permission of Oxford University Press).

[2] M. Khoh, 'Un gouvernement mondial dans l'ombre', *Le Monde Diplomatique*, May 1997.

[3] G. de Jonquières, 'The WTO's Capacity to Arouse Controversy Highlights a Growing Public Awareness of Its Role', *Financial Times*, 24 September 1999.

[4] G. de Jonquières, 'Prime Target for Protests: WTO Ministerial Conference', *Financial Times*, 24 September 1999.

> concerns of anti-globalization protestors, while neutralizing their more dubious criticisms. International institutions are too important to be left to demagogues, no matter how well-meaning.[5]

Developing-country Members criticise the WTO and object to what they consider to be their 'marginalisation' within the WTO's negotiation and rule-making processes.

This chapter deals with the WTO as the primary international intergovernmental organisation for international trade and trade-related matters. It first explores the origins of the WTO, a young institution with a long history. Subsequently, it examines:

- the mandate of the WTO, i.e., its objectives and functions;
- the membership of the WTO and the accession process;
- the institutional structure of the WTO; and
- the WTO's decision-making procedures, with particular attention to the role of developing-country Members and NGOs therein.

In general, this chapter seeks to address the issue of the legitimacy and effectiveness of the WTO as the main international organisation for managing and regulating international trade.

2.2. THE ORIGINS OF THE WTO

The origins of the WTO lie in the GATT 1947. The study of these origins is relevant because the decisions, procedures and customary practices of the GATT guide the WTO in its actions. Article XVI:1 of the *WTO Agreement* states:

> Except as otherwise provided under this Agreement or the Multilateral Trade Agreements, the WTO shall be guided by the decisions, procedures and customary practices followed by the CONTRACTING PARTIES to GATT 1947 and the bodies established in the framework of GATT 1947.

This section will discuss:

- the genesis of the GATT 1947 and its operation as the *de facto* international organisation for international trade until the end of 1994;
- the GATT Uruguay Round of Multilateral Trade Negotiations (1986–94) and the emergence of the WTO, operational as of 1 January 1995.

2.2.1. The General Agreement on Tariffs and Trade 1947

2.2.1.1. The GATT 1947 and the International Trade Organization

The history of the GATT begins in December 1945 when the United States invited its war-time allies to enter into negotiations to conclude a multilateral

---

[5] J. Nye, 'Take Globalization Protests Seriously', *International Herald Tribune*, 25 November 2000.

agreement for the reciprocal reduction of tariffs on trade in goods. In July 1945, the US Congress had granted President Truman the authority to negotiate and conclude such an agreement. These multilateral tariff negotiations took place in the context of a more ambitious project on international trade. At the proposal of the United States, the United Nations Economic and Social Committee adopted a resolution, in February 1946, calling for a conference to draft a charter for an 'International Trade Organization' (ITO).[6] At the 1944 Bretton Woods Conference, where the International Monetary Fund (IMF) and the International Bank for Reconstruction and Development (the 'World Bank') were established, the problems of trade had not been taken up as such, but the Conference did recognise the need for a comparable international institution for trade to complement the IMF and the World Bank.[7] A Preparatory Committee was established in February 1946 and met for the first time in London in October 1946 to work on the charter of an international organisation for trade.[8] The work was continued from April to November 1947 in Geneva. As John Jackson explained:

> The 1947 Geneva meeting was actually an elaborate conference in three major parts. One part was devoted to continuing the preparation of a charter for a major international trade institution, the ITO. A second part was devoted to the negotiation of a multilateral agreement to reduce tariffs reciprocally. A third part concentrated on drafting the 'general clauses' of obligations relating to the tariff obligations. These two latter parts together would constitute the General Agreement on Tariffs and Trade. The 'general clauses' of the draft GATT imposed obligations on nations to refrain from a variety of trade-impeding measures.[9]

The negotiations on the General Agreement on Tariffs and Trade (GATT) advanced well in Geneva, and by October 1947 the negotiators had reached an agreement on the GATT. The negotiations on the ITO, however, were more difficult and it was clear, towards the end of the 1947 Geneva meeting, that the ITO Charter would not be finished before 1948. Although the GATT was intended to be attached to the ITO Charter, many negotiators felt that it was not possible to wait until the ITO Charter was finished to bring the GATT into force. According to Jackson, there were two main reasons for this:

> First, although the tariff concessions were still secret, the negotiators knew that the content of the concessions would begin to be known. World trade patterns could thus be seriously disrupted if a prolonged delay occurred before the tariff concessions came into force.
>
> Second, the US negotiators were acting under the authority of the US trade legislation which had been renewed in 1945 ... But the 1945 Act expired in mid-1948. Thus,

---

[6] 1 UN ECOSOC Res. 13, UN Doc. E/22 (1946). For an overview of the negotiations of the GATT 1947 and the ITO with references to official documents, see *Guide to GATT Law and Practice* (WTO, 1995), 3–6.

[7] J. Jackson, *The World Trade Organization: Constitution and Jurisprudence* (Royal Institute of International Affairs, 1998), 15–16, who refers to United Nations Monetary and Financial Conference (Bretton Woods, NH, 1–22 July 1944), Proceedings and Documents 941 (US Department of State Publications No. 2866, 1948).

[8] The work in London proceeded on the basis of a proposal by the United States entitled 'Suggested Charter for an International Trade Organization'.

[9] J. Jackson, *The World Trade Organization: Constitution and Jurisprudence* (Royal Institute of International Affairs, 1998), 16.

> there was a strong motivation on the part of the United States to bring the GATT into force before this Act expired.[10]

It was therefore decided to bring the provisions of the GATT into force immediately. However, this created a new problem. Under the provisions of their constitutional law, some countries could not agree to parts of the GATT without submitting this agreement to their parliaments. Since they anticipated the need to submit the final draft of the ITO Charter to their parliaments in late 1948 or the following year, they feared that 'to spend the political effort required to get the GATT through the legislature might jeopardise the later effort to get the ITO passed'.[11] Therefore, they preferred to take the ITO Charter and the GATT to their legislatures as a package.

To resolve this problem, on 30 October 1947, eight of the twenty-three countries that had negotiated the GATT 1947 signed the 'Protocol of Provisional Application of the General Agreement on Tariffs and Trade' (PPA). Pursuant to this Protocol, these Contracting Parties undertook:

> to apply provisionally on and after 1 January 1948:
>
> a. Parts I and III of the General Agreement on Tariffs and Trade; and
> b. Part II of that Agreement to the fullest extent not inconsistent with existing legislation.[12]

As from 1 January 1948, the GATT 1947 was thus applied through the PPA. The other fifteen of the original twenty-three Contracting Parties also soon agreed to the provisional application of the GATT 1947 through the PPA. Pursuant to the PPA, Part I (containing the MFN obligation and the tariff concessions) and Part III (containing procedural provisions) would apply in full, while Part II (containing most of the substantive provisions, the application of which could require the modification of national legislation and thus the involvement of the legislature) only applied to the extent that it was not inconsistent with existing legislation. According to the PPA, a GATT Contracting Party was entitled to retain any provision of its legislation which was inconsistent with a GATT Part II obligation.[13] The PPA thus provided for an 'existing legislation exception', also referred to as 'grandfather rights'. This was quite convenient and explains why the GATT 1947 itself was never adopted by the Contracting Parties. Until 1995, the provisions of the GATT 1947 were applied through the PPA of 30 October 1947.

In March 1948, the negotiations on the ITO Charter were successfully completed in Havana. The Havana Charter provided for the establishment of the ITO, and sets out basic rules and disciplines for international trade and other international economic matters. The ITO Charter, however, never entered into force. While repeatedly submitted to the United States Congress, it was never approved. Therefore, in 1951, President Truman

---

[10] *Ibid.*, 17–18.   [11] *Ibid.*, 18.   [12] GATT BISD, Vol. IV, 77.
[13] J. Jackson, *The World Trade Organization: Constitution and Jurisprudence* (Royal Institute of International Affairs, 1998), 18.

eventually decided that he would no longer seek Congressional approval of the ITO Charter. Since no State was interested in establishing an international organisation for trade of which the United States, the world's leading economy and trading nation, would not be a member, the ITO was 'still-born'. As the ITO was intended to complete the Bretton Woods structure of international economic institutions, its demise left a significant gap in that structure.

2.2.1.2. *The GATT as a de facto international organisation for trade*

In the absence of an international organisation for trade, countries turned, from the early fifties, to the only existing multilateral international institution for trade, the GATT 1947, to handle problems concerning their trade relations.[14] Although the GATT was conceived as a multilateral *agreement* for the reduction of tariffs, and *not* an international *organisation*, it would over the years successfully 'transform' itself – in a pragmatic and incremental manner – into a *de facto* international organisation. The 'institutional' provisions in the GATT 1947 were very scant. Article XXV of the GATT 1947, entitled 'Joint Action by the Contracting Parties' stated:

> 1. Representatives of the contracting parties shall meet from time to time for the purpose of giving effect to those provisions of this Agreement which involve joint action and, generally, with a view to facilitating the operation and furthering the objectives of this Agreement. Wherever reference is made in this Agreement to the contracting parties acting jointly they are designated as the CONTRACTING PARTIES.
> 2. The Secretary-General of the United Nations is requested to convene the first meeting of the CONTRACTING PARTIES, which shall take place not later than March 1, 1948.
> 3. Each contracting party shall be entitled to have one vote at all meetings of the CONTRACTING PARTIES.
> 4. Except as otherwise provided for in this Agreement, decisions of the CONTRACTING PARTIES shall be taken by a majority of the votes cast.
> 5. In exceptional circumstances not elsewhere provided for in this Agreement, the CONTRACTING PARTIES may waive an obligation imposed upon a contracting party by this Agreement; *Provided* that any such decision shall be approved by a two-thirds majority of the votes cast and that such majority shall comprise more than half of the contracting parties.

Nevertheless, over the years, through experimentation and trial and error, the GATT evolved to include some fairly elaborate procedures for conducting its business. Some of these procedures were 'contrary' to Article XXV. For example, in practice, under the GATT voting was very uncommon; decisions were taken by consensus.

In spite of its scant institutional framework,[15] the GATT was very successful in reducing tariffs on trade in goods, in particular on industrial goods from

---

[14] A second and more modest attempt in 1955 to establish an 'Organization for Trade Cooperation' also failed because the US Congress was again unwilling to give its approval.

[15] On the institutional shortcomings of the GATT, see e.g., P. Van den Bossche, 'The Establishment of the World Trade Organization: The Dawn of a New Era in International Trade?', *Maastricht Journal of European and Comparative Law*, 1994, 398–400.

developed countries. In eight negotiating rounds between 1947 and 1994, the average level of tariffs of developed countries on industrial products was brought down from over 40 per cent to less than 4 per cent. The first five negotiating rounds ((Geneva (1947), Annecy (1949), Torquay (1951), Geneva (1956) and Dillon (1960–1)) focused on the reduction of tariffs. As from the Kennedy Round (1964–7) onwards, however, the negotiations would increasingly focus on non-tariff barriers (which were rapidly becoming a more serious barrier to trade than tariffs). With respect to the reduction of non-tariff barriers, the GATT was notably less successful than it was with the reduction of tariffs. Negotiations on the reduction of non-tariff barriers were much more complex and, therefore, required, *inter alia*, a more 'sophisticated' institutional framework than that of the GATT. The Kennedy Round produced very few results on non-tariff barriers. The Tokyo Round (1973–9) produced better results; however, a number of the agreements or codes decided upon clearly showed a lack of real consensus among the negotiators and proved to be difficult to implement. Moreover, the Tokyo Round agreements were plurilateral, rather than multilateral, in nature and did not bind many Contracting Parties.[16] In the early 1980s, it was clear that a new round of trade negotiations would be necessary. As Jackson noted:

> the world was becoming increasingly complex and interdependent, and it was becoming more and more obvious that the GATT rules were not satisfactorily providing the measure of discipline that was needed to prevent tensions and damaging national activity.[17]

The United States and a few other countries were in favour of a round with a very broad agenda including new subjects such as trade in services and the protection of intellectual property rights. Other countries objected to such a broad agenda or were opposed to the starting of a round altogether. However, in September 1986, at Punta del Este, Uruguay, the GATT Contracting Parties eventually agreed to the start of a new round.

Questions and Assignments 2.1

Briefly outline the historical origins of the GATT. Explain how the constitutional law of the United States and of other countries played a decisive role in the genesis of the GATT. Did the GATT 1947 ever enter into force? How did the PPA solve the problem faced by those countries that needed parliamentary approval of the GATT 1947? Has the GATT been a success?

---

[16] On the distinction between multilateral and plurilateral agreements, see above, pp. 53–4.
[17] J. Jackson, *The World Trade Organization: Constitution and Jurisprudence* (Royal Institute of International Affairs, 1998), 24.

2.2.2. Uruguay Round of Multilateral Trade Negotiations

2.2.2.1. *Ministerial Declaration of Punta del Este*

The Punta del Este Declaration contained a very broad and ambitious mandate for negotiations. The Uruguay Round negotiations would cover, *inter alia*, trade in goods, including trade in agricultural products and trade in textiles and clothing, as well as – for the first time in history – trade in services. The establishment of a new international organisation for trade was not, however, among the Uruguay Round's initial objectives. The Punta del Este Declaration explicitly recognised the need for institutional reforms in the GATT system but the ambitions were limited in this respect. The Declaration stated in relevant part:

> Negotiations shall aim to develop understandings and arrangements:
>
> i.   to enhance the surveillance in the GATT to enable regular monitoring of trade policies and practices of contracting parties and their impact on the functioning of the multilateral system;
>
> ii. to improve the overall effectiveness and decision-making of the GATT as an institution, including *inter alia*, through involvement of Ministers;
>
> iii. to increase the contribution of the GATT to achieving greater coherence in global economic policy-making through strengthening its relationship with other international organizations responsible for monetary and financial matters.[18]

2.2.2.2. *Negotiations on a new international organisation for trade*

During the first years of the Uruguay Round negotiations, major progress was made with respect to all of the institutional issues identified in the Ministerial Declaration. In December 1988, at the Montreal Ministerial Mid-Term Review Conference, it was decided in principle to implement, on a provisional basis, a Trade Policy Review Mechanism to improve adherence to GATT rules.[19] This Mid-Term Review also resulted in an agreement attempting to create greater cooperation between the GATT, the IMF and the World Bank as 'a first step to explore ways to achieve greater coherence in global economic policy making'.[20] In April 1989, it was agreed that in order to improve the functioning of the GATT, the Contracting Parties would meet at least once every two years at ministerial level.[21] At the time, however, the establishment of a new international trade organisation had not been discussed. It was the then Italian Trade Minister Renato Ruggiero (later the second Director-General of the WTO) who, in February 1990, first floated the idea of establishing a new international organisation for trade. A few months later, in April 1990, Canada formally proposed the establishment of what it called a 'World Trade Organization', a

---

[18] Ministerial Declaration on the Uruguay Round, GATT MIN.DEC, dated 20 September 1986, Part I, Section E, 'Functioning of the GATT System'.
[19] In April 1989, the CONTRACTING PARTIES formally established the Trade Policy Review Mechanism.
[20] T. Stewart, *The GATT Uruguay Round* (Klumer Law and Taxation,1993), Vol. III, 1927.
[21] See *ibid.*, 1928.

fully fledged international organisation which was to administer the different legal instruments related to international trade, including the GATT, the GATS and other multilateral instruments which were being developed in the context of the ongoing negotiations.[22] Along the same lines, the European Community submitted a proposal, in July 1990, calling for the establishment of a 'Multilateral Trade Organization'. The European Community argued that the GATT needed a sound institutional framework 'to ensure the effective implementation of the results of the Uruguay Round'.[23]

The reactions to these proposals for a new international trade organisation were mixed. The United States and most developing countries were all but enthusiastic.[24] At the time, the possibility of a major institutional overhaul was, in fact, thought to be unlikely. Such a major overhaul was – it was said – unlikely to gain much political support.[25] Fear of supranationalism, the reluctance of major trading nations to give in to voting equality and the traditional worry of national leaders about 'tying their hands', were thought to inhibit the possibility of reconstructing GATT into an international organisation for trade.[26]

The December 1990 Brussels Draft Final Act, discussed at what was initially planned to be the closing conference of the Uruguay Round, did not contain an agreement with regard to a new international organisation for trade.[27] Albeit for very different reasons, this conference was a total failure, and the Uruguay Round was subsequently suspended.[28] In April 1991, however, the negotiations were taken up again, and, in November 1991, the European Community, Canada and Mexico drafted a joint proposal for an international trade organisation. This joint proposal served as the basis for further negotiations which resulted, in December 1991, in the draft *Agreement Establishing the Multilateral Trade Organization*. The latter agreement was part of the 1991 Draft Final Act, commonly referred to as the Dunkel Draft, after the then Director-General of the GATT.[29]

For many of the reasons already referred to above, the United States remained opposed to the establishment of a Multilateral Trade Organization and actively campaigned against the idea throughout 1992. In spite of the

[22] See *ibid.*, 1942–3.
[23] See Communication from the European Community, GATT Doc. No. MTN.GNG/NG14/W/42, dated 1 July 1990, 2.
[24] Many developing countries were hostile to the idea of an international trade organisation, unless this organisation was instituted within the framework of the United Nations. UNCTAD tried to present itself as a possible multilateral trade organisation. See T. Stewart, *The GATT Uruguay Round* (Kluwer Law and Taxation, 1993), vol. III, 1944.
[25] J. Jackson, 'Strengthening the International Legal Framework of the GATT-MTN System: Reform Proposals for the New GATT Round 1991', in E. U. Petersmann and M. Hilf (eds.), *The New GATT Round of Multilateral Trade Negotiations: Legal and Economic Problems* (Kluwer, 1991), 17, 21 and 22. See also P. VerLoren van Themaat, in *ibid.*, 29: 'It is highly unlikely that the world's government leaders would be willing, at this point in history, to even start serious discussions about such a new institution.'
[26] See J. Jackson, 'Strengthening the International Legal Framework of the GATT-MTN System: Reform Proposals for the New GATT Round 1991', in *ibid.*, 21.
[27] Draft Final Act Embodying the Results of the Uruguay Round of Multilateral Trade Negotiations, GATT Doc. MTN.TNC/W/35/Rev.1, dated 3 December 1990.
[28] The negotiations broke down because of the fundamental disagreement between the European Community and the United States on the issue of agricultural subsidies.
[29] Draft Final Act Embodying the Results of the Uruguay Round of Multilateral Trade Negotiations, GATT Doc. MTN.TNC/W/FA, dated 20 December 1991.

United States' efforts at dissuasion, by early 1993 most participants in the Round were prepared to agree to the establishment of a Multilateral Trade Organization, and the United States became increasingly isolated on this issue. This perhaps explains the turnabout in the US position in the course of 1993 when the new Clinton Administration dropped its outspoken opposition to a new international trade organisation. Nevertheless, uncertainty about US support for such a new international organisation persisted until the last days of the Round.[30] The United States formally agreed to the establishment of the new organisation on 15 December 1993. To the surprise of many, however, the United States demanded a change of name as a condition for giving its consent. The United States suggested that the name of the new organisation should be the 'World Trade Organization' as had originally been proposed by Canada. The proponents of an international trade organisation had opted for 'Multilateral Trade Organization', as was proposed by the European Community, in the hope that this rather technical and therefore less menacing name would appease the United States and others opposed to an international organisation perceived as a threat to national sovereignty. Reportedly, the United States did not want to give the European Community the satisfaction of having given the new organisation its name, and further considered that an organisation with such a tongue-twisting and unappealing name as the 'Multilateral Trade Organization' would have a hard time winning the hearts and minds of the American people.[31] The *Agreement Establishing the World Trade Organization* was signed in Marrakesh in April 1994, and entered into force on 1 January 1995.[32] A perceptive observer, Gary Sampson, noted:

> Those who constructed the WTO are proud of having created what has been described as the greatest ever achievement in institutionalized global economic cooperation.[33]

Questions and Assignments 2.2

Did the Punta del Este Ministerial Declaration recognise the need for a new international organisation for trade? Briefly outline the events between 1990 and 1993 that led to an agreement on the establishment of a new international trade organisation in December 1993. Which countries or international entities were the driving forces behind the establishment of the WTO? Which countries were less enthusiastic and why?

---

[30] Withholding its consent to a new international trade organisation proved a useful bargaining chip in negotiations with the European Community. See *Financial Times*, 16 December 1993, 5.

[31] See *ibid*. The World Trade Organization and the World Tourism Organization concluded an agreement on the use of the acronym 'WTO'. To avoid confusion, the World Trade Organization agreed to use a distinct logo and will avoid using the acronym in the context of tourism. See GATT Doc. MTN.TNC/W/146, 4.

[32] Note that, after the entry into force of the *WTO Agreement* and the establishment of the WTO on 1 January 1995, the WTO and the GATT existed side by side for one year. The GATT 1947 was terminated only at the end of 1995.

[33] G. Sampson, *Overview*, in G. Sampson (ed.), *The Role of the World Trade Organization in Global Governance* (United Nations University Press, 2001), 5.

2.3. MANDATE OF THE WTO

The WTO was formally established and became operational on 1 January 1995 when the *WTO Agreement* entered into force. Pursuant to the *WTO Agreement*, the WTO has a broad and ambitious mandate. This section examines two main aspects of this mandate:

- the objectives of the WTO; and
- the functions of the WTO.

2.3.1. Objectives of the WTO

The reasons for establishing the WTO and the policy objectives of this international organisation are set out in the Preamble to the *WTO Agreement*. According to the Preamble, the Parties to the *WTO Agreement* agreed to the terms of this agreement and the establishment of the WTO:

> *Recognizing* that their relations in the field of trade and economic endeavour should be conducted with a view to raising standards of living, ensuring full employment and a large and steadily growing volume of real income and effective demand, and expanding the production of and trade in goods and services, while allowing for the optimal use of the world's resources in accordance with the objective of sustainable development, seeking both to protect and preserve the environment and to enhance the means for doing so in a manner consistent with their respective needs and concerns at different levels of economic development . . .
>
> *Recognizing* further that there is need for positive efforts designed to ensure that developing countries, and especially the least developed among them, secure a share in the growth in international trade commensurate with the needs of their economic development . . .

The ultimate objectives of the WTO are thus:

- the increase of standards of living;
- the attainment of full employment;
- the growth of real income and effective demand; and
- the expansion of production of, and trade in, goods and services.

However, it is clear from the Preamble that in pursuing these objectives the WTO must take into account the need for preservation of the environment and the needs of developing countries. The Preamble stresses the importance of *sustainable* economic development and of the *integration* of developing countries, and in particular least-developed countries, in the world trading system. Both of these aspects were absent from the Preamble to the GATT 1947.

The statements in the Preamble to the *WTO Agreement* on the objectives of the WTO are not without legal significance. In *US – Shrimp*, the Appellate Body stated:

> [The language to the Preamble to the *WTO Agreement*] demonstrates a recognition by WTO negotiators that optimal use of the world's resources should be made in

accordance with the objective of sustainable development. As this preambular language reflects the intentions of negotiators of the *WTO Agreement*, we believe it must *add colour, texture and shading to our interpretation of the agreements* annexed to the *WTO Agreement*, in this case, the GATT 1994. We have already observed that Article XX(g) of the GATT 1994 is appropriately read with the perspective embodied in the above preamble.[34]

[Emphasis added]

The preambular statements of the objectives of the WTO contradict the contention that the WTO is only about trade liberalisation without regard to environmental degradation and global poverty.

The Preamble also states how these objectives are to be achieved:

Being desirous of contributing to these objectives by entering into reciprocal and mutually advantageous arrangements directed to the substantial reduction of tariffs and other barriers to trade and to the elimination of discriminatory treatment in international trade relations ...

Resolved, therefore, to develop an integrated, more viable and durable multilateral trading system encompassing the General Agreement on Tariffs and Trade, the results of past trade liberalization efforts, and all of the results of the Uruguay Round of Multilateral Trade Negotiations, ...

Determined to preserve the basic principles and to further the objectives underlying this multilateral trading system ...

According to the Preamble to the *WTO Agreement*, the two main instruments, or means, to achieve the objectives of the WTO are reciprocal and mutually advantageous arrangements on:

- the reduction of trade barriers; and
- the elimination of discrimination.

These were also the two main instruments of the GATT 1947, but the *WTO Agreement* aims at constituting the basis of an *integrated*, *more viable* and *more durable* multilateral trading system.

In the Doha Ministerial Declaration of 14 November 2001, the WTO Members stated, with regard to the objectives of the WTO and its instruments for achieving these objectives:

We ... strongly reaffirm the principles and objectives set out in the Marrakesh Agreement Establishing the World Trade Organization, and pledge to reject the use of protectionism.

International trade can play a major role in the promotion of economic development and the alleviation of poverty. We recognize the need for all our peoples to benefit from the increased opportunities and welfare gains that the multilateral trading system generates. The majority of WTO Members are developing countries. We seek to place their needs and interests at the heart of the Work Programme adopted in this Declaration. Recalling the Preamble to the Marrakesh Agreement, we shall continue to make positive efforts designed to *ensure that developing countries*, and especially the least-developed among them, *secure a share in the growth of world trade* commensurate with the needs of their economic development ...

---

[34] Appellate Body Report, *US – Shrimp*, para. 153.

> We strongly reaffirm our commitment to the objective of *sustainable development*, as stated in the Preamble to the Marrakesh Agreement. We are convinced that the aims of upholding and safeguarding an open and non-discriminatory multilateral trading system, and acting for the protection of the environment and the promotion of sustainable development can and must be mutually supportive.[35]
>
>   [Emphasis added]

Questions and Assignments 2.3

What are the objectives of the WTO? Are development cooperation and environmental protection objectives of the WTO? Explain. What is the legal significance of the Preamble to the *WTO Agreement*? What are the main instruments, or means, of the WTO for achieving its objectives?

2.3.2. Functions of the WTO

In the broadest of terms, the primary function of the WTO is to:

> provide the common institutional framework for the conduct of trade relations among its Members in matters related to the agreements and associated legal instruments included in the Annexes to [the WTO] Agreement.[36]

More specifically, the WTO has been assigned six widely defined functions. Article III of the *WTO Agreement* states:

> 1. The WTO shall *facilitate the implementation*, administration and operation, and further the objectives, of this Agreement and of the Multilateral Trade Agreements, and shall also provide the framework for the implementation, administration and operation of the Plurilateral Trade Agreements.
> 2. The WTO shall provide the *forum for negotiations* among its Members concerning their multilateral trade relations in matters dealt with under the agreements in the Annexes to this Agreement. The WTO may also provide a forum for further negotiations among its Members concerning their multilateral trade relations, and a framework for the implementation of the results of such negotiations, as may be decided by the Ministerial Conference.
> 3. The WTO shall administer the Understanding on Rules and Procedures Governing the *Settlement of Disputes* (hereinafter referred to as the "Dispute Settlement Understanding" or "DSU") in Annex 2 to this Agreement.
> 4. The WTO shall administer the *Trade Policy Review Mechanism* (hereinafter referred to as the "TPRM") provided for in Annex 3 to this Agreement.
> 5. With a view to achieving greater coherence in global economic policy-making, the WTO shall *cooperate*, as appropriate, with the International Monetary Fund and with the International Bank for Reconstruction and Development and its affiliated agencies. [Emphasis added]

In addition to the functions of the WTO explicitly referred to in Article III of the *WTO Agreement*, technical assistance to developing-country Members, to

---

[35] Doha Ministerial Declaration, WT/MIN(01)/DEC/1, 20 November 2001, paras. 1, 2 and 6.
[36] Article II:1 of the WTO Agreement.

allow the latter to integrate into the world trading system is, undisputedly, also an important function of the WTO.

This section will examine the following functions of the WTO:

- the implementation of the WTO agreements;
- the negotiation of new agreements;
- the settlement of disputes;
- trade policies review;
- cooperation with other organisations; and
- technical assistance to developing countries.

2.3.2.1. *Implementation of the WTO agreements*

A first function of the WTO is to facilitate the implementation, administration and operation of the *WTO Agreement* and the manifold multilateral and plurilateral agreements annexed to it.[37] The WTO is also entrusted with the task of furthering the objectives of these agreements. For two concrete examples of what this function of 'facilitating' and 'furthering' entails, we refer to the work of the WTO Committee on Sanitary and Phytosanitary Measures (the 'SPS Committee') and the work of the WTO Committee on Safeguards. Article 12, paragraph 2, of the *SPS Agreement* states that the SPS Committee shall, *inter alia*:

> encourage and facilitate ad hoc consultations or negotiations among Members on specific sanitary or phytosanitary issues. The Committee shall encourage the use of international standards, guidelines or recommendations by all Members and, in this regard, shall sponsor technical consultation and study with the objective of increasing coordination and integration between international and national systems and approaches for approving the use of food additives or for establishing tolerances for contaminants in foods, beverages or feedstuffs.

Pursuant to Article 13 of the *Agreement on Safeguards*, the tasks of the Committee on Safeguard include:

> a. to monitor, and report annually to the Council for Trade in Goods on, the general implementation of this Agreement and make recommendations towards its improvement;
> b. to find, upon request of an affected Member, whether or not the procedural requirements of this Agreement have been complied with in connection with a safeguard measure, and report its findings to the Council for Trade in Goods;
> c. to assist Members, if they so request, in their consultations under the provisions of this Agreement; ...

This function of facilitating the implementation, administration and operation of the WTO agreements and furthering the objectives of these agreements is an essential function of the WTO. It involves most of its bodies and takes up much of their time.[38]

---

[37] For an overview of these agreements, see above, pp. 45–54.
[38] For a list and a description of these WTO bodies, see below, pp. 120–30.

Pursuant to Article III:1 of the *WTO Agreement*, the WTO also provides the 'framework for the implementation, administration and operation' of the plurilateral agreements. It has been suggested that the wording of Article III:1 indicates that plurilateral agreements will not get the same level of support as the multilateral agreements but there is little evidence of this in practice.

Questions and Assignments 2.4

Give two concrete examples of how the WTO facilitates the implementation, administration and operation of the *WTO Agreement* other than the examples given in this section.

2.3.2.2. Negotiation of new agreements

A second function of the WTO is to provide a permanent forum for negotiations amongst its Members. These negotiations may concern matters already dealt with in the WTO agreements but may also concern matters currently not yet addressed in WTO law. With regard to negotiations on matters already covered, the WTO is 'the' forum for negotiations while, with regard to negotiations on matters not yet addressed, it is 'a' forum among others.

To date, WTO Members have negotiated and concluded five trade agreements, in the framework of the WTO, providing for:

- further market access commitments for specific services and service providers (on financial services in 1995 and 1997,[39] on basic telecommunications services in 1997[40] and on the movement of natural persons in 1995[41]); and
- the liberalisation of trade in information technology products in 1996.[42]

Since the conclusion of these specific agreements in the first years of the WTO, no further agreements have been negotiated and concluded in the framework of the WTO. While the WTO provides a *permanent* forum for negotiations, in practice Members seem to require the political momentum, and the opportunity for package deals, brought by an old GATT-type round of negotiations covering a wide range of matters.

---

[39] Second Protocol to the General Agreement on Trade in Services, S/L/11, dated 24 July 1995; and Fifth Protocol to the General Agreement on Trade in Services, S/L/45, dated 3 December 1997.
[40] Fourth Protocol to the General Agreement on Trade in Services, S/L/20, dated 30 April 1996.
[41] Third Protocol to the General Agreement on Trade in Services, S/L/12, dated 24 July 1995.
[42] Ministerial Declaration on Trade in Information Technology Products (ITA), adopted on 13 December 1996 and entered into force on 1 July 1997; the ITA was agreed at the close of the Singapore Session of the Ministerial Conference in December 1996; the ITA provides for the elimination of customs duties and other duties and charges on information technology products by the year 2000 on an MFN basis; the implementation of the ITA, however, was contingent on approx. 90% of world trade in IT products being covered by the ITA; on 26 March 1997 that criterion was met; world trade in IT products was about $600 billion annually, or about 10.2 per cent of world merchandise. In 2004, sixty-three Members were party to the ITA.

After failing dismally to do so at the Seattle Session of the Ministerial Conference in November–December 1999, the WTO decided at the Doha Session of the Ministerial Conference in November 2001 to start a new round of multilateral trade negotiations, commonly referred to as the 'Doha Development Round'. In the Doha Ministerial Declaration, the WTO Members stressed their

> commitment to the WTO as the unique forum for global trade rule-making and liberalization.[43]

The Ministerial Declaration provides for an ambitious agenda for negotiations. These negotiations include matters on which, in the *WTO Agreement*, WTO Members had already agreed to continue negotiations, such as:

- trade in agricultural products;[44] and
- trade in services.[45]

In fact, negotiations on these matters had already started in early 2000. Furthermore, the Doha Development Round negotiations include negotiations on matters such as:

- problems of developing-country Members with the implementation of the existing WTO agreements (the so-called 'implementation issues');
- market access for non-agricultural products;
- TRIPS issues such as access for developing countries to essential medicines and the protection of geographical indications;
- rules on anti-dumping duties, subsidies and regional trade agreements;
- dispute settlement; and
- special and differential treatment for developing-country Members and least-developed-country Members.[46]

Pursuant to the Doha Ministerial Declaration, the Round must be concluded no later than 1 January 2005. When the results of the negotiations in all areas have been established, a Special Session of the Ministerial Conference will be held to take decisions regarding the adoption and implementation of those results.[47] With respect to the negotiations, the Ministerial Declaration further stated:

> With the exception of the improvements and clarifications of the Dispute Settlement Understanding, the conduct, conclusion and entry into force of the outcome of the negotiations shall be treated as parts of a *single undertaking*. However, agreements reached at an early stage may be implemented on a provisional or a definitive basis. Early agreements shall be taken into account in assessing the overall balance of the negotiations.[48]
>
> [Emphasis added]

---

[43] Doha Ministerial Declaration, WT/MIN(01)/DEC/1, dated 20 November 2001, para. 4.
[44] Article 20 of the *Agreement on Agriculture*.   [45] Article XIX of the GATS.
[46] For a complete list of the matters on the agenda of the Doha Development Round, see Ministerial Conference, Doha Ministerial Declaration, WT/MIN(01)/DEC/1, dated 20 November 2001.
[47] *Ibid.*, para. 45.   [48] *Ibid.*, para. 47.

Moreover, the Doha Ministerial Declaration provides that:

> The negotiations shall be conducted in a transparent manner among participants, in order to facilitate the effective participation of all. They shall be conducted with a view to ensuring benefits to all participants and to achieving an overall balance in the outcome of the negotiations.[49]

The Doha Development Round negotiations are conducted by the Trade Negotiations Committee (TNC) and its negotiating bodies. The TNC is established especially for the Round and endures until its completion. It supervises the overall conduct of the negotiations under the authority of the General Council. The Director-General of the WTO chairs the TNC *ex officio*. The actual negotiations take place either in Special Sessions of existing WTO bodies[50] or in especially established negotiating groups.[51] The TNC and its negotiating bodies consist of all the WTO Members and countries negotiating membership. Decisions on the results of the negotiations shall, however, be taken only by WTO Members.[52]

All publicly available documents, reports and position papers relating to the Doha Development Round are available on the *Documents Online* database of the WTO as TN/ ... documents.[53]

Some WTO Members, and in particular the European Communities, wanted a broader agenda for the Doha Development Round. They also wanted the WTO to start negotiations on, for example, the relationship between trade and investment, the relationship between trade and competition law and the relationship between trade and core labour standards. There was, however, strong opposition, especially among developing-country Members, to the inclusion of some or all of these matters on the agenda of negotiations. At the Doha Session of the Ministerial Conference, WTO Members decided that there will be no negotiations, within the context of the WTO, on the relationship between trade and core labour standards. However, with respect to what is commonly referred to as the 'Singapore issues',[54] namely:

- the relationship between trade and investment,
- the relationship between trade and competition law,
- transparency in government procurement, and
- trade facilitation,

the WTO Members decided in Doha that negotiations would start after they had agreed, by 'explicit consensus', on the modalities of these negotiations.[55] This agreement was to be reached at the Cancún Ministerial Conference in

---

[49] *Ibid.*, para. 49.
[50] E.g., the negotiations on the DSU take place in Special Sessions of the DSB.
[51] E.g., negotiations on market access for non-agricultural products take place in a Negotiating Group on Market Access established for that purpose.
[52] For further details on the institutional arrangements for the Doha Development Round, see below, pp. 130–1.
[53] See http://docsonline.wto.org/gen_home.asp?language=1&_=1, visited on 15 May 2004.
[54] At the Singapore Session of the Ministerial Conference in December 1996, these issues were first identified as possible issues for further negotiations within the WTO.
[55] Note that the concept of 'explicit consensus' was a *novum* in WTO law. For a further discussion, see below, p. 142.

September 2003. In the meantime, the relevant WTO bodies 'prepared' these negotiations by discussing, and attempting to clarify, the matters that would be addressed in the negotiations.

To date, the Doha Development Round has not been very successful. Important intermediate deadlines (for example, the modalities of the negotiations on trade in agricultural products, and on reform of the dispute settlement system) were not met.[56] The Cancún Session of the Ministerial Conference in September 2003, at which Members were to take stock of the progress made in the negotiations thus far and decide on how to proceed with the negotiations, was a failure. Nothing was agreed upon. The two principal stumbling blocks were the negotiations on trade in agricultural products and the start of the negotiations on the Singapore issues. On trade in agricultural products, the European Communities, the United States and other developed-country Members with protectionist agricultural policies were, in the opinion of developing countries, not willing to lower their import duties and export and domestic subsidies sufficiently.[57] On the Singapore issues, developing countries were unwilling to agree to the demand of the European Communities and others to start negotiations on these issues. In diplomatic language masking the deep sense of failure and disappointment, the Ministerial Statement adopted at the close of the Cancún Session on 14 September 2003 reads:

> All participants have worked hard and constructively to make progress as required under the Doha mandates. We have, indeed, made considerable progress. However, more work needs to be done in some key areas to enable us to proceed towards the conclusion of the negotiations in fulfilment of the commitments we took at Doha.[58]

The deadlock in the negotiations resulting from the failure of the Cancún Session was only overcome when, following weeks of intense discussions, a new Doha Work Programme was adopted by the General Council on 1 August 2004.

Thus, the negotiations in the context of the WTO Doha Development Round continue. The Doha Development Round negotiations currently proceed on the basis of this new Work Programme. In its decision of 1 August 2004, the General Council called on all Members 'to redouble their efforts towards the conclusion of a balanced overall outcome of the Doha Development Agenda'. Note that the General Council agreed to continue the negotiations beyond 1 January 2005, the time originally set out in the Doha Declaration.

Questions and Assignments 2.5

Has the WTO thus far been successful as a forum for the negotiations of new multilateral trade agreements? What is on the agenda of the Doha Development Round? What is not (or not yet) on the agenda? Find out

---

[56] Note that in the meantime an agreement on access to essential medicines for developing countries was reached. See below, pp. 149–50.
[57] See below, pp. 390–2, 583–6.   [58] WT/MIN(03)/20, dated 23 September 2003, para. 3.

exactly what the Doha Ministerial Declaration of November 2001 says
about the relationship between trade and core labour standards.

2.3.2.3. *Dispute settlement*

A third and very important function of the WTO is the administration of the
WTO dispute settlement system. As stated in Article 3.2, first sentence, of the
DSU:

> The dispute settlement system of the WTO is a central element in providing security
> and predictability to the multilateral trading system.

The prompt settlement of disputes under the WTO agreements is essential for
the effective functioning of the WTO and for maintaining a proper balance
between the rights and obligations of Members.[59] The WTO dispute settlement
system serves:

- to preserve the rights and obligations of Members under the WTO agreements; and
- to clarify the existing provisions of those agreements.[60]

The dispute settlement system is explicitly proscribed from adding to or
diminishing the rights and obligations provided in the WTO agreements.[61]

The WTO dispute settlement system, referred to as the 'jewel in the
crown' of the WTO, has been operational for nine years now, and has
arguably been the most prolific of all intergovernmental dispute settlement
systems in that period. Since 1 January 1995, more than 314 disputes have
been brought to the WTO system for resolution.[62] Some of these disputes,
involving, for example, national legislation on public health or environmental protection, were politically sensitive and have attracted considerable
attention from the media. With its compulsory jurisdiction, its strict timeframes, its confidential and closed nature, the possibility of appellate review
and the detailed mechanism to ensure compliance with recommendations
and rulings, the WTO dispute settlement system is unique among international dispute settlement systems. Chapter 3 examines in detail the origins,
basic principles, institutions and proceedings of the WTO dispute settlement
system.

2.3.2.4. *Trade policy review*

A fourth function of the WTO is the administration of the trade policy review
mechanism (TPRM).[63] The TPRM provides for the regular *collective* appreciation

---

[59] Article 3.3 of the DSU.   [60] Article 3.2, second sentence, of the DSU.
[61] Article 3.2, last sentence, of the DSU.
[62] See www.wto.org/english/tratop_e/dispu_status_e.htm, visited on 27 August 2004.
[63] Annex 3 to the *WTO Agreement*, entitiled 'Trade Policy Review Mechanism'.

and evaluation of the full range of *individual* Members' trade policies and practices and their impact on the functioning of the multilateral trading system.[64] The purpose of the TPRM is:

- to achieve greater transparency in, and understanding of, the trade policies and practices of Members; and
- to contribute, in this way, to improved adherence by all Members to rules, disciplines and commitments made under the WTO agreements.[65]

Under the TPRM, the trade policies and practices of all Members are subject to *periodic review*. The frequency of review is determined by reference to each Member's share of world trade in a recent representative period.[66] The four largest trading entities, i.e., the European Communities,[67] the United States, Japan and Canada, are subject to review every two years. The next sixteen are reviewed every four years. Other Members are reviewed every six years, except that a longer period may be fixed for least-developed-country Members.[68]

The trade policy reviews are carried out by the Trade Policy Review Body (TPRB)[69] on the basis of two reports: a report supplied by the Member under review, in which the Member describes the trade policies and practices it pursues; and a report, drawn up by the WTO Secretariat, based on the information available to it and that provided by the Member under review.[70] These reports, together with the concluding remarks by the TPRB Chairperson on a Member's review and the minutes of the meeting of the TPRB are published shortly after the review and are a valuable source of information on a WTO Member's trade policy. The TPR reports and the minutes of the TPRB are available on the *Documents Online* database of the WTO as WT/TPR/ ... documents.[71]

By the end of 2003, a total of 182 reviews had been conducted, covering ninety-six Members,[72] representing around 87 per cent of world trade.[73]

---

[64] See *Trade Policy Review Mechanism*, para. A(i).
[65] Note that it is explicitly stated that the TPRM is *not* intended to be used as a basis for the enforcement of specific objectives under the WTO agreements or for dispute settlement procedures. See *ibid.*
[66] See *ibid.*, para. C(ii).
[67] It is understood that the review of entities having a common external policy covering more than one Member shall cover all components of policy affecting trade including relevant policies and practices of the individual Members.
[68] Exceptionally, in the event of changes in a Member's trade policies or practices that may have a significant impact on its trading partners, the Member concerned may be requested by the TPRB, after consultation, to bring forward its next review.
[69] See below, p. 126.
[70] The two reports cover all aspects of the Member's trade policies, including its domestic laws and regulations, the institutional framework, bilateral, regional and other preferential agreements, the wider economic needs and the external environment.
[71] See http://docsonline.wto.org/gen_home.asp?language=1&_=1, visited on 15 May 2004. Press releases on trade policy reviews are available as PRESS/TPRB/ ... documents.
[72] Note that the European Communities and the Member States of the European Union are counted as one.
[73] See Report of the Trade Policy Review Body for 2003, WT/TPR/140, dated 31 October 2003, 1. The trade policies of Burundi, Bulgaria, Guyana, Haiti, Honduras, the Maldives and Niger were reviewed for the first time in 2003. The trade policies of the United States, the European Communities, Japan and Canada have been reviewed six times since 1995. For a statistical overview, see Report of the Trade Policy Review Body for 2003, WT/TPR/140, dated 31 October 2003, Annex I.

During 2003, the TPRB carried out reviews of sixteen Members. The programme for the year 2004 again includes sixteen reviews, including reviews of the trade policies of the United States and the European Communities.[74] Over the past few years, greater focus has been placed on the review of the trade policies of least-developed-country Members.

It is important to note that the TPRM is not intended to serve as a basis for the enforcement of specific obligations under the WTO agreements or for dispute settlement procedures, or to impose new policy commitments on Members. However, by *publicly* deploring inconsistencies with WTO law of a Member's trade policy or practices inconsistent with WTO law, the TPRM intends to 'shame' Members into compliance and to bolster domestic opposition to trade policy and practices inconsistent with WTO law. Likewise, by *publicly* praising WTO-consistent trade policies, the TPRM bolsters, both internationally and domestically, support for such policies.

By way of example, note the first trade policy review of Malawi, which the TPRB concluded on 6 and 8 February 2002. In his concluding remarks, the TPRB Chairperson stated:

> Members welcomed Malawi's commitment to the multilateral trading system and appreciated the substantial effort this requires from Malawi, a small landlocked least-developed country with no representation in Geneva. They were encouraged by the Government's economic reforms, including trade and investment liberalization efforts to foster increased efficiency and private sector development ...
>
> Members appreciated Malawi's on-going efforts to refrain from using non-tariff measures and its reliance on relatively low average tariffs as the main trade instrument. ...
>
> Members expressed some concern about Malawi's dependence on tobacco, which was subject to international price fluctuations and to the adverse effects of the anti-smoking campaigns in major developed markets. Members pointed out that Malawi's agricultural policies aimed at food security and rural development. They questioned the impact of communal land ownership on agricultural development and planned reforms in the sector, mainly in land tenure.

Trade policy reviews of developing-country Members also give an opportunity to identify the needs of these countries in terms of technical and other assistance.[75]

The final remarks of the TPRB Chairperson at the meeting of 23 and 25 January 2002, when the TPRB concluded the trade policy review of Pakistan, are also noteworthy:

> Purely as an aside, and as much a comment on the review process as on this Review, I was struck by [Pakistan's] Secretary Beg's remarks that questions had given his delegation food for considerable thought and that sources of information had been found of which he was unaware. This goes to the heart of our work: not only do we learn a lot about the Member, but often the Member learns a lot about itself. Moreover, this is put into a multilateral setting, thus serving to strengthen our system. Increasingly our work highlights the value of the Trade Policy Review Body.[76]

---

[74] *Ibid.*, Annexes II and III.

[75] See e.g. Trade Policy Review Body – Review of Malawi – TPRB's Evaluation, PRESS/TPRB/189, dated 8 February 2002.

[76] Trade Policy Review Body – Review of Pakistan – TPRB's Evaluation, PRESS/TPRB/187, dated 25 January 2002.

Apart from carrying out individual trade policy reviews, the TPRB also undertakes an *annual overview* of developments in the international trading environment which have an impact on the multilateral trading system. To assist the TPRB with this review, the Director-General presents an *annual report* setting out the major activities of the WTO and highlighting significant policy issues affecting the trading system.[77]

Questions and Assignments 2.6

What is the objective of the Trade Policy Review Mechanism? Is trade policy review under the WTO comparable with WTO dispute settlement? Find the latest trade policy review reports concerning the European Communities and the United States on the WTO website. Find also the latest Annual Report by the Director-General on the *Overview of Developments in the International Trading Environment.*

2.3.2.5. *Cooperation with other organisations*

A fifth function of the WTO is to cooperate with international organisations and non-governmental organisations.

Article III:5 of the WTO Agreement refers specifically to cooperation with the IMF and the World Bank. Such cooperation is mandated by the need for greater coherence in global economic policy-making. The 'linkages' between the different aspects of global economic policy (financial, monetary and trade) require that the international institutions with responsibilities in these areas follow coherent and mutually supportive policies. It is therefore stated in the Uruguay Round *Declaration on the Contribution of the World Trade Organization to Achieving Greater Coherence in Global Economic Policymaking*, commonly referred to as the *Declaration on Coherence*, that the WTO should:

> pursue and develop cooperation with the international organizations responsible for monetary and financial matters, while respecting the mandate, the confidentiality requirements and the necessary autonomy in decision-making procedures of each institution, and avoiding the imposition on governments of cross-conditionality or additional conditions. Ministers further invite the Director-General of the WTO to review with the Managing Director of the International Monetary Fund and the President of the World Bank, the implications of the WTO's responsibilities for its cooperation with the Bretton Woods institutions, as well as the forms such cooperation might take, with a view to achieving greater coherence in global economic policymaking.[78]

---

[77] See e.g *Overview of Developments in the International Trading Environment*, Annual Report by the Director-General (2002), WT/TPR/OV/8, dated 15 November 2002.

[78] *Declaration on the Contribution of the World Trade Organization to Achieving Greater Coherence in Global Economic Policymaking*, Final Act Embodying the Results of the Uruguay Round of Multilateral Trade Negotiations, para. 5.

The WTO has concluded agreements with both the IMF and the World Bank to give form to the cooperation required by Article III:5 of the *WTO Agreement*.[79] These agreements provide for consultations and the exchange of information between the WTO Secretariat and the staff of the IMF and the World Bank. The WTO, the IMF and the World Bank now cooperate quite closely on a day-to-day basis, in particular in the area of technical assistance to developing countries. Along with three other international organisations,[80] the IMF and the World Bank participate actively in a WTO-led Integrated Framework to help the least-developed countries expand their exports.[81] Furthermore, the IMF and the World Bank have observer status in the WTO and the WTO attends the meetings of the IMF and the World Bank. Officials of the three organisations meet regularly to discuss issues of global economic policy coherence.

Pursuant to Article V:1 of the *WTO Agreement*, the WTO is also to cooperate with other international organisations. Article V, which is entitled 'Relations with Other Organizations', states in its first paragraph:

> The General Council shall make appropriate arrangements for effective cooperation with other intergovernmental organizations that have responsibilities related to those of the WTO.

The WTO has made cooperation arrangements with, *inter alia*, the World Intellectual Property Organization (WIPO) and the United Nations Conference on Trade and Development (UNCTAD). In these and other international organisations the WTO has observer status.[82] The WTO and UNCTAD cooperate in a joint venture, the International Trade Centre (ITC). The ITC works with developing countries and economies in transition to set up effective trade promotion programmes to expand their exports and improve their import operations.

In addition, the WTO Secretariat has concluded a large number of so-called Memoranda of Understanding (MOUs) with other international secretariats. These MOUs provide mainly for technical assistance from the WTO to these other secretariats or the geographical regions in which they work. In September 2003, for example, the WTO Director-General, Supachai Panitchpakdi, and the Secretary General of the ACP Group, Jean-Robert Goulongana, signed an MOU committing both organisations to cooperate more closely to provide training, technical assistance and support to negotiators of the ACP member states in the Doha Development Round.[83]

---

[79] *Agreement between the International Monetary Fund and the World Trade Organization*, contained in Annex I to WT/GC/W/43, dated 4 November 1996; and the *Agreement between the International Bank for Reconstruction and Development and the World Trade Organization*, contained in Annex II to WT/GC/W/43, dated 4 November 1996.

[80] UNCTAD, the ITC and the UNDP.   [81] See below, p. 101.

[82] See WTO Annual Report 2003, Annex III.3(B) and (C), 124–5.

[83] The ACP (African, Caribbean and Pacific) Group comprises seventy-nine members, forty of which are least-developed countries, most of them from Africa. The objective of the ACP Group is to contribute to the economic development and social progress of its member States. See also below, pp. 107–8.

International governmental organisations are also invited to attend sessions of the WTO Ministerial Conference. Representatives of seventy-six international governmental organisations therefore attended the Cancún Session of the Ministerial Conference in September 2003.[84]

In addition to cooperating with intergovernmental international organisations, the WTO also cooperates with non-governmental organisations (NGOs). Article V:2 of the *WTO Agreement* states:

> The General Council may make appropriate arrangements for consultation and cooperation with non-governmental organizations concerned with matters related to those of the WTO.

On 18 July 1996, the General Council therefore adopted a set of guidelines clarifying the framework for relations with NGOs.[85] In these guidelines, the General Council:

> recognize the role NGOs can play to increase the awareness of the public in respect of WTO activities ...

It is important for the WTO to maintain a positive dialogue with the various components of civil society. To date, 'cooperation' with NGOs has essentially focused on:

- the attendance by NGOs at sessions of the Ministerial Conference;
- symposia for NGOs on specific issues;[86]
- regular briefings for NGOs on the work of WTO committees and working groups; and
- the frequent contact between the WTO Secretariat and NGOs.

The WTO Secretariat also regularly forwards a list to WTO Members of documents, position papers and newsletters submitted by NGOs. This list is made available on a special section of the WTO's website, devoted to NGOs' issues and WTO activities organized for the benefit of NGOs.[87] In the Doha Ministerial Declaration, Members stated:

> we are committed to making the WTO's operations more transparent, including through more effective and prompt dissemination of information, and to improve dialogue with the public.[88]

The extent and focus of cooperation between the WTO and NGOs is discussed in more detail later in this chapter.[89]

---

[84] WTO Annual Report 2004, 77 and Table III.9.

[85] Guidelines for Arrangements on Relations with Non-Governmental Organizations, Decision adopted by the General Council on 18 July 1996, WT/L/162, dated 23 July 1996. See below, pp. 157–8.

[86] The WTO Secretariat organised symposia for NGOs on issues such as the relationship between trade and the environment.

[87] See http://www.wto.org/english/forums_e/ngo_e/ngo_e.htm, visited on 6 February 2004.

[88] Ministerial Conference, Doha Ministerial Declaration, WT/MIN(01)/DEC/1, dated 20 November 2001, para. 10.

[89] See below, pp. 154–62.

2.3.2.6. *Technical assistance to developing countries*

The functions of the WTO listed in Article III of the *WTO Agreement* do not
explicitly include technical assistance to developing-country Members. Yet
this is, in practice, an important function of the WTO. Of course, it could be
argued that this function is implied in the other functions discussed above, in
particular the function of facilitating the implementation, administration and
operation, and of furthering the objectives, of the *WTO Agreement*. However, in
view of its importance, it deserves to be mentioned separately.

In order to exercise their rights and obligations under the *WTO Agreement*, to
reap the benefits of their membership of the WTO and to participate fully and
effectively in trade negotiations, most developing-country Members need to
have significantly more expertise in the area of trade law and policy. This is
recognised in many WTO agreements, including the *SPS Agreement*, the *TBT
Agreement*, the *TRIPS Agreement*, the *Customs Valuation Agreement* and the *DSU*,
which all specifically provide for technical assistance to developing-country
Members. This technical assistance may take the form of bilateral assistance,
given by developed-country Members, or multilateral assistance, given by the
WTO Secretariat.[90]

At its Doha Session in November 2001, the Ministerial Conference declared
that:

> technical cooperation and capacity building are core elements of the development
> dimension of the multilateral trading system.[91]

As an essential element of the Doha Development Agenda, in 2002, the WTO
embarked on a programme of greatly enhanced support for developing
countries.[92]

In his 2003 report on technical cooperation and capacity-building at the
Cancún Session of the Ministerial Conference, the WTO Director-General,
Supachai Panitchpakdi, stated:

> the challenges for the Secretariat in the area of technical cooperation and training were
> unprecedented. This was due to the high number of requests for assistance, the ever
> expanding priorities, increasing cooperation with all stakeholders, an ever growing
> interest in the WTO on the part of all layers of society, a rapidly evolving multilateral

---

[90] Note that Article 9 of the *SPS Agreement* also refers to assistance by other international organisations.
[91] Ministerial Conference, Doha Ministerial Declaration, WT/MIN(01)/DEC/1, dated 20 November 2001, para. 38.
[92] *Ibid.*, para. 41.

trading system, and the complexity of the subject matter of the negotiations and work programme.[93]

As from 2002, there was a notable increase in the WTO's budget to allow for more technical co-operation and capacity-building activities.[94] Furthermore, in 2002, WTO Members contributed almost 20 million Swiss Francs to the Doha Development Agenda Global Trust Fund.[95] In 2003 and 2004, Members continued to make contributions to the Global Trust Fund.[96] The Global Trust Fund has significantly complemented the regular budget as a source of funding for the WTO Secretariat's training and technical assistance activities.[97]

The WTO has also significantly improved co-ordination with other international organisations (World Bank, IMF, UNCTAD, etc.), with regional banks and regional organisations and with bilateral governmental donors. The coordination with the World Bank, the IMF and other international organisations takes place in the context of the Integrated Framework for Trade-Related Technical Assistance (IF). The IF has two objectives:

- to integrate trade priorities into LDCs' national development plans and poverty reduction strategies; and
- to assist in the coordinated delivery of trade-related assistance.

The IF currently applies to nineteen least-developed countries and a number of other least-developed countries have expressed an interest in joining the IF.[98] The WTO also takes a leading role in the Joint Integrated Technical Assistance Programme (JITAP) for Selected African and Least-Developed Countries. The JITAP is a major capacity-building programme put in place by the WTO, UNCTAD and the ITC to address trade-related capacity constraints of African countries. Sixteen African countries are currently involved in the JITAP.[99]

The WTO Secretariat organises, mostly in response to a specific request from one or more developing-country Members:

- *general seminars* on the multilateral trading system and the WTO;
- *technical seminars and workshops* focusing on a particular area of trade law or policy; and

---

[93] WT/MIN(03)/3, dated 14 August 2003, para. 7.

[94] See below, pp. 164–5. For the latest information on WTO technical co-operation and capacity building, see WTO, Annual Report 2003 on Training and Technical Cooperation, WT/COMTD/W/127, dated 17 April 2004.

[95] WT/MIN(03)/3, dated 14 August 2003, Annex II.

[96] For example, on 13 September 2003, Belgium committed itself to contribute €2 million over four years (2004–7) to the Global Trust Fund. See http://www.wto.org/english/news_e/pres03_e/pr359_e.htm, visited on 6 February 2004. On 19 November 2003, the Netherlands pledged a contribution of €1.4 million to the Global Trust Fund. See http://www.wto.org/english/news_e/pres03_e/pr367_e.htm, visited on 6 February 2004.

[97] See below, p. 166.   [98] See WT/MIN(03)/3, dated 14 August 2003, paras. 18 and 19.

[99] See WT/MIN(03)/3, dated 14 August 2003, paras. 20–2. An evaluation carried out in April 2002 concluded that JITAP had made an important contribution by enabling many of the participating countries to play a fuller role in the multilateral trading system and the ongoing negotiations, and that it had also contributed to developing a more holistic and comprehensive view of trade issues in participating countries. It was viewed as a model for possible replication elsewhere. See *ibid.*

- *technical missions* to assist developing-country Members on specific tasks related to the implementation of obligations under the WTO agreements (such as the adoption of trade legislation or notifications) and to provide support to mainstream trade into national plans for economic development and to assist in their strategies for poverty reduction.

In 2003, the WTO Secretariat organised 451 technical cooperation activities.[100] In 2002 and the first half of 2003, some 700 technical assistance and training activities, covering all topics and all regions, were implemented involving thousands of mission days of WTO staff members and other officials of partner institutions, and reaching an audience of approximately 25,000 participants.[101]

Furthermore, the WTO Secretariat organises *training courses* for developing-country government officials at the WTO headquarters in Geneva. These courses, introductory, general or advanced in nature, run from a few days to three months and cover the full range of WTO issues. In view of the interest in the three-month-long, general WTO *Trade Policy Course*, the WTO decided, in 2002, to organise this course not only in Geneva but also in developing countries in cooperation with local universities. The first of such trade policy courses took place in Africa: two in Nairobi for English-speaking African countries and one in Casablanca for French-speaking African countries.[102] While in general highly regarded, note that one African diplomat reportedly stated, with respect to those WTO training courses and seminars:

> the Secretariat attempts to put us through university in a period of three days; as a result I come out even more confused than when I started. These are complex issues that must be addressed in layers. We can't do the whole thing together.[103]

The WTO also organises a programme known as 'Geneva Week', a special week-long event bringing together representatives of developing-country Members and Observers that do not have permanent missions in Geneva.[104] The objectives of the Geneva Week are to introduce participants to WTO issues and work processes, and to provide information about the range of technical assistance available. During their stay in Geneva, participants have an opportunity to be involved in the work of WTO bodies; they also have the opportunity to interact with officials from other Geneva-based agencies, and with Geneva-based delegations. Geneva Week was initiated in 1999, and has since been held at least once a year.

---

[100] See WTO Annual Report 2004, 5.
[101] See WT/MIN(03)/3, dated 14 August 2003, para. 11. Reportedly, the evaluation and feedback mechanisms that have been established clearly suggest that, in most cases, the set objectives of the assistance and training provided were attained (*ibid.*).
[102] See WT/MIN(03)/3, dated 14 August 2003, para. 13.
[103] Reported by Shefali Sharma, *WTO Decision Making: A Broken Process*, WTO Cancún Series Paper No. 4 (Institute for Agriculture and Trade Policy, 2003), 10.
[104] See below, p. 109.

Since 1997, the WTO Secretariat has set up 'Reference Centres' in developing countries.[105] These Reference Centres allow government officials, as well as the local business and academic communities, to access essential documents instantly via the WTO's website. To date, more than 140 Reference Centres have been established all over the world. Priority has been given to least-developed countries.[106]

In November 2002, the OECD and the WTO established a database which gives details of the trade-related technical-assistance and capacity-building activities of all donors (bilateral, regional and multilateral). This database gives an overall picture of technical development activities, which helps the coordination of such activities and aims to avoid costly overlap.[107]

For a detailed overview of the WTO's current efforts regarding technical assistance to developing countries, refer to the Technical Assistance and Training Plan 2004.[108]

Questions and Assignments 2.8

Give a brief overview of the technical assistance efforts of the WTO. How does the WTO coordinate its technical assistance efforts with the efforts of other organisations and donors? Look up how much of the 2004 WTO budget was earmarked for technical co-operation, trade policy courses and the WTO contribution to the ITC.

2.4. MEMBERSHIP OF THE WTO

On 1 September 2004, the WTO had 147 Members and more than 25 countries were negotiating their accession to the WTO. This section will examine:

- the universality and diversity of the current membership;
- accession to the WTO;
- the obligations of WTO membership; and
- withdrawal and expulsion from the WTO.

2.4.1. Current membership

The membership of the WTO is quasi-universal. It includes all major trading powers and most developing countries. The Members of the WTO represent 92 per cent of the global population and 95 per cent of world trade. On 15 October 2004, the 148 Members of the WTO included:

---

[105] The WTO Secretariat provides governments with computers and other hardware, software and the training required for the operation of these Reference Centres.
[106] See WT/MIN(03)/3, dated 14 August 2003, paras. 74 and 75.
[107] See http://tcbdb.wto.org.
[108] WT/COMTD/W/119/Rev.3, dated 18 February, 2004. See also below, pp. 700–2.

Albania, 8 September 2000; **Angola**, 23 November 1996; **Antigua and Barbuda**, 1 January 1995; **Argentina**, 1 January 1995; **Armenia**, 5 February 2003; **Australia**, 1 January 1995; **Austria**, 1 January 1995; **Bahrain**, 1 January 1995; **Bangladesh**, 1 January 1995; **Barbados**, 1 January 1995; **Belgium**, 1 January 1995; **Belize**, 1 January 1995; **Benin**, 22 February 1996; **Bolivia**, 12 September 1995; **Botswana**, 31 May 1995; **Brazil**, 1 January 1995; **Brunei Darussalam**, 1 January 1995; **Bulgaria**, 1 December 1996; **Burkina Faso**, 3 June 1995; **Burundi**, 23 July 1995; **Cambodia**, 13 October 2004; **Cameroon**, 13 December 1995; **Canada**, 1 January 1995; **Central African Republic**, 31 May 1995; **Chad**, 19 October 1996; **Chile**, 1 January 1995; **China**, 11 December 2001; **Colombia**, 30 April 1995; **Congo**, 27 March 1997; **Costa Rica**, 1 January 1995; **Côte d'Ivoire**, 1 January 1995; **Croatia**, 30 November 2000; **Cuba**, 20 April 1995; **Cyprus**, 30 July 1995; **Czech Republic**, 1 January 1995; **Democratic Republic of the Congo**, 1 January 1997; **Denmark**, 1 January 1995; **Djibouti**, 31 May 1995; **Dominica**, 1 January 1995; **Dominican Republic**, 9 March 1995; **Ecuador**, 21 January 1996; **Egypt**, 30 June 1995; **El Salvador**, 7 May 1995; **Estonia**, 13 November 1999; **European Communities**, 1 January 1995; **Fiji**, 14 January 1996; **Finland**, 1 January 1995; **Former Yugoslav Republic of Macedonia**, 4 April 2003; **France**, 1 January 1995; **Gabon**, 1 January 1995; **The Gambia**, 23 October 1996; **Georgia**, 14 June 2000; **Germany**, 1 January 1995; **Ghana**, 1 January 1995; **Greece**, 1 January 1995; **Grenada**, 22 February 1996; **Guatemala**, 21 July 1995; **Guinea**, 25 October 1995; **Guinea Bissau**, 31 May 1995; **Guyana**, 1 January 1995; **Haiti**, 30 January 1996; **Honduras**, 1 January 1995; **Hong Kong, China**, 1 January 1995; **Hungary**, 1 January 1995; **Iceland**, 1 January 1995; **India**, 1 January 1995; **Indonesia**, 1 January 1995; **Ireland**, 1 January 1995; **Israel**, 21 April 1995; **Italy**, 1 January 1995; **Jamaica**, 9 March 1995; **Japan**, 1 January 1995; **Jordan**, 11 April 2000; **Kenya**, 1 January 1995; **Korea, Republic of**, 1 January 1995; **Kuwait**, 1 January 1995; **Kyrgyz Republic**, 20 December 1998; **Latvia**, 10 February 1999; **Lesotho**, 31 May 1995; **Liechtenstein**, 1 September 1995; **Lithuania**, 31 May 2001; **Luxembourg**, 1 January 1995; **Macao, China**, 1 January 1995; **Madagascar**, 17 November 1995; **Malawi**, 31 May 1995; **Malaysia**, 1 January 1995; **Maldives**, 31 May 1995; **Mali**, 31 May 1995; **Malta**, 1 January 1995; **Mauritania**, 31 May 1995; **Mauritius**, 1 January 1995; **Mexico**, 1 January 1995; **Moldova**, 26 July 2001; **Mongolia**, 29 January 1997; **Morocco**, 1 January 1995; **Mozambique**, 26 August 1995; **Myanmar**, 1 January 1995; **Namibia**, 1 January 1995; **Nepal**, 23 April 2004, **Netherlands** (including the Netherlands Antilles), 1 January 1995; **New Zealand**, 1 January 1995; **Nicaragua**, 3 September 1995; **Niger**, 13 December 1996; **Nigeria**, 1 January 1995; **Norway**, 1 January 1995; **Oman**, 9 November 2000; **Pakistan**, 1 January 1995; **Panama**, 6 September 1997; **Papua New Guinea**, 9 June 1996; **Paraguay**, 1 January 1995; **Peru**, 1 January 1995; **Philippines**, 1 January 1995; **Poland**, 1 July 1995; **Portugal**, 1 January 1995; **Qatar**, 13 January 1996; **Romania**, 1 January 1995; **Rwanda**,

22 May 1996; **Saint Kitts and Nevis**, 21 February 1996; **Saint Lucia**, 1 January 1995; **Saint Vincent and the Grenadines,** 1 January 1995; **Senegal**, 1 January 1995; **Separate Customs Territory of Taiwan, Penghu, Kinmen and Matsu**, 1 January 2002; **Sierra Leone**, 23 July 1995; **Singapore**, 1 January 1995; **Slovak Republic**, 1 January 1995; **Slovenia**, 30 July 1995; **Solomon Islands**, 26 July 1996; **South Africa,** 1 January 1995; **Spain**, 1 January 1995; **Sri Lanka**, 1 January 1995; **Suriname**, 1 January 1995; **Swaziland**, 1 January 1995; **Sweden**, 1 January 1995; **Switzerland**, 1 July 1995; **Tanzania**, 1 January 1995; **Thailand**, 1 January 1995; **Togo**, 31 May 1995; **Trinidad and Tobago**, 1 March 1995; **Tunisia**, 29 March 1995; **Turkey**, 26 March 1995; **Uganda**, 1 January 1995; **United Arab Emirates**, 10 April 1996; **United Kingdom**, 1 January 1995; **United States of America**, 1 January 1995; **Uruguay**, 1 January 1995; **Venezuela**, 1 January 1995; **Zambia**, 1 January 1995; **Zimbabwe**, 5 March 1995.[109]

2.4.1.1. *States and customs territories*

The WTO membership does not include only States. Separate customs territories possessing full autonomy in the conduct of their external commercial relations and in the other matters covered by the *WTO Agreement* can also be WTO Members.[110] Two examples of such WTO Members, which are not States but separate customs territories, are Hong Kong, China (commonly referred to as Hong Kong), and the Separate Customs Territory of Taiwan, Penghu, Kinmen and Matsu (commonly referred to as Chinese Taipei).

2.4.1.2. *The European Communities*

The European Communities is also a WTO Member but this is a case apart, specifically provided for in the *WTO Agreement*.[111] Both the European Communities and all the Member States of the European Union are Members of the WTO. This reflects the division of competence between the European Communities and the Member States in the various areas covered by the *WTO Agreement* (trade in goods; trade in services; and the protection of intellectual property rights). As is clear from Articles IX, XI and XIV of the *WTO Agreement*, it

---

[109] See http://www.wto.org/english/thewto_e/whatis_e/tif_e/org6_e.htm, visited on 1 September 2004. The date after the name of the country or separate customs territory refers to the date on which the country or separate customs territory became a Member of the WTO. Note that, on 11 September 2003, at the Cancún Session of the Ministerial Conference, the WTO Members approved the Protocols of Accession of Cambodia and Nepal. Nepal became the 147th Member in April 2004 and Cambodia became the 148th Member in October 2004.

[110] See Article XII of the *WTO Agreement*. The Explanatory Notes attached to the *WTO Agreement* stipulate that the terms 'country' or 'countries' as used in this Agreement and the Multilateral Trade Agreements are to be understood to include any separate customs territory Member of the WTO. In the case of a separate customs territory Member of the WTO, where an expression in this Agreement and the Multilateral Trade Agreements is qualified by the term 'national', such expression shall be read as pertaining to that customs territory, unless otherwise specified.

[111] See Article XI of the *WTO Agreement*.

is the European Communities, and not the European Community or the European Union, which is a Member of the WTO. The reason for this also lies in EU constitutional law. The European Communities, and not the European Community, is a WTO Member because at the time of the negotiations it was unclear whether the European Community, one of the then three Communities, had the necessary competence to conclude the *WTO Agreement*. In *Opinion 1/94*, the European Court of Justice established that, of the then three European Communities (EC, ECSC and Euratom), only the European Community needed to be involved in the WTO. However, the ECJ's clarification of the legal situation came after the *WTO Agreement* had been signed. The European Communities, and not the European Union, is a WTO Member, because in 1994 – the time of the conclusion of the *WTO Agreement* – the European Union did not yet have *any* competence to conclude international agreements. Note that both the European Communities and all Member States of the European Union are *full* Members of the WTO and that all obligations of the *WTO Agreement* apply equally to all of them. Irrespective of the internal division of competence between the European Communities and the Member States of the European Union, they can all be held responsible for compliance with all the obligations under the *WTO Agreement*.

2.4.1.3. Developing-country Members

Three-quarters of the 148 Members of the WTO are developing countries. There is no WTO definition of a 'developing country'. The status of 'developing-country Member' is based, to a large extent, on self-selection. Members announce whether they are 'developed' or 'developing' countries.

In recent years, and in particular since the failure of the Seattle Session of the Ministerial Conference at the end of 1999, developing-country Members have played an increasingly important role in the WTO, not only because of their numbers but also because of their increasing importance in the global economy.[112] Because of the size of their economies and the fact that they often act as spokespersons for other developing countries, China, Brazil, India and South Africa are today undoubtedly the most influential and 'activist' Members among the developing-country Members. While their interests do not always converge, these countries are formidable champions of the cause of the developing-country Members within the WTO.

As discussed further in this book, developing-country Members benefit from special and differential treatment under many of the WTO agreements and receive WTO technical assistance.[113] Other Members can, and occasionally do, challenge the decision of a Member to make use of special and differential treatment provisions available to developing countries.[114]

---

[112] See above, p. 8.   [113] See e.g. below, pp. 660–1, 665–6, 669–70, 700–2.
[114] Note that, for the Generalised System of Preferences (GSP), it is the preference-giving Member that decides which countries qualify for the preferential tariff treatment.

On 1 June 2004, there were thirty-one least-developed countries among the developing-country Members. The WTO recognises as least-developed countries those countries which have been designated as such by the United Nations.[115] Least-developed countries benefit from additional special and differential treatment. The least-developed countries among the WTO Members are Angola, Bangladesh, Benin, Burkina Faso, Burundi, Central African Republic, Chad, Democratic Republic of the Congo, Djibouti, Gambia, Guinea, Guinea Bissau, Haiti, Lesotho, Madagascar, Malawi, Maldives, Mali, Mauritania, Mozambique, Myanmar, Nepal, Niger, Rwanda, Senegal, Sierra Leone, Solomon Islands, Tanzania, Togo, Uganda and Zambia.[116]

2.4.1.4. Groups and alliances within the WTO

The developing-country Members and the least-developed-country Members are not the only distinguishable groups within the WTO membership. Other formal or informal groups and alliances exist in the WTO.

Some of these groups have been formed to defend common interests and advance common positions; they coordinate (or try to coordinate) positions and, when appropriate, speak in unison. This category of groups includes the *Association of South East Asian Nations* (ASEAN);[117] the *Caribbean Community* (CARICOM) and the *African, Caribbean and Pacific Group* (ACP). However, the *North American Free Trade Agreement* (NAFTA)[118] and the *Southern Common Market* (MERCOSUR),[119] while constituting significant efforts at regional economic integration, have not, or have hardly ever, spoken with one voice within the WTO. A well-known and quite effective alliance of a different kind is the Cairns group of seventeen agricultural-produce-exporting developed and developing countries.[120] This group was set up in the mid-1980s to campaign for agricultural trade liberalisation and is an important force in negotiations on trade in agricultural products. However, at the Cancún Session of the Ministerial Conference in September 2003, the Cairns group seemed to have all but disappeared. In the run-up to, and at, the Cancún Session, a new influential group of developing countries, including China, India, Brazil, Egypt, Argentina and South Africa, emerged. This group, commonly referred to as the 'G-20', forcefully demanded the dismantling of the trade distorting and protectionist agricultural policies of the European Communities, the

---

[115] Note that the share of world trade of the least-developed countries is around 0.5 per cent of the total and, therefore, marginal. See also above, p. 8.

[116] Nine other least-developed countries are in the process of accession to the WTO and therefore have Observer status. They are: Bhutan, Cape Verde, Ethiopia, Laos, Samoa, Sudan, Vanuatu and Yemen. See http://www.wto.org/english/thewto_e/whatis_e/tif_e/org7_e.htm, visited on 1 June 2004.

[117] I.e. Cambodia, Malaysia, Myanmar, Indonesia, Singapore, the Philippines, Thailand and Brunei Darussalam. Other Members of ASEAN, namely Laos and Vietnam, are negotiating their accession to the WTO.

[118] I.e. Canada, the US and Mexico.

[119] I.e. Brazil, Argentina, Paraguay and Uruguay.

[120] I.e. Argentina, Australia, Bolivia, Brazil, Canada, Chile, Colombia, Costa Rica, Guatemala, Indonesia, Malaysia, New Zealand, Paraguay, the Philippines, South Africa, Thailand and Uruguay. See http://www.cairnsgroup.org/introduction.html, visited on 6 February 2004.

United States and other industrialised countries. Also in Cancún, a new group known as the ACP/LDC/AU alliance (an alliance made up of the ACP countries, the least-developed countries and the countries of the African Union), emerged as the 'representative' of the interests of the poorest countries.[121]

Other groups have been formed to allow for discussion in small(er) groups of Members, to agree on new initiatives, to break deadlocks and to achieve compromises. The best-known example of such a group is the Quad, the group of the four largest trading entities, i.e. Canada, the European Communities, Japan and the United States. The Quad plays a central role in any negotiation in the context of the WTO. In the summer of 2004, a new key grouping, referred to as the 'Five Interested Parties', consisting of Australia, Brazil, the European Communities, India and the United States, played a crucial role in breaking the deadlock in the Doha Development Round negotiations and reaching an agreement on the new Doha Work Programme.

2.4.1.5. Observers

The WTO also has thirty Observer Governments. With the exception of the Holy See, these Observer Governments must start accession negotiations within five years of becoming an Observer. Occasionally, the decision on granting Observer status leads to controversy. For example, in January 2004, the European Communities agreed to back a US-sponsored request by Iraq's Governing Council for Observer status. However, the European Communities stressed that it also wanted to extend this status to Iran and Syria, an initiative opposed by the United States.[122] At its meeting on 11 February 2004, the General Council granted Iraq Observer status.[123] At the same meeting, the General Council also considered Iran's request to begin accession negotiations. The European Communities, China, India, Indonesia and other Members supported this request. However, as the United States was opposed, the General Council decided to postpone a decision on Iran's request.[124]

In 1997, the General Council granted permanent Observer status to the UN, UNCTAD, the FAO, WIPO and the OECD.[125] The IMF and the World Bank have permanent Observer status under their respective agreements with the WTO.[126] Other international organisations have Observer status in the WTO bodies that deal in particular with the matters within their mandate. As such, the WHO/FAO Joint Codex Alimentarius Commission has Observer status in the WTO SPS Committee; and the Convention on International Trade in

---

[121] This group is also referred to as the 'G-90'.
[122] See T. Buck and G. de Jonquières, 'EU Backs Iraqi Plea for WTO Status', *Financial Times*, 26 January 2004.
[123] See BRIDGES, *Weekly Trade News Digest*, 12 February 2004.
[124] See *ibid.*
[125] See WT/GC/M/18. Also, the ITC, a joint subsidiary of the WTO and UNCTAD, was granted permanent Observer status. See WT/GC/M/25.
[126] See above, pp. 97–8.

Endangered Species (CITES) in the WTO Committee on Trade and Environment.[127]

2.4.1.6. Representation in Geneva

Most Members have a permanent diplomatic mission in Geneva.[128] This is often a mission to all Geneva-based international organisations; however, some Members have a separate mission to the WTO. This is the case, for example, for the United States, the European Communities, India, Honduras, Hungary and Malaysia. The meetings of WTO bodies are attended by diplomats from the mission, but, increasingly, government officials specialising in a specific matter are flown in to attend meetings in Geneva and present their governments' views.

Questions and Assignments 2.9

Can non-State entities become Members of the WTO? Explain why both the European Communities and all the Member States of the European Union are Members of the WTO? Why is the European Communities, and not the European Community or the European Union, a Member of the WTO? When will a country 'qualify' as a developing-country Member or as a least-developed-country Member? Discuss briefly the various groups and alliances that exist within the WTO membership.

2.4.2. Accession

Becoming a Member of the WTO is not an easy matter. This section discusses the accession process and looks at some recent and future accessions.

2.4.2.1. The accession process

The *WTO Agreement* initially provided for two ways of becoming a WTO Member. The first, 'original membership', was provided for in Article XI of the *WTO Agreement*, and allowed Contracting Parties to the GATT 1947 (and the European Communities) to join the WTO by:

- accepting the terms of the *WTO Agreement* and the Multilateral Trade Agreements; and

---

[127] For an exhaustive list of all international organisations having Observer status in the WTO and in one or more WTO bodies, see WTO Annual Report 2004, Tables II.9(A) and (B), 79–82. These tables also list the many international organisations that have requested Observer status but have not yet been granted this status. Table II.9(C) lists the international organisations that were granted Observer status in committees under the Plurilateral Trade Agreements. Table III.9 lists the international organisations that were granted Observer status at the Doha Session of the Ministerial Conference.

[128] There are, however, twenty-four WTO Members (and twelve Observers) that do not have any form of representation in Geneva. See also above, p. 102.

- making concessions and commitments for both trade in goods and services (embodied in national schedules annexed to the GATT 1994 and the GATS respectively).[129] This way of becoming a WTO Member was only available until March 1997.[130] All but one of the GATT Contracting Parties became WTO Members in this way.[131] Of the 148 WTO Members, 123 are 'original Members' in that they became Members pursuant to Article XI. It should be stressed, however, that 'original Members' have exactly the same membership rights as other Members.

The second way of becoming a WTO Member is through accession, and this way is open indefinitely. The procedure for accession is set out in Article XII of the *WTO Agreement*. This provision states:

> 1. Any State or separate customs territory possessing full autonomy in the conduct of its external commercial relations and of the other matters provided for in this Agreement and the Multilateral Trade Agreements may accede to this Agreement, on terms to be agreed between it and the WTO. Such accession shall apply to this Agreement and the Multilateral Trade Agreements annexed thereto.
> 2. Decisions on accession shall be taken by the Ministerial Conference. The Ministerial Conference shall approve the agreement on the terms of accession by a two-thirds majority of the Members of the WTO.
> 3. Accession to a Plurilateral Trade Agreement shall be governed by the provisions of that Agreement.

To become a WTO Member through accession, a country or customs territory has to negotiate the terms of accession with those countries and customs territories that are already Members. The candidate for membership must always accept the terms of the *WTO Agreement* and all Multilateral Trade Agreements. This is not up for negotiation. The subject of the accession negotiations are the market access commitments and concessions the candidate for membership has to make. A 'ticket of admission' is negotiated. When a State or customs territory accedes to the WTO, it instantly benefits from all the efforts that WTO Members have undertaken to date to reduce barriers to trade and increase market access. In return for the access to the markets of current Members that a new Member will obtain, that new Member will itself have to open up its market for the current Members. The extent of the market access commitments and concessions that a candidate for membership will be expected to make will depend to a large extent on its economic development.

Generally speaking, there are four phases in the accession process. In the first phase – the 'tell us about yourself' phase – the country or customs territory applying for membership has to report on all aspects of its trade and economic policies that are relevant to the obligations under the WTO agreements, and to

---

[129] The term 'original membership' is an unfortunate misnomer. It suggests that there are two sorts of membership with different rights. This is not the case. All Members have the same membership rights (and obligations). The term 'original membership' is used merely to distinguish between the different ways of acquiring membership.

[130] The General Council had initially set the deadline for becoming a WTO Member in this way at 1 January 1997 but later agreed on a short extension.

[131] Yugoslavia is the only GATT Contracting Party which did not become a WTO Member in this way.

submit a memorandum on these policies to the WTO. A WTO working party established especially to deal with the request for accession, will examine this memorandum.[132]

When the working party has made satisfactory progress with its examination of the trade and economic policies, the second phase is initiated. In this phase – the 'work out with us individually what you have to offer' phase – parallel bilateral negotiations on market access begin between the candidate for membership and individual Members. These negotiations are bilateral because different Members have different trading interests, but it should be recalled that the new Member's market access commitments and concessions will eventually apply equally to all WTO Members as a result of the MFN treatment obligation. These bilateral market access negotiations can be very difficult.

Once the working party has fully completed its examination of the trade and economic policies of the candidate, and the parallel bilateral market access negotiations are successfully concluded, the third phase of the accession process can start. In this phase – the 'let's draft membership terms' phase – the working party finalises the terms of accession which are set out in a report, a draft membership treaty ('protocol of accession') and lists ('schedules') of the market access commitments and concessions of the candidate for membership. This package is submitted to the Ministerial Conference or the General Council.

In the fourth and final phase of the accession process – the 'decision' phase – the Ministerial Conference or the General Council decides by consensus or, if consensus cannot be achieved, by a two-thirds majority of WTO Members on the application for membership. In case of a positive decision, the candidate for membership accedes to the WTO thirty days after it has deposited its instrument of ratification of the membership treaty (i.e. the protocol of accession).

Even when no major problems are encountered, accession negotiations are typically long. The shortest accession process to date took just under three years. The accession negotiations with Algeria have now been going on since 1987. The delays in completing accession negotiations have been severely criticised. However, this situation is not only the result of hard bargaining on the part of WTO Members or political facts. It is also a result of the tardy supply of information and making the necessary policy adjustments on the part of the candidate for membership. Adapting to WTO rules usually requires significant changes in national legislation and practices. It can take years to draft, approve and apply new legislation required for accession to the WTO. Least-developed countries, in particular, often lack the administrative capacity to conduct the complex negotiations and to develop and apply the necessary changes in national legislation and practices. In December 2002, the General Council

---

[132] See *Members and Accession: Becoming a Member of the WTO*, Cancún WTO Ministerial 2003 Briefing Notes. See http://www.wto.org/english/thewto_e/minist_e/min03_e/brief_e/brief23_e.htm, visited 12 February 2004.

agreed on guidelines to facilitate the accession of least-developed countries to the WTO, in accordance with a mandate given at the Doha Session of the Ministerial Conference in November 2001.[133] These guidelines concern, *inter alia*, technical assistance and capacity-building.

2.4.2.2. Past and future accessions

On 1 September 2004, there were more than twenty-five countries negotiating their accession to the WTO. The most important ongoing accession negotiations, in both economic and political terms, are those with Russia, Ukraine and Saudi Arabia.[134] In March 2002, Robert Cottrell and Stefan Wagstyl of the *Financial Times* reported on the accession of Russia:

> Russian President Vladimir Putin's bid to take his country into the World Trade Organization as early as next year has split the country's business community.
> While few business leaders dare to openly criticise the president, a strong lobby has formed seeking to delay accession to give Russian industry more time to prepare for international competition.

A major issue in the negotiations on accession was the low energy prices in Russia. The European Communities considered these low energy prices to be the result of an unfair State subsidy which distorts global competition. It required Russia to raise its energy prices. In October 2003, President Putin reportedly said on this divisive issue:

> EU bureaucrats either don't understand it or deliberately put unacceptable conditions for Russia to join the WTO. We cannot move to world energy prices in a single day. It will ruin the country's economy.[135]

In response, a spokesperson for Trade Commissioner Lamy stated:

> the WTO's adhesion process is not political, it's a process that consists in fulfilling rules and regulations that exist already at the WTO ... When a country doesn't meet them, it doesn't join.[136]

In addition to the sensitive issue of Russia's domestic energy prices, progress in the accession negotiations was, and is, hindered by issues such as Russia's restrictions on imported beef, pork and poultry and its reluctance to open up its services market to foreign firms.[137] On 21 May 2004, Russia reached a bilateral agreement on market access concessions with the European Communities, its biggest trade partner, thus clearing a major hurdle in the accession process. Currently, Russia is still in bilateral negotiations with its other main trading partners.

---

[133] Interim Report by the Director-General: Paragraph 43 of the Doha Ministerial Declaration, Decision of the General Council, WT/GC/W/485, dated 4 December 2002.
[134] For an overview of the accession negotiations in 2002, see the Annual Report of the General Council (2002), WT/GC/70, dated 14 February 2003, 28ff.
[135] See WTO Forum, *WTO Newsletter*, 10 October 2003.   [136] *Ibid.*
[137] BRIDGES, *Weekly Trade News Digest*, 12 February 2004, 8.

On the accession of Saudi Arabia, Supachai Panitchpakdi stated in January 2004, that:

> After over ten years of negotiations, the prospect of Saudi Arabia's accession to the WTO is no longer a dim light at the end of the tunnel, but an imminent reality. If all goes well, there is a realistic chance that Saudi Arabia will accede to the WTO before the end of this year.[138]

As of the end of August 2004, the United States was the only WTO Member country with which Saudi Arabia had not yet concluded a bilateral agreement.[139] Sticking points in the market access negotiations with these countries reportedly are issues related to insurance, financial services, telecommunications, intellectual property protection and non-tariff barriers.[140]

Since 2000, Albania, Armenia, Cambodia, China, Croatia, the Former Yugoslav Republic of Macedonia, Georgia, Jordan, Lithuania, Moldova, Oman, Nepal and the Separate Customs Territory of Taiwan, Penghu, Kinmen and Matsu successfully completed their accession negotiations.[141] In 2003, Cambodia and Nepal became the first least-developed countries to successfully complete accession negotiations.

The most difficult and most important accession negotiations ever conducted were those with the People's Republic of China.[142] China was one of the twenty-three original signatories of the GATT 1947 but after China's revolution in 1949, the Chinese nationalist government in Chinese Taipei announced that China would leave the GATT system. The government of the People's Republic of China in Beijing never recognised this withdrawal decision and, in 1986, it notified the GATT of its wish to resume its status as a GATT Contracting Party. The GATT Contracting Parties considered, however, that China would have to negotiate its re-accession. In 1987, a GATT Working Party on the Accession of China was established and in 1995 this Working Party was converted into a WTO Working Party. On 16 November 1999, Frances Williams and Neil Buckley of the *Financial Times* reported at a crucial moment of these protracted negotiations as follows:

> Completion of negotiations with Washington does not mean China can now join the WTO, though it is an essential step in the process. Beijing has to conclude market-opening negotiations on goods and services with each of its main trading partners and its terms of entry must then be approved by all WTO members. The first half of 2000 is the earliest realistic date for entry ... China has now completed membership talks with 13 nations, including Japan, Australia, Chile and Hungary. However, it has yet to

---

[138] Speech by Supachai Panitchpakdi, *The Future of the WTO and Its Role in Global Economic Growth*, Jeddah Economic Forum, 19 January 2004, see http://www.wto.org/english/news_e/spsp_e/spsp20_e.htm, visited on 6 February 2004.

[139] See P. K. Abdul Ghafour, 'Saudi Team in US for WTO Talks', at www.arabnews.com, visited on 27 August 2004.

[140] See BRIDGES, *Weekly Trade News Digest*, 4 March 2004, 9.

[141] Source: www.wto.org, visited on 1 September 2003.

[142] See E. Wu, 'China Today: Why Its Accession to the World Trade Organization is Inevitable and Good for the International Community', *Journal of International Economic Law*, 2002, 689–718 (reproduced by permission of Oxford University Press); and Q. Kong, 'China's WTO Accession: Commitments and Implications', *Journal of International Economic Law*, 2000, 655–90 (reproduced by permission of Oxford University Press).

conclude negotiations with the European Union and 23 other trading partners, among them Canada, Brazil, India and Switzerland. Of those, the EU is the most crucial for China's hopes of entry. Officials suggested yesterday that senior European Commission negotiators might depart for China within days, followed later by Pascal Lamy, the EU's new trade commissioner. The deal with the US was broadly welcomed in Brussels yesterday, where officials said about 80 per cent of the package was in common with the EU's aims ... In the 20 per cent of the package where the EU has differences, officials said there were three main areas of concern. First, there are differences on certain tariffs. The EU has specific requirements on between 300 and 400 lines where it exports more than the US, including some agricultural equipment, as well as ceramics and glassware, cosmetics, leather goods and shoes. In some areas where the EU and US have similar interests, Brussels has been pressing for bigger tariff reductions, such as on cars. Secondly, the EU has particular demands in services. In life insurance, seen as a big growth area, it wants to secure the same number of operating licences as the US, and a similar possibility to set-up wholly-owned operations in China – something Beijing has so far not been prepared to give. In telecoms, it wants to ensure the possibility of eventually owning more than 50 per cent of operators, not just in fixed-line services, but in mobile telephony, paging and satellite phones ... The EU also has concerns on some "horizontal" issues, such as export performance requirements – where foreign companies manufacturing in China are required to export as much as 70 per cent of turnover – and conditions on technology transfer. It is pressing for commitments to non-discrimination and transparency in government procurement. Under the WTO's Most Favoured Nation rule the best terms negotiated by any one member must be extended to all. So the US, which has wide-ranging trade interests in China, can set the pace for the rest. However, other countries may want to hold out for a better deal in certain sectors to which they attach more importance than the US.[143]

The accession negotiations with China eventually took almost fifteen years and resulted in a legal text of some 900 pages. At its Doha Session in November 2001, the Ministerial Conference approved by consensus the text of the agreement for China's entry into the WTO. On 11 December 2001, China formally became a Member of the WTO.[144]

In order to join the WTO, China has agreed to undertake a series of important market access commitments and concessions and to offer a more predictable environment for trade and foreign investment in accordance with WTO rules. While China reserves the right of exclusive State trading for products such as cereals, tobacco, fuels and minerals and maintains some restrictions on transportation and distribution of goods inside the country, many of the restrictions on foreign companies, currently imposed by China, were to be eliminated or considerably eased after a three-year phase-out period.

During a twelve-year period starting from the date of accession, a special transitional safeguard mechanism applies. This mechanism allows other WTO Members to restrict – more easily than under the normal rules on safeguard measures[145] – imports of products of Chinese origin that cause or threaten to cause market disruption to their domestic producers. On the other hand,

---

[143] F. Williams, 'Europe the Next Stop on the Negotiation Trail', *Financial Times*, 16 November 1999.
[144] China Accession Protocol, WT/ACC/CHN/49, dated 1 October 2001.
[145] See below, pp. 633–49.

prohibitions, quantitative restrictions or other measures maintained against imports from China, in a manner inconsistent with the *WTO Agreement*, are phased out or otherwise dealt with in accordance with mutually agreed terms and timetables specified in an annex to the Protocol of Accession.[146]

Questions and Assignments 2.10

Is the country of which you are a national an 'original Member' of the WTO? Does it matter whether it is or not? Why does the WTO, as do other international organisations, not automatically allow any country willing to accept the obligations of membership to join the WTO? Discuss the various steps in the process of accession to the WTO.

2.4.3. Obligations of membership

Article XVI:4 of the *WTO Agreement* provides that:

> Each Member shall ensure the conformity of its laws, regulations and administrative procedures with its obligations as provided in the annexed Agreements.

Article XIV:5 of the *WTO Agreement* provides that:

> No reservations may be made in respect of any provision of this Agreement. Reservations in respect of any of the provisions of the Multilateral Trade Agreements may only be made to the extent provided for in those Agreements. Reservations in respect of a provision of a Plurilateral Trade Agreement shall be governed by the provisions of that Agreement.

One should note, however, the possibility of obtaining a waiver of obligations under the WTO agreements (Article IX:3 and 4 of the *WTO Agreement*) and the 'non-application' clause, both discussed below.[147]

2.4.3.1. Waiver of WTO obligations

When a Member finds it difficult, if not impossible, to meet an obligation under one of the WTO agreements, that Member can request the WTO to waive the 'problematic' obligation. Pursuant to Article IX:3 of the *WTO Agreement*, 'exceptional circumstances' may justify such a waiver.[148] The decision of the Ministerial Conference (or the General Council) granting the waiver shall state the exceptional circumstances, the terms and conditions governing the

---

[146] 'WTO Successfully Concludes Negotiations on China's Entry', WTO Press/243, dated 17 September 2001.

[147] Note that there are a number of exceptions to the general rule of Article XVI:5 of the *WTO Agreement* that no reservations can be made to the provisions of the Multilateral Trade Agreements. See, e.g. Article 15.1 of the *TBT Agreement* and Article 32.2 of the *SCM Agreement*. To date, however, no reservation has been made under these exceptions.

[148] Note that, for waivers of GATT 1994 obligations, provisions of the *Understanding in Respect of Waivers of Obligations under the General Agreement on Tariffs and Trade 1994* also apply.

application of the waiver and the date on which the waiver shall be terminated.[149] The procedure for taking this decision is examined below.[150]

As is provided in Article IX:4 of the *WTO Agreement*, any waiver granted for a period of more than one year shall be reviewed annually. The General Council shall examine whether the exceptional circumstances justifying the waiver still exist and whether the terms and conditions attached to the waiver have been met. On the basis of this annual review, the waiver may be extended, modified or terminated. Until now, these annual reviews have, however, been largely *pro forma*.[151]

One of the most important waivers currently in force is a waiver of the MFN treatment obligation under Article I:1 of the GATT 1994, granted to the European Communities, with respect to preferential tariff treatment given to products of African, Caribbean and Pacific countries under the terms of the Cotonou *ACP–EC Partnership Agreement*.

Another waiver worth noting is the waiver granted to Australia, Brazil, Canada, Israel, Japan, Korea, Philippines, Sierra Leone, Thailand, the United Arab Emirates and the United States to allow these Members to take domestic measures under the Kimberley Process aimed at banning trade in conflict diamonds, also referred to as 'blood diamonds'.[152] The WTO waiver decision of the General Council of 15–16 May 2003 exempts – from 1 January 2003 until 31 December 2006 – trade measures taken under the Kimberley Process by these eleven Members (and other Members that join subsequently) from the MFN treatment obligation (Article I:1 of the GATT 1994), from the prohibition of quantitative restrictions (Article XI:1 of the GATT 1994) and from the obligation of non-discriminatory administration of quantitative restrictions (Article XIII:1 of the GATT 1994).

With regard to trade in essential medicines for HIV, malaria and other life-threatening diseases, note the Decision of the General Council of 30 August 2003, which waives obligations under Article 31(f) and (h) of the *TRIPS Agreement* to give developing countries access to these essential medicines.

The Annual Report of the General Council gives an overview every year of all Article IX:3 decisions on new waivers and Article IX:4 reviews of existing waivers.[153]

In *EC – Bananas III*, the European Communities argued that the Lomé Waiver, which waived the provisions of Article I:1 of the GATT 1994, should also be interpreted to waive the provisions of Article XIII of the GATT 1994. In that case, the Panel accepted this argument to the extent that 'the scope of

---

[149] Article IX:4 of the *WTO Agreement*.   [150] See below, pp. 145–6.

[151] For an overview of waivers granted and reviewed in 2002, see the Annual Report of the General Council (2002), WT/GC/70, dated 14 February 2003, 33ff.

[152] Decision of the General Council of 15–16 May 2003, WT/GC/W/498, dated 13 May 2003. In November 2002, the participants in the Kimberley Process issued the Interlaken Declaration expressing their intent to implement an international scheme of certification for rough diamonds to help break the link between armed conflict and the trade in rough diamonds. The Kimberley Process provides that each participant should 'ensure that no shipment of rough diamonds is imported or exported to a non-Participant'.

[153] See e.g. General Council, *Annual Report* (2003), WT/GC/76, dated 6 January 2004, 6–7.

Figure 2.1 Decision of 14 November 2001 of the Ministerial Conference on a Waiver for the ACP–EC Partnership Agreement[154]

World Trade Organization

WT/MIN(01)/15
14 November 2001
(01–5786)

Ministerial Conference
Fourth Session
Doha, 9–14 November 2001

European Communities – The ACP–EC Partnership Agreement

Decision of 14 November 2001

The Ministerial Conference,

Having regard to paragraphs 1 and 3 of Article IX of the Marrakech Agreement Establishing the World Trade Organisation (the "WTO Agreement"), the Guiding Principles to be followed in considering applications for waivers adopted on 1 November 1956 (BISD 5S/25), the Understanding in Respect to Waivers of Obligations under the General Agreement on Tariffs and Trade 1994, paragraph 3 of Article IX of the WTO Agreement, and Decision-Making Procedures under Articles IX and XII of the WTO Agreement agreed by the General Council (WT/L/93);

Taking note of the request of the European Communities (EC) and of the Governments of the ACP States which are also WTO members (hereinafter also the "Parties to the Agreement") for a waiver from the obligations of the European Communities under paragraph 1 of Article I of the General Agreement with respect to the granting of preferential tariff treatment for products originating in ACP States as required by Article 36.3, Annex V and its Protocols of the ACP–EC Partnership Agreement (hereinafter also referred to as "the Agreement")[155]

Considering that, in the field of trade, the provisions of the ACP–EC Partnership Agreement requires preferential tariff treatment by the EC of exports of products originating in the ACP States;

Considering that the Agreement is aimed at improving the standard of living and economic development of the ACP States, including the least developed among them;

Considering also that the preferential tariff treatment for products originating in ACP States as required by Article 36.3, Annex V and its Protocols of the Agreement is designed to promote the expansion of trade and economic development of beneficiaries in a manner consistent with the objectives of the WTO and with the trade, financial and development needs of the beneficiaries and not to raise undue barriers or to create undue difficulties for the trade of other members;

. . .

Considering that, in light of the foregoing, the exceptional circumstances justifying a waiver from paragraph 1 of Article I of the General Agreement exist;

Decides as follows:

1. Subject to the terms and conditions set out hereunder, Article I, paragraph 1 of the General Agreement shall be waived, until 31 December 2007, to the extent necessary to permit the European Communities to provide preferential tariff treatment for products originating in ACP States as required by Article 36.3, Annex V and its Protocols of the ACP–EC Partnership Agreement, without being required to extend the same preferential treatment to like products of any other member . . .

Article XIII:1 is identical with that of Article I'.[156] The Appellate Body reversed this finding and noted, with regard to the nature and the interpretation of waivers, the following:

> Although the *WTO Agreement* does not provide any specific rules on the interpretation of waivers, Article IX of the *WTO Agreement* and the *Understanding in Respect of Waivers of Obligations under the General Agreement on Tariffs and Trade 1994*, which provide requirements for granting and renewing waivers, stress the exceptional nature of waivers and subject waivers to strict disciplines. Thus, waivers should be interpreted with great care.[157]

---

[154] WT/MIN(01)/15, dated 14 November 2001.

[155] As contained in the following documents: Request for a WTO Waiver – New ACP-EC Partnership Agreement, G/C/W/187, dated 2 March 2000; Request for a WTO Waiver – New ACP-EC Partnership Agreement, G/C/W/204, dated 4 March 2000; Request for a WTO Waiver – New ACP-EC Partnership Agreement G/C/W/254 dated 12 March 2001; and Council for Trade in Goods – Requests for a GATT Article I and a GATT Article XIII Waiver – New ACP-EC Partnership Agreement, G/C/W/269, dated 27 June 2001.

[156] Panel Reports, *EC – Bananas III*, para. 7.107.

[157] Appellate Body Report, *EC – Bananas III*, para. 185.

2.4.3.2. 'Non-application' clause

For political or other reasons (including economic reasons), certain Members may not want the WTO rules to apply *between* them. Article XIII of the *WTO Agreement*, entitled 'Non-Application of Multilateral Trade Agreements between Particular Members', states:

1. This Agreement and the Multilateral Trade Agreements in Annexes 1 and 2 shall not apply as between any Member and any other Member if either of the Members, at the time either becomes a Member, does not consent to such application.
2. Paragraph 1 may be invoked between original Members of the WTO which were contracting parties to GATT 1947 only where Article XXXV of that Agreement had been invoked earlier and was effective as between those contracting parties at the time of entry into force for them of this Agreement.
3. Paragraph 1 shall apply between a Member and another Member which has acceded under Article XII only if the Member not consenting to the application has so notified the Ministerial Conference before the approval of the agreement on the terms of accession by the Ministerial Conference.
4. The Ministerial Conference may review the operation of this Article in particular cases at the request of any Member and make appropriate recommendations.
5. Non-application of a Plurilateral Trade Agreement between parties to that Agreement shall be governed by the provisions of that Agreement.

It is thus possible for a Member to prevent WTO rules from applying to its trade relations with another Member. However, the 'non-application' or 'opt-out' clause has to be invoked at the time that this Member, or the other, joins the WTO. The 'opt-out' clause cannot be invoked at any later time. The decision to opt out must be notified to the Ministerial Conference (or the General Council) before the latter decides on the accession.[158]

In practice, the importance of the 'non-application' clause under the *WTO Agreement* has been limited. Only the United States has made use of this clause in respect of some former Communist countries.[159] Currently, no WTO Member invokes the 'non-application' clause.

Questions and Assignments 2.11

What is a 'waiver' of WTO obligations and under what conditions can it be granted? Find out how many and which waivers currently apply in favour of the European Communities. Can the European Communities invoke the 'non-application' clause against a WTO Member that is guilty of gross violations of human rights or acts of aggression against other countries?

---

[158] Between the Contracting Parties of the GATT 1947 which joined the WTO as original Members, an opt-out is only possible to the extent that such opt-out already existed under the GATT 1947.

[159] Between 1 January 1995 and 30 June 2001, the United States invoked the 'non-application' clause of Article XIII:1 of the *WTO Agreement* with respect to Georgia, Kyrgyz Republic, Moldova, Mongolia and Romania. See WTO Analytical Index, Vol. 1, 97.

2.4.4. **Withdrawal and expulsion**

Article XV of the *WTO Agreement* states:

> 1. Any Member may withdraw from this Agreement. Such withdrawal shall apply both to this Agreement and the Multilateral Trade Agreements and shall take effect upon the expiration of six months from the date on which written notice of withdrawal is received by the Director-General of the WTO.
> 2. Withdrawal from a Plurilateral Trade Agreement shall be governed by the provisions of that Agreement.

Any Member may, at any time, unilaterally withdraw from the WTO. A withdrawal only takes effect, however, upon the expiration of six months from the notification of the decision to withdraw.[160] It should be noted that, when a Member withdraws from the WTO, it cannot remain a party to the Multilateral Trade Agreements. To date, no Member has ever withdrawn from the WTO. A group of Caribbean banana-producing countries, very disappointed with the outcome of the *EC – Bananas III* dispute, 'threatened' at one point to withdraw from the WTO but did not do so.

The *WTO Agreement* does not provide for a general procedure for the expulsion of a Member. There is no procedure to exclude States from the WTO that systematically breach their obligations under the WTO agreements. There are also no rules or procedures for the expulsion of Members that are guilty of gross violations of human rights or acts of aggression.[161] The expulsion of a Member is, however, provided for as a possibility in the specific case of the non-acceptance of an amendment.[162]

Questions and Assignments 2.12

Can a Member withdraw from the WTO? If so, how? Has any Member ever withdrawn from the WTO? Can a WTO Member, guilty of gross violations of human rights or acts of aggression against other countries, be expelled from the WTO?

2.5. INSTITUTIONAL STRUCTURE OF THE WTO

To carry out the functions and tasks entrusted to the WTO, the *WTO Agreement* provides for a manifold of bodies. This section examines:

---

[160] The notification to withdraw is made to the WTO Director-General.
[161] Note, however, that the UN Security Council could impose trade sanctions or a trade embargo on such Members and that, pursuant to Article XXI of the GATT 1994 and Article XIV *bis* of the GATS, other Members would be able to apply these sanctions or that embargo. See below, pp. 628–33.
[162] See below, pp. 146–7.

- the basic institutional structure;
- the Ministerial Conference;
- the General Council, the DSB and the TPRB;
- specialised councils, committees and working parties;
- the Trade Negotiating Committee;
- political bodies lacking in the WTO structure;
- quasi-judicial and other non-political bodies of the WTO; and
- the WTO Secretariat.

2.5.1. Basic structure

The basic institutional structure of the WTO is set out in Article IV of the *WTO Agreement*. Subordinate committees and working groups have been added to this structure by later decisions.

There are, at present, a total of seventy WTO bodies, of which thirty-four are standing bodies.[163] Many of these WTO bodies meet on a regular basis, making for a heavy workload for WTO diplomats. In 2001, WTO bodies held nearly 1,000 formal and informal meetings.[164] Sometimes as many as four or five formal meetings were convened at the same time.[165] For many developing-country Members, with no or a very small permanent delegation in Geneva, this is a serious problem.[166] The schedule of meetings at the WTO is posted on the WTO's website.[167] Consider the schedule of meetings for March 2003, as shown in Figure 2.3.

The institutional structure of the WTO includes, at the highest level, the Ministerial Conference, at a second level, the General Council, the DSB and the TPRB and, at lower levels, specialised councils, committees and working parties. Furthermore, this structure includes quasi-judicial and other non-political bodies, as well as the WTO Secretariat. We note, however, that, unlike other international organisations, the WTO does not have any permanent body through which the 'dialogue' between the WTO, NGOs and civil society can take place.[168] Furthermore, the WTO does not have an executive body, comprising of only a core group of WTO Members, to facilitate the process of deliberation and decision-making.

---

[163] See Statement by Miguel Rodriguez Mendoza, WTO Deputy Director-General, to the General Council on 13 February 2002, WT/GC/M/73. This number includes the TNC and the two negotiating groups established by the TNC. See below, pp. 130–1. The *ad hoc* bodies (i.e. the non-standing bodies) are comprised of the TNC, the two TNC negotiating groups, twenty-eight accession working groups and five plurilateral bodies.

[164] See *ibid.* In 2001, there were nearly 400 formal meetings, 500 informal meetings and some 90 other meetings such as symposia, workshops and seminars organised under the auspices of WTO bodies. The number of meetings is calculated on the basis of half-day units.

[165] See *ibid.*   [166] See below, p. 109.

[167] See http://www.wto.org/english/news_e/news_e.htm#whatson, visited on 7 February 2004.

[168] On the involvement of NGOs and civil society in WTO decision-making, see below, pp. 154–62.

Figure 2.2 WTO organisation chart[169]

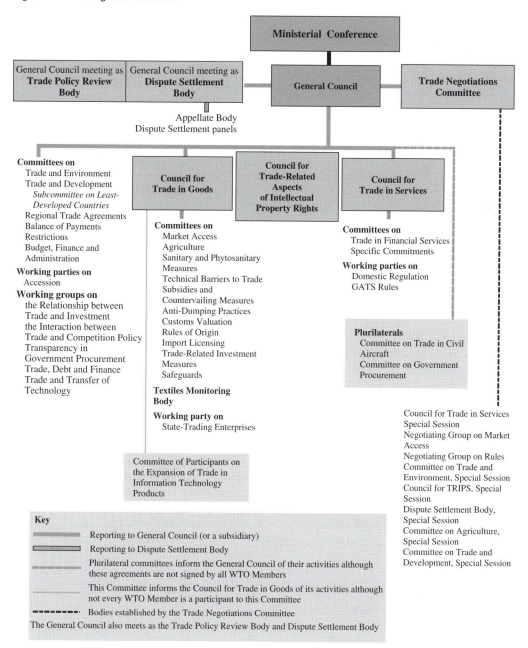

Figure 2.3 Programme of meetings in March 2003[170]

Date	Time	Meeting
3	10:00	Special Session of the Council for Trade in Services
3	10:00	Working Group on Trade and Transfer of Technology
4 & 5	10:00	Trade Negotiations Committee
6	15:00	Special Session of the Council for Trade in Services
6	15:00	Working Party on the Accession of the Russian Federation
7	10:00	Committee on Trade and Development
10	10:00	Committee on Trade and Development
10		Committee on Trade and Development on Small Economies
10 & 11		Special Session of the Dispute Settlement Body
11	09:30	WTO Introduction Day
12 & 13	10:00	Council for Trade in Goods – Trade Facilitation
12	09:30	Trade Policy Review Body – Canada
13		Council for Trade in Goods
14	10:00	Integrated Framework Steering Committee
14	09:30	Trade Policy Review Body – Canada
18		Dispute Settlement Body
18		Workshop on Technical Barriers to Trade
20		Committee on Technical Barriers to Trade
24 & 25		Special Session of the Committee on Agriculture
24 & 25	10:00	Textiles Monitoring Body
26		Committee on Market Access
26		Special Session of the Committee on Agriculture
26	10:00	Textiles Monitoring Body
27		Committee on Agriculture
28		Special Session of the Committee on Agriculture
28		Working Group on Trade, Debt and Finance
31		Special Session of the Committee on Agriculture
31 & 1		Working Group on the relationship between Trade and Investment

Questions and Assignments 2.13

Briefly describe the basic institutional structure of the WTO. Is the list of WTO bodies prescribed in Article IV of the *WTO Agreement* an exhaustive list? Look up the programme of meetings at the WTO for this month. Which of these meetings would you definitely want to attend if you were a small, sugar-exporting, least-developed-country Member (with a diplomatic staff of two for all international organisations in Geneva)?

2.5.2. Ministerial Conference

Article IV:1 of the *WTO Agreement* states:

> There shall be a Ministerial Conference composed of representatives of all the Members, which shall meet at least once every two years. The Ministerial Conference shall carry out the functions of the WTO and take actions necessary to this effect. The Ministerial Conference shall have the authority to take decisions on all matters under any of the Multilateral Trade Agreements, if so requested by a Member,

---

[170] See http://www.wto.org/english/news_e/meets.pdf, visited on 13 March 2003.

> in accordance with the specific requirements for decision-making in this Agreement
> and in the relevant Multilateral Trade Agreement.

The Ministerial Conference is the 'supreme' body of the WTO. It is composed of minister-level representatives from *all* Members and has decision-making powers on *all* matters under *any* of the multilateral WTO agreements.[171] However, it is not clear whether this very broad power to make decisions, in fact, enables the Ministerial Conference to take decisions which are *legally binding* on WTO Members.[172] With regard to the Decision of 15 December 2000 regarding Implementation-Related Issues and Concerns,[173] a decision based, *inter alia*, on Article IV:1 and containing several clauses which begin with the words 'Members shall . . .', Pieter-Jan Kuijper, then Director of the WTO Legal Affairs Division, noted that:

> It is as yet unclear whether this is taken by Members as laying down a political or a
> legal commitment.[174]

In addition to this very broad decision-making power, the Ministerial Conference has been explicitly granted a number of specific powers, such as:

- adopting authoritative interpretations of the WTO agreements;[175]
- granting waivers;[176]
- adopting amendments;[177]
- decisions on accession;[178] and
- appointing the Director-General and adopting staff regulations.[179]

The Ministerial Conference is not often in session. Since 1995, there have only been five sessions of the Ministerial Conference, each lasting only a few days: Singapore (1996),[180] Geneva (1998),[181] Seattle (1999),[182] Doha (2001)[183]

---

[171] For the Rules of Procedure for the Ministerial Conference, see WT/L/161.

[172] See, in this respect, P. J. Kuijper, 'Some Institutional Issues Presently Before the WTO', in D. Kennedy and J. Southwick (eds.), *The Political Economy of International Trade Law: Essays in Honor of Robert E. Hudec* (Cambridge University Press, 2002), 82.

[173] General Council, *Implementation-Related Issues and Concerns*, Decision of 15 December 2000, WT/L/384, dated 19 December 2000. This was a Decision by the General Council exercising the authority of the Ministerial Conference in between sessions of the Ministerial Conference. See below, p. ##.

[174] P. J. Kuijper, 'Some Institutional Issues Presently Before the WTO', in D. Kennedy and J. Southwick (eds.), *The Political Economy of International Trade Law: Essays in Honor of Robert E. Hudec* (Cambridge University Press, 2002), 82, footnote 3.

[175] Article IX:2 of the *WTO Agreement*. See below, pp. 144–5.

[176] Article IX:3 of the *WTO Agreement*. See below, pp. 145–6.

[177] Article X of the *WTO Agreement*. See below, pp. 146–7.

[178] Article XII of the *WTO Agreement*. See below, p. 145.

[179] Article VI:2 and VI:3 of the *WTO Agreement*. See below, pp. 135–7, 139–40. Note also that, pursuant to Article XII:5(b) and XII:6 of the GATS, the Ministerial Conference also has the power to establish certain procedures in connection with balance-of-payments restrictions (see below, pp. 667–75). Pursuant to Article 64.3 of the *TRIPS Agreement*, the Ministerial Conference has the power to extend the non-application of non-violation complaints to the *TRIPS Agreement* (see below, p. 192).

[180] For the Ministerial Declarations adopted at the Singapore Session of the Ministerial Conference in 1996, see WT/MIN(96)/DEC, dated 18 December 1996 and WT/MIN(96)/16, dated 13 December 1996.

[181] For the Ministerial Declarations adopted at the Geneva Session of the Ministerial Conference in 1998, see WT/MIN(98)/DEC/1 and WT/MIN(98)/DEC/2.

[182] No Ministerial Declaration was adopted at the Seattle Session of the Ministerial Conference in 1999.

[183] For the Ministerial Declarations and Decisions adopted at the Doha Session of the Ministerial Conference in 2001, see WT/MIN(01)/DEC/1, WT/MIN(01)/DEC/2, WT/MIN(01)/15, WT/MIN(01)/16 and WT/MIN(01)/17.

and Cancún (2003).[184] The next session of the Ministerial Conference will be held in Hong Kong, China.

Sessions of the Ministerial Conference are major media events and therefore focus the minds of the political leaders of WTO Members on the current challenges to, and the future of, the multilateral trading system. They offer a much needed bi-annual opportunity to give political leadership and guidance to the WTO and its actions.

Questions and Assignments 2.14

Discuss the composition and the scope of the decision-making competence of the Ministerial Conference.

2.5.3. General Council, DSB and TPRB

2.5.3.1. *General Council*

Article IV:2 of the *WTO Agreement* states:

> There shall be a General Council composed of representatives of all the Members, which shall meet as appropriate. In the intervals between meetings of the Ministerial Conference, its functions shall be conducted by the General Council. The General Council shall also carry out the functions assigned to it by this Agreement. The General Council shall establish its rules of procedure and approve the rules of procedure for the Committees provided for in paragraph 7.

The General Council is composed of ambassador-level diplomats and normally meets once every two months.[185] All WTO Members are represented in the General Council. As with all other WTO bodies, except the Ministerial Conference, the General Council normally meets on the premises of the WTO Secretariat in Geneva. Each year, the General Council elects its Chairperson from the members of the Council. The Chairperson of the General Council holds the highest elected office within the WTO. In February 2004, the General Council elected Ambassador Shotaro Oshima of Japan as its Chairperson for 2004.[186]

The General Council is responsible for the continuing, 'day-to-day' management of the WTO and its many activities. In between sessions of the Ministerial Conference, the General Council exercises the full powers of the Ministerial Conference.[187]

---

[184] No Ministerial Declaration was adopted at the Cancún Session of the Ministerial Conference in 2003. However, the Ministerial Conference did issue a Ministerial Statement. See WT/MIN(03)/20.

[185] For the Rules of Procedures of the General Council, see WT/L/161.

[186] The list of the 2004 chairpersons of all WTO bodies can be found on the WTO's website, at http://www.wto.org/english/thewto_e/whatis_e/tif_e/org2_e.htm, visited on 13 February 2004.

[187] Note that, when the Ministerial Conference is in session, it will typically focus on other issues than the exercise of the specific powers entrusted to it. See also P. J. Kuijper, 'Some Institutional Issues Presently Before the WTO', in D. Kennedy and J. Southwick (eds.), *The Political Economy of International Trade Law: Essays in Honor of Robert E. Hudec* (Cambridge University Press, 2002), 83.

Figure 2.4 Excerpt from the minutes of the meeting of the General Council of 21 October 2003[188]

WORLD TRADE ORGANIZATION	RESTRICTED wt/gc/m/**83** 17 November 2003 (03–6154)

General Council
21 October 2003

MINUTES OF MEETING
Held in the Centre William Rappard
on 21 October 2003
Chairman: Mr. Carlos Pérez del Castillo (Uruguay)
[…]
Subjects discussed
1. Iran – Request for Accession
2. Work Programme on Small Economies – Report by the Chairman of the Dedicated Sessions of the Committee on Trade and Development
3. Report by the Chairman of the Trade Negotiations Committee
4. Review of Chairmanships of WTO bodies under the TNC – Statement by the Chairman
5. Sixth Session of the Ministerial Conference – Communication from Hong Kong, China
6. Widening of EC textiles quota restrictions following accession of new member States
7. Eleventh APEC Economic Leaders' Declaration
8. Trade in textiles and clothing – Developing Members' concerns about potential reduction in market (quota) access in 2003
9. Review of the exemption provided under Paragraph 3 of GATT 1994
10. Chairmanship of the Working Party on the Accession of Kazakhstan

In addition, the General Council also carries out some functions specifically assigned to it. The General Council is responsible for:

- adopting the annual budget and the financial regulations; and[189]
- making appropriate arrangements for effective cooperation with international organisations and NGOs.[190]

By way of example of the matters dealt with by the General Council, consider the list of matters discussed at the General Council meeting of 21 October 2003, set out in Figure 2.4.

Rule 37 of the *Rules of Procedure for the Meetings of the General Council* states:

> The meeting of the General Council shall ordinarily be held in private. It may be decided that a particular meeting or meetings should be held in public.

In practice, the General Council always meets behind closed doors. After the meeting, the Chairperson may issue a *communiqué* to the press.[191] The Chairperson and/or the Director-General, assisted by the WTO spokesperson, usually hold a press conference after the meeting. The minutes of a meeting of the General Council (as are the minutes of meetings of all WTO bodies except the TPRB) are 'restricted' documents, i.e. not available to the public, until they are 'de-restricted' under the rules on the de-restriction of official

---

[188] See WT/GC/M/83, dated 17 November 2003, 1–2.   [189] Article VII:3 of the *WTO Agreement*.
[190] Article V:1 of the *WTO Agreement*.
[191] Rule 38 of the Rules of Procedure for the Meetings of the General Council.

documents.[192] Later in this chapter, the alleged lack of transparency and openness of the General Council and other WTO bodies is discussed in more detail.[193]

2.5.3.2. DSB and TPRB

The functions specifically assigned to the General Council also cover dispute settlement and trade policy review.

Article IV: 3 and 4 of the *WTO Agreement* state respectively:

> 3. The General Council shall convene as appropriate to discharge the responsibilities of the Dispute Settlement Body provided for in the Dispute Settlement Understanding. The Dispute Settlement Body may have its own chairman and shall establish such rules of procedure as it deems necessary for the fulfilment of those responsibilities.
>
> 4. The General Council shall convene as appropriate to discharge the responsibilities of the Trade Policy Review Body provided for in the TPRM. The Trade Policy Review Body may have its own chairman and shall establish such rules of procedure as it deems necessary for the fulfilment of those responsibilities.

The General Council, the Dispute Settlement Body (DSB) and the Trade Policy Review Body (TPRB) are, in fact, the same body. The DSB and the TPRB are the *alter ego* of the General Council; they are two emanations of the General Council. When the General Council administers the WTO dispute settlement system, it convenes and acts as the DSB. When the General Council administers the WTO trade policy review mechanism, it convenes and acts as the TPRB. To date, the DSB and the TPRB have always had a different Chairperson than the General Council, and both the DSB and the TPRB have developed their own Rules of Procedure, which take account of the special features of their work.[194]

The DSB has a regular meeting once a month, but may have additional meetings in between. In 2003, the DSB met twenty-two times.[195] The TPRB also meets at least once a month. In February 2004, Ambassadors Amina Mohamed of Kenya and Puangrat Asavapisit of Thailand were elected as Chairpersons for 2004 of the DSB and the TPRB respectively.

Questions and Assignments 2.15

What is the relationship between the Ministerial Conference and the General Council? What is the relationship between the General Council and the DSB? Look up who serves this year as the Chairperson of the General Council, the DSB and the TPRB. Find the minutes of the last

---

[192] Procedures for the Circulation and Derestriction of WTO Documents, WT/L/452, dated 16 May 2002. For a discussion on the rules of derestriction, see below, p. 161.

[193] See below, pp. 152–4, 159–62.

[194] For the Rules of Procedure for the TPRB, see WT/TPR/6. For the Rules of Procedure for the DSB, see below, pp. 228–31. Note that the TPRB and the DSB follow, *mutatis mutandis* and with certain deviations, the Rules of Procedure for the General Council (WT/L/160).

[195] WTO Annual Report, 2004, 49.2004, 49.

meeting of the General Council. What issues were on the agenda of this meeting?

2.5.4. Specialised councils, committees and working parties

2.5.4.1. *Specialised councils*

At the level below the General Council, the DSB and the TPRB, there are three so-called specialised councils: the Council for Trade in Goods (CTG);[196] the Council for Trade in Services (CTS);[197] and the Council for TRIPS.[198] Article IV:5 of the *WTO Agreement* states:

> There shall be a Council for Trade in Goods, a Council for Trade in Services and a Council for Trade-Related Aspects of Intellectual Property Rights (hereinafter referred to as the "Council for TRIPS"), which shall operate under the general guidance of the General Council. The Council for Trade in Goods shall oversee the functioning of the Multilateral Trade Agreements in Annex 1A. The Council for Trade in Services shall oversee the functioning of the General Agreement on Trade in Services (hereinafter referred to as "GATS"). The Council for TRIPS shall oversee the functioning of the Agreement on Trade-Related Aspects of Intellectual Property Rights (hereinafter referred to as the "Agreement on TRIPS"). These Councils shall carry out the functions assigned to them by their respective agreements and by the General Council. They shall establish their respective rules of procedure subject to the approval of the General Council. Membership in these Councils shall be open to representatives of all Members. These Councils shall meet as necessary to carry out their functions.

In 2003, for example, the CTG met five times in formal session and so did the CTS.[199] Furthermore, these specialised councils also met informally. All WTO Members are represented in these specialised councils although some Members, in particular developing-country Members, may find it difficult to attend all of the meetings. Under the general guidance of the General Council, these specialised councils oversee the functioning of the multilateral agreements in Annex 1A, 1B and 1C respectively. They assist the General Council and the Ministerial Conference in carrying out their functions. They carry out both:

- the tasks which the General Council delegates to them; and
- the tasks which the *WTO Agreement*, the GATS or the *TRIPS Agreement* explicitly confer on them.

For example, in May 2000, the General Council decided:

> to direct the Council on Trade in Goods to give positive consideration to individual requests presented in accordance with Article 5.3 by developing countries for extension to transition periods for implementation of the TRIMs Agreement.[200]

---

[196] For the Rules of Procedure for the CTG, see W/L/79.
[197] For the Rules of Procedure for the CTS, see S/L/15.
[198] For the Rules of Procedure for the Council for TRIPS, see IP/c/1.
[199] WTO Annual Report 2004, 37 and 48.
[200] See WT/GC/M/55, section 8(b) and Annex II, third bullet point.

The *WTO Agreement* itself explicitly stipulates, for example, that the Ministerial Conference and the General Council may only exercise their authority to adopt authoritative interpretations of the multilateral trade agreements of Annex 1 on the basis of a recommendation from the specialised council overseeing the functioning of the agreement at issue.[201] The specialised councils also play a role in the procedure for the adoption of waivers and the amendment procedure.[202] The GATS explicitly empowers the CTS to develop disciplines on domestic regulation under Article VI:4 and the power to establish rules and procedures for the rectification and modification of schedules under Article XXI. The *TRIPS Agreement* empowers the TRIPS Council to extend, upon a duly motivated request, the ten-year transition period for the implementation of the *TRIPS Agreement* granted to the least-developed-country Members.[203]

Overall, however, few specific powers have been entrusted to the specialised councils, and their general power to *oversee* the functioning of relevant agreements does not explicitly include the power to take any decision, political or legal.[204]

There are instances in which WTO bodies go beyond their powers. An often cited example is the extension of the deadline for the entry into force of the result of negotiations on emergency safeguard measures in the field of services, adopted by the CTS. Article X of the GATS sets this deadline explicitly at 'not later than three years from the date of entry into force of the WTO Agreement', i.e. on 1 January 1998. This treaty-mandated deadline was extended three times by three successive decisions by the CTS although the CTS clearly did not have any legal mandate to do so.[205] The political need to extend the deadline prevailed over any concern about the CTS acting *ultra vires*.

2.5.4.2. Committees and working parties

In addition to the three specialised councils, there are a number of committees and working parties that assist the Ministerial Conference and the General Council in carrying out their functions. The committees include the important Committee on Trade and Development. Article IV:7 of the *WTO Agreement* states in relevant part:

> The Ministerial Conference shall establish a Committee on Trade and Development, a Committee on Balance-of-Payments Restrictions and a Committee on Budget, Finance and Administration, which shall carry out the functions assigned to them by this Agreement and by the Multilateral Trade Agreements, and any additional functions assigned to them by the General Council, and may establish such additional

---

[201] Article IX:2 of the *WTO Agreement*.
[202] Article IX:3(b) and Article X:1 of the *WTO Agreement*.   [203] Article 66.1 of the *TRIPS Agreement*.
[204] See also P. J. Kuijper, 'Some Institutional Issues Presently Before the WTO', in D. Kennedy and J. Southwick (eds.), *The Political Economy of International Trade Law: Essays in Honor of Robert E. Hudec* (Cambridge University Press, 2002), 84.
[205] See Decision on Negotiations on Emergency Safeguard Measures, S/L/43, dated 2 December 1997; Second Decision on Negotiations on Emergency Safeguard Measures, S/L/73, dated 5 July 1999; and Third Decision on Negotiations on Emergency Safeguard Measures, S/L/90, dated 8 December 2000.

Committees with such functions as it may deem appropriate. ... Membership in these Committees shall be open to representatives of all Members.

In exercising the power conferred on it in Article IV:7, the General Council established:

- the Committee on Trade and Environment in 1995;[206] and
- the Committee on Regional Trade Agreements in 1996.[207]

Furthermore, all but one of the Multilateral Agreements on Trade in Goods provide for a committee to carry out certain functions relating to the implementation of the particular agreement.[208] All of these committees are under the authority of, and report to, the CTG. In practice, however, they tend to be relatively independent, arguably due to the technical nature of their work. Note, by way of example, the SCM Committee. Article 24.1 of the *SCM Agreement* states:

> There is hereby established a Committee on Subsidies and Countervailing Measures composed of representatives from each of the Members. The Committee shall elect its own Chairman and shall meet not less than twice a year and otherwise as envisaged by relevant provisions of this Agreement at the request of any Member. The Committee shall carry out responsibilities as assigned to it under this Agreement or by the Members and it shall afford Members the opportunity of consulting on any matter relating to the operation of the Agreement or the furtherance of its objectives. The WTO Secretariat shall act as the secretariat to the Committee.[209]

Note that under Article 27.4 of the *SCM Agreement*, the SCM Committee has the power to determine whether a request to extend the special transitional period, for the maintenance of export subsidies by developing countries, is justified.[210] Such specific decision-making powers to add to, or diminish, the obligations of certain Members are, however, quite exceptional.[211]

Furthermore, Article IV:6 of the *WTO Agreement* provides that the specialised Councils may also establish subsidiary bodies as required. For example, the Council for Trade in Services created the Working Party on Professional Services. A number of committees also have this power to establish subordinate bodies where necessary.[212]

---

[206] This Committee was established at the same meeting of the General Council on 31 January 1995, at which the Committee on Trade and Development, the Committee on Balance-of-Payment Restrictions and the Committee on the Budget, Finance and Administration were established (see WT/GC/M/1). The establishment of the Committee on Trade and Development was provided for in the *Marrakesh Ministerial Decision on Trade and Development*.

[207] See WT/GC/M/10, para. 11.

[208] The exception is the *Agreement on Preshipment Inspection*. However, the CTG established a Committee on Preshipment Inspection.

[209] The powers of the Committee on Anti-Dumping (AD) Practices, the Committee on Customs Valuation (CV) and the Committee on Technical Barriers to Trade (TBT) are worded in similar terms.

[210] Furthermore, Article 29.4 of the *SCM Agreement* gives the SCM Committee the power to allow Members in the process of transformation into a market economy to derogate from their notified programmes and measures and their timeframes.

[211] Another example is the power given to the TBT Committee under Article 12.8 of the *TBT Agreement* relating to granting exceptions from TBT obligations to developing country Members.

[212] See e.g. Article 13.2 of the *TBT Agreement*.

Temporary subsidiary bodies, set up to study and report on a particular issue, are usually referred to as 'working parties'. In February 2002, there were twenty-eight working parties on the accession of candidate Members.

When a working party, a committee or a specialised council is called upon to take a decision but is unable to do so, the applicable Rules of Procedure commonly require the matter to be referred to a higher body if a Member so requests.

The Plurilateral Agreements, the *Agreement on Trade in Civil Aircraft* and the *Agreement on Government Procurement*, provide for a Committee on Trade in Civil Aircraft and a Committee on Government Procurement respectively. These bodies carry out the functions assigned to them under those agreements. They operate within the institutional framework of the WTO, keeping the General Council informed of their activities on a regular basis.[213]

Questions and Assignments 2.16

What role do the specialised councils have? Which committees are explicitly provided for in the *WTO Agreement*?

2.5.5. Trade Negotiations Committee

The Doha Development Round negotiations are conducted by the Trade Negotiations Committee (TNC) and its subordinate negotiating groups. The TNC was established by the Ministerial Conference at its Doha Session in November 2001.[214] This body supervises the overall conduct of the negotiations under the authority of the General Council. The TNC reports on the progress of the negotiations to each regular meeting of the General Council. The 'detailed' negotiations take place either in special sessions of standing WTO bodies or in specially created negotiating groups. At its first meeting on 28 January and 1 February 2002, the TNC established two such new negotiating groups, one on market access and one on rules. Most of the negotiations, however, take place in special sessions of standing WTO bodies (such as the Dispute Settlement Body, the Council for Trade in Services and the Committee on Agriculture). The TNC and its negotiating bodies consist of all the WTO Members and all countries negotiating membership. However, decisions on agreements that would result from the negotiations are taken by WTO Members only.

On 1 February 2002, the TNC elected the WTO Director-General *ex officio* to chair the TNC. The TNC is the only political WTO body chaired by an international official, rather than a diplomat of a Member country. Note that the

---

[213] See Article IV:8 of the *WTO Agreement*.
[214] Doha Ministerial Declaration, WT/MIN(01)/DEC/1, dated 20 November 2001, para. 46.

choice of the WTO Director-General as Chairperson of the TNC was contro-versial among WTO Members.

Questions and Assignments 2.17

What is the composition and function of the TNC? To whom does the TNC report?

2.5.6. Political bodies lacking in the WTO structure

Unlike other international organisations, such as the IMF or the World Bank, the WTO does not have an executive body or organ consisting of the most important Members and a selection of other Members. In other international organisations having such a large membership, an executive body facilitates decision-making by concentrating discussions in a smaller but representative group of members.[215] Also, unlike other international organisations such as the OECD and the ILO, the WTO does not have any permanent body in which entities other than governments are represented.

2.5.6.1. A WTO executive body?

As discussed above, all political WTO bodies are comprised of the 147 WTO Members. However, it is clear that it is impossible to negotiate effectively with such a large number. Therefore, in the GATT 1947 and now the WTO, mechan-isms have been developed to reduce the number of countries actively partici-pating in the deliberations of WTO bodies. Hoekman and Kostecki noted in this respect:

> The first and most important device is to involve only 'principals', at least initially. To some extent this is a natural process – a country that has no agricultural sector is unlikely to be interested in discussions centering on the reduction of agricultural trade barriers. In general the quad – Canada, the EU, Japan and the US – are part of any group that forms to discuss any topic. They are supplemented by countries that have a principal supplying interest in a product, and the major (potential) importers whose policies are the subject of interest. Finally a number of countries that have established a reputation as spokespersons tend to be involved in most major meetings. Historically, such countries have included India ... Egypt, and the former Yugoslavia.[216]

In the days of the GATT 1947, contentious issues were often hotly debated in 'green room meetings', named after a conference room next to the office of the Director-General. These green room meetings, bringing together about twenty or so delegations at the invitation of the Director-General,

---

[215] B. Hoekman and M. Kostecki, *The Political Economy of the World Trading System: The WTO and Beyond*, 2nd edition (Oxford University Press, 2001), 60.

[216] *Ibid.*

> were part of a consultative process through which the major countries and a representative set of developing countries ... tried to hammer out the outlines of acceptable proposals or negotiating agendas. Such meetings generally involved the active participation and input of the Director-General ... Once a deal has emerged, it is submitted to the general ... membership. Although amendments may be made, these are usually marginal.[217]

Green room meetings (i.e. inner circle meetings) comprise of usually no more than twenty Members, including the Quad, Members deemed to have a vital interest in the issue under discussion and developing-country Members that play a leading role such as Brazil, India, China and South Africa. The least-developed-country Members are frequently represented by Bangladesh.

After the establishment of the WTO, the practice of green room meetings continued. However, this practice was one of the reasons for the dismal failure of the Seattle Session of the Ministerial Conference in 1999. At Seattle, major trading powers and selected developing countries tried to agree on the agenda for a new round in green room meetings. Many developing-country Members, excluded from these meetings, revolted because they felt that they were not kept informed and that their views were not considered. The problem of full and effective participation of developing countries in the WTO decision-making process is discussed in more detail below.[218]

In this context, the Heads of Delegation Meetings (HODs) should also be mentioned. These are informal meetings which ambassadors alone (i.e., the heads of delegation) are invited to attend. However, as *all* ambassadors are invited, these meetings may still be too 'crowded' for effective deliberation.[219]

There have been a number of proposals to create an executive body, or a 'Security Council for Trade' type of body, within the WTO institutional structure to facilitate decision-making. To date, however, such proposals have not received much support from WTO Members.[220]

2.5.6.2. WTO consultative bodies

The WTO does not have any permanent consultative body in which representatives of national parliaments or NGOs are represented. As is the case in other international organisations, such a body could serve as a forum for 'dialogue' between the WTO and civil society.

The European Communities has proposed the establishment of a WTO Parliamentary Consultative Assembly. While there seems to be little support for the establishment of such an assembly, it should be noted that, in recent years, contacts with national parliamentarians have been greatly enhanced through regular visits to capitals by the WTO Director-General and through various seminars and briefings with the Inter-Parliamentary Union, the European Parliament and the US Congress.

---

[217] *Ibid.*, 60–1.   [218] See below, pp. 151–4.
[219] The 'HOD plus One' are meetings where the ambassador can also select another senior diplomat to attend the meeting with him or her.
[220] See General Council, *Minutes of Meeting*, WT/GC/M/57, dated 14 September 2000, paras. 132–70.

While strongly supporting the principle that only WTO Members have the authority to make decisions in the WTO, Canada, for example, has argued that 'outside voices', such as expert NGOs, can provide valuable advice to Members. To manage this process of obtaining specialised advice, the WTO could set up *ad hoc* advisory boards to provide non-binding advice on WTO-related issues. These boards could be composed of individuals and/or NGOs, and should reflect a broad range of views and interests. However, suggestions to establish such consultative bodies comprising of representatives of NGOs have received little support from members to date.

In 2003, the WTO Director-General established the Consultative Board on the Future of the Multilateral Trading System, composed of eminent persons, chaired by Peter Sutherland, the former GATT and WTO Director-General. This Board advises Supachai Panitchpakdi on the challenges and opportunities confronting the organisation and the multilateral trading system.[221]

In 2003, the WTO Director-General also established two other advisory bodies: the Informal NGO Advisory Body and the Informal Business Advisory Body. The Informal NGO Advisory Body, which is made up of eleven high-level representatives from NGOs, provides a platform for dialogue with NGOs from around the world. The Informal Business Advisory Body, which comprises fourteen captains of industry, provides a platform for dialogue with international business organisations and leading companies from developed as well as developing-country Members. Both advisory bodies advise the WTO Director-General, channel the positions and constraints of civil society and global business on trade issues to the WTO and ultimately aim at facilitating mutual understanding. These advisory bodies are expected to meet twice a year.[222]

Questions and Assignments 2.18

In your opinion, should the WTO have an executive body and/or a consultative assembly?

2.5.7. Quasi-judicial and other non-political bodies

All the WTO bodies discussed above are political in nature. The WTO also has a number of quasi-judicial and other non-political bodies. The most prominent among the quasi-judicial bodies are the *ad hoc* dispute settlement panels and the standing Appellate Body, which are discussed in detail in Chapter 3.

The WTO also has other non-political bodies. An example of such a body is the Textile Monitoring Body (TMB). The TMB is a non-political body in view of its mandate and the fact that its members discharge their function

---

[221] See WTO Press/ 345, 19 June 2003, www.wto.org/English/news_e/pres03_e/pr345_e.htm, visited on 1 September 2004.

[222] Note that the WTO website does not yet include any information on these advisory bodies. See www.wto.org, visited on 1 September 2004.

independently and on an *ad personam* basis (not as the representative of a WTO Member). Article 8.1 of the *Agreement on Textiles and Clothing* states:

> In order to supervise the implementation of this Agreement, to examine all measures taken under this Agreement and their conformity therewith, and to take the actions specifically required of it by this Agreement, the Textiles Monitoring Body ("TMB") is hereby established. The TMB shall consist of a Chairman and 10 members. Its membership shall be balanced and broadly representative of the Members and shall provide for rotation of its members at appropriate intervals. The members shall be appointed by Members designated by the Council for Trade in Goods to serve on the TMB, discharging their function on an *ad personam* basis.[223]

At the request of any WTO Member, the TMB shall promptly review any particular matter which that Member considers to be detrimental to its interests under the *Agreement on Textiles and Clothing*. The TMB may formulate recommendations, findings and observations as it deems appropriate. Pursuant to Article 8.9 of the *Agreement on Textiles and Clothing*, WTO Members must 'endeavour' to accept, in full, the recommendations of the TMB. The TMB supervises the implementation of such recommendations. If a Member considers itself unable to comply with the recommendations of the TMB, it must provide the TMB with valid reasons. Following a thorough consideration of the reasons given, the TMB shall immediately issue any further recommendations it considers appropriate. If, following such further recommendations, the matter remains unresolved, either Member may request the Dispute Settlement Body to establish a panel to hear and decide the dispute.[224] Note that, when the implementation of the *Agreement on Textiles and Clothing*, i.e. the elimination of all quantitative restrictions on textiles, is achieved at the end of 2004, the TMB would normally cease to exist.

Another non-political body which deserves to be mentioned is the Permanent Group of Experts provided for under the *SCM Agreement*. Paragraphs 3 and 4 of Article 24 of the *SCM Agreement* state:

> 1. The [SCM] Committee shall establish a Permanent Group of Experts composed of five independent persons, highly qualified in the fields of subsidies and trade relations. The experts will be elected by the Committee and one of them will be replaced every year. The PGE may be requested to assist a panel, as provided for in paragraph 5 of Article 4. The Committee may also seek an advisory opinion on the existence and nature of any subsidy.
> 2. The PGE may be consulted by any Member and may give advisory opinions on the nature of any subsidy proposed to be introduced or currently maintained by that Member. Such advisory opinions will be confidential and may not be invoked in proceedings under Article 7.

---

[223] Note that para. 1.4 of the *Working Procedures for the Textiles Monitoring Body* states: 'In discharging their functions in accordance with paragraph 1.1 above, TMB members and alternates undertake not to solicit, accept or act upon instructions from governments, nor to be influenced by any other organisations or undue extraneous factors. They shall disclose to the Chairman any information that they may consider likely to impede their capacity to discharge their functions on an *ad personam* basis.' See *Working Procedures for the Textiles Monitoring Body*, adopted on 26 July 1995, G/TMB/R/1. Note also para. V of the *Rules of Conduct for the Understanding on Rules and Procedures Governing the Settlement of Disputes*, WT/ DSB/RC/1, dated 11 December 1996.

[224] See Article 8.10 of the *Agreement on Textiles and Clothing*.

It should be noted that to date no use has been made of this Permanent Group of Experts.

Questions and Assignments 2.19

How is the TMB composed and what is its function? Find the latest annual report of the TMB.

2.5.8. WTO Secretariat

The WTO Secretariat is based in Geneva, and has a staff of about 600 persons.[225] This makes it undoubtedly the smallest Secretariat of any of the major international organisations. Note that in the mid-1990s the FAO cut staff, at its headquarters in Rome, by more jobs than there were at the time in the whole WTO Secretariat.[226] However, as Hoekman and Kostecki observed:

> The small size of the secretariat is somewhat misleading … [T]he WTO is a network-based organization. The WTO secretariat and the national delegates in Geneva work in close cooperation with numerous civil servants in their respective capitals … The total size of the network is impossible to determine, but certainly spans at least 5,000 people.[227]

As discussed below, the Secretariat's prime function is to keep the WTO network operating smoothly.

2.5.8.1. Appointment of the Director-General

The Secretariat is headed by a Director-General, who is appointed by the Ministerial Conference.[228] The Ministerial Conference adopts regulations setting out the powers, duties, conditions of service and the term of office of the Director-General.

In the brief history of the WTO, the appointment of the Director-General has often been a contentious matter.[229] In particular, the appointments of the current Director-General, Dr Supachai Panitchpakdi, and his predecessor,

---

[225] Article VI:1 of the *WTO Agreement*. The WTO Secretariat has its offices in Geneva at the Centre William Rappard (154, rue de Lausanne), along the lac Léman. Note that the Secretariat of the WTO Appellate Body, which is independent of the WTO Secretariat, is also housed in the Centre William Rappard. See below, pp. 248–9.

[226] J. Madeley, 'UN Farm Aid Agency Wins Renewed Pledges of Funding', *Financial Times*, 25 February 1997. The FAO cut more than 560 jobs at its Rome headquarters.

[227] B. Hoekman and M. Kostecki, *The Political Economy of the World Trading System*, 2nd edition (Oxford University Press, 2001), 55.

[228] Article VI:2 of the *WTO Agreement*.

[229] Only the appointment of Mr Peter Sutherland, the last Director-General of the GATT, to become the first Director-General of the WTO was not contentious. To date, the following persons have served as WTO Director-General:

- Mr Peter Sutherland from Ireland (January 1995–April 1995):
- Mr Renato Ruggiero from Italy (May 1995–April 1999);
- Mr Mike Moore from New Zealand (September 1999–August 2002); and
- Dr Supachai Panitchpakdi from Thailand (September 2002–August 2005).

Mr Mike Moore, were divisive. In March 1999, Frances Williams of the *Financial Times* reported on the search for a replacement for Mr Renato Ruggiero, the WTO's second Director-General, as follows:

> The search for a new head of the World Trade Organization appeared to have reached an impasse yesterday, raising fears of an interregnum when Renato Ruggiero, the present director-general, steps aside at the end of April. After missing two deadlines for the selection of Mr. Ruggiero's successor, the WTO members last week set March 12 as their new target date, but this, too, looks in danger of slipping. Consultations with members over the past months have not changed the rankings of the four candidates, according to a report yesterday to the WTO's general council. Among the 118 members which have now expressed a view, Supachai Panitchpakdi, Thailand's deputy premier, continues to lead the field with 39 first preferences, followed closely by Hassan Abuyoub, a former Moroccan trade minister, who has significantly improved his relative position at 35. Roy MacLaren, former Canadian trade minister, is third with 23 first preferences, just in front of Mike Moore, former New Zealand premier, with 21. However, Mr. Moore had the most second preferences (32) compared with 23 for Mr. Supachai, 11 for Mr. Abuyoub and eight for Mr. MacLaren. Several countries yesterday called for weaker candidates to drop out to make it easier to reach consensus, while some developing countries urged a vote if consensus is not achieved by the end of the month. A vote is opposed by many WTO members, however, because they argue that the next director-general should clearly be acceptable to all 134 member countries. On a purely arithmetic basis, Mr. MacLaren would seem to be in the weakest position but he has some influential backers including the US which claims to be supporting him alongside Mike Moore. Sir Leon Brittan, the European Union trade commissioner, also favours Mr. MacLaren though EU Members are split between all four candidates.[230]

After a year-long effort to appoint a successor to Renato Ruggiero, WTO Members finally agreed on 22 July 1999 to an unprecedented term-sharing arrangement under which Mr Moore, of New Zealand, was appointed as Director-General for a term of three years, beginning on 1 September 1999, and Dr Supachai Panitchpakdi, of Thailand, was appointed for a three-year term beginning 1 September 2002.[231] Mike Moore, a former printer, social worker and trade union researcher, was the youngest member of Parliament ever elected in New Zealand. In the 1980s, he served six years as New Zealand's Minister of Overseas Trade and Marketing, and was New Zealand's Prime Minister for a brief period in 1990. When he took office as Director General of the WTO, a few weeks before the fated Seattle Session of the Ministerial Conference, Mr Moore, the first non-European to head the WTO (or the GATT), stated that he intended to defend the WTO as an organisation 'where the little guy not only has a say but where he can protect and defend his trading rights', and pledged to make the expansion of trading opportunities for the world's poorest countries a top priority during his three-year term.[232]

---

[230] F. Williams, 'Impasse in Search for World Trade Chief', *Financial Times*, 2 March 1999.

[231] In its decision on this 'double' appointment, the General Council stressed that this arrangement did not constitute a precedent for future appointments of the Director-General and agreed to work towards establishing 'a comprehensive set of rules and procedures for such appointments' by the end of September 2000.

[232] F. Williams, 'Moore Takes up WTO Post with Pledge on Poor', *Financial Times*, 2 September 1999.

On 1 September 2002, Dr Supachai Panitchpakdi took over from Mr Moore. Dr Supachai held a range of senior government positions in Thailand and was directly in charge of Thailand's participation in the final stages of the Uruguay Round negotiations. At the time of his appointment to the post of WTO Director-General for the period 2002–5, Dr Supachai served as Thailand's Deputy Prime Minister and Minister of Commerce.

At its meeting of 10–11 November 2002, the General Council adopted new procedures for the appointment of a Director-General.[233] Under these new procedures, the appointment process shall start nine months prior to the expiry of the term of an incumbent Director-General. The various steps of the process are carefully set out. The process shall be conducted by the Chair of the General Council, assisted by the Chairs of the Dispute Settlement Body and the Trade Policy Review Body acting as facilitators. Only WTO Members may nominate candidates. Candidates should have extensive experience in international relations, encompassing economic, trade and/or political experience; a firm commitment to the work and objectives of the WTO; proven leadership and managerial ability; and demonstrable communications skills. The overriding objective of Members is to reach a decision on the appointment of a Director-General by consensus. However, note that the new procedures explicitly state:

> If, after having carried out all the procedures set out above, it has not been possible for the General Council to take a decision by consensus by the deadline provided for the appointment, Members should consider the possibility of recourse to a vote as a last resort by a procedure to be determined at that time. Recourse to a vote for the appointment of a Director-General shall be understood to be an exceptional departure from the customary practice of decision-making by consensus, and shall not establish any precedent for such recourse in respect of any future decisions in the WTO.[234]

2.5.8.2. Role of the Director-General and the WTO Secretariat

The WTO is a 'Member-driven' organisation. The Members – and not the Director-General or the WTO Secretariat – set the agenda and take decisions. Neither the Director-General nor the WTO Secretariat has any decision-making powers. The Director-General and the WTO Secretariat act primarily as an 'honest broker' in, or a 'facilitator' of, the decision-making processes within the WTO. They seldom act as initiators of proposals for action or reform. In such a seemingly modest role, the Director-General and the WTO Secretariat can, however, make an important contribution to helping Members to come to an agreement or decision. Note, in this respect, that in February 2002 the Trade Negotiations Committee (TNC), the body overseeing the Doha Development Round negotiations, elected the Director-General *ex officio* to chair the TNC.

In a speech in January 2003, Dr Supachai Panitchpakdi, speaking about his role and that of the WTO Secretariat, noted:

---

[233] Procedures for the Appointment of Directors-General – Communication from the Chairman, WT/GC/W/482, dated 28 November 2002.
[234] *Ibid.*, para. 21.

> As you know the WTO is, if I may use the cliché, a 'member-driven' organization. In the negotiations, Member governments negotiate directly with each other. As Chairman of the TNC, I shall be doing my utmost to keep all Members on board, facilitate their discussions, mediate in their problems and consult with all. And the WTO Secretariat, through its technical assistance work programme, is working hard to help developing and least-developed-country Members prepare effectively for the negotiations. But we cannot make any decisions on behalf of Members, we cannot unplug blockages when Members' positions are intractable and we cannot force consensus. It is Members who have the very difficult responsibility of developing policy positions, negotiating concessions and deciding how far they are able to go in any given area.[235]

However, developing-country Members are reported to be apprehensive regarding the role of the Director-General and the WTO Secretariat. In a joint communication, addressing, *inter alia*, the issue of their role at sessions of the Ministerial Conference, fifteen developing-country Members, led by India, stated:

> The Secretariat and the Director-General of the WTO … should assume a neutral/impartial and objective role. They shall not express views explicitly or otherwise on the specific issues being discussed in the Ministerial Conference.[236]

The main duties of the WTO Secretariat are:

- to provide technical and professional support for the various WTO bodies;
- to provide technical assistance to developing-country Members;
- to monitor and analyse developments in world trade;
- to advise governments of countries wishing to become Members of the WTO; and
- to provide information to the public and the media.

Furthermore, the Secretariat also provides administrative support and legal assistance for WTO dispute settlement panels. The Appellate Body has its own Secretariat which is independent of the WTO Secretariat but which shares the same facilities and makes use of the general support services of the WTO Secretariat (translation, library, etc.).

With regard to the status of the Director-General and WTO staff as independent and impartial international officials, Article VI:4 of the *WTO Agreement* states:

> The responsibilities of the Director-General and of the staff of the Secretariat shall be exclusively international in character. In the discharge of their duties, the Director-General and the staff of the Secretariat shall not seek or accept instructions from any government or any other authority external to the WTO. They shall refrain from any action which might adversely reflect on their position as international officials. The Members of the WTO shall respect the international character of the responsibilities of the Director-General and of the staff of the Secretariat and shall not seek to influence them in the discharge of their duties.

---

[235] Supachai Panitchpakdi, *Build Up: The Road to Mexico*, speech on 8 January 2003 at Plenary Session XI of the Partnership Summit 2003 in Hyderabad: see www.wto.org/english/news_e/spsp09_e.htm, visited on 1 September 2004.

[236] Preparatory Process in Geneva and Negotiating Procedure at the Ministerial Conferences – Communication from Cuba, Dominican Republic, Egypt, Honduras, India, Indonesia, Jamaica, Kenya, Malaysia, Mauritius, Pakistan, Sri Lanka, Tanzania, Uganda and Zimbabwe, WT/GC/W/471, dated 24 April 2002, para. i.

2.5.8.3. The structure and composition of the WTO Secretariat

As noted above, the WTO Secretariat is headed by the WTO Director-General. The Director-General is assisted by four Deputy Directors-General (DDGs), also political appointees, serving for a limited period of time. They are appointed by the Director-General – in consultation with WTO Members – and form, together with the Director-General, the senior management of the WTO Secretariat. Currently, Roderick Abbott (a former EC ambassador to the WTO), Kipkorir Aly Azad Rana (a former ambassador of Kenya to the UN and the WTO), Francisco Thompson-Flôres (a former ambassador of Brazil) and Rufus H. Yerxa (a former US ambassador to the GATT) serve as DDGs under Dr Supachai. The number of DDGs has been the subject of discussions in the General Council.[237] While it is argued that the number could be less than four, having four DDGs makes it possible for the main regions of the world to be represented in senior management.

The WTO Secretariat is organised into Divisions with a functional role (e.g. the Rules Division, the Services Division and the Market Access Division), an information and liaison role (e.g. the Information and Media Relations Division) and a supporting role (e.g. the Administration and General Services Division and the Language Services and Documentation Division). Divisions are normally headed by a Director who reports to one of the WTO's four Deputy Directors-General or directly to the Director-General. In addition to Divisions, the WTO Secretariat also includes the Institute for Training and Technical Cooperation (ITTC), often referred to as the Training Institute, which was established in 2003 to ensure a coherent and coordinated approach to capacity-building and technical assistance.[238]

The Director-General appoints the staff and determines their duties and conditions of service in accordance with the *Staff Regulations* adopted by the Ministerial Conference.[239]

About sixty different nationalities are represented in the staff of the WTO Secretariat. Nationals of France, the United Kingdom, Spain, Switzerland, Canada and the United States (in order of importance) are best represented among the staff. The representation of developing-country nationals in the staff is growing but remains a matter of concern. Only nationals of WTO Members can be officials of the WTO Secretariat but there are no formal or informal national quotas.[240] Most of the professional staff

---

[237] See Statement by Ambassador Ali Mchumo, Chairman of the General Council at the Meeting on 6 October 1999, WT/GC/27, dated 12 October 1999.

[238] Also note in this respect the Technical Assistance Management Committee (TAMC) in which all relevant WTO Divisions are represented.

[239] Article VI:3 of the *WTO Agreement*. According to the Staff Regulations, the paramount objective in the determination of conditions of service is to secure staff members of the highest standards of competence, efficiency and integrity and to meet the requirements of the WTO taking into account the needs and aspirations of the staff members. The Director-General has established and administers Staff Rules. The Staff Rules implement the provisions of the Staff Regulations. The Director-General furthermore issues Staff Administrative Memoranda in elaboration of the Staff Rules.

[240] Vacancies are the subject of open competition. The final selection of professional staff is done on the basis of a written exam and an interview. The recruitment process is highly competitive. Vacancies

Figure 2.5 WTO Secretariat organisation chart[241]

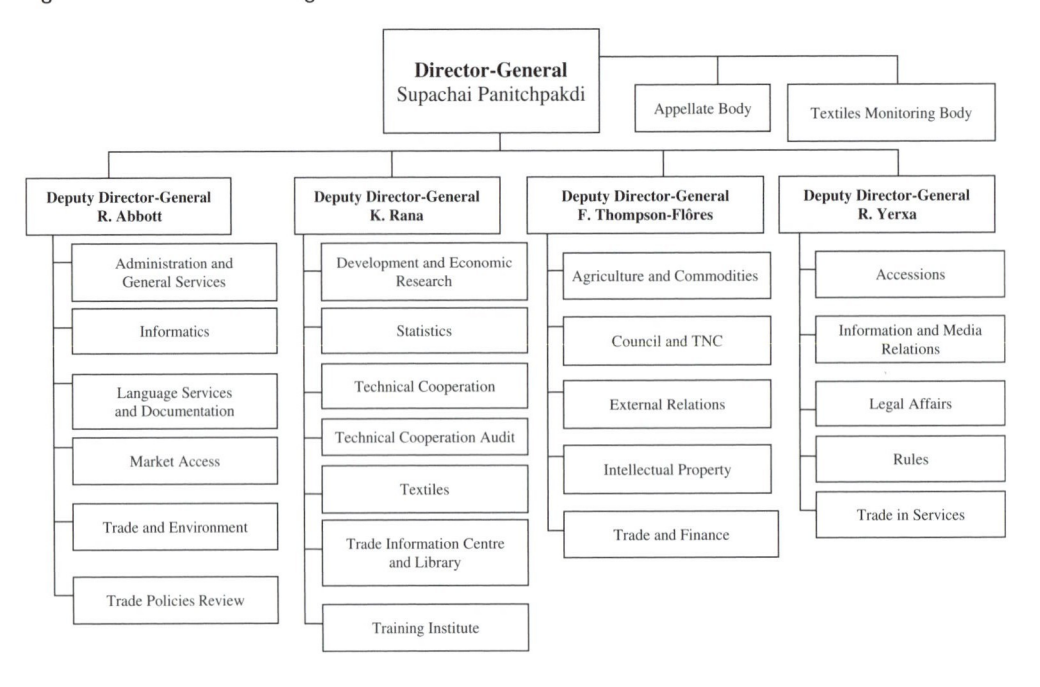

are lawyers or economists. The working languages within the WTO Secretariat are English, French and Spanish, with English being the language most frequently used.

The WTO Secretariat has an internship programme for postgraduate university students wishing to gain practical experience and deeper knowledge of the activities of the WTO and the multilateral trading system. Only a limited number of such internship posts are available. The eligibility requirements, as well as the terms and conditions of the internship and the application procedure, are set out on the WTO's website.

Questions and Assignments 2.20

Is the WTO controlled by 'faceless international bureaucrats'? Discuss the role and the powers of the WTO Director-General and the WTO Secretariat.

---

are advertised by means of vacancy notices, the distribution of which is made to all WTO Members. They are also posted on the WTO's website (www.wto.org) and where appropriate advertised in the international press.
[241] See http://www.wto.org/english/thewto_e/whatis_e/tif_e/org4_e.htm.

2.6. DECISION-MAKING IN THE WTO

There has been much criticism of the WTO decision-making process as being undemocratic, non-transparent and accountable to none. The NGO War on Want noted:

> The International Monetary Fund and World Bank, which hold increasing amounts of power in the globalised world, are blatantly undemocratic organisations – with rich nations holding far more votes than poorer nations. The World Trade Organisation (WTO) is theoretically democratic – all countries are equal and have one vote. But in reality, poor countries cannot afford the lawyers and representatives to send to the WTO, and lack the economic clout to give them a proper voice in the WTO. More importantly than all of this, however, is that ordinary citizens are told little about the proceedings of these important organisations, despite the fact that every one of us is affected by their decisions.[242]

This section will examine:

- the normal decision-making procedure, which applies as the default procedure;
- a number of special procedures for specific decisions;
- WTO decision-making in practice;
- the participation of developing-country Members in WTO decision-making;
- the involvement of NGOs; and
- the form and legal basis of WTO decisions.

2.6.1. Normal procedure

The normal decision-making procedure for WTO bodies is set out in Article IX:1 of the *WTO Agreement*, which states:

> The WTO shall continue the practice of decision-making by consensus followed under GATT 1947. Except as otherwise provided, where a decision cannot be arrived at by consensus, the matter at issue shall be decided by voting. At meetings of the Ministerial Conference and the General Council, each Member of the WTO shall have one vote ... Decisions of the Ministerial Conference and the General Council shall be taken by a majority of the votes cast, unless otherwise provided in this Agreement or in the relevant Multilateral Trade Agreement.

2.6.1.1. Decision-making by consensus

Pursuant to Article IX:1 of the *WTO Agreement*, Members first try to take decisions *by consensus*. Footnote 1 to Article IX defines consensus decision-making by WTO bodies as follows:

> The body concerned shall be deemed to have decided by consensus on a matter submitted for its consideration, if no Member, present at the meeting when the decision is taken, *formally* objects to the proposed decision.
>
> [Emphasis added]

---

[242] Excerpt from 'The Global Workplace', a project of War on Want, www.globalworkplace.org, visited on 13 August 2003.

In other words, unless a Member *explicitly* objects to the proposed decision, that decision is taken. No voting takes place.[243]

Note that the Doha Ministerial Declaration of November 2001 introduced the concept of 'explicit consensus' (for decisions on the inclusion of 'Singapore issues' in the agenda of the Doha Development Round).[244] It is not clear what is meant by 'explicit consensus'. The inclusion of this concept in the Doha Ministerial Declaration was, however, a condition of India and other developing-country Members for agreeing to adopt the Declaration. At the close of the Doha Session of the Ministerial Conference, the Conference Chair, the Qatari Finance, Economy and Trade Minister Youssef Hussain Kamal, stated that his understanding of the requirement of 'explicit consensus' was that it would:

> give each member the right to take a position on modalities that would prevent negotiations from proceeding after the Fifth Session of the Ministerial Conference until that member is prepared to join in an explicit consensus.[245]

If this is indeed the meaning of the concept of 'explicit consensus', the question arises whether an 'explicit' consensus differs from a 'normal' consensus.

Decision-making by consensus gives all Members *veto power*. John Jackson noted, however, in this respect:

> the practice … is that some countries that have difficulty with a particular decision will nevertheless remain silent out of deference to countries with a substantially higher stake in the pragmatic economic consequences of a decision.[246]

As Jackson observed, decision-making by consensus in practice involves a degree of deference to economic power. It is only when important national, economic or other interests are at stake that a WTO Member would consider blocking consensus.

As Hoekman and Kostecki noted, decision-making by consensus is a useful device to ensure that only decisions which have a good chance of being implemented are adopted because the decisions adopted are all decisions to which there was no major opposition. However, Hoekman and Kostecki also observed that decision-making by consensus:

> reinforces conservative tendencies in the system. Proposals for change can be adopted only if unopposed, creating the potential for paralysis.[247]

2.6.1.2. Decision-making by majority voting

If consensus cannot be achieved, Article IX:1 of the *WTO Agreement* provides for voting on a one-country/one-vote basis. Under the normal procedure, decisions

---

[243] Unlike under decision-making by unanimity.   [244] See above, pp. 92–3.

[245] See http://www.wto.org/english/thewto_e/minist_e/min01_e/min01_chair_speaking_e.htm#clarification, visited on 2 January 2004.

[246] J. Jackson, *The World Trade Organization: Constitution and Jurisprudence* (Royal Institute of International Affairs, 1998), 46.

[247] B. Hoekman and M. Kostecki, *The Political Economy of the World Trading System*, 2nd edition (Oxford University Press, 2001), 57.

are then taken by a majority of the votes cast. The Rules of Procedure of the various WTO bodies set out the quorum requirement. For example, Rule 16 of the *Rules of Procedure for the Meetings of the General Council* states:

> A simple majority of the Members shall constitute a quorum.

Most WTO bodies have the same quorum requirement.[248] Currently, seventy-four of the WTO Members must be present at the meeting in order to take valid decisions. However, in the meetings of the subordinate WTO bodies seventy-four Members are seldom, if ever, present. In practice, the quorum is never checked. At many meetings no more than approximately forty Members will be present.

Whereas each WTO Member has one vote, Article IX:1 of the *WTO Agreement* provides in relevant part:

> Where the European Communities exercise their right to vote, they shall have a number of votes equal to the number of their member States which are Members of the WTO.

In a footnote to this sentence, it is further explained that the number of votes of the European Communities and their Member States shall in no case exceed the number of the Member States of the European Union. It is thus clear that either the European Communities *or* the Member States of the European Union will participate in a vote. Who participates in a vote is not a matter of WTO law but of EU constitutional law. For reasons relating to the practice of WTO decision-making, discussed below, the fact that the European Communities currently has twenty-five votes and the United States, China and India only one, does not have much, if any, impact on the political decision-making processes at the WTO.[249]

It should be pointed out that, as a rule, the European Commission speaks for the European Communities *and* the Member States of the European Union at meetings of WTO bodies, even if those bodies deal with matters that are not within the exclusive competence of the European Community. Delegates from the EU Member States attend the meetings but do not speak. The EU Member States speak (and vote, if a vote is called) only with regard to budgetary matters and organisational matters (e.g. the election of the Director-General). Furthermore, the Ministers of the EU Member States make short formal statements at the biannual sessions of the Ministerial Conference.

Questions and Assignments 2.21

What is decision-making by consensus? In practice, does it amount to a veto power for each WTO Member? Can WTO bodies take decisions by voting? Do all WTO Members have the same number of votes? How many votes do the United States, the European Communities, China, Belgium and Saint Lucia

---

[248] Note, however, that the TPRB does not have a quorum requirement to conduct trade policy review.
[249] See below, pp. 148–9.

have? In your opinion, should the number of votes of Members be related to the size of their population or their share of world trade?

2.6.2. Special procedures

The *WTO Agreement* sets out a number of decision-making procedures which deviate from the normal procedure discussed above. This section deals with:

- decision-making by the DSB;
- authoritative interpretations;
- accessions;
- waivers;
- amendments; and
- the annual budget and financial regulations.[250]

2.6.2.1. Decision-making by the DSB

Footnote 3 to Article IX of the *WTO Agreement* provides:

> Decisions by the General Council when convened as the Dispute Settlement Body shall be taken only in accordance with the provisions of paragraph 4 of Article 2 of the Dispute Settlement Understanding.

Article 2.4 of the DSU states:

> Where the rules and procedures of this Understanding provide for the DSB to take a decision, it shall do so by consensus.[251]

As discussed in detail in Chapter 3, the DSB takes certain decisions, such as decisions on the establishment of a panel or decisions on the adoption of dispute settlement reports, by reverse consensus. Other decisions, such as the appointment of Members of the Appellate Body, are taken by a normal consensus.

2.6.2.2. Authoritative interpretations

Article IX:2 of the *WTO Agreement* states:

> The Ministerial Conference and the General Council shall have the exclusive authority to adopt interpretations of this Agreement and of the Multilateral Trade Agreements. In the case of an interpretation of a Multilateral Trade Agreement in Annex 1, they shall exercise their authority on the basis of a recommendation by the Council overseeing the functioning of that Agreement. The decision to adopt an interpretation shall be taken by a three-fourths majority of the Members. This paragraph shall not be used in a manner that would undermine the amendment provisions in Article X.

---

[250] Note that this is not an exhaustive list of special decision-making procedures. See e.g. Article 12.1 of the *SPS Agreement*, which is not dealt with in this section. According to this provision, the SPS Committee always takes its decisions by consensus.

[251] Footnote 1 to Article 2.4 of the DSU stipulates: 'The DSB shall be deemed to have decided by consensus on a matter submitted for its consideration, if no Member, present at the meeting of the DSB when the decision is taken, formally objects to the proposed decision.'

Article IX:2 explicitly states that the Ministerial Conference and the General Council have the *exclusive* authority to adopt interpretations of provisions of the WTO agreements. This may appear surprising since we noted in Chapter 1 that, pursuant to Article 3.2 of the DSU, the WTO dispute settlement system serves to 'clarify', i.e. interpret, the provisions of the WTO agreements. However, these interpretations by panels or the Appellate Body cannot and may not – also pursuant to Article 3.2 of the DSU – add to or diminish the rights and obligations of Members. Furthermore, these interpretations are, in principle, only binding on the parties to the dispute. The interpretation referred to in Article IX:2 of the *WTO Agreement*, which is also referred to as an 'authoritative interpretation', is of a different nature. This interpretation, by the highest political bodies of the WTO, is binding on all WTO Members and may affect their rights and obligations (although the right of interpretation should not be used so as to undermine the amendment provisions).

To date, the WTO has not made any *explicit* use of the possibility to adopt 'authoritative interpretations'. The Decision of the Ministerial Conference on *Implementation-Related Issues and Concerns,* taken at the Doha Session on 14 November 2001, contains a number of provisions which are obviously interpretations of provisions of the WTO agreements. However, in its preamble, the Decision does not explicitly refer to Article IX:2.

2.6.2.3. Accessions

As already discussed above and provided for in Article XII:2 of the *WTO Agreement*, decisions on the accession of new Members are taken by the Ministerial Conference or, in between sessions of the latter, the General Council. Decisions on accession are taken by consensus or, if consensus cannot be achieved, by a two-thirds majority of WTO Members. The decision on the accession of Ecuador was taken by majority vote.

2.6.2.4. Waivers

As discussed above, a Member unable to meet an obligation under one of the WTO agreements, may request the WTO to waive that obligation.[252] With respect to the decision-making procedure to be followed, Article IX:3 of the *WTO Agreement* states, in relevant part:

> the Ministerial Conference may decide to waive an obligation imposed on a Member by this Agreement or any of the Multilateral Trade Agreements, provided that any such decision shall be taken by three fourths of the Members unless otherwise provided for in this paragraph.
>
> a. A request for a waiver concerning this Agreement shall be submitted to the Ministerial Conference for consideration pursuant to the practice of decision-making

---

[252] With respect to the conditions under which waivers of WTO obligations can be granted, see above, pp. 115–17.

> by consensus. The Ministerial Conference shall establish a time-period, which shall not exceed 90 days, to consider the request. If consensus is not reached during the time-period, any decision to grant a waiver shall be taken by three fourths of the Members.
> b. A request for a waiver concerning the Multilateral Trade Agreements in Annexes 1A or 1B or 1C and their annexes shall be submitted initially to the Council for Trade in Goods, the Council for Trade in Services or the Council for TRIPS, respectively, for consideration during a time-period which shall not exceed 90 days. At the end of the time-period, the relevant Council shall submit a report to the Ministerial Conference.

Although explicitly provided for, decisions on waivers are, in practice, not taken by a three-fourths majority of the Members. WTO Members decided, in 1995, not to apply the provisions allowing for a vote, but to continue to take decisions on waivers by consensus.[253]

2.6.2.5. Amendments

The most complex of all special decision-making procedures are the procedures for amending the WTO agreements. Article X:1 of the *WTO Agreement* states:

> Any Member of the WTO may initiate a proposal to amend the provisions of this Agreement or the Multilateral Trade Agreements in Annex 1 by submitting such proposal to the Ministerial Conference. The Councils listed in paragraph 5 of Article IV may also submit to the Ministerial Conference proposals to amend the provisions of the corresponding Multilateral Trade Agreements in Annex 1 the functioning of which they oversee. Unless the Ministerial Conference decides on a longer period, for a period of 90 days after the proposal has been tabled formally at the Ministerial Conference any decision by the Ministerial Conference to submit the proposed amendment to the Members for acceptance shall be taken by consensus ... If consensus is reached, the Ministerial Conference shall forthwith submit the proposed amendment to the Members for acceptance. If consensus is not reached at a meeting of the Ministerial Conference within the established period, the Ministerial Conference shall decide by a two-thirds majority of the Members whether to submit the proposed amendment to the Members for acceptance ...

Generally speaking, the amendment procedure is as follows. Individual Members or one of the three Specialised Councils initiate the amendment procedure by submitting an amendment proposal to the Ministerial Conference or the General Council. In the first period of at least ninety days, the Ministerial Conference or the General Council tries to reach consensus on the proposal for amendment. If consensus cannot be reached, the Ministerial Conference or the General Council resorts to voting. To be adopted, the proposal for amendment requires a two-thirds majority of the Members. Once adopted by consensus or by a two-thirds majority, the proposal is forthwith submitted to the Members for acceptance in accordance with their

---

[253] Decision-Making Procedures under Articles IX and XII of the WTO Agreement, WT/L/93, dated 24 November 1995.

national constitutional requirements and procedures. The amendment is effective only in respect of those Members that have accepted it.[254]

However, Article X:2 lists a number of fundamental provisions (concerning the MFN treatment obligation under the GATT 1994, the GATS and the *TRIPS Agreement*, the GATT 1994 tariff schedules and WTO decision-making and amendment) which have to be accepted by all Members before they can take effect. Moreover, a decision to amend the DSU must be made by consensus, and amendments to the DSU take effect for all Members upon approval by the Ministerial Conference. These amendments are not submitted to the Members for acceptance.[255] Article X:4 also provides that amendments that do not alter the rights and obligations of the Members take effect for all Members upon acceptance by two-thirds of the Members.

Finally, Article X:3 states in relevant part:

> The Ministerial Conference may decide by a three-fourths majority of the Members that any amendment made effective under this paragraph is of such a nature that any Member which has not accepted it within a period specified by the Ministerial Conference in each case shall be free to withdraw from the WTO or to remain a Member with the consent of the Ministerial Conference.

While conveyed in very diplomatic language, this means, in effect, that a Member who refuses to accept certain amendments may be expelled from the WTO. The actual importance of this provision, however, seems limited. Note that this power also existed under the GATT 1947 but was never used.[256] It is likely that this will also be the case in the WTO.

To date, the *WTO Agreement* has not been amended.[257]

2.6.2.6. *Annual budget and financial regulations*

Finally, the adoption of the annual budget and financial regulations also entails a special decision-making procedure. Pursuant to Article VII:3 of the *WTO Agreement*, the General Council adopts the annual budget and the financial regulations by a two-thirds majority comprising of more than half of the Members of the WTO. For a more detailed discussion, refer to the last section of this chapter.

Questions and Assignments 2.22

How does the WTO decide on waivers of WTO obligations? What is the difference between 'authoritative interpretations' under Article IX:2 and interpretation by panels and the Appellate Body? What is the difference between 'authoritative interpretations' under Article IX:2 and 'amendments' under Article X? Should Members want to amend Article III

---

[254] Article X:3 of the *WTO Agreement*.   [255] Article X:8 of the *WTO Agreement*.
[256] *Guide to GATT Law and Practice*, 6th edition (GATT, 1994), 934.
[257] A number of proposals to amend, in particular, the DSU have been tabled but none of these proposals has been adopted (see, for example, WT/MIN(99)/8 and Corr.1).

of the GATT 1994 or Article 5 of the DSU, what are the procedural
requirements for such amendments?

2.6.3. WTO decision-making in practice

2.6.3.1. Decision-making by consensus versus voting

As was the case under the GATT 1947, it is exceptional for WTO bodies to vote.
In 1999, when discussion on the selection of a new Director-General became
deadlocked, some developing countries suggested that the decision on the new
Director-General should be taken by vote (as provided for in Article IX:1 of the
WTO Agreement). However, this suggestion was not well received, in particular
by the developed countries, who argued that this was 'contrary to the way
things were done in the WTO'. Jackson wrote:

> the spirit and practice of the GATT has always been to try to accommodate through
> consensus negotiation procedures the views of as many countries as possible, but
> certainly to give weight to the views of countries that have power in the trading system.
> This is not likely to change.[258]

In a speech in February 2000 at UNCTAD X in Bangkok, a few weeks after the
dismal failure of the Seattle Session of the Ministerial Conference, Mike
Moore, the then WTO Director-General, stated:

> the consensus principle which is at the heart of the WTO system – and which is a
> fundamental democratic guarantee – is not negotiable.[259]

It cannot be disputed that decisions taken by consensus, i.e. decisions taken
collectively, have more 'democratic legitimacy' than decisions taken by majority
vote. At the same time, it should be noted that the consensus requirement does,
of course, make decision-making in the WTO difficult and susceptible to paralysis.

After the failure of the Cancún Session of the Ministerial Conference in
September 2003, the *Financial Times* reported on the frustration of the European
Communities with the consensus requirement as follows:

> Mr Lamy [the EU's trade commissioner] also expanded on his calls for a sweeping
> overhaul of the way in which the 146-strong WTO operates, and promised that the EU
> would come up with a set of reform proposals. His comments made clear that he is
> primarily concerned with the body's consensus-driven approach. "I think it's above
> dispute that the principle of the permanent sit-in of 146 trade ministers in order to take
> a number of very detailed decisions ... is a theory that visibly does not work", he said.
> A Commission official said Mr Lamy was not yet in a position to come up with a set of
> rounded proposals but that they were likely to address the WTO's most obvious
> shortfalls. "Everything needs to be done by consensus. Even the agenda needs to be
> decided by consensus. And the powers of the WTO director-general are very limited",
> the official said. "All that is incredibly complicated with 146 members."[260]

---

[258] *Ibid.*, 45.
[259] M. Moore, *Back on Track for Trade and Development*, keynote address at the UNCTAD X, Bangkok, on
16 February 2000, www.wto.org/english,news_e/spmm_e/spmm24_e.htm, visited on 30 August 2004.
[260] T. Buck, 'EU May Rethink Multilateral Trade Role', FT.com, 16 September 2003.

Even though the *WTO Agreement* provides for the possibility to vote, the current political reality is that voting is an exceptional event in WTO bodies. When it occasionally does take place, it is typically with regard to decisions for which the special procedures, discussed below, apply.

Questions and Assignments 2.23

Why are WTO Members so hesitant to resort to decision-making by voting? Would decision-making by voting be to the advantage of the developing-country Members?

2.6.3.2. *The process of WTO decision-making in practice*

At the Doha Session of the Ministerial Conference in November 2001, it was decided that the General Council would reach an agreement, before the end of 2002, to improve the access to essential medicines for developing countries with insufficient or no manufacturing capacities in the pharmaceutical sector.[261] In December 2002, the WTO came very close to reaching such an agreement (referred to as the 'December 16 text') but the United States refused to join the consensus. In August 2003, the United States was finally willing to agree to the December 16 text if it was adopted together with a Statement of the Chair of the TRIPS Council on the interpretation of the December 16 text. At first, it seemed that this would finally resolve this thorny issue of access for developing countries to essential medicines. However, the other WTO Members then raised further concerns. Tahir Hasnain, a well-informed WTO observer of the Network for Consumer Protection, reported as follows on this remarkable (but not a-typical) process of WTO decision-making:

> It is understood that a number of developing countries had indicated that they had reservations about the statement of understanding, drafted by TRIPS Council Chair, as an interpretative note to the December 16 text. It is widely known that the statement of understanding is intended to provide "comfort language" that would enable the US to join consensus on the December 16 text.
>
> The failure to reach agreement is a surprising turn of events. Agreement on the Chair's statement of understanding had seemed close at hand, when Members met on Wednesday August 27 at an informal TRIPS Council meeting. Several countries (both developed and developing) had then indicated their general support (subject to confirmation of instructions from capitals) for the statement of understanding.
>
> However, as the hours passed in the afternoon and evening of August 28, it became more and more apparent that the expected easy passage of an agreement was not going to take place. An informal TRIPS Council meeting, which had been scheduled for 4.30pm was suspended/postponed several times during the course of the evening. Reportedly, one or more of the members, including Kenya, were waiting for further instructions from their capital and in the meanwhile could not endorse the Chairman's statement.

---

[261] Ministerial Conference, *Declaration on the TRIPS Agreement and Public Health*, WT/MIN(01)/DEC/2, dated 20 November 2001, para. 6.

A formal TRIPS Council meeting was convened at around 11.30pm, during which the Philippines made an intervention outlining their understanding of the Chair's statement. This prompted a number of other Members (apparently about 14–15) to indicate their intention to make interventions. At this point, before further interventions from members were made, it was decided that the TRIPS Council meeting would end, and that both the December 16 text and the Chair's statement of understanding would be transmitted to the General Council for consideration and approval. It is understood that a number of Members had made it known that they intended to make statements at the General Council before the adoption of the texts.

However, the General Council meeting did not take place until 1.00am on the morning of Friday 29 August. It is understood that the delay had been due to informal consultations held with some of the Members, apparently to dissuade them from making their statements at the General Council. According to trade officials, it became clear during the consultations that a large number (about two dozen or more) of Members had concerns about the Chair's statement as it stood and would like to make statements about their interpretation of it. They had different interpretations on almost all elements of the text, and on the relationship between the Chair's understanding and the December 16/Motta text.

When the General Council finally met at 1.10am on Friday morning (29 August), it was in an informal mode wherein the Chair informed Members of the problem with differing interpretations, which went well beyond one or two countries. The General Council Chairman, Carlos Pérez del Castillo, reportedly said that while all delegations were willing to join a consensus in adopting the decision and chair's statement, several delegations said this would have to be based on their own declared interpretation of these texts. This would clash with the purpose of the proposed chair's statement, which says it (the statement) "represents several key shared understandings of Members regarding the Decision to be taken and the way in which it will be interpreted and implemented".

A subject as important as this could not be treated lightly and could not be settled with different interpretations, Amb[assador] Pérez del Castillo said. He therefore asked for more time to hold consultations. The General Council was therefore suspended and he will reconvene it when he feels important elements are ready for consensus, he concluded.

The Chair is expected to hold open-ended consultations on Friday 29 August.[262]

Hasnain's comments clearly show the complexity of decision-making within the WTO. Note the respective roles of the TRIPS Council, the Chair of the TRIPS Council, the General Council and the Chair of the General Council. Note as well the role of consultations (open-ended or otherwise), the difference between formal and informal meetings, the need for diplomats to receive instructions from their governments and the late (or early) hour of some of the meetings.

After two extra days of intense consultations, the General Council was eventually able to reach agreement on the Decision on *Implementation of Paragraph 6 of the Doha Declaration on the TRIPS Agreement and Public Health*, concerning access for developing countries to essential medicines.[263] A statement of the Chairman of the General Council describing Members' 'shared understanding' on how the decision is to be interpreted and implemented is attached to the Decision.

---

[262] As reported by Tahir Hasnain, Project Coordinator, International Trade, The Network for Consumer Protection, Islamabad, Pakistan, www.thenetwork.org.pk.
[263] See WT/L/540.

2.6.4. Participation of developing-country Members

As already discussed above, the WTO commonly takes decisions by consensus and, in the exceptional instance where a vote is called, each Member has one vote. As such, decision-making within the WTO seems to ensure the participation of all Members, including developing-country Members and, hence, appears *democratic*. Every Member formally enjoys an equal say. Nevertheless, many developing-country Members feel marginalised within the WTO decision-making process.

2.6.4.1. *Marginalisation of developing-country Members*

As discussed above, it will often be impossible for Members, and especially developing-country Members, to block consensus decision-making when a critical mass of other Members favours the decision.[264] Moreover, it is obviously not possible or practical to involve all 147 Members in discussions aimed at reaching deals on controversial issues. It is likely that such broad participation would make these discussions ineffective. As Robert Keohane and Joseph Nye observed in 2000, the legitimacy of international organisations flows not only from 'inputs' in the form of procedures and accountability, but also from 'outputs', that is, their capacity to deliver results.[265] Mechanisms have, therefore, been developed to reduce the number of countries actively participating in the deliberations in the WTO and to allow the WTO to come to decisions. One such mechanism, already discussed above, is the 'green room' meetings.[266] This mechanism brings the major trading powers and a select group of developing-country Members together to try to reach preliminary agreements which are then presented to the rest of the membership. As noted above, this mechanism was much criticised at the ill-fated Seattle Session of the Ministerial Conference.[267] Peter Sutherland wrote in this respect:

> Ironically, in Seattle, WTO Director-General Mike Moore and US Trade Representative Charlene Barshefsky, the co-chairs of the Ministerial Meeting, made a concerted, good-faith effort to broaden the participation of delegations in the negotiations. They divided the Ministerial agenda into several sections, created working groups for each, and invited all delegations to participate in all the working groups. Their goal was to keep Green Rooms to a minimum. But developing country delegations, in particular, had difficulty covering all of the working groups, and as the Ministerial week proceeded and agreements remained elusive, the temptation to pull together smaller groups of countries for harder bargaining – Green Rooms, in other words – understandably grew. In communiqués released towards the end of the week, large

---

[264] See above, p. 142.
[265] R. Keohane and J. Nye, 'The Club Model of Multilateral Cooperation and the World Trade Organization: Problems of Democratic Legitimacy', in R. Porter, P. Sauvé, A. Subramanian and A. Beviglia Zampetti (eds.), *Efficiency, Equity and Legitimacy: The Multilateral Trading System at the Millennium* (Brookings Institutions Press, 2001), 286.
[266] See above, pp. 131–2.   [267] *Ibid.*

groupings of African and Latin American countries denounced what they described as the Ministerial's exclusive and non-democratic negotiating structure.[268]

A small group of influential developing-country Members, including Argentina, Brazil, Mexico, Egypt, India, South Africa and the ASEAN Members, actively participate in the work of the WTO. However, many other developing and low income countries lack the staff and expertise to participate effectively in the many, often highly specialised meetings and discussions within the WTO. These countries are frequently confronted with 'take-it-or-leave-it' decisions agreed upon during informal meetings of a selective group of developed and developing countries.

2.6.4.2. The 'internal transparency' debate

In the first half of 2000, after the debacle of the Seattle Session of the Ministerial Conference in 1999, Members conducted intensive consultations on what was referred to as the issue of 'internal transparency', i.e. the issue of the effective participation of developing countries in WTO decision-making. At the General Council meeting of 17–19 July 2000, the Chairman of the General Council summarised the outcome of the consultations as follows:

> First, within the framework of the WTO Agreement it seemed that Members generally did not see the need for any major institutional reform which could alter the basic character of the WTO as a Member-driven organization and its decision-making process. There was also a strong commitment of the Members to reaffirm the existing practice of taking decisions by consensus. Second, Members seemed to recognize that interactive open-ended informal consultation meetings played an important role in facilitating consensus decision-making. As a complement to, but in no way a replacement of this open-ended consultation process, consultations might also take place with individual Members or groups of Members. In such cases, in order to ensure that the consultations contribute to the achievement of a durable consensus, it was important that Members were advised of the intention to hold such consultations, that those Members with an interest in the specific issue under consideration were given the opportunity to make their views known, that no assumption should be made that one Member represented any other Members except where the Members concerned had agreed on such an arrangement, and that the outcome of such consultations was reported back to the full membership expeditiously for consideration.[269]

The consultations of 2000 on internal transparency did not result in any formal change to the WTO's institutional structure or its decision-making process. They did, however, serve to 'clear the air' and rebuild a degree of confidence in the process. There was specific emphasis on the need:

- to inform all Members of consultations conducted by a select group of Members;

---

[268] P. Sutherland, J. Sewell and D. Weiner, 'Challenges Facing the WTO and Policies to Address Global Governance', in G. Sampson, *The Role of the World Trade Organization in Global Governance* (United Nations University Press, 2001), 87–8.

[269] Minutes of Meeting, WT/GC/M/57, dated 14 September 2000, para. 134.

- to allow all interested Members to make their views known in such consultations;
- not to make any assumptions on the representation of Members by other Members in such consultations; and
- to report back promptly on the results of the consultations to all Members.

The consultations on internal transparency also made clear that the WTO needed:

- to schedule its meetings carefully so as to avoid overlapping meetings as much as possible; and
- to ensure prompt and efficient dissemination of information and documents to Members, and, in particular, to non-resident Members and Members with small missions.

Since 2000, improvements along these lines have been made to the WTO decision-making process. The success of the Doha Session of the Ministerial Conference and the launch of the Doha Development Round is testimony to the progress made since the Seattle debacle. Nevertheless, the improvements made still fall short of the expectations of some Members. Members continue the discussion with a view to identifying and agreeing on further improvements in the decision-making process within the WTO. In 2002, Members held consultations on internal transparency and effective participation of Members in sessions of the Ministerial Conference and the preparatory process leading up to these sessions.[270]

The main challenge is to *balance* the interests of inclusiveness with the interests of efficiency. Disparities in economic and political power will of course always affect, if not determine, the weight of Members in the WTO decision-making process. No institutional mechanism can ever totally 'undo' these differences. Neither would this be desirable. It is clear that an obvious response to the problem of the 'marginalisation' of many developing-country Members in the WTO is technical assistance and human capacity-building. As discussed above, considerable efforts in that respect are currently undertaken as part of the Doha Development Agenda.[271]

Furthermore, as Rubens Ricupero, a former Ambassador of Brazil to the GATT and Chairman of the GATT Council and now Secretary-General of UNCTAD, noted:

> developing countries needed to draw up a "positive agenda" in which they would systematically identify their interests and set realistic objectives with respect to all issues, not only those where they were *demandeurs*, and would pursue these objectives by formulating explicit and technically sound proposals in alliance with other like-

---

[270] Minutes of Meetings, WT/GC/M/73, dated 11 March 2002; WT/GC/M/74, dated 1 July 2002; WT/GC/M/75, dated 27 September 2002; and WT/GC/M/77, dated 13 February 2002. See also Communication from Cuba, Dominican Republic, Egypt, Honduras, India, Indonesia, Jamaica, Kenya, Malaysia, Mauritius, Pakistan, Sri Lanka, Tanzania, Uganda and Zimbabwe, Preparatory Process in Geneva and Negotiating Procedure at the Ministerial Conferences, WT/GC/W/471, dated 24 April 2002.

[271] See above, pp. 100–3.

> minded countries. This would be a concrete way of both strengthening the multilateral trading system and enhancing the participation of developing countries in the decision-making process.[272]

By developing a common 'positive agenda' and coordinating their actions, it is possible for developing-country Members to exercise considerable influence in the WTO through their numbers and their growing importance in the world economy. Developing countries undisputedly played a determining role in 1999, 2001 and 2003 at the Seattle, Doha and Cancún Sessions of the Ministerial Conference.

The Doha Ministerial Declaration of November 2001 explicitly stated:

> Recognizing the challenges posed by an expanding WTO membership, we confirm our collective responsibility to ensure internal transparency and the effective participation of all Members.[273]

The success of the Doha Development Round depends, to a large extent, on whether Members will be able to meet that collective responsibility of ensuring internal transparency and the effective participation of all Members.

Questions and Assignments 2.24

Can developing-country Members effectively participate in the WTO decision-making process? If not, why? What are 'green room' meetings? Could the WTO function without green room or similar meetings? How can the effective participation of developing-country Members best be ensured?

2.6.5. Involvement of NGOs

The WTO is portrayed, by many, as a secretive organisation in which the governments (of a few major trading nations), unsupervised by parliaments or civil society, set the agenda and push through rules that affect the welfare of people worldwide. WTO decision-making has been described as undemocratic and lacking transparency.

2.6.5.1. *Requirements of democratic decision-making*

To the extent that rule-making, as a result of globalisation, is shifting from the national to the international level, international rule-making must meet the standards of democratic decision-making. For decision-making to be democratic, it must involve either directly, but more likely through representation,

---

[272] R. Ricupero, 'Rebuilding Confidence in the Multilateral Trading System: Closing the Legitimacy Gap', in G. Sampson (ed.), *The Role of the World Trade Organization in Global Governance* (United Nations University Press, 2001), 39–40.
[273] WT/MIN(01)/DEC/1, dated 20 November 2001, para. 10.

those that will be affected by the decisions taken. Furthermore, decisions must be reached as a result of an open and transparent exchange of rational arguments which allows those represented to 'watch-dog' the representatives.[274]

If these standards of democratic decision-making are applied to WTO decision-making, one could argue that, in a narrow, formal sense, those affected by WTO decisions are involved, through representation, in the decision-making process. At least for democratic WTO Members, it is true that diplomats act in the WTO under the instructions of their governments, and that these governments are controlled by parliaments which represent the people. In practice, however, the so-called 'legitimacy chain', the chain between those affected by the decision and those making the decision, is too long and not transparent.[275] Parliamentary participation in, and control over, WTO processes is very weak in most Members.

With regard to the other standard of democratic decision-making, namely, that decisions are reached as a result of an open and transparent exchange of rational arguments, the WTO's performance is particularly poor. WTO decision-making is characterised by its non-transparent, selective and secretive nature. Moreover, it has been said that WTO decision-making is dominated by bargaining (and sometimes irrational trade-offs) instead of arguing (and exchanging rational arguments).[276]

2.6.5.2. Article V:2 of the WTO Agreement

Over the last decade, NGOs have demanded a greater role in WTO decision-making in order to make this process more democratic and to give it more legitimacy. As was discussed above, Article V:2 of the *WTO Agreement* empowers the General Council to:

> make appropriate arrangements for consultations and cooperation with non-governmental organizations concerned with matters related to those of the WTO.

It is interesting to note that the 1948 Havana Charter on the International Trade Organization (ITO) contained a similarly-worded provision.[277] As discussed above, the ITO never became operational, and the GATT 1947 filled the gap left by the ITO for almost fifty years. The GATT, however, did not have any provision relating to cooperation with NGOs.[278] Under the GATT, informal and *ad hoc* contacts existed with NGOs. However, NGOs were denied accreditation and access to meetings and conferences.

---

[274] See M. Krajewski, 'Democratic Legitimacy and Constitutional Perspectives of WTO Law', *Journal of World Trade*, 2001, 167–86.
[275] See *ibid.*, 170.   [276] See *ibid.*, 177.
[277] Article 87.2 of the Final Act of the United Nations Conference on Trade and Employment (the *Havana Charter for an International Trade Organization*).
[278] The GATT did allow business NGOs to participate in GATT working parties in the 1950s. See S. Charnovitz, 'Two Centuries of Participation: NGOs and International Governance', *Michigan Journal of International Law*, 1997, 255.

That was also the case for the Marrakesh Conference at which the *WTO Agreement* was signed. NGOs as such were not invited to Marrakesh; those NGOs present were registered as members of the press.

2.6.5.3. Arguments for and against greater NGO involvement

The debate on the desirability of greater involvement of NGOs in the work of the WTO is multi-faceted, as the abundant literature on the issue clearly shows. Summarising that literature, this section gives a brief overview of the arguments for and against greater involvement of NGOs.

There are four arguments *in favour* of greater NGO involvement. First, NGO participation will enhance the WTO decision-making process because NGOs will provide information, arguments and perspectives that governments do not bring forward. NGOs have a wealth of specialised knowledge, resources and analytical capacity. As Daniel Esty noted, NGOs can and should function as 'intellectual competitors' to governments in the quest for optimal policies.[279] In fact, governments often lack the resources and very specific expertise necessary to investigate certain issues. NGOs may frequently be of help, enhancing the resources and expertise available and enriching the policy debate.

Secondly, NGO participation will increase the legitimacy of the WTO. Public confidence in the WTO will increase when NGOs have the opportunity to be heard and to observe the decision-making process. NGOs will contribute to ensuring that decisions result from the open and transparent exchange of rational arguments rather than from shady bargaining. Moreover, NGOs can play an important role in disseminating information at the national level, ensuring broader public support and understanding.

Thirdly, transnational interests and concerns may not be adequately represented by any national government. By allowing NGO involvement in WTO discussions, the WTO would hear about important issues which are international in nature.

Finally, civil society participation in the debate at the national level is only an option for those WTO Members with open and democratic processes at the national level. This is not the case for all WTO Members. Hearing NGOs at the WTO can compensate for the fact that NGOs are not always and everywhere heard at the national level.

There are equally four main arguments *against* greater involvement of NGOs in the work of the WTO. First, NGO involvement may lead the decision-making process to be captured by special interests.[280] Trade liberalisation produces diffuse and hard-to-quantify benefits for the general public while producing

---

[279] See D. Esty, 'Non-Governmental Organizations at the World Trade Organization: Cooperation, Competition, or Exclusion', *Journal of International Economic Law*, 1998, 136 (reproduced by permission of Oxford University Press).

[280] See J. Dunoff, 'The Misguided Debate over NGO Participation at the WTO', *Journal of International Economic Law*, 1998, 437 (reproduced by permission of Oxford University Press).

visible harm to specific and well-organised interests.[281] The NGOs seeking access to the WTO are often entities representing special interests, not the interests of the general public. Thus, special interests may gain undue influence.

Secondly, many NGOs lack legitimacy. They are neither accountable to an electorate nor representative in a general way. NGOs typically advocate relatively narrow interests. Unlike governments, they do not balance all of society's interests. It is legitimate to ask questions regarding the actual constituency of an NGO and its financial backing.

Thirdly, most developing-country Members object to greater involvement of NGOs in the WTO because they view most NGOs, and in particular NGOs focusing on environmental or labour issues, as inimical to their interests. Moreover, NGOs of industrialised Members tend to be well organised and well financed. Allowing NGOs a bigger role may therefore further marginalise developing-country Members within the WTO decision-making process. In other words, it may tilt the negotiating balance further to their disadvantage.

Finally, WTO decision-making, with its consensus requirement, is already very difficult. NGO involvement will make negotiations and decision-making even more difficult. Further transparency will enable private interest groups to frustrate the negotiating powers of governments in WTO fora. Gary Sampson noted in this respect:

> national representatives must on occasion subordinate certain national interests in order to achieve marginally acceptable or sub-optimal compromises that, by definition, require trade-offs. Doubt is expressed whether such a system could continue to work effectively if these trade-offs were open to scrutiny by precisely those special interest groups that would have opposed them.[282]

2.6.5.4. The 1996 Guidelines of the General Council

Pursuant to Article V:2 of the *WTO Agreement*, the General Council adopted a set of Guidelines, in July 1996, regarding the relations of the WTO with non-governmental organisations.[283] In deciding on these Guidelines, Members recognised 'the role NGOs can play to increase the awareness of the public in respect of WTO activities'.[284] Members agreed to improve transparency by making documents available more promptly. NGOs were recognised to be 'a valuable resource' that can 'contribute to the accuracy and richness of the public debate'.[285] In the 1996 Guidelines, it was agreed that interaction with NGOs should be developed through various means such as:

---

[281] See above, pp. 25–6.
[282] G. Sampson, 'Overview', in G. Sampson (ed.), *The Role of the World Trade Organization in Global Governance* (United Nations University Press, 2001), 11.
[283] General Council, *Guidelines for Arrangements on Relations with Non-Governmental Organizations*, WT/L/162, dated 23 July 1996.
[284] *Ibid.*, para. II. See also above, p. 99.   [285] *Ibid.*, para. IV.

- the organisation of symposia for NGOs on specific WTO-related issues;
- informal arrangements to receive the information NGOs may wish to make available for consultation by interested delegations;
- the continuation of the past practice of the WTO Secretariat of responding to requests for general information and briefings about the WTO; and
- participation of chairpersons of WTO councils and committees in discussions and meetings with NGOs in their personal capacity.

The 1996 Guidelines also make the limits of NGO involvement clear. In the concluding paragraph of the Guidelines, the General Council refers to the special character of the WTO which is both a legally binding intergovernmental treaty of rights and obligations among its Members *and* a forum for negotiations. The General Council then concludes:

> As a result of extensive discussions, there is currently a broadly held view that it would not be possible for NGOs to be directly involved in the work of the WTO or its meetings. Closer consultation and cooperation with NGOs can also be met constructively through appropriate processes at the national level where lies primary responsibility for taking into account the different elements of public interest which are brought to bear on trade policy-making.[286]

In 1996, the position of the General Council was clearly that NGOs could not be *directly* involved in the work of the WTO.

Subsequent to the 1996 Guidelines, the External Relations Division was created within the WTO Secretariat to deal with contacts with civil society and NGOs in particular. In July 1996, the General Council adopted the Decision on De-restriction introducing the principle of immediate, unrestricted circulation of WTO documents. Unfortunately this principle was, at the time, still subject to important exceptions. Minutes of WTO meetings and WTO Secretariat background papers were de-restricted, and thus made available to the public, only after the lapse of eight to nine months. A breakthrough of sorts was realised in Singapore in December 1996, when NGOs were invited to attend the plenary sessions of the First Session of the Ministerial Conference and an NGO Centre with facilities for organising meetings and workshops was set up alongside the official Conference Centre. However, the 108 NGOs that attended did not have observer status. They were not allowed to make any statements and could only attend the plenary meetings of the Session. The WTO Secretariat accredited all non-profit organisations that could point to activities related to those of the WTO and did not examine the representativeness and/or legitimacy of the NGOs wishing to attend the Ministerial Conference. Since the Singapore Session, the number of NGO's represented has increased with each Session, with the exception of the Doha Session when limited local facilities did not allow a large number of NGOs.

Almost 800 NGOs were represented at the Cancún Session in September 2003. Note, however, that the NGOs' 'participation' remains limited to the

---

[286] *Ibid.*, para. VI.

Figure 2.6 Trend in NGO representation at Ministerial Conference sessions[287]

	Number of eligible NGOs	NGOs represented	Number of registered participants
Singapore 1996	159	108	235
Geneva 1998	153	128	362
Seattle 1999	776	686	approx 1,500
Doha 2001	651	370	370
Cancún 2003	961	795	1,578

formal plenary sessions when heads of government and trade ministers read out short prepared statements. Access to the working meetings is denied. During the sessions, NGOs are kept informed about the issues under discussion through regular briefings by the WTO Secretariat.

Over the years, the WTO Secretariat has also organised a number of symposia for NGOs and delegations of Members pursuant to the 1996 Guidelines. At the WTO Public Symposium of May 2004 on 'Multilateralism at the Crossroads', there were almost 1,200 registered participants and 150 speakers. At this three-day event, financed by Norway, twenty-five of the twenty-nine workshops were organised by NGOs, Members, international organisations and academic institutions; four workshops were organised by the WTO Secretariat.[288] The lukewarm participation of Members in these symposia has been a source of frustration for NGOs. Furthermore, large symposia, involving NGOs with very different agendas, are likely to lead to poorly focused discussions and overly general conclusions. Issue-specific symposia with a limited agenda and a limited number of participants may therefore be preferable and are more likely to produce constructive results.[289] However, budgetary and staff constraints limit the number of symposia that can be organised.

In the autumn of 1998, a special section for NGOs, the 'NGO Room', was created on the WTO's website.[290] Furthermore, the WTO Secretariat began to compile a monthly list of position papers of NGOs received by the Secretariat and to circulate them to WTO Members. Members can obtain a copy of these papers from the Secretariat or on the WTO's website.[291] In September 1998, the WTO Secretariat also initiated regular briefings for NGOs on specific issues.

2.6.5.5. The 'external transparency' debate after the Seattle debacle

In autumn of 2000, one year after the Seattle debacle, the General Council held informal but intensive consultations on what was referred to as the issue of 'external transparency', i.e. the issue of the participation of civil society/NGOs

---

[287] See http://www.wto.org/english/news_e/news03_e/ngo_minconf_ 6oct03_e.htm, visited on 8 February 2004.

[288] See www.wto.org/english/tratop_e/dda_e/sym_devagenda_prog_04_e.htm, visited on 31 May 2004.

[289] G. Marceau and P. Pedersen, 'Is the WTO Open and Transparent?: A Discussion of the Relationship of the WTO with Non-Governmental Organisations and Civil Society's Claims for More Transparency and Public Participation', *Journal of World Trade*, 1999, 18.

[290] See http://www.wto.org/english/forums_e/ngo_e/ngo_e.htm, visited on 8 February 2004.

[291] See http://www.wto.org/english/forums_e/ngo_e/pospap_e.htm, visited on 8 February 2004.

in the work of the WTO. A number of Members, including the European Communities, the United States, Canada, Australia and Hong Kong, submitted position papers for these informal consultations.

From these position papers, it is clear that no Member wishes to undermine the government-to-government, or intergovernmental, character of the WTO. Moreover, most, if not all, Members are of the opinion that the dialogue with civil society is first and foremost a responsibility for Member governments. The primary responsibility for synthesising the views and concerns of all domestic stakeholders (NGOs, special interest groups, etc.) into an overall national position must fall on the national governments. Furthermore, while recognising the importance of confidentiality in negotiations and intergovernmental discussions, many Members are in favour of a more liberal policy regarding the de-restriction (i.e. making available to the general public) of documents, in particular the minutes of meetings of WTO bodies and Secretariat background notes. Many Members also called for improving the user-friendliness of the WTO's website.

However, on whether NGOs can and should play a more important role in the work of the WTO, the positions of Members differ significantly. On the one hand, the position championed by many of the industrialised Members is that the involvement of NGOs in the work of the WTO should be a 'two way street'. The involvement of NGOs should be a 'give and take' relationship; it involves not only informing NGOs about the work and activities of the WTO but also being informed by NGOs on issues of relevance to the WTO. On the other hand, the position of many developing-country Members, a position well reflected in the submission of Hong Kong, is that the relationship between the WTO and NGOs can only be a 'one-way street'. Hong Kong insists that a distinction is made between enhancing transparency to the civil society (i.e. informing the public about the WTO) *and* making provision for their direct participation in the decision-making process (including a right to make representations of interest in WTO meetings and thus influence the outcome of discussions). Hong Kong is 'not convinced of the desirability of adopting proposals which seek to make provisions for direct participation of civil society'.[292] Indeed, it would be very difficult, if not impossible, for the WTO to function as a negotiating forum, should it be required to reconcile the interests and positions of different political factions and domestic constituencies of individual Members.

The United States takes the most radical position in favour of participation of NGOs in the work of the WTO. It has argued that some of the WTO council and committee meetings should be opened to NGOs. It has proposed that WTO bodies would hold an annual meeting to which NGOs would be invited and at which they would be allowed to make submissions. The United States has also suggested opening the meetings of the Trade Policy Review Body to the public, perhaps by web-casting these meetings. Finally, the United States has proposed

---

[292] Submission from Hong Kong, 'General Council Informal Consultations on External Transparency', WT/GC/W/418, dated 31 October 2000, para. 9.

organising symposia and other forms of informal dialogue with civil society on a broader range of WTO issues and on a more regular basis.[293]

Along the same lines but less radical, the European Communities has proposed that the meetings of the Trade Policy Review Body be opened (on a voluntary basis) to parliamentarians and NGOs of the Member reviewed. It has also suggested that the WTO could hold an annual open meeting at ministerial or senior official level combined with a symposium for dialogue with civil society as well as a meeting of parliamentarians of WTO Members. As already mentioned above, the European Communities has also proposed the establishment of a WTO Parliamentary Consultative Assembly as a forum for inter-parliamentary dialogue on WTO issues.[294]

In view of the sharply opposing positions of Members on the appropriate role of civil society in the WTO, it is not surprising that the consultations and discussions of 2000 have not resulted in any substantial changes allowing for the direct participation of NGOs in the work of the WTO. However, symposia for and with NGOs have been held, and the WTO's website has been improved. In its *Global Accountability Report 2003*, the One World Trust, a British NGO, reported on the access to online information about the WTO:

> Information on the WTO's trade activities is excellent. The WTO provides access to the legal texts of its agreements by topic, alongside a full, non-technical description of the law. This is very important given the technical nature of much of the work it covers. The public are able to review the extent to which members have implemented agreements and view the process and documentation surrounding any decisions taken by the disputes panel. The information available from the committees is standardised. Each committee produces an annual report of its work for the General Council outlining its activities.[295]

With respect to access to official documents, WTO Members finally agreed in May 2002, after years of discussion, to accelerate the de-restriction of official WTO documents. Pursuant to the Decision of the General Council of 14 May 2002 on Procedures for the Circulation and De-restriction of WTO Documents, most WTO documents are now immediately available to the public and those documents that are initially restricted are de-restricted much faster.[296] Under the new rules, the time period for de-restriction has been reduced to an average of six to twelve weeks from the previous time period of eight to nine months.

Stepping on thin ice, the then WTO Director-General, Mike Moore, noted in March 2002 with regard to the role of NGOs in the WTO:

> We plan special workshops where both critics and friends will have time put aside to make their case. This includes the environmentalists, the ICFTU, the Chamber of Commerce, the Third World Network, other development NGOs like Oxfam,

---

[293] See Submission from the United States, 'General Council Informal Consultations on External Transparency', WT/GC/W/413/Rev.1, dated 13 October 2000.

[294] See Discussion Paper from the European Community to the WTO General Council on 'Improving the Functioning of the WTO System', WT/GC/W/412, dated 6 October 2000.

[295] H. Kovach, C. Neligan and S. Burall, *Power Without Accountability: The Global Accountability Report 2003* (One World Trust, 2003), 15.

[296] General Council, *Procedures for the Circulation and Derestriction of WTO Documents*, WT/L/452, dated 16 May 2002.

Parliamentarians, and hopefully Party Political Internationals. I believe these kinds of exchanges are all very healthy and can be a constructive opportunity to learn and improve upon our performance, the better to serve our Member Governments and the people.

The WTO will always remain an Inter-governmental organization, because ultimately it is always our member Governments and Parliaments that must ratify any agreements we conclude. We need to encourage better-focused and more constructive inputs from civil society. *They should be given a voice, but not a vote.* But in return, we should seek from civil society and its representatives a formal code of conduct, and much greater transparency and accountability from them to us and to their membership.[297]

[Emphasis added]

Questions and Assignments 2.25

Describe how the WTO currently communicates with civil society and the role NGOs play within the WTO. How would the United States and the European Communities like to change this role? Would the WTO benefit from a greater role for NGOs in WTO decision-making processes?

2.6.6. Form and legal basis of WTO decisions

Having addressed the two most controversial issues regarding WTO decision-making, namely, the effective participation of developing-country Members and the role of NGOs in the process of WTO decision-making, this section finally examines an aspect of WTO decision-making which is often overlooked: the form and legal basis of WTO decisions. Consistency regarding the form of WTO decisions and the systematic and reasoned reference in decisions to their legal basis would:

- enhance the transparency of WTO decision-making; and
- contribute to the democratic accountability of the WTO.

However, the old GATT legacy of diplomacy and pragmatism is still clearly visible in the formal aspects of the decisions taken by WTO bodies. As Pieter-Jan Kuijper, then Director of the WTO Legal Affairs Division, noted:

it is very often unclear whether any decision in the legal sense of the term has been taken. The WTO presently abounds in "decisions" which have no legal basis whatsoever, are not presented in a standard legal format, but nevertheless purport to be "decisions". Many of such decisions are taken by a mere tap of the gavel. Moreover, the WTO organs are somewhat addicted to Chairman's statements. It must be admitted that they often present a useful way out of a dilemma. The Chairman pronounces them from the chair, usually after painstaking consultations with many

---

[297] M. Moore, *How Trade Liberalization Impacts on Employment*, Speech to the International Labour Organization, 18 March 2002, www.wto.org/english/news_e_spmm_e/spmm80_e.htm visited on 31 August 2004.

delegations, but in principle they are not fully negotiated. Nobody contradicts them, but nobody has accepted them either and everybody can live in the illusion that this statement is the Chair's responsibility alone, does not really represent a true consensus or decision but, as if by magic, will still be followed and respected by everyone. Except in the end, of course, in the dispute settlement procedure, as the Appellate Body made only too clear when it treated the various "decisions" and "Chairman's statements" in the Foreign Sales Corporation case.[298]

To avoid the demise of such 'decisions' at the hands of panels or of the Appellate Body, Pieter-Jan Kuijper suggested that it would be useful to have a clear distinction between:

- *decisions* which have binding legal effect and which should be based on a specific legal basis giving the power for such binding decisions; and
- *recommendations* which are just that: mere recommendations with no binding effect.

Furthermore, Kuijper suggested that it might also be useful to make a distinction between:

- *decisions with external effect*, i.e. imposing legal obligations or legal rights on Members; and
- *decisions with internal effect*, i.e. binding only the WTO organs.[299]

Kuijper has also pointed out that it is often unclear *who* takes the decision. General Council decisions in certain instances still begin with the words, 'the Members'. Kuijper argued:

Showing clearly that WTO decisions, though as a political matter of course still taken by the Members, are legal acts of the Ministerial Conference or one of the Councils is the simple consequence of the fact that an international organization like the WTO has a separate (legal) life from that of its Members.[300]

Finally, it is quite obvious that in the past little attention was given to the legal form of the text of decisions. As a result:

decisions are highly variegated in this respect: some state no legal basis, some have the legal basis at the beginning, some at the end of the preamble, sometimes there is no consistent reference to proposals made or reports forming the basis of the decision, often there is no consistent pattern of building the reasoning (the *motifs*) underpinning the decision, etc.; a consistent way of presenting the operational clauses is also often lacking.[301]

Recently, some degree of uniformity with respect to the legal form of the text of decisions has been achieved. This is an important step towards more transparency and accountability of WTO decision-making. However, much work remains to be done.

---

[298] P. J. Kuijper, 'Some Institutional Issues Presently Before the WTO', in D. Kennedy and J. Southwick (eds.), *The Political Economy of International Trade Law: Essays in Honor of Robert E. Hudec* (Cambridge University Press, 2002), 106.
[299] *Ibid.*, 106–7.   [300] *Ibid.*, 107.   [301] *Ibid.*

Questions and Assignments 2.26

Does the WTO give sufficient attention to the form and legal basis of its decisions? If not, how could this be improved and why would such improvement be welcome?

2.7. OTHER ISSUES

2.7.1. Status of the WTO

Article VIII of the *WTO Agreement* states:

1. The WTO shall have legal personality, and shall be accorded by each of its Members such legal capacity as may be necessary for the exercise of its functions.
2. The WTO shall be accorded by each of its Members such privileges and immunities as are necessary for the exercise of its functions.
3. The officials of the WTO and the representatives of the Members shall similarly be accorded by each of its Members such privileges and immunities as are necessary for the independent exercise of their functions in connection with the WTO.
4. The privileges and immunities to be accorded by a Member to the WTO, its officials, and the representatives of its Members shall be similar to the privileges and immunities stipulated in the Convention on the Privileges and Immunities of the Specialised Agencies, approved by the General Assembly of the United Nations on 21 November 1947.
5. The WTO may conclude a headquarters agreement.

The *WTO Headquarters Agreement* with Switzerland addresses the matter of the privileges and immunities of the WTO, its officials and the representatives of WTO Members in great detail.[302]

It deserves to be mentioned that the WTO is *not* part of the UN 'family'. It is a fully independent international organisation with its own particular 'corporate' culture. John Jackson noted with regard to the question of 'specialised agency of the UN' status for the WTO, that this question:

was explicitly considered and explicitly rejected by the WTO members, possibly because of the skepticism of some members about the UN budgetary and personnel policies and their alleged inefficiencies.[303]

2.7.2. The WTO budget

The total WTO budget for 2004 amounted to 162 million Swiss francs.[304] In recent years, the WTO budget has been steadily increased to allow the WTO

---

[302] For the *WTO Headquarters Agreement*, see WT/GC/1 and Add.1.
[303] J. Jackson, *The World Trade Organization: Constitution and Jurisprudence* (Royal Institute of International Affairs, 1998), 52.
[304] See http://www.wto.org/english/thewto_e/secre_e/budget04_e.htm, visited on 1 September 2004. CHF162 million is equivalent to €105 million.

Secretariat to give more technical assistance to developing countries and contribute more to capacity-building in these countries.[305] However, in comparison with the annual budget of other international organisations or some NGOs, the WTO's annual budget remains quite modest. In 2001, the then WTO Director-General, Mike Moore, noted that the World Wildlife Fund had three times the resources of the WTO.[306] The modest budget of the WTO reflects the small size of the Secretariat and the relatively limited scope of the WTO's activities outside Geneva. Peter Sutherland has, however, criticised the limited size of the WTO budget:

> Lacking either the courage of their own convictions or confidence in their ability to prevail over domestic opposition, the chief financial backers of the WTO have failed to provide adequate funding for a WTO Secretariat (by far the smallest of all the major multilateral institutions) that is already overburdened by technical assistance demands as well as dispute settlement cases and new accessions.[307]

Article VII:1 of the *WTO Agreement* sets out the basic rules applicable to the draft WTO budget presented by the Director-General:

> The Director-General shall present to the Committee on Budget, Finance and Administration the annual budget estimate and financial statement of the WTO. The Committee on Budget, Finance and Administration shall review the annual budget estimate and the financial statement presented by the Director-General and make recommendations thereon to the General Council. The annual budget estimate shall be subject to approval by the General Council.

With respect to the financial contributions to be made by Members to the budget of the WTO, Article VII:2 of the *WTO Agreement* states:

> The Committee on Budget, Finance and Administration shall propose to the General Council financial regulations which shall include provisions setting out:
>
> a. the scale of contributions apportioning the expenses of the WTO among its Members; and
> b. the measures to be taken in respect of Members in arrears.

The financial regulations are based, as far as practicable, on the regulations and practices of GATT 1947. In November 1995, the General Council adopted the WTO Financial Regulations and the Financial Rules.[308]

Pursuant to Article VII:4 of the *WTO Agreement* and as elaborated in the Financial Regulations, each Member shall promptly contribute to the WTO its share in the expenses of the WTO in accordance with the financial regulations adopted by the General Council.

---

[305] In 2001, the WTO budget amounted to €92 million. Between 2001 and 2004, the WTO budget was therefore increased by 14 per cent.

[306] Reported by F. Lewis, 'The Anti-Globalization Spoilers Are Going Global', *International Herald Tribune*, 6 July 2001.

[307] P. Sutherland, J. Sewell and D. Weiner, 'Challenges Facing the WTO and Policies to Address Global Governance', in G. Sampson (ed.), *The Role of the World Trade Organization in Global Governance* (United Nations University Press, 2001), 82.

[308] For the Financial Regulations, see WT/L/156; for the Financial Rules, see WT/L/157.

The contributions of Members to the WTO budget are established according to a formula based on their share of international trade in goods and services for the last three years for which data are available. Members whose share in the total trade is less than 0.015 per cent make a minimum contribution to the budget of 0.015 per cent. The Member States of the European Union are by far the largest contributors to the WTO budget. The European Communities itself does not contribute to the WTO budget. In the calculation of the contribution of the EU Member States, the intra-Community trade is also taken into account, which explains the high level of their contributions. Altogether, the EU Member States contributed, in 2003, 39.6 per cent of the WTO budget; the United States 15.9 per cent; Japan 6.4 per cent; Canada 3.9 per cent; China 3.2 per cent; Hong Kong 3.2 per cent; Korea 2.4 per cent; Mexico 2.3 per cent; Chinese Taipei 2 per cent; Singapore 2 per cent, Malaysia 1.3 per cent; Australia 1.2 per cent; Brazil 0.9 per cent; India 0.9 per cent; and Indonesia 0.8 per cent.

As already discussed, Article VII:3 of the *WTO Agreement* provides that the annual budget and the financial regulations, setting out the contributions to be paid, are adopted by the General Council by a two-thirds majority comprising of more than half of the Members of the WTO.

In addition to the budget, the WTO also manages a number of trust funds, which have been contributed to by Members. Trust funds such as the Doha Development Agenda Global Trust Fund are used in support of special activities for technical cooperation and training meant to enable least-developed and developing countries to make better use of the WTO and draw greater benefit from the multilateral trading system. In March 2002, WTO Members pledged €20.5 million to the Doha Development Agenda Global Trust Fund.[309]

The General Council adopted guidelines, in December 2000, and reviewed them in January 2003, with respect to 'Voluntary Contributions, Gifts or Donations from Non-Governmental Donors'.[310]

Questions and Assignments 2.27

How is the WTO financed? How is the decision on the annual budget and on the contributions of Members to that budget taken? Who is the biggest contributor to the WTO budget?

2.8. SUMMARY

The WTO is a young international organisation with a long history. The origins of the WTO lie in the GATT 1947, which for almost fifty years was – after the 'still-birth' of the ITO in the late 1940s – the *de facto* international organisation

[309] Press/279, dated 11 March 2002, at www.wto.org.   [310] See WT/L/386, dated 15 January 2000.

for trade. While the GATT was successful with respect to the reduction of tariffs, effectively addressing the problems of international trade in goods and services in the era of economic globalisation would require a more 'sophisticated' institutional framework. The Uruguay Round negotiations resulted, in December 1993, in an agreement on the establishment of the World Trade Organization which was subsequently signed in Marrakesh, Morocco, in April 1994. The WTO has been operational since 1 January 1995.

Pursuant to the Preamble to the *WTO Agreement*, the ultimate objectives of the WTO are:

- the increase of standards of living;
- the attainment of full employment;
- the growth of real income and effective demand; and
- the expansion of production of, and trade in, goods and services.

However, it is clear from the Preamble that, in pursuing these objectives, the WTO must take into account the need for environmental protection and the needs of developing countries. The two main instruments, or means, to achieve the objectives of the WTO are reciprocal and mutually advantageous arrangements on:

- the reduction of trade barriers; and
- the elimination of discrimination.

The primary function of the WTO is to provide the common institutional framework for the conduct of trade relations among its Members. More specifically, the WTO has been assigned six widely defined functions:

- to facilitate the implementation, administration and operation of the WTO agreements;
- to be a forum for negotiations of new trade agreements;
- to settle trade disputes between its Members;
- to review the trade policies of its Members;
- to cooperate with other international organisations and non-governmental organisations; and
- to give technical assistance to developing-country Members to allow them to integrate into the world trading system and reap the benefits from international trade.

Since the accession of the People's Republic of China in December 2001, the WTO has been a quasi-universal organisation. Its 147 Members account for almost all international trade. Three out of every four WTO Members are developing countries. It is noteworthy that not only States but also autonomous customs territories can be, and are, Members of the WTO. Equally noteworthy is that both the European Communities *and* all Member States of the European Union are Members of the WTO. Accession to the WTO is a difficult process since candidates for membership have to negotiate an 'entrance ticket' of market access concessions, in addition to bringing their national legislation and practice into conformity with the obligations under the *WTO Agreement*. Members can, and do, in exceptional circumstances obtain temporary, partial waivers of their WTO obligations; they can also, but have not done so to date, withdraw from the WTO. In limited circumstances, a Member may – for political or other reasons – opt out of WTO treaty relations with another Member. With one exception of minor importance, the *WTO Agreement* does not provide for the possibility to expel Members from the WTO. There is no procedure to expel States, from the WTO, which systematically act inconsistently with their obligations under the WTO agreements or which are guilty of systematic gross violations of human rights or acts of aggression.

The WTO has a complex institutional structure which includes:

- at the *highest* level, the Ministerial Conference, which is in session only for a few days every two years;
- at a *second* level, the General Council, which exercises the powers of the Ministerial Conference in between its sessions; and the Dispute Settlement Body (DSB) and the Trade Policy Review Body (TPRB), which are both emanations of the General Council; and
- at *lower* levels, specialised councils and a manifold of committees and working parties.

The current Doha Development Round negotiations are conducted in special sessions of existing WTO bodies and in two, specially created, negotiating groups. The conduct of these negotiations is supervised by the Trade Negotiations Committee (TNC), which regularly reports to the General Council. Furthermore, the institutional structure of the WTO includes quasi-judicial and other non-political bodies as well as the WTO Secretariat, headed by the WTO Director-General. The WTO is a 'Member-driven' organisation. The Members – and not the Director-General or the WTO Secretariat – set the agenda, make proposals and take decisions. The Director-General and the WTO Secretariat act primarily as an 'honest broker' in, or a 'facilitator' of, the political decision-making processes in the WTO. Unlike other international organisations, the WTO does not have a permanent body through which the 'dialogue' between the WTO and civil society can take place. Furthermore, all WTO bodies (except for the non-political bodies) comprise all the 147 Members of the WTO. Unlike other international organisations with a large membership, the WTO does not have an executive body, comprising of only core WTO Members, to facilitate the process of deliberation and decision-making. To date, proposals for the establishment of a WTO consultative body, comprising of representatives of civil society, and/or a WTO executive body, comprising of core WTO Members, have received little support from WTO Members.

With respect to decision-making by WTO bodies, one can distinguish between the normal decision-making procedure, which applies as the default procedure, and a number of special procedures for specific decisions. In theory, WTO Members, under both the normal and most of the special procedures, take decisions by consensus, and, if that is not possible, by majority voting. Every Member has one vote, except the European Communities which has as many votes as the European Union has Member States. In practice, however, the WTO seldom resorts to voting. WTO decisions are made almost exclusively by consensus. Decision-making by consensus is at the heart of the WTO system and is regarded as a fundamental democratic guarantee. However, the consensus requirement renders decision-making by the WTO difficult and susceptible to paralysis.

While decision-making by consensus should, in principle, ensure the participation in the decision-making process of all Members, including developing-country Members, many developing-country Members feel marginalised. The effective participation of developing-country Members in WTO decision-making has become one of the principal institutional challenges of the WTO. It is generally recognised that it is not possible to negotiate effectively in bodies comprising of all 147 WTO Members. Therefore, in the GATT and now the WTO, mechanisms have been developed that allow for negotiations on difficult issues among a restricted number of Members. While they are indispensable, these mechanisms, and in particular the 'green room' meetings, have triggered much criticism from developing-country Members. Discussions among WTO Members since the ill-fated Seattle Session of the Ministerial Conference have led to informal agreement on a number of checks on negotiations among a restricted number of Members. Furthermore, it has been recognised that to ensure a more effective involvement of developing-country Members in WTO decision-making, the lack of expertise and resources of these Members has to be addressed. At present, a considerable effort to help developing-country Members with capacity-building is being undertaken by the WTO as well as by individual developed-country Members.

Apart from the effective involvement of developing-country Members in WTO decision-making, another aspect of WTO decision-making that has given rise to considerable controversy is the role of NGOs in the decision-making process. Over the last decade, NGOs have demanded a bigger role in the WTO decision-making process in order to make this process more democratic and to give it more legitimacy. The response of Members to the demands of NGOs has been mixed. No Member wishes to undermine the intergovernmental character of the WTO. Most, if not all, Members are of the opinion that the dialogue with civil society is first and foremost a responsibility for Member governments and needs to be conducted at the national level. However, a number of developed-country Members have supported NGOs in their demand for a bigger role at the international level. They have campaigned for more transparency in the work of the WTO and for some degree of direct involvement of NGOs in the WTO decision-making process. On the other hand, many developing-country Members have strongly objected to NGO involvement. They fear that granting NGOs a bigger role may further marginalise developing-country Members within the WTO decision-making process. Positions on the appropriate role of NGOs in the WTO decision-making process thus sharply diverge. In recent years, however, NGOs have been given more of a voice through WTO symposia organised for and with NGOs and through the systematic transfer by the WTO Secretariat of NGO position papers to WTO Members. Furthermore, public access to WTO official documents and information on WTO policies and activities has been enhanced by the 2002 Decision on De-restriction and by improvements to the WTO's website. Also, the regular briefings of NGOs by the WTO Secretariat and frequent, informal contacts between the Secretariat and NGOs have contributed to the dialogue between the WTO and civil society.

In the Doha Ministerial Declaration of November 2001, the Ministerial Conference stated:

> Recognizing the challenges posed by an expanding WTO membership, we confirm our collective responsibility to ensure internal transparency and the effective participation of all members. While emphasizing the intergovernmental character of the organization, we are committed to making the WTO's operations more transparent, including through more effective and prompt dissemination of information, and to improve dialogue with the public.[311]

WTO Members thus clearly acknowledge the institutional problems confronting the WTO:

- the effective participation of developing-country Members; and
- the 'dialogue' of the WTO with civil society, and in particular NGOs.

These institutional problems are without easy solutions but WTO Members are willing to address them. They realise that, if left unaddressed, these problems will undermine the legitimacy and/or the effectiveness of the WTO as an international organisation to promote trade, to balance trade with other societal values and interests, and to advance the integration of developing countries in the world trading system.

2.9. EXERCISE: TO JOIN OR NOT TO JOIN?

The Parliament of the Republic of Newland has approved – by a narrow margin – the Government's plans to start negotiations on accession to the WTO. However, the opposition continues its campaign against Newland's accession to the WTO in the hope of turning public opinion in Newland against WTO membership. In a series of interviews and speeches the charismatic leader of the opposition claims that:

- for many years Newland's best diplomats and negotiators will be caught up in never-ending, very complex negotiations on accession;
- Newland will have to make many amendments to its domestic legislation;

---

[311] WT/MIN(01)/DEC/1, dated 20 November 2001, para. 10.

- should Newland be unable to meet some of its obligations under the *WTO Agreement*, it will have no other option than to withdraw from the WTO;
- as a Member, Newland will have to grant market access to goods and services from Evilland, an original WTO Member, but a country with a notoriously bad human rights record;
- the WTO is controlled by the European Communities (which holds no less than twenty-five votes) and the United States;
- Newland, as a developing country, will not be able to participate effectively in WTO decision-making;
- the WTO is directed by a powerful group of faceless international bureaucrats, headed by the WTO Director-General, who is handpicked by the Quad;
- the confidentiality of government-to-government negotiations on trade matters is not guaranteed as special interest groups have access to meetings of WTO bodies and have immediate access to all official documents; and
- NGOs, none of which is friendly to the economic and trade interests of Newland, have a voice in WTO decision-making.

A recent poll showed that the opposition's campaign against WTO accession is succeeding and that public opinion in Newland is turning against accession. To reverse the tide, Newland's Government decides to engage in a Parliamentary debate with the opposition. The Minister of Foreign Affairs has taken it upon herself to reply to each of the claims of the opposition leader. She does so with legal, rather than political, arguments. A sharp debate between the Minister and the opposition leader ensues.

Group A: You are the opposition leader.

Group B: You are Newland's Minister of Foreign Affairs.

WTO dispute settlement

Contents

3.1. INTRODUCTION

The WTO agreements provide for many wide-ranging rules concerning international trade in goods, trade in services and trade-related aspects of intellectual property rights.[1] In view of the importance of their impact, economic and otherwise, it is not surprising that WTO Members do not always agree on the correct interpretation and application of these rules. Members frequently argue about whether or not a particular law or practice of a Member constitutes a violation of a right or obligation provided for in a WTO agreement. The WTO disposes of a remarkable system to settle such disputes between WTO Members concerning their rights and obligations under the WTO agreements.

The WTO dispute settlement system has been operational for ten years now. In that period it has arguably been the most prolific of all international dispute settlement systems. Between 1 January 1995 and 1 September 2004, a total of 314 disputes had been brought to the WTO system for resolution.[2] That is more than were brought to the GATT, the WTO's predecessor, in the forty-seven years between 1948 and 1995. In almost a quarter of the disputes brought to the WTO system, the parties were able to reach an amicable solution through consultations, or the dispute was otherwise resolved without recourse to adjudication.[3] In other disputes, parties have resorted to adjudication.[4]

Some of the disputes brought to the WTO dispute settlement system have triggered considerable controversy and public debate and have attracted much

---

[1] For an overview, see above, pp. 45–52.
[2] I.e. the number of requests for consultations notified to the DSB on 1 September 2004. See below, pp. 183–4, 255–9, and see www.wto.org/english/tradtop_e/dispu_e/dispu_status_e.htm, visited on 1 September 2004.
[3] See below, pp. 183–4, 258–9.   [4] *Ibid.*

media attention. This has been the case, for example, for disputes on national legislation for the protection of public health or the environment, such as:

- the *EC – Hormones* dispute on the European Communities' import ban on meat from cattle treated with growth hormones;[5]
- the *US – Shrimp* dispute on the US import ban on shrimp harvested with nets that kill sea turtles;[6]
- the *EC – Asbestos* dispute on a French ban on asbestos and asbestos-containing products;[7] and
- the *EC – Biotech Products* dispute on measures affecting the approval and marketing of genetically modified products in the European Union.[8]

Also, the *EC – Bananas III* dispute on the European Communities' preferential import regime for bananas was, for many years, headline news.[9]

This chapter deals with the WTO dispute settlement system. It discusses:

- the origins of the WTO dispute settlement system;
- the principles of WTO dispute settlement;
- the institutions of WTO dispute settlement;
- WTO dispute settlement proceedings;
- WTO dispute settlement practice to date; and
- challenges and proposals for reform.

3.2. THE ORIGINS OF THE WTO DISPUTE SETTLEMENT SYSTEM

The WTO dispute settlement system, which has been in operation since 1 January 1995, was not established out of the blue. It is not a novel system. On the contrary, this system is based on, and has taken on board, almost fifty years of experience in the resolution of trade disputes in the context of the GATT 1947. Article 3.1 of the DSU states:

> Members affirm their adherence to the principles for the management of disputes heretofore applied under Articles XXII and XXIII of GATT 1947, and the rules and procedures as further elaborated and modified herein.

In order to understand the WTO dispute settlement system, a brief discussion of its origins is indispensable.

---

[5] *EC – Hormones*, complaints by the US and Canada.
[6] *US – Shrimp*, complaint by India, Malaysia, Pakistan and Thailand.
[7] *EC – Asbestos*, complaint by Canada.
[8] *EC – Biotech Products*, complaint by the United States, Canada and Argentina.
[9] *EC – Bananas III*, complaint by Ecuador, Guatemala, Honduras, Mexico and the United States.

Figure 3.1 Dispute resolution methods compared[10]

METHOD	CONS	PROS
DUELING	- OUT OF FASHION - MIGHT GET KILLED	- USUALLY DONE AT DAWN - SO WON'T INTERFERE WITH WORKDAY
COIN TOSS	- ARBITRARY	- CHEAP - SIMPLE
WAR	- MIGHT GET KILLED - WORLD MIGHT END	- GOOD FOR BUSINESS - CAN TELL GRAND-CHILDREN ABOUT IT
"ALTERNATIVE DISPUTE RESOLUTION"	- SEEN AS FLAKEY - NO ONE UNDERSTANDS IT	- CHEAPER THAN LITIGATION - QUICKER THAN LITIGATION
LITIGATION	- EXPENSIVE - DRAGS ON FOREVER	- RESPECTABLE - MIGHT GET IN LAWYERS WEEKLY
RARE FISTS	- MIGHT NEED COSMETIC SURGERY AFTERWARDS	- GOOD EXERCISE - CHEAP

3.2.1. Settlement of disputes between States

Historically, as well as today, disputes in society have been and are 'resolved' in different ways.

Article 2.3 of the *UN Charter* requires that all Members of the United Nations:

> settle their international disputes by peaceful means in such a manner that international peace and security, and justice, are not endangered.

Article 33.1 of Chapter VI, entitled 'Pacific settlement of disputes', of the *UN Charter* further states:

> The parties to any dispute, the continuance of which is likely to endanger the maintenance of international peace and security, shall, first of all, seek a solution by negotiation, enquiry, mediation, conciliation, arbitration, judicial settlement, resort to regional agencies or arrangements, or other peaceful means of their own choice.

---

[10] From *The Lawyers Weekly*, 27 August 1993.

There are essentially two methods of peaceful resolution of international disputes. An international dispute can be resolved:

- through diplomatic negotiations between the disputing States (with varying degrees of third party intervention and assistance); or
- through adjudication by an independent entity (arbitration and judicial settlement).

In recent years, there has been a remarkable increase in the importance and effectiveness of international dispute settlement through adjudication. There has been a clear proliferation of international courts and tribunals and an exponential growth in international litigation.[11] The WTO dispute settlement system is at the forefront of this significant evolution in international relations between States. The GATT dispute settlement system evolved between the late 1940s and the early 1990s, from a system that was primarily a system of dispute settlement through diplomatic negotiations into a system of dispute settlement through adjudication. The WTO system is a further step in the evolution of international trade dispute settlement.

3.2.2. Dispute settlement under the GATT 1947

For reasons explained in Chapter 2, the GATT 1947 did not provide for an elaborate dispute settlement system.[12] The GATT 1947 contained only two brief provisions relating to dispute settlement: Articles XXII and XXIII. Note that neither provision explicitly referred to 'dispute settlement' or provided for detailed procedures to handle disputes. Article XXII, entitled 'Consultations', stated:

> 1. Each contracting party shall accord sympathetic consideration to, and shall afford adequate opportunity for consultation regarding, such representations as may be made by another contracting party with respect to any matter affecting the operation of this Agreement.
> 2. The CONTRACTING PARTIES may, at the request of a contracting party, consult with any contracting party or parties in respect of any matter for which it has not been possible to find a satisfactory solution through consultation under paragraph 1.

Article XXIII, entitled 'Nullification or Impairment', stated:

> 1. If any contracting party should consider that any benefit accruing to it directly or indirectly under this Agreement is being nullified or impaired or that the attainment of any objective of the Agreement is being impeded as the result of
>   a. the failure of another contracting party to carry out its obligations under this Agreement, or
>   b. the application by another contracting party of any measure, whether or not it conflicts with the provisions of this Agreement, or
>   c. the existence of any other situation,

---

[11] P. Sands *et al.*, *Manual on International Courts and Tribunals* (Butterworths, 1999), xxv–xxvi.
[12] See above, pp. 78–81. Note, however, that the Havana *ITO Charter* set out detailed dispute settlement procedures.

> the contracting party may, with a view to the satisfactory adjustment of the matter, make written representations or proposals to the other contracting party or parties which it considers to be concerned. Any contracting party thus approached shall give sympathetic consideration to the representations or proposals made to it.
>
> 2. If no satisfactory adjustment is effected between the contracting parties concerned within a reasonable time, or if the difficulty is of the type described in paragraph 1 (c) of this Article, the matter may be referred to the CONTRACTING PARTIES. The CONTRACTING PARTIES shall promptly investigate any matter so referred to them and shall make appropriate recommendations to the contracting parties which they consider to be concerned, or give a ruling on the matter, as appropriate ... If the CONTRACTING PARTIES consider that the circumstances are serious enough to justify such action, they may authorize a contracting party or parties to suspend the application to any other contracting party or parties of such concessions or other obligations under this Agreement as they determine to be appropriate in the circumstances. ...

When consultations under Articles XXII or XXIII:1 of the GATT 1947 failed to resolve a dispute arising under the GATT 1947, the dispute was initially 'handled' by working parties, set up pursuant to Article XXIII:2. These working parties consisted of representatives of all interested Contracting Parties, including the parties to the dispute, and made decisions on the basis of consensus.[13] Very soon, however, this 'method' of resolving disputes was abandoned. From the early 1950s onwards, disputes were usually first heard by so-called 'panels' of three to five independent experts from GATT Contracting Parties not involved in the dispute. These panels reported to the GATT Council, consisting of all Contracting Parties, which would have to adopt the recommendations and rulings of the panel by consensus before they would become legally binding on the parties to the dispute. In the 1950s, this 'panel procedure' worked well. In those days, the GATT was essentially a small 'club' of like-minded trade officials, working together since the 1946–8 ITO/GATT negotiations; they 'all knew what they had meant to say' in the GATT 1947.[14] After an impressive record of disputes settled in the 1950s, the GATT dispute settlement system was used much less in the 1960s.[15] As a result of the establishment of the European Economic Community and the significant increase in the number of developing countries among the Contracting Parties, the 'conventional wisdom of GATT was that lawsuits were a non-productive way to approach any problem'.[16] In response to the proliferation of non-tariff barriers in the 1970s, the Contracting Parties slowly 'rediscovered' the GATT dispute settlement system. However, by the 1970s, the 'club' of the

---

[13] See e.g. the Report of the Working Party in Brazil Internal Taxes, adopted by the CONTRACTING PARTIES on 30 June 1949, GATT/CP.3/42; or the Report on the Withdrawal by the United States of a Tariff Concession under Article XIX of the General Agreement on Tariffs and Trade (Hatter's Fur), adopted by the CONTRACTING PARTIES on 22 October 1951, CP/106. Both documents are available at www.worldtradelaw.net, visited on 1 February 2004.

[14] R. Hudec, 'The New WTO Dispute Settlement Procedure', *Minnesota Journal of Global Trade*, 1999, 6.

[15] Of particular importance for the further development of the GATT dispute settlement system was, however, the Panel Report in *Uruguayan Recourse to Article XXIII*, adopted on 3 March 1965, L/2074, BISD 13S/35. The Panel, in this report, introduced a *prima facie* presumption of nullification or impairment of benefits whenever there was a violation of a GATT obligation. See below, pp. 192–3.

[16] R. Hudec, 'The New WTO Dispute Settlement Procedure', *Minnesota Journal of Global Trade*, 1999, 6.

1950s had gone and had been replaced by a much more contentious group of Contracting Parties, represented by a new generation of trade diplomats for whom the ITO/GATT negotiations were ancient history.[17] Robert Hudec, the leading authority on the GATT dispute settlement system, noted:

> The inadequacy of the diplomatic approach was demonstrated rather vividly in a few embarrassingly poor decisions rendered in the late 1970s and early 1980s. In contrast, a few well-reasoned legal rulings at this time received a favorable reception from governments. The GATT Secretariat recognized that, in this new and more difficult setting, the dispute settlement procedure would need to rely more heavily on the authority of "law" itself.[18]

As a result, the Contracting Parties agreed to the addition of legal staff to the GATT Secretariat and, in 1983, to the establishment of a Legal Office within the GATT Secretariat, to help panels, often composed of trade diplomats without legal training, with the drafting of panel reports. Consequently, the legal quality of panel reports improved and the confidence Contracting Parties had in the panel system increased.[19] During the 1980s, previous panel reports were increasingly used as a sort of 'precedent' and the panels started using customary rules of interpretation of public international law.

Discussing the evolution in GATT dispute settlement, Hudec noted:

> during the first thirty years of GATT history, roughly 1948–1978, the GATT disputes procedure did exhibit a distinctly diplomatic character. Its operating procedures were quite ill-defined, its legal rulings were written in vague language that suggested more than it said, and both its procedures and its rulings left plenty of room for negotiation. In 1970, the artful ambiguity of this early GATT procedure led this author to christen its methods "A Diplomat's Jurisprudence" ... After 1980, the GATT dispute settlement procedure transformed itself into an institution based primarily on the authority of legal obligations.[20]

In the context of the Tokyo Round in the late 1970s and during the early 1980s, the Contracting Parties codified, as well as modified, emerging dispute settlement procedures.[21] The GATT dispute settlement system gradually evolved, from a power-based system of dispute settlement through diplomatic negotiations, into a system that had many of the features of a rules-based system of dispute settlement through adjudication. Ernst-Ulrich Petersmann wrote with respect to this evolution in GATT dispute settlement:

> The economic, political and legal advantages of this progressive "judicialization" of GATT dispute settlement procedures are obvious. For example:

---

[17] *Ibid.*, 7.

[18] *Ibid.* In a footnote, Hudec referred to the 1977 Panel Report, *US – DISC*; the 1979 Panel Report, *EEC – Minimum Import Prices*; and the 1983 Panel Report, *US – Spring Assemblies*.

[19] R. Hudec *et al.*, 'A Statistical Profile of the GATT Dispute Settlement Cases: 1948–1989', *Minnesota Journal of Global Trade*, 1993, 138.

[20] R. Hudec, 'The New WTO Dispute Settlement Procedure', *Minnesota Journal of Global Trade*, 1999, 4.

[21] These efforts find reflection in the Tokyo Round 'Understanding Regarding Notification, Consultation, Dispute Settlement and Surveillance', 28 November 1979 (BISD 26S/210) (including an Agreed Description of the Customary Practice of the GATT in the field of disputes settlement); the Decision on Dispute Settlement Procedures of 29 November 1982 (BISD 29S/13); and the Decision on Dispute Settlement Procedures of 30 November 1984 (BISD 31S/9).

a. Rules, and their "rule-oriented" rather than "power-oriented" interpretation and application, enhance predictability and legal security, limit the risks of abuse of power, reduce transaction costs of traders and producers, increase the scope for decentralized decision-making and thereby promote liberty and economic welfare. It is an everyday experience that traders, investors and consumers prefer to do business where rules are observed and enforced.

b. Legal dispute settlement and enforcement mechanisms render international treaties more effective and credible and are essential to maintain confidence in the GATT system.

c. Panel reports, dispute settlement rulings, arbitration awards and court decisions, generally build up consistent case law and evolve into time tested precedents, generally accepted interpretations and new rules which may fill "gaps" in existing treaty law and progressively transform multilateral treaties into more consistent legal systems.[22]

Petersmann also noted that the GATT dispute settlement system appeared less 'protection-biased' than many domestic courts. He furthermore observed that:

Many "GATT disputes" tend to be "secondary disputes" brought to the international level after the "primary conflicts" of interests – for example between domestic consumers and domestic import-competing producers, or between the US President and protectionist lobbies in the US Congress – could not be settled in a transparent and non-discriminatory manner in conformity with GATT law. Governments know very well this "domestic policy nature" of most GATT disputes ... Many governments value this "domestic policy function" of GATT rules to assist governments in overcoming protectionist pressures at home. They regularly agree to the adoption of panel reports because they know very well that:

– the GATT commitments for the use of transparent, non-discriminatory and welfare-increasing policy instruments ... do not impose any economic "sacrifices": from an economic point of view, a government hardly ever "loses" a GATT dispute settlement proceeding;
– any GATT dispute settlement ruling against the use of non-transparent, discriminatory or disproportionately harmful policy instruments can be used by governments against the same trade restrictions by all other [GATT Contracting Parties] ...[23]

The GATT dispute settlement system has generally been considered to be quite successful in fully or partially resolving disputes to the satisfaction of the complaining party.[24] John Jackson noted:

these procedures worked better than might have been expected, and some could argue that in fact they worked better than those of the World Court and many other international dispute settlement procedures.[25]

---

[22] E.-U. Petersmann, *The GATT/WTO Dispute Settlement System: International Law, International Organisations and Dispute Settlement* (Kluwer Law International, 1998), 85–6.

[23] *Ibid.*, 86.

[24] Hudec's 1993 statistical analysis of the results of GATT dispute settlement until the end of the 1980s indicates an overall success rate of almost 90 per cent (see R. Hudec *et al.*, 'A Statistical Profile of GATT Dispute Settlement Cases; 1948–1989', *Minnesota Journal of Global Trade*, 1993, 285–7) and, as Hudec noted, 'accomplishments to this point, if not unique, are at least rare in the history of international legal institutions'. See *ibid.*, 353.

[25] J. Jackson, *The World Trade Organization: Constitution and Jurisprudence* (Royal Institute of International Affairs, 1998), 64. In a footnote, Jackson referred to L. Gross (ed.), *The Future of the International Court of Justice* (Oceana, 1976); and D. Partan, 'Increasing the Effectiveness of the International Court', *Harvard International Law Journal*, 1977, 559.

However, the GATT dispute settlement system had some serious shortcomings which became acute in the 1980s and the early 1990s. The most important shortcoming of the system related to the manner in which key decisions were taken. These key decisions on:

- the establishment and composition of a panel,
- the adoption of a panel report, and
- the authorisation of the suspension of concessions,

were all to be taken by the GATT Council by *consensus*. The responding party could thus delay or block any of these decisions and paralyse or frustrate the operation of the dispute settlement system. In particular, the adoption of panel reports became a real problem from the late 1980s onwards. Moreover, the fact that the losing party could prevent the adoption of the panel report meant that panels were often tempted to arrive at a conclusion that would be acceptable to all parties, regardless of whether that conclusion was legally sound and convincing. Furthermore, the Contracting Parties regarded the dispute settlement process as being unable to handle many of the politically sensitive trade disputes, since the assumption was that the losing party would prevent the adoption of the panel report. Finally, some of the agreements concluded at the Tokyo Round (1973–9), such as the *Anti-Dumping Code*, included special procedures for the settlement of disputes arising under these agreements. As a result, dispute settlement procedures (as well as substantive obligations) became fragmented and disputes arose over which procedure – the GATT procedure or the Tokyo Round Code procedure – applied with respect to a specific dispute.

3.2.3. Uruguay Round negotiations and the Dispute Settlement Understanding

The improvement of the GATT dispute settlement system was high on the agenda of the Uruguay Round negotiations. The 1986 Punta del Este Ministerial Declaration on the Uruguay Round stated with regard to dispute settlement:

> In order to ensure prompt and effective resolution of disputes to the benefit of all contracting parties, negotiations shall aim to improve and strengthen the rules and the procedures of the dispute settlement process, while recognizing the contribution that would be made by more effective and enforceable GATT rules and disciplines. Negotiations shall include the development of adequate arrangements for overseeing and monitoring of the procedures that would facilitate compliance with adopted recommendations.[26]

Already in December 1988, the negotiators had agreed on a number of improvements to the GATT dispute settlement system.[27] These improvements included the recognition of the right of a complainant to bring a case before

---

[26] Punta del Este Ministerial Declaration on the Uruguay Round, 20 September 1986, BISD 33S/25.
[27] See Improvements to the GATT Dispute Settlement Rules and Procedures, BISD 36S/61–67.

a panel and strict timeframes for panel proceedings. No agreement was reached, however, on the most difficult issue, namely, the issue of the adoption of panel reports by consensus. As Robert Hudec noted:

> The sentiment at the time was that dispute settlement worked better on the whole if defendant governments participated on a voluntary basis, and that it would not be productive to try to force governments into adjudicatory rulings they were not prepared to accept voluntarily.[28]

However, in the course of 1989, the general sentiment of the Contracting Parties changed dramatically. The cause for this change was the *US Trade and Competitiveness Act* of 1988, which considerably extended and intensified section 301 of the *US Trade Act* of 1974. Section 301 provides for the imposition of unilateral trade sanctions against other countries which the United States considers to be in violation of their GATT obligations. The 1988 *Trade and Competitiveness Act* created a new 'Super 301' and several other 'Special 301s'. The other GATT Contracting Parties were greatly alarmed by this new legislation and the system of 'vigilante justice' it strengthened. They demanded that the United States change its legislation. The United States, however, argued that the existing GATT dispute settlement system, as a result of the consensus requirement, was too weak to protect US trade interests effectively. Hudec noted:

> This United States counter-attack against the procedural weakness of the existing dispute settlement system led other governments to propose a deal. In exchange for a US commitment not to employ its Section 301-type trade restrictions, the other GATT governments would agree to create a new and procedurally tighter dispute settlement system that would meet US complaints.[29]

In this way, agreement was eventually reached on the *Understanding on Rules and Procedures Governing the Settlement of Disputes*, commonly referred to as the *Dispute Settlement Understanding* or DSU. The DSU is attached to the *WTO Agreement* as Annex 2, and constitutes an integral part of that Agreement. The DSU provides for an elaborate dispute settlement system, and is often referred to as one of the most important achievements of the Uruguay Round negotiations. The most significant innovations introduced by the new dispute settlement system concern:

- the quasi-automatic adoption of requests for the establishment of panels, of panel reports and of requests for the authorisation to suspend concessions;
- the strict timeframes for various stages of the dispute settlement process; and
- the possibility of appellate review of panel reports.

The latter innovation is closely linked to the quasi-automatic adoption of panel reports, and reflects the concern of Members to ensure high-quality panel reports.

---

[28] Robert Hudec, 'The New WTO Dispute Settlement Procedure', *Minnesota Journal of Global Trade*, 1999, 12.
[29] *Ibid.*, 13.

Much more than the GATT dispute settlement system, the WTO dispute settlement system is rules-based dispute settlement through adjudication. Note, however, that the WTO dispute settlement system has retained a few characteristics of power-based dispute settlement through diplomatic negotiations.[30]

Questions and Assignments 3.1

How did the GATT dispute settlement system evolve between the late 1940s and the early 1990s? What was the most important shortcoming of the GATT dispute settlement system and how did this shortcoming affect the recourse to the system and the quality and nature of dispute settlement reports? What are the most significant innovations in the GATT dispute settlement system introduced by the DSU? In your opinion, why did governments agree, during the Uruguay Round, to the progressive 'judicialisation' of the settlement of international trade disputes?

3.3. PRINCIPLES OF WTO DISPUTE SETTLEMENT

As noted above, the dispute settlement system of the WTO is arguably the most prolific of all international dispute settlement systems.[31] The WTO does indeed possess a remarkable system for the resolution of trade disputes between its Members. This section deals with the basic principles of WTO dispute settlement. It examines:

- the object and purpose of the WTO dispute settlement system;
- the various methods of WTO dispute settlement;
- the jurisdiction of the WTO dispute settlement system;
- access to the WTO dispute settlement system;
- the steps in, and timeframe for, the WTO dispute settlement process;
- rules on interpretation and the burden of proof applicable in WTO dispute settlement;
- the confidentiality of, and rules of conduct for, WTO dispute settlement;
- remedies for breach of WTO law; and
- special rules and assistance for developing-country Members.

3.3.1. Object and purpose of the WTO dispute settlement system

The prime object and purpose of the WTO dispute settlement system is the prompt settlement of disputes between WTO Members concerning their

---

[30] See below, pp. 255–9 (regarding consultations), pp. 228–31 (regarding the role of the DSB) and pp. 213–14 (regarding the confidentiality of proceedings).
[31] See above, pp. 94, 173.

respective rights and obligations under WTO law. As stated in Article 3.3 of the DSU, the prompt settlement of such disputes is:

> essential to the effective functioning of the WTO and the maintenance of a proper balance between the rights and obligations of Members.

Article 3.2 of the DSU states:

> The dispute settlement system of the WTO is a central element in providing security and predictability to the multilateral trading system. The Members recognize that it serves to preserve the rights and obligations of Members under the covered agreements, and to clarify the existing provisions of those agreements in accordance with customary rules of interpretation of public international law.

According to the Panel in *US – Section 301 Trade Act*, the DSU is one of the most important *instruments* of the WTO in protecting the security and predictability of the multilateral trading system.[32]

3.3.1.1. *Settlement of disputes through multilateral procedures*

The object and purpose of the dispute settlement system is for Members to settle disputes with other Members through the *multilateral* procedures of the DSU, rather than through *unilateral* action.[33] Article 23.1 of the DSU states:

> When Members seek the redress of a violation of obligations or other nullification or impairment of benefits under the covered agreements or an impediment to the attainment of any objective of the covered agreements, they shall have recourse to, and abide by, the rules and procedures of this Understanding.

Pursuant to Article 23.2 of the DSU, WTO Members may not make a *unilateral* determination that a violation of WTO law has occurred and may not take retaliation measures *unilaterally* in the case of a violation of WTO law. As noted above, concerns regarding unilateral actions by the United States against what it considered to be violations of GATT law were a driving force behind the negotiations of the DSU.[34]

3.3.1.2. *Settlement of disputes through consultations if possible*

Article 3.7 of the DSU states, in relevant part:

> The aim of the dispute settlement mechanism is to secure a positive solution to a dispute. A solution mutually acceptable to the parties to a dispute and consistent with the covered agreements is clearly to be preferred.

The DSU thus expresses a clear preference for solutions mutually acceptable to the parties reached through negotiations, rather than solutions resulting from adjudication. Accordingly, each dispute settlement proceeding must start with consultations (or an attempt to have consultations) between the

---

[32] Panel Report, *US – Section 301 Trade Act*, para. 7.75.   [33] See Article 23 of the DSU.
[34] See above, p. 181.

Figure 3.2 Success of consultations: totals 1995–2003[35]

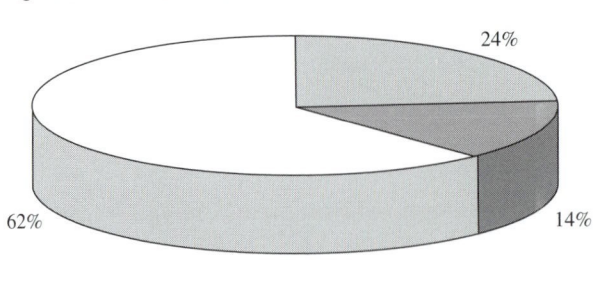

24%

62%   14%

□ Mutually agreed solutions   ■ Otherwise settled   □ Adjudication

parties to the dispute, with a view to reaching a mutually agreed solution. To resolve disputes through consultations is obviously cheaper and more satisfactory for the long-term trade relations with the other party to the dispute than adjudication by a panel. Note that any mutually agreed solution reached through consultations needs to be consistent with WTO law.[36]

In 24 per cent of disputes, it has indeed been possible to resolve the dispute amicably as the parties succeeded in reaching a solution acceptable to all. In 14 per cent, the dispute was otherwise amicably resolved without resort to adjudication.[37] In other disputes, however, recourse to adjudication was necessary in order to secure actual resolution of the dispute (62 per cent).[38]

3.3.1.3. Settlement of disputes and the clarification of WTO law

Article 3.2 of the DSU, as quoted above, states that the dispute settlement system serves not only 'to preserve the rights and obligations of Members under the covered agreements', but also 'to clarify the existing provisions of those agreements'. As the covered agreements are full of gaps and 'constructive ambiguity', there is much need for clarification of the existing provisions. However, the last sentence of Article 3.2 provides:

> Recommendations and rulings of the DSB cannot add to or diminish the rights and obligations provided in the covered agreements.

Article 19.2 of the DSU states:

> In accordance with paragraph 2 of Article 3, in their findings and recommendations, the panel and Appellate Body cannot add to or diminish the rights and obligations provided in the covered agreements.

While allowing the WTO dispute settlement system to clarify WTO law, Articles 3.2 and 19.2 explicitly preclude the system from adding to or

---

[35] See 'Update of WTO Dispute Settlement Cases', WT/DS/OV/14, dated 30 June 2003, ii.
[36] See Articles 3.5 and 3.7 of the DSU.   [37] See below, pp. 258–9.
[38] Data calculated on the basis of the number of requests for consultations which have led to adopted reports or mutually agreed solutions or were otherwise settled.

diminishing the rights and obligations of Members. The DSU thus explicitly cautions the WTO dispute settlement system against 'judicial activism', i.e. against taking on the role of 'legislator'. Furthermore, as noted in Chapter 2, pursuant to Article IX:2 of the *WTO Agreement*, it is the exclusive competence of the Ministerial Conference and the General Council to adopt 'authoritative' interpretations of the provisions of the *WTO Agreement* and the Multilateral Trade Agreements. Article 3.9 of the DSU stipulates that the provisions of the DSU are without prejudice to the rights of Members to seek such 'authoritative' interpretation.[39] In *US – Certain EC Products*, the Appellate Body held:

> we observe that it is certainly not the task of either panels or the Appellate Body to amend the DSU or to adopt interpretations within the meaning of Article IX:2 of the *WTO Agreement*. Only WTO Members have the authority to amend the DSU or to adopt such interpretations. Pursuant to Article 3.2 of the DSU, the task of panels and the Appellate Body in the dispute settlement system of the WTO is "to preserve the rights and obligations of Members under the covered agreements, and to *clarify the existing provisions* of those agreements in accordance with customary rules of interpretation of public international law." Determining what the rules and procedures of the DSU ought to be is not our responsibility nor the responsibility of panels; it is clearly the responsibility solely of the Members of the WTO.[40]
>
> [Emphasis added]

3.3.1.4. Settlement of disputes in good faith

Finally, Article 3.10 of the DSU provides that the use of the dispute settlement procedures:

> should not be intended or considered as contentious acts

and that all Members must:

> engage in these procedures in good faith in an effort to resolve the dispute.

Engaging in dispute settlement *in good faith*, i.e. with the genuine intention to see the dispute resolved, is part of the object and purpose of the WTO dispute settlement system.[41]

Questions and Assignments 3.2

What is the object and purpose of the WTO dispute settlement system? What is the WTO dispute settlement system's preferred method of dispute settlement? Is it part of the object and purpose of the WTO dispute settlement system 'to make' law?

---

[39] See also above, pp. 144–5.   [40] Appellate Body Report, *US – Certain EC Products*, para. 92.
[41] On the role of good faith in such efforts, see Appellate Body Report, *US – FSC*, para. 166.

3.3.2. Methods of WTO dispute settlement

The DSU provides for more than one method to settle disputes between WTO Members. In fact, the DSU provides for:

- consultations or negotiations;
- adjudication by panels and the Appellate Body;
- arbitration; and
- good offices, conciliation and mediation.

As noted above, the DSU expresses a clear preference for resolving disputes through *consultations*, i.e. negotiations, between the parties to the dispute. Therefore, consultations, or at least an attempt to have consultations, must always precede resort to adjudication. The rules and procedures for consultations are set out in Article 4 of the DSU.[42]

If consultations fail to resolve the dispute, the complaining party may resort to *adjudication* by a panel and, if either party to the dispute appeals the findings of the panel, adjudication by the Appellate Body. The rules and procedures for adjudication by a panel and the Appellate Body are set out in Articles 6 to 20 of the DSU.[43]

The dispute settlement methods provided for in Articles 4 and 6 to 20 of the DSU (consultations and adjudication by panels and the Appellate Body) are by far the methods most frequently used. However, the WTO dispute settlement system provides for expeditious *arbitration* as an alternative means of dispute settlement.[44] Pursuant to Article 25 of the DSU, parties to a dispute arising under a covered agreement may decide to resort to arbitration, rather than follow the procedure set out in Articles 4 and 6 to 20 of the DSU. In that case, the parties must clearly define the issues referred to arbitration and agree on the particular procedure to be followed.[45] The parties must also agree to abide by the arbitration award.[46] Pursuant to Article 3.5 of the DSU, the arbitration award must be consistent with the covered agreements. In the latter part of 2001, WTO Members used the Article 25 arbitration procedure for the first time.[47]

Finally, the DSU also provides, in Article 5 of the DSU, for the possibility for the parties to a dispute – if they all agree to do so – to use good offices, conciliation or mediation to settle a dispute.[48] Good offices, conciliation or mediation may be requested by any party at any time. Also, they may begin and be terminated at any time.[49] If the parties agree, procedures for good

---

[42] For a detailed discussion of consultations, see below, pp. 255–9.

[43] For a detailed discussion of panel and appellate review proceedings, see below, pp. 259–77.

[44] See Article 25 of the DSU.   [45] Articles 25.1 and 25.2 of the DSU.

[46] Article 25.3 of the DSU.

[47] Award of the Arbitrators, *US – Section 110(5) Copyright Act (Article 25.3)*, recourse to arbitration under Article 25 of the DSU, WT/DS160/ARB25/1, 9 November 2001. The DSU also provides for arbitration in Articles 21.3(c) and 22.6 of the DSU, but this arbitration is not 'an alternative means of dispute settlement'. See below, pp. 278–9, 283.

[48] Pursuant to Article 5.6 of the DSU, the Director-General of the WTO may, acting in an *ex officio* capacity, offer good offices, conciliation or mediation. See below, p. 187.

[49] Article 5.3 of the DSU.

offices, conciliation or mediation may continue while the panel process proceeds.[50] The Director-General may, acting in an *ex officio* capacity, offer good offices, conciliation or mediation with a view to assisting Members to settle a dispute.[51] In July 2001, the Director-General reminded Members of his availability to help to settle disputes through good offices, mediation or conciliation.[52] Formally speaking, to date, WTO Members have not yet made use of the dispute settlement methods provided for in Article 5 of the DSU. However, on 4 September 2002, the Philippines, Thailand and the European Communities jointly requested – albeit not on the basis of Article 5 of the DSU – mediation by the Director-General, or by a mediator designated by him with their agreement, in a matter concerning the tariff treatment of canned tuna.[53] The requesting Members had held three rounds of consultations, but could not reach a mutually acceptable solution. The Director-General accepted the request for mediation and, with the agreement of the requesting Members, nominated Deputy Director-General Rufus Yerxa as mediator. On 20 December 2002, Yerxa informed the Director-General that he had completed his work.[54] He also informed the Director-General that the requesting Members had agreed that the mediator's conclusions would remain confidential.[55] In July 2003, the European Communities, the Philippines and Thailand informed the Director-General that an amicable outcome had been reached based on the mediator's conclusions.[56]

Questions and Assignments 3.3

Briefly discuss the various dispute settlement methods provided for in the DSU.

3.3.3. Jurisdiction of the WTO dispute settlement system

The WTO dispute settlement system stands out by virtue of the broad scope of its jurisdiction as well as by the compulsory, exclusive and contentious nature of that jurisdiction. This section examines these two aspects – scope and nature – of the jurisdiction of the WTO dispute settlement system.

---

[50] Article 5.5 of the DSU.   [51] Article 5.6 of the DSU.

[52] Communication from the Director-General, Article 5 of the Dispute Settlement Understanding, WT/DSB/25, dated 17 July 2001.

[53] Note that the request stated that the requesting Members did not consider the matter at issue to be a 'dispute' within the terms of the DSU, but nevertheless agreed that the WTO Director-General or the mediator designated by him could be guided by procedures similar to those envisaged for mediation under Article 5 of the DSU. See WT/GC/66, dated 16 October 2002.

[54] See WT/GC/66/Add.1, dated 23 December 2002.   [55] *Ibid.*

[56] See WT/GC/71, dated 1 August 2003.

3.3.3.1. One integrated system for all WTO disputes

The WTO dispute settlement system has jurisdiction over any dispute between WTO Members arising under the 'covered agreements'.[57] Article 1.1 of the DSU states, in relevant part:

> The rules and procedures of this Understanding shall apply to disputes brought pursuant to the consultation and dispute settlement provisions of the agreements listed in Appendix 1 to this Understanding (referred to in this Understanding as the "covered agreements").

The covered agreements, listed in Appendix 1 to the DSU, include the *WTO Agreement*, the GATT 1994 and all other multilateral agreements on trade in goods, the GATS, the *TRIPS Agreement* and the DSU.[58]

Article 1.1 of the DSU establishes 'an integrated dispute settlement system' which applies to all the covered agreements.[59] The DSU provides for a *single, coherent system* of rules and procedures for dispute settlement, applicable to disputes arising under any of the covered agreements. However, some of the covered agreements provide for a few special and additional rules and procedures 'designed to deal with the particularities of dispute settlement relating to obligations arising under a specific covered agreement'.[60] Article 1.2 of the DSU provides, in relevant part:

> The rules and procedures of this Understanding shall apply subject to such special or additional rules and procedures on dispute settlement contained in the covered agreements as are identified in Appendix 2 to this Understanding.

Pursuant to Article 1.2 of the DSU, these special or additional rules and procedures *prevail* over the DSU rules and procedures to the extent that there is a 'difference' between them. The Appellate Body in *Guatemala – Cement I* ruled:

> if there is no "difference", then the rules and procedures of the DSU apply *together with* the special or additional provisions of the covered agreement. In our view, it is only where the provisions of the DSU and the special or additional rules and procedures of a covered agreement *cannot* be read as *complementing* each other that the special or additional provisions are to *prevail*. A special or additional provision should only be found to *prevail* over a provision of the DSU in a situation where adherence to the one provision will lead to a violation of the other provision, that is, in the case of a *conflict* between them.[61]

The special and additional rules and procedures of a particular covered agreement combine with the generally applicable rules and procedures of the DSU 'to form a comprehensive, integrated dispute settlement system for the *WTO Agreement*'.[62]

---

[57] For the concept of 'covered agreements', see below, p. 188.

[58] The only multilateral trade agreement which is not a covered agreement is the Trade Policy Review Mechanism, Annex 3 to the *WTO Agreement*. Whether plurilateral trade agreements are covered agreements is subject to the adoption of a decision by the parties to these agreements setting out the terms for the application of the DSU (see Appendix 1 to the DSU). Of the two plurilateral agreements currently in force, only the *Agreement on Government Procurement* is a covered agreement.

[59] Appellate Body Report, *Guatemala – Cement I*, para. 64.   [60] *Ibid.*, para. 66.

[61] *Ibid.*, para. 65.   [62] *Ibid.*, para. 66.

Questions and Assignments 3.4

The WTO dispute settlement system has been defined as 'an integrated dispute settlement system'. What does this mean and why is this important? Which of the agreements forming part of the *WTO Agreement* are not 'covered agreements'? Identify the special or additional rules and procedures contained in the *Anti-Dumping Agreement* and discuss whether these rules and procedures prevail over the rules and procedures of the DSU.

3.3.3.2. Compulsory jurisdiction

The jurisdiction of the WTO dispute settlement system is compulsory in nature. Article 23.1 of the DSU states:

> When Members seek the redress of a violation of obligations or other nullification or impairment of benefits under the covered agreements or an impediment to the attainment of any objective of the covered agreements, they shall have recourse to, and abide by, the rules and procedures of this Understanding.

Pursuant to this provision, a complaining Member is obliged to bring any dispute arising under the covered agreements to the WTO dispute settlement system. On the other hand, a responding Member has, as a matter of law, no choice but to accept the jurisdiction of the WTO dispute settlement system. With regard to the latter, we note that Article 6.1 of the DSU states:

> *If* the complaining party *so requests*, a *panel* shall *be established* at the latest at the DSB meeting following that at which the request first appears as an item on the DSB's agenda, unless at that meeting the DSB decides by consensus not to establish a panel.
> [Emphasis added]

Unlike in other international dispute settlement systems, there is no need for the parties to a dispute, arising under the covered agreements, to accept, in a separate declaration or separate agreement, the jurisdiction of the WTO dispute settlement system to adjudicate that dispute. Membership of the WTO constitutes consent to, and acceptance of, the compulsory jurisdiction of the WTO dispute settlement system.

3.3.3.3. Exclusive jurisdiction

The Panel, in *US – Section 301 Trade Act*, ruled that Article 23.1 of the DSU (as quoted above):

> imposes on all Members [a requirement] to "have recourse to" the multilateral process set out in the DSU when they seek the redress of a WTO inconsistency. In these circumstances, Members have to have recourse to the DSU dispute settlement system to the exclusion of any other system, in particular a system of unilateral enforcement of

> WTO rights and obligations. This, what one could call "exclusive dispute resolution clause", is an important new element of Members' rights and obligations under the DSU.[63]

Members shall thus have recourse to the WTO dispute settlement system to the exclusion of any other system. As Article 23.2(a) of the DSU provides, Members are prohibited from making a determination to the effect that a violation has occurred, that benefits have been nullified or impaired, or that the attainment of any objective of the covered agreements has been impeded, *except* through recourse to dispute settlement in accordance with the rules and procedures of the DSU.[64]

3.3.3.4. Contentious jurisdiction

The WTO dispute settlement system only has contentious, and not advisory, jurisdiction. In *US – Wool Shirts and Blouses*, the Appellate Body held:

> Given the explicit aim of dispute settlement that permeates the DSU, we do not consider that Article 3.2 of the DSU is meant to encourage either panels or the Appellate Body to "make law" by clarifying existing provisions of the WTO Agreement *outside the context of resolving a particular dispute.*[65]
>
> [Emphasis added]

The WTO dispute settlement system is only called upon to clarify WTO law in the context of an actual dispute.

Questions and Assignments 3.5

Does the WTO dispute settlement system have compulsory, as well as exclusive, jurisdiction? Could a WTO Member submit a dispute arising under one of the covered agreements to the International Court of Justice? In your opinion, would it be useful for the WTO dispute settlement system to have advisory jurisdiction?

3.3.4. Access to the WTO dispute settlement system

Access to, or the use of, the WTO dispute settlement system is limited to Members of the WTO. The Appellate Body ruled in *US – Shrimp*:

> It may be well to stress at the outset that access to the dispute settlement process of the WTO is limited to Members of the WTO. This access is not available, under the *WTO Agreement* and the covered agreements as they currently exist, to individuals

---

[63] Panel Report, *US – Section 301 Trade Act*, para. 7.43.
[64] Article 23.2 also stipulates that, to determine the reasonable period of time for implementation (see below, pp. 278–9) or to determine the level of suspension of concessions or other obligations and to obtain DSB authorisation for such suspension (see below, p. 283), Members must also follow the rules and procedures set out in the DSU.
[65] Appellate Body Report, *US – Wool Shirts and Blouses*, 340.

or international organizations, whether governmental or non-governmental. Only Members may become parties to a dispute of which a panel may be seized, and only Members "having a substantial interest in a matter before a panel" may become third parties in the proceedings before that panel. Thus, under the DSU, only Members who are parties to a dispute, or who have notified their interest in becoming third parties in such a dispute to the DSB, have a *legal right* to make submissions to, and have a *legal right* to have those submissions considered by, a panel.[66]

The WTO dispute settlement system is a *government-to-government* dispute settlement system for disputes concerning rights and obligations of WTO Members .

This section discusses when Members can use the WTO dispute settlement system. It looks at the causes of action, i.e. the grounds for action, in WTO dispute settlement. Furthermore, this section examines whether legislation *as such*, i.e. independent from its application in specific cases, can be challenged and found to be inconsistent with WTO law. This section also addresses the controversial issue of *amicus curiae* briefs submitted to panels and the Appellate Body by legal and natural persons seeking some degree of access to the WTO dispute settlement system. Finally, this section discusses the 'indirect' access that companies and industry associations have to the WTO dispute settlement system.

3.3.4.1. Causes of action

Each covered agreement contains one or more consultation and dispute settlement provisions. These provisions set out when a Member can have recourse to the WTO dispute settlement system. For the GATT 1994, the relevant provisions are Articles XXII and XXIII. Of particular importance is Article XXIII:1 of the GATT 1994, which states:

> If any Member should consider that any benefit accruing to it directly or indirectly under this Agreement is being nullified or impaired or that the attainment of any objective of the Agreement is being impeded as the result of
>
> a. the failure of another Member to carry out its obligations under this Agreement, or
> b. the application by another Member of any measure, whether or not it conflicts with the provisions of this Agreement, or
> c. the existence of any other situation,
>
> the Member may, with a view to the satisfactory adjustment of the matter, make written representations or proposals to the other Member or Members which it considers to be concerned.

In *India – Quantitative Restrictions*, the Appellate Body held:

> This dispute was brought pursuant to, *inter alia*, Article XXIII of the GATT 1994. According to Article XXIII, any Member which considers that a benefit accruing to it directly or indirectly under the GATT 1994 is being nullified or impaired as a result of the failure of another Member to carry out its obligations, may resort to the dispute settlement procedures of Article XXIII. The United States considers that a benefit accruing to it under the GATT 1994 was nullified or impaired as a result of India's

---

[66] Appellate Body Report, *US – Shrimp*, para. 101.

> alleged failure to carry out its obligations regarding balance-of-payments restrictions under Article XVIII:B of the GATT 1994. Therefore, the United States was entitled to have recourse to the dispute settlement procedures of Article XXIII with regard to this dispute.[67]

The consultation and dispute settlement provisions of most other covered agreements incorporate, by reference, Articles XXII and XXIII of the GATT 1994. For example, Article 11.1 of the *SPS Agreement*, entitled 'Consultations and Dispute Settlement', states:

> The provisions of Articles XXII and XXIII of GATT 1994 as elaborated and applied by the Dispute Settlement Understanding shall apply to consultations and the settlement of disputes under this Agreement, except as otherwise specifically provided herein.

As was the case in *India – Quantitative Restrictions*, the nullification or impairment of a benefit (or the impeding of the realisation of an objective) may, and most often will, be the result of a violation of an obligation prescribed by a covered agreement. Nullification or impairment may, however, also be the result of 'the application by another Member of any measure, whether or not it conflicts with the provisions' of a covered agreement.[68] Nullification or impairment may equally be the result of 'the existence of any other situation'.[69]

Unlike other international dispute settlement systems, the WTO system thus provides for three types of complaint:

- 'violation' complaints;
- 'non-violation' complaints; and
- 'situation' complaints.[70]

In the case of a 'non-violation' complaint or a 'situation' complaint, the complainant must demonstrate that there is nullification or impairment of a benefit or that the achievement of an objective is impeded.[71] In the case of a 'violation' complaint, however, there is a presumption of nullification or impairment when the complainant demonstrates the existence of the 'violation'. Article 3.8 of the DSU states:

> In cases where there is an infringement of the obligations assumed under a covered agreement, the action is considered *prima facie* to constitute a case of nullification or impairment. This means that there is normally a presumption that a breach of the rules

---

[67] Appellate Body Report, *India – Quantitative Restrictions*, para. 84.

[68] Article XXIII:1(b) of the GATT 1994 and Article 26.1 of the DSU.

[69] Article XXIII:1(c) of the GATT 1994 and Article 26.2 of the DSU.

[70] Pursuant to Article XXIII:3 of the GATS, situation complaints are not possible in disputes arising under the GATS. Pursuant to Article 64.2 of the *TRIPS Agreement*, non-violation complaints and situation complaints were not possible in disputes arising under the *TRIPS Agreement* during a period of five years from the date of entry into force of the *WTO Agreement*. Article 64.3 provides that the Ministerial Conference can only extend this period by consensus. At the Doha Session of the Ministerial Conference in November 2001, it was agreed that the TRIPS Council would continue to discuss the scope and modalities of non-violation complaints under the *TRIPS Agreement*. It was also agreed that, in the meantime, Members would not file non-violation complaints under the *TRIPS Agreement*.

[71] Articles 26.1 (for non-violation complaints) and 26.2 (for situation complaints) of the DSU. Articles 26.1 and 26.2 set out a few special rules for these types of complaint. With regard to what a complainant must show in a non-violation complaint, see Panel Report, *Japan – Film*, para. 9.5. With respect to non-violation complaints, see also Appellate Body Report, *EC – Asbestos*, paras. 38 and 185–6.

> has an adverse impact on other Members parties to that covered agreement, and in such cases, it shall be up to the Member against whom the complaint has been brought to rebut the charge.

In only a few cases to date has the respondent argued that the alleged violation of WTO law did not nullify or impair benefits accruing to the complainant.[72] In no case has the respondent been successful in rebutting the presumption of nullification or impairment. It is doubtful whether this presumption really is rebuttable.

Violation complaints are by far the most common type of complaint. To date, there have, in fact, been few non-violation complaints.[73] There have been no situation complaints. The difference between the WTO system and other international dispute settlement systems on this point may, therefore, be 'of little practical significance'.[74]

There is no explicit provision in the DSU requiring a Member to have a 'legal interest' in order to have recourse to the WTO dispute settlement system. It has been held that such a requirement is not implied either in the DSU or in any other provision of the *WTO Agreement*.[75] In *EC – Bananas III*, the Appellate Body held:

> we believe that a Member has broad discretion in deciding whether to bring a case against another Member under the DSU. The language of Article XXIII:1 of the GATT 1994 and of Article 3.7 of the DSU suggests, furthermore, that a Member is expected to be largely self-regulating in deciding whether any such action would be "fruitful".[76]

The Appellate Body explicitly agreed with the statement of the Panel in *EC – Bananas III* that:

> with the increased interdependence of the global economy, ... Members have a greater stake in enforcing WTO rules than in the past since any deviation from the negotiated balance of rights and obligations is more likely than ever to affect them, directly or indirectly.[77]

In *EC – Bananas III*, the Appellate Body decided that the United States could bring a claim under the GATT 1994 despite the fact that the United States does not export bananas. In coming to this decision, the Appellate Body considered the fact that the United States is a producer and a *potential* exporter of bananas, the effects of the EC banana regime on the US internal market for bananas and the fact that the US claims under the GATS and the GATT 1994 were inextricably interwoven. The Appellate Body subsequently concluded:

> Taken together, these reasons are sufficient justification for the United States to have brought its claims against the EC banana import regime under the GATT 1994.[78]

---

[72] See Appellate Body Report, *EC – Bananas III*, paras. 250–3, in which the Appellate Body referred to the GATT Panel Report, *US – Superfund*, para. 5.1.9. See also Panel Report, *Turkey – Textiles*, para. 9.204; and Panel Report, *Guatemala – Cement II*, para. 8.25.

[73] See e.g. Panel Report, *Japan – Film*; and Panel Report, *Korea – Procurement*.

[74] F. Feliciano and P. Van den Bossche, 'The Dispute Settlement System of the World Trade Organization: Institutions, Process and Practice', in N. Blokker and H. Schermers (eds.), *Proliferation of International Organizations* (Kluwer Law International, 2001), 308.

[75] Appellate Body Report, *EC – Bananas III*, paras. 132 and 133.

[76] *Ibid.*, para. 135.　　[77] *Ibid.*, para. 136.　　[78] *Ibid.*, para. 138.

The Appellate Body added, however, that:

> This does not mean, though, that one or more of the factors we have noted in this case would necessarily be dispositive in another case.[79]

In *Mexico – Corn Syrup (Article 21.5 – US)*, the Appellate Body ruled with respect to recourse by Members to the WTO dispute settlement system:

> Given the "largely self-regulating" nature of the requirement in the first sentence of Article 3.7, panels and the Appellate Body must presume, whenever a Member submits a request for establishment of a panel, that such Member does so in good faith, having duly exercised its judgement as to whether recourse to that panel would be "fruitful". Article 3.7 neither requires nor authorizes a panel to look behind that Member's decision and to question its exercise of judgement.[80]

A Member's decision to start WTO dispute settlement proceedings is thus largely beyond judicial review.

In *Argentina – Poultry*, Argentina requested that the Panel refrain from ruling on the claims raised by Brazil because Brazil had already challenged the measure at issue, albeit unsucsessfully, before a MERCOSUR Ad Hoc Arbitral Tribunal. Argentina did not invoke the principle of *res judicata* but asserted that Brazil failed to act in good faith and in conformity with the principle of estoppel. The Panel rejected Argentina's arguments, and did consider Brazil's claims.[81]

Questions and Assignments 3.6

Who has access to the WTO dispute settlement system? When do WTO Members have access to the WTO dispute settlement system? List the different causes of action provided for in Article XXIII:1 of the GATT 1994. Can the presumption of nullification or impairment, provided for in Article 3.8 of the DSU, be rebutted? In your opinion, why have there been so few 'non-violation' complaints? Can a Member bring a case against another Member regardless of its 'interest' in the outcome of the case?

3.3.4.2. Challenges to legislation and/or its application

It is clear that the WTO consistency of the actual application of specific national legislation can be challenged in WTO dispute settlement proceedings. However, can national legislation as such, i.e. independently from its application in specific cases, be challenged in WTO dispute settlement procedures? In *US – 1916 Act*, the Appellate Body recalled the GATT practice in this respect as follows:

> Prior to the entry into force of the *WTO Agreement*, it was firmly established that Article XXIII:1(a) of the GATT 1947 allowed a Contracting Party to challenge

---

[79] *Ibid.*   [80] Appellate Body Report, *Mexico – Corn Syrup (Article 21.5 – US)*, para. 74.
[81] See Panel Report, *Argentina – Poultry*, paras. 7.33–7.42.

legislation as such, independently from the application of that legislation in specific instances. While the text of Article XXIII does not expressly address the matter, panels consistently considered that, under Article XXIII, they had the *jurisdiction* to deal with claims against legislation as such. In *examining* such claims, panels developed the concept that mandatory and discretionary legislation should be distinguished from each other, reasoning that only legislation that mandates a violation of GATT obligations can be found as such to be inconsistent with those obligations.[82]

The practice of GATT panels was summed up in *US – Tobacco* as follows:

panels had consistently ruled that legislation which mandated action inconsistent with the General Agreement could be challenged as such, whereas legislation which merely gave the discretion to the *executive authority* of a contracting party to act inconsistently with the General Agreement could not be challenged as such; only the actual application of such legislation inconsistent with the General Agreement could be subject to challenge.[83]

[Emphasis added]

WTO panels, as well as the Appellate Body, have followed the same practice. However, the Panel, in *US – Section 301 Trade Act*, considerably 'refined' the existing jurisprudence. The Panel, in *US – Section 301 Trade Act*, rejected the presumption, implicit in the argument of the United States, that no WTO provision ever prohibits discretionary legislation. The Panel explicitly stated that, in rejecting this presumption, it did not imply a reversal of the classical test in the existing jurisprudence that only legislation mandating a WTO inconsistency or precluding WTO consistency, could, as such, violate WTO provisions.[84] On the contrary, that was the very test which the Panel applied. The Panel argued:

It simply does not follow from this test, as sometimes has been argued, that legislation with discretion could never violate the WTO. If, for example, it is found that the specific obligations in Article 23 [of the DSU] prohibit a certain type of legislative discretion, the existence of such discretion in the statutory language of Section 304 would presumptively preclude WTO consistency.[85]

The Panel then examined Article 23 of the DSU, the obligation at issue, in great detail. In this examination, the Panel observed with regard to the nature of the obligation of Article 23 of the DSU:

It may have been plausible if one considered a strict Member-Member matrix to insist that the obligations in Article 23 [of the DSU] do not apply to legislation that threatens unilateral determinations but does not actually mandate them. It is not, however, plausible to construe Article 23 in this way if one interprets it in the light of the indirect effect such legislation has on individuals and the market-place, the protection of which is one of the principal objects and purposes of the WTO.

To be sure, in the cases referred to above, whether the risk materialised or not depended on certain market factors such as fluctuating reference prices on which the taxation of the imported product was based by virtue of the domestic legislation. In this case, whether the risk materializes depends on a decision of a government agency.

---

[82] Appellate Body Report, *US – 1916 Act*, para. 60. In a footnote, the Appellate Body referred, for example, to the GATT Panel Reports in *US – Superfund*, *US – Section 337*, *Thailand – Cigarettes* and *US – Malt Beverages*.
[83] GATT Panel Report, *US – Tobacco*, para. 118.
[84] Panel Report, *US – Section 301 Trade Act*, para. 7.54.   [85] *Ibid.*

> From the perspective of the individual economic operator, however, this makes little difference. Indeed, it may be more difficult to predict the outcome of discretionary government action than to predict market conditions, thereby exacerbating the negative economic impact of the type of domestic law under examination here.
>
> When a Member imposes unilateral measures in violation of Article 23 in a specific dispute, serious damage is created both to other Members and the market place. However, in our view, the creation of damage is not confined to actual conduct in specific cases. A law reserving the right for unilateral measures to be taken contrary to DSU rules and procedures, may – as is the case here – constitute an ongoing threat and produce a "chilling effect" causing serious damage in a variety of ways.[86]

According to the Panel, the duty of Members under Article 23 to abstain from unilateral determinations of inconsistency is meant to guarantee Members, as well as the marketplace and those who operate in it, that no such determinations in respect of WTO rights and obligations will be made.[87] The Panel subsequently ruled with regard to the measure at issue:

> The *discretion* given to the [US Trade Representative] to make a determination of inconsistency creates a real risk or threat for both Members and individual economic operators that determinations prohibited under Article 23.2(a) will be imposed. The USTR's *discretion* effectively to make such determinations removes the guarantee which Article 23 is intended to give not only to Members but indirectly also to individuals and the market place.[88]
>
> [Emphasis added]

The Panel concluded, therefore, that the statutory language of Section 304 of the Trade Act of 1974, although it was not mandatory but discretionary in nature, was *prima facie* inconsistent with Article 23 of the DSU (in view of the particular nature of the obligation in Article 23).[89] The Panel report in *US – Section 301 Trade Act* was not appealed.

Questions and Assignments 3.7

Can a Member challenge national legislation as such, i.e. independently from any application of this legislation in specific cases? Does the Panel in *US – Section 301 Trade Act* deviate from the established GATT/WTO practice on this issue?

3.3.4.3. *The amicus curiae brief issue*

As noted above, the WTO dispute settlement system is a government-to-government dispute settlement system for disputes concerning rights and obligations of WTO Members. Individuals, companies, international organisations and non-governmental organisations (including environmental and human rights NGOs, labour unions and industry associations) have no direct

---

[86] *Ibid.*, paras. 7.86–7.88.   [87] *Ibid.*, para. 7.95.   [88] *Ibid.*, para. 7.96.
[89] *Ibid.*, para. 7.97.

access to the WTO dispute settlement system. They cannot bring claims of violation of WTO rights or obligations. Under the current rules, they do not have the *right* to be heard or to participate, in any way, in the proceedings. However, under Appellate Body case law, panels and the Appellate Body have the authority to accept and consider written briefs submitted by individuals, companies or organisations. The acceptance by panels and the Appellate Body of these briefs, which are commonly referred to as *amicus curiae* briefs ('friend of the court' briefs), has been controversial and criticised by most WTO Members.[90]

In *US – Shrimp*, the Appellate Body noted with respect to the authority of panels to accept and consider *amicus curiae* briefs:

> The comprehensive nature of the authority of a panel to "seek" information and technical advice from "any individual or body" it may consider appropriate, or from "any relevant source", should be underscored. This authority embraces more than merely the choice and evaluation of the *source* of the information or advice which it may seek. A panel's authority includes the authority to decide *not to seek* such information or advice at all. We consider that a panel also has the authority to *accept or reject* any information or advice which it may have sought and received, or to *make some other appropriate disposition* thereof. It is particularly within the province and the authority of a panel to determine *the need for information and advice* in a specific case, to ascertain the *acceptability* and *relevancy* of information or advice received, and to decide *what weight to ascribe to that information or advice* or to conclude that no weight at all should be given to what has been received. It is also pertinent to note that Article 12.1 of the DSU authorizes panels to depart from, or to add to, the Working Procedures set forth in Appendix 3 of the DSU, and in effect to develop their own Working Procedures, after consultation with the parties to the dispute. Article 12.2 goes on to direct that "[p]anel procedures should provide *sufficient flexibility* so as to *ensure high-quality panel reports* while *not unduly delaying the panel process*".
>
> [Emphasis added]

> The thrust of Articles 12 and 13, taken together, is that the DSU accords to a panel established by the DSB, and engaged in a dispute settlement proceeding, ample and extensive authority to undertake and to control the process by which it informs itself both of the relevant facts of the dispute and of the legal norms and principles applicable to such facts. That authority, and the breadth thereof, is indispensably necessary to enable a panel to discharge its duty imposed by Article 11 of the DSU to "make an objective assessment of the matter before it, including an *objective assessment of the facts of the case* and the *applicability of and conformity with the relevant covered agreements*".[91]
>
> [Emphasis added]

On the basis of Articles 13, 12 and 11 of the DSU, the Appellate Body thus came to the conclusion that panels have the authority to accept and consider *amicus curiae* briefs, and reversed the Panel's finding to the contrary. A few panels in later disputes did, on the basis of this ruling of the Appellate Body in *US – Shrimp*, accept and consider *amicus curiae* briefs. This was the case, for example,

---

[90] Only *amicus curiae* briefs that were attached to the submissions of the parties or third parties have generally been accepted.

[91] Appellate Body Report, *US – Shrimp*, paras. 104, 105 and 106.

in *Australia – Salmon (Article 21.5 – Canada)*, in which the Panel accepted and considered a letter from 'Concerned Fishermen and Processors' in South Australia. This letter addressed the treatment by Australia of, on the one hand, imports of pilchard for use as bait or fish feed and, on the other hand, imports of salmon. The Panel considered the information submitted in the letter as relevant to its procedures and accepted this information as part of the record.[92] In many other disputes, however, panels refused to accept or consider *amicus curiae* briefs submitted to them.

In *US – Lead and Bismuth II*, the Appellate Body ruled with respect to its own authority to accept and consider *amicus curiae* briefs submitted in appellate review proceedings:

> In considering this matter, we first note that nothing in the DSU or the *Working Procedures* specifically provides that the Appellate Body may accept and consider submissions or briefs from sources other than the participants and third participants in an appeal. On the other hand, neither the DSU nor the *Working Procedures* explicitly prohibit acceptance or consideration of such briefs. However, Article 17.9 of the DSU provides:
>
> > Working procedures shall be drawn up by the Appellate Body in consultation with the Chairman of the DSB and the Director-General, and communicated to the Members for their information.
>
> This provision makes clear that the Appellate Body has broad authority to adopt procedural rules which do not conflict with any rules and procedures in the DSU or the covered agreements. Therefore, we are of the opinion that as long as we act consistently with the provisions of the DSU and the covered agreements, we have the legal authority to decide whether or not to accept and consider any information that we believe is pertinent and useful.[93]

In this case, the Appellate Body did not find it necessary to take the two *amicus curiae* briefs filed into account in rendering its decision.[94]

In October 2000, the Appellate Body Division hearing the appeal in *EC – Asbestos* adopted an Additional Procedure to deal with *amicus curiae* briefs which the Division expected to receive in great numbers in that dispute.[95] This Additional Procedure, which was adopted pursuant to Rule 16(1) of the *Working Procedures for Appellate Review* in the interests of fairness and orderly procedure in the conduct of this appeal, stipulated:

> 1. Any person, whether natural or legal, other than a party or a third party to this dispute, wishing to file a written brief with the Appellate Body, must apply for leave to file such a brief from the Appellate Body *by noon* on *Thursday, 16 November 2000*.
> 2. An application for leave to file such a written brief shall:
>
>   . . .

---

[92] Panel Report, *Australia – Salmon (Article 21.5 – Canada)*, paras. 7.8–7.9.

[93] Appellate Body Report, *US – Lead and Bismuth II*, para. 39. In support of its reasoning, the Appellate Body referred, in a footnote to this paragraph, to Rule 16(1) of the *Working Procedures for Appellate Review*. Rule 16(1) allows a Division hearing an appeal to develop an appropriate procedure in certain specified circumstances where a procedural question arises that is not covered by the *Working Procedures*. See below, pp. 270–1.

[94] *Ibid.*, para. 42.

[95] See Appellate Body Report, *EC – Asbestos*, paras. 51–2. Note that the Division adopted this Additional Procedure after consultations among several Members of the Appellate Body.

d. specify the nature of the interest the applicant has in this appeal;
e. identify the specific issues of law covered in the Panel Report and legal interpretations developed by the Panel that are the subject of this appeal, as set forth
   in the Notice of Appeal (WT/DS135/8) dated 23 October 2000, which the
   applicant intends to address in its written brief;
f. state why it would be desirable, in the interests of achieving a satisfactory
   settlement of the matter at issue, in accordance with the rights and obligations
   of WTO Members under the DSU and the other covered agreements, for the
   Appellate Body to grant the applicant leave to file a written brief in this appeal;
   and indicate, in particular, in what way the applicant will make a contribution to
   the resolution of this dispute that is not likely to be repetitive of what has been
   already submitted by a party or third party to this dispute; . . .
3. The Appellate Body will review and consider each application for leave to file a written
   brief and will, without delay, render a decision whether to grant or deny such leave.

With regard to these persons that would be granted leave to file an *amicus curiae*
brief, the Additional Procedure further stipulated:

4. The grant of leave to file a brief by the Appellate Body does not imply that the
   Appellate Body will address, in its Report, the legal arguments made in such a brief.
5. Any person, other than a party or a third party to this dispute, granted leave to file a
   written brief with the Appellate Body, must file its brief with the Appellate Body
   Secretariat *by noon* on *Monday, 27 November 2000.*
6. A written brief filed with the Appellate Body by an applicant granted leave to file
   such a brief shall:
      . . .
      (b) be concise and in no case longer than 20 typed pages, including any appen-
          dices; and
      (c) set out a precise statement, strictly limited to legal arguments, supporting the
          applicant's legal position on the issues of law or legal interpretations in the
          Panel Report with respect to which the applicant has been granted leave to
          file a written brief.

The Appellate Body received eleven applications for leave to file a written brief
in the *EC – Asbestos* appeal within the time limits specified in paragraph 2 of the
Additional Procedure. It reviewed and considered each of these applications in
accordance with the Additional Procedure and, in each case, decided to deny
leave to file a written brief for failure to comply sufficiently with all the
requirements set forth in paragraph 3 of the Additional Procedure.

While, in the end, the Appellate Body did not accept and consider any *amicus
curiae* brief in the *EC – Asbestos* appeal, many WTO Members were infuriated by
the Appellate Body's adoption of the Additional Procedure and its apparent
willingness to accept and consider *amicus curiae* briefs where certain requirements are fulfilled. On 20 November 2000, a Special Meeting of the General
Council was convened to discuss this issue. The discussion at this meeting
reflected the deep division between the vast majority of WTO Members opposing the Appellate Body's case law on this issue and the United States, which
fully supported this case law. At the end of this tumultuous meeting, the
Chairman of the General Council made the following observations:

There was a broad agreement that the rights and obligations under the DSU belonged
to WTO Members. It had been repeatedly stated that the WTO was a Member-driven

organization. Therefore, most delegations had concluded that since there was no specific provision regarding *amicus* briefs such briefs should not be accepted. Some delegations were of the view that *amicus* briefs could be used in some cases and there was at least one delegation who believed that there was both a legal and a substantive reason to use *amicus* briefs. There was no agreement on this point.

... [M]any Members had made reference to the shrimp case and the decision to interpret Article 13 of the DSU in such a way so as to accept *amicus* briefs. The majority of delegations had stated that they did not agree with that decision which served as a basis for subsequent decisions on *amicus* briefs by panels and the Appellate Body. At the same time, at least one delegation had stated that there was nothing wrong with that kind of procedure.

Finally, many Members had made the point that the issue under discussion was not a transparency issue, but rather a legal issue and concerned the question of who should participate in the legal system.[96]

The Chairman of the General Council concluded that he believed that there had been a large sentiment, expressed by almost all delegations, that there was a need to put clear rules in place for *amicus curiae* briefs. He called for further consultations on both the substantive content of the rules and what procedure should be used for putting them in place. The Chairman finally also stated:

in light of the views expressed and in the absence of clear rules, he believed that the Appellate Body should exercise extreme caution in future cases until Members had considered what rules were needed.[97]

There are two main reasons for the antagonism of many Members, especially developing-country Members, against *amicus curiae* briefs. First, Members fear that the need to consider and react to *amicus curiae* briefs will take up scarce legal resources and will further bend the WTO dispute settlement procedures in favour of Members with more legal resources at their disposal. Secondly, developing-country Members, in particular, note that the most vocal and best funded NGOs (such as Greenpeace, WWF and labour unions) often take positions that are considered 'unfriendly' to the interests and policies of developing-country Members.[98]

To date, WTO Members have been unable to adopt any clear rules on *amicus curiae* briefs. The Appellate Body has repeatedly confirmed its case law on the authority of panels and the Appellate Body to accept and consider *amicus curiae* briefs. In no appellate proceedings thus far, however, has the Appellate Body considered it useful in deciding on an appeal to accept and consider *amicus curiae* briefs submitted to it.[99]

---

[96] Minutes of the General Council Meeting of 22 November 2000, WT/GC/M/60, dated 23 January 2001, paras. 114–15 and 118.

[97] *Ibid.*, para. 120.

[98] Note that it has also been argued that persons submitting an *amicus curiae* brief would have more rights than third parties. This argument is mistaken. In fact, persons submitting an *amicus curiae* brief have *no* right to have this brief considered (see above, p. 197). By contrast, third parties do have a right to have their brief considered (see above, pp. 190–1). See also Appellate Body Report, *US – Steel Safeguards*, para. 268.

[99] Even in *US – Countervailing Measures on Certain EC Products*, a complaint by the EC, in which both the complainant and the respondent explicitly agreed that the Appellate Body had the authority to accept and consider an *amicus curiae* brief from an industry association received in the course of the appeal, the Appellate Body decided not to take the brief into account 'as we do not find it to be of assistance in this appeal'. See Appellate Body Report, *US – Countervailing Measures on Certain EC Products*, paras. 10 and 76.

Note that, in *US – Steel Safeguards*, the Appellate Body ruled, in response to a question from the European Communities whether the Appellate Body intended to accept and take account of the *amicus curiae* brief from the American Institute of International Steel, that this determination would be made after the Division had considered all submissions by the participants in the appeal, including the submissions at the oral hearing.[100]

The *amicus curiae* brief filed by Morocco in the appellate proceedings in *EC – Sardines* was of particular interest. Morocco was the first WTO Member to file an *amicus curiae* brief. Peru, the complainant in the *EC – Sardines* dispute, argued that the Appellate Body should not accept or consider this brief. In considering the issue, the Appellate Body first recalled its case law on *amicus curiae* briefs and then noted:

> We have been urged by the parties to this dispute not to treat Members less favourably than non-Members with regard to participation as *amicus curiae*. We agree. We have not. And we will not. As we have already determined that we have the authority to receive an *amicus curiae* brief from a private individual or an organization, *a fortiori* we are entitled to accept such a brief from a WTO Member, provided there is no prohibition on doing so in the DSU. We find no such prohibition.[101]

The Appellate Body therefore concluded that it was entitled to accept the *amicus curiae* brief submitted by Morocco, and consider it.[102] However, the Appellate Body emphasised that, in accepting the brief filed by Morocco in this appeal, it was not suggesting that each time a Member filed such a brief it would be required to accept and consider it. The Appellate Body noted:

> To the contrary, acceptance of any *amicus curiae* brief is a matter of discretion, which we must exercise on a case-by-case basis. We recall our statement that:
>
>> The procedural rules of WTO dispute settlement are designed to promote ... the fair, prompt and effective resolution of trade disputes.
>
> Therefore, we could exercise our discretion to reject an *amicus curiae* brief if, by accepting it, this would interfere with the "fair, prompt and effective resolution of trade disputes." This could arise, for example, if a WTO Member were to seek to submit an *amicus curiae* brief at a very late stage in the appellate proceedings, with the result that accepting the brief would impose an undue burden on other participants.[103]

Having concluded that it had the authority to accept the *amicus curiae* brief filed by Morocco, the Appellate Body then considered whether this brief could assist it in this appeal. Morocco's *amicus curiae* brief provided mainly factual information.[104] The Appellate Body therefore ruled on the relevance of these parts of Morocco's brief:

---

[100] Appellate Body Report, *US – Steel Safeguards*, paras. 9 and 10.
[101] Appellate Body Report, *EC – Sardines*, para. 164.   [102] *Ibid.*, para. 167.   [103] *Ibid.*
[104] Morocco's brief referred to the scientific differences between *Sardina pilchardus Walbaum* ('*Sardina pilchardus*') and *Sardinops sagax sagax* ('*Sardinops sagax*'), and it also provided economic information about the Moroccan fishing and canning industries.

> As Article 17.6 of the DSU limits an appeal to issues of law and legal interpretations developed by the panel, the factual information provided in Morocco's *amicus curiae* brief is not pertinent in this appeal.[105]

Morocco also put forward arguments relating to legal issues.[106] However, the Appellate Body decided not to make findings on these specific issues and, therefore, Morocco's arguments on these issues did not assist the Appellate Body in this appeal.[107] If the Appellate Body had made findings on these issues, it would arguably have accepted and considered the relevant part of Morocco's *amicus curiae* brief.

Questions and Assignments 3.8

Do panels and the Appellate Body have the authority to accept and consider *amicus curiae* briefs? Do NGOs have a right to submit *amicus curiae* briefs? Should an *amicus curiae* brief filed by a WTO Member be treated differently from briefs filed by NGOs? Did panels and the Appellate Body ever consider *amicus curiae* briefs in their deliberations? Why are most WTO Members highly critical of the Appellate Body's approach to the *amicus curiae* brief issue? Do you consider their criticism justified?

3.3.4.4. 'Indirect access' for non-Members

Many, if not most, of the disputes heard by the WTO are disputes brought by governments *at the instigation of* an industry or a company. It is well known that in *Japan – Film*, it was Kodak which masterminded and actively supported the US claims against Japan. In *EC – Bananas III*, Chiquita played a central role in the United States' involvement in this dispute. As Quentin Peel reported in the *Financial Times*:

> Even in the incestuous world of trade politics in Washington, where deals are done behind closed doors and lobbyists reign supreme, they talk of Carl Lindner in hushed tones.
>
> If the present words between the US and the European Union over bananas comes to real blows, his influence will certainly be seen as critical. This veteran financier, 80 next year, has succeeded almost single-handedly in turning a row about someone else's exports, and other people's jobs into an issue of principle for the US Government, and the possible cause of a serious rift in relations with its biggest trading partner.
>
> And yet no one admits to surprise. "It is a textbook case of how trade policy works in this city", says a diplomat closely involved in trade talks. "It is driven by very narrow interest groups. And nobody is prepared to stand up to this."
>
> Mr Lindner is a banana baron, although a thoroughly unlikely one. He is chairman and chief executive of Chiquita Brands International, the largest banana producer and trader in the world, with some 26 per cent of the market.

---

[105] Appellate Body Report, *EC – Sardines*, para. 169.
[106] Morocco's brief contained arguments relating to Article 2.1 of the *TBT Agreement* and the GATT 1994.
[107] Appellate Body Report, *EC – Sardines*, para. 314.

> In 1993, the EU introduced new rules to discriminate in favour of buying Caribbean bananas, and therefore squeezed the share of Chiquita's "dollar bananas" from one of its most lucrative markets. Since then, Mr Lindner has lined up a remarkable bipartisan battery of political heavy-weights to gun for him in the capital.
>
> Headed by Bob Dole, the former Senate majority leader, and Trent Lott, his successor as majority leader, it includes Newt Gingrich, the former Speaker of the House of Representatives, Senator John Glenn of Ohio and space fame, and Congressman Richard Gephardt, the House Democratic leader. All wrote letters to President Bill Clinton and Mickey Kantor, then US Trade Representative, urging tough counter-measures against the EU. They also tried to bring down the wrath of the US on any Central American country that dared to break ranks and join the EU cartel.[108]

Companies or industry associations will not only lobby governments to bring dispute settlement cases to the WTO, they (and their law firms) will often also play an important, 'behind-the-scenes' role in planning the legal strategy and drafting the submissions.

The legal system of some WTO Members explicitly provides for the possibility for industry associations and/or companies to bring violation of WTO obligations, by another WTO Member, to the attention of their government and to 'induce' their government to start WTO dispute settlement proceedings against that Member. In EC law, this possibility is provided for under the Trade Barriers Regulation;[109] in US law, under section 301 of the 1974 Trade Act.[110] In many other Members, this process of lobbying the government to bring WTO cases has not been regulated and institutionalised in the same manner, but the process is no less present. In this respect, industry associations and individual companies have 'indirect' access to the WTO dispute settlement system.

Questions and Assignments 3.9

Find the full text of the EC Trade Barriers Regulation and section 301 of the US 1974 Trade Act. Determine who can make use of the procedures set out in these legislative acts.

3.3.5. The WTO dispute settlement process

3.3.5.1. *Steps in the WTO dispute settlement process*

The WTO dispute settlement process entails four major steps:

- consultations;
- panel proceedings;

---

[108] Quentin Peel, 'Man in the News Carl Lindner, Banana Republican', *Financial Times*, 14–15 November 1998.
[109] Council Regulation (EC) No. 3286/94 on Community procedures for the exercise of rights under international trade rules, in particular those established under the WTO, OJ 1994, L349, 71, as amended by Council Regulation (EC) No. 356/95, OJ 1995, L41, 3.
[110] Section 301(a)(1) of the Trade Act 1974, 19 USC § 2411(a)(1).

- appellate review proceedings; and
- implementation and enforcement.

As already indicated above, the process always starts with *consultations*, or at least an attempt by the complainant to involve the respondent in consultations, to resolve the dispute amicably.[111] If that is not possible, the complainant can refer the dispute to a panel for adjudication. The *panel proceedings* will result in a panel report.[112] This report can be appealed to the Appellate Body. The *appellate review proceedings* will result in an Appellate Body report upholding, modifying or reversing the panel report.[113] The panel report, or in the case of an appeal, the Appellate Body report *and* the panel report, will be adopted by the DSB. After the adoption of the reports, the respondent, if found to be in breach of WTO law, will have to implement the recommendations and rulings adopted by the DSB. This *implementation and enforcement* of the adopted recommendations and rulings constitute the last major step in the WTO dispute settlement process.[114]

Figure 3.3, a flowchart prepared by the WTO Secretariat, reflects the four major steps, adding additional elements which are discussed below.[115]

3.3.5.2. *Timeframe for the WTO dispute settlement process*

One of the most striking features of the WTO dispute settlement system is the short timeframes within which the proceedings of both panels and the Appellate Body must be completed. The timeframes for consultations and implementation are also strictly regulated. In principle, panel proceedings should in no case exceed nine months.[116] In practice, however, panel proceedings often exceed this time limit. On average, panel proceedings last approximately twelve months.[117] Appellate Body proceedings shall not exceed ninety days.[118] In practice, the Appellate Body keeps to this time limit.[119] No other international court or tribunal operates under such severe time limits. These time limits, and in particular the time limits for appellate review, have been criticised as excessively short and demanding for both the parties to the dispute and the Appellate Body. As a result of these time limits, however, there is no backlog of cases at either the panel or appellate level.

Accelerated procedures with even shorter time limits (generally half of the normal time limits) apply for both panel and appellate review proceedings

---

[111] See above, pp. 183–4. For a detailed discussion on the initiation, conduct and possible outcome of consultations, see below, pp. 255–9.
[112] For a detailed discussion of panel proceedings, see below, pp. 259–70.
[113] For a detailed discussion of appellate review proceedings, see below, pp. 270–7.
[114] For a detailed discussion of implementation and enforcement proceedings, see below, pp. 278–83.
[115] See below, p. 205.   [116] Article 12.9 of the DSU.
[117] For a detailed discussion on the duration of the panel proceedings and the reasons for delays in these proceedings, see below, pp. 269–70.
[118] Article 17.5 of the DSU.
[119] For a detailed discussion of the duration of the appellate review proceedings, see below, p. 277.

Figure 3.3 Flowchart of the WTO dispute settlement process[120]

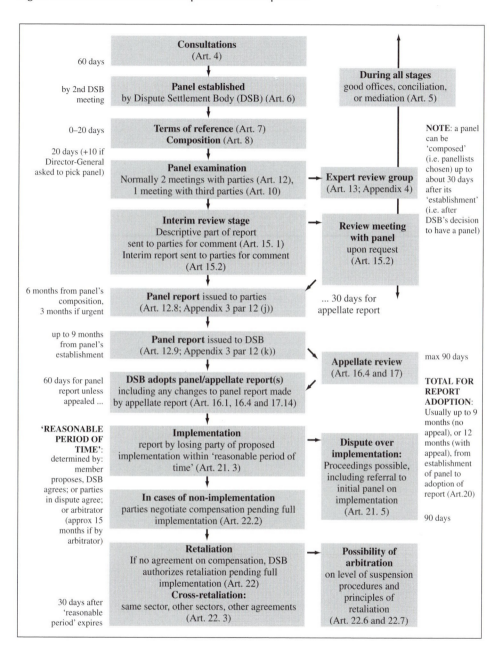

with respect to disputes regarding prohibited subsidies under the *SCM Agreement*.[121]

Questions and Assignments 3.10

Briefly describe the successive steps in the WTO dispute settlement process. In your opinion, are the time limits on the WTO dispute settlement process excessively short?

3.3.6. Rules of interpretation and burden of proof

Central to any dispute settlement system are the rules of interpretation and the rules on burden of proof. This section discusses these rules as applied in WTO dispute settlement.

3.3.6.1. *Rules of interpretation*

Article 3.2 of the DSU stipulates in relevant part that the dispute settlement system serves:

> to clarify the existing provisions of [the covered] agreements in accordance with *customary rules of interpretation of public international law*.
>
> [Emphasis added]

In *US – Gasoline*, the Appellate Body noted:

> The "general rule of interpretation" (set out in Article 31(1) of the Vienna Convention on the Law of Treaties) has attained the status of a rule of customary or general international law. As such, it forms part of the "customary rules of interpretation of public international law" which the Appellate Body has been directed, by Article 3(2) of the *DSU*, to apply in seeking to clarify the provisions of the *General Agreement* and the other "covered agreements" of the *Marrakesh Agreement Establishing the World Trade Organization* (the "*WTO Agreement*"). That direction reflects a measure of recognition that the *General Agreement* is not to be read in clinical isolation from public international law.[122]

In *Japan – Alcoholic Beverages II*, the Appellate Body added:

> There can be no doubt that Article 32 of the *Vienna Convention*, dealing with the role of supplementary means of interpretation, has also attained the same status [of a rule of customary international law].[123]

Article 31 of the *Vienna Convention on the Law of Treaties*, entitled 'General Rule of Interpretation', states:

---

[121] Article 4 of the *SCM Agreement*. A panel must, for example, circulate its report within ninety days of the date of its composition (Article 4.6 of the *SCM Agreement*). Pursuant to Article 7 of the *SCM Agreement*, disputes regarding actionable subsidies are also subject to some specific deadlines. A panel must, for example, circulate its report to all Members within 120 days of the date of its composition (Article 7.5 of the *SCM Agreement*).

[122] Appellate Body Report, *US – Gasoline*, 16.

[123] Appellate Body Report, *Japan – Alcoholic Beverages II*, 104.

1. A treaty shall be interpreted in good faith in accordance with the ordinary meaning to be given to the terms of the treaty in their context and in the light of its object and purpose.
2. The context for the purpose of the interpretation of a treaty shall comprise, in addition to the text, including its preamble and annexes:
   a. any agreement relating to the treaty which was made between all the parties in connection with the conclusion of the treaty;
   b. any instrument which was made by one or more parties in connection with the conclusion of the treaty and accepted by the other parties as an instrument related to the treaty.
3. There shall be taken into account together with the context:
   a. any subsequent agreement between the parties regarding the interpretation of the treaty or the application of its provisions;
   b. any subsequent practice in the application of the treaty which establishes the agreement of the parties regarding its interpretation;
   c. any relevant rules of international law applicable in the relations between the parties.
4. A special meaning shall be given to a term if it is established that the parties so intended.

Article 32 of the *Vienna Convention*, entitled 'Supplementary Means of Interpretation', states:

> Recourse may be had to supplementary means of interpretation, including the preparatory work of the treaty and the circumstances of its conclusion, in order to confirm the meaning resulting from the application of article 31, or to determine the meaning when the interpretation according to article 31:
>
> a. leaves the meaning ambiguous or obscure; or
> b. leads to a result which is manifestly absurd or unreasonable.

Consequently, panels and the Appellate Body interpret provisions of the covered agreements in accordance with the ordinary meaning of the words of the provision taken in their context and in the light of the object and purpose of the agreement involved. If necessary and appropriate, panels and the Appellate Body have recourse to supplementary means of interpretation.

As the Panel in *US – Section 301 Trade Act* observed:

> Text, context and object-and-purpose correspond to well established textual, systemic and teleological methodologies of treaty interpretation, all of which typically come into play when interpreting complex provisions in multilateral treaties. For pragmatic reasons the normal usage, and we will follow the normal usage, is to start the interpretation from the ordinary meaning of the "raw" text of the relevant treaty provisions and then seek to construe it in its context and in the light of the treaty's object and purpose. However, the elements referred to in Article 31 – text, context and object-and-purpose as well as good faith – are to be viewed as one holistic rule of interpretation rather than a sequence of separate tests to be applied in a hierarchical order. Context and object-and-purpose may often appear simply to confirm an interpretation seemingly derived from the "raw" text. In reality it is always some context, even if unstated, that determines which meaning is to be taken as "ordinary" and frequently it is impossible to give meaning, even "ordinary meaning", without looking also at object-and-purpose.[124]

---

[124] Panel Report, *US – Section 301 Trade Act*, para. 7.22.

The Panel in *US – Section 301 Trade Act* thus stressed that the elements of Article 31 of the *Vienna Convention* – text, context, object and purpose – constitute 'one holistic rule of interpretation', and not 'a sequence of separate tests to be applied in a hierarchical order'. To determine the ordinary meaning of a term, it makes sense to start with the dictionary meaning of that term but, as the Appellate Body noted more than once, a term often has several dictionary meanings and dictionary meanings thus leave many interpretative questions open.[125] The ordinary meaning of a term cannot be determined outside the context in which the term is used and without consideration of the object and purpose of the agreement at issue.

In *Japan – Alcoholic Beverages II*, the Appellate Body stated:

> Article 31 of the *Vienna Convention* provides that the words of the treaty form the foundation for the interpretive process: "interpretation must be based above all upon the text of the treaty". The provisions of the treaty are to be given their ordinary meaning in their context. The object and purpose of the treaty are also to be taken into account in determining the meaning of its provisions.[126]

The duty of an interpreter is to examine the words of the treaty to determine the *common* intentions of the parties.[127]

One of the corollaries of the 'general rule of interpretation' of Article 31 of the *Vienna Convention* is that interpretation must give meaning and effect to *all* the terms of a treaty (i.e. the interpretive principle of effectiveness). An interpreter is not free to adopt a reading that would result in reducing whole clauses or paragraphs of a treaty to redundancy or inutility.[128] Furthermore, the Appellate Body in *EC – Hormones* cautioned interpreters as follows:

> The fundamental rule of treaty interpretation requires a treaty interpreter to read and interpret the words actually used by the agreement under examination, not words the interpreter may feel should have been used.[129]

In *India – Patents (US)*, the Appellate Body ruled that the principles of treaty interpretation 'neither require nor condone' the importation into a treaty of 'words that are not there' or 'concepts that were not intended'.[130]

With regard to the use of 'supplementary means of interpretation', the Appellate Body held in *EC – Computer Equipment*:

> The application of ... [the] rules in Article 31 of the *Vienna Convention* will usually allow a treaty interpreter to establish the meaning of a term. However, if after applying Article 31 the meaning of the term remains ambiguous or obscure, or leads to a result which is manifestly absurd or unreasonable, Article 32 allows a treaty interpreter to

---

[125] See Appellate Body Report, *Canada – Aircraft*, para. 153; and Appellate Body Report, *EC – Asbestos*, para. 92.

[126] Appellate Body Report, *Japan – Alcoholic Beverages II*, 105–6.

[127] See, e.g. Appellate Body Report, *India – Patents (US)*, para. 45; and Appellate Body Report, *EC – Computer Equipment*, para. 84. Note that, in both these cases, the Appellate Body rejected the relevance of the 'legitimate expectations' of one of the parties in the interpretation of the meaning of the provision at issue.

[128] Appellate Body Report, *US – Gasoline*, 21.

[129] Appellate Body Report, *EC – Hormones*, para. 181.

[130] Appellate Body Report, *India – Patents (US)*, para. 45.

> have recourse to ... supplementary means of interpretation, including the preparatory work of the treaty and the circumstances of its conclusion.
>
> With regard to "the circumstances of [the] conclusion" of a treaty, this permits, in appropriate cases, the examination of the historical background against which the treaty was negotiated.[131]

In this case, the Appellate Body considered that the tariff classification practice in the European Communities during the Uruguay Round was part of 'the circumstances of [the] conclusion' of the *WTO Agreement* and could therefore be used as a supplementary means of interpretation within the meaning of Article 32 of the *Vienna Convention*.[132] In *EC – Poultry*, the Appellate Body considered a pre-WTO bilateral agreement between the parties to the dispute (i.e. the Oilseeds Agreement) to be part of the historical background to be taken into account when interpreting the provision at issue.[133] In *Canada – Dairy*, the Appellate Body based its interpretation of the scope of the tariff quota commitment by Canada on its 'reading of the circumstances surrounding the conclusion of the *WTO Agreement*'.[134]

As there is no official record of the Uruguay Round negotiations leading up to the *WTO Agreement*, recourse to the 'preparatory work' of the *WTO Agreement* is not possible.

With regard to the degree of 'flexibility' and 'interpretability' of the *WTO Agreement*, the Appellate Body noted in *Japan – Alcoholic Beverages II*:

> WTO rules are reliable, comprehensible and enforceable. WTO rules are not so rigid or so inflexible as not to leave room for reasoned judgements in confronting the endless and ever-changing ebb and flow of real facts in real cases in the real world. They will serve the multilateral trading system best if they are interpreted with that in mind. In that way, we will achieve the "security and predictability" sought for the multilateral trading system by the Members of the WTO through the establishment of the dispute settlement system.[135]

Questions and Assignments 3.11

Why are Articles 31 and 32 of the *Vienna Convention on the Law of Treaties* relevant to the interpretation and clarification of the provisions of the covered agreements? How do panels and the Appellate Body have to interpret provisions of the covered agreements? Can panels or the Appellate Body base their interpretation of a provision of the covered agreements on the 'legitimate expectations' of one of the parties to the dispute? What does the 'principle of effectiveness' require panels and the Appellate Body to do when they interpret provisions of the covered agreements? What can panels and the Appellate Body use as supplementary means of interpretation and when can they do so?

---

[131] Appellate Body Report, *EC – Computer Equipment*, para. 86. See also Appellate Body Report, *Canada – Dairy*, para. 138.
[132] Appellate Body Report, *EC – Computer Equipment*, para. 92.
[133] Appellate Body Report, *EC – Poultry*, para. 83.
[134] Appellate Body Report, *Canada – Dairy*, para. 139.
[135] Appellate Body Report, *Japan – Alcoholic Beverages II*, 122–3.

3.3.6.2. Burden of proof

The DSU does not contain any specific rules concerning the burden of proof in the WTO dispute settlement system. However, in *US – Wool Shirts and Blouses*, the Appellate Body noted:

> we find it difficult, indeed, to see how any system of judicial settlement could work if it incorporated the proposition that the mere assertion of a claim might amount to proof. It is, thus, hardly surprising that various international tribunals, including the International Court of Justice, have generally and consistently accepted and applied the rule that the party who asserts a fact, whether the claimant or the respondent, is responsible for providing proof thereof. Also, it is a generally accepted canon of evidence in civil law, common law and, in fact, most jurisdictions, that the burden of proof rests upon the party, whether complaining or defending, who asserts the affirmative of a particular claim or defence. If that party adduces evidence sufficient to raise a presumption that what is claimed is true, the burden then shifts to the other party, who will fail unless it adduces sufficient evidence to rebut the presumption.[136]

The burden of proof in WTO dispute settlement proceedings is thus on the party, the complainant or the respondent, that asserts the affirmative of a particular claim or defence. The burden of proof shifts to the other party when sufficient evidence is adduced to raise a presumption that what is claimed is true. Precisely how much and precisely what kind of evidence is required to establish such a presumption 'will necessarily vary from measure to measure, provision to provision, and case to case'.[137]

In *EC – Hormones*, the Appellate Body further clarified the burden of proof in WTO dispute settlement proceedings and stated with respect to disputes under the *SPS Agreement*:

> The initial burden lies on the complaining party, which must establish a *prima facie* case of inconsistency with a particular provision of the *SPS Agreement* on the part of the defending party, or more precisely, of its SPS measure or measures complained about. When that *prima facie* case is made, the burden of proof moves to the defending party, which must in turn counter or refute the claimed inconsistency.
>
> ... It is also well to remember that a *prima facie* case is one which, in the absence of effective refutation by the defending party, requires a panel, as a matter of law, to rule in favour of the complaining party presenting the *prima facie* case.[138]

The above should not be understood as imposing a requirement on panels to make an explicit ruling on whether the complainant has established a *prima facie* case of violation before a panel may proceed to examine the respondent's defence and evidence.[139] The jurisprudence of the Appellate Body regarding the rules on burden of proof is well summarised by the Panel in *US – Section 301 Trade Act*, where it is stated:

---

[136] Appellate Body Report, *US – Wool Shirts and Blouses*, 335.
[137] *Ibid.*   [138] Appellate Body Report, *EC – Hormones*, paras. 98 and 104.
[139] See Appellate Body Report, *Korea – Dairy*, para. 145. In *Thailand – H-Beams*, the Appellate Body ruled that a panel is not required to make a separate and specific finding, in each and every instance, that a party has met its burden of proof in respect of a particular claim, or that a party has rebutted a *prima facie* case. See Appellate Body Report, *Thailand – H-Beams*, para. 134.

In accordance with this jurisdiction, both parties agreed that it is for the EC, as the complaining party, to present arguments and evidence sufficient to establish a *prima facie* case in respect of the various elements of its claims regarding the inconsistency of Sections 301–310 with US obligations under the WTO. Once the EC has done so, it is for the US to rebut that *prima facie* case. Since, in this case, both parties have submitted extensive facts and arguments in respect of the EC claims, our task will essentially be to balance all evidence on record and decide whether the EC, as party bearing the original burden of proof, has convinced us of the validity of its claims. In case of uncertainty, i.e. in case all the evidence and arguments remain in equipoise, we have to give the benefit of the doubt to the US as defending party.[140]

As stated by the Panel in *US – Section 301 Trade Act*, the task of a panel is essentially to *balance all evidence* on record and decide whether the party bearing the original burden of proof has convinced it of the validity of its claims. The Panel in the same case furthermore noted:

the party that alleges a specific fact – be it the EC or the US – has the burden to prove it. In other words, it has to establish a *prima facie* case that the fact exists. Following the principles set out in the previous paragraph, this *prima facie* case will stand unless sufficiently rebutted by the other party.

The factual findings in this Report were reached [by] applying these principles. Of course, when it comes to deciding on the correct interpretation of the covered agreements a panel will be aided by the arguments of the parties but not bound by them; its decisions on such matters must be in accord with the rules of treaty interpretation applicable to the WTO.[141]

With regard to the burden of establishing the correct legal interpretation of provisions of the covered agreements, the Appellate Body further clarified in *EC – Tariff Preferences*:

Consistent with the principle of *jura novit curia*, it is not the responsibility of the European Communities to provide us with the legal interpretation to be given to a particular provision in the Enabling Clause; instead, the burden of the European Communities is to adduce sufficient evidence to substantiate its assertion that the Drug Arrangements comply with the requirements of the Enabling Clause.[142]

Thus, the burden of establishing what the applicable rule of WTO law is, and how that rule must be interpreted, is not on the parties but on the panel and the Appellate Body.

The relationship between the rules on burden of proof, discussed here, and the authority of panels to seek out expert advice is examined in detail below.[143]

---

[140] Panel Report, *US – Section 301 Trade Act*, para. 7.14.   [141] *Ibid.*, paras. 7.15 and 7.16.
[142] Appellate Body Report, *EC – Tariff Preferences*, para. 105. In a footnote, the Appellate Body added that the principle of *jura novit curia* was articulated by the International Court of Justice as follows: 'it being the duty of the Court itself to ascertain and apply the relevant law in the given circumstances of the case, the burden of establishing or proving rules of international law cannot be imposed upon any of the parties, for the law lies within the judicial knowledge of the Court.' International Court of Justice, Merits, *Case Concerning Military and Paramilitary Activities in and against Nicaragua (Nicaragua v. United States of America)*, 1986 ICJ Reports, 14, para. 29.
[143] See below, pp. 266–7.

Note that in *EC – Tariff Preferences*, the Appellate Body introduced the concept of the legal responsibility to *raise* a defence as an issue in dispute settlement proceedings. With regard to the Enabling Clause, and in view of the specific characteristics of the Enabling Clause,[144] the Appellate Body ruled that:

> although a responding party must defend the consistency of its preference scheme with the conditions of the Enabling Clause and must prove such consistency, a *complaining* party has to define the parameters within which the *responding* party must make that defence.[145]

The Appellate Body thus concluded that it is the responsibility of the complaining party to identify those provisions of the Enabling Clause with which the scheme is allegedly inconsistent. The Appellate Body emphasised, however, that the responsibility of the complaining party in such an instance should not be overstated. The Appellate Body noted that the responsibility of the complaining party:

> is merely to *identify* those provisions of the Enabling Clause with which the scheme is allegedly inconsistent, without bearing the burden of *establishing* the facts necessary to support such inconsistency.[146]

The latter burden remains on the responding party invoking the Enabling Clause as a defence.

Questions and Assignments 3.12

Who has the burden of proof in WTO dispute settlement proceedings? Does the burden of proof ever shift between the parties? When has a *prima facie* case of inconsistency been made? Will a panel consider the arguments and evidence advanced by the respondent before the complainant has made a *prima facie* case with respect to its claims?

3.3.7. Confidentiality and Rules of Conduct

This section discusses the confidential – some say secretive – nature of WTO dispute settlement. It also examines the Rules of Conduct that apply to all those involved in WTO dispute settlement.

---

[144] The Appellate Body noted that every measure undertaken pursuant to the Enabling Clause would necessarily be inconsistent with Article I, if assessed on that basis alone, but it would be exempted from compliance with Article I because it meets the requirements of the Enabling Clause. The Appellate Body noted that: 'under these circumstances, we are of the view that a complaining party challenging a measure taken pursuant to the Enabling Clause must allege more than mere inconsistency with Article I:1 of the GATT 1994, for to do only that would not convey the "legal basis of the complaint sufficient to present the problem clearly". In other words, it is insufficient in WTO dispute settlement for a complainant to allege inconsistency with Article I:1 of the GATT 1994 if the complainant seeks also to argue that the measure is not justified under the Enabling Clause'. See Appellate Body Report, *EC – Tariff Preferences*, para. 110.

[145] Appellate Body Report, *EC – Tariff Preferences*, para. 114.   [146] *Ibid.*, para. 115.

3.3.7.1. *Confidentiality of the proceedings*

The WTO dispute settlement proceedings are characterised by their confidentiality. Consultations, panel proceedings and appellate review proceedings are all confidential. The meetings of the DSB also take place behind closed doors.[147] All written submissions to a panel or to the Appellate Body by the parties and third parties to a dispute are confidential.[148] Parties *may* make their *own* submissions available to the public.[149] While a few Members do so in a systematic manner (e.g. the United States and the European Communities), most parties choose to keep their submissions confidential. The DSU provides that a party to a dispute must, upon request of any WTO Member, provide a non-confidential summary of the information contained in its submissions to the panel that could be disclosed to the public.[150] However, this provision does not provide for a deadline by which such a non-confidential summary must be made available. In the few instances in which WTO Members requested such a summary, it was usually made available too late to be of any practical relevance.

The interim report of the panel and the final panel report, as long as it is only issued to the parties to the dispute, are also confidential. The final panel report only becomes a public document when it is circulated to all WTO Members. In reality, however, the interim report and the final report issued to the parties do not remain confidential very long and are usually 'leaked' to the media. Unlike panel reports, Appellate Body reports are not first issued to the parties and then, weeks later, circulated to all WTO Members. In principle, they are issued to the parties and circulated to all WTO Members at the same time and are as of that moment a public document.

Recognising that parties have a legitimate interest in protecting sensitive and confidential business information submitted to a panel, the Panels, in *Canada – Aircraft* and *Brazil – Aircraft*, adopted special procedures governing confidential business information that go beyond the protection afforded by Article 18.2 of the DSU.[151] In *Canada – Aircraft*, the Appellate Body ruled, after carefully considering all the confidentiality requirements already provided for in the DSU, and in particular in Articles 17.10 and 18.2:

> we do not consider that it is necessary, under all the circumstances of this case, to adopt *additional* procedures for the protection of business confidential information in these appellate proceedings.[152]

The Appellate Body considered the protection offered by the confidentiality requirements of Article 17.10 and 18.2 of the DSU more than sufficient.

---

[147] See above, p. 125, and below, p. 230.
[148] Articles 18.2 and 17.10 of and Appendix 3, para. 3, to the DSU.
[149] See, for a further complication, Panel Report, *Argentina – Poultry*, paras. 7.13–7.16.
[150] Article 18.2 of the DSU.
[151] See Panel Report, *Canada – Aircraft*, Annex 1; and Panel Report, *Brazil – Aircraft*, Annex 1. For a further discussion of the special procedures, see below, p. 267.
[152] Appellate Body Report, *Canada – Aircraft*, para. 147. See also Appellate Body Report, *Brazil – Aircraft*, para. 125.

The meetings of the panel with the parties as well as the hearings of the Appellate Body take place behind closed doors.[153] Nobody except the parties themselves and the officials of the WTO Secretariat, assisting the panel, are allowed to attend all meetings of the panel with the parties. Third parties are usually invited to attend only one session of the first substantive panel meeting.[154] The hearings of the Appellate Body may only be attended by the participants and third-party participants in the appellate review proceedings as well as the staff of the Appellate Body Secretariat.

The DSU does not explicitly address the issue of representation of the parties before panels of the Appellate Body. In *EC – Bananas III*, the issue arose whether private counsel, not employed by government, may represent a party or third party (such as Saint Lucia) before the Appellate Body. In its ruling, the Appellate Body noted that nothing in the *WTO Agreement* or the DSU, or in customary international law or the prevailing practice of international tribunals, prevents a WTO Member from determining the composition of its own delegation in WTO dispute settlement proceedings.[155] A party can, therefore, decide that private counsel forms part of its delegation and will represent it in WTO dispute settlement proceedings. While the ruling of the Appellate Body concerned the proceedings before this body, the reasoning of this ruling is equally relevant for panel proceedings. This was confirmed in the Panel Report in *Indonesia – Autos*, adopted one year after the Appellate Body Report in *EC – Bananas III*. The Panel in *Indonesia – Autos* rejected the request of the United States to exclude Indonesia's private lawyers from the Panel meetings, stating:

> it is for the Government of Indonesia to nominate the members of its delegation to meetings of this Panel, and we find no provision in the WTO Agreement or the DSU, including the standard rules of procedure included therein, which prevents a WTO Member from determining the composition of its delegation to WTO panel meetings.[156]

Private counsel now routinely appear in panel as well as appellate review proceedings as part of the delegation of a party or third party. The parties and third parties are responsible for all members of their delegations and must ensure that all members of the delegation, private counsel included, act in accordance with the rules of the DSU and the Working Procedures of the panel, particularly with respect to the confidentiality of the proceedings.[157]

Questions and Assignments 3.13

Under WTO law, do citizens have a right of access to the submissions made by their and other governments to panels and the Appellate Body? Do WTO Members have a right of access to the submissions made by other

---

[153] Appendix 3, para. 2, to and Article 17.10 of the DSU.   [154] See below, pp. 263–4.
[155] Appellate Body Report, *EC – Bananas III*, para. 10.
[156] Panel Report, *Indonesia – Autos*, para. 14.1.
[157] See, in this respect, Appellate Body Report, *Thailand – H-Beams*, paras. 62–78. In this case, Hogan & Hartson LLP withdrew as Poland's legal counsel after Thailand's appellant submission had been 'leaked' and the Appellate Body had instituted an investigation into this breach of the confidentiality of the appellate review proceedings.

Members in panel or Appellate Body proceedings? Are meetings of panels or the hearing of the Appellate Body open to the public? Are they open to WTO Members that are not a party to the dispute? In your opinion, should panel meetings and Appellate Body hearings be open to the public? In your opinion, should confidential business information, submitted by the parties to a panel or the Appellate Body, be given *additional* protection? Are panel and Appellate Body reports confidential documents? Can WTO Members be represented by private counsel in WTO dispute settlement proceedings?

3.3.7.2. Rules of Conduct

When hearing and deciding a WTO dispute, panellists, arbitrators and Appellate Body members are subject to the *Rules of Conduct for the Understanding on Rules and Procedures Governing the Settlement of Disputes* (the '*Rules of Conduct*').[158] To preserve the integrity and impartiality of the WTO dispute settlement system, the *Rules of Conduct* require that panellists, arbitrators and Appellate Body members:[159]

> shall be independent and impartial, shall avoid direct or indirect conflicts of interest and shall respect the confidentiality of proceedings.[160]

Also the staff of the WTO Secretariat and the staff of the Appellate Body Secretariat as well as experts consulted by panels are subject to these *Rules of Conduct*.

To ensure compliance with the *Rules of Conduct*, all persons to whom the rules apply must disclose:

> the existence or development of any interest, relationship or matter that person could reasonably be expected to know and that is likely to affect, or give rise to justifiable doubts as to, that person's independence or impartiality.[161]

This disclosure obligation includes information on financial, professional and other active interests as well as considered statements of public opinion and employment or family interests.[162]

Parties can request the disqualification of a panellist on the ground of *material* violation of the obligations of independence, impartiality, confidentiality or the avoidance of direct or indirect conflicts of interests.[163] The evidence of such material violation is provided to the Chairman of the DSB, who will, in consultation with the Director-General of the WTO and the chairpersons of the relevant WTO bodies, decide whether a material violation has occurred. If it has, the panellist is replaced. Parties can also request the disqualification of an Appellate Body member on the ground of a material

---

[158] WT/DSB/RC/1, dated 11 December 1996.
[159] Note that the *Rules of Conduct* also apply to the members of the TMB. See above, pp. 133–4.
[160] Para. II(1) of the *Rules of Conduct*.   [161] Para. III(1) of the *Rules of Conduct*.
[162] Annex 2 to the *Rules of Conduct*.   [163] Para. VIII of the *Rules of Conduct*.

violation of the obligations of the *Rules of Conduct*. It is, however, for the Appellate Body, and not for the Chairman of the DSB, to decide whether a material violation has occurred and, if so, to take appropriate action.[164] To date, no panellist or Appellate Body member has ever been found to have committed a material violation of the *Rules of Conduct*. However, in a few instances, a panellist withdrew, on his or her own initiative, after a party raised concerns about a possible conflict of interests.

With respect to the issue of the rules of conduct applicable to private counsel acting for a party or third party, note that in *EC – Tariff Preferences*, the European Communities objected to the 'joint representation' by the Advisory Centre on WTO Law (ACWL) of both India, the complainant, and Paraguay, a third party. The Panel was therefore confronted with the question of whether the same legal counsel could represent simultaneously a complaining party and a third party.[165] In response to this question, the Panel first noted that:

> the WTO has not itself elaborated any rules governing the ethical conduct of legal counsel representing WTO Members in particular disputes.[166]

The Panel subsequently noted, however, that:

> As a general matter ... it is the responsibility of legal counsel to ensure that it is not placing itself in a position of actual or potential conflict of interest when agreeing to represent, and thereafter representing, one or more WTO Members in a dispute under the DSU.[167]

As the Panel observed, bar associations in many jurisdictions have elaborated rules of conduct dealing explicitly with conflicts of interest through joint representation. Common to all such ethical rules of conduct are:

- the principle that counsel shall not accept or continue representation of more than one client in a matter in which the interests of the clients actually or potentially conflict;
- the possibility for clients, when faced with counsel being subject to actual or potential conflict of interest as the result of joint representation, to consent to such joint representation, but only following full disclosure by counsel; and
- that counsel shall nevertheless discontinue such joint representation at such time as counsel becomes aware that the interests of the two (or more) clients are directly adverse.[168]

As India and Paraguay had been fully informed about their joint representation by the ACWL and had given their written consent to such representation, the Panel did not see any problem with the joint representation in this case.[169]

---

[164] ibid.   [165] Panel Report, *EC – Tariff Preferences*, para. 7.3.
[166] Ibid., para. 7.5.   [167] Ibid., para. 7.9.   [168] Ibid., para. 7.10.
[169] Ibid., para. 7.13. The European Communities also raised the question of whether the ACWL's joint representation of a party and a third party may be inconsistent with the DSU rules on confidentiality. As the Panel in this case granted the third parties 'additional rights' (see below, p. 264), the Panel found that the confidentiality issue did not arise in this dispute. See Panel Report, *EC – Tariff Preferences*, para. 7.17.

3.3.8. Remedies for breach of WTO law

The DSU provides for three types of remedy for breach of WTO law:

- one final remedy, namely, the withdrawal (or amendment) of the WTO-inconsistent measure; and
- two temporary remedies which can be applied awaiting the withdrawal (or amendment) of the WTO-inconsistent measure, namely, compensation and suspension of concessions or other obligations (commonly referred to as 'retaliation').

This section discusses these three types of remedy. It also briefly examines whether other types of remedy may be available.

3.3.8.1. *Withdrawal of the WTO-inconsistent measure*

Article 3.7 of the DSU states, in relevant part:

> In the absence of a mutually agreed solution, the first objective of the dispute settlement mechanism is usually to secure the withdrawal of the measures concerned if these are found to be inconsistent with the provisions of any of the covered agreements.

Furthermore, Article 3.7 suggests that the withdrawal of the WTO-inconsistent measure should normally be 'immediate'.[170]

Article 19.1 of the DSU provides:

> Where a panel or the Appellate Body concludes that a measure is inconsistent with a covered agreement, it shall recommend that the Member concerned bring the measure into conformity with that agreement. ...

Such a recommendation, once adopted by the DSB, is legally binding on the Member concerned.[171] With regard to recommendations and rulings adopted by the DSB, Article 21.1 of the DSU provides that:

> *Prompt* compliance with recommendations or rulings of the DSB is essential in order to ensure effective resolution of disputes to the benefit of all Members.
>
> [Emphasis added]

---

[170] As discussed below, Article 3.7 provides: 'The provision of compensation should be resorted to only if the immediate withdrawal of the measure is impracticable ...'.

[171] See below, p. 243.

While Article 3.7 of the DSU refers to the withdrawal of the measure found to be WTO-inconsistent, the withdrawal or the amendment of the WTO-inconsistent aspects or elements of such a measure usually suffices to bring the measure into conformity with WTO law pursuant to the recommendations or rulings of the DSB. Prompt or immediate compliance with the DSB recommendations and rulings, i.e. prompt or immediate withdrawal or amendment of the WTO-inconsistent measure, is essential to the effective functioning of the WTO and the primary obligation.

However, if it is impracticable to comply immediately with the recommendations and rulings, and this may often be the case, the Member concerned has, pursuant to Article 21.3 of the DSU, a reasonable period of time in which to do so. The 'reasonable period of time for implementation' may be:

- determined by the DSB;
- agreed on by the parties to the dispute; or
- determined through binding arbitration at the request of either party.[172]

The parties to the dispute often succeed in agreeing on what constitutes a 'reasonable period of time for implementation'. Parties agreed on the 'reasonable period of time for implementation' in, for example, *Canada – Periodicals* (fifteen months), *India – Patents (US)* (fifteen months), *US – Shrimp* (thirteen months), *Japan – Agricultural Products II* (nine months and twelve days) and *US – DRAMS* (eight months).[173] In sixteen cases to date, the 'reasonable period of time for implementation' was decided through binding arbitration under Article 21.3(c) of the DSU.[174] The latter provision states:

> In such arbitration, a guideline for the arbitrator should be that the reasonable period of time to implement panel or Appellate Body recommendations should not exceed 15 months from the date of the adoption of a panel or Appellate Body report. However, that time may be shorter or longer, depending upon the particular circumstances.

The Arbitrator in *US – Hot Rolled Steel* explained the following with regard to the 'reasonable period of time for implementation':

> It is useful to recall the essential principle and rule that WTO Members are committed to "prompt compliance" with DSB recommendations and rulings and that "prompt compliance" translates into "immediate" compliance. When, however, such "immediate" compliance is "*impracticable*", then the Member bound to comply becomes entitled to "a reasonable period of time" within which to comply. It is similarly salutary to recall that the 15-month period mentioned in Article 21.3(c) of the DSU is expressly designated as "a *guideline* for the arbitrator": the "reasonable period of time" to implement panel or Appellate Body recommendations "should not exceed 15 months" from the date of adoption of the panel or Appellate Body Report, which period may, however, be "shorter or longer", "depending upon the particular circumstances". I do not see any basis for reading the 15-month guideline as establishing a fixed maximum

---

[172] Article 21.3(a), (b) and (c) of the DSU.
[173] Note that, to date, the reasonable period of time has never been determined by the DSB pursuant to Article 21.3(a) of the DSU.
[174] See www.worldtradelaw.net, visited on 1 March 2004. This number does not include *US – Line Pipe*, in which the parties reached an agreement on the reasonable period of time during the Article 21.3(c) proceedings.

or "*outer*" limit" for "a reasonable period of time". Neither, of course, does the 15-month guideline constitute a *floor* or "*inner* limit" of "a reasonable period of time".[175]

[Emphasis added]

In *EC – Hormones*, the Arbitrator ruled that the 'reasonable period of time for implementation', as determined under Article 21.3(c), should be:

the shortest period possible within the legal system of the Member to implement the recommendations and rulings of the DSB.[176]

However, as the Arbitrator in *Korea – Alcoholic Beverages* ruled, a Member is not required to utilise extraordinary legislative procedures, rather than the normal procedure, in order to shorten the period of implementation.[177] In *EC – Hormones*, the Arbitrator also noted that, when implementation does not require changes in legislation but can be effected by administrative means, the reasonable period of time 'should be considerably less than 15 months'.[178] In *Canada – Pharmaceutical Patents*, the Arbitrator listed a number of other 'particular circumstances' that can influence what the shortest period possible for implementation may be within the legal system of the implementing Member. Apart from the means of implementation (legislative or administrative), this Arbitrator referred to the complexity of the proposed implementation and the legally binding, as opposed to the discretionary, nature of the component steps in the process leading to implementation.[179] Political and economic circumstances are irrelevant in determining the 'reasonable period of time for implementation'. The absence of a political majority to adopt implementing measures or economic hardship resulting from implementation, for example, are not taken into consideration by the arbitrator in determining the 'reasonable period of time for implementation'. However, Article 21.2 of the DSU requires that, in determining the 'reasonable period of time for implementation', particular attention should be paid to matters affecting the interests of developing-country Members. On that legal basis, the Arbitrator in *Indonesia – Autos* ruled:

Indonesia is not only a developing country; it is a developing country that is currently in a dire economic and financial situation. Indonesia itself states that its economy is "near collapse". In these very particular circumstances, I consider it appropriate to give full weight to matters affecting the interests of Indonesia as a developing country pursuant to the provisions of Article 21.2 of the DSU. I, therefore, conclude that an additional period of six months over and above the six-month period required for the completion of Indonesia's domestic rule-making process constitutes a reasonable period of time for implementation of the recommendations and rulings of the DSB in this case.[180]

---

[175] Arbitration Award, *US – Hot Rolled Steel*, para. 25.
[176] Arbitration Award, *EC – Hormones*, para. 26.
[177] Arbitration Award, *Korea – Alcoholic Beverages*, para. 42.
[178] Arbitration Award, *EC – Hormones*, para. 25. See also Arbitration Award, *Australia – Salmon*, para. 38.
[179] Arbitration Award, *Canada – Pharmaceutical Patents*, paras. 48–52.
[180] Arbitration Award, *Indonesia – Autos*, para. 24. See, however, Arbitration Award, *Chile – Alcoholic Beverages*, para. 45, in which the Arbitrator noted: 'It is not necessary to assume that the operation of Article 21.2 will essentially result in the application of "criteria" for the determination of "the reasonable period of time" … that would be "qualitatively" different for developed and for developing-country Members.'

The 'reasonable period of time for implementation' determined through arbitration to date ranges between six months (*Canada – Pharmaceutical Patents*) and fifteen months and one week (*EC – Bananas III*) from the date of adoption of the report(s) by the DSB.[181]

Note that, in more than four out of five disputes in which the responding party had to bring its disputed measure or legislation into conformity with WTO law, this was done within the 'reasonable period of time for implementation'. In most cases, therefore, the responding party implements the recommendations and rulings adopted by the DSB, in a timely and correct manner. The media and academic interest tends to focus on disputes in which this was, or is, not the case, such as *EC – Bananas III*, *EC – Hormones*, *US – FSC*, *US – Offset Act (Byrd Amendment)*, *Canada – Aircraft II* and *Brazil – Aircraft*. However, the overall record of compliance with the recommendations and rulings adopted by the DSB is quite positive and encouraging.

Questions and Assignments 3.15

What are the remedies for breach of WTO law? Must Members comply with the recommendations and rulings adopted by the DSB 'immediately' or within a 'reasonable period of time'? Who determines the 'reasonable period of time for implementation'? How is the 'reasonable period of time for implementation' determined?

3.3.8.2. Compensation and retaliation

Only the withdrawal (or amendment) of the WTO-inconsistent measure constitutes a final remedy for breach of WTO law. However, if a Member has not withdrawn or amended the WTO-inconsistent measure by the end of the 'reasonable period of time for implementation', the DSU provides for the possibility of recourse to *temporary* remedies:

- compensation: or
- suspension of concessions or other obligations.

Article 22.1 states, in relevant part:

> Compensation and the suspension of concessions or other obligations are temporary measures available in the event that the recommendations and rulings are not implemented within a reasonable period of time. However, neither compensation nor the suspension of concessions or other obligations is preferred to full implementation of a recommendation to bring a measure into conformity with the covered agreements.

The DSU leaves no doubt that compensation and/or the suspension of concessions or other obligations are *not* alternative remedies which Members may want to apply *instead of* complying with the recommendations and rulings.

---

[181] Arbitration Award, *Canada – Pharmaceutical Patents*, paras. 62–4; and Arbitration Award, *EC – Bananas III*, paras. 18–20.

Compensation and suspension of concessions are remedies which are only applied until implementation takes place.[182]

Compensation within the meaning of Article 22 of the DSU is voluntary and forward looking, i.e. both parties have to agree on the compensation and the compensation concerns only damages that will be suffered in the future. Compensation must be consistent with the covered agreements.[183] To date, parties have been able to agree on compensation in very few cases. In *Japan – Alcoholic Beverages II*, for example, the parties agreed on compensation which took the form of temporary, additional market access concessions for certain products of export interest to the original complainants.

The suspension of concessions or other obligations – commonly referred to as 'retaliation' – is very different in nature from compensation. There is no need for the parties to agree. When the 'reasonable period of time for implementation' has expired and the parties have not been able to agree on compensation, the injured party may request authorisation from the DSB to retaliate against the offending party by suspending concessions or other obligations with respect to that offending party. Since the DSB decides on such a request by reverse consensus, the granting of authorisation is automatic.[184]

Retaliation usually takes the form of a drastic increase in the customs duties on strategically selected products of export interest to the offending party.[185] Retaliation thus puts economic and political pressure on the offending party to comply with the recommendations and rulings. The producers and traders of the products hit by the increased duties – typically not beneficiaries of the WTO-inconsistent measure – will lobby furiously for the withdrawal or amendment of the WTO-inconsistent measure.

With regard to the concessions or other obligations that may be suspended, Article 22.3 provides, in relevant part:

> In considering what concessions or other obligations to suspend, the complaining party shall apply the following principles and procedures:
>
> a. the general principle is that the complaining party should first seek to suspend concessions or other obligations with respect to the same sector(s) as that in which the panel or Appellate Body has found a violation or other nullification or impairment;
> b. if that party considers that it is not practicable or effective to suspend concessions or other obligations with respect to the same sector(s), it may seek to suspend concessions or other obligations in other sectors under the same agreement;
> c. if that party considers that it is not practicable or effective to suspend concessions or other obligations with respect to other sectors under the same agreement, and that the circumstances are serious enough, it may seek to suspend concessions or other obligations under another covered agreement.[186]

---

[182] Articles 22.1 and 22.8 of the DSU.   [183] Article 22.1 of the DSU.

[184] See below, pp. 229–30.

[185] In the *EC – Bananas III* case, for example, the United States increased the customs duties on carefully selected products from the European Communities to 100 per cent *ad valorem*. See Panel Report, *EC – Regime for the Importation, Sale and Distribution of Bananas – Recourse to Article 21.5 by the European Communities*, WT/DS27/RW/EEC, dated 12 April 1999, para. 2.3. Retaliation can also take the form of an import quota on certain products from the Member that failed to implement the recommendations and rulings of the DSU.

[186] For definitions of e.g. the concept of 'sectors', and further rules, see Article 22.3(d) to (g) of the DSU.

In other words, if the violation of WTO law concerns an obligation regarding trade in goods, or regarding trade in financial services, or regarding the protection of patents, suspension of concessions or other obligations should first be sought in the *same* sector. If this is not 'practicable' or 'effective', then suspension may be sought in another sector or under another agreement.[187]

With regard to the level of suspension of concessions or other obligations, Article 22.4 of the DSU provides:

> The level of the suspension of concessions or other obligations authorized by the DSB shall be equivalent to the level of the nullification or impairment.

Disputes between the parties on the level of suspension or on whether the rules set out in Article 22.3 have been complied with are resolved through arbitration by the original panel.[188]

In the period from January 1995 to August 2004, the DSB authorised the taking of retaliatory measures in seven instances.[189] Particularly noteworthy is that in *US – FSC*, the DSB authorised the European Communities to suspend concessions or other obligations for the very significant amount of US$4 billion a year. However, in only four out of the seven instances in which the DSB authorised retaliation, the injured parties actually suspended concessions or other obligations. This was the case in *EC – Bananas III* (retaliation by the United States for an amount of US$191.4 million a year), in *EC – Hormones* (retaliation by the United States and Canada for an amount of US$116.8 million and C$11.3 million a year respectively) and in *US – FSC* (retaliation by the European Communities for an initial amount of US$4,043 million per year).

As noted above, retaliation measures usually take the form of a drastic *increase* in the customs duties (e.g. up to an additional 100 per cent *ad valorem*) on selected products of export interest to the offending party. In *US – FSC*, however, the European Communities opted for retaliation measures on selected products consisting of an additional customs duty of 5 per cent, increased each month by 1 per cent up to a maximum of 17 per cent.[190]

Retaliation measures can also take the form of the suspension of 'obligations' rather than the suspension of tariff 'concessions'. In *US – 1916 Act*, the European Communities requested the DSB to authorise the suspension of

---

[187] In *EC – Bananas III*, the DSB authorised Ecuador to suspend concessions or other obligations under another agreement (the *TRIPS Agreement*) than the agreements at issue in that dispute (the GATT 1994 and the GATS).

[188] See below, p. 283. On the problems that arise when the suspension takes the form of a suspension of obligations rather than a suspension of concessions, see Decision by the Arbitrators, *US – 1916 Act (Article 22.6 – US)*.

[189] See 'Update of WTO Dispute Settlement Cases', WT/DS/OV/21, dated 30 June 2004, www.wto.org. The DSB authorised retaliatory measures in *EC – Bananas III* (US and Ecuador), *EC – Hormones* (US and Canada), *Brazil – Aircraft* (Canada), *US – FSC* (EC) and *Canada – Aircraft* (Brazil).

[190] If the United States does not comply with the *US – FSC* recommendations and rulings in the meantime, the maximum additional customs duty of 17 per cent will be reached on 1 March 2005. At that time, the retaliation measures will be re-examined in the light of the then applicable circumstances. However, the need for this may not arise as, during the summer of 2004, the US legislature was close to reaching agreement on legislation repealing the WTO-inconsistent FSC/ETI. See www.europa.eu.int/comm/trade/issues/respectrules/dispute/pr270204_en.htm, visited on 31 August 2004.

the application of the obligations under GATT 1994 and the *Anti-Dumping Agreement* in order to adopt an equivalent regulation to the 1916 Act (i.e. the WTO-inconsistent US measure at issue) against imports from the United States[191]

Retaliation measures are *trade destructive* and the injured party imposing these measures is also negatively affected by these measures. In particular for developing-country Members, applying retaliation measures is often not a genuine option. In *EC – Bananas III*, Ecuador was authorised to apply retaliation measures for an amount of US$201.6 million a year but found it impossible to make use of this possibility without causing severe damage to its own economy. Doubts exist as to the effectiveness of retaliation as a temporary remedy for breach of WTO law. However, in *EC – Bananas III*, the retaliation measures imposed by the United States on the European Communities have arguably contributed to the eventual compliance by the European Communities with the recommendations and rulings in that dispute.

It is much debated whether a Member authorised to take retaliation measures may periodically (e.g. every six months) change the products or services on which these retaliation measures are applied. This issue, commonly referred to as the 'carousel' issue, arose because US legislation provides for a periodic shift in the focus of retaliation measures to maximise their impact. To date, the United States has not applied this legislation. Other Members have argued that a periodic change in the products and services 'hit' by the retaliation measure cannot be allowed since it would result in retaliation measures going beyond the level of nullification or impairment caused.[192]

Questions and Assignments 3.16

What are the rules applicable to compensation within the meaning of Article 22 of the DSU? What are the rules applicable to the suspension of concessions or other obligations? Has the suspension of concessions or other obligations been an effective temporary remedy for breach of WTO law?

3.3.8.3. *Other remedies for breach of WTO law*

Under general international law, a breach of an international obligation leads to responsibility entailing certain legal consequences. The first legal consequence of international responsibility is the obligation to cease the illegal conduct.[193]

---

[191] See WT/DS136/15, 11 January 2002. This EC regulation would allow the European Communities to impose on United States companies found to dump their products in the European Communities additional duties corresponding to three times the amount of the damage suffered by companies in the European Communities when certain specific intents analogous to those required under the 1916 Act are established. See also the Article 22.6 Arbitration on the level of the proposed suspension of obligations, Decision by the Arbitrators, *US – 1916 Act (Article 22.6 – US)*.
[192] See further below, pp. 290, 296.   [193] ILC Articles on State Responsibility, Part 2, Article 6.

According to the ILC Articles on State Responsibility, the injured State is further-more entitled to claim 'full reparation' in the form of:

- restitution in kind;
- compensation;
- satisfaction; and,
- assurances and guarantees of non-repetition.[194]

Restitution in kind means that the wrong-doing State has to re-establish the situation that existed before the illegal act was committed.[195] If restitution in kind is not available, compensation for the damage caused by the act must be paid. Compensation covers any economically assessable damage suffered by the injured State and may include interest, and also, under certain circum-stances, lost profits.[196] The DSU does not explicitly provide for the compensa-tion of damage suffered.[197] However, the question is whether the rules of general international law on State responsibility, as reflected in the ILC Articles, apply to breaches of WTO law. Are the only possible remedies for breaches of WTO law, the remedies explicitly provided for in the provisions of the DSU quoted above? Or, in the absence of a specific rule in the DSU on the compensation of damage suffered, is the general international law rule on compensation applicable? It could be argued that by providing a detailed set of rules regarding the legal consequences of a breach of WTO law, the DSU has contracted out of general economic law on State responsibility and the rule on compensation for damage suffered would thus not apply.[198] Most, if not all, WTO Members seem to share this view.

While controversial, in very specific circumstances, repayment of sums illegally received may also constitute a remedy for breach of WTO law. Article 4.7 of the *SCM Agreement* states that, if a measure is found to be a prohibited subsidy, the panel shall recommend that the subsidising Member withdraw the subsidy without delay. In *Australia – Automotive Leather II (Article 21.5 – US)*, the Panel examined whether the recommendation to 'withdraw the subsidy' in Article 4.7 of the *SCM Agreement* can properly be understood to encompass repayment. The Panel concluded that:

> in the circumstances of this case, repayment is necessary in order to "withdraw" the prohibited subsidies found to exist. As discussed above, we do not find any basis for repayment of anything less than the full subsidy. We therefore conclude that repay-ment in full of the prohibited subsidy is necessary in order to "withdraw the subsidy" in this case.

---

[194] *Ibid.*, Article 6 *bis.*

[195] *Ibid.*, Article 7. Restitution in kind is not required in a number of situations set out in this provision such as the situation in which the restitution would 'seriously jeopardize the political independence or economic stability of the State which has committed the internationally wrongful act, whereas the injured State would not be similarly affected if it did not obtain restitution in kind'.

[196] *Ibid.*, Article 8. See also P. Malanczuk, *Akehurst's Modern Introduction to International Law*, 7th revised edition. (Routledge, 1997), 269–71.

[197] Compensation under Article 22 of the DSU concerns only damages that will be suffered in the future. See above, pp. 220–1.

[198] See also above, p. 57.

> In our view, the required repayment does not include any interest component. We believe that withdrawal of the subsidy was intended by the drafters of the SCM Agreement to be a specific and effective remedy for violations of the prohibition in Article 3.1(a). However, we do not understand it to be a remedy intended to fully restore the *status quo ante* by depriving the recipient of the prohibited subsidy of the benefits it may have enjoyed in the past. Nor do we consider it to be a remedy intended to provide reparation or compensation in any sense. A requirement of interest would go beyond the requirement of repayment encompassed by the term "withdraw the subsidy", and is therefore, we believe, beyond any reasonable understanding of that term.[199]

The Panel insisted on the specificity of this ruling by stating:

> That a "retrospective" remedy might not be permissible under Article 19.1 of the DSU (a question which we do not here decide) does not preclude us from concluding, on the basis of the text of Article 4.7 of the SCM Agreement, that "withdraw the subsidy" is **not** limited to purely prospective action, but may encompass repayment of prohibited subsidies.[200]

The Panel's ruling that, at least with regard to prohibited subsidies, the DSU not only provides for a 'prospective' but also for a 'retrospective' remedy was criticised by many WTO Members, including *both* parties to this dispute.[201]

Questions and Assignments 3.17

Do WTO rules on remedies deviate from general international law on remedies? If so, does general international law nevertheless apply? In your opinion, should a Member that causes significant damage to the economy of another Member as a result of a breach of WTO law compensate this damage? Should customs duties which were imposed in violation of obligations under WTO law be repaid to the importer?

3.3.9. Special rules and assistance for developing-country Members

As noted above, developing-country Members have made much use of the WTO dispute settlement system. In 1995 and in every year since 2000, developing-country Members, as a group, have brought more disputes to the WTO than developed-country Members.[202] Brazil and India are among the biggest users of the system.

Developing-country Members have often used the WTO dispute settlement system to bring cases against the economic superpowers and have done so successfully. *US – Underwear*, a complaint by Costa Rica, is a well-known

---

[199] Panel Report, *Australia – Automotive Leather II (Article 21.5 – US)*, paras. 6.48 and 6.49.
[200] *Ibid.*, para. 6.42.
[201] The Panel Report was not appealed because the parties to this dispute, the United States and Australia, had agreed at the start of the Article 21.5 panel proceedings not to appeal the panel report.
[202] See below, pp. 284–6.

example of a successful 'David versus Goliath' use of the system. Developing-country Members have also used the system against other developing-country Members. Examples of such use of the system are *Chile – Price Band System*, a complaint by Argentina, and *Egypt – Import Prohibition on Canned Tuna with Soybean Oil*, a complaint by Thailand.

Thus far, least-developed-country Members have used the WTO dispute settlement system only once. In February 2004, Bangladesh requested consultations with India on the imposition of anti-dumping duties by India on batteries from Bangladesh.[203] To date, the WTO dispute settlement system has never been used 'against' least-developed-country Members. Note in this respect that Article 24.1 of the DSU requires Members to 'exercise due restraint' in using the WTO dispute settlement system in disputes involving a least-developed-country Member.

The DSU contains a number of other provisions providing for special treatment or consideration for developing-country Members involved in WTO dispute settlement. This section examines these provisions. This section also discusses the legal assistance available to developing-country Members involved in WTO dispute settlement.

3.3.9.1. Special rules for developing-country Members

The DSU recognises the difficulties developing-country Members may encounter when they are involved in WTO dispute settlement. Therefore, the DSU contains some special rules for developing-country Members. Such special DSU rules are found in Article 3.12 (regarding the application of the 1966 Decision),[204] Article 4.10 (regarding consultations), Article 8.10 (regarding the composition of panels), Article 12.10 (regarding consultations and the time to prepare and present arguments), Article 12.11 (regarding the content of panel reports), Article 24 (regarding least-developed countries) and Article 27 (assistance of the WTO Secretariat). For the most part, however, these special rules have not been used much to date. Developing-country Members criticise the fact that many of these provisions are merely hortatory in nature. A number of these provisions will be discussed in greater detail below.[205]

---

[203] Request for Consultations by Bangladesh, *India – Anti-Dumping Measure on Batteries from Bangladesh*, WT/DS306/1, dated 2 February 2004.

[204] Decision of 5 April 1966 on Procedures under Article XXIII, BISD 14S/18. Article 3.12 of the DSU allows a developing-country Member that brings a complaint against a developed-country Member to invoke the provisions of the Decision of 5 April 1966 of the GATT Contracting Parties. These provisions may be invoked as an 'alternative' to the provisions contained in Articles 4, 5, 6 and 12 of the DSU. To date, no developing country has invoked the provisions of the 1966 Decision. The reason for this lack of enthusiasm for the provisions of the 1966 Decision is undoubtedly that the DSU provisions afford developing country complaining parties treatment at least as favourable as, if not more favourable than, the treatment afforded by the 1966 Decision.

[205] See below, pp. 227, 235, 242, 259, 263.

3.3.9.2. *Legal assistance for developing-country Members*

Many developing-country Members do not have the 'in-house' legal expertise to participate effectively in WTO dispute settlement. As discussed above, since the Appellate Body ruling in *EC – Bananas III*, it is clear that WTO Members can be assisted and represented by private counsel in WTO dispute settlement proceedings. The Appellate Body noted in its ruling:

> that representation by counsel of a government's own choice may well be a matter of particular significance – especially for developing-country Members – to enable them to participate fully in dispute settlement proceedings.[206]

However, assistance and representation by private counsel has its costs, and these costs may be quite burdensome for developing-country Members.

The WTO Secretariat assists all Members in respect of dispute settlement when they so request. However, the DSU recognises that there may be a need to provide additional legal advice and assistance to developing-country Members.[207] To meet this additional need, Article 27.2 of the DSU requires that the WTO Secretariat make qualified legal experts available to help any developing-country Member that so requests. The extent to which the Secretariat can assist developing-country Members is, however, severely limited by the requirement that the Secretariat's experts give assistance in a manner 'ensuring the continued impartiality of the Secretariat'.[208] The experts cannot therefore act on behalf of a developing-country Member in a dispute with another Member and their assistance is necessarily limited to the preliminary phases of a dispute.

Effective legal assistance for developing-country Members, in dispute settlement proceedings, is given by the Geneva-based Advisory Centre on WTO Law (ACWL). The ACWL is an independent, intergovernmental organisation (fully independent from the WTO), which functions essentially as a law office specialising in WTO law, providing legal services and training exclusively to developing country and economy-in-transition Members of the ACWL *and* all least-developed countries. The ACWL provides support at all stages of WTO dispute settlement proceedings at discounted rates. The ACWL currently has thirty-two members: nine developed countries and twenty-three developing countries and economies-in-transition.[209]

On the occasion of the official opening of the ACWL on 5 October 2001, Mike Moore, then WTO Director-General, said:

> The International Court of Justice has a small fund out of which costs of legal assistance can be paid for countries who need such help. But today marks the first time a true legal aid centre has been established within the international legal system, with a view to combating the unequal possibilities of access to international justice as between States.[210]

---

[206] Appellate Body Report, *EC – Bananas III*, para. 12.   [207] Article 27.2 of the DSU.
[208] Article 27.2, final sentence, of the DSU. Moreover, the WTO Secretariat has only two part-time experts available for this task.
[209] For up-to-date information on the ACWL, see www.acwl.ch.
[210] See www.acwl.ch, visited on 19 July 2003.

At the same occasion, Claus-Dieter Ehlermann, then Chairman of the Appellate Body, noted:

> By providing low-cost, high-quality legal services, the Centre will enable the greater participation of developing-country Members. The Centre will, therefore, benefit its Members. It will benefit panels, the Appellate Body, and the WTO. Ultimately, the Centre will benefit the "rules-based" multilateral trading system, and strengthen the notion that the dispute settlement system of the WTO is available to the economically weak as much as it is available to the economically strong.[211]

In the summer of 2001, the ACWL, for the first time, assisted a WTO developing-country Member in a dispute settlement procedure when it assisted Pakistan in the Appellate Body proceedings in *US – Cotton Yarn*. A significant success for the ACWL thus far was the *EC – Sardines* dispute in which the ACWL represented Peru, the complainant in this dispute.

Questions and Assignments 3.18

Does the DSU take the particular situation of developing-country Members into account? Do developing-country Members involved in WTO dispute settlement benefit from legal assistance? By whom and under what conditions is this assistance granted?

3.4. INSTITUTIONS OF WTO DISPUTE SETTLEMENT

Among the institutions involved in WTO dispute settlement, one can distinguish between *political institutions*, such as the Dispute Settlement Body, and independent, *judicial-type institutions*, such as the dispute settlement panels and the standing Appellate Body. While the WTO has entrusted the adjudication of disputes, at the first instance to panels, and at the appellate level to the Appellate Body, the Dispute Settlement Body continues to play an active role in the WTO dispute settlement system. This section briefly examines the Dispute Settlement Body, the panels and the Appellate Body.

3.4.1. The Dispute Settlement Body

The WTO dispute settlement system is administered by the Dispute Settlement Body (DSB).[212] Article IV:3 of the *WTO Agreement* states, in relevant part:

> The General Council shall convene as appropriate to discharge the responsibilities of the Dispute Settlement Body provided for in the Dispute Settlement Understanding. The Dispute Settlement Body may have its own chairman and shall establish such rules of procedure as it deems necessary for the fulfilment of those responsibilities.

---

[211] *Ibid.*   [212] Article 2.1 of the DSU.

As already noted in Chapter 2, the DSB is an emanation, or an *alter ego*, of the WTO's General Council.[213] When the General Council administers the WTO dispute settlement system, it convenes and acts as the DSB. As the General Council, the DSB is composed of ambassador-level diplomats of all WTO Members.[214]

With respect to the functions of the DSB, Article 2.1 of the DSU broadly defines these functions as the administration of the dispute settlement system and then specifies them by stating:

> Accordingly, the DSB shall have the authority to establish panels, adopt panel and Appellate Body reports, maintain surveillance of implementation of rulings and recommendations, and authorize suspension of concessions and other obligations under the covered agreements.

However, the administration of the dispute settlement system is not limited to these functions. They also include, for example, the appointment of the Members of the Appellate Body[215] and the adoption of the Rules of Conduct for WTO dispute settlement.[216]

Article 2.4 of the DSU stipulates that, where the DSU provides for the DSB to take a decision, such a decision is always taken by consensus.[217] It is important to note, however, that, for some key decisions, such as:

- the decision on the establishment of panels,
- the adoption of panel and Appellate Body reports and
- the authorisation of suspension of concession and other obligations,

the consensus requirement is in fact a 'reverse' or 'negative' consensus requirement.[218] With respect to the DSB's decision to adopt an Appellate Body report for example, Article 17.14 of the DSU states, in relevant part:

> An Appellate Body report shall be adopted by the DSB ... unless the DSB decides by consensus not to adopt the Appellate Body report within 30 days following its circulation to the Members.

The 'reverse' consensus requirement means that the DSB is deemed to take a decision unless there is a consensus among WTO Members *not* to take that decision. Since there will usually be at least one Member with a strong interest in the establishment of a panel, the adoption of the panel and/or Appellate Body reports or the authorisation to suspend concessions, it is unlikely that there will be a consensus *not* to adopt these

---

[213] See above, p. 126.
[214] See Article IV:2 of the WTO Agreement. Where the DSB administers the dispute settlement provisions of a WTO plurilateral trade agreement, only those WTO Members that are parties to that agreement may participate in the decisions or actions taken by the DSB with respect to that dispute. See Article 2.1 of the DSU.
[215] See below, p. 246.   [216] See above, pp. 215–16.
[217] Footnote 1 to the DSU states: 'The DSB shall be deemed to have decided by consensus on a matter submitted for its consideration, if no Member, present at the meeting of the DSB when the decision is taken, formally objects to the proposed decision.'
[218] See Articles 6.1, 16.4, 17.14 and 22.6 of the DSU. Other decisions of the DSB, such as the appointment of the Members of the Appellate Body, are taken by 'normal' consensus.

Figure 3.4 Agenda of the DSB meeting of 18 March 2003[219]

1. Surveillance of implementation of recommendations adopted by the DSB
    (a) United States – Section 110(5) of the US Copyright Act: Status report by the
        United States
    (b) United States – Anti-Dumping Act of 1916: Status report by the United States
    (c) United States – Section 211 Omnibus Appropriations Act of 1998: Status report by the
        United States
    (d) United States – Anti-dumping measures on certain hot-rolled steel products from Japan: Status
        report by the United States
2. United States – Subsidies on upland cotton
    (a) Request for the establishment of a panel by Brazil
3. Canada – Measures relating to exports of wheat and treatment of imported grain
    (a) Request for the establishment of a panel by the United States
4. Canada – Export credits and loan guarantees for regional aircraft
    (a) Recourse by Brazil to Article 22.7 of the DSU and Article 4.10 of the SCM Agreement
5. Proposed nomination for the indicative list of governmental and non-governmental panelists
6. United States – Definitive safeguard measures on imports of circular welded carbon quality line pipe
   from Korea
    (a) Statement by the United States

decisions.[220] As a result, decision-making by the DSB on these matters is, for all practical purposes, automatic and a matter of course. Furthermore, it should be noted that the DSU provides for strict timeframes within which decisions on these matters must be taken.[221]

The DSB meets as often as necessary to carry out its functions within the timeframes provided in the DSU. In practice, the DSB has one scheduled meeting per month and, in addition, special meetings convened when the need for a meeting arises. In 2003, the DSB met twenty-two times.[222]

By way of example, consider the agenda of the DSB meeting of 18 March 2003, as shown in Figure 3.4.

Meetings of the DSB are always held in Geneva, usually last a few hours and are well attended. About fifty WTO Members will normally attend, and these Members will, as a rule, be represented by their highest-ranking resident diplomat, the Permanent Representative of that Member in Geneva. In February 2004, Ambassador Amina Mohamed of Kenya was elected as Chairperson for 2004. With minor deviations regarding Observers (Chapter IV) and the Chairperson (Chapter V), the Rules of Procedure for the General Council apply to the meetings of the DSB.

---

[219] See WT/DSB/M/145, dated 7 May 2003.
[220] Note, however, that, in very exceptional circumstances, it is possible that no Member puts the adoption of the report on the agenda of the DSB and that the report therefore remains unadopted. This happened with the Panel Report, *EC – Bananas III (Article 21.5 – EC)*, circulated on 12 April 1999.
[221] For example, the decision to adopt an Appellate Body report shall be taken within thirty days following its circulation to the Members (see Article 17.14 of the DSU). If there is no meeting of the DSB scheduled during this period, such a meeting shall be held for this purpose (see footnote 8 to the DSU).
[222] *WTO Annual* Report (2004), 87. See www.wto.org/english/res_e/booksp_e/anrep04_e.pdf, visited on 31 August 2004.

As a result of the fact that the DSB takes the core dispute settlement decisions referred to above by reverse consensus, the DSB's impact on, and influence over, WTO dispute settlement is limited. The involvement of the DSB is, to a large extent, a legacy of the past in which trade dispute settlement was more diplomatic and political than judicial in nature.[223] Nevertheless, the involvement of the DSB in each major step of a dispute fulfils two useful purposes:

- it keeps all WTO Members directly informed of WTO dispute settlement; and
- it gives WTO Members a designated political forum in which issues arising from the use of the dispute settlement system can be debated.

Questions and Assignments 3.19

What are the functions of the DSB in the WTO dispute settlement system? Is it common for political institutions to play an active role in dispute settlement systems? Does the DSB play a significant role in WTO dispute settlement or is its role more a 'symbolic' one?

3.4.2. WTO dispute settlement panels

The actual adjudication of disputes brought to the WTO is carried out, at the first-instance level, by *ad hoc* dispute settlement panels. This section discusses:

- the request for the establishment of a panel;
- the establishment of a panel;
- the composition of a panel;
- a panel's terms of reference;
- the standard of review applied by panels;
- the exercise of judicial economy by panels;
- characteristics of a panel report; and
- the role of the WTO Secretariat in supporting panels.

3.4.2.1. *Request for the establishment of a panel*

WTO dispute settlement panels are not standing bodies. They are *ad hoc* bodies established for the purpose of adjudicating a particular dispute and are dissolved once they have accomplished this task. The complainant must request the DSB to establish a panel. Pursuant to Article 6.2 of the DSB, the 'request for

---

[223] See above, pp. 176–80.

the establishment of a panel', also referred to as the 'panel request', must be made in writing and must:

- indicate *whether* consultations were held;
- identify the *specific* measures at issue; and
- provide a brief summary of the legal basis of the complaint *sufficient* to present the problem clearly.[224]

In *EC – Bananas III*, the Appellate Body found that:

> It is important that a panel request be sufficiently precise for two reasons: first, it often forms the basis for the terms of reference of the panel pursuant to Article 7 of the DSU; and, second, it informs the defending party and the third parties of the legal basis of the complaint.[225]

Whether or not the 'specific measure at issue' is sufficiently identified in the panel request depends on the ability of the respondent to defend itself given the actual reference to the measure at issue. If the respondent can reasonably be found to have received adequate notice of the measure at issue, that measure is then regarded as sufficiently identified.[226]

With regard to the requirement that the panel request must 'provide a brief summary of the legal basis of the complaint sufficient to present the problem clearly', the Appellate Body noted that the DSU demands only a brief summary of the legal basis of the complaint.[227] The summary must, however, be one 'sufficient to present the problem clearly'.[228] The claims, but not the arguments, must all be specified sufficiently in the panel request.[229] In *EC – Bananas III*, the Appellate Body found that, in view of the particular circumstances of that case, the listing of the articles of the agreements alleged to have been breached satisfied the minimum requirements of the DSU.[230] In *Korea – Dairy*, however, the Appellate Body noted that, where the articles listed establish not one single, distinct obligation but, rather, multiple obligations, the listing of articles of an agreement, in and of itself, may fall short of the standard of

---

[224] Article 6.2 of the DSU   [225] Appellate Body Report, *EC – Bananas III*, para. 142.

[226] See Panel Report, *Japan – Film*, para. 10.8; Panel Report, *Argentina – Footwear (EC)*, para. 8.35 (on subsidiary or implementing measures or later modifications to measures which were not explicitly identified); and Appellate Body Report, *EC – Computer Equipment*, para. 70 (on the identification of the products to which the measure at issue applied). The 'measure' referred to in Article 6.2 of the DSU must be a governmental measure. On the issue of whether a private action can be classified as a governmental measure, see below, pp. 351–2, and Panel Report, *Japan – Film*, paras. 10.55–10.56. With regard to the issue of 'terminated measures', see Panel Report, *Japan – Film*, para. 10.58; Panel Report, *Argentina – Textiles and Apparel*, paras. 6.14–6.15 (on the danger of a re-introduction of the terminated measure); and Panel Report, *EC – Poultry*, paras. 250–2 (on terminated measures with lingering effects).

[227] Appellate Body Report, *Korea – Dairy*, para. 120.   [228] *Ibid*.

[229] Appellate Body Report, *EC – Bananas III*, para. 143. Note that the Appellate Body ruled in *EC – Tariff Preferences* that in the particular circumstances of that case 'a complaining party challenging a measure taken pursuant to the Enabling Clause must allege more than mere inconsistency with Article I:1 of the GATT 1994, for to do only that would not convey the "legal basis of the complaint sufficient to present the problem clearly".' See Appellate Body Report, *EC – Tariff Preferences*, para. 110. See also above, p. 212.

[230] Appellate Body Report, *EC – Bananas III*, para. 141.

Article 6.2 of the DSU. The Appellate Body concluded that the question of whether the mere listing of the articles suffices must be examined on a case-by-case basis. Furthermore, it ruled that, in resolving that question:

> we take into account whether the ability of the respondent to defend itself was prejudiced, given the actual course of the panel proceedings, by the fact that the panel request simply listed the provisions claimed to have been violated.[231]

The Appellate Body thus set forth the standard of the 'ability of the respondent to defend itself'. In *EC – Tube or Pipe Fittings*, the Panel examined whether the ability to defend itself was prejudiced by an alleged lack of specificity in the text of the panel request. The Panel found that it was evident from the participation of the European Communities in asserting its views in various phases of the panel proceedings that the abilitiy of the European Communities to defend itself had not been prejudiced over the course of the proceedings.[232]

Note that Article 6.2 of the DSU requires that the *claims* must be specified in the panel request. The panel request must not, and typically will not, specify the arguments supporting the claims. The arguments are set out and progressively clarified in the written submissions to the panel and at the panel meetings.[233]

Questions and Assignments 3.20

What are the requirements that a panel request must meet? Why is it important that a panel request is sufficiently precise? How does one determine whether a panel request is sufficiently precise?

3.4.2.2. Establishment of a panel

The panel is established *at the latest* at the DSB meeting following the meeting at which the request for the establishment first appeared as an item on the agenda. At this stage, the panel is established *unless* the DSB decides by consensus *not* to establish a panel ('reverse consensus').[234] Since this is unlikely, the establishment of a panel by the DSB is 'quasi-automatic'. A panel can be, and occasionally is, established at the first DSB meeting at which the panel request is considered. At this meeting, the establishment of the panel requires a 'normal consensus' decision of the DSB. The panel can thus only be established at the first DSB meeting if the respondent does not object to its establishment. Often, however, the respondent objects to the establishment of the panel at the first DSB meeting, arguing that it 'hopes' and 'believes' that a mutually agreed solution to the dispute can still be found.

---

[231] Appellate Body Report, *Korea – Dairy*, para. 127.
[232] See Panel Report, *EC – Tube or Pipe Fittings*, paras. 7.22–7.24.
[233] See Appellate Body Report, *EC – Bananas III*, paras. 141–3.
[234] Article 6.1 of the DSU. See also above, pp. 229–30.

The decision of the DSB on the establishment of a panel is usually preceded by short statements by the parties to the dispute setting forth their respective positions. The routine decisions to establish a panel very seldom give rise to much debate within the DSB. A practice has evolved whereby, immediately after the DSB's decision to establish the panel (or within ten days of this decision), other Members may notify their interest in the dispute and reserve their third party rights.

Where more than one Member requests the establishment of a panel related to the same matter, Article 9.1 of the DSU states that:

> a single panel may be established to examine these complaints taking into account the rights of all Members concerned.

Whenever feasible, a single panel *should* be established to examine such complaints.[235]

In *US – Steel Safeguards*, the DSB at first established multiple panels to hear and decide on similar complaints by the European Communities, Japan, Korea, China, Switzerland, Norway, New Zealand and Brazil. Subsequently, the United States and the complainants reached an agreement on the establishment of a single panel, under Article 9.1, to hear the matter at issue. The United States, however, requested that the Panel issue eight separate reports rather than one single report.[236] On the basis of Article 9.2, which explicitly provides for the right of parties to have separate reports, the Panel decided 'to issue its Reports in the form of one document constituting eight Panel Reports' with a common cover page and a common descriptive part.

Note that in *US – Offset Act (Byrd Amendment)* concerning complaints by Australia, Brazil, Chile, the European Communities, India, Indonesia, Japan, Korea and Thailand, the Appellate Body upheld the Panel's refusal to issue, at the request of the United States, a separate report for the complaint brought by Mexico. The United States had made its request for a separate report two months after the issuance of the descriptive part of the Panel report and more than seven months after the Panel had been composed. As the Appellate Body observed, Article 9.2 of the DSU refers to the rights of *all* the parties to the dispute and the Panel correctly based its decision on an assessment of the rights of *all* the parties.[237]

---

[235] Article 9.1 of the DSU. For further rules on single panels, see Article 9.2 of the DSU. For rules on multiple panels examining complaints relating to the same matter (for example, the panels in *EC – Hormones* and *US – 1916 Act*), see Article 9.3 of the DSU.

[236] The United States argued that by doing so it wanted to protect its rights under the DSU, including the right to seek a solution with one or more of the complainants without adoption of a report or without an appeal.

[237] See Appellate Body Report, *US – Offset Act (Byrd Amendment)*, paras. 305–17. The Appellate Body also considered that the United States was not claiming that it suffered any prejudice as a result of the Panel's denial of its request.

Questions and Assignments 3.21

Who establishes a panel? How are panels established? What happens in case more than one Member requests the establishment of a panel related to the same matter?

3.4.2.3. *Composition of a panel*

As set forth in Article 8.5 of the DSU, panels are normally composed of three persons. The parties to the dispute can agree, within ten days from the establishment of the panel, to a panel composed of five panellists.[238] However, to date, this has never occurred.

Pursuant to Article 8.1 of the DSU, panels must be composed of well-qualified governmental and/or non-governmental individuals. By way of guidance, the DSU indicates that these individuals can be:

> persons who have served on or presented a case to a panel, served as a representative of a Member or of a contracting party to GATT 1947 or as a representative to the Council or Committee of any covered agreement or its predecessor agreement, or in the Secretariat, taught or published on international trade law or policy, or served as a senior trade policy official of a Member.[239]

Article 8.2 of the DSU stipulates that panel members should be selected with a view to ensuring the independence of the members, providing a sufficiently diverse background and a wide spectrum of experience. Nationals of Members that are parties or third parties to the dispute shall not serve on a panel concerned with that dispute unless the parties to the dispute agree otherwise.[240] While this is not common, parties have in some cases agreed on a panellist who is a national of one of the parties. When a dispute occurs between a developing-country Member and a developed-country Member, the panel shall, if the developing-country Member so requests, include at least one panellist from a developing-country Member.[241] In many panels dealing with disputes involving a developing-country Member, at least one of the panellists has been a national of a developing-country Member.

Panellists are predominantly current or retired government trade officials with a background in law. Many among them are Geneva-based diplomats of WTO Members not involved in the dispute before the panel. The DSU explicitly provides, however, that panellists shall serve in their individual capacities and not as government representatives, nor as representatives of any organisation. Members shall therefore not give government officials serving as panellists any instructions nor seek to influence them as individuals with regard to matters before a panel.[242] In recent years, there has been an increase in the

---

[238] Article 8.5 of the DSU.   [239] Article 8.1 of the DSU.   [240] Article 8.3 of the DSU.
[241] Article 8.10 of the DSU.   [242] Article 8.9 of the DSU.

number of academics and legal practitioners serving as panellists. It is also significant that at least half of the panellists have already served on a GATT or WTO panel before their selection.

Panellists' expenses, including travel and subsistence allowances, are covered by the WTO budget. Non-governmental individuals serving as panellists receive, in addition to travel and subsistence allowances, a fee for their service.[243] However, this fee is low compared to fees ordinarily paid in international arbitration or the fees of most of the private lawyers representing Members in WTO dispute settlement proceedings.

Once a panel is established by the DSB, the parties to the dispute will try to reach an agreement on the composition of the panel. The Secretariat shall propose nominations for the panel to the parties to the dispute. The DSU requires the parties to the dispute not to oppose nominations except for compelling reasons.[244] However, parties often reject the nominations initially proposed by the WTO Secretariat without much justification. In practice, the composition of the panel is often a difficult and contentious process, which may take many weeks. If the parties are unable to agree on the composition of the panel within twenty days of its establishment by the DSB, either party *may* request the Director-General of the WTO to determine the composition of the panel.[245] Within ten days of such a request, the Director-General shall – after consulting the parties to the dispute and the Chair of the DSB and of the relevant council or committee – appoint the panellists whom he considers most appropriate. In recent years, the Director-General has determined the composition of about half of the panels.

To assist in the selection of panellists, the Secretariat maintains a list of governmental and non-governmental individuals possessing the required qualifications to serve as panellists.[246] Members periodically suggest names of individuals for inclusion on this list, and those names are added to the list upon approval by the DSB. However, this list is merely *indicative* and individuals not included in this list may be selected as panellists. In fact, most first-time panellists were not on the list at the time of their selection.

Questions and Assignments 3.22

Who decides on the composition of panels? Describe the relevant procedure. What are the required qualifications for a panellist? Is it, in your opinion, inappropriate for a national of a party or third party to the dispute to sit on the panel?

---

[243] Article 8.11 of the DSU.   [244] Article 8.6 of the DSU.
[245] Article 8.7 of the DSU. Often, however, parties will allow more time to reach an agreement on the composition of a panel instead of requesting the Director-General to decide on the composition.
[246] Article 8.4 of the DSU.

3.4.2.4. *Terms of reference of a panel*

Article 7.1 of the DSU states that, unless the parties agree otherwise within twenty days from the establishment of the panel, a panel is given the following *standard* terms of reference:

> To examine in the light of the relevant provisions in (name of the covered agreement(s) cited by the parties to the dispute), the matter referred to the DSB by (name of party) in document ... and make such findings as will assist the DSB in making the recommendations or in giving the rulings provided for in that/those agreement(s).

The document referred to in these standard terms of reference is usually the panel request. Hence, a claim falls within the panel's terms of reference, i.e. within the mandate of the panel, only if that claim is identified in the panel request. In *EC–Tube or Pipe Fittings*, the Panel found that Brazil's claims under Articles 6.9, 6.13, 9.3 and 12.1 of the *Anti-Dumping Agreement* were not within its terms of reference as these provisions 'do not appear in the list of provisions' in the panel request, 'nor are they referred to in the ensuing description of allegations in that document'.[247]

As the Appellate Body stated in *Brazil – Desiccated Coconut*, the terms of reference of the panel are important for two reasons:

> First, terms of reference fulfil an important due process objective – they give the parties and third parties sufficient information concerning the claims at issue in the dispute in order to allow them an opportunity to respond to the complainant's case. Second, they establish the jurisdiction of the panel by defining the precise claims at issue in the dispute.[248]

A panel may consider only those claims that it has authority to consider under its terms of reference.[249] Therefore, a panel is *bound* by its terms of reference.[250]

Within twenty days of the establishment of the panel, the parties to the dispute *can* agree on special terms of reference for the panel.[251] However, this rarely occurs.[252] In establishing a panel, the DSB may authorise its Chairperson to draw up the terms of reference of the panel in consultation with the parties to the dispute.[253] However, if no agreement on special terms of reference is reached within twenty days of the establishment of the panel, the panel shall have standard terms of reference.

Note that, in case of a broadly phrased panel request, it may be necessary to examine the complainant's submissions closely to determine precisely which claims have been made and fall under the terms of reference of the panel.[254]

---

[247] Panel Report, *EC – Tube or Pipe Fittings*, para. 7.14. Note also the Panel in *Argentina – Poultry*, which found that 'there is no reference to this claim in Brazil's Request of Establishment of this Panel' and therefore concluded that this claim falls outside its terms of reference. See Panel Report, *Argentina – Poultry*, para. 7.157.

[248] Appellate Body Report, *Brazil – Desiccated Coconut*, 186.

[249] Appellate Body Report, *India – Patents (US)*, para. 92. A panel cannot assume jurisdiction that it does not have (*ibid.*).

[250] *Ibid.*, para. 93.   [251] Article 7.1 of the DSU.   [252] See, e.g. *Brazil – Desiccated Coconut*.

[253] Article 7.3 of the DSU.   [254] Appellate Body Report, *Chile – Price Band System*, para. 165.

Questions and Assignments 3.23

What are, and where do we find, the terms of reference of a panel? Why are the terms of reference of a panel important?

3.4.2.5. *Standard of review for panels*

A panel is called upon to review the consistency of a challenged measure with WTO law. Both the measure at issue and the relevant provisions of WTO law allegedly violated are determined by the terms of reference of the panel. But what is the standard of review a panel has to apply in reviewing the WTO consistency of the challenged measure? Article 11 of the DSU stipulates:

> The function of panels is to assist the DSB in discharging its responsibilities under this Understanding and the covered agreements. Accordingly, a panel should make an objective assessment of the matter before it, including an objective assessment of the facts of the case and the applicability of and conformity with the relevant covered agreements, and make such other findings as will assist the DSB in making the recommendations or in giving the rulings provided for in the covered agreements.

In *EC – Hormones*, the Appellate Body noted that Article 11 of the DSU:

> articulates with great succinctness but with sufficient clarity the appropriate standard of review for panels in respect of both the ascertainment of facts and the legal characterization of such facts under the relevant agreements.[255]

As far as fact-finding is concerned, the appropriate standard is neither a *de novo* review of the facts nor 'total deference' to the factual findings of national authorities. Rather, pursuant to Article 11 of the DSU, panels have 'to make an objective assessment of the facts'. With regard to legal questions, i.e. the consistency or inconsistency of a Member's measure with the specified provisions of the relevant agreement, Article 11 imposes the same standard on panels, i.e. 'to make an objective assessment' of the applicability of and conformity with the relevant covered agreement.

In a number of appeals from panel reports, the Appellate Body addressed the question of whether a panel had failed to discharge its duty under Article 11 of the DSU 'to make an objective assessment of the matter before it'. Certain statements made by the Appellate Body indicate that the threshold for a finding that a panel has not made an objective assessment of the matter is high. In *EC – Hormones*, the Appellate Body explained that:

> not every error in the appreciation of the evidence (although it may give rise to a question of law) may be characterized as a failure to make an objective assessment of the facts ... The duty to make an objective assessment of the facts is, among other things, an obligation to consider the evidence presented to a panel and to make factual findings on the basis of that evidence. The deliberate disregard of, or refusal to consider, the evidence submitted to a panel is incompatible with a panel's duty to

---

[255] Appellate Body Report, *EC – Hormones*, para. 116. See Panel Report, *US – Underwear*, paras. 7.10, 7.12 and 7.13; and Panel Report, *US – Wool Shirts and Blouses*, paras. 7.16 and 7.17.

make an objective assessment of the facts. The wilful distortion or misrepresentation of the evidence put before a panel is similarly inconsistent with an objective assessment of the facts. "Disregard" and "distortion" and "misrepresentation" of the evidence, in their ordinary signification in judicial and quasi-judicial processes, imply not simply an error of judgment in the appreciation of evidence but rather an egregious error that calls into question the good faith of a panel.[256]

According to the Appellate Body in *EC – Hormones*, a panel must make an *egregious* error in the assessment of the evidence before the Appellate Body will come to the conclusion that the panel failed to make an objective assessment of the facts. As the Appellate Body noted in *EC – Poultry*:

An allegation that a panel has failed to conduct the "objective assessment of the matter before it" required by Article 11 of the DSU is a very serious allegation. Such an allegation goes to the very core of the integrity of the WTO dispute settlement process itself.[257]

The party losing a case may be tempted to argue that the panel failed to make an objective assessment. However, as the Appellate Body observed in *Korea – Alcoholic Beverages*, it is not an error, let alone an egregious error, for a panel to fail to accord to the evidence the weight that one of the parties believes should be accorded to it.[258]

In *US – Wheat Gluten*, the Appellate Body considered the following:

in view of the distinction between the respective roles of the Appellate Body and panels, we have taken care to emphasize that a panel's appreciation of the evidence falls, in principle, "within the *scope of the panel's discretion as the trier of facts*". In assessing the panel's appreciation of the evidence, we cannot base a finding of inconsistency under Article 11 simply on the conclusion that we might have reached a different factual finding from the one the panel reached. Rather, we must be satisfied that the panel has exceeded the bounds of its discretion, as the trier of facts, in its appreciation of the evidence. As is clear from previous appeals, we will not interfere lightly with the panel's exercise of its discretion.[259]

[Emphasis added]

For the Appellate Body to find that a panel has acted inconsistently with Article 11 of the DSU, it must be satisfied that the panel has *exceeded the bounds of its discretion* in adjudicating the facts. To date, the Appellate Body found that the Panel had acted inconsistently with its obligation under Article 11 in, for example, *US – Wheat Gluten* and *US – Lamb*.[260]

In *US – Steel Safeguards*, the Appellate Body noted that a challenge under Article 11 of the DSU 'must not be vague or ambiguous', but, rather, must be clearly articulated and substantiated with specific arguments.[261] A claim that a panel failed to conduct an objective assessment of the matter is, according to the Appellate Body:

---

[256] Appellate Body Report, *EC – Hormones*, para. 133. See also Appellate Body Report, *Japan –Agricultural Products II*, para. 141.
[257] Appellate Body Report, *EC – Poultry*, para. 133.
[258] Appellate Body Report, *Korea – Alcoholic Beverages*, para. 164.
[259] Appellate Body Report, *US – Wheat Gluten*, para. 151.
[260] *Ibid.*, paras. 161–3; and Appellate Body Report, *US – Lamb*, paras. 147–9.
[261] See Appellate Body Report, *US – Steel Safeguards*, para. 498.

> not to be made lightly, or merely as a subsidiary argument or claim in support of a claim of a panel's failure to construe or apply correctly a particular provision of a covered agreement.[262]

A claim of inconsistency with Article 11 of the DSU 'must stand by itself and be substantiated, as such, and not as subsidiary to another alleged violation'.[263]

Article 11 of the DSU sets forth the appropriate standard of review for panels for all but one of the covered agreements. The only exception is the *Anti-Dumping Agreement* in which a specific provision, Article 17.6, sets out a special standard of review for disputes arising under that Agreement.[264]

Questions and Assignments 3.24

What is the standard of review a panel has to apply in reviewing the WTO consistency of a measure challenged by the complainant? When does a panel *not* meet the requirement of Article 11 to make an objective assessment of the matter before it?

3.4.2.6. Judicial economy and acts ultra petita

Complainants often assert numerous violations under various agreements. It is well-established case law that panels are not required to examine each and every one of the legal claims that a complainant makes. The aim of dispute settlement is to secure a positive solution to a dispute. The Appellate Body in *US – Wool Shirts and Blouses* ruled that panels:

> need only address those claims which must be addressed in order to resolve the matter in issue in the dispute.[265]

A panel has discretion to determine the claims it must address in order to resolve the dispute between the parties effectively.[266] The Appellate Body has, however, cautioned panels to be careful when exercising judicial economy. To provide only a partial resolution of the matter at issue may be false judicial economy since the unanswered issues may well give rise to a new dispute.[267] As the Appellate Body stated in *Australia – Salmon*, a panel has to address:

---

[262] *Ibid.*   [263] *Ibid.*

[264] Article 17.6(i) requires a panel in a dumping case to examine whether the establishment and evaluation of the facts by the competent national authorities was proper, unbiased and objective. If so, the panel shall not overturn the findings of the national authorities, even though it might itself have come to a different conclusion. Article 17.6(ii) requires a panel to uphold a decision by the competent national authorities if that decision is based on a 'permissible' interpretation of the relevant provision of the *Anti-Dumping Agreement*. As interpreted by the Appellate Body, however, this special standard of review does not fundamentally differ from the standard of review of Article 11 of the DSU.

[265] Appellate Body Report, *US – Wool Shirts and Blouses*, 340.

[266] Appellate Body Report, *India – Patents (US)*, para. 87. A panel is never required to exercise judicial economy (see Appellate Body Report, *US – Lead and Bismuth II*, para. 71), but when it does exercise judicial economy, it should state so explicitly for the purposes of transparency and fairness to the parties (see Appellate Body Report, *Canada – Autos*, para. 117).

[267] The Appellate Body found that the panels had erred in exercising judicial economy in, for example, Appellate Body Report, *Japan – Agricultural Products II* and Appellate Body Report, *Australia – Salmon*.

those claims on which a finding is necessary in order to enable the DSB to make sufficiently precise recommendations and rulings so as to allow for prompt compliance by a Member with those recommendations and rulings "in order to ensure effective resolution of disputes to the benefit of all Members".[268]

In *Argentina – Preserved Peaches*, Chile requested that the Panel rule on all the claims presented 'in order to ensure that Argentina does not continue to violate these agreements as it has done'. The Panel observed, however, that Chile did not offer any explanation as to why ruling on *all* claims would achieve this objective. Having concluded that the measure at issue was inconsistent with various WTO provisions and that further findings on the other Chilean claims would not alter that conclusion and would not further assist the DSB in making sufficiently precise recommendations (to allow for prompt compliance by Argentina), the Panel chose to exercise judicial economy on these other claims.[269]

If a panel makes a finding on a claim that does not fall within its terms of reference, i.e. acts *ultra petita*, the panel does not make an objective assessment *of the matter before it*, and thus acts inconsistently with Article 11 of the DSU.[270] However, if a panel makes a finding on a *claim* which does fall within its terms of reference it is not restricted to considering only those *legal arguments* made by the parties to the dispute.[271] The Appellate Body ruled in *EC – Hormones* that:

nothing in the DSU limits the faculty of a panel freely to use arguments submitted by any of the parties – or to develop its own legal reasoning – to support its own findings and conclusions on the matter under its consideration.[272]

A panel which uses arguments or reasoning that have not been submitted or developed by any of the parties to the dispute does not act *ultra petita*. Panels are restricted to the claims falling within their terms of reference but they are not restricted to the arguments and reasoning submitted or developed by the parties.

Questions and Assignments 3.25

Does a panel have to address and decide on every claim of the complainant? Can the panel ignore an explicit request of the complainant to rule on a particular claim? Can a panel develop an 'original' legal reasoning in its report that is not in any way based on legal arguments made by any of the parties to the dispute?

---

[268] Appellate Body Report, *Australia – Salmon*, para. 223. See also Appellate Body Report, *Japan – Agricultural Products II*, para. 111.

[269] See Panel Report, *Argentina – Preserved Peaches*, paras. 7.141–7.142.

[270] Appellate Body Report, *Chile – Price Band System*, para. 173.

[271] Also note, however, in this respect, the rules on the burden of proof. See above, pp. 210–12.

[272] Appellate Body Report, *EC – Hormones*, para. 156. See also Panel Report, *Australia – Automotive Leather II (Article 21.5 – US)*, para. 6.19.

3.4.2.7. Characteristics of a panel report

A panel submits its findings and conclusions on the WTO consistency of the measure at issue in the form of a written report to the DSB. This report typically includes a section on the following:

- procedural aspects of the dispute;
- factual aspects of the dispute (in which the measure at issue is discussed);
- the claims of parties;
- summary of the arguments of the parties and third parties;[273]
- the interim review;
- the panel's findings; and
- the panel's conclusions.

A panel report must, at a minimum, set out the findings of fact, the applicability of relevant provisions and the basic rationale behind any findings and recommendations that it makes.[274] In a few cases to date, parties have challenged a panel report before the Appellate Body for lack of a basic rationale behind the panel's findings and recommendations. In *Argentina – Footwear (EC)*, the Appellate Body found as follows:

> In this case, the Panel conducted *extensive* factual and legal analyses of the competing claims made by the parties, set out numerous factual findings based on detailed consideration of the evidence before the Argentine authorities as well as other evidence presented to the Panel, and provided extensive explanations of how and why it reached its factual and legal conclusions. Although Argentina may not agree with the rationale provided by the Panel, and we do not ourselves agree with all of its reasoning, we have no doubt that the Panel set out, in its Report, a "basic rationale" consistent with the requirements of Article 12.7 of the DSU.[275]

In a dispute involving a developing-country Member, the panel report must explicitly indicate how the panel has taken account of any special or differential treatment provision that the developing-country Member has invoked before the panel. In *India – Quantitative Restrictions*, for example, the Panel specifically referred to this requirement and noted:

> In this instance, we have noted that Article XVIII:B as a whole, on which our analysis throughout this section is based, embodies the principle of special and differential treatment in relation to measures taken for balance-of-payments purposes. This entire part G therefore reflects our consideration of relevant provisions on special

---

[273] The practice on this point varies. Most panels have included a summary of the arguments drafted on the basis of an 'executive summary' of the arguments provided by the parties and third parties. Other panels have not included a separate section in their report summarising the arguments but have attached the executive summaries received from the parties and third parties to the report. Some parties have attached the submissions of the parties and third parties in full to the panel report. In *EC – Tube or Pipe Fittings*, Brazil, the complainant, requested that the complete text of its first and second written submissions, rather than its executive summaries, be included in Annexes A and C to the Panel Report. The Panel rejected this request as it had been provided for in the *ad hoc* working procedures that the 'executive summary approach' would be followed. See Panel Report, *EC – Tube or Pipe Fittings*, paras. 7.48–7.55.

[274] Article 12.7 of the DSU. Note the special requirements for panel reports in cases where parties reached a mutually acceptable solution during the panel proceedings (see Article 12.7 of the DSU).

[275] Appellate Body Report, *Argentina – Footwear (EC)*, para. 149.

and differential treatment, as does Section VII of our report (suggestions for implementation).[276]

Where a panel concludes that a Member's measure is inconsistent with a covered agreement, it shall recommend that the Member concerned bring that measure into conformity with that agreement.[277] The recommendations and rulings of a panel are *not* legally binding by themselves. They become legally binding only when they are adopted by the DSB and thus have become the recommendations and rulings of the DSB.[278] In addition to making recommendations and rulings, the panel may suggest ways in which the Member concerned could implement those recommendations.[279] These suggestions are not legally binding on the Member concerned. However, because the panel making the suggestions might later be called upon to assess the sufficiency of the implementation of the recommendations, such suggestions are likely to have a certain impact.[280] To date, few panels have made use of this authority to make suggestions regarding implementation of their recommendations.[281]

Panellists can express a separate opinion in the panel report, be it dissenting or concurring. However, if they do, they must do so *anonymously*.[282] To date, there have been few panel reports setting out a separate opinion of one of the panellists.[283]

Panel reports are always circulated to WTO Members, and made available to the public, in English, French and Spanish. Reports are not circulated until all three language versions are available. Most reports are written in English and then translated into French and Spanish. However, in recent years, there have been a few panel reports written in Spanish and at least one written in French.[284]

Questions and Assignments 3.26

What are the (formal) requirements that a panel report must meet under the DSU? Can a panellist have his or her dissenting opinion noted in the panel report? What is the difference between a recommendation of a panel and a suggestion of a panel?

3.4.2.8. Role of the WTO Secretariat

Pursuant to Article 27.1 of the DSU, the WTO Secretariat has the responsibility of assisting panels, especially on the legal, historical and procedural aspects of

[276] Panel Report, *India – Quantitative Restrictions*, para. 5.157.
[277] Article 19.1 of the DSU.
[278] On the adoption of panel reports, see above, pp. 229–30, and below, p. 269.
[279] Article 19.1 of the DSU.　　[280] See below, pp. 281–2.
[281] See e.g. Panel Report, *US – Underwear*, paras. 8.1–8.3; Panel Report, *India – Quantitative Restrictions*, paras. 7.1–7.7; and Panel Report, *Guatemala – Cement II*, paras. 9.3–9.7.
[282] Article 14.3 of the DSU.
[283] See, e.g., Panel Report, *EC – Poultry*, paras. 289–92; and Panel Report, *EC – Tariff Preferences*, paras. 9.1–9.21.
[284] See e.g. Panel Report, *EC – Asbestos*.

the matters dealt with, and of providing secretarial and technical support. The Legal Affairs Division and the Rules Division are the main divisions of the WTO Secretariat that assist dispute settlement panels. However, a significant number of staff from other 'operational divisions' of the WTO Secretariat are also involved.

Depending on the agreement principally at issue in the dispute, a panel will be assisted by an interdisciplinary team (i.e. economists and lawyers) drawn from the Legal Affairs Division and other divisions of the WTO Secretariat. For example, for a dispute concerning an SPS measure, a team composed of staff from the Agriculture and Commodities Division and staff from the Legal Affairs Division will assist the panel. Panels considering cases relating to State trading, subsidies, countervailing duties and anti-dumping are assisted by staff from the Rules Division. As already noted above, officials of the WTO Secretariat assigned to assist panels are also subject to the *Rules of Conduct* and bound by the obligations of independence, impartiality, confidentiality and the avoidance of direct or indirect conflicts of interests.[285]

Questions and Assignments 3.27

What is the role of the WTO Secretariat in panel proceedings? In your opinion, can this role be problematic? If so, how?

3.4.3. The Appellate Body

Article 17.1 of the DSU provides for the establishment of an Appellate Body to hear appeals from reports of dispute settlement panels. The DSB established the Appellate Body in February 1995.[286] Unlike panels, the Appellate Body is a standing, i.e. permanent, international tribunal.[287] This section discusses:

- the membership of the Appellate Body;
- the institutional structure of the Appellate Body;
- access to appellate review;
- the scope of appellate review; and
- the mandate of the Appellate Body.

3.4.3.1. *Membership of the Appellate Body*

The Appellate Body is composed of seven persons referred to as 'Members' of the Appellate Body. With respect to the required qualifications of Members of the Appellate Body, Article 17.3 of the DSU states in relevant part:

---

[285] See above, pp. 215–16.
[286] Dispute Settlement Body, *Decision Establishing the Appellate Body*, 10 February 1995, WT/DSB/1, dated 19 June 1995.
[287] Article 17.1 of the DSU.

> The Appellate Body shall comprise persons of recognized authority, with demonstrated expertise in law, international trade and the subject matter of the covered agreements generally. They shall be unaffiliated with any government.

It is understood that the expertise of Appellate Body Members should be of a type that allows them to resolve 'issues of law covered in the panel report and legal interpretations developed by the panel'.[288] While the overriding concern is to provide highly qualified members for the Appellate Body,[289] Article 17.3 also requires that:

> The Appellate Body membership shall be broadly representative of membership in the WTO.

Therefore, factors such as different geographical areas, levels of development, and legal systems are taken into account.[290] In its *Decision Establishing the Appellate Body*, the DSB stated:

> The success of the WTO will depend greatly on the proper composition of the Appellate Body, and persons of the highest calibre should serve on it.[291]

Since January 2004, the composition of the Appellate Body has been as follows:[292]

- Professor Georges Abi-Saab (Egypt)
- Professor Merit Janow (United States)
- Professor Luiz Olavo Baptista (Brazil)
- Mr A. V. Ganesan (India)
- Judge John Lockhart (Australia)
- Professor Giorgio Sacerdoti (Italy)
- Professor Yasuhei Tanigushi (Japan)

Appellate Body Members are not required to reside permanently or continuously in Geneva and most do not. However, Article 17.3 of the DSU requires that they 'be available at all times and on short notice'. To this end, Members keep the Appellate Body Secretariat informed of their whereabouts at all times.[293]

---

[288] WT/DSB/1, dated 19 June 1995, para. 5.   [289] *Ibid.*, para. 6.   [290] *Ibid.*   [291] *Ibid.*, para. 4.

[292] During its first four years (December 1995–December 1999), the composition of the Appellate Body was as follows: James Bacchus (US), Christopher Beeby (New Zealand), Claus-Dieter Ehlermann (Germany), Said El Naggar (Egypt), Florentino Feliciano (the Philippines), Julio Lacarte-Muró (Uruguay), and Mitsuo Matsushita (Japan). In 1997, the DSB determined by lot that Ehlermann, Feliciano and Lacarte-Muró would, pursuant to Article 17.2 of the DSU, serve a first term of two years and decided subsequently to appoint these three Members for a second term (ending in December 2001). At the end of their first four-year term in December 1999, El-Naggar and Matsushita did not seek a second term while Bacchus and Beeby were re-elected for a second term of four years. In March 2000, Beeby died, shortly after having started his second term. In April 2000, the DSB appointed Georges Abi-Saab (Egypt), A. V. Ganesan (India) and Yasuhei Tanigushi (Japan) to the Appellate Body. During the period June 2000 to December 2001, the composition of the Appellate Body was as follows: James Bacchus (US), Georges Abi-Saab (Egypt), A. V. Ganesan (India), Yasuhei Tanigushi (Japan), Claus-Dieter Ehlermann (Germany), Said El Naggar (Egypt), Florentino Feliciano (the Philippines), and Julio Lacarte-Muró (Uruguay). To replace Ehlermann, Feliciano and Lacarte-Muró, whose second and last term would expire in December 2001, the DSB appointed in September 2001 Luiz Olavo Baptista (Brazil), Judge John Lockhart (Australia) and Giorgio Sacerdoti (Italy). In January 2004, Merit Janow (US) replaced James Bacchus (US), after the latter had completed the maximum of two terms of four years.

[293] Rule 2(4) of the *Working Procedures*.

Article 17.2 of the DSU states with respect to the appointment of Appellate Body Members and their term of office:

> The DSB shall appoint persons to serve on the Appellate Body for a four-year term, and each person may be reappointed once … Vacancies shall be filled as they arise. A person appointed to replace a person whose term of office has not expired shall hold office for the remainder of the predecessor's term.

The Members of the Appellate Body thus serve a term of four years which can be renewed once.[294] Pursuant to Article 2.4 of the DSU, the DSB takes the decision on the appointment of Appellate Body Members by consensus. It takes this decision on the recommendation of a Selection Committee, composed of the chairpersons of the General Council, the DSB, the Councils for Goods and for Services, the TRIPS Council and the WTO Director-General. The Selection Committee selects among candidates nominated by WTO Members.

As already noted, Appellate Body Members must not be affiliated with any government.[295] They must exercise their office without accepting or seeking instructions from any international, governmental or non-governmental organisation or any private source.[296] During their term of office, Members must not accept any employment nor pursue any professional activity that is inconsistent with their duties and responsibilities.[297] As already noted above, the Members of the Appellate Body are subject to the *Rules of Conduct* and are required 'to disclose the existence or development of any interest, relationship or matter' that is 'likely to affect, or give rise to justifiable doubts' as to his or her 'independence or impartiality'.[298] They may not participate in the consideration of any appeal that would create a direct or indirect conflict of interest.

Appellate Body Members are remunerated on a part-time basis. Their remuneration consists of a monthly retainer[299] plus a fee for actual days worked either in their home country or in Geneva.[300] This contractual arrangement reflects the expectation on the part of WTO Members, in 1995, that the Appellate Body would, in fact, not be so 'busy' as to justify a full-time employment arrangement. As of 1998, however, Appellate Body membership has often been more than a full-time job. The demands of the job have been such that it is difficult, and at times impossible, for Appellate Body Members to pursue other professional activities. In 2001, the employment arrangement of Appellate Body Members came under review by the DSB to determine whether a move to full-time employment was warranted. WTO Members failed, however, to agree on such a change.[301]

---

[294] In order to stagger the terms of office of the Members of the Appellate Body, three of the original seven Members (Ehlermann, Feliciano and Lacarte-Muró) served an initial term of two, rather than four, years. See above, footnote 292.

[295] Article 17.3 of the DSU.   [296] Rule 2(3) of the *Working Procedures*.

[297] Rule 2(2) of the *Working Procedures*.   [298] See above, pp. 215–16.

[299] See WT/DSB/1, dated 19 June 1995, para. 11.

[300] Members are also paid travel expenses and a daily subsistence allowance for the days that they work in Geneva.

[301] WT/DSB/M/101, dated 8 April 2001, para. 119.

Questions and Assignments 3.28

How and by whom are Members of the Appellate Body appointed? Is the current composition of the Appellate Body consistent with the relevant DSU provisions? What requirements apply to Appellate Body Members during their term in office?

3.4.3.2. Institutional structure of the Appellate Body

The Appellate Body does not hear or decide appeals *en banc*. It hears and decides appeals in divisions of three Members.[302] Rule 6 of the *Working Procedures for Appellate Review* (the '*Working Procedures*'), entitled 'Divisions', provides:

1. In accordance with paragraph 1 of Article 17 of the DSU, a division consisting of three Members shall be established to hear and decide an appeal.
2. The Members constituting a division shall be selected on the basis of rotation, while taking into account the principles of random selection, unpredictability and opportunity for all Members to serve regardless of their national origin.
3. A Member selected pursuant to paragraph 2 to serve on a division shall serve on that division, unless:
   i. he/she is excused from that division pursuant to Rules 9 or 10;
   ii. he/she has notified the Chairman and the Presiding Member that he/she is prevented from serving on the division because of illness or other serious reasons pursuant to Rule 12; or
   iii. he/she has notified his/her intentions to resign pursuant to Rule 14.

The Members constituting the division hearing and deciding a particular appeal are selected on the basis of *rotation* taking into account the principles of random selection and unpredictability and opportunity for all Members to serve, regardless of their nationality.[303] Unlike in the process for panellist selection, the nationality of Appellate Body Members is irrelevant. Appellate Body Members can, and will, sit in cases in which their countries of origin are a party.

The Members of a division select their Presiding Member.[304] Pursuant to Rule 7(2), the responsibilities of the Presiding Member shall include:

- coordinating the overall conduct of the appeal proceeding;
- chairing all oral hearings and meetings related to that appeal; and
- coordinating the drafting of the appellate report.

---

[302] Article 17.1 of the DSU and Rule 6(1) of the *Working Procedures*.

[303] A Member unable to serve on a division for a reason set out in Rule 6(3), shall be replaced by another Member selected pursuant to Rule 6(2). In *US – Softwood Lumber IV* and *US – Offset Act (Byrd Amendment)*, for example, Professor G. Sacerdoti was selected to replace Mr A. V. Ganesan, who had to step down for 'serious personal reasons'. See Appellate Body Report, *US – Softwood Lumber IV*, para. 10; and Appellate Body Report, *US – Offset Act (Byrd Amendment)*, para. 8.

[304] Rule 7 of the *Working Procedures*.

Decisions relating to an appeal are taken by the division assigned to that appeal. However, to ensure consistency and coherence in its case law and to draw on the individual and collective expertise of all seven Members, the division responsible for deciding an appeal exchanges views with the other Members on the issues raised by the appeal.[305] This exchange of views, which may take two to three days, is held before the division has come to any definitive views on the issues arising in the appeal.

A division makes every effort to take its decision on the appeal by consensus. However, if a decision cannot be reached by consensus, the *Working Procedures* provide that the matter at issue be decided by a majority vote.[306] Individual Members may express dissenting opinions in the report. However, Article 17.11 of the DSU requires in this respect:

> Opinions expressed in the Appellate Body report by individuals serving on the Appellate Body shall be anonymous.

To date, only once, in *EC – Asbestos*, did an Appellate Body Member express an individual opinion in an Appellate Body report.[307]

All seven Appellate Body Members convene on a regular basis to discuss matters of policy, practice and procedure.[308] These meetings are usually held either before or after the exchange of views in a particular appeal. If the Appellate Body is called upon to take a decision, it will try to do so by consensus. However, if it fails to reach a consensus, the decision will be taken by majority vote.

Each year the Appellate Body Members elect a Chairperson from among them.[309] Rule 5(3) of the *Working Procedures* states that:

> The Chairman shall be responsible for the overall direction of the Appellate Body business. His/her responsibilities shall include:
>
> • the supervision of the internal functioning of the Appellate Body; and
> • any such other duties as the Members may agree to entrust to him/her.

While the term of office of the Chairperson is one year, the Appellate Body may decide to extend the term of office for an additional period of up to one year.[310] However, in order to ensure rotation of the chairmanship, no Member can serve as Chairperson for more than two consecutive terms.

The Appellate Body has its own Secretariat which is separate and independent from the WTO Secretariat.[311] The Appellate Body Secretariat provides the Appellate Body with legal and administrative support.[312] As noted above,

---

[305] Rule 4(3) of the *Working Procedures*. Each Member therefore receives all documents filed in an appeal. A Member who has a conflict of interest shall not take part in the exchange of views.
[306] Rule 3(2) of the *Working Procedures*.
[307] On the separate opinion in *EC – Asbestos*, see below, p. 358.
[308] Rule 4 of the *Working Procedures*.   [309] Rule 5(1) of the *Working Procedures*.
[310] To date, Mr Julio Lacarte-Muró (1996, 1997) and Mr James Bacchus (2002, 2003) served two years as Chairman.
[311] *Decision Establishing the Appellate Body*, WT/DSB/1, para. 17.
[312] Article 17.7 of the DSU. While for many years notoriously understaffed, the Appellate Body Secretariat now consists of a director who heads a team of ten lawyers and four secretariat support staff. See www.wto.org/english/tratop_e/dispu_e/ab_secretariat_bio_e.htm, visited on 31 August 2004.

the *Rules of Conduct* and their requirements of independence, impartiality and confidentiality apply to the staff of the Appellate Body Secretariat.[313] The Appellate Body Secretariat has its offices in the Centre William Rappard, the lakeside premises of the WTO Secretariat in Geneva. All meetings of the Appellate Body or of divisions of the Appellate Body, as well as the oral hearings in appeals, are also held on these premises.

Questions and Assignments 3.29

How are the Appellate Body divisions that hear and decide particular appeals composed? In your opinion, is it appropriate that a Member of the Appellate Body with the nationality of one of the participants may sit on the division hearing and deciding the appeal? How has the Appellate Body been able to maintain consistency in its case law in spite of the fact that appeals are never heard or decided *en banc*?

3.4.3.3. *Access to appellate review*

Only parties to the dispute may appeal a panel report.[314] Third parties or other WTO Members cannot appeal a panel report. However, third parties, i.e. WTO Members which have notified the DSB of a substantial interest in the dispute at the time of the establishment of the panel, can participate in the appellate review proceedings.[315]

In appellate review proceedings, the parties are referred to as 'participants'. The participant that appeals a panel report is called the 'appellant', while the participant responding to an appeal is called the 'appellee'. Once one of the participants has appealed certain aspects of a panel report, it is not uncommon for other participants to 'cross-appeal' other aspects of the report. A participant cross-appealing is known as an 'other appellant'. Third parties choosing to participate in the appellate review proceedings are referred to as 'third participants'.

During the first years of the WTO dispute settlement system, all panel reports were appealed. The first panel report *not* appealed was the report in *Japan – Film*, circulated on 31 March 1998. Of all panel reports circulated since 1995, 70 per cent were appealed. See Figure 3.5.

This high rate of appeal is not necessarily a reflection of the quality of the panel reports but rather of the fact that appealing an unfavourable panel report does not 'cost' the appellant anything. On the contrary, an appeal – even if eventually unsuccessful – will allow a party, found to have acted inconsistently with WTO law, to delay the moment at which it has to bring

---

[313] See above, pp. 215–16.   [314] Article 17.4 of the DSU.
[315] For a detailed discussion, see below, p. 275.

Figure 3.5 Rate of appeal: total 1995–2003[316]

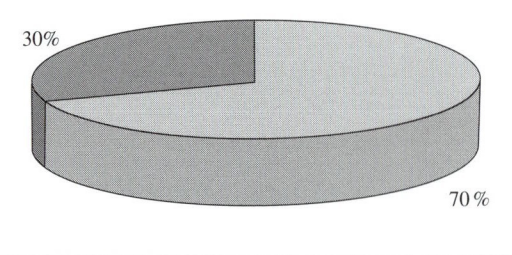

30%

70%

☐ Panel Reports Appealed   ■ Panel Reports Not Appealed

its measure into consistency. An appeal will also demonstrate to domestic constituencies that a Member has exhausted all legal means available.

> *Questions and Assignments 3.30*
>
> Can third parties or other WTO Members which are directly and adversely affected by a panel report appeal that report? What is an 'other appellant'? What explains the high rate of appeals of panel reports?

3.4.3.4. *Scope of appellate review*

The scope of review in appeals to the WTO Appellate Body is defined primarily in Article 17.6 of the DSU, which states:

> An appeal shall be limited to issues of law covered in the panel report and legal interpretations developed by the panel.

In *EC – Hormones*, the Appellate Body found that factual findings of panels are, in principle, excluded from the scope of appellate review. The Appellate Body stated:

> Under Article 17.6 of the DSU, appellate review is limited to appeals on questions of law covered in a panel report and legal interpretations developed by the panel. Findings of fact, as distinguished from legal interpretations or legal conclusions, by a panel are, in principle, not subject to review by the Appellate Body.[317]

In some cases, the characterisation of specific issues before the panel as issues of fact, rather than as issues of law or legal interpretations, is fairly straightforward. In *EC – Hormones*, the Appellate Body noted that:

> The determination of whether or not a certain event did occur in time and space is typically a question of fact.[318]

---

[316] See www.worldtradelaw.net, visited on 15 January 2004.
[317] Appellate Body Report, *EC – Hormones*, para. 132.   [318] *Ibid.*

In that case, the Appellate Body found that the Panel's findings regarding whether or not international standards had been adopted by the *Codex Alimentarius* Commission were findings on issues of fact and were, therefore, not subject to appellate review.

In other cases, the task of distinguishing between issues of fact and issues of law can be a complex exercise. The Appellate Body has made it clear, however, that findings involving the application of a legal rule to a specific fact or a set of facts are findings on issues of law and thus fall within the scope of appellate review. As stated in *EC – Hormones*:

> The consistency or inconsistency of a given fact or set of facts with the requirements of a given treaty provision is … a legal characterization issue. It is a legal question.[319]

The Appellate Body used similar reasoning in *Canada – Periodicals* to explain why the panel's determination of 'like products', for the purposes of Article III:2 of the GATT 1994, was reviewable:

> The determination of whether imported and domestic products are "like products" is a process by which legal rules have to be applied to facts.[320]

As a panel's factual determinations are, in principle, not subject to appellate review, a panel's weighing and assessment of evidence before it is also, in principle, not subject to appellate review.[321] In *EC – Hormones*, the Appellate Body found:

> Determination of the credibility and weight properly to be ascribed to (that is, the appreciation of) a given piece of evidence is part and parcel of the fact finding process and is, in principle, left to the discretion of a panel as the trier of facts.[322]

In *Korea – Alcoholic Beverages*, in which Korea sought to cast doubt on certain studies relied on by the Panel in that case, the Appellate Body stated:

> The Panel's examination and weighing of the evidence submitted fall, in principle, within the scope of the Panel's discretion as the trier of facts and, accordingly, outside the scope of appellate review. This is true, for instance, with respect to the Panel's treatment of the Dodwell Study, the Sofres Report and the Nielsen Study. *We cannot second-guess the Panel in appreciating either the evidentiary value of such studies or the consequences, if any, of alleged defects in those studies.* Similarly, it is not for us to review the relative weight ascribed to evidence on such matters as marketing studies.[323]
>
> [Emphasis added]

---

[319] *Ibid.*   [320] Appellate Body Report, *Canada – Periodicals*, 468.

[321] In *US – Offset Act (Byrd Amendment)*, Canada argued on appeal that Article 17.6 of the DSU prohibited the United States from challenging 'the credibility and weight the Panel attached' to two letters that had been in evidence before it. The Appellate Body, however, rejected Canada's claim. It found that the comments by the United States formed part of the latter's challenge to the Panel's legal findings. Whether these findings were supported by those letters was, according to the Appellate Body, an issue of law on which it had the authority to rule. See Appellate Body Report, *US – Offset Act (Byrd Amendment)*, para. 220.

[322] Appellate Body Report, *EC – Hormones*, para. 132.

[323] Appellate Body Report, *Korea – Alcoholic Beverages*, para. 161.

Panels thus have wide-ranging discretion in the consideration and weight they give to the evidence before them.[324] However, such discretion is *not* unlimited.[325] A panel's factual determinations must be consistent with Article 11 of the DSU. Article 11, which is quoted and discussed above, defines the mandate of panels.[326] As noted by the Appellate Body in *EC – Hormones*:

> Whether or not a panel has made an objective assessment of the facts before it, as required by Article 11 of the DSU, is also a legal question which, if properly raised on appeal, would fall within the scope of appellate review.[327]

Therefore, a factual finding may be subject to appellate review when the appellant alleges that this finding was not reached in a manner consistent with the requirements of Article 11 of the DSU.

Note that, in *US – Offset Act (Byrd Amendment)*, the Appellate Body held that, as Article 17.6 is clear in limiting the scope of appellate review to issues of law and legal interpretations, the Appellate Body has no authority to consider 'new facts' on appeal, even if these new facts are contained in documents that are 'available on the public record'.[328]

Questions and Assignments 3.31

What can be appealed? How does one distinguish between issues of law and issues of fact? Can factual findings ever be the subject of appeal? Can the weighing of evidence by a panel be reviewed by the Appellate Body?

3.4.3.5. *The mandate of the Appellate Body*

The mandate of the Appellate Body is primarily set out in Article 17.13 of the DSU, which states:

> The Appellate Body may uphold, modify or reverse the legal findings and conclusions of the panel.

When the Appellate Body agrees with both the panel's reasoning and the conclusion regarding the WTO-consistency of a measure, it *upholds* the relevant findings. When the Appellate Body agrees with the conclusion but not with the reasoning leading to that conclusion, it *modifies* the relevant findings. If the Appellate Body disagrees with the conclusion regarding the WTO-consistency of a measure, it *reverses* the relevant findings.[329]

---

[324] See also Appellate Body Report, *Australia – Salmon*, para. 261; and Appellate Body Report, *India – Quantitative Restrictions*, para. 143; and Appellate Body Report, *Korea – Dairy*, para. 137.
[325] Appellate Body Report, *Korea – Alcoholic Beverages*, para. 162.
[326] See above, pp. 238–40.
[327] Appellate Body Report, *EC – Hormones*, para. 132. See also Appellate Body Report, *Korea – Alcoholic Beverages*, para. 162.
[328] See Appellate Body Report, *US – Offset Act (Byrd Amendment)*, paras. 221–2.
[329] The distinction between 'upholding' and 'modifying' a panel's finding has not always been clear. Occasionally, the Appellate Body has 'upheld' a panel's finding while criticising and disagreeing to some extent with the panel's reasoning. See e.g. Appellate Body Report, *US – Hot-Rolled Steel*, paras. 90 and 158; and Appellate Body Report, *US – Lamb*, para. 188.

Figure 3.6 Results of appellate review: total 1995–2003[330]

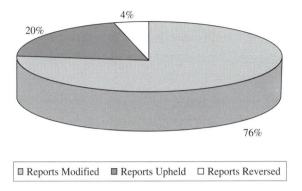

| ☐ Reports Modified | ■ Reports Upheld | ☐ Reports Reversed |

In around 20 per cent of all panel reports appealed, the Appellate Body upheld all findings appealed and thus upheld the panel report as a whole. The Appellate Body agreed with all the panel's reasoning and with its conclusions. In less than 5 per cent of all panel reports appealed the Appellate Body found such fundamental error that it could not but reverse the whole report.[331] In more than 75 per cent of all appeals, the results of the appellate review were mixed. Some of the findings appealed were upheld, some modified and/or some reversed. The panel report as a whole therefore was modified. See Figure 3.6.

Although Article 17.13 of the DSU allows the Appellate Body only to uphold, modify or reverse the panel's findings appealed, the Appellate Body has, in a number of cases, gone beyond that mandate. In those cases, the Appellate Body has, explicitly or implicitly, 'completed the legal analysis'.[332] As noted above, a complainant often makes claims of violation of multiple provisions of WTO law with regard to the measure at issue. After the panel has found a violation of one or some of these provisions, the panel may decide, for reasons of judicial economy, not to make findings with respect to the claims of violation of other provisions. However, if the panel report is appealed and the Appellate Body reverses the panel's findings of violation, the question arises as to what the Appellate Body can do with regard to the claims of violation which the panel, in its exercise of judicial economy, did not address. A similar question arises in cases in which a panel concludes that a provision or provisions of WTO law (e.g. the *TBT Agreement* as in *EC – Asbestos*) is not applicable in the case at hand but in which, on appeal of this finding of inapplicability, the Appellate Body comes to the opposite conclusion. What can the Appellate Body subsequently do in such situation?

---

[330] See www.worldtradelaw.net, visited on 15 January 2004.
[331] The two panel reports reversed to date are the reports in *Guatemala – Cement I* and *Canada – Dairy (Article 21.5 – New Zealand and US)*.
[332] The Appellate Body has completed the legal analysis of one or more issues in e.g. *Canada – Periodicals, EC – Hormones, EC – Poultry, US – Shrimp, Japan – Agricultural Products II, US – FSC, Canada – Aircraft (Article 21.5 – Brazil), US – Wheat Gluten* and *EC – Asbestos*.

In many domestic judicial systems, the appeals court would in similar situations 'remand' the case to the court of first instance. However, the DSU does not provide the Appellate Body with the authority to remand a dispute to the panel. In the absence of a remand authority, the Appellate Body is left with two options:

- either to leave the dispute unresolved; or
- to go on to 'complete the legal analysis'.

In *Canada – Periodicals*, the Appellate Body stated:

> We believe the Appellate Body *can, and should*, complete the analysis of Article III:2 of the GATT 1994 in this case by examining the measure with reference to its consistency with the second sentence of Article III:2, *provided that there is a sufficient basis in the Panel Report to allow us to do so.*[333]
>
> [Emphasis added]

In the circumstances of that case, the Appellate Body considered that it would be 'remiss in not completing the analysis of Article III:2'.[334] However, the Appellate Body has 'completed the legal analysis' only in cases in which there were sufficient factual findings in the panel report or undisputed facts in the panel record to enable it to carry out the legal analysis.[335] In practice, the Appellate Body has often found it impossible to 'complete the legal analysis' due to insufficient factual findings in the panel report or a lack of undisputed facts in the panel record. In addition, the Appellate Body has also declined to complete the legal analysis because of the novel character of the claims which the Panel did not address. Claims are 'novel' when they concern issues which have not yet been dealt with in the WTO case law. In *EC – Asbestos*, the Appellate Body stated:

> In light of their novel character, we consider that Canada's claims under the *TBT Agreement* have not been explored before us in depth. As the Panel did not address these claims, there are no "issues of law" or "legal interpretations" regarding them to be analyzed by the parties, and reviewed by us under Article 17.6 of the DSU. We also observe that the sufficiency of the facts on the record depends on the reach of the provisions of the *TBT Agreement* claimed to apply – a reach that has yet to be determined.[336]

Questions and Assignments 3.32

When does the Appellate Body uphold, when does it modify and when does it reverse the legal findings and conclusions of the panel under appellate review? Why and when does the Appellate Body 'complete the legal analysis'? In your opinion, should the Appellate Body have the power to remand cases to the panel? How do you interpret the data on the results of appellate review in Figure 3.6 above?

---

[333] Appellate Body Report, *Canada – Periodicals*, 469.   [334] *Ibid.*
[335] Appellate Body Report, *Australia – Salmon*, para. 118.
[336] Appellate Body Report, *EC – Asbestos*, para. 82.

3.4.4. Other bodies and persons involved in WTO dispute settlement

Apart from the DSB, panels and the Appellate Body, there are a number of other bodies and persons involved in the WTO's efforts to resolve disputes between its Members. These bodies and persons include, in no particular order:

- arbitrators under Articles 21.3, 22.6 and 25 of the DSU;[337]
- the Textile Monitoring Body;[338]
- the Permanent Group of Experts under Article 4.5 of the *SCM Agreement*;[339]
- the Facilitator under Annex V.4 of the *SCM Agreement*;[340]
- experts under Articles 13.1 and 13.2 of the DSU, Article 11.2 of the *SPS Agreement*, and Article 14 of the *TBT Agreement*;[341]
- Expert Review Groups under Article 13.2 of and Appendix 4 to the DSU;[342]
- Technical Expert Groups under Article 14.3 of and Annex 2 to the *TBT Agreement*;[343]
- the Chairman of the DSB;[344] and
- the WTO Director-General.[345]

Note also the role of the WTO Secretariat, the Appellate Body Secretariat and the Advisory Centre on WTO Law, as discussed above.[346]

3.5. WTO DISPUTE SETTLEMENT PROCEEDINGS

In WTO dispute settlement proceedings four separate stages can be distinguished:

- consultations;
- panel proceedings;
- appellate review proceedings; and
- implementation and enforcement of the recommendations and rulings of the panel and/or the Appellate Body, as adopted by the DSB.

In this section, each of these stages of the WTO dispute settlement proceedings will be examined.

3.5.1. Consultations

As noted above, the DSU expresses a clear preference for resolving disputes amicably rather than through adjudication.[347] To that end, WTO dispute

---

[337] See below, pp. 186–7, 278–9, 283.   [338] See above, pp. 133–4.   [339] See above, pp. 134–5, 565.
[340] See below, p. 573.   [341] See below, pp. 265–7.   [342] See below, p. 266.
[343] See below, p. 461.   [344] See above, pp. 215–16, 230, 236, 237, 246, and below, pp. 259, 271.
[345] See above, pp. 187, 215, 236, 246, and below, pp. 271, 278.
[346] See above, pp. 135–41 and 243–4 (on the WTO Secretariat), pp. 248–9 (on the Appellate Body Secretariat) and p. 227 (on the ACWL). Recall that the ACWL is *not* a WTO body or institution.
[347] See above. pp. 183–4.

settlement proceedings always start with consultations (or, at least, an attempt to have consultations) between the parties to the dispute.[348] In *Mexico – Corn Syrup (Article 21.5 – US)*, the Appellate Body stressed the importance of consultations in WTO dispute settlement as follows:

> Through consultations, parties exchange information, assess the strengths and weaknesses of their respective cases, narrow the scope of the differences between them and, in many cases, reach a mutually agreed solution in accordance with the explicit preference expressed in Article 3.7 of the DSU. Moreover, even where no such agreed solution is reached, consultations provide the parties an opportunity to define and delimit the scope of the dispute between them. Clearly, consultations afford many benefits to complaining and responding parties, as well as to third parties and to the dispute settlement system as a whole.[349]

As already noted above, the resolution of disputes, through consultations, is obviously more cost-effective and more satisfactory for the long-term trade relations with the other party to the dispute than adjudication by a panel.[350] Consultations enable the disputing parties to understand better the factual situation and the legal claims in respect of the dispute. Such understanding may allow them to resolve the matter without further proceedings and, if not, will at least allow a party to learn more about the facts and the legal arguments that the other party is likely to use when the dispute goes to adjudication. In this way, the consultations *can* serve as an informal pre-trial discovery mechanism. Their primary object and purpose, however, is to settle the dispute amicably.

This section discusses the following issues that arise with respect to consultations:

- initiation of consultations;
- conduct of consultations; and
- outcome of consultations.

3.5.1.1. *Initiation of consultations*

Any WTO Member considering that a benefit accruing to it under the *WTO Agreement* is being impaired or nullified by measures taken by another WTO Member may request consultations with that other Member. WTO Members are required to accord sympathetic consideration to, and afford adequate opportunity for, consultations.[351] A request for consultations, giving the reasons for the request, must be submitted in writing and must identify:

- the measure at issue; and
- the legal basis for the complaint.[352]

---

[348] Article 4 of the DSU. Note in particular Article 4.5 but also Articles 4.3 and 4.7 of the DSU.
[349] Appellate Body Report, *Mexico – Corn Syrup (Article 21.5 – US)*, para. 54.
[350] See above, pp. 183–4.   [351] Article 4.2 of the DSU.
[352] Article 4.4 of the DSU. With respect to the relationship between the request for consultations and the later request for the establishment of a panel, the Appellate Body noted, in *Brazil – Aircraft*, that Articles 4 and 6 of the DSU do not require a *precise and exact identity* between the specific measures that were the subject of consultations and the specific measures that were identified in the request for the establishment of a panel. See Appellate Body Report, *Brazil – Aircraft*, para. 132.

All requests for consultations are to be notified to the DSB (and the relevant councils and committees) by the Member requesting consultations.[353]

3.5.1.2. Conduct of consultations

Parties have broad discretion as regards the manner in which consultations are to be conducted. The DSU provides few rules on the conduct of consultations. The consultation process is essentially a *political-diplomatic process*, 'without prejudice to the rights of any Member in further legal proceedings'.[354]

Unless otherwise agreed, the Member to which a request for consultation is made must *reply* to the request within ten days of the date of its receipt, and enter into consultations within a period of no more than thirty days after the date of receipt of the request.[355] It must enter into consultations in good faith and with a view to reaching a mutually satisfactory solution. If the Member does not respond within ten days after the date of receipt of the request, or does not enter into consultations within a period of no more than thirty days (or a period otherwise mutually agreed), then the Member that requested the consultations may proceed directly to request the establishment of a panel. As the Appellate Body noted in *Mexico – Corn Syrup (Article 21.5 – US)*, in such a case the respondent, by its own conduct, relinquishes the potential benefits that could be derived from consultations.[356]

While the request for consultations is notified to the DSB, the consultations themselves are confidential.[357] Generally, consultations are held in Geneva and involve Geneva-based diplomats as well as capital-based trade officials of the parties to the dispute. The WTO Secretariat is neither present, nor in any other way associated with, the consultations.

Consultations can be requested:

- pursuant to Article XXII of the GATT 1994, or the corresponding provisions in other covered agreements; or
- pursuant to Article XXIII of the GATT 1994, or the corresponding provisions in other covered agreements.

---

[353] Article 4.4 of the DSU.
[354] Article 4.6 of the DSU. Therefore, evidence pertaining to settlement offers made during the consultations are 'of no legal consequence to the later stages' of WTO dispute settlement proceedings. See Panel Report, *US – Underwear*, para. 7.27.
[355] Article 4.3 of the DSU.
[356] See Appellate Body Report, *Mexico – Corn Syrup (Article 21.5 – US)*, para. 59.
[357] Article 4.6 of the DSU. Note that the requirement of confidentiality does not mean that information acquired during consultations may not be used during the panel proceedings. It means that the information acquired may not be disclosed to anyone not involved in the consultations (see Panel Report, *Korea – Alcoholic Beverages*, para. 10.23; and Panel Report, *EC – Bed Linen*, paras. 6.39–6.40).

The Member requesting consultations is free to choose either type of consultations. There is only one difference, albeit significant, between these two types
of consultations. Only in the context of consultations pursuant to Article XXII
or corresponding provisions can a Member other than the consulting Members
be allowed to participate in the consultations. A Member that considers that it
has a 'substantial trade interest' may notify the consulting Members and the
DSB of such interest within ten days after the date of the circulation of the
request for consultations.[358] Provided that the respondent to the dispute
agrees the claim of substantial interest to be well founded, this Member shall
join in the consultations. If consultations are conducted pursuant to Article
XXIII, or corresponding provisions, it is not possible for other Members to join
in the consultations.

Occasionally, respondents have argued that the consultations held had not
been adequate or meaningful or that the complainant had not engaged in
consultations in good faith.[359] The Panel, in *Korea – Alcoholic Beverages*, ruled
in this respect that it was not for panels to assess the 'adequacy' of consultations.[360] Consultations are a matter reserved for the parties and nobody but
the parties is to be involved in the consultations. What takes place in these
consultations is not the concern of panels. Panels may only ascertain whether
consultations were held or at least were requested.[361] Note that, if a panel were
to find that consultations had not been held or requested prior to its establishment, it would have to conclude that it has no authority to hear and decide the
dispute.[362]

3.5.1.3. Outcome of consultations

If consultations are successful and lead to a mutually agreed solution to the
dispute, these solutions must be notified to the DSB and other relevant WTO
bodies.[363] Any Member may raise any point relating to these notified solutions
at meetings of the DSB or other WTO bodies. Note that mutually agreed
solutions must be consistent with WTO law.[364] As discussed above, consultations have often been successful in resolving disputes.

If consultations between the parties fail to settle the dispute within
sixty days of the receipt of the request for consultations, the complainant
may request the DSB to establish a panel to adjudicate the dispute.[365] In
many cases, however, the complainant will not, immediately upon the

[358] Article 4.11 of the DSU.
[359] See the requirements in Articles 3.10 and 4.2. Also note Article 4.10 which provides that during
    consultations Members 'should' give special attention to the particular problems and interests of
    developing-country Members.
[360] Panel Report, *Korea – Alcoholic Beverages*, para. 10.19.
[361] See also Panel Reports, *EC – Bananas III*, para. 7.19.
[362] The lack of prior consultations is, however, not a defect that a panel must examine on its own motion.
    See Appellate Body Report, *Mexico – Corn Syrup (Article 21.5 – US)*, para. 64.
[363] Article 3.6 of the DSU.   [364] Article 3.5 of the DSU.
[365] The complainant may request a panel during the sixty-day period if the consulting parties jointly
    consider that consultations have failed to settle the dispute. See Article 4.7 of the DSU.

expiration of the sixty-day period, request the establishment of a panel but will allow for considerably more time to settle the dispute through consultations.

For consultations involving a measure taken by a developing-country Member, Article 12.10 of the DSU explicitly provides that the parties may agree to extend the sixty-day period. If, after the sixty-day period has elapsed, the consulting parties cannot agree that the consultations have concluded, the Chairman of the DSB shall decide, after consultation with the parties, whether to extend this period and, if so, for how long. To date, the Chairman of the DSB has never been called upon to exercise this authority.

Consultations between the parties with the aim of settling the dispute can, and do, continue *during* the panel proceedings. The DSU provides that panels should consult the parties to the dispute regularly and give them an adequate opportunity to develop a mutually satisfactory solution.[366] There have been a number of disputes in which a mutually agreed solution was reached while the dispute was already before a panel.[367]

Questions and Assignments 3.34

What is the 'sanction' for not holding (or requesting) consultations before requesting the establishment of a panel? Will consultations always last at least sixty days? Can consultations last longer than sixty days? Can a panel find that the complainant did not engage in consultation in good faith as required by Article 3.10 of the DSU? Can other Members join consultations between the parties to a dispute? May WTO Members resolve a dispute amicably by *agreeing* to a solution which deviates from the *WTO Agreement*? Does the DSU provide any special rules for developing-country Members engaged in consultations?

3.5.2. Panel proceedings

As outlined above, when consultations are unsuccessful, the complainant may request the establishment of a panel. As discussed earlier in this chapter, the DSB will usually establish the panel by reverse consensus at the meeting following that at which the panel request first appeared on the DSB's agenda.[368] Subsequently, the parties will agree on the composition of the panel or, if they fail to do so, the composition of the panel will be decided on by the WTO Director-General.[369] This section discusses the following issues which arise with respect to panel proceedings:

---

[366] See Article 11 of the DSU.
[367] See e.g. *EC – Scallops*, complaints by Canada, Peru and Chile; and *EC – Butter Products*, complaint by New Zealand.
[368] See above, pp. 233–4.   [369] See above, pp. 235–6.

- working procedures for panel proceedings;
- written submissions and panel meetings;
- rights of third parties;
- submission and admission of evidence;
- use of experts;
- protection of confidential business information;
- panel deliberations and interim review;
- adoption or appeal of the panel report; and
- duration of panel proceedings.

3.5.2.1. Working procedures for panel proceedings

The basic rules governing panel proceedings are set out in Article 12 of the DSU. Article 12.1 of the DSU directs a panel to follow the *Working Procedures* contained in Appendix 3 to the DSU, while at the same time authorising a panel to do otherwise after consulting the parties to the dispute. In *EC – Hormones*, the Appellate Body noted that panels enjoy:

> a margin of discretion to deal, always in accordance with due process, with specific situations that may arise in a particular case.[370]

In *India – Patents (US)*, however, the Appellate Body cautioned panels as follows:

> Although panels enjoy some discretion in establishing their own working procedures, this discretion does not extend to modifying the substantive provisions of the DSU. To be sure, Article 12.1 of the DSU says: "Panels shall follow the Working Procedures in Appendix 3 unless the panel decides otherwise after consulting the parties to the dispute." Yet that is *all* that it says. Nothing in the DSU gives a panel the authority either to disregard or to modify other explicit provisions of the DSU.[371]

Article 12.2 of the DSU requires that panel procedures provide sufficient flexibility so as to ensure high-quality panel reports while not unduly delaying the panel process. Since the *Working Procedures* contained in Appendix 3 to the DSU are rudimentary, most panels now find it useful, if not necessary, to adopt more detailed *ad hoc* working procedures.

Appendix 3 to the DSU provides for 'a proposed timetable for panel work'.[372] On the basis of this proposed timetable, the panel will – whenever possible within a week of its composition – fix the timetable for its work.[373] The panel may at that time also decide on detailed *ad hoc* working procedures.

---

[370] Appellate Body Report, *EC – Hormones*, footnote 138.
[371] Appellate Body Report, *India – Patents (US)*, para. 92. In this case, the Appellate Body reversed a decision by the Panel that it would consider all claims made prior to the end of the first substantive meeting. All parties had agreed with this Panel decision.
[372] See para. 12 of Appendix 3 to the DSU.
[373] Article 12.3 of the DSU. The timetable includes precise deadlines for written submissions by the parties, which the parties must respect (see Article 12.5 of the DSU). In determining the timetable, the panel must provide sufficient time for the parties to prepare their submissions (see Article 12.4 of the DSU).

The panel will do so after consulting the parties to the dispute at what is called the 'organisational meeting'.[374]

Generally speaking, the parties to a dispute enjoy a high degree of discretion to argue before panels in the manner they deem appropriate. This discretion, however, does not detract from their obligation under the DSU to engage in dispute settlement proceedings 'in good faith in an effort to resolve the dispute'.[375] Both the complaining and the responding Members must comply with the requirements of the DSU in good faith. In *US – FSC*, the Appellate Body held:

> By good faith compliance, complaining Members accord to the responding Members the full measure of protection and opportunity to defend, contemplated by the letter and spirit of the procedural rules. The same principle of good faith requires that responding Members seasonably and promptly bring claimed procedural deficiencies to the attention of the complaining Member, and to the DSB or the Panel, so that corrections, if needed, can be made to resolve disputes. The procedural rules of WTO dispute settlement are designed to promote, not the development of litigation techniques, but simply the fair, prompt and effective resolution of trade disputes.[376]

Note that, in *EC – Tube or Pipe Fittings*, Brazil's first written submission did not contain paragraph or line numbering. The Panel noted in this respect that it 'would appreciate efforts on the part of the parties to facilitate the task of the Panel in examining the matter referred to [it]', and 'invite[d] Brazil to submit a paragraph-numbered version of its first submission to facilitate referencing by the Panel and the parties'.[377] Brazil accordingly submitted a revised, paragraph-numbered version of its first written submission to the Panel.[378]

Questions and Assignments 3.35

Who decides on the working procedures for the panels and on the timetable for the panel's work? Which requirements do the working procedures and the timetable have to meet? Is a panel free to deviate from Appendix 3 to the DSU as well as other provisions of the DSU if all parties to the dispute agree? How much discretion do parties enjoy regarding the manner in which they argue before panels?

3.5.2.2. *Written submissions and substantive panel meetings*

Each of the parties to a dispute submit two written submissions to the panel:

- a 'first written submission'; and
- a 'rebuttal submission'.

---

[374] Articles 12.3 and 12.5 of the DSU.   [375] Article 3.10 of the DSU.
[376] Appellate Body Report, *US – FSC*, para. 166. See also Appellate Body Report, *US – Lamb*, para. 115.
[377] Panel Report, *EC – Tube or Pipe Fittings*, para. 7.40.   [378] *Ibid.*, para. 7.41.

In their first written submissions, the parties present the facts of the case and their arguments.[379] In their rebuttal submissions, they reply to the arguments and evidence submitted by the other party.[380] The first written submission of the complainant is usually filed two to three weeks in advance of the first written submission of the respondent.[381] The rebuttal submissions are filed simultaneously.[382] As the Appellate Body ruled in *US – Shrimp*, the parties have a *legal right* to make the above-mentioned submissions to the panel, and the panel in turn is *obliged in law* to accept and give due consideration to these submissions.[383]

After the first written submissions of the parties have been filed, the panel holds its first substantive meeting with the parties.[384] At this meeting, the panel asks the complainant to present its case. At the same meeting, the respondent is also asked to present its point of view.[385] The panel holds a second substantive meeting with the parties after the rebuttal submissions have been filed. At this meeting, the respondent party is given the right to take the floor first, to be followed by the complainant.[386] While not mandatory, panel meetings are always held on the premises of the WTO Secretariat in Geneva. A panel meeting may take one or more days. While initially less formal and less 'court-like' than the oral hearings of the Appellate Body, WTO panel meetings have become more formal and 'court-like' in recent years.[387] All *ex parte* communications with the panel, on matters under consideration, are explicitly proscribed.[388] As already discussed above, the panel always meets in closed session with only the delegations of the parties present.[389]

The panel may, at any time, put questions to the parties and ask them for explanations either in the course of a meeting or in writing.[390] The DSU provides panels with discretionary authority to request and obtain information from *any* Member, including *a fortiori* a Member which is a party to a dispute before the panel.[391] The parties are under an obligation to provide the panel with the information or the documents that the panel requests. Article 13.1 of the DSU states, in relevant part:

> A Member *should* respond promptly and fully to any request by a panel for such information as the panel considers necessary and appropriate.
>
> [Emphasis added]

---

[379] Note that, even if the complainant fails to include any arguments on certain claims in its first written submission, these claims, when properly identified in the panel request, remain within the terms of reference of the panel. See Appellate Body Report, *EC – Bananas III*, para. 145.

[380] However, on the 'late' submission of evidence, see below, pp. 264–5.

[381] Article 12.6 of, and para. 12 of Appendix 3 to, the DSU.

[382] *Ibid.*

[383] Appellate Body Report, *US – Shrimp*, para. 101. This is also the case for submissions by third parties but not for submissions by any other Member or person (*amicus curiae* briefs). See above, pp. 196–202.

[384] Para. 4 of Appendix 3 to the DSU.   [385] Para. 5 of Appendix 3 to the DSU.

[386] Para. 7 of Appendix 3 to the DSU. Additional meetings with the parties may be scheduled if required (para. 12 of Appendix 3 to the DSU). In practice, however, very few panels have had additional meetings with the parties.

[387] See below, p. 274.   [388] Article 18.1 of the DSU.   [389] See above, pp. 213–14.

[390] Para. 8 of Appendix 3 to the DSU. During panel proceedings, parties may also question each other.

[391] Article 13.1 of the DSU.

In *Canada – Aircraft*, the Appellate Body ruled that the word 'should' in Article 13.1 is used in a normative sense.[392]

For the benefit of a developing-country Member, Article 12.10 of the DSU provides, in relevant part:

> in examining a complaint against a developing-country Member, the panel shall accord sufficient time for the developing country to prepare and present its argumentation.

In *India – Quantitative Restrictions*, India requested additional time from the Panel in order to prepare its first written submission. Referring to the DSU's strict timeframe for the panel process, the United States objected to this request. Referring to Article 12.10, the Panel ruled as follows:

> In light of this provision, and considering the administrative reorganization taking place in India as a result of the recent change in government, the Panel has decided to grant an additional period of time to India to prepare its submission. However, bearing in mind also the need to respect the time frames of the DSU and in light of the difficulties of rescheduling the meeting of 7 and 8 May, the Panel considers that an additional period of ten days would represent "sufficient time" within the meaning of Article 12.10 of the DSU. India is therefore granted until 1 May 1998 (5 p.m.) to submit its first written submission to the Panel. The original date of the first meeting remains unchanged as 7 and 8 May.[393]

Questions and Assignments 3.36

Briefly describe the content of the various written submissions of the parties to the panel. When does the panel meet with the parties? Are *ex parte* communications with the panel allowed? Are parties to a dispute obliged to provide the panel with the information or the documents that the panel requests? Can developing-country Members request additional time to prepare their written submissions?

3.5.2.3. Rights of third parties

As discussed above, any WTO Member having a substantial interest in a matter before a panel and having notified its interest in a timely manner to the DSB shall have an opportunity to be heard by the panel and to make written submissions to the panel.[394] These third parties to the dispute are invited by the panel to present their views during a special session of the first substantive meeting.[395] Their written submissions to the panel are given to the parties to

---

[392] Appellate Body Report, *Canada – Aircraft*, para. 187. As the Appellate Body ruled in this case, it is within the discretion of panels to draw adverse inferences from the fact that a party had refused to provide information requested by the panel. However, the Appellate Body stressed that panels must draw inferences on the basis of all the facts of record (and not only the refusal to provide information). See Appellate Body Report, *Canada – Aircraft*, paras. 204–5; and Appellate Body Report, *US – Wheat Gluten*, paras. 173–6.

[393] Panel Report, *India – Quantitative Restrictions*, para. 5.10.

[394] Article 10.2 of the DSU. See also above, pp. 190–1, 234.

[395] Articles 10.2 and 10.3 of, and para. 6 of Appendix 3 to, the DSU.

the dispute.[396] Third parties, however, only receive the first written submissions of the parties. The rights of third parties to participate in the panel proceedings are quite limited.

In some cases, however, third parties have sought and obtained enhanced third party rights. In *EC – Bananas III*, for example, third party developing-country Members having a major interest in the outcome of this case were allowed to attend the entire first and second substantive meetings of the panel with the parties as well as make statements at both meetings.[397] Note that the grant of enhanced third party rights is within 'the sound discretion' of the panel, although '[s]uch discretionary authority is, of course, not unlimited and is circumscribed, for example, by the requirements of due process'.[398]

Questions and Assignments 3.37

What are the rights of third parties in panel proceedings?

3.5.2.4. Submission and admission of evidence

The DSU does not establish precise rules or deadlines for the submission of evidence by a party to the dispute. In *Argentina – Textiles and Apparel*, the Panel allowed the United States to submit certain evidence two days before the second substantive meeting. Argentina appealed the Panel's decision to admit this evidence. The Appellate Body rejected the appeal on the basis of the following reasoning:

> Article 11 of the DSU does not establish time limits for the submission of evidence to a panel. Article 12.1 of the DSU directs a panel to follow the Working Procedures set out in Appendix 3 of the DSU, but at the same time authorizes a panel to do otherwise after consulting the parties to the dispute. The Working Procedures in Appendix 3 also do not establish precise deadlines for the presentation of evidence by a party to the dispute. It is true that the Working Procedures "do not prohibit" submission of additional evidence after the first substantive meeting of a panel with the parties.[399]

The Appellate Body recognised that the DSU clearly contemplates two distinguishable stages in panel proceedings: a first stage during which the parties should set out their case in chief, including a full presentation of the facts on the basis of submission of supporting evidence; and a second stage which is generally designed to permit 'rebuttals' by each party of the arguments and evidence submitted by the other party.[400] Nevertheless, unless specific

---

[396] Article 10.2 of the DSU. These submissions are reflected in, or attached to, the panel report.
[397] The Panel did, however, refuse the third parties participation in the interim review process: see Panel Reports, *EC – Bananas III*, para. 7.9. For a recent example of the granting of 'additional rights' to third parties, see Panel Report, *EC – Tariff Preferences*, para. 1.10. The Panel in *EC – Tariff Preferences* allowed third parties some participation in the interim review process by allowing them to review the summary of their respective arguments in the draft descriptive part of the Panel Report.
[398] Appellate Body, *US – 1916 Act*, paras. 149 and 150.
[399] Appellate Body Report, *Argentina – Textiles and Apparel*, para. 79.   [400] *Ibid.*

deadlines for the submission of evidence are set out in the *ad hoc* working procedures of the panel, parties can submit new evidence as late as the second meeting with the panel. The panel must, of course, always be careful to observe due process which, *inter alia*, entails providing the parties with adequate opportunity to respond to the evidence submitted.[401] Most panels now have *ad hoc* working procedures that set out precise deadlines for the submission of evidence.[402]

Questions and Assignments 3.38

Can parties submit new evidence to the panel at any stage of the panel proceedings?

3.5.2.5. *Use of experts*

Disputes brought to panels for adjudication often involve complex factual, technical and scientific issues. These issues frequently play a central role in WTO dispute settlement proceedings. Article 13 of the DSU gives panels the authority to seek information and technical advice from any individual or body which it deems appropriate.[403] Panels may consult experts to obtain their opinion on certain aspects of the matter under consideration. As the Appellate Body ruled in *Argentina – Textiles and Apparel*, '[t]his is a grant of discretionary authority'.[404] In *US – Shrimp*, the Appellate Body further stated:

> a panel ... has the authority to *accept or reject* any information or advice which it may have sought and received, or to *make some other appropriate disposition* thereof. It is particularly within the province and the authority of a panel to determine the *need for information and advice* in a specific case, to ascertain the *acceptability* and *relevancy* of information or advice received, and to decide *what weight to ascribe* to that information or advice or to conclude that no weight at all should be given to what has been received.[405]

This authority is 'indispensably necessary' to enable a panel to discharge its duty under Article 11 of the DSU to 'make an objective assessment of the matter before it'.[406]

To date, panels have consulted experts in, for example, *EC – Hormones*, *Australia – Salmon*, *Japan – Agricultural Products II*, *EC – Asbestos* and *Japan – Apples*, all disputes involving complex scientific issues. In these cases, the panels typically selected the experts in consultation with the parties;

---

[401] *Ibid.*, paras. 80–1; and Appellate Body Report, *Australia – Salmon*, para. 272.
[402] Under these rules, the submission of evidence after the deadline will nevertheless be allowed when there is 'good cause' to do so. See e.g. Panel Report, *US – Offset Act (Byrd Amendment)*, para. 7.2.
[403] In addition to Article 13 of the DSU, panels have either the possibility or the obligation to consult experts under a number of other covered agreements: see Article XV:2 of the GATT 1994; Article 11.2 of the *SPS Agreement*; Articles 14.2 and 14.3 of the *TBT Agreement*; Articles 19.3 and 19.4 of and Annex II to the *Agreement on Customs Valuation*; and Articles 4.5 and 24.3 of the *SCM Agreement*.
[404] Appellate Body Report, *Argentina – Textiles and Apparel*, para. 84.
[405] Appellate Body Report, *US – Shrimp*, para. 104.   [406] *Ibid.*, para. 106.

presented the experts with a list of questions to which each expert individually responded in writing; and finally called a special meeting with the experts at which these and other questions were discussed with the panellists and the parties. The panel report usually contained both the written responses of the experts to the panel's questions as well as a transcript of the discussions at the meeting with the panel. However, confidential information which is provided must not be revealed without formal authorisation from the individual, body or authorities of the Member providing the information.

Apart from consulting individual experts, a panel can, with respect to a factual issue concerning a scientific or other technical matter, request an advisory report in writing from an expert review group.[407] Rules for the establishment of such a group and its procedures are set forth in Appendix 4 to the DSU. Expert review groups are under the authority of the panel and report to the panel. The panel decides their terms of reference. The report of an expert review group is advisory only; it does not bind the panel. To date, panels have made no use of this possibility to request an advisory report from an expert review group. Panels have preferred to seek information from experts directly and on an individual basis.[408]

It should be noted that, while a panel has broad authority to consult experts to help it to understand and evaluate the evidence submitted and the arguments made by the parties, a panel may not – with the help of its experts – make the case for one or the other party. In *Japan – Agricultural Products II*, the Appellate Body held:

> Article 13 of the DSU and Article 11.2 of the *SPS Agreement* suggest that panels have a significant investigative authority. However, this authority cannot be used by a panel to rule in favour of a complaining party which has not established a *prima facie* case of inconsistency based on specific legal claims asserted by it. A panel is entitled to seek information and advice from experts and from any other relevant source it chooses, pursuant to Article 13 of the DSU and, in an SPS case, Article 11.2 of the *SPS Agreement*, to *help it to understand and evaluate the evidence* submitted and the arguments made by the parties, but not to make the case for a complaining party.[409]
>
> [Emphasis added]

In *Japan – Apples*, Japan referred to this finding by the Appellate Body to challenge on appeal the Panel's use of experts. Japan argued that the US had not made claims or submitted evidence in respect of the risk of transmission of

---

[407] Article 13.2 of the DSU.

[408] The DSU also leaves it to the sound discretion of a panel to determine whether the establishment of an expert review group is necessary or appropriate (Appellate Body Report, *EC – Hormones*, para. 147).

[409] Appellate Body Report, *Japan – Agricultural Products II*, para. 129. In *Japan – Agricultural Products II*, the Panel was correct to seek information and advice from experts to help it to understand and evaluate the evidence submitted and the arguments made by the United States and Japan with regard to the alleged violation of Article 5.6 of the *SPS Agreement*. The Panel erred, however, when it used that expert information and advice as the basis for a finding of inconsistency with Article 5.6, since the United States did not establish a *prima facie* case of inconsistency with Article 5.6 based on claims relating to the 'determination of sorption levels'. The United States did not even argue that the 'determination of sorption levels' is an alternative measure which meets the three elements under Article 5.6 (see Appellate Body Report, *Japan – Agricultural Products II*, para. 130). See further Appellate Body Report, *Japan – Apples*, para. 158.

fire blight by apples other than mature symptomless apples, yet the Panel had made findings of fact with regard to these 'other' apples. Japan claimed that the Panel had thus exceeded the bounds of its investigative authority. The Appellate Body rejected Japan's argument, finding that the Panel had acted within the limits of its investigative authority, as:

> it did nothing more than assess the relevant allegations of fact asserted by Japan, in the light of the evidence submitted by the parties and the opinions of the experts.[410]

It thus clarified that a panel may use the evidence of its experts to assist it in assessing not only the claims of the complaining Member, but also the allegations of the responding Member. In doing so, it cannot be said to be exceeding its authority under Article 11.2.

Questions and Assignments 3.39

When can panels make use of experts? Which experts may panels consult? Who selects the experts? Do panels have broad investigative authority? What are the limits of this authority? Find in a panel report a section dealing with the testimony and questioning of experts.

3.5.2.6. *Protection of confidential business information*

As mentioned above, panel proceedings are confidential. However, the Panels in *Canada – Aircraft* and *Brazil – Aircraft* considered that parties have a legitimate interest in additional protection for sensitive business information submitted to a panel. Thus, special procedures governing this information were adopted.[411] Under the Procedures Governing Business Confidential Information adopted by the Panel in *Canada – Aircraft*, the confidential business information was to be stored in a safe in a locked room at the premises of the relevant Geneva missions, with restrictions imposed on access. The Procedures also provided for either party to visit the other party's Geneva mission and review the proposed location of the safe and suggest any changes. Finally, the Procedures provided for the return or the destruction of the confidential business information after completion of the panel process. In spite of these Procedures adopted by the Panel, Canada nevertheless refused to submit certain confidential business information because these Procedures did not, according to Canada, provide the requisite level of protection.[412]

---

[410] *Ibid.*
[411] Panel Report, *Canada – Aircraft*, Annex 1; and *Brazil – Aircraft*, Annex 1.
[412] On the consequences of such a refusal to submit information requested by the Panel, see above, pp. 262–3.

Questions and Assignments 3.40

Which documents are confidential in panel proceedings? Are there any exceptions? Describe the additional procedures adopted by the Panel in *Canada – Aircraft* to protect confidential business information. In your opinion, is there a need for such procedures?

3.5.2.7. Panel deliberations and interim review

As with a court or tribunal, panel deliberations are confidential.[413] The reports of panels are drafted without the presence of the parties to the dispute; they are drafted in the light of the information provided and the statements made during the proceedings.[414]

Having completed a draft of the descriptive (i.e. facts and argument) sections of its report, the panel issues this draft to the parties for their comments.[415] Following the expiration of the time period for comments, the panel subsequently issues an interim report to the parties including both the descriptive sections and the panel's findings and conclusions.[416] A party may submit a written request to the panel to review particular aspects of the interim report. At the request of a party, the panel may hold a further meeting with the parties on the issues identified in the written comments.[417] The final panel report must include a discussion of the arguments made at the interim review stage.[418]

The comments made by the parties at the interim review frequently give rise to corrections of technical errors or unclear drafting. However, panels have seldom changed the conclusions reached in their reports in any substantive way as a result of the comments made by parties. Parties may also prefer to comment only on minor factual issues during the interim review stage, saving their legal arguments for a later appeal to the Appellate Body.

Interim review is an unusual feature in judicial or quasi-judicial dispute settlement procedures. The need for and utility of this interim review procedure has been the subject of debate.

Questions and Assignments 3.41

In your opinion, is interim review of panel reports useful and/or appropriate in the current WTO dispute settlement system?

---

[413] Article 14.1 of the DSU.   [414] Article 14.2 of the DSU.
[415] Article 15.1 of the DSU. Note that recently some panels attached the submissions, the written versions of oral statements and answers to questions, to their report, rather than a summary of these documents in the descriptive sections of the report. See e.g. Panel Report, *US – Lead and Bismuth II*. See also above, pp. 242–3.
[416] Article 15.2 of the DSU.   [417] *Ibid.*
[418] Article 15.3 of the DSU. If no comments are received from any party within the comment period, the interim report shall be considered the final panel report (Article 15.3 of the DSU).

3.5.2.8. *Adoption or appeal of the panel report*

The final panel report is first issued to the parties to the dispute, and some weeks later, once the report is available in the three working languages of the WTO, it is circulated to the general WTO membership. Once circulated to WTO Members, the panel report is an unrestricted document available to the public. On the day of its circulation, a panel report is posted on the WTO's website. Panel reports are also included in the official WTO *Dispute Settlement Reports*, published by Cambridge University Press.

Within sixty-days after the date of circulation of the panel report to the Members, the report is adopted at a DSB meeting unless:

- a party to the dispute formally notifies the DSB of its decision to appeal; or
- the DSB decides by consensus not to adopt the report.[419]

If a panel report is appealed, it is not discussed by the DSB until the appellate review proceedings are completed and the Appellate Body report – together with the panel report – comes before the DSB for adoption.

When the DSB does consider and debate a panel report, all Members have the right to comment on the report. In order to provide sufficient time for the Members to review panel reports, the reports shall not be considered for adoption by the DSB until twenty days after they have been circulated. The parties have the right to participate fully in the consideration of panel reports by the DSB, and their views shall be fully recorded.[420]

Questions and Assignments 3.42

Is a panel report that is appealed, considered by the DSB for adoption? Do parties have an opportunity to comment on a panel report prior to its adoption by the DSB? Within what period can and must a panel report be adopted or rejected by the DSB? Can the adoption of a panel report be blocked? Look up what Members had to say on the Panel report in *US – Shrimp*.

3.5.2.9. *Duration of panel proceedings*

The period in which a panel must conduct its examination, from the date that the composition and terms of reference of the panel have been agreed upon until the date the final report is issued to the parties, shall, as a general rule, not exceed six months.[421] When a panel considers that it cannot issue its report within six months, it shall inform the DSB in writing of the reasons for the delay, together with an estimate of the period within which it will issue

---

[419] Article 16.4 of the DSU.   [420] Article 16.1 and 16.3 of the DSU.
[421] Article 12.8 of the DSU. In cases of urgency, including those relating to perishable goods, the panel aims to issue its report to the parties within three months and makes every effort to accelerate the proceedings to the greatest extent possible (Articles 12.9 and 4.9 of the DSU).

its report. In no case should the period from the establishment of the panel to the circulation of the report to the Members exceed nine months.[422]

In practice, however, the panel process often exceeds this time limit. On average, a panel process – from the establishment of the panel until the circulation of the panel report – lasts 371 days.[423] The reasons for exceeding the nine-month time limit include: the complexity of the case; the need to consult experts; the availability of experts; problems with scheduling meetings; and the time taken to translate the report.

Note that, at the request of the complaining party, the panel may, at any time during the panel proceedings, suspend its work for a maximum period of twelve months.[424] While not common, this does happen occasionally.[425] The authority of the panel lapses if the work of the panel is suspended for more than twelve months.[426]

Questions and Assignments 3.43

Describe the various steps in panel proceedings? Do you consider the rules on the duration of panel proceedings too strict or too liberal? Can panel proceedings be suspended indefinitely?

3.5.3. Appellate review

Seventy per cent of the panel reports circulated to date were appealed to the Appellate Body. This section discusses key aspects of the appellate review proceedings and issues that arise with respect to these proceedings:

- working procedures for appellate review;
- initiation of appellate review;
- written submissions and the oral hearing;
- rights of third participants;
- exchange of views, deliberations and the adoption of the Appellate Body report; and
- duration of appellate review proceedings.

3.5.3.1. Working procedures for appellate review

In contrast to panels, the Appellate Body has detailed standard working procedures set out in the *Working Procedures for Appellate Review* (the 'Working

---

[422] Article 12.9 of the DSU.
[423] See www.worldtradelaw.net/dsc/database/paneltiming.asp, visited on 31 August 2004. The period between the establishment of the panel and the adoption of the panel report by the DSB (in cases where there is no appeal) is on average 420 days. See www.worldtradelaw.net/dsc/database/adoptiontiming1.asp.
[424] Article 12.12 of the DSU.
[425] See e.g. *EC – Butter Products*, para. 12, in which New Zealand requested the Panel to suspend its work.
[426] The authority of the panel lapsed in, for example, *US – Helms-Burton Act*, complaint by the EC.

Procedures').[427] Pursuant to Article 17.9 of the DSU, these *Working Procedures* were drawn up by the Appellate Body itself, in consultation with the Chairman of the DSB and the WTO Director-General. In addition, where a procedural question arises that is not covered by the *Working Procedures*, the division hearing the appeal may, 'in the interest of fairness and orderly procedure in the conduct of the appeal', adopt an appropriate procedure for the purpose of that appeal.[428] The Additional Procedure adopted in the context of the *EC – Asbestos* case in respect of the filing of *amicus curiae* briefs, partially quoted and discussed above, is the best known example of the use of this authority.[429]

> **Questions and Assignments 3.44**
>
> How are the *Working Procedures for Appellate Review* established? What can a division hearing an appeal do when a procedural question arises that is not covered by the *Working Procedures*?

3.5.3.2. Initiation of appellate review

Pursuant to Rule 20(1) of the *Working Procedures*, appellate review proceedings commence with a party's notification in writing to the DSB of its decision to appeal *and* the simultaneous filing of a notice of appeal with the Appellate Body. The notice of appeal must adequately identify the findings or legal interpretations of the panel which are being appealed as erroneous. In addition to the title of the panel report under appeal, the name of the appellant and the service address, Rule 20(2)(d) states that a Notice of Appeal will include:

> a brief statement of the nature of the appeal, including the allegations of errors in the issues of law covered in the panel report and legal interpretations developed by the panel.[430]

---

[427] *Working Procedures for Appellate Review*, WT/AB/WP/7, dated 1 May 2003. This is a consolidated, revised version of the original *Working Procedures for Appellate Review*, WT/AB/WP/1, dated 15 February 1996. Note that, by a communication from the Chairman of the Appellate Body to the Chairman of the DSB, dated 7 October 2004 (WT/AB/WP/W/9), the Chairman of the Appellate Body informed the DSB that the Appellate Body was adopting a number of amendments to the *Working Procedures*. The communication of 7 October 2004 set out the adopted amendments as well as a new consolidated version of the *Working Procedures*, to be applied to appeals initiated after 1 January 2005. The amendments concern chiefly the introduction of the 'Notice of Other Appeal' (see below, p. 273, footnote 441), the new requirements regarding the content of the notice of appeal and notice of other appeal (see below, pp. 271–2, footnote 431), procedures for amending notices of appeal (see below, pp. 272, 273, footnote 431,441), and the date to conduct an oral hearing (see below, p. 274, footnote 445).

[428] Rule 16(1) of the *Working Procedures*. Such procedure must, however, be consistent with the DSU, the other covered agreements and the *Working Procedures*.

[429] See above, pp. 198–200.

[430] For early case law on the scope of this requirement, see Appellate Body Report, *US – Shrimp*, paras. 92–7; and Appellate Body Report, *EC – Bananas III*, paras. 151–2. Note that, according to the amendments to the *Working Procedures* coming into effect on 1 January 2005, the requirements as to the content of the notice of appeal are becoming more precise. Specifically, the modified Rule 20(2)(d) requires a notice of appeal to include:
> (i) identification of the alleged errors in the issues of law covered in the panel report and legal interpretations developed by the panel;
> (ii) a list of the legal provision(s) of the covered agreements that the panel is alleged to have erred in interpreting or applying; and

In *US – Countervailing Measures on Certain EC Products*, the Appellate Body ruled with respect to this requirement:

> [O]ur previous rulings have underscored the important balance that must be main-tained between the right of Members to exercise the right of appeal meaningfully and effectively, and the right of appellees to receive notice through the Notice of Appeal of the findings under appeal, so that they may exercise their right of defence effectively … [The] requirements under Rule 20(2) serve to ensure that the appellee also receives notice, albeit brief, of the "nature of the appeal" and the "allegations of errors" by the panel.[431]

The underlying rationale of Rule 20(2)(d) is thus to require the appellant to provide notice of the alleged error that the appellant intends to argue on appeal.[432] As the Appellate Body noted in *US – Shrimp*, the 'nature of the appeal' and the 'allegations of errors' are, in principle, sufficiently set out where the notice of appeal adequately identifies the findings or legal inter-pretations of the panel that are being appealed as erroneous. The notice of appeal is not expected to contain the reasons why the appellant regards those findings or interpretations as erroneous.[433] If the notice of appeal fails to give the appellee sufficient notice of a claim of error, that claim cannot and will not be considered by the Appellate Body.[434] Note that the Appellate Body, in *US – Offset Act (Byrd Amendment)*, held that the issue of a panel's jurisdiction is so:

> fundamental that it is appropriate to consider claims that a panel has exceeded its jurisdiction even if such claims were not raised in the Notice of Appeal.[435]

In the interest of due process, it would of course be preferable for the appellant to raise such important issues in the Notice of Appeal.

A party can appeal a panel report as soon as the report is circulated to WTO Members, and it can do so as long as the report has not yet been adopted by the DSB. In practice, parties usually appeal shortly before the meeting of the DSB that would consider the adoption of the report.

Upon the commencement of an appeal, the Appellate Body division respon-sible for deciding the appeal draws up an appropriate working schedule in

---

(iii) without prejudice to the ability of the appellant to refer to other paragraphs of the panel report in the context of its appeal, an indicative list of the paragraphs of the panel report containing the alleged errors.

New Rule 23 *bis* of the *Working Procedures* further introduces the possibility of amending a notice of appeal, if authorized by the division. See WT/AB/WP/W/9, dated 7 October 2004, Annex B.

[431] Appellate Body Report, *US – Countervailing Measures on Certain EC Products*, para. 62.

[432] Appellate Body Report, *US – Offset Act (Byrd Amendment)*, para. 195.

[433] The legal arguments in support of the allegations of error are to be set out and developed in the appellant's submission. See Appellate Body Report, *US – Shrimp*, paras. 92–7; and Appellate Body Report, *EC – Bananas III*, paras. 148–52. Note the special situation of a claim that the Panel has violated Article 11 of the DSU (see *US – Offset Act (Byrd Amendment)*, paras. 199–201).

[434] See e.g. *US – Offset Act (Byrd Amendment)*, para. 206; see also *Japan – Apples* and *Chile – Price Band System*. In both of these cases, the Appellate Body found that the appellee could not have been aware that the appellant intended to raise an Article 11 challenge with respect to certain findings of the Panel because the notice of appeal did not refer to Article 11 or to the 'objective assessment' standard with respect to these findings. The Appellate Body therefore concluded that the Article 11 claim of error was not reviewable in these appeals. See Appellate Body Report, *Japan – Apples*, paras. 120–8 and Appellate Body Report, *Chile – Price Band System*, paras. 151–65.

[435] Appellate Body Report, *US – Offset Act (Byrd Amendment)*, para. 208.

accordance with the time periods stipulated in the *Working Procedures*.[436] The working schedule sets forth precise dates for the filing of documents and includes a timetable of the division's work.[437] In exceptional circumstances, where strict adherence to a time period would result in manifest unfairness, a party or third party to the dispute may request modification of that time period. This possibility is provided for in Rule 16(2) of the *Working Procedures* and has been used occasionally.

Questions and Assignments 3.45

How and when can an appellate review proceeding be initiated? At what point in time are appellate review proceedings most frequently initiated? When is a notice of appeal sufficiently precise?

3.5.3.3. *Written submissions and the oral hearing*

Within ten days after filing the notice of appeal the appellant must file a written submission.[438] The written submission sets out a precise statement of the grounds of appeal, including the specific allegations of legal errors in the panel report, and the legal arguments in support of these allegations.[439] Within fifteen days of the filing of the notice of appeal, other parties to the dispute may, by filing 'other appellant's submission', join in the original appeal or appeal on the basis of other alleged legal errors in the panel report ('cross appeal').[440] Within twenty-five days of the filing of the notice of appeal, any party that wishes to respond to allegations of legal errors, whether raised in the submission of the original appellant or in the submission(s) of other appellants, may file an appellee's submission.[441] The appellee's submission sets out a precise statement of the grounds for opposing the specific allegations of legal errors raised in the appellant's submission and includes legal arguments in support thereof.[442] Should a participant fail to file a submission

---

[436] Rule 26(1) of the *Working Procedures*. The Appellate Body Secretariat shall serve forthwith a copy of the working schedule on the appellant, the parties to the dispute and any third parties (Rule 26(4) of the *Working Procedures*).

[437] Rule 26(2) of the *Working Procedures*.

[438] Rule 21(1) of the *Working Procedures*. Note that, according to the amendments to the *Working Procedures* coming into effect on 1 January 2005, this period is shortened to seven days. See WT/AB/WP/W/9, dated 7 October 2004, Annex B.

[439] Rule 21(2) of the *Working Procedures*. The submission also includes a precise statement of the provisions of the covered agreements and other legal sources relied on, as well as the nature of the decision or ruling sought.

[440] Rule 23(1) of the *Working Procedures*. Note that, according to the amendments to the *Working Procedures* coming into effect on 1 January 2005, Rule 23(1) requires the other appellant to file first a notice of other appeal (requirements as to the content of the notice of other appeal are set out in new Rule 23(2) and are similar to those relating to the notice of appeal). It is only after filing the notice of other appeal that the other appellant may file a written submission. New Rule 23 *bis* of the *Working Procedures* further envisages the possibility of amending a notice of other appeal, if authorised by the division. See WT/AB/WP/W/9, dated 7 October 2004, Annex B.

[441] Rules 22(1) and 23(3) of the *Working Procedures*.

[442] For written submissions of third participants, see below, p. 275.

within the required time periods, the division, after hearing the views of the participants, issues such order, including dismissal of the appeal, as it deems appropriate.[443]

The division responsible for deciding the appeal holds an oral hearing. According to the *Working Procedures*, the oral hearing is, as a general rule, held thirty days after the notice of appeal is filed.[444] However, for practical and organisational reasons, the hearing is often held at a later date. The purpose of the oral hearing is to provide participants with an opportunity to present and argue their case before the division, in order to clarify the legal issues in the appeal. At the hearing, the appellant(s) and appellee(s) first make brief oral presentations focusing on the core legal issues raised in the appeal.[445] After the oral presentations, the participants answer detailed questions posed by Members of the Division regarding the issues raised in the appeal. At the end of the oral hearing, the participants are given the opportunity to make a brief concluding statement. The oral hearing is usually completed in one day. In complex cases, however, the oral hearing may take longer. In *EC – Bananas III* and *EC – Hormones*, for example, the oral hearing took two and a half days and two days, respectively.

At any time during the appellate proceedings, the division may address questions to, or request additional memoranda from, any participant or third participant and specify the time periods by which written responses or memoranda shall be received.[446] Any such questions, responses or memoranda are made available simultaneously to the other participants and third participants in the appeal who are then given an opportunity to respond.[447] Neither the DSU nor any other covered agreement explicitly grants the Appellate Body the authority to appoint and consult experts. However, to the extent advice from experts would be necessary to comprehend better the arguments made by the participants and to decide the appeal, such authority is implied and cannot be denied to the Appellate Body.

Throughout the proceedings, the participants and third participants are precluded from having *ex parte* communications with the Appellate Body in respect of matters concerning the appeal. Neither a division nor any of its Members may meet with or contact a participant or third participant in the absence of the other participants and third participants.[448]

---

[443] Rule 29 of the *Working Procedures*. To date, there has been no need for such an order.

[444] Rule 27(1) of the *Working Procedures*. It has been quite common for the hearing to be held around day 40 of the appellate review process. This practice led to the amendment to Rule 27(1) of the *Working Procedures*. The modified Rule 27(1), effective as of 1 January 2005, requires the oral hearing to be held, as a general rule, between thirty-five and forty-five days after the date of the filing of a notice of appeal. See WT/AB/WP/W/9, dated 7 October 2004, Annex B.

[445] Rule 27(3) of the *Working Procedures*. Any third participant may also make an oral presentation and may be questioned at the oral hearing (see below, p. 275). The Presiding Member may, as necessary, set time limits for oral arguments (Rule 27(4) of the *Working Procedures*). Typically, the appellant and appellee are given thirty minutes each and the third participants fifteen minutes each for their oral arguments. Any time limit imposed is strictly enforced.

[446] Rule 28(1) of the *Working Procedures*.   [447] Rule 28(2) of the *Working Procedures*.

[448] Article 18.1 of the DSU and Rule 19(1) of the *Working Procedures*. Also, a Member of the Appellate Body who is not assigned to the division hearing the appeal shall not discuss any aspect of the subject matter of the appeal with any participant or third participant (Rule 19(3) of the *Working Procedures*).

3.5.3.4. *Rights of third participants*

As discussed above, the rights of third parties in panel proceedings are limited. Normally, third parties only attend, and are heard at, a special session of the first substantive meeting of the panel, and receive the first written submissions of the parties only. Third participants, i.e. third parties participating in appellate review proceedings, have much broader rights.

In appellate review proceedings, all third parties have a right to file a written submission, within twenty-five days of the date of the filing of the notice of appeal, containing the grounds and legal arguments in support of their position.[449] A third party has the right to participate in the oral hearing when:

- it has filed a written submission; or
- it has notified the Appellate Body Secretariat of its intention to participate in the oral hearing within twenty-five days of the notice of appeal.[450]

A third party that has neither filed a written submission nor has notified its intention to participate in the oral hearing may still participate in the oral hearing. It may, at the discretion of the division and taking into account the requirements of due process, be allowed to make an oral statement at the hearing and respond to questions asked by the division.[451]

---

[449] Rule 24(1) of the *Working Procedures*.
[450] Rule 24(1) of the *Working Procedures*. Third participants are encouraged to file written submissions to facilitate their positions being taken into account (see Rule 24(3) of the Working Procedures).
[451] Rule 27(3)(b) and (c) of the *Working Procedures*.

3.5.3.5. *Exchange of views, deliberations and the adoption of the report*

As noted above, the division responsible for deciding an appeal will exchange views on issues raised by the appeal with the other Members of the Appellate Body, before finalising its report.[452] The exchange of views puts into practice the principle of collegiality set out in the *Working Procedures*.[453] Depending on the number and complexity of the issues under discussion, this process usually takes place over two or more days.

Following the exchange of views, the division continues its deliberations and drafts the report. When finalised, the report is signed by the three Members of the division. The report is then translated so that it is available in all three languages of the WTO.[454] After translation, the report is circulated to the WTO Members as an unrestricted document available to the public.[455]

Note that the appellant can, pursuant to Rule 30(1) of the *Working Procedures*, withdraw its appeal at any time. In *India – Autos*, India withdrew its appeal the day before the oral hearing. The Appellate Body immediately informed the DSB of the withdrawal and, a few days later, circulated a short report in which it briefly described the measure at issue, the conclusions of the Panel, the issues of law appealed by India, and the steps in the appellate review proceedings up to the moment of the withdrawal. The Appellate Body concluded this report by noting that 'in view of India's withdrawal of the appeal … the Appellate Body hereby completes its work in this appeal'.[456] In *US – Softwood Lumber IV*, the United States filed a notice of appeal on 2 October 2003 and withdrew this notice the following day 'for scheduling reasons'. The withdrawal was conditional upon the right to re-file the notice of appeal at a later date, and, on 21 October 2003, the United States re-filed a 'substantively identical' notice of appeal.[457]

Within thirty days following circulation of the Appellate Body report, the Appellate Body report *and* the panel report as upheld, modified or reversed by the Appellate Body, are adopted by the DSB *unless* the DSB decides by consensus not to adopt the reports.[458] The adopted Appellate Body report is accepted unconditionally by the parties to the dispute. The adoption procedure is, however, without prejudice to the right of Members to express their views on an Appellate Body report.[459] WTO Members often take full advantage of this opportunity to comment on the reports at the meeting of the DSB at which they are adopted. Generally, the winning party briefly praises the Appellate Body (and/or the panel) while the losing party is more critical, often repeating

---

[452] See above, p. 248.   [453] Rule 4 of the *Working Procedures*.
[454] During the period 1995–2003, in all appellate review proceedings English has been the working language of the Appellate Body, and the Appellate Body reports were all drafted in English and then translated into French and Spanish. In a few appellate review proceedings, participants or third participants filed submissions or made oral statements in French and Spanish. When requested, interpretation is provided at the oral hearing.
[455] See www.wto.org.   [456] Appellate Body Report, *India – Autos*, para. 18.
[457] Appellate Body Report, *US – Softwood Lumber IV*, para. 6.
[458] Article 17.14 of the DSU. On the reverse consensus requirement, see above, pp. 229–30.
[459] *Ibid.*

the arguments submitted to, but rejected by, the Appellate Body (and/or the panel). The views of Members on the Appellate Body report (and/or the panel report) are fully recorded in the minutes of the DSB meeting.

Questions and Assignments 3.48

When is an Appellate Body report considered by the DSB for adoption? Is a panel report that has been reversed by the Appellate Body adopted by the DSB? Can an appeal pending before the Appellate Body be withdrawn? Look up what Members had to say at the time of DSB adoption of the Appellate Body and panel reports in *US – Shrimp*.

3.5.3.6. *Duration of appellate review proceedings*

With regard to the appellate review proceedings, the DSU provides that, as a general rule, the proceedings shall not exceed sixty-days from the date a party to the dispute formally notifies its decision to appeal to the date the Appellate Body circulates its report.[460] When the Appellate Body believes that it cannot render its report within sixty-days, it shall inform the DSB in writing of the reasons for the delay together with an estimate of the period within which it will submit its report. In no case shall the proceedings exceed ninety days.[461]

In practice, the Appellate Body has, in most cases, taken more than sixty-days to complete the appellate review.[462] In all but four cases, however, the Appellate Body has been able to complete the proceedings within the ninety-day time limit.[463] The reasons for the delay in the appellate review proceedings included the complexity of the appeal, an overload of work, a hold-up in translation and the death of an Appellate Body Member hearing the appeal.

Questions and Assignments 3.49

Describe the various steps in appellate review proceedings. Do you consider the rules on the duration of appellate review proceedings too strict or too liberal?

---

[460] Article 17.5 of the DSU. In cases of urgency, including those which concern perishable foods, the Appellate Body makes every effort to accelerate the proceedings to the greatest extent possible (Articles 17.5 and 4.9 of the DSU). Also, for disputes involving prohibited subsidies, there are accelerated proceedings. See below, p. 565.

[461] Article 17.5 of the DSU. Note that this ninety-day time limit also includes the time needed for translation.

[462] Especially during the first years of its operation, the Appellate Body succeeded a few times in completing appellate review proceedings within the sixty-day time limit. See e.g. *Japan – Alcoholic Beverages II*, *US – Wool Shirts and Blouses*, *Canada – Periodicals*, *Brazil – Aircraft (Article 21.5 – Canada)* and *Canada – Aircraft (Article 21.5 – Brazil)*. It has not done so again since May 2000. For *India – Autos*, see above, p. 276.

[463] The four cases in which the ninety-day time limit was exceeded were *EC – Hormones* (114 days), *US – Lead and Bismuth II* (104 days), *EC – Asbestos* (140 days) and *Thailand – H-Beams* (140 days).

3.5.4. Implementation and enforcement

At a DSB meeting held within thirty days of the adoption of the panel and/or Appellate Body report, the Member concerned must inform the DSB of its intentions in respect of the implementation of the recommendations and rulings.[464] This section discusses the following procedural issues which arise with respect to the implementation and enforcement of recommendations and rulings:

- arbitration on the 'reasonable period of time for implementation';
- the surveillance of implementation by the DSB;
- the 'sequencing' issue;
- disagreement on implementation; and
- arbitration on, and authorisation of, suspension of concessions or other obligations.

3.5.4.1. Arbitration on the 'reasonable period of time for implementation'

As discussed above, prompt or immediate compliance with the DSB'S recommendations and rulings, i.e. prompt or immediate withdrawal or amendment of the WTO-inconsistent measure, is essential for the effective functioning of the WTO and the primary obligation of the Member concerned.[465] However, if it is impracticable to comply with the recommendations and rulings immediately – and this may often be the case – the Member concerned has a reasonable period of time in which to do so pursuant to Article 21.3 of the DSU.[466]

If no agreement between the parties can be reached on the 'reasonable period of time for implementation' within forty-five days of the adoption of the recommendations and rulings, the original complainant can refer the matter to arbitration under Article 21.3(c) of the DSU. The parties must agree on an arbitrator; in most cases they are able to do so. However, if they cannot agree on an arbitrator within ten days, either party may request the Director-General of the WTO to appoint an arbitrator.[467] The Director-General will consult the parties and appoint an arbitrator within ten days. The DSU does not provide for any rule or guideline as to the professional or other requirements persons should meet to serve as an Article 21.3(c) arbitrator. However, a practice has developed that Members of the Appellate Body serve as Article 21.3(c) arbitrators.[468] They do so not as Appellate Body Members but in a personal capacity.

While not set out in the DSU, the arbitration proceedings involve the filing of written submissions and a meeting of the parties with the arbitrator. The

---

[464] Article 21.3 of the DSU.   [465] See above, pp. 217–18.   [466] Article 21.3(a), (b) and (c) of the DSU.
[467] In all but three cases, up to February 2004, the parties agreed on the arbitrator. In the other three cases, the Director-General appointed the arbitrator.
[468] To date, all Article 21.3(c) arbitrators have been Members of the Appellate Body. In *EC – Hormones*, the Director-General initially appointed two arbitrators: an Appellate Body Member and a senior diplomat of a WTO Member. However, for reasons unrelated to the arbitration, the senior diplomat withdrew at the start of the arbitration proceedings.

DSU does require that the arbitration proceedings do not exceed ninety days commencing on the date of the adoption of the panel and Appellate Body reports by the DSB. As this requirement is often not realistic, it is – with the express agreement of the parties – commonly set aside.

The mandate of an Article 21.3(c) arbitrator is narrow in scope. The Arbitrator in *Korea – Alcoholic Beverages* stated as follows:

> My mandate in this arbitration relates exclusively to determining the reasonable period of time for implementation under Article 21.3(c) of the DSU. It is not within my mandate to suggest ways and means to implement the recommendations and rulings of the DSB.[469]

It is not for the Article 21.3(c) arbitrator to rule on the WTO-consistency of the proposed implementing measures.[470]

The arbitration award indicating the 'reasonable period of time for implementation' is issued to the parties and circulated to all WTO Members. Note that, unlike panel or Appellate Body reports, an Article 21.3(c) arbitration award is *not* adopted by the DSB. An arbitration award is circulated to WTO Members and posted as a WT/DS document on the WTO's website.

Questions and Assignments 3.50

Who can serve as an Article 21.3(c) arbitrator? Briefly discuss the steps in Article 21.3(c) proceedings. What is the mandate of Article 21.3(c) arbitrators? Find the Article 21.3(c) award in *EC – Hormones*. What was the ruling of the Arbitrator in that case?

3.5.4.2. *Surveillance of implementation by the DSB*

During the 'reasonable period of time for implementation', the DSB keeps the implementation of adopted recommendations and rulings under surveillance.[471] At any time following adoption of the recommendations or rulings, any WTO Member may raise the issue of implementation at the DSB. Starting six months after establishment of the reasonable period of time, the issue of implementation is placed on the agenda of each DSB meeting and remains on the DSB's agenda until the issue is resolved. At least ten days prior to such a DSB meeting, the Member concerned must provide the DSB with a status report on its progress in the implementation of the recommendations or rulings.[472]

---

[469] Award of the Arbitrator, *Korea – Alcoholic Beverages*, para. 45.
[470] Award of the Arbitrator, *Canada – Pharmaceutical Patents*, para. 41.
[471] Article 21.6 of the DSU. Note also that, after the DSB has authorised retaliation measures (see below, p. 283), the DSB shall 'continue to keep under surveillance the implementation of adopted recommendations or rulings' (see Article 22.8 of the DSU).
[472] *Ibid.* The status reports under Article 21.6 of the DSU are posted on the WTO's website as WT/DS · · · documents. For the debate on these reports, see the minutes of the relevant DSB meeting (WT/DSB/M/ · · ·).

3.5.4.3. *The 'sequencing' issue*

As discussed above, if the respondent fails to implement the recommendations
and rulings within the 'reasonable period of time' and agreement on compensation cannot be reached, the complainant may request authorisation from the
DSB to suspend concessions or other obligations.[473] However, it is clear that
such retaliation is only called for when the respondent failed to implement the
recommendations and rulings. As the complainant and the respondent may
often disagree on whether the respondent did indeed fail to implement the
recommendations and rulings, Article 21.5 of the DSU provides:

> Where there is disagreement as to the existence or consistency with a covered agree-
> ment of measures taken to comply with the recommendations and rulings such dispute
> shall be decided through recourse to these dispute settlement procedures, including
> wherever possible resort to the original panel.

The so-called Article 21.5 'compliance' panel must circulate its report within
ninety days after the date of referral of the matter to it.[474] However, due to
careless drafting of the DSU, there is a conflict between the timeframe for this
Article 21.5 procedure and the timeframe within which authorisation for the
suspension of concessions and other obligations must be requested and
obtained from the DSB. Pursuant to Article 22.6, the authorisation for retaliation
must be granted by the DSB within thirty days of the expiry of the reasonable
period of time. It is clear that it is not possible to obtain authorisation for
retaliation within thirty days, where the complainant first must submit the
disagreement on implementation to an Article 21.5 'compliance' panel. In the
EC – Bananas III dispute, this inconsistency led to a serious institutional crisis in
which the United States insisted on its right to obtain authorisation for retaliation and the European Communities asserted that an Article 21.5 'compliance'
panel first had to establish that the implementing measures taken by the
European Communities were not WTO-consistent. Eventually, a pragmatic
compromise was found to unblock the situation. However, the problem of
the relationship between these two procedures (often referred to as the
'sequencing issue') remains, and a change to the DSU is required to resolve
the problem. In the meantime, parties commonly agree, on an *ad hoc* basis, that
the procedure of examining the WTO consistency of the implementing

---

[473] See above, pp. 220–3.
[474] Article 21.5 of the DSU. If the panel considers that it cannot provide its report within ninety days, it
must inform the DSB of the reasons for the delay together with an estimate of the period within which
the report will be submitted.

measures will need to be terminated before the authorisation for retaliation measures may be granted.[475] As the European Communities noted in a communication of March 2002:

> In light of the practice followed consistently since [1999], it would appear that Members now broadly agree that completing the procedure established under Article 21.5 DSU is a pre-requisite for invoking the provisions of Article 22 DSU, in case of disagreement among the parties about implementation.[476]

However, this does not mean that the DSU does not need to be clarified on this point in order to ensure legal certainty and predictability of the system for all its Members.

Questions and Assignments 3.52

Explain briefly what the so-called 'sequencing issue' is and how it is 'handled' now. In your opinion, can the DSB authorise the suspension of concessions or other obligations before a panel, under Article 21.5 of the DSU, has established that there has not been proper implementation?

3.5.4.4. Disagreement on the implementation

As noted above, the complainant and the respondent may disagree as to whether the respondent did indeed fail to implement the recommendations and rulings. Article 21.5 of the DSU provides that such disagreement as to the existence, or consistency with WTO law, of implementing measures shall be decided:

> through recourse to these dispute settlement procedures, including wherever possible resort to the original panel.

Recourse to 'these dispute settlement procedures' means recourse to the procedures set out in Articles 4 to 20 of the DSU.[477] The normal procedures discussed in previous sections apply with one important exception. Article 21.5 requires that the panel circulate its report within ninety days after the date of the referral of the matter to it. However, this timeframe is not realistic as is demonstrated by the fact that the average duration of an Article 21.5 compliance procedure is now 170 days, i.e. almost double the time allowed.[478]

The mandate of an Article 21.5 'compliance' panel is to examine the WTO-consistency of implementing measures, i.e. measures taken to comply with

---

[475] See e.g. in *US – Shrimp*, or in *US – FSC*.   [476] TN/DS/W/1, 4.

[477] While Article 21.5 refers to 'these procedures', it is disputed by some WTO Members whether this also includes consultations pursuant to Article 4 of the DSU. It is now generally accepted that 'these procedures' include appellate review pursuant to Article 17 of the DSU.

[478] See www.worldtradelaw.net/dsc/database/paneltiming1.asp, visited on 31 August 2004.

the recommendations and rulings of the DSB. As the Appellate Body ruled in *Canada – Aircraft (Article 21.5 – Brazil)*:

> in carrying out its review under Article 21.5 of the DSU, a panel is not confined to examining the "measures taken to comply" from the perspective of the claims, arguments and factual circumstances that related to the measure that was the subject of the original proceedings. Although these may be of some relevance in the proceedings under Article 21.5 of the DSU, Article 21.5 proceedings involve, in principle, not the original measure, but rather a new and different measure which was not before the original panel.[479]

If an Article 21.5 panel were restricted to examining the new measure from the perspective of the claims, arguments and factual circumstances that related to the original measure, the effectiveness of an Article 21.5 review would be seriously undermined because an Article 21.5 panel would then be unable to examine fully the 'consistency with a covered agreement of the measures taken to comply', as required by Article 21.5 of the DSU.[480]

To date, there have been thirteen such Article 21.5 'compliance' procedures.[481] In one dispute, *Canada – Dairy (Article 21.5 – New Zealand and US)*, there were two successive Article 21.5 'compliance' procedures. In all Article 21.5 procedures thus far, the original panel served as the compliance panel. Eight of the thirteen Article 21.5 panel reports were appealed.

Like 'normal' panel and Appellate Body reports, Article 21.5 compliance panel and Appellate Body reports become legally binding on the parties only after adoption by the DSB. The DSB adopts these reports by reverse consensus.

An important difference between the recommendations and rulings of 'normal' reports and Article 21.5 reports is that the respondent does not benefit from a reasonable period of time to implement the recommendations and rulings of Article 21.5 reports. Immediately after the adoption of these report(s), the complainant can request authorisation from the DSB to take retaliatory measures.

Questions and Assignments 3.53

When will an Article 21.5 procedure be initiated? What are the differences between the 'normal' DSU proceedings and the Article 21.5 proceedings? What is the mandate of an Article 21.5 'compliance' panel? Will an Article 21.5 'compliance' panel examine whether the respondent has adopted a measure which implements the recommendations and rulings of the DSB or a measure which is consistent with WTO law?

---

[479] Appellate Body Report, *Canada – Aircraft (Article 21.5 – Brazil)*, para. 41.
[480] *Ibid.*
[481] See www.worldtradelaw.net/dsc/database/paneltiming1.asp, visited on 2 September 2004.

3.5.4.5. *Arbitration on and authorisation of suspension of concessions or other obligations*

If the respondent fails to implement the recommendations and rulings adopted by the DSB correctly within the reasonable period of time agreed by the parties or determined by an arbitrator, the respondent will, at the request of the complainant, enter into negotiations with the latter party in order to come to an agreement on mutually acceptable compensation.[482] If satisfactory compensation is not agreed upon within twenty days of the expiry of the reasonable period of time, the complainant may request the authorisation from the DSB to suspend the application of concessions or other obligations to the respondent, under the covered agreements.[483] In other words, it may seek authorisation to retaliate. The DSB must decide on the authorisation to retaliate within thirty days of the expiry of the reasonable period of time.[484] As discussed above, the DSB decides on the authorisation to retaliate by reverse consensus; the authorisation is thus quasi-automatic.[485]

However, if the non-complying Member objects to the level of suspension proposed, or claims that the principles and procedures for suspension have not been followed, the matter may be referred to arbitration before the DSB takes a decision.[486] This arbitration under Article 22.6 of the DSU is carried out by the original panel, if the same members are available, or by an arbitrator appointed by the Director-General.[487] The arbitration must be completed within sixty days of expiry of the reasonable period of time,[488] and a second arbitration or appeal is not possible.[489] The DSB is informed promptly of the decision of the arbitrator and grants, by reverse consensus, the requested authorisation to suspend concessions or other obligations where the request is consistent with the decision of the arbitrator.[490] Decisions by the arbitrators under Article 22.6 of the DSU are circulated to WTO Members, and posted on the WTO's website as WT/DS documents.

Note that the DSU currently does not provide for a procedure for the withdrawal or termination of the authorisation to retaliate.

Questions and Assignments 3.54

When *must* the respondent enter into negotiations on compensation? When may the complainant request the DSB to authorise retaliation measures? How is the level of retaliation decided on?

---

[482] Article 22.2 of the DSU. On compensation under Article 22, see above, pp. 220–1.
[483] Article 22.2 of the DSU. On the specificity of the request for suspension, see the Award of the Arbitrators, *EC – Hormones (US)* (Article 22.6 – EC), para. 16; and Award by the Arbitrators, *EC – Bananas III (Ecuador)* (Article 22.6 – EC), para. 24.
[484] Article 22.6 of the DSU.   [485] See above, p. 221.
[486] Article 22.6 of the DSU. On the appropriate level of suspension and on the principles and procedures of suspension, see above, pp. 221–3.
[487] Article 22.6 of the DSU.   [488] Article 22.6 of the DSU.
[489] Article 22.7 of the DSU.
[490] Article 22.7 of the DSU. Note that the Decision of the Arbitrators under Article 22.6 is notified to the DSB but is not adopted by it.

3.6. WTO DISPUTE SETTLEMENT PRACTICE TO DATE

The WTO dispute settlement system became operational when the *WTO Agreement* entered into force on 1 January 1995. In the decade since January 1995, the WTO dispute settlement system has been much and widely used, and its 'output' in terms of the number of dispute settlement reports has been remarkable.

3.6.1. Disputes

To illustrate the use made of the WTO dispute settlement system to date, this section examines:

* the number of disputes brought to the WTO;
* the identity of the WTO Members acting as complainant or respondent; and
* the agreements at issue in the disputes brought to the WTO.

The data analysed relate to the period 1995–2003 but some comments concern subsequent developments.

3.6.1.1. *Number of disputes*

Between 1 January 1995 and 1 September 2004, WTO Members brought 314 disputes to the WTO for resolution under the multilateral rules and procedures of the DSU.[491] As already noted above, this is more than in almost half a century of GATT dispute settlement. The WTO dispute settlement system is arguably the most used international dispute settlement system.[492] The number of disputes brought to the WTO was at its highest in 1997 and at its lowest in 2001. The number of disputes tends to go up and down from year to year, often without a clear reason for either the increase or the decrease in the number of disputes. See Figure 3.7.

3.6.1.2. *Complainants and respondents*

Unlike the GATT dispute settlement system, which was rarely used by developing-country Members, the WTO dispute settlement system has been used by developed and developing-country Members alike. In fact, in 1995 and from 2000 to 2003, developing-country Members (i.e. upper middle-income countries,[493] lower

---

[491] See www.worldtradelaw.net/dsc/database/searchcomplaints.asp, visited on 2 September 2004. This number refers to the number of requests for consultations notified to the DSB.
[492] See above, pp. 94, 173–4.
[493] Upper middle income countries include, for example, Argentina, Brazil, Mexico, Poland and Slovakia. The classification of countries in four categories (high income, upper middle income, lower middle income and low income) indicates that the following number of complaints have been brought against each category: 202, 71, 34 and 23.

Figure 3.7 Requests for consultations: trend 1995–2003[494]

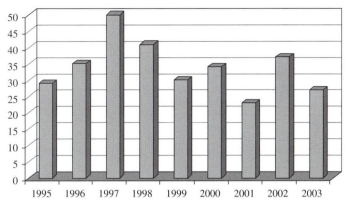

Figure 3.8 Complainants per income category: trend 1995–2003[495]

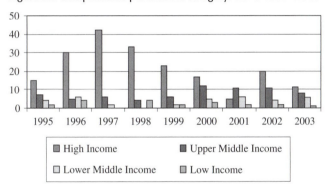

middle-income countries[496] and low-income countries[497]) brought more dis-putes to the WTO than the developed-country Members (i.e. high-income countries). See Figure 3.8.

Over the period from 1995 to 2003, high-income countries have been the most prolific users of the WTO dispute settlement system. In 61 per cent of all disputes, high-income countries, such as the United States and the European Communities, were the complainant. In view of their share of world trade, this is not surprising. However, in 39 per cent of all disputes, developing-country Members, and in particular upper middle-income countries (22 per cent), were complainants. The United States has been the single most active complainant (in seventy-five disputes), followed by the European Communities (in sixty-two

[494] See www.worldtradelaw.net, visited on 1 January 2004.
[495] See www.worldtradelaw.net, visited on 1 January 2004.
[496] Lower middle income countries include, for example, China, Colombia, the Philippines, Romania and Turkey.
[497] Low income countries include, for example, India, Indonesia, Nicaragua and Pakistan.

Figure 3.9 Complainants per income category: totals 1995–2003[498]

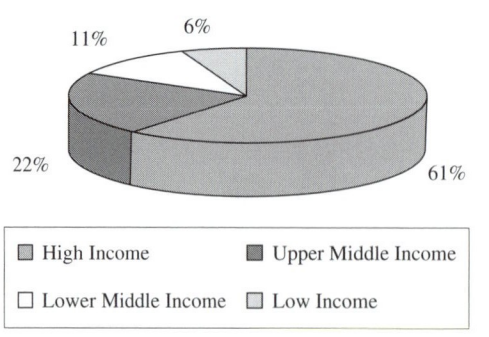

- High Income
- Upper Middle Income
- Lower Middle Income
- Low Income

disputes), Canada (in twenty-four disputes) and Brazil (in twenty-two disputes). It is remarkable that India, a low-income country, has been a complainant in fifteen disputes. Low-income countries were complainants in a total of twenty disputes. Thus far, Bangladesh is the only least-developed-country Member that has brought a dispute to the WTO. In January 2004, it requested consultations with India on the imposition by India of an anti-dumping measure on batteries from Bangladesh.[499] See Figure 3.9.

Sixty-two per cent of all disputes thus far related, or relate, to measures of developed-country Members; and 38 per cent related, or relate, to measures of developing-country Members. Cases brought against measures of developing-country Members have often been brought by other developing-country Members. Small developing-country Members have brought cases, and won cases, against large developed-country Members. A classic example of this is *US – Underwear*, a complaint by Costa Rica.[500] The United States was the single most important respondent (in eighty-one disputes), followed by the European Communities (in forty-five disputes), India (in fourteen disputes), Japan (in thirteen disputes) and Canada, Korea and Brazil (in twelve disputes each). To date, there has been no case against a measure of a least-developed-country Member.[501] See Figure 3.10.

3.6.1.3. WTO agreements at issue in disputes

While a number of disputes concern limited economic interests, other disputes raise important and politically sensitive issues relating, for example, to the conflict between trade liberalisation and the protection of public health or the protection of the environment, or the conflict between liberalised trade and economic development. The disputes brought to the WTO to date concerned,

[498] See www.worldtradelaw.net, visited on 1 January 2004.
[499] Request for Consultations by Bangladesh, *India – Anti-Dumping Measure on Batteries from Bangladesh*, WT/DS306/1, dated 2 February 2004.
[500] See also above, pp. 225–6.
[501] See www.worldtradelaw.net, visited on 15 January 2004. Note that a number of these disputes concern the same measure. E.g. *India – Quantitative Restrictions* which is counted six times (complaints by the EC, Switzerland, New Zealand, Canada, Australia and the US).

Figure 3.10 Respondents per income category: totals 1995–2003[502]

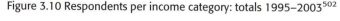
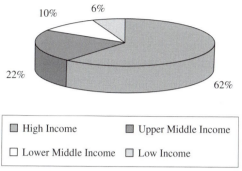

| ◼ High Income | ◼ Upper Middle Income |
| ☐ Lower Middle Income | ☐ Low Income |

and concern, all the covered agreements. There has been dispute settlement on a very broad scope of rights and obligations. However, in 39 per cent of all disputes, the complainant argued that the respondent had violated a provision of the GATT 1994. The GATT 1994 was, and is, by far the most invoked covered agreement. In 10 per cent of the disputes, the complainant argued a violation of the *Anti-Dumping Agreement*, in 9 per cent a violation of the *Agreement on Agriculture*, and in 9 per cent a violation of the *SCM Agreement*. The number of disputes in which a violation of the GATS or the *TRIPS Agreement* was argued has been relatively low to date. See Figure 3.11.

3.6.2. Reports and awards

In the period from 1 January 1995 to 1 September 2004, panels and the Appellate Body circulated 103 and 63 reports respectively.[503] Panel reports in particular tend to be quite voluminous. Furthermore, the WTO dispute settlement system also produced a number of arbitration awards.[504] When compared with the 'output' of the International Court of Justice or the International Tribunal for the Law of the Sea, the WTO dispute settlement system has been remarkably 'industrious'. See Figure 3.12.

The number of panel reports peaked in 2000 (with twenty-three reports), an exceptional year partly reflecting the high number of requests for consultations in 1997. The number of panel reports dropped in 2001 (twelve reports) and was at sixteen in 2003. The number of Appellate Body reports peaked in

---

[502] Seewww.worldtradelaw.net, visited on 1 January 2004.

[503] See www.worldtradelaw.net/dsc/database/wtopanels.asp and www.worldtradelaw.net/dsc/database/abreports.asp, visited on 2 September 2004. Four panel reports in cases where a mutually agreed solution was reached are not included. The Appellate Body report in *India – Autos*, in which the appeal was withdrawn, is also not included. Note, however, that, in *US – Steel Safeguards*, eight reports were circulated (in one document). See above, p. 234.

[504] Sixteen arbitration awards under Article 21.3(c) of the DSU on the reasonable period of time for implementation, not including the award in *US – Line Pipe Safeguards* in which the parties reached an agreement on the reasonable period of time for implementation (see above, pp. 278–9); seven arbitration decisions under Article 22.6 of the DSU on the suspension of concessions or other obligations (see above, p. 283); and one arbitration award under Article 25 of the DSU (see above, p. 186). See www.worldtradelaw.net/reports/wtopanels/us-linepipesafeguards(panel).pdf, visited on 2 September 2004.

Figure 3.11 WTO agreements at issue: totals 1995–2003[505]

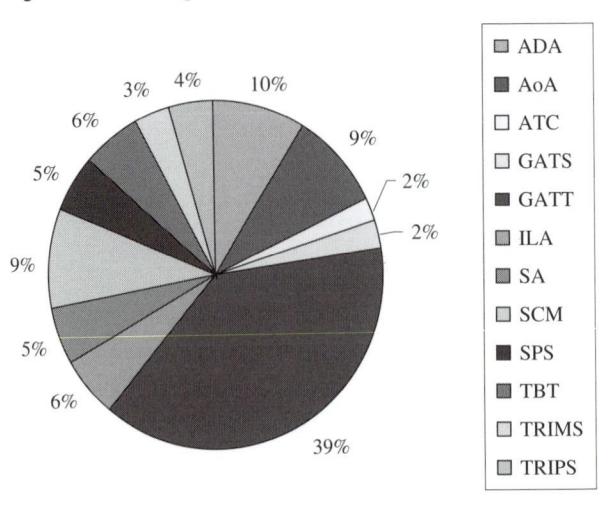

Figure 3.12 Number of reports: trend 1995–2003[506]

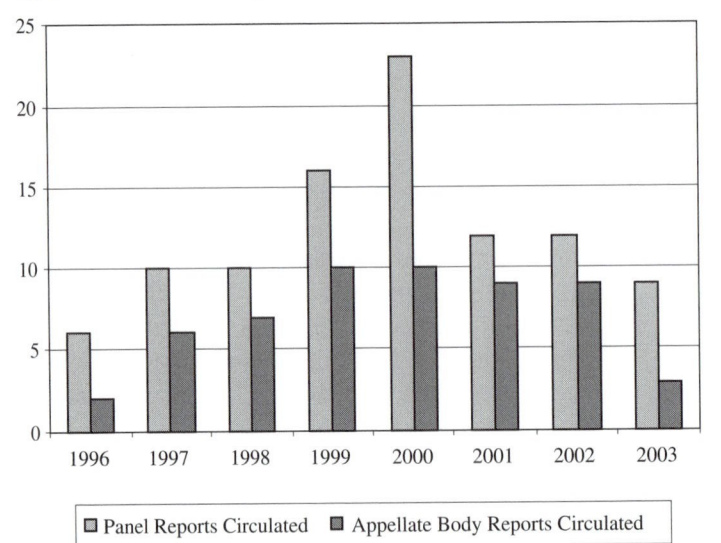

☐ Panel Reports Circulated   ■ Appellate Body Reports Circulated

1999 and 2000 (with ten reports) but has decreased since.[507] In 2003, the number of Appellate Body reports circulated dropped to seven.

505 See www.worldtradelaw.net, visited on 1 January 2004. ADA stands for *Anti-Dumping Agreement*; AoA for *Agreement on Agriculture*; ATC for *Agreement on Textiles and Clothing*; ILA for *Agreement on Import Licensing Procedures*; SA for *Agreement on Safeguards*; and TRIMS for *Agreement on Trade-Related Investment Measures*. Covered agreements under which less than five disputes were brought to the WTO are not included in this figure. E.g. the disputes under the *Agreement on Public Procurement*.
506 See www.worldtradelaw.net, visited on 1 January 2004.
507 On the issue of how many panel reports were appealed, see above, pp. 249–50. The data used here do not give a good picture of the 'appeal rate'.

Note that, in WTO dispute settlement proceedings, the complaining party is usually successful. The percentage of adopted reports in which at least one violation was found is 85 per cent; in other words, in only 15 per cent of all disputes do the responding parties 'walk free'.[508]

3.7. CHALLENGES AND PROPOSALS FOR REFORM

The WTO system for resolving trade disputes between WTO Members has been a remarkable success in many respects. However, the current system can undoubtedly be further improved. This section first briefly discusses past and current attempts to amend the dispute settlement system, from the DSU review (1998–9) to the current negotiations on the DSU in the context of the Doha Development Round. It then examines a number of key proposals of Members for institutional, procedural and systemic changes to the DSU. This section concludes with an analysis of the main challenge to the WTO dispute settlement system, i.e. the imbalance in terms of effectiveness and impact between the political, rule-making bodies and processes *and* the quasi-judicial, dispute settlement bodies and processes of the WTO.

3.7.1. From DSU review to DSU negotiations

3.7.1.1. The DSU review and beyond

As agreed at the time of the adoption of the *WTO Agreement*, the WTO Members reviewed the DSU in 1998 and 1999.[509] Although at the start of this review Members expressed the opinion that the dispute settlement system was working satisfactorily, a large number of proposals for further improvement of the system were nevertheless made by Members. After January 1999, most Members were convinced that, if anything, the review should address and resolve the 'sequencing' issue concerning the relationship between Articles 21.5 and 22 of the DSU, a serious systemic problem that had just surfaced.[510] However, despite the best efforts of Members, the DSU review was concluded in July 1999 without agreement on any amendment to the DSU. Discussions on amendments to the DSU continued on an informal basis in the run-up to the Seattle Session of the Ministerial Conference in December 1999. These discussions resulted in a proposal for reform to the Ministerial Conference by a group of developed-country and developing-country Members including the European Communities, but without the United States.[511] While also addressing a number of minor technical issues, this proposal focused primarily on

---

[508] See www.worldtradelaw.net, visited on 15 January 2004.
[509] *Decision on the Application and Review of the Understanding on Rules and Procedures Governing the Settlement of Disputes*, published in *The Legal Texts: The Results of the Uruguay Round of Multilateral Trade Negotiations* (Cambridge University Press, 1999), 465.
[510] See above, pp. 280–1.   [511] See WT/MIN(99)/8.

resolving the 'sequencing' issue. At the Seattle Session of the Ministerial Conference, agreement on this proposal might have been possible, but fell victim to the overall failure of that Session.[512]

3.7.1.2. The Doha Development Round and DSU negotiations

In 2000 and 2001, informal efforts, outside the DSB, to reach agreement on amendments to the DSU continued. These efforts resulted in October 2001 in a revised proposal for amending the DSU tabled by a group of fourteen WTO Members, chaired by Japan but not including the European Communities or the United States.[513] This proposal again focused on the 'sequencing' issue but also addressed the timeframes for panel proceedings, third party rights and the 'carousel' retaliation issue. However, Members failed to reach agreement on this proposal.

In November 2001, at the Doha Session of the Ministerial Conference, Members decided to open formal negotiations on the DSU in January 2002.[514] These negotiations, based on the work on DSU reform done so far as well as on any additional proposals by Members, are currently still under way. The Doha Ministerial Declaration clearly states that the negotiations on the DSU will not be part of the single undertaking, i.e. that they will not be tied to the overall success or failure of the other negotiations mandated by the Ministerial Declaration. As the improvement of the dispute settlement system is in the interest of all Members, it was considered inappropriate to make the DSU negotiations part of the 'give and take' of the overall negotiations. The desire to keep the DSU negotiations 'separate' from the rest of the Doha Development Round is also reflected in the timeframe for the DSU negotiations. Unlike the Doha Development Round, which was initially scheduled to be concluded in January 2005, the deadline for the DSU negotiations was initially set at May 2003.[515]

The negotiations on the DSU are conducted by the Special Session of the DSB. Between February 2002 and May 2003, the initial deadline for the negotiations, the Special Session of the DSB met formally thirteen times to carry out negotiations on the DSU. In addition, it also met many times informally. While the prevailing view of Members was that 'the DSU has generally functioned well to date', in total forty-two proposals for clarifications and amendments to the DSU were submitted.[516] These proposals

---

[512] The only major issue of disagreement left was the 'carousel' retaliation issue. See above, p. 223.

[513] *Proposal to Amend Certain Provisions of the Understanding on Rules and Procedures Governing the Settlement of Disputes (DSU) Pursuant to Article X of the Marrakesh Agreement Establishing the World Trade Organization,* Submission by Bolivia, Canada, Chile, Colombia, Costa Rica, Ecuador, Japan, Korea, New Zealand, Norway, Peru, Switzerland, Uruguay and Venezuela for Examination and Further Consideration by the General Council, WT/GC/W/410/Rev.1, dated 26 October 2001.

[514] Ministerial Conference, Doha Ministerial Declaration, WT/MIN(01)/DEC/1, dated 20 November 2001, para. 30.

[515] *Ibid.*

[516] Special Session of the Dispute Settlement Body, *Report by the Chairman to the Trade Negotiations Committee,* TN/DS/9, dated 6 June 2003, para. 3.

touched on almost all DSU provisions and were submitted by developed-country as well as developing-country Members. Unsurprisingly, the major users of the dispute settlement system such as the United States, the European Communities, Canada, India and Brazil, all tabled proposals for reform. Of these proposals, the proposal by the European Communities was undoubtedly the most elaborate and far reaching. Surprisingly, however, Members who had not used the dispute settlement system to that date also tabled proposals for reform. Note in this respect the proposals by Jordan and Kenya, the proposal by the African Group and the proposal by the Group of least-developed-country Members (the 'LDC Group'). Also noteworthy are the proposals for reform submitted by the 'new' Members, China and Chinese Taipei.

Due to the large number and the complexity of the proposals for reform, it took until the end of March 2003 merely to complete an initial review of the proposals.[517] The then Chairman of the Special Session of the DSB, Ambassador Péter Balás, subsequently put draft legal texts forward in April 2003.[518] This work eventually culminated in the so-called 'Chairman's Text', issued on 16 May 2003.[519]

The 'Chairman's Text' contained proposals for reform on a significant number of issues, including:

- the extension of third party rights;
- improved conditions for Members seeking to be joined in consultations;
- the introduction of remand and interim review in appellate review proceedings;
- the 'sequencing' issue and other problems concerning the suspension of concessions or other obligations;
- the enhancement of compensation as a temporary remedy for breach of WTO law;
- the strengthening of notification requirements for mutually agreed solutions; and
- the strengthening of special and differential treatment for developing-country Members.[520]

In the absence of a sufficiently high level of support, other proposals by Members were not included in the 'Chairman's Text'. These 'rejected' proposals included proposals on:

- accelerated procedures for certain disputes;
- a list of permanent panellists or a permanent panel body;

---

[517] The WTO Secretariat made a very useful compilation of the proposals made by the Members. This compilation is contained in Job(03)/10/Rev.3.

[518] The draft legal texts were contained in the so-called 'Framework Document', which can be found in Job(03)/69/Rev.2.

[519] The 'Chairman's Text' can be found in Job(03)/91.

[520] Special Session of the Dispute Settlement Body, *Report by the Chairman to the Trade Negotiations Committee*, TN/DS/9, dated 6 June 2003, para. 5.

- increased control of Members over panel and Appellate Body reports;
- the treatment of *amicus curiae* briefs; and
- collective and monetary retaliation.

During the intensive discussions on the 'Chairman's Text' at the end of May 2003, Members generally welcomed this document. However, in spite of a number of amendments, they were eventually unable to agree to the proposals for reform it contained.[521] Certain Members had conceptual problems with some of these proposals or objected to the fact that other proposals had been excluded from the 'Chairman's Text'.[522]

Members were therefore unable to meet the May 2003 deadline for the DSU negotiations provided for in the Doha Ministerial Declaration. While there was general recognition of the need for the Special Session of the DSB to continue its work, Members were divided over whether further work should build on the 'Chairman's Text' only *or* on other proposals by Members as well. At its meeting on 24 July 2003, the General Council, acknowledging the fact that Members needed more time to conclude the negotiations on the DSU, agreed to extend the negotiating mandate of the Special Session of the DSB by one year, to May 2004. In May 2004, there was, however, still no agreement on the amendment of the DSU, and, in July 2004, the General Council decided once more to extend the negotiating mandate of the Special Session of the DSB.[523]

3.7.2. Proposals for DSU reform

Among the proposals for DSU reform currently on the negotiating table, one must distinguish between proposals with respect to:

- the institutions of WTO dispute settlement;
- the proceedings of WTO dispute settlement; and
- systemic issues, such as transparency of WTO dispute settlement, the *amicus curiae* brief issue and special and differential rights for developing-country Members.

This section will briefly discuss the most significant of these proposals. Some of these proposals were included in the 'Chairman's Text', indicating a wide support among Members. Other proposals discussed below were not included in the 'Chairman's Text' but nevertheless deserve attention as these proposals indicate how the WTO dispute settlement system may develop in the future.

---

[521] The amended version of the 'Chairman's Text' can be found in the annex to Special Session of the Dispute Settlement Body, *Report by the Chairman to the Trade Negotiations Committee*, TN/DS/9, dated 6 June 2003.

[522] *Ibid.*, paras. 10 and 11.

[523] General Council, Doha Work Programme, Decision adopted on 1 August 2004, WT/L/579, dated 2 August 2004, para. 1(f).

3.7.2.1. *Key proposals with respect to the institutions of WTO dispute settlement*

A far-reaching proposal not included in the 'Chairman's Text' is the proposal by the European Communities to move from the current system of *ad hoc* panellists to a system of permanent panellists.[524] According to the European Communities, such a change will lead to faster procedures and increase the quality of the panel reports. In the opinion of the European Communities, there is currently a growing quantitative discrepancy between the need for panellists and the availability of qualified *ad hoc* panellists. Not only is the number of disputes much higher than under the old GATT, the actual conduct of a dispute settlement procedure has become much more sophisticated than before. The workload of panellists has substantially increased since the substance of the cases, from both a factual and a legal point of view, has become significantly more complex. For the European Communities, it is, therefore, necessary to introduce a system of permanent panellists. Under the proposal by the European Communities, panels shall be composed of individuals included on a roster of permanent panellists established by the DSB.[525] The panellists shall be appointed by the Director-General on a random basis within five days from the establishment of the panel. The parties may agree, however, at the time of the establishment of the panel that the panel may include two individuals from outside the roster with particular expertise on the subject matter of the dispute. The chairperson of the panel must always be an individual included in the roster of permanent panellists. If within ten days of the establishment of the panel the parties have not agreed on the panellists from outside the roster or the Director-General has not been requested to nominate such panellist from outside the roster, the panellists shall be drawn from the roster by the Director-General on a random basis. Under the proposal of the European Communities, the DSB shall include persons on the roster for six-year terms, non-renewable. The roster shall be broadly representative of membership in the WTO. This radical proposal, if adopted, would constitute another significant step in the process of 'judicialisation' of WTO dispute settlement. To date, however, the proposal has received little open support. One concern of Members is the additional budgetary cost of a roster of permanent panellists. Currently, there seems to be more support for a less radical proposal by Thailand for a 'roster of panel chairs' comprised of individuals who may be appointed as chair of a panel by random selection.[526] However, this proposal was also not included in the 'Chairman's Text'.

With regard to the Appellate Body and, in particular, to ensure the capability of the Appellate Body to meet its workload, the European Communities

---

[524] Communication from the European Union, TN/DS/W/1, dated 13 March 2002, 3; and Communication from the European Union, TN/DS/W/38, dated 23 January 2003, 3. On the current system, see above, pp. 235–6.

[525] It is for the DSB to decide on the number of such permanent panellists, but the European Communities has suggested a number ranging from sixteen to twenty-five.

[526] Communication from Thailand, TN/DS/W/ 31, dated 22 January 2003, 2.

suggested that the DSB should be given the power to modify – when necessary – the number of Appellate Body Members, now set at seven by Article 17.1 of the DSU.[527] This proposal has been included in the 'Chairman's Text'.[528] The European Communities and India proposed that Appellate Body Members be appointed for a non-renewable term of six years rather than the current renewable term of four years.[529] However, this proposal has not been included in the 'Chairman's Text'.

3.7.2.2. *Key proposals with respect to the proceedings of WTO dispute settlement*

A number of Members, including the European Communities, proposed that the parties to a dispute have the authority to extend the time limits set forth in the DSU by mutual agreement. This proposal, clearly intended to give Members more control over dispute settlement proceedings again, is included in the 'Chairman's Text'. Proposals by Australia and China for accelerated timeframes for disputes on safeguard measures and anti-dumping actions are not included.[530]

With respect to consultations, the European Communities, Japan and China have proposed to reduce the minimum period for consultations from sixty days to thirty days.[531] However, this proposal did not receive sufficient support to be included in the 'Chairman's Text'. The LDC Group proposed that in disputes involving a least-developed-country Member consultations must, at the request of that member, be held in the capital of that Member rather than in Geneva. This proposal has been included in the 'Chairman's Text'. Jamaica, Costa Rica and Chinese Taipei have all submitted proposals to facilitate Members to join consultations between other Members.[532] The 'Chairman's Text', in this respect, includes wording that is largely based on the proposal by Chinese Taipei. Finally, Jordan and the European Communities proposed that a request for consultations be deemed to have been withdrawn by the complainant if that party has not submitted a panel request within twelve or eighteen months after the request for consultations. The proposal for a time limit on consultations of eighteen months has been included in the 'Chairman's Text'.

---

[527] Communication from the European Union, TN/DS/W/1, dated 13 March 2002, 12. According to the European Communities, it would also appear 'desirable' – in view of the workload of the Appellate Body and on the basis of past experience – to convert the mandate of the Appellate Body Members into a full-time appointment. *Ibid.*, 8. On the current arrangement, see above, pp. 244–6.

[528] Note that Thailand proposed to increase the number of the Appellate Body Members by at least two to four persons. Communication from Thailand, TN/DS/W/2, dated 20 March 2002, 1.

[529] Proposal on DSU by Cuba, Honduras, India, Malaysia, Pakistan, Sri Lanka, Tanzania and Zimbabwe, TN/DS/W/18, dated 7 October 2002, 4–5; and Communication from the European Union, TN/DS/W/1, dated 23 January 2003, 5.

[530] Communication from Australia, TN/DS/W/49, dated 17 February 2003, 1; and Communication from China, TN/DS/W/29, dated 22 January 2003, 2.

[531] Communication from the European Union, TN/DS/W/1, dated 13 March 2002, 9; Proposal by Japan, TN/DS/W/32, dated 22 January 2003, 9; and Communication from China (Revision), TN/DS/W/51/Rev.1, dated 13 March 2003, 1.

[532] Communication from Jamaica, TN/DS/W/21, dated 10 October 2002, 2; Communication from the Separate Customs Territory of Taiwan, Penghu, Kinmen and Matsu, TN/DS/W/25, dated 27 November 2002, 3; and Communication from Costa Rica, TN/DS/W/12, dated 24 July 2002, 2.

With respect to panel proceedings, Japan and the European Communities proposed that the DSB establish a panel by reverse consensus at the meeting at which the panel request *first* appears as an item on the DSB's agenda. Currently, the DSB can only establish a panel by reverse consensus at the meeting at which the request appears on the agenda for the second time. This proposal was included in the 'Chairman's Text'. However, reflecting a proposal by China, the 'Chairman's Text' provides that, in cases against developing-country Members, the establishment of the panel will be postponed to the next DSB meeting if the developing-country Member so requests.[533] Costa Rica and the African Group proposed a significant extention of the rights of third parties in panel proceedings.[534] The 'Chairman's Text' contains a proposal for allowing third parties to participate in all substantive panel meetings and to receive a copy of all written submissions of the parties to the panel.[535] With respect to the non-confidential summary of submissions which parties must provide at the request of any WTO Member, it has been proposed that such non-confidential summary must be provided within fifteen days of the request. This proposal was taken up in the 'Chairman's Text'. A proposal by Mexico, which provided for an interim relief procedure in case the measure at issue in a dispute is causing or threatening to cause harm which would be difficult to repair, was not included in the 'Chairman's Text'.[536]

With respect to appellate review proceedings, the United States and Chile jointly proposed to introduce interim review in appellate review proceedings. They also proposed that the timeframe for appellate review be extended from a maximum of 90 days to 120 days.[537] Both proposals are reflected in the 'Chairman's Text'. The European Communities submitted a proposal to introduce a remand procedure, under which any party can request, within ten days after the adoption of the Appellate Body report by the DSB, the remand to the original panel of those issues on which the Appellate Body could not rule.[538] The 'Chairman's Text' incorporates this proposal of the European Communities to a large degree. A proposal by Jordan to give the Appellate Body remand authority was not retained.[539]

The LDC Group and the African Group proposed that, in panel and Appellate Body reports, *each* panellist and *each* Appellate Body Member should make findings and deliver a fully reasoned separate opinion on all issues; that such opinions should no longer be *anonymous*; and that the opinions clearly state which party has prevailed. The opinion of the majority of panellists or Appellate Body Members would determine the decision of the panel or the

---

[533] Communication from China (Revision), TN/DS/W/51/Rev.1, dated 13 March 2003, 1.
[534] Communication from Costa Rica, TN/DS/W/12, dated 24 July 2002; and Proposal by the African Group, TN/DS/W/15, dated 25 September 2002, 4.
[535] On the current situation, see above, pp. 263–4.   [536] Proposal by Mexico, TN/DS/W/23, 4.
[537] Textual Contribution by Chile and United States, TN/DS/W/52, dated 14 March 2003, 1.
[538] Communication from the European Communities, TN/DS/W/38, dated 23 January 2003, 6.
[539] Communication from Jordan, TN/DS/W/43, dated 28 January 2003, 6. In May 2003, however, Jordan replaced its proposal to grant the Appellate Body remand authority with a proposal to provide a remand procedure similar to the remand procedure proposed by the European Communities. Communication from Jordan, TN/DS/W/56, dated 19 May 2003, 2.

Appellate Body. These proposals are not reflected in the 'Chairman's Text'. The same is true for a proposal by Chile and the United States that the DSB may decide by consensus *not* to adopt a specific finding of the panel or the Appellate Body or not to adopt the basic rationale behind a specific finding.

With respect to the implementation and enforcement of recommendations and rulings, the European Communities and Japan proposed the inclusion of an Article 21 *bis* on 'Determination of Compliance'. According to this proposed Article 21 *bis*, disputes on the existence or WTO-consistency of implementing measures will be heard by a compliance panel consisting of the members of the original panel. While the procedure set forth in Article 21 *bis* reflects the current practice under Article 21.5 to a large extent, it elaborates and clarifies the latter provision considerably. The European Communities and Japan also proposed that Article 22 of the DSU be amended. According to the amended Article 22 of the DSU, the complainant may only request authorisation from the DSB to retaliate *after* the compliance panel or the Appellate Body finds that the respondent has failed to bring the measures found to be WTO-inconsistent into compliance with the *WTO Agreement*. Both proposals (on Article 21 *bis* and on Article 22) have been included in the 'Chairman's Text'. If adopted, the amended Article 22 would resolve the 'sequencing' issue in an unambiguous manner.

The European Communities and Japan also proposed a procedure for the termination of retaliation measures. According to this proposed procedure, the respondent may request the DSB to authorise the termination of retaliation measures on the grounds that it has taken the necessary WTO-consistent measures.[540] This proposal on a termination procedure is included in the 'Chairman's Text'. A proposal by Mexico to allow Members to transfer, i.e. to sell, the right to suspend concessions or other obligations has not been retained in the 'Chairman's Text'. The same is true for proposals by the African Group and the LDC Group for collective retaliation, i.e. the suspension of concessions or other obligations by all Members, rather than only by the complainant(s) in the dispute.[541] Other proposals on, for example, the withdrawal of membership rights or compulsory monetary compensation in case of failure to implement have received little support.

3.7.2.3. *Key proposals with respect to systemic issues*

With respect to the transparency of the WTO dispute settlement system, the European Communities and Canada submitted a proposal to allow panel meetings and Appellate Body hearings to be open to the public (if the parties to the dispute agree).[542] These proposals were not included in the 'Chairman's Text'.

---

[540] Communication from Japan, TN/DS/W/22, dated 28 October 2002, 6; and Communication from the European Communities, TN/DS/W/38, dated 23 January 2003, 7.
[541] Proposal by the African Group, TN/DS/W/15, dated 15 September 2002, 3; and Proposal by the LDC Group, TN/DS/W/17, dated 9 October 2003, 4.
[542] Communication from the European Communities, TN/DS/W/1, dated 13 March 2003, 6; and Communication from Canada, TN/DS/W/41, dated 24 January 2003, 5.

With respect to the *amicus curiae* brief issue, the African Group and India have proposed an amendment to the wording of Article 13 of the DSU that would explicitly prohibit panels and the Appellate Body to accept and consider unsolicited information and advice.[543] By contrast, the European Communities made a detailed proposal to give panels and the Appellate Body the right to accept and consider unsolicited information and advice provided that this information or advice is directly relevant to the factual and legal issues under consideration.[544] None of the proposals on *amicus curiae* briefs were retained in the 'Chairman's Text'.

Finally, with respect to special and differential treatment for developing-country Members, a number of specific proposals were made to 'strengthen' DSU provisions relating to special attention given to the needs of developing-country Members by replacing 'should' by 'shall'. Most of these proposals have been taken up in the 'Chairman's Text'. Also, proposals to strengthen the rights of developing-country Members regarding the prolongation of consultations, the composition of panels and the timetable for panel proceedings, panel reports and assistance by the WTO Secretariat were all included in the 'Chairman's Text'. This is also the case for the proposal to make it possible for panels and the Appellate Body to award, upon request, 'an amount for litigation costs'.[545] Not included in the 'Chairman's Text', however, are:

- a proposal by the African Group to establish a 'WTO Fund on Dispute Settlement' to facilitate the effective utilisation of the WTO dispute settlement system by developing and least-developed-country Members;[546] and
- a proposal by China to require that developed-country Members exercise due restraint in cases against developing-country Members and limit the number of cases brought against a particular developing-country Member to a maximum of two in one calendar year.[547]

Questions and Assignments 3.55

Is the current effort to amend the DSU the first attempt since 1995 to improve the dispute settlement system? Discuss the key proposals for reform currently on the negotiating table. Which of these proposals would strengthen the judicial, rules-based nature of the WTO dispute settlement system, if adopted? Which proposals would weaken the current system?

---

[543] Proposal by the African Group, TN/DS/W/15, dated 15 September 2002, 5; and Proposal on DSU by India *et al.*, TN/DS/W/18, dated 7 October 2002, 2.

[544] Communication from the European Communities, TN/DS/W/1, dated 13 March 2002, 11. Note that the European Communities in fact proposed to include in the DSU a procedure very similar to the Additional Procedure adopted by the Appellate Body in *EC – Asbestos* (see above, pp. 198–200).

[545] While this proposal does not exclude the possibility that panels and the Appellate Body would award litigation costs to developed-country Members, it is clearly intended to facilitate the use of the dispute settlement system by developing-country Members. See, in this respect, the Communication from China, TN/DS/W/29, dated 22 January 2003, 1–2.

[546] Proposal by the African Group, TN/DS/W/15, 25 September 2002, 2.

[547] Communication from China, TN/DS/W/29, dated 22 January 2003, 1.

3.7.3. Main challenge to the WTO dispute settlement system

While the WTO dispute settlement system is definitely still open to improvement, it currently already constitutes an effective and efficient system for the peaceful resolution of trade disputes. It brings a degree of security and predictability in international trade to all its Members and their citizens. The WTO dispute settlement system offers an opportunity for economically weak countries to challenge trade measures taken by economically stronger countries. The system works to the advantage of all Members, but it especially gives security to the weaker Members that have often, in the past, lacked the political or economic clout to enforce their rights and to protect their interests.[548] Special dispute settlement rules and procedures for developing-country Members and the Advisory Centre on WTO Law must help developing-country Members to make use of this opportunity. As a result of the dispute settlement system, right perseveres over might in the WTO. According to Peter Sutherland, a former EC Commissioner and GATT/WTO Director-General and now Chairman of BP and Goldman Sachs International, the WTO dispute settlement system is 'the greatest advance in multilateral governance since Bretton Woods'.[549]

However, there is a genuine danger that Members overburden, and thus undermine, the dispute settlement system as a result of their inability to agree on (clearer) rules governing politically sensitive issues concerning international trade. Since 1995, the WTO dispute settlement system has been severely put to the test by politically sensitive disputes over issues touching on public health (*EC – Hormones* and *EC – Asbestos*), environmental protection (*US – Gasoline* and *US – Shrimp*), cultural identity (*Canada – Periodicals*), taxation (*US – FSC*) and foreign and development policy (*EC – Bananas III* and *EC – Tariff Preferences*). Although the WTO dispute settlement system has performed very well so far,[550] the task may become steadily more difficult as the WTO is drawn more deeply into politically controversial issues. Some observers fear that the system may be overwhelmed. Claude Barfield of the Washington-based American Enterprise Institute has stirred keen debate in the international trade policy community by suggesting that the WTO dispute settlement system is 'substantively and politically unsustainable'. Barfield suggests that governments may only continue to obey its rulings if its powers are curbed.[551] While disagreeing with Barfield's prescription, others have also warned against excessive reliance by WTO Members on adjudication, instead of political

---

[548] J. Lacarte and P. Gappah, 'Developing Countries and the WTO Legal and Dispute Settlement System', *Journal of International Economic Law*, 2000, 400 (reproduced by permission of Oxford University Press).

[549] As quoted by Guy de Jonquieres, 'Rules to Fight By', *Financial Times*, 24 March 2002.

[550] As discussed in this chapter, the WTO dispute settlement system has been widely used by developed as well as developing-country Members (see above, pp. 173, 225–6, 284–6). In 85 per cent of the disputes in which a WTO-inconsistent measure had to be withdrawn or amended, the Member concerned did so within a reasonable period of time (see above, pp. 217–20, 289). The conclusions of the Appellate Body have generally been well received and accepted by the WTO memberships.

[551] See C. Barfield, *Free Trade, Sovereignty, Democracy: The Future of the World Trade Organization* (American Enterprise Institute Press, Washington DC, 2001), 111–48.

solutions, to resolve problems arising in trade relations. Claus-Dieter Ehlermann, a former Chairman of the Appellate Body, has noted that the system is threatened by a dangerous imbalances between the WTO's highly efficient judicial arm and its far less effective political arm.[552]

To preserve the effectiveness and efficiency of the WTO dispute settlement system, Members will need to improve the ability of the political institutions of the WTO to address the major issues confronting the multilateral trading system. As Hugo Paemen, a former senior EU trade negotiator and EU Ambassador to the US, noted:

> the strains on the system can be relieved only if governments seek to deal with conflicts through more active diplomacy, rather than expecting disputes adjudicators to do the job for them.[553]

3.8. SUMMARY

The WTO dispute settlement system is based on the dispute settlement system of the GATT. The latter system evolved between the late 1940s and the early 1990s from a system that was primarily a power-based system of dispute settlement, through diplomatic negotiations, into a rules-based system of dispute settlement through adjudication. The WTO dispute settlement system, one of the most significant achievements of the Uruguay Round, is a further step in that process of progressive 'judicialisation' of the settlement of international trade disputes.

Since January 1995, the WTO dispute settlement system has been widely used and its 'output', in terms of the number of dispute settlement reports, has been remarkable. Both developed and developing-country Members have frequently used the system to resolve their trade disputes, and these disputes have concerned a very broad range of matters under WTO law.

Among the institutions involved in WTO dispute settlement one can distinguish between a political institution, the DSB, and two independent, judicial-type institutions, the dispute settlement panels and the Appellate Body. The DSB, which is composed of all WTO Members, administers the dispute settlement system. It has the authority to establish panels, adopt panel and Appellate Body reports, and authorise suspension of concessions and other obligations under the covered agreements. It takes decisions on these important matters by reverse consensus. As a result, the DSB decisions on these matters are, for all practical purposes, automatic.

The actual adjudication of disputes brought to the WTO is done, at the first-instance level, by dispute settlement panels and, at the appellate level, by the standing Appellate Body. Panels are *ad hoc* bodies established for the purpose of adjudicating a particular dispute and are dissolved once they have

---

[552] C.-D. Ehlermann, *Some Personal Experiences as Member of the Appellate Body of the WTO*, Policy Papers, RSC No. 02/9 (European University Institute, 2002), 14.

[553] As quoted by Guy de Jonquieres, 'Rules to Fight By', *Financial Times*, 25 March 2002.

accomplished this task. Panels are established by the DSB at the request of the complainant. At the second DSB meeting at which the panel request is discussed, the panel is established by reverse consensus. The parties decide on the composition of the panel. However, if they fail to do so within twenty days after the establishment of the panel, the complainant can ask the Director-General of the WTO to appoint the panellists. As a rule, panels are composed of three well-qualified governmental and/or non-governmental individuals, who are not nationals of the parties or third parties to the dispute. Almost all panels have standard terms of reference, which refer back to the complainant's request to establish a panel. Hence, a claim falls within the panel's terms of reference, i.e. within the mandate of the panel, only if that claim is identified in the panel request. The standard of review of panels, as set forth in Article 11 of the DSU, is 'to make an objective assessment of the matter'. Panels may exercise judicial economy; they need only to address those claims which must be addressed in order to resolve the matter at issue in the dispute. A panel report must, at a minimum, set out the findings of fact, the applicability of relevant provisions and the basic rationale behind any findings and recommendations it makes. Where a panel concludes that a Member's measure is inconsistent with WTO law, it shall recommend that the Member concerned bring that measure into conformity with WTO law. The recommendations and rulings of the panel are *not* legally binding by themselves. They become legally binding only when they are adopted – by reverse consensus – by the DSB.

The Appellate Body is a standing, i.e. permanent, international tribunal of seven independent individuals of recognised authority, appointed by the DSB for a term of four years. The composition of the Appellate Body is representative of WTO membership. The Appellate Body hears and decides appeals in divisions of three of its Members. Only parties to the dispute can appeal a panel report. An appeal is limited to issues of law covered in the panel report and legal interpretations developed by the panel. Issues of fact cannot be appealed. However, the treatment of the facts or evidence by a panel may raise the question of whether the panel acted consistently with Article 11 of the DSU. This is a legal issue and can therefore be examined by the Appellate Body. The Appellate Body may uphold, modify or reverse the legal findings and conclusions of the panel that were appealed. On occasion, the Appellate Body has also, in the absence of the authority to remand a case to the panel, felt compelled to 'complete the legal analysis' on issues not addressed by the panel.

The prime object and purpose of the WTO dispute settlement system is the prompt settlement of disputes through multilateral proceedings. The system prefers to resolve a dispute through consultations rather than adjudication. The WTO dispute settlement system serves to preserve the rights and obligations of Members under the covered agreements, and to clarify the existing provisions of those agreements. The system may not, however, add to or diminish the rights and obligations of the WTO Members. The DSU provides for four different methods to settle disputes between WTO Members: consultations or negotiations (Article 11 of the DSU); adjudication by panels and the Appellate Body

(Articles 6 to 20 of the DSU); arbitration (Articles 21.3(c), 22.6 and 25 of the DSU); and good offices, conciliation and mediation (Article 5 of the DSU).

The jurisdiction of the WTO dispute settlement system is very broad in scope. It covers disputes arising under the *WTO Agreement*, the DSU, all multi-lateral agreements on trade in goods, the GATS and the *TRIPS Agreement*. Furthermore, the jurisdiction of the WTO dispute settlement system is compulsory, exclusive and contentious in nature.

Access to the WTO dispute settlement system is limited to WTO Members. A WTO Member can use the system when it claims that a benefit accruing to it under one of the covered agreements is nullified or impaired. A complainant will almost always argue that the respondent violated a provision of WTO law (violation complaint). If the violation is shown, there is a presumption of nullification or impairment of a benefit.

NGOs, industry associations or individuals have no access to the WTO dispute settlement system. However, it should be noted that most disputes are brought to the WTO system for resolution at the instigation of companies and industry associations. Moreover, panels and the Appellate Body have the right to accept and consider *amicus curiae* briefs submitted by NGOs.

The WTO dispute settlement process entails four major steps: consultations; the panel proceedings; appellate review proceedings; and implementation and enforcement of the recommendations and rulings adopted by the DSB. The WTO dispute settlement process is subject to strict time limits.

WTO dispute settlement bodies interpret provisions of the covered agreements in accordance with the ordinary meaning of the words of the provision taken in their context and in the light of the object and purpose of the agreement involved. If necessary and appropriate, they have recourse to supplementary means of interpretation. The burden of proof in WTO dispute settlement proceedings is on the party, the complainant or the respondent, that asserts the affirmative of a particular claim or defence.

The WTO dispute settlement proceedings are characterised by their confidentiality. Written submissions by the parties are confidential. Panel meetings or the oral hearing of the Appellate Body take place behind closed doors. The *Rules of Conduct* require panellists and Appellate Body Members to be independent and impartial, to avoid direct and indirect conflicts of interest and to respect the confidentiality of proceedings.

The DSU provides for three types of remedy for breach of WTO law: one final remedy, namely, the withdrawal (or amendment) of the WTO-inconsistent measure; and two temporary remedies, namely, compensation and suspension of concessions or other obligations (commonly referred to as 'retaliation'). Compliance with the recommendations or rulings of the DSB must be immediate, or, if that is impracticable, within a 'reasonable period of time'. In most disputes, the Member concerned complies with the recommended actions and rulings in a timely and correct fashion. If not, the DSB will, by reverse consensus, authorise the original complainant to take retaliation measures when requested. Retaliation measures (usually in the form of a drastic increase in custom duties of strategically selected products) put economic and political pressure on Members to withdraw or amend their WTO-inconsistent measures. However, doubts exist as to the effectiveness of retaliation as a temporary remedy for breach of WTO law.

In recognition of the difficulties developing-country Members may encounter when they are involved in WTO dispute settlement, the DSU contains some special rules for developing-country Members. Most of these rules are, however, of limited significance. Effective legal assistance to developing-country Members in dispute settlement proceedings is given by the Geneva-based Advisory Centre on WTO Law, an independent, international organisation that offers legal advice and representation to its developing-country Members and to least-developed countries.

WTO dispute settlement proceedings always begin with consultations (or, at least, an attempt to have consultations) between the parties to the dispute. The consultations enable the disputing parties to understand the factual situation and the legal claims in respect of the dispute better. Parties have broad discretion regarding the manner in which consultations are to be conducted. The consultation process is essentially a *political-diplomatic* process and has often been successful in resolving disputes. However, if consultations do not resolve the dispute within sixty days after the request for consultations, the complainant may request the DSB to establish a panel.

The basic rules governing panel proceedings are set out in Article 12 of the DSU. Article 12.1 of the DSU directs a panel to follow the *Working Procedures* contained in Appendix 3 to the DSU, but at the same time authorises a panel to do otherwise. A panel will – whenever possible within one week of its composition – fix the timetable for its work and decide on detailed *ad hoc* working procedures. Each party to a dispute normally submits two written submissions to the panel: a 'first written submission'; and a 'rebuttal submission'. Shortly after the filing of each of these submissions, the panel meets with the parties. During the proceedings, the panel will meet with the parties twice, first after the filing of the 'first written submissions' and then after the filing of the 'rebuttal submissions'. Unless specific deadlines for the submission of evidence are set out in the *ad hoc* working procedures of the panel, parties can submit new evidence as late as the second meeting with the panel. The panel must of course always be careful to observe due process. Panels have the discretionary authority to seek information and technical advice from experts in order to help them to understand and evaluate the evidence submitted and the arguments made by the parties. The parties are under an obligation to provide the panel with the information or the documents that the panel requests at any time during the proceedings. The rights of third parties to participate in the panel proceedings are quite limited. Panels submit their draft reports to the parties for a so-called 'interim review'. After this interim review, the panel finalises the report, issues it to the parties and eventually – when the report is available in the three official languages – makes the report public by circulating it to all WTO Members. Panel proceedings in theory should not exceed nine months, but in practice panel proceedings take, on average, twelve months. Within sixty days of its circulation, a panel report is either adopted by the DSB or appealed to the Appellate Body.

In contrast to panels, the Appellate Body has detailed standard working procedures set out in the *Working Procedures for Appellate Review*. Appellate review proceedings are initiated by a notice of appeal. The appellant's submission, the other (or cross) appellants' submission(s) and the appellee's submission(s) are due within, respectively ten, fifteen and twenty-five days after the date of the notice of appeal. An oral hearing is, in practice, held usually around day forty of the appellate review process. Unlike in panel proceedings, third parties have broad rights to participate in appellate review proceedings. After the oral hearing and before finalising its report, the division responsible for deciding an appeal will always exchange views on the issues raised by the appeal with the Members of the Appellate Body not sitting on the division. When the report is available in the three official languages, it is circulated to all WTO Members and made public. Appellate review proceedings shall not exceed ninety days, and they very seldom do exceed this time limit. Within thirty days of its circulation, the Appellate Body report, together with the panel report, as upheld, modified or reversed by the Appellate Body, is adopted by the DSB.

Recommendations and rulings of panels and/or the Appellate Body, as adopted by the DSB, must be implemented promptly. If that is impracticable, the Member concerned must implement them within a 'reasonable period of time'. If the parties are unable to agree on the duration of that period, it can – at the request of either party – be determined through binding arbitration (under Article 21.3(c) of the DSU). During the 'reasonable period of time for implementation', the DSB keeps the implementation of adopted recommendations and rulings under surveillance. If the respondent fails to implement the recommendations and rulings within the 'reasonable period of time' and agreement on compensation cannot be reached, the complainant may request authorisation from the DSB to suspend concessions or other obligations. If there is disagreement as to the existence or the WTO-consistency of the implementing measures, a practice has developed under which the complainant will first resort to the Article 21.5 compliance procedure before obtaining authorisation from the DSB to retaliate. Under the Article 21.5 compliance procedure, disagreement as to the existence or consistency with WTO law of implementing measures shall be decided through recourse to the DSU dispute settlement procedures, including, wherever possible, resort to the original panel. If the respondent did indeed fail to implement or adopted WTO-inconsistent implementing measures, the DSB can at the request of the complainant authorise the suspension of concessions or other obligations by reverse consensus. If the non-complying Member objects to the level of suspension proposed or claims that the principles and procedures for suspension have not been followed, the matter may be referred to arbitration (under Article 22.6 of the DSU) before the DSB takes a decision.

The WTO system for resolving trade disputes between WTO Members has been a remarkable success in many respects. However, the current system can undoubtedly be further improved. In the context of the Doha Development Round, WTO Members are currently negotiating on proposals for clarification and amendment of the DSU. Since early 2002, a large number of WTO Members have made proposals for reform relating to the institutions of WTO dispute settlement, its proceedings and more general systemic issues. These negotiations on the reform of the DSU should have been completed by May 2003 but are still ongoing. Note that some of the proposals for reform would, if adopted, further strengthen the judicial, rules-based nature of the WTO dispute settlement system while other proposals would weaken that nature. The main challenge to the WTO dispute settlement system at present is the imbalance in terms of effectiveness and impact between the political, rule-making bodies and processes *and* the quasi-judicial, dispute settlement bodies and processes of the WTO. This imbalance, however, must not be fixed by weakening the WTO dispute settlement system but by strengthening the WTO political system.

3.9. EXERCISE: NEWLAND SEEKS JUSTICE

To protect its ailing steel industry from import competition, the Kingdom of Richland, a WTO Member, imposed a quota on imports of steel from the Republic of Newland, a recent WTO Member. After intense lobbying by FerMetal, Newland's major steel producer, and the Newland Brotherhood of Steel Workers, the Government of Newland decided to challenge the WTO consistency of Richland's import quota.

As a lawyer in the Brussels-based law firm, Dupont, Bridge & Brucke, you have been asked by the Government of Newland to advise on the procedural and systemic issues arising in the course of the dispute settlement proceedings in Geneva. In the course of the proceedings, the following situations arise on which your advice is requested.

To mitigate the damage to Newland's steel exports and employment in the steel industry, it is important to act quickly against Richland's steel quota. Newland's Minister of Foreign Affairs therefore instructs Newland's Permanent Representative to the WTO, Ambassador Rita Montesdeoca de Murillo, to request the establishment of a panel, at the next meeting of the DSB. Does Newland act in accordance with the DSU by requesting the establishment of a panel in this way? If not, could the DSB refuse to establish the panel?

Richland's Permanent Representative to the WTO, Ambassador Dr Heinrich Schiller, reportedly receives instructions from his Government to block or, if that is impossible, to delay the establishment *and* composition of a panel as much as possible. What can the Permanent Representative of Richland do? Can he refuse to accept the jurisdiction of the WTO to settle this dispute and suggest that Richland and Newland take the dispute to the International Court of Justice?

The Government of Richland announces that it will insist that the panel includes five members, of which at least one is a national of Richland and none are nationals of developing-country Members. Among the five panellists, it wants two economists and one engineer. None of the panellists should be a former or current Geneva diplomat. The instructions of the Government of Richland are not to agree to a panel, the composition of which does not meet these 'requirements'. The Government of Newland cannot agree to Richland's 'requirements' and instructs its Permanent Representative to expedite the process of establishing *and* composing the panel. What can the Permanent Representative of Newland do?

Poorland, a neighbour of Newland, would like to be a third party in this dispute. Is this possible? Can Richland prevent Poorland from becoming a third party in this dispute?

In its first written submission, Newland requests the Panel to examine not only the quota on steel (the measure at issue identified in the panel request) but an import quota on cement that was also recently introduced by Richland. Moreover, Newland wants the Panel to find that the import quota on steel is not only in breach of Article XIX of the GATT 1994 and the *Agreement on Safeguards* (as it had stated in its panel request) but also in violation of the *Agreement on Import Licensing Procedures.* Finally, Newland calls upon the Panel to examine *de novo* whether the imports of steel from Newland did indeed cause or threaten to cause serious injury to the domestic steel industry of Richland. How will the Panel react to these demands by Newland?

Newland also argues in its first written submission that the burden is on Richland to demonstrate that it has acted consistently with its obligations under Article XIX of the GATT 1994 since Article XIX constitutes an exception to the basic prohibition of quantitative restrictions set out in Article XI of the GATT 1994. On whom does the burden of proof rest in this dispute?

The Newland Brotherhood of Steel Workers, the National Association of Steel Producers of Richland and 'Fair Deal', a non-governmental organisation that focuses on the problems of developing countries, all send *amicus curiae* briefs to the Chairman of the Panel. The brief of the National Association of Steel Producers of Richland was published in the *Financial Times* and the *Wall Street Journal* a week earlier and received a lot of attention. The Chairman of the Panel also receives a brief from Southland, a developing-country Member with important interests in steel. What should the Panel do with these unsolicited briefs? The Newland Brotherhood of Steel Workers and the National Association of Steel Producers of Richland have expressed a wish to receive all the briefs submitted by the parties to the Panel and to attend the panel meetings. Is this possible? Will you, as a private lawyer, be allowed to attend the panel meetings and speak for Newland?

Newland argues in its rebuttal submission that the Panel should interpret the provisions of the *Agreement on Safeguards* in the light of the object and purpose of the *WTO Agreement* and in the light of the alleged intention of the negotiators to limit the use of safeguard measures. One week before the second substantive meeting with the Panel, Newland submits to the Panel a 100-page document on the Uruguay Round negotiations, which it claims supports its position. The Panel would like to get the advice of a number of eminent international trade law scholars and of former Uruguay Round negotiators on this issue. What can the Panel do?

In its interim report, the Panel finds in favour of Newland and recommends that the DSB requests that Richland bring the measure at issue in this dispute into conformity with its obligations under the GATT 1994 and the *Agreement on Safeguards*. The Panel suggests that this can best be achieved by prompt removal of the quota. Richland's Minister of Trade denounces the Panel's ruling as a legal travesty and announces that Richland will appeal as soon as possible. When and how can Richland appeal the panel report? When will it need to submit its appellant's submission? Under what circumstances will Richland also need to submit an appellee's submission? When can it expect a ruling of the Appellate Body?

Richland appeals the Panel's interpretation of Article XIX of the GATT 1994 and several provisions of the *Agreement on Safeguards*. It also appeals the Panel's finding that the imports of steel from Newland did not cause or threaten to cause serious injury to the domestic steel industry of Richland. In its notice of appeal, Richland also calls upon the Appellate Body 'to complete the legal analysis when required'. Does the Appellate Body have the mandate to review the findings appealed by Richland? Can the Appellate Body complete the legal analysis?

Newland objects to the composition of the Division of the Appellate Body that hears the appeal. One of the Appellate Body Members is a national of Richland and has acted in the past as counsel to a Richland steel company. Newland also insists that it needs more time to prepare its appellee's submission and argues that the date set for the oral hearing is not convenient. What can Newland do?

The Appellate Body upholds the Panel report. After the DSB adopts the Appellate Body report and the Panel report as upheld, Richland announces that it will comply with the DSB's recommendations and rulings but that it is unable to do so immediately. Newland contends that it is possible to withdraw the quota promptly. What can Newland do next?

After the expiry of the reasonable period of time for implementation, (determined at five months), Richland claims that it has implemented the recommendations and rulings of the Panel. Newland is baffled by this claim since the import quota is still in force. Can Newland take retaliatory measures?

Principles of non-discrimination

Contents

4.1. INTRODUCTION

Non-discrimination is a key concept in WTO law and policy. As already noted in Chapter 1, there are two main principles of non-discrimination in WTO law: the most-favoured-nation (MFN) treatment obligation and the national treatment obligation. In simple terms, the MFN treatment obligation prohibits a country from discriminating *between* countries; the national treatment obligation prohibits a country from discriminating *against* other countries. This chapter examines these two principles of non-discrimination as they apply to trade in goods and trade in services.[1]

Discrimination between, as well as against, other countries was an important characteristic of the protectionist trade policies pursued by many countries during the economic crisis of the 1930s. Historians now regard these discriminatory policies as an important contributing cause of the economic and political crises that resulted in the Second World War. Discrimination in trade matters breeds resentment among the countries, manufacturers, traders and workers discriminated against. Such resentment poisons international relations and may lead to economic and political confrontation and conflict. In addition, discrimination makes scant economic sense, generally speaking, since it distorts the market in favour of products and services that are more expensive and/or of a lesser quality. Eventually, it is the citizens of the discriminating country that end up 'paying the bill' for the discriminatory trade policies pursued.

The importance of eliminating discrimination in the context of the WTO is highlighted in the Preamble to the *WTO Agreement*, where the 'elimination of discriminatory treatment in international trade relations' is identified as one of the two main means by which the objectives of the WTO may be attained.[2]

The key provisions of the GATT 1994 dealing with non-discrimination in trade in goods are:

- Article I, on the MFN treatment obligation; and
- Article III, on the national treatment obligation.

The key provisions on non-discrimination in the GATS are:

- Article II, on the MFN treatment obligation; and
- Article XVII, on the national treatment obligation.

The MFN and national treatment obligations of the GATT 1994 and the GATS prohibit discrimination on the basis of 'nationality' or the 'national origin or destination' of a product, service or service supplier. It should be noted, however, that, in a few situations, WTO law also prohibits discrimination based on criteria other than 'nationality' or 'national origin or destination'. Most notable in this

---

[1] As briefly discussed in Chapter 1, these principles of non-discrimination are also relevant in the context of trade-related aspects of intellectual property rights. See above, pp. 51–2.

[2] See above, pp. 40–1, 87.

respect is Article X:3(a) of the GATT 1994, which requires that laws, regulations, judicial decisions and administrative rulings of general application pertaining to trade be administered in 'a uniform, impartial and reasonable manner'. It has been suggested that this requirement of Article X:3(a) has the effect of imposing a general non-discrimination obligation.[3] In the GATS, Article VI arguably provides for a similar obligation. This chapter, however, focuses exclusively on the MFN treatment obligation and the national treatment obligation.

As noted in Chapter 1, WTO law provides for exceptions to its basic rules, including the MFN treatment obligation and the national treatment obligation. These exceptions are important in WTO law and policy because they allow for the 'reconciliation' of trade liberalisation with other economic and non-economic values and interests. This chapter explores the obligations of non-discrimination but does not address the exceptions thereto. The exceptions to the obligations of MFN treatment and national treatment are dealt with in detail in Chapter 7.[4]

This chapter addresses:

- the MFN treatment obligations under the GATT 1994 and the GATS; and
- the national treatment obligations under the GATT 1994 and the GATS.

With respect to each of these fundamental non-discrimination obligations, this chapter first examines the nature and then the constituent elements of these obligations.

Questions and Assignments 4.1

Why is non-discrimination such an important concept in WTO law and policy? What are the key non-discrimination provisions in the GATT 1994 and the GATS?

4.2. MOST-FAVOURED-NATION TREATMENT UNDER THE GATT 1994

Article I of the GATT 1994, entitled 'General Most-Favoured-Nation Treatment', states in paragraph 1:

> With respect to customs duties and charges of any kind imposed on or in connection with importation or exportation or imposed on the international transfer of payments for imports or exports, and with respect to the method of levying such duties and

---

[3] Note by the GATT Director-General, L/3149, dated 11 November 1968. See also below, p. 311, footnote 11.

[4] See below, pp. 596–691. The relevant exceptions to the MFN treatment obligation and the national treatment obligation dealt with in Chapter 7 are the general exceptions (Article XX of the GATT 1994 and Article XIV of the GATS), the security exceptions (Article XXI of the GATT 1994 and Article XIV *bis* of the GATS), the regional integration exceptions (Article XXIV of the GATT 1994 and Article V of the GATS) and the economic development exception (Enabling Clause).

> charges, and with respect to all rules and formalities in connection with importation and exportation, and with respect to all matters referred to in paragraphs 2 and 4 of Article III, any advantage, favour, privilege or immunity granted by any [Member] to any product originating in or destined for any other country shall be accorded immediately and unconditionally to the like product originating in or destined for the territories of all other [Members].[5]

The GATT 1994 contains a number of other provisions requiring MFN or MFN-like treatment:

- Article III:7 (regarding internal quantitative regulations);
- Article V (regarding freedom of transit);
- Article IX:1 (regarding marking requirements);
- Article XIII (regarding the non-discriminatory administration of quantitative restrictions); and
- Article XVII (regarding State trading enterprises).

Article XX of the GATT 1994, the 'general exceptions provision', also contains an MFN-like obligation.[6] The very existence of these MFN-type clauses demonstrates the pervasive character of the MFN principle of non-discrimination.[7] Other multilateral agreements on trade in goods such as the *TBT Agreement*, the *SPS Agreement* and the *Agreement on Import Licensing Procedures* likewise require MFN treatment. However, this section is only concerned with the MFN treatment obligation set out in Article I:1 of the GATT 1994.

4.2.1. Nature of the MFN treatment obligation of Article I:1 of the GATT 1994

As the Appellate Body stated in *EC – Tariff Preferences*, it is well settled that the MFN treatment obligation set out in Article I:1 of the GATT 1994 is a 'cornerstone of the GATT' and 'one of the pillars of the WTO trading system'.[8] In *US – Section 211 Appropriations Act*, the Appellate Body ruled:

> For more than fifty years, the obligation to provide most-favoured-nation treatment in Article I of the GATT 1994 has been both central and essential to assuring the success of a global rules-based system for trade in goods.[9]

Article I:1 of the GATT 1994 prohibits discrimination *between* like products originating in, or destined for, different countries.[10] The principal purpose of the MFN treatment obligation is to ensure *equality of opportunity* to import from, or to export to, all WTO Members. In *EC – Bananas III*, the Appellate Body stated,

---

[5] Article I:2 to I:4 of the GATT 1994 deals with so-called colonial preferences and allow the continuation of such preferences albeit within certain limits. While important and controversial when the GATT 1947 was negotiated, these colonial preferences are now of very little significance and will not therefore be discussed.
[6] See below, pp. 618–22.   [7] Appellate Body Report, *Canada – Autos*, para. 82.
[8] See Appellate Body Report, *EC – Tariff Preferences*, para. 101.
[9] Appellate Body Report, *US – Section 211 Appropriations Act*, para. 297. See also Appellate Body Report, *Canada – Autos*, para. 69; and Appellate Body Report, *EC – Tariff Preferences*, para. 101.
[10] Appellate Body Report, *Canada – Autos*, para. 84.

with respect to WTO non-discrimination obligations (such as the obligation set out in Article I:1):

> The essence of the non-discrimination obligations is that like products should be treated equally, irrespective of their origin. As no participant disputes that all bananas are like products, the non-discrimination provisions apply to *all* imports of bananas, irrespective of whether and how a Member categorizes or subdivides these imports for administrative or other reasons.[11]

In *EC – Bananas III*, the measure at issue was the import regime for bananas of the European Communities under which bananas from Latin American countries ('dollar bananas'), were treated less favourably than bananas from, broadly speaking, former European colonies ('ACP bananas').

Article I:1 covers not only 'in law', or *de jure*, discrimination but also 'in fact', or *de facto*, discrimination.[12] In *Canada – Autos*, the Appellate Body rejected, as the Panel had done, Canada's argument that Article I:1 does not apply to measures which appear, on their face, to be 'origin-neutral'.[13] Also, measures which appear, on their face, to be 'origin-neutral' can give certain countries more opportunity to trade than others and can, therefore, be in violation of the non-discrimination obligation of Article I:1. The measure at issue in *Canada – Autos* was an import duty exemption accorded by Canada to imports of motor vehicles by certain manufacturers. Formally speaking, there were no restrictions on the origin of the motor vehicles that were eligible for this exemption. In practice, however, the manufacturers imported only their own make of motor vehicle and those of related companies. As a result, only motor vehicles originating in a small number of countries benefited *de facto* from the exemption.

Previously, the GATT Panel in *EEC – Imports of Beef* found that EC regulations making the suspension of an import levy conditional on the production of a certificate of authenticity were inconsistent with the MFN obligation of Article I:1 after it was established that the only certifying agency authorised to produce a certificate of authenticity was an agency in the United States.[14]

Questions and Assignments 4.2

What is the principal purpose of the MFN treatment obligation of Article I:1 of the GATT 1994? Does Article I:1 cover both *de jure* and *de facto* discrimination? Give two examples of *de facto* discrimination from the WTO/GATT case law.

---

[11] Appellate Body Report, *EC – Bananas III*, para. 190. Note that the Appellate Body also referred to the non-discrimination obligations set out in Articles X:3(a) and XIII of GATT 1994 and Article 1.3 of the *Import Licensing Agreement*.

[12] A measure may be said to discriminate in law (or *de jure*) in a case in which it is clear from reading the text of the law, regulation or policy that it discriminates. If the measure does not appear on the face of the law, regulation or policy to discriminate, it may still be determined to discriminate *de facto* if, on reviewing all the facts relating to the application of the measure, it becomes obvious that it discriminates in practice or in fact.

[13] Appellate Body Report, *Canada – Autos*, para. 78.

[14] GATT Panel Report, *EEC – Imports of Beef*, paras. 4.2 and 4.3.

4.2.2. Consistency with Article I:1 of the GATT 1994

Article I:1 of the GATT 1994 sets out a three-tier test of consistency. There are three questions which must be answered to determine whether there is a violation of the MFN treatment obligation of Article I:1, namely:

- whether the measure at issue confers a trade 'advantage' of the kind covered by Article I:1;
- whether the products concerned are 'like' products; and
- whether the advantage at issue is granted 'immediately and unconditionally' to all like products concerned.

4.2.2.1. 'Any advantage with respect to ...'

The MFN treatment obligation concerns 'any advantage, favour, privilege or immunity' granted by any Member to any product originating in, or destined for, any other country with respect to: (1) customs duties; (2) charges of any kind imposed *on* importation or exportation (e.g. import surcharges or consular taxes); (3) charges of any kind imposed *in connection with* importation or exportation (e.g. customs fees or quality inspection fees); (4) charges imposed on the international transfer of payments for imports or exports; (5) the method of levying such duties and charges, such as the method of assessing the base value on which the duty or charge is levied; (6) all rules and formalities in connection with importation and exportation; (7) internal taxes or other internal charges; and (8) laws, regulations and requirements affecting internal sale, offering for sale, purchase, transportation, distribution or use of any product.

In brief, the MFN treatment obligation concerns any advantage granted by any Member with respect to:

- customs duties, other charges on imports and exports and other customs matters;
- internal taxes; and
- internal regulation affecting the sale, distribution and use of products.

Note that the MFN treatment obligation not only concerns advantages granted to other WTO Members, but advantages granted to all other countries (including non-WTO Members). If a Member grants an advantage to a non-Member, Article I:1 obliges the Member to grant that advantage also to all WTO Members.

Generally, there has been little debate about the kind of measures covered by Article I:1. Both panels and the Appellate Body have recognised that Article I:1 clearly casts a very wide net.[15] In *US – MFN Footwear*, also referred to as *US – Non-Rubber Footwear*, the Panel found:

---

[15] Already in August 1948, the CONTRACTING PARTIES adopted a ruling by the Chairman that consular taxes would be covered by the phrase 'charges of any kind' in Article I:1 of the GATT 1947. See BISD II/12.

> the rules and formalities applicable to countervailing duties, including those applicable to the revocation of countervailing duty orders, are rules and formalities imposed in connection with importation, within the meaning of Article I:1.[16]

The Panel in *US – Customs User Fee* stated:

> The merchandise processing fee was a "charge imposed on or in connection with importation" within the meaning of Article I:1. Exemptions from the fee fell within the category of "advantage, favour, privilege or immunity" which Article I:1 required to be extended unconditionally to all other contracting parties.[17]

As already mentioned, in *EEC – Imports of Beef*, the Panel applied Article I:1 to EC regulations making the suspension of an import levy conditional on the production of a certificate of authenticity.[18]

In *EC – Bananas III*, the European Communities contended before the Appellate Body that the Panel had erred in concluding that the EC's 'activity function rules' for the allocation of import licences for bananas violated Article I:1. The Appellate Body upheld the Panel's finding of a violation of Article I:1 as follows :

> the Panel found that the procedural and administrative requirements of the activity function rules for importing third-country and non-traditional ACP bananas differ from, and go significantly beyond, those required for importing traditional ACP bananas. This is a factual finding. Also, a broad definition has been given to the term "advantage" in Article I:1 of the GATT 1994 by the panel in *United States – Non-Rubber Footwear* ... For these reasons, we agree with the Panel that the activity function rules are an "advantage" granted to bananas imported from traditional ACP States, and not to bananas imported from other Members, within the meaning of Article I:1.[19]

In *Canada – Autos*, the Appellate Body usefully clarified the scope of Article I:1 by ruling:

> Article I:1 requires that "*any advantage*, favour, privilege or immunity granted by any Member to *any product* originating in or destined for any other country shall be accorded immediately and unconditionally to the like product originating in or destined for the territories of *all other Members*". [Emphasis added] The words of Article I:1 refer not to *some* advantages granted "with respect to" the subjects that fall within the defined scope of the Article, but to "*any advantage*"; not to *some* products, but to "*any product*"; and not to like products from *some* other Members, but to like products originating in or destined for "*all other*" Members.[20]

In other words, the MFN treatment obligation requires that *any* advantage granted by a Member to any product from or for another country be granted to *all* like products from or for *all other* Members.

In the past, there has been some debate on the applicability of Article I:1 to safeguard measures, anti-dumping duties and countervailing duties. With regard to safeguard measures, the *Agreement on Safeguards* makes it clear that

---

[16] GATT Panel Report, *US – MFN Footwear*, para. 6.8.
[17] GATT Panel Report, *US – Customs User Fee*, para. 122.   [18] See above, p. 311.
[19] Appellate Body Report, *EC – Bananas III*, para. 206.   [20] Appellate Body Report, *Canada – Autos*, para. 79.

the MFN treatment obligation normally applies to safeguard measures. However, the *Agreement* does allow, under certain conditions, the discriminatory use of safeguard measures.[21] With regard to anti-dumping duties and countervailing duties which are, in principle, within the scope of Article I:1, it should be noted that the facts concerning dumped or subsidised exports will more often than not differ from country to country. However, where all the relevant facts are the same, anti-dumping duties and countervailing duties should be applied without discrimination.[22] In a 1960 Report of the Group of Experts on Anti-Dumping and Countervailing Duties, it is stated:

> In equity, and having regard to the most-favoured-nation principle the Group considered that where there was dumping to the same degree from more than one source and where that dumping caused or threatened material injury to the same extent, the importing country ought normally to be expected to levy anti-dumping duties equally on all the dumping imports.[23]

Article I:1 applies also, in principle, to advantages granted under the Plurilateral Agreements. Advantages granted by a party to other parties to the *Agreement on Civil Aircraft* or to the *Agreement on Government Procurement* should, pursuant to Article I:1, at least in principle, be accorded 'immediately and unconditionally' to all WTO Members.

Questions and Assignments 4.3

What are the constituent elements of the Article I:1 test? To which kind of 'advantages', generally speaking, does Article I:1 apply? Does Article I:1 apply to 'advantages' granted to non-WTO Members? Does the MFN treatment obligation apply to safeguard measures, anti-dumping duties and countervailing duties?

4.2.2.2. *'Like products'*

Article I:1 concerns any product originating in or destined for any other country and requires that an advantage granted to such products shall be accorded to 'like products' originating in or destined for the territories of all other Members. It is only between 'like products' that the MFN treatment obligation applies and that discrimination is prohibited. Products that are not 'like' may be treated differently.

The concept of 'like products' is used not only in Article I:1 but also in Article II:2(a), III:2, III:4, VI:1(a), IX:1, XI:2(c), XIII:1, XVI:4 and XIX:1 of the GATT 1994. Nevertheless, the concept of 'like products' is not defined in the GATT 1994. As the Appellate Body considered in *EC – Asbestos* in its examination of the concept of 'like products' under Article III:4, the dictionary meaning of 'like'

---

[21] See below, pp. 638–9.   [22] See below, pp. 543, 580.
[23] Report of the Group of Experts on Anti-Dumping and Countervailing Duties, BISD 9S/194 at 198.

suggests that 'like products' are products that share a number of identical or similar characteristics. The reference to 'similar' as a synonym of 'like' also echoes the language of the French version of Article III:4, '*produits similaire*', and the Spanish version, '*productos similares*'.[24] However, as the Appellate Body noted in *Canada – Aircraft*, 'dictionary meanings leave many interpretative questions open'.[25] With regard to the concept of 'like products', there are three questions of interpretation that need to be resolved:

(1) which characteristics or qualities are important in assessing 'likeness';
(2) to what degree or extent must products share qualities or characteristics in order to be 'like products'; and
(3) from whose perspective should 'likeness' be judged.[26]

It is generally accepted that the concept of 'like products' has different meanings in the different contexts in which it is used. In *Japan – Alcoholic Beverages II*, the Appellate Body illustrated the possible differences in the scope of the concept of 'like products' between different provisions of the *WTO Agreement* by evoking the image of an accordion:

> The accordion of "likeness" stretches and squeezes in different places as different provisions of the *WTO Agreement* are applied. The width of the accordion in any one of those places must be determined by the particular provision in which the term 'like' is encountered as well as by the context and the circumstances that prevail in any given case to which that provision may apply.[27]

The meaning of the phrase 'like products' in Article I:1 was addressed in a number of GATT working party and panel reports.[28] In *Spain – Unroasted Coffee*, the Panel had to decide whether various types of unroasted coffee ('Colombian mild', 'other mild', 'unwashed Arabica', 'Robusta' and 'other') were 'like products' within the meaning of Article I:1. Spain did not apply customs duties on 'Colombia mild' and 'other mild', while it imposed a 7 per cent customs duty on the other three types of unroasted coffee. Brazil, which exported mainly 'unwashed Arabica', claimed that the Spanish tariff regime was inconsistent with Article I:1. In examining whether the various types of unroasted coffee were 'like products' to which the MFN treatment obligation applied, the Panel considered:

- the characteristics of the products;
- their end-use; and
- tariff regimes of other Members.

---

[24] Appellate Body Report, *EC – Asbestos*, para. 91. Note that the French and Spanish versions of the GATT 1994 are equally authentic.
[25] Appellate Body Report, *Canada – Aircraft*, para. 153. See also Appellate Body Report, *EC – Asbestos*, para. 92.
[26] See Appellate Body Report, *EC – Asbestos*, para. 92.
[27] Appellate Body Report, *Japan – Alcoholic Beverages II*, 114.
[28] See e.g. Working Party Report, *Australian Subsidy on Ammonium Sulphate*, para. 8; and GATT Panel Report, *EEC – Animal Feed Proteins*, para. 4.2. In the latter case, the Panel decided, on the basis of 'such factors as the number of products and tariff items carrying different duty rates and tariff bindings, the varying protein contents and the different vegetable, animal and synthetic origin of the protein products', that the various protein products at issue could not be considered as 'like products' within the meaning of Articles I and III of the GATT 1947.

The Panel stated as follows:

> The Panel examined all arguments that had been advanced during the proceedings for the justification of a different tariff treatment for various groups and types of unroasted coffee. It noted that these arguments mainly related to organoleptic differences resulting from geographical factors, cultivation methods, the processing of the bean, and the genetic factor. The Panel did not consider that such differences were sufficient reason to allow for a different tariff treatment. It pointed out that it was not unusual in the case of agricultural products that the taste and aroma of the end-product would differ because of one or several of the above-mentioned factors.
>
> The Panel furthermore found relevant to its examination of the matter that unroasted coffee was mainly, if not exclusively, sold in the form of blends, combining various types of coffee, and that coffee in its end-use, was universally regarded as a well-defined and single product intended for drinking.
>
> The Panel noted that no other contracting party applied its tariff régime in respect of unroasted, non-decaffeinated coffee in such a way that different types of coffee were subject to different tariff rates.
>
> In the light of the foregoing, the Panel concluded that unroasted, non-decaffeinated coffee beans listed in the Spanish Customs Tariff ... should be considered as "like products" within the meaning of Article I:1.[29]

In addition to the characteristics of the products, their end-use and the tariff regimes of other Members – the criteria used by the GATT Panel in *Spain – Unroasted Coffee* – a WTO panel examining whether products are 'like' within the meaning of Article I:1 would now definitely also consider consumers' tastes and habits, a criterion or factor not referred to in *Spain – Unroasted Coffee*.[30]

It is much debated whether, under current WTO law, the process or production method (PPM) by which a product is produced is relevant in determining whether products are 'like' if the process or production method does not affect the physical characteristics of the products. The prevailing view is that the PPM is not relevant.[31] Consequently, products produced in an environmentally unfriendly manner cannot be treated differently than products produced in an environmentally friendly manner on the sole basis of the difference in process or production methods.[32]

Finally, note that Article I:1 also applies to products that are not subject to a tariff binding.[33] As the Panel in *Spain – Unroasted Coffee* ruled, Article I:1 applies equally to bound and unbound tariff items.[34]

Questions and Assignments 4.4

According to the Appellate Body in *EC – Asbestos,* which three questions of interpretation need to be answered to clarify the concept of 'likeness'? Is there one concept of 'likeness' in WTO law? What criteria have been used

---

[29] GATT Panel Report, *Spain – Unroasted Coffee*, paras. 4.6–4.9.
[30] With respect to the criteria that can be used in determining 'likeness' within the meaning of Article I:1, see the discussion on the criteria used to determine whether products are 'like' within the meaning of Article III:2, first sentence, and Article III:4. See below, pp. 334–40, 354–60.
[31] Note, however, the discussion of the concept of 'likeness' in Article III:4 in the context of the *EC – Asbestos* dispute. See below, pp. 354–9.
[32] GATT Panel Report, *US – Tuna (Mexico)*, para. 5.15.   [33] See below pp. 419–22.
[34] GATT Panel Report, *Spain – Unroasted Coffee*, para. 4.3.

by GATT panels to determine whether products were 'like' within the meaning of Article I:1? Are differences in the way in which products are produced (e.g. an environmentally friendly versus a polluting production method, or production involving child labour versus production not involving child labour) relevant to the determination of the 'likeness' of products under Article I:1?

4.2.2.3. Advantage granted 'immediately and unconditionally'

Article I:1 requires that any advantage granted by a WTO Member to imports from any country must be granted 'immediately and unconditionally' to imports from all other WTO Members.[35] Once a WTO Member has granted an advantage to imports from a country, it cannot make the granting of that advantage to imports of other WTO Members conditional upon those other WTO Members 'giving something in return' or 'paying' for the advantage.

In a legal opinion of 1973 in the context of the accession of Hungary to the GATT, the GATT Secretariat noted that:

> the prerequisite of having a cooperation contract in order to benefit from certain tariff treatment appeared to imply conditional most-favoured-nation treatment and would, therefore, not appear to be compatible with the General Agreement.[36]

In *Indonesia – Autos*, the Panel found with respect to the requirement under Article I:1 that advantages are granted 'unconditionally and immediately', as follows:

> under the February 1996 car programme the granting of customs duty benefits to parts and components is conditional to their being used in the assembly in Indonesia of a National Car. The granting of tax benefits is conditional and limited to the only Pioneer company producing National Cars. And there is also a third condition for these benefits: the meeting of certain local content targets. Indeed under all these car programmes, customs duty and tax benefits are conditional on achieving a certain local content value for the finished car. The existence of these conditions is inconsistent with the provisions of Article I:1 which provides that tax and customs duty advantages accorded to products of one Member (here on Korean products) be accorded to imported like products from other Members "immediately and unconditionally".[37]

In *Canada – Autos*, the Appellate Body also discussed the concepts of 'immediately and unconditionally', and found:

> The measure maintained by Canada accords the import duty exemption to certain motor vehicles entering Canada from certain countries. These privileged motor vehicles are imported by a limited number of designated manufacturers who are required to meet certain performance conditions. In practice, this measure does not accord the same import duty exemption immediately and unconditionally to like motor vehicles of *all* other Members, as required under Article I:1 of the GATT 1994. The advantage

---

[35] Note that Article I:1 also requires that any advantage granted by a WTO Member to exports to any country must be accorded 'immediately and unconditionally' to exports to all other WTO Members. This has, however, seldom been a problem.

[36] Working Party Report on the 'Accession of Hungary', L/3889, adopted on 30 July 1973, BISD 20S/34, para. 12.

[37] Panel Report, *Indonesia – Autos*, para. 14.146.

> of the import duty exemption is accorded to some motor vehicles originating in certain countries without being accorded to like motor vehicles from *all* other Members. Accordingly, we find that this measure is not consistent with Canada's obligations under Article I:1 of the GATT 1994.[38]

The granting of an advantage within the meaning of Article I:1 may not be conditional on whether a Member has certain characteristics, has certain legislation or undertakes certain action. In the *Belgium – Family Allowances* case, a dispute of 1952 concerning a Belgian law providing for an exemption from a levy on products purchased from countries which had a system of family allowances similar to that of Belgium, the Panel held that the Belgian law at issue:

> introduced a discrimination between countries having a given system of family allowances and those which had a different system or no system at all, and made the granting of the exemption dependent on certain conditions.[39]

The Panel concluded that the advantage – the exemption from a levy – was not granted 'unconditionally' and that the Belgian law was, therefore, inconsistent with the MFN treatment obligation of Article I:1.

Questions and Assignments 4.5

Give a few examples where panels found that an advantage was not accorded 'unconditionally' to like products of all WTO Members.

4.3. MOST-FAVOURED-NATION TREATMENT UNDER THE GATS

As mentioned above, the MFN treatment obligation is also one of the basic provisions of the GATS. This section examines:

- the nature of the MFN treatment obligation provided for in Article II:1 of the GATS;
- the test of consistency with Article II:1; and
- the exemptions from the MFN treatment obligation of Article II:1 of the GATS.

4.3.1. Nature of the MFN treatment obligation of Article II:1 of the GATS

Article II:1 of the GATS prohibits discrimination *between* like services and service suppliers from different countries. Accordingly:

---

[38] Appellate Body Report, *Canada – Autos*, para. 85.
[39] GATT Panel Report, *Belgium – Family Allowances*, para. 3.

> With respect to any measure covered by this Agreement, each Member shall accord immediately and unconditionally to services and service suppliers of any other Member treatment no less favourable than that it accords to like services and service suppliers of any other country.[40]

As is the case with the MFN treatment obligation under the GATT 1994, the principal purpose of the MFN treatment obligation of Article II:1 of the GATS is to ensure *equality of opportunity*, *in casu*, for services and service suppliers from *all* WTO Members.

The MFN treatment obligation of Article II:1 of the GATS applies both to *de jure* and to *de facto* discrimination. This was the ruling of the Appellate Body in *EC – Bananas III*.[41] The Appellate Body disagreed in this case with the European Communities, which had argued that, if the negotiators of the GATS wanted Article II:1 to cover also *de facto* discrimination, it would have explicitly said so.[42] The Appellate Body ruled, however:

> The obligation imposed by Article II is unqualified. The ordinary meaning of this provision does not exclude *de facto* discrimination. Moreover, if Article II was not applicable to *de facto* discrimination, it would not be difficult – and, indeed, it would be a good deal easier in the case of trade in services, than in the case of trade in goods – to devise discriminatory measures aimed at circumventing the basic purpose of that Article.[43]

In *EC – Bananas III*, various rules for the allocation of import licences for bananas were at issue. According to the complainants, these rules, which on their face were origin-neutral, discriminated against distributors of Latin American and non-traditional ACP bananas in favour of distributors of EC and traditional ACP bananas.

Questions and Assignments 4.6

Are the MFN clauses of the GATS and of the GATT 1994 similar in wording? Are they similar in nature? Does Article II:1 of the GATS also prohibit *de facto* discrimination? Explain.

---

[40] Article II:1 of the GATS.
[41] With respect to the concepts of *de jure* and *de facto* discrimination, see above, p. 311, footnote 12.
[42] The European Communities noted that, unlike Article II:1, Article XVII of the GATS on the national treatment obligation states explicitly that it applies both to *de jure* and to *de facto* discrimination (see below, pp. 368–9).
[43] Appellate Body Report, *EC – Bananas III*, para. 233. While the Appellate Body agreed with the Panel that Article II of the GATS also covers *de facto* discrimination, it found the Panel's reasoning on this issue 'to be less than fully satisfactory' (Appellate Body Report, *EC – Bananas III*, para. 231). The Panel interpreted Article II of the GATS in the light of panel reports interpreting the national treatment obligation of Article III of the GATT. The Panel also referred to Article XVII of the GATS, which is also a national treatment obligation. The Appellate Body observed, however, that Article II of the GATS relates to MFN treatment, not to national treatment. Therefore, provisions elsewhere in the GATS relating to national treatment obligations, and previous GATT practice relating to the interpretation of the national treatment obligation of Article III of the GATT 1994, are not necessarily relevant to the interpretation of Article II of the GATS. According to the Appellate Body, the Panel would have been on safer ground had it compared the MFN obligation in Article II of the GATS with the MFN and MFN-type obligations in the GATT 1994. The Appellate Body referred, in particular, to the GATT Panel Report in *EEC – Imports of Beef*. See Appellate Body Report, *EC – Bananas III*, paras. 231 and 232. For comments on *EEC – Imports of Beef*, see above, p. 311.

4.3.2. Consistency with Article II:1 of the GATS

As is the case with Article I:1 of the GATT 1994, Article II:1 of the GATS sets out a three-tier test of consistency. There are three questions which need to be answered to determine whether or not a measure violates the MFN treatment obligation of Article II:1. These three questions are whether:

- the measure is a measure covered by the GATS;
- the services or service suppliers concerned are 'like' services or service suppliers; and
- less favourable treatment is accorded to the services or service suppliers of a Member.

4.3.2.1. 'Measures covered by this Agreement'

Article I:1 of the GATS states:

> This Agreement applies to measures by Members affecting trade in services.

For a measure to be covered by the GATS, that measure must therefore be:

- a measure by a Member; and
- a measure affecting trade in services.

A 'measure by a Member' is a very broad concept. As stated in Article I:3(a) of the GATS, a 'measure by a Member' is not limited to measures taken by the central government or central government authorities. Measures taken by regional or local governments and authorities are also 'a measure by a Member' within the meaning of Article I:1 of the GATS. Measures taken by non-governmental bodies are 'a measure by a Member' when these measures are taken in the exercise of powers delegated by governments or authorities.[44] A 'measure by a Member' can be a law, regulation, rule, procedure, decision or administrative action, but can also take any other form.[45] A 'measure by a Member' within the meaning of Article I:1 can therefore be a national parliamentary law as well as municipal decrees or rules adopted by professional bodies.[46]

The concept of a 'measure affecting the trade in services' has been clarified by the Appellate Body in *Canada – Autos*. The measure at issue in that case was an import duty exemption accorded by Canada to imports of motor vehicles by certain manufacturers. The European Communities and Japan, the complainants, argued that this measure was inconsistent with Article II:1 of the GATS as

---

[44] Article I:3(a) of the GATS. It follows that measures of private persons, companies or organisations, which do not exercise any delegated governmental powers, will not be considered to be a 'measure by a Member'.

[45] Article XXVIII(a) of the GATS.

[46] Note that, pursuant to Article I:3(a) of the GATS, Members have the obligation to take all reasonable measures to ensure that 'sub-national' levels of government and non-governmental bodies with delegated governmental powers comply with the obligations under the GATS. See also above, pp. 65–6.

it accorded 'less favourable treatment' to certain Members' services and service suppliers than to those of other Members. The Panel found that the import duty exemption was indeed inconsistent with Article II:1 of the GATS. Canada appealed this finding of inconsistency and, in addition, as a threshold matter, appealed the Panel's finding that the measure at issue fell within the scope of Article II:1 of the GATS. According to Canada, the measure at issue was not a measure 'affecting trade in services'. The Appellate Body stated that two key issues must be examined to determine whether a measure is one 'affecting trade in services', namely:

- whether there is 'trade in services' in the sense of Article I:2; and
- whether the measure in issue 'affects' such trade in services within the meaning of Article I:1.[47]

With respect to the question of whether there is 'trade in services', note that the GATS does not define what a service is. Article I:3(b) of the GATS, however, states that the term 'services' includes:

> any service in any sector except services supplied in the exercise of governmental authority.

'Services supplied in the exercise of governmental authority' are defined as any service which is supplied neither on a commercial basis nor in competition with one or more service suppliers.[48] Examples of such a service may be health care, police protection, penitentiary services and basic education. However, in a growing number of Members, some of the services that are traditionally considered to be services supplied in the exercise of government authority have in recent years been subject to privatisation and may now fall within the scope of the GATS.[49]

While the GATS does not define 'services', Article I:2 thereof defines 'trade in services' as 'the supply of a service' within one of four defined 'modes of supply'. Article I:2 states:

> For the purpose of this Agreement, trade in services is defined as the supply of a service:
>
> a. from the territory of one Member into the territory of any other Member;
> b. in the territory of one Member to the service consumer of any other Member;
> c. by a service supplier of one Member, through commercial presence in the territory of any other Member;
> d. by a service supplier of one Member, through presence of natural persons of a Member in the territory of any other Member.

---

[47] Appellate Body Report, *Canada – Autos*, para. 155. Note that the Appellate Body eventually reversed the Panel's conclusion that the import duty exemption was inconsistent with the requirements of Article II:1 of the GATS. However, it did so, not because it came to the conclusion that Canada acted consistently with its MFN treatment obligation, but because the Panel failed to substantiate its conclusion that the import duty exemption was inconsistent with Article II:1 of the GATS. See Appellate Body Report, *Canada – Autos*, paras. 182 and 184.

[48] Article I:3(c) of the GATS.

[49] Note also that many measures affecting services in the air transport sector do not fall within the scope of application of the GATS. See GATS Annex on Air Transport Services, para. 2.

These four modes of supply of services are commonly referred to as:

- the '*cross border*' mode of supply (for example, legal advice given by a lawyer established in country A to a client in country B);
- the '*consumption abroad*' mode of supply (for example, medical treatment given by a doctor established in country A to a patient from country B who comes to country A for medical treatment);
- the '*commercial presence*' mode of supply (for example, financial services supplied in country B by a bank from country A through a branch office established in country B);[50] and
- the '*presence of natural persons*' mode of supply (for example, the services supplied in country B by a computer programmer from country A, who travels to country B to supply his services).[51]

Clearly, the concept of 'trade in services' within the meaning of Article I:1 is very broad.

With respect to the question of whether the measure at issue *affects* trade in services within the meaning of Article I:1, the Appellate Body clarified in *EC – Bananas III* the term 'affecting' as follows:

> In our view, the use of the term "affecting" reflects the intent of the drafters to give a broad reach to the GATS. The ordinary meaning of the word "affecting" implies a measure that has "an effect on", which indicates a broad scope of application. This interpretation is further reinforced by the conclusions of previous panels that the term "affecting" in the context of Article III of the GATT is wider in scope than such terms as "regulating" or "governing".[52]

For a measure to affect trade in services, this measure is not required to regulate or govern the trade in, i.e. the supply of, services. A measure is covered by the GATS if it *affects* trade in services, even though the measure may regulate other matters.[53] A measure affects trade in services when the measure bears upon 'the conditions of competition in supply of a service'.[54]

Article XXVIII of the GATS gives a number of examples of 'measures by Members affecting trade in services'. This non-exhaustive list includes measures in respect of:

- the purchase, payment or use of a service;
- the access to and use of – in connection with the supply of a service – services which are required by those Members to be offered to the public generally; and

---

[50] Note that, pursuant to Article XXVIII(d) of the GATS, 'commercial presence' means any type of business or professional establishment, including through the constitution, acquisition or maintenance of a juridical person, or the creation or maintenance of a branch or a representative office, within the territory of a Member for the purpose of supplying a service.

[51] It is estimated that cross-border supply of services and supply through commercial presence each represent around 40 per cent of total world trade in services; consumption abroad represents around 20 per cent. Supply through the presence of natural persons is, to date, insignificant. See WTO Secretariat, *Market Access: Unfinished Business*, Special Studies 6 (WTO, 2001), 105.

[52] Appellate Body Report, *EC – Bananas III*, para. 220.

[53] See Panel Reports, *EC – Bananas III*, para. 7.285.   [54] See *ibid.*, para. 7.281.

- the presence, including commercial presence, of persons of a Member for the supply of a service in the territory of another Member.

In brief, the concept of 'measures by Members affecting trade in services' is, in all respects, a concept with a broad meaning. Consequently, the scope of measures covered by the GATS, i.e. the scope of measures to which the MFN treatment obligation applies, is likewise broad.

Questions and Assignments 4.7

What are the elements of the test of consistency with Article II:1 of the GATS? What measures are covered by the GATS and therefore subject to the MFN treatment obligation under Article II:1 of the GATS? What measures are not covered? In your opinion, are measures affecting basic education and health care in your country subject to the MFN treatment obligation of Article II:1 of the GATS? Give an example (other than those given above) of each mode of supply of services. Can an import prohibition on products containing asbestos be a measure covered by the GATS?

4.3.2.2. 'Like services or service suppliers'

Once it has been established that the measure at issue is covered by the GATS, the second element of the three-tier test of consistency concerning Article II:1 comes into play, namely, whether the services or service suppliers concerned are 'like' services or service suppliers. It is only between 'like' services or service suppliers that the MFN treatment obligation applies and that discrimination is prohibited. Services or service suppliers that are not 'like' may be treated differently.

As noted above, the term 'services' is not defined in the GATS, but Article I:3(c) states that 'services' includes 'any service in any sector except services supplied in the exercise of governmental authority'. The concept of 'service supplier' is defined in the GATS. Article XXVIII(g) provides that a 'service supplier' is 'any person who supplies a service', including natural and legal persons as well as service suppliers providing their services through forms of commercial presence, such as a branch or a representative office. The concept of 'like services' and 'like service suppliers' are not defined in the GATS and, to date, there is almost no relevant case law on the meaning of these terms.[55] A determination of the 'likeness' of services and service suppliers should clearly be based – among other relevant factors – on:

- the characteristics of the service or the service supplier;
- the classification and description of the service in the United Nations Central Product Classification (CPC) system; and

---

[55] Note Panel Report, *EC – Bananas III*, para. 7.322; and Panel Report, *Canada – Autos*, para. 10.248. In the latter case, the Panel stated that 'to the extent that the service suppliers concerned supply the same services, they should be considered "like" for the purposes of this case'.

- consumer habits and preferences regarding the service or the service supplier.

Note that two service suppliers that supply a like service are not necessarily 'like service suppliers'. Factors such as the size of the companies, their assets, their use of technology and the nature and extent of their expertise must all be taken into account.

The case law on the concept of 'like product' used in the GATT 1994 can serve as a useful source of inspiration but it is clear that the concepts of 'like services' and 'like service suppliers' raise much more difficult conceptual problems than does the concept of 'like product'.

Questions and Assignments 4.8

How does one determine whether services or service suppliers are 'like' within the meaning of Article II:1 of the GATS? Are all banking services 'like services'? Are all law firms 'like service suppliers'?

4.3.2.3. Treatment no less favourable

The third and final element of the test of consistency with Article II:1 of the GATS concerns the treatment accorded to 'like services' or 'like service suppliers'. Members must accord, immediately and unconditionally, to services or service suppliers of Members 'treatment no less favourable' than the treatment they accord to 'like services' or 'like service suppliers' of any other country. Article II of the GATS does not provide for any guidance as to the meaning of the concept of 'treatment no less favourable'. However, as discussed below, Article XVII of the GATS on the national treatment obligation contains guidance on the meaning of the concept of 'treatment no less favourable'.[56] Article XVII:3 states:

> Formally identical or formally different treatment shall be considered to be less favourable if it modifies the conditions of competition in favour of services or service suppliers of the Member compared to the like services or service suppliers of any other Member.

In the context of Article XVII, a measure constitutes less favourable treatment if it *modifies* the *conditions of competition*. The Appellate Body ruled in *EC – Bananas III* that, in interpreting Article II:1, and in particular the concept of 'treatment no less favourable', it should not be assumed that the guidance of Article XVII equally applies to Article II. However, as noted above, the Appellate Body has already concluded that the concept of 'treatment no less favourable' in Article II:1 and Article XVII of the GATS should be interpreted to include both *de facto*, as well as *de jure*, discrimination although only Article XVII states so explicitly.[57]

---

[56] See below, pp. 368–9.   [57] See Appellate Body Report, *EC – Bananas III*, para. 234. See above, p. 319.

When is treatment accorded to services or service suppliers of any other Member *less favourable* than that accorded to like services or like service suppliers of any other country? Can formally identical treatment be considered to be *less favourable* treatment within the meaning of Article II:1 of the GATS?

4.3.3. Exemptions from the MFN treatment obligation under Article II:1 of the GATS

Unlike under the GATT 1994, the GATS allows Members to schedule exemptions from the MFN treatment obligation in Article II:1. Article II:2 of the GATS provides:

> A Member may maintain a measure inconsistent with paragraph 1 provided that such a measure is listed in, and meets the conditions of, the Annex on Article II Exemptions.

Members could list measures in the Annex on Article II Exemptions *until* the date of entry into force of the *WTO Agreement*, i.e. 1 January 1995.[58] Around two-thirds of WTO Members have listed MFN exemptions. These exemptions concern mainly transport (especially maritime), communications (mostly audiovisual), financial and business services.[59]

A Member's notification of an exemption had to contain:

- a description of the sector or sectors in which the exemption applies;
- a description of the measure, indicating why it is inconsistent with Article II;
- the country or countries to which the measure applies;
- the intended duration of the exemption; and
- the conditions creating the need for the exemption.

In principle, exemptions *should* not exceed a period of ten years.[60] In January 2005, all exemptions under Article II:2 should have come to an end.[61] In the meantime, all exemptions granted for a period of more than five years are reviewed after five years by the Council for Trade in Services. In such a review, the Council examines whether the conditions that created the need for the exemption still prevail and sets a date for any further review.[62] In any case, the

---

[58] Since 1 January 1995, a Member can only exempt a measure from the application of the MFN obligation under Article II:1 by obtaining a waiver from the MFN obligation pursuant to Article IX:3 of the *WTO Agreement* (see paragraph 2 of the Annex on Article II Exemptions). On waivers, see above, pp. 115–17, 145–6.

[59] WTO Secretariat, *Market Access: Unfinished Business*, Special Studies 6 (WTO, 2001), 100.

[60] Para. 6 of the Annex on Article II Exemptions.

[61] Many Members, however, have stated in their exemption list that particular exemptions would last for more than ten years. Note that para. 6 of the Annex on Article II Exemptions states that the exemptions *should* not exceed ten years; it does not state that they *shall* not exceed ten years.

[62] Paras. 3 and 4 of the Annex on Article II Exemptions. If the Council concludes that these conditions are no longer present, the Member concerned would arguably be obliged to accord MFN treatment in respect of the measure previously exempted from this obligation.

exemption terminates on the date provided for in the exemption.[63] It is important to note that the exemption list may not identify Members that would not benefit from MFN treatment; the exemption list may only identify Members which would benefit from more market access than other Members.

Note, by way of example, that the European Communities included the following exemptions from the MFN treatment obligation in the *Annex of Article II Exemptions*:

- with regard to audiovisual services (production and distribution of television programmes and cinematographic works), measures granting the benefit for any support programmes (such as the Action Plan for Advanced Television Services, MEDIA and EURIMAGES) to audiovisual works and suppliers of such works, meeting certain European origin criteria;
- with regard to publishing, foreign participation in Italian companies exceeding 49 per cent of the capital and voting rights, subject to a condition of reciprocity; and
- with regard to inland waterways transport, regulations implementing the Mannheim Convention on Rhine Shipping.[64]

The lists of measures which individual Members have included in the *Annex of Article II Exemptions* can be found on the WTO's website.[65]

Questions and Assignments 4.10

Can Members exempt measures affecting trade in services from the application of the MFN treatment obligation under Article II:1 of the GATS? Give two examples (other than those referred to above) of measures of the European Communities, or of the Member of whom you are a national, which are exempted from the MFN treatment obligation pursuant to Article II:2 of the GATS.

4.4. NATIONAL TREATMENT UNDER THE GATT 1994

Article III of the GATT 1994, entitled 'National Treatment on Internal Taxation and Regulation', states, in relevant part:

> 2. The [Members] recognize that internal taxes and other internal charges, and laws, regulations and requirements affecting the internal sale, offering for sale, purchase, transportation, distribution or use of products, and internal quantitative regulations requiring the mixture, processing or use of products in specified amounts or

---

[63] Para. 5 of the Annex on Article II Exemptions.
[64] See European Communities and Their Members States, *Final List of Article II (MFN) Exemptions*, GATS/EL/31, dated 15 April 1994.
[65] See www.wto.org/english/tratop_e/serv_e/serv_commitments_e.htm, visited on 1 September 2004.

> proportions, should not be applied to imported or domestic products so as to afford protection to domestic production.
> 3. The products of the territory of any [Member] imported into the territory of any other [Member] shall not be subject, directly or indirectly, to internal taxes or other internal charges of any kind in excess of those applied, directly or indirectly, to like domestic products. Moreover, no [Member] shall otherwise apply internal taxes or other internal charges to imported or domestic products in a manner contrary to the principles set forth in paragraph 1.
> 4. ...
> 5. The products of the territory of any [Member] imported into the territory of any other [Member] shall be accorded treatment no less favourable than that accorded to like products of national origin in respect of all laws, regulations and requirements affecting their internal sale, offering for sale, purchase, transportation, distribution or use.

The other paragraphs of Article III deal with particular measures such as internal quantitative regulations relating to the mixture, processing or use of products in specific amounts (paragraphs 5 to 7); government procurement (paragraph 8(a)); subsidies to domestic producers (paragraph 8(b)); internal maximum price control measures (paragraph 9); and internal quantitative regulations relating to cinematographic films (paragraph 10). This chapter does not discuss the rules relating to these specific measures in any detail. It is sufficient to mention here that, pursuant to paragraph 5, local content requirements are prohibited,[66] and that, pursuant to paragraphs 8(a) and 8(b) respectively, the national treatment obligation does not apply to laws, regulations or requirements governing government procurement and that the national treatment obligation does not prevent the payment of subsidies exclusively to domestic producers.[67] The provisions of Article III, quoted above, should always be read together with the provisions of the *Ad* Article III Note contained in Annex I, entitled 'Notes and Supplementary Provisions', of the GATT 1994.

Other multilateral agreements on trade in goods, such as the *TBT Agreement*, the *SPS Agreement* and the *Agreement on Trade-Related Investment Measures*, require national treatment.[68] However, this section is only concerned with the national treatment obligation set out in Article III of the GATT 1994.

4.4.1. Nature of the national treatment obligation of Article III of the GATT 1994

4.4.1.1. *The object and purpose of Article III*

Article III of the GATT 1994 prohibits discrimination against imported products. Generally speaking, it prohibits Members from treating imported

---

[66] Local content requirements are direct or indirect requirements that any specific amount or proportion of any product must be supplied from domestic sources.
[67] With regard to subsidies to domestic producers, it should be noted that the GATT Panel in *Italy – Agricultural Machinery* in 1958 had already given a narrow interpretation to the Article III:8(b) exemption from the MFN treatment obligation. If this provision were to be interpreted broadly, any discrimination against imports could be qualified as a subsidy to domestic producers and thus render the discipline of Article III meaningless.
[68] See below, pp. 459–60, 463.

products less favourably than like domestic products once the imported product has entered the domestic market. In 1958, in *Italy – Agricultural Machinery*, a dispute concerning an Italian law providing special conditions for the purchase on credit of Italian-produced agricultural machinery, the Panel stated with regard to Article III:

> that the intention of the drafters of the Agreement was clearly to treat the imported products in the same way as the like domestic products once they have been cleared through customs. Otherwise indirect protection could be given.

In *US – Section 337*, the Panel noted that:

> the purpose of Article III … is to ensure that internal measures "not be applied to imported or domestic products so as to afford protection to domestic production' (Article III:1).[69]

In *Japan – Alcoholic Beverages II*, the Appellate Body stated with respect to the purpose of the national treatment obligation of Article III:

> The broad and fundamental purpose of Article III is to avoid protectionism in the application of internal tax and regulatory measures. More specifically, the purpose of Article III "is to ensure that internal measures "not be applied to imported or domestic products so as to afford protection to domestic producers". Toward this end, Article III obliges Members of the WTO to provide equality of competitive conditions for imported products in relation to domestic products. "[T]he intention of the drafters of the Agreement was clearly to treat the imported products in the same way as the like domestic products once they had been cleared through customs. Otherwise indirect protection could be given."[70]

In *Korea – Alcoholic Beverages*, the Appellate Body identified the objectives of Article III as 'avoiding protectionism, requiring equality of competitive conditions and protecting expectations of equal competitive relationships'.[71]

Panels and scholars have affirmed that one of the main purposes of Article III is to guarantee that internal measures of WTO Members do not undermine their commitments regarding tariffs under Article II.[72] Note, however, that the Appellate Body stressed in *Japan – Alcoholic Beverages II* that the purpose of Article III is broader. The Appellate Body stated:

> The broad purpose of Article III of avoiding protectionism must be remembered when considering the relationship between Article III and other provisions of the *WTO Agreement*. Although the protection of negotiated tariff concessions is certainly one purpose of Article III, the statement in Paragraph 6.13 of the Panel Report that 'one of the main purposes of Article III is to guarantee that WTO Members will not

---

[69] GATT Panel Report, *US – Section 337*, para. 5.10.

[70] Appellate Body Report, *Japan – Alcoholic Beverages II*, 109. In a footnote, the Appellate Body refers to GATT Panel Report, *US – Section 337*, para. 5.10 (for the first quote); GATT Panel Report, *US – Superfund*, para. 5.1.9; Panel Report, *Japan – Alcoholic Beverages II*, para. 5.5(b); and GATT Panel Report, *Italy – Agricultural Machinery*, para. 11 (for the second quote). See also Appellate Body Report, *Korea – Alcoholic Beverages*, para. 119; Appellate Body Report, *Chile – Alcoholic Beverages*, para. 67; Appellate Body Report, *EC – Asbestos*, para. 97; and Panel Report, *Indonesia – Autos*, para. 14.108.

[71] Appellate Body Report, *Korea – Alcoholic Beverages*, para. 120. In *Canada – Periodicals*, the Appellate Body stated: 'The fundamental purpose of Article III of the GATT 1994 is to ensure equality of competitive conditions between imported and like domestic products.' See Appellate Body Report, *Canada–Periodicals*, 8. See also Panel Report, *Argentina – Hides and Leather*, para. 11.182.

[72] See e.g. Panel Report, *Japan – Alcoholic Beverages II*, para. 6.13.

undermine through internal measures their commitments under Article II' should not be overemphasized. The sheltering scope of Article III is not limited to products that are the subject of tariff concessions under Article II. The Article III national treatment obligation is a general prohibition on the use of internal taxes and other internal regulatory measures so as to afford protection to domestic production. This obligation clearly extends also to products not bound under Article II. This is confirmed by the negotiating history of Article III.[73]

4.4.1.2. Internal measures versus border measures

Article III only applies to internal measures, not to border measures. Other GATT provisions, such as Article II on tariff concessions and Article XI on quantitative restrictions, apply to border measures. Since Articles III and Articles II and XI provide for very different rules, it is important to determine whether a measure is an internal or a border measure. It is not always easy to distinguish an internal measure from a border measure when the measure is applied to imported products at the time or point of importation. The *Ad* Article III Note clarifies:

> Any internal tax or other internal charge, or any law, regulation or requirement of the kind referred to in paragraph 1 which applies to an imported product and to the like domestic product and is collected or enforced in the case of the imported product at the time or point of importation, is nevertheless to be regarded as an internal tax or other internal charge, or a law, regulation or requirement of the kind referred to in paragraph 1, and is accordingly subject to the provisions of Article III.

It follows that, if the import of a product is barred at the border because that product fails, for example, to meet a public health or consumer safety requirement that applies equally to domestic products, consistency of this import ban with the GATT is to be examined under Article III, not under Article XI.[74]

In *EC – Asbestos*, the Panel examined the question as to whether Article III applies also when there is no 'domestic product' due to a general ban on a particular product. Canada argued that 'as France neither produces nor mines asbestos fibres on its territory, the ban on manufacturing, processing, selling and domestic marketing is, in practical terms, equivalent to a ban on importing chrysotile asbestos fibre', and would therefore fall within the scope of Article XI:1. The Panel stated, however, that 'the fact that France no longer produces asbestos or asbestos-containing products does not suffice to make the Decree [banning these products] a measure falling under Article XI:1' since, as the Panel pointed out, '[t]he cessation of French production is the consequence of the Decree and not the reverse'.[75]

In *India – Autos*, the Panel had occasion to illustrate the difference between measures falling within the scope of Article III:4 (internal measures) and measures falling within the scope of Article XI (border measures). The Panel

---

[73] Appellate Body Report, *Japan – Alcoholic Beverages II*, 110.
[74] See also GATT Panel Report, *Canada – FIRA*, para. 5.14.
[75] Panel Report, *EC – Asbestos*, paras. 8.89 and 8.91.

ruled that India acted inconsistently with Article III:4 by imposing an obligation on automotive manufacturers to use a certain proportion of local parts and components in the manufacture of cars and automotive vehicles and by imposing an obligation to offset the amount of their *purchases* of *previously imported* kits and components, already on the Indian market, by exports of equivalent value. According to the Panel, however, India also acted inconsistently with Article XI by imposing a further obligation on automotive manufacturers to balance their *importation* of kits and components with exports of equivalent value.[76]

4.4.1.3. Articles III:1, III:2 and III:4

As stated above, and as explicitly noted by the Appellate Body in *Japan – Alcoholic Beverages II*, Article III:1 articulates a general principle that internal measures should not be applied so as to afford protection to domestic production. According to the Appellate Body in *Japan – Alcoholic Beverages II*:

> This general principle informs the rest of Article III. The purpose of Article III:1 is to establish this general principle as a guide to understanding and interpreting the specific obligations contained in Article III:2 and in the other paragraphs of Article III, while respecting, and not diminishing in any way, the meaning of the words actually used in the texts of those other paragraphs.[77]

The general principle that internal measures should not be applied so as to afford protection to domestic production is elaborated on in Article III:2 with regard to internal taxation and in Article III:4 with regard to internal regulation. In Article III:2, two non-discrimination obligations can be distinguished: one obligation is set out in the first sentence of Article III:2, relating to internal taxation of 'like products'; and the other obligation is set out in the second sentence of Article III:2, relating to internal taxation of 'directly competitive or substitutable products'. The sections below will discuss:

- the constituent elements of Article III:2, first sentence;
- the constituent elements of Article III:2, second sentence; and
- the constituent elements of Article III:4.

Questions and Assignments 4.11

What is the purpose of the national treatment obligation set out in Article III? Does Article III apply to border measures? How does one distinguish between border measures and internal measures? What is the function of Article III:1?

---

[76] Panel Report, *India – Autos*, para. 8.1.
[77] Appellate Body Report, *Japan – Alcoholic Beverages II*, 111.

4.4.2. Consistency with Article III:2, first sentence, of the GATT 1994

Article III:2, first sentence, states:

> The products of the territory of any [Member] imported into the territory of any other [Member] shall not be subject, directly or indirectly, to internal taxes or other internal charges of any kind in excess of those applied, directly or indirectly, to like domestic products.

This provision sets out a two-tier test of consistency of internal taxation. In *Canada – Periodicals*, the Appellate Body found:

> [T]here are two questions which need to be answered to determine whether there is a violation of Article III:2 of the GATT 1994: (a) whether imported and domestic products are like products; and (b) whether the imported products are taxed in excess of the domestic products. If the answers to both questions are affirmative, there is a violation of Article III:2, first sentence.[78]

In brief, the two-tier test of consistency of internal taxation with Article III:2, first sentence, therefore requires the examination of:

- whether the imported and domestic products are *like products*; and
- whether the imported products are *taxed in excess* of the domestic products.

Recall that Article III:1 provides that internal taxation must not be applied so as to afford protection to domestic production. However, according to the Appellate Body in *Japan – Alcoholic Beverages II*, the presence of a protective application need not be established separately from the *specific* requirements of Article III:2, first sentence. The Appellate Body stated:

> Article III:1 informs Article III:2, first sentence, by establishing that if imported products are taxed in excess of like domestic products, then that tax measure is inconsistent with Article III. Article III:2, first sentence does not refer specifically to Article III:1. There is no specific invocation in this first sentence of the general principle in Article III:1 that admonishes Members of the WTO not to apply measures so as to afford protection. This omission must have some meaning. We believe the meaning is simply that the presence of a protective application need not be established separately from the specific requirements that are included in the first sentence in order to show that a tax measure is inconsistent with the general principle set out in the first sentence. However, this does not mean that the general principle of Article III:1 does not apply to this sentence. To the contrary, we believe the first sentence of Article III:2 is, in effect, an application of this general principle.[79]

The Panel in *Argentina – Hides and Leather* further clarified the relevance of Article III:1 and the general principle of 'not affording protection to domestic production' by stating:

> As we understand it, the presence of a protective application need be established neither separately nor together with the specific requirements contained in Article III:2, first sentence. The quoted passage from the Appellate Body report in

---

[78] Appellate Body Report, *Canada – Periodicals*, 468.
[79] Appellate Body Report, *Japan – Alcoholic Beverages II*, 111–12.

> *Japan – Alcoholic Beverages II* makes clear that Article III:2, first sentence, is, in effect, an application of the general principle stated in Article III:1. Accordingly, whenever imported products from one Member's territory are subject to taxes in excess of those applied to like domestic products in the territory of another Member, this is deemed to "afford protection to domestic production" within the meaning of Article III:1.[80]

However, before applying the test under Article III:2, first sentence, it has to be determined whether the measure at issue is an 'internal tax or other internal charge of any kind' within the meaning of that provision.

Questions and Assignments 4.12

What are the constituent elements of the test under Article III:2, first sentence?

4.4.2.1. 'Internal tax ...'

Article III:2, first sentence concerns 'internal taxes and other charges of any kind' which are applied 'directly or indirectly' on products. Examples of such internal taxes on products are value added taxes (VAT), sales taxes and excise duties. Income taxes or import duties are not covered since they are not *internal* taxes on *products*. The words 'applied *directly or indirectly* on products' should be understood to mean 'applied *on or in connection with* products'. It has been suggested that a tax applied 'indirectly' is a tax applied, not on a product as such, but on the processing of the product.[81]

In *US – Tobacco*, the Panel examined the question of whether penalty provisions under US law, consisting of a non-refundable marketing assessment and a requirement to purchase additional quantities of domestic burley and flue-cured tobacco could be qualified as 'internal taxes or other charges of any kind' within the meaning of Article III:2, first sentence. The Panel stated:

> It was thus the Panel's understanding that the US Government treated these DMA [Domestic Marketing Assessment] provisions as penalty provisions for the enforcement of a domestic content requirement for tobacco, not as separate fiscal measures, and that such interpretation corresponded to the ordinary meaning of the terms used in the relevant statute and proposed rules. Further, it appeared that these penalty provisions had no separate raison d'être in the absence of the underlying domestic content requirement. The above factors suggested to the Panel that it would not be appropriate to analyze the penalty provisions separately from the underlying domestic content requirement.[82]

According to the Panel in *US – Tobacco*, a penalty provision for the enforcement of a domestic law is not an 'internal tax or charge of any kind' within the meaning of Article III:2, first sentence.

---

[80] Panel Report, *Argentina – Hides and Leather*, para. 11.137.   [81] GATT Analytical Index, 141.
[82] GATT Panel Report, *US – Tobacco*, para. 80.

Also, the Panel in *EEC – Animal Feed Proteins* did not consider a security deposit to be a fiscal measure although this deposit accrued to the EEC when the buyers of vegetable proteins failed to fulfil the obligation to purchase milk powder. The Panel considered the security deposit, including any associated cost, to be only an enforcement mechanism for the purchase requirement and, as such, should be examined with the purchase obligation.[83]

The issue of border tax adjustment must also be mentioned in this context. Border tax adjustments are:

> any fiscal measures which put into effect, in whole or in part, the destination principle (i.e. which enable exported products to be relieved of some or all of the tax charged in the exporting country in respect of similar domestic products sold to consumers on the home market and which enable imported products sold to consumers to be charged with some or all of the tax charged in the importing country in respect of similar domestic products).[84]

Such a fiscal measure waiving or reimbursing taxes by the exporting country and an *imposition of taxes* by the importing country is obviously a fiscal measure which falls within the scope of application of Article III:2. In 1968–70, the Working Party on Border Tax Adjustments examined whether border tax adjustments were consistent with Article III:2 and other GATT disciplines. The Working Party concluded:

> there was convergence of views to the effect that taxes directly levied on products were eligible for tax adjustment. Examples of such taxes comprised specific excise duties, sales taxes and cascade taxes and the tax on value added.
> ... Furthermore, the Working Party concluded that there was convergence of views to the effect that certain taxes that were not directly levied on products were not eligible for tax adjustment. Examples of such taxes comprised social security charges whether on employers or employees and payroll taxes.[85]

Note that the regulatory objective pursued by the tax measure is of no relevance to the question of whether the measure is an internal tax within the meaning of Article III:2 and the consistency of that measure with the national treatment requirement. In *Japan – Alcoholic Beverages II*, the Appellate Body stated that Members may pursue, through their tax measures, any given policy objective *provided* they do so in compliance with Article III:2. In *Argentina – Hides and Leather*, the Panel rejected Argentina's contention that the tax legislation at issue in that case was designed to achieve efficient tax administration and collection and as such did not fall under Article III:2. The Panel stated:

> We agree that Members are free, within the outer bounds defined by such provisions as Article III:2, to administer and collect internal taxes as they see fit. However, if, as here, such "tax administration" measures take the form of an internal charge and are applied to products, those measures must, in our view, be in conformity with Article III:2. There is nothing in the provisions of Article III:2 to suggest a different conclusion. If it were accepted that "tax administration" measures are categorically

---

[83] See GATT Panel Report, *EEC – Animal Feed Proteins*, para. 4.4.
[84] See 1970 Report of the Working Party on Border Tax Adjustments, BISD 18S/97, para. 4.
[85] *Ibid.*, para. 14.

excluded from the ambit of Article III:2, this would create a potential for abuse and circumvention of the obligations contained in Article III:2.[86]

In *US – Malt Beverages*, a measure preventing imported products from being sold in a manner that would enable them to avoid taxation was considered to be a measure within the scope of Article III:2, first sentence, because it assigned a higher tax rate to the imported products.[87]

Questions and Assignments 4.13

Does income tax fall within the scope of application of Article III:2? What is border tax adjustment and does it fall within the scope of application of Article III:2? Does Article III:2 affect the freedom of Members to administer and collect internal taxes on products as they see fit?

4.4.2.2. 'Like products'

Similar to the concept of 'like products' in Article I:1 of the GATT 1994, the concept of 'like products' in Article III:2, first sentence, is not defined in the GATT 1994. The GATT 1994 does not give any guidance as to the characteristics of products that must be taken into account in determining 'likeness' either. There are, however, a considerable number of GATT and WTO dispute settlement reports that shed light on the meaning of the concept of 'like products' in Article III:2, first sentence.

Under the Japanese tax system at issue in *Japan – Alcoholic Beverages II*, the internal tax imposed on domestic *shochu* was the same as that imposed on imported *shochu*; the higher tax imposed on imported vodka was also imposed on domestic vodka. Identical products (not considering brand differences) were thus taxed identically. However, the question was whether *shochu* and vodka should be considered to be 'like products'. If *shochu* and vodka were found to be 'like', vodka could not be taxed in excess of *shochu*. The Appellate Body in *Japan – Alcoholic Beverages II* addressed the scope of the concept of 'like products' within the meaning of Article III:2, first sentence. The Appellate Body first stated that this concept should be interpreted narrowly because of the existence of the concept of 'directly competitive or substitutable products' used in the second sentence of Article III:2. The Appellate Body ruled:

> Because the second sentence of Article III:2 provides for a separate and distinctive consideration of the protective aspect of a measure in examining its application to a broader category of products that are not "like products" as contemplated by the first sentence, we agree with the Panel that the first sentence of Article III:2 must be construed narrowly so as not to condemn measures that its strict terms are not

---

[86] Panel Report, *Argentina – Hides and Leather*, para. 11.144.
[87] See GATT Panel Report, *US – Malt Beverages*, paras. 5.21 and 5.22.

meant to condemn. Consequently, we agree with the Panel also that the definition of "like products" in Article III:2, first sentence, should be construed narrowly.[88]

Subsequently, the Appellate Body expressly agreed with the basic approach for determining 'likeness' set out in the 1970 report of the Working Party on Border Tax Adjustments.[89] This Working Party found that:

> the interpretation of the term should be examined on a case-by-case basis. This would allow a fair assessment in each case of the different elements that constitute a "similar" product. Some criteria were suggested for determining, on a case-by-case basis, whether a product is "similar": the product's end-uses in a given market; consumers' tastes and habits, which change from country to country; the product's properties, nature and quality.[90]

This basic approach was followed in almost all GATT panel reports adopted after the Working Group's report involving a GATT provision in which the concept of 'like products' was used.[91] According to the Appellate Body in *Japan – Alcoholic Beverages II*, this approach should be helpful in identifying on a case-by-case basis the range of 'like products' that fall within the limits of Article III:2, first sentence of the GATT 1994. However, the Appellate Body added:

> Yet this approach will be most helpful if decision makers keep ever in mind how narrow the range of "like products" in Article III:2, first sentence is meant to be as opposed to the range of "like" products contemplated in some other provisions of the GATT 1994 and other Multilateral Trade Agreements of the *WTO Agreement*. In applying the criteria cited in [the report of the Working Group on] Border Tax Adjustments to the facts of any particular case, and in considering other criteria that may also be relevant in certain cases, panels can only apply their best judgement in determining whether in fact products are "like". This will always involve an unavoidable element of individual, discretionary judgement.[92]

The criteria listed in the report of the Working Group on Border Tax Adjustments did not include the tariff classification of the products concerned. Yet tariff classification has been used as a criterion for determining 'like products' in several panel reports.[93] The Appellate Body acknowledged in *Japan – Alcoholic Beverages II* that uniform classification in tariff nomenclatures based on the Harmonised System can be of help in determining 'likeness', but cautioned against the use of tariff bindings since there are sometimes very broad bindings that do not necessarily indicate similarity of the products

---

[88] Appellate Body Report, *Japan – Alcoholic Beverages II*, 112–13.
[89] The Working Party considered the concept of 'like' or 'similar' products as used throughout the GATT.
[90] Report of the Working Party on Border Tax Adjustments, BISD 18S/97, para. 18.
[91] See e.g. GATT Panel Report, *Australia – Ammonium Sulphate*; GATT Panel Report, *EEC – Animal Proteins*; GATT Panel Report, *Spain – Unroasted Coffee*; GATT Panel Report, *Japan – Alcoholic Beverages I*; and GATT Panel Report, *US – Superfund*.
[92] Appellate Body Report, *Japan – Alcoholic Beverages II*, 113. The Appellate Body disagreed with the Panel's observation in para. 6.22 of the Panel Report that distinguishing between 'like products' and 'directly competitive or substitutable products' under Article III:2 is 'an arbitrary decision'. According to the Appellate Body, it is 'a discretionary decision that must be made in considering the various characteristics of products in individual cases'. Appellate Body Report, *Japan – Alcoholic Beverages II*, 114.
[93] Note that the tariff classification of the products concerned by other countries was a factor considered by the GATT Panel in *Spain – Unroasted Coffee*. See above, pp. 315–16. Also, the Panel in *US – Gasoline* referred to the tariff classification in its determination of 'likeness'.

covered by those bindings. Rather, tariff bindings represent the results of trade concessions negotiated among WTO Members.[94]

In *US – Malt Beverages*, the Panel held that national legislation giving special tax exemptions to products of *small* firms (whether domestic or foreign) would constitute discrimination against imports from a *larger* foreign firm and therefore infringe Article III because its products would be treated less favourably than the like products of a small domestic firm.[95] The fact that products were produced by small or large firms was irrelevant in the determination of 'likeness'.

The same Panel also considered, however, with regard to the determination of 'likeness' that:

> the like product determination under Article III:2 also should have regard to the purpose of the Article … The purpose is … not to prevent contracting parties from using their fiscal and regulatory powers for purposes other than to afford protection to domestic production. Specifically, the purpose of Article III is not to prevent contracting parties from differentiating between different product categories for policy purposes unrelated to the protection of domestic production … Consequently, in determining whether two products subject to different treatment are like products, it is necessary to consider whether such product differentiation is being made "so as to afford protection to domestic production".[96]

The Panel found domestic wine containing a particular local variety of grape 'like' imported wine not containing this variety of grape after considering that the purpose of differentiating between the wines was to afford protection to the local production of wine. The Panel noted that the United States did not advance any alternative policy objective for the differentiation. According to the Panel in *US – Malt Beverages*, the reason for the product differentiation was to be considered when deciding on the 'likeness' of products.

In a dispute concerning, *inter alia*, special tax levels for luxury vehicles, *US – Taxes on Automobiles*, the Panel elaborated on this approach of determining 'likeness'.[97] The United States imposed a retail excise tax on cars over US$30,000 and the Panel had to determine whether cars with prices above and below US$30,000 were 'like products'. The complainant in this dispute, the European Communities, argued before the Panel that 'likeness' should be determined on the basis of factors such as the end-use of the products, their physical characteristics and tariff classification. The United States, however, contended that the key factor in determining 'likeness' should be whether the measure was applied 'so as to afford protection to domestic industry'. The Panel reasoned that the determination of 'likeness' would, in all but the most straightforward cases, have to include an examination of the *aims and effects* of the particular tax measure. According to the Panel in *US – Taxes on Automobiles*, 'likeness' should be examined in terms of whether the less favourable treatment was based on a regulatory distinction taken so as to afford protection to domestic production. *In casu*, the Panel decided that the luxury tax was not

---

[94] Appellate Body Report, *Japan – Alcoholic Beverages II*, 114–15.
[95] GATT Panel Report, *US – Malt Beverages*, para. 5.19.   [96] *Ibid.*, paras. 5.24–5.25.
[97] GATT Panel Report, *US – Taxes on Automobiles*, paras. 5.8ff. This report was never adopted.

implemented to afford protection to the domestic production of cars and that cars above and below US$30,000 could not, for the purpose of the luxury tax, be considered as 'like products' under Article III:2, first sentence.[98]

The 'aim-and-effect' test for determining 'likeness' was, however, explicitly rejected in 1996 by the Panel in *Japan – Alcoholic Beverages II*. The Panel found as follows:

> The Panel noted, in this respect, that the proposed aim-and-effect test is not consistent with the wording of Article III:2, first sentence. The Panel recalled that the basis of the aim-and-effect test is found in the words "so as to afford protection" contained in Article III:1. The Panel further recalled that Article III:2, first sentence, contains no reference to those words. Moreover, the adoption of the aim-and-effect test would have important repercussions on the burden of proof imposed on the complainant. The Panel noted in this respect that the complainants, according to the aim-and-effect test, have the burden of showing not only the effect of a particular measure, which is in principle discernible, but also its aim, which sometimes can be indiscernible. The Panel also noted that very often there is a multiplicity of aims that are sought through enactment of legislation and it would be a difficult exercise to determine which aim or aims should be determinative for applying the aim-and-effect test. Moreover, access to the complete legislative history, which according to the arguments of the parties defending the aim-and-effect test, is relevant to detect protective aims, could be difficult or even impossible for a complaining party to obtain. Even if the complete legislative history is available, it would be difficult to assess which kinds of legislative history (statements in legislation, in official legislative reports, by individual legislators, or in hearings by interested parties) should be primarily determinative of the aims of the legislation. The Panel recalled in this respect the argument by the United States that the aim-and-effect test should be applicable only with respect to origin-neutral measures. The Panel noted that neither the wording of Article III:2, nor that of Article III:1 support a distinction between origin-neutral and origin-specific measures.[99]

In support of its rejection of the aim-and-effect test in determining 'likeness' in the context of Article III:2, the Panel in *Japan – Alcoholic Beverages II* further noted:

> the list of exceptions contained in Article XX of GATT 1994 could become redundant or useless because the aim-and-effect test does not contain a definitive list of grounds justifying departure from the obligations that are otherwise incorporated in Article III. The purpose of Article XX is to provide a list of exceptions, subject to the conditions that they "are not applied in a manner which would constitute a means of arbitrary or unjustifiable discrimination between countries where the same conditions prevail, or a disguised restriction of international trade", that could justify deviations from the obligations imposed under GATT. Consequently, in principle, a WTO Member could, for example, invoke protection of health in the context of invoking the aim-and-effect test. The Panel noted that if this were the case, then the standard of proof established in Article XX would effectively be circumvented. WTO Members would not have to prove that a health measure is "necessary" to achieve its health objective. Moreover, proponents of the aim-and-effect test even shift the burden of proof, arguing that it would be up to the complainant to produce a *prima facie* case that a measure has both the aim and effect of affording protection to domestic production and, once the complainant has demonstrated that this is the case, only then would the defending party have to present evidence to rebut the claim. In sum, the Panel concluded that for

---

[98] Note that the GATT Panel Report *in US – Taxes on Automobiles* was never adopted by the CONTRACTING PARTIES.
[99] Panel Report, *Japan – Alcoholic Beverages II*, para. 6.16.

reasons relating to the wording of Article III as well as its context, the aim-and-effect test proposed by Japan and the United States should be rejected.[100]

The Appellate Body in *Japan – Alcoholic Beverages II* implicitly affirmed the Panel's rejection of the aim-and-effect test.[101]

Questions and Assignments 4.14

Why must the concept of 'like products' in Article III:2, first sentence, be interpreted narrowly? What is the basic approach followed by most panels and the Appellate Body in determining 'likeness' within the meaning of Article III:2, first sentence? Can it be that products considered to be 'like' under Article I:1 are not 'like' under Article III:2, first sentence? What is the 'aim-and-effect' test in the determination of 'likeness'? Why did the Panel in *Japan – Alcoholic Beverages II* reject this test?

4.4.2.3. Taxes 'in excess of'

Pursuant to Article III:2, first sentence, internal taxes on imported products should not be 'in excess of' the internal taxes applied to 'like' domestic products. In *Japan – Alcoholic Beverages II*, the Appellate Body established a strict benchmark for the 'in excess of' requirement. The Appellate Body ruled:

> Even the smallest amount of "excess" is too much. The prohibition of discriminatory taxes in Article III:2, first sentence, is not conditional on a 'trade effects test' nor is it qualified by a *de minimis* standard.[102]

On the absence of a 'trade effects test', the Appellate Body stated in the same case, *Japan – Alcoholic Beverages II*:

> it is irrelevant that the "trade effects" of the tax differential between imported and domestic products, as reflected in the volumes of imports, are insignificant or even non-existent; Article III *protects expectations* not of any particular trade volume but rather of the *equal competitive relationship* between imported and domestic products.[103]
>
> [Emphasis added]

With respect to the absence of a *de minimis* standard, note that the Panel in *US – Superfund* had already ruled in 1987:

> The rate of tax applied to the imported products is 3.5 cents per barrel higher than the rate applied to the like domestic products... The tax on petroleum is ... inconsistent with the United States' obligations under Article III:2, first sentence.[104]

---

[100] *Ibid.*, para. 6.17.
[101] Appellate Body Report, *Japan – Alcoholic Beverages II*, 115. The Appellate Body stated: 'With these modifications to the legal reasoning in the Panel Report, we affirm the legal conclusions and the findings of the Panel with respect to "like products" in all other respects.'
[102] *Ibid.* See also Panel Report, *Argentina – Hides and Leather*, para. 11.244.
[103] Appellate Body Report, *Japan – Alcoholic Beverages II*, 110.
[104] GATT Panel Report, *US – Superfund*, para. 5.1.1.

In *Argentina – Hides and Leather*, the Panel rejected Argentina's argument that the tax burden differential between imported and domestic products would only exist for a thirty-day period and therefore was *de minimis*.[105] Furthermore, the Panel ruled that the identity and circumstances of the persons involved in sales transactions could not serve as a justification for tax burden differentials.[106]

In the same case, the Panel also emphasised that Article III:2, first sentence, requires a comparison of *actual* tax burdens rather than merely of *nominal* tax burdens. The Panel ruled:

> It is necessary to recall the purpose of Article III:2, first sentence, which is to ensure "equality of competitive conditions between imported and like domestic products". Accordingly, Article III:2, first sentence, is not concerned with taxes or charges as such or the policy purposes Members pursue with them, but with their economic impact on the competitive opportunities of imported and like domestic products. It follows, in our view, that what must be compared are the tax burdens imposed on the taxed products.
>
> We consider that Article III:2, first sentence, requires a comparison of actual tax burdens rather than merely of nominal tax burdens. Were it otherwise, Members could easily evade its disciplines. Thus, even where imported and like domestic products are subject to identical tax rates, the actual tax burden can still be heavier on imported products. This could be the case, for instance, where different methods of computing tax bases lead to a greater actual tax burden for imported products.[107]

With respect to the methods of computing tax bases, the Panel in *Japan – Alcoholic Beverages I* stated:

> in assessing whether there is tax discrimination, account is to be taken not only of the rate of the applicable internal tax but also of the taxation methods (e.g. different kinds of internal taxes, direct taxation of the finished product or indirect taxation by taxing the raw materials used in the product during the various stages of its production) and of the rules for the tax collection (e.g. basis of assessment).[108]

While it is the *actual* tax burden on the 'like products' which must be examined, it should be noted that the Panel in *EEC – Animal Feed Proteins* ruled that an internal regulation which merely exposed imported products to a risk of discrimination constitutes, by itself, a form of discrimination and therefore less favourable treatment within the meaning of Article III.[109]

A Member which applies higher taxes on imported products in some situations but 'balances' this by applying lower taxes on the imported products in other situations also acts inconsistently with the national treatment obligation of Article III:2, first sentence. The Panel in *Argentina – Hides and Leather* ruled:

---

[105] Panel Report, *Argentina – Hides and Leather*, para. 11.245.
[106] *Ibid.*, para. 11.220. See also Panel Report, *US – Gasoline*, para. 6.11. As the Panel in *Argentina – Hides and Leather* noted in a footnote, the disciplines of Article III:2, first sentence, are of course subject to whatever exceptions a Member may justifiably invoke.
[107] Panel Report, *Argentina – Hides and Leather*, paras. 11.182–11.183.
[108] GATT Panel Report, *Japan – Alcoholic Beverages I*, para. 5.8.
[109] GATT Panel Report, *EEC – Animal Feed Proteins*, para. 141. See also GATT Panel Report, *US – Tobacco*, paras. 95–7.

> Article III:2, first sentence, is applicable to each individual import transaction. It does not permit Members to balance more favourable tax treatment of imported products in some instances against less favourable tax treatment of imported products in other instances.[110]

If differences in taxes are based only upon the nationality of producers or the origin of the parts and components contained in the products, these tax differences are – as the Panel in *Indonesia – Autos* found – necessarily inconsistent with the national treatment obligation of Article III:2, first sentence.[111]

Questions and Assignments 4.15

Is the size of the tax differential important under Article III:2, first sentence? Does Article III:2, first sentence, require equality of the nominal or the actual tax burden on like products? Does Article III:2, first sentence, allow balancing more favourable tax treatment of imported products in some instances against less favourable tax treatment of imported products in other instances?

4.4.3. Consistency with Article III:2, second sentence, of the GATT 1994

The second sentence of Article III:2 states:

> Moreover, no Member shall otherwise apply internal taxes or other internal charges to imported or domestic products in a manner contrary to the principles set forth in paragraph 1.

As discussed above, the relevant leading principle set forth in Article III:1 is that internal taxes and other internal charges:

> should not be applied to imported or domestic products so as to afford protection to domestic production.

Furthermore, the *Ad* Article III Note provides with respect to Article III:2:

> A tax conforming to the requirements of the first sentence of paragraph 2 would be considered to be inconsistent with the provisions of the second sentence only in cases where competition was involved between, on the one hand, the taxed product and, on the other hand, a directly competitive or substitutable product which was not similarly taxed.

The relationship between the first and the second sentence of Article III:2 was addressed by the Appellate Body in *Canada – Periodicals*, a dispute concerning, *inter alia*, the Canadian excise tax on magazines. The Appellate Body considered:

> there are two questions which need to be answered to determine whether there is a violation of [the first sentence of] Article III:2 of the GATT 1994: (a) whether imported

---

[110] Panel Report, *Argentina – Hides and Leather*, para. 11.260. See already in GATT Panel Report, *US – Tobacco*, para. 98.
[111] Panel Report, *Indonesia – Autos*, para. 14.112.

and domestic products are like products; and (b) whether the imported products are taxed in excess of the domestic products. If the answers to both questions are affirmative, there is a violation of Article III:2, first sentence.

If the answer to one question is negative, there is a need to examine further whether the measure is consistent with Article III:2, second sentence.[112]

As the Appellate Body stated in *Japan – Alcoholic Beverages II* and again in *Canada – Periodicals*, Article III:2, second sentence, contemplates a 'broader category of products' than Article III:2, first sentence.[113] Furthermore, Article III:2, second sentence, sets out a different test of inconsistency. In *Japan – Alcoholic Beverages II*, the Appellate Body stated:

> Unlike that of Article III:2, first sentence, the language of Article III:2, second sentence, specifically invokes Article III:1. The significance of this distinction lies in the fact that whereas Article III:1 acts implicitly in addressing the two issues that must be considered in applying the first sentence, it acts explicitly as an entirely separate issue that must be addressed along with two other issues that are raised in applying the second sentence. Giving full meaning to the text and to its context, three separate issues must be addressed to determine whether an internal tax measure is inconsistent with Article III:2, second sentence. These three issues are whether:
>
> 1. the imported products and the domestic products are *"directly competitive or substitutable products" which are in competition with each other*;
> 2. the directly competitive or substitutable imported and domestic products are *"not similarly taxed"*; and
> 3. the dissimilar taxation of the directly competitive or substitutable imported and domestic products is *"applied ... so as to afford protection to domestic production"*.
>
> Again, these are three separate issues. Each must be established separately by the complainant for a panel to find that a tax measure imposed by a Member of the WTO is inconsistent with Article III:2, second sentence.[114]

In brief, the test of consistency of internal taxation with Article III:2, second sentence, thus requires an examination of:

- whether the imported and domestic products are *directly competitive or substitutable*;
- whether these products are *not similarly taxed*; and
- whether the dissimilar taxation is *applied so as to afford protection* to domestic production.

However, before this test of consistency of internal taxation can be applied, it must be established that the measure at issue is an 'internal tax or other internal charge' within the meaning of Article III:2, second sentence.

---

[112] Appellate Body Report, *Canada – Periodicals*, 486.   [113] *Ibid.*, 470.
[114] Appellate Body Report, *Japan – Alcoholic Beverages II*, 116. This part was later cited and endorsed by the Appellate Body, in Appellate Body Report, *Canada – Periodicals*, 470, and in Appellate Body Report, *Chile – Alcoholic Beverages*, para. 47.

4.4.3.1. 'Internal taxes …'

As is the case with Article III:2, first sentence, Article III:2, second sentence, is also concerned with 'internal taxes or other internal charges'. For a discussion on the meaning and the scope of these concepts, recall the discussion above in the section dealing with Article III:2, first sentence. With regard to this constituent element, there is no difference between the first and second sentence of Article III:2.

4.4.3.2. 'Directly competitive or substitutable products'

The national treatment obligation of Article III:2, second sentence, applies to 'directly competitive or substitutable products'. In *Canada - Periodicals*, the Appellate Body ruled that to be 'directly competitive or substitutable' within the meaning of Article III:2, second sentence, products do not – contrary to what Canada had argued – have to be perfectly substitutable. The Appellate Body noted:

> A case of perfect substitutability would fall within Article III:2, first sentence, while we are examining the broader prohibition of the second sentence.[115]

With regard to the relationship between the concept of 'like products' of Article III:2, first sentence, and the concept of 'directly competitive or substitutable' products of Article III:2, second sentence, the Appellate Body stated in *Korea - Alcoholic Beverages*:

> "Like" products are a subset of directly competitive or substitutable products: all like products are, by definition, directly competitive or substitutable products, whereas not all 'directly competitive or substitutable' products are "like". The notion of like products must be construed narrowly but the category of directly competitive or substitutable products is broader. While perfectly substitutable products fall within Article III:2, first sentence, imperfectly substitutable products can be assessed under Article III:2, second sentence.[116]

As to the meaning of the concept of 'directly competitive or substitutable products', the Appellate Body stated in *Korea - Alcoholic Beverages*:

> The term "directly competitive or substitutable" describes a particular type of relationship between two products, one imported and the other domestic. It is evident from the wording of the term that the essence of that relationship is that the products are in

---

[115] Appellate Body Report, *Canada - Periodicals*, 473.
[116] Appellate Body Report, *Korea - Alcoholic Beverages*, para. 118. In a footnote, the Appellate Body referred to the Appellate Body Report, *Japan - Alcoholic Beverages II* and Appellate Body Report, *Canada - Periodicals*.

> competition. This much is clear both from the word "competitive" which means "characterized by competition", and from the word "substitutable" which means "able to be substituted". The context of the competitive relationship is necessarily the marketplace since this is the forum where consumers choose between different products. Competition in the market place is a dynamic, evolving process. Accordingly, the wording of the term "directly competitive or substitutable" implies that the competitive relationship between products is *not* to be analyzed *exclusively* by reference to *current* consumer preferences. In our view, the word "substitutable" indicates that the requisite relationship *may* exist between products that are not, at a given moment, considered by consumers to be substitutes but which are, nonetheless, *capable* of being substituted for one another.[117]

The Appellate Body also noted:

> according to the ordinary meaning of the term, products are competitive or substitutable when they are interchangeable or if they offer, as the Panel noted, "alternative ways of satisfying a particular need or taste". Particularly in a market where there are regulatory barriers to trade or to competition, there may well be latent demand.
>
> The words "competitive or substitutable" are qualified in the *Ad* Article by the term "directly". In the context of Article III:2, second sentence, the word "directly" suggests a degree of proximity in the competitive relationship between the domestic and the imported products. The word "direct" does not, however, prevent a panel from considering both latent and extant demand.[118]

In brief, the Appellate Body considers products to be 'directly competitive or substitutable' when they are interchangeable, in that they offer alternative ways of satisfying a particular need or taste. The Appellate Body also considers that, in examining whether products are 'directly competitive or substitutable', an analysis of *latent* as well as *extant* demand is required since 'competition in the market place is a dynamic, evolving process'. As the Appellate Body in *Korea – Alcoholic Beverages* stated, in justification of its dynamic view of the concept of 'directly competitive or substitutable products':

> In view of the objectives of avoiding protectionism, requiring equality of competitive conditions and protecting expectations of equal competitive relationships, we decline to take a static view of the term "directly competitive or substitutable". The object and purpose of Article III confirms that the scope of the term "directly competitive or substitutable" cannot be limited to situations where consumers *already* regard products as alternatives. If reliance could be placed only on current instances of substitution, the object and purpose of Article III:2 could be defeated by the protective taxation that the provision aims to prohibit.[119]

As the Appellate Body recalled in *Korea – Alcoholic Beverages*, past panels have acknowledged that consumer behaviour might be influenced, in particular, by protectionist internal taxation. Citing the Panel in *Japan – Alcoholic Beverages I*,[120] the Panel in *Japan – Alcoholic Beverages II* observed:

> a tax system that discriminates against imports has the consequence of creating and even freezing preferences for domestic goods.[121]

---

[117] Appellate Body Report, *Korea – Alcoholic Beverages*, para. 114.
[118] *Ibid.*, paras. 115–16.   [119] *Ibid.*, para. 120.
[120] GATT Panel Report, *Japan – Alcoholic Beverages I*, para. 5.9.
[121] Panel Report, *Japan – Alcoholic Beverages II*, para. 6.28.

The same Panel also stated:

> consumer surveys in a country with ... a [protective] tax system would likely under-state the degree of *potential* competitiveness between substitutable products.[122]
>
> [Emphasis added]

The Appellate Body in *Korea – Alcoholic Beverages* thus concluded that it may be highly relevant to examine latent demand.[123]

With respect to the factors to be taken into account in establishing whether products are 'directly competitive or substitutable', the Appellate Body, in *Japan – Alcoholic Beverages II*, agreed with the Panel in that case that these factors include, in addition to their physical characteristics, common end-use and tariff classifications, the nature of the compared products and the competitive conditions in the relevant market.[124] The Appellate Body held:

> The GATT 1994 is a commercial agreement, and the WTO is concerned, after all, with markets. It does not seem inappropriate to look at competition in the relevant markets as one among a number of means of identifying the broader category of products that might be described as "directly competitive or substitutable".
>
> Nor does it seem inappropriate to examine elasticity of substitution as one means of examining those relevant markets. The Panel did not say that cross-price elasticity of demand is "*the* decisive criterion" for determining whether products are "directly competitive or substitutable".[125]

The Appellate Body thus considered an examination of the competitive conditions in the market, and, in particular, the cross-price elasticity of demand in that market, as a means of establishing whether products are 'directly competitive or substitutable'. In *Korea – Alcoholic Beverages*, the Appellate Body further clarified:

> studies of cross-price elasticity, which in our Report in *Japan – Alcoholic Beverages* were regarded as one means of examining a market, involve an assessment of latent demand. Such studies attempt to predict the change in demand that would result from a change in the price of a product following, *inter alia*, from a change in the relative tax burdens on domestic and imported products.[126]

However, in that case, *Korea – Alcoholic Beverages*, the Appellate Body was careful to stress that cross-price elasticity of demand for products is not the decisive criterion in determining whether these products are 'directly competitive or substitutable'. The Appellate Body agreed with the Panel's emphasis on the 'quality' or 'nature' of competition rather than the 'quantitative overlap of competition'. The Appellate Body shared the Panel's reluctance to rely unduly on quantitative analyses of the competitive relationship. In its view, an approach that focused solely on the quantitative overlap of competition would, in essence, make cross-price elasticity the decisive criterion in deter-mining whether products are 'directly competitive or substitutable'.[127]

---

[122] *Ibid.*, para. 6.28.   [123] Appellate Body Report, *Korea – Alcoholic Beverages*, para. 120.
[124] Appellate Body Report, *Japan – Alcoholic Beverages II*, 117.
[125] *Ibid.*   [126] Appellate Body Report, *Korea – Alcoholic Beverages*, para. 121.   [127] *Ibid.*, para. 134.

In establishing whether products are 'directly competitive or substitutable', the market situation in *other* Members may be relevant and can be taken into consideration. In *Korea – Alcoholic Beverages*, the Appellate Body stated:

> It is, of course, true that the "directly competitive or substitutable" relationship must be present in the market at issue, in this case, the Korean market. It is also true that consumer responsiveness to products may vary from country to country. This does not, however, preclude consideration of consumer behaviour in a country other than the one at issue. It seems to us that evidence from other markets may be pertinent to the examination of the market at issue, particularly when demand on that market has been influenced by regulatory barriers to trade or to competition. Clearly, not every other market will be relevant to the market at issue. But if another market displays characteristics similar to the market at issue, then evidence of consumer demand in that other market may have some relevance to the market at issue. This, however, can only be determined on a case-by-case basis, taking account of all relevant facts.[128]

The question has arisen as to whether, in examining whether products are 'directly competitive or substitutable', it is necessary to examine products on an item-by-item basis or whether it is permitted to group products together for the purpose of this examination. In *Korea – Alcoholic Beverages*, the Panel compared distilled and diluted *soju* (the domestic Korean liquor at issue in this case) with imported liquor products on a group basis, rather than on an item-by-item basis. The Appellate Body, rejecting Korea's appeal of the Panel's method of comparison, ruled:

> Whether, and to what extent, products can be grouped is a matter to be decided on a case-by-case basis. In this case, the Panel decided to group the imported products at issue on the basis that:
>
> > ... on balance, all of the imported products specifically identified by the complainants have sufficient common characteristics, end-uses and channels of distribution and prices ... ".
>
> As the Panel explained in the footnote attached to this passage, the Panel's subsequent analysis of the physical characteristics, end-uses, channels of distribution and prices of the imported products confirmed the correctness of its decision to group the products for analytical purposes. Furthermore, where appropriate, the Panel did take account of individual product characteristics. It, therefore, seems to us that the Panel's grouping of imported products, complemented where appropriate by individual product examination, produced the same outcome that individual examination of each imported product would have produced. We, therefore, conclude that the Panel did not err in considering the imported beverages together.[129]

Questions and Assignments 4.17

When are products 'directly competitive or substitutable' within the meaning of Article III:2, second sentence? In determining whether products are 'directly competitive or substitutable', does one consider only extant demand or also latent demand? What factors can be taken into account in determining whether products are 'directly competitive or substitutable'? How important is

---

[128] *Ibid.*, para. 137.   [129] *Ibid.*, paras. 143–4.

the cross-price elasticity of demand of products in determining whether such products are 'directly competitive or substitutable'?

4.4.3.3. 'Not similarly taxed'

The next element or requirement of the test under Article III:2, second sentence, is whether the products at issue are 'not similarly taxed'. While under Article III:2, first sentence, even the slightest tax differential leads to the conclusion that the internal tax imposed on imported products is inconsistent with the national treatment obligation, under Article III:2, second sentence, the tax differential has to be more than *de minimis* to support a conclusion that the internal tax imposed on imported products is WTO-inconsistent. In *Japan – Alcoholic Beverages II*, the Appellate Body explained:

> To interpret "in excess of" and "not similarly taxed" identically would deny any distinction between the first and second sentences of Article III:2. Thus, in any given case, there may be some amount of taxation on imported products that may well be "in excess of" the tax on domestic "like products" but may not be so much as to compel a conclusion that "directly competitive or substitutable" imported and domestic products are "not similarly taxed" for the purposes of the *Ad* Article to Article III:2, second sentence. In other words, there may be an amount of excess taxation that may well be more of a burden on imported products than on domestic "directly competitive or substitutable products" but may nevertheless not be enough to justify a conclusion that such products are "not similarly taxed" for the purposes of Article III:2, second sentence. We agree with the Panel that this amount of differential taxation must be more than *de minimis* to be deemed "not similarly taxed" in any given case. And, like the Panel, we believe that whether any particular differential amount of taxation is *de minimis* or is not *de minimis* must, here too, be determined on a case-by-case basis. Thus, to be "not similarly taxed", the tax burden on imported products must be heavier than on "directly competitive or substitutable" domestic products, and that burden must be more than *de minimis* in any given case.[130]

The 'not similarly taxed' requirement is met even if only some imported products are not taxed similarly to domestic products, while other imported products are taxed similarly. The Appellate Body stated in *Canada – Periodicals* that:

> dissimilar taxation of even some imported products as compared to directly competitive or substitutable domestic products is inconsistent with the provisions of the second sentence of Article III:2.[131]

To support this conclusion, the Appellate Body referred to the Panel in *US – Section 337* which found:

> that the 'no less favourable' treatment requirement of Article III:4 has to be understood as applicable to each individual case of imported products. The Panel rejected any notion of balancing more favourable treatment of some imported products against less favourable treatment of other imported products.[132]

---

[130] Appellate Body Report, *Japan – Alcoholic Beverages II*, 118. On the *de minimis* standard, see also Appellate Body Report, *Canada – Periodicals*, 474; Appellate Body Report, *Chile –Alcoholic Beverages*, para. 49; and Panel Report, *Indonesia – Autos*, para. 14.115.

[131] Appellate Body Report, *Canada – Periodicals*, 474.   [132] GATT Panel Report, *US – Section 337*, para. 5.14.

Questions and Assignments 4.18

Is the size of the tax differential important under Article III:2, second sentence?

4.4.3.4. *'So as to afford protection to domestic production'*

The last element or requirement of the test under Article III:2, second sentence, is whether the internal taxes are applied 'so as to afford protection to domestic production'. This requirement must be distinguished from the second requirement of 'not similarly taxed'. In *Japan – Alcoholic Beverages II*, the Appellate Body noted:

> [T]he Panel erred in blurring the distinction between [the issue of whether the products at issue were "not similarly taxed"] and the entirely separate issue of whether the tax measure in question was applied "so as to afford protection". Again, these are separate issues that must be addressed individually. If "directly competitive or substitutable products" are *not* "not similarly taxed", then there is neither need nor justification under Article III:2, second sentence, for inquiring further as to whether the tax has been applied "so as to afford protection". But if such products are "not similarly taxed", a further inquiry must necessarily be made.[133]

As to how to establish whether a tax measure was applied so as to afford protection to domestic production, the Appellate Body noted in *Japan – Alcoholic Beverages II* :

> As in [the GATT Panel Report on *Japan – Customs Duties, Taxes and Labelling Practices on Imported Wines and Alcoholic Beverages*, BISD 34S/83], we believe that an examination in any case of whether dissimilar taxation has been applied so as to afford protection requires a comprehensive and objective analysis of the structure and application of the measure in question on domestic as compared to imported products. We believe it is possible to examine objectively the underlying criteria used in a particular tax measure, its structure, and its overall application to ascertain whether it is applied in a way that affords protection to domestic products.
>
> Although it is true that the aim of a measure may not be easily ascertained, nevertheless its protective application can most often be discerned from the design, the architecture, and the revealing structure of a measure.[134]

To determine whether the application of a tax measure affords protection to domestic production, it is the application criteria, the structure and the overall application rather than the subjective intent of the legislator or regulator that must be examined. For example, if the tax measure operates in such a way that the lower tax brackets cover almost exclusively domestic production, whereas the higher tax brackets embrace almost exclusively imported products, the implication is that the tax measure is applied so as to afford protection to domestic production.

---

[133] Appellate Body Report, *Japan – Alcoholic Beverages II*, 119.   [134] *Ibid.*, 120.

As the Appellate Body acknowledged in *Japan – Alcoholic Beverages II*, the very magnitude of the tax differential may be evidence of the protective application of a tax measure. Most often, however, other factors will also be considered.

With regard to the relevance of the intent of the legislator or regulator, the Appellate Body in *Japan – Alcoholic Beverages II* noted:

> [Whether a tax measure is applied so as to afford protection to domestic production] is not an issue of intent. It is not necessary for a panel to sort through the many reasons legislators and regulators often have for what they do and weigh the relative significance of those reasons to establish legislative or regulatory intent. If the measure is applied to imported or domestic products so as to afford protection to domestic production, then it does not matter that there may not have been any desire to engage in protectionism in the minds of the legislators or the regulators who imposed the measure. It is irrelevant that protectionism was not an intended objective if the particular tax measure in question is nevertheless, to echo Article III:1, "*applied* to imported or domestic products so as to afford protection to domestic production". This is an issue of how the measure in question is *applied*.[135]

In *Chile – Alcoholic Beverages*, Chile argued that the internal taxation on alcoholic beverages at issue in that case was aimed at, among other things, reducing the consumption of alcoholic beverages with higher alcohol content. The Appellate Body held:

> We recall once more that, in *Japan – Alcoholic Beverages*, we declined to adopt an approach to the issue of "so as to afford protection" that attempts to examine "the many reasons legislators and regulators often have for what they do". We called for examination of the design, architecture and structure of a tax measure precisely to permit identification of a measure's objectives or purposes as revealed or objectified in the measure itself. Thus, we consider that a measure's purposes, objectively manifested in the design, architecture and structure of the measure, *are* intensely pertinent to the task of evaluating whether or not that measure is applied so as to afford protection to domestic production. In the present appeal, Chile's explanations concerning the structure of the New Chilean System – including, in particular, the truncated nature of the line of progression of tax rates, which effectively consists of two levels (27 per cent *ad valorem* and 47 per cent *ad valorem*) separated by only 4 degrees of alcohol content – might have been helpful in understanding what *prima facie* appear to be anomalies in the progression of tax rates. The conclusion of protective application reached by the Panel becomes very difficult to resist, in the absence of countervailing explanations by Chile. The mere statement of the four objectives pursued by Chile does not constitute effective rebuttal on the part of Chile.[136]

Note, however, that, in *Canada – Periodicals*, the Appellate Body did seem to give at least some importance to statements of representatives of the Canadian Government about the policy objectives of the tax measure at issue.[137]

Questions and Assignments 4.19

How does one establish whether internal taxes on directly competitive or substitutable products have been applied so as to afford protection to

---

[135] *Ibid.*,119.   [136] Appellate Body Report, *Chile – Alcoholic Beverages*, para. 71.
[137] See Appellate Body Report, *Canada – Periodicals*, 475–6.

domestic production? Is the intent of the legislator relevant in deciding whether an internal tax is inconsistent with the national treatment obligation of Article III:2, second sentence?

4.4.4. Consistency with the national treatment obligation of Article III:4 of the GATT 1994

The national treatment obligation of Article III of the GATT 1994 does not only concern internal taxation dealt with in Article III:2. Article III also concerns internal regulation, dealt with primarily in Article III:4.

Article III:4 states, in relevant part:

> The products of the territory of any [Member] imported into the territory of any other [Member] shall be accorded treatment no less favourable than that accorded to like products of national origin in respect of all laws, regulations and requirements affecting their internal sale, offering for sale, purchase, transportation, distribution or use.

This provision sets out a three-tier test for the consistency of internal regulation. In *Korea – Various Measures on Beef*, the Appellate Body stated:

> For a violation of Article III:4 to be established, three elements must be satisfied: that the imported and domestic products at issue are "like products"; that the measure at issue is a "law, regulation, or requirement affecting their internal sale, offering for sale, purchase, transportation, distribution, or use"; and that the imported products are accorded "less favourable" treatment than that accorded to like domestic products.[138]

In other words, the three-tier test of consistency of internal regulation with Article III:4 thus requires the examination of whether:

- the measure at issue is a *law, regulation or requirement* covered by Article III:4;
- the imported and domestic products are *like products*; and
- the imported products are accorded *less favourable treatment*.

In *EC – Bananas III*, the Appellate Body, in its examination of the constituent elements of Article III:4, ruled with regard to the phrase 'so as afford protection to domestic production' of Article III:1, as follows:

> Article III:4 does *not* specifically refer to Article III:1. Therefore, a determination of whether there has been a violation of Article III:4 does *not* require a separate consideration of whether a measure "afford[s] protection to domestic production".[139]

As the Appellate Body found in *EC – Asbestos*, Article III:1, nevertheless, has 'particular contextual significance in interpreting Article III:4, as it sets forth the "general principle" pursued by that provision'.[140]

---

[138] Appellate Body Report, *Korea – Various Measures on Beef*, para. 133.

[139] Appellate Body Report, *EC – Bananas III*, para. 216. We note, however, that, in *Canada – Periodicals*, the Panel did examine whether a measure at issue 'afford[ed] protection to domestic production' to determine the consistency of that measure with Article III:4. (para. 5.38).

[140] Appellate Body Report, *EC – Asbestos*, para. 93.

Questions and Assignments 4.20

What are the constituent elements of the test of consistency with Article III:4? In this context, what is the importance of the general principle, set out in Article III:1, that internal measures may not be applied so as to afford protection to domestic production?

4.4.4.1. *'Laws, regulations and requirements ...'*

Article III:4 concerns 'all laws, regulations and requirements affecting [the] internal sale, offering for sale, purchase, transportation, distribution or use [of products]'. Broadly speaking, the national treatment obligation of Article III:4 applies to regulations affecting the sale and use of products.

In 1958, the Panel in *Italy – Agricultural Machinery* ruled:

> the text of paragraph 4 referred both in English and French to laws and regulations and requirements *affecting* internal sale, purchase, etc., and not to laws, regulations and requirements governing the conditions of sale or purchase. The selection of the words "affecting" would imply, in the opinion of the Panel, that the drafters of the Article intended to cover in paragraph 4 not only laws and regulations which directly governed the conditions of sale or purchase but also any laws or regulations which might adversely modify the conditions of competition between the domestic and imported products on the internal market.[141]

The Panel thus interpreted the scope of application of Article III:4 broadly as including all measures that may modify the conditions of competition. Later GATT panels built on this broad interpretation of the scope of Article III:4. In *US – Section 337*, for example, the Panel, referring back to the paragraph from *Italy – Agricultural Machinery* quoted above, addressed the issue of whether only substantive laws, regulations and requirements or also procedural laws, regulations and requirements can be regarded as 'affecting' the internal sale of imported goods. The Panel, in *US – Section 337*, found:

> In the Panel's view, enforcement procedures cannot be separated from the substantive provisions they serve to enforce. If the procedural provisions of internal law were not covered by Article III:4, contracting parties could escape the national treatment standard by enforcing substantive law, itself meeting the national treatment standard, through procedures less favourable to imported products than to like products of national origin. The interpretation suggested by the United States would therefore defeat the purpose of Article III, which is to ensure that internal measures "not be applied to imported or domestic products so as to afford protection to domestic production" (Article III:1).[142]

According to GATT case law, Article III:4 applies, *inter alia*, to:

- minimum price requirements applicable to domestic and imported beer;[143]

---

[141] GATT Panel Report, *Italy – Agricultural Machinery*, para. 12.
[142] GATT Panel Report, *US – Section 337*, para. 5.10.
[143] See GATT Panel Report, *Canada – Provincial Liquor Boards (US)*, para. 5.30.

- limitations on points of sale for imported alcoholic beverages;[144]
- the practice of limiting listing of imported beer to the six-pack size;[145]
- the requirement that imported beer and wine be sold only through in-State wholesalers or other middlemen;[146]
- a ban on all cigarette advertising;[147]
- additional marking requirements such as an obligation to add the name of the producer or the place of origin or the formula of the product;[148]
- practices concerning internal transportation of beer;[149]and
- trade-related investment measures.[150]

In *EC – Bananas III*, the Appellate Body agreed with the Panel that Article III:4 was applicable to the EC import licensing requirements at issue. This was contested by the European Communities on the ground that import licensing was a border measure and not an internal measure within the scope of Article III:4. However, the Appellate Body ruled:

> At issue in this appeal is not whether *any* import licensing requirement, as such, is within the scope of Article III:4, but whether the EC procedures and requirements for the *distribution* of import licences for imported bananas among eligible operators *within* the European Communities are within the scope of this provision ... These rules go far beyond the mere import licence requirements needed to administer the tariff quota for third-country and non-traditional ACP bananas or Lomé Convention requirements for the importation of bananas. These rules are intended, among other things, to cross-subsidize distributors of EC (and ACP) bananas and to ensure that EC banana ripeners obtain a share of the quota rents. As such, these rules affect "the internal sale, offering for sale, purchase ... " within the meaning of Article III:4, and therefore fall within the scope of this provision.[151]

In *Canada – Autos*, the Panel held that a measure can be considered to be a measure affecting, i.e. having an effect on, the internal sale or use of imported products even if it is not shown that *under the current circumstances* the measure has an impact on the decisions of private parties to buy imported products. The Panel noted:

> With respect to whether the CVA [Canadian Value Added] requirements affect the "internal sale ... or use" of products, we note that, as stated by the Appellate Body, the ordinary meaning of the word "affecting" implies a measure that has "an effect on" and thus indicates a broad scope of application. The word "affecting" in Article III:4 of the GATT has been interpreted to cover not only laws and regulations which directly govern the conditions of sale or purchase but also any laws or regulations which *might* adversely modify the conditions of competition between domestic and imported products.

---

[144] See GATT Panel Report, *Canada – Provincial Liquor Boards (EEC)*, para. 4.26.
[145] See GATT Panel Report, *Canada – Provincial Liquor Boards (US)*, para. 5.4.
[146] See GATT Panel Report, *US – Malt Beverages*, para. 5.32.
[147] See GATT Panel Report, *Thailand – Cigarettes*, para. 77.
[148] See Working Party Report, *Certificates of Origin, Marks of Origin, Consular Formalities*, para. 13.
[149] See GATT Panel Report, *Canada – Provincial Liquor Boards (US)*, para. 5.12; and GATT Panel Report, *US – Malt Beverages*, para. 5.50.
[150] See GATT Panel Report, *Canada – FIRA*, paras. 5.12 and 6.1.
[151] Appellate Body Report, *EC – Bananas III*, para. 211.

> The idea that a measure which distinguishes between imported and domestic products can be considered to affect the internal sale or use of imported products only if such a measure is shown to have an impact *under current circumstances* on decisions of private firms with respect to the sourcing of products is difficult to reconcile with the concept of the "no less favourable treatment" obligation in Article III:4 as an obligation addressed to governments to ensure effective equality of competitive opportunities between domestic and imported products, and with the principle that a showing of trade effects is not necessary to establish a violation of this obligation.[152]
>
> [Emphasis added]

While, to date, most cases involving Article III:4 concerned *generally applicable* 'laws' and 'regulations', Article III:4 also covers 'requirements' which may apply to *isolated cases only*.[153] Article III:4 covers both measures that apply across the board and measures that apply in isolated cases only. The Panel in *Canada – FIRA* noted:

> The Panel could not subscribe to the Canadian view that the word "requirements" in Article III:4 should be interpreted as "mandatory rules applying across-the-board" because this latter concept was already more aptly covered by the term "regulations" and the authors of this provision must have had something different in mind when adding the word 'requirements" ... The Panel also considered that, in judging whether a measure is contrary to obligations under Article III:4, it is not relevant whether it applies across-the-board or only in isolated cases. Any interpretation which would exclude case-by-case action would, in the view of the Panel, defeat the purposes of Article III:4.[154]

The question has arisen whether a 'requirement' within the meaning of Article III:4 necessarily needs to be a government-imposed requirement, or whether an action by a private party can constitute a 'requirement' to which Article III:4 applies. In *Canada – Autos*, the Panel examined commitments by Canadian car manufacturers to increase the value added to cars in their Canadian plants. These commitments were communicated in letters addressed to the Canadian Government. The Panel qualified these commitments as 'requirements' subject to Article III:4.[155] The Panel found:

> To qualify a private action as a "requirement" within the meaning of Article III:4 means that in relation to that action a Member is to provide no less favourable treatment to imported products than to domestic products. A determination of

---

[152] Panel Report, *Canada – Autos*, paras. 10.80 and 10.84. In a footnote to para. 10.80, the Panel referred to Appellate Body Report, *EC – Bananas III*, para. 220. Note that the Appellate Body in this report did not discuss the word 'affecting' within the meaning of Article III:4 but within the meaning of Article I:1 of the GATS. The Panel in *Canada – Autos* also referred to GATT Panel Report, *Italy – Agricultural Machinery*, para. 12, quoted above.

[153] See GATT Panel Report, *Canada – FIRA*.

[154] *Ibid.*, para. 5.5. The measures at issue in *Canada – FIRA* were written undertakings by investors to purchase goods of Canadian origin in preference to imported goods or in specified amounts or proportions, or to purchase goods from Canadian sources.

[155] The question of whether actions of private parties can qualify as 'requirements' within the meaning of Article III:4 was previously addressed in GATT Panel Report, *Canada – FIRA*, para. 5.4 and GATT Panel Report, *EEC – Parts and Components*, para. 5.21. The Panel in *Canada – Autos* explicitly refers to this case law and takes it further. Note that, in *Canada – FIRA*, Canada argued that the purchase of undertakings should be considered as private contractual obligations of particular foreign investors *vis-à-vis* the Canadian Government. The Panel felt, however, that, even if this was so, private contractual obligations entered into by investors should not adversely affect the rights which Members possess under Article III:4 of the GATT. See GATT Panel Report, *Canada – FIRA*, para. 5.6.

> whether private action amounts to a "requirement" under Article III:4 must therefore necessarily rest on a finding that there is a nexus between that action and the action of a government such that the government must be held responsible for that action. We do not believe that such a nexus can exist only if a government makes undertakings of private parties legally enforceable, as in the situation considered by the Panel on *Canada – FIRA*, or if a government conditions the grant of an advantage on undertakings made by private parties, as in the situation considered by the Panel on *EEC – Parts and Components* … The word "requirements" in its ordinary meaning and in light of its context in Article III:4 clearly implies government action involving a demand, request or the imposition of a condition but in our view this term does not carry a particular connotation with respect to the legal form in which such government action is taken. In this respect, we consider that, in applying the concept of "requirements" in Article III:4 to situations involving actions by private parties, it is necessary to take into account that there is a broad variety of forms of government action that can be effective in influencing the conduct of private parties.[156]

In brief, private action can be a 'requirement' within the meaning of Article III:4 if, and only if, there is such a *nexus*, i.e. a close link, between that action and the action of a government, that the government must be held responsible for that private action.

Note that the *Agreement on Trade-Related Investment Measures* contains an illustrative list of TRIMs that are inconsistent with Article III:4.[157] The illustrative list includes, for example, measures that:

- are mandatory or enforceable under domestic law or compliance with which is necessary to obtain an advantage; and
- require the purchase or use by an enterprise of products of domestic origin; or require that an enterprise's purchases or use of imported products be limited to an amount related to the volume or value of local products that it exports.

Questions and Assignments 4.21

What laws, regulations and requirements fall within the scope of application of Article III:4? Can a measure be considered to be a measure affecting the internal sale of imported products within the meaning of Article III:4 if it is not shown that *under current circumstances* the measure has an impact on the decisions of private parties to buy imported products? Is the national treatment obligation of Article III:4 also applicable to measures that apply only to isolated cases? Can an action by a private person, company or organization constitute a measure within the meaning of Article III:4? Does the national treatment obligation of Article III apply to regulations concerning government procurement or to subsidies to domestic producers?

---

[156] Panel Report, *Canada – Autos*, paras. 10.106–10.107.
[157] See Article 2.2 of, and the Annex to, the *Agreement on Trade-Related Investment Measures*.

4.4.4.2. 'Like products'

As with Articles I:1 and III:2, first sentence, both discussed above, the non-discrimination obligation of Article III:4 only applies to 'like products'. The Appellate Body considered the meaning of the concept of 'like products' in Article III:4 in *EC – Asbestos*. In its report in that case, the Appellate Body first noted that the concept of 'like products' was also used in Article III:2, first sentence, and that, in previous reports, it had held that the scope of 'like products' was to be construed 'narrowly' in that provision.[158] The Appellate Body then examined whether this interpretation of 'like products' in Article III:2 could be taken to suggest a similarly narrow reading of 'like products' in Article III:4, since both provisions form part of the same Article. The Appellate Body reasoned as follows:

> we observe that, although the obligations in Articles III:2 and III:4 both apply to "like products", the text of Article III:2 differs in one important respect from the text of Article III:4. Article III:2 contains *two separate* sentences, each imposing *distinct* obligations: the first lays down obligations in respect of "like products", while the second lays down obligations in respect of "directly competitive or substitutable" products. By contrast, Article III:4 applies only to "like products" and does not include a provision equivalent to the second sentence of Article III:2.[159]

The Appellate Body considered that this textual difference between Article III:2 and Article III:4 had considerable implications for the meaning of the concept of 'like products' in these two provisions. The Appellate Body recalled:

> In *Japan – Alcoholic Beverages*, we concluded, in construing Article III:2, that the two separate obligations in the two sentences of Article III:2 must be interpreted in a harmonious manner that gives meaning to *both* sentences in that provision. We observed there that the interpretation of one of the sentences necessarily affects the interpretation of the other. Thus, the scope of the term "like products" in the first sentence of Article III:2 affects, and is affected by, the scope of the phrase "directly competitive or substitutable" products in the second sentence of that provision. We said in *Japan – Alcoholic Beverages*:
>
>> Because the second sentence of Article III:2 provides for a separate and distinctive consideration of the protective aspect of a measure in examining its application to a broader category of products that are not "like products" as contemplated by the first sentence, we agree with the Panel that the first sentence of Article III:2 must be construed narrowly so as not to condemn measures that its strict terms are not meant to condemn. Consequently, we agree with the Panel also that the definition of "like products" in Article III:2, first sentence, should be construed narrowly.[160]

The Appellate Body, after considering the reasoning underlying its interpretation of 'like products' in Article III:2, first sentence, subsequently observed:

> In construing Article III:4, the same interpretive considerations do not arise, because the "general principle" articulated in Article III:1 is expressed in Article III:4, not through two distinct obligations, as in the two sentences in Article III:2, but instead

---

[158] The Appellate Body referred in a footnote to Appellate Body Report, *Japan – Alcoholic Beverages II*, 112 and 113 and Appellate Body Report, *Canada – Periodicals*, 473.

[159] Appellate Body Report, *EC – Asbestos*, para. 94.   [160] *Ibid.*, para. 95.

through a single obligation that applies solely to "like products". Therefore, the harmony that we have attributed to the two sentences of Article III:2 need not and, indeed, cannot be replicated in interpreting Article III:4. Thus, we conclude that, given the textual difference between Articles III:2 and III:4, the "accordion" of "likeness" stretches in a different way in Article III:4.[161]

Having distinguished the concept of 'like products' in Article III:4 from the concept in Article III:2, first sentence, the Appellate Body then proceeded to examine the meaning of this concept in Article III:4. It first recalled that, in *Japan – Alcoholic Beverages II*, it ruled that the broad and fundamental purpose of Article III is to avoid protectionism in the application of internal tax and regulatory measures. As is explicitly stated in Article III:1, the purpose of Article III is to ensure that internal measures 'not be applied to imported and domestic products so as to afford protection to domestic production'. To this end, Article III obliges Members of the WTO to provide *equality of competitive conditions for imported products in relation to domestic products*.[162] This 'general principle' is not explicitly invoked in Article III:4. Nevertheless, it does 'inform' that provision.[163] The Appellate Body in *EC – Asbestos* thus reasoned:

> the term "like product" in Article III:4 must be interpreted to give proper scope and meaning to this principle. In short, there must be consonance between the objective pursued by Article III, as enunciated in the "general principle" articulated in Article III:1, and the interpretation of the specific expression of this principle in the text of Article III:4. This interpretation must, therefore, reflect that, in endeavouring to ensure "equality of competitive conditions", the "general principle" in Article III seeks to prevent Members from applying internal taxes and regulations in a manner which affects the competitive relationship, in the marketplace, *between the domestic and imported products involved*, "so as to afford protection to domestic production".[164]

This reasoning led the Appellate Body to the following conclusion with respect to the meaning of 'like products' in Article III:4:

> As products that are in a competitive relationship in the marketplace could be affected through treatment of *imports* "less favourable" than the treatment accorded to *domestic* products, it follows that the word "like" in Article III:4 is to be interpreted to apply to products that are in such a competitive relationship. Thus, a determination of "likeness" under Article III:4 is, fundamentally, a determination about the nature and extent of a competitive relationship between and among products. In saying this, we are mindful that there is a spectrum of degrees of "competitiveness" or "substitutability" of products in the marketplace, and that it is difficult, if not impossible, in the abstract, to indicate precisely where on this spectrum the word "like" in Article III:4 of the GATT 1994 falls. We are not saying that *all* products which are in *some* competitive relationship are "like products" under Article III:4. In ruling on the measure at issue, we also do not attempt to define the precise scope of the word "like" in Article III:4. Nor do we wish to decide if the scope of "like products" in Article III:4 is co-extensive with the combined scope of "like" and "directly competitive or substitutable" products in Article III:2 ... In view of [the] different language [of Articles III:2 and III:4], and although we need not rule, and do not rule, on the precise product scope of Article III:4, we do conclude that the product scope of Article III:4, although

---

[161] *Ibid.*, para. 96.
[162] See Appellate Body Report, *Japan – Alcoholic Beverages II*, 109–10.
[163] *Ibid.*, 111.   [164] Appellate Body Report, *EC – Asbestos*, para. 98.

broader than the *first* sentence of Article III:2, is certainly *not* broader than the *combined* product scope of the *two* sentences of Article III:2 of the GATT 1994.[165]

In brief, the determination of whether products are 'like products' under Article III:4 is, fundamentally, a determination about the nature and extent of the competitive relationship between these products. Precisely what the nature and extent of the competitive relationship needs to be for products to be 'like' within the meaning of Article III:4 cannot be indicated in the abstract. Nevertheless, it can be said that the concept of 'like products' in Article III:4 has a relatively broad scope. Its scope is broader than that of the concept of 'like products' in Article III:2, first sentence. However, it is no broader than the combined scope of the concepts of 'like product' and 'directly competitive or substitutable products' of Article III:2, first and second sentence, respectively.

Having reached this conclusion, the Appellate Body in *EC – Asbestos* then turned to the question of how it should determine whether products are 'like' within the meaning of Article III:4. The Appellate Body noted:

> As in Article III:2, in this determination, "[n]o one approach ... will be appropriate for all cases". Rather, an assessment utilizing "an unavoidable element of individual, discretionary judgement" has to be made on a case-by-case basis. The Report of the Working Party on Border Tax Adjustments outlined an approach for analyzing "likeness" that has been followed and developed since by several panels and the Appellate Body. This approach has, in the main, consisted of employing four general criteria in analyzing "likeness": (i) the properties, nature and quality of the products; (ii) the end-uses of the products; (iii) consumers' tastes and habits – more comprehensively termed consumers' perceptions and behaviour – in respect of the products; and (iv) the tariff classification of the products. We note that these four criteria comprise four categories of "characteristics" that the products involved might share: (i) the physical properties of the products; (ii) the extent to which the products are capable of serving the same or similar end-uses; (iii) the extent to which consumers perceive and treat the products as alternative means of performing particular functions in order to satisfy a particular want or demand; and (iv) the international classification of the products for tariff purposes.[166]

The Appellate Body in *EC – Asbestos* hastened to add, however, that, while these general criteria, or groupings of potentially shared characteristics, provide a framework for analysing the 'likeness' of particular products, they are 'simply tools to assist in the task of sorting and examining the relevant evidence'.[167] The Appellate Body stressed that these criteria are 'neither a treaty-mandated nor a closed list of criteria that will determine the legal characterisation of products'.[168] In each case, *all* pertinent evidence, whether related to one of these criteria or not, must be examined and considered by

---

[165] *Ibid.*, paras. 99–100.

[166] *Ibid.*, para. 101. In a footnote, the Appellate Body referred to Appellate Body Report, *Japan – Alcoholic Beverages II*, 113 and 114; it also referred to Panel Report, *US – Gasoline*, para. 6.8, where the approach set out in the Border Tax Adjustments report was adopted in a dispute concerning Article III:4 of the GATT 1994. The Appellate Body noted in a footnote that the fourth criterion, tariff classification, was not mentioned by the Working Party on Border Tax Adjustments, but was included by subsequent panels (see e.g. GATT Panel Report, *EEC – Animal Feed Proteins*, para. 4.2; and GATT Panel Report, *Japan – Alcoholic Beverages I*, para. 5.6).

[167] Appellate Body Report, *EC – Asbestos*, para. 102.   [168] *Ibid.*

panels to determine whether products are 'like'. With regard to these general criteria, the Appellate Body in *EC – Asbestos* finally noted:

> under Article III:4 of the GATT 1994, the term "like products" is concerned with competitive relationships between and among products. Accordingly, whether the *Border Tax Adjustments* framework is adopted or not, it is important under Article III:4 to take account of evidence which indicates whether, and to what extent, the products involved are – or could be – in a competitive relationship in the marketplace.[169]

In its appeal in *EC – Asbestos*, the European Communities argued that the Panel erred in its consideration of 'likeness', in particular because it: adopted an exclusively 'commercial or market access approach' to the comparison of allegedly 'like products'; placed excessive reliance on a single criterion, namely, end-use; and failed to include consideration of the health 'risk' factors relating to asbestos.[170]

The Appellate Body was highly critical of the manner in which the Panel examined the 'likeness' of *chrysotile asbestos fibres* and *PCG fibres* [171] as well as the 'likeness' of *cement-based products containing chrysotile asbestos fibres* and *cement-based products containing PCG fibres*.[172] The Appellate Body criticised the Panel for not examining each of the criteria set forth in the report of the Working Group on Border Tax Adjustments[173] and for not examining these criteria separately.[174] The Appellate Body also disagreed with the Panel's refusal to consider the health risks posed by asbestos in the determination of 'likeness', stating:

> neither the text of Article III:4 nor the practice of panels and the Appellate Body suggest that any evidence should be excluded *a priori* from a panel's examination of "likeness". Moreover, as we have said, in examining the "likeness" of products, panels must evaluate *all* of the relevant evidence. We are very much of the view that evidence relating to the health risks associated with a product may be pertinent in an examination of "likeness" under Article III:4 of the GATT 1994. We do not, however, consider that the evidence relating to the health risks associated with chrysotile asbestos fibres need be examined under a *separate* criterion, because we believe that this evidence can be evaluated under the existing criteria of physical properties, and of consumers' tastes and habits.[175]

In the opinion of the Appellate Body, the carcinogenic or toxic nature of chrysotile asbestos fibres constitutes a defining aspect of the physical properties of those fibres and must therefore be considered when determining 'likeness' under Article III:4.[176] According to the Appellate Body, 'evidence relating

---

[169] *Ibid.*, para. 103.
[170] The European Communities was an 'other appellant' pursuant to Rule 23(1) of the *Working Procedures for Appellate Review*.
[171] PCG fibres are PVA, cellulose and glass fibres.
[172] Appellate Body Report, *EC – Asbestos*, para. 109.
[173] The Panel declined to examine the third criterion (consumers' tastes and habits) and dismissed the fourth criterion (tariff classification) as non-decisive.
[174] In the course of the examination of the first criterion (the properties, nature and quality of the products), the Panel relied on the second criterion (end-use) to come to the 'conclusion' that the products were like.
[175] Appellate Body Report, *EC – Asbestos*, para. 113.   [176] *Ibid.*, para. 114.

to health risks may be relevant in assessing the *competitive relationship in the market place* between allegedly "like" products'.[177]

In a concurring opinion, one of the Members of the Appellate Body in *EC – Asbestos* went further and considered that, in view of the nature and the quantum of the scientific evidence showing that the physical properties and qualities of chrysotile asbestos fibres include or result in carcinogenicity, there is ample basis for a 'definitive characterisation' of such fibres as not 'like' PCG fibres. The Member suggested that this 'definitive characterisation' may and should be made even in the absence of evidence concerning end-uses and consumers' tastes and habits. As this Member explained:

> It is difficult for me to imagine what evidence relating to economic competitive relationships as reflected in end-uses and consumers' tastes and habits could outweigh and set at naught the undisputed deadly nature of chrysotile asbestos fibres, compared with PCG fibres, when inhaled by humans, and therefore compel a characterisation of "likeness" of chrysotile asbestos and PCG fibres.[178]

The Member who wrote this separate opinion clearly did not share the position taken by the two other Appellate Body Members that the competitive relationship in the market is decisive in the determination of the 'likeness' of products under Article III:4.[179] In the opinion of this Member, 'the necessity or appropriateness of adopting a "fundamentally" economic interpretation of the "likeness" of products under Article III:4 of the GATT 1994 does not appear to me to be free from substantial doubts'.[180] This separate opinion reflects a very significant and fundamental difference of views on how to interpret the concept of 'likeness' under Article III:4.

With regard to the second and third criterion set out in the report of the Working Group on Border Tax Adjustments, i.e. end-uses and consumers' tastes and habits, the Appellate Body found in *EC – Asbestos*:

> Evidence of this type is of particular importance under Article III of the GATT 1994, precisely because that provision is concerned with competitive relationships in the marketplace. If there is – or could be – *no* competitive relationship between products, a Member cannot intervene, through internal taxation or regulation, to protect domestic production. Thus, evidence about the extent to which products can serve the same end-uses, and the extent to which consumers are – or would be – willing to choose one product instead of another to perform those end-uses, is highly relevant evidence in assessing the "likeness" of those products under Article III:4 of the GATT 1994.
>
> We consider this to be especially so in cases where the evidence relating to properties establishes that the products at issue are physically quite different. In such cases, in order to overcome this indication that products are *not* "like", a higher burden is placed on complaining Members to establish that, despite the pronounced physical differences, there is a competitive relationship between the products such that *all* of the evidence, taken together, demonstrates that the products are "like" under Article III:4 of the GATT 1994.[181]

---

[177] *Ibid.*, para. 115.   [178] *Ibid.*, para. 152.   [179] *Ibid.*, para. 153, *in fine.*
[180] *Ibid.*, para. 154.   [181] *Ibid.*, paras. 117 and 118.

With respect to end-uses, the Appellate Body found that, while it is certainly relevant that products have similar end-uses for a 'small number of … applications', a panel must also consider the other, *different* end-uses for products. As the Appellate Body stated in *EC – Asbestos*:

> It is only by forming a complete picture of the various end-uses of a product that a panel can assess the significance of the fact that products share a limited number of end-uses.[182]

With respect to consumers' tastes and habits, the Appellate Body was very critical of the Panel for declining to examine this criterion because, as the Panel stated, 'this criterion would not provide clear results'.[183] Furthermore, the Appellate Body noted that, in its opinion, consumers' tastes and habits regarding asbestos fibres or PCG fibres, even in the case of commercial parties such as manufacturers, are very likely to be shaped by the health risks associated with a product which is known to be highly carcinogenic (as asbestos fibres are).[184]

After reversing the Panel's findings, in *EC – Asbestos*, on the 'likeness' of chrysotile asbestos fibres and PCG fibres, the Appellate Body itself examined the 'likeness' of these products and came to the conclusion that the evidence was certainly far from sufficient to satisfy the complainant's burden of proving that chrysotile asbestos fibres are 'like' PCG fibres under Article III:4. The Appellate Body considered that the evidence tended rather to suggest that these products are not 'like products'.[185]

As the Appellate Body stated in *Japan – Alcoholic Beverages II*, the concept of 'like products' in WTO law is indeed like an accordion whose width varies depending on the provision under which the term is interpreted. As discussed above, the interpretation of the concept of 'like product' in Article III:4 is relatively broad. However, it is not so broad that chrysotile asbestos fibres and PCG fibres would be 'like products'.

In 1992, in *US – Malt Beverages*, the Panel considered the question of whether low alcohol beer and high alcohol beer should be considered 'like products' within the meaning of Article III:4. In this regard, the Panel recalled its earlier statement on like product determinations under Article III:2, first sentence,[186] and considered that:

> in the context of Article III, it is essential that such determinations be made not only in the light of such criteria as the products' physical characteristics, but also in the light of the purpose of Article III, which is to ensure that internal taxes and regulations "not be applied to imported or domestic products so as to afford protection to domestic production".[187]

---

[182] *Ibid.*, para. 119.   [183] Panel Report, *EC – Asbestos*, para. 8.139.
[184] Appellate Body Report, *EC – Asbestos*, para. 122.
[185] *Ibid.*, para. 141. Also, with regard to the products containing asbestos and PCG fibres, the Appellate Body concluded that Canada had not satisfied the burden of proof that these products were 'like' (see Appellate Body Report, *EC – Asbestos*, para. 147).
[186] See above, p. 336.   [187] GATT Panel Report, *US – Malt Beverages*, para. 5.71.

The Panel noted that, on the basis of their 'physical characteristics', low and high alcohol beers were 'similar'. However, in order to determine whether low and high alcohol beers were 'like products' under Article III:4, the Panel considered that it had to examine whether the purpose of the distinction between low and high alcohol beers was 'to afford protection to domestic production'. The Panel noted that the United States argued that the distinction was made to encourage the consumption of low rather than high alcohol beer. The Panel eventually concluded that the purpose of the regulatory distinction was not to afford protection to domestic production and that low and high alcoholic beers were, therefore, not 'like products'.[188]

For reasons discussed above, this 'aim-and-effect' approach to the determination of 'likeness' has been discredited and abandoned by WTO panels and the Appellate Body.[189] A first indication that WTO panels would not follow this 'aim-and-effect' approach was given in *US – Gasoline*, in which the Panel found that chemically identical imported and domestic gasoline were 'like products' because 'chemically identical imported and domestic gasoline by definition have exactly the same physical characteristics, end-uses, tariff classification, and are perfectly substitutable'.[190] The aim and effect of the regulatory distinction made was not given any consideration in determining 'likeness'.

Finally, note that the Panel in *US – Tuna (Mexico)* found that differences in process and production methods (PPMs) of products are not relevant in determining 'likeness'. The Panel stated:

> Article III:4 calls for a comparison of the treatment of imported tuna *as a product* with that of domestic tuna *as a product*. Regulations governing the taking of dolphins incidental to the taking of tuna could not possibly affect tuna as a product. Article III:4 therefore obliges the United States to accord treatment to Mexican tuna no less favourable than that accorded to United States tuna, whether or not the incidental taking of dolphins by Mexican vessels corresponded to that of United States vessels.[191]

Questions and Assignments 4.22

Should the concept of 'like products' in Article III:4 be interpreted in the same manner as in Article III:2, first sentence? What is the relevance of the general principle of Article III:1 to the interpretation of the concept of 'like products' in Article III:4? How does the scope of the concept of 'likeness' in Article III:2 and Article III:4 compare? Which factors should be taken into account in determining whether products are 'like' within the meaning of Article III:4? What is the ultimate basis for determining the 'likeness' of products? Can two products that have totally different physical characteristics be 'like products' within the meaning of Article III:4? Would the Appellate Body Member who wrote the 'concurring opinion' in *EC – Asbestos* agree?

---

[188] *Ibid.*, paras. 5.25–5.26 and 5.71–5.76.   [189] See above, pp. 336–8.
[190] Panel Report, *US – Gasoline*, para. 6.9.
[191] GATT Panel Report, *US – Tuna (Mexico)*, para. 5.15. Note that this report was never adopted.

4.4.4.3. 'Treatment no less favourable'

The fact that a measure distinguishes between 'like products' does not suffice to permit the conclusion that this measure is inconsistent with Article III:4. As the Appellate Body noted in *EC – Asbestos*:

> there is a second element that must be established before a measure can be held to be inconsistent with Article III:4 ... A complaining Member must still establish that the measure accords to the group of "like" *imported* products "less favourable treatment" than it accords to the group of "like" *domestic* products.[192]

The Panel in *US – Section 337* explained the 'treatment no less favourable' element of the Article III:4 test in clear terms, noting that:

> the "no less favourable" treatment requirement set out in Article III:4, is unqualified. These words are to be found throughout the General Agreement and later Agreements negotiated in the GATT framework as *an expression of the underlying principle of equality of treatment* of imported products as compared to the treatment given either to other foreign products, under the most favoured nation standard, or to domestic products, under the national treatment standard of Article III. The words "treatment no less favourable" in paragraph 4 call for *effective equality of opportunities* for imported products in respect of the application of laws, regulations and requirements affecting the internal sale, offering for sale, purchase, transportation, distribution or use of products. This clearly sets a minimum permissible standard as a basis.[193]
>
> [Emphasis added]

The Panel in *US – Section 337* thus clearly interpreted 'treatment no less favourable' as requiring 'effective equality of competitive opportunities'. In later GATT and WTO reports, the Appellate Body and panels have consistently interpreted 'treatment no less favourable' in the same way.[194]

In *US – Gasoline*, a dispute concerning legislation designed to prevent and control air pollution, the Panel found that the measure at issue afforded less favourable treatment to imported gasoline than to domestic gasoline because, for domestic refiners of gasoline, an individual baseline (representing the quality of gasoline produced by that refiner in 1990) was established while, for importers of gasoline, the more onerous statutory baseline applied. The Panel observed, *inter alia*:

> This resulted in less favourable treatment to the imported product, as illustrated by the case of a batch of imported gasoline which was chemically identical to a batch of domestic gasoline that met its refiner's individual baseline, but not the statutory baseline levels. In this case, sale of the imported batch of gasoline on the first day of an annual period would require the importer over the rest of the period to sell on the whole cleaner gasoline in order to remain in conformity with the Gasoline Rule. On the other hand, sale of the chemically identical batch of domestic gasoline on the first

---

[192] Appellate Body Report, *EC – Asbestos*, para. 100.
[193] GATT Panel Report, *US – Section 337*, para. 5.11.
[194] See e.g. GATT Panel Report, *Canada – Provincial Liquor Boards (US)*, paras. 5.12–5.14 and 5.30–5.31; GATT Panel Report, *US – Malt Beverages*, para. 5.30; Panel Report, *US – Gasoline*, para. 6.10; Panel Report, *Canada – Periodicals*, 75; Panel Reports, *EC – Bananas III*, paras. 7.179–7.180; and Panel Report, *Japan – Film*, para. 10.379.

> day of an annual period would not require a domestic refiner to sell on the whole cleaner gasoline over the period in order to remain in conformity with the Gasoline Rule.[195]

Recalling the ruling of the Panel in *US – Section 337* that the words 'treatment no less favourable' in paragraph 4 call for effective equality of opportunities for imported products, the Panel in *US – Gasoline* thus concluded:

> since, under the baseline establishment methods, imported gasoline was effectively prevented from benefiting from as favourable sales conditions as were afforded domestic gasoline by an individual baseline tied to the producer of a product, imported gasoline was treated less favourably than domestic gasoline.[196]

Although in *EC – Asbestos* the Appellate Body was not called upon to examine the 'no less favourable treatment' finding of the Panel, the Appellate Body noted:

> The term "less favourable treatment" expresses the general principle, in Article III:1, that internal regulations "should not be applied … so as to afford protection to domestic production" If there is "less favourable treatment" of the group of "like" imported products, there is, conversely, "protection' of the group of "like' domestic products.[197]

In *Korea – Various Measures on Beef*, a dispute concerning a dual retail distribution system for the sale of beef under which imported beef was, *inter alia*, to be sold in specialised stores selling only imported beef or in separate sections of supermarkets, the Appellate Body stressed that the formal difference in treatment between domestic and imported products is neither necessary nor sufficient for a violation of Article III:4. Formally different treatment of imported products did not necessarily constitute less favourable treatment while the absence of formal difference in treatment did not necessarily mean that there was no less favourable treatment.[198] The Appellate Body in *Korea – Various Measures on Beef* stated:

> We observe … that Article III:4 requires only that a measure accord treatment to imported products that is "no less favourable" than that accorded to like domestic products. A measure that provides treatment to imported products that is *different* from that accorded to like domestic products is not necessarily inconsistent with Article III:4, as long as the treatment provided by the measure is "no less favourable". According "treatment no less favourable" means, as we have previously said, according *conditions of competition* no less favourable to the imported product than to the like domestic product.
>
> This interpretation, which focuses on the *conditions of competition* between imported and domestic like products, implies that a measure according formally *different* treatment to imported products does not *per se*, that is, necessarily, violate Article III:4.[199]

---

[195] Panel Report, *US – Gasoline*, para. 6.10.   [196] *Ibid.*, para. 6.10.
[197] Appellate Body Report, *EC – Asbestos*, para. 100. The Appellate Body did not examine the requirement of 'treatment no less favourable' any further since the Panel's findings on this requirement had not been appealed.
[198] See also GATT Panel Report, *US – Section 337*, para. 5.11; and Panel Report, *US – Gasoline*, para. 6.25.
[199] Appellate Body Report, *Korea – Various Measures on Beef*, paras. 135–6.

The Appellate Body recalled that this point was persuasively made in *US – Section 337*. The Panel in that case had to determine whether United States patent enforcement procedures, which were formally different for imported and for domestic products, violated Article III:4. The Panel ruled:

> On the one hand, contracting parties may apply to imported products *different* formal legal requirements if doing so would accord imported products more favourable treatment. On the other hand, it also has to be recognised that there may be cases where the application of formally *identical* legal provisions would in practice accord less favourable treatment to imported products and a contracting party might thus have to apply different legal provisions to imported products to ensure that the treatment accorded them is in fact no less favourable. For these reasons, the mere fact that imported products are subject under Section 337 to legal provisions that are different from those applying to products of national origin is in itself not conclusive in establishing inconsistency with Article III:4.[200]
>
> [Emphasis added]

From this, the Appellate Body concluded in *Korea – Various Measures on Beef*:

> A formal difference in treatment between imported and like domestic products is thus neither necessary, nor sufficient, to show a violation of Article III:4. Whether or not imported products are treated "less favourably" than like domestic products should be assessed instead by examining whether a measure modifies the *conditions of competition* in the relevant market to the detriment of imported products.[201]

In *US – Gasoline*, the Panel rejected the US argument that the requirements of Article III:4 were met because imported gasoline was treated similarly to domestic gasoline from *similarly situated* domestic parties.[202] The Panel pointed out, *inter alia*, that '[the] wording [of Article III:4] does not allow less favourable treatment dependent on the characteristics of the producer'.[203] In *US – Gasoline*, the Panel also rejected the US contention that the regulation at issue treated imported products 'equally overall' and was therefore not inconsistent with Article III:4.[204] The Panel noted that:

> the argument that on average the treatment provided was equivalent amounted to arguing that less favourable treatment in one instance could be offset provided that there was correspondingly more favourable treatment in another. This amounted to claiming that less favourable treatment of particular imported products in some instances would be balanced by more favourable treatment of particular products in others.[205]

Under Article III:4, as under Articles I:1 and III:2, 'balancing' less favourable treatment by more favourable treatment does not 'excuse' the less favourable treatment.[206]

GATT and WTO panels and the Appellate Body have found a wide variety of measures inconsistent with the national treatment obligation of Article III:4. In addition to the measures at issue in *US – Section 337*, *Korea – Various Measures*

---

[200] GATT Panel Report, *US – Section 337*, para. 5.11.
[201] Appellate Body Report, *Korea – Various Measures on Beef*, para. 137.
[202] Panel Report, *US – Gasoline*, para. 6.11. The Appellate Body did not address this finding of the Panel.
[203] *Ibid.*   [204] See *ibid.*, para. 6.14.   [205] *Ibid.*
[206] See GATT Panel Report, *US – Section 337*, para. 5.14.

on Beef and *US – Gasoline*, all discussed above, measures found to be inconsistent include:

- minimum price requirements (*Canada – Provincial Liquor Boards (US)*);
- a general ban on all cigarette advertising (*Thailand – Cigarettes*); and
- regulations concerning internal transportation (*US – Malt Beverages*).

With respect to minimum price requirements, it deserves to be noted that the Panel in *Canada – Provincial Liquor Boards (US)* ruled in 1992 that the fact that

> minimum prices applied equally to imported and domestic beer did not necessarily accord equal conditions of competition to imported and domestic beer. Whenever they prevented imported beer from being supplied at a price lower than that of domestic beer, they accorded in fact treatment to imported beer less favourable than that accorded to domestic beer: when they were set at the level at which domestic brewers supplied beer – as was presently the case in New Brunswick and Newfoundland – they did not change the competitive opportunities accorded to domestic beer but did affect the competitive opportunities of imported beer which could otherwise be supplied below the minimum price.[207]

With respect to a general ban on all cigarette advertising, the Panel in *Thailand – Cigarettes* argued:

> It might be argued that such a general ban on all cigarette advertising would create unequal competitive opportunities between the existing Thai supplier of cigarettes and new, foreign suppliers and was therefore contrary to Article III:4.[208]

The Panel in *US – Malt Beverages* found that:

> the requirement for imported beer and wine to be transported by common carrier, whereas domestic in-state beer and wine is not so required, may result in additional charges to transport these imported products and therefore prevent imported products from competing on an equal footing with domestic like products.[209]

Questions and Assignments 4.23

Can a Member treat 'like' products differently without being inconsistent with Article III:4? What does 'treatment no less favourable' require? Give three examples of internal regulations which panels and/or the Appellate Body found to be inconsistent with Article III:4 of the GATT 1994.

---

[207] GATT Panel Report, *Canada – Provincial Liquor Boards (US)*, para. 5.30.
[208] GATT Panel Report, *Thailand – Cigarettes*, para. 78. We note that such a general ban on cigarette advertising was not the measure at issue in this case but a suggested alternative measure of which the Panel considered the GATT-consistency. The Panel further stated: 'Even if this argument were accepted, such an inconsistency would have to be regarded as unavoidable and therefore necessary within the meaning of Article XX(b) because additional advertising rights would risk stimulating demand for cigarettes.'
[209] GATT Panel Report, *US – Malt Beverages*, para. 5.50.

4.5. NATIONAL TREATMENT UNDER THE GATS

Article XVII of the GATS, which is entitled 'National Treatment', states, in paragraph 1:

> In the sectors inscribed in its Schedule, and subject to any conditions and qualifications set out therein, each Member shall accord to services and service suppliers of any other Member, in respect of all measures affecting the supply of services, treatment no less favourable than that it accords to its own like services and service suppliers.

This section first explores the nature of the national treatment obligation of Article XVII of the GATS and then discusses the test of consistency with this obligation.

4.5.1. Nature of the national treatment obligation of Article XVII of the GATS

The national treatment obligation of Article XVII of the GATS is different from the national treatment obligation of Article III of the GATT 1994. As discussed above, for trade in goods, the national treatment obligation has *general* application to all trade. On the contrary, the national treatment obligation for trade in services does not have such general application; it does not apply generally to all measures affecting trade in services. The national treatment obligation applies only to the extent that WTO Members have explicitly committed themselves to grant 'national treatment' in respect of specific service sectors.[210] Members set out such commitments in the national treatment column of their 'Schedule of Specific Commitments'. These specific commitments to grant national treatment are often made subject to certain conditions, qualifications and limitations, which are also set out in the Schedules. Members can, for example, grant national treatment in a specific service sector only with respect to certain modes of supply (such as cross-border supply) and not others (such as commercial presence). Typical national treatment limitations included in Schedules relate to:

- nationality or residence requirements for executives;
- requirements to invest a certain amount of assets in local currency;
- restrictions on the purchase of land by foreign service suppliers;
- special subsidy or tax privileges granted to domestic suppliers; and
- differential capital requirements and special operational limits applying only to operations of foreign suppliers.[211]

Note, by way of example, the national treatment column of the Schedule of the European Communities and its Member States with respect to higher education services, as included in Figure 4.1. It appears from this Schedule that the

---

[210] A list of the services sectors is contained in GATT Secretariat, Note by the Secretariat, *Services Sectoral Classification List*, MTN.GNS/W/120, dated 10 July 1991.
[211] See WTO Secretariat, *Market Access: Unfinished Business*, Special Studies 6 (WTO, 2001), 103.

Figure 4.1 Excerpt from the Schedule of Specific Commitments of the European Communities and their Member States[212]

Sector or Sub-Sector	Limitations on Market Access	Limitations on National Treatment	Additional Commitments	Notes
C. Higher Education Services (CPC 923)	5. PRIVATELY FUNDED EDUCATION SERVICES 1) F: Condition of nationality. However, third country nationals can have authorization from competent authorities to establish and direct an education institution and to teach. 2) None 3) E, I: Needs test for opening of private universities authorised to issue recognised diplomas or degrees; procedure involves an advice of the Parliament. GR: Unbound for education institutions granting recognised State diplomas. 4) Unbound except as indicated in the horizontal section and subject to the following specific limitations: DK: Condition of nationality for professors. F: Condition of nationality. However, third country nationals may obtain authorization from competent authorities to establish and direct an education institution and to teach. I: Condition of nationality for service providers to be authorised to issue State recognised diplomas.	1) I: Condition of nationality for service providers to be authorised to issue State recognised diplomas. 2) None 3) None 4) Unbound except as indicated in the horizontal section		

European Communities and its Member States have agreed to accord national treatment to higher education services supplied in mode 1 ('cross-border supply') (with a qualification by Italy), mode 2 ('consumption abroad') and mode 3 ('commercial presence'). However, no commitment to accord national treatment was made with regard to mode 4 ('presence of persons'), except the commitment made for all service sectors. The Schedules of Specific Commitments of Members can be found on the WTO's website.[213] For an explanation on how to 'read' these Schedules, refer to Chapter 5 on Rules on Market Access.[214]

To determine the scope of the national treatment obligation of a Member, or to determine whether, in respect of a specific service, a Member must grant national treatment to services and service suppliers of other Members, it is necessary to examine the commitments, conditions, qualifications and limitations set out in the Member's Schedule very carefully.

Questions and Assignments 4.24

In your country, are measures affecting basic education and health care subject to the national treatment obligation of Article XVII:1 of the GATS? Are they in the United States, the European Communities, India and Brazil?

---

[212] GATS/SC/31, dated 15 April 1994.   [213] www.wto.org, visited on 15 May 2004.
[214] See below, pp. 487–92.

4.5.2. Consistency with Article XVII of the GATS

In the sectors inscribed in its Schedule and subject to the conditions, qualifications and limitations set out therein, a Member must accord treatment no less favourable, to services and service suppliers of any other Member, in respect of all measures affecting the supply of services, than that it accords to its own like services and service suppliers. Article XVII of the GATS sets out a three-tier test of consistency. In brief, this three-tier test of consistency with Article XVII of the GATS requires the examination of whether:

- the measure at issue affects trade in services;
- the foreign and domestic services or service suppliers are 'like' services or service suppliers; and
- the foreign services or service suppliers are granted treatment no less favourable.

4.5.2.1. *'Measures affecting trade in services'*

As discussed above in the context of the MFN treatment obligation of Article II of the GATS, the concept of a 'measure affecting trade in services' has been clarified by the Appellate Body in *Canada – Autos*, where it stated that two key issues must be examined to determine whether a measure is one 'affecting trade in services', namely:

- first, whether there is 'trade in services' in the sense of Article I:2; and
- secondly, whether the measure at issue 'affects' such trade in services within the meaning of Article I:1.[215]

Recall, with respect to the first question, the broad scope of the concept of 'trade in services', including all services except services supplied in the exercise of governmental authority and including services supplied in any of the four distinct modes of supply (cross-border supply, consumption abroad, commercial presence and the presence of natural persons).[216] With respect to the second question, recall that, for a measure to 'affect' trade in services, this measure must not regulate or govern the trade in, i.e. the supply of, services. A measure affects trade in services when the measure bears 'upon the conditions of competition in supply of a service'.[217]

Questions and Assignments 4.25

What are the elements of the test of consistency with the national treatment obligation of Article XVII:1 of the GATS? Which measures are 'measures affecting trade in services'?

---

[215] Appellate Body Report, *Canada – Autos*, para. 155. See above, pp. 320–1.
[216] See above, pp. 321–2.   [217] See above, pp. 322–3.

4.5.2.2. 'Like services and service suppliers'

The second element of the three-tier test of consistency with the national treatment obligation of Article XVII of the GATS is whether the foreign and domestic services or service suppliers are 'like' services or service suppliers. The concept of 'like' services or service suppliers is discussed above in the context of the MFN treatment obligation of Article II of the GATS. As for 'likeness' under Article II, there is almost no relevant case law to date on the meaning of 'likeness' under Article XVII.[218] However, a determination of the 'likeness' of services and service suppliers should clearly be based, among other relevant factors, on:

- the characteristics of the service or the service supplier;
- the classification and description of the service in the United Nations Central Product Classification (CPC) system; and
- consumers' habits and preferences regarding the service or the service supplier.

As is the case in Article II, Article XVII provides that two service suppliers that supply a like service are not necessarily 'like service suppliers'. Factors such as the size of the companies, their assets, their use of technology and the nature and extent of their expertise must all be taken into account.[219]

Questions and Assignments 4.26

How does one determine whether services or service suppliers are 'like' within the meaning of Article XVII:1 of the GATS? Are all banking services 'like services' within the meaning of Article XVII:1? Are all law firms 'like service suppliers' within the meaning of Article XVII:1?

4.5.2.3. 'Treatment no less favourable'

The third and final element of the test of consistency with the national treatment obligation of Article XVII:1 of the GATS is whether the foreign services or service suppliers are granted treatment no less favourable. Paragraphs 2 and 3 of Article XVII clarify the requirement of 'treatment no less favourable' set out in paragraph 1 by stating:

> 2. A Member may meet the requirement of paragraph 1 by according to services and service suppliers of any other Member, either formally identical treatment or formally different treatment to that it accords to its own like services and service suppliers.
>
> 3. Formally identical or formally different treatment shall be considered to be less favourable if it modifies the conditions of competition in favour of services or service suppliers of the Member compared to like services or service suppliers of any other Member.

---

[218] Note Panel Report, *EC – Bananas III*, para. 7.322.   [219] See above, pp. 323–4.

It follows from this that a Member that gives formally identical treatment to foreign and domestic services or service suppliers may nevertheless be in breach of the national treatment obligation if that Member, by giving formally identical treatment, modifies the conditions of competition in favour of the domestic services or service suppliers. Also, a Member that gives formally different treatment to foreign and domestic services or service suppliers does not act in breach of the national treatment obligation if that Member, by giving formally different treatment, does not modify the conditions of competition in favour of the domestic services and service suppliers. The latter would obviously be the case if the different treatment would be in favour of the foreign services or service suppliers but it may also be that a formally different treatment has no impact on the conditions of competition.

With respect to inherent competitive disadvantages resulting from the fact that the service or service supplier is foreign and not domestic, footnote 10 to Article XVII states:

> Specific commitments assumed under this Article shall not be construed to require any Member to compensate for any inherent competitive disadvantages which result from the foreign character of the relevant services or service suppliers.

The Panel in *Canada – Autos*, however, stressed the limited scope of this provision as follows:

> Footnote 10 to Article XVII only exempts Members from having to compensate for disadvantages due to the foreign character in the application of the national treatment provision; it does not provide cover for actions which might modify the conditions of competition against services or service suppliers which are already disadvantaged due to their foreign character.[220]

Questions and Assignments 4.27

When is treatment less favourable within the meaning of Article XVII:1 of the GATS? Can a measure which grants a subsidy to both domestic and foreign service suppliers be in breach of the national treatment obligation of Article XVII:1 of the GATS? Give an example of formally different treatment of domestic and foreign services which does not constitute a breach of Article XVII:1 of the GATS.

4.6. SUMMARY

There are two main principles of non-discrimination in WTO law: the most-favoured-nation (MFN) treatment obligation and the national treatment obligation. In simple terms, the MFN treatment obligation prohibits a country from

---

[220] Panel Report, *Canada – Autos*, para. 10.300.

discriminating *between* other countries; the national treatment obligation prohibits a country from discriminating *against* other countries. These principles of non-discrimination apply – albeit not in the same manner – with respect to trade in goods, as well as to trade in services. The key provisions of the GATT 1994 that deal with non-discrimination in trade in goods are Article I, on the MFN treatment obligation, and Article III, on the national treatment obligation. The key provisions on non-discrimination in the GATS are Article II, on the MFN treatment obligation, and Article XVII, on the national treatment obligation.

The principal purpose of the MFN treatment obligation of Article I of the GATT 1994 is to ensure *equality of opportunity* to import from, or to export to, *all* WTO Members. There are three questions which must be answered to determine whether or not there is a violation of the MFN treatment obligation of Article I:1, namely:

- Whether the measure at issue confers a trade 'advantage' of the kind covered by Article I:1;
- Whether the products concerned are 'like' products; and
- Whether the advantage at issue is granted 'immediately and unconditionally' to all like products concerned.

As is the case with the MFN treatment obligation under the GATT 1994, the principal purpose of the MFN treatment obligation of Article II:1 of the GATS is to ensure *equality of opportunity*, *in casu*, for services and service suppliers of *all* other WTO Members. There are three questions which must be answered to determine whether or not a measure violates the MFN treatment obligation of Article II:1, namely:

- Whether the measure at issue affects trade in services;
- Whether the services or service suppliers concerned are 'like' services or service suppliers; and
- Whether less favourable treatment is accorded to the services or service suppliers of a Member.

The principal purpose of the national treatment obligations of Article III of the GATT 1994 is to *avoid protectionism* in the application of internal tax and regulatory measures. As is explicitly stated in Article III:1, the purpose of Article III is to ensure that internal measures 'not be applied to imported and domestic products so as to afford protection to domestic production'. To this end, Article III obliges Members of the WTO to provide *equality of competitive conditions* for imported products in relation to domestic products. The test of consistency of internal taxation with the national treatment obligation of Article III:2, first sentence, of the GATT 1994 requires the examination of:

- whether the measure at issue is an 'internal tax';
- whether the imported and domestic products are 'like' products; and
- whether the imported products are not taxed in excess of the domestic products.

Article III:2, second sentence, also concerns national treatment with respect to internal taxation, but it contemplates a 'broader category of products' than Article III:2, first sentence. It applies not only to 'like products' but also to 'directly competitive or substitutable products'. Article III:2, second sentence, sets out a different test of inconsistency, which requires the examination of:

- whether the measure at issue is an 'internal tax';
- whether the imported and domestic products are directly competitive or substitutable;
- whether these products are not similarly taxed; and
- whether the dissimilar taxation is applied so as to afford protection to domestic production.

The national treatment obligation of Article III concerns not only internal taxation, but also internal regulation. The national treatment obligation for internal regulation is set out in Article III:4. To determine whether a measure is consistent with the national treatment obligations of Article III:4, there is a three-tier test which requires the examination of:

- whether the measure at issue is a law, regulation or requirement covered by Article III:4;
- whether the imported and domestic products are 'like' products; and
- whether the imported products are accorded less favourable treatment.

The national treatment obligation, with respect to measures affecting trade in services, is set out in Article XVII of the GATS. The national treatment obligation of Article XVII is different from the national treatment obligation of Article III of the GATT 1994. While, for trade in goods, the national treatment obligation has *general* application to all trade, the national treatment obligation for trade in services applies only to the extent WTO Members have explicitly committed themselves to grant 'national treatment' in respect of specific service sectors. Often such national treatment commitments are subject to conditions and qualifications limiting the scope of the commitment. Where a Member has made a specific commitment to grant 'national treatment', it must fulfil the 'national treatment' obligations of Article XVII of the GATS. To determine whether a measure is consistent with the national treatment obligations of Article XVII, there is a three-tier test which requires the examination of:

- whether the measure at issue affects trade in services;
- whether the foreign and domestic services or service suppliers are 'like' services or service suppliers; and
- whether the foreign services or service suppliers are granted treatment no less favourable.

The non-discrimination obligations of Articles I:1, III:2, first sentence, and III:4 of the GATT 1994 and Articles II:1 and XVII:1 of the GATS only apply to products, services or service suppliers which are 'like'. As the Appellate Body noted, the concept of 'like' products is like an accordion whose width varies depending on the provision under which the term is interpreted. However, the determination of whether products are 'like products' is, fundamentally, a determination of the nature and extent of the competitive relationship between these products. The same can be said of the determination of whether services or service suppliers are 'like'. The factors that must be considered in determining 'likeness' are, among other relevant factors:

- the characteristics of the products, services and service suppliers;
- the classification of the products, services and service suppliers;
- consumer habits and preferences regarding the products, services and service supplier; and
- for products, their end-use.

4.7. EXERCISE: BEER IN NEWLAND

Traditionally, Newland is a wine-drinking country. However, recent market research has shown that demand for beer in Newland is now high and likely to grow further in the future. Superbrew Inc. of Richland, one of the world's largest beer producers, therefore wants to increase its exports of lager beer, speciality beers and non-alcoholic beer to Newland. Before its accession to the WTO, Newland limited the importation of beer of any kind to a meagre 50,000 hectolitres per year. This quantitative restriction was put in place in the late 1950s to protect the many winegrowers in Newland from competition from imported beer. The National Association of Wineries (NAW) was, and still is, a powerful lobby in Newland's politics. On accession to the WTO, Newland abolished the quantitative restriction on the importation of beer and introduced customs duties instead.

Since 1995, Newland imposes the following *ad valorem* customs duties:

- 10 per cent on wine;
- 20 per cent on lager beer and non-alcoholic beer; and
- 30 per cent on speciality beers.

Newland has exempted the following beverages from customs duties:

- speciality beers produced in the United States; and
- speciality beers produced in micro-breweries.

Since last year, when a case of serious customs fraud was discovered, Newland has required that all beer be imported through two designated ports only.

This requirement does not apply, however, to beer imported from neighbouring Nearland, a country currently negotiating accession to the WTO.

Shortly after Newland joined the WTO, it also revised its tax regime for alcoholic and non-alcoholic beverages. The following VAT rates apply:

- 2 per cent on domestically produced non-alcoholic beverages and non-alcoholic beverages produced in the United States; and
- 5 per cent on all other imported non-alcoholic beverages.

The following excise tax rates apply:

- 15 per cent on wine;
- 15.5 per cent on lager beer and non-alcoholic beer; and
- 30 per cent on speciality beers.

Newland also imposes a security deposit equivalent to €0.02 per bottle of imported beer. This deposit accrues to Newland if the importer fails to recycle the beer bottles.

In Newland, beer, whether domestic or imported, may only be sold by licensed beer merchants and may not be sold in supermarkets. No such restrictions exist on the sales of domestic or imported wine. In addition, they do not apply to Australian lager beer. Superbrew Inc. not only wants to sell its beer in Newland's supermarkets, it also wants to establish a wholesale trade company in Newland as well as a network of retail shops to handle the distribution of its beer. Superbrew has been told it can do neither.

Pursuant to the Fair Competition Act of 1991, imported as well as domestic beer is subject to a minimum price requirement, annually set by the Ministry of Commerce of Newland. Furthermore, Newland prohibits the use of additives in beer while leaving the use of additives in wine unregulated.

Many municipalities in Newland prohibit the consumption of beer in public on Sundays. Sunday is a divine day and therefore a day for wine. Furthermore, in support of the national wine industry, Newland's National Federation of Restaurateurs, a government-sponsored organisation, has instructed its 10,000 members not to serve beer with traditional Newland dishes. Note also that, since the Armed Forces Reform Act of 1996, the armed forces of Newland are required by law to buy domestic alcoholic beverages.

Finally, CoolBrew Inc., a subsidiary of Superbrew Inc. specialising in the maintenance of beer-cooling installations, wants to employ in Newland engineers from Richland for short-term repair jobs. However, CoolBrew Inc. has been informed that, under Newland's Regulated Professions Act of 1997, only engineers with a degree obtained in Newland or the United States are allowed to work in Newland.

Note that Newland's Schedule of Specific Commitments contains national treatment commitments for 'wholesale trade' services and 'maintenance and repair of equipment' services with respect to all modes of supply. For 'wholesale trade' services, however, 'commercial presence' is subject to the limitation that foreigners may never own more than 70 per cent of wholesale trade companies established in Newland. Newland's Schedule does not refer to retailing services. Finally, Newland did not include any measures relating to distribution or other business services in the Annex on Article II Exemptions.

You are an associate with the Brazilian law firm, Nogueira Neto Avogados. Your firm has been hired by Superbrew Inc. to give an objective legal assessment of all the issues raised above. You have been instructed to limit your legal brief to the question of whether there are violations of the non-discrimination obligations under WTO law. At present, you will not address the question of whether a possible violation can be justified under the 'general' or other exceptions provided for in the GATT 1994 or the GATS as discussed in Chapter 7 of this book.

5
Rules on market access

Contents

5.1. INTRODUCTION

There can be no international trade without access to the domestic market of other countries. It is of the highest importance for countries, traders and service suppliers to have predictable and growing access to markets of other countries for their goods and services. Rules on market access are, therefore, at the core of WTO law.

Market access for goods and services from other countries is frequently impeded or restricted in various ways. There are two main categories of barriers to market access:

- tariff barriers; and
- non-tariff barriers.

The category of tariff barriers primarily includes customs duties, i.e. tariffs. Tariff barriers are particularly relevant for trade in goods; they are of marginal importance for trade in services. The category of non-tariff barriers includes quantitative restrictions (such as quotas) and 'other non-tariff barriers' (such as lack of transparency of trade regulation, unfair and arbitrary application of trade regulation, customs formalities, technical barriers to trade and government procurement practices). These 'other non-tariff barriers' undoubtedly constitute the largest and most diverse sub-category of non-tariff barriers.

As set out in the Preamble to the *WTO Agreement*, WTO Members pursue the objectives of higher standards of living, full employment, growth and sustainable economic development by:

> entering into reciprocal and mutually advantageous arrangements directed to the substantial reduction of tariffs and other barriers to trade.

The substantial reduction of tariff and non-tariff barriers to market access is, together with the elimination of discrimination, the key instrument of the WTO to achieve its overall objectives. Few economists and trade policy-makers dispute that further trade liberalisation can make a significant contribution to the economic development of most developed and developing countries. If tariffs were eliminated, the range of estimated economic benefits would be between US$80 billion and US$500 billion.[1] The estimates of the share of these economic benefits going to developing countries range from 40 to 60 per cent. Potential gains from the liberalisation of trade in services are estimated to be between two to four times the gains from liberalising trade in goods.

As already noted in Chapter 1, some barriers to market access, such as quantitative restrictions on goods, are prohibited, while other barriers, such as customs duties, are allowed in principle and are only limited to the extent of

---

[1] See *Some Facts for the 'Fifth'*, Cancún WTO Ministerial 2003 Briefing Notes, http://www.wto.org/english/thewto_e/minist_e/min03_e/brief_e/brief24_e.htm, visited on 10 May 2003.

a Member's specific agreement. Different rules apply to different forms of barriers. This difference in rules reflects a difference in the negative effects they have on trade and on the economy.

This chapter on the rules on market access addresses the rules on:

- tariff barriers to trade in goods;
- non-tariff barriers to trade in goods; and
- barriers to trade in services.

The section on non-tariff barriers to trade in goods discusses both quantitative restrictions and other non-tariff barriers.

5.2. TARIFF BARRIERS TO TRADE IN GOODS

The most common and widely used barrier to market access for goods is customs duties, also referred to as tariffs. Furthermore, market access for goods is impeded by other duties and charges. This section discusses:

- customs duties or tariffs;
- negotiations on tariff reductions;
- tariff concessions or bindings;
- the imposition of customs duties; and
- duties and charges other than customs duties.

Since tariffs are normally not imposed on trade in services, this section will only address tariffs on trade in goods.

5.2.1. Customs duties or tariffs

5.2.1.1. Definition and types

A customs duty, or tariff, is a financial charge, in the form of a tax, imposed on products at the time of, and/or because of, their importation.[2] Market access is conditional upon the payment of the customs duty.

Customs duties are specific, *ad valorem* or mixed. A specific customs duty on a product is an amount based on the weight, volume or quantity of that product, for example a duty of €100 per hectolitre of vegetable oil or a duty of €3,000 on each car. An *ad valorem* customs duty on a good is an amount based on the value of that good. It is a percentage of the value of the imported product, for example a 15 per cent *ad valorem* duty on computers. In that case, the duty on a computer worth €1,000 will be €150. A mixed, or compound, duty is a customs duty comprising of an *ad valorem* duty to which a specific duty is added or, less frequently, subtracted, for example a customs

---

[2] Note that governments can also impose customs duties on products at the time of, and/or because of, their exportation. However, this is uncommon and, therefore, not addressed in this chapter.

duty on wool of 10 per cent *ad valorem* and €50 per ton. In that case, the duty on three tons of wool worth €1,000 per ton will be €450.

Ad valorem customs duties are by far the most common type of customs duties. They are preferable to specific and mixed duties for several reasons. First, *ad valorem* duties are more transparent than specific duties. The protectionist impact and the negative effect on prices for consumers are easier to assess for *ad valorem* duties than for specific duties. The lack of transparency of specific duties makes it easier for special interest groups to obtain governmental support for high levels of protection.[3] Secondly, by definition, *ad valorem* customs duties are indexed. In times of inflation, the government's tariff revenue will keep up with price increases and the level of protection will remain the same. By contrast, specific duties will constantly have to be increased to maintain the same real tariff revenue or maintain the same level of protection.[4] Overall, with respect to industrial products, specific duties as well as mixed duties are unusual.[5] With respect to agricultural products, however, non-*ad valorem* duties, and in particular mixed duties, are still quite common.[6]

Ad valorem, specific or mixed customs duties can be MFN duties, preferential duties or neither of the two. *MFN duties* are the 'standard' customs duties applicable to all other WTO Members in compliance with the non-discrimination MFN treatment obligation of Article I:1 of the GATT 1994.[7] *Preferential duties* are customs duties applied to specific countries pursuant to conventional or autonomous arrangements under which products from these countries are subject to duties lower than MFN duties. For example, the customs duties applied by the European Communities on products from ACP countries under the terms of the *Cotonou Agreement* are conventional preferential duties.[8] The customs duties applied by the European Communities on products from all developing countries under the EC's Generalised System of Preferences (GSP) are autonomous preferential duties.[9] Finally, there are customs duties that are neither MFN duties nor preferential duties. These are the duties applicable on goods from countries which are not WTO Members and do not benefit from MFN treatment.[10] The number of such countries is small and the latter category of customs duties is therefore of limited importance.

[3] See WTO Secretariat, *Market Access: Unfinished Business*, Special Studies 6 (WTO, 2001), 9.
[4] Note that specific customs duties have the advantage that they are easier to impose as they do not require customs authorities to determine the value of the imported products (see below, pp. 429–32).
[5] Switzerland, and to a lesser extent Sri Lanka and Thailand, are exceptions in this respect. Over 80 per cent of Switzerland's customs duties are non-*ad valorem* duties. See WTO Secretariat, *Market Access: Unfinished Business*, Special Studies 6 (WTO, 2001), 9. Note that the General Council, in its Decision of 1 August 2004 on the Doha Work Programme, decided that 'all non-*ad valorem* duties shall be converted to *ad valorem* equivalents on the basis of a methodology to be determined' (WT/L/579, dated 2 August 204, Annex B, para. 5).
[6] *Ibid.*, 46 and 47.   [7] See above, pp. 309–18.
[8] See *Partnership Agreement between the Members of the African, Caribbean and Pacific Group of States of the One Part and the European Community and Its Member States, of the Other Part*, signed in Cotonou, Benin, on 23 June 2000. Under Article 1 of Annex V to the Agreement, industrial products from ACP countries shall be imported into the European Communities free of customs duties; agricultural products benefit from a lower rate than normal.
[9] See below, pp. 679–80.
[10] Note that non-WTO Members may benefit from MFN treatment under the terms of bilateral or regional trade agreements.

5.2.1.2. Purpose of customs duties or tariffs

Customs duties or tariffs serve three different purposes. First, customs duties are a source of revenue for governments. This purpose is less important for industrialised countries with a well-developed system of direct and indirect taxation. For many developing countries, however, customs duties are an important source of government revenue. In comparison with income taxes and sales taxes, customs duties are easy to collect. Imports are relatively easy to monitor and the collection of customs duties can be concentrated in a few ports of entry. Secondly, customs duties are used to protect domestic industries. The customs duties imposed on imported products make the like domestic products relatively cheaper, giving them a price advantage and thus some degree of protection from import competition. Thirdly, customs duties can be used to promote a *rational* allocation of scarce foreign exchange. To promote the use of foreign exchange for the importation of capital goods (e.g. industrial machinery) and discourage its use for the importation of luxury goods (e.g. perfume), a country can impose high customs duties on the latter and lower customs duties on the former. Customs duties can thus be an instrument of an economic development policy.

5.2.1.3. National tariff

As stated above, the terms 'customs duties' and 'tariffs' are synonyms. However, the term 'tariff' has a second meaning. A 'tariff' is also a structured list of product descriptions and their corresponding customs duty. The customs duties or tariffs, which are due on importation, are set out in a country's tariff. Most national tariffs now follow or reflect the structure set out in the Harmonised Commodity Description and Coding System, usually referred to as the Harmonised System or HS, discussed in detail later in this chapter.[11]

The national tariff of the European Communities is referred to as the Common Customs Tariff.[12] Its structure follows the HS, but is more detailed, as is the case for the tariffs of many industrialised countries. Every year the European Commission adopts a Regulation reproducing a complete version of the Common Customs Tariff, taking into account Council and Commission amendments of that year. The Regulation is published in the *Official Journal* no later than 31 October. It applies from 1 January of the following year.[13] See Figures 5.1 and 5.2.

---

[11] See below, pp. 425–9.

[12] See Council Regulation (EEC) No. 2658/87 of 23 July 1987 on the tariff and statistical nomenclature and on the Common Customs Tariff, OJ 1987, L256, 7 September 1987. In addition to the applicable customs duties, the Common Customs Tariff is usually understood to include also all other Community legislation that has an effect on the level of customs duty payable on a particular import. Note that the Member States of the European Union, as constituent members of the customs union of the European Union, do not have separate national tariffs. Their common external tariff is the Common Customs Tariff.

[13] For 2004, see Commission Regulation (EC) No. 1789/2003 of 11 September 2003, amending Annex I to Council Regulation (EEC) No. 2658/87 on the tariff and statistical nomenclature and on the Common Customs Tariffs, OJ 2003, L281, 30 October 2003.

Figure 5.1 Excerpt from Chapter 18 of the EC Common Customs Tariff (cocoa and cocoa preparations)[14]

---

134   EN   30.10.2003

CHAPTER 18

COCOA AND COCOA PREPARATIONS

Notes

1. This chapter does not cover the preparations of heading 0403, 1901, 1904, 1905, 2105, 2202, 2208, 3003 or 3004.

2. Heading 1806 includes sugar confectionery containing cocoa and, subject to none 1 to this chapter, other food preparations containing cocoa.

Additional notes

1. *When imported in the form of an assortment, goods of subheadings 1806 20, 1806 31, 1806 32 and 1806 90 are subject to an agricultural component (EA) fixed according to the average content in milk fats, milk proteins, sucrose, isoglucose, glucose and starch of the assortment as a wide.*

2. Subheadings 1806 90 11 and 1806 90 19 do not cover chocolates made entirely of one type of chocolate.

CN code	Description	Conventional rate of duty (%)	Supplementary unit
1	2	3	4
1801 00 00	**Cocoa beans, whole or broken, raw or roasted**	Free	–
1802 00 00	**Cocoa shells, husks, skins and other cocoa waste**	Free	–
1803	**Cocoa paste, whether or not defatted:**		
1803 10 00	**– Not defatted**	9.6	–
1803 20 00	**– Wholly or partly defatted**	9.6	–
1804 00 00	**Cocoa butter, fat and oil**	7.7	–
1805 00 00	**Cocoa powder, not containing added sugar or other sweetening matter**	8	–
1806	**Chocolate and other food preparations containing cocoa:**		
1806 10	**– Cocoa powder, containing added sugar or other sweetening matter:**		
1806 10 15	– – Containing no sucrose or containing less than 5% by weight of sucrose (including invert sugar expressed as sucrose) or isoglucose expressed as sucrose	8	–
1806 10 20	– – Containing 5% or more but less than 65% by weight of sucrose (including invert sugar expressed as sucrose) or isoglucose expressed as sucrose	8 + 25.2 €/ 100 kg/net	–
1806 10 30	– – Containing 65% or more but less than 80% by weight of sucrose (including invert sugar expressed as sucrose) or isoglucose expressed as sucrose	8 + 31.4 €/ 100 kg/net	–
1806 10 90	– – Containing 80% or more by weight of sucrose (including invert sugar expressed as sucrose) or isoglucose expressed as sucrose..	8 + 41.9 €/ 100 kg/net	–
1806 20	**– Other preparations in blocks, slabs or bars weighing more than 2kg or in liquid, paste, powder, granular or other bulk form in containers or immediate packings, of a content exceeding 2 kg.**		
1806 20 10	– – Containing 31% or more by weight of cocoa butter or containing a combined weight of 31% or more of cocoa butter and milk fat	8.3 + EA MAX 18.7 + AD S/Z (¹)	–

(¹) See Annex 1.

14 *Official Journal of the European Communities*, L281, 30 October 2003, 134–5.

Figure 5.2 Excerpt from Chapter 78 of the EC Common Customs Tariff (vehicles ...)[15]

| 30.10.2003 | EN | Official Journal of the Europeon Union | 589 |

CHAPTER 87
Vehicles other than railway or tramway rolling stock, and parts and
accessories thereof

Notes

1. This chapter does not cover railway or tramway rolling stock designed solely for running on rails.
2. For the purposes of this chapter, 'tractors' means vehicles constructed essentially for hauling or pushing another vehicle, appliance or load, whether or not they contain subsidiary provision for the transport, in connection with the use of the tractor, of tools, seeds, fertilisers or other goods.

   Machines and working tools designed for fitting to tractors of heading 8701 as interchangeable equipment remain classified in their respective headings even if presented with the tractor, and whether or not mounted on it.

3. Motor chassis lined with cabs fall in headings 8702 to 8704, and not within heading 8706.
4. Heading 8712 includes all children's bicycles. Other children's cycles fall in heading 9501.

CN code	Description	Conventional rate of duty (%)	Supplementary unit
1	2	3	4
8701	**Tractors (other than tractors of heading 8709):**		
8701 10 00	– **Pedestrian-controlled tractors**....................................	3	p/st
8701 20	– **Road tractors for semi-trailers**		
8701 20 10	– – New..	16	p/st
8701 20 90	– – Used...	16	p/st
8701 30	– **Track-laying tractors**		
8701 30 10	– – Snowgroupers	Free	p/st
8701 30 90	– – Other	Free	p/st
8701 90	– **Other:**		
	– – Agricultural tractors excluding pedestrian-controlled tractors and forestry tractors, wheeled:		
	– – – New, of an engine power:		
8701 90 11	– – – – Not exceeding 18kw	Free	p/st
8701 90 20	– – – – Exceeding 18kw but not exceeding 37 kw	Free	p/st
8701 90 25	– – – – Exceeding 37kw but not exceeding 59 kw	Free	p/st
8701 90 31	– – – – Exceeding 59kw but not exceeding 75 kw	Free	p/st
8701 90 35	– – – – Exceeding 75kw but not exceeding 90 kw	Free	p/st
8701 90 39	– – – – Exceeding 90kw	Free	p/st
8701 90 50	– – – Used	Free	p/st
8701 90 90	– – Other...	7	p/st
8702	**Motor vehicles for the transport of 10 or more persons, including the driver.**		
8702 10	– **With compression-ignition internal combustion piston engine (diesel or semi-diesel):**		
	– – Of a cylinder capacity exceeding 2 500^2 cm.		
8702 10 11	– – – New..	16	p/st

The third column of Figures 5.1 and 5.2, entitled 'Conventional rate of duty (%)', lists the 'standard', MFN customs duties.[16] Some of these duties are *ad valorem* (see, for example, CN 1803 10 00 or CN 8702 10 11),[17] and others are mixed (see, for example, CN 1806 10 20 or CN 1806 20 10).[18]

---

[15] *Official Journal of the European Communities*, L281, 30 October 2003, 589.
[16] In the past, the Common Customs Tariff had an additional column for the customs duties applicable to goods from countries that were not WTO Members and with which the European Community had not concluded agreements providing for MFN treatment. Now, MFN duties are, as a rule, also applicable to

Compare the customs duties imposed by the European Communities on cocoa powder and tractors to the customs duties imposed on these products by the United States,[19] India,[20] Mercosur (Argentina, Brazil, Paraguay and Uruguay) and China, as set out in Figures 5.3 to 5.10.[21]

Note that the Harmonized Tariff Schedule of the United States is structured in the same manner as the EC Common Customs Tariff; both follow the Harmonised System.[22] The fifth column of the US Harmonized Tariff Schedule, entitled 'Rates of Duty – 1 – General', sets out the MFN customs duties; the sixth column, entitled 'Rates of Duty – 1 – Special', sets out the preferential customs duties.[23] The seventh column, entitled 'Rates of duty – 2', sets out the customs duties applicable on goods from Cuba, Laos and North Korea.[24]

The excerpts from India's First Schedule to the Customs Tariff Act may give the impression that *all* India's customs duties are 30 per cent *ad valorem*. While many are indeed 30 per cent, others are higher and a few are lower. The customs duty on, for example, tariff item 1704 10 00 ('Chewing gum … ') is 45 per cent *ad valorem* and the customs duty on tariff item 8703 21 10 ('Vehicles principally designed for the transport of more than seven persons, including the driver') is 105 per cent *ad valorem*. The customs duty on tariff item 2501 00 10 ('Common salt … ') is 25 per cent *ad valorem*. When compared to the customs duties imposed by the European Communities and the United States, the duties imposed by India are definitively high.[25]

goods from any of these countries. However, when the duties on goods from these countries are lower than the MFN duties, these duties, shown by means of a footnote, are applicable. For example, see the footnote to CN 0802 90 50 (pine nuts) which states: 'Autonomous rate of duty: 2'.

[17] With respect to CN 8702 10 11, note that 'p/st' in the fourth column, entitled 'Supplementary unit', stands for 'number of items'.

[18] With respect to CN 1806 20 10, note that the symbol 'EA' indicates that the goods concerned are chargeable with an 'agricultural component' fixed in accordance with Annex 1 to the Common Customs Tariff. The symbol 'AD S/Z' indicates that the maximum rate of duty consists of an *ad valorem* duty plus an additional duty for certain forms of sugar. This additional duty is *fixed* in accordance with Annex 1. An agricultural component and the additional duty on sugar are expressed in € per 100 kilograms net.

[19] See Harmonized Tariff Schedule of the United States (2004), at http://dataweb.usitc.gov/SCRIPTS/tariff/toc.html, visited on 28 December 2003.

[20] See First Schedule to the Customs Tariff Act, 1975, of India, as amended, at http://www.cbec.gov.in/cae/customs/cs-abc.html, visited on 28 December 2003.

[21] See Common External Tariff of Mercosur, http://www.desenvolvimento.gov.br/sitio/secex/negInternacionais/tec/apresentacao.php, visited on 1 September 2004; and Customs Tariff of China, http://www.apectariff.org/tdb.cgi/ff3236/apecfind.cgi?form_name=CHAPTER&maER&max_chapter=10&Country=CN&Country=18&csearch.x=90&csearch.y=27, visited on 1 September 2004.

[22] See below, pp. 425–9.

[23] The symbols in this column refer to the conventional or autonomous arrangements providing for the preferential tariff treatment. These arrangements include the Generalised System of Preferences (A, A* or A+); the Automotive Products Trade Act (B); the Agreement on Trade in Civil Aircraft (C); the North American Free Trade Agreement (CA or MX); the African Growth and Opportunity Act (D); the Caribbean Basin Economic Recovery Act (E or E*); the United States–Israel Free Trade Area (IL), etc.

[24] For more details, see Harmonized Tariff Schedule of the United States, General Notes, at http://dataweb.usitc.gov/SCRIPTS/tariff/0400gn.pdf, GNs 1–3(a)(iv)(C).

[25] See below, p. 385.

Figure 5.3 Excerpt from Chapter 18 of the Harmonized Tariff Schedule of the United States (cocoa and cocoa preparations)[26]

				Rates of Duty		
			Unit	1		2
Heading/ Subheading	Stat Suffix	Article Description	of Quantity	General	Special	
		Harmonized Tariff Schedule of the United States (2004) **Annotated for Statistical Reporting Purposes** IV 18-2				
1801.00.00	00	Cocoa beans, whole or broken, raw or roasted	kg	Free		Free
1802.00.00	00	Cocoa shells, husks, skins and other cocoa waste	kg	Free		10%
1803		Cocoa paste, whether or not defatted:				
1803.10.00	00	Not defatted	kg	Free		6.6ø/kg
1803.20.00	00	Wholly or partly defatted............	kg	0.2ø/kg	Free (A.CA.E, IL, J. JO, MX)	6.6ø/kg
1804.00.00	00	Cocoa butter, fat and oil	kg	Free		25%
1805.00.00	00	Cocoa powder, not containing added sugar or other sweetening matter	kg	0.52ø/kg	Free (A.CA.E, IL, J. JO, MX)	5.6ø/kg
1806		Chocolate and other food preparations containing cocoa:				
1806.10		Cocoa powder, containing added sugar or other sweetening matter:				
		Containing less than 65 percent by weight of sugar:				
1806.10.05	00	Described in general note 15 of the tariff schedule and entered pursuant to its provisions	kg	Free		40%
1806.10.10	00	Described in additional U.S. note to this chapter and entered pursuant to its provisions	kg	Free		40%
1806.10.15	00	Other1/	kg	21.7ø/kg	Free (MX) See 9909.04.05. 9909.04.39 (JO)	25.5ø/kg
		Containing 65 percent or more but less than 90 percent by dry weight of sugar:				
180610.22	00	Described in general note 15 of the tariff schedule and entered pursuant to its provisions	kg	10%	Free (A*, CA, E, IL, J, JO, MX)	20%
		Articles containing over 65 percent by dry weight of sugar described in additional U.S. note 2 to chapter 17:				
1806.10.24	00	Described in additional U.S. note 7 to chapter 17 and entered pursuant to its provisions	kg	10%		20%
1806.10.28	00	Other2/	kg	33.6ø/kg	Free (MX) See 9909.17.05 9909.17.40 (JO)	39.5ø/kg
		Other:				
1806.10.34	00	Described in additional U.S. note 1 to this chapter and entered pursuant to its provisions	kg	10%	Free (A*, CA, E, IL, J, JO)	20%
1806.10.38	00	Other1/	kg	33.6ø/kg	Free (MX) See 9909.17.05 9909.17.40 (JO)	39.5ø/kg

1/ See subheadings 9904.18.01-9904.18.08.
2/ See subheadings 9904.17.17-9904.17.48.

[26] Harmonized Tariff Schedule of the United States (2004), at http://dataweb.usitc.gov/SCRIPTS/tariff/0400c18.pdf, visited on 28 December 2003, IV 18-2.

Figure 5.4 Excerpt from Chapter 87 of the Harmonized Tariff Schedule of the United States (vehicles ...)[27]

Heading/ Subheading	Stat Suffix	Article Description	Unit of Quantity	Rates of Duty		2
				1		
				General	Special	
8701		Tractors (other than tractors of heading 8709):				
8701.10.00	00	Pedestrian controlled tractors............	No	Free		Free
8701.20.00		Road tractors for semi-trailers............	....	4%	Free (A+, B,CA, D, E, IL, J, JO, MX)	25%
		New:				
	15	G.V.W. not exceeding 36.287 kg ...	No.			
	45	G.V.W. exceeding 36.287 kg	No.			
	80	Used.......................................	No.			
8701.30		Track-laying tractors:				
8701.30.10		Suitable for agricultural use	....	Free		Free
		New:				
	15	With a net engine power of less than 93.3 kW..................	No.			
	30	With a net engine power of 93.3 kW or more but less than 119.4 kW...........................	No.			
	45	With a net engine power of 119.4 kW or more but less than 194 kW..............................	No.			
	60	With a net engine power of 194 kW or more but less than 257.4 kW...........................	No.			
	75	With a net engine power of 257.4 kW or more	No.			
	90	Used	No.			
8701.30.50		Other..	....	Free		27.5%
		New:				
	15	With a net engine power or less than 93.3 kW	No.			
	30	With a net engine power of 93.3 kW or more but less than 119.4 kW...........................	No.			
	45	With a net engine power of 119.4 kW or more but less than 194 kW..............................	No.			
	60	With a net engine power of 194 kW or more but less than 257.4 kW...........................	No.			
	75	With a net engine power of 257.4 kW or more	No.			
	90	Used	No.			

Harmonized Tariff Schedule of the United States (2004) — Annotated for Statistical Reporting Purposes — XVII 87-2

[27] Harmonized Tariff Schedule of the United States (2004), at http://dataweb.usitc.gov/SCRIPTS/tariff/0400c87.pdf, visited on 28 December 2003, XVII 87-2.

Figure 5.5 Excerpt from Chapter 18 of the First Schedule to the Customs Tariff Act, 1975, of India (cocoa and cocoa preparations)[28]

CHAPTER 18
Cocoa and cocoa preparations
NOTES

1. This Chapter does not cover the preparations of headings 0403, 1901, 1904, 1905, 2105, 2202, 2208, 3003 or 3004.
2. Heading 1806 includes sugar confectionery containing cocoa and, subject to Note 1 to this Chapter, other food preparations containing cocoa.

Tariff Item	Description of Goods		Unit	Rate of Duty	
				Standard	Preferential Areas
(1)	(2)		(3)	(4)	(5)
1801 00 00	COCOA BEANS, WHOLE OR BROKEN, RAW OR ROASTED		kg.	30%	–
1802 00 00	COCOA SHELLS, HUSKS, SKINS AND OTHER COCOA WASTE		kg.	30%	–
1803	COCOA PASTE, WHETHER OR NOT DEFATTED				
1803 10 00	–	Not defatted	kg.	30%	–
1803 20 00	–	Wholly or partly defatted	kg.	30%	–
1804 00 00	COCOA BUTTER, FAT AND OIL		kg.	30%	–
1805 00 00	COCOA POWDER, NOT CONTAINING ADDED SUGAR OR OTHER SWEETENING MATTER		kg.	30%	–
1806	CHOCOLATE AND OTHER FOOD PREPARATIONS CONTAINING COCOA				
1806 10 00	–	**Cocoa powder, containing added sugar or other sweetening matter**	kg.	30%	–
1806 20 00	–	**Other preparations in blocks, slabs or bars weighing more than 2 kg. or in liquid, paste, powder, granular or other bulk form in containers or immediate packings, of a content exceeding 2 kg.**	kg.	30%	–
	–	*Other, in blocks, slabs or bars:*			
1806 31 00	– –	**Filled**	kg.	30%	–
1806 32 00	– –	**Not filled**	kg.	30%	–
1806 90	–	*Other:*			
1806 90 10	– – –	**Chocolate and chocolate products**	kg.	30%	–
1806 90 20	– – –	**Sugar confectionery containing cocoa**	kg.	30%	–
1806 90 30	– – –	**Spreads containing cocoa**	kg.	30%	–
1806 90 40	– – –	**Preparations containing cocoa for making beverages**	kg.	30%	–
1806 90 90	– – –	Other	kg.	30%	–

The customs duties imposed by Brazil on cocoa powder as well as on tractors are higher than those imposed by the European Communities (and, possibly, the specific duties imposed by the United States). They are lower, however, than those imposed by India. 'BK' stands for 'Bens de Capital' or capital goods.

The customs duties applied by China to other WTO Members are included in the 'MFN Rate' column. Note that the Customs Tariff of China also includes information on the applicable VAT and excise rates. The customs duties imposed by China on cocoa powder as well as tractors are higher than those

---

[28] First Schedule to the Customs Tariff Act, 1975, of India, as amended, at http://www.cbec.gov.in/cae/customs/cs-abc.html, visited on 28 December 2003, 58.

Figure 5.6 Excerpt from Chapter 87 of the First Schedule to the Customs Tariff Act, 1975, of India (vehicles ...)[29]

CHAPTER 87

Vehicles other than railway or tramway rolling-stock, and parts and accessories thereof

NOTES

1. This Chapter does not cover railway or tramway rolling-stock designed solely for running on rails.
2. For the purposes of this Chapter, "tractors" means vehicles constructed essentially for hauling or pushing another vehicle, appliance or load, whether or not they contain subsidiary provision for the transport, in connection with the main use of the tractor, of tools, seeds, fertilizers or other goods. Machines and working tools designed for fitting to tractors of heading 8701 as interchangeable equipment remain classified in their respective headings even if presented with the tractor, and whether or not mounted on it.
3. Motor chassis fitted with cabs fall in headings 8702 to 8704, and not in heading 8706.
4. Heading 8712 includes all children's bicycles. Other children's cycles fall in heading 9501.

Tariff Item	Description of goods	Unit	Rate of duty	
			Standard	Preferential Areas
(1)	(2)	(3)	(4)	(5)
8701	TRACTORS (OTHER THAN TRACTORS OF HEADING 8709)			
8701 10 00 –	Pedestrian controlled tractors	ll	30%	–
8701 20 –	*Road tractors for semi-trailers:*			
8701 20 10 – – –	Of engine capacity not exceeding 1,800 cc	ll	30%	–
8701 20 90 – – –	Other	ll	30%	–
8701 30 –	*Track-laying tractors:*			
– – –	*Garden tractors:*			
8701 30 11 – – –	Of engine capacity not exceeding 1,800 cc	ll	30%	–
8701 30 19 – – –	Other	ll	30%	–
– – –	*Other:*			
8701 30 91 – – –	Of engine capacity not exceeding 1,800 cc	ll	30%	–
8701 30 99 – – –	Other	ll	30%	–
8701 90 –	*Other:*			
8701 90 10 – – –	Of engine capacity not exceeding 1,800 cc	ll	30%	–
8701 9090 – – –	Other	ll	30%	–
8702	MOTOR VEHICLES FOR THE TRANSPORT OF TEN OR MORE PERSONS, INCLUDING THE DRIVER			
8702 10 –	*With compression-ignition internal combustion piston engine (diesel or semi-diesel).*			
–	*Vehicles for transport of not more than 13 persons, including the driver:*			
8702 10 11 – – –	Integrated monocoque vehicle	ll	30%	–
8702 10 12 – – –	Air-conditioned vehicle	ll	30%	–
8702 10 19 – – –	Other	ll	30%	–
– – –	*Other:*			
8702 10 91 – – –	Integrated monocoque vehicle	ll	30%	–
8702 10 92 – – –	Air-conditioned vehicle	ll	30%	–
8702 10 99 – – –	Other	ll	30%	–
8702 90 –	*Other:*			
– – –	*Vehicles for transport of not more than 13 persons, including the driver:*			
8702 90 11 – – –	Integrated monocoque vehicle	ll	30%	–
8702 90 12 – – –	Air-conditioned vehicle	ll	30%	–
8702 90 13 – – –	Electrically operated	ll	30%	–

[29] *Ibid.*, 538.

Figure 5.7 Excerpt from Chapter 18 of the Common External Tariff of Mercosur (cocoa and cocoa preparations)[30]

CÓDIGO NCM	DESCRIÇÃO	ALÍQUOTA DO II (%)
1801.00.00	CACAU INTEIRO OU PARTIDO, EM BRUTO OU TORRADO	10
1802.00.00	CASCAS, PELÍCULAS E OUTROS DESPERDÍCIOS DE CACAU	10
18.03	PASTA DE CACAU, MESMO DESENGORDURADA	
1803.10.00	-Não desengordurada	12
1803.20.00	-Total ou parcialmente desengordurada	12
1804.00.00	MANTEIGA, GORDURA E ÓLEO, DE CACAU	12
1805.00.00	CACAU EM PÓ, SEM ADIÇÃO DE AÇÚCAR OU DE OUTROS EDULCORANTES	14
18.06	CHOCOLATE E OUTRAS PREPARAÇÕES ALIMENTÍCIAS CONTENDO CACAU	
1806.10.00	-Cacau em pó, com adição de açúcar ou de outros edulcorantes	18
1806.20.00	-Outras preparações em blocos ou em barras, com peso superior a 2kg, ou no estado líquido, em pasta, em pó, grânulos ou formas semelhantes, em recipientes ou embalagens imediatas de conteúdo superior a 2kg	18
1806.3	-Outros, em tabletes, barras e paus	
1806.31	–Recheados	
1806.31.10	Chocolate	20
1806.31.20	Outras preparações	20
1806.32	–Não recheados	
1806.32.10	Chocolate	20
1806.32.20	Outras preparações	20
1806.90.00	-Outros	20

Figure 5.8 Excerpt from Chapter 87 of the Common External Tariff of Mercosur (vehicles ...)[31]

CÓDIGO NCM	DESCRIÇÃO	ALÍQUOTA DO II (%)
87.01	TRATORES (EXCETO OS CARROS-TRATORES DA POSIÇÃO 87.09)	
8701.10.00	-Motocultores	14BK
8701.20.00	-Tratores rodoviários para semi-reboques	35
8701.30.00	-Tratores de lagartas	14BK
8701.90	-Outros	
8701.90.10	Tratores especialmente concebidos para arrastar troncos ("log skidders")	0BK
8701.90.90	Outros	14BK
87.02	VEÍCULOS AUTOMÓVEIS PARA TRANSPORTE DE 10 PESSOAS OU MAIS, INCLUINDO O MOTORISTA	
8702.10.00	-Com motor de pistão, de ignição por compressão (diesel ou semidiesel)	35
8702.90	-Outros	
8702.90.10	Trolebus	35
8702.90.90	Outros	35

imposed by the European Communities and Brazil (and, possibly, the specific duties imposed by the United States). They are, however, lower than those imposed by India.

Many WTO Members have an on-line database of the customs duties they apply. The website of the World Customs Organization, www.wcoomd.org,

---

[30] Common External Tariff of Mercosur, http://www.desenvolvimento.gov.br/sitio/secex/negInternacionais/tec/apresentacao.php, visited on 1 September 2004.
[31] Common External Tariff of Mercosur, http://www.desenvolvimento.gov.br/sitio/secex/negInternacionais/tec/apresentacao.php, visited on 1 September 2004.

Figure 5.9 Excerpt from Chapter 18 of the Customs Tariff of China (cocoa and cocoa preparations)

TARIFF NUMBER	GOODS DESCRIPTION	M.F.N. RATE	GENERAL TARIFF RATE	VAT RATE	EXCISE RATE	COMBINED DUTY AND TAX RATE
1801 18010000	Cocoa beans, whole or broken, raw or roasted: Cocoa beans, whole or broken, raw or roasted	9.6	30	17		28.23
1802 18020000	Cocoa shells, husks, skins and other cocoa waste Cocoa shells, husks, skins and other cocoa waste:	10	30	17		28.7
1803 18031000 18032000	Cocoa paste, whether or not defatted: - Not defatted - Wholly or partly defatted	10 10	30 30	17 17		28.7 28.7
1804 18040000	Cocoa butter, fat and oil: Cocoa butter, fat and oil	35	70	17		57.95
1805 18050000	Cocoa powder, not containing added sugar or other sweetening matter: Cocoa powder, not containing added sugar or other sweetening matter	19	40	17		39.23
1806 18061000	Chocolate and other food preparations containing cocoa: - Cocoa powder, containing added sugar or other sweetening matter	10	50	17		28.7
18062000	- Other preparations in blocks, slabs or bars weighing more than 2kg or in liquid, paste, powder, granular or other bulk form in containers or immediate packing, of a content exceeding 2 kg	12	50	17		31.04
18063100	- Other, in blocks, slabs or bars: – Filled	12	50	17		31.04
18063200	– Not Filled	12	50	17		31.04
18069000	- Other	12	50	17		31.04

gives easy access to a number of these databases, including the TARIC database of the European Communities.[32]

Alternatively, the EU Market Access Database, a service offered by the Directorate-General for Trade of the European Commission, also gives up-to-date information on the customs duties imposed by about ninety other countries or customs territories.[33] This database also includes a convenient link to the TARIC database.

Questions and Assignments 5.1

What are specific customs duties and how do they differ from *ad valorem* customs duties? What are MFN customs duties? What is a

[32] See http://europa.eu.int/comm/taxation_customs/dds/en/tarhome.htm. The TARIC database shows the various rules applying to specific products when imported into the European Union. Apart from the MFN duties, it also incorporates tariff quotas; preferential customs duties (under the EC's Generalised System of Preferences), under the *Cotonou Agreement* for ACP countries; under the *European Economic Area Agreement* for Iceland, Liechtenstein and Norway; and under a number of bilateral trade agreements with, for example, Algeria, Egypt, Israel, the Occupied Palestinian Territory and South Africa. The TARIC database also incorporates anti-dumping and countervailing duties; import prohibitions; and import restrictions. See OJ 2003, C103, 30 April 2003.

[33] See http://mkaccdb.eu.int, visited on 12 May 2004. This database also gives information on non-tariff barriers to trade maintained by other countries, general information on the trade policies of these countries and statistics on trade.

Figure 5.10 Excerpt from Chapter 87 of the Customs Tariff of China (vehicles …)

Tariff Heading	Description Tractors (other than tractors of heading No. 8709):					
TARIFF NUMBER	GOODS DESCRIPTION	M.F.N. RATE	GENERAL TARIFF RATE	VAT RATE	EXCISE RATE	COMBINED DUTY AND TAX RATE
8701	Tractors (other than tractors of heading No.8709)					
87011000	-Pedestrian controlled tractors	13	20	13		27.69
87012000	-Road tractors for semi-trailers	15	20	17		34.55
87013000	-Track-laying tractors	15	20	13 / 17		29.95 / 34.55
87019000	-Other	15	20	13 / 17		29.95 / 34.55

tariff? Why do countries impose customs duties on imports? Find out what the MFN customs duties imposed by the European Communities, the United States, China and Poland on chewing gum and common salt are. If you are a national of a WTO Member other than those Members referred to in this section, find out what the MFN customs duties which your government imposes on cocoa powder and tractors are.

5.2.2. Negotiations on tariff reductions

5.2.2.1. Tariffs as a lawful instrument of protection

In principle, WTO Members are free to impose customs duties on imported products. WTO law and, in particular, the GATT 1994, does not prohibit the imposition of customs duties. This is in sharp contrast to the general prohibition on quantitative restrictions.[34] Customs duties, unlike quantitative restrictions, represent an instrument of protection against imports generally allowed by the GATT 1994. The reasons behind the GATT's preference for customs duties are discussed below.

5.2.2.2. A call for tariff negotiations

While WTO law does not prohibit customs duties, it does recognise that customs duties often constitute significant obstacles to trade. Article XXVIII *bis* of the GATT 1994, therefore, calls upon WTO Members to negotiate the reduction of customs duties. This article provides, in relevant part:

> thus negotiations on a reciprocal and mutually advantageous basis, directed to the substantial reduction of the general level of tariffs and other charges on imports and exports and in particular to the reduction of such high tariffs as discourage the importation even of minimum quantities, and conducted with due regard to the objectives of this Agreement and the varying needs of individual Members, are of great importance to the expansion of international trade. The Members may therefore sponsor such negotiations from time to time.

[34] See below, pp. 444–6.

Figure 5.11 Fifty years of tariff reduction negotiations[35]

Implementation period	Round covered	Weighted tariff reduction
1948–63	First five GATT rounds (1947–62)	-36
1968–72	Kennedy Round (1964–7)	-37
1980–7	Tokyo Round (1973–9)	-33
1995–9	Uruguay Round (1986–94)	-38

Note that Article XXXVII:1 of the GATT 1994 calls upon developed-country Members to accord, in the interest of the economic development of developing-country Members,

> high priority to the reduction and elimination of barriers to products currently or potentially of particular export interest to [developing-country Members] ... [36]

5.2.2.3. Success of past tariff negotiations

Under the GATT 1947, negotiations on the reduction of tariff duties took place primarily in the context of eight successive 'Rounds' of trade negotiations. In fact, the first five of these Rounds (Geneva, Annecy, Torquay, Geneva and Dillon) were exclusively dedicated to the negotiation of the reduction of tariffs. The sixth, seventh and eighth Rounds (Kennedy, Tokyo and Uruguay) had an increasingly broader agenda although the negotiation of tariff reductions remained an important element on the agenda of these Rounds.

The eight GATT Rounds of trade negotiations have been very successful in reducing customs duties. In the late 1940s, the average duty on industrial products imposed by developed countries was about 40 per cent *ad valorem*.

As a result of the eight GATT Rounds, the average duty of developed-country Members on industrial products is now as low as 3.9 per cent *ad valorem*. See Figure 5.11.

5.2.2.4. Customs duties remain important trade barriers

Economists often consider a customs duty, or tariff, below 5 per cent to be a nuisance rather than a barrier to trade. Nevertheless, customs duties remain an important barrier in international trade for several reasons. First, most developing-country Members still maintain high customs duties. See Figure 5.12. Many of them have an average duty for industrial products ranging between 25 and 50 per cent *ad valorem*.[37] For India, the average duty for industrial products is almost 60 per cent.[38] Secondly, among developed-country Members average duties for industrial products vary largely, from a

---

[35] www.wto.org, visited on 6 September 2003. The tariff reductions concern MFN tariffs of developed countries on industrial products, excluding petroleum.

[36] Note, however, that Article XXXVII qualifies its call to give high priority to the reduction and elimination of barriers with the words 'except when compelling reasons ... make it impossible'.

[37] See WTO Secretariat, *Market Access: Unfinished Business*, Special Studies 6 (WTO, 2001), 10. In this section, the concept of 'average duty' refers to the 'simple average bound customs duty'.

[38] *Ibid.*

Figure 5.12 Average customs duties by Member and product category

Import markets	1 Wood, pulp, paper & furniture	2 Textiles and clothing	3 Leather, rubber, footwear & travel goods	4 Metals	5 Chemicals & photographic supplies	6 Transport equipment	7 Non-electric machinery	8 Electric machinery	9 Mineral products & precious stones & precious metals	10 Manufactured articles not elsewhere specified	11 Fish & fish product
Developing Countries											
Brazil	22.7	34.9	34.7	33.4	22.7	33.6	32.6	31.9	33.5	33.5	33.4
Mexico	34.0	35.0	34.8	34.7	35.2	35.8	35.0	34.1	34.4	34.6	35.0
Hong Kong, China	0.0	0.0	0.0	0.0	0.0	0.0	0.0	0.0	0.0	0.0	0.0
India	56.4	87.8	67.8	58.3	44.1	53.9	36.2	44.8	47.2	72.4	68.6
South Africa	9.2	27.7	23.1	14.1	13.9	23.3	12.0	17.4	11.5	14.8	22.5
Developed Countries											
Canada	1.3	12.4	7.6	2.8	4.5	6.8	3.6	5.2	3.1	4.2	1.8
United States	0.6	8.9	8.4	1.8	3.7	2.7	1.2	2.1	3.3	3.0	2.2
European Union	0.7	7.9	4.8	1.6	4.8	4.7	1.8	3.3	2.4	2.7	11.8
Australia	7.0	28.8	17.5	4.5	9.2	15.1	9.1	13.3	7.0	7.0	0.8
Japan	1.2	6.8	15.7	0.9	2.4	0.0	0.0	0.2	1.0	1.1	6.2

low 1.8 per cent for Switzerland to a comparatively high 14.2 per cent for Australia.[39] Thirdly, developed-country Members still have high, to very high, duties on specific groups of 'sensitive' industrial and agricultural products. With respect to industrial products, these so-called 'tariff peaks'[40] are quite common for textiles and clothing, leather and, to a lesser extent, transport equipment.[41] With respect to agricultural products, note that, under the WTO *Agreement on Agriculture*, all non-tariff barriers on trade in agricultural products have been eliminated and substituted by customs duties at often very high levels.[42] Fourthly, and finally, in very competitive markets and in trade between neighbouring countries, a very low duty may still constitute a barrier.

In addition, customs duties may also impede the economic development of developing-country Members to the extent that duties increase with the level of processing that products have undergone. The duties on processed and semi-processed products are often higher than the duties on non-processed products and raw materials. This phenomenon is referred to as 'tariff escalation'. Tariff escalation discourages manufacturing or processing in developing countries.[43] The customs duties of Canada and Australia increase at each production stage. US customs duties increase significantly only between raw materials and semi-processed products. The same is true for the customs duties of Japan. In general, the customs duties of the European Communities appear to de-escalate, i.e. they are higher on raw materials than on semi-processed or processed products.[44] However, consider the above excerpt from Chapter 18 of the EC Common Customs Tariff, which provides for:

- zero duties on cocoa beans;
- an *ad valorem* duty of 9.6 per cent on cocoa paste; and
- a mixed duty of 8 per cent and €31.40 per 100 kg net on cocoa powder containing added sugar.[45]

Questions and Assignments 5.2

Is the imposition of customs duties or tariffs on products imported into the territory of a Member prohibited under WTO law? What does Article XXVIII

---

[39] See WTO Secretariat, *Market Access: Unfinished Business*, Special Studies 6 (WTO, 2001), 10. Among the Quad countries, Japan has the lowest average duty (3.5 per cent) while Canada has the highest (5.2 per cent).

[40] Tariff peaks are tariffs that exceed a selected reference level. The OECD distinguishes between 'national peaks' and 'international peaks'. 'National peaks' are tariffs which are three times or more the national mean tariff. 'International peaks' are tariffs of 15 per cent or more. See WTO Secretariat, *Market Access: Unfinished Business,* Special Studies 6 (WTO, 2001), 12.

[41] See WTO Secretariat, *Market Access: Unfinished Business*, Special Studies 6 (WTO, 2001), 12. Note that the European Communities does not have tariff peaks in the textiles and clothing sector.

[42] See below, pp. 447–8.

[43] Note that Article XXXVII of the GATT 1994 calls upon developed-country Members to accord 'high priority to the reduction and elimination of barriers to products currently or potentially of particular export interest to [developing-country Members], including customs duties and other restrictions *which differentiate unreasonably between such products in their primary and in their processed forms*' [emphasis added]. See, in this respect, however, also footnote 36, p. 390.

[44] See WTO Secretariat, *Market Access: Unfinished Business*, Special Studies 6 (WTO, 2001), 12 and 13.

[45] See above, p. 380.

bis of the GATT 1994 provide for? Have past efforts to reduce customs duties through negotiations been successful? Are customs duties still a major barrier to trade? Give reasons for your answer. What is 'tariff escalation' and why is it a problem?

5.2.2.5. *Basic principles and rules governing tariff negotiations*

As noted above, Article XXVIII *bis* of the GATT 1994 calls for '[tariff] negotiations on a reciprocal and mutually advantageous basis'. As discussed in Chapter 4, Article I:1 of the GATT 1994 requires that '[w]ith respect to customs duties ... any advantage ... granted by any [Member] to any product originating in ... any other country shall be accorded immediately and unconditionally to the like product originating in ... all other [Members]'. The basic principles and rules governing tariff negotiations are thus:

- the principle of reciprocity and mutual advantage; and
- the most-favoured-nation (MFN) treatment obligation.

The principle of reciprocity and mutual advantage, as applied in tariff negotiations, entails that, when a Member requests another Member to reduce its customs duties on certain products, it must be ready to reduce its own customs duties on products which the other Member exports, or wishes to export. For tariff negotiations to succeed, the tariff reductions requested must be considered to be of equivalent value to the tariff reductions offered. There is no agreed method to establish or measure reciprocity. Each Member determines for itself whether the economic value of the tariff reductions received is equal to the value of the tariff reductions granted. Although some Members apply rather sophisticated economic methods to measure reciprocity, in general the methods applied are basic. The final assessment of the 'acceptability' of the outcome of tariff negotiations is primarily political in nature.[46]

The principle of reciprocity does not apply, at least not to its full extent, to tariff negotiations between developed and developing-country Members. Article XXXVI:8 of Part IV ('Trade and Development') of the GATT 1994 provides:

> The [developed-country Members] do not expect reciprocity for commitments made by them in trade negotiations to reduce or remove tariffs and other barriers to the trade of [developing-country Members].

This is further elaborated on in the 1979 Tokyo Round *Decision on Differential and More Favourable Treatment, Reciprocity and Fuller Participation of Developing Countries*, commonly referred to as the *Enabling Clause*, which provides, in paragraph 5:

---

[46] Note that the principle of reciprocity applies not only to tariff negotiations adopting a product-by-product request-and-offer approach but also to tariff negotiations adopting a linear reduction approach, a harmonisation formula approach or a sector approach. See below, pp. 395–8.

> [Developed-country Members] shall ... not seek, neither shall [developing-country Members] be required to make, concessions that are inconsistent with the latter's development, financial and trade needs.

In tariff negotiations between developed and developing Members, the principle of *relative* reciprocity applies. In tariff negotiations with developed-country Members, developing-country Members are expected to 'reciprocate' only to the extent consistent with their development, financial and trade needs.

With respect to least-developed-country Members, paragraph 6 of the *Enabling Clause* furthermore instructs developed-country Members to exercise the 'utmost restraint' in seeking any concessions for commitments made by them to reduce or remove tariffs.

Note, however, that paragraph 7 of the *Enabling Clause* states, in relevant part:

> [Developing-country Members] expect that their capacity to make contributions or negotiated concessions ... would improve with the progressive development of their economies and improvement in their trade situation and they would accordingly expect to participate more fully in the framework of rights and obligations under the General Agreement.

Because of the principle of relative reciprocity, few developing-country Members agreed to any reductions of their customs duties up to and including the Tokyo Round. Before the Uruguay Round, tariff negotiations were, in practice, primarily conducted between developed-country Members. This changed in the Uruguay Round when almost all developing-country Members agreed to a reduction of their customs duties, albeit that this reduction – in accordance with the principle of relative reciprocity – was smaller than the reduction agreed to by developed-country Members.

The increased willingness of developing-country Members to participate actively in tariff reduction negotiations during the Uruguay Round can be attributed to two factors. First, a number of developing-country Members had made significant progress in their economic development. Secondly, a fundamental change had occurred in the trade policy of many developing-country Members. In the 1980s, many developing-country Members moved away from protectionist trade policies to open and liberal trade policies.[47]

As noted above, tariff negotiations are governed not only by the principle of reciprocity (full or relative), but also by the MFN treatment obligation set out in Article I:1 of the GATT 1994. Any tariff reduction a Member would grant to any country, as the result of tariff negotiations with that country, must be granted to all other Members, immediately and unconditionally. This considerably complicates tariff negotiations. Member A, interested in exporting product *a* to Member B, will request Member B to reduce its customs duties on product *a*. In return for such a reduction, Member A will offer Member B, interested in

---

[47] *Business Guide to the World Trading System* (International Trade Centre/Commonwealth Secretariat, 1999), 59.

exporting product *b* to Member A, a reduction of its customs duties on product *b*. As a result of the MFN treatment obligation, the tariff reductions to which Members A and B would agree would also benefit all other Members. However, Members A and B will be hesitant to give other Members the benefit of the tariff reductions 'without getting something in return'. Member A is therefore likely to put a hold on the agreement to reduce the customs duty on product *b* until it has been able 'to get something in return' from, for example, Member C which also exports product *b* to Member A and would thus also benefit from the reduction of the customs duty on product *b*. Likewise, Member B will be hesitant to reduce the customs duty on product *a* as long as Member D which also has an interest in exporting product *a* to Member B, has not given Member B 'something in return' for this reduction. In tariff negotiations, Members may try to benefit from tariff reductions agreed between other Members without giving anything in return. If their export interests are small, they are likely to succeed and will therefore be 'free-riders'. The free-rider problem can be mitigated by opting for an approach to tariff negotiations other than the product-by-product request-and-offer approach. Other approaches to tariff negotiations include the linear reduction approach, the harmonisation formula approach and the sector approach, all discussed below.

Questions and Assignments 5.3

What are the basic principles and rules governing tariff negotiations? Does the principle of reciprocity also apply to tariff negotiations between developed- and developing-country Members? Why does the MFN treatment obligation complicate tariff negotiations? What does the term 'free-rider' refer to in tariff negotiations?

5.2.2.6. *Organisation of tariff negotiations*

Tariff negotiations can be organised in different ways. As Article XXVIII *bis* of the GATT 1994 provides, tariff negotiations may be carried out:

- on a selective product-by-product basis; or
- by the application of such multilateral procedures as may be accepted by the Members concerned.

During the first GATT Rounds (up to and including the 1961–2 Dillon Round), negotiators opted for a *product-by-product request-and-offer approach* to tariff negotiations. Under this approach, each of the participants in the tariff negotiations submits first its request list and then its offer list, identifying respectively the products with regard to which they are seeking and are willing to make tariff reductions. The negotiations take place between the principal suppliers and importers of each product. However, the product-by-product approach has one major disadvantage. For practical reasons, the number of products that can be subject to this kind of tariff negotiation is necessarily limited, and the product coverage of the tariff reductions that can be achieved is thus 'restricted'.

The product-by-product request-and-offer approach to tariff negotiations is still used, in bilateral or plurilateral negotiations outside a Round, both for Article XXVIII re-negotiations and for tariff negotiations in the context of the accession of new Members to the WTO. However, since the 1963–7 Kennedy Round, the product-by-product request-and-offer approach has no longer been used in multilateral tariff negotiations. A *linear reduction approach* to tariff negotiations was adopted for the Kennedy Round tariff negotiations. Under this approach, the negotiations aim at agreeing on a reduction of customs duties across the board, i.e. a reduction of the customs duties on all products, by for example 50 per cent. By agreement, certain products are excluded from the linear reduction, and, with respect to these products, the tariff negotiations are conducted on a product-by-product request-and-offer basis. While successful, the linear reduction approach also presented problems. Members with low customs duties on average argued that it was not reasonable to expect them to cut these duties by the same percentage as Members with high customs duties. It is clear that a 50 per cent reduction of a customs duty of 40 per cent still leaves a 20 per cent customs duty in place, i.e. a significant degree of protection from import competition. However, a 50 per cent reduction of a customs duty of 10 per cent leaves only a 5 per cent customs duty. To mitigate this problem, the negotiators in the Tokyo Round applied a *harmonisation formula approach* to tariff negotiations. A harmonisation formula approach is a non-linear reduction approach which requires larger cuts of higher customs duties than of lower customs duties. The negotiations aim at reaching agreement on the formula *and* on the products excluded from the application of the formula.

In the Uruguay Round tariff negotiations, both old and new approaches to tariff negotiations were applied. Under the new *sector approach*, the negotiators aimed at the elimination (or harmonisation) of customs duties in a given sector (such as the pharmaceuticals, construction equipment, medical equipment and beer sectors).[48] Other approaches applied in the Uruguay Round tariff negotiations were the harmonisation formula approach, a 50 per cent reduction in tariff peaks, and a linear reduction of 33 per cent on residual products.

Between the end of the Uruguay Round and the start of the current Doha Development Round, Members of the WTO agreed to eliminate all customs duties on information technology products (i.e. computers, telecommunications equipment, semiconductors, etc.). At the Singapore Session of the Ministerial Conference in 1996, twenty-nine Members adopted the *Ministerial Declaration on Trade in Information Technology Products* (ITA).[49] The ITA provided for participants to eliminate duties completely on information technology products

---

[48] See A. Hoda, *Tariff Negotiations and Renegotiations under the GATT and the WTO: Procedures and Practice* (WTO/ Cambridge University Press, 2001), 37.
[49] Ministerial Conference, *Singapore Ministerial Declaration on Trade in Information Technology Products*, WT/ MIN(96)/16, dated 13 December 1996.

by 1 January 2000. The ITA entered into force in 1997 when forty Members had adopted the agreement, and the agreement covered more than 90 per cent of world trade in information technology products. As a result of the ITA, almost all trade in information technology products is now free from customs duties.

The Doha Ministerial Declaration of November 2001, in which the WTO Members agreed to start the Doha Development Round, provides little guidance with respect to the approach to be taken to the tariff negotiations in the Doha Development Round. The Doha Ministerial Declaration states, in relevant part:

> We agree to negotiations which shall aim, *by modalities to be agreed*, to reduce or as appropriate eliminate tariffs, including the reduction or elimination of tariff peaks, high tariffs, and tariff escalation, as well as non-tariff barriers, in particular on products of export interest to developing countries. Product coverage shall be comprehensive and without *a priori* exclusions. The negotiations shall take fully into account the special needs and interests of developing and least-developed country participants, including through less than full reciprocity in reduction commitments.[50]
> [Emphasis added]

In August 2003, the Chair of the Negotiating Group on Market Access proposed with regard to the tariff negotiations on non-agricultural products:

> All non-agricultural tariffs shall be reduced on a line-by-line basis using the formula applied to the base rates outlined in paragraph 6:
>
> $$t_1 = \frac{B \times t_a \times t_0}{B \times t_a + t_0}$$
>
> where,
> t_1 is the final rate, to be bound in *ad valorem* terms
> t_0 is the base rate
> t_a is the average of the base rates
> B is a coefficient with a unique value to be determined by the participants.[51]

The Chair thus proposed a *harmonisation formula approach* to the Doha Development Round tariff negotiations.[52] In addition to the application of the formula, the Chair proposed a *sector elimination approach* in order to eliminate, in three phases, all customs duties on products of particular export interest to developing and least-developed country participants. The following sectors were proposed: electronics and electrical goods; fish and fish products; footwear; leather goods; motor vehicle parts and components; stones, gems and precious metals; and textiles and clothing.[53] The Chair's proposal furthermore included additional provisions for developing and least-developed-country

---

[50] Ministerial Conference, *Doha Ministerial Declaration*, WT/MIN(1)/DEC/1, dated 20 November 2001, para. 16.
[51] Draft Elements of Modalities for Negotiations on Non-Agricultural Products, TN/MA/W/35/Rev.1, dated 19 August 2003, para. 7.
[52] As an exception to the harmonisation formula approach, the Chair proposed that participants with a binding coverage of non-agricultural tariff lines of less than 35 per cent would be exempt from making tariff reductions through the formula. Instead, they would be expected to bind 100 per cent of non-agricultural tariff lines at an average level that does not exceed the overall average of bound tariffs for all developing countries after full implementation of current concessions (27.5 per cent). See Draft Elements of Modalities for Negotiations on Non-Agricultural Products, TN/MA/W/35/Rev.1, dated 19 August 2003, para. 8.
[53] *Ibid.*, para. 9.

Members participating in the tariff negotiations. For example, for developing country participants, longer implementation periods for tariff reductions would be applicable, and least-developed country participants would not be required to undertake tariff reduction commitments.

The Chair's proposals for tariff negotiations on non-agricultural products were not received with much enthusiasm. Many developing-country Members, in particular African Members, have grave concerns regarding both the harmonisation formula approach and the sector elimination approach. They consider that the specific interests of developing countries are not sufficiently taken into account. Developed-country Members are also dissatisfied with the Chair's proposals, as these proposals are not, in their opinion, sufficiently ambitious in reducing customs duties. In September 2004, WTO Members had still not reached agreement on the modalities for the Doha Development Round tariff negotiations. However, on 1 August 2004, the General Council did agree on the 'initial elements' for future work on modalities by the Negotiating Group on Market Access and instructed the Negotiating Group to address the outstanding issues expeditiously, using the Chair's proposals as a reference. The General Council stated:

> We recognize that a formula approach is key to reducing tariffs, and reducing or eliminating tariff peaks, high tariffs, and tariff escalation. We agree that the Negotiating Group should continue its work on a non-linear formula applied on a line-by-line basis which shall take fully into account the special needs and interests of developing and least-developed country participants, including through less than full reciprocity in reduction commitments.
>
> . . .
>
> We recognize that a sectoral tariff component, aiming at elimination or harmonization is another key element to achieving the objectives of paragraph 16 of the Doha Ministerial Declaration with regard to the reduction or elimination of tariffs, in particular on products of export interest to developing countries.[54]

Questions and Assignments 5.4

Discuss the different approaches to tariff negotiations applied since 1947. Which approach to tariff negotiations is applied in the Doha Development Round tariff negotiations?

5.2.3. Tariff concessions and Schedules of Concessions

5.2.3.1. *Tariff concessions or tariff bindings*

The results of tariff negotiations are referred to as 'tariff concessions' or 'tariff bindings'. A tariff concession, or a tariff binding, is a commitment not to raise

---

[54] See General Council, *Doha Work Programme, Framework for Establishing Modalities in Market Access for Non-Agricultural Products*, WT/L/597, dated 2 August 2004, Annex B, paras. 4 and 7. See paras. 5, 6 and 8–13 for further details on the 'initial elements' for future work on the modalities for the Doha Development Round tariff negotiations.

the customs duty on a certain product above an agreed level. As a result of the Uruguay Round tariff negotiations, all, or almost all, customs duties imposed by developed-country Members are now 'bound', i.e. are subject to a maximum level.[55] Most Latin American developing-country Members have bound all customs duties; however, for Asian and African developing-country Members the situation is more varied.[56] While Members such as Indonesia and South Africa have bound more than 90 per cent of the customs duties on industrial products, India and Thailand have bound about 60 per cent, Hong Kong, China, 23 per cent, Zimbabwe, 9 per cent and Cameroon, 0.1 per cent.[57] Cameroon has made tariff concessions with regard to only three products.

5.2.3.2. Schedules of Concessions

The tariff concessions or bindings of a Member are set out in that Member's Schedule of Concessions. Each Member of the WTO has a schedule, except when the Member is part of a customs union in which case the Member has a common schedule with the other members of the customs union. The Schedules resulting from the Uruguay Round negotiations are all annexed to the *Marrakesh Protocol* to the GATT 1994. Pursuant to Article II:7 of the GATT 1994, the Schedules of Members are an integral part of the GATT 1994.

Each Schedule of Concessions contains four parts. The most important part, Part I, sets out the MFN concessions with respect to agricultural products (tariffs (Section 1A) and tariff quotas (Section 1B)) and with respect to non-agricultural products (tariffs only (Section 2)). Furthermore, a schedule sets out preferential concessions (Part II), concessions on non-tariff measures (Part III) and specific commitments on domestic support and export subsidies on agricultural products (Part IV).

It is not possible for Members to agree in their Schedules to treatment which is inconsistent with the basic GATT obligations. In *EC – Bananas III*, the Appellate Body addressed the question of whether the allocation of tariff quotas agreed to and inscribed in the EC's Schedule was inconsistent with Article XIII of the GATT 1994. The Appellate Body referred first to the headnote to the report of the Panel in *US – Sugar*, which stated, *inter alia*:

> Article II permits contracting parties to incorporate into their Schedules acts yielding rights under the General Agreement but not acts diminishing obligations under that Agreement.[58]

---

[55] For the European Communities, 100 per cent of the tariff lines for both agricultural products and industrial products are bound. For the United States, 100 per cent of the tariff lines for agricultural products and 99.9 per cent of the tariff lines for industrial products are bound. See WTO Secretariat, *Market Access: Unfinished Business*, Special Studies 6 (WTO, 2001), 49.

[56] Note that many Latin American Members apply a 'uniform ceiling binding', i.e. they have bound their customs duties to a single maximum level. For Chile, for example, this uniform maximum level is 25 per cent.

[57] See WTO Secretariat, *Market Access: Unfinished Business*, Special Studies 6 (WTO, 2001), 7 and 8. Note that these percentages are not weighted according to trade volume or value. Note, with regard to Hong Kong, China, that, while a high percentage of customs duties is unbound, the applied duties are zero.

[58] GATT Panel Report, *US – Sugar (US – Restrictions on Imports of Sugar)*, para. 5.2.

Subsequently, the Appellate Body ruled in *EC – Bananas III*:

> This principle is equally valid for the market access concessions and commitments for agricultural products contained in the Schedules annexed to the GATT 1994. The ordinary meaning of the term "concessions" suggests that a Member may yield rights and grant benefits, but it cannot diminish its obligations.[59]

All schedules are structured according to the Harmonised Commodity Description and Coding System ('Harmonised System' or 'HS'), discussed below, and contain the following information for each product subject to tariff concessions:

- HS tariff item number;
- description of the product;
- rate of duty;
- present concession established;
- initial negotiating rights (INR);[60]
- other duties and charges;[61] and
- for agricultural products only, special safeguards.[62]

Consider by way of example Figures 5.13 to 5.17, which reproduce excerpts from the Uruguay Round Schedules of Concessions of the European Communities (Schedule LXXX), the United States (Schedule XX), India (Schedule XII) and Brazil (Schedule III), annexed to the *Marrakesh Protocol* to the GATT 1994. Consider also the Schedule of Concessions of China (Schedule CLII), annexed to the Accession Protocol of China.

Note that the Schedules of the major trading entities such as the European Communities and the United States, which have made tariff concessions on virtually all products, are lengthy and detailed. The file containing the Schedule of the European Communities on the WTO's website is 759KB in size. By contrast, the Schedules of many developing-country Members are short. The files containing the Schedules of Botswana and the Dominican Republic are only 12 and 13KB respectively.[63]

5.2.3.3. Interpretation of tariff schedules and concessions

Since the tariff schedules are an integral part of the GATT 1994, they constitute a 'covered agreement' under the DSU. Article 3.2 of the DSU applies to the interpretation of tariff schedules and the concessions set out therein. As discussed in Chapter 3, Article 3.2 of the DSU provides that the function of the WTO dispute settlement system is to 'clarify the existing provisions of [the covered agreements] in accordance with customary rules of interpretation of public international law'. Accordingly, the tariff schedules and tariff

---

[59] Appellate Body Report, *EC – Bananas III*, para. 154. The Appellate Body confirmed this ruling in *EC – Poultry*, para. 98.

[60] See below, pp. 423–4. The schedule may also set out the concession first incorporated in a GATT schedule.

[61] See below, pp. 436–41. The schedule may also set out INRs on earlier occasions.

[62] See below, p. 634.

[63] See http://www.wto.org/english/tratop_e/schedules_e/goods_schedules_e.htm, visited on 10 May 2004.

concessions must be interpreted in accordance with the customary rules of interpretation of public international law as codified in Articles 31 and 32 of the *Vienna Convention on the Law of Treaties*. In *EC – Computer Equipment*, at issue was a dispute between the United States and the European Communities on whether the EC's tariff concessions regarding automatic data processing equipment applied to local area network (LAN) computer equipment.[64] The Panel based its interpretation of the EC's tariff concessions on the 'legitimate expectations' of the exporting Member, *in casu*, the United States. On appeal, the Appellate Body rejected this approach to the interpretation of tariff concessions, ruling as follows:

> The purpose of treaty interpretation under Article 31 of the *Vienna Convention* is to ascertain the *common* intentions of the parties. These *common* intentions cannot be ascertained on the basis of the subjective and unilaterally determined "expectations" of *one* of the parties to a treaty. Tariff concessions provided for in a Member's Schedule – the interpretation of which is at issue here – are reciprocal and result from a mutually advantageous negotiation between importing and exporting Members. A Schedule is made an integral part of the GATT 1994 by Article II:7 of the GATT 1994. Therefore, the concessions provided for in that Schedule are part of the terms of the treaty. As such, the only rules which may be applied in interpreting the meaning of a concession are the general rules of treaty interpretation set out in the *Vienna Convention*.[65]

The Appellate Body furthermore noted with respect to the lack of clarity of tariff concessions and tariff schedules:

> Tariff negotiations are a process of reciprocal demands and concessions, of "give and take". It is only normal that importing Members define their offers (and their ensuing obligations) in terms which suit their needs. On the other hand, exporting Members have to ensure that their corresponding rights are described in such a manner in the Schedules of importing Members that their export interests, as agreed in the negotiations, are guaranteed … [T]he fact that Member's Schedules are an integral part of the GATT 1994 indicates that, while each Schedule represents the tariff commitments made by *one* Member, they represent a common agreement among *all* Members.
>
> For the reasons stated above, we conclude that the Panel erred in finding that "the United States was not required to clarify the scope of the European Communities' tariff concessions on LAN equipment". We consider that any clarification of the scope of tariff concessions that may be required during the negotiations is a task for *all* interested parties.[66]

Note that, at the very end of the Uruguay Round, a special arrangement was made to allow the negotiators to check and control, through consultations with their negotiating partners, the scope of tariff concessions agreed to. This 'process of verification' took place from 15 February to 25 March 1994.[67]

As discussed above, all schedules are structured according to the Harmonised System. The Uruguay Round tariff negotiations were held on the

---

[64] In the context of the Uruguay Round tariff negotiations, the European Communities agreed to a tariff binding for automatic data processing equipment of 4.9 per cent (to be reduced to 2.5 per cent for some products or duty-free for others). According to the United States, during and shortly after the Uruguay Round, the European Communities classified LAN computer equipment as automatic data processing equipment. Later, however, it started classifying LAN computer equipment as telecommunications equipment, a product category subject to generally higher duties, in the range of 4.6 to 7.5 per cent (to be reduced to 3 to 3.6 per cent).

[65] Appellate Body Report, *EC – Computer Equipment*, para. 84.

[66] Appellate Body Report, *EC – Computer Equipment*, paras. 109 and 110.

[67] See MTN.TNC/W/131, dated 21 January 1994.

Figure 5.13 Excerpt from Chapter 18 of the Schedule of Concessions of the European Communities (cocoa and cocoa preparations).[68]

Tariff item number	Description of products	Base rate of duty			Bound rate of duty		Implementation period from/to	Special safeguard	Initial negotiating right	Other duties and charges	Comments
		Ad valorem (%)	Other	U/B/C	Ad valorem (%)	Other					
1	2	3			4		5	6	7	8	9
1801.00.00	Cocoa beans, whole or broken, raw or roasted	3.0			0.0						
1802.00.00	Cocoa shells, husks, skins and other cocoa waste	3.0			0.0						
1803	Cocoa pastes, whether or not defatted										
1803.10.00	-Not defatted	15.0			9.6						
1803.20.00	-Wholly or partly defatted	15.0			9.6						
1804.00.00	Cocoa butter, fat and oil	12.0			7.7						
1805.00.00	Cocoa powder, not containing added sugar or other sweetening matter	16.0			8.0						
1806	Chocolate and other food preparations containing cocoa:										
1806.10	-Cocoa powder, containing added sugar or other sweetening matter:										
1806.10.10	Containing no more or less than 5% by weight of sucrose (including invert sugar expressed as sucrose) or isoglucose expressed as sucrose	10.0	+ 315 ECU/T		8.0	+ 252 ECU/T					
	Containing 5% or more but less than 65% by weight of sucrose (including invert sugar expressed as sucrose) or isoglucose expressed as sucrose										
1806.10.30	—Containing 65 % or more but less than 80 % by weight of sucrose (including invert sugar expressed as sucrose) or isoglucose expressed as sucrose	10.0	+ 393 ECU/T		8.0	+ 314 ECU/T					

1806.10.90	--Containing 80 % or more by weight of sucrose (including invert sugar expressed as sucrose) or isoglucose expressed as sucrose	10.0	+ 524 ECU/T	8.0	+ 419 ECU/T
1806.20	-Other preparations in block slabs or bars weighing more than 2 kg or in liquid, paste, powder, granular or other bulk form in containers or immediate packings, of a content exceeding 2 kg:				
1806.20.70	--Chocolate milk crumb, containing a combined weight of less than 25% of cocoa butter and milkfat and containing less than 18% by weight of cocoa butter	22.3	*	15.4	*	* see annex 1
1806.20.80	--Other	12.0	8.3	* MAX 18.7% + AD S/Z		* see annex 1
	Other, in blocks, slabs or bars:				
1806.31.00	--Filled	12.0	8.3	* MAX 18.7% + AD S/Z	* see annex 1
1806.32.50	--Not filled	12.0	8.3	* MAX 18.7% + AD S/Z	* see annex 1
1806.90.49	-Other	12.0	8.3	* MAX 18.7% + AD S/Z	* see annex 1

68 Schedule LXXX, European Communities, Part I, Most-Favoured-Nation Tariff, Section I, Agricultural Products, Section I–A, Tariffs. See www.wto.org/english/ tratop_e/schedules_e/goods_schedules_e.htm, visited on 1 September 2004.

Figure 5.14 Excerpt from Chapter 18 of the Schedule of Concessions of the United States (cocoa and cocoa preparations)[69]

Tariff item number	Description of products	Base rate of duty			Bound rate of duty		Implementation period from/to	Special safeguard	Initial negotiating right
		Ad valorem (%)	Other	U/B	Ad valorem (%)	Other			
1	**2**	**3**			**4**		**5**	**6**	**7**
1806.10.28	Other.............	39.5¢/kg*				33.6¢/kg		SSG	
	Other:								
1806.10.34	Described in additional U.S. note 1 to this Chapter and entered pursuant to its provisions.	10.0			10.0		1995		
1806.10.38	Other.............		39.5¢/kg*			33.6¢/kg		SSG	
	Containing 90 per cent or more by dry weight of sugar: Articles containing over 65 per cent by dry weight of sugar described in additional U.S. note 3 to Chapter 17:								
1806.10.45	Described in additional U.S. note 4 to Chapter 17 and entered pursuant to its provisions............	10.0			10.0		1995		
1806.10.55	Other.............		39.5¢/kg*			33.6¢/kg	1995	SSG	
	Other:								
1806.10.65	Described in additional U.S. note 1 to this Chapter and entered pursuant to its provisions.	10.0			10.0		1995		
1806.10.75	Other.............		39.5¢/kg*			33.6¢/kg		SSG	

Heading	Article Description	Rates of Duty 1 General	Special		Rates of Duty 2
1806.20	Other preparations in blocks, slabs or bars weighing more than 2 kg or in liquid, paste, powder, granular or other bulk form in containers or immediate packings, of a content exceeding 2 kg: Preparations consisting wholly of ground cocoa beans, with or without added cocoa fat, flavoring or emulsifying agents, and containing not more than 32 percent by weight of butterfat or other milk solids and not more than 60 percent by weight of sugar:				
1806.20.20	In blocks or slabs weighing 4.5 kg or more each...............	0.0			0.0
	Other:				
	Containing butterfat or other milk solids: Containing over 5.5 per cent by weight of butterfat:				
1806.20.24	Described in additional U.S. note 2 to this Chapter and its provisions...............	5.0		1995	5.0
	Other:				

1806.20.26	Containing less than 21 per cent by weight of milk solids........	5.0	+ 43.8¢/kg*		4.3	+ 37.2¢/kg		SSG
1806.20.28	Other........	5.0	+ 62.1¢/kg*		4.3	+ 52.8¢/kg		SSG
	Other:							
1806.20.34	Described in additional U.S. note 3 to this Chapter and entered pursuant to its provisions........	5.0			5.0		1995	
1806.20.36	Containing less than 21 per cent by weight of milk solids........	5.0	+ 43.8¢/kg*		4.3	+ 37.2¢/kg		SSG
1806.20.38	Other........	5.0	+ 62.1¢/kg*		4.3	+ 52.8¢/kg		SSG
1806.20.50	Other........	5.0			4.3			
1806.20.60	Confectioners coatings and other products (except confectionery) containing by weight not less than 6.8 per cent non-fat solids of the cocoa bean nib and not less than 15 per cent of vegetable fats other than cocoa butter.	2.5			2.0			
	Other:							
	Containing more than 65 per cent by weight of sugar: Articles containing over 65 per cent by dry weight of sugar described in additional U.S. note 3 to Chapter 17:							

1806.20.71	Described in additional U.S. note 4 to Chapter 17 and entered pursuant to its provisions....	10.0		10.0		1995	
1806.20.73	Other................	10.0	+ 35.9¢/kg*	8.5	+ 30.5¢/kg		SSG
	Articles containing over 10 per cent by dry weight of sugar described in additional U.S. note 5 to Chapter 17:						
1806.20.75	Described in additional U.S. note 6 to Chapter 17 and entered pursuant to its provisions...	10.0		10.0		1995	
1806.20.77	Other....................	10.0	+ 35.9¢/kg*	8.5	+ 30.5¢/kg		SSG
1806.20.79	Other....................	10.0		8.5			
	Other: Dairy products described in additional U.S. note 8 to Chapter 4:						
1806.20.81	Described in additional U.S. note 9 to Chapter 4 and entered pursuant to its provisions............	10.0		10.0		1995	
	Other:						
1806.20.82	Containing less than 21 per cent by weight of milk solids...........	10.0	+ 43.8¢/kg*	8.5	+ 37.2¢/kg		SSG
1806.20.83	Other....................	10.0	+ 62.1¢/kg	8.5	+ 52.8¢/kg		SSG
	Low fat chocolate crumb:						

1806.20.85	Described in additional U.S. note 3 to this Chapter and entered pursuant to its provisions.....	10.0		10.0		
	Other:					
1806.20.87	Containing less than 21 per cent by weight of milk solids.....	10.0	+ 43.8¢/kg*	8.5	+ 37.2¢/kg	SSG
1806.20.89	Other......	10.0	+ 62.1¢/kg*	8.5	+ 52.8¢/kg	SSG
	Other:					
1806.20.91	Described in additional U.S. note 7 to Chapter 17 and entered pursuant to its provisions......	10.0		10.0		1995
	Blended syrups described in additional U.S. note 4 to Chapter 18:					
	Other:					
1806.20.92	Containing less than 21 per cent by weight of milk solids.....	10.0	+ 43.8¢/kg*	8.5	+ 37.2¢/kg	SSG
1806.20.93	Other......	10.0	+ 62.1¢/kg*	8.5	+ 52.8¢/kg	SSG
	Articles containing over 10 per cent by dry weight of sugar described in additional U.S. note 5 to Chapter 17:					

		General			Special			
1806.20.95	Described in additional U.S. note 6 to Chapter 17 and entered pursuant to its provisions.............	10.0			10.0			
	Other:							
1806.20.96	Containing less than 21 per cent by weight of milk solids.............	10.0 + 43.8¢/kg*			8.5 + 37.2¢/kg		1995	SSG
1806.20.97	Other.............	10.0 + 62.1¢/kg*			8.5 + 52.8¢/kg			SSG
1806.20.99	Other.............	10.0			8.5			
	Other, in blocks, slabs or bars:							
1806.31.00	Filled.................	7.0			5.6			
1806.32	Not filled: Preparations consisting wholly of ground cocoa beans, with or without added cocoa fat, flavoring or emulsifying agents, and containing not more than 32 per cent by weight of butterfat or other milk solids and not more than 60 per cent by weight							
1806.32.04	Described in additional U.S. note 2 to this Chapter and entered pursuant to its provisions.............	5.0			5.0		1995	
	Other:							

1806.32.06	Containing less than 21 per cent by weight of milk solids............	5.0	+ 43.8¢/kg*	4.3	+ 37.2¢/kg	SSG
1806.32.08	Other.............	5.0	+ 62.1¢/kg*	4.3	+ 52.8¢/kg	SSG
	Other:					
1806.32.14	Described in additional U.S. note 3 to this Chapter and entered pursuant to its provisions............	5.0		5.0		1995
	Other:					
1806.32.16	Containing less than 21 per cent by weight of milk solids............	5.0	+ 43.8¢/kg*	4.3	+ 37.2¢/kg	SSG
1806.32.18	Other.............	5.0	+ 62.1¢/kg*	4.3	+ 52.8¢/kg	SSG
1806.32.30	Other.............	5.0		4.3		
1806.32.60	Described in additional U.S. note 8 to Chapter 4:	7.0		7.0		1995
	Other: Dairy products described in additional U.S. note 9 to Chapter 4 and entered pursuant to its provisions............					
1806.32.70	Containing less than 21 per cent by weight of milk solids............	7.0	+ 43.8¢/kg*	6.0	+ 37.2¢/kg	SSG
	Other:					
1806.32.80	Other.............	7.0	+ 62.1¢/kg*	6.0	+ 52.8¢/kg	SSG
1806.32.90	Other.............	7.0		6.0		
1806.90	Other:					

HTS No.	Article Description						
	Dairy products described in additional U.S. note 8 to Chapter 4:						
1806.90.05	Described in additional U.S. note 9 to Chapter 4 and entered pursuant to its provisions............	7.0		3.5			
	Other:............						
1806.90.08	Containing less than 21 per cent by weight of milk solids........	7.0	+ 43.8¢/kg*	6.0	+ 37.2¢/kg		SSG
1806.90.10	Other:............	7.0	+ 62.1¢/kg*	6.0	+ 52.8¢/kg		SSG
	Other:						
	Containing butterfat or other milk solids: Containing over 5.5 per cent by weight of						
1806.90.15	Described in additional U.S. note 2 to this Chapter and entered pursuant to its provisions............	7.0		3.5			
	Other:						
1806.90.18	Containing less than 21 per cent by weight of milk solids.........	7.0	+ 43.8¢/kg*	6.0	+ 37.2¢/kg		SSG
1806.90.20	Other:......	7.0	+ 62.1¢/kg*	6.0	+ 52.8¢/kg		SSG

411

	Other:					
1806.90.25	Described in additional U.S. note 3 to this Chapter and entered pursuant to its provisions......	7.0		3.5		
	Other:					
1806.90.28	Containing less than 21 per cent by weight of milk solids......	7.0	+ 43.8¢/kg*	6.0	+ 37.2¢/kg	SSG
1806.90.30	Other.........	7.0	+ 62.1¢/kg*	6.0	+ 52.8¢/kg	SSG
	Other:					
1806.90.35	Described in additional U.S. note 7 to Chapter 17 and entered pursuant to its provisions......	7.0		3.5		
	Blended syrups described in additional U.S. note 4 to chapter 18:					
	Other:					
1806.90.38	Containing less than 21 per cent by weight of milk solids......	7.0	+ 43.8¢/kg*	6.0	+ 37.2¢/kg	SSG
1806.90.40	Other......	7.0	+ 62.1¢/kg*	6.0	+ 52.8¢/kg	SSG
	Articles containing over 65 per cent by dry weight of sugar described in additional U.S. note 3 to Chapter 17:					

1806.90.45	Described in additional U.S. note 4 to Chapter 17 and entered pursuant to its provisions........	7.0		3.5		
	Other:					
1806.90.48	Containing less than 21 per cent by weight of milk solids.........	7.0	+ 43.8¢/kg*	6.0	+ 37.2¢/kg	SSG
1806.90.50	Other................ ...	7.0	+ 62.1¢/kg*	6.0	+ 52.8¢/kg	SSG
	Articles containing over 10 per cent by dry weight of suga described in additional U.S. note 5 to Chapter 17:					
1806.90.55	Described in additional U.S. note 6 to Chapter 17 and entered pursuant to its provisions.......	7.0		3.5		
	Other:					
1806.90.58	Containing less than 21 per cent by weight of milk solids.........	7.0	+ 43.8¢/kg*	6.0	+ 37.2¢/kg	SSG
1806.90.60	Other................ ...	7.0	+ 62.1¢/kg*	6.0	+ 52.8¢/kg	SSG
1806.90.90	Other..............	7.0		6.0		

[69] Schedule XX, United States, Part I, Most-Favoured-Nation Tariff, Section I, Agricultural Products, Section I-A, Tariffs. See www.wto.org/english/tratop_e/schedules_e/goods_schedules_e.htm, visited on 1 September 2004.

Figure 5.15 Excerpt from Chapter 18 of the Schedule of Concessions of India (cocoa and cocoa preparations)[70]

Tariff item number	Description of products	Base rate of duty			Bound rate of duty		Implementation period from/to	Special safeguard	Initial negotiating right	Other duties and charges
		Ad valorem (%)	Other	U/B	Ad valorem (%)	Other				
1	2	3			4		5	6	7	8
1801.00	Cocoa beans, whole or broken, raw or roasted	140			100					
1802.00	Cocoa shells, husks, skins and other cocoa waste	140			100					
1803.10	-Not defatted	140			100					
1803.20	-Wholly or partly defatted	140			100					
1804.00	Cocoa butter, fat and oil	140			100					
1805.00	Cocoa powder, not containing added sugar or other sweetening matter	140			150					
1806.10	-Cocoa powder, containing added sugar or other sweetening matter	140			150					

		140		150			
1806.20	-Other preparations in block slabs or bars weighing more than 2 kg orin liquid, paste, powder, granular or other bulk form in containers or immediate packings,of a content exceeding 2 kg	140		150			
1806.31	--Filled	140		150			
1806.32	--Not filled	140		150			
1806.90	-Other	140		150			

[70] Schedule XII, India, Part I, Most-Favoured-Nation Tariff, Section I, Agricultural Products, Section I-A Tariffs. See www.wto.org/english/ tratop_e/schedules_e/goods_schedules_e.htm, visited on 1 September 2004.

Figure 5.16 Excerpt from Chapter 18 of the Schedule of Concessions of Brazil (cocoa and cocoa preparations)[71]

Numéro du tarif	Désignation des produits	Taux de base du droit			Taux consolidé du droit		Période de mise en oeuvre, de/à	Sauvegarde spéciale
		Ad valorem (%)	Autre	C/NC	Ad valorem (%)	Autre		
1	2	3			4		5	6
1801	Cacao en fèves et brisures de fèves, bruts ou torréfiés:							
1801.01.00	brut	55.0			35.0		1995/2004	
1801.02.00	torréfiés	55.0			35.0		1995/2004	
1802	Coques, pellicules (pelures) et autres déchets de cacao	55.0			35.0		1995/2004	
1803	Pâte de cacao, même dégraissée:							
1803.10	non dégraissée:							
1803.10.0100	Pâte de cacao, raffinée (liqueur de cacao), en flocons ou en blocs	85.0			35.0		1995/2004	
1803.10.9900	autres	85.0			35.0		1995/2004	
1803.20	complètement ou partiellement dégraissée:							
1803.20.0100	Pâte de cacao, raffinée (liqueur de cacao), en flocons ou en blocs	85.0			35.0		1995/2004	
1803.20.9900	autres	85.0			35.0		1995/2004	
1804	Beurre, graisse et huile de cacao	85.0			35.0		1995/2004	
1805	Poudre de cacao, sans addition de sucre ou d'autres édulcorants	85.0			35.0		1995/2004	
1806	Chocolat et autres préparations alimentaires contenant du cacao:							
1806.10.0000	Poudre de cacao, avec addition de sucre ou d'autres édulcorants	85.0			35.0		1995/2004	
1806.20	autres préparations présentées soit en blocs ou en barres d'un poids excédant 2 kg, soit à l'état liquide ou pâteux ou en pou dres, granulés ou formes similaires, en récipients ou en emballages immédiats, d'un contenu excédant 2 kg							
1806.20.01	Chocolat:							
1806.20.0101	en poudre	85.0			35.0		1995/2004	
1806.20.0102	en granulés	85.0			35.0		1995/2004	
1806.20.0103	sous forme de pâte	85.0			35.0		1995/2004	
1806.20.0199	autres	85.0			35.0		1995/2004	
1806.20.0200	Préparations pour l'alimentation des enfants ou à usage diététique ou culinaire, fabriquées à base de farines, d'amidons, de fécules ou d'extraits de malt, contenant au moins 50 % de cacao	85.0			35.0		1995/2004	

1806.20.0300	Sucreries au lait	85.0	35.0	1995/2004
1806.20.0400	Gelées et pâtes de fruits	85.0	35.0	1995/2004
1806.20.9900	autres	85.0	35.0	1995/2004
1806.31	autres, présentés en tablettes, barres ou bâtons:			
	fourrés:			
1806.31.0100	Chocolat	85.0	25.0	1995/2004
1806.31.0200	Sucreries au lait	85.0	25.0	1995/2004
1806.31.0300	Nougat	85.0	25.0	1995/2004
1806.31.9900	autres	85.0	25.0	1995/2004
1806.32	non fourrés:			
1806.32.0100	Chocolat	85.0	25.0	1995/2004
1806.32.0200	Sucreries au lait	85.0	25.0	1995/2004
1806.32.0500	Nougat	85.0	25.0	1995/2004
1806.32.9900	autres	85.0	25.0	1995/2004
1806.90	autres:			
1806.90.01	Chocolat:			
1806.90.0101	en poudre	85.0	25.0	1995/2004
1806.90.0102	en granulés	85.0	25.0	1995/2004
1806.90.0103	sous forme de pâte	85.0	25.0	1995/2004
1806.90.0199	autres	85.0	25.0	1995/2004
1806.90.0200	Préparations pour l'alimentation des enfants ou à usage diététique ou culinaire, fabriquées à base de farines, d'amidons, de fécules ou d'extraits de malt, contenant au moins 50 % de cacao	85.0	35.0	1995/2004
1806.90.0300	Sucreries au lait	85.0	25.0	1995/2004
1806.90.0400	Bonbons	85.0	35.0	1995/2004
1806.90.0500	Caramels	85.0	35.0	1995/2004
1806.90.0600	Gelées et pâtes de fruits	85.0	35.0	1995/2004
1806.90.0700	Arachides confites enrobées de chocolat	85.0	25.0	1995/2004
1806.90.9900	autres	85.0	25.0	1995/2004

[71] Schedule III, Brazil, Part I, Most-Favoured-Nation Tariff, Section I, Agricultural Products, Section I-A, Tariffs. See www.wto.org/english/tratop_e/schedules_e/goods_schedules_e.htm, visited on 1 September 2004.

Figure 5.17 Excerpt from Chapter 18 of the Schedule of Concessions of China (cocoa and cocoa preparations)[72]

HS	Description	Bound rate at date of accession	Final Bound rate	Implementation	Present concession established	INR LV,MX,US	Concession first incorporated in a GATT Schedule INRs	Earlier INRs	ODCs
1801	Cocoa beans, whole or broken, raw or roasted:								
18010000	Cocoa beans, whole or broken, raw or roasted	9.2	8	2004			BO,CO,DO,EC,HN,MY, NI,PA,US		0
1802	Cocoa shells, husks, husks, skins and other cocoa waste:								
18020000	Cocoa shells, husks, skins and other cocoa waste	10					US		0
1803	Cocoa paste, whether or not defatted:								
18031000	- Not defatted	10					US		0
18032000	- Wholly or partly defatted	10					SG,US		0
1804	Cocoa butter, fat and oil:								
18040000	Cocoa butter, fat and oil	29.8	22	2004			MY,US		0
1805	Cocoa powder, not containing added sugar								
18050000	Cocoa powder, not containing added sugar or other sweetening matter:	18	15	2004			MY,US		0
1806	Chocolate and other food preparations containing cocoa:								
18061000	- Cocoa powder, containing added sugar or other sweetening matter	10					CO,MY,US		0
18062000	- Other preparations in blocks, slabs or bars weighing more than 2kg or in liquid, paste, powder, granular or other bulk form in containers or immediate packings, of a content exceeding 2 kg	11.2	10	2004			AU,CH,US		0
	- Other, in blocks, slabs or bars:								
18063100	– Filled	10.4	8	2004			AU,CH,EC,LV,US		0
18063200	– Not filled	11.2	10	2004			CH,LV,US		0
18069000	– Other	10.4	8	2004			AU,CH,EC,JP,LV,SG,U		0

[72] Schedule CLII, People's Republic of China, WT/ACC/CHN/49/Add.1, WT/MIN(01)/3/Add.1, http://www.wto.org/english/thewto_e/acc_e/completeacc_e.htm, and http://www.mofcom.gov.cn/table/wto/02B.doc, visited on 1 September 2004.

basis of the Harmonised System's nomenclature; requests for, and offers of, concessions were normally made in terms of this nomenclature. For that reason, the Appellate Body expressed surprise in *EC – Computer Equipment* that neither the European Communities nor the United States argued before the Panel that the Harmonised System and its Explanatory Notes were relevant in the interpretation of Schedule LXXX of the European Communities. The Appellate Body ruled:

> We believe ... that a proper interpretation of Schedule LXXX should have included an examination of the *Harmonized System* and its *Explanatory Notes*.[73]

According to the Appellate Body, decisions of the World Customs Organization regarding the Harmonised System may also be relevant to the interpretation of tariff concessions and should therefore be examined.[74]

Finally, note that the consistent classification practice at the time of the tariff negotiations is also relevant to the interpretation of tariff concessions.[75] As the Appellate Body noted in *EC – Computer Equipment*, the classification practice during the Uruguay Round is part of 'the circumstances of [the] conclusion' of the *WTO Agreement*. Therefore, this practice may be used as a supplementary means of interpretation within the meaning of Article 32 of the *Vienna Convention*.[76]

Questions and Assignments 5.5

What are tariff concessions or tariff bindings? Where can you find the tariff concessions or tariff bindings agreed to by a Member? Do Argentina, Mali, Thailand and the Netherlands each have a tariff schedule? Find out what, if any, is the tariff binding of your country on photographic cameras and on goat meat. How are tariff schedules and tariff concessions to be interpreted? Whose obligation is it to ensure that the scope of tariff concessions is unambiguous?

5.2.4. Protection of tariff concessions

As noted above, under WTO law, customs duties are not prohibited. This does not mean, however, that there are no rules on customs duties. WTO rules on customs duties relate primarily to the protection of tariff concessions or bindings agreed to in the context of tariff negotiations. The basic rules are set out in Article II:1 of the GATT 1994.

---

[73] Appellate Body Report, *EC – Computer Equipment*, para. 89.
[74] *Ibid.*, para. 90.   [75] On tariff classification, see below, pp. 425–9.
[76] See above, pp. 208–9. See also Appellate Body Report, *EC –Computer Equipment*, paras. 92 and 95. Note that, while the prior classification practice of only *one* of the parties may be relevant, it is clearly of more limited value than the practice of all parties. See *ibid.*, para. 93.

5.2.4.1. Articles II:1(a) and II:1(b), first sentence, of the GATT 1994

Article II:1 of the GATT 1994 states:

> a. Each [Member] shall accord to the commerce of the other [Members] treatment no less favourable than that provided for in the appropriate Part of the appropriate Schedule annexed to this Agreement.
> b. The products described in Part I of the Schedule relating to any [Member], which are the products of territories of other [Members], shall, on their importation into the territory to which the Schedule relates, and subject to the terms, conditions or qualifications set forth in that Schedule, be exempt from ordinary customs duties in excess of those set forth and provided therein ...

Article II:1(a) provides that Members shall accord to products imported from other Members *treatment no less favourable* than that provided for in their Schedule. Article II:1(b), first sentence, provides that products described in Part I of the Schedule of any Member shall, on importation, be *exempt from ordinary customs duties in excess of* those set out in the Schedule. This means that products may not be subjected to customs duties above the tariff concessions or bindings. With respect to the relationship between Article II:1(a) and Article II:1(b), first sentence, the Appellate Body noted in *Argentina – Textiles and Apparel*:

> Paragraph (a) of Article II:1 contains a general prohibition against according treatment less favourable to imports than that provided for in a Member's Schedule. Paragraph (b) prohibits a specific kind of practice that will always be inconsistent with paragraph (a): that is, the application of ordinary customs duties in excess of those provided for in the Schedule.[77]

The requirement of Article II:1(b), first sentence, that a Member may not impose customs duties *in excess of* the duties set out in its Schedule was at issue in *Argentina – Textiles and Apparel*. In its Schedule, Argentina has bound its customs duties on textiles and apparel to 35 per cent *ad valorem*. In practice, however, these products were subject to the higher of *either* a 35 per cent *ad valorem* duty *or* a minimum specific import duty (the so-called 'DIEM'). The Panel found the DIEM to be inconsistent with Argentina's obligations under Article II:1(b) of the GATT 1994 for two reasons:

- first, because Argentina applied a different *type* of import duty (a specific duty) than that set out in its Schedule (an *ad valorem* duty); and
- secondly, because the DIEM would, in certain cases, be in excess of the binding of 35 per cent *ad valorem*.

On appeal, the Appellate Body agreed with the Panel that the DIEM was inconsistent with Argentina's obligations under Article II:1(b), but it considerably modified the Panel's reasoning. The Appellate Body first noted:

> The principal obligation in the first sentence of Article II:1(b) ... requires a Member to refrain from imposing ordinary customs duties *in excess of* those provided for in that Member's Schedule. However, the text of Article II:1(b), first sentence, does not

---

[77] Appellate Body Report, *Argentina – Textiles and Apparel*, para. 45.

address whether applying a *type* of duty different from the *type* provided for in a Member's Schedule is inconsistent, in itself, with that provision.[78]

According to the Appellate Body, the application of a type of duty different from the type provided for in a Member's Schedule is only inconsistent with Article II:1(b) *to the extent that* it results in customs duties being imposed in excess of those set forth in that Member's Schedule.[79] In *Argentina – Textiles and Apparel*, the Appellate Body concluded:

> In this case, we find that Argentina has acted inconsistently with its obligations under Article II:1(b), first sentence, of the GATT 1994, because the DIEM regime, by its structure and design, results, with respect to a certain range of import prices in any relevant tariff category to which it applies, in the levying of customs duties in excess of the bound rate of 35 per cent *ad valorem* in Argentina's Schedule.[80]

As Article II:1(b), first sentence, explicitly states, the obligation to exempt products from customs duties in excess of those set forth in the Schedule is 'subject to the terms, conditions or qualifications set forth in that Schedule'. In *Canada – Dairy*, the Appellate Body ruled in this respect:

> In our view, the ordinary meaning of the phrase "subject to" is that such concessions are without prejudice to and are *subordinated to*, and are, therefore, *qualified by*, any "terms, conditions or qualifications" inscribed in a Member's Schedule … A strong presumption arises that the language which is inscribed in a Member's Schedule under the heading "Other Terms and Conditions", has some *qualifying* or *limiting* effect on the substantive content or scope of the concession or commitment.[81]

Consider the example of 'terms, conditions and qualifications' in the 'comments' column of the EC Schedule, which limit the content or scope of tariff concessions on seeds, as shown in Figure 5.18.

5.2.4.2. *Tariff concessions and customs duties actually applied*

Finally, a note on the difference between tariff concessions or bindings and the customs duties actually applied. As the Appellate Body noted in *Argentina – Textiles and Apparel*:

> A tariff binding in a Member's Schedule provides an upper limit on the amount of duty that may be imposed, and a Member is permitted to impose a duty that is less than that provided for in its Schedule.[82]

[78] *Ibid.*, para. 46.   [79] *Ibid.*, para. 55.   [80] *Ibid.*
[81] Appellate Body Report, *Canada – Dairy*, para. 134. At issue in *Canada – Dairy* was a tariff quota (see below, p. 443) for fluid milk of 64,500 tonnes included in Canada's Schedule. In the column 'Other Terms and Conditions' of Canada's Schedule, it states that 'this quantity [64,500 tonnes] represents the estimated annual cross-border purchases imported by Canadian consumers'. In practice, Canada restricted imports under the 64,500 tonnes tariff quota to dairy products for the personal use of the importer and his household not exceeding C\$20 in value for each importation. The United States contested that the restriction of access to imports for personal use not exceeding C\$20 in value constituted a violation of Article II:1(b) of the GATT 1994. The Panel agreed with the United States. The Panel found that the 'condition' in Canada's Schedule is *descriptive* and does not establish restrictions on access to the tariff quota for fluid milk. The Appellate Body disagreed with the Panel that the 'condition' was merely descriptive, and concluded that the limitation of cross-border purchases to 'Canadian consumers' referred to in Canada's Schedule justifies Canada's effective limitation of access to the tariff quota to imports for 'personal use'.
[82] Appellate Body Report, *Argentina – Textiles and Apparel*, para. 46.

Figure 5.18 Terms, conditions and qualifications in the EC Schedule

Tariff item number	Description of products	Base rate of duty		Bound rate of duty	Implementa-tion period from/to	Special safeguard	Initial negotiating right	Other duties and charges	Comments
		Ad valorem (%)	Other	Ad valorem (%)					
1	2	3		4	5	6	7	8	9
1209.21.00	--Lucerne (alfalfa) seed	5.0		2.5	*				* 2.5% to be applied from 1995
1209.22.50	--Clover (Trifolium spp.) seed	4.0		0.0	*				* 2% to be applied during 1995 and 1996
1209.23	--Fescue seed:								
1209.23.10	---Meadow fescue (Festuca pratensis Huds.) seed and red fescue (Festuca rubra L.) seed	4.0		0.0	*				* 2% to be applied during 1995 and 1996
1209.23.60	---Other	5.0		2.5	*				* 2.5% to be applied from 1995
1209.24.00	--Kentucky blue grass (Poa pratensis L.) seed	4.0		0.0	*				* 2% to be applied during 1995 and 1996

For many Members, tariff bindings for industrial products are considerably higher than the customs duties actually applied to these products. This means that the customs duties applied are significantly lower than the maximum levels agreed upon. For example, the simple average bound tariff of Costa Rica is about 45 per cent, while its average applied tariff is just above 6 per cent.[83] Likewise, the simple average bound tariff of Turkey is around 43 per cent, while its average applied tariff is 8 per cent.[84] To the extent that this reflects a unilateral lowering of tariff barriers and thus allows for more trade, the difference between bound tariffs and the lower applied tariffs is to be welcomed. However, this difference also gives the importing Members concerned ample opportunity to increase the applied tariffs, namely, up to the level of the tariff binding. The tariff bindings thus do not give exporting Members and traders much security and predictability with respect to the level of the customs duties that will actually be applied on the imported products.

Questions and Assignments 5.6

Which provisions of the GATT 1994 prohibit the imposition of customs duties higher than the tariff concession? What is the relationship between Article II:1(a) and Article II:1(b), first sentence? Is the application of a type

[83] See WTO Secretariat, *Market Access: Unfinished Business*, Special Studies 6 (WTO, 2001), 2.
[84] *Ibid.*

of duty different from the type provided for in a Member's Schedule inconsistent with Article II:1(b), first sentence? Can tariff concessions be subject to terms and conditions? Can a Member impose customs duties lower than the tariff concession? Is this a problem?

5.2.5. Modification or withdrawal of tariff concessions

As discussed above, Members may not apply customs duties above the tariff concessions or bindings agreed to in tariff negotiations. However, the GATT 1994 provides a procedure for the modification or withdrawal of the agreed tariff concessions. Article XXVIII:1 of the GATT 1994 states, in relevant part:

> a [Member] ... may, by negotiation and agreement ... modify or withdraw a concession included in the appropriate schedule annexed to this Agreement.

The negotiations on the modification or withdrawal of tariff concessions are to be conducted with:

- the Members that hold so-called 'Initial Negotiating Rights' (INRs); and
- any other Member that has a 'principal supplying interest'.

The Members holding INRs are those Members with which the concession was bilaterally negotiated, initially. As mentioned above, INRs are commonly specified in the Schedule of the Member granting the concession but can also be determined on the basis of the negotiation records. Due to the approach to tariff negotiations adopted during the Uruguay Round,[85] most tariff concessions did not result from bilateral negotiations and thus INRs are virtually non-existent in respect of concessions agreed during the Uruguay Round.[86] It was therefore agreed in the Uruguay Round *Understanding on Article XXVIII* that:

> Any Member having a principal supplying interest ... in a concession which is modified or withdrawn shall be accorded an initial negotiating right.[87]

A Member has a 'principal supplying interest' if, as provided in Note *Ad* Article XXVIII, paragraph 1.4:

> that [Member] has had, over a reasonable period of time prior to the negotiations, a larger share in the market of the applicant [Member] than a Member with which the concession was initially negotiated or would ... have had such a share in the absence of discriminatory quantitative restrictions maintained by the applicant [Member].

Furthermore, the Note *Ad* Article XXVIII, paragraph 1.5, states:

> the [Ministerial Conference] may exceptionally determine that a [Member] has a principal supplying interest if the concession in question affects trade which constitutes a major part of the total exports of such [Member].

---

[85] See above, p. 396.
[86] A. Hoda, *Tariff Negotiations and Renegotiations under the GATT and the WTO: Procedures and Practice* (WTO/ Cambridge University Press, 2001), 136.
[87] *Understanding on the Implementation of Article XXVIII of the GATT 1994*, para. 7.

Finally, the *Understanding on Article XXVIII*, paragraph 1, provides with respect to the concept of 'principal supplying interest':

> the Member which has the highest ratio of exports affected by the concession (i.e. exports of the product to the market of the Member modifying or withdrawing the concession) to its total exports shall be deemed to have a principal supplying interest if it does not already have an initial negotiating right or a principal supplying interest as provided for in paragraph 1 of Article XXVIII.

Pursuant to Article XXVIII, the *negotiations* on the modification or withdrawal of a tariff concession are to be conducted only with the Members holding INRs or those having a principal supplying interest. However, the Member wishing to modify or withdraw a tariff concession must *consult* any other Member that has a substantial interest in such concession.[88] The Note *Ad* Article XXVIII, paragraph 1.7, states:

> The expression "substantial interest" is not capable of a precise definition and accordingly may present difficulties ... It is, however, intended to be construed to cover only those [Members] which have, or in the absence of discriminatory quantitative restrictions affecting their exports could reasonably be expected to have, a significant share in the market of the [Member] seeking to modify or withdraw the concession.

A 'significant share', required to claim a 'substantial interest', has generally been considered to be 10 per cent of the market of the Member seeking to modify or withdraw a tariff concession. With respect to the objective of the negotiations and agreement on the modification or withdrawal of tariff concessions, Article XXVIII:2 provides:

> In such negotiations and agreement ... the [Members] concerned shall endeavour to maintain a general level of reciprocal and mutually advantageous concessions not less favourable to trade than that provided for in this Agreement prior to such negotiations.

When a tariff concession is modified or withdrawn, compensation in the form of new concessions needs to be granted to maintain a general level of concessions not less favourable to trade.

It follows from the above that the modification or withdrawal of a tariff binding is based on the principle of renegotiation and compensation. However, if the negotiations fail to lead to an agreement, Article XXVIII:3(a) provides, in relevant part, that:

> the [Member] which proposes to modify or withdraw the concession shall, nevertheless, be free to do so.

In that case, any Member holding an INR, any Member having a principal supplying interest *and* any Member having a substantial interest shall be free to withdraw substantially equivalent concessions.[89]

---

[88] See Article XXVIII:1 of the GATT 1994. The Ministerial Conference determines which Members have a 'substantial interest'; see *ibid*.

[89] See Article XXVIII:3 of the GATT 1994.

Can tariff concessions or bindings, set forth in a Member's Schedule, be modified or withdrawn? Which Members hold INRs? Which Members have a 'principal supplying interest' and which Members have a 'substantial interest' in the concession to be modified or withdrawn? Why is this important? Can a tariff concession or binding be modified or withdrawn without agreement on compensation?

5.2.6. Imposition of customs duties

In addition to rules for the protection of tariff concessions, WTO law also provides for rules on the manner in which customs duties must be imposed. The imposition of customs duties may require three determinations to be made:

- the determination of the proper classification of the imported good;
- the determination of the customs value of the imported good; and
- the determination of the origin of the imported good.

The need for these determinations follows from the fact that customs duties differ from good to good; are *ad valorem* duties and thus calculated on the basis of the value of the products concerned; and may differ depending on the exporting country.

5.2.6.1. *Customs classification*

The WTO agreements do not specifically address the issue of customs classification. In *spain – Unroasted Coffee*, the Panel ruled:

> that there was no obligation under the GATT to follow any particular system for classifying goods, and that a contracting party had the right to introduce in its customs tariff new positions or sub-positions as appropriate.[90]

However, in classifying products for customs purposes, Members have of course to consider their general obligations under the WTO agreements, such as the MFN treatment obligation. As discussed in Chapter 4, the Panel in *Spain – Unroasted Coffee* ruled that:

> whatever the classification adopted, Article I:1 required that the same tariff treatment be applied to "like products".[91]

Specific rules on classification can be found in the *International Convention on the Harmonised Commodity Description and Coding System*, which entered into force on

---

[90] GATT Panel Report, *Spain – Unroasted Coffee*, para. 4.4.
[91] *Ibid.* See also above, pp. 314–16; and GATT Panel Report, *Japan – SPF Dimension Lumber*, para. 5.9.

1 January 1988 and to which most WTO Members are a party.[92] The Harmonised Commodity Description and Coding System, commonly referred to as the 'Harmonised System' or HS, is an *international commodity classification system*, developed under the auspices of the Brussels-based Customs Cooperation Council (CCC), known today as the World Customs Organization (WCO).[93]

The Harmonised System consists of 21 sections covering 99 Chapters, 1,241 headings and over 5,000 commodity groups. The sections and chapters are:

- Section I (Chapters 1–5, live animals and animal products);
- Section II (Chapters 6–14, vegetable products);
- Section III (Chapter 15, animal or vegetable fats and oils);
- Section IV (Chapters 16–24, prepared foodstuffs, beverages and spirits, tobacco);
- Section V (Chapters 25–27, mineral products);
- Section VI (Chapters 28–38, chemical products);
- Section VII (Chapters 39–40, plastics and rubber);
- Section VIII (Chapters 41–43, leather and travel goods);
- Section IX (Chapters 44–46, wood, charcoal, cork);
- Section X (Chapters 47–49, wood pulp, paper and paperboard articles);
- Section XI (Chapters 50–63, textiles and textile products);
- Section XII (Chapters 64–67, footwear, umbrellas, artificial flowers);
- Section XIII (Chapters 68–70, stone, cement, ceramic, glass);
- Section XIV (Chapter 71, pearls, precious metals);
- Section XV (Chapters 72–83, base metals);
- Section XVI (Chapters 84–85, electrical machinery);
- Section XVII (Chapters 86–89, vehicles, aircraft, vessels);
- Section XVIII (Chapters 90–92, optical instruments, clocks and watches, musical instruments);
- Section XIX (Chapter 93, arms and ammunition);
- Section XX (Chapters 94–96, furniture, toys, miscellaneous manufactured articles); and
- Section XXI (Chapter 97, works of art, antiques).[94]

By way of example, look at Chapter 97 of Section XXI of the Harmonised System, set out in Figure 5.19. Each commodity group has a six-digit HS code. For example, the HS Code for 'paintings, drawings and pastels' is 9701.10. Of this code, the first two digits refer to the Chapter, in this case Chapter 97 ('Works of art, collectors' pieces and antiques'), while the first four digits refer to the heading, in this case Heading 97.01 ('Paintings, drawings and pastels, entirely executed by hand ...').

---

[92] *International Convention on the Harmonised Commodity Description and Coding System*, Brussels, 14 June 1983, as amended by the Protocol of Amendment of 24 June 1986, *www.wcoomd.org/ie/En/Conventions/ conventions.html*, visited on 22 December 2003.

[93] The Harmonised System was developed not only for customs classification purposes, but also for the collection of trade statistics and for use in the context of various types of transactions in international trade (such as insurance and transport).

[94] Chapters 98 and 99 are reserved for special use by contracting parties.

Figure 5.19 Excerpt from the Harmonised System[95]

Chapter 97
Works of art, collectors' pieces and antiques

Notes.

1.-   This Chapter does not cover:

     (a)   Unused postage or revenue stamps, postal stationery (stamped paper) or the like, of heading 49.07;

     (b)   Theatrical scenery, studio back-cloths or the like, of painted canvas (heading 59.07) except if they may be classified in heading 97.06; or

     (c)   Pearls, natural or cultured, or precious or semi-precious stones (headings 71.01 to 71.03).

2.-   For the purposes of heading 97.02, the expression "original engravings, prints and lithographs" means impressions produced directly, in black and white or in colour, of one or of several plates wholly executed by hand by the artist, irrespective of the process or of the material employed by him, but not including any mechanical or photomechanical process.

3.-   Heading 97.03 does not apply to mass-produced reproductions or works of conventional craftsmanship of a commercial character, even if these articles are designed or created by artists.

4.-   (a)   Subject to Notes 1 to 3 above, articles of this Chapter are to be classified in this Chapter and not in any other Chapter of the Nomenclature.

     (b)   Heading 97.06 does not apply to articles of the preceding headings of this Chapter.

5.-   Frames around paintings, drawings, pastels, collages or similar decorative plaques, engravings, prints or lithographs are to be classified with those articles, provided they are of a kind and of a value normal to those articles. Frames which are not of a kind or of a value normal to the articles referred to in this Note are to be classified separately.

Heading	H.S. Code	
97.01		**Paintings, drawings and pastels, executed entirely by hand, other than drawings of heading 49.06 and other than hand-painted or hand-decorated manufactured articles; collages and similar decorative plaques**
	9701.10	- Paintings, drawings and pastels
	9701.90	- Other
97.02	9702.00	**Original engravings, prints and lithographs.**
97.03	9703.00	**Original sculptures and statuary, any material.**
97.04	9704.00	**Postage or revenue stamps, stamp-postmarks, first-day covers, postal stationery (stamped paper), and the like, used or unused, other than those of heading 49.07.**
97.05	9705.00	**Collections and collectors' pieces of zoological, botanical, mineralogical, anatomical, historical, archaeological, palaeontological, ethnographic or numismatic interest.**
97.06	9706.00	**Antiques of an age exceeding one hundred years.**

[95] http://www.wcoomd.org/ie/En/Topics_Issues/HarmonizedSystem/DocumentDB/2197E.pdf, visited on 23 December 2003.

To keep the Harmonised System up to date, to include new products (resulting from new technologies) and to take account of new developments in international trade, the Harmonised System is revised every four to six years.[96]

To allow for a systematic and uniform classification of goods, the Harmonised System provides not only for a structured list of commodity descriptions but also includes:

- General Rules for the Interpretation of the Harmonised System; and
- Explanatory Notes.

The General Rules for the Interpretation of the Harmonised System provide that the classification of goods shall be governed, *inter alia*, by the following principles:

- Incomplete or unfinished goods are classified as finished goods (in the event that they do not have their own line) when the goods already have the essential character of the complete or finished goods.[97]
- When goods are, *prima facie*, classifiable under two or more headings, classification shall be effected as follows:
  a. the heading which provides the most specific description shall be preferred to headings providing a more general description;[98]
  b. when goods cannot be classified as provided under (a), mixtures, composite goods consisting of different materials or made up of different components, and goods put up in sets for retail sale, shall be classified as if they consisted of the material or component which gives them their essential character;[99]
  c. when goods cannot be classified as provided under (a) or (b), they shall be classified under the heading which occurs last in numerical order among those which equally merit consideration.[100]
- Goods which cannot be classified in accordance with the above rules shall be classified under the heading appropriate to the goods to which they are most akin, i.e. with which they bear most likeness.[101]

The Explanatory Notes give the official interpretation of the Harmonised System as agreed by the WCO.[102]

WTO Members were not obliged under the GATT 1994, or under any other WTO agreement, to adopt the Harmonised System. However, as already noted, most WTO Members are a party to the *International Convention on the Harmonised System*. Article 3.1(a) of this Convention provides, in relevant part, that a party to the Convention:

---

[96] See Article 16 of the *International Convention on the Harmonised System*. To date, there have been revisions in 1992, 1996 and 2002.
[97] See General Rules for the Interpretation of the Harmonised System, para. 2(a).
[98] *Ibid.*, para. 3(a).   [99] *Ibid.*, para. 3(b).   [100] *Ibid.*, para. 3(c).
[101] *Ibid.*, para. 4.
[102] They are published in four volumes in English and French but are also available on CD-ROM, as part of a database giving the HS classification of more than 200,000 goods.

> undertakes that, in respect of its Customs tariff and statistical nomenclatures:
>   i. it shall use all the headings and subheadings of the Harmonized System without addition or modification, together with their related numerical codes;
>   ii. it shall apply the General Rules for the Interpretation of the Harmonized System and all the Section, Chapter and Subheading Notes, and shall not modify the scope of the Sections, Chapters, headings or subheadings of the Harmonized System; and
>   iii. it shall follow the numerical sequence of the Harmonized System.

Consequently, most WTO Members use the Harmonised System, its General Rules for the Interpretation of the Harmonised System and its Explanatory Notes in their national tariffs and for the customs classification of goods.

Although the Harmonised System is not part of WTO law, it can be relevant to the interpretation and application of WTO obligations. As discussed above, in *EC – Computer Equipment*, the Appellate Body expressed surprise that:

> Neither the European Communities nor the United States argued before the Panel that the *Harmonized System* and its *Explanatory Notes* were relevant in the interpretation of the terms of Schedule LXXX. We believe, however, that a proper interpretation of Schedule LXXX should have included an examination of the *Harmonized System* and its *Explanatory Notes*.[103]

Disputes between the importer and the relevant customs authorities on proper classification are resolved by national courts (see Article X of the GATT 1994 on access to courts). Parties to the *International Convention on the Harmonised System* may bring a dispute to the WCO for settlement.

Questions and Assignments 5.8

Are there any WTO rules on tariff classification? What is the Harmonised System? Discuss the key principles that govern the classification of goods set forth in the Rules for the Interpretation of the Harmonised System? Are these rules of any relevance in disputes on WTO rights and obligations?

5.2.6.2. Valuation for customs purposes

As previously explained, most customs duties are *ad valorem*. The customs administrations must therefore determine the value of the imported goods in order to be able to calculate the applicable duty.

Unlike for customs classification, the *WTO Agreement* provides for rules on customs valuation. These rules are set out in:

- Article VII of the GATT 1994, entitled 'Valuation for Customs Purposes';
- the Note *Ad* Article VII; and
- the WTO *Agreement on the Implementation of Article VII of the GATT 1994*.[104]

---

[103] Appellate Body Report, *EC – Computer Equipment*, para. 89. See above, pp. 400–1, 419.

[104] The WTO *Agreement on the Implementation of Article VII of the GATT 1994* replaced the 1979 Tokyo Round *Agreement on the Implementation of Article VII of the GATT*, but is not significantly different from this 1979 Agreement.

The latter agreement, commonly referred to as the *Customs Valuation Agreement*, elaborates the provisions of Article VII in order to provide greater uniformity and certainty in their implementation.

The core provision of Article VII on customs valuation is found in paragraph 2(a), which states:

> The value for customs purposes of imported merchandise should be based on the *actual value* of the imported merchandise on which duty is assessed, or of like merchandise, and should *not* be based on the value of merchandise of national origin or on arbitrary or fictitious values.
>
> [Emphasis added]

Paragraph 2(b) of Article VII defines the concept of the 'actual value' of goods as the price at which such or like goods are sold or offered for sale in the ordinary course of trade under fully competitive conditions.

Elaborating on and elucidating Article VII:2 of the GATT 1994, Article 1.1 of the *Customs Valuation Agreement* provides:

> The customs value of imported goods shall be the *transaction value*, that is the price actually paid or payable for the goods when sold for export to the country of importation adjusted in accordance with the provisions of Article 8, provided ... [105]
>
> [Emphasis added]

The primary basis for the customs value is thus the 'transaction value' of the imported goods, i.e. the price actually paid or payable for the goods. This price is normally shown in the invoice, contract or purchase order.[106] Article 1.1 is to be read together with Article 8 which provides for *adjustments* to be made to the price actually paid or payable, as discussed below.

Articles 2 to 7 of the *Customs Valuation Agreement* provide methods for determining the customs value whenever it cannot be determined under the provisions of Article 1. These methods to determine the customs value, other than the 'transaction value' method, are:

- the transaction value of identical goods (Article 2);[107]
- the transaction value of similar goods (Article 3);[108]

---

[105] Note that, in the proviso to Article 1.1, a number of situations are identified in which the transaction value cannot be used to determine the customs value. This is, for example, the case when there are certain restrictions on the use or disposition of the goods. Furthermore, as a rule, the buyer and seller should not be related (within the meaning of Article 15) but, if they are, the use of the transaction value is still acceptable if this relationship did not influence the price (see Article 1.2(a)) or the transaction value closely approximates a test value (see Article 1.2(b)).

[106] Pursuant to Article 17 of the *Customs Valuation Agreement*, customs administrations have the right to 'satisfy themselves as to the truth or accuracy of any statement, document or declaration'. In cases of doubt as to the truth or accuracy, customs administrations will first request the importer to provide further information and clarification. If reasonable doubt persists, the customs administration will not determine the customs value on the basis of the transaction value but will apply a different method of valuation (see below, pp. 430–1).

[107] Goods are 'identical' if they are the same in all respects, including physical characteristics, quality and reputation. 'Similar goods' means goods which, although not alike in all respects, have like characteristics and like component materials which enable them to perform the same functions and to be commercially interchangeable. In addition, goods shall not be regarded as 'similar' or 'identical' unless they are produced in the same country as the goods being valued. See Article 15.2 of the *Customs Valuation Agreement*.

[108] See above, footnote 107, p. 430.

- the deductive value method (Article 5);
- the computed value method (Article 6); and
- the fall-back method (Article 7).

These methods to determine the customs value of imported goods are to be applied in the above order.[109] Under the *deductive value method*, the customs value of imported goods is determined on the basis of the unit price at which the imported goods, or identical or similar imported goods, are sold at the greatest aggregate quantity to an unrelated buyer in the country of importation. The greatest aggregate quantity is the greatest number of units sold at one price.[110] Since the deductive value method uses the sale price in the country of importation as a basis for the calculation of the customs value, a number of deductions (for profits, general expenses, transport, etc.) are necessary to reduce the sale price to the relevant customs value. Under the *computed value method*, the customs value is determined on the basis of the computed value. The computed value is the sum of the production cost (i.e. the cost of materials and fabrication), profit and general expenses and other expenses (e.g. transport costs to the place or port of importation).[111]

The *fallback method*, set out in Article 7, applies when the customs value cannot be determined under any of the other four methods. Under this method, the customs value shall be:

> determined using reasonable means consistent with the principles and general provisions of this Agreement and of Article VII of the GATT 1994 and on the basis of the data available in the country of importation.[112]

However, the customs value of imported goods may never be determined on the basis of, for example:

- the selling price in the country of importation of goods produced in that country;
- the price of goods on the domestic market of the country of exportation;
- minimum customs values; or
- arbitrary or fictitious values.[113]

As mentioned above, the customs value of imported goods is – if possible and, usually, this is possible – determined on the basis of the transaction value of these goods. This transaction value must, however, be adjusted as provided for in Article 8 of the *Customs Valuation Agreement*. Pursuant to Article 8.1, the following costs and values, for example, must be added to the price actually paid or payable for the imported products:

---

[109] Article 4 of and Annex I, General Note, to the *Customs Valuation Agreement*. Note, however, that at the request of the importer the order of application of the deductive method (Article 5) and the computed method (Article 6) may be reversed (*ibid.*).

[110] Article 5 of and Annex I, Note to Article 5, to the *Customs Valuation Agreement*.

[111] Article 6 of and Annex I, Note to Article 6, to the *Customs Valuation Agreement*.

[112] Article 7.1 of the *Customs Valuation Agreement*.

[113] See Article 7.2 of the *Customs Valuation Agreement*.

- commissions and brokerage;[114]
- the cost of packing;[115]
- royalties and licence fees related to the goods being valued that the buyer must pay;[116] and
- the value of any part of the proceeds of any subsequent resale that accrues to the seller.[117]

Pursuant to Article 8.2, each Member is free either to include or to exclude from the customs value of imported goods:

- the cost of transport to the port or place of importation;
- loading, unloading and handling charges associated with the transport to the port or place of importation; and
- the cost of insurance.

Note in this respect that the European Communities and most other Members take the CIF price as the basis for determining the customs value, while the United States takes the FOB price.[118]

Questions and Assignments 5.9

Why must customs administrations determine the value of imported goods? Which provisions set out the WTO rules on customs valuation? What is the principal, and most common, method for determining the customs value of imported goods? Briefly discuss other methods for determining the customs value of imported products. Must the cost of the packaging and/or the cost of transport to the port or place of importation be included in the customs value of imported goods?

5.2.6.3. Determination of origin

The customs duties applied to imported goods may differ depending on the country from which the goods were exported. For example, goods *from* developing-country Members commonly benefit from lower import duties in developed-country Members than goods from other developed-country Members; and on goods *from* Members that are a party to the same free trade agreement, no customs duties apply. Moreover, only the goods *from* WTO Members benefit under WTO law from MFN treatment with respect to customs duties. It is, therefore, important to determine the origin of imported goods

---

[114] See Article 8.1(a)(i) of the *Customs Valuation Agreement*.
[115] See Article 8.1(a)(iii) of the *Customs Valuation Agreement*.
[116] See Article 8.1(c) of the *Customs Valuation Agreement*.
[117] See Article 8.1(d) of the *Customs Valuation Agreement*.
[118] CIF (cost, insurance and freight) and FOB (free on board) are INCO terms. CIF means that the seller must pay the costs and freight necessary to bring the goods to the named port of destination. FOB means that the buyer has to bear all costs and risks of loss of or damage to the goods from the point that the goods pass the ship's rail at the named port of shipment.

and, surprisingly perhaps, this is not always an easy determination to make. Most industrial products, available on the market today, are produced in more than one country. For example, in the case of cotton shirts, it is possible that the cotton used in their production is manufactured in country A, the textile woven, dyed and printed in country B, the cloth cut and stitched in country C and the shirts packed for retail in country D before being exported to country E.[119]

The rules to determine the origin of imported goods differ from Member to Member and many Members use different rules of origin depending on the purpose for which the origin is determined.[120] However, generally speaking, the rules of origin currently applied by Members are based on:

- the principle of value added; or
- the principle of change in tariff classification.

Under rules of origin based on the principle of value added, an imported good will be considered to have originated in country X if in that country a specified percentage (for example, 50 per cent) of the value of the good was added. Under rules of origin based on the principle of change in tariff classification, a good will be considered to have originated in country X, if, as a result of processing in that country, the tariff classification of the product changes.

The GATT 1947 had no specific rules on the determination of the origin of imported goods, and the GATT 1994 still provides no specific rules on this matter. However, the negotiators during the Uruguay Round recognised the need for multilateral disciplines on rules of origin in order to prevent these rules from being a source of uncertainty and unpredictability in international trade. The consensus on the need for such disciplines resulted in the WTO *Agreement on Rules of Origin*. This Agreement makes a distinction between:

- non-preferential rules of origin; and
- preferential rules of origin.

Pursuant to Article 1 of the *Agreement on Rules of Origin*, most of the multilateral disciplines set forth therein (i.e. Parts I to IV) concern only *non-preferential* rules of origin. Non-preferential rules of origin are rules of origin used in non-preferential trade policy instruments (relating to, *inter alia*, MFN treatment, anti-dumping and countervailing duties, safeguard measures, origin marking or tariff quotas).[121] However, Annex II to the *Agreement on Rules of Origin* provides some multilateral disciplines for *preferential* rules of origin. Preferential rules of origin are rules of origin applied by Members to determine whether goods qualify for preferential treatment under contractual or autonomous trade regimes (leading to the granting of tariff preferences going beyond the

---

[119] See *Business Guide to the World Trading System*, second edition (International Trade Centre, 1999), 155.
[120] E.g. whether the origin of imported products is determined for the imposition of ordinary customs duties, anti-dumping duties or the administration of country-specific tariff quota shares.
[121] See Article 1.2 of the *Agreement on Rules of Origin*.

application of MFN treatment obligation).[122] Note that around 45 per cent of world trade is conducted on a preferential basis.[123]

With respect to *non-preferential rules of origin*, the *Agreement on Rules of Origin* provides for a work programme on the harmonisation of these rules.[124] Pursuant to Article 9.2 of the *Agreement on Rules of Origin*, this Harmonisation Work Programme should have been completed by July 1998. However, due to the complexity of the matter, the WTO Members failed to meet this deadline. In fact, work on the harmonisation of non-preferential rules of origin is still not completed.[125]

The failure of WTO Members to agree, to date, on harmonised rules of origin does not mean, however, that no WTO disciplines apply to non-preferential rules of origin. Article 2 of the *Agreement on Rules of Origin* contains a rather extensive list of multilateral disciplines for rules of origin already applicable during the 'transition period', i.e. the period until the Harmonisation Work Programme is completed. These multilateral disciplines applicable during the transitional period include:

- a transparency requirement: the rules of origin must clearly and precisely define the criteria they apply;
- a prohibition on using rules of origin as instruments to pursue trade objectives;
- a requirement that rules of origin shall not themselves create restrictive, distorting or disruptive effects on international trade;
- a national treatment requirement, namely, that the rules of origin applied to imported products shall not be more stringent than the rules of origin applied to determine whether or not a good is domestic;
- an MFN requirement, namely, that rules of origin shall not discriminate between other Members, irrespective of the affiliation of the manufacturers of the good concerned;
- a requirement that rules of origin shall be administered in a consistent, uniform, impartial and reasonable manner;
- a requirement that rules of origin state what *does* confer origin (positive standard) rather than state what does *not* confer origin (negative standard);
- a requirement to publish laws, regulations, judicial decisions, etc., relating to rules of origin, as required under Article X of the GATT 1994;
- requirements regarding the issuance of assessments of origin (no later than 150 days after the request) and the validity of the assessments (in principle, three years);

---

[122] See Article 1.1 of and Annex II.2 to the *Agreement on Rules of Origin*.
[123] See above, p. 378, and below, pp. 652–62, 679–82.
[124] Article 9.1 of the *Agreement on Rules of Origin*. This work programme is to be undertaken in conjunction with the WCO.
[125] Ninth Annual Review of the Implementation and Operation of the Agreement on Rules of Origin, Note by the Secretariat, G/RO/57, dated 9 December 2003.

- a prohibition on the retroactive application of new or amended rules of origin;
- a requirement that any administrative action relating to the determination of origin is reviewable promptly by independent tribunals; and
- a requirement to respect the confidentiality of information provided on a confidential basis.[126]

Once the Harmonisation Work Programme is completed, all Members will apply only one set of non-preferential rules of origin for all purposes.[127] As provided for in Article 3 of the *Agreement on Rules of Origin*, the disciplines set out in Article 2, already applicable, will continue to apply.[128] In addition, Article 3 provides that Members must ensure that under the harmonised rules of origin:

> the country to be determined as the origin of a particular good is either the country where the good has been wholly obtained or, when more than one country is concerned in the production of the good, the country where the last substantial transformation has been carried out.[129]

Once the harmonisation is achieved, WTO Members will therefore be required to determine as the country of origin of imported goods:

- the country where the goods have been wholly obtained; or
- the country where the last substantial transformation to the goods has been carried out.

To date, Members have been unsuccessful in achieving full consensus either on detailed rules regarding the requirements for a good to be 'wholly obtained' in one country,[130] or on the criteria for a 'substantial transformation' (a change in tariff classification and/or a specific percentage of value added).

The disciplines on rules of origin discussed above concern, pursuant to Article 1 of the *Agreement on Rules of Origin*, only non-preferential rules of origin. However, as already noted, Annex II to the *Agreement on Rules of Origin* provides – in the form of a 'Common Declaration' – for some multilateral disciplines applicable to preferential rules of conduct. Pursuant to Annex II, the general principles and requirements set out in the *Agreement on Rules of Origin* in respect of transparency, positive standards, administrative assessments, judicial review, non-retroactivity of changes and confidentiality apply also to *preferential* rules of origin. The results of the Harmonisation Work Programme, however, will not apply to preferential rules of origin.

---

[126] See Article 2(a) to (k) of the *Agreement on Rules of Origin*.
[127] See Article 3(a) of the *Agreement on Rules of Origin*.
[128] See Article 3(c) to (i) and Article 9(c) to (g) of the *Agreement on Rules of Origin*.
[129] Article 3(b) of the *Agreement on Rules of Origin*.
[130] Under debate is, for example, the question of which minimal operations or processes can and cannot, by themselves, confer origin on a good.

5.2.7. Other duties and charges

In addition to 'ordinary customs duties', tariff barriers can also take the form of 'other duties and charges'. This section discusses this form of tariff barrier.

5.2.7.1. *Definition and types*

'Other duties and charges' are financial charges, *other than* ordinary customs duties, imposed on, or in the context of, the importation of a good. 'Other duties and charges' form a residual category. They are import-related financial charges which are not ordinary customs duties. Unfortunately, the GATT 1994 does not define the concept of 'ordinary customs duties' and the relevant case law is not very helpful. In *Chile – Price Band System*, the Panel found that 'ordinary customs duties':

> always relate to either the value of the imported goods, in the case of *ad valorem* duties, or the volume of the imported goods, in the case of specific duties. Such ordinary customs duties, however, do not appear to involve the consideration of any other, exogenous, factors, such as, for instance, fluctuating world market prices. We therefore consider that … an "ordinary" customs duty, that is, a customs duty *senso strictu*, is to be understood as referring to a customs duty which is not applied on the basis of factors of an exogenous nature.[131]

On appeal, the Appellate Body disagreed with the Panel and reversed its finding that the concept of 'ordinary customs duty' is to be understood as referring to a customs duty which is not applied on the basis of factors of an exogenous nature.[132] The Appellate Body, however, did not give an alternative definition of 'ordinary customs duties'.

Examples of 'other duties and charges' are:

- an import surcharge, i.e. a duty imposed on an imported product in addition to the ordinary customs duty;[133]

---

[131] Panel Report, *Chile – Price Band System*, para. 7.52. See also *ibid.*, para. 7.104.
[132] See Appellate Body Report, *Chile – Price Band System*, para. 278.
[133] See e.g. the surcharges on imported beef at issue in *Korea – Beef (Australia)*, GATT Panel Report, adopted 7 November 1979, BISD 36S/202.

- a security deposit to be made on the importation of goods;[134]
- a statistical tax imposed to finance the collection of statistical information;[135] or
- a customs fee, i.e. a financial charge imposed for the processing of imported goods by the customs authorities.[136]

5.2.7.2. *Rules regarding 'other duties or charges'*

To protect the tariff bindings set forth in the Schedules and to prevent 'circumvention' of the prohibition of Article II:1(b), first sentence, of the GATT 1994, to impose ordinary customs duties in excess of the bindings, the WTO law provides for rules on 'other duties and charges'. With regard to products subject to a tariff binding, Article II:1(b), second sentence, of the GATT 1994 states:

> Such products shall also be exempt from all other duties or charges of any kind imposed on or in connection with the importation in excess of those imposed on the date of this Agreement or those directly and mandatorily required to be imposed thereafter by legislation in force in the importing territory on that date.

Article II:1(b), second sentence, thus requires that, on products subject to a tariff binding, *no* other duties or charges may be imposed *in excess of* those duties or charges:

- already imposed at the 'date of this Agreement'; or
- provided for in mandatory legislation in force on that date.

However, under the GATT 1947 regime, the 'date of this Agreement' was not necessarily the date of the GATT 1947, i.e. 30 October 1947, but could also be the date of a later tariff protocol to the GATT 1947.[137] As is explained in the *Guide to GATT Law and Practice*:

> in the GATT 1947, each concession would have its own "date of this Agreement" for the purpose of the binding on "other duties and charges" under Article II:1(b) ... and in a Schedule with a number of concessions there could be a number of different and coexisting such "dates of this Agreement".[138]

As a result, there was considerable uncertainty and confusion regarding the maximum level of 'other duties or charges' that could be imposed. Therefore, the Uruguay Round negotiators agreed on the *Understanding on the Interpretation of Article II:1(b) of the GATT 1994*, commonly referred to as the *Understanding on Article II:1(b)*. This Understanding states, in relevant part:

> In order to ensure transparency of the legal rights and obligations deriving from paragraph 1(b) of Article II, the nature and level of any "other duties or charges"

---

[134] See e.g. the security deposits at issue in *EEC – Programme of Minimum Import Prices, Licences and Surety Deposits for Certain Processed Fruits and Vegetables* (see GATT Panel Report, adopted 18 October 1978, BISD 25S/68) and *EEC – Animal Feed Proteins* (see GATT Panel Report, adopted 14 March 1978, BISD 25S/49).
[135] See e.g. the statistical tax at issue in *Argentina – Textiles and Apparel*, WT/DS56.
[136] See e.g. *United States – Customs User Fee* (see GATT Panel Report, adopted 2 February 1988, BISD 35S/245).
[137] *Analytical Index to the GATT*, 1995, 84.   [138] *Ibid.*, 85.

> levied on bound tariff items, as referred to in that provision, shall be recorded in the Schedules of Concessions annexed to GATT 1994 against the tariff item to which they apply.[139]

The *Understanding on Article II:1(b)* thus requires Members to record in their Schedules all 'other duties or charges' imposed on products subject to a tariff binding. As noted above, the Uruguay Round Schedules have a special column for 'other duties or charges'.[140] The 'other duties or charges' must be recorded in the Schedules at the levels applying on 15 April 1994.[141] The 'other duties or charges' are 'bound' at these levels.[142]

It follows from Article II:1(b), second sentence, and from the *Understanding on Article II:1(b)*, that Members may:

- impose only 'other duties and charges' that have been properly recorded in their Schedules; and
- impose 'other duties and charges' only at a level that does not exceed the level recorded in their Schedules.

In *Chile – Price Band System*, the Panel, having found that the Chilean Price Band System (PBS) duties were not 'ordinary customs duties' but were 'other duties or charges', examined whether these duties were inconsistent with Article II:1(b), second sentence. The Panel ruled:

> Pursuant to the Uruguay Round Understanding on the Interpretation of Article II:1(b), such other duties or charges had to be recorded in a newly created column "other duties and charges" in the Members' Schedules ...
>
> Other duties or charges must not exceed the binding in this "other duties and charges" column of the Schedule. If other duties or charges were not recorded but are nevertheless levied, they are inconsistent with the second sentence of Article II:1(b), in light of the Understanding on the Interpretation of Article II:1(b). We note that Chile did not record its PBS in the "other duties and charges" column of its Schedule.
>
> We therefore find that the Chilean PBS duties are inconsistent with Article II:1(b) of GATT 1994.[143]

5.2.7.3. Exceptions to the rule

There are a number of exceptions to the rule that Members may not impose 'other duties or charges' in excess of the recorded level. Pursuant to Article II:2

---

[139] *Understanding on the Interpretation of Article II:1(b) of the GATT 1994* (hereinafter '*Understanding on Article II:1(b)*'), para. 1.

[140] See above, pp. 399–400.

[141] *Understanding on Article II:1(b)*, para. 2. Note, however, that paragraph 4 of the *Understanding on Article II:1(b)* states: 'Where a tariff item has previously been the subject of a concession, the level of "other duties or charges" recorded in the appropriate Schedule shall not be higher than the level obtaining at the time of the first incorporation of the concession in that Schedule.'

[142] Note that paragraph 1 of the *Understanding on Article II:1(b)* states that the recording in the Schedules does not change the legal character of the 'other duties or charges' and that paragraphs 4 and 5 provide that – with certain restrictions in time – the Members can challenge the GATT-consistency of recorded 'other duties or charges'.

[143] Panel Report, *Chile – Price Band System*, paras. 7.105 and 7.107–7.108. On appeal, the Appellate Body found that the Panel's finding on Article II:1(b), second sentence, related to a claim that had not been made, and this finding was therefore in violation of Article 11 of the DSU. As a result, the Appellate Body reversed the finding. See above, p. 436.

of the GATT 1994, Members may – despite their obligations under Article II:1(b), second sentence – impose on imported products:

- any financial charge that is not in excess of the internal tax imposed on the like domestic product;
- WTO-consistent anti-dumping or countervailing duties; or
- fees or other charges 'commensurate' with, i.e. matching, the cost of the services rendered.

With respect to the latter category of 'other duties or charges', note that the requirement that these fees or other charges are commensurate with the cost of the services, is also reflected in Article VIII:1(a) of the GATT 1994. This article requires that:

> All fees and charges of whatever character (other than import or export duties and other than taxes within the purview of Article III) imposed by [Members] on or in connection with importation or exportation shall be limited in amount to the approximate cost of services rendered and shall not represent an indirect protection to domestic products or a taxation of imports or exports for fiscal purposes.[144]

The fees and charges for services rendered at issue in Articles II:2(c) and VIII:1(a) include, pursuant to Article VIII:4, fees and charges relating to:

- consular transactions, such as consular invoices and certificates;
- quantitative restrictions;
- licensing;
- exchange control;
- statistical services;
- documents, documentation and certification;
- analysis and inspection; and
- quarantine, sanitation and fumigation.

With respect to the concept of 'services' used in this context, the GATT Panel in *US – Customs User Fee* stated, not without wit:

> Granted that some government regulatory activities can be considered as "services" in an economic sense when they endow goods with safety or quality characteristics deemed necessary for commerce, most of the activities that governments perform in connection with the importation process do not meet that definition. They are not desired by the importers who are subject to them. Nor do they add value to the goods in any commercial sense. Whatever governments may choose to call them, fees for such government regulatory activities are, in the Panel's view, simply taxes on imports. It must be presumed, therefore, that the drafters meant the term "services" to be used in a more artful political sense, i.e. government activities closely enough connected to the processes of customs entry that they might, with no more than the customary artistic licence accorded to taxing authorities, be called a "service" to the importer in question.[145]

---

[144] Note that there is a slight difference in wording between the two 'cost of services' limitations stated in Articles II:2(c) and VIII:1(a), i.e. 'commensurate with the cost of services rendered' and 'limited in amount to the approximate cost of services rendered'. However, the GATT Panel in *US – Customs User Fee*, after reviewing both the drafting history and the subsequent application of these provisions, concluded that no difference of meaning had been intended.

[145] GATT Panel Report, *US – Customs User Fee*, para. 77.

In *US – Customs User Fee*, the financial charge at issue was a merchandise-processing fee, in the form of an *ad valorem* charge without upper limits. The complainants, the European Communities and Canada, challenged the GATT-consistency of an *ad valorem* charge without upper limit. Before turning to the specific claim of inconsistency, the Panel noted that the requirement of Article VIII:1(a) that a fee or charge be 'limited in amount to the approximate cost of services rendered' is in fact a dual requirement:

- the fee or charge in question must first involve a 'service' rendered; and
- the level of the charge must not exceed the approximate cost of that 'service'.[146]

With respect to the first element of this dual requirement, the Panel further clarified that the fee or charge in question must involve a 'service' rendered to the *individual* importer in question.[147] Services rendered to foreign trade operators in general and foreign trade as an activity *per se* would fail to meet this first element of the dual requirement.[148] With respect to the second element of the dual requirement, the Panel stated:

> that the term "cost of services rendered" in Articles II:2(c) and VIII:1(a) must be interpreted to refer to the cost of the customs processing for the individual entry in question and accordingly that the *ad valorem* structure of the United States merchandise processing fee was inconsistent with the obligations of Articles II:2(c) and VIII:1(a) to the extent that it caused fees to be levied in excess of such costs.[149]

In *Argentina – Textiles and Apparel*, the Panel found that Argentina's 3 per cent *ad valorem* statistical tax on imports was inconsistent with Article VIII:1(a) of the GATT 1994

> to the extent it results in charges being levied in excess of the approximate costs of the services rendered.[150]

As the Panel explained, an *ad valorem* charge with no maximum limit, as was the case with Argentina's statistical tax,

> by its very nature, is not "limited in amount to the approximate cost of services rendered". For example, high-price items necessarily will bear a much higher tax burden than low-price goods, yet the service accorded to both is essentially the same. An unlimited *ad valorem* charge on imported goods violates the provisions of Article VIII because such a charge cannot be related to the cost of the service rendered.[151]

Note that the Panel in *Argentina – Textiles and Apparel* also found that the statistical tax was inconsistent with Article VIII:1(a) because this tax – according to Argentina's own admission – was imposed for 'fiscal purposes', which is explicitly prohibited under Article VIII:1(a).

---

[146] *Ibid.*, para. 69. See also Panel Report, *Argentina – Textiles and Apparel*, para. 6.74; and Panel Report, *US – Certain EC Products*, para. 6.69.
[147] GATT Panel Report, *US – Customs User Fee*, para. 80.
[148] Panel Report, *Argentina – Textiles and Apparel*, para. 6.74.
[149] GATT Panel Report, *US – Customs User Fee*, para. 86.
[150] Panel Report, *Argentina – Textiles and Apparel*, para. 6.80.
[151] *Ibid.*, para. 6.75.

Questions and Assignments 5.11

What are 'other duties or charges' within the meaning of Article II:1(b), second sentence, of the GATT 1994? Give three examples of such 'other duties or charges'. Are 'other duties or charges' permitted in the same way as customs duties are, in principle, permitted? Which 'other duties or charges' are permitted under the GATT 1994? Find an example of a product on which the European Communities imposes an 'other duty or charge'. Which 'other duties or charges' are allowed on imported products irrespective of a Member's obligations under Article II:1(b), second sentence, of the GATT 1994? When are customs fees or charges covered by Article II:2(c) of the GATT 1994?

5.3. NON-TARIFF BARRIERS TO TRADE IN GOODS

Trade in goods is not only restricted by customs duties and other duties and charges, but also by non-tariff barriers. This section deals with both main categories of non-tariff barriers, i.e. quantitative restrictions and other non-tariff barriers. It discusses:

- quantitative restrictions;
- rules on quantitative restrictions;
- the administration of quantitative restrictions; and
- other non-tariff barriers.

5.3.1. Quantitative restrictions

5.3.1.1. Definition and types

A quantitative restriction, also referred to as a 'QR', is a measure which *limits the quantity* of a product that may be imported or exported. There are different types of quantitative restriction:

- a *prohibition*, or ban, of a product; such a prohibition may be absolute or conditional, i.e. only applicable when certain defined conditions are *not* fulfilled;
- a *quota*, i.e. a measure indicating the quantity that may be imported or exported; a quota can be a global quota, a global quota allocated among countries, or a bilateral quota;
- automatic and non-automatic *licensing*;[152] and

---

[152] See below, pp. 455–7.

- *other* quantitative restrictions, such as a quantitative restriction made effective through State trading operations; a mixing regulation; a minimum price, triggering a quantitative restriction; and a voluntary export restraint.[153]

A typical example of a quantitative restriction, and in particular a quota, is a measure allowing the importation of a maximum of 1,000 tonnes of cocoa powder a year or a measure allowing the importation of a maximum of 450 tractors. While usually based on the number of units, weight or volume, quantitative restrictions can also be based on value, for example a limit on the importation of flowers to €12 million per year.

WTO Members are required to notify the WTO Secretariat of any quantitative restrictions which they maintain and of any changes in these restrictions, as and when they occur.[154] The notifications must indicate:

- the products affected by the QR;
- the type of QR (prohibition, quota, licensing, etc.);
- an indication of the grounds and WTO justification for the QR; and
- a statement on the trade effects of the QR.

With this information, the WTO Secretariat maintains a QR database, which Members may consult.[155]

5.3.1.2. *Customs duties versus quantitative restrictions*

The WTO has a clear preference for customs duties over quantitative restrictions and this preference is reflected in the relevant provisions of the GATT 1994, discussed below.[156] In comparing customs duties with quantitative restrictions, the Panel in *Turkey – Textiles* noted:

> A basic principle of the GATT system is that tariffs are the preferred and acceptable form of protection ... The prohibition against quantitative restrictions is a reflection that tariffs are GATT's border protection "of choice".[157]

The reasons for this preference are both economic and political in nature. First, customs duties are more transparent. The economic impact of customs duties on imported products, i.e. how much more expensive imported products are as a result of customs duties, is immediately clear. Quantitative restrictions also increase the price of the imported products. As supply of the imported product is limited, the price increases. However, it is not immediately clear by how much quantitative restrictions increase the price of imported products. Secondly, while the price increase resulting from customs duties goes to the government, the price increase resulting from quantitative restrictions

---

[153] For an illustrative list of quantitative restrictions, see Council for Trade in Goods, *Decision on Notification Procedures for Quantitative Restrictions*, G/L/59, dated 10 January 1996, Annex.
[154] See Council for Trade in Goods, *Decision on Notification Procedures for Quantitative Restrictions*, G/L/59, dated 10 January 1996,
[155] This database is not accessible for the general public.
[156] See below, pp. 444–6. See also above, p. 389.   [157] Panel Report, *Turkey – Textiles*, para. 9.63.

ordinarily benefits the importers. The importers will be able to sell at higher prices because of the limits on the supply of the product. The 'extra profit' is commonly referred to as the 'quota rent' and, unless a quota is auctioned (which is seldom done), no part of this quota rent goes to the government. Thirdly, the administration of quantitative restrictions is more open to corruption than the administration of customs duties. This is because quantitative restrictions, and, in particular, quotas, are usually administered through an import licensing system and decisions by government officials to award an import licence are not necessarily based on the general interest.[158] Fourthly, and arguably most importantly, quantitative restrictions impose absolute limits on imports, while customs duties do not. While customs duties are surmountable (at least, if they are not set at prohibitively high levels), quantitative restrictions cannot be surmounted. If a foreign producer is sufficiently more efficient than a domestic producer, the customs duty will not prevent imported products from competing with domestic products. By contrast, once the limit of a quantitative restriction is reached, no more products can be imported. Even the most efficient foreign producer cannot 'overcome' the quantitative restriction. Above the quota, domestic products have no competition from imported products.

5.3.1.3. Tariff quotas

A tariff (rate) quota, or 'TRQ', is *not* a quota; it is *not* a quantitative restriction.[159] A tariff quota is a quantity which can be imported at a certain duty. Any quantity above that amount is subject to a higher tariff. For example, a Member may allow the importation of 5,000 tractors at 10 per cent *ad valorem* and any tractor imported above this quantity at 30 per cent *ad valorem*. Tariff quotas are not quantitative restrictions since they do not directly prohibit or restrict the quantity of imports. They only subject the imports to varying duties. The European Communities' intricate import regime for bananas, at issue in *EC – Bananas III*, provided for tariff quotas. Under this regime, the European Communities granted, for example, duty-free access to 90,000 tonnes of non-traditional ACP bananas; the out-of-quota tariff rate for these same bananas was 693 ECU per tonne.

Questions and Assignments 5.12

What is a quantitative restriction? Discuss the different types of quantitative restriction. Why does the WTO prefer customs duties to quantitative restrictions? Are tariff quotas quantitative restrictions or quotas?

---

[158] On import licensing procedures, see below, pp. 455–7.
[159] See the unadopted GATT Panel Report, *EEC – Bananas II*, DS38/R, paras. 138–9.

5.3.2. Rules on quantitative restrictions

5.3.2.1. *General prohibition on quantitative restrictions*

Article XI:1 of the GATT 1994, entitled 'General Elimination of Quantitative Restrictions', sets out a general prohibition on quantitative restrictions, whether on imports or exports. As the Panel in *Turkey – Textiles* stated:

> The prohibition on the use of quantitative restrictions forms one of the cornerstones of the GATT system.[160]

Article XI:1 provides, in relevant part:

> No prohibitions or restrictions other than duties, taxes or other charges, whether made effective through quotas, import or export licences or other measures, shall be instituted or maintained by any [Member] on the importation of any product of the territory of any other [Member] or on the exportation or sale for export of any product destined for the territory of any other [Member].

As the Panel in *Japan – Semi-Conductors* noted, the wording of Article XI:1

> was comprehensive: it applied to *all measures* instituted or maintained by a contracting party *prohibiting or restricting* the importation, exportation or sale for export of products *other than* measures that take the form of duties, taxes or other charges.[161]
> [Emphasis added]

As an illustration of the broad scope of the prohibition on quantitative restrictions, consider the following examples of measures that were found to be inconsistent with Article XI:1:

- In *US – Shrimp*, the Panel found that the United States acted inconsistently with Article XI:1 by imposing an import ban on shrimp and shrimp products harvested by vessels of foreign nations where the exporting country had not been certified by the US authorities as using methods not leading to the accidental killing of sea turtles above certain levels.[162]
- In *EEC – Minimum Import Prices*, the Panel found that the prohibition on quantitative restrictions in Article XI:1 applied to a system of minimum import prices.[163]
- In *Japan – Agricultural Products I*, the Panel ruled that the prohibition of Article XI:1 applied to import restrictions made effective through an import monopoly, or more broadly through State trading operations.[164]

---

[160] Panel Report, *Turkey – Textiles*, para. 9.63.
[161] GATT Panel Report, *Japan – Semi-Conductors*, para. 104.
[162] See Panel Report, *US – Shrimp*, paras. 7.17 and 8.1. Previous GATT panels in *US – Tuna (EEC)*, para. 5.10, and *US – Tuna (Mexico)*, paras. 5.17–5.18, found similar measures also to be 'restrictions' within the meaning of Article XI.
[163] See GATT Panel Report, *EEC – Minimum Import Prices*, para. 4.14. Also, restrictions on exports below a certain price fall within the scope of application of Article XI:1 (see GATT Panel Report, *Japan – Semi-Conductors*, para. 117).
[164] See GATT Panel Report, *Japan – Restrictions on Imports of Certain Agricultural Products*, para. 5.2.2.2. The Panel noted that its finding was confirmed by the Note *Ad* Articles XI, XII, XIII, XIV and XVIII, according to which the concept of 'import restrictions' throughout these Articles covers restrictions made effective through State trading operations. Note, however, that the mere fact that imports are affected through State trading enterprises does not in itself constitute a restriction within the meaning of

- In *India – Quantitative Restrictions*, the Panel held that non-automatic import licensing systems are import restrictions prohibited by Article XI:1.[165]

Unlike other GATT provisions, Article XI refers not to laws or regulations but more broadly to measures. A measure instituted or maintained by a Member which restricts imports or exports is covered by Article XI, *irrespective* of the legal status of the measure.[166] In *Japan – Semi-Conductors*, the Panel therefore ruled that *non-mandatory* measures of the Japanese Government, restricting the export of certain semiconductors at below-cost price, were nevertheless 'restrictions' within the meaning of Article XI:1.[167]

Note that, in addition, quantitative restrictions which do not *actually* impede trade are nevertheless prohibited under Article XI:1 of the GATT 1994.[168] The Panel in *EEC – Oilseeds I* ruled in this respect in 1990:

> the CONTRACTING PARTIES have consistently interpreted the basic provisions of the General Agreement on restrictive trade measures as provisions establishing conditions of competition. Thus they decided that an import quota constitutes an import restriction within the meaning of Article XI:1 whether or not it actually impeded imports.[169]

On the other hand, the Panel in *EEC – Minimum Import Prices* found in 1978 that automatic import licensing does not

> constitute a restriction of the type meant to fall under the purview of Article XI:1.[170]

In *EC – Asbestos*, the question arose whether a French ban on the manufacturing, import and export, and domestic sales and transfer of certain asbestos and asbestos-containing products fell under the scope of the prohibition of quantitative restrictions in Article XI or the national treatment obligation of Article III. Recall in this respect the discussion on the respective scopes of Articles III and XI of the GATT 1994 in Chapter 4.[171]

Finally, note that restrictions of a *de facto* nature are also prohibited under Article XI:1 of the GATT 1994. In *Argentina – Hides and Leather*, the issue arose whether Argentina violated Article XI:1 by authorising the presence of domestic tanners' representatives in the customs inspection procedures for

---

Article XI. For such a restriction to be found to exist, it should be shown that the operation of this State trading entity is such as to result in a restriction (see Panel Report, *India – Quantitative Restrictions*, para. 5.134).

[165] See Panel Report, *India – Quantitative Restrictions*, para. 5.130. For an explanation of a 'non-automatic import licensing system', see below, pp. 456–7.

[166] See GATT Panel Report, *Japan – Semi-Conductors*, para. 106.

[167] See GATT Panel Report, *Japan – Semi-Conductors*, paras. 104–17. The Panel considered that, in order to determine whether the *non-mandatory* measures were measures falling within the scope of Article XI, it needed to be satisfied on two essential criteria. First, there were reasonable grounds to believe that sufficient incentives or disincentives existed for non-mandatory measures to take effect. Secondly, the operation of the measures was essentially dependent on government action or intervention. The Panel considered that, if these two criteria were met, the measures would be operating in a manner equivalent to mandatory requirements such that the difference between the measures and mandatory requirements was only one of form and not one of substance, and that there could therefore be no doubt that they fell within the scope of Article XI:1.

[168] Such non-biting quotas, i.e. quotas above current levels of trade, cause increased transaction costs and create uncertainties which could affect investment plans. See GATT Panel Report, *Japan – Leather II (US)*, para. 55.

[169] GATT Panel Report, *EEC – Oilseeds I*, para. 150.

[170] GATT Panel Report, *EEC – Minimum Import Prices*, para. 4.1.

[171] See above, pp. 329–30.

hides destined for export operations. According to the complainant (the European Communities), Argentina thus imposed a *de facto* restriction on the exportation of hides inconsistent with Article XI:1. The Panel ruled:

> There can be no doubt, in our view, that the disciplines of Article XI:1 extend to restrictions of a *de facto* nature.[172]

However, the Panel concluded with respect to the Argentinean regulation providing for the presence of the domestic tanners' representatives in the customs inspection procedures that there was insufficient evidence that this regulation really operated as an export restriction inconsistent with Article XI:1 of the GATT 1994.[173]

The general prohibition on quantitative restrictions set out in Article XI:1 of the GATT 1994 is, however, not without exceptions. The many and broad exceptions discussed in Chapter 7 are most important in this respect.[174] In addition, note that Article XI itself provides for a few exceptions in its second paragraph. However, the latter exceptions are no longer of much importance.[175]

Questions and Assignments 5.13

Are quantitative restrictions allowed under WTO law? To which measures does Article XI:1 of the GATT 1994 apply? Give four examples of quantitative restrictions which panels and/or the Appellate Body have found to be inconsistent with Article XI:1 of the GATT. Is a quantitative restriction which does not actually impede trade inconsistent with Article XI:1 of the GATT 1994? Give an example of a *de facto* quantitative restriction. Is such a restriction consistent with Article XI:1 of the GATT 1994?

5.3.2.2. *Rules on quantitative restrictions on specific products*

Under the GATT 1947, the prohibition against quantitative restrictions was often *not* respected. The Panel in *Turkey – Textiles* noted:

> From early in the GATT, in sectors such as agriculture, quantitative restrictions were maintained and even increased to the extent that the need to restrict their use became central to the Uruguay Round negotiations. In the sector of textiles and clothing, quantitative restrictions were maintained under the Multifibre Agreement ... Certain contracting parties were even of the view that quantitative restrictions had gradually been tolerated and accepted as negotiable and that Article XI could not be and had

---

[172] Panel Report, *Argentina – Hides and Leather*, para. 11.17. In support of this finding, the Panel referred to the GATT Panel Report in *Japan – Semi-Conductors*, paras. 105–9.
[173] Panel Report, *Argentina – Hides and Leather*, para. 11.55.
[174] See below, pp. 596–691.
[175] Note that, to the extent Article XI:2 allows the use of quantitative restrictions with regard to agricultural products, this provision has been set aside by Article 4.2 of the *Agreement on Agriculture* (see, on the relationship between the GATT 1994 and the *Agreement on Agriculture*, Article 21.1 of the *Agreement on Agriculture*).

> never been considered to be, a provision prohibiting such restrictions irrespective of the circumstances specific to each case.[176]

However, the overall detrimental effect of these quantitative restrictions in the sectors of agriculture and textiles was generally recognised. Therefore, the elimination of these quantitative restrictions was high on the agenda of the Uruguay Round negotiations (1986–93). As a result, the *Agreement on Agriculture* and the *Agreement on Textiles and Clothing* contain specific rules regarding the elimination of quantitative restrictions on agricultural products and textile products respectively.

The *Agreement on Agriculture* provides that quantitative restrictions and voluntary export restraints, *inter alia*, must be converted into tariffs and that no new quantitative restrictions can be adopted. Article 4.2 of the *Agreement on Agriculture* states:

> Members shall not maintain, resort to, or revert to any measures of the kind which have been required to be converted into ordinary customs duties, except as otherwise provided for in Article 5 and Annex 5.

In footnote 1 to this provision, the measures which had to be converted into tariffs (or tariff quotas) were identified as: quantitative import restrictions, variable import levies, minimum import prices, discretionary import licensing, non-tariff measures maintained through State trading enterprises, voluntary export restraints, and similar border measures other than ordinary customs duties.[177] The process of converting these non-tariff measures into tariffs is commonly referred to as the 'tariffication process'. As this process provided for the replacement of non-tariff measures with a tariff which afforded *an equivalent level of protection*, many of the tariffs resulting from the 'tariffication process' are high.[178] However, by introducing a system of tariff quotas, it was possible to guarantee:

- that the quantities imported before Article 4.2 of the *Agreement on Agriculture* took effect could continue to be imported; and
- that some new quantities were subject to tariffs that were not prohibitive.

Under this system of tariff quotas, lower tariffs applied to specified quantities (in-quota quantities), while higher (often prohibitive) tariffs applied to quantities that exceed the quota (over-quota quantities).[179]

---

[176] Panel Report, *Turkey – Textiles*, para. 9.64. Note that the argument of certain contracting parties that Article XI could not be a provision prohibiting quantitative restrictions irrespective of the circumstances in which they were imposed, was explicitly rejected by the GATT Panel in *EEC – Import Restrictions*.

[177] Note that measures maintained under balance-of-payments provisions or under other general, non-agriculture-specific provisions of the GATT 1994 or of the other Multilateral Trade Agreements in Annex 1A to the *WTO Agreement*, did not need to be converted to tariffs.

[178] The tariffs resulting from the 'tariffication process' concern, on average, one-fifth of the total number of agricultural tariff lines in the tariffs of developed-country Members.

[179] Note that developed-country Members also agreed during the Uruguay Round negotiations to reduce all tariffs on agricultural products (and the over-quota tariffs in the case of tariff quotas) by an average of 36 per cent, in equal steps over six years. Developing-country Members agreed to reduce these tariffs by 24 per cent over ten years. See Uruguay Round Schedules of Concessions.

With respect to the relationship between Article 4.2 of the *Agreement on Agriculture* and Article XI of the GATT 1994, the Panel in *Korea – Various Measures on Beef* stated that:

> when dealing with measures relating to agricultural products which should have been converted into tariffs or tariff-quotas, a violation of Article XI of GATT ... would necessarily constitute a violation of Article 4.2 of the *Agreement on Agriculture* and its footnote.[180]

As mentioned above, trade in textiles and clothing largely 'escaped' from the GATT 1947 rules and disciplines, and in particular the prohibition of Article XI on quantitative restrictions. Under the *Multifiber Agreement* (MFA), in effect from 1974, developed and developing countries, respectively importing and exporting textiles, entered into bilateral agreements requiring the exporting developing countries to limit their exports of certain categories of textiles and clothing. In 1995, the main importing countries had eighty-one such restraint agreements with exporting countries, comprising over a thousand individual quotas.[181] The MFA, which was negotiated within the framework of the GATT, provided a 'legal cover' for the GATT-inconsistency of these quotas.[182] The *Agreement on Textiles and Clothing* (ATC) negotiated during the Uruguay Round, seeks to address this situation and contains specific rules for quantitative restrictions on textiles and clothing. The Panel in *US – Underwear* stated:

> the overall purpose of the ATC is to integrate the textiles and clothing sector into GATT 1994. Article 1 of the ATC makes this point clear. To this effect, the ATC requires notification of all existing quantitative restrictions (Article 2 of the ATC) and provides that they will have to be terminated by the year 2004 (Article 9 of the ATC).[183]

The integration process, provided for in the ATC, is to be carried out in four stages. At each stage, products amounting to a certain minimum percentage of the volume of a Member's 1990 imports of textiles and clothing must be made fully subject to the disciplines of the GATT 1994, including the prohibition on quantitative restrictions of Article XI.[184] Note, however, that this integration process applied to *all* textile products listed in the ATC, including products on which there were no quantitative restrictions. This allowed the United States and the European Communities, during the first stages, to integrate mainly products on which there were *no* quantitative restrictions, into the GATT

---

[180] Panel Report, *Korea – Various Measures on Beef*, para. 762.
[181] In addition, there were also a number of non-MFA (Multifiber Agreement) agreements or unilateral measures restricting the imports of textiles and clothing. See *Business Guide to the World Trading System* (Commonwealth Secretariat, 2000), 164.
[182] *Ibid.*, para. 165.   [183] Panel Report, *US – Underwear*, para. 7.19.
[184] The minimum percentages of the volume of imports that must be made subject to the GATT 1994 disciplines are:
- 16 per cent on the date of entry into force of the *Agreement on Textiles and Clothing* (1 January 1995);
- 17 per cent at the end of the third year (1 January 1998);
- 18 per cent at the end of the seventh year (1 January 2002); and
- the balance, up to 49 per cent, at the end of the tenth year (1 January 2005).

See Articles 2.6 and 2.7 of the *Agreement on Textiles and Clothing*.

1994.[185] To the discontent and disappointment of the textile exporting Members, the two major importing Members could thus meet their obligations under the ATC without significantly removing quantitative restrictions. They will remove most of the quantitative restrictions only in the fourth and last stage, ending on 1 January 2005.[186]

As the last stage of the implementation of the ATC drew to an end in 2004, a number of smaller, textile-producing developing-country Members, which thus far enjoyed guaranteed quota access, feared that they would encounter serious adjustment problems as their textile exports cannot compete with the textile exports of the large textile-producing developing-country Members, such as China, India and Brazil.

5.3.2.3. *Voluntary export restraints*

Voluntary export restraints (VERs) are actions taken by exporting countries involving a self-imposed *quantitative restriction* of exports. VERs are taken either unilaterally or under the terms of an agreement or arrangement between two or more countries. As the term indicates, in theory VERs are entered into on a voluntary basis, i.e. the exporting country *voluntarily* limits the volume of its exports. However, in reality this is usually not the case. A 1984 GATT report correctly observed:

> It appeared ... that exporting countries which accepted so-called "grey-area" actions did so primarily because ... they felt that they had little choice and that the alternative was, or would have been, unilateral action in the form of quantitative restrictions, harassment by anti-dumping investigations, countervailing action ... involving greater harm to their exports in terms of quantity or price.[187]

Under the GATT 1947, the legality of voluntary export restraints was a much-debated issue. Since the entry into force of the *WTO Agreement*, this issue has been definitively decided. The WTO *Agreement on Safeguards* specifically prohibits voluntary export restraints.[188] Article 11.1(b) of the *Agreement on Safeguards* provides:

> a Member shall not seek, take or maintain any voluntary export restraints, orderly marketing arrangements or any other similar measures on the export or the import side.[189]

---

[185] Note that the percentage of imports of products on which there were no quantitative restrictions in the reference year, 1990, was 34 per cent for the United States and 37 per cent for the European Communities. See *Business Guide to the World Trading System* (Commonwealth Secretariat, 2000), 165.

[186] The quotas were increased by 16 per cent per year from 1995 to 1997, by 25 per cent per year from 1998 to 2001 and by 27 per cent per year from 2002 to 2004. In 2005, all quotas will have been terminated. Note that Article 2 of the *Agreement on Textiles and Clothing* also provides for an annual, escalating increase in the quotas on products that had not yet been integrated into the GATT 1994. See Articles 2.13 and 2.14 of the *Agreement on Textiles and Clothing*.

[187] Report of the Chairman of the Safeguards Committee, BISD 30S/216, 218.

[188] For a more detailed discussion of the *Agreement on Safeguards*, see below, pp. 633–49.

[189] Footnote 4 to this provision contains an illustrative list of 'similar measures' including export moderation, export-price or import-price monitoring systems, export or import surveillance, compulsory import cartels and discretionary export or import licensing schemes, any of which afford protection.

Article 11.1(b) of the *Agreement on Safeguards* furthermore provides:

> Any such measure in effect on the date of entry into force of the WTO Agreement shall be brought into conformity with this Agreement or phased out in accordance with paragraph 2.

Pursuant to Article 11.2, all voluntary export restraints had to be phased out (or brought into compliance with the *Agreement on Safeguards*) before the end of 1999.

5.3.3. Administration of quantitative restrictions

Article XI:1 of the GATT 1994 prohibits quantitative restrictions. There are, however, as noted above, many exceptions to this prohibition of Article XI:1. Article XIII of the GATT 1994 bears testimony to this by setting out rules on the *administration* of quantitative restrictions. This section will address:

- the rule of non-discrimination; and
- the rules on the distribution of trade.

While tariff quotas are not quantitative restrictions, the rules on the administration of quantitative restrictions set out in Article XIII and discussed in this section, also apply to the administration of tariff quotas. Article XIII:5 of the GATT 1994 states, in relevant part:

> The provisions of this Article shall apply to any tariff quota instituted or maintained by any [Member].

Note that many of the disputes on Article XIII were in fact related to the administration of tariff quotas.[190] This section therefore includes some examples of tariff quotas applied by the European Communities.

5.3.3.1. *Rule of non-discrimination*

Article XIII:1 of the GATT 1994 provides that quantitative restrictions, when applied, should be administered in a non-discriminatory manner. Article XIII:1 states:

> No prohibition or restriction shall be applied by any [Member] on the importation of any product of the territory of any other [Member] or on the exportation of any product destined for the territory of any other [Member], unless the importation of the like product of all third countries or the exportation of the like product to all third countries is *similarly prohibited or restricted*.
>
> [Emphasis added]

What Article XIII:1 requires is that, if a Member imposes a quantitative restriction on products to or from another Member, products to or from all other countries are 'similarly restricted'. This requirement of Article XIII:1 is an

---

[190] See e.g. the controversial administration of the tariff quotas under the EC's import regime for bananas (*EC – Bananas III*) or for poultry (*EC – Poultry*).

MFN-like obligation. As the Appellate Body noted in *EC – Bananas III*, the essence of the non-discrimination obligations of Articles I:1 *and* XIII of the GATT 1994 is that:

> like products should be treated equally, irrespective of their origin.[191]

The GATT Panel in *EEC – Apples I (Chile)* found that the European Communities had acted inconsistently with the non-discrimination obligation of Article XIII:1. The importation of apples from Argentina, Australia, New Zealand and South Africa had been restricted through voluntary restraint agreements negotiated and concluded with these countries. The European Communities tried to agree on a similar voluntary restraint agreement with Chile but the negotiations failed. The European Communities subsequently adopted measures restricting the importation of Chilean apples to approximately 42,000 tonnes. The Panel found that the measures applied to imports from Chile by the European Communities were *not* a restriction *similar* to the voluntary restraint agreements negotiated with the other countries and therefore were a violation of Article XIII:1. The Panel came to this conclusion primarily on the basis that:

- there was a difference in transparency between the two types of action;
- there was a difference in the administration of the restrictions, the one being an import restriction, the other an export restraint; and
- the import restriction was unilateral and mandatory while the other was voluntary and negotiated.[192]

5.3.3.2. *Rules on the distribution of trade*

If quantitative restrictions, other than a prohibition or ban, are applied on the importation of a product, the question arises how the trade that is still allowed will be distributed among the different Members exporting that product. The chapeau of Article XIII:2 of the GATT 1994 provides in this respect:

> In applying import restrictions to any product, [Members] shall aim at a distribution of trade in such product approaching as closely as possible the shares which the various [Members] might be expected to obtain in the absence of such restrictions.

The GATT 1994 thus favours a distribution of trade as close as possible to that which would have been the distribution of trade in the absence of the quantitative restriction.

Furthermore, Article XIII:2 sets out a number of requirements to be met when imposing quantitative restrictions. Article XIII:2(a) states:

> Wherever practicable, quotas representing the total amount of permitted imports (whether allocated among supplying countries or not) shall be fixed, and notice given of their amount in accordance with paragraph 3(b) of this Article.

---

[191] Appellate Body Report, *EC – Bananas III*, para. 190.
[192] GATT Panel Report, *EEC – Apples I (Chile)*, para. 4.11.

When imposing a quantitative restriction, a quota – whether global or allocated among the supplying countries – is preferred.[193] In cases in which a quota is allocated among supplying countries, Article XIII:2(d) provides:

> the [Member] applying the restrictions may seek agreement with respect to the alloca-
> tion of shares in the quota with all other [Members] having a substantial interest in
> supplying the product concerned.

However, when this method of allocating the shares in the quota 'is not reasonably practicable', i.e. when no agreement can be reached with *all* the Members having a substantial interest, the Member applying the quota:

> shall allot to [Members] having a substantial interest in supplying the product shares
> based upon the proportions, supplied by such [Members] during a previous represen-
> tative period, of the total quantity or value of imports of the product, due account
> being taken of any special factors which may have affected or may be affecting the
> trade in the product.

In other words, if no agreement can be reached, the quota must be allocated among the Members having a substantial interest on the basis of their share of the trade during a previous representative period. It is normal GATT practice to use a three-year period prior to the imposition of the quota as the 'representative period'.[194]

Quotas allocated among supplying countries *must* be allocated among all Members having a *substantial interest* in supplying the product.[195] There is no additional obligation to allocate a part of the quota to Members *without* a substantial interest in supplying the product concerned. While the require-ment of Article XIII:2(d) is not expressed as an exception to the basic non-discrimination requirement of Article XIII:1, it may be regarded, to the extent that its practical application is inconsistent with it, as a *lex specialis*.[196] It allows for the discrimination between Members with and Members without a sub-stantial interest in supplying the product at issue. Their imports of that prod-uct are not 'similarly' restricted.

In *EC – Bananas III*, the Panel addressed the question of whether quota shares or tariff quota shares (as they were *in casu*) can also be allocated to Members that do not have a substantial interest in supplying the product at issue. According to the Panel, quota shares and tariff quota shares *can* be allocated to these Members with minor market shares. The Panel ruled:

> we note that the first sentence of Article XIII:2(d) refers to allocation of a quota "among
> supplying countries". This could be read to imply that an allocation may also be made to
> Members that do not have a substantial interest in supplying the product.[197]

---

[193] In cases in which a quota is not practicable, Article XIII:2(b) provides that the quantitative restrictions may be applied by means of import licences or permits without a quota.

[194] See GATT Panel Report, *EEC – Apples I (Chile)*, para. 4.16; and GATT Panel Report, *EEC – Dessert Apples*, para. 12.22.

[195] As discussed above, a share of 10 per cent of the market of the Member applying the quota has generally been considered to be a 'significant share' of the market, required to claim a 'substantial interest'. See above, p. 424.

[196] See Panel Reports, *EC – Bananas III*, para. 7.75.

[197] Panel Reports, *EC – Bananas III*, para. 7.73.

However, if a Member wishes to allocate quota shares or tariff quota shares to some suppliers with minor market shares, then such shares must be allocated to all such suppliers. If not, imports from Members would not be 'similarly restricted' as required by Article XIII:1 of the GATT 1994.[198] Moreover, it would be required to use the same method as was used to allocate the shares to the Members having a substantial interest in supplying the product. Otherwise, the non-discrimination obligation of Article XIII:1 would not be met.[199]

If a Member wishes to allocate a part of the quota or tariff quota to Members with minor market shares, then this is best done by providing – next to country-specific quota shares for Members with a substantial interest – for an 'others' category for all Members not having a substantial interest in supplying the product.[200] The use of an 'others' category is in conformity with the object and purpose of Article XIII (as expressed in the chapeau of Article XIII:2) to achieve a distribution of trade as close as possible to that which would have been the distribution of trade in the absence of the quantitative restriction.[201] The Panel in *EC – Bananas III* noted:

> When a significant share of a tariff quota is assigned to "others", the import market will evolve with a minimum amount of distortion. Members not having a substantial supplying interest will be able, if sufficiently competitive, to gain market share in the "others" category and possibly achieve "substantial supplying interest" status ... New entrants will be able to compete in the market, and likewise have an opportunity to gain "substantial supplying interest" status.[202]

5.3.3.3. *Examples of the allocation of quotas and tariff quotas*

As examples of the manner in which quotas and tariff quotas can be allocated, as discussed above, consider the tariff quotas on various agricultural products applied by the European Communities, as set out in Figure 5.20. Note that some of these tariff quotas are global tariff quotas (see CN 0701 90 50 (Potatoes ...)) while others are allocated among the supplying countries (see CN 0703 20 00 (Garlic)).

Questions and Assignments 5.14

How should quantitative restrictions be administered? Are the rules set out in Article XIII also applicable to the administration of measures other than quantitative restrictions? If the importation of a product is subject to a quota, how then shall the trade that is still allowed be distributed among the different Members exporting that product? Can a Member applying a quota, or tariff quota, allocate part of that quota, or tariff quota, to Members

---

[198] See above, pp. 450–1.   [199] See *ibid.*

[200] The alternative is to allocate to all supplying countries, including Members with minor market shares, country-specific tariff quota shares. This method, however, is more likely to lead to a long-term freezing of market shares and a less competitive market. See also Panel Report, *EC – Bananas II*, para. 7.76.

[201] See *ibid.*, para. 7.76.   [202] Panel Reports, *EC – Bananas III*, para. 7.76.

Figure 5.20 Excerpt from Annex 7 to the EC Common Customs Tariff (quotas)[203]

30.10.2003	EN	Official Journal of the European Union			867

Annex 7

Order No	CN Code	Description	Quota quantity	Rate of duty (%)	Other terms and conditions
1	2	3	4	5	6
45	0407 00 30	Other poultry eggs	135 000 t	152€/ 1 000 kg/net	Import under the Europe Agreements may be taken into account when implementing this quota
46	0408 11 80	Egg yolks	7 000 t (shell egg equivalent)	711€/ 1 000 kg/net	Import under the Europe Agreements may be taken into account when implementing this quota
	0408 19 81			711€/ 1 000 kg/net	
	0408 19 89			331€/ 1 000 kg/net	
	0408 91 80	Birds' eggs not in shell		687€/ 1 000 kg/net	
	0408 99 80			176€/ 1 000 kg/net	
47	0701 90 50	Potatoes from 1 January to 15 May	4 000 t	3	
48	0703 20 00	Garlic	38 370 t	9.6	Allocated to supplying countries as follows: — Argentina 19 147 t — China 13 200 t — Other countries 6 023 t
49	0706 10 00	Carrots and turnips	1 200 t	7	
50	0707 00 05	Cucumbers, from 1 November to 15 May	1 100 t	Ad valorem duty reduced to 2.5	
51	0709 60 10 0711	Sweet peppers See order No 86	500 t	1.5	
52	0712 20 00	Dried onions	12 000 t	10	
53	0714 10 0714 10 91 0714 10 99	Manioc	5 500 000 t	6	Within maximum quantity of 21 million t over each four-year period Allocated to Thailand as supplying country Qualification for this quota is subject to conditions laid down in the relevant Community provisions

54	0714 10 91
	
	 0714 90 11
	
	 0714 90 19
		Manioc
		
		 Arrowroot, salep and similar roots and
		 tubers with high starch content
			1 352 590 t	6	Allocated to supplying countries as follows:
					
					 — Indonesia 825 000 t
					 — Other GATT countries except
					   Thailand 145 590 t
					 — China 350 000 t
					 — Other non-GATT contries 32000 t
					   of which 2 000 t shall be of a kind used for human consumption, in immediate packings of a net content not exceeding 28 kg. either fresh and whole or without skin and frozen. whether or not sliced

[203] For 2004, see Commission Regulation (EC) No. 1789/2003 of 11 September 2003, amending Annex I to Council Regulation (EEC) No. 2658/87 on the tariff and statistical nomenclature and the Common Customs Tariffs, OJ 2003, L281, 867, 30 October 2003.

with minor market shares? If so, how is this done best? Give two examples other than those referred to above of the administration of tariff quotas by allocating country-specific tariff quota shares.

5.3.3.4. *Import-licensing procedures*

Quotas and tariff quotas are habitually administered through import-licensing procedures. Article 1.1 of the *Import Licensing Agreement* defines import-licensing procedures as:

> administrative procedures ... requiring the submission of an application or other documentation (other than that required for customs purposes) to the relevant administrative body as a prior condition for importation into the customs territory of the importing Member.[204]

A trader who wishes to import a product that is subject to a quota or tariff quota must apply for an import licence, i.e. a permit to import. Whether this import licence will be granted depends on whether the quota is already filled or not, and on whether the trader meets the requirements for an import licence.[205]

Economists agree that a first-come, first-served distribution rule for import licences is the most economically efficient licensing method.[206] However, import-licensing rules and procedures are often much more complex, as was illustrated by the import licensing system for bananas at issue in *EC – Bananas III*.[207]

Article 1 of the *Import Licensing Agreement* sets out rules on the *application* and *administration* of import-licensing rules. The most important of these rules is set out in Article 1.3, which reads:

> The rules for import licensing procedures shall be neutral in application and administered in a fair and equitable manner.[208]

Moreover, Article 1.4 of the *Import Licensing Agreement* requires that the rules and all information concerning procedures for the submission of applications for import licences must be published in such a manner as to enable Members and traders to become acquainted with them.[209] In no event shall such a

---

[204] While Article 1.1 of the *Import Licensing Agreement* does not explicitly state that import licensing procedures for tariff quotas are import-licensing procedures within the meaning of Article 1.1, the Appellate Body in *EC – Bananas III* ruled that a careful reading of that provision 'leads inescapably to that conclusion'. As the Appellate Body noted, import-licensing procedures for tariff quotas require 'the submission of an application' for import licences as 'a prior condition for importation' of a product at the lower in-quota tariff rate (see Appellate Body Report, *EC – Bananas III*, para. 193).

[205] This would be an example of non-automatic import licensing. As discussed below, there is also automatic import licensing, but this would not occur with respect to the importation of a product that is subject to a quota or tariff quota. See below, p. 456.

[206] See P. Lindert and T. Pugel, *International Economics*, 10th edition (McGraw Hill, 1996).

[207] Panel Reports, *EC – Bananas III*, paras. 7.142–7.273.

[208] On this provision, see Appellate Body Report, *EC – Bananas III*, para. 197.

[209] Article 1.4(a) of the *Import Licensing Agreement*. The rules and information concerned include rules and information on the eligibility of persons, firms and institutions to make such applications and the administrative body(ies) to be approached.

publication be later than the date on which the licence requirement becomes effective.[210] Any exceptions, derogations or changes in or from the rules concerning licensing procedures or the list of products subject to import licensing shall also be published in the same manner and within the same period.[211] In *EC – Poultry*, Brazil argued that frequent changes to the EC licensing rules and procedures regarding the poultry tariff quota made it difficult for Members and traders to become familiar with the rules, contrary to the provisions of Article 1.4 and other provisions of the *Import Licensing Agreement*. The Panel rejected this complaint as follows:

> We note that the transparency requirement under the cited provisions is limited to publication of rules and other information. While we have sympathy for Brazil regarding the difficulties caused by the frequent changes to the rules, we find that changes in rules *per se* do not constitute a violation of Articles 1.4, 3.3, 3.5(b), 3.5(c) or 3.5(d).[212]

Articles 1.7 and 1.8 of the *Import Licensing Agreement* require that, in the administration and application of licensing rules, 'common sense' prevails. Small errors or variations may not have major adverse consequences. For example, an application for an import licence shall not be refused for minor documentation errors, which do not alter basic data contained therein.[213]

The *Import Licensing Agreement* distinguishes between automatic and non-automatic import licensing. *Automatic import licensing* is defined as import licensing where approval of the application is granted *in all cases*.[214] Automatic import licensing may be maintained to collect statistical and other information on imports. Article 2.2 of the *Import Licensing Agreement* requires that automatic import-licensing procedures shall not be administered in such a manner as to have 'restricting effects on imports subject to automatic licensing'. *Non-automatic import licensing* is import licensing where approval is *not* granted in all cases. Import-licensing procedures for quotas and tariff quotas are by definition non-automatic import-licensing procedures. Article 3.2 of the *Import Licensing Agreement* requires that-

> Non-automatic licensing shall not have trade-restrictive or distortive effects on imports additional to those caused by the imposition of the restriction.

Other requirements relating to non-automatic import licensing concern:

- the non-discrimination among applicants for import licences;[215]
- the obligation to give reasons for refusing an application;[216]
- the right of appeal or review of the decisions on applications;[217]
- time–limits for processing applications;[218]

---

[210] Article 1.4(a) of the *Import Licensing Agreement*. Whenever practicable, the publication shall take place twenty-one days prior to the effective date.
[211] *Ibid.*   [212] Panel Report, *EC – Poultry*, para. 246.
[213] See Article 1.7 of the *Import Licensing Agreement*.
[214] See Article 2.1 of the *Import Licensing Agreement*.
[215] Article 3.5(e) of the *Import Licensing Agreement*.   [216] *Ibid.*
[217] *Ibid.*   [218] Article 3.5(f) of the *Import Licensing Agreement*.

- the validity of import licences;[219] and
- the desirability of issuing licences for products in economic quantities.[220]

Questions and Assignments 5.15

What are import-licensing procedures and how do they relate to quotas and tariff quotas? How are import licensing rules to be applied and administered? What is the difference between automatic and non-automatic import licensing? Are they subject to different requirements?

5.3.4. Other non-tariff barriers

In addition to customs duties and other duties and charges (i.e. tariff barriers) and quantitative restrictions (i.e. the first subcategory of non-tariff barriers), trade in goods is also impeded by 'other non-tariff barriers'. As the term indicates, this is a *residual* category of measures and actions that restrict, to various degrees, market access of goods.[221] The category of 'other non-tariff barriers' covers numerous rather different measures and actions, such as technical barriers to trade, customs formalities and procedures, and government procurement practices. With regard to technical barriers to trade, one must distinguish between:

- the general category of technical barriers to trade, for which rules have been set out in the *TBT Agreement*; and
- a special category of technical barriers to trade, namely, sanitary and phytosanitary measures, for which rules are provided in the *SPS Agreement*.

Note, however, that not only action but also the absence of action, and in particular the failure to inform about the applicable trade laws, regulations, procedures and practices, timely and accurately, may constitute a formidable barrier to trade.

This section addresses the following other 'non-tariff barriers' to trade in goods:

- technical regulations, standards and conformity assessment procedures;
- sanitary and phytosanitary measures;
- lack of transparency;
- unfair and arbitrary application of trade measures;
- customs formalities and procedures; and
- other measures or actions, such as preshipment inspection; marks of origin; government procurement practices; and measures relating to transit shipments.

---

[219] Article 3.5(g) of the *Import Licensing Agreement*.
[220] Article 3.5(h) of the *Import Licensing Agreement*.
[221] See e.g. *Table of Contents of the Inventory of Non-Tariff Measures*, Note by the Secretariat, TN/MA/S/5/Rev.1, dated 28 November 2003.

5.3.4.1. *Technical regulations, standards and conformity assessment procedures*

In modern society, products are often subject to technical requirements relating to their characteristics and/or the manner in which they are produced. The purpose of these requirements may be the protection of life or health, the protection of the environment, the prevention of deceptive practices or to ensure the quality of products. These requirements may constitute formidable barriers to trade. Moreover, procedures set up to verify whether a product meets certain requirements may obstruct trade. These barriers to trade are referred to as *technical barriers to trade*. As stated above, the rules applicable to the general category of technical barriers to trade are set out in the *Agreement on Technical Barriers to Trade*, commonly referred to as the *TBT Agreement*. The rules applicable to the special category of technical barriers to trade known as sanitary and phytosanitary measures will be discussed later.[222]

The rules of the *TBT Agreement* apply to technical regulations, standards and conformity assessment procedures relating to:

- products (both industrial and agricultural); and
- *related* processes and production methods (PPMs).

A measure is a 'technical regulation' within the meaning of the *TBT Agreement* if:

- the measure applies to an identifiable product or group of products;
- the measure lays down product characteristics; and
- compliance with the product characteristics laid down in the measure is mandatory.[223]

A standard differs from a technical regulation in that compliance with a standard is not mandatory.[224] A conformity assessment procedure is a procedure, such as inspection, sampling or testing, used to verify compliance with the requirements set out in technical regulations or standards.[225]

Although the *TBT Agreement* is mainly addressed to central government bodies, it extends its application also to local government bodies and non-governmental bodies by imposing on WTO Members the obligation:

- to take measures in order to ensure compliance with the *TBT Agreement* by local government bodies and non-governmental bodies; and
- to refrain from taking measures that could encourage actions by these other bodies that are inconsistent with the provisions of the *TBT Agreement*.

---

[222] See below, pp. 462–6.
[223] See the definition of a 'technical regulation' in Annex 1.1 to the *TBT Agreement*. See also Appellate Body Report, *EC – Asbestos*, paras. 67–70; and Appellate Body Report, *EC – Sardines*, para. 176.
[224] See the definition of a 'Standard' in Annex 1.2 to the *TBT Agreement*.
[225] See the definition of 'Conformity assessment procedures' in Annex 1.3 to the *TBT Agreement*.

It does so with respect to the obligations related to technical regulations, standards and procedures for assessment of conformity.[226] Note, in particular, the 'Code of Good Practice' in Annex 3 to the *TBT Agreement*. This 'Code of Good Practice' applies to the preparation, adoption and use of standards. Members have to ensure that their central government standardising bodies accept and comply with the 'Code of Good Practice'. In addition, Members are obliged, pursuant to Article 4 of the *TBT Agreement*, to take such reasonable measures as are available to them to ensure that local and non-governmental standardising bodies also accept and comply with the Code.

With regard to the relationship between the *TBT Agreement* and other WTO agreements, note that the applicability of the *SPS Agreement* or the *Agreement on Government Procurement* to a specific measure excludes the applicability of the *TBT Agreement* to that measure.[227] However, the *TBT Agreement* and the GATT 1994 can both be applicable to a specific measure.[228] Note, in general, that the relationship between the GATT 1994 and the other multilateral agreements on trade in goods (including the *TBT Agreement*) is governed by the *General Interpretative Note* to Annex 1A of the *WTO Agreement*.[229] This provides that, in case of conflict between a provision of the GATT 1994 and a provision of another multilateral agreement on trade in goods, the latter will prevail to the extent of the conflict. However, such a conflict between the *TBT Agreement* and the GATT 1994 is rather unlikely.

The basic substantive provisions of the *TBT Agreement* contain several principles that are also found in the GATT 1994, such as the MFN treatment obligation, the national treatment obligation and the obligation to refrain from creating unnecessary obstacles to international trade. In *EC – Asbestos*, the Appellate Body observed that the *TBT Agreement* intends to further the objectives of the GATT 1994. However, it immediately noted that the *TBT Agreement* does so through a specialised legal regime, containing different and additional obligations to those of the GATT 1994.[230]

The *TBT Agreement* requires that, in respect of TBT measures, Members accord national treatment and MFN treatment to products imported from other Members.[231] The *TBT Agreement* also requires that TBT measures do not

---

[226] See Articles 3.1 and 3.4 of the *TBT Agreement* (for technical regulations), Article 4.1 of the *TBT Agreement* (for standards) and Articles 7.1, 7.4 and 8.1 of the *TBT Agreement* (for conformity assessment procedures).

[227] See Articles 1.4 and 1.5 of the *TBT Agreement*.

[228] Note that the Panel in *EC – Asbestos* held that, in a case where both the GATT 1994 and the *TBT Agreement* appear to apply to a given measure, a panel must first examine whether the measure at issue is consistent with the *TBT Agreement*, since this agreement deals 'specifically and in detail' with technical barriers to trade. Should the measure be consistent with the *TBT Agreement*, a panel would have to determine whether the measure is GATT-consistent. See Panel Report, *EC – Asbestos*, para. 8.16.

[229] See above, p. 49.

[230] See Appellate Body Report, *EC – Asbestos*, para. 80. Therefore, caution needs to be used when transposing interpretations given to these obligations under GATT 1994 to the similar provisions in the *TBT Agreement*. The different context, structure and formulation of the *TBT Agreement*'s provisions can result in an interpretation that deviates from previously pronounced interpretations under the GATT 1994.

[231] See Article 2.1 of the *TBT Agreement* (for technical regulations), Article 5.1.1 of the *TBT Agreement* (for conformity assessment procedures) and Annex 3D to the *TBT Agreement* (for standards).

create unnecessary obstacles to international trade.[232] To this end, Article 2.2 further requires that:

> technical regulations shall not be more trade-restrictive than necessary to fulfil a legitimate objective, taking account of the risks non-fulfilment would create.

Article 2.2 proceeds to enumerate several legitimate objectives, such as the protection of human life or health or the protection of the environment.[233] In determining the necessity of their regulations, Members are explicitly obliged to 'take account of the risks non-fulfilment would create'. In assessing such risks, Article 2.2 lists relevant considerations, including available scientific and technical information, related processing technology and intended end-uses of products.

Harmonisation of national technical regulations, standards and conformity assessment procedures around international standards and procedures greatly facilitate the conduct of international trade, by minimising the variety of requirements exporters have to meet on their export markets. Thus, Article 2.4 of the *TBT Agreement* requires that:

> Where technical regulations are required and relevant international standards exist or their completion is imminent, Members shall use them, or the relevant parts of them, as a basis for their technical regulations.[234]

The meaning of the obligation to use a relevant international standard 'as a basis' for a technical regulation was addressed by the Panel in *EC – Sardines*.[235] It concluded that the concept of 'based on' is not equivalent to the concept of 'conform to', but imposes the obligation to 'employ or apply' the international standard as 'the principal constituent or fundamental principle for the purpose of enacting the technical regulation'.[236] According to the Appellate Body in *EC – Sardines*, this comes down to an analysis of 'whether there is a contradiction' between the international standard and the national regulation.[237]

According to Article 2.4, a technical regulation does not have to be based on the relevant international standards if:

> such international standards or relevant parts would be an ineffective or inappropriate means for the fulfilment of the legitimate objectives pursued, for instance because of fundamental climatic or geographical factors or fundamental technological problems.[238]

---

[232] See Article 2.2 of the *TBT Agreement* (for technical regulations), Article 5.1.2 of the *TBT Agreement* (for conformity assessment procedures) and Annex 3E to the *TBT Agreement* (for standards).

[233] See the list contained in Article 2.2 of the *TBT Agreement*. The list of legitimate objectives enumerated in Article 2.2 is not exhaustive. It will be up to panels and the Appellate Body to assess whether policy objectives other than those listed in Article 2.2 are, in a particular case, *legitimate* policy objectives.

[234] Article 2.4 of the *TBT Agreement*. See also Annex 3F to the *TBT Agreement* (for standards) and Article 5.4 of the *TBT Agreement* (for conformity assessment procedures).

[235] The Panel followed the case law on the meaning of 'based on' in the *SPS Agreement*; see below, p. 465.

[236] Panel Report, *EC – Sardines*, para. 7.110.

[237] Appellate Body Report, *EC – Sardines*, para. 249.

[238] Article 2.4 of the *TBT Agreement*. See also Annex 3F to the *TBT Agreement* (for standards), and Article 5.4 of the *TBT Agreement* (for conformity assessment procedures). Note, however, that, unlike Article 2.4 and Annex 3F, the criterion of effectiveness of the international standard is not mentioned in Article 5.4.

According to the Appellate Body in *EC – Sardines*, it is for the complainant to demonstrate that the international standard in question is both an effective *and* an appropriate means to fulfil the legitimate objective.[239] The difference between effectiveness and appropriateness is that:

> the question of effectiveness bears upon the results of the means employed, whereas the question of appropriateness relates to the nature of the means employed.[240]

In other words, the international standard:

- would be *effective* if it had the capacity to accomplish all objectives pursued; and
- would be *appropriate* if it were suitable for the fulfilment of all objectives pursued.[241]

Furthermore, the *TBT Agreement* requires WTO Members to consider accepting, as equivalent, the technical regulations of other Members if they are satisfied that the foreign technical regulations *adequately* fulfil the legitimate objectives pursued by their own technical regulations.[242] The *TBT Agreement* subjects Members to a number of detailed transparency and notification obligations.[243]

Members consult, regarding any matters pertaining to the operation or objectives of the *TBT Agreement*, in the TBT Committee, which is composed of all WTO Members and meets several times a year.[244] The WTO dispute settlement rules and procedures, discussed in Chapter 3, apply to disputes concerning the *TBT Agreement*.[245] The *TBT Agreement* contains a few special or additional rules and procedures, primarily with regard to the possibility for panels to consult technical experts.[246] Finally, in recognition of the difficulties developing-country Members may face in implementing the obligations under the *TBT Agreement*, the *TBT Agreement* provides for technical assistance and some special and differential treatment for developing-country Members.[247]

Questions and Assignments 5.16

What types of measure fall within the scope of the *TBT Agreement*? What does the necessity test of Article 2.2 of the *TBT Agreement* entail? Under what circumstances may Members adopt or maintain a technical regulation that is not based on an existing international standard? What special rules with regard to dispute settlement are provided for in the *TBT Agreement*?

---

[239] See Appellate Body Report, *EC – Sardines*, para. 287.
[240] See Panel Report, *EC – Sardines*, para. 7.116.
[241] Appellate Body Report, *EC – Sardines*, para. 288.
[242] See Article 2.7 of the *TBT Agreement*. See also Article 6.1 of the *TBT Agreement* (for conformity assessment procedures). In addition, Article 9 of the *TBT Agreement* encourages the adoption of, and participation in, international and regional systems for conformity assessment.
[243] See Articles 2.9 to 2.12 of the *TBT Agreement* (for technical regulations), Annex 3L to 3O of the *TBT Agreement* (for standards) and Article 5.8 of the *TBT Agreement* (for conformity assessment procedures).
[244] See Article 13 of the *TBT Agreement*.   [245] See Article 14 of the *TBT Agreement*.
[246] See Articles 14.2 and 14.3 of and Annex 2 to the *TBT Agreement*.
[247] See Article 12 of the *TBT Agreement*.

5.3.4.2. *Sanitary and phytosanitary measures*

A specific category of measures can be identified within the general category of technical barriers to trade, namely, sanitary and phytosanitary measures ('SPS measures'). These are measures aimed at the protection of human, animal or plant life or health from certain specified risks. The negotiators of the WTO agreements considered that these measures merited special attention for two reasons. First, these measures are closely linked to agricultural trade, a sector notoriously difficult to liberalise. Secondly, these measures fall within a politically sensitive area of government policy, namely, the protection of health. A separate agreement, the *SPS Agreement*, was therefore considered necessary to balance the goal of trade liberalisation with the right of governments to regulate for the protection of health in their territories.

The substantive scope of application of the *SPS Agreement* is set out in Article 1.1. For a measure to be subject to the *SPS Agreement*, it must be:

- an SPS measure; and
- a measure that may affect international trade.

Not all measures for the protection of health are 'SPS measures' for the purposes of the *SPS Agreement*. Whether a measure is an 'SPS measure' as defined in Annex A1 of the *SPS Agreement* depends on its purpose or aim. In broad terms, an 'SPS measure' is a measure that:

- aims at the protection of human or animal life or health from food-borne risks; or
- aims at the protection of human, animal or plant life or health from risks from pests or diseases.

Note that the definition in Annex A1 refers specifically to the protection of human, animal or plant life or health 'within the territory of the Member', thus excluding measures aimed at extra-territorial health protection from the scope of application of the *SPS Agreement*.

The adoption and implementation of SPS measures are sometimes in the hands of bodies other than central government, such as regulatory agencies, regional bodies and sub-federal governments. The *SPS Agreement* takes this into account by providing that Members are fully responsible for the implementation of the Agreement and must enact and implement positive measures to ensure the observance of its rules by other than central government bodies.[248]

With regard to the relationship between the *SPS Agreement* and other WTO agreements, note that, when a measure is an 'SPS measure' as defined in Annex A1 of the *SPS Agreement*, the *SPS Agreement* applies to the exclusion of

---

[248] See Article 13 of the *SPS Agreement*. This Article was applied by the Panel in *Australia – Salmon (Article 21.5)* to find that measures taken by the Government of Tasmania were subject to the *SPS Agreement* and fell under the responsibility of Australia. See Panel Report, *Australia – Salmon (Article 21.5)*, para. 7.13.

the *TBT Agreement*.[249] However, no relationship of mutual exclusivity exists between the *SPS Agreement* and the GATT 1994.[250] However, Article 2.4 of the *SPS Agreement* contains a presumption of consistency with the relevant provisions of the GATT 1994 for all measures that are in conformity with the *SPS Agreement*. It would therefore be logical, in a dispute involving an SPS measure, to begin by examining the measure under the *SPS Agreement*.[251]

One of the motives behind the negotiation of the *SPS Agreement* was the need to flesh out and clarify the exception for health measures in Article XX(b) of the GATT 1994. However, the *SPS Agreement* goes much further than a mere elaboration of this exception and imposes a new and comprehensive set of rules.[252]

The basic principles of the *SPS Agreement*, contained in Article 2, reflect the underlying aim of balancing the need to increase market access for food and agricultural products with the recognition of the sovereign right of governments to take measures to protect human, animal and plant life and health. The *SPS Agreement*, in Article 2.1, explicitly acknowledges the sovereign right of WTO Members to take SPS measures.[253] At the same time, however, the *SPS Agreement* subjects Members to a number of disciplines regarding their SPS measures. Besides incorporating some familiar GATT rules relevant to health measures, these disciplines introduce science as the touchstone against which SPS measures are judged.

The basic disciplines are:

- the obligation to take or maintain only those SPS measures *necessary* to protect human, animal or plant life or health;[254]
- the obligation to take or maintain only SPS measures 'based on' scientific principles and on sufficient scientific evidence;[255] and
- the obligation not to adopt or maintain SPS measures that arbitrarily or unjustifiably discriminate or constitute a disguised restriction on trade.[256]

The *SPS Agreement* further contains rules, in Article 3, encouraging, but not obliging, Members to harmonise their SPS measures around international standards.[257] The aim of Article 3 of the *SPS Agreement* was expressed as follows by the Appellate Body in *EC – Hormones*:

---

[249] Article 1.5 of the *TBT Agreement*; see above, p. 459.
[250] Just as is the case for the *TBT Agreement*, the relationship between the GATT 1994 and the *SPS Agreement* is governed by the *General Interpretative Note* to Annex 1A to the *WTO Agreement*, discussed above, p. 49.
[251] The Panel in *EC – Hormones* held that, in a dispute involving an SPS measure, the consistency of the measure with the *SPS Agreement* should be examined first, as this agreement 'specifically addresses the type of measure in dispute'. See Panel Report, *EC – Hormones (Canada)*, para. 8.45; and Panel Report, *EC – Hormones (US)*, para. 8.42.
[252] This was recognised by the Panel in *EC – Hormones*. See Panel Report, *EC – Hormones (Canada)*, para. 8.41; and Panel Report, *EC – Hormones (US)*, para. 8.38.
[253] This differs from the position of health measures under GATT rules where discriminatory measures or quantitative restrictions are in principle prohibited. Justification for such measures must be found under Article XX(b). This has important implications for the burden of proof in dispute settlement proceedings.
[254] See Article 2.2 of the *SPS Agreement*.   [255] See Article 2.2 of the *SPS Agreement*.
[256] See Article 2.3 of the *SPS Agreement*.
[257] Article 3 refers to 'international standards, guidelines or recommendations'. For reasons of convenience, the concept of 'international standards' will be used in this section to refer to 'international standards, guidelines or recommendations'. Annex A3 to the *SPS Agreement* defines international standards as

> In generalized terms, the object and purpose of Article 3 is to promote the harmoniza-
> tion of the SPS measures of Members on as wide a basis as possible, while recognizing
> and safeguarding, at the same time, the right and duty of Members to protect the life
> and health of their people.[258]

Under Article 3, Members have three autonomous options with regard to international standards, each with its own consequences. Members may choose to:

- *base* their SPS measures *on* international standards according to Article 3.1;
- *conform* their SPS measures to international standards under Article 3.2; or
- impose SPS measures resulting in a *higher level* of protection than would be achieved by the relevant international standard in terms of Article 3.3.

In *EC – Hormones*, the Appellate Body confirmed that these are equally available options and there is no rule–exception relationship between them.[259] Thus, a Member is not penalised for choosing the Article 3.3 alternative. However, the three options have different consequences. If a Member chooses to conform its measure to an international standard, it benefits from a presumption of consistency with the *SPS Agreement* and the GATT 1994.[260] If a Member chooses to deviate from the international standard, it must have scientific justification for this deviation, in the form of a risk assessment.[261]

The substantive obligations provided for in the *SPS Agreement* also include obligations with respect to risk analysis, i.e. risk assessment and risk management. The concept of 'risk assessment' refers to the scientific process of identifying the existence of a risk and establishing the likelihood that the risk may actually materialise according to the measures that could be applied to address the risk. 'Risk management', by contrast, is the policy-based process of determining the level of protection a country wants to ensure in its territory and choosing the measure that will be used to achieve that level of protection. In risk management decision-making, not only are the scientific results of the risk assessment taken into account but also societal value considerations such as consumer preferences, industry interests and relative costs.

With regard to risk assessment, Article 5.1 of the *SPS Agreement* states:

> Members shall ensure that their sanitary or phytosanitary measures are based on an
> assessment, as appropriate to the circumstances, of the risks to human, animal or plant
> life or health, taking into account risk assessment techniques developed by the relevant
> international organizations.[262]

---

those set by the following three international standard-setting organisations: the Codex Alimentarius Commission, for food safety; the International Plant Protection Convention, for plant health; and the International Office of Epizootics, for animal health.

[258] Appellate Body Report, *EC – Hormones*, para. 177.   [259] *Ibid.*, para. 104.

[260] Article 3.2 of the *SPS Agreement*.

[261] Article 3.3 of the *SPS Agreement*. Note that Article 3.3 lays down two alternative conditions for deviation from international standards. However, the difference between them is not clear, and in *EC – Hormones* the Appellate Body found that in both cases a risk assessment is required. See Appellate Body Report, *EC – Hormones*, paras. 175–6.

[262] Article 5.1 of the *SPS Agreement*. There are *two* types of risk assessment, each with different requirements applicable to risks from pests and diseases on the one hand and food-borne risks on the other. These are defined in Annex A4 to the *SPS Agreement*.

The meaning of the requirement that measures be 'based on' a risk assessment was clarified by the Appellate Body in *EC – Hormones*. The Appellate Body in that case held that, for an SPS measure to be 'based on' a risk assessment, there must be a 'rational relationship' between the measure and the risk assessment, and the risk assessment must 'reasonably support' the measure.[263]

Some general observations can be made with respect to the requirements for risk assessments as identified in the case law. First, the Appellate Body has held that a risk assessment must show proof of an actual risk, not just a theoretical uncertainty.[264] Secondly, the Appellate Body has recognised that a risk assessment may go beyond controlled laboratory conditions and take account of the actual potential for adverse effects in the 'real world where people live and work and die'.[265] Thirdly, the risk assessment must be specific to the particular type of risk at issue in the case and not merely show a general risk of harm.[266] Fourthly, a risk assessment may evaluate the risk quantitatively or qualitatively.[267] Fifthly, Article 5.1 does not oblige Members to carry out their own risk assessments. Instead, they may rely on risk assessments carried out by other Members or by an international organisation.[268]

Although the *SPS Agreement* does not lay down any methodology of risk assessment to be followed by Members, it does specify certain factors that Members must take into account in their risk assessments. Article 5.2 lists certain scientific and technical factors that Members must consider when assessing risks, and Article 5.3 lays down certain economic factors that those Members must take into account.

With regard to risk management, the *SPS Agreement* primarily requires that Members must:

- avoid arbitrary or unjustifiable distinctions in the levels of protection deemed appropriate in different situations, if these distinctions lead to discrimination or disguised restrictions on trade;[269] and
- ensure that SPS measures are not more trade-restrictive than required to achieve the appropriate level of protection.[270]

While the *SPS Agreement* uses science as the touchstone against which SPS measures are judged, it also recognises the fact that science does not always have clear answers to regulatory problems. Situations may arise where there is insufficient scientific evidence regarding the existence and extent of the relevant risk, but where governments nonetheless consider they need to act promptly and take measures to avoid possible harm. Thus, governments act with precaution without waiting for the collection of sufficient scientific information to conclusively assess the risks. This is commonly referred to as

---

[263] Appellate Body Report, *EC – Hormones*, para. 193.   [264] *Ibid.*, para. 186.
[265] *Ibid.*, para. 187.   [266] *Ibid.*, para. 200.
[267] With regard to the first definition of risk assessment, see Appellate Body Report, *Australia – Salmon*, para. 124. In respect of the second definition, see Appellate Body Report, *EC – Hormones*, para. 186.
[268] Appellate Body Report, *EC – Hormones*, para. 190.   [269] See Article 5.5 of the *SPS Agreement*.
[270] See Article 5.6 of the *SPS Agreement*.

acting in accordance with the 'precautionary principle'. Under certain conditions, Article 5.7 of the *SPS Agreement* allows Members to take *provisional* SPS measures where scientific evidence is insufficient. Article 5.7 provides:

> In cases where relevant scientific evidence is insufficient, a Member may provisionally adopt sanitary or phytosanitary measures on the basis of available pertinent information, including that from the relevant international organizations as well as from sanitary or phytosanitary measures applied by other Members. In such circumstances, Members shall seek to obtain the additional information necessary for a more objective assessment of risk and review the sanitary or phytosanitary measure accordingly within a reasonable period of time.[271]

The *SPS Agreement* also provides for substantive provisions relating to: the recognition of equivalence of SPS measures of other Members;[272] the obligation of Members to adapt their SPS measures to regional conditions;[273] control, inspection and approval procedures;[274] and transparency and notification obligations regarding SPS measures.[275]

Members consult regarding any matters pertaining to the operation or objectives of the *SPS Agreement* in the SPS Committee. This Committee is composed of all WTO Members and meets several times a year.[276] The WTO dispute settlement rules and procedures, discussed in Chapter 3, apply to disputes concerning the *SPS Agreement*.[277] The *SPS Agreement* contains one special or additional dispute settlement rule, providing panels with the possibility to consult scientific experts.[278] Finally, the *SPS Agreement* acknowledges the difficulties developing-country Members may face in implementing the obligations under the *SPS Agreement*, and thus provides for technical assistance and some special and differential treatment for developing-country Members.[279]

Questions and Assignments 5.17

What requirements must be met for the *SPS Agreement* to apply to a specific measure? If a measure falls under both the *SPS Agreement* and the GATT 1994, how should a panel proceed? How does the treatment of health measures under the *SPS Agreement* differ from that under Article XX(b) of the GATT 1994? What three options do Members have with regard to international harmonised standards? When is an SPS measure 'based on' a risk assessment? Which obligations regarding risk management does the *SPS Agreement* provide for? When can Members invoke the 'precautionary principle' in justification of SPS measures that are not based on scientific evidence?

---

[271] The requirements of Article 5.7 were clarified by panels and the Appellate Body in *Japan – Agricultural Products* and *Japan – Apples*.
[272] See Article 4 of the *SPS Agreement*.   [273] See Article 6 of the *SPS Agreement*.
[274] See Article 8 of the *SPS Agreement*.   [275] See Article 7 of the *SPS Agreement*.
[276] See Article 12 of the *SPS Agreement*.   [277] See Article 11.1 of the *SPS Agreement*.
[278] See Article 11.2 of the *SPS Agreement*.   [279] See Articles 9 and 10 of the *SPS Agreement*.

5.3.4.3. *Lack of transparency*

As discussed above, ignorance, uncertainty or confusion with respect to the trade laws, regulations and procedures applicable in actual or potential export markets is an important barrier to trade. Therefore, WTO law provides for rules and procedures to ensure a high level of transparency of its Members' trade laws, regulations and procedures.

There are four kinds of relevant WTO rules and procedures:

- the *publication* requirement;
- the *notification* requirement;
- the requirement to establish *enquiry points*; and
- the trade policy *review* process.

Article X of the GATT 1994, entitled 'Publication and Administration of Trade Regulations', states in its first paragraph:

> Laws, regulations, judicial decisions and administrative rulings of general application, made effective by any [Member], pertaining to the classification or the valuation of products for customs purposes, or to rates of duty, taxes or other charges, or to requirements, restrictions or prohibitions on imports or exports or on the transfer of payments therefor, or affecting their sale, distribution, transportation, insurance, warehousing, inspection, exhibition, processing, mixing or other use, shall be published promptly in such a manner as to enable governments and traders to become acquainted with them. Agreements affecting international trade policy which are in force between the government or a governmental agency of any [Member] and the government or governmental agency of any other [Member] shall also be published.

Article X:1 thus requires Members to publish their laws, regulations, judicial decisions, administrative rulings of general application and international agreements relating to trade matters. Article X:1 does not prescribe in any detail how the laws, regulations, etc. have to be published but it does state that they have to be published 'promptly' and 'in such a manner as to enable governments and traders to become acquainted with them'.[280] In *EEC – Apples (US)*, the United States claimed that the European Communities acted inconsistently with, *inter alia*, Article X:1 by not giving 'adequate public notice' of the import quotas on the product at issue, apples. These import quotas applied to the period from 15 February to 31 August 1988, but the European Communities adopted the regulation setting forth these import quotas only on 20 April 1988 and published the regulation on the following day.[281] The Panel noted that:

---

[280] Note that these requirements do not explicitly apply to the publication of the international agreements, but it may be assumed that they also apply in this context. Moreover, note that Article X:1 does not require Members to disclose confidential information which would impede law enforcement or otherwise be contrary to the public interest or which would prejudice the legitimate commercial interests of particular enterprises, public or private. See Article X:1, last sentence.

[281] GATT Panel Report, *EEC – Apples (US)*, para. 3.41.

> the EEC had observed the requirement of Article X:1 to publish the measures under examination "promptly in such a manner as to enable governments and traders to become acquainted with them" through their publication in the Official Journal of the European Communities. It noted that no lapse of time between publication and entry into force was specified by this provision.[282]

The Panel, however, subsequently interpreted the requirements of Article X:2 of the GATT as prohibiting backdated quotas, and concluded therefore that the European Communities acted inconsistently with Article X:2 since it gave public notice of the quotas only about two months after the quota period had begun.[283]

In *Canada – Provincial Liquor Boards (EEC)*, the Panel noted that Article X:2 required the prompt publication of trade regulations but did not require the publication of trade regulations *in advance* of their entry into force.[284] The Panel also noted that Article X:2 did not require that information affecting trade be made available to domestic and foreign suppliers at the same time.[285]

With regard to the concept of 'administrative ruling of general application', note that, to the extent that an administrative ruling is addressed to a specific company or applied to a specific shipment, it cannot be qualified as an administrative ruling of general application. However, to the extent that an administrative ruling affects an unidentified number of economic operators, it can be qualified as a ruling of general application. The fact that a measure is country-specific does not preclude the possibility of it being an administrative ruling of general application.[286]

In addition to Article X:1, Article X:2 of the GATT 1994 also concerns the publication of trade measures of general application. Article X:2 provides:

> No measure of general application taken by any [Member] effecting an advance in a rate of duty or other charge on imports under an established and uniform practice, or imposing a new or more burdensome requirement, restriction or prohibition on imports, or on the transfer of payments therefor, shall be enforced before such measure has been officially published.

Pursuant to Article X:2, publication is therefore a condition of enforcement. Members may not enforce trade measures of general application, imposing restraints, requirements or other burdens, *before* they are published. Such

---

[282] *Ibid.*, para. 5.21.
[283] The Panel's reasoning was in fact based on its interpretation of Article XIII:3(b) and (c) as prohibiting backdated quotas. The Panel merely stated that it interpreted Article X:1 'likewise'. See GATT Panel Report, *EEC – Apples (US)*, para. 5.23.
[284] GATT Panel Report, *Canada – Provincial Liquor Boards*, para. 5.34. Note, however, that Article 2.12 of the *TBT Agreement* requires that 'Members shall allow a reasonable interval between the publication of technical regulations and their entry into force in order to allow time for producers in exporting Members … to adapt their products or methods of production to the requirements of the importing Member'.
[285] *Ibid.*
[286] See Appellate Body Report, *US – Underwear*, 21. See also Appellate Body Report, *EC – Poultry*, paras. 111–13. Note that the Panel in *Japan – Film* stated that: 'it stands to reason that inasmuch as the Article X:1 requirement applies to all administrative rulings of general application, it also should extend to administrative rulings in individual cases where such rulings establish or revise principles or criteria applicable in future cases.' See Panel Report, *Japan – Film*, para. 10.388.

measures will only take effect *after* publication.[287] With respect to the rationale of Article X:2, the Appellate Body noted in *US – Underwear*:

> Article X:2, *General Agreement*, may be seen to embody a principle of fundamental importance – that of promoting full disclosure of governmental acts affecting Members and private persons and enterprises, whether of domestic or foreign nationality. The relevant policy principle is widely known as the principle of transparency and has obviously due process dimensions. The essential implication is that Members and other persons affected, or likely to be affected, by governmental measures imposing restraints, requirements and other burdens, should have a reasonable opportunity to acquire authentic information about such measures and accordingly to protect and adjust their activities or alternatively to seek modification of such measures.[288]

Note that the GATT 1994 and other WTO agreements also require Members to publish, or give public notice of, certain *specific* trade measures of general application.[289]

As noted above, WTO law also provides for a *notification* requirement. Almost all WTO agreements require Members to notify the WTO of measures or actions covered by these agreements.[290] A typical example of such a notification requirement is found in Article 12.6 of the *Agreement on Safeguards*, which states:

> Members shall notify promptly the Committee on Safeguards of their laws, regulations and administrative procedures relating to safeguard measures as well as any modifications made to them.

A number of WTO agreements also provide for the possibility for a Member to notify measures or actions of other Members, which the latter failed to notify. Article 12.8 of the *Agreement on Safeguards*, for example, provides:

> Any Member may notify the Committee on Safeguards of all laws, regulations, administrative procedures and any measures or actions dealt with in this Agreement that have not been notified by other Members that are required by this Agreement to make such notifications.

The following list, annexed to the *Decision on Notification Procedures* of 1993, contains measures and actions, which Members must notify to the WTO:

- Tariffs (including range and scope of bindings, GSP provisions, rates applied to members of free trade areas/customs unions, other preferences)
- Tariff quotas and surcharges

---

[287] Note that, with respect to the issue of the retroactive effect of measures, the Appellate Body ruled in *US – Underwear* that prior publication as required by Article X:2 of the GATT 1994 cannot, in and of itself, justify the retroactive effect of a trade-restrictive measure. Article X:2 does not speak to, and hence does not resolve, the permissibility of giving retroactive effect to trade-restrictive measures. Where no authority exists to give retroactive effect to a trade-restrictive measure, that deficiency is not cured by publishing the measure sometime before its actual application. See Appellate Body Report, *US – Underwear*, 21.

[288] *Ibid.*

[289] See e.g. Article XIII:3 of the GATT 1994 (concerning quotas and tariff quotas) and Article 2.11 of the *TBT Agreement* (concerning technical regulations).

[290] In addition, see also the *Decision on Notification Procedures*, adopted by the Trade Negotiations Committee on 15 December 1993 and annexed to the Final Act Embodying the Results of the Uruguay Round of Multilateral Trade Negotiations, in *The Legal Texts: Results of the Uruguay Round of Multilateral Trade Negotiations* (Cambridge University Press, 1999), 388.

- Quantitative restrictions, including voluntary export restraints and orderly marketing arrangements affecting imports
- Other non-tariff measures such as licensing and mixing requirements; variable levies
- Customs valuation
- Rules of origin
- Government procurement
- Technical barriers
- Safeguard actions
- Anti-dumping actions
- Countervailing actions
- Export taxes
- Export subsidies, tax exemptions and concessionary export financing
- Free trade zones, including in-bond manufacturing
- Export restrictions, including voluntary export restraints and orderly marketing arrangements
- Other government assistance, including subsidies, tax exemptions
- Role of State trading enterprises
- Foreign exchange controls related to imports and exports
- Government-mandated countertrade
- Any other measure covered by the Multilateral Trade Agreements in Annex 1A to the *WTO Agreement*.[291]

To improve the operation of the WTO notification requirements and thereby contribute to the transparency of Members' trade policies and measures, a *central registry of notifications* has been established under the responsibility of the WTO Secretariat. This central registry records the measures notified and the information provided by Members with respect to the purpose of the measure, its trade coverage, and the requirement under which it has been notified. The central registry cross-references its records of notifications by Members and their obligations.[292] Information in the central registry regarding individual notifications is made available, on request, to any Member entitled to receive the notification concerned. The central registry informs each Member annually of the regular notification obligations to which that Member will be expected to respond in the course of the following year.

In addition to a publication requirement and a notification requirement, some WTO agreements also require Members to establish national *enquiry points* where further information on certain trade laws and regulations can be obtained. Article 10.1 of the *TBT Agreement*, for example, provides:

> Each Member shall ensure that an enquiry point exists which is able to answer all reasonable enquiries from other Members and interested parties in other Members as well as to provide the relevant documents regarding:

---

[291] *Ibid.*, 390.   [292] *Ibid.*, 388.

> ... any technical regulations adopted or proposed ...
> ... any standards adopted or proposed ...
> ... any conformity assessment procedures, or proposed conformity assessment procedures ...

Note also that Article 10.4 of the *TBT Agreement* requires that Members take all reasonable measures available to them to ensure that where *copies of documents* are requested by other Members or by interested parties, they are supplied, and are supplied at an equitable price (if any).

Finally, the transparency of Members' trade policies, legislation and procedures is also advanced considerably by the periodic trade policy reviews under the *Trade Policy Review Mechanism.* This mechanism is discussed in detail in Chapter 2.[293]

Questions and Assignments 5.18

Why is the lack of transparency with respect to a country's trade laws, regulations and other measures of general application, a formidable barrier to trade in goods? How does WTO law seek to ensure transparency with respect to its Members' trade measures of general application?

5.3.4.4. *Unfair and arbitrary application of trade measures*

It is clear that the unfair and arbitrary application of national trade measures, and the degree of uncertainty and unpredictability this generates for other Members and traders, constitute a significant barrier to trade – in the same way as the lack of transparency discussed above. To ensure a fair and correct application of national trade measures, WTO law provides for:

- a requirement of uniform, impartial and reasonable administration of national trade rules; and
- a requirement for procedures for the objective and impartial review of the administration of national customs rules.

Article X:3(a) of the GATT provides:

> Each [Member] shall administer in a uniform, impartial and reasonable manner all its laws, regulations, decisions and rulings of the kind described in paragraph 1 of this Article.

As the words of Article X:3(a) clearly indicate, the requirements of 'uniformity, impartiality and reasonableness' do not apply to the laws, regulations, decisions and rulings *themselves*, but rather to the *administration* of those laws, regulations, decisions and rulings.[294] To the extent that the laws, regulations, decisions and rulings themselves are discriminatory, they may be found inconsistent with, for example, Articles I:1, III:2 or III:4 of the GATT 1994.[295]

---

[293] See above, pp. 94–7. [294] See Appellate Body Report, *EC – Bananas III*, para. 200.
[295] See above, pp. 309–18, 326–64.

Moreover, Article X:3(a) applies *not only* in situations where it is established that a Member, in the administration of its trade laws, regulations, decisions and rulings, discriminates between Members. In fact, the test under Article X:3(a) generally will not be whether there has been discriminatory treatment in favour of imports to, or exports from, one Member relative to another.[296] According to the Panel in *Argentina – Hides and Leather*:

> the focus is on the treatment accorded by government authorities to the *traders* in question.[297]
>
> [Emphasis added]

As stated above, Article X:3(a) concerns the *administration* of national trade rules, and not the trade rules themselves. However, this does not mean that a violation of Article X:3(a) can only be found in the administration of a regulation, and not in its substance. As the Panel in *Argentina – Hides and Leather* concluded, administrative regulations, i.e. regulations providing for a certain manner of applying substantive rules, *can* also be found consistent with Article X:3(a).[298] At issue in that case was an Argentinean regulation providing for the participation of representatives of the domestic tanners' association, ADICMA, in the customs inspection procedures for hides destined for export operations.[299] The representatives of ADICMA 'assisted' Argentina's customs authorities in the application and enforcement of the rules on customs classification, valuation and export duties.[300] The European Communities, the complainant in *Argentina – Hides and Leather*, claimed that the presence of 'partial and interested' representatives of the domestic tanning industry made the application of the Argentinean customs rules in a 'uniform, impartial and reasonable manner' impossible.[301]

The Panel first noted that:

> Article X:3(a) requires an examination of the real effect that a measure might have on traders operating in the commercial world. This, of course, does not require a showing of trade damage, as that is generally not a requirement with respect to violations of the GATT 1994. But it can involve an examination of whether there is a possible *impact on the competitive situation* due to alleged partiality, unreasonableness or lack of uniformity in the application of customs rules, regulations, decisions, etc.[302]
>
> [Emphasis added]

With regard to the requirement that national trade rules be applied in a uniform manner (the requirement of 'uniform administration'), the Panel found that there was no evidence that Argentina had applied the regulation at issue in a non-uniform manner with respect to hides.[303]

---

[296] Panel Report, *Argentina – Hides and Leather*, para. 11.76.
[297] *Ibid.*   [298] *Ibid.*, paras. 11.71–11.72.   [299] See also above, pp. 445–6.
[300] ADICMA stands for 'Association of Industrial Producers of Leather, Leather Manufactures and Related Products'.
[301] Panel Report, *Argentina – Hides and Leather*, para. 11.58.
[302] *Ibid.*, para. 11.77.
[303] See *ibid.*, para. 11.85. Note that the Panel stated in this context that Article X:3(a) should not be read as a broad anti-discrimination provision. According to the Panel, this provision does not require that all products be treated identically. There are many variations in products that might require differential treatment. See Panel Report, *Argentina – Hides and Leather*, para. 11.84.

However, with respect to the requirement that national trade rules be applied in a reasonable manner (the requirement of 'reasonable administration'), the Panel found that:

> a process ... which inherently contains the possibility of revealing confidential business information, is an unreasonable manner of administering the laws, regulations and rules identified in Article X:1 and therefore is inconsistent with Article X:3(a).[304]

With respect to the requirement that national trade rules be applied in an impartial manner (the requirement of 'impartial administration'), the Panel found:

> Whenever a party with a contrary commercial interest, but no relevant legal interest, is allowed to participate in an export transaction such as this, there is an inherent danger that the Customs laws, regulations and rules will be applied in a partial manner so as to permit persons with adverse commercial interests to obtain confidential information to which they have no right.[305]

While adequate safeguards could remedy such a situation, these safeguards were – according to the Panel – not in place. The Panel, therefore, ruled that the regulation at issue could not be considered an impartial administration of the customs laws and was, also for that reason, inconsistent with Article X:3(a) of the GATT 1994.

In *US – Stainless Steel*, Korea, the complainant, argued that the United States had violated Article X:3(a) by departing from its own established policy with respect to an important aspect of its anti-dumping investigation. The Panel rejected this claim of inconsistency. The Panel held that Article X:3(a) is:

> not ... intended to function as a mechanism to test the consistency of a Member's particular decisions or rulings with the Member's own domestic law and practice; that is a function reserved for each Member's domestic judicial system.[306]

With regard to the requirements of 'uniform administration' and 'reasonable administration', the Panel in *US – Stainless Steel* stated:

> the requirement of uniform administration of laws and regulations must be understood to mean uniformity of treatment in respect of persons similarly situated; it cannot be understood to require identical results where relevant facts differ. Nor do we consider that the requirement of reasonable administration of laws and regulations is violated merely because, in the administration of those laws and regulations, different conclusions were reached based upon differences in the relevant facts.[307]

The requirements of uniform, impartial and reasonable administration with regard to specific trade rules are also reflected in WTO agreements other than the GATT 1994. Article 1.3 of the *Import Licensing Agreement*, for example, provides:

> The rules for import licensing procedures shall be neutral in application and administered in a fair and equitable manner.[308]

---

[304] *Ibid.*, para. 11.94.   [305] *Ibid.*, para. 11.100.
[306] Panel Report, *US – Stainless Steel*, para. 6.50.   [307] *Ibid.*, para. 6.51.
[308] See also above, pp. 455–7.

The Appellate Body ruled in *EC – Bananas III* that Article 1.3 of the *Import Licensing Agreement* and Article X:3(a) of the GATT 1994 have 'identical coverage'.[309] In disputes involving the administration of import licensing procedures, Article 1.3 of the *Import Licensing Agreement* should be applied *first* since the *Import Licensing Agreement* deals specifically, and in detail, with the administration of import licensing procedures.[310]

Apart from the requirements of Article X:3(a) that national trade rules be administered in a uniform, impartial and reasonable manner, WTO law contains – as noted above – a second rule to ensure the fair and correct application of national trade rules, namely, the requirement of procedures for the *objective and impartial review*, and possible correction, of the administration of national customs rules. Article X:3(b) of the GATT 1994 provides:

> Each [Member] shall maintain, or institute as soon as practicable, judicial, arbitral or administrative tribunals or procedures for the purpose, *inter alia*, of the prompt review and correction of administrative action relating to customs matters.

Article X:3(b) requires that these tribunals or procedures be independent of the agencies entrusted with administrative enforcement.[311] Their decisions must be implemented by, and shall govern the practice of, administrative enforcement agencies (unless an appeal is lodged with a court or tribunal of superior jurisdiction).[312]

Note that Article X:3(b) refers to 'administrative action relating to customs matters', i.e. the administration of *customs rules*, and *not* to the administration of the broader category of 'laws, regulations, decisions and rulings relating to trade matters' or, in short, the administration of *trade rules*. However, it could be argued that, with respect to trade rules other than customs rules, Members should also provide for procedures for the objective and impartial review of the administration of these rules.

5.3.4.5. *Customs formalities and procedures*

Another important type of 'other non-tariff barrier' to trade is customs formalities and procedures, i.e. administrative barriers to trade. The losses that traders suffer through delays at borders, complicated and/or unnecessary documentation requirements and lack of automation of customs trade procedures are estimated to exceed, in many cases, the costs of tariffs. A 2001 UNCTAD study estimated that the average customs transaction involves:

- 20–30 different parties;
- 40 documents;

---

[309] Appellate Body Report, *EC – Bananas III*, para. 203. The Appellate Body noted the difference in wording between Article 1.3 of the *Import Licensing Agreement* and Article X:3(a) of the GATT 1994, but considered that 'the two phrases are, for all practical purposes, interchangeable'.

[310] *Ibid.*, para. 204.

[311] For situations in which the procedures are not fully or formally independent of the agencies entrusted with administrative enforcement, see Article X:3(c) of the GATT 1994.

[312] See Article X:3(b) of the GATT 1994.

- 200 data elements (30 of which are repeated at least 30 times); and
- the re-keying of 60–70 per cent of all data at least once.[313]

At present, many small and medium-size companies are not active players in international trade and it is argued that this has more to do with red tape rather than tariff barriers.[314] The administrative barriers for companies who do not regularly export large quantities are often simply too high to make foreign markets appear attractive.[315]

Article VIII:1(c) of the GATT 1994 states:

> The [Members] … recognize the need for minimizing the incidence and complexity of import and export formalities and for decreasing and simplifying import and export documentation requirements.

Nevertheless, WTO law currently contains few rules on customs formalities and procedures aimed at mitigating their adverse impact on trade. Article VIII:2 requires Members, in very general terms, to 'review' the operation of their laws and regulations in the light of the acknowledged need for:

- minimising the incidence and complexity of customs formalities; and
- decreasing and simplifying documentation requirements.

Article VIII:3 of the GATT 1994 furthermore requires penalties for breaches of customs regulations and procedural requirements to be *proportional*. Article VIII:3 provides:

> No [Member] shall impose substantial penalties for minor breaches of customs regulations or procedural requirements. In particular, no penalty in respect of any omission or mistake in customs documentation which is easily rectifiable and obviously made without fraudulent intent or gross negligence shall be greater than necessary to serve merely as a warning.

In view of the paucity of, and the need for, substantive WTO rules with respect to customs formalities and procedures, the Ministerial Conference directed the Council for Trade in Goods, at its Singapore Session in 1996, 'to undertake exploratory and analytical work … on the simplification of trade procedures in order to assess the scope for WTO rules in this area'.[316] In 2001, at its Doha Session, the Ministerial Conference agreed with regard to the simplification of trade procedures, commonly referred to as 'trade facilitation':

---

[313] See *Trade Facilitation: Cutting Red Tape at the Border*, Briefing Note, Ministerial Conference, December 2001, at http://www.wto.org/english/thewto_e/minist_e/min01_e/brief_e/brief15_e.htm, visited on 1 January 2004.

[314] Note that, in many economies, small and medium-sized companies account for up to 60 per cent of GDP creation.

[315] See *Trade Facilitation: Cutting Red Tape at the Border*, Briefing Note, Ministerial Conference, December 2001, at http://www.wto.org/english/thewto_e/minist_e/min01_e/brief_e/brief15_e.htm, visited on 1 January 2004.

[316] Ministerial Conference, *Singapore Ministerial Declaration*, adopted 13 December 1996, WT/MIN(96)/DEC, para. 21.

that negotiations will take place after the Fifth Session of the Ministerial Conference on the basis of a decision to be taken, by explicit consensus, at that session on modalities of negotiations.[317]

However, at the Fifth Session of the Ministerial Conference, i.e. the Cancún Session in September 2003, Members failed to agree on the modalities of negotiations on any of the Singapore issues, including trade facilitation. Only in the summer of 2004 were Members able to agree on including trade facilitation on the agenda of the Doha Development Round.[318] Note that many developing-country Members are very hesitant to take on new WTO obligations regarding customs formalities and procedures. They are worried that, without a substantial increase of technical assistance to strengthen their administrative capacities and to support their national reform efforts, additional WTO rules on customs formalities and procedures will exceed their implementation capacities.

Questions and Assignments 5.19

Are customs procedures and formalities significant barriers to trade? Are there any *specific* WTO rules on customs procedures and formalities? Does the Doha Development Round include negotiations on multilateral rules on customs procedures and formalities?

5.3.4.6. Other measures or actions

In addition to technical barriers to trade, lack of transparency, unfair and arbitrary application of trade rules, and customs formalities and procedures, the category of 'other non-tariff barriers' to trade in goods also includes many other measures or actions, or the lack thereof. This section briefly addresses the following 'other non-tariff barriers':

- preshipment inspection;
- marks of origin;
- government procurement practices; and
- measures relating to transit shipments.[319]

Preshipment inspection is the practice of employing private companies to check the price, quantity, quality and/or the customs classification of goods *before* their shipment to the importing country.[320] Preshipment inspection is

---

[317] Ministerial Conference, *Doha Ministerial Declaration*, adopted 14 November 2001, WT/MIN(01)/DEC/1, para. 27.

[318] See General Council, *Doha Work Programme*, Decision adopted on 1 August 2004, WT/L/579, dated 2 August 2004, para. g.

[319] In addition, exchange controls or exchange restrictions (see Article XV:9 of the GATT 1994) and the operations of State trading enterprises (see Article XVII of the GATT 1994) can also constitute or create serious barriers to trade.

[320] See Article 1 of the *Agreement on Preshipment Inspection*.

used by developing-country Members to prevent commercial fraud and evasion of customs duties. Preshipment inspection is used to compensate for inadequacies in national customs administrations. While certainly beneficial, the problem with preshipment inspection is that it may give rise to unnecessary delays or unequal treatment, and thus constitute a barrier to trade. The WTO *Agreement on Preshipment Inspection* sets out obligations for both importing (developing-country) Members using preshipment inspection and the exporting Members on whose territory the inspection is carried out. The importing Members using preshipment inspection must ensure, *inter alia*, that:

- preshipment inspection activities are carried out in a non-discriminatory manner;[321]
- preshipment inspection activities are carried out in a transparent manner;[322]
- the companies carrying out the inspection respect the confidentiality of business information received in the course of the preshipment inspection;[323] and
- the companies carrying out the inspection avoid unreasonable delays in the inspection of shipments.[324]

The exporting Members on whose territory the preshipment inspection is carried out must ensure non-discrimination and transparency with regard to their laws and regulations relating to preshipment inspection activities.[325] The *Agreement on Preshipment Inspection* also provides for rules on procedures for independent review of disputes between the companies carrying out the inspection and the exporters.[326]

With respect to *marks of origin* 'attached' to imported goods, Article IX:2 of the GATT 1994 states:

> The [Members] recognize that, in adopting and enforcing laws and regulations relating to marks of origin, the difficulties and inconveniences which such measures may cause to the commerce and industry of exporting countries should be *reduced to a minimum*, due regard being had to the necessity of protecting consumers against fraudulent or misleading indications.
>
> [Emphasis added]

Note that marking requirements are, of course, subject to all relevant WTO rules and disciplines, such as the MFN treatment obligation.

National laws and/or practices relating to the *procurement of goods* by a government for its own use are often significant barriers to trade. Under such laws or practices, governments frequently buy domestic products rather

---

[321] See Articles 2.1 and 2.2 of the *Agreement on Preshipment Inspection*.
[322] See Articles 2.5 to 2.8 of the *Agreement on Preshipment Inspection*.
[323] See Articles 2.9 to 2.13 of the *Agreement on Preshipment Inspection*.
[324] See Articles 2.15 to 2.19 of the *Agreement on Preshipment Inspection*.
[325] See Articles 3.1 and 3.2 of the *Agreement on Preshipment Inspection*. These Members must also provide to user Members, if requested, technical assistance directed towards the achievement of the objectives of this agreement on mutually agreed terms. See Article 3.3 of the *Agreement on Preshipment Inspection*.
[326] See Article 4 of the *Agreement on Preshipment Inspection*.

than imported products.[327] However, as discussed above, the national treatment obligation of Article III:4 of the GATT 1994 does not apply to government procurement laws and practices.[328] In fact, these laws and practices are outside the scope of the multilateral WTO rules. As government procurement typically represents between 10 and 15 per cent of GDP, it is clear that the absence of such multilateral rules represents a significant gap in the multilateral trading system and leaves a considerable source of barriers to trade unaddressed.

The plurilateral WTO *Agreement on Government Procurement* provides for some disciplines with respect to government procurement. However, it does so only for the twenty-six Members that are currently a party to this Agreement.[329] The *Agreement on Government Procurement* applies to the laws, regulations, procedures and practices regarding procurement by the government bodies which a Member listed in Appendix I to the Agreement.[330] Furthermore, for the Agreement to apply, the government procurement contract must be worth more than a specified threshold value.[331] The key discipline provided for in the plurilateral *Agreement on Government Procurement* is non-discrimination. Article III, entitled 'National Treatment and Non-Discrimination', states, in paragraph 1:

> With respect to all laws, regulations, procedures and practices regarding government procurement covered by this Agreement, each Party shall provide immediately and unconditionally to the products, services and suppliers of other Parties offering products or services of the Parties, treatment no less favourable than:
>
> a. that accorded to domestic products, services and suppliers; and
> b. that accorded to products, services and suppliers of any other Party.

Furthermore, in order to ensure that the national treatment and MFN treatment obligations under Articles III:1(a) and (b) quoted above, are abided by, the plurilateral *Agreement on Government Procurement* provides for procedures to ensure that laws, regulations, procedures and practices regarding government procurement are transparent.[332] However, it deserves to be stressed again that all of these disciplines and rules only apply to the twenty-six Members which are party to the *Agreement on Government Procurement*.

---

[327] It is undisputed that a government can most effectively ensure 'best value for money' by purchasing goods (and services) through an open and non-discriminatory procurement process. However, governments often use public procurement to support the domestic industry or to promote employment.

[328] See Article III:8(a) of the GATT 1994; and above, p. 327.

[329] The parties to the *Agreement on Government Procurement* currently are Austria, Belgium, Canada, Denmark, the European Communities, Finland, France, Germany, Greece, Hong Kong China, Iceland, Ireland, Israel, Italy, Japan, Korea, Liechtenstein, Luxembourg, the Netherlands, the Netherlands with respect to Aruba, Norway, Portugal, Singapore, Spain, Sweden, Switzerland, the United Kingdom and the United States. Accession negotiations are under way with Bulgaria, Estonia, Jordan, the Kyrgyz Republic, Latvia, Panama and Chinese Taipei. See http://www.wto.org/english/tratop_e/gproc_e/memobs_e.htm, visited on 2 January 2004.

[330] See, in this respect, Panel Report, *Korea – Procurement*, in which the question arose whether the Korean Airport Construction Authority, the Korean Airports Authority and the Inchon International Airport Corporation were within the scope of Korea's list of 'central government entities' as specified in Korea's Schedule in Appendix I to the *Agreement on Government Procurement*.

[331] See Article I.4 of the *Agreement on Government Procurement*. In Appendix I to the Agreement, each party specifies relevant thresholds.

[332] See Articles VII to XVI of the *Agreement on Government Procurement*.

At the Singapore Session in 1996, the Ministerial Conference agreed to establish a working group to conduct a study on transparency in government procurement practices and, based on this study, to develop elements for inclusion in an appropriate *multilateral* agreement.[333] In 2001, in Doha, the Ministerial Conference expressly recognised the case for a *multilateral* agreement on transparency in government procurement and agreed:

> that negotiations will take place after the Fifth Session of the Ministerial Conference on the basis of a decision to be taken, by explicit consensus, at that session on modalities of negotiations.[334]

It is important to note that these negotiations will be:

> limited to the transparency aspects and therefore will not restrict the scope for countries to give preference to domestic supplies and suppliers.[335]

As discussed above, the current plurilateral *Agreement on Government Procurement* prohibits discrimination and limits the scope for preference for domestic goods. The wished-for *multilateral agreement* would thus be far less 'ambitious' than the current plurilateral agreement (which will continue to exist in parallel). The new agreement would focus on transparency as such, rather than on transparency as a vehicle for monitoring market access commitments (as does the current plurilateral agreement).[336]

Between the 2001 Doha Session and the 2003 Cancún Session of the Ministerial Conference, Members prepared the start of the negotiations in the Working Group on Transparency in Government Procurement. However, as already discussed, the Members failed to agree on the modalities of the negotiations on any of the Singapore issues, including government procurement, at the Cancún Session. In the summer of 2004, the General Council eventually decided not to start negotiations on transparency in government procurement in the context of the Doha Development Round.[337] Although Members have explicitly committed themselves in the Doha Ministerial Declaration 'to ensuring adequate technical assistance and support for capacity-building both during the negotiations and after their conclusion',[338] many developing-country Members were concerned about their ability to engage 'successfully' in negotiations and to implement the new international commitments resulting from these negotiations.

---

[333] Ministerial Conference, *Singapore Ministerial Declaration*, adopted 13 December 1996, WT/MIN(96)/DEC, para. 21.

[334] Ministerial Conference, *Doha Ministerial Declaration*, adopted 14 November 2001, WT/MIN(01)/DEC/1, para. 26.

[335] *Ibid.*

[336] See Transparency in Government Procurement: Applying the Fundamental WTO Principle of Transparency to How Governments Buy Goods and Services, Briefing Note, Ministerial Conference, December 2001, http://www.wto.org/english/thewto_e/minist_e/min01_e/brief_e/brief14_e.htm, visited on 2 January 2004.

[337] See General Council, *Doha Work Programme*, Decision adopted on 1 August 2004, WT/L/579, dated 2 August 2004, para. 1(g).

[338] Ministerial Conference *Doha Ministerial Declaration*, adopted 14 November 2001, WT/MIN(01)/DEC/1, para. 26.

Finally, with respect to measures concerning *traffic in transit*, Article V of the GATT 1994, entitled 'Freedom of Transit', sets out a number of obligations on Members not to impede this traffic. Traffic in transit is the traffic of goods from country A to country C, through the territory of country B. It is clear that any restriction or impediment that country B would impose on the transit of the goods concerned would constitute a barrier to trade. Article V:2 of the GATT 1994 provides:

> There shall be freedom of transit through the territory of each [Member], via the routes most convenient for international transit, for traffic in transit to or from the territory of other [Members]. No distinction shall be made which is based on the flag of vessels, the place of origin, departure, entry, exit or destination, or on any circumstances relating to the ownership of goods, of vessels or of other means of transport.

Traffic in transit shall not be subject to any unnecessary delays or restrictions and shall be exempt from customs duties and from all transit duties or other charges imposed in respect of transit, except charges for transportation or those commensurate with administrative expenses entailed by transit or with the cost of services rendered.[339] All charges, regulations and formalities in connection with transit shall be reasonable and be subject to the MFN treatment obligation.[340]

Questions and Assignments 5.20

Explain how government procurement laws and practices, marks of origin, measures relating to traffic in transit and preshipment inspection can constitute barriers to trade in goods. In your opinion, which of these measures or actions is the most significant barrier to trade? Does WTO law regulate these types of other non-tariff barriers? Name at least two other measures or actions, not discussed in this chapter, that may constitute other non-tariff barriers to trade in goods.

5.4. BARRIERS TO TRADE IN SERVICES

This chapter on barriers to trade has dealt thus far with tariff and non-tariff barriers to trade in *goods*. This section deals with barriers to trade in *services*. As already discussed, the production and consumption of services are a principal economic activity in virtually all countries, developed and developing, alike.[341] Services play an increasingly central role in the world economy.

---

[339] Article V:3 of the GATT 1994.   [340] Article V:4 and 5 of the GATT 1994.
[341] Financial, telecommunications and transport services are the backbone of a modern economy, and economic development and prosperity are dependent on the availability and efficiency of these, and other, services. See WTO Secretariat, *Market Access: Unfinished Business*, Special Studies 6 (WTO, 2001), 98.

They now represent 60 per cent of world GDP.[342] However, the importance of services in the world economy is *not* reflected in their share of world trade. Services account for no more than 20 per cent of global cross-border trade.[343]

Trade in services is often subject to restrictions. For trade in services, unlike trade in goods, trade-restrictive measures applied at the border are barely significant. The production and consumption of services are subject to a vast range of domestic regulations. Barriers to trade in services are primarily resulting from these domestic regulations. Examples of such domestic regulations that may constitute barriers to trade in services are:

- a restriction on the number of drugstores allowed within a geographical area;
- an obligation for all practising lawyers to be a member of the local bar association;
- sanitation standards for restaurants;
- technical safety requirements for airline companies;
- a requirement that all professional services are offered in the national language;
- professional qualification requirements for accountants; and
- a prohibition on banks to sell life insurance.

WTO law, and the GATS in particular, provides for rules and disciplines on barriers to trade in services. Note, however, that – as explained below – most domestic regulation of services does not constitute GATS-inconsistent barriers to trade in services.[344] The production and consumption of services are often subject to domestic regulation for good reasons, including the protection of consumers and the protection of public health and safety. The Preamble to the GATS explicitly recognises:

> the right of Members to regulate, and to introduce new regulations on, the supply of services within their territories in order to meet national policy objectives.

It is important to stress that the objective of the GATS is *not* the *deregulation* of services.

This section addresses:

- the GATS rules on market access barriers; and
- the GATS rules on other barriers to trade in services.[345]

---

[342] See *ibid.*, 97. There is, however, significant variation across different country groupings. In 1998, services accounted for 38 per cent of GDP in low income countries and 65 per cent in high income countries (*ibid.*).
[343] *Ibid.*   [344] See below, pp. 497–8.
[345] Recall that Chapter 4 already discussed the scope of application of the GATS and the GATS non-discrimination provisions, i.e. Article II (MFN) and Article XVII (national treatment). See above, pp. 318–26, 365–9.

5.4.1. Market access barriers to trade in services

The GATS provides for specific rules on market access barriers and their progressive reduction. This section discusses:

- the definition and types of market access barriers;
- rules on market access barriers;
- negotiations on market access;
- schedules of specific commitments;
- modification and withdrawal of commitments; and
- market access commitments agreed to thus far.

5.4.1.1. Definition and types of market access barriers

The GATS does not explicitly define the concept of 'market access barriers'. However, Article XVI:2 (a) to (f) of the GATS provides for an *exhaustive* list of such measures. This list includes:

- limitations on the *number of service suppliers* whether in the form of numerical quotas, monopolies, exclusive service suppliers or the requirements of an economic needs test (see Article XVI:2(a)); for example, licences for fast food restaurants subject to an economic needs test based on population density;
- limitations on the *total value of service transactions* or assets in the form of numerical quotas or the requirement of an economic needs test (see Article XVI:2(b)); for example, limitation of the activities of subsidiaries of foreign insurance companies to 40 per cent of the domestic insurance market;
- limitations on the *total number of service operations* or on the *total quantity of service output* expressed in terms of designated numerical units in the form of quotas or the requirement for an economic needs test (see Article XVI:2(c)); for example, restrictions on the broadcasting time available for foreign movies;
- limitations on the *total number of natural persons* that may be employed in a particular service sector or that a service supplier may employ and who are *necessary* for, and directly related to, the *supply of a specific service* in the form of numerical quotas or the requirement of an economic needs test (see Article XVI:2(d)); for example, a cap on the percentage of foreign workers employed by construction companies;
- measures which restrict or require *specific types of legal entity or joint venture* through which a service supplier may supply a service (see Article XVI:2(e)); for example, all foreign subsidiaries must be in the form of a joint venture in which the domestic partner(s) remain in control; and
- limitations on the *participation of foreign capital* in terms of maximum percentage limits on foreign shareholding or the total value of individual or aggregate foreign investment (see Article XVI:2(f)); for example, foreign banks may never hold more than 49 per cent of the capital of domestic banks.

In short, the market access barriers listed in Article XVI:2 of the GATS include:

- four types of quantitative restrictions;[346]
- limitations on forms of legal entity;[347] and
- limitations on foreign equity participation.[348]

These market access barriers can be discriminatory *or* non-discriminatory against foreign services or service suppliers. Of the examples included above, a restriction on the broadcasting time available for foreign movies is obviously a *discriminatory* market access barrier, while a licence for a fast food restaurant subject to an economic needs test based on population density is a *non-discriminatory* market access barrier.[349] Article XVI:2 covers both discriminatory and non-discriminatory market access barriers.

Note that the four types of quantitative restrictions can be expressed numerically, *or* through the criteria specified in Article XVI:2(a) to (d), such as an economic needs test. It is important to note, however, that these criteria do *not* relate:

- to the quality of the service supplied; or
- to the ability of the supplier to supply the service (i.e. technical standards or qualification of the supplier).[350]

A requirement, for example, that services be offered in the national language or a requirement for engineers to have specific professional qualifications may impede trade in services but are *not* market access barriers within the meaning of Article XVI:2 of the GATS.

Also note that the quantitative restrictions specified in sub-paragraphs (a) to (d) refer to *maximum* limitations. Minimum requirements such as those common to licensing criteria (for example, minimum capital requirements for the establishment of a corporate entity) do not fall within the scope of Article XVI of the GATS.[351]

The GATS does not provide for a general prohibition of the market access barriers discussed in the above paragraphs. Whether a Member may maintain or adopt these market access barriers with regard to a specific service depends on whether, and if so to what extent, that Member has, in its Services Schedule, made market access commitments with regard to that service or the relevant service sector. Article XVI of the GATS, entitled 'Market Access', provides, in paragraph 1:

---

[346] See Article XVI:2(a) to (d) of the GATS.   [347] See Article XVI:2(e) of the GATS.
[348] See Article XVI:2(f) of the GATS.
[349] See *Guidelines for the Scheduling of Specific Commitments under the General Agreement on Trade in Services (GATS)*, adopted by the Council for Trade in Services on 23 March 2001, http://tsdb.wto.org/wto/Public.nsf/What U Get Frm Set? Open Frameset, visited on 20 January 2004. As stated in an explanatory note, these Guidelines were based on two documents which were produced and circulated during the Uruguay Round negotiations: MTN.GNS/W/164, *Scheduling of Initial Commitments in Trade in Services: Explanatory Note*, dated 3 September 1993; and MTN.GNS/W/164, Add.1, *Scheduling of Initial Commitments in Trade in Services: Explanatory Note, Addendum*, dated 30 November 1993.
[350] *Ibid.*   [351] *Ibid.*

> With respect to market access through the modes of supply identified in Article I, each Member shall accord services and service suppliers of any other Member *treatment no less favourable* than that provided for under the terms, limitation and conditions agreed and specified in its Schedule.
>
> [Emphasis added]

Furthermore, the chapeau of Article XVI:2 of the GATS states:

> In sectors where market-access commitments are undertaken, the measures which a Member shall not maintain or adopt either on the basis of a regional subdivision or on the basis of its entire territory, unless otherwise specified in its Schedule, are defined as: ...

Paragraphs (a) to (f) of Article XVI:2 then provide for the list of market access barriers discussed above. In other words, when a Member has undertaken a market access commitment in a service sector, it may not maintain or adopt any of the listed market access barriers with regard to trade in services in that sector, unless otherwise specified in its Schedule. A Member can specify in its Schedule that it maintains, or reserves the right to adopt, certain market access barriers.

When a Member makes a market access commitment, it *binds* the level of market access specified in the Schedule (see Article XVI:1) and agrees not to impose any market access barrier that would restrict access to the market beyond the level specified (see Article XVI:2).

Questions and Assignments 5.21

Are the following measures inconsistent with Article XVI of the GATS: a governmental measure prohibiting the broadcasting of American and Australian television soaps; a law limiting the number of foreign workers employed by construction companies; a law stating that foreign banks may not hold more than 49 per cent of the capital of domestic banks? What must you know in order to answer these questions?

5.4.1.2. Negotiations on market access

The GATS aims at achieving *progressively* higher levels of liberalisation of trade in services through *successive* rounds of negotiations. The Uruguay Round negotiations on the liberalisation of trade in services were only a first step in what will definitely be a long process of progressive liberalisation. Article XIX of the GATS, entitled 'Negotiation of Specific Commitments', states, in its first paragraph:

> In pursuance of the objectives of this Agreement, Members shall enter into successive rounds of negotiations ... with a view to achieving a progressively higher level of liberalization.

With regard to the negotiations on the progressive liberalisation of trade in services, Article XIX:1 furthermore provides:

> Such negotiations shall be directed to the reduction or elimination of the adverse effects on trade in services of measures as a means of providing effective market access. This process shall take place with a view to promoting the interests of all participants on a mutually advantageous basis and to securing an overall balance of rights and obligations.

The objective of the negotiations is thus to provide effective *market access* for services. In these market access negotiations, Members strive for a 'mutually advantageous' outcome, i.e. 'reciprocity'.[352] The approach to negotiations on the liberalisation of services is a request-and-offer approach.[353] At the initial stage of negotiations, Members first make requests for the liberalisation of trade in specific services.[354] The exchange of requests, as a process, is purely bilateral. It is simply a process of letters being addressed from the requesting participants to their negotiating partners.[355] After Members participating in the negotiations have made requests, they submit offers.[356] A Member submits an offer in response to all the requests that it has received, but does not necessarily have to address each element contained in those requests in its offer.[357] Unlike a request, which is usually presented in the form of a letter, an offer is normally presented in the form of a draft schedule of commitments.[358] While requests are addressed bilaterally to negotiating partners, offers are circulated multilaterally.[359] Offers are to be open to consultations and negotiation by all negotiating partners; not only to those who have made requests to the Member concerned but also any other participant in the negotiations.[360] In fact, offers are a signal of the real start of the advanced stage of bilateral negotiations, i.e. when negotiators come to Geneva to hold many bilateral talks with various different delegations. The submission of offers may also trigger the submission of further requests and then the process continues and becomes a succession of requests and offers.[361]

Article XIX:2 of the GATS explicitly requires that the process of liberalisation of trade in services takes place with due respect for:

---

[352] Note, in this respect, that, while perhaps economically dubious, striving for 'reciprocity' in market access negotiations is 'one of the most deep-rooted … compulsions in international trade policy-making'. See WTO Secretariat, *Market Access: Unfinished Business*, Special Studies 6 (WTO, 2001), 99.

[353] On approaches to *tariff* negotiations, see above, pp. 393–8.

[354] There are possibly four types of contents in a request, which are not mutually exclusive: (i) the addition of new service sectors; (ii) the removal of existing limitations or the introduction of bindings in modes which have so far been unbound; (iii) the undertaking of additional commitments under Article XVIII; and (iv) the termination of MFN exemptions. See *Technical Aspects of Requests and Offers*, Summary of Presentation by the WTO Secretariat at the WTO Seminar on the GATS, 20 February 2002, 1, at http://www.wto.org/english/tratop_e/serv_e/requests_offers_approach_e.doc, visited on 20 January 2004. For further clarification, see below, pp. 487–92.

[355] See *Technical Aspects of Requests and Offers*, Summary of Presentation by the WTO Secretariat at the WTO Seminar on the GATS, 20 February 2002, 2, at http://www.wto.org/english/tratop_e/serv_e/requests_offers_approach_e.doc, visited on 20 January 2004.

[356] In terms of content, offers normally address the same four types referred to in footnote 354 above.

[357] See *Technical Aspects of Requests and Offers*, Summary of Presentation by the WTO Secretariat at the WTO Seminar on the GATS, 20 February 2002, 3, at http://www.wto.org/english/tratop_e/serv_e/requests_offers_approach_e.doc, visited on 20 January 2004.

[358] *Ibid.*, 3.

[359] *Ibid.*, 3. The multilateral circulation is not only useful from a transparency point of view but also from a functional point of view since, in an offer, a participant is actually responding to *all* the requests that it has received.

[360] *Ibid.*, 3.　[361] *Ibid.*, 3.

- national policy objectives; and
- the level of development of individual Members, both overall and in individual sectors.

Consequently, Article XIX:2 further provides with respect to the position of developing-country Members in the negotiations on the liberalisation of trade in services that:

> There shall be appropriate flexibility for individual developing-country Members for opening fewer sectors, liberalizing fewer types of transactions, progressively extending market access in line with their development situation and, when making access to their markets available to foreign service suppliers, attaching to such access conditions aimed at achieving the objectives referred to in Article IV.

It is thus accepted that developing-country Members undertake fewer and more limited market access commitments than developed-country Members. 'Full reciprocity' is not required from developing-country Members. These Members are only expected to undertake market access commitments commensurate with their level of development.

As provided in Article XIX:3 of the GATS, for each round of multilateral negotiations on the liberalisation of trade in services, negotiating guidelines and procedures shall be established.[362] For the current negotiations, initiated pursuant to Article XIX:1 of the GATS in January 2000 and now conducted in the context of the Doha Development Round, the *Guidelines and Procedures for the Negotiations on Trade in Services* were adopted on 28 March 2001 by the Council for Trade in Services.[363] The Doha Ministerial Declaration of November 2001 stated with respect to the current negotiations:

> The negotiations on trade in services shall be conducted with a view to promoting the economic growth of all trading partners and the development of developing and least-developed countries. We recognize the work already undertaken in the negotiations, initiated in January 2000 under Article XIX of the General Agreement on Trade in Services, and the large number of proposals submitted by members on a wide range of sectors and several horizontal issues, as well as on movement of natural persons. We reaffirm the Guidelines and Procedures for the Negotiations adopted by the Council for Trade in Services on 28 March 2001 as the basis for continuing the negotiations.[364]

Members have been exchanging bilateral initial requests since 30 June 2002 and between 31 March and 30 October 2003, thirty-nine Members have submitted initial offers.[365]

However, there is widespread disappointment regarding the progress made in the negotiations. In April 2004, the Chairman of the Special Session of the Council for Trade in Services reported to the Trade Negotiations Committee as follows:

---

[362] For the purposes of establishing such guidelines, the Council for Trade in Services carries out an assessment of trade in services in overall terms and on a sectoral basis with reference to the objectives of the GATS. Negotiating guidelines, *inter alia*, establish modalities for the treatment of liberalisation undertaken autonomously by Members since previous negotiations, as well as for the special treatment for least-developed-country Members. See Article XIX:3 of the GATS.

[363] S/L/93, dated 29 March 2001.

[364] Ministerial Conference, *Doha Ministerial Declaration*, adopted 14 November 2001, WT/MIN(01)/DEC/1, dated 20 November 2001, para. 15.

[365] On the request-and-offer approach to the negotiations on trade in services, see above, p. 485.

there was a feeling among Members that, in the light of the passage of one year since the benchmark date for the circulation of initial offers, far too few offers had been submitted and that the minimalist character of many of these offers was disappointing.[366]

In its Decision of 1 August 2004 on the *Doha Work Programme*, the General Council reaffirmed the Members' commitment to progress in this area of the negotiations in line with the Doha mandate. A deadline of May 2005 was set for tabling revised offers.[367]

Questions and Assignments 5.22

What is the objective of negotiations pursuant to Article XIX of the GATS? How are these negotiations conducted? How is the special situation of developing-country Members taken into consideration in these negotiations?

5.4.1.3. *Schedules of Specific Commitments*

The terms, limitations and conditions on market access agreed to in the negotiations on the liberalisation of trade in services are set out in Schedules of Specific Commitments, already referred to above as Services Schedules.[368] As discussed elsewhere in this and the previous chapter, the conditions and qualifications on national treatment and undertakings relating to additional commitments are set out in the Schedules of Specific Commitments.[369] Each Member has a Schedule of Specific Commitments. In fact, each Member *must* have a Schedule, albeit that there is no minimum requirement as to the scope or depth of the commitments set out in that Schedule. All Schedules of Specific Commitments are annexed to the GATS and form an integral part thereof.[370] The online WTO Services Database gives information on all commitments undertaken by all Members that joined the WTO before 2000.[371] All Schedules of Specific Commitments are also available on the WTO's website.[372]

Schedules of Specific Commitments have two parts:

- a part containing the *horizontal commitments*; and
- a part containing the *sectoral commitments*.

---

[366] Council for Trade in Services, *Report by the Chairman to the Trade Negotiations Commitee*, TN/S/15, dated 14 April 2004, para. 5.

[367] See General Council, *Doha Work Programme*, Decision adopted on 1 August 2004, WT/L/579, dated 2 August 2004, para. 1(e). The General Council adopted the recommendations agreed by the Special Session, set out in Annex C to the General Council Decision, based on which further progress in the services negotiations will be pursued.

[368] See above, p. 485.   [369] See above, pp. 365–6, and below, pp. 489–92.

[370] Article XX:3 of the GATS.

[371] WTO Services Database Online, at http://tsdb.wto.org/wto/WTO Homepublic.htm, visited on 20 January 2004.

[372] See http://www.wto.org/english/tratop_e/serv_e/serv_commitments_e.htm, visited on 20 January 2004.

Horizontal commitments apply to all sectors included in the Schedule. Schedules include horizontal commitments *to avoid repeating* in relation to each sector contained in the Schedule the same information regarding limitations, conditions or qualifications of commitments. They often concern two modes of supply in particular, namely, supply through commercial presence (mode 3) and supply through the presence of natural persons (mode 4).[373] For example, the Schedule of Specific Commitments of the European Communities and their Member States mentions with regard to mode 4 supply of all services scheduled:

> Unbound except for measures concerning the entry into and temporary stay within a Member State, without requiring compliance with an economic needs test, of the following categories of natural persons providing services: ...[374]

Sectoral commitments, or sector-specific commitments, are, as the term indicates, commitments made regarding specific services sectors or sub-sectors. For scheduling commitments, WTO Members distinguish twelve broad service sectors:

- business services;
- communication services;
- construction and related engineering services;
- distribution services;
- educational services;
- environmental services;
- financial services;
- health-related and social services;
- tourism and travel-related services;
- recreational, cultural and sporting services;
- transport services; and
- other services not included elsewhere.

These twelve broad service sectors are further divided into more than 150 sub-sectors. For example, the 'business services' sector includes:

- professional services (including, for example, legal services, accounting, architectural services, engineering services, and medical and dental services);
- computer and related services;
- research and development services;
- real estate services;

---

[373] On the four modes of supply of services (cross-border supply, consumption abroad, supply through commercial presence and supply through the presence of natural persons), see above, pp. 321–2.

[374] GATS/SC/31, dated 15 April 1994, 7–10. For the categories of persons subsequently listed (including intra-corporate transferees and representatives of a service supplier seeking temporary entry for the purpose of negotiating for the sale of services), the measures concerning entry and temporary stay will not require compliance with an economic needs test. However, all other requirements of Community and Member States' laws and regulations regarding entry, stay, work and social security measures continue to apply, including regulations concerning the period of stay, minimum wages as well as collective wage agreements.

- rental/leasing services without operators; and
- other business services (including, for example, building cleaning services and publishing).

The 'communication services' sector includes:

- postal services;
- courier services;
- telecommunications services (including, for example, voice telephone services, electronic mail, voice mail and electronic data interchange); and
- audiovisual services (including, for example, motion picture and video tape production and distribution services, radio and television services and sound recording).

This WTO classification of service sectors, set out in the Services Sectoral Classification List of the WTO Secretariat,[375] is based on the Central Product Classification (CPC) of the United Nations. In the Secretariat's List each sector is identified by the corresponding CPC number. The CPC gives a detailed explanation of the services covered by each of the sectors and sub-sectors.[376]

In scheduling their commitments, most Members follow the WTO Services Sectoral Classification List. Thus, most Schedules have the same structure. A service sector or sub-sector is of course only included in a Member's Services Schedule if that Member undertakes commitments in that sector or sub-sector.

As shown by the excerpts included below, Services Schedules have four columns:

1. a first column identifying the services sector or sub-sector which is the subject of the commitment;
2. a second column containing the terms, limitations and conditions on market access;
3. a third column containing the conditions and qualifications on national treatment; and
4. a fourth column for undertakings relating to additional commitments.

With regard to market access commitments, Members indicate, in the second column of their Schedule, the presence or absence of limitations on market access. They do so for each service sector scheduled *and* with regard to each of the four modes of supply:

- cross-border supply (mode 1);
- consumption abroad (mode 2);
- supply through commercial presence (mode 3); and
- supply through presence of natural persons (mode 4).

---

[375] See MTN.GNS/W/120, dated 10 July 1991.
[376] A breakdown of the CPC, including explanatory notes for each sub-sector, is contained in the UN Provisional Central Product Classification, at http://unstats.un.org/unsd/cr/registry/regcst.asp?Cl=9&Lg=1, visited on 20 January 2004. To determine the coverage of the service sectors and sub-sectors of the WTO Services Sectoral Classification List, the detailed explanation of the CPC system can be used. Entries in Schedules often include CPC numbers.

Figure 5.21 Excerpt from the Schedule of Specific Commitments of the European Communities and their Members States (engineering services)[377]

Modes of supply: (1) Cross-border supply (2) Consumption abroad (3) Commercial presence (4) Presence of natural persons

Sector or subsector	Limitations on market access	Limitations on national treatment	Additional commitments

e) Engineering services (CPC 8672)	1. GR, I, P: Unbound.
	2. None
	3. E: Access is restricted to natural persons.
	   I, P: Access is restricted to natural persons. Professional association (no incorporation) among natural persons permitted.
	4. Unbound except as indicated in the horizontal section and subject to the following specific limitations:
	
	   GR: Condition of nationality.
		1. GR, I, P: Unbound.
		2. None
		3. None
		
		4. Unbound except as indicated in the horizontal section and subject to the following specific limitations:
		
		   I, P: Residence requirement.	

Figure 5.22 Excerpt from the Schedule of Specific Commitments of the United States (engineering services)[378]

Modes of supply: (1) Cross-border supply (2) Consumption abroad (3) Commercial presence (4) Presence of natural persons

Sector or subsector	Limitations on market access	Limitations on national treatment	Additional commitments
e) Engineering Services f) Integrated Engineering Services	1. None 2. None 3. None 4. Unbound, except as indicated in the horizontal section. In addition, US citizenship is required for licensure in the District of Columbia.	1. None 2. None 3. None 4. In-state residency is required for licensure in: Idaho, Iowa, Kansas, Maine, Mississippi, Nevada, Oklahoma, South Carolina, South Dakota, Tennessee, Texas, and West Virginia.	

Figures 5.21 to 5.25 are excerpts from the Schedules of Specific Commitments of respectively the European Communities and their Member States, the United States, Brazil, India and China. As the excerpts illustrate, for each market access commitment with respect to each mode of supply, four different situations can occur:[379]

- *full commitment*, i.e. the situation in which a Member does not seek in any way to limit market access in a given sector and mode of supply through market access barriers inconsistent with Article XVI:2; a Member in this situation records in the second column of its Schedule the word 'none';[380]

---

[377] GATS/SC/31, dated 15 April 1994, 21. Note that I is Italy, E is Spain, P is Portugal and GR is Greece.
[378] GATS/SC/90, dated 15 April 1994, 36.
[379] See Council for Trade in Services, *Guidelines for the Scheduling of Specific Commitments under the General Agreement on Trade in Services (GATS)*, adopted by the Council for Trade in Services on 23 March 2001, at http://tsdb.wto.org/wto/Public.nsf/WhatUGetFrmSet?OpenFrameset, visited on 20 January 2004.
[380] Note, however, that any relevant limitations listed in the 'horizontal commitments' part of the Schedule still apply. See above, pp. 487–8.

Figure 5.23 Excerpt from the Schedule of Specific Commitments of Brazil (engineering services)[381]

Modes of supply: (1) Cross-border supply (2) Consumption abroad (3) Commercial presence (4) Presence of natural persons

Sector or sub-sector	Limitations on market access	Limitations on national treatment	Additional commitments
e) Engineering Services			
Advisory and consultative engineering services (CPC 86721)	1. Unbound 2. Unbound 3. Same conditions as in Architectural services 4. Unbound except as indicated in the horizontal section	1. Unbound 2. Unbound 3. None 4. Unbound except as indicated in the horizontal section	
Industrial engineering (CPC 86725)	1. Unbound 2. Unbound 3. Same conditions as in Architectural services 4. Unbound except as indicated in the horizontal section	1. Unbound 2. Unbound 3. None 4. Unbound except as indicated in the horizontal section	
Engineering design (CPC 86722, CPC 86723, CPC 86724)	1. Unbound 2. Unbound 3. Same conditions as in Architectural services 4. Unbound except as indicated in the horizontal section	1. Unbound 2. Unbound 3. None 4. Unbound except as indicated in the horizontal section	
Other engineering services (CPC 86729)	1. Unbound 2. Unbound 3. Same conditions as in Architectural services 4. Unbound except as indicated in the horizontal section	1. Unbound 2. Unbound 3. None 4. Unbound except as indicated in the horizontal section	

Figure 5.24 Excerpt from the Schedule of Specific Commitments of India (engineering services)[382]

Modes of supply: (1) Cross-border supply (2) Consumption abroad (3) Commercial presence (4) Presence of natural persons

Sector or subsector	Limitations on market access	Limitations on national treatment	Additional commitments
1) BUSINESS SERVICES A) Professional Services e) Engineering Services (CPC 8672)	1. Unbound 2. Unbound 3. Only through incorporation with a foreign equity ceiling of 51 per cent 4. Unbound except as indicated in the horizontal section	1. Unbound 2. Unbound 3. None 4. Unbound except as indicated in the horizontal section	

- *commitment with limitations*, i.e. the situation in which a Member wants to limit market access in a given sector and mode of supply through market access barriers inconsistent with Article XVI:2; a Member in this situation describes in the second column of its Schedule the market access barrier(s) that are maintained;[383]

---

[381] GATS/SC/13, dated 15 April 1994, 7. [382] GATS/SC/42, dated 15 April 1994, 4.
[383] Two main possibilities can be envisaged in such a situation: the first is the binding of an existing situation ('standstill'); the second is the binding of a more liberal situation where some, but not all, of the access barriers inconsistent with Article XVI:2 will be removed ('rollback').

Figure 5.25 Excerpt from the Schedule of Specific Commitments of China (engineering services)

Modes of supply: (1) Cross-border supply (2) Consumption abroad (3) Commercial presence (4) Presence of natural persons

Sector or sub-sector	Limitations on market access	Limitations on national treatment	Additional commitments
e) Engineering services (CPC 8672)	1. None for scheme design Co-operation with Chinese professional organisations is required except scheme design 2. None 3. Only in the form of joint ventures, with foreign majority ownership permitted. Within five years after China's accession to the WTO, wholly foreign-owned enterprises will be permitted 4. Unbound, except as indicated in Horizontal Commitments	1. None 2. None 3. Foreign service suppliers shall be registered architects/engineers, or enterprises engaged in architectural/engineering/urban planning services, in their home country 4. Unbound, except as indicated in Horizontal Commitments	

- *no commitment*, i.e. the situation in which a Member wants to remain free in a given sector and mode of supply to introduce or maintain market access barriers inconsistent with Article XVI:2; a Member in this situation records in the second column of its Schedule the word 'unbound';[384] and

- *no commitment technically feasible*, i.e. the situation in which a particular mode of supply is not technically possible, such as the cross-border supply of hairdressing services; a Member in this situation records in the second column of its Schedule 'unbound*'.[385]

As discussed in Chapter 4, and as is evident from the excerpts from the Services Schedules in Figures 5.21 to 5.25, national treatment commitments and limitations thereof are inscribed in the third column of the Schedules in the same way as market access commitments and limitations thereof are inscribed. It is possible that a measure is both a market access barrier prohibited under Article XVI:2 and a measure inconsistent with the national treatment obligation of Article XVII. For this type of situation, Article XX:2 of the GATS provides that:

> Measures inconsistent with both Articles XVI and XVII shall be inscribed in the column relating to Article XVI. In this case the inscription will be considered to provide a condition or qualification to Article XVII as well.

Questions and Assignments 5.23

What is the difference between horizontal and sectoral commitments?
What is the function of the WTO Services Sectoral Classification List?
Examine the excerpts from the Schedules of Specific Commitments of the

---

[384] Note that this situation will only occur when a Member made a commitment in a sector with respect to at least one mode of supply. Where all modes of supply are 'unbound', and no additional commitments have been undertaken in the sector, the sector should not appear on the schedule.

[385] The asterisk refers to a footnote which states: 'Unbound due to lack of technical feasibility'.

European Communities and their Member States, the United States, Brazil, China and India and draw conclusions as to the extent of market access commitments in the engineering services sector. Find out whether Mexico and South Africa, as well as the WTO Member of which you are a national, have made market access commitments in the engineering services sector.

5.4.1.4. *Modification or withdrawal of commitments*

As is the case with tariff concessions for goods, market access commitments for services can also be modified or withdrawn.[386] According to Article XXI of the GATS, a Member may modify or withdraw any commitment in its Schedule, at any time after three years have elapsed from the date on which that commitment entered into force, in accordance with the provisions of this Article.[387] A Member wishing to 'unbind' a market access commitment must first notify its intention to do so to the Council for Trade in Services. Subsequently, it must – if so requested – enter into negotiations with a view to reaching agreement on any necessary compensatory adjustment. The purpose of these negotiations on compensatory adjustment is to maintain a general level of mutually advantageous commitments not less favourable to trade than that provided for in the Schedule.

If no agreement on compensatory adjustment can be reached between the modifying Member and any affected Member, the affected Member may refer the matter to arbitration.[388] Recall that this possibility to refer to arbitration is not provided for in the context of the modification or withdrawal of tariff concessions.[389] If no arbitration is requested, the modifying Member is free to implement the intended modification or withdrawal.[390] If arbitration is requested, however, the modifying Member may not modify or withdraw its commitment until it has made compensatory adjustments in conformity with the findings of the arbitration.[391] In case the modifying Member does not comply with the findings of the arbitration, any affected Member that participated in the arbitration may modify or withdraw *substantially equivalent benefits* in conformity with those findings.[392]

Note that any compensatory adjustment made by the Member 'unbinding' a commitment must be made on an MFN basis. However, the modification or withdrawal of substantially equivalent benefits by affected Members in case of non-compliance with the arbitration findings may be implemented solely with respect to the modifying Member.[393]

---

[386] On tariff concessions, see Article XXVIII of the GATT 1994, and above, pp. 423–4.
[387] In certain exceptional circumstances, the period of three years is reduced to one year. See Article X of the GATS.
[388] See Article XXI:3(a) of the GATS. Any affected Member that wishes to enforce a right that it may have to compensation must participate in the arbitration. See *ibid.*
[389] See above, pp. 423–4.   [390] See Article XXI:3(b) of the GATS.
[391] See Article XXI:4(a) of the GATS.   [392] See Article XXI:4(b) of the GATS.
[393] See Article XXI:2(b) of the GATS (for the compensatory adjustment) and Article XXI:4(b) of the GATS (for the modification or withdrawal of substantially equivalent benefits).

5.4.1.5. *Market access commitments agreed to thus far*

The market access commitments agreed on during the Uruguay Round negotiations on the liberalisation of trade in services are, in general, modest. On
average, WTO Members have only undertaken market access commitments on
about 25 sub-sectors, i.e. 15 per cent of the total.[394] Only one-third of the
Members have undertaken commitments on more that 61 sub-sectors.[395]
Furthermore, the market access commitments rarely go beyond the *status
quo*, i.e. they bind the degree of market access already existing. The value of
these bindings, also referred to as standstill bindings, is that they give traders
and investors a degree of security and predictability with respect to market
access in the service sectors of interest to them.

In a number of important sectors, such as financial services, telecommunications, maritime transport, professional services, and with respect to the
movement of natural persons, the Uruguay Round negotiators were unable
to complete the market access negotiations and the GATS made provision for
further negotiations. These further negotiations led in 1997 to agreements
providing for significant market access commitments in the sectors of basic
telecommunications and financial services. Further negotiations on market
access for maritime transport failed, while further negotiations on the movement of natural persons were completed in July with very modest results. To
the dissatisfaction of developing-country Members, the agreement reached on
the movement of natural persons was largely confined to business visitors (to
establish business contacts or negotiate contracts) and intra-corporate transfers of managers and technical staff.

Thus far, tourism has been the service sector in which most market access
commitments were made. After this come financial and business services. In
the health and education sectors, Members have made the fewest market
access commitments, but few commitments were also made in the sector of
distribution services.

On the whole, developed-country Members have made market access commitments with regard to nearly all sectors, except health and education. Note,
however, that the United States and the European Communities did not make
any market access commitments with respect to maritime transport services;

---

[394] See WTO Secretariat, *Market Access: Unfinished Business*, Special Studies 6 (WTO, 2001), 104.
[395] *Ibid.* This group of Members includes Australia, Canada, the European Communities, Hong Kong China,
Japan, Korea, Mexico, New Zealand, Norway, South Africa, Switzerland, Thailand, Turkey and the
United States (*ibid.*, 106).

Figure 5.26 WTO Members' market access commitments by sector[396]

Max. 140						Service Sectors					
Tourism	Financial	Business	Commu-nication	Transport	Construc-tion	Recreation	Environmental	Distribu-tion	Health	Education
128	106	103	99	84	74	63	54	52	48	46

and that the European Communities, Canada and Switzerland made no commitments with regard to audiovisual services.[397]

Market access commitments with respect to 'consumption abroad' (mode 2) are much less subject to limitations than market access commitments with respect to other modes of supply of services.[398] Presumably, governments feel no need to restrict their nationals' consumption abroad or consider it impracticable to enforce such restrictions.[399] Market access commitments with respect to 'supply through the presence of natural persons' (mode 4), however, are usually subject to broad limitations. Many Members have horizontal limitations, i.e. limitations to market access applicable to all scheduled sectors, with respect to mode 4. All Members, developed and developing alike, are clearly hesitant to undertake any commitments involving the entry of natural persons onto their territory. They are unwilling to expose their labour markets to competition from foreign workers.

Questions and Assignments 5.25

Discuss the extent of market access commitments agreed to in the context of the WTO thus far.

5.4.2. Other barriers to trade in services

In addition to the market access barriers, discussed above, trade in services can also be impeded by a wide array of other barriers. With regard to a number of these other barriers, WTO law, and in particular the GATS, provides for specific rules. Some of these rules have general application.[400] Other rules apply only in sectors where specific market access commitments were made.[401] This section discusses:

---

[396] See WTO Secretariat, *Market Access: Unfinished Business*, Special Studies 6 (WTO, 2001), 107.
[397] *Ibid.*, 104.
[398] On the relative importance of each of the four modes of supply in the total world services trade, see above, p. 322, footnote 51.
[399] *Ibid.*, 105.
[400] For example, the requirement to publish promptly measures affecting trade in services. See Article III of the GATS, and below, pp. 496–7.
[401] For example, the requirement to administer measures affecting trade in services in a reasonable, objective and impartial manner. See Article VI:1 of the GATS, and below, p. 497.

- lack of transparency;
- unfair or arbitrary application of measures affecting trade in services;
- domestic legislation;
- lack of recognition of diplomas and professional certificates; and
- other measures and actions.

5.4.2.1. Lack of transparency

Ignorance, uncertainty or confusion with respect to the relevant laws and regulations applicable in actual or potential foreign markets, are formidable barriers to trade in services. Effective market access is impossible without transparency regarding the laws and regulations affecting the services concerned. Service suppliers must have accurate information concerning the rules with which they must comply.

As in Article X of the GATT 1994, Article III of the GATS also requires that Members *publish* all measures of general application affecting trade in services.[402] Publication must take place promptly and at the latest by the time the measure enters into force.[403]

Since the end of 1997, each Member is required to establish one or more *enquiry points* to provide information on laws and regulations affecting trade in services.[404] Members have an obligation to respond promptly to all requests by any other Member for specific information on any of its measures of general application.[405] For the benefit of developing-country Members, developed-country Members have a special obligation to establish 'contact points' to facilitate the access of service suppliers from developing-country Members to information of special interest to them.[406]

Article III of the GATS also requires a Member to *notify* the Council for Trade in Services of any new, or changes to, laws, regulations or administrative guidelines, which significantly affect trade in sectors where that Member has made specific commitments. Members must do so at least once a year.[407]

Members are required to maintain procedures allowing service suppliers to *appeal* against administrative decisions. These procedures may be administrative or judicial but must be objective and impartial. Moreover, they must provide for prompt review and, where necessary, appropriate remedies.

---

[402] Where publication is not practicable, the information must be made otherwise publicly available (see Article III:2 of the GATS). Note that this transparency obligation applies to *all* service sectors, not only to those sectors with regard to which a Member has made specific commitments.

[403] See Article III:1 of the GATS. This obligation can be waived in emergency situations. This publication obligation also applies to international agreements pertaining or affecting trade in services to which a Member is a signatory.

[404] Article III:4 of the GATS.   [405] *Ibid.*

[406] See Article IV:2 of the GATS. Such information includes information on registration, recognition and obtaining of professional qualifications; and the availability of services technologies.

[407] See Article III:3 of the GATS. Members are not required, however, to supply confidential information. See Article III *bis* of the GATS.

The obligations concerning publication, enquiry points, notification and procedures for appeal apply also to service sectors with regard to which no specific commitments have been made.

5.4.2.2. *Unfair and arbitrary application of measures affecting trade in services*

In sectors where specific commitments are undertaken, Article VI:1 of the GATS requires a Member to ensure:

> that all measures of general application affecting trade in services are administered in a reasonable, objective and impartial manner.

This obligation is the counterpart of Article X:3(a) of the GATT 1994, discussed above, for trade in services.[408] Moreover, where authorisation is required for the supply of a service on which a commitment has been made, the competent authorities of a Member must, within a reasonable period of time, inform the applicant of the decision concerning the application.[409]

5.4.2.3. *Domestic regulation*

As discussed above, trade in services is primarily impeded or restricted by domestic regulation. For scheduled services, certain domestic regulations may constitute market access barriers within the meaning of Article XVI:2 and, as discussed above, are prohibited unless otherwise specified in the Schedule.[410] However, most domestic regulations do not constitute market access barriers within the meaning of Article XVI:2. Examples of such domestic regulations include, for example, qualification requirements, technical standards and licensing requirements for services or service suppliers as well as price controls imposing minimum or maximum prices on services.[411] Apart from the rules concerning transparency and the rules on unfair and arbitrary application, discussed above, the GATS does not provide for rules on domestic regulations in general. Nevertheless, it is clear that domestic regulations of the sort described here can seriously undermine any market access commitments made with regard to a service sector. Therefore, Article VI:5(a) of the GATS provides:

> In sectors in which a Member has undertaken specific commitments … the Member shall not apply licensing and qualification requirements and technical standards that nullify or impair such specific commitments in a manner which:
>
> i. does not comply with the criteria outlined in subparagraphs 4(a), (b) or (c); and
> ii. could not reasonably have been expected of that Member at the time the specific commitments in those sectors were made.

According to the criteria of Article VI:4(a), (b) and (c) to which the above provision refers, licensing requirements, qualification requirements and

---

[408] See above, pp. 471–4.   [409] See Article VI:3 of the GATS.   [410] See above, pp. 482–4.
[411] For the scope of the concept of 'market access barrier' within the meaning of Article XVI:2 of the GATS, see above, pp. 482–3.

technical standards relating to service sectors in which specific commitments are undertaken, must:

- be based on objective and transparent criteria such as competence and the ability to supply the service;
- not be more burdensome than necessary to ensure the quality of the service; and
- in the case of licensing procedures, not be, in themselves, a restriction on the supply of the service.

If licensing requirements, qualification requirements or technical standards relating to service sectors, in which specific commitments are undertaken, do not meet these criteria *and*, furthermore, nullify or impair the specific commitments undertaken in a manner which could not reasonably have been expected at the time the commitments were made, the Member acts inconsistent with its obligations under Article VI:5(a) of the GATS.[412] The Member must then amend the licensing requirement, qualification requirement or technical standard at issue.

Note that Article VI:4 of the GATS gives the Council for Trade in Services a broad and ambitious mandate to develop the multilateral disciplines necessary to ensure that licensing requirements, qualification requirements and procedures and technical standards do not constitute *unnecessary barriers* to trade in services. To date, such disciplines have only been successfully developed with regard to accountancy.[413]

Note also that Article XVIII, entitled 'Additional Commitments', provides:

> Members may negotiate commitments with respect to measures affecting trade in services not subject to scheduling under Articles XVI or XVII, including those regarding qualifications, standards or licensing matters. Such commitments shall be inscribed in a Member's Schedule.

Members may therefore make commitments with respect to measures which are neither market access barriers (Article XVI) nor inconsistent with the national treatment obligation (Article XVII). These *additional* commitments are recorded in the fourth column of a Member's Schedule. In practice, such commitments are exceptional.

5.4.2.4. *Lack of recognition of foreign diplomas and professional certificates*

Foreign service suppliers, such as doctors, engineers, nurses, lawyers and accountants, will usually have obtained their diplomas and professional certificates in their country of origin and will not have diplomas or professional certificates of the country in which they wish to be active. Members are

---

[412] Note that, in determining whether a Member is in conformity with the obligation under Article VI:5(a), account shall be taken of international standards of relevant international organisations applied by that Member. See Article VII:5(b) of the GATS.
[413] See Council for Trade in Services, *Disciplines on Domestic Regulation in the Accountancy Sector*, Press 118, 14 December 1998.

required to provide for adequate procedures, in sectors where specific commitments regarding professional services are undertaken, to *verify the competence* of professionals from any other Member.[414] However, it is clear that even with these procedures, having only a foreign diploma or professional certificate may constitute an important impediment for persons to supply services in other Members.

WTO law does not require that Members recognise foreign diplomas or professional certificates. However, the GATS *encourages the recognition* of foreign diplomas and professional certificates, by allowing Members to deviate, under certain conditions, from the basic MFN treatment obligation of Article II of the GATS. Article VII:1 of the GATS provides in relevant part:

> a Member may recognize the education or experience obtained, requirements met, or licences or certifications granted in *a particular country*.
>
> [Emphasis added]

Pursuant to Article VII:1, such recognition:

- may be achieved through harmonisation *or* otherwise; and
- may be based upon an agreement with the country concerned *or* may be accorded autonomously.

However, the recognition must be based on objective criteria, and may not discriminate among Members where similar conditions prevail. Members who are parties to recognition agreements are required to afford adequate opportunity for other interested Members to negotiate their accession to such agreements or negotiate comparable agreements with them. If recognition is accorded on an autonomous basis, the Member concerned must give adequate opportunity for any other Member concerned to demonstrate that qualifications acquired in its territory should be recognised. Members must notify the Council for Trade in Services of all existing recognition measures.[415]

In the long term, Members aim at adopting common standards for the recognition of diplomas and professional qualifications. A first effort in this respect has been the *Guidelines for Mutual Recognition Agreements or Arrangements in the Accountancy Sector*, agreed upon by the Council for Trade in Services in May 1997.[416]

5.4.2.5. *Other measures and actions*

In addition to lack of transparency, unfair or arbitrary application of measures affecting trade in services, domestic regulation and lack of recognition, trade

---

[414] See Article VII:6 of the GATS.

[415] Article VII:4 of the GATS. They must also inform the Council of the opening of negotiations on a recognition agreement in order to give any other Member the opportunity to indicate an interest in participating in the negotiations.

[416] See S/L/38, dated 28 May 1997. Negotiations on these guidelines were conducted in the WTO Working Party on Professional Services. See WPPS/W/12/Rev.1, dated 20 May 1997.

Figure 5.27 Excerpt from the Schedule of Specific Commitments of the European Communities and their Member States (legal services)[417]

Modes of supply: 1) Cross-border supply 2) Consumption abroad 3) Commercial presence 4) Presence of natural persons

Sector or subsector	Limitations on market access	Limitations on national treatment	Additional commitments
a)Legal advice home country law and public international law (excluding EC law)	1) F, P: Unbound for drafting of legal documents.	1) F, P: Unbound for drafting of legal documents. DK: Marketing of legal advice activities is restricted to lawyers with a Danish licence to practise and law firms registered in Denmark.	
	2) None	2) None	F: Host country law and international law (including EC law) are opened to the Members of the regulated legal and judicial profession.*
	3) D: Access subject to acceptance into a Bar Association according to the "Federal Lawyers Act" which requires establishment which is restricted to sole proprietorship or partnership only. F: Provision through SEL (anonyme, à responsabilité limitée ou en commandite par actions) or SCP only.	3) DK: Marketing of legal advice activities is restricted to law firms registered in Denmark. Only lawyers with a Danish licence to practise and law firms registered in Denmark may own shares in a Danish law firm. Only lawyers with a Danish licence to practise may sit on the board or be part of the management of a Danish law firm.	

in services is impeded by a number of other measures or actions. This section briefly addresses the following:

- monopolies and exclusive service providers;
- international payments and transfers; and
- government procurement laws and practices.

While *monopolies* or the *exclusive right* to supply a service can obviously impede trade in services, they are not prohibited by WTO law in general or by the GATS in particular. It is common for governments to grant entities an exclusive right to supply certain services, such as rail transport, telecommunications, sanitation, etc. However, pursuant to Article VIII:1 of the GATS, a Member must ensure that:

> any monopoly supplier of a service in its territory does not, in the supply of the monopoly service in the relevant market, act in a manner inconsistent with that Member's obligations under Article II and specific commitments.

A Member must also ensure that, when a monopoly supplier competes in the supply of a service outside the scope of its monopoly rights, the Member does not *abuse* its monopoly position inconsistent with its commitments regarding that service.[418]

---

[417] Article VII:4 of the GATS. They must also inform the Council of the opening of negotiations on a recognition agreement in order to give any other Member the opportunity to indicate an interest in participating in the negotiations.

[418] Article VIII:2 of the GATS.

Business practices, other than monopolies, may also hinder competition and thereby restrict trade in services. Article IX of the GATS requires Members, at the request of any other Member, to enter into consultations with a view to eliminating such practices.

It is obvious that restrictions on *international transfers and payments for services* can constitute a barrier to trade in services. Article XI of the GATS requires Members to allow international transfers and payments relating to services covered by specific commitments. A Member is also required to allow incoming transfers related to the establishment of commercial presence whenever commitment is undertaken with respect to that mode of supply.

As discussed above in the context of trade in goods, *government procurement laws and practices* often constitute significant barriers to trade as governments give preference to domestic services or service suppliers over foreign services or service suppliers. The GATS, like the GATT 1994 with regard to government procurement of goods, does not set forth any multilateral disciplines on the procurement of services for governmental purposes. Article XIII:1 of the GATS provides:

> Articles II, XVI and XVII shall not apply to laws, regulations or requirements governing the procurement by governmental agencies of services purchased for governmental purposes and not with a view to commercial resale or with a view to use in the supply of services for commercial sale.

The general MFN treatment obligation (of Article II) and specific commitments on market access and national treatment (of Article XVI and XVII respectively) do not, generally speaking, apply to laws, regulations or requirements governing public procurement of services.

Note, however, that the plurilateral WTO *Agreement on Government Procurement*, discussed above, applies not only to government procurement of goods but also to government procurement of services. The plurilateral disciplines set forth in that Agreement also apply to laws and regulations on the government procurement of services.[419]

Questions and Assignments 5.26

Briefly describe the GATS rules on transparency and the unfair and arbitrary application of measures affecting trade in services. Does the GATS lay down rules with respect to domestic regulation other than market access barriers? Are there any GATS rules regarding the recognition of diplomas and professional qualifications? Are there any WTO rules on government procurement of services?

---

[419] See above, pp. 477–9.

5.5. SUMMARY

Market access for goods and services from other countries can be, and frequently is, impeded or restricted in various ways. There are two main categories of barriers to market access:

- tariff barriers; and
- non-tariff barriers.

The category of tariff barriers includes customs duties (i.e. tariffs) and other duties and charges. The category of non-tariff barriers includes quantitative restrictions (such as quotas) and other non-tariff barriers (such as lack of transparency of trade regulation, unfair and arbitrary application of trade regulation, customs formalities, technical barriers to trade and government procurement practices). Different rules apply to the different forms of barrier. This difference in rules reflects a difference in the negative effects the barriers have on trade and on the economy.

A customs duty, or tariff, is a financial charge, i.e. a tax, imposed on products at the time of, and/or because of, their importation. Market access is conditional upon the payment of the customs duty. Customs duties are either specific, *ad valorem* or mixed. *Ad valorem* customs duties are by far the most common type of customs duties. The customs duties or tariffs, which are due on importation, are set out in a country's tariff. Most national tariffs follow or reflect the structure set out in the Harmonised Commodity Description and Coding System, usually referred to as the Harmonised System.

WTO law and, in particular, the GATT 1994, does not prohibit the imposition of customs duties. Customs duties, unlike quantitative restrictions, represent an instrument of protection against imports generally allowed by the GATT 1994. Article XXVIII *bis* of the GATT 1994 does, however, call upon WTO Members to negotiate the reduction of customs duties. The eight GATT Rounds of trade negotiations have been very successful in reducing customs duties. Nevertheless, customs duties remain an important barrier in international trade for several reasons and further negotiations on the reduction of tariffs are therefore necessary. The basic principles and rules governing tariff negotiations are:

- the principle of reciprocity and mutual advantage; and
- the most-favoured-nation treatment (MFN) obligation.

The principle of reciprocity does not apply in full to tariff negotiations between developed and developing-country Members. Members can adopt different approaches to tariff negotiations including the product-by-product request-and-offer approach, the linear reduction approach, the formula approach or the sectoral elimination approach.

The results of tariff negotiations are referred to as 'tariff concessions' or 'tariff bindings'. A tariff concession, or tariff binding, is a commitment not to raise the customs duty on a certain product above an agreed level. The tariff concessions or bindings of a Member are set out in that Member's Schedule of Concessions. The Schedules resulting from the Uruguay Round negotiations are all annexed to the *Marrakesh Protocol* to the GATT 1994 and are an integral part thereof. Accordingly, the tariff schedules and tariff concessions must be interpreted in accordance with the general rules of interpretation set out in the *Vienna Convention on the Law of Treaties*.

Article II:1(a) of the GATT 1994 provides that Members shall accord to products imported from other Members *treatment no less favourable* than that provided for in their Schedules. Article II:1(b), first sentence, of the GATT 1994 provides that products described in Part I of the Schedule of any Member shall, on importation, be *exempt from ordinary customs duties in excess of* those set out in the Schedule. This means that products may not be subjected to customs duties above the tariff concessions or bindings. Note, however, that Article XXVIII of the GATT 1994 provides a procedure for the modification or withdrawal of the agreed tariff concessions.

In addition to the rules to protect tariff concessions, WTO law also provides for some rules on the manner in which customs duties must be imposed. The imposition of customs duties may require three determinations to be made:

- the determination of the proper classification of the imported good;
- the determination of the customs value of the imported good; and
- the determination of the origin of the imported good.

The WTO agreements do not specifically address the issue of customs classification. However, in classifying products for customs purposes, Members have of course to consider their general obligations under the WTO agreements, such as the MFN treatment obligation. *Specific* rules on classification can be found in the *International Convention on the Harmonised Commodity Description and Coding System*, to which most WTO Members are a party.

Unlike for customs classification, the *WTO Agreement* provides for rules on customs valuation. These rules are set out in:

- Article VII of the GATT 1994, entitled 'Valuation for Customs Purposes';
- the Note *Ad* Article VII; and
- the WTO *Customs Valuation Agreement*.

The primary basis for the customs value is the 'transaction value' of the imported goods, i.e. the price actually paid or payable for the goods. This price is normally shown in the invoice, contract or purchase order, albeit that a number of adjustments usually have to be made. If the customs value cannot be established in this manner, it must be established pursuant to the alternative methods set out in the *Customs Valuation Agreement*.

The GATT 1994 provides no specific rules on rules of origin. However, the negotiators during the Uruguay Round recognised the need for multilateral disciplines on rules of origin in order to prevent these rules from being a source of uncertainty and unpredictability in international trade. The consensus on the need for such disciplines resulted in the WTO *Agreement on Rules of Origin*. With respect to *non-preferential rules of origin*, the *Agreement on Rules of Origin* provides for a work programme on the harmonisation of these rules. Until the successful completion of this work programme, Article 2 of the *Agreement on Rules of Origin* contains a rather extensive list of multilateral disciplines for rules of origin applicable during the current 'transition period'. After harmonised rules of origin have been agreed on, these disciplines will continue to apply. Article 3 provides that Members must ensure that, under the harmonised rules of origin currently negotiated, the country of origin of a good for customs purposes is:

- the country where the goods were wholly obtained; or
- the country where the last substantial transformation to the goods was carried out.

In addition to 'ordinary customs duties', tariff barriers can also take the form of 'other duties and charges'. 'Other duties and charges' are financial charges, *other than* ordinary customs duties, imposed on, or in the context of, the importation of a good. Pursuant to Article II:1(b), second sentence, of the GATT 1994 and the *Understanding on Article II:1(b)*, Members may:

- impose only 'other duties and charges' that have been properly recorded in their Schedules; and
- impose 'other duties and charges' only at a level that does not exceed the level recorded in their Schedules.

There are, however, a number of exceptions to the rule that Members may not impose 'other duties or charges' in excess of the recorded level. Pursuant to Article II:2 of the GATT 1994, Members may – in spite of their obligations under Article II:1(b), second sentence – impose on imported products:

- any financial charge that is not in excess of the internal tax imposed on the like domestic product;
- WTO-consistent anti-dumping or countervailing duties; or
- fees or other charges 'commensurate' with, i.e. matching, the cost of the services rendered.

Trade in goods is not only restricted by customs duties and other duties and charges, but also by non-tariff barriers, i.e. quantitative restrictions and other non-tariff barriers. A quantitative restriction is a measure which *limits the quantity* of a product that may be imported or exported. Article XI:1 of the GATT 1994, entitled 'General Elimination of Quantitative Restrictions', sets out a general prohibition on quantitative restrictions, whether on imports or exports. Unlike other GATT provisions, Article XI refers not to laws or regulations but more broadly to measures. A measure instituted or maintained by a Member which restricts imports or exports is covered by Article XI, *irrespective* of the legal status of the measure. Furthermore, quantitative restrictions which do not *actually* impede trade are nevertheless prohibited under Article XI:1 of the GATT 1994. According to firmly established case law, the basic provisions of the GATT on restrictive trade measures are 'provisions establishing equality of conditions of competition'. Also note that restrictions of a *de facto* nature are also prohibited under Article XI:1 of the GATT 1994.

As quantitative restrictions were widely used in the sectors of agriculture and textiles, specific rules on their elimination were negotiated during the Uruguay Round negotiations and set out in the *Agreement on Agriculture* and the *Agreement on Textiles and Clothing*. The *Agreement on Agriculture* provides for the immediate 'tariffication' of all quantitative restrictions, while the *Agreement on Textiles and Clothing* provides for the gradual elimination of quantitative restrictions over a period of ten years, ending on 1 January 2005. WTO law also regulates voluntary export restraints (VERs). VERs are actions taken by exporting countries involving a self-imposed quantitative restriction of exports. The *Agreement on Safeguards* specifically prohibits VERs.

While quantitative restrictions are, as a rule, prohibited, there are many exceptions to this prohibition. Article XIII of the GATT 1994 sets out rules on the *administration* of these GATT-consistent quantitative restrictions (and tariff quotas). Article XIII:1 of the GATT 1994 provides that quantitative restrictions, when applied, should be administered in a non-discriminatory manner. Article XIII:1 requires that, if a Member imposes a quantitative restriction on products to or from another Member, 'like' products to or from all other countries should be 'similarly restricted'. According to Article XIII:2 of the GATT 1994, the distribution of trade still allowed should be as close as possible to what would have been the distribution of trade in the absence of the quantitative restriction (or tariff quota). Furthermore, Article XIII:2 sets out a number of requirements to be met when imposing quotas (or tariff quotas). Article XIII:2(d) provides that, if no agreement can be reached with all Members having a substantial interest in supplying the product concerned, the quota (or tariff quota) must be allocated among these Members on the basis of their share of the trade during a previous representative period.

Quotas and tariff quotas are habitually administered through import licensing procedures. A trader, who wishes to import a product that is subject to a quota or tariff quota must apply for an import licence, i.e. a permit to import. The *Import Licensing Agreement* sets out rules on the *application* and *administration* of import licensing rules. The most important of these rules, set out in Article 1.3, is that the rules for import-licensing procedures shall be neutral in application and administered in a fair and equitable manner. Furthermore, Article 3.2 of the *Import Licensing Agreement* requires that non-automatic licensing shall not have trade-restrictive or distortive effects on imports additional to those caused by the imposition of the restriction.

In addition to customs duties and other duties and charges (i.e. tariff barriers) and quantitative restrictions (i.e. the first category of non-tariff barriers), trade in goods is also impeded by 'other non-tariff barriers', including:

- technical barriers to trade in goods;
- lack of transparency;
- unfair and arbitrary application of trade laws and regulations; and
- customs formalities and procedures.

With regard to technical barriers to trade, one must distinguish between:

- the general category of technical barriers to trade, namely, technical regulations, standards and conformity assessment procedures, for which rules have been set out in the *TBT Agreement*; and
- a special category of technical barriers to trade, namely, sanitary and phytosanitary measures, for which rules are provided in the *SPS Agreement*.

The rules of the *TBT Agreement* apply to technical regulations, standards and conformity assessment procedures relating to:

- products (both industrial and agricultural); and
- *related* processes and production methods (PPMs).

A measure is a 'technical regulation' within the meaning of the *TBT Agreement* if:

- the measure applies to an identifiable product or group of products;
- the measure lays down product characteristics; and
- compliance with the product characteristics laid down in the measure is mandatory.

A standard differs from a technical regulation in that compliance with a standard is not mandatory. A conformity assessment procedure is a procedure, such as inspection, sampling or testing, used to verify compliance with the requirements set out in technical regulations or standards. The *TBT Agreement* requires that, in respect of TBT measures, Members accord national treatment and MFN treatment to products imported from other Members. The *TBT Agreement* also requires that TBT measures do not create unnecessary obstacles to international trade. To this end, Article 2.2 further requires that technical regulations shall not be more trade-restrictive than necessary to fulfil a legitimate objective, taking account of the risks non-fulfilment would create. The legitimate objectives enumerated in Article 2.2 include the protection of human life or health or the protection of the environment. Harmonisation of national technical regulations, standards and conformity assessment procedures around international standards and procedures greatly facilitates the conduct of international trade, by minimising the variety of requirements exporters have to meet on their export markets. Thus, Article 2.4 of the *TBT Agreement* requires that, where technical regulations are required and relevant international standards exist or their completion is imminent, Members must use them as a basis for their technical regulations. However, a technical regulation does not have to be based on the relevant international standard if such international standards would be 'an ineffective or inappropriate means for the fulfilment of the legitimate objectives pursued'.

SPS measures are measures aimed at the protection of human, animal or plant life or health from certain specified risks. Not all measures for the protection of health are 'SPS measures' for the purposes of the *SPS Agreement*. Whether a measure is an 'SPS measure' as defined in Annex A1 to the *SPS Agreement* depends on its purpose or aim. In broad terms, an 'SPS measure' is a measure that:

- aims at the protection of human or animal life or health from food-borne risks; or
- aims at the protection of human, animal or plant life or health from risks from pests or diseases.

The basic principles of the *SPS Agreement*, contained in Article 2, reflect the underlying aim of balancing the need to increase market access for food and agricultural products with the recognition of the sovereign right of governments to take measures to protect human, animal and plant life and health. The *SPS Agreement*, in Article 2.1, explicitly acknowledges the sovereign right of WTO Members to take SPS measures. At the same time, however, the *SPS Agreement* subjects Members to the following basic disciplines:

- the obligation to take or maintain only SPS measures *necessary* to protect human, animal or plant life or health;
- the obligation to take or maintain only SPS measures 'based on' scientific principles and on sufficient scientific evidence; and
- the obligation not to adopt or maintain SPS measures that arbitrarily or unjustifiably discriminate or constitute a disguised restriction on trade.

The *SPS Agreement* further contains rules, in Article 3, encouraging, but not obliging, Members to harmonise their SPS measures around international standards. Members may choose to:

- *base* their SPS measures on international standards according to Article 3.1;
- *conform* their SPS measures to international standards under Article 3.2; or
- impose SPS measures resulting in a *higher level* of protection than would be achieved by the relevant international standard in terms of Article 3.3.

The substantive obligations provided for in the *SPS Agreement* also include obligations with respect to risk analysis, i.e. risk assessment and risk management. With regard to risk assessment, Article 5.1 of the *SPS Agreement* requires that Members ensure that their SPS measures are 'based on' an assessment of the risks to human, animal or plant life or health. With regard to risk management, the *SPS Agreement* primarily requires that Members must:

- avoid arbitrary or unjustifiable distinctions in the levels of protection deemed appropriate in different situations, if these distinctions lead to discrimination or disguised restrictions on trade (Article 5.5 of the *SPS Agreement*); and
- ensure that SPS measures are not more trade-restrictive than required to achieve the appropriate level of protection (Article 5.6 of the *SPS Agreement*).

Article 5.7 of the *SPS Agreement* allows Members, under certain conditions, to take provisional SPS measures where scientific evidence is insufficient.

Ignorance, uncertainty or confusion with respect to the trade laws, regulations and procedures applicable in actual or potential export markets is an important barrier to trade in goods. To ensure a high level of transparency of its Members' trade laws, regulations and procedures, WTO law requires their *publication* and the *notification* as well as the establishment of *enquiry points*. The unfair and arbitrary application of national trade measures, and the degree of uncertainty and unpredictability this generates for other Members and traders, also constitutes a significant barrier to trade in goods. Therefore, WTO law provides for:

- a requirement of uniform, impartial and reasonable administration of national trade rules; and
- a requirement of procedures for the objective and impartial review of the administration of national customs rules.

The losses that traders suffer through delays at borders and complicated and/or unnecessary documentation requirements and other customs procedures and formalities are estimated to exceed the costs of tariffs in many cases. However, WTO law currently contains few rules on customs formalities and procedures aimed at mitigating their adverse impact on trade.

As with trade in goods, trade in services is also often subject to restrictions. Unlike for trade in goods, however, trade-restrictive measures applied at the border are barely significant for trade in services. The production and consumption of services are subject to a vast range of domestic regulations. Barriers to trade in services primarily result from these domestic regulations. WTO law, and the GATS in particular, provide for rules and disciplines on barriers to trade in services. A distinction must be made between market access barriers and other barriers to trade in services.

Article XVI:2 of the GATS contains an *exhaustive* list of *market access barriers*. This list includes:

- four types of quantitative restrictions (Article XVI:2(a) to (d));
- limitations on forms of legal entity (Article XVI:2(e)); and
- limitations on foreign equity participation (Article XVI:2(f)).

These market access barriers can be discriminatory *or* non-discriminatory against foreign services or service suppliers. Note that the four types of quantitative restrictions can be expressed numerically, *or* through the criteria specified in Article XVI:2(a) to (d), such as an economic needs test. It is important, however, that these criteria do *not* relate:

- to the quality of the service supplied; or
- to the ability of the supplier to supply the service (i.e. technical standards or qualification of the supplier).

Also note that the quantitative restrictions specified in Article XVI:2(a) to (d) refer to *maximum* limitations.

The GATS does not provide for a general prohibition of these market access barriers. Whether a Member may maintain or adopt such market access barriers with regard to a specific service depends on whether, and if so to what extent, that Member has made market access commitments with regard to that service or relevant service sector in its Schedule of Specific Commitments. When a Member makes a market access commitment, it *binds* the level of market access specified in the Schedule (see Article XVI:1) and agrees not to impose any market access barrier that would restrict access to the market beyond the level specified (see Article XVI:2).

To achieve *progressively* higher levels of liberalisation of trade in services, the GATS provides for *successive* rounds of negotiations. The approach to negotiations on the liberalisation of services is a request-and-offer approach. It is accepted that developing-country Members undertake fewer and more limited market access commitments than developed-country Members. The terms, limitations and conditions on *market access* agreed to in the negotiations on the liberalisation of trade in services are set out in the second column of the Schedules of Specific Commitments. Each Member has a Schedule of Specific Commitments, and these Schedules, all annexed to the GATS, form an integral part thereof. Like tariff concessions for goods, market access commitments for services can also be modified or withdrawn. To do so, the procedure set out in Article XXI of the GATS must be followed.

In addition to market access barriers, trade in services can also be impeded by a wide array of other barriers. With regard to a number of these other barriers, WTO law, and in particular the GATS, provides for specific rules. The GATS requires the prompt *publication* of all measures of general application affecting trade in services. It also requires Members to establish *enquiry points* to provide information on laws and regulations affecting trade in services. Furthermore, the GATS requires Members to ensure that all measures of general application affecting trade in services are administered in a *reasonable, objective and impartial* manner. As noted above, trade in services is primarily impeded or restricted by domestic regulation. Most domestic regulation does not constitute market access barriers within the meaning of Article XVI:2. Apart from the rules concerning transparency and the rules on unfair and arbitrary application, the GATS does not provide for general rules on domestic regulation. The GATS, however, does provide for certain disciplines for licensing and qualification requirements and technical standards relating to service sectors in which specific commitments are undertaken. These requirements and standards must:

- be based on objective and transparent criteria such as competence and the ability to supply the service;
- not be more burdensome than necessary to ensure the quality of the service; and
- in the case of licensing procedures, not be, in themselves, a restriction on the supply of the service.

5.6. EXERCISE: CARLIE® GOES TO EUROPE

Dolls Я Us is a toys manufacturer from Goldtown, Richland, with production facilities in both Richland and Newland. Dolls Я Us produces a wide range of toys but is best known for a doll named Carlie®. In view of its success in the United States, Dolls Я Us wants to explore the possibility of marketing Carlie® in the United Kingdom. However, Dolls Я Us does not merely want to export Carlie® to the United Kingdom. It also wants to distribute its dolls to retail shops in the United Kingdom and set up its own chain of Carlie® shops for the London area. In the United States, a daughter company of Dolls Я Us, BuyItNow, has acquired significant expertise in advertising Carlie® and it intends to offer advertising services to UK toy retailers, either via the internet or by sending its experts to the UK.

Carlie® is a Barbie-like doll with a plastic body, artificial hair and three sets of clothes. The plastic body parts, the hair and the clothes are produced in Newland. Carlie® is only assembled and packaged in Richland. It is expected to sell at £10 per doll in the United Kingdom.

Her Majesty's Customs Service has informed Dolls Я Us that the customs duty on Carlie® will amount to 15 per cent *ad valorem* and that the value will be determined on the basis of the sales price on the domestic market in Richland. Dolls Я Us challenges both the level of the duty and the manner in which the Customs Service intends to determine the value of the dolls for customs purposes. It also disagrees with the Customs Service that the country of origin of Carlie® is Richland and not Newland . Furthermore, Dolls Я Us considers that Carlie® is not really a toy but rather a collector's item. Finally, it wonders whether, for the customs classification of Carlie®, it makes a difference whether Carlie® is imported as a finished product or in parts still to be assembled.

The Customs Service also informed Dolls Я Us that the European Communities only allows the importation of 500,000 dolls per year. This quota has been divided among China (400,000 dolls), Vietnam (90,000 dolls) and others (10,000 dolls). In the past, neither Richland nor Newland has been significant exporters of dolls to the European Communities. Dolls Я Us, however, hopes to sell at least 100,000 dolls per year in the United Kingdom within two years.

Finally, Her Majesty's Customs Service informs Dolls Я Us that all dolls must be imported through the port of Plymouth and that a special customs-handling fee of 0.2 per cent *ad valorem* is imposed on foreign toys upon their importation. This fee goes to the Customs Service's Fund for Disfavoured Children.

With respect to Dolls Я Us' plans to distribute Carlie® to retail shops in the United Kingdom itself and to set up – for the London area – a chain of Carlie® shops, the UK Ministry of Trade and Industry informed Dolls Я Us that:

- under the Toys Act of 1935, foreign companies are not allowed to act as wholesale distributors of toys in the United Kingdom; and

- under the Small Shopkeepers Protection Act of 1976, the number of retail shops in a specific area is limited on the basis of an economic needs test.

The Ministry of Trade and Industry also informs Dolls Я Us that only persons holding European professional qualifications or qualifications recognised as equivalent by the United Kingdom can supply advertising services in the United Kingdom.

Dolls Я Us is very disappointed by the information received from the Customs Service and the Ministry of Trade and Industry. It has asked its law firm, Gandhi, Rao & Ganesan, an Indian law firm with offices in London, to contact both the Customs Service and the Ministry of Trade and Industry to discuss the information given by them. Dolls Я Us considers that much of the legislation at issue in this case is not transparent and that its application is arbitrary and unfair. Dolls Я Us has announced that, if it is not allowed to market Carlie® in the United Kingdom on more 'favourable' terms, it will lobby the governments of Richland and Newland to bring a case against the European Communities *and* the United Kingdom at the WTO in Geneva. Lawyers of Gandhi, Rao & Ganesan and British Government's lawyers have agreed to meet.

Group A plays the role of the lawyers of Gandhi, Rao & Ganesan. Group B plays the role of the British Government's lawyers.

All lawyers are well advised to consult the Goods and Services Schedules of the European Communities and the TARIC database.

6 Rules on unfair trade

Contents

6.1. INTRODUCTION

While professing support for trade liberalisation, trade policy-makers often insist that international trade should at the same time be 'fair'.

'Unfair' trade comes in many forms and guises. Unfair trade practices include cartel agreements, price fixing, and the abuse of a dominant position on the market. WTO law, at present, does not provide for rules on these and many other particular forms of unfair trade. It does provide, however, for relatively detailed rules with respect to dumping and certain types of subsidisation – two specific practices commonly considered to be unfair trade practices. This chapter examines the WTO rules on dumping and subsidisation.[1]

6.2. DUMPING AND ANTI-DUMPING MEASURES

As already discussed in Chapter 1, 'dumping' is the bringing of a product onto the market of another country (or customs territory) at a price less than the normal value of that product.[2] In WTO law, dumping is not prohibited.[3] However, dumping is to be 'condemned' if it causes injury to the domestic industry of the importing country. The essence of the WTO rules on dumping is that Members are allowed to take certain measures, which are otherwise WTO-inconsistent, to protect their domestic industry from the injurious effects of dumping.

During the first six months of 2004, eighteen WTO Members imposed a total of fifty-two new definitive anti-dumping measures against exports from twenty-four countries or customs territories.[4] This represents a significant decline from the 114 measures imposed during the corresponding period of 2003.[5]

From 1995 to 2004, India was the most frequent user of anti-dumping measures, with a total of 279. The United States was second, with 211 measures and the European Communities was third with 193.[6] In the first semester of 2004, the European Communities, India and the United States imposed the most new final measures (six each). Canada was a close second in the number of final measures imposed during the period, with five, followed by China, Peru and Turkey with four each. Other Members imposed three or fewer measures each during this period. The days when anti-dumping measures were taken almost exclusively by developed-country Members are gone. Developing-country Members have 'discovered' this trade policy instrument and some have become avid users of it. For example, in the first semester of 2004, developed countries imposed only nineteen of a total of fifty-two measures.[7] The overall use of anti-dumping measures fluctuates from year to year but was definitely higher in the 1980s than at present.

---

[1] The section on dumping and anti-dumping measures was written in collaboration with Dr Julie Soloway. It is largely based on a text by Julie Soloway, adapted to fit the format, focus and approach of this book. I am much indebted to her for her contribution to this chapter.
[2] See above, p. 42. For a more detailed definition, see below, pp. 518–26.
[3] See below, p. 516.
[4] See www.wto.org/english/news_e/pres04_e/pr387_e.htm, visited on 3 November 2004.
[5] *Ibid.*
[6] See www.wto.org/english/tratop_e/adp_e/adp_stattab7_e.xls, visited on 3 November 2004.
[7] See www.wto.org/english/news_e/pres04_e/pr387_e.htm, visited on 3 November 2004.

China has been by far the biggest target of anti-dumping measures, with 272 such measures having been taken against it between 1995 and 2004.[8] Also, in the first semester of 2004, exports from China were once more the subject of the largest number of anti-dumping measures (sixteen).[9] However, this represents a slight decrease from the eighteen measures imposed against Chinese exports during the first semester of 2003. Korea, Malaysia, Russia and Thailand were distant seconds, with three measures each on their exports.[10]

This section on the WTO rules on dumping and anti-dumping addresses:

- the basic elements of the anti-dumping regime;
- the determination of dumping;
- the determination of injury and causation; and
- the national procedures for taking anti-dumping measures.

Questions and Assignments 6.1

What is the essence of the WTO rules on dumping? Is all dumping to be 'condemned'? How has the use of anti-dumping measures evolved over the years?

6.2.1. Basic elements of WTO law on dumping

Before entering into a more detailed, and often technical, discussion of the rules on dumping and anti-dumping measures, this section addresses in general terms:

- the history of the law on dumping;
- the concept of 'dumping';
- WTO treatment of dumping; and
- the response to injurious dumping.

6.2.1.1. History of the law on dumping

Current WTO law on dumping and anti-dumping measures is set out in Article VI of the GATT 1994 and in the WTO *Agreement on Implementation of Article VI of the GATT 1994*, commonly referred to as the *Anti-Dumping Agreement*. When the GATT was negotiated in 1947, participants could not immediately agree on whether a provision allowing anti-dumping duties should even be included.[11]

---

[8] See www.wto.org/english/tratop_e/adp_e/adp_stattab6_e.xls, visited on 3 November 2004.
[9] See www.wto.org/english/news_e/pres04_e/pr387_e.htm, visited on 3 November 2004.
[10] *Ibid.*
[11] The United Kingdom and others argued that anti-dumping laws were a hindrance to free trade and that the GATT should actually prohibit the imposition of anti-dumping duties. See B. Blonigen and T. Prusa, 'Antidumping', in *Handbook of International Economics* (Basil Blackwell, forthcoming). Available at http://www.sice.oas.org/geograph/antidumping/prusa-bl.pdf, visited on 28 October 2004.

However, largely at US insistence, Article VI was included to provide a basic framework as to how nations could respond to cases of dumping. In the years following its negotiation, Article VI by itself proved to be inadequate in dealing with the anti-dumping issue. The Article was vague and was interpreted and applied in an inconsistent manner.[12] Many GATT contracting parties began to feel that other contracting parties were applying anti-dumping laws in a manner that effectively raised new barriers to trade.[13] While Article VI remains at the heart of today's anti-dumping regime,[14] its inadequacies dictated that it would have to be fleshed out in further agreements. This was done, in 1967, by the Kennedy Round Anti-Dumping Code, which was later replaced, in 1979, by the Tokyo Round Anti-Dumping Code. However, in spite of the clarification and elaboration of Article VI by the Tokyo Round Anti-Dumping Code, there was even more criticism of the anti-dumping regime in the 1980s. At that time, there was a genuine proliferation of anti-dumping activity, with developed countries being the dominant user of the regime and developing countries a significant target.[15] This naturally led to growing tension between North and South. Not surprisingly, therefore, the anti-dumping regime was one of the most controversial issues on the agenda of the Uruguay Round. The positions taken by the participants in the negotiations varied greatly. Some participants wanted to facilitate the taking of anti-dumping measures (the United States and the European Communities) while others wanted to impose stricter disciplines (Japan, Korea and Hong Kong, China). At the end of the Uruguay Round, a compromise was reached which found its reflection in the WTO *Anti-Dumping Agreement* and which, together with Article VI of the GATT 1994, sets out the current rules on dumping and anti-dumping measures. As will be noted in this chapter, the conflicting, and sometimes even opposing, interests at stake in the negotiations resulted in provisions with ambiguous language. Some of these provisions have already been 'clarified' by the case law. Others still await clarification.

Note that, at the Doha Session of the Ministerial Meeting in November 2001, WTO Members agreed to place anti-dumping rules on the agenda of the Doha Development Round:

> In the light of experience and of the increasing application of these instruments by Members, we agree to negotiations aimed at clarifying and improving disciplines under the Agreements on Implementation of Article VI of the GATT 1994 and on Subsidies and Countervailing Measures, while preserving the basic concepts, principles and effectiveness of these Agreements and their instruments and objectives, and taking into account the needs of developing and least-developed participants.[16]

---

[12] M. Trebilcock and R. Howse, *The Regulation of International Trade* (Routledge, 1999), 167.

[13] J. Jackson, *The World Trading System: Law and Policy of International Economic Relations*, 2nd edition (MIT, 1997), 256.

[14] *Ibid.*

[15] Between July 1980 and June 1988, nearly 1,200 anti-dumping actions were initiated. See M. Trebilcock and R. Howse, *The Regulation of International Trade* (Routledge, 1999), 166.

[16] Ministerial Conference, *Doha Ministerial Declaration*, WT/MIN(01)/DEC/1, dated 20 November 2001, para. 28.

6.2.1.2. Concept of 'dumping'

'Dumping' is a situation of *international price discrimination* involving the price and cost of a product in the exporting country in relation to its price in the importing country. Article VI of the GATT 1994 and Article 2.1 of the *Anti-Dumping Agreement* define dumping as the introduction of a product into the commerce of another country at less than its 'normal value'. Thus, a product can be considered 'dumped' where the export price of that product is less than its normal value, that is, the comparable price in the ordinary course of trade for the 'like product' destined for consumption in the exporting country.[17]

6.2.1.3. WTO treatment of dumping

WTO law does *not* prohibit dumping. In fact, since prices of products are ordinarily set by private companies, 'dumping' in and of itself is *not* regulated by WTO law. As discussed above, WTO law in general only imposes obligations on and regulates the measures and actions of WTO Members. It does not directly regulate the actions of private companies. Therefore, WTO law does not prohibit dumping. However, as dumping may cause injury to the domestic industry of the importing country, Article VI of the GATT 1994 states, in relevant part, that:

> The [Members] recognize that dumping ... is to be *condemned* if it causes or threatens material injury to an established industry in the territory of a [Member] or materially retards the establishment of a domestic industry.
>
> [Emphasis added]

Consequently, Article VI of the GATT 1994 and the *Anti-Dumping Agreement* provide a framework of substantive and procedural rules to govern how a Member may counteract or 'remedy' dumping, through the imposition of 'anti-dumping' measures.

It is not mandatory for a WTO Member to enact anti-dumping legislation or to have in place a system for conducting anti-dumping investigations and for imposing anti-dumping measures. However, if the government of a Member makes the policy choice to have the option of imposing anti-dumping measures, Article 1 of the *Anti-Dumping Agreement* specifies that:

> An anti-dumping measure shall be applied only under the circumstances provided for in Article VI of GATT 1994 and pursuant to investigations initiated and conducted in accordance with the provisions of this Agreement. The following provisions govern the application of Article VI of GATT 1994 in so far as action is taken under anti-dumping legislation or regulations.

Pursuant to Article VI of the GATT 1994 and the *Anti-Dumping Agreement*, WTO Members are entitled to impose anti-dumping measures if, after an investigation initiated and conducted in accordance with the Agreement, on the basis of

---

[17] Article 2.1 of the *Anti-Dumping Agreement*. For a more detailed analysis of the concept of dumping, see below, pp. 518–26.

pre-existing legislation that has been properly notified to the WTO, a determination is made that:

- there is dumping;
- the domestic industry producing the like product in the importing country is suffering injury; and
- there is a causal link between the dumping and the injury.

6.2.1.4. *Response to injurious dumping*

In response to injurious dumping, Members may take anti-dumping measures. However, Article VI, and in particular Article VI:2, read in conjunction with the *Anti-Dumping Agreement*, limits the permissible responses to dumping to:

- definitive anti-dumping duties;
- provisional measures; and
- price undertakings.[18]

Article 18.1 of the *Anti-Dumping Agreement* provides:

> No specific action against dumping of exports from another Member can be taken except in accordance with the provisions of GATT 1994, as interpreted by this Agreement.[19]

In *US – 1916 Act*, the Appellate Body indicated that this provision clarifies the scope of application of Article VI of the GATT 1994. This provision requires that any 'specific action against dumping' be in accordance with the provisions of Article VI of the GATT 1994 concerning dumping, as those provisions are interpreted by the *Anti-Dumping Agreement*. Article VI of the GATT 1994 is thus applicable to any:

> "specific action against dumping" of exports, i.e. action that is taken in response to situations presenting the constituent elements of "dumping".[20]

In *US – 1916 Act*, the Appellate Body upheld the Panel's findings that the United States legislation at issue – which provided for civil and criminal proceedings and penalties for conduct which presented the constituent elements of dumping – fell within the scope of application of Article VI of the GATT 1994 and the *Anti-Dumping Agreement* was inconsistent with Article VI:2 and the *Anti-Dumping Agreement* to the extent that it provided for 'specific action against dumping' in the form of civil and criminal proceedings and penalties.

In *US – Offset Act (Byrd Amendment)*, the measure at issue was the United States Continued Dumping and Subsidy Offset Act of 2000 (CDSOA).[21] This Act provided, in relevant part, that the United States Customs shall *distribute* duties

---

[18] See Appellate Body Report, *US – 1916 Act*, para. 137.
[19] Footnote 24 to this provision reads: 'This is not intended to preclude action under other relevant provisions of GATT 1994, as appropriate.'
[20] Appellate Body Report, *US – 1916 Act*, para. 126.
[21] The CDSOA amends Title VII of the US Tariff Act of 1930 by adding a new section 754 entitled 'Continued Dumping and Subsidy Offset' and is often referred to as the 'Byrd Amendment'.

assessed pursuant to an anti-dumping duty order to 'affected domestic producers' for 'qualifying expenditures'.[22] Recalling its ruling in *US – 1916 Act* that Article VI:2, read in conjunction with the *Anti-Dumping Agreement*, limits the permissible responses to dumping to definitive anti-dumping duties, provisional measures and price undertakings,[23] the Appellate Body concluded in *US – Offset Act (Byrd Amendment)*:

> As CDSOA offset payments are not definitive anti-dumping duties, provisional measures or price undertakings, we conclude, in the light of our finding in *US – 1916 Act*, that the CDSOA is not "in accordance with the provisions of the GATT 1994, as interpreted by" the *Anti-Dumping Agreement*. It follows that the CDSOA is inconsistent with Article 18.1 of that Agreement.[24]

Questions and Assignments 6.2

Has the WTO *Anti-Dumping Agreement* set aside and replaced Article VI of the GATT 1947? What is 'dumping' in simple terms? Why does WTO law not prohibit dumping? Why and when do Members recognise that dumping is to be 'condemned'? Is it mandatory for WTO Members to enact anti-dumping legislation? To which measures do Article VI of the GATT 1994 and the *Anti-Dumping Agreement* apply? What forms can an anti-dumping measure take? Is it WTO-consistent for a measure against dumping to take the form of civil and criminal proceedings and penalties? What was the Appellate Body's ruling in *US – Offset Act (Byrd Amendment)*?

6.2.2. Determination of dumping

As already discussed above, Article VI:1 of the GATT 1994 and Article 2.1 of the *Anti-Dumping Agreement* define 'dumping' as the introduction of a product into the commerce of another country at less than its 'normal value'. In other words, 'dumping' exists where the 'normal value' of the product exceeds the 'export price'. This section explains:

- how the 'normal value' of the product concerned is determined; and
- how the relevant 'export price' is determined.

Ordinarily, dumping is discerned through a price-to-price comparison of the 'normal value' with the 'export price'. However, the *Anti-Dumping Agreement* envisages circumstances in which such a straightforward price-to-price comparison may not be possible or appropriate, and provides for alternative methods of calculation.

---

[22] Appellate Body Report, *US – Offset Act (Byrd Amendment)*, para. 12. On the concepts of 'affected domestic producer' and 'qualifying expenditure', see section 754(b)(1) and (4) of the US Tariff Act of 1930 respectively.

[23] See above, p. 517.   [24] Appellate Body Report, *US – Offset Act (Byrd Amendment)*, para. 265.

Before engaging in this discussion of how to determine the existence of dumping, it is important to recall that only dumping causing injury is condemned and potentially subject to anti-dumping measures under Article VI of the GATT 1994 and the *Anti-Dumping Agreement*. However, in determining whether dumping exists, the injurious effect that 'dumping' may have on a Member's domestic industry is not a constituent element of 'dumping'.[25] In addition, the intent of the persons engaging in 'dumping' is irrelevant in the determination of whether dumping exists.[26]

6.2.2.1. Determination of the 'normal value'

Article 2.1 of the *Anti-Dumping Agreement* defines the 'normal value' of a product as:

> the comparable price, in the ordinary course of trade, for the like product when destined for consumption in the exporting country.

In other words, the 'normal value' is the price of the like product in the home market of the exporter or producer. According to the Appellate Body in *US – Hot-Rolled Steel*, the text of Article 2.1 expressly imposes four conditions on domestic sales transactions so that they may be used to determine 'normal value':

- first, the sale must be 'in the ordinary course of trade';
- secondly, it must be of the 'like product';
- thirdly, the product must be 'destined for consumption in the exporting country'; and
- fourthly, the price must be 'comparable'.[27]

The first of the four conditions imposed on sales transactions so that they may be used to determine the 'normal value' is that the sale must be 'in the ordinary course of trade'. The decision as to whether sales in the domestic market of the exporting Member are made 'in the ordinary course of trade' can be a complex one. One basis on which investigating authorities may determine that sales are not in the ordinary course of trade – and thus disregard them in determining normal value – is if sales are at prices below the cost of production, in the specific circumstances identified in the *Anti-Dumping Agreement*.[28]

Sales not made in the ordinary course of trade, including sales below cost meeting these criteria, may be *disregarded* in determining normal value, which would then be determined on the basis of the remaining sales.[29] As the Appellate Body stated in *US – Hot-Rolled Steel*:

---

[25] See Appellate Body Report, *US – 1916 Act*, para. 107..   [26] *Ibid.*
[27] See Appellate Body Report, *US – Hot-Rolled Steel*, para. 165. Other provisions in the *Anti-Dumping Agreement*, such as Article 2.4, discussed below, permit the domestic investigating authorities to take account of considerations that may not be expressly identified in Article 2.1, such as the identity of the seller in a particular sales transaction.
[28] See Article 2.2.1 of the *Anti-Dumping Agreement*. Note that pricing below cost alone is not sufficient. Such sales must be made within an extended period of time, in substantial quantities, and at prices which do not provide for recovery of costs within a reasonable period of time.
[29] See Appellate Body Report, *US – Hot-Rolled Steel*, para. 139. However, where the exclusion of such below-cost sales results in a level of sales that is so low as not to permit a proper comparison with export price, an alternative method of calculation may arguably be used.

> ... Article 2.1 requires investigating authorities to exclude sales not made "in the ordinary course of trade", from the calculation of normal value, precisely to ensure that normal value is, indeed, the "normal" price of the like product, in the home market of the exporter.[30]

There could be many situations that *may* form a reason to determine that transactions were not made 'in the ordinary course of trade', such as:

- sales to affiliated parties;
- abberationally high priced sales, or abnormally low priced sales; or
- sales below cost.

As the Appellate Body found in *US – Hot-Rolled Steel*, the *Anti-Dumping Agreement* affords WTO Members discretion to determine how to ensure that normal value is not distorted through the inclusion of sales that are not 'in the ordinary course of trade'. However, the Appellate Body noted at the same time that this discretion is not without limits. The Appellate Body ruled:

> In particular, the discretion must be exercised in an *even-handed* way that is fair to all parties affected by an anti-dumping investigation. If a Member elects to adopt general rules to prevent distortion of normal value through sales between affiliates, those rules must reflect, even-handedly, the fact that both high and low-priced sales between affiliates might not be "in the ordinary course of trade".[31]

The second of the four conditions imposed on sales transactions so that they may be used to determine the 'normal value' is that the sale must be of the 'like product'. The determination of what constitutes a 'like product' involves:

- first examining the imported product or products that is or are alleged to be dumped; and
- then establishing the product that is 'like'.

Article 2.6 of the *Anti-Dumping Agreement* defines the 'like product' as:

> a product which is identical, i.e. alike in all respects to the product under consideration, or in the absence of such a product, another product which, although not alike in all respects, has characteristics closely resembling those of the product under consideration.

A 'like product' is thus an identical product or a product with a close resemblance.

Recall that the third and fourth condition imposed on sales transactions, so that they may be used to determine the 'normal value', is that the product must be 'destined for consumption in the exporting country' *and* that the price must be 'comparable'. With respect to the latter condition, note that Article 2.4 of the *Anti-Dumping Agreement* requires that a 'fair comparison' be made between export price and normal value. This comparison 'shall be made at the same level of trade, normally at the ex-factory level'. In making a 'fair comparison', Article 2.4 mandates that due account be taken of 'differences

---

[30] *Ibid.*, para. 140.   [31] *Ibid.*, para. 148.

which affect price comparability', such as differences in the 'levels of trade' at which normal value and the export price are calculated'.[32]

Questions and Assignments 6.3

What is the 'normal value' of a product within the meaning of Article 2.1 of the *Anti-Dumping Agreement*? What four conditions must sales transactions fulfil in order to be used to determine the 'normal value'? What is the 'ordinary course of trade' and why is it important? What is a 'like product' within the meaning of the *Anti-Dumping Agreement*? What differences may, according to Article 2.4 of the *Anti-Dumping Agreement*, affect the price comparability and what should be done about this?

6.2.2.2. *Alternative rules for the determination of the 'normal value'*

The *Anti-Dumping Agreement* acknowledges that in certain circumstances consideration of the domestic price in the exporting country does not produce an appropriate 'normal value' for the purposes of comparison with the export price. Such circumstances may arise when there are no sales of the like product in the 'ordinary course of trade' in the domestic market of the exporting country; or when, because of the low volume of sales in that market, such sales do not permit a proper comparison.[33]

The *Anti-Dumping Agreement* also recognises that the domestic price in the exporting country market may not produce an appropriate normal value for the purposes of comparison with the export price because of 'a particular market situation', but does not offer any criteria to aid domestic investigating authorities in determining whether such a particular market situation exists.[34]

The second Supplementary Provision to paragraph 1 of Article VI of the GATT 1994, to which Article 2.7 of the *Anti-Dumping Agreement* also refers, acknowledges that a straight comparison with the home market price may not always be appropriate in the case of imports from a country which has a complete or substantially complete monopoly of its trade and where all domestic prices are fixed by the State, often referred to as a 'non-market economy'. In practice, this means that investigating authorities in the importing Member have in such a situation considerable discretion in determining normal value since it no longer rests on the regular rules that govern such determinations.

---

[32] *Ibid.*, para. 167.

[33] Footnote 2 to Article 2.2 of the *Anti-Dumping Agreement* provides that the level of sales in the domestic market of the exporting country shall normally be considered 'sufficient' for the purposes of calculating normal value if such sales constitute 5 per cent or more of the sales of the like product under consideration to the importing Member.

[34] A panel established under the Tokyo Round Anti-Dumping Code, when considering a similar provision in that Code, found that the combined circumstance created by hyper-inflation and a frozen exchange rate in Brazil did not constitute such a particular market situation and therefore did not render home market prices an inappropriate basis for normal value. See Panel Report, *EC – Imposition of Anti-Dumping Duties on Cotton Yarn from Brazil*, ADP/137, para. 479.

Where the domestic price in the exporting country market may not produce an appropriate normal value for the purposes of comparison with the export price, Article 2.2 of the *Anti-Dumping Agreement* provides that an importing Member may select one of two alternative methods for determining an appropriate normal value for comparison with the export price:

- using a third country price as the normal value; or
- constructing the normal value.

No preference or hierarchy between these alternatives is expressed in the Agreement.

First, Article 2.2 of the *Anti-Dumping Agreement* permits the determination of 'normal value' through consideration of the comparable price of the like product when exported to an 'appropriate' third country, provided that this price is representative. Note, however, that the Agreement does not offer any criteria for determining whether a third country is 'appropriate'.

Secondly, Article 2.2 of the *Anti-Dumping Agreement* permits a Member to construct the normal value on the basis of:

> the cost of production in the country of origin plus a reasonable amount for administrative, selling and general costs and for profits.

The amounts for administrative, selling and general costs and for profits shall be based on actual data pertaining to production and sales in the ordinary course of trade of the like product by the exporter or producer under investigation.[35] If the amounts for administrative, selling and general costs and for profits cannot be determined in this way, they may be determined in one of the three ways discussed in Article 2.2.2(i) to (iii) of the *Anti-Dumping Agreement*.[36]

Questions and Assignments 6.4

Under what circumstances does consideration of the domestic price in the exporting country market not produce an appropriate normal value? In such cases, how can the 'normal value' be determined?

6.2.2.3. Determination of the 'export price'

The export price is ordinarily based on the transaction price at which the producer in the exporting country sells the product to an importer in the importing country.

However, the *Anti-Dumping Agreement* recognises that the transaction price may not be an appropriate export price. For example, there may be no export price where the transaction involves an internal transfer or barter.

[35] Article 2.2.2 of the *Anti-Dumping Agreement*.
[36] On the interpretation and application of these provisions, see Panel Report, *EC – Bed Linen*, paras. 6.59–6.62; and Appellate Body Report, *EC – Bed Linen*, paras. 74–83.

Additionally, an association or a compensatory arrangement between the exporter and the importer or a third party may affect the transaction price. Article 2.3 of the *Anti-Dumping Agreement* therefore provides for an alternative method to calculate, or 'construct', an appropriate export price. The 'constructed export price' is based on the price at which the product is first sold to an independent buyer. Where it is not possible to construct the export price on this basis, the investigating authorities may determine a reasonable basis on which to calculate the export price.

Questions and Assignments 6.5

When is the transaction price at which the producer in the exporting country sells to the importer in the importing country not an appropriate export price? In such a case, how is the export price to be determined?

6.2.2.4. *Comparison between the export price and the 'normal value'*

To determine whether dumping, as defined above, exists, the export price is compared with the normal value. Article 2.4 of the *Anti-Dumping Agreement* provides in relevant part:

> A fair comparison shall be made between the export price and the normal value. This comparison shall be made at the same level of trade, normally at the ex-factory level, and in respect of sales made at as nearly as possible the same time.

In order to ensure a fair comparison between the export price and normal value, Article 2.4 of the *Anti-Dumping Agreement* requires that adjustments be made to the normal value, the export price, or both. Thus, Article 2.4 requires that:

> Due allowance shall be made in each case, on its merits, for differences which affect price comparability, including differences in conditions and terms of sale, taxation, levels of trade, quantities, physical characteristics, and any other differences which are also demonstrated to affect price comparability.[37]

As the reference to 'any other differences' indicates, this provision does not exhaustively identify differences which may affect price comparability. One difference that is identified is a difference 'in conditions and terms of sale', which refers to such considerations as, for example, transport costs or credit terms associated with particular transactions involving the product concerned. In *US – Stainless Steel*, the question arose as to whether differences resulting from the unforeseen bankruptcy of a customer and consequent failure to pay for certain sales fell within 'differences in the conditions and terms of sale' for which due allowance is to be made. The Panel in this case stated that:

---

[37] Footnote 7 to the *Anti-Dumping Agreement* notes that: 'It is understood that some of the above factors may overlap, and authorities shall ensure that they do not duplicate adjustments that have been already made under this provision.'

> the requirement to make due allowance for differences that affect price comparability is intended to neutralise differences in a transaction that an exporter could be expected to have reflected in his pricing. A difference that could not reasonably have been anticipated and thus taken into account by the exporter when determining the price to be charged for the product in different markets or to different customers is not a difference that affects the comparability of *prices* within the meaning of Article 2.4.[38]

The Panel in *US – Stainless Steel* therefore ruled that an unanticipated failure of a customer to pay for certain sales cannot be considered to be a 'difference in conditions and terms of sale', requiring adjustment to the export price, the normal value or both, to ensure price comparability.[39]

Where the export price is constructed, Article 2.4 of the *Anti-Dumping Agreement* contains special rules regarding adjustments. An allowance must be made for costs, including duties and taxes, incurred *between* the importation of the product and its resale to the first independent purchaser, as well as for profits. Where the comparison of the 'normal value' with the export price requires conversion of currency, Article 2.4.1 of the *Anti-Dumping Agreement* provides specific rules governing that conversion.[40]

The question of making a *fair* comparison is often one of the most contentious aspects of an anti-dumping investigation as there will always be adjustments that arguably should be made. Frequently the extent of the adjustments allowed will have an important impact on the outcome of the anti-dumping investigation.

Questions and Assignments 6.6

Which differences may affect price comparability and may therefore require adjustment of the export price, the 'normal value' or both? How can price comparability be ensured?

6.2.2.5. *Calculation of the margin of dumping*

The margin of dumping is the difference between the export price and the 'normal value'. This would appear simple enough. However, the methodology to be applied when calculating the difference between the export price and the 'normal value' may raise difficult and controversial issues.

As provided in Article 2.4.2 of the *Anti-Dumping Agreement*, the calculation of the dumping margin *generally* requires:

- either the *comparison of the weighted average* 'normal value' to the weighted average of prices of all comparable export transactions; or
- a *transaction-to-transaction comparison* of 'normal value' and export price.

---

[38] Panel Report, *US – Stainless Steel*, para. 6.77.   [39] *Ibid.*
[40] See on the interpretation of this provision, Panel Report, *US – Stainless Steel*, paras. 6.11–6.12. The Panel in that case concluded that it was inconsistent with Article 2.4.1 of the *Anti-Dumping Agreement* to undertake currency conversions in instances where the prices being compared were in the same currency.

However, a comparison of the weighted average normal value to export prices in individual transactions may occur if:

- there is 'targeted dumping' (i.e., a pattern of export prices differing significantly among different purchasers, regions or time periods); and
- the investigating authorities provide an explanation as to why such differences cannot be taken into account appropriately in weighted-average-to-weighted-average or transaction-to-transaction comparisons.[41]

It is important to note that, where a weighted-average-to-weighted-average comparison is conducted, the *entirety of the prices* for all comparable transactions involving the product that is the subject of the investigation must be included in the calculation of the dumping margin. For this reason, the Appellate Body found in *EC – Bed Linen* that the practice of 'zeroing' is inconsistent with the *Anti-Dumping Agreement*. The Appellate Body described the practice of 'zeroing' as follows:

> The practice of "zeroing", as applied in this dispute, can briefly be described as follows: first, the European Communities identified with respect to the product under investigation – cotton-type bed linen – a certain number of different "models" or "types" of that product. Next, the European Communities calculated, for each of these models, a *weighted average* normal value and a *weighted average* export price. Then, the European Communities compared the weighted average normal value with the weighted average export price for each model. For some models, normal value was *higher* than export price; by subtracting export price from normal value for these models, the European Communities established a "*positive* dumping margin" for each model. For other models, normal value was *lower* than export price; by subtracting export price from normal value for these other models, the European Communities established a "*negative* dumping margin" for each model. Thus, there is a "positive dumping margin" where there *is* dumping, and a "negative dumping margin" where there *is not*. The "positives" and "negatives" of the amounts in this calculation are an indication of precisely *how much* the export price is above or below the normal value. Having made this calculation, the European Communities then added up the amounts it had calculated as "dumping margins" for each model of the product in order to determine an *overall* dumping margin for the product *as a whole*. However, in doing so, the European Communities treated any "negative dumping margin" as zero – hence the use of the word "zeroing". Then, finally, having added up the "positive dumping margins" and the zeroes, the European Communities divided this sum by the cumulative total value of all the export transactions involving all types and models of that product. In this way, the European Communities obtained an overall margin of dumping for the product under investigation.[42]

Examining this practice of the European Communities under Article 2.4.2 of the *Anti-Dumping Agreement*, the Appellate Body stated:

> We see nothing in Article 2.4.2 or in any other provision of the *Anti-Dumping Agreement* that provides for the establishment of "the existence of margins of dumping" for *types or models* of the product under investigation; to the contrary, all references to the establishment of "the existence of margins of dumping" are references to the *product* that is the subject of the investigation ... Whatever the method used to

---

[41] See Article 2.4.2 of the *Anti-Dumping Agreement*.
[42] Appellate Body Report, *EC – Bed Linen*, para. 47.

> calculate the margins of dumping, in our view, these margins must be, and can only be, established for the *product* under investigation as a whole.
>
> . . .
>
> . . . [T]he investigating authorities are required to compare the weighted average normal value with the weighted average of prices of *all* comparable export transactions. Here, we emphasize that Article 2.4.2 speaks of "all" comparable export transactions . . . By "zeroing" the "negative dumping margins", the European Communities, therefore, did *not* take fully into account the entirety of the prices of *some* export transactions, namely, those export transactions involving models of cotton-type bed linen where "negative dumping margins" were found.[43]

Questions and Assignments 6.7

How is the dumping margin to be calculated under the *Anti-Dumping Agreement*? Explain the practice of 'zeroing' as applied by the European Communities. Why did the Appellate Body in *EC – Bed Linen* consider this practice to be inconsistent with Article 2.4.2 of the *Anti-Dumping Agreement*?

6.2.3. Determination of injury

As noted above, only dumping that causes, or threatens to cause, injury to the domestic industry is condemned and potentially subject to anti-dumping measures under Article VI of the GATT 1994 and the *Anti-Dumping Agreement*. Therefore, after having determined the existence of dumping, the competent authorities must establish:

- the existence, or threat, of injury to the domestic industry; and
- the causal link between the dumping and the injury.

This section addresses the determination of injury to the domestic industry.

6.2.3.1. *Concept of 'domestic industry'*

The concept of 'domestic industry' flows from the definition of the 'like product'. It establishes who may file a petition requesting the initiation of an anti-dumping investigation.[44] It also delineates the scope of the data to be taken into account in the injury determination, in that the domestic industry with respect to which injury is considered and determined must be the domestic industry defined in accordance with Article 4.1. Article 4.1 of the *Anti-Dumping Agreement* defines the 'domestic industry' generally as:

---

[43] *Ibid.*, paras. 53 and 55. Note that the issue of 'zeroing' has also been addressed more recently in *US – Softwood Lumber V*.

[44] See below, pp. 536–8.

the domestic producers as a whole of the like products or ... those of them whose collective output of the products constitutes a major proportion of the total domestic production of those products.[45]

The domestic industry may presumably consist of one *or* multiple producers. The Panel in *EC – Bed-Linen* stated:

Article 4.1 of the [Anti-Dumping] Agreement defines the domestic industry in terms of "domestic producers" in the plural. Yet we consider it indisputable that a single domestic producer may constitute the domestic industry under the [Anti-Dumping] Agreement, and that the provisions concerning domestic industry under Article 4 continue to apply in such a factual situation.[46]

The *Anti-Dumping Agreement* recognises that it may not be appropriate to include *all* producers of the like product in the domestic industry when producers are 'related' to the exporters or importers or are themselves importers of the allegedly dumped product.[47] Related producers may not entirely share the interests of purely domestic producers. A producer is deemed to be 'related' to exporters or importers only if:

- one of them directly or indirectly controls the other; or
- both of them are directly or indirectly controlled by a third person; or
- together they directly or indirectly control a third person,

provided that there are grounds for believing or suspecting that the effect of the relationship is such as to cause the producer concerned to behave differently from non-related producers.[48]

Note that, in limited circumstances, a *regional industry*, instead of the total domestic industry, may be defined as the basis for the injury analysis.[49]

Questions and Assignments 6.8

What is the 'domestic industry' within the meaning of Article 4 of the *Anti-Dumping Agreement*? Which producers, established in a Member, may be excluded from the relevant 'domestic industry' of that Member?

---

[45] Article 3.6 of the *Anti-Dumping Agreement* addresses the situation where information concerning the production of the like product, such as producers' profits and sales, cannot be separately identified. In such cases, Article 3.6 allows the authorities to consider information concerning production of a broader product group than the like product produced by the domestic industry, which includes the like product, in evaluating the effect of imports.

[46] Panel Report, *EC – Bed Linen*, para. 6.72.

[47] See Article 4.1(i) of the *Anti-Dumping Agreement*.

[48] See footnote 11 to the *Anti-Dumping Agreement*. Note that one is deemed to control another 'when the former is legally or operationally in a position to exercise restraint or direction over the latter'.

[49] See Article 4.1(ii) of the *Anti-Dumping Agreement*. On the application of anti-dumping measures in that case, see Article 4.2 of the *Anti-Dumping Agreement*.

6.2.3.2. Determination of injury

An affirmative determination of injury to the domestic industry is a fundamental pre-condition for the imposition of anti-dumping measures, along with
a determination of the causal link between the dumped imports and the
injury. The *Anti-Dumping Agreement* defines 'injury' to mean one of three things:

- material injury to a domestic industry;
- threat of material injury to a domestic industry; or
- material retardation of the establishment of a domestic industry.

The *Anti-Dumping Agreement* provides further details and guidance relating to
the consideration of material injury and threat of material injury, but provides
no further specific guidance on the consideration of material retardation of
the establishment of a domestic industry.

Article 3.1 of the *Anti-Dumping Agreement* requires that a determination of
injury to the domestic industry:

> be based on positive evidence and involve an objective examination of both: (*a*) the
> volume of dumped imports and the effect of the dumped imports on prices in the
> domestic market for like products; and (*b*) the consequent impact of these imports on
> domestic producers of such products.

In *Thailand – H-Beams*, the Appellate Body referred to Article 3.1 as an overarching provision that sets forth a Member's fundamental, substantive obligation with respect to the determination of injury.[50] Article 3.1 informs the more
detailed obligations in succeeding paragraphs. These obligations concern:

- the determination of the volume of dumped imports, and their effect on
  prices (Article 3.2);
- investigations of imports from more than one country (Article 3.3);
- the impact of dumped imports on the domestic industry (Article 3.4);
- causality between dumped imports and injury (Article 3.5);
- the assessment of the domestic production of the like product (Article 3.6); and
- the determination of the threat of material injury (Articles 3.7 and 3.8).

The Appellate Body in *Thailand – H-Beams* emphasised that the focus of Article 3
is thus on *substantive* obligations that a Member must fulfil in making an injury
determination.[51]

In *US – Hot-Rolled Steel*, the Appellate Body held that the thrust of the investigating authorities' obligation, in Article 3.1, lies in the requirement that they:

- base their determination on 'positive evidence'; and
- conduct an 'objective examination'.

According to the Appellate Body, the concept of 'positive evidence' relates to the
quality of the evidence that authorities may rely on in making a determination.

---

[50] Appellate Body Report, *Thailand – H-Beams*, para. 106.   [51] *Ibid.*

The word 'positive' means that the evidence must be of an affirmative, objective and verifiable character, and that it must be credible.[52] The concept of 'objective examination' aims at a different aspect of the investigating authorities' determination. The word 'objective', which qualifies the word 'examination', indicates essentially that the 'examination' process must conform to the dictates of the basic principles of good faith and fundamental fairness.[53] In short, an 'objective examination' requires that the domestic industry, and the effects of dumped imports, be investigated in an unbiased manner, without favouring the interests of any interested party, or group of interested parties, in the investigation.[54] If an examination is to be 'objective', the identification, investigation and evaluation of the relevant factors must be *even-handed*. Thus, investigating authorities are not entitled to conduct their investigation in such a way that it becomes more likely that, because of the fact-finding or evaluation process, they will determine that the domestic industry is injured.[55]

As noted above, Article 3.1 requires that a determination of injury to the domestic market must involve an examination of both:

- the volume of dumped imports and the effect of the dumped imports on prices in the domestic market for like products (first requirement); and
- the consequent impact of these imports on domestic producers of such products (second requirement).

With regard to the first requirement, the Panel in *EC – Bed Linen* rejected the argument that 'dumped imports' must be understood to refer only to imports which are the subject of transactions in which the export price was below normal value. Instead, the Panel stated:

> We consider that dumping is a determination made with reference to a *product* from a particular producer/exporter, and not with reference to individual transactions. That is, the determination of dumping is made on the basis of consideration of transactions involving a particular product from particular producers/exporters. If the result of that consideration is a conclusion that the product in question from particular producers/exporters is dumped, we are of the view that the conclusion applies to all imports of that product from such source(s), at least over the period for which dumping was considered. Thus, we consider that the investigating authorities are entitled to consider all such imports in their analysis of "dumped imports" under Articles 3.1, 3.4, and 3.5 of the [Anti-Dumping] Agreement.[56]

The Appellate Body in *EC – Bed Linen (Article 21.5 – India)* made clear, however, that imports from those *exporters* who were not found to be dumping may *not* be included in the volume of dumped imports from a country:

---

[52] Appellate Body Report, *US – Hot-Rolled Steel*, para. 192. [53] *Ibid.*, para. 193. [54] *Ibid.*
[55] *Ibid.*, para. 196. Note that the Appellate Body in *US – Hot-Rolled Steel* ruled that an examination of only certain parts of a domestic industry does not ensure a proper evaluation of the state of the domestic industry as a whole, and does not, therefore, satisfy the requirements of 'objectiv[ity]' in Article 3.1 of the *Anti-Dumping Agreement*. See Appellate Body Report, *US – Hot-Rolled Steel*, para. 206.
[56] Panel Report, *EC – Bed Linen*, para. 6.136.

It is clear from the text of Article 3.1 that investigating authorities must ensure that a "determination of injury" is made on the basis of "positive evidence" and an "objective examination" of the volume and effect of imports that *are dumped* – and to the exclusion of the volume and effect of imports that *are not dumped*. It is clear from the text of Article 3.2 that investigating authorities must consider whether there has been a significant increase in *dumped* imports, and that they must examine the effect of *dumped* imports on prices resulting from price undercutting, price depression, or price suppression.

Article 3.5 continues in the same vein as the initial paragraphs of Article 3 by requiring a demonstration that dumped imports are causing injury to the domestic industry "through the *effects of dumping*", which, of course, depends upon there being imports from producers or exporters that *are dumped*. In addition, Article 3.5 lists "volume and prices of imports *not* sold at dumping prices" as an example of "known factors *other than the dumped* imports" that are injuring the domestic industry at the same time as the dumped imports. Article 3.5 requires that this injury *not* be attributed to the dumped imports. Thus, injury caused by "volume and prices of imports *not* sold at dumping prices" must be *separated and distinguished* from injury caused by the "dumped imports". None of these provisions of the *Anti-Dumping Agreement* can be construed to suggest that Members may include in the volume of *dumped* imports the imports from producers that are *not* found to be dumping.[57]

[Emphasis in the original]

With regard to the first requirement, note also that the injury enquiry focuses on developments in the domestic market of the importing Member. Article 3.2 of the *Anti-Dumping Agreement* requires the investigating authorities to consider whether there has been a *significant increase* in the dumped imports, either in absolute terms or relative to production or consumption, in the domestic market. The investigating authorities must also consider whether there has been *significant price undercutting* by the dumped imports as compared with the price of a like product of the importing Member, or whether the effect is otherwise to *depress prices to a significant degree* or prevent price increases, which would otherwise have occurred, to a significant degree.

With regard to the second requirement referred to above, Article 3.4 of the *Anti-Dumping Agreement* states:

The examination of the impact of the dumped imports on the domestic industry concerned shall include an evaluation of all relevant economic factors.

Article 3.4 then lists the following relevant economic factors that must be evaluated:

- factors and indices having a bearing on the state of the industry (such as: an actual or potential decline in sales; profits; output; market share; productivity; return on investments; or utilisation of capacity);
- factors affecting the domestic prices;
- the magnitude of the margin of dumping;
- actual or potential negative effects on cash flow; inventories; employment; wages; growth; ability to raise capital; or investments.

---

[57] Appellate Body Report, *EC – Bed Linen (Article 21.5 – India)*, paras. 111–12.

Article 3.4 of the *Anti-Dumping Agreement* explicitly states that this list is not exhaustive. It also stresses that one or more of these factors, no matter how pronounced, will not necessarily give decisive guidance as to the existence of injury to the domestic industry.

While not exhaustive, it is widely accepted that the list of factors in Article 3.4 is a *mandatory* minimum, and that investigating authorities must therefore collect and analyse data relating to each of these individual enumerated factors.[58] In addition, investigating authorities must also collect and analyse data relating to *any other relevant factors* that may have a bearing on the state of a domestic industry in a particular case.[59]

Article 3.1 of the *Anti-Dumping Agreement* permits investigating authorities, making an injury determination, to base their determination on all relevant reasoning and facts before it, including all confidential and non-confidential information on the record of the investigation.[60]

Questions and Assignments 6.9

What does the term 'injury' in the *Anti-Dumping Agreement* mean? What is the thrust of the investigating authorities' obligation under Article 3 of the *Anti-Dumping Agreement* relating to the determination of injury? What is 'positive evidence' and an 'objective examination' within the meaning of Article 3.1 of the *Anti-Dumping Agreement*? Can the total volume of dumped imports legally include imports from exporters that were not found to be dumping?

6.2.3.3. *Determination of a threat of material injury*

As discussed above, the term 'injury' in the *Anti-Dumping Agreement* refers not only to material injury but also to the *threat of material injury*. Article 3.7 of the *Anti-Dumping Agreement* relates to the determination of a threat of material injury. It provides:

> A determination of a threat of material injury shall be based on facts and not merely on allegation, conjecture or remote possibility. The change in circumstances which would create a situation in which the dumping would cause injury must be clearly foreseen and imminent.

Article 3.7 further provides that, in making a determination regarding the existence of a threat of material injury, the investigating authorities should consider, *inter alia*, such factors as:

---

[58] Panel Report, *Thailand – H-Beams*, paras. 7.224–7.225. The Appellate Body upheld this aspect of the Panel Report, stating: 'We agree with the Panel's analysis in its entirety, and with the Panel's interpretation of the mandatory nature of the factors mentioned in Article 3.4 of the *Anti-Dumping Agreement*.' See Appellate Body Report, *Thailand – H-Beams*, para. 125.
[59] Panel Report, *Thailand – H-Beams*, para. 7.225.
[60] Appellate Body Report, *Thailand – H-Beams*, para. 111.

- a significant rate of increase of dumped imports into the domestic market indicating the likelihood of substantially increased importation;
- sufficient freely disposable, or an imminent substantial increase in, capacity of the exporter indicating the likelihood of substantially increased dumped exports to the importing Member's market, taking into account the availability of other export markets to absorb any additional exports;
- whether imports are entering at prices that will have a significant depressing or suppressing effect on domestic prices, and would be likely to increase demand for further imports; and
- inventories of the product being investigated.

However, no one of these factors by itself can necessarily give decisive guidance. The totality of the factors considered must lead to the conclusion that further dumped exports are imminent and that, unless protective action is taken, material injury would occur.[61]

In respect of the nature of the analysis required under Article 3.7 of the *Anti-Dumping Agreement*, the Panel in *Mexico – Corn Syrup* considered whether a specific analysis of the consequent impact of the dumped imports on the domestic industry is required in a 'threat of injury' determination. Referring to Article 3.7, the Panel stated that:

> This language, in our view, recognizes that factors other than those set out in Article 3.7 itself will necessarily be relevant to the determination.[62]

The Panel in *Mexico – Corn Syrup* further stated that it is clear that in making a determination regarding the threat of material injury, investigating authorities must conclude that *material injury would occur* in the absence of an anti-dumping measure. However, a determination that material injury would occur cannot be made solely on the basis of consideration of the Article 3.7 factors. Therefore, the Panel in *Mexico – Corn Syrup* ruled that:

> consideration of the Article 3.4 factors in examining the consequent impact of imports is required in a case involving threat of injury in order to make a determination consistent with the requirements of Articles 3.1 and 3.7.[63]

The Appellate Body ruled in *Mexico – Corn Syrup (Article 21.5 – US)* that:

> In determining the existence of a *threat* of material injury, the investigating authorities will necessarily have to make assumptions relating to "the occurrence of future events" since such *future* events "can never be definitively proven by facts". Notwithstanding this intrinsic uncertainty, a "proper establishment" of facts in a determination of threat of material injury must be based on events that, although they have not yet occurred, must be "clearly foreseen and imminent", in accordance with Article 3.7 of the *Anti-Dumping Agreement*.[64]

Not surprisingly, Article 3.8 of the *Anti-Dumping Agreement* requires that the application of anti-dumping measures shall be considered and decided with

---

[61] See Article 3.7 of the *Anti-Dumping Agreement*.
[62] Panel Report, *Mexico – Corn Syrup*, para. 7.124.   [63] *Ibid.*, para. 7.127.
[64] Appellate Body Report, *Mexico – Corn Syrup (Article 21.5 – US)*, para. 85.

'special care' where a determination of threat of material injury is involved. While the provision offers no further guidance as to the meaning of 'special care', it is clear that the provision cautions against the 'automatic' imposition of measures in such cases.

Questions and Assignments 6.10

When does a 'threat of material injury' within the meaning of Article 3.7 of the *Anti-Dumping Agreement* exist? Which factors should investigating authorities consider in order to establish a 'threat of material injury'?

6.2.3.4. *Determination of material retardation*

Beyond specifying that the term 'injury' as used in the *Anti-Dumping Agreement* also includes 'material retardation', the Agreement contains no further specific language pertaining to this concept. Some guidance may perhaps be derived from the 1967 Anti-Dumping Code,[65] which refers to the retardation of the establishment of a new industry, and indicates that a finding must be based on 'convincing evidence' that such a new industry is actually forthcoming. Examples of such evidence include plans for an industry being at an advanced stage, a factory under construction or new capital equipment already having been ordered.

6.2.4. Demonstration of a causal link

Article 3.5 of the *Anti-Dumping Agreement* requires the demonstration of a *causal link* between:

- the dumped imports; and
- the injury to the domestic industry.

As with the determinations of dumping and injury to the domestic industry, the demonstration of a causal link between these two elements shall be based on an examination of all relevant evidence before the investigating authorities. Article 3.5 also contains a *'non-attribution' requirement*. According to this requirement, investigating authorities must examine any known factors other than the dumped imports that are injuring the domestic industry at the same time *and* they must not attribute the injury caused by these other factors to the dumped imports. It is important to note that the *Anti-Dumping Agreement* does *not* require that the dumped imports are the *principal cause* of the injury to the domestic injury.[66] The *Anti-Dumping Agreement* only requires that the dumped imports be a

---

[65] See above, p. 515.
[66] Note that this was the requirement under Article 3 of the Kennedy Round Anti-Dumping Code, BISD 15S/74. As discussed above, the Kennedy Round *Anti-Dumping Code* was superseded by the Tokyo Round *Anti-Dumping Code* in which this requirement was already dropped.

cause of the injury and that other causes of injury not be attributed to the dumping.

6.2.4.1. Relevant factors

Article 3.5 of the *Anti-Dumping Agreement* identifies several factors which 'may be relevant' in demonstrating a causal link between dumped imports and injury *and* in ensuring non-attribution to the dumped imports of injury being caused by other factors. These factors include:

- the volume and prices of imports not sold at dumping prices;
- contraction in demand or changes in the patterns of consumption;
- trade-restrictive practices of and competition between the foreign and domestic producers;
- developments in technology; and
- the export performance and productivity of the domestic industry.

However, Article 3.5 does not *require* examination of any particular factors or *give clear guidance* on the manner in which the investigating authorities should evaluate relevant evidence in order to establish the causal link *and* to ensure non-attribution to the dumped imports of injury being caused by other factors. The Panel in *Thailand – H-Beams* made clear its view that, in contrast to the mandatory list of factors in Article 3.4, the list of factors in Article 3.5 was merely *illustrative*. Thus, while the listed factors in Article 3.5 might be relevant in many cases, and while the list contains useful guidance as to the kinds of factors other than imports that might cause injury to the domestic industry, the specific list in Article 3.5 is not itself mandatory.[67]

6.2.4.2. 'Non-attribution' requirement

The Appellate Body in *US – Hot-Rolled Steel* clarified the 'non-attribution' requirement of Article 3.5 of the *Anti-Dumping Agreement* as follows:

> The non-attribution language in Article 3.5 of the *Anti-Dumping Agreement* applies solely in situations where dumped imports and other known factors are causing injury to the domestic industry *at the same time*. In order that investigating authorities, applying Article 3.5, are able to ensure that the injurious effects of the other known factors are not "attributed" to dumped imports, they must appropriately assess the injurious effects of those other factors. Logically, such an assessment must involve separating and distinguishing the injurious effects of the other factors from the injurious effects of the dumped imports. If the injurious effects of the dumped imports are not appropriately separated and distinguished from the injurious effects of the other factors, the authorities will be unable to conclude that the injury they ascribe to dumped imports is actually caused by those imports, rather than by the other factors. Thus, in the absence of such separation and distinction of the different injurious effects, the investigating authorities would have no rational basis to conclude that

---

[67] Panel Report, *Thailand – H-Beams*, para. 7.274.

> the dumped imports are indeed causing the injury which, under the *Anti-Dumping Agreement*, justifies the imposition of anti-dumping duties.[68]

In short, in order to comply with the 'non-attribution' requirement of Article 3.5, investigating authorities must make an appropriate *assessment* of the injury caused to the domestic industry by the other known factors, and they must *separate and distinguish* the injurious effects of the dumped imports from the injurious effects of those other factors.

Note that, under the GATT 1947 practice, there was no need to 'identify' the injury caused by the other factors. According to the GATT Panel in *US – Norwegian Salmon AD*, such separate identification of the injurious effects of the other causal factors was not required.[69] The Appellate Body in *US – Hot-Rolled Steel* reversed this case law although it did recognise that the different causal factors operating on a domestic industry may interact, and their effects may well be interrelated, such that they produce a *combined* effect on the domestic industry. Therefore, it may not be easy, as a practical matter, to separate and distinguish the injurious effects of different causal factors. The Appellate Body noted:

> However, although this process may not be easy, this is precisely what is envisaged by the non-attribution language. If the injurious effects of the dumped imports and the other known factors remain lumped together and indistinguishable, there is simply no means of knowing whether injury ascribed to dumped imports was, in reality, caused by other factors. Article 3.5, therefore, requires investigating authorities to undertake the process of assessing appropriately, and separating and distinguishing, the injurious effects of dumped imports from those of other known causal factors.[70]

6.2.4.3. Cumulation

A cumulative analysis is the consideration of the effects of dumped imports from more than one country in determining whether dumped imports are causing injury to the domestic industry. As such an analysis will necessarily increase the volume of imports whose impact is being considered, it will clearly augment the possibility of an affirmative injury determination. A controversial negotiation topic in the Uruguay Round, the conditions for cumulative analysis of the effects of imports from more than one country are now set forth in Article 3.3 of the *Anti-Dumping Agreement*. Cumulation is *not mandatory* under any circumstances, and is *permitted only* when the investigating authorities determine that:

- the margin of dumping established in relation to the imports from each country is more than *de minimis* (i.e. more than 2 per cent of the export price) and the volume of imports from each country is not negligible (i.e. normally, more than 3 per cent of imports of the like product in the importing Member, unless countries accounting for less than 3 per cent *individually*

---

[68] Appellate Body Report, *US – Hot-Rolled Steel*, para. 223.
[69] GATT Panel Report, *US – Norwegian Salmon Anti-Dumping*, 550.
[70] Appellate Body Report, *US – Hot-Rolled Steel*, para. 228.

account *collectively* for more than 7 per cent of imports of the like product in the importing Member);

- a cumulative analysis is appropriate in light of the conditions of competition among imported products and between the imported products and the like domestic products.

Questions and Assignments 6.11

Does the *Anti-Dumping Agreement* require that the dumped imports are the principal cause of the injury to the domestic industry? What does the 'non-attribution' requirement of Article 3.5 entail? What is the purpose or relevance of the list of economic factors contained in Article 3.5 of the *Anti-Dumping Agreement*? Why must the investigating authorities separate and distinguish the injurious effects of dumped imports from those of other known causal factors of the injury? What is a cumulative analysis within the meaning of Article 3.3 of the *Anti-Dumping Agreement*? Are investigating authorities permitted to apply such analysis?

6.2.5. Anti-dumping investigation

The *Anti-Dumping Agreement* sets out, in considerable detail, how investigating authorities of WTO Members have to initiate and conduct an anti-dumping investigation. This section addresses:

- the initiation of an anti-dumping investigation;
- the period of an investigation; and
- the conduct of an investigation.

6.2.5.1. Initiation of an investigation

Article 5 of the *Anti-Dumping Agreement* contains numerous requirements concerning the initiation of an anti-dumping investigation. The domestic investigating authorities can instigate an investigation on their own initiative. However, the *Anti-Dumping Agreement* specifies that investigations must *generally* be initiated on the basis of a written application submitted 'by or on behalf of' a domestic industry. This 'standing' requirement is informed by numerical thresholds to determine whether there exists sufficient support for the application among domestic producers to warrant initiation. The *Anti-Dumping Agreement* contains guidance relating to the required contents of the initiation request, including:

- evidence of dumping;
- evidence of injury to the domestic industry; and
- evidence of a causal link between the dumped imports and the injury to the domestic industry.

The application must contain information that is 'reasonably available' to the applicant in accordance with Article 5.2. Simple assertion, unsubstantiated by relevant evidence, cannot be considered to meet the requirements of this provision. In considering the nature and extent of the information that must be provided in an application pursuant to Article 5.2(iv), the Panel in *Mexico – Corn Syrup* stated:

> Obviously, the quantity and quality of the information provided by the applicant need not be such as would be required in order to make a preliminary or final determination of injury. Moreover, the applicant need only provide such information as is "reasonably available" to it with respect to the relevant factors. Since information regarding the factors and indices set out in Article 3.4 concerns the state of the domestic industry and its operations, such information would generally be available to applicants. Nevertheless, we note that an application which is consistent with the requirements of Article 5.2 will not necessarily contain sufficient evidence to justify initiation under Article 5.3.[71]

Article 5.3 of the *Anti-Dumping Agreement* requires that the investigating authorities examine the accuracy and adequacy of the evidence provided in the application to determine whether there is sufficient evidence to justify the initiation of the investigation. However, in determining whether there is sufficient evidence to initiate an investigation, the investigating authorities are not limited to the information contained in the application. The Panel in *Guatemala – Cement II* noted:

> We have expressed the view that Articles 5.2 and 5.3 contain different obligations. One of the consequences of this difference in obligations is that investigating authorities need not content themselves with the information provided in the application but may gather information on their own in order to meet the standard of sufficient evidence for initiation in Article 5.3.[72]

With respect to the nature and extent of the evidence required to initiate an anti-dumping investigation, the Panel in *Guatemala – Cement II* ruled:

> We do not of course mean to suggest that an investigating authority must have before it at the time it initiates an investigation evidence of dumping within the meaning of Article 2 of the quantity and quality that would be necessary to support a preliminary or final determination. An anti-dumping investigation is a process where certainty on the existence of all the elements necessary in order to adopt a measure is reached gradually as the investigation moves forward. However, the evidence must be such that an unbiased and objective investigating authority could determine that there was sufficient evidence of dumping within the meaning of Article 2 to justify initiation of an investigation.[73]

The same is true for the evidence on injury to the domestic industry and the causal link between the dumped imports and the injury.[74]

---

[71] Panel Report, *Mexico – Corn Syrup*, para. 7.74.
[72] Panel Report, *Guatemala – Cement II*, para. 8.62.   [73] *Ibid.*, para. 8.35.
[74] Where an investigation is self-initiated by the authorities, the authorities may proceed only if they have sufficient evidence of dumping, injury and a causal link to justify the initiation of the investigation. See Article 5.6 of the *Anti-Dumping Agreement*.

Article 5.5 of the *Anti-Dumping Agreement* requires that the investigating authorities 'avoid, unless a decision has been made to initiate an investigation, any publicizing of the application for the initiation of an investigation'. However, 'after receipt of a properly documented application and before proceeding to initiate an investigation, the authorities shall notify the government of the exporting Member concerned'.[75] There are also public notice requirements concerning the initiation of an investigation in Article 12.1 of the *Anti-Dumping Agreement*.

An application to initiate an anti-dumping investigation shall be rejected, and an investigation shall be terminated, *promptly* as soon as the investigating authorities are satisfied that there is not enough evidence either of dumping or of injury.[76] Moreover, in order to ensure that an unwarranted investigation is not continued, Article 5.8 provides for prompt termination of investigations in the event that:

- the margin of dumping is *de minimis* (i.e. less than 2 per cent of the export price); and
- the volume of imports from each country is *negligible* (i.e. normally, less than 3 per cent of imports of the like product in the importing Member, unless countries accounting for less than 3 per cent *individually* account *collectively* for more than 7 per cent of imports of the like product in the importing Member).

6.2.5.2. *Period of investigation*

It is the common practice of WTO Members to conduct an anti-dumping investigation using data for a fixed 'investigation period' which precedes the date of initiation of an investigation. Measures are then imposed on the basis of the determinations on dumping and injury made using the data from the 'investigation period'. The *Anti-Dumping Agreement* refers to the concept of a 'period of investigation', and the use of such an investigation period appears to be implicit in several provisions of the Agreement.[77]

The WTO Committee on Anti-Dumping Practices has adopted a *Recommendation Concerning the Periods of Data Collection for Anti-Dumping Investigations*.[78] Pursuant to this Recommendation, the period of data collection for *dumping investigations* normally should not exceed twelve months and, in any case, be no less than six months, ending as close to the date of initiation as is practicable. Furthermore, the period of data collection for *injury investigations* normally should be at least three years, unless a party from

---

[75] See Article 5.5 of the *Anti-Dumping Agreement*. Several panels (*Thailand – H-Beams*; *Guatemala – Cement I*; *Guatemala – Cement II*) have considered the nature and extent of the obligation imposed by Article 5.5. See also *Recommendation Concerning the Timing of the Notification under Article 5.5*, adopted by the Committee on Anti-Dumping Practices on 29 October 1998, G/ADP/5, dated 3 November 1998.
[76] See Article 5.8 of the *Anti-Dumping Agreement*.
[77] For example, Articles 2.4.2 and 2.2.1 of the *Anti-Dumping Agreement*.
[78] G/ADP/6, adopted by the Committee on Anti-Dumping Practices on 5 May 2000.

whom data is being gathered has existed for a shorter period, and should include the entirety of the period of data collection for the dumping investigation.

Questions and Assignments 6.12

How is an anti-dumping investigation initiated? On what basis do the investigating authorities of a Member decide to initiate an investigation? How does the *Anti-Dumping Agreement* ensure that unwarranted investigations are not continued? What is the 'period of investigation' in anti-dumping investigations? Can or should the period of investigation differ from case to case depending on the facts?

6.2.5.3. *Conduct of the investigation*

Article 6 of the *Anti-Dumping Agreement* contains detailed rules concerning the process of the investigation, including evidentiary, informational and procedural elements.

Article 6.1 requires that all interested parties in an anti-dumping investigation be given *notice* of the information which the authorities require and ample *opportunity to present* in writing all evidence which they consider relevant in respect of the investigation. In practice, investigating authorities typically send interested parties questionnaires in which they identify the information that they require in order to conduct the investigation. Article 6.1 sets 'flexible' thirty-day minimum time limits for submissions and responses to questionnaires from interested parties.[79]

Pursuant to Article 6.6 of the *Anti-Dumping Agreement*, investigating authorities must *generally* satisfy themselves as to the accuracy of the information supplied by interested parties upon which their findings are based. The investigating authorities will often verify the information supplied by on-site visits to review the records of the companies involved. In this regard, the Panel in *US – DRAMS* stated the following in support of its position that the text of Article 6.6 does *not* explicitly require verification of all information relied upon:

> Article 6.6 simply requires Members to "satisfy themselves as to the accuracy of the information". In our view, Members could "satisfy themselves as to the accuracy of the information" in a number of ways without proceeding to some type of formal verification, including for example reliance on the reputation of the original source of the information. Indeed, we consider that anti-dumping investigations would become totally unmanageable if investigating authorities were required to actually verify the accuracy of all information relied on.[80]

---

[79] See Appellate Body Report, *US – Hot-Rolled Steel*, paras. 73–5, where the Appellate Body states that Article 6.1.1 establishes that investigating authorities may impose time limits for questionnaire responses, that these time limits are not necessarily absolute and immutable and that in appropriate circumstances these time limits must be extended.

[80] Panel Report, *US – DRAMS*, para. 6.78.

The Panel questioned, for example, 'whether investigating authorities should be required to verify import statistics from a different government office' and 'whether investigating authorities should be required to verify "official" exchange rates obtained from a central bank'.[81]

To ensure the transparency of the anti-dumping investigation and proceedings, the investigating authorities must, according to Article 6.4 of the *Anti-Dumping Agreement*, provide timely opportunities for all interested parties to see all relevant information.[82] Note, however, that Article 6.5 of the *Anti-Dumping Agreement* requires that investigating authorities preserve the confidentiality of sensitive business information relating to the exporting firms and the domestic industry involved in the investigation.[83]

All interested parties enjoy certain rights to participate in the proceedings and to make presentations.[84] In addition, investigating authorities must provide opportunities for industrial users of the product under investigation and for representative consumer organisations, in cases where the product is commonly sold at the retail level, to provide information which is relevant to the investigation regarding dumping, injury and causation.[85]

Article 6 is supplemented by two Annexes to the *Anti-Dumping Agreement* that provide further guidance relating to the conduct of the investigation. These Annexes concern rules for on-site investigations to verify information obtained from foreign parties as well as use of 'best information available' in the event a party refuses access or does not provide requested information, or significantly impedes the investigation. With respect to the use of 'best information available' under Article 6.8 of and Annex II to the *Anti-Dumping Agreement*, the Appellate Body stated in *US – Hot-Rolled Steel*:

> Article 6.8 identifies the circumstances in which investigating authorities may overcome a lack of information, in the responses of the interested parties, by using "facts" which are otherwise "available" to the investigating authorities. According to Article 6.8, where the interested parties do not "significantly impede" the investigation, recourse may be had to facts available only if an interested party fails to submit necessary information "within a reasonable period". Thus, if information is, in fact, supplied "within a reasonable period", the investigating authorities *cannot* use facts available, but must use the information submitted by the interested party.[86]
>
> In determining whether information is submitted within a reasonable period of time, it is proper for investigating authorities to attach importance to the time limit fixed for questionnaire responses, and to the need to ensure the conduct of the investigation in an orderly fashion.[87]

[81] *Ibid.*, para. 6.78, footnote 513.
[82] Article 6.4 of the *Anti-Dumping Agreement* defines what information is 'relevant' for the purposes of this provision.
[83] Article 6.5 of the *Anti-Dumping Agreement* protects information which is by its nature confidential (i.e. information of which the disclosure would, for example, be of significant competitive advantage to a competitor or would have a significantly adverse effect upon a person supplying the information) *or* information which has been supplied on a confidential basis by the parties to the investigation.
[84] Article 6.13 of the *Anti-Dumping Agreement* requires investigating authorities to take due account of the difficulties interested parties, in particular small companies, may experience in supplying information. Investigating authorities must provide interested parties with any assistance practicable.
[85] Article 6.12 of the *Anti-Dumping Agreement*.
[86] Appellate Body Report, *US – Hot-Rolled Steel*, para. 77.   [87] *Ibid.*, para. 86.

Paragraph 7 of Annex II to the *Anti-Dumping Agreement* indicates that a lack of 'cooperation' by an interested party may, by virtue of the use made of facts available, lead to a result that is 'less favourable' to the interested party than would have been the case had that interested party cooperated. In *US – Hot-Rolled Steel*, the Appellate Body cautioned, however, that investigating authorities should not arrive at a 'less favourable' outcome simply because an interested party fails to furnish requested information if, in fact, the interested party has 'cooperated' with the investigating authorities. Parties may very well 'cooperate' to a high degree, even though the requested information is, ultimately, not obtained.[88] The Appellate Body noted:

> In order to complete their investigations, investigating authorities are entitled to expect a very significant degree of effort – to the "best of their abilities" – from investigated exporters. At the same time, however, the investigating authorities are not entitled to insist upon *absolute* standards or impose *unreasonable* burdens upon those exporters.[89]

Article 5.10 of the *Anti-Dumping Agreement* specifies that an anti-dumping investigation must be completed within one year, and in no cases more than eighteen months, after initiation.

Questions and Assignments 6.13

How are interested parties involved in an anti-dumping investigation? Are there any specific rules on the involvement of consumer organisations? When may investigating authorities make use of 'best information available' within the meaning of Article 6.8 of and Annex II to the *Anti-Dumping Agreement*? Is it recommendable for an interested party not to cooperate with the investigating authorities in the context of an anti-dumping investigation? Within what timeframe must investigating authorities complete an anti-dumping investigation?

6.2.6. Anti-dumping measures

The *Anti-Dumping Agreement* provides for three kinds of anti-dumping measures:

- provisional measures;
- price undertakings; and
- definitive anti-dumping duties.

This section will discuss the rules on the imposition of each of these measures. It will also address the issues of the duration, termination and review of anti-dumping measures.

---

[88] *Ibid.*, para. 99.   [89] *Ibid.*, para. 102.

6.2.6.1. *Imposition of provisional anti-dumping measures*

Article 7 of the *Anti-Dumping Agreement* contains rules relating to the imposition of provisional measures. To apply a provisional anti-dumping measure, investigating authorities must make a *preliminary* affirmative determination of dumping, injury and causation.[90] Furthermore, the investigating authorities must judge that such a measure is *necessary* to prevent injury being caused during the investigation.[91] A provisional measure cannot be applied earlier than sixty days following the initiation of the investigation.[92] Provisional measures may take the form of a provisional duty or, preferably, a security, by cash deposit or bond, equal to the amount of the preliminarily determined margin of dumping.[93]

With regard to the time period for application of the provisional measure, Article 7.4 of the *Anti-Dumping Agreement* states that it:

> shall be limited to as short a period as possible, not exceeding four months or, on decision of the authorities concerned, upon request by exporters representing a significant percentage of the trade involved, to a period not exceeding six months.

Where the Member applies the 'lesser duty rule' in its administration of anti-dumping duties, the period of provisional application is generally six months, with the possibility of extension to nine months upon request of the exporters.[94]

6.2.6.2. *Price undertakings*

Article 8 of the *Anti-Dumping Agreement* provides for the possibility of offering and accepting price undertakings as an alternative to the imposition of anti-dumping duties. Undertakings to revise prices or cease exports at the dumped price may be entered into only after the investigating authorities have made an affirmative preliminary determination of dumping, injury and causation. Such undertakings are voluntary on the part of both exporters and investigating authorities. An exporter may request the continuation of an investigation after the acceptance of an undertaking. The undertaking would then automatically lapse in the event of a negative final determination of dumping, injury or causation.

Questions and Assignments 6.14

When can provisional anti-dumping measures be imposed according to the *Anti-Dumping Agreement*? What form can these anti-dumping measures take? For how long can provisional anti-dumping measures be applied? What are price undertakings within the meaning of Article 8 of the *Anti-Dumping Agreement*? When can such price undertakings be made?

---

[90] Article 7.1(ii) of the *Anti-Dumping Agreement*.   [91] Article 7.1(iii) of the *Anti-Dumping Agreement*.
[92] Article 7.3 of the *Anti-Dumping Agreement*.   [93] Article 7.2 of the *Anti-Dumping Agreement*.
[94] On the 'lesser duty rule', see below, p. 543.

6.2.6.3. *Imposition and collection of anti-dumping duties*

Article 9 of the *Anti-Dumping Agreement* governs the imposition and collection of anti-dumping duties. This provision establishes the general principle that 'it is desirable' that, even where all the requirements for imposition of duties have been fulfilled, the imposition of anti-dumping duties remains *optional*. Article 9 also contains the so-called 'lesser duty rule', under which 'it is desirable' that the duty imposed be *less* than the margin of dumping *if* such lesser duty would be *adequate* to remove the injury to the domestic industry.

Members are required to collect duties on a *non-discriminatory* basis on imports from all sources found to be dumped and causing injury.[95] The competent national authorities should name the supplier or suppliers of the products affected by the anti-dumping duty. However, if several suppliers from the same country are involved, and it is impracticable to name all these suppliers, the authorities may just name the supplying country concerned. If several suppliers from more than one country are involved, the authorities may either name all the suppliers involved or, if this is impracticable, all the supplying countries involved.[96]

The anti-dumping duty collected *may not exceed* the dumping margin.[97] Article 9.3 of the *Anti-Dumping Agreement* provides for two mechanisms to ensure that excessive duties are not collected.[98] These mechanisms are further discussed in Articles 9.3.1 and 9.3.2.

When anti-dumping duties are imposed, the investigating authorities must, in principle, calculate a dumping margin for each exporter.[99] However, the *Anti-Dumping Agreement* recognises that this may not always be possible.[100] When it is not possible to calculate a dumping margin for each exporter, the investigating authorities may limit the number of exporters considered individually (i.e. sampling). In accordance with Article 9.4 of the *Anti-Dumping Agreement*, an anti-dumping duty is then imposed on *uninvestigated* sources on the basis of the *weighted average dumping margin* actually established for investigated sources (sometimes referred to as the 'all others' rate). However, the investigating authorities:

---

[95] See Article 9.2 of the *Anti-Dumping Agreement*. Note, however, that the anti-dumping duty will *not* be applied to imports from sources from which a price undertaking has been put in place. See *ibid.*

[96] See Article 9.2 of the *Anti-Dumping Agreement*.

[97] See Article 9.3 of the *Anti-Dumping Agreement*.

[98] Which mechanism a Member opts to use will depend on whether the Member collects the anti-dumping duties on a *prospective basis* (i.e. where a Member collects the duty at the time of importation – as is the case for the European Communities) or on a *retrospective basis* (i.e. where a Member calculates a specific amount of anti-dumping duty to be paid only after permitting importation and collecting an estimated duty – as the United States does). See further, Articles 9.3.1 and 9.3.2 of the *Anti-Dumping Agreement*.

[99] See Article 6.10 of the *Anti-Dumping Agreement*.

[100] This will be the case when the number of exporters, producers, importers or types of products concerned is considerable. See Article 6.10 of the *Anti-Dumping Agreement*.

- must not include in this weighted average calculation any dumping margins that are *de minimis*, zero or based on the 'facts available';[101] and
- must calculate an individual margin for any exporter or producer who provides the necessary information during the course of the investigation.[102]

With respect to the 'all others' rate applied to uninvestigated sources, the Appellate Body stated in *US – Hot-Rolled Steel*:

> Article 9.4 does not prescribe any method that WTO Members must use to establish the "all others" rate that is actually applied to exporters or producers that are not investigated. Rather, Article 9.4 simply identifies a maximum limit, or ceiling, which investigating authorities "*shall not exceed*" in establishing an "all others" rate.[103]

With respect to the individual margin of dumping for producers or exporters who were not sources of imports considered during the period of investigation (i.e. 'new shippers'), Article 9.5 of the *Anti-Dumping Agreement* provides that:

> the authorities shall promptly carry out a review for the purpose of determining individual margins of dumping.

The investigating authorities must therefore conduct an expedited review to determine a specific margin of dumping for exports from such 'new shippers'. No anti-dumping duties may be levied on imports from such exporters or producers while the review is being carried out.[104]

Article 10 of the *Anti-Dumping Agreement* establishes the general principle that both provisional and definitive duties may be applied only as of the date on which the determinations of dumping, injury and causation have been made.[105] *Retroactive application* of anti-dumping duties is thus, in principle, prohibited. However, Article 10 contains rules for the retroactive application of anti-dumping duties in specific circumstances. Where the imposition of the anti-dumping duty is based on a determination of material injury – as opposed to a threat thereof, or material retardation – the duties may be collected as of the date of imposition of the provisional measures. If provisional duties were collected in an amount greater than the amount of the final duty or if the imposition of duties is based on a finding of threat of material injury or of material retardation, a refund of provisional duties is necessary. In exceptional circumstances, Article 6.10 permits retroactive application of final anti-dumping duties. These exceptional circumstances involve:

---

[101] Also when a dumping margin was calculated, only to a very limited extent, on the basis of 'facts available' pursuant to Article 6.8 of the *Anti-Dumping Agreement*, this dumping margin may not be used to calculate the 'all others' rate. See Appellate Body Report, *US – Hot-Rolled Steel*, paras. 122–3.

[102] See Article 9.4 of the *Anti-Dumping Agreement*. Note that Article 9.4 of the *Anti-Dumping Agreement* does not expressly address the issue of how the 'all others' rate should be calculated in the event that all margins are to be excluded from the calculation, under the prohibitions. See Appellate Body Report, *US – Hot-Rolled Steel*, para. 126.

[103] Appellate Body Report, *US – Hot-Rolled Steel*, para. 116.

[104] See Article 9.5 of the *Anti-Dumping Agreement*. The authorities may, however, withhold appraisal and/or request guarantees to ensure that, if necessary, anti-dumping duties can be levied retroactively to the date of the initiation of the review. See Article 9.5 of the *Anti-Dumping Agreement*.

[105] See Article 10.1 of the *Anti-Dumping Agreement*.

- a history of dumping which caused injury; *or* a situation in which the importer was, or should have been, aware that the exporter practices injurious dumping, *and*
- the injury is caused by massive dumped imports in a short time which is likely to undermine the remedial effect of the definitive anti-dumping duty (this may be the case because of a rapid and massive build-up of stocks of the imported product).[106]

In these circumstances, Article 10.6 permits retroactive application of final duties to a date not more than ninety days prior to the application of provisional measures.[107]

Questions and Assignments 6.15

What is the 'lesser duty rule' of Article 9 of the *Anti-Dumping Agreement*? Are Members required to collect anti-dumping duties on imports from all sources found to be dumped and causing injury? Will the competent authority name the supplier or suppliers of the products affected by the anti-dumping duty *or* will it name the supplying country concerned? Must investigating authorities calculate a dumping margin for each exporter? What is the maximum anti-dumping duty that may pursuant to Article 9.4 of the *Anti-Dumping Agreement* be imposed on 'uninvestigated sources'? Can anti-dumping duties be applied retroactively? Can anti-dumping duties be levied prior to the date of initiation of an anti-dumping investigation?

6.2.6.4. *Duration, termination and review of anti-dumping measures*

Responding to the concern of some Members that some countries were leaving anti-dumping measures in place indefinitely, Article 11 of the *Anti-Dumping Agreement* establishes rules governing the duration of anti-dumping measures and a requirement for the periodic review of any continuing necessity for the imposition of anti-dumping measures.

With respect to the duration of anti-dumping duties, Article 11.1 of the *Anti-Dumping Agreement* provides:

> An anti-dumping duty shall remain in force only as long as and to the extent necessary to counteract dumping which is causing injury.

The Panel in *US – DRAMS* stated that:

---

[106] See Article 10.6 of the *Anti-Dumping Agreement*.

[107] Note that Article 10.7 of the *Anti-Dumping Agreement* provides that: 'The authorities may, after initiating an investigation, take such measures … *as may be necessary to collect* anti-dumping duties retroactively, as provided for in paragraph 6 …' [emphasis added]. Once the authorities have 'sufficient evidence' that the conditions of Article 10.6 are satisfied, they may take the *conservatory or precautionary measures* provided for in Article 10.7. On what constitutes 'sufficient evidence', and other issues relating to Articles 10.6 and 10.7, see Panel Report, *US – Hot-Rolled Steel*, paras. 7.143–7.144.

> the need for the continued imposition of the duty must be demonstrable on the basis of the evidence adduced.[108]

With respect to the periodic review of anti-dumping duties applied, Article 11.2, first sentence, requires the competent authorities to:

> review the need for the continued imposition of the duty, where warranted, on their own initiative or, provided that a reasonable period of time has elapsed since the imposition of the definitive anti-dumping duty, upon request by any interested party which submits positive information substantiating the need for a review.

The second sentence of Article 11.2 requires investigating authorities to examine whether the 'continued imposition' of the duty is necessary to offset dumping. The Panel in *US – DRAMS* interpreted this requirement as follows:

> The word "continued" covers a temporal relationship between past and future. In our view, the word "continued" would be redundant if the investigating authority were restricted to considering only whether the duty was necessary to offset *present* dumping. Thus, the inclusion of the word "continued" signifies that the investigating authority is entitled to examine whether imposition of the duty may be applied henceforth to offset dumping.[109]

Furthermore, with regard to injury, Article 11.2, second sentence, provides for a review of 'whether the injury would be likely to continue or recur if the duty were removed or varied'. The Panel in *US – DRAMS* stated in this respect that:

> In conducting an Article 11.2 injury review, an investigating authority may examine the causal link between injury and dumped imports. If, in the context of a review of such a causal link, the only injury under examination is injury that may recur following revocation (i.e. future rather than present injury), an investigating authority must necessarily be examining whether that future injury would be caused by dumping with a commensurately prospective timeframe. To do so, the investigating authority would first need to have established a status regarding the prospects of dumping. For these reasons, we do not agree that Article 11.2 precludes *a priori* the justification of continued imposition of anti-dumping duties when there is no present dumping.
>
> In addition, we note that there is nothing in the text of Article 11.2 of the [Anti-Dumping] Agreement that explicitly limits a Member to a "present" analysis, and forecloses a prospective analysis, when conducting an Article 11.2 review.[110]

In other words, Article 11.2 does not preclude *a priori* continued imposition of anti-dumping duties in the *absence* of present dumping. However, it may also be clear from the plain meaning of the text of Article 11.2 that the continued imposition must still satisfy the 'necessity' standard, even where the need for the continued imposition of an anti-dumping duty is tied to the *recurrence* of dumping.[111] Note also that the Panel in *US – DRAMS* found that, with regard to injury, an absence of dumping during the preceding three years and six months is not in and of itself indicative of the likely state of the relevant domestic industry if the duty were removed or varied. Likewise, with regard to causality, an absence of dumping during the preceding three years and six months is not in and of itself indicative of causal factors other than the absence of dumping.[112]

---

[108] Panel Report, *US – DRAMS*, para. 6.42.   [109] *Ibid.*, para. 6.27.
[110] *Ibid.*, paras. 6.28–6.29.   [111] *Ibid.*, para. 6.43.   [112] *Ibid.*, para. 6.59.

If, as a result of the review, the authorities determine that the anti-dumping duty is no longer warranted, it shall be terminated immediately.[113]

In any case, pursuant to Article 11.3 of the *Anti-Dumping Agreement* (the so-called 'sunset clause'), any definitive anti-dumping duty shall be *terminated* on a date not later than *five years* from its imposition,[114] *unless* the authorities determine, in a review initiated before that date, that the expiry of the duty 'would be likely to lead to continuation or recurrence of dumping and injury'.[115] Such a review is commonly referred to as a 'sunset review'. It can be initiated:

- at the initiative of the competent authorities; or
- upon a duly substantiated request made by or on behalf of the domestic industry.[116]

Any such review shall be carried out expeditiously and shall normally be concluded within twelve months of the date of initiation of the review.[117]

The Panel in *US – DRAMS* made the following observations with regard to the 'sunset review' under Article 11.3 of the *Anti-Dumping Agreement*:

> We note that Article 11.3 provides for termination of a definitive anti-dumping duty five years from its imposition. However, such termination is conditional. First, the terms of Article 11.3 itself lay down that this should occur unless the authorities determine that the expiry would be "likely to lead to continuation or recurrence of dumping and injury". Where there is a determination that both are likely, the duty may remain in force, and the five year clock is reset to start again from that point. Second, Article 11.3 provides also for another situation whereby this five year period can be otherwise effectively extended, viz in a situation where a review under paragraph 2 covering both dumping and injury has taken place. If, for instance, such a review took place at the four year point, it could effectively extend the sunset review until 9 years from the original determination. In the first case, we note that the provisions of Article 11.3 explicitly conditions the prolongation of the five year period on a finding that there is *likelihood* of dumping and injury continuing or recurring. In the second case, where there is reference to review under Article 11.2, there is no such explicit reference.[118]

However, since both instances of review have the same practical effect of prolonging the application of anti-dumping duties beyond five years, the Panel in *US – DRAMS* argued that the investigating authorities are entitled to apply the same test concerning the likelihood of recurrence or the continuation of dumping for both Article 11.2 and 11.3 reviews. With respect to both Article 11.2 and 11.3 reviews, the Panel in *US – DRAMS* noted that:

---

[113] Article 11.2 of the *Anti-Dumping Agreement*.

[114] Or, alternatively, from the date of the most recent review under Article 11.2, if that review has covered both dumping and injury, or the date of the most recent review under Article 11.3.

[115] The duty may remain in force pending the outcome of such a review. See Article 11.3 of the *Anti-Dumping Agreement*.

[116] *Ibid*.

[117] See Article 11.4 of the *Anti-Dumping Agreement*. The provisions of Article 6 of the *Anti-Dumping Agreement* regarding evidence and procedure shall apply to any review carried out under Article 11.

[118] Panel Report, *US – DRAMS*, para. 6.48, footnote 494.

> "likelihood" or "likely" carries with it the ordinary meaning of "probable". That being so, it seems to us that a "likely standard" amounts to the view that where recurrence of dumping is found to be probable as a consequence of revocation of an anti-dumping duty, this probability would constitute a proper basis for entitlement to maintain that anti-dumping duty in force.[119]

Note that the sunset review in Article 11.3 has more recently been the subject of WTO dispute settlement proceedings.[120]

Questions and Assignments 6.16

How long can an anti-dumping duty remain in force? When, and on whose initiative, will the national investigating authorities review the continued need for the imposition of an anti-dumping duty? On what basis will the investigating authorities decide on the continued need for the imposition of an anti-dumping duty? What is a 'sunset review'? Describe two ways in which the imposition of an anti-dumping duty can be prolonged beyond the period of five years provided for in Article 11.3 of the *Anti-Dumping Agreement*.

6.2.6.5. Problem of circumvention of anti-dumping duties

As explained above, anti-dumping duties are typically levied on a specific product of a specific exporter or producer from a specific country. An exporter or producer may try to change the characteristics of the product concerned so that it no longer responds to the characteristics of the product subjected to an anti-dumping duty. An exporter or producer may move part of its assembly or manufacturing operations to another country so that the product arguably no longer originates in the country whose products are subjected to an anti-dumping duty. In short, the exporter or producer may attempt to 'circumvent' the anti-dumping duties imposed. Members have different ways of handling this problem and of answering the question to what extent the 'new' products may be subjected to the existing anti-dumping duties.[121] The problem of circumvention and anti-circumvention measures was on the agenda of the Uruguay Round but no agreement on specific rules was reached.

6.2.6.6. Public notice and judicial review

In order to increase the transparency of the determinations made by the investigating authorities and to encourage solid and thorough reasoning underlying such determinations, Article 12 of the *Anti-Dumping Agreement* contains detailed requirements for public notice by investigating authorities of

---

[119] *Ibid.*
[120] See e.g. Panel Report and Appellate Body Report, *US – Corrosion-Resistant Steel Sunset Review*.
[121] The rules of the European Communities on anti-circumvention were found inconsistent with Article III:2 of the GATT 1947 because they provided for an internal tax not applied to like products of EC origin. See GATT Panel Report, *EEC – Parts and Components*, BISD 37S/132.

the initiation of an investigation, preliminary and final determinations and price undertakings. For example, the public notice of a final determination *must* set forth, or otherwise make available through a separate report, in sufficient detail, the findings and conclusions reached on all issues of fact and law considered material by the investigating authorities.[122] In particular, the notice or report *must* contain:

- the names of the suppliers, or, when this is impracticable, the supplying countries involved;
- a description of the product which is sufficient for customs purposes;
- the margins of dumping established and a full explanation of the reasons for the methodology used in the establishment and comparison of the export price and the normal value under Article 2;
- considerations relevant to the injury determination as set out in Article 3; and
- the main reasons leading to the determination.[123]

Furthermore, the notice or report *must* set out the reasons for the acceptance or rejection of relevant arguments or claims made by the exporters and importers.[124]

As provided for in Article 13 of the *Anti-Dumping Agreement*, entitled 'Judicial Review', each Member whose national legislation contains provisions on anti-dumping measures must maintain judicial, arbitral or administrative tribunals or procedures for the purpose, *inter alia*, of the prompt review of administrative actions relating to final determinations and reviews of determinations. Such tribunals or procedures must be independent of the authorities responsible for the determination or review in question.[125]

6.2.7. Special and differential treatment for developing-country Members

As with many other WTO agreements, the *Anti-Dumping Agreement* contains a provision relating to special and differential treatment for developing-country Members. Article 15 of the *Anti-Dumping Agreement* states:

> It is recognized that special regard must be given by developed-country Members to the special situation of developing-country Members when considering the application of anti-dumping measures under this Agreement. Possibilities of constructive remedies provided for by this Agreement shall be explored before applying anti-dumping duties where they would affect the essential interests of developing-country Members.

With respect to the meaning of the phrase 'constructive remedies provided for by this Agreement', the Panel in *EC – Bed Linen* rejected the argument that a 'constructive remedy' might be a decision not to impose anti-dumping duties at all. The Panel stated that:

---

[122] Article 12.2.2 of the *Anti-Dumping Agreement*. Note, however, that Article 12.2.2 does require that due regard be paid to the requirement for the protection of confidential information.
[123] Article 12.2.2 in conjunction with Article 12.2.1 of the *Anti-Dumping Agreement*.
[124] Article 12.2.2 of the *Anti-Dumping Agreement*.
[125] See Article 13 of the *Anti-Dumping Agreement*.

> Article 15 refers to "remedies" in respect of injurious dumping. A decision not to impose an anti-dumping duty, while clearly within the authority of a Member under Article 9.1 of the [Anti-Dumping] Agreement, is not a "remedy" of any type, constructive or otherwise.[126]

Addressing what the phrase 'constructive remedies provided for by this Agreement' might encompass, the Panel in *EC – Bed Linen* stated:

> The Agreement provides for the imposition of anti-dumping duties, either in the full amount of the dumping margin, or desirably, in a lesser amount, or the acceptance of price undertakings, as a means of resolving an anti-dumping investigation resulting in a final affirmative determination of dumping, injury, and causal link. Thus, in our view, imposition of a lesser duty, or a price undertaking would constitute "constructive remedies" within the meaning of Article 15. We come to no conclusions as to what other actions might in addition be considered to constitute "constructive remedies" under Article 15, as none have been proposed to us.[127]

The Panel in *EC – Bed Linen* understood the phrase 'before applying anti-dumping duties' to mean before the application of definitive (as opposed to provisional) anti-dumping measures, at the end of the investigative process.[128]

Furthermore, the Panel in *EC – Bed Linen* interpreted the term 'explore' as follows:

> In our view, while the exact parameters of the term are difficult to establish, the concept of "explore" clearly does not imply any particular outcome. We recall that Article 15 does not require that "constructive remedies" must be explored, but rather that the "possibilities" of such remedies must be explored, which further suggests that the exploration may conclude that no possibilities exist, or that no constructive remedies are possible, in the particular circumstances of a given case. Taken in its context, however, and in light of the object and purpose of Article 15, we do consider that the "exploration" of possibilities must be actively undertaken by the developed country authorities with a willingness to reach a positive outcome. Thus, in our view, Article 15 imposes no obligation to actually provide or accept any constructive remedy that may be identified and/or offered. It does, however, impose an obligation to actively consider, with an open mind, the possibility of such a remedy prior to imposition of an anti-dumping measure that would affect the essential interests of a developing country.[129]

There is no obligation to accept or apply a 'constructive remedy'. There is merely an obligation to 'explore' possibilities of constructive remedies, in particular, where the possibility of an undertaking has already been broached by the developing country concerned.[130] However, when a Member fails to respond, in some manner other than bare rejection that Member fails to 'explore constructive remedies'. That is certainly the case when the developing-country Member concerned has expressed its willingness to enter into an undertaking.

At the Doha Session of the Ministerial Conference in November 2001, WTO Members recognised the following, concerning Article 15 of the *Anti-Dumping Agreement*:

> while Article 15 ... is a mandatory provision, the modalities for its application would benefit from clarification. Accordingly, the Committee on Anti-Dumping Practices is

---

[126] Panel Report, *EC – Bed Linen*, para. 6.228.   [127] *Ibid.*, para. 6.229.
[128] See *ibid.*, paras. 6.231–6.232.   [129] *Ibid.*, para. 6.233.   [130] See *ibid.*, para. 6.238.

instructed, through its working group on implementation, to examine this issue and to draw up appropriate recommendations within twelve months on how to operationalize this provision.[131]

Questions and Assignments 6.17

What does the 'special and differntial treatment' provision of Article 15 of the *Anti-Dumping Agreement* require from developed-country Members?

6.3. SUBSIDIES AND COUNTERVAILING MEASURES

In addition to rules on dumping and anti-dumping duties, WTO law also includes rules on another so-called 'unfair' trade practice, subsidisation. Subsidies are a very sensitive matter in international trade relations. On the one hand, subsidies are evidently used by governments to pursue and promote important and fully legitimate objectives of economic and social policy. On the other hand, however, subsidies may have adverse effects on the interests of trading partners whose industry may suffer, in its domestic or export markets, from the unfair competition from subsidised products.

As already discussed in Chapter 1, subsidies are subject to an intricate set of rules.[132] Some subsidies, such as export subsidies, are, as a rule, prohibited, while other subsidies are not prohibited but must be withdrawn (or their adverse effects removed) when they cause adverse effects to the interests of other Members. Furthermore, if a subsidy causes or threatens to cause material injury to the domestic industry of a Member, that Member is authorised to impose countervailing duties on the subsidised products to offset the subsidisation.

In the period from 1 July 2002 to 30 June 2003, fourteen definitive countervailing duties were imposed, of which nine were imposed by the United States. South Africa and Peru imposed one countervailing duty each, and the European Communities three.[133] On 30 June 2003, a total of 103 definitive countervailing measures were in force, of which 57 were taken by the United States and 20 by the European Communities.[134]

Questions and Assignments 6.18

Compare the use made of countervailing duties with that of anti-dumping duties.

---

[131] Ministerial Conference, *Decision on Implementation, Implementation-Related Issues and Concerns*, WT/MIN(01)/W/10, para. 7.2.
[132] See above, p. 42.
[133] See *WTO Annual Report 2004*, 45, available at www.wto.org/English/res_e/booksp_e/anrep04_e.pdf.
[134] *Ibid.*

6.3.1. Basic elements of WTO law on subsidies and subsidised trade

Before entering into a more detailed, and often technical, discussion of the rules on subsidies and countervailing measures, this section addresses in general terms:

- the history of the law on subsidies;
- the concept of 'subsidies';
- WTO treatment of subsidies; and
- the response to injurious subsidised trade.

6.3.1.1. The history of the law on subsidies and subsidised trade

The WTO rules on subsidies and subsidised trade are set out in Articles VI and XVI of the GATT 1994 but also, and more importantly, in the WTO *Agreement on Subsidies and Countervailing Measures*, commonly referred to as the *SCM Agreement*. The GATT 1947 did not contain clear and comprehensive rules on subsidies. In fact, Article XVI of the GATT 1947, entitled 'Subsidies', did not even define the concept of 'subsidies'. Moreover, with regard to subsidies in general, Article XVI merely provides that Contracting Parties to the GATT should notify subsidies that have an effect on trade and should be prepared to discuss limiting such subsidies if they cause serious damage to the interests of other Contracting Parties.[135] With regard to export subsidies, Article XVI provides that Contracting Parties were to 'seek to avoid' using subsidies on exports of primary products.[136] In 1962, Article XVI was amended to add a provision prohibiting Contracting Parties from granting export subsidies to non-primary products which would reduce the sales price on the export market below the sales price on the domestic market.[137] Note, however, that this amendment did not apply to developing countries. In addition, Article VI of the GATT 1947, which dealt with measures taken to offset any subsidy granted to an imported product (i.e. countervailing duties), did not provide for clear and comprehensive rules. In order to elaborate on the GATT rules on subsidies and countervailing duties and to provide greater uniformity and certainty in their implementation, the GATT Contracting Parties, during the Tokyo Round (1973–9), negotiated and concluded the *Agreement on Interpretation and Application of Articles VI, XVI and XXIII of the General Agreement*, commonly referred to as the Tokyo Round Subsidies Code.[138] Less than twenty-five Contracting Parties accepted this plurilateral agreement,[139] including the European Communities and the United States.[140] The Subsidies Code certainly did not

---

[135] See Article XVI:1 of the GATT 1947.
[136] See Article XVI:3 of the GATT 1947. Contracting parties 'should not' give a subsidy which results in the exporting country gaining 'more than an equitable share of world export trade in that product'.
[137] See Article XVI:4 of the GATT 1947, as amended.   [138] See BISD 26S/56.
[139] See the list of acceptances of Tokyo Round agreements in *Analytical Index of the GATT* (WTO, 1995), 1147–50.
[140] *Ibid.*

bring the degree of clarification and elaboration of the rules on subsidies and countervailing duties sought by some of the Contracting Parties. During the 1970s and 1980s, the lack of clear rules on subsidies and countervailing duties led to many disputes between the GATT Contracting Parties. It was therefore not surprising that the Punta del Este Ministerial Declaration on the Uruguay Round of September 1986 instructed the negotiators to review Articles VI and XVI of the GATT 1947 as well as the Tokyo Round Subsidies Code:

> with the objective of improving GATT disciplines relating to all subsidies and counter-vailing measures that affect international trade.[141]

The Uruguay Round negotiations eventually resulted in the *SCM Agreement*, which forms part of Annex 1A to the *WTO Agreement*. The multilateral rules on subsidies and subsidised trade are now set out in Articles VI and XVI of the GATT 1994 and, most importantly, in the *SCM Agreement*. With respect to the object and purpose of this Agreement, the Panel in *Brazil – Aircraft* clarified that:

> The object and purpose of the SCM Agreement is to impose multilateral disciplines on subsidies which distort international trade.[142]

The Panel in *Canada – Aircraft* also stated that:

> The object and purpose of the SCM Agreement could more appropriately be sum-marised as the establishment of multilateral disciplines on the premise that some forms of government intervention distort international trade [or] have the potential to distort [international trade].[143]

Questions and Assignments 6.19

Briefly discuss the origins of the *SCM Agreement*. What is the object and purpose of the *SCM Agreement*?

6.3.1.2. *The concept of 'subsidy'*

The *SCM Agreement* contains, for the first time in the GATT/WTO context, a detailed and comprehensive definition of the concept of 'subsidy'. As the Panel in *US – FSC* stated:

> the inclusion of this detailed and comprehensive definition of the term "subsidy" is generally considered to represent one of the most important achievements of the Uruguay Round in the area of subsidy disciplines.[144]

Broadly speaking, Article 1.1 of the *SCM Agreement* defines a subsidy as a financial contribution by a government or public body, which confers a benefit.[145]

---

[141] Punta del Este Ministerial Declaration on the Uruguay Round, BISD 33S/25.
[142] Panel Report, *Brazil – Aircraft*, para. 7.26.
[143] Panel Report, *Canada – Aircraft*, para. 9.119.   [144] Panel Report, *US – FSC*, para. 7.80.
[145] On this definition and its constituent elements, see below, pp. 555–61. See also Panel Report, *US – Export Restraints*, paras. 8.22–8.24.

Furthermore, Article 2 of the *SCM Agreement* provides that the WTO rules on subsidies and subsidised trade only apply to 'specific' subsidies, i.e. subsidies granted to an enterprise or industry, or a group of enterprises or industries. The concepts of 'subsidy' and 'specificity' are examined in detail below.[146]

6.3.1.3. *WTO treatment of subsidies*

Article XVI of the GATT 1994 and Articles 3 to 9 of the *SCM Agreement* deal with the WTO treatment of subsidies.[147] As discussed above, dumping is not prohibited. It is merely condemned if it causes injury. The WTO treatment of subsidies is different. Certain subsidies are prohibited, and many other subsidies, at least when they are specific rather than general, may be challenged when they cause adverse effects to the interests of other Members.[148] WTO law distinguishes between prohibited subsidies, actionable subsidies and non-actionable subsidies.[149] Each of these kinds of subsidy has its own substantive and procedural rules. Moreover, subsidies on agricultural products are subject to certain rules set out in the *Agreement on Agriculture*.

6.3.1.4. *Response to injurious subsidised trade*

Article VI of the GATT 1994 and Articles 10 to 23 of the *SCM Agreement* concern the manner in which WTO Members may respond to subsidised trade which causes injury to the domestic industry. Members may, in these situations, impose countervailing duties on the subsidised imports to offset, i.e. cancel out, the subsidisation. However, like the anti-dumping measures discussed above, countervailing duties may only be imposed when it is properly established that there are subsidised imports, that there is injury to a domestic industry and that there is a causal link between the subsidisation and the injury. As with the conduct of anti-dumping investigations, the conduct of countervailing investigations is also subject to relatively strict procedural requirements. Note that the substantive and procedural rules on the imposition and maintenance of countervailing measures are similar to (albeit somewhat less detailed than) the rules on anti-dumping measures.

---

[146] See below, pp. 555–60.

[147] The obligations and procedures set out in Article XVI of the GATT 1994, with respect to subsidies, must be taken together with the *SCM Agreement*. As the Appellate Body concluded in *Brazil – Desiccated Coconut*, Article XVI of the GATT 1994 cannot be invoked independently from the *SCM Agreement*. See Appellate Body Report, *Brazil – Desiccated Coconut*, 16–17. In fact, the provisions of the *SCM Agreement* are so wide and detailed that they leave very little scope for application of the provisions of Article XVI of the GATT 1994.

[148] For a full discussion of the WTO treatment of subsidies, see below, pp. 561–74.

[149] As further discussed below, the 'non-actionable' category of subsidies was originally addressed in the Agreement. However, the provisions governing non-actionable subsidy lapsed at the end of 1999, by virtue of the operation of Article 31 of the *SCM Agreement*. Currently, the Agreement regulates two types of subsidy within its scope of application: prohibited and actionable.

Questions and Assignments 6.20

Explain briefly how WTO law regulates subsidisation and the response to injurious subsidised trade.

6.3.2. Determination of subsidisation

Article 1.1 of the *SCM Agreement* provides, in relevant part:

> For the purpose of this Agreement, a subsidy shall be deemed to exist if:
>
> (a)(1) there is a financial contribution by a government or any public body within the territory of a Member ...
>
>   or
>
> (a)(2) there is any form of income or price support in the sense of Article XVI of GATT 1994 and
>
> (b) a benefit is thereby conferred.

Article 1.2 of the *SCM Agreement* furthermore provides:

> A subsidy as defined in paragraph 1 shall be subject to the provisions of Part II or shall be subject to the provisions of Part III or V only if such a subsidy is specific in accordance with the provisions of Article 2.

This section first examines the three constituent elements of the concept of 'subsidy':

- a *financial contribution*;
- a financial contribution *by a government or any public body*; and
- a financial contribution *conferring a benefit*.

Subsequently, this section discusses the concept of 'specificity'.

6.3.2.1. *Financial contribution*

For a measure to be a subsidy within the meaning of Article 1.1 of the *SCM Agreement*, that measure must constitute a 'financial contribution' or take the form of income or price support in the sense of Article XVI of the GATT 1994. Article 1.1 provides for an exhaustive list of types of financial contributions. This list includes:

- direct transfers of funds, such as grants, loans and equity infusions (Article 1.1(a)(1)(i));
- potential direct transfers of funds or liabilities, such as loan guarantees (Article 1.1(a)(1)(i));
- government revenue, otherwise due, that is foregone or not collected (Article 1.1(a)(1)(ii));
- the provision by a government of goods or services other than general infrastructure (Article 1.1(a)(1)(iii));

- the purchase by a government of goods (Article 1.1(a)(1)(i)); and
- government payments to a funding mechanism or entrustment or direction of a private body (Article 1.1(a)(1)(iv)).

A financial contribution exists not only when a direct transfer of funds or a potential direct transfer of funds has actually been effectuated. Pursuant to Article 1.1(a)(1)(i), it is sufficient that there is a 'government practice' involving the transfer of funds. The Panel in *Brazil – Aircraft* noted in this respect:

> If subsidies were deemed to exist only once a direct or potential direct transfer of funds had actually been effectuated, the Agreement would be rendered totally ineffective and even the typical WTO remedy (i.e. the cessation of the violation) would not be possible.[150]

As provided in Article 1.1(a)(1)(ii), government revenue, otherwise due, that is foregone or not collected is also a financial contribution within the meaning of Article 1.1. In *US – FSC*, the Appellate Body held:

> In our view, the "*foregoing*" of revenue "*otherwise*" due" implies that less revenue has been raised by the government than would have been raised in a different situation, or, that is, "otherwise". Moreover, the word "foregone" suggests that the government has given up an entitlement to raise revenue that it could "otherwise" have raised. This cannot, however, be an entitlement in the abstract, because governments, in theory, could tax *all* revenues. There must, therefore, be some defined, normative benchmark against which a comparison can be made between the revenue actually raised and the revenue that would have been raised "otherwise". We, therefore, agree with the Panel that the term "otherwise due" implies some kind of comparison between the revenues due under the contested measure and revenues that would be due in some other situation. We also agree with the Panel that the basis of comparison must be the tax rules applied by the Member in question ... A Member, in principle, has the sovereign authority to tax any particular categories of revenue it wishes. It is also free *not* to tax any particular categories of revenues. But, in both instances, the Member must respect its WTO obligations. What is "otherwise due", therefore, depends on the rules of taxation that each Member, by its own choice, establishes for itself.[151]

The term 'otherwise', as used in 'government revenue, otherwise due, that was foregone', refers to a normative benchmark as established by the tax rules applied by the Member concerned.[152] The Panel in *US – FSC* explained that the term 'otherwise due' refers to the situation that would prevail *but for* the measure at issue.[153]

---

[150] Panel Report, *Brazil – Aircraft*, para. 7.13.   [151] Appellate Body Report, *US – FSC*, para. 90.

[152] The Appellate Body in *US – FSC (Article 21.5)* clarified that Article 1.1(a)(1)(ii) does *not* require panels to identify a general rule of taxation and exceptions to that general rule, but rather they should compare the domestic fiscal treatment of 'legitimately' comparable income 'to determine whether the contested measure involves the foregoing of revenue that is "otherwise due" '. See Appellate Body Report, *US – FSC (Article 21.5)*, paras. 88–92.

[153] Panel Report, *US – FSC*, para. 7.45. Note, however, that the Appellate Body stated that, although the Panel's 'but for' test works in this case, it may not work in other cases. The Appellate Body had 'certain abiding reservations' about applying any legal standard, such as this 'but for' test, in place of the actual treaty language. See Appellate Body Report, *US – FSC*, para. 91.

Questions and Assignments 6.21

Give five examples of 'financial contributions' within the meaning of the *SCM Agreement.* When does the non-taxation of income constitute a 'financial contribution'? Is a temporary waiver of environmental standards on a company in financial and economic difficulty a 'financial contribution' within the meaning of Article 1.1(a) of the *SCM Agreement*?

6.3.2.2. *A financial contribution by a government*

For a financial contribution to be a subsidy within the meaning of Article 1.1 of the *SCM Agreement*, the financial contribution must be made by a government or a public body, including regional and local authorities as well as State-owned companies. Pursuant to Article 1.1(a)(1)(iv), a financial contribution made by a *private body* is considered to be a 'financial contribution by a government' when the government entrusts or directs the private body to carry out one or more of the type of functions illustrated in Article 1.1(a)(1)(i) to (iii).[154]

Questions and Assignments 6.22

Can a financial contribution by a local authority or a private body be a 'subsidy' within the meaning of Article 1.1 of the *SCM Agreement*? Is financial assistance given by an NGO to cotton growers in African countries a 'financial contribution by a government'?

6.3.2.3. *A financial contribution conferring a benefit*

A financial contribution by a government is a subsidy within the meaning of Article 1.1 of the *SCM Agreement* only if the financial contribution *confers a benefit*. If a government gives a sum of money to a company, it seems clear that this financial contribution would generally confer a benefit. However, it may be less clear whether a loan to that same company, the purchase of goods or services by the government from the company or an equity infusion by the government in the company, confer a benefit. In *Canada – Aircraft*, Canada argued that 'cost to government' is one way of conceiving of 'benefit'. The Appellate Body rejected this argumentation as follows:

> A "benefit" does not exist in the abstract, but must be received and enjoyed by a beneficiary or a recipient. Logically, a "benefit" can be said to arise only if a person, natural or legal, or a group of persons, has in fact received something. The term "benefit", therefore, implies that there must be a recipient. This provides textual

[154] See above, pp. 555–6. In *US – Export Restraints*, the Panel stated that the ordinary meanings of 'entrusts' and 'directs' require an explicit and affirmative action of delegation or command. See Panel Report, *US – Export Restraints*, para. 8.44.

> support for the view that the focus of the inquiry under Article 1.1(b) of the *SCM Agreement* should be on the recipient and not on the granting authority. The ordinary meaning of the word "confer", as used in Article 1.1(b), bears this out. "Confer" means, *inter alia*, "give", "grant" or "bestow". The use of the past participle "conferred" in the passive form, in conjunction with the word "thereby", naturally calls for an inquiry into *what was conferred on the recipient*. Accordingly, we believe that Canada's argument that "cost to government" is one way of conceiving of "benefit" is at odds with the ordinary meaning of Article 1.1(b), which focuses on the *recipient* and not on the *government* providing the "financial contribution".[155]

This reading of the term 'benefit' is confirmed by Article 14 of the *SCM Agreement*, which sets forth guidelines for calculating the amount of a subsidy in terms of 'the benefit to the recipient'.[156] The guidelines set forth in Article 14 apply to the calculation of the 'benefit to the recipient conferred pursuant to paragraph 1 of Article 1'. The reference to 'benefit to the recipient' in Article 14 also implies that the word 'benefit', as used in Article 1.1, is concerned with the 'benefit to the recipient' and not with the 'cost to government'.[157]

In *Canada – Aircraft*, the Appellate Body further held with regard to the term 'benefit' that:

> the word "benefit", as used in Article 1.1(b), implies some kind of comparison. This must be so, for there can be no "benefit" to the recipient unless the "financial contribution" makes the recipient "better off" than it would otherwise have been, absent that contribution. In our view, the marketplace provides an appropriate basis for comparison in determining whether a "benefit" has been "conferred", because the trade-distorting potential of a "financial contribution" can be identified by determining whether the recipient has received a "financial contribution" on terms more favourable than those available to the recipient in the market.[158]

In brief, a 'benefit' arises if the recipient has received a 'financial contribution' on terms more favourable than those available to any recipient in the market.[159] In other words, a government loan is a financial contribution conferring a benefit, i.e., a subsidy, *only* if the terms of the loan are more favourable than the terms of a comparable commercial loan.

The *SCM Agreement* leaves Members wide discretion in deciding on the particular method used to calculate the subsidy in terms of the benefit that the recipient has received. However, Article 14 of the *SCM Agreement*, already referred to above, provides, *inter alia*, for the following guidelines:

---

[155] Appellate Body Report, *Canada – Aircraft*, para. 154.
[156] See *ibid.*, para. 155. Although Article 14 explicitly states that its guidelines apply '[f]or the purposes of Part V' of the *SCM Agreement*, which relates to 'countervailing measures', the Appellate Body was of the opinion that Article 14, nonetheless, constitutes a relevant context for the interpretation of 'benefit' in Article 1.1(b).
[157] See *ibid.*, para. 155.
[158] *Ibid.*, para. 157. Note also that, in *US – CVDs on EC Products*, the Appellate Body stated that, if 'fair market value' is paid in a privatisation transaction, the subsidies previously provided to the State-owned producer 'may' extinguish the benefit to the privatised producer. The Appellate Body, however, reversed the conclusion that a fair market value privatisation 'must' lead to the conclusion that there is no benefit. See Appellate Body Report, *US – CVDs on EC Products*, paras. 103–5.
[159] See also Panel Report, *US – Lead and Bismuth II*, para. 6.66.

- government provision of equity capital shall not be considered as conferring a benefit when the investment decision can be regarded as consistent with the usual investment practice of private investors;[160]
- governmental loans shall not be considered as conferring a benefit, unless (and to the extent that) there is a difference between the amount that the firm receiving the loan pays on the government loan and the amount the firm would pay on a comparable commercial loan which the firm could actually obtain on the market;[161] and
- the provision of goods or services or the purchase of goods by a government shall not be considered as conferring a benefit unless the provision is made for less than adequate remuneration, or the purchase is made for more than adequate remuneration.[162]

Questions and Assignments 6.23

Why is 'cost to government' an invalid method of conceiving of 'benefit' within the meaning of Article 1.1 of the *SCM Agreement*? When does a financial contribution confer a benefit?

6.3.2.4. *Requirement of 'specificity' of the subsidy*

The WTO rules on subsidies do not apply to all 'financial contributions by the government that confer a benefit'. In other words, these rules do not apply to all subsidies. They apply only to *specific* subsidies. Article 1.2 of the *SCM Agreement*, already quoted above, states:

> A subsidy as defined in paragraph 1 shall be subject to the provisions of Part II or shall be subject to the provisions of Part III or V only if such a subsidy is specific in accordance with the provisions of Article 2.

According to Article 2, a subsidy is *specific* when it has been specifically provided to an enterprise, an industry or a group of enterprises or industries. A subsidy that is widely available within an economy is presumed not to distort the allocation of resources within that economy and, therefore, does not require or justify any action.

The *SCM Agreement* distinguishes between four types of specificity:

- *enterprise specificity*, i.e. a situation in which a government targets a particular company or companies for subsidisation;[163]

---

[160] See Article 14(a) of the *SCM Agreement*.
[161] See Article 14(b) of the *SCM Agreement*. The same is true for loan guarantees. See Article 14(c) of the *SCM Agreement*.
[162] Article 14(d) of the *SCM Agreement*. The adequacy of the remuneration shall be determined in relation to prevailing market conditions for the good or service in question in the country of provision or purchase (including price, quality, availability, marketability, transportation and other conditions of purchase or sale).
[163] See Article 2.1 of the *SCM Agreement*.

- *industry specificity*, i.e. a situation in which a government targets a particular sector or sectors for subsidisation;[164]
- *regional specificity*, i.e. a situation in which a government targets producers in specified parts of its territory for subsidisation;[165] and
- *prohibited subsidies*, i.e. a situation in which a government targets export goods or goods using domestic inputs for subsidisation.[166]

For a subsidy to fall within the scope of application of the *SCM Agreement*, it has to be *specific* in one of the above four ways.

If the criteria and conditions governing eligibility for, and the amount of, a subsidy are objective, the subsidy is *not specific*, provided that eligibility is automatic and the criteria and conditions are strictly applied.[167] Pursuant to footnote 2 to the *SCM Agreement*, objective criteria and conditions are:

> criteria or conditions which are neutral, which do not favour certain enterprises over others, and which are economic in nature and horizontal in application, such as number of employees or size of enterprise.

Often, a subsidy may not be specific, on its face, but, in fact, operates in a specific manner. The *SCM Agreement* applies to both *de jure* and *de facto* specific subsidies. Article 2.1(c) of the *SCM Agreement* states:

> If, notwithstanding any appearance of non-specificity resulting from the application of the principles laid down in subparagraphs (a) and (b), there are reasons to believe that the subsidy may in fact be specific, other factors may be considered.

These 'other factors' on the basis of which *de facto* subsidies may be identified include:

- the use of a subsidy programme by a limited number of certain enterprises;
- the predominant use of a subsidy programme by certain enterprises;
- the granting of disproportionately large subsidies to certain enterprises;
- the manner in which discretion has been exercised by the granting authority in the decision to grant a subsidy; the frequency with which applications for a subsidy are refused or approved and the reasons for such decisions are of particular relevance in this context.[168]

The extent of diversification of economic activities within the jurisdiction of the granting authority and the length of time during which the subsidy programme has been in operation will also be taken into account when determining whether a subsidy, which is not specific *de jure*, is specific *de facto*.[169]

---

[164] *Ibid.*   [165] See Article 2.2 of the *SCM Agreement*.   [166] See Article 2.3 of the *SCM Agreement*.
[167] See Article 2.1(b) of the *SCM Agreement*.
[168] See Article 2.1(c) of and footnote 3 to the *SCM Agreement*.
[169] See Article 2.1(c) of the *SCM Agreement*.

Questions and Assignments 6.24

Do the rules of the *SCM Agreement* apply to all 'financial contributions by the government that confer a benefit'? Discuss the various types of 'specificity' within the meaning of Article 2.1 of the *SCM Agreement*? When is a subsidy not specific? Does the *SCM Agreement* apply also to *de facto* specific subsidies? How is a *de facto* specific subsidy identified?

6.3.2.5. *Transparency and notification requirement*

As transparency is essential for the effective operation of the *SCM Agreement*, Article 25 requires that Members notify all specific subsidies by 30 June of each year. Currently, there is an understanding in the SCM Committee that there is an emphasis on new and full subsidy notifications to be submitted every two years, while updating notifications in the interim years are de-emphasised. As of 29 October 2003, thirty-four Members[170] had submitted their 2001 new and full notifications indicating that they provided specific subsidies within the meaning of the *SCM Agreement*. Eleven Members had notified that they provided no notifiable specific subsidies. Eighty-six Members did not submit any notification.[171]

6.3.3. **Prohibited subsidies**

The *SCM Agreement* distinguishes between prohibited subsidies, actionable subsidies and non-actionable subsidies.[172] This section will discuss the rules relating to prohibited subsidies.

Article 3 of the *SCM Agreement*, entitled 'Prohibition', states, in its first paragraph:

> Except as provided in the Agreement on Agriculture, the following subsidies, within the meaning of Article 1, shall be prohibited:
>
> a. subsidies contingent, in law or in fact, whether solely or as one of several conditions, upon export performance, including those illustrated in Annex I;
> b. subsidies contingent, whether solely or as one of several conditions, upon the use of domestic over imported products.

In short, WTO Members may not grant or maintain:

- export subsidies; or
- import substitution subsidies.[173]

---

[170] For this purpose, the European Communities and its Member States were counted as a single Member.
[171] The 2003 notifications may be found in document series G/SCM/N/95/. See also Report (2003) of the Committee on Subsidies and Countervailing Measures, G/L/655, dated 4 November 2003, 2. The WTO Secretariat is scheduled to circulate to Members after 21 June 2004 a list of the 2003 new and full subsidy notifications (which were due no later than 30 June 2003).
[172] Note, however, that, since 1 January 2000, this category of 'non-actionable subsidies' only contains non-specific subsidies. See below, p. 574.
[173] See Article 3.2 of the *SCM Agreement*.

These subsidies, which are often referred to as 'red light' subsidies, are prohibited because they aim at affecting trade and are most likely to cause adverse effects to other Members.

6.3.3.1. Export subsidies

As defined in Article 3.1(a) of the *SCM Agreement*, quoted above, export subsidies are subsidies contingent upon export performance.[174] Annex I to the *SCM Agreement* contains an 'Illustrative List of Export Subsidies'. This non-exhaustive list includes eleven types of export subsidy, including:

- direct export subsidies;
- export retention schemes which involve a bonus on exports;
- export-related exemption, remission or deferral of direct taxes and social welfare charges;
- excess exemption, remission or deferral of indirect taxes or import duties;
- provision of goods or services for use in the production of exported goods on terms more favourable than those for the production of goods for domestic consumption; and
- provision of certain forms of export financing extended at rates below those which the government actually had to pay for the funds (subject to certain considerations).

Article 3.1(a) of the *SCM Agreement* prohibits subsidies contingent upon export performance, whether that subsidy is contingent *de jure* or *de facto*. In *Canada – Aircraft*, the Appellate Body stated:

> The Uruguay Round negotiators have, through the prohibition against export subsidies that are contingent *in fact* upon export performance, sought to prevent circumvention of the prohibition against subsidies contingent *in law* upon export performance.[175]

Pursuant to footnote 4 to the *SCM Agreement*, a subsidy is contingent *de facto* upon export performance:

> when the facts demonstrate that the granting of a subsidy, without having been made legally contingent upon export performance, is in fact tied to actual or anticipated exportation or export earnings. The mere fact that a subsidy is granted to enterprises which export shall not for that reason alone be considered to be an export subsidy within the meaning of this provision.

While the legal standard expressed by the term 'contingent' is the same for both *de jure* and *de facto* contingency, there is an important difference in what evidence may be employed to demonstrate that a subsidy is export contingent.[176] *De jure* export contingency is demonstrated on the basis of the words of

---

[174] As the Panel in *Australia – Automotive Leather II* noted, the ordinary meaning of 'contingent' is 'dependent for its existence on something else', 'conditional; dependent on, upon'. See Panel Report, *Australia – Automotive Leather II*, para. 9.55. See also Appellate Body Report, *Canada – Aircraft*, para. 166.

[175] Appellate Body Report, *Canada – Aircraft*, para. 167.   [176] *Ibid.*

the relevant legislation, regulation or other legal instrument. In *Canada – Autos*, the Appellate Body held:

> The simplest, and hence, perhaps, the uncommon, case is one in which the condition of exportation is set out expressly, in so many words, on the face of the law, regulation or other legal instrument. We believe, however, that a subsidy is also properly held to be *de jure* export contingent where the condition to export is clearly, though implicitly, in the instrument comprising the measure.[177]

According to the Appellate Body, for a subsidy to be *de jure* export contingent, the underlying law, regulation or other legal instrument does *not* have to provide *expressis verbis* that the subsidy is available only upon the fulfilment of the condition of export performance.[178] The *de jure* export contingency can also 'be derived by necessary implication from the words actually used in the measure'.[179]

With respect to *de facto* export contingency, footnote 4 to the *SCM Agreement* states that the standard of 'in fact' contingency is met if the facts demonstrate that the subsidy is:

> in fact tied to actual or anticipated exportation or export earnings.[180]

As the Panel in *Australia – Automotive Leather II* established, *de facto* export contingency requires there to be a 'close connection' between the granting of, or maintenance of, a subsidy *and* export performance.[181]

De facto export contingency is much more difficult to demonstrate than *de jure* export contingency.[182] It must be inferred from the *total* configuration of the facts constituting and surrounding the granting of the subsidy.[183] None of these facts on its own is likely to be decisive. In combination, however, they may lead to the conclusion that there is *de facto* export contingency in a given case. Note that a subsidy to an export-oriented company is not *per se* an export subsidy. The export orientation of a recipient may be taken into account but it will be only one of several facts which are considered and cannot be the only fact supporting a finding of *de facto* export contingency.[184]

To illustrate the wide scope of the prohibition on export subsidies, consider the subsidies at issue in, for example, *Brazil – Aircraft*, *Australia – Automotive Leather II* and *US – FSC*. The WTO-inconsistent export subsidies at issue in these disputes concerned:

---

[177] Appellate Body Report, *Canada – Autos*, para. 100.   [178] *Ibid.*   [179] *Ibid.*

[180] The Panel in *Australia – Automotive Leather II* noted that the ordinary meaning of 'tied to' is 'restrain or constrain to or from an action; limit or restrict as to behaviour, location, conditions, etc.'. See Panel Report, *Australia – Automotive Leather II*, para. 9.55. For a further discussion of the concept of 'tied to', see Appellate Body Report, *Canada – Aircraft*, para. 171.

[181] See Panel Report, *Australia – Automotive Leather II*, para. 9.55.

[182] Note that, as the Appellate Body stressed in *Canada – Aircraft*, the legal standard expressed by the word 'contingent' is the same for both *de jure* and *de facto* contingency. The difference is in what evidence may be employed to prove that a subsidy is export contingent. See Appellate Body Report, *Canada – Aircraft*, para. 167.

[183] *Ibid.*

[184] See footnote 4, second sentence, to the *SCM Agreement*; and Panel Report, *Australia – Automotive Leather II*, para. 9.56.

- payments by the Government of Brazil, related to the export of regional aircraft made under the interest rate equalisation component of the 'PROEX', an export financing programme, which cover, at most, the difference between the interest charges contracted with the buyer and the cost to the financing party of raising the required funds (*Brazil – Aircraft*);
- grants for a total of A$30 million and a loan of A$25 million (on 'non-commercial' terms), provided by the Australian Government to Howe, the only producer and exporter of automotive leather in Australia (*Australia – Automotive Leather II*); and
- exemption from United States income tax of a portion of export-related income of 'foreign sales corporations' (FSCs), i.e. foreign corporations in charge of specific activities with respect to the sale or lease of goods produced in the United States for export outside the United States (*US – FSC*).

Questions and Assignments 6.25

Which subsidies are 'prohibited' under the *SCM Agreement*? Define an export subsidy. Give three examples of an export subsidy. When is a subsidy *de jure* contingent on export performance? Is a subsidy that is *de facto* export contingent an export subsidy? How is *de facto* export contingency demonstrated?

6.3.3.2. *Import substitution subsidies*

In addition to export subsidies, the category of prohibited subsidies also includes import substitution subsidies. As defined in Article 3.1(b) of the *SCM Agreement*, quoted above, import substitution subsidies are subsidies contingent upon the use of domestic over imported goods.[185] The Appellate Body in *Canada – Autos* ruled that the prohibition of import substitution subsidies of Article 3.1(b) covers both *de jure* and *de facto* contingency upon the use of domestic over imported goods. The Panel in that case found that 'contingency' under Article 3.1(b) extended only to *de jure* contingency.[186] Reversing this finding of the Panel, the Appellate Body held:

> we believe that a finding that Article 3.1(b) extends only to contingency "in law" upon the use of domestic over imported goods would be contrary to the object and purpose of the *SCM Agreement* because it would make circumvention of obligations by Members too easy.[187]

---

[185] Note that 'import substitution subsidies' are also referred to as 'local content subsidies'.
[186] In making this finding, the Panel relied on the wording of Article 3.1(b), which, unlike Article 3.1(a), did not refer explicitly to both subsidies contingent '*in law* or *in fact*'. See Panel Report, *Canada – Autos*, para. 10.220–10.222. Note the relationship of this concept to the cornerstone principle of national treatment in Article III:4 of the GATT 1994.
[187] Appellate Body Report, *Canada – Autos*, para. 142.

6.3.3.3. *Multilateral remedies for prohibited subsidies*

The multilateral remedies for prohibited subsidies, be it export subsidies or import substitution subsidies, are set out in Article 4 of the *SCM Agreement*. Pursuant to Article 4, consultations may be requested with any Member believed to be granting or maintaining a prohibited subsidy. If such consultations fail to resolve the dispute, the dispute may be referred to a dispute settlement panel, and then to the Appellate Body, for adjudication. The rules applicable to consultations and adjudication are primarily those of the DSU, discussed in detail in Chapter 3 above.[188] However, Article 4 of the *SCM Agreement* sets out a number of 'special or additional rules and procedures' which prevail over the DSU rules in cases of conflict.[189] The most notable difference between the rules and procedures of Article 4 of the *SCM Agreement* and the DSU rules and procedures relates to the difference in timeframes. The timeframes under Article 4 are half as long as the timeframes provided for under the DSU.[190] For example, the timeframe for 'ordinary' panel proceedings is six months;[191] under Article 4 of the *SCM Agreement* the time limit for panel proceedings concerning prohibited subsidies is three months. Note also that a panel established for a 'prohibited subsidy' dispute may ask a Permanent Group of Experts (PGE) whether the measure at issue is a prohibited subsidy.[192] The determination of the PGE is binding on the panel. To date, panels have not yet made use of this possibility.

If a panel finds a measure to be a prohibited subsidy, Article 4.7 of the *SCM Agreement* states that:

> the panel shall recommend that the subsidizing Member withdraw the subsidy without delay. In this regard, the panel shall specify in its recommendation the time period within which the measure must be withdrawn.

Prohibited subsidies must therefore be withdrawn without delay. As the Appellate Body clarified in *Brazil – Aircraft (Article 21.5 – Canada)*, withdrawal of the prohibited subsidy involves the removal of the subsidy.[193] The Panel in

---

[188] See above, pp. 182–283.   [189] See above, p. 188.

[190] Note, however, that parties can, and regularly do, agree on an extension of these special timeframes. See Article 4.12 of the *SCM Agreement*. Also, when a complainant brings claims under both the *SCM Agreement* and other WTO agreements, the shorter timeframes under the *SCM Agreement* do not apply.

[191] See Article 12.8 of the DSU. See also above, pp. 269–70.

[192] See Article 4.5 of the *SCM Agreement*. See also above, pp. 134–5.

[193] See Appellate Body Report, *Brazil – Aircraft (Article 21.5 – Canada)*, para. 45.

Australia – Automotive Leather II (Article 21.5 – US) concluded that the obligation to withdraw the prohibited subsidy, in that case, could only be met by repayment of the subsidy received. In general, remedies for breaches of WTO law are only prospective, but, according to the Panel in *Australia – Automotive Leather II (Article 21.5 – US)*, Article 4.7 of the *SCM Agreement* provides for a retrospective remedy and requires the company that received a one-time prohibited subsidy to repay that subsidy to the subsidising Member. The Panel in *Australia – Automotive Leather II (Article 21.5 – US)* reasoned as follows:

> We believe it is incumbent upon us to interpret "withdraw the subsidy" so as to give it effective meaning. A finding that the term "withdraw the subsidy" may not encompass repayment would give rise to serious questions regarding the efficacy of the remedy in prohibited subsidy cases involving one-time subsidies paid in the past whose retention is not contingent upon future export performance.[194]

This ruling of the Panel in *Australia – Automotive Leather II (Article 21.5 – US)* was heavily criticised by WTO Members because of its retroactive character (and because it was felt to violate the principle of *non ultra petita*).[195] To date, no other panel has followed this ruling of the Panel in *Australia – Automotive Leather II (Article 21.5 – US)*.[196]

Panels in 'prohibited subsidy' disputes specify the time period within which the prohibited subsidy must be withdrawn, i.e. they specify what is meant by 'withdraw without delay' as required by Article 4.7 of the *SCM Agreement*.[197] To date, several panels have specified a period of three months for the withdrawal of a prohibited subsidy. In *US – FSC*, however, the Panel specified a period of more than a year to allow the United States to adopt the necessary fiscal legislation.[198]

If a recommendation for withdrawal is not followed within the time period set by the panel, the DSB must, upon the request of the original complainant(s) and by reverse consensus, authorise 'appropriate countermeasures'. In 'prohibited subsidies' disputes, these 'appropriate countermeasures' replace the suspension of concessions or other obligations, i.e. retaliation measures, available in case of non-implementation in WTO disputes.[199] 'Appropriate countermeasures' and 'retaliation measures' may differ in that the level of 'appropriate countermeasures' could be the amount of the prohibited subsidy rather than the level of any trade effects or the nullification or impairment that has been caused.[200]

---

[194] Panel Report, *Australia – Automotive Leather II (Article 21.5 – US)*, para. 6.35.

[195] See Minutes of the DSB Meeting of 11 February 2000, WT/DSB/M/75. See also above, pp. 224–5. Note that the United States, the original complainant in this dispute, had not requested the repayment of the export subsidy at issue.

[196] Note that the Panels in *Canada – Aircraft (Article 21.5 – Brazil)* and *Brazil – Aircraft (Article 21.5 – Canada)* did not rule on the repayment of subsidies because repayment had not been requested by the complainant and the Panels considered that their findings should be restricted to the scope of the disagreement between the parties. See Panel Report, *Canada – Aircraft (Article 21.5 – Brazil)*, para. 5.48; and Panel Report, *Brazil – Aircraft (Article 21.5 – Canada)*, footnote 17.

[197] Recall that 'ordinary' panels do not set a time period within which a WTO-inconsistent measure must be brought into consistency. The reasonable period of time for implementation is agreed on by the parties or is determined through binding arbitration under Article 21.3(c) of the DSU. See above, pp. 278–9.

[198] See Panel Report, *US – FSC*, para. 8.8.   [199] See above, pp. 220–3.

[200] The Arbitrators in *Brazil – Aircraft (Article 22.6)* accepted the view of the parties that the term 'countermeasures', as used in these provisions, includes suspension of concessions or other obligations. It was concluded that, when dealing with a prohibited export subsidy, an amount of

6.3.4. Actionable subsidies

Unlike export subsidies and import substitution subsidies, most subsidies are not prohibited but are 'actionable', i.e. they are subject to challenge in the event that they cause adverse effects to the interests of another Member. To the extent that these subsidies do not cause adverse effects, or the adverse effects are removed, they cannot, or can no longer, be challenged. Article 5 of the *SCM Agreement* provides:

> No Member should cause, through the use of any subsidy referred to in paragraphs 1 and 2 of Article 1, adverse effects to the interests of other Members.

Article 5(a) to (c) distinguishes between three types of 'adverse effect' to the interests of other Members:

- *injury* to the domestic industry of another Member (Article 5(a));
- *nullification or impairment* of benefits accruing directly or indirectly to other Members under the GATT 1994 (Article 5(b)); and
- *serious prejudice*, including a threat thereof, to the interests of another Member (Article 5(c)).

6.3.4.1. *Subsidies causing injury*

Subsidies have adverse effects on the interests of other Members within the meaning of Article 5(a) of the *SCM Agreement* – and are therefore 'actionable' – when the subsidised imports cause injury to the domestic industry producing the like product. This section examines, in turn, the concepts of 'like product',

---

countermeasures that corresponds to the total amount of the subsidy is appropriate. See Decision of the Arbitrators, *Brazil – Aircraft (Article 22.6)*, paras. 3.28, 3.29 and 3.33–3.40. See also Decision of the Arbitrators, *US – FSC (Article 22.6)*. There, the Arbitrators held that the amount of the countermeasures proposed exhibited a manifest relationship of proportionality with regard to the amount of the export subsidy granted. The Arbitrators also observed that trade effects are not *a priori* to be ruled out as relevant in a particular case, and stated that *even if* one addressed the matter of trade effects in this case, they found no reason to reach a different conclusion after examining the arguments presented by the United States in respect of the trade effects of the FSC/ETI [Foreign Sales Corporation/Extraterritorial Income Exclusion Act] scheme on the European Communities.

'domestic industry', 'injury' and causation as generally applied in the *SCM Agreement*.[201]

The concept of 'like product' is defined in footnote 46 to the *SCM Agreement* as:

> a product which is identical, i.e. alike in all respects to the product under consideration, or in the absence of such a product, another product which, although not alike in all respects, has characteristics closely resembling those of the product under consideration.[202]

When compared to the definitions of 'like products' resulting from the case law on Articles I and III of the GATT 1994 or the definition of 'like products' in the *Agreement on Safeguards*, the definition in the *SCM Agreement* seems narrower. The approach to establishing 'likeness' under the *SCM Agreement* is, however, in fact similar to the approach under the GATT 1994.[203] In *Indonesia – Autos*, the Panel found:

> Although we are required in this dispute to interpret the term "like product" in conformity with the specific definition provided in the SCM Agreement, we believe that useful guidance can nevertheless be derived from prior analysis of "like product" issues under other provisions of the WTO Agreement.[204]

The provisions of the *WTO Agreement* referred to are, of course, Articles I:1, III:2 and III:4 of the GATT 1994. In establishing 'likeness', the same elements (physical characteristics as well as end uses, consumer habits and preferences, substitutability and tariff classification) will be of importance. In *Indonesia – Autos*, in which the product, allegedly subsidised by Indonesia, was a car called the 'Timor', the Panel noted:

> we do not see that the SCM Agreement precludes us from looking at criteria other than physical characteristics, where relevant to the like product analysis. The term "characteristics closely resembling" in its ordinary meaning includes but is not limited to physical characteristics, and we see nothing in the context or object and purpose of the SCM Agreement that would dictate a different conclusion.[205]

In *Indonesia – Autos*, the European Communities argued before the Panel that *all* passenger cars should be considered 'like products' to the Timor. The Panel disagreed and ruled:

> While it is true that all passenger cars "share the same basic physical characteristics and share an identical end-use", we agree with Indonesia that passenger cars are highly differentiated products ... [A]ll drivers know that passenger cars may differ greatly in terms of size, weight, engine power, technology, and features. The significance of these extensive physical differences, both in terms of the cost of producing the cars and in consumer perceptions regarding them, is manifested in huge differences in price between

---

[201] Note that footnote 11 to the *SCM Agreement* stipulates that the term "injury to the domestic industry" is used in Article 5(a) in the same sense as it is used in Part V of that Agreement. They are addressed here together, although it may be important to note that considerations may differ under certain provisions of Part III and Part V of the Agreement.

[202] Note that this definition applies throughout the *SCM Agreement* and not merely in the context of the determination of material injury. It also applies, for example, in the context of the serious prejudice determination of Article 6 of the *SCM Agreement* (see below, pp. 572–3).

[203] See above, pp. 314–16, 334–8, 354–60.   [204] Panel Report, *Indonesia – Autos*, para. 14.174.

[205] *Ibid.*, para. 14.173.

> brands and models. It is evident that the differences, both physical and non-physical, between a Rolls Royce and a Timor are enormous, and that the degree of substitutability between them is very low. Viewed from the perspective of the SCM Agreement, it is almost inconceivable that a subsidy for Timors could displace or impede imports of Rolls Royces, or that any meaningful analysis of price undercutting could be performed between these two models. In short, we do not consider that a Rolls Royce can reasonably be considered to have "characteristics closely resembling" those of the Timor.[206]

The Panel eventually decided that the Ford Escort, Peugeot 306 and Opel Optima were 'like products' to the Timor within the meaning to footnote 46 to the *SCM Agreement*.[207]

The definition of 'domestic industry' in the *SCM Agreement* is quite similar to the definition of that concept in the *Anti-Dumping Agreement*.[208] Article 16.1 of the *SCM Agreement* defines the 'domestic industry' as:

> the domestic producers as a whole of the like products or ... those of them whose collective output of the products constitutes a major proportion of the total domestic production of those products.

There are two exceptions to this definition of 'domestic industry'. First, domestic producers that are related to exporters or importers or which themselves import the subsidised products may be excluded from the relevant 'domestic industry'.[209] Secondly, in exceptional circumstances, the territory of a Member may be divided into two or more competitive markets and the producers within each market may be regarded as a separate industry. A regional industry then constitutes the relevant 'domestic industry'.[210]

The concept of 'injury' to a domestic industry in the *SCM Agreement* covers:

- material injury, i.e. genuine injury, to a domestic industry;
- a threat of material injury to a domestic industry; and
- material retardation of the establishment of a domestic industry.[211]

Note that the *SCM Agreement*, as with the *Anti-Dumping Agreement*, requires *material injury*, or a threat thereof, rather than serious injury as required under the *Agreement on Safeguards*.[212] As already mentioned, the Appellate Body in *US – Lamb* noted that the standard of 'serious injury' is higher than that of 'material injury'.[213]

The determination of 'injury' to the domestic industry must, pursuant to Article 15.1 of the *SCM Agreement*, be based on positive evidence and involve an objective examination of:

- the volume of the subsidised imports and the effect of the subsidised imports on prices in the domestic market for like products; and

---

[206] *Ibid.*, para. 14.175.
[207] *Ibid.*, para. 14.193. For the purposes of its further analysis, the Panel assumed, *arguendo*, that the Chrysler Neon is also a 'like product' to the Timor.
[208] See above, pp. 526–7.   [209] See Article 16.1 of the *SCM Agreement*.
[210] See Article 16.2 of the *SCM Agreement*.   [211] See footnote 45 to the *SCM Agreement*.
[212] See above, pp. 528–33, and below, pp. 645–7.
[213] Appellate Body Report, *US – Lamb*, para. 124.

- the consequent impact of these imports on the domestic producers of such products.[214]

With respect to the volume of the subsidised imports, it must be examined whether there has been a significant increase of the subsidised imports.[215] With respect to the effect of the subsidised imports on prices, it must be examined whether there has been a significant price undercutting by the subsidised imports, or whether these imports otherwise depress or suppress prices to a significant degree.[216] The examination of the consequent impact of the subsidised imports on the domestic industry must include an evaluation of all *relevant economic factors and indices* having a bearing on the state of the industry.[217] Article 15.4 lists the following specific factors:

- an actual and potential decline in the output, sales, market share, profits, productivity, return on investments, or utilisation of capacity;
- factors affecting domestic prices; and
- actual and potential negative effects on cash flow, inventories, employment, wages, growth or the ability to raise capital or investments.[218]

The examination of all factors on this list is mandatory in each case.[219] However, this list is not exhaustive and *other* relevant factors must also be considered. Furthermore, note that no single factor, or combination of factors, listed in Article 15.4 necessarily gives decisive guidance.[220]

The determination of a 'threat of material injury' must be based on facts and not merely on allegations, conjecture or remote possibility.[221] For there to be a 'threat of material injury':

> the change in circumstances which would create a situation in which the subsidy would cause injury must be clearly foreseen and imminent.[222]

Article 15.7 lists a number of factors to be considered in making a determination regarding the existence of a 'threat of material injury'. This non-exhaustive list of factors includes:

---

[214] Note in this regard that the Panel in *US – Lumber ITC Investigation* recalled the definitions of the Appellate Body with respect to 'positive evidence' and 'objective examination' (as in *US – Hot Rolled Steel*). See Panel Report, *US – Lumber ITC Investigation*, para. 7.28.

[215] See Article 15.2 of the *SCM Agreement*. This increase may be an increase in absolute terms or relative to production or consumption in the importing country.

[216] See Article 15.2 of the *SCM Agreement*. Note that to 'suppress' prices is to prevent price increases that would otherwise occur.

[217] See Article 15.4 of the *SCM Agreement*.

[218] Note that, in the case of agriculture, the investigating authorities must also consider whether there has been an increased burden on government support programmes.

[219] The existence of an obligation to examine all the factors of the Article 15.4 list can be established by analogy to panel and Appellate Body reports interpreting similar provisions in the *Anti-Dumping Agreement* and the *Agreement on Safeguards*. See above, pp. 530–1, and below, pp. 646–7.

[220] See Article 15.4 of the *SCM Agreement*.

[221] See Article 15.7 of the *SCM Agreement*. Note that the Panel in *US – Lumber ITC Investigation* stated that a *threat* determination is made against the background of an evaluation of the condition of the industry in light of the Article 15.4 factors: once such an analysis has been carried out in the context of an investigation of material injury, however, the Panel said that none of the relevant provisions of Article 15 require a second analysis of the injury factors in cases involving a threat of material injury. See Panel Report, *US – Lumber ITC Investigation*, paras. 7.97–7.112.

[222] Article 15.7, second sentence, of the *SCM Agreement*.

- the nature of the subsidy and the trade effects likely to arise from it;
- a significant rate of increase of subsidised imports; and
- whether imports are entering at prices that will have a significant depressing or suppressing effect on domestic prices.[223]

All relevant factors (including the injury factors listed in Article 15.4, discussed above)[224] must be considered in order to establish whether further subsidised imports are imminent and whether, unless protective action is taken, material injury would occur.[225] In addition, as in the case of dumping, Article 15.8 requires 'special care' when considering and deciding on the application of countervailing measures in the case of a threat of material injury. In this regard, the Panel in *US – Lumber ITC Investigation* considered the phrase 'special care' to mean:

> a degree of attention over and above that required of investigating authorities in all [other] [anti-dumping] and [countervailing duty] injury cases.[226]

When the subsidised imports originate in several countries and several countries are therefore subject to the anti-subsidy investigations, the effects of the subsidised imports may be assessed *cumulatively* establishing injury to the domestic industry.[227] It is quite common for WTO Members to apply a cumulative assessment of the effects of subsidised imports. However, pursuant to Article 15.3 of the *SCM Agreement* such cumulative assessment is only allowed when:

- the amount of subsidisation is more than *de minimis* (i.e. more than 1 per cent *ad valorem*);[228]
- the volume of the imports of each country is not negligible; and
- the cumulative assessment of the effects of the imports is appropriate in light of the conditions of competition between the imported products and the conditions of competition between the imported products and the like domestic products.[229]

Article 15.5 of the *SCM Agreement* provides:

> It must be demonstrated that the subsidized imports are, through the effects of subsidies, causing injury within the meaning of this Agreement.

A causal link between the subsidised imports and the injury to the domestic industry must therefore be established. The injury suffered by the domestic industry may be caused not only by the subsidised imports. Other factors may also cause injury to the domestic industry, including: the volumes and prices of *non-subsidised* imports of the product in question; a contraction in demand or changes in the

---

[223] See the factors mentioned in Article 15.7(i), (ii) and (iv) of the *SCM Agreement*.
[224] See, by analogy, Panel Report, *Mexico – Corn Syrup*, para. 7.133, which concerned an identical provision in the *Anti-Dumping Agreement*. See above, pp. 530–1.
[225] See Article 15.7, last sentence, of the *SCM Agreement*.
[226] Panel Report, *US – Lumber ITC Investigation*, paras. 7.29–7.37.
[227] Article 15.3 of the *SCM Agreement*.
[228] See Article 11.9 of the *SCM Agreement*. The amount of the subsidy is considered *de minimis* if the subsidy is less than 1 per cent of the value of the subsidised product.
[229] Article 15.3 of the *SCM Agreement*.

patterns of consumption; trade-restrictive practices of, and competition between, the foreign and domestic producers; developments in technology; and the export performance and productivity of the domestic industry. The injury caused by these other factors may not be attributed to the subsidised imports.

Questions and Assignments 6.29

What are 'like products' in the context of the *SCM Agreement*? What is the relevant 'domestic industry' in the context of the *SCM Agreement*? What does the concept of 'injury', within the meaning of Article 15 of the *SCM Agreement*, cover? How is 'injury' to the domestic industry established? When is there a 'threat of material injury'? May the effects of subsidised imports from different countries be assessed *cumulatively* for the purpose of establishing injury to the domestic industry? Explain the non-attribution requirement provided for in Article 15.5 of the *SCM Agreement*.

6.3.4.2. *Subsidies causing nullification or impairment*

Subsidies have adverse effects on the interests of other Members within the meaning of Article 5(b) of the *SCM Agreement* – and are therefore 'actionable' – when the subsidised imports cause the nullification or impairment of benefits accruing directly or indirectly to other Members under the GATT 1994. This may be the case, in particular, with respect to the benefits from tariff concessions bound under Article II:1 of the GATT 1994. Subsidisation may undercut improved market access resulting from a tariff concession.[230]

6.3.4.3. *Subsidies causing serious prejudice*

Subsidies have adverse effects on the interests of other Members within the meaning of Article 5(c) of the *SCM Agreement* – and are therefore 'actionable' – when the subsidised imports cause serious prejudice to the interests of another Member. Pursuant to Article 6.3 of the *SCM Agreement*, 'serious prejudice' *may* arise where a subsidy has one or more of the following effects:

- the subsidy displaces or impedes imports of a like product of another Member into the market of the subsidising Member (Article 6.3(a));
- the subsidy displaces or impedes the export of a like product of another Member from a third country market (Article 6.3(b));
- the subsidy results in a significant price undercutting by the subsidising product in comparison to the like product of another Member in the same market, or significant price suppression, price depression or lost sales in the same market (Article 6.3(c)); or

---

[230] The existence of nullification or impairment is established in accordance with the practice of application of Article XXIII of the GATT 1994. See footnote 12 of the *SCM Agreement*.

- the subsidy leads to an increase in the world market share of the subsidising Member in a particular primary product or commodity in comparison to the average share it had during the previous period of three years (Article 6.3(d)).

If a complaining Member can show that a subsidy has any of these effects, then 'serious prejudice' may be found to exist.[231] On the other hand, if the subsidising Member can show that subsidies do not result in any of these effects, these subsidies will *not* be found to cause serious prejudice.[232] Note that the concept of 'serious prejudice' includes a 'threat of serious prejudice', i.e. a situation in which the serious prejudice is imminent.[233]

The existence of serious prejudice must be determined on the basis of the information submitted to, or obtained by, the panel. Specific procedures for developing information on serious prejudice are set out in Annex V to the *SCM Agreement*. If a Member fails to cooperate in the information-gathering process, the panel may rely on the 'best information available', and it may draw adverse inferences from the lack of cooperation.[234]

Questions and Assignments 6.30

When will a subsidy be found to cause 'serious prejudice' within the meaning of Article 6 of the *SCM Agreement*? Can a WTO Member bring a claim that *another* Member has suffered serious prejudice?

6.3.4.4. *Multilateral remedies for actionable subsidies*

The multilateral remedies for actionable subsidies are set out in Article 7 of the *SCM Agreement*. Like the remedies for prohibited subsidies, the remedies for actionable subsidies also differ from the remedies provided for in the DSU. Compared with the remedies for prohibited subsidies, however, the time-frames are longer and the Permanent Group of Experts is not involved.[235] If a panel concludes that a subsidy causes adverse effects to the interests of another Member (be it injury, nullification or impairment, or serious prejudice), the subsidising Member must:

> take appropriate steps to remove the adverse effect or … withdraw the subsidy.[236]

---

[231] Note that, if the list in Article 6.3(c) is illustrative and non-exhaustive, it may be possible to establish serious prejudice on grounds other than those in the list.

[232] Article 6.2 of the *SCM Agreement*. Note that Article 6.1 of the *SCM Agreement* lists several situations in which subsidies are deemed to cause 'serious prejudice'. However, this provision lapsed on 31 December 1999. See Article 31 of the *SCM Agreement*.

[233] See footnote 13 to the *SCM Agreement*. Compare also the Panel in *Indonesia – Autos* which considered that products not originating in a complaining Member cannot be the subject of a claim of serious prejudice and that Members cannot bring a claim that *another Member* has suffered serious prejudice. See Panel Report, *Indonesia – Autos*, paras. 14.201–14.202.

[234] Annex V, paras. 6 and 7, to the *SCM Agreement*.

[235] Several of the timeframes provided for under Article 7 are, however, still shorter than the 'ordinary' timeframes provided for in the DSU. For example, the timeframe for the panel proceedings is four months. See Article 7.5 of the *SCM Agreement*.

[236] Article 7.8 of the *SCM Agreement*.

The subsidising Member must do so within six months from the adoption of the report by the DSB.[237] Instead of withdrawing the subsidy at issue or removing its adverse effects, the subsidising Member can also agree with the complaining Member on compensation.[238] If, within six months from the adoption of the report, the subsidy is not withdrawn, its adverse effects are not removed or no agreement on compensation is reached, the DSB must, at the request of the complaining Member and by reverse consensus, grant authorisation to the complaining Member to take countermeasures. These countermeasures must be commensurate with the degree and nature of the adverse effects of the subsidies granted.[239]

Questions and Assignments 6.31

What happens when a panel finds that a subsidy granted by a Member causes adverse effects to the interests of other Members?

6.3.4.5. *Note on non-actionable subsidies*

As already mentioned, in addition to prohibited subsidies and actionable subsidies, the *SCM Agreement* provides for a third category of subsidies: non-actionable subsidies. These are subsidies, which are allowed and therefore were referred to as 'green light' subsidies. This group of subsidies includes those non-specific subsidies, to which, as discussed above, the disciplines of the *SCM Agreement* do not apply.[240] Until 31 December 1999, this category of non-actionable subsidies also included certain types of specific subsidy, such as certain narrowly defined regional subsidies, environmental subsidies and research and development subsidies. As from 1 January 2000, however, these subsidies, provided that they are specific, have been actionable.[241]

6.3.5. Countervailing measures

Prohibited and actionable subsidies which cause injury to the domestic industry cannot only be challenged multilaterally but can also be offset by the application of a countervailing measure.[242] A Member, whose domestic industry is injured because of subsidised imports, has the choice between:

- challenging the subsidy concerned *multilaterally*, pursuant to Article 4 or 7 of the *SCM Agreement*, as discussed in detail above; and
- *unilaterally* imposing countervailing duties on the subsidised imports.

---

[237] See Article 7.9 of the *SCM Agreement*.
[238] *Ibid.* Note that, in this specific context, compensation is a permanent alternative for bringing the measure into consistency with WTO law. This is not the case under the DSU. See above, pp. 220–1.
[239] Article 7.9 of the *SCM Agreement*.   [240] See above, pp. 559–60.
[241] See Article 31 of the *SCM Agreement*.
[242] A countervailing measure is also sometimes referred to as an 'anti-subsidy measure'.

A countervailing duty is defined in Article VI of the GATT 1994 and footnote 36 to the *SCM Agreement* as:

> a special duty levied for the purpose of offsetting ... any subsidy bestowed, directly, or indirectly, upon the manufacture, production or export of any merchandise.

Article 10 of the *SCM Agreement* provides with respect to countervailing duties:

> Members shall take all necessary steps to ensure that the imposition of a countervailing duty on any product of the territory of any Member imported into the territory of another Member is in accordance with the provisions of Article VI of GATT 1994 and the terms of this Agreement. Countervailing duties may only be imposed pursuant to investigations initiated and conducted in accordance with the provisions of this Agreement and the Agreement on Agriculture.

This section examines:

- under what conditions countervailing duties may be imposed on subsidised imports;
- how the investigations leading up to the imposition of countervailing duties should be conducted; and
- how countervailing duties must be applied.

6.3.5.1. *Conditions for the imposition of countervailing duties*

It follows from Article VI of the GATT 1994 and Article 10 of the *SCM Agreement* that WTO Members may only impose countervailing duties when three conditions are fulfilled:

- there are *subsidised imports*, i.e. imports of products from producers who benefited from specific subsidies within the meaning of Articles 1, 2 and 14 of the *SCM Agreement*, as discussed in detail above;[243]
- there is *injury* to the domestic industry of the like products within the meaning of Articles 15 and 16 of the *SCM Agreement*, as discussed in detail above;[244] and
- there is a *causal link* between the subsidised imports and the injury to the domestic industry *and* injury caused by other factors is *not attributed* to the subsidised imports.[245]

Questions and Assignments 6.32

When may a Member impose countervailing duties under the terms of the *SCM Agreement*? Compare the conditions for imposing countervailing

---

[243] On the concept of 'subsidies' and the specificity of subsidies, see above, pp. 555–61.
[244] On the concepts of 'like products', 'domestic industry' and 'injury' (including 'material injury', 'threat of material injury' and 'material retardation'), see above, pp. 568–71.
[245] See above, pp. 571–2. All the conditions for the imposition of countervailing duties, including the causal link and non-attribution requirements, are discussed above.

duties on subsidised imports to the conditions for a successful multilateral challenge of subsidies pursuant to Article 4 or 7 of the *SCM Agreement*.

6.3.5.2. *Conduct of countervailing investigations*

The *SCM Agreement* provides for detailed procedural requirements regarding the initiation and conduct of a countervailing investigation by the competent authorities of the Member imposing the countervailing duties on the subsidised imports. These requirements are set out in Articles 11 to 13 of the *SCM Agreement*. The main objective of these requirements is to ensure that:

- the investigations are conducted in a transparent manner;
- all interested parties have the opportunity to defend their interests; and
- the investigating authorities adequately explain the basis for their determinations.

The Appellate Body and panels have interpreted these requirements strictly and have given little discretion to the investigating authorities as to how they conduct countervailing investigations. Note that the procedural requirements for countervailing investigations set out in the *SCM Agreement* are largely the same as the procedural requirements for anti-dumping investigations set out in the *Anti-Dumping Agreement* and discussed above.[246] This is true, in particular, for that part of the investigation dealing with injury and the general notification and explanation requirements. The rest of the investigation, not dealing with injury, of course has a different substantive focus. In a countervailing investigation, the focus is on establishing the extent to which countervailable subsidies are granted and the measurement of the amount of such subsidisation, while in an anti-dumping investigation, the focus is on the measurement of a dumping margin.

A countervailing investigation normally starts with the submission of a so-called application, i.e. a written complaint that injurious subsidisation is taking place. This application is submitted by, or on behalf of, the domestic industry allegedly injured by the subsidised imports.[247] Pursuant to Article 11.2 of the *SCM Agreement*, the application must contain sufficient evidence of the existence of:

- a subsidy and, if possible, its amount;
- injury to the domestic industry; and
- a causal link between the subsidised imports and the alleged injury.[248]

---

[246] See above, pp. 536–41.
[247] See Article 11.1 of the *SCM Agreement*. The application shall be considered to have been made 'by or on behalf of the domestic industry' if it is supported by those domestic producers whose collective output constitutes more than 50 per cent of the total production of the like product produced by that portion of the domestic industry expressing either support for or opposition to the application. However, no investigation shall be initiated when domestic producers expressly supporting the application account for less than 25 per cent of total production of the like product produced by the domestic industry. See Article 11.4 of the *SCM Agreement*.

Simple assertion, unsubstantiated by relevant evidence, is not considered to meet the requirement of 'sufficient evidence' under Article 11.2. Before initiating a countervailing investigation, the investigating authorities must examine the adequacy and accuracy of the evidence in the application to determine whether this evidence justifies the initiation of an investigation.[249]

When the investigating authorities concerned are satisfied that there is *not* sufficient evidence of either subsidisation or of injury to justify proceeding with the case, they must reject the application for the initiation of an investigation, or, if the investigation has already been initiated, promptly terminate that investigation.[250] There shall be immediate termination in cases where the amount of a subsidy is *de minimis* (i.e. less than 1 per cent *ad valorem*), or where the volume of subsidised imports, actual or potential, or the injury, is negligible.[251]

In special circumstances, domestic authorities can also initiate countervailing investigations of their own accord.[252] However, they may only do so when they have sufficient evidence of the existence of a subsidy, injury and causal link to justify the initiation of an investigation.

When the investigating authorities decide to initiate an investigation, several obligations must then be fulfilled to provide adequate protection for those potentially affected by such an investigation. First, a public notice of the initiation must be issued,[253] and as soon as the investigation is initiated[254] the application for the initiation of an investigation must be made available to the known exporters of the subsidised products and the exporting Member.[255] Secondly, interested Members and all interested parties in the investigation, including, of course, the exporter(s) of the subsidised products and the domestic producer(s) of the like product,[256] must be given:

- notice of the information which the authorities require; and
- ample opportunity to present in writing all evidence which they consider relevant.[257]

Thirdly, Members and interested parties must then be given at least thirty days to reply to the questionnaire they receive from the investigating

---

[248] Article 11.2 of the *SCM Agreement* sets out in significant detail the information the application must contain.

[249] See Article 11.3 of the *SCM Agreement*. Note, however, that Article 11.3 of the *SCM Agreement* does not specify how this examination is to be carried out. Note also that 'sufficient evidence' is, of course, not the same as 'full proof'; it is clearly a lower standard.

[250] Article 11.9 of the *SCM Agreement*.   [251] *Ibid.*   [252] Article 11.6 of the *SCM Agreement*.

[253] See Article 22.1 of the *SCM Agreement*. Article 22.2 sets out the information which this public notice must contain.

[254] Note that, before the investigation is actually initiated, the investigating authorities must invite the subsidising Member for consultations. Such consultations will continue throughout the investigation. See Articles 13.1 and 13.2 of the *SCM Agreement*.

[255] Article 12.1.3 of the *SCM Agreement*. The application shall also be made available, upon request, to other interested parties involved.

[256] For a definition of 'interested parties', see Article 12.9 of the *SCM Agreement*. Note that domestic or foreign parties other than those mentioned above may be considered to be 'interested parties'.

[257] Article 12.1 of the *SCM Agreement*.

authorities.[258] Fourthly, the investigating authorities must provide opportunities for industrial users of the product under investigation, and for representative consumer organisations in cases where the product is commonly sold at the retail level, to provide information.[259] Fifthly, all interested parties must be invited to participate in the hearings held by the investigating authorities.[260] Finally, the investigating authorities are obliged to make all information that is not confidential available to all interested Members and interested parties.[261] However, any information the disclosure of which would be of significant competitive advantage to a competitor or would have significant adverse effects on those supplying the information (i.e. any confidential information or other information which is provided on a confidential basis), must, where good cause is shown, be treated as such by the investigating authorities.[262] Such confidential information may only be disclosed with the specific permission of the party submitting it.[263]

During the course of an investigation, the investigating authorities must satisfy themselves as to the accuracy of the information supplied by interested Members or interested parties upon which their findings are based.[264]

Investigating authorities, that, in spite of their best efforts, fail to obtain all relevant information, may take decisions on the basis of the 'best information available'. Article 12.7 of the *SCM Agreement* provides:

> In cases in which any interested Member or interested party refuses access to, or otherwise does not provide, necessary information within a reasonable period or significantly impedes the investigation, preliminary and final determinations, affirmative or negative, may be made on the basis of the facts available.

This possibility for investigating authorities to base their decisions on the 'best information available' is important to avoid investigations being frustrated and deadlocked because of the lack of cooperation from an interested party holding the relevant information. However, this possibility may evidently also potentially give rise to abuse on the part of investigating authorities.

Investigations must normally be concluded within one year,[265] and in no case should an investigation take longer than eighteen months.[266]

---

[258] Article 12.1.1 of the *SCM Agreement*. Where cause is shown, a thirty-day extension period should be granted whenever practicable.

[259] Article 12.10 of the *SCM Agreement*.

[260] Article 12.2 of the *SCM Agreement*. Note, however, that any decision of the investigating authorities can only be based on such information and arguments as were on the written record of these authorities. Therefore, information provided orally must also be submitted in writing.

[261] Article 12.3 of the *SCM Agreement*.   [262] Article 12.4 of the *SCM Agreement*.

[263] *Ibid.* Investigating authorities may, however, be asked to provide non-confidential summaries that provide a reasonable understanding of the substance of the information submitted in confidence. See Article 12.4.1 of the *SCM Agreement*.

[264] Article 12.5 of the *SCM Agreement*.   [265] Article 11.11 of the *SCM Agreement*.   [266] *Ibid.*

Describe the key features of a countervailing investigation. What is the main objective of the procedural requirements set out in Articles 11 to 13 of the *SCM Agreement*? How is a countervailing investigation initiated? When are investigating authorities obliged to terminate a countervailing investigation immediately? How does the *SCM Agreement* ensure all interested parties get a chance to be heard in a countervailing investigation? Discuss how confidential information is handled in a countervailing investigation. Can investigating authorities base their conclusions on the 'best information available'?

6.3.5.3. *Application of countervailing measures*

The *SCM Agreement* provides for three types of countervailing measure:

- provisional countervailing measures;
- voluntary undertakings; and
- definitive countervailing duties.

After making a preliminary determination that a subsidy is causing or threatening to cause injury to a domestic industry, an importing Member can impose *provisional countervailing measures* on the subsidised imports.[267] However, such provisional countervailing measures cannot be applied earlier than sixty days from the date of initiation of the investigation. Furthermore, their application must be limited to as short a period as possible and in no case may they be applied for more than four months.[268]

Investigations may be suspended or terminated without the imposition of provisional measures or countervailing duties upon receipt of satisfactory *voluntary undertakings* under which:

- the government of the exporting Member agrees to eliminate or limit the subsidy or to take other measures concerning its effects; or
- the exporter agrees to revise its prices so that the investigating authorities are satisfied that the injurious effect of the subsidy is eliminated.[269]

Members may impose *definitive countervailing duties* only after making a final determination that:

---

[267] Article 17 of the *SCM Agreement*.   [268] Articles 17.3 and 17.4 of the *SCM Agreement*.
[269] Article 18.1 of the *SCM Agreement*. Note that, pursuant to Article 18.2 of the *SCM Agreement*, undertakings may not be sought or accepted unless the investigating authorities have made a preliminary affirmative determination of subsidisation and injury caused by such subsidisation. In case of undertakings from exporters, the consent of the exporting Member must be obtained. Article 18.4 provides that, if an undertaking is accepted, the investigation of subsidisation and injury shall nevertheless be completed if the exporting Member so desires or the importing Member so decides.

- a countervailable subsidy exists; and
- the subsidy causes, or threatens to cause, injury to the domestic industry.[270]

With respect to the amount of the countervailing duty imposed on subsidised imports, Article 19.4 of the *SCM Agreement* provides:

> No countervailing duty shall be levied on any imported product in excess of the amount of the subsidy found to exist, calculated in terms of subsidization per unit of the subsidized and exported product.

Thus, a countervailing duty must never exceed the amount of the subsidy. Moreover, if the amount of the injury caused is less than the amount of the subsidy, the definitive countervailing duty should preferably be limited to the amount necessary to counteract the injury caused.[271]

Countervailing duties must be collected on a non-discriminatory basis. Article 19.3 of the *SCM Agreement* states:

> When a countervailing duty is imposed in respect of any product, such countervailing duty shall be levied ... on a non-discriminatory basis on imports of such product from all sources found to be subsidized and causing injury.

As discussed above, the MFN treatment obligation applies to countervailing duties.[272] Such duties must be applied to all imports from all countries found to be granting a countervailable subsidy.

Note that any exporter whose exports are subject to a definitive countervailing duty but who was not actually investigated is entitled to an expedited review so that the investigating authorities can promptly establish an individual countervailing duty rate for that exporter.[273]

Countervailing duties may not be applied retroactively, i.e. they may only be applied to products imported after the decision to impose countervailing duties entered into force.[274] Where a final determination is negative, any cash deposit made during the period of the application of provisional measures shall be refunded and any bonds released in an expeditious manner.[275]

With respect to the duration of countervailing measures, Article 21.1 of the *SCM Agreement* states as a rule:

> A countervailing duty shall remain in force only as long as and to the extent necessary to counteract subsidization which is causing injury.

---

[270] See Article 19.1 of the *SCM Agreement*. Before a final determination is made, the investigating authorities inform all interested Members and interested parties of the essential facts under consideration which form the basis for the decision whether to apply definitive measures. Such disclosure should take place in sufficient time for the parties to defend their interests. See Article 12.8 of the *SCM Agreement*.

[271] Article 19.2 of the *SCM Agreement*.

[272] See above, p. 314. The MFN treatment obligation also applies to anti-dumping duties. See above, p. 543.

[273] Article 19.3 of the *SCM Agreement*. This does not apply to exporters for which no individual countervailing duty was established due to their refusal to cooperate with the investigating authorities.

[274] See Article 20.1 of the *SCM Agreement*. Note, however, that in specific circumstances the retroactive application of countervailing duties is possible. See Articles 20.2 and 20.6 of the *SCM Agreement*.

[275] Article 20.5 of the *SCM Agreement*. However, if the definitive countervailing duty is higher than the amount guaranteed by the cash deposit or bond, the difference shall not be collected. See Article 20.3 of the *SCM Agreement*.

Upon their own initiative or upon a request from an interested party, the investigating authorities shall review the need for the continued imposition of the duty.[276] Interested parties may request such review once a reasonable period has elapsed since the imposition of the definitive countervailing duty. The interested parties must then submit positive information substantiating the need for a review.[277] During the review, the investigating authorities examine:

- whether the continued imposition of the duty is necessary to offset subsidisation;
- whether the injury would be likely to continue or recur if the duty were removed or varied; or
- both.[278]

If, because of a review, the investigating authorities determine that the countervailing duty is no longer warranted, it shall be terminated immediately. Should the investigating authorities conclude that the countervailing duty remains warranted, it will continue to apply, albeit possibly at a different level.

Article 21.3 of the *SCM Agreement* provides for a so-called 'sunset' clause under which all definitive countervailing duties must be terminated, at the latest, five years after their imposition or the latest review. However, where the investigating authorities determine that the expiry of the countervailing duty would be likely to lead to continuation or recurrence of subsidisation and injury, the duty will not be terminated.[279] In this regard, the Appellate Body in *US – Carbon Steel* upheld the Panel's finding that there are no evidentiary standards for self initiation of sunset reviews under Article 21.3.[280]

Note that Article 32.1 of the *SCM Agreement* states:

> No specific action against a subsidy of another Member can be taken except in accordance with the provisions of GATT 1994, as interpreted by this Agreement.

In *US – Offset Act (Byrd Amendment)*, the Appellate Body ruled that it follows from this provision that countervailing duties must be in one of the four forms provided for in provisions of the GATT 1994 and the *SCM Agreement*.[281] As discussed above, the GATT 1994 and the *SCM Agreement* provide four responses to a countervailable subsidy: definitive countervailing duties; provisional measures; price undertakings; and multilaterally sanctioned countermeasures under the dispute settlement system. No other response to subsidisation is permitted. In *US – Offset Act (Byrd Amendment)*, the measure at issue was the United States Continued Dumping and Subsidy Offset Act of 2000 (CDSOA).[282] This Act provided, in relevant part, that the United States Customs shall *distribute* duties assessed pursuant to a countervailing duty order to 'affected

---

[276] Article 21.2 of the *SCM Agreement*.   [277] *Ibid.*

[278] *Ibid.* The review must be conducted pursuant to the same procedural rules as those that applied to the original investigation. See Article 21.4 of the *SCM Agreement*.

[279] Article 21.3 of the *SCM Agreement*.

[280] Appellate Body Report, *US – German Steel Countervailing Duties*, para. 112.

[281] Appellate Body Report, *US – Offset Act (Byrd Amendment)*, para. 269.

[282] Appellate Body Report, *US – Offset Act (Byrd Amendment)*, paras. 11–14.

domestic producers' for 'qualifying expenditures'.[283] The Appellate Body concluded:

> As the CDSOA does not correspond to any of the responses to subsidization envisaged by the GATT 1994 and the *SCM Agreement*, we conclude that it is not in accordance with the provisions of the GATT 1994, as interpreted by the *SCM Agreement*, and that, therefore, the CDSOA is inconsistent with Article 32.1 of the *SCM Agreement*.[284]

Questions and Assignments 6.34

Discuss briefly the three types of countervailing measure. When can a Member impose a provisional countervailing duty? When can a Member impose a definitive countervailing measure? Is a Member allowed to impose a countervailing duty in excess of the subsidy found to exist? Is a Member allowed to impose a countervailing duty in excess of the amount necessary to counteract the injury caused? Discuss whether the MFN treatment obligation applies to countervailing duties. Can countervailing duties be applied retroactively? What is the maximum duration of a countervailing duty? What is the object and purpose of the review procedure of Article 21.2 of the *SCM Agreement*?

6.3.5.4. *Public notice and judicial review*

In order to increase the transparency of decisions taken by investigating authorities and to encourage solid and thorough reasoning underlying such decisions, Article 22 of the *SCM Agreement* contains detailed requirements for public notice by investigating authorities of decisions on the initiation of an investigation, provisional countervailing duties, voluntary undertakings or definitive countervailing duties. For example, the public notice issued when the investigating authorities decide to impose a definitive countervailing duty *must* set forth, or otherwise make available through a separate report, all relevant information on the matters of fact, law and reasons which have led to the imposition of the countervailing duty.[285] In particular, the notice or report *must* contain:

- the names of the suppliers or, when this is impracticable, the supplying countries involved;
- a description of the product which is sufficient for customs purposes;
- the amount of subsidy established and the basis on which the existence of a subsidy has been determined;
- considerations relevant to the injury determination as set out in Article 15 and discussed above; and
- the main reasons leading to the determination.[286]

---

[283] *Ibid.*   [284] *Ibid.*, para. 273.
[285] Article 22.5 of the *SCM Agreement*. Note, however, that Article 22.5 requires that due regard be paid to the requirement for the protection of confidential information.
[286] Article 22.5 of the *SCM Agreement*, referring to Article 22.4 thereof.

Furthermore, the notice or report *must* set out the reasons for the acceptance or rejection of relevant arguments or claims made by interested Members and by the exporters and importers.[287]

As provided for in Article 23 of the *SCM Agreement*, entitled 'Judicial Review', each Member whose national legislation contains provisions on countervailing measures must maintain judicial, arbitral or administrative tribunals or procedures for the purpose of, *inter alia*, the prompt review of administrative actions relating to final determinations and reviews of determinations. Such tribunals or procedures must be independent of the authorities responsible for the determination or review in question, and must provide all interested parties who participated in the administrative proceeding, and are affected directly and individually by the administrative actions, with access to review.[288]

Questions and Assignments 6.35

Why is the public notice requirement of Article 22 of the *SCM Agreement* important? What must the public notice, issued when the investigating authorities decide to impose a definitive countervailing duty, set forth, or otherwise make available through a separate report? What does Article 23 of the *SCM Agreement* require from Members?

6.3.5.5. *Countervailing duties or countermeasures*

Note that the provisions relating to prohibited and actionable subsidies, discussed above, may be invoked, and relied upon, *in parallel with* the provisions relating to countervailing duties. However, with regard to the effects of a particular subsidy, only *one* form of remedy (either a countervailing duty *or* a countermeasure) may be applied.[289]

Questions and Assignments 6.36

Can countervailing duties and countermeasures be applied simultaneously with regard to the same instance of subsidisation?

6.3.6. Agricultural subsidies

Agricultural subsidies have traditionally been, and continue to be, a very contentious issue in international trade. Agricultural subsidies were a major topic during the Uruguay Round and are again high on the agenda of the Doha Development Round. Agricultural export subsidies and domestic agricultural

---

[287] Article 22.5 of the *SCM Agreement*.   [288] See Article 23 of the *SCM Agreement*.
[289] See footnote 35 to the *SCM Agreement*.

support measures are indispensable instruments of the current agricultural policies of a number of developed-country Members (such as the European Communities). At the same time, the trade interests and the economic development of many other Members are severely affected by these agricultural subsidies. The particularly sensitive nature of the issue of agricultural subsidies explains why the rules of the *SCM Agreement* do not apply in full to agricultural subsidies.[290] The *Agreement on Agriculture* provides for special rules on agricultural subsidies and, in case of conflict, these special rules prevail over the rules of the *SCM Agreement*.[291] This section briefly discusses the special rules of the *Agreement on Agriculture* on:

- agricultural export subsidies; and
- domestic agricultural support measures.

Questions and Assignments 6.37

Do the rules of the *SCM Agreement* apply to agricultural subsidies?

6.3.6.1. *Agricultural export subsidies*

The *SCM Agreement*'s prohibition on export subsidies applies on agricultural export subsidies except as provided otherwise in the *Agreement on Agriculture*. While export subsidies on non-agricultural products are prohibited, with respect to export subsidies on agricultural products, a distinction must be made between export subsidies on:

- agricultural products that are specified in Section II of Part IV of a Member's GATT Schedule of Concessions; and
- agricultural products that are not specified in that section.

With respect to the agricultural products specified in the relevant section of their Schedule, the export subsidies, defined in Article 9.1(a) to (f) of the *Agreement on Agriculture*, are subject to reduction commitments.[292] As set out in the relevant section of their Schedule, developed-country Members agreed to reduce the export subsidies on these products by an average of 36 per cent by value (budgetary outlay) and 21 per cent by volume (subsidised quantities). Developing-country Members agreed to reduce the export subsidies by an average of 24 per cent by value and 14 per cent by volume. Members may *not*

---

[290] See also above, p. 554.

[291] See Article 21 of the *Agreement on Agriculture*, which states: 'The provisions of GATT 1994 and of other Multilateral Trade Agreements in Annex 1A to the WTO Agreement shall apply subject to the provisions of this Agreement.'

[292] Note also Article 10 of the *Agreement on Agriculture*, which deals with the circumvention of the export subsidy commitments.

provide listed export subsidies *in excess of* the budgetary outlay and quantitative commitment levels specified in their Schedules.[293]

Members may not apply export subsidies that are not listed in the *Agreement on Arrgriculture* in a manner which results in or threatens to lead to circumvention of export subsidy commitments. This effectively prohibits any other export subsidies. Thus, with respect to agricultural products not specified in the relevant section of their Schedule, Members shall not provide export subsidies.[294]

In *Canada – Dairy*, the measure at issue was a government scheme under which the price for milk used in manufacturing dairy products destined for export was set at a lower level than the price for milk destined for domestic consumption. On appeal, the Appellate Body upheld the Panel's finding that Canada acted:

> inconsistently with its obligations under Article 3.3 and Article 8 of the *Agreement on Agriculture* by providing export subsidies as listed in Article 9.1(c) of that Agreement in excess of the quantity commitment levels specified in Canada's Schedule.[295]

Questions and Assignments 6.38

Are agricultural export subsidies prohibited under the *Agreement on Agriculture*?

6.3.6.2. *Domestic agricultural support measures*

With respect to domestic agricultural support measures, Members have agreed to reduce the level of support. Under the terms of the *Agreement on Agriculture*, developed-country Members agreed to reduce between 1995 and 2000 their 'aggregate measurement of support', or 'AMS', by 20 per cent. Developing-country Members agreed to reduce their AMS by 13.3 per cent in the period 1995–2004.[296] The commitments of Members on the reduction of domestic agricultural support measures are set out in Part IV of their GATT Schedule of Concessions. Members may *not* provide domestic support *in excess of* the commitment levels specified in their Schedules.[297]

Domestic agricultural support measures that do not have the effect of providing price support to producers are exempt from the reduction commitments. These exempted domestic support measures are commonly referred to

---

[293] Article 3.3 of the *Agreement on Agriculture*. See also Article 8 of the *Agreement on Agriculture*, which states that a Member must undertake *not* to provide export subsidies *otherwise than* in conformity with the Agreement and with the commitments as specified in that Member's Schedule.
[294] *Ibid.*   [295] See Appellate Body Report, *Canada – Dairy*, para. 144.
[296] See Article 15.2 of the *Agreement on Agriculture*. Least-developed-country Members are not required to undertake reduction commitments. *Ibid.*
[297] Article 3.2 of the *Agreement on Agriculture*.

as 'green box' and 'blue box' measures.[298] 'Green box' measures include support for agricultural research and infrastructure, training and advisory services and domestic food aid.[299] 'Blue box' subsidies include certain developing-country subsidies designed to encourage agricultural production, certain *de minimis* subsidies, and certain direct payments aimed at limiting agricultural production.[300]

Questions and Assignments 6.39

What are the obligations of Members with respect to domestic agricultural support measures? What are 'amber box', 'green box', and 'blue box' measures?

6.3.6.3. Note on the 'peace' clause

Until the end of the nine-year implementation period,[301] agricultural export subsidies that conformed fully to the requirements of the *Agreement on Agriculture*, and domestic agricultural support that was within commitment levels and fulfilled certain other conditions, benefited from the 'due restraint' or 'peace' clause of Article 13 of the *Agreement on Agriculture*.[302] Pursuant to Article 13, the consistency of many agricultural subsidies with the *SCM Agreement* could not be challenged. Furthermore, 'green box' subsidies could not be subjected to countervailing duties.

Since the end of the implementation period in 2004, however, the 'peace' clause no longer applies. The consistency of agricultural subsidies with the *SCM Agreement* can be challenged and countervailing duties can be imposed on 'green box' subsidies. As already mentioned above, in case of conflict between the rules of the *SCM Agreement* and those of the *Agreement on Agriculture*, the rules of the *Agreement on Agriculture* prevail.

6.3.7. Special and differential treatment for developing-country Members

Subsidies can play an important role in the economic development programmes of developing-country Members. Article 27 of the *SCM Agreement*

---

[298] Note that domestic support measures that *are* subject to reduction commitments are commonly referred to as 'amber box' subsidies.

[299] See Annex 2 to the *Agreement on Agriculture*. Article 7 provides that Members must ensure that any 'green box' subsidies are maintained in conformity with the criteria set out in Annex 2, which justify their exemption from reduction commitments.

[300] See Article 6 of the *Agreement on Agriculture*.

[301] This period began in 1995. By virtue of Article 1(i) of the *Agreement on Agriculture*, the term "year" refers to the calendar, financial or marketing year specified in the Schedule relating to that Member.

[302] With respect to the requirements to be fulfilled for agricultural export subsidies, see Articles 9, 10 and 11 of the *Agreement on Agriculture*; for 'amber box' subsidies, see Article 7 (not in excess of the reduction commitments); for 'green box' subsidies, see Annex 2; and for 'blue box' subsidies, see Article 6.

recognises this and provides for some rules and disciplines for developing-country Members that are less strict than the general rules and disciplines.

Pursuant to Article 27, the prohibition of export subsidies under Article 3 of the *SCM Agreement* does not apply to least-developed countries and to countries with a per capita annual income of less than US$1,000.[303] The remedies available against these export subsidies are those available against actionable subsidies as set out in Article 7 of the *SCM Agreement*.[304]

Furthermore, certain subsidies which are normally actionable are not actionable when granted by developing-country Members in the context of privatisation programmes. This is the case, for example, for direct forgiveness of debts and subsidies to cover social costs.[305]

With respect to countervailing duties, Article 27.2 of the *SCM Agreement* provides that any countervailing investigation of a product originating in a developing-country Member must be terminated as soon as the investigating authorities determine that:

- the overall level of subsidies granted upon the product in question does not exceed 2 per cent *ad valorem*; or
- the volume of the subsidised imports represents less than 4 per cent of the total imports of the like product of the importing Member.

Note, however, that the latter rule does not apply when the imports from developing-country Members whose individual shares of total imports represent less than 4 per cent, collectively account for more than 9 per cent of the total imports of the like product of the importing Member.[306]

Questions and Assignments 6.40

To what extent does the *SCM Agreement* provide special and differential treatment for developing-country Members?

---

[303] See Article 27.2 of the *SCM Agreement*. Note that, until 2003, the prohibition on export subsidies did not apply to the remaining developing-country Members either, albeit that these Members had to phase out their export subsidies progressively. Their export subsidies could not be increased and had to come to an end even *before* 2003 when their use had become inconsistent with the Member's development needs. See Article 27.4 of the *SCM Agreement* and the Panel and Appellate Body Reports in *Brazil – Aircraft*. The SCM Committee was empowered, under certain conditions and for certain countries, to extend the period of non-application of the prohibition export subsidies of Article 3 beyond 2003. Accordingly, in 2002, the SCM Committee granted extensions of the transition period for exemption from the prohibition on export subsidies in respect of a number of programmes of twenty-one developing-country Members. These extensions are time limited and programme-specific. They were granted on the basis of Article 27.4, in most cases in conjunction with procedures (G/SCM/39) endorsed by Ministers at the Doha Session of the Ministerial Conference and/or paragraph 10.6 of the *Doha Decision on Implementation Issues* (WT/MIN(01)/17). The SCM Committee granted continuations of some of these extensions in 2003. Note that the prohibition on import substitution subsidies applies to least-developed-country Members since 2003 and to other developing-country Members since 2000. See Article 27.3 of the *SCM Agreement*.
[304] See above, pp. 573–4.
[305] See Article 27.13 of the *SCM Agreement*. Note also the limitation in Article 27.9 of the *SCM Agreement* on remedies for actionable subsidies granted by developing countries.
[306] Article 27.10 of the *SCM Agreement*.

6.4. SUMMARY

WTO law provides for detailed rules with respect to dumping and subsidisation – two specific practices commonly considered to be unfair trade practices.

'Dumping' is the bringing of a product onto the market of another country at a price less than the normal value of that product. In WTO law, dumping is not prohibited. However, WTO Members are allowed to take measures to protect their domestic industry from the injurious effects of dumping. Pursuant to Article VI of the GATT 1994 and the *Anti-Dumping Agreement*, WTO Members are entitled to impose anti-dumping measures if:

- there is dumping;
- the domestic industry producing the like product in the importing country is suffering injury; and
- there is a causal link between the dumping and the injury.

First, dumping is generally determined through a price-to-price comparison of the 'normal value' with the 'export price'. The 'normal value' is the price of the like product in the domestic market of the exporter or producer. Where this price in the exporting country market is not an 'appropriate' normal value, an importing Member may determine the normal value by:

- using the export price to a third country as the normal value; or
- constructing the normal value.

The export price is ordinarily based on the transaction price at which the producer in the exporting country sells the product to an importer in the importing country. Where the transaction price is not an 'appropriate' export price, the importing Member may calculate, or 'construct', an export price. In order to ensure a fair comparison between the export price and normal value, the *Anti-Dumping Agreement* requires that adjustments be made to either the normal value, the export price, or both.

The dumping margin is the difference between the export price and the 'normal value'. The calculation of the dumping margin *generally* requires:

- either the *comparison of the weighted average* 'normal value' to the weighted average of prices of all comparable export transactions; or
- a *transaction-to-transaction comparison* of 'normal value' and export price.

However, in particular circumstances, a comparison of the weighted average normal value to export prices in individual transactions may be used.

Secondly, the domestic industry producing the like product in the importing country must be suffering injury. The *Anti-Dumping Agreement* defines 'injury' to mean one of three things:

- material injury to a domestic industry;
- the threat of material injury to a domestic industry; or
- material retardation of the establishment of a domestic industry.

The *Anti-Dumping Agreement* defines the 'domestic industry' generally as 'the domestic producers as a whole of the like products or ... those of them whose collective output of the products constitutes a major proportion of the total domestic production of those products'. The concept of 'material injury' is not defined but is understood to mean 'genuine injury' and to be a less demanding standard than the 'serious injury' required for the imposition of a safeguard measure. The *Anti-Dumping Agreement* requires that a determination of injury to the domestic industry 'be based on positive evidence and involve an objective examination of both:

- the volume of dumped imports and the effect of the dumped imports on prices in the domestic market for like products; and
- the consequent impact of these imports on domestic producers of such products'.

A determination of a threat of material injury shall be based on facts and not merely on allegation, conjecture or remote possibility. A threat of material injury exists when a change in circumstances, creating a situation in which the dumping would cause injury, is clearly foreseen and imminent.

Thirdly, the *Anti-Dumping Agreement* requires the demonstration of a *causal link* between:

- the dumped imports; and
- the injury to the domestic industry.

As with the determinations of dumping and injury to the domestic industry, the demonstration of a causal link between these two elements must be based on an examination of all relevant evidence before the investigating authorities. The *Anti-Dumping Agreement* also contains a *'non-attribution' requirement*. According to this requirement, investigating authorities must examine any known factors other than the dumped imports that are injuring the domestic industry at the same time *and* must not attribute the injury caused by these other factors to the dumped imports.

The *Anti-Dumping Agreement* contains detailed rules on the initiation of an anti-dumping investigation, the process of the investigation (including evidentiary issues) and requirements for public notice of the initiation of an investigation, preliminary and final determinations and price undertakings. The main objectives of these procedural rules are to ensure that:

- the investigations are conducted in a transparent manner;
- all interested parties have the opportunity to defend their interests; and
- the investigating authorities adequately explain the basis for their determinations.

The *Anti-Dumping Agreement* provides for three kinds of anti-dumping measure:

- provisional measures;
- price undertakings; and
- definitive anti-dumping duties.

To apply a provisional anti-dumping measure, investigating authorities must make a *preliminary* affirmative determination of dumping, injury and causation. Furthermore, the investigating authorities must judge that such a measure is *necessary* to prevent injury being caused during the investigation.

The *Anti-Dumping Agreement* provides for an alternative to the imposition of anti-dumping duties, affording exporters the possibility to offer, and investigating authorities the possibility to accept, price undertakings. These voluntary undertakings to revise prices or cease exports at the dumped price may be entered into only after the investigating authorities have made an affirmative preliminary determination of dumping, injury and causation.

The amount of the anti-dumping duty *may not exceed* the dumping margin, although it may be a lesser amount. Members are required to collect duties, on a *non-discriminatory* basis, on imports from all sources found to be dumped and causing injury. When anti-dumping duties are imposed, the investigating authorities must, in principle, calculate a dumping margin for each exporter. However, the *Anti-Dumping Agreement* recognises that this may not always be possible. When it is not possible to calculate a dumping margin for each exporter, the investigating authorities may limit the number of exporters considered individually.

An anti-dumping duty shall remain in force only as long as and to the extent necessary to counteract dumping which is causing injury. The need for the continued imposition of an anti-dumping duty must be periodically reviewed by the competent authorities, where warranted, on their own initiative or upon a request by any interested party. In any case, any definitive anti-dumping duty shall be *terminated* at a date not later than *five years* from its imposition, *unless* the authorities determine that the expiry of the duty 'would be likely to lead to continuation or recurrence of dumping and injury'.

As with many other WTO agreements, the *Anti-Dumping Agreement* contains a provision relating to special and differential treatment for developing-country Members. Article 15 of the *Anti-Dumping Agreement* requires developed-country Members to explore 'possibilities of constructive remedies' provided for by the *Anti-Dumping Agreement* before applying anti-dumping duties, where such duties would affect the essential interests of developing-country Members.

In addition to rules on dumping, WTO law also includes rules on subsidies and subsidised trade. The *SCM Agreement* defines a subsidy as a financial contribution by a government or public body which confers a benefit. Both the *SCM Agreement* as well as case law work out and clarify each element of this definition. Furthermore, the *SCM Agreement* provides that the WTO rules on subsidies and subsidised trade only apply to 'specific' subsidies.

Article XVI of the GATT 1994 and Parts II, III and IV of the *SCM Agreement* concern the WTO treatment of subsidies. The WTO treatment of subsidies is different from the treatment of dumping. Under WTO law, certain subsidies are prohibited and many other subsidies may be challenged as WTO-inconsistent when they cause adverse effects to the interests of other Members. Article VI of the GATT 1994 and Part V of the *SCM Agreement* concern the manner in which WTO Members may respond to subsidised trade which causes injury to the domestic industry. Members may, in these situations, impose countervailing duties on the subsidised imports to offset, i.e. to cancel out, the subsidisation.

The *SCM Agreement* distinguishes between prohibited subsidies and actionable subsidies. The prohibited subsidies are:

- export subsidies; and
- import substitution subsidies.

Export subsidies are subsidies contingent upon export performance. Annex I of the *SCM Agreement* contains an 'Illustrative List of Export Subsidies'. Import substitution subsidies are subsidies contingent upon the use of domestic over imported goods. Both export subsidies and import substitution subsidies are prohibited regardless of whether the subsidy is contingent (whether *de jure* or *de facto*) upon exportation or the use of domestic over imported goods.

The rules applicable to consultations and adjudication concerning allegedly prohibited subsidies are primarily those of the DSU. However, the timeframes under Article 4 are half as long as the timeframes provided for under the DSU. Moreover, if a panel finds a measure to be a prohibited subsidy, that subsidy must be withdrawn, i.e. removed, without delay. If a recommendation for withdrawal is not followed within the time period set by the panel, the DSB must, upon the request of the original complainant(s) and by reverse consensus, authorise 'appropriate countermeasures' (rather than the 'suspension of concessions or other obligations').

Unlike export subsidies and import substitution subsidies, most subsidies are not prohibited but are 'actionable', i.e. they are subject to challenge in the event that they cause adverse effects to the interests of another Member. There are three types of 'adverse effect' to the interests of other Members:

- *injury* to the domestic industry of another Member;
- *nullification or impairment* of benefits accruing directly or indirectly to other Members under the GATT 1994; and
- *serious prejudice*, including a threat thereof, to the interests of another Member.

The concept of 'injury' to a domestic industry in the *SCM Agreement* covers:

- material injury to the domestic industry of a like product;
- a threat of material injury to a domestic industry; and
- material retardation of the establishment of a domestic industry.

While the concept of 'like product' in this context is specifically defined in the *SCM Agreement*, it should be noted that the approach to establishing 'likeness' under the *SCM Agreement* is, in fact, similar to the approach under the GATT 1994. The definition of 'domestic industry' in the *SCM Agreement* is quite similar to the definition of this concept in the *Anti-Dumping Agreement*. There is also a high degree of similarity between the concepts of 'material injury' and the 'threat of material injury' in the *Anti-Dumping Agreement* and the *SCM Agreement*. Note that it must be demonstrated that the subsidised imports are causing injury to the domestic industry because of the effects of subsidies and that injury caused by factors, other than the subsidies, may not be attributed to the dumped imports.

'Serious prejudice' *may arise* where a subsidy has one or more of the effects described in the *SCM Agreement*, including the impediment of imports of another Member into the market of the subsidising Member or the significant price undercutting by the subsidised product in comparison to the like product of another Member in the same market. If a complaining Member can show that a subsidy has any of the effects listed in the *SCM Agreement*, serious prejudice may be found to exist. Note that the concept of 'serious prejudice' includes a 'threat of serious prejudice', i.e. a situation in which the serious prejudice is imminent.

As is the case with multilateral remedies for prohibited subsidies, the multilateral remedies for actionable subsidies are principally, but not entirely, the remedies for breach of WTO law provided for in the DSU. If a panel concludes that a subsidy causes adverse effects to the interests of another Member (be it injury, nullification or impairment, or serious prejudice), the subsidising Member must take appropriate steps to remove the adverse effect or withdraw the subsidy. The subsidising Member must do so within six months from the adoption of the report by the DSB. Instead of withdrawing the subsidy at issue or removing its adverse effects, the subsidising Member can also agree with the complaining Member on compensation. If within six months from the adoption of the report, the subsidy is not withdrawn, its adverse effects are not removed or no agreement on compensation is reached, the DSB shall, at the request of the complaining Member and by reverse consensus, grant authorisation to the complaining Member to take countermeasures.

Prohibited and actionable subsidies, which cause injury to the domestic industry, not only can be challenged multilaterally but can also be offset by the application of a countervailing duty. WTO Members may impose countervailing duties when three conditions are fulfilled:

- there are *subsidised imports*, i.e. imports of products from producers who benefited from specific subsidies;
- there is *injury* to the domestic industry of the like products; and
- there is a *causal link* between the subsidised imports and the injury to the domestic industry *and* injury caused by other factors is *not attributed* to the subsided imports.

The *SCM Agreement* provides for detailed procedural requirements regarding the initiation and conduct of a countervailing investigation by the competent authorities of the Member imposing the countervailing duties on the subsidised imports. Note that the procedural requirements for countervailing investigations set out in the *SCM Agreement* are largely the same as the procedural requirements for anti-dumping investigations set out in the *Anti-Dumping Agreement*. The main objectives of these requirements are also the same.

The *SCM Agreement* provides for three types of countervailing measure:

- provisional countervailing measures;
- voluntary undertakings; and
- definitive countervailing duties.

After making a preliminary determination that a subsidy is causing or threatening to cause injury to a domestic industry, an importing Member can impose *provisional countervailing measures* on the subsidised imports. Investigations may be suspended or terminated without the imposition of provisional measures or countervailing duties upon receipt of satisfactory *voluntary undertakings* under which:

- the government of the exporting Member agrees to eliminate or limit the subsidy or take other measures concerning its effects; or
- the exporter agrees to revise its prices so that the investigating authorities are satisfied that the injurious effect of the subsidy is eliminated.

Members may impose *definitive countervailing duties* only after making a final determination that a countervailable subsidy exists; and the subsidy causes, or threatens to cause, injury to the domestic industry. The amount of a countervailing duty must never exceed the amount of the subsidy. Moreover, if the amount of the injury caused is less than the amount of the subsidy, the definitive countervailing duty should preferably be limited to the amount necessary to counteract the injury caused.

Countervailing duties must be collected on a non-discriminatory basis. Note that any exporter whose exports are subject to a definitive countervailing duty but who was not actually investigated is entitled to an expedited review so that the investigating authorities promptly establish an individual countervailing duty rate for that exporter.

Countervailing duties may not be applied retroactively, except in certain very specific circumstances.

A countervailing duty shall remain in force only as long as and to the extent necessary to counteract subsidisation which is causing injury. Upon their own initiative or upon a request from an interested party, the investigating authorities shall review the need for the continued imposition of the duty. All definitive countervailing duties must be terminated, at the latest, five years after their imposition or the latest review. However, where the investigating authorities determine that the expiry of the countervailing duty would be likely to lead to a continuation or recurrence of subsidisation and injury, the duty will not be terminated.

Note that countervailing duties and countermeasures cannot be applied simultaneously with regard to the same instance of subsidisation.

The *Agreement on Agriculture* provides for special rules on agricultural export subsidies and domestic agricultural support measures. In case of conflict, these special rules prevail over the rules of the *SCM Agreement*. Export subsidies on agricultural products specified in Section II of Part IV of a Member's GATT Schedule of Concessions are not prohibited but are subject to reduction commitments. Members may *not* provide export subsidies *in excess of* the budgetary outlay and quantitative commitment levels specified in the Schedule. Also with respect to domestic agricultural support measures, Members have agreed to reduce the level of support. Members may *not* provide domestic support *in excess of* the commitment levels specified in their Schedules. However, domestic agricultural support measures that do not have the effect of providing price support to producers are exempt from the reduction commitments.

Subsidies can play an important role in the economic development programmes of developing-country Members. Article 27 of the *SCM Agreement*, therefore, provides some rules and disciplines for developing-country Members that are less strict than the general rules on subsidies of the *SCM Agreement*.

6.5. EXERCISE: DIRTY PLAY, BUT BY WHOM?

Newland has three important manufacturers of furniture, AEKI, Schoeder and StyleMark. Together, they represent 70 per cent of the domestic furniture industry. Many small manufacturers make up the rest of the industry. Over the last few years, all manufacturers of furniture in Newland have been exporting an ever increasing part of their production to Richland, as the trendy but cheap furniture from Newland is quite popular with consumers in Richland.

The furniture industry in Richland is not happy with this development. The market share of the domestic furniture manufacturers has steadily decreased over recent years and many of the smaller manufacturers are going out of business. The six major furniture manufacturers, which together represent about 60 per cent of total furniture production in Richland, want to take action against the imports of furniture from Newland. They want the government of Richland to impose anti-dumping and/or countervailing duties on the furniture imported from Newland or to take any other action that would reduce the flow of furniture from Newland. They are convinced that the furniture from Newland is sold on the market of Richland at prices far below the cost of production. They claim that this is the case in particular for bedroom furniture produced by AEKI and StyleMark. They also note that the furniture manufacturers of Newland get electricity from the state-owned Newland Power Corporation at preferential rates. In addition, the small furniture manufacturers of Newland get a significant tax rebate if they hire a number of unemployed workers each year. Small manufacturers can also get technical advice and financial support from the Export Promotion Board of Newland, a government agency, to market their furniture abroad.

Alarmed by reports in the *Financial Times* on the calls of the Richland furniture industry for action against imports of furniture from Newland, the Government of Newland turns to the Advisory Centre on WTO Law (ACWL) for legal advice on whether, and under what conditions, Richland may, consistent with WTO law:

- impose anti-dumping duties;
- impose countervailing duties; or
- take any other action.

Newland also wants to know what procedures WTO law prescribes for the imposition of anti-dumping or countervailing duties.

Should Richland be allowed to impose such duties, Newland wants to know:

- whether duties may be imposed on all furniture imported from Newland;
- the maximum level of duties that may be applied; and
- the maximum length of time duties may be imposed.

The Executive Director of the ACWL has instructed you, a junior lawyer at the Centre, to prepare a presentation for a group of Newland trade officials and representatives of the Newland furniture industry addressing the concerns and queries put forward by the Government of Newland.

Trade liberalisation versus other societal values and interests

7.1. INTRODUCTION

The promotion and protection of public health, consumer safety, the environment, employment, economic development and national security are *core* tasks of governments. Often, trade liberalisation and the resulting availability of better and cheaper products and services facilitate the promotion and protection of these and other economic and non-economic societal values and interests. Through trade, environmentally friendly products or life-saving medicines, that would not be available otherwise, become available to consumers and patients respectively. At a more general level, trade generates the degree of economic activity and economic welfare indispensable for the effective promotion and protection of the societal values and interests referred to above.

In order to protect and promote these societal values and interests, however, governments also frequently adopt legislation or take measures that inadvertently or deliberately constitute barriers to trade. Members are often politically and/or economically 'compelled' to adopt legislation or measures which are inconsistent with the rules of WTO law and, in particular, with the principles of non-discrimination and the rules on market access as discussed in Chapters 4 and 5. Trade liberalisation, and its principles of non-discrimination and rules on market access, often conflict with other important societal values and interests.

This chapter will discuss the rules provided for in WTO law to reconcile trade liberalisation with other societal values and interests. This chapter will address the wide-ranging *exceptions* to the basic WTO rules, allowing Members to adopt trade-restrictive legislation and measures that pursue these other societal values and interests. This chapter deals with:

- the 'general exceptions' of Article XX of the GATT 1994 and Article XIV of the GATS;
- the 'security exceptions' of Article XXI of the GATT 1994 and Article XIV *bis* of the GATS;
- the 'economic emergency exceptions' of Article XIX of the GATT 1994 and the *Agreement on Safeguards*;
- the 'regional integration exceptions' of Article XXIV:5 of the GATT 1994 and Article V of the GATS;

- the 'balance of payments exceptions' of Articles XII and XVIII:B of the GATT 1994 and Article XII of the GATS; and
- the 'economic development exceptions' of Article XVIII:A of the GATT 1994 and the 'Enabling Clause'.

These exceptions differ in scope and nature. Some allow deviation from all other GATT or GATS obligations; others allow deviation from specific obligations only; some are of indefinite duration; others temporary; some can be invoked by all Members; others only by a specific category of Members. However, while different in scope and nature, all the exceptions have something in common: they allow Members, under specific conditions, to adopt and maintain legislation and measures that protect other important societal values and interests, even though this legislation or these measures are inconsistent with substantive disciplines imposed by the GATT 1994 or the GATS. These exceptions clearly allow Members, under specific conditions, to give *priority* to certain societal values and interests *over* trade liberalisation, and its principles of non-discrimination and rules on market access.

7.2. GENERAL EXCEPTIONS UNDER THE GATT 1994

Article XX of the GATT 1994, entitled 'General Exceptions', states:

> Subject to the requirement that such measures are not applied in a manner which would constitute a means of arbitrary or unjustifiable discrimination between countries where the same conditions prevail, or a disguised restriction on international trade, nothing in this Agreement shall be construed to prevent the adoption or enforcement by any [Member] of measures:
>
> a. necessary to protect public morals;
> b. necessary to protect human, animal or plant life or health;
> c. ...
> d. necessary to secure compliance with laws or regulations which are not inconsistent with the provisions of this Agreement, including those relating to customs enforcement, the enforcement of monopolies operated under paragraph 4 of Article II and Article XVII, the protection of patents, trade marks and copyrights, and the prevention of deceptive practices;
> e. relating to the products of prison labour;
> f. imposed for the protection of national treasures of artistic, historic or archaeological value;
> g. relating to the conservation of exhaustible natural resources if such measures are made effective in conjunction with restrictions on domestic production or consumption; ...

Thus, Article XX allows for, *inter alia*, the protection of some important non-economic societal values, such as public health and the environment. Note that paragraphs (c), (h), (i) and (j) are not included above. These paragraphs relate to trade in gold and silver; obligations under international commodities agreements; efforts to ensure essential quantities of materials to a domestic processing industry; and products in general or local short supply. These paragraphs have been, and still are, of less importance in international trade law and practice than the other paragraphs of Article XX. Therefore, they are not discussed in this chapter.

7.2.1. The nature and function of Article XX of the GATT 1994

The Panel in *US – Section 337* noted, with respect to the nature and function of Article XX:

> that Article XX is entitled "General Exceptions" and that the central phrase in the introductory clause reads: "nothing in this Agreement shall be construed to prevent the adoption or enforcement ... of measures ...". Article XX(d) thus provides for a limited and conditional exception from obligations under other provisions. The Panel therefore concluded that Article XX(d) applies only to measures inconsistent with another provision of the General Agreement, and that, consequently, the application of Section 337 has to be examined first in the light of Article III:4. If any inconsistencies with Article III:4 were found, the Panel would then examine whether they could be justified under Article XX(d).[1]

In general, Article XX is relevant and will be invoked by a Member only when a measure of that Member has been found to be inconsistent with another GATT provision. In such a case, Article XX will be invoked to justify the GATT-inconsistent measure. As the Panel in *US – Section 337* noted, the central phrase in the first sentence of Article XX is that 'nothing in this Agreement shall be construed to prevent the adoption or enforcement by any Member of measures ...'. Measures satisfying the conditions set out in Article XX are thus permitted, even if they are inconsistent with other provisions of the GATT 1994. As noted by the Panel in *US – Section 337*, Article XX provides, however, for *limited and conditional exceptions* from obligations under other GATT provisions. The exceptions are 'limited' as the list of exceptions in Article XX is exhaustive. The exceptions are 'conditional' in that Article XX only provides for justification of an otherwise illegal measure when the conditions set out in Article XX – and discussed in detail below – are fulfilled. While Article XX allows Members to adopt or maintain measures promoting or protecting other important societal values, it provides an exception to, or limitation of, affirmative commitments under the GATT 1994. In this light, it is not surprising that Article XX has played a central role in many GATT and WTO disputes.

   While it could be argued that it is an accepted principle of interpretation that exceptions are to be construed narrowly (*singularia non sunt extendenda*) and that Article XX should, therefore, be construed narrowly, the Appellate Body has not adopted this approach. Instead, it has advocated in *US – Gasoline* and *US – Shrimp* a kind of balancing between the general rule and the exception. It stated, with regard to Article XX(g), the exception at issue in these cases:

---

[1] GATT Panel Report, *US – Section 337*, para. 5.9.

The context of Article XX(g) includes the provisions of the rest of the *General Agreement*, including in particular Articles I, III and XI; conversely, the context of Articles I and III and XI includes Article XX. Accordingly, the phrase "relating to the conservation of exhaustible natural resources" may not be read so expansively as seriously to subvert the purpose and object of Article III:4. Nor may Article III:4 be given so broad a reach as effectively to emasculate Article XX(g) and the policies and interests it embodies. The relationship between the affirmative commitments set out in, e.g. Articles I, III and XI, and the policies and interests embodied in the "General Exceptions" listed in Article XX, can be given meaning within the framework of the *General Agreement* and its object and purpose by a treaty interpreter only on a case-to-case basis, by careful scrutiny of the factual and legal context in a given dispute, without disregarding the words actually used by the WTO Members themselves to express their intent and purpose.[2]

Clearly, therefore, the Appellate Body considers a *narrow* interpretation of the exceptions of Article XX, i.e. the exceptions allowing for, *inter alia*, trade-restrictive measures to protect public health or the environment, to be inappropriate. The Appellate Body advocates a *balance* between trade liberalisation and other societal values.

With regard to the kind of measure that can be justified under Article XX, the Panel in *US – Shrimp* ruled that Article XX could not justify measures that 'undermine the WTO multilateral trading system'[3] and that a measure of a Member 'conditioning access to its market for a given product upon the adoption by the exporting Member of certain policies' would undermine the multilateral trading system.[4] On appeal, however, the Appellate Body categorically rejected this ruling by the Panel on the scope of measures that Article XX could justify. The Appellate Body held:

conditioning access to a Member's domestic market on whether exporting Members comply with, or adopt, a policy or policies unilaterally prescribed by the importing Member may, to some degree, be a common aspect of measures falling within the scope of one or another of the exceptions (a) to (j) of Article XX. Paragraphs (a) to (j) comprise measures that are recognized as *exceptions to substantive obligations* established in the GATT 1994, because the domestic policies embodied in such measures have been recognized as important and legitimate in character. It is not necessary to assume that requiring from exporting countries compliance with, or adoption of, certain policies (although covered in principle by one or another of the exceptions) prescribed by the importing country, renders a measure *a priori* incapable of justification under Article XX. Such an interpretation renders most, if not all, of the specific exceptions of Article XX inutile, a result abhorrent to the principles of interpretation we are bound to apply.[5]

Measures requiring that exporting countries comply with, or adopt, certain policies prescribed by the importing country are, in fact, typical of the measures that Article XX *can* justify. They are definitely not *a priori* excluded from the scope of Article XX.

To date, the Appellate Body has yet to rule whether measures that protect, or purport to protect, a societal value or interest outside the territorial jurisdiction of the Member taking the measure, can be justified under Article XX. There

---

[2] Appellate Body Report, *US – Gasoline*, 18.   [3] Panel Report, *US – Shrimp*, para. 7.44.
[4] *Ibid.*, para. 7.45.   [5] Appellate Body Report, *US – Shrimp*, para. 121.

is no explicit jurisdictional limitation in Article XX. However, the question is whether there is an *implied* jurisdictional limitation, in that Article XX cannot be invoked to protect non-economic values *outside* the territorial jurisdiction of the Member concerned. In *US – Shrimp*, a case involving an import ban on shrimp harvested through methods resulting in the incidental killing of sea turtles, the Appellate Body noted that sea turtles migrate to or traverse waters subject to the jurisdiction of the United States, and subsequently stated:

> We do not pass upon the question of whether there is an implied jurisdictional limitation in Article XX(g), and if so, the nature or extent of that limitation. We note only that in the specific circumstances of the case before us, there is a sufficient nexus between the migratory and endangered marine populations involved and the United States for purposes of Article XX(g).[6]

Questions and Assignments 7.1

When can a Member invoke Article XX of the GATT 1994? Which societal values are covered by Article XX? Give at least two examples of non-economic, societal values that are not explicitly referred to in Article XX. Does Article XX provide for an exhaustive list of grounds of exception? If so, what are the advantages and the disadvantages of such a closed-list approach? What did the Appellate Body rule in *US – Shrimp* regarding the kinds of measure that may be justified under Article XX? Are measures aimed at protecting societal values outside the territorial jurisdiction of the Member taking the measure, within the scope of application of Article XX?

7.2.2. The two-tier test under Article XX of the GATT 1994

Article XX sets out a two-tier test for determining whether a measure, otherwise inconsistent with GATT obligations, can be justified. In *US – Gasoline*, the Appellate Body stated:

> In order that the justifying protection of Article XX may be extended to it, the measure at issue must not only come under one or another of the particular exceptions – paragraphs (a) to (j) – listed under Article XX; it must also satisfy the requirements imposed by the opening clauses of Article XX. The analysis is, in other words, two-tiered: first, provisional justification by reason of characterization of the measure under Article XX(g); second, further appraisal of the same measure under the introductory clauses of Article XX.[7]

Thus, for a GATT-inconsistent measure to be justified under Article XX, it must meet:

- the requirements of one of the exceptions listed in paragraphs (a) to (j) of Article XX; *and*
- the requirements of the chapeau of Article XX.

---

[6] *Ibid.*, para. 133.   [7] Appellate Body Report, *US – Gasoline*, 22.

In *US – Shrimp*, the Appellate Body clarified the relationship between these two elements or steps of the Article XX test as follows:

> The sequence of steps indicated above in the analysis of a claim of justification under Article XX reflects, not inadvertence or random choice, but rather the fundamental structure and logic of Article XX. [...] The task of interpreting the chapeau so as to prevent the abuse or misuse of the specific exemptions provided for in Article XX is rendered very difficult, if indeed it remains possible at all, where the interpreter (like the Panel in this case) has not first identified and examined the specific exception threatened with abuse. The standards established in the chapeau are, moreover, necessarily broad in scope and reach: the prohibition of the *application* of a measure "in a manner which would constitute a means of *arbitrary* or *unjustifiable discrimination* between countries where the same conditions prevail" or "a *disguised restriction* on international trade". When applied in a particular case, the actual contours and contents of these standards will vary as the kind of measure under examination varies. What is appropriately characterizable as "arbitrary discrimination" or "unjustifiable discrimination", or as a "disguised restriction on international trade" in respect of one category of measures, need not be so with respect to another group or type of measures. The standard of "arbitrary discrimination", for example, under the chapeau may be different for a measure that purports to be necessary to protect public morals than for one relating to the products of prison labour.[8]
>
> [Emphasis added]

In examining whether a measure can be justified under Article XX, one must always examine, first, whether this measure can be provisionally justified under one of the specific exceptions listed in paragraphs (a) to (j) of Article XX and, if so, whether the application of this measure meets the requirements of the chapeau of Article XX. The following paragraphs will, therefore, first discuss the specific exceptions and their requirements provided for in Article XX before analysing the requirements of the chapeau of Article XX.

Questions and Assignments 7.2

What are the main elements of the Article XX test? Does the sequence in which the constituent elements of the Article XX test are examined matter?

7.2.3. Specific exceptions under Article XX of the GATT 1994

Article XX sets out, in paragraphs (a) to (j), specific grounds of justification for measures which are otherwise inconsistent with provisions of the GATT 1994. These grounds of justification relate, *inter alia*, to the protection of economic and non-economic societal values such as human, animal or plant life or health, exhaustible natural resources, national treasures of artistic, historic or archaeological value and public morals. Comparing the terms used in the different paragraphs of Article XX, the Appellate Body stated in *US – Gasoline*:

---

[8] Appellate Body Report, *US – Shrimp*, paras. 119–20.

> In enumerating the various categories of governmental acts, laws or regulations which WTO Members may carry out or promulgate in pursuit of differing legitimate state policies or interests outside the realm of trade liberalization, Article XX uses different terms in respect of different categories: "necessary" – in paragraphs (a), (b) and (d); "essential" – in paragraph (j); "relating to" – in paragraphs (c), (e) and (g); "for the protection of"' – in paragraph (f); "in pursuance of" – in paragraph (h); and "involving" – in paragraph (i).
>
> It does not seem reasonable to suppose that the WTO Members intended to require, in respect of each and every category, the same kind or degree of connection or relationship between the measure under appraisal and the state interest or policy sought to be promoted or realized.[9]

Thus, the paragraphs of Article XX contain different requirements regarding the relationship between the measure at issue and the societal value pursued. Some measures need to be 'necessary' for the protection or promotion of the societal value they pursue (e.g. the protection of life and health of humans, animals and plants), while for other measures it suffices that they 'relate to' the societal value they pursue (e.g. the conservation of exhaustible natural resources). Therefore the grounds of justification, and the accompanying requirements provided for in Article XX, will be examined separately.

7.2.3.1. Article XX(b): 'measures necessary to protect human, animal or plant life or health'

Article XX(b) concerns measures which are 'necessary to protect human, animal or plant life or health'. It sets out a two-tier test to determine whether a measure is *provisionally* justified under this provision. The Panel in *US – Gasoline* stated that the United States, as the party invoking Article XX(b), had to establish:

> 1. that the *policy* in respect of the measures for which the provision was invoked fell within the range of policies designed to protect human, animal or plant life or health; [and]
> 2. that the inconsistent measures for which the exception was being invoked were *necessary* to fulfil the policy objectives . . . [10]

In other words, for a GATT-inconsistent measure to be provisionally justified under Article XX(b):

- the policy objective pursued by the measure must be the protection of life or health of humans, animals or plants; and
- the measure must be necessary to fulfil that policy objective.

The first element of this test under Article XX(b) is relatively easy to apply and has not given rise to major interpretative problems. In *Thailand – Cigarettes*, for example, the Panel ruled with regard to this element of the test under Article XX(b):

---

[9] Appellate Body Report, *US – Gasoline*, 17–18.   [10] *Ibid.*, para. 6.20.

> the Panel accepted that smoking constituted a serious risk to human health and that consequently measures designed to reduce the consumption of cigarettes fell within the scope of Article XX(b).[11]

In *EC – Asbestos*, Canada appealed the Panel's finding that 'the EC have shown that the policy of prohibiting chrysotile asbestos implemented by the Decree falls within the range of policies designed to protect human life or health'.[12] However, Canada's appeal on this point was, in fact, not related to the Panel's interpretation of the first element of the Article XX(b) test. Instead, it challenged the Panel's assessment of the credibility and weight to be ascribed to the scientific evidence before it. Canada contested the conclusions drawn by the Panel both from the evidence of the scientific experts and from scientific reports before it. The Appellate Body, however, rejected this ground of appeal because it found that the Panel had remained well within the bounds of its discretion in finding that chrysotile-cement products pose a risk to human life or health.[13] Note that the policies covered by Article XX(b) include public health policies as well as environmental policies.

The second element of the test under Article XX(b), the 'necessity' requirement, is more problematic. In *Thailand – Cigarettes*, the Panel examined whether Thailand's import prohibition of cigarettes – inconsistent with Article XI of the GATT 1947 – was justified under Article XX(b), and ruled as follows:

> The Panel noted that this provision clearly allowed contracting parties to give priority to human health over trade liberalization; however, for a measure to be covered by Article XX(b) it had to be "necessary".
>
> The Panel concluded … that the import restrictions imposed by Thailand could be considered to be "necessary" in terms of Article XX(b) only if there were no alternative measure consistent with the General Agreement, or less inconsistent with it, which Thailand could reasonably be expected to employ to achieve its health policy objectives.[14]

The principal health objectives advanced by Thailand to justify its import restrictions on cigarettes were twofold: first, to ensure the quality of cigarettes by protecting the public from harmful ingredients in imported cigarettes; and, secondly, to reduce the consumption of cigarettes in Thailand. Applying its 'necessity' test defined above, the Panel in *Thailand – Cigarettes* therefore examined:

> whether the Thai concerns about the *quality* of cigarettes consumed in Thailand could be met with measures consistent, or less inconsistent, with the General Agreement. It noted that other countries had introduced strict, non-discriminatory labelling and ingredient disclosure regulations which allowed governments to control, and the public to be informed of, the content of cigarettes. A non-discriminatory regulation implemented on a national treatment basis in accordance with Article III:4 requiring complete disclosure of ingredients, coupled with a ban on unhealthy substances, would

---

[11] GATT Panel Report, *Thailand – Cigarettes*, para. 73.
[12] Panel Report, *EC – Asbestos*, para. 8.194.
[13] Appellate Body Report, *EC – Asbestos*, para. 162. On the discretionary authority of panels to assess the credibility and weight to be ascribed to the evidence before it, see above, pp. 238–40.
[14] GATT Panel Report, *Thailand – Cigarettes*, paras. 73 and 75.

be an alternative consistent with the General Agreement. The Panel considered that Thailand could reasonably be expected to take such measures to address the quality-related policy objectives it now pursues through an import ban on all cigarettes whatever their ingredients.[15]

With regard to the second health objective of the import restriction at issue, namely, the reduction of the consumption of cigarettes:

> The Panel then considered whether Thai concerns about the *quantity* of cigarettes consumed in Thailand could be met by measures reasonably available to it and consistent, or less inconsistent, with the General Agreement...
>
> ... A ban on the advertisement of cigarettes of both domestic and foreign origin would normally meet the requirements of Article III:4 [or] ... would have to be regarded as unavoidable and therefore necessary within the meaning of Article XX(b) because additional advertising rights would risk stimulating demand for cigarettes.[16]

The Panel in *Thailand – Cigarettes* thus came to the conclusion that there were in fact various measures consistent with the GATT which were reasonably available to Thailand to control the quality and quantity of cigarettes smoked and which, taken together, could achieve the health policy goals pursued by the Thai government. The import restrictions on cigarettes were therefore not 'necessary' within the meaning of Article XX(b).[17]

In short, for the Panel in *Thailand – Cigarettes*, a measure is 'necessary' within the meaning of Article XX(b) only when there exists no alternative measure that is GATT-consistent or less inconsistent, and that a Member could reasonably be expected to employ to achieve the public health objective pursued. It is clear that a Member can only be reasonably expected to employ an alternative measure when that measure is at least *as effective* in achieving the policy objective pursued.

In *US – Gasoline*, the Panel made an important clarification as to the requirement of 'necessity' under Article XX(b): it is not the necessity of the policy objective but the necessity of the disputed measure *to achieve* that objective which is at issue. The Panel stated:

> it was not the necessity of the policy goal that was to be examined, but whether or not it was necessary that imported gasoline be effectively prevented from benefiting from as favourable sales conditions as were afforded by an individual baseline tied to the producer of a product. It was the task of the Panel to address whether these inconsistent measures were necessary to achieve the policy goal under Article XX(b). It was therefore not the task of the Panel to examine the necessity of the environmental objectives of the Gasoline Rule, or of parts of the Rule that the Panel did not specifically find to be inconsistent with the General Agreement.[18]

In this case, the Panel then examined whether measures existed that were 'consistent or less inconsistent' with the GATT 1994 and 'reasonably available to the United States to further its policy objectives of protecting human, animal and plant life or health'.[19]

In *EC – Asbestos*, a dispute between Canada and the European Communities on the French ban on asbestos and asbestos products, Canada argued on appeal

---

[15] *Ibid.*, para. 77.   [16] *Ibid.*, para. 78.   [17] *Ibid.*, para. 81.
[18] Panel Report, *US – Gasoline*, para. 6.22.   [19] *Ibid.*, para. 6.25.

that the Panel erred in applying the 'necessity' test under Article XX(b) of the GATT 1994. In addressing Canada's arguments in support of its appeal, the Appellate Body clarified the 'necessity' test under Article XX(b) in three important respects.

First, the Appellate Body noted:

> it is undisputed that WTO Members have the right to determine the level of protection of health that they consider appropriate in a given situation. France has determined, and the Panel accepted,[20] that the chosen level of health protection by France is a "halt" to the spread of *asbestos*-related health risks. By prohibiting all forms of amphibole asbestos, and by severely restricting the use of chrysotile asbestos, the measure at issue is clearly designed and apt to achieve that level of health protection.[21]

It is therefore for WTO Members to determine the *level* of protection of health or the environment they consider appropriate. Other Members cannot challenge the level of protection chosen; they can only argue that the measure at issue is not 'necessary' to achieve that level of protection.

Secondly, in *EC – Asbestos*, the Appellate Body clarified the meaning of the requirement, formulated in *Thailand – Cigarettes* and *US – Gasoline*, that there is 'no alternative to the measure at issue that the Member could *reasonably* be expected to employ'. Canada asserted, before the Appellate Body, that the Panel had erred in finding that 'controlled use' is not a reasonably available alternative to the import ban on asbestos. According to Canada, an alternative measure is only excluded as a 'reasonably available' alternative if implementation of that measure is 'impossible'. The Appellate Body stated that in determining whether a suggested alternative measure is 'reasonably available', several factors must be taken into account, alongside the difficulty of implementation. The Appellate Body subsequently referred to its earlier findings on the 'necessity' test under Article XX(d) in *Korea – Various Measures on Beef*.[22] As discussed below, the interpretation by the Appellate Body in *Korea – Various Measures on Beef*, of the term 'necessary' in Article XX(d) refers to a 'range of degrees of necessity', so it may be assumed that the same is true for Article XX(b). In *EC – Asbestos*, the Appellate Body noted with respect to 'necessary' in Article XX(b):

> We indicated in *Korea – Beef* that one aspect of the "weighing and balancing process ... comprehended in the determination of whether a WTO-consistent alternative measure" is reasonably available is the extent to which the alternative measure "contributes to the realization of the end pursued". In addition, we observed, in that case, that "[t]he more vital or important [the] common interests or values" pursued, the easier it would be to accept as "necessary" measures designed to achieve those ends. In this case, the objective pursued by the measure is the preservation of human life and health through the elimination, or reduction, of the well-known, and life-threatening, health risks posed by asbestos fibres. The value pursued is both vital and important in the highest degree.[23]

---

[20] Panel Report, *EC – Asbestos*, para. 8.204.
[21] Appellate Body Report, *EC – Asbestos*, para. 168.
[22] It was held that there is no reason to interpret the 'necessity' requirement in Article XX(b) differently from that in Article XX(d) in the GATT.
[23] Appellate Body Report, *EC – Asbestos*, para. 172.

In deciding whether a measure is necessary, the Appellate Body therefore also considers the *importance* of the societal value pursued by the measure at issue, as well as the *extent* to which the alternative measure will contribute to the protection or promotion of that value.

Thirdly, instead of the requirement in *Thailand – Cigarettes* that the alternative measure needs to be GATT-consistent or less inconsistent, the Appellate Body in *EC – Asbestos* puts forward another requirement, namely, that the alternative measure must be *less trade-restrictive* than the measure at issue. In summarising the test under Article XX(b), the Appellate Body held in *EC – Asbestos*:

> The … question … is whether there is an alternative measure that would achieve the same end and that is less restrictive of trade than a prohibition.[24]

Canada, the complainant in *EC – Asbestos*, had asserted that 'controlled use' of asbestos and asbestos products represented a 'reasonably available' measure that would serve the same end than the ban on asbestos and asbestos products. The issue for the Appellate Body was, therefore, whether France could reasonably be expected to employ 'controlled use' practices to achieve its chosen level of health protection – a halt in the spread of asbestos-related health risks. The Appellate Body concluded that this was not the case. It reasoned as follows:

> In our view, France could not reasonably be expected to employ *any* alternative measure if that measure would involve a continuation of the very risk that the Decree seeks to "halt". Such an alternative measure would, in effect, prevent France from achieving its chosen level of health protection. On the basis of the scientific evidence before it, the Panel found that, in general, the efficacy of "controlled use" remains to be demonstrated. Moreover, even in cases where "controlled use" practices are applied "with greater certainty", the scientific evidence suggests that the level of exposure can, in some circumstances, still be high enough for there to be a "significant residual risk of developing asbestos-related diseases". The Panel found too that the efficacy of "controlled use" is particularly doubtful for the building industry and for DIY enthusiasts, which are the most important users of cement-based products containing chrysotile asbestos. Given these factual findings by the Panel, we believe that "controlled use" would not allow France to achieve its chosen level of health protection by halting the spread of asbestos-related health risks. "Controlled use" would, thus, not be an alternative measure that would achieve the end sought by France.[25]

Note also that the Appellate Body stated with regard to the evaluation of the 'necessity' of a measure that:

> In justifying a measure under Article XX(b) of the GATT 1994, a Member may also rely, in good faith, on scientific sources which, at that time, may represent a divergent, but qualified and respected, opinion. A Member is not obliged, in setting health policy, automatically to follow what, at a given time, may constitute a majority scientific opinion. Therefore, a panel need not, necessarily, reach a decision under Article XX(b) of the GATT 1994 on the basis of the "preponderant" weight of the evidence.[26]

---

[24] *Ibid.*   [25] *Ibid.*, para. 174.   [26] *Ibid.*, para. 178.

Questions and Assignments 7.3

Questions and Assignments 7.3

What are the constituent elements of the test under Article XX(b) of the GATT 1994? When is a measure 'necessary' within the meaning of Article XX(b)? What factors are to be taken into account in determining whether there is a 'reasonably available alternative' within the meaning of the case law on Article XX(b)? Must a Member invoking Article XX(b) justify the *level* of protection of public health or the environment it has chosen to pursue? Can a Member consider a measure to be 'necessary' to achieve a health or environmental policy objective when the prevailing view among scientists is that such a measure is *not* necessary? Briefly describe the measures at issue in *Thailand – Cigarettes* and *EC – Asbestos* and explain how the GATT panel and the Appellate Body concluded that these measures respectively were not and were provisionally justified under Article XX(b).

7.2.3.2. Article XX(d): "measures necessary to secure compliance with ..."

As mentioned above, Article XX(d) concerns and can justify measures:

> necessary to secure compliance with laws or regulations which are not inconsistent with the provisions of this Agreement, including those relating to customs enforcement, the enforcement of monopolies operated under paragraph 4 of Article II and Article XVII, the protection of patents, trade marks and copyrights, and the prevention of deceptive practices.

Article XX(d) sets out a two-tier test for the provisional justification of GATT-inconsistent measures. In *Korea – Various Measures on Beef*, a dispute concerning the regulation of retail sales of both domestic and imported beef products (the dual retail system) designed to secure compliance with a consumer protection law, the Appellate Body ruled:

> For a measure, otherwise inconsistent with GATT 1994, to be justified provisionally under paragraph (d) of Article XX, two elements must be shown. First, the measure must be one designed to "secure compliance" with laws or regulations that are not themselves inconsistent with some provision of the GATT 1994. Secondly, the measure must be "necessary" to secure such compliance. A Member who invokes Article XX(d) as a justification has the burden of demonstrating that these two requirements are met.[27]

Thus, for a GATT-inconsistent measure to be provisionally justified under Article XX(d):

- the measure must be designed to *secure compliance* with national law, such as customs law or intellectual property law, which, in itself, is not GATT-inconsistent; and
- the measure must be *necessary* to ensure compliance.

---

[27] Appellate Body Report, *Korea – Various Measures on Beef*, para. 157. See also Panel Report, *US – Gasoline*, para. 6.31.

With respect to the first element of the Article XX(d) test, namely, that the measure must be 'designed to secure compliance' with GATT-consistent laws and regulations, note that the Panel in *US – Gasoline* found that:

> maintenance of discrimination between imported and domestic gasoline contrary to Article III:4 under the baseline establishment methods did not "secure compliance" with the baseline system. These methods were not an enforcement mechanism. They were simply rules for determining the individual baselines. As such, they were not the type of measures with which Article XX(d) was concerned.[28]

With respect to the second element of the Article XX(d) test, namely, the 'necessity' test, the Appellate Body stated in *Korea – Various Measures on Beef*:

> It seems to us that a treaty interpreter assessing a measure claimed to be necessary to secure compliance of a WTO-consistent law or regulation may, in appropriate cases, take into account the relative importance of the common interests or values that the law or regulation to be enforced is intended to protect. The more vital or important those common interests or values are, the easier it would be to accept as "necessary" a measure designed as an enforcement instrument.
>
> There are other aspects of the enforcement measure to be considered in evaluating that measure as "necessary". One is the extent to which the measure contributes to the realization of the end pursued, the securing of compliance with the law or regulation at issue. The greater the contribution, the more easily a measure might be considered to be "necessary". Another aspect is the extent to which the compliance measure produces restrictive effects on international commerce, that is, in respect of a measure inconsistent with Article III:4, restrictive effects *on imported goods*. A measure with a relatively slight impact upon imported products might more easily be considered as "necessary" than a measure with intense or broader restrictive effects.[29]

The Appellate Body subsequently held in *Korea – Various Measures on Beef*:

> In sum, determination of whether a measure, which is not "indispensable", may nevertheless be "necessary" within the contemplation of Article XX(d), involves in every case a process of weighing and balancing a series of factors which prominently include the contribution made by the compliance measure to the enforcement of the law or regulation at issue, the importance of the common interests or values protected by that law or regulation, and the accompanying impact of the law or regulation on imports or exports.[30]

Thus, an evaluation of whether a measure is 'necessary', as required by the second element of the test under Article XX(d), involves, in every case, the weighing and balancing of factors such as:

- the relative importance of the common interests or values that the law or regulation to be enforced is intended to protect;
- the extent to which the measure contributes to the securing of compliance with the law or regulation at issue; and
- the extent to which the compliance measure produces restrictive effects on international trade.

---

[28] Panel Report, *US – Gasoline*, para. 6.33. The Panel referred in a footnote to GATT Panel Report, *EEC – Parts and Components*, paras. 5.12–5.18.

[29] Appellate Body Report, *Korea – Various Measures on Beef*, paras. 162–3. In *ibid*., para. 165, the Appellate Body cited GATT Panel Report, *US – Section 337*, para. 5.26.

[30] *Ibid*., para. 164.

Questions and Assignments 7.4

What are the constituent elements of the test under Article XX(d) of the GATT 1994? How does one establish whether a measure is 'necessary' within the meaning of Article XX(d)? Briefly describe the measure at issue in *Korea – Various Measures on Beef* and explain how the Appellate Body concluded that this measure was not provisionally justified under Article XX(d).

7.2.3.3. Article XX(g): 'measures relating to the conservation of exhaustible natural resources ...'

Article XX(g) concerns measures relating to the conservation of exhaustible natural resources. Article XX(g) is fundamentally important because, together with Article XX(b), it permits measures that depart from core GATT rules for environmental protection purposes.

Article XX(g) sets out a three-tier test requiring that a measure:

- relate to the *conservation of exhaustible natural resources*;
- *relate to* the conservation of exhaustible natural resources; and
- be made effective *in conjunction with* restrictions on domestic production or consumption.[31]

With respect to the first element of the test under Article XX(g), namely, that the measure must relate to the 'conservation of exhaustible natural resources', the Appellate Body, in *US – Shrimp*, adopted a broad, 'evolutionary' interpretation of the concept of 'exhaustible natural resources'. In this case, the complainants had taken the position that Article XX(g) was limited to the conservation of 'mineral' or 'non-living' natural resources. Their principal argument was rooted in the notion that 'living' natural resources are 'renewable' and therefore cannot be 'exhaustible' natural resources. The Appellate Body disagreed. It noted:

> We do not believe that "exhaustible" natural resources and "renewable" natural resources are mutually exclusive. One lesson that modern biological sciences teach us is that living species, though in principle, capable of reproduction and, in that sense, "renewable", are in certain circumstances indeed susceptible of depletion, exhaustion and extinction, frequently because of human activities. Living resources are just as "finite" as petroleum, iron ore and other non-living resources.[32]

---

[31] See above, pp. 602–3.
[32] Appellate Body Report, *US – Shrimp*, para. 128. In a footnote the Appellate Body noted that the World Commission on Environment and Development stated: 'The planet's species are under stress. There is growing scientific consensus that species are disappearing at rates never before witnessed on the planet.' World Commission on Environment and Development, *Our Common Future* (Oxford University Press, 1987), 13.

The Appellate Body further noted with regard to the appropriate interpretation of the concept of 'exhaustible natural resources':

> The words of Article XX(g), "exhaustible natural resources", were actually crafted more than 50 years ago. They must be read by a treaty interpreter in the light of contemporary concerns of the community of nations about the protection and conservation of the environment. While Article XX was not modified in the Uruguay Round, the preamble attached to the *WTO Agreement* shows that the signatories to that Agreement were, in 1994, fully aware of the importance and legitimacy of environmental protection as a goal of national and international policy. The preamble of the *WTO Agreement* – which informs not only the GATT 1994, but also the other covered agreements – explicitly acknowledges "the objective of *sustainable development*".
>
> ... From the perspective embodied in the preamble of the *WTO Agreement*, we note that the generic concept of "natural resources" in Article XX(g) is not "static" in its content or reference but is rather "by definition, evolutionary". It is, therefore, pertinent to note that modern international conventions and declarations make frequent references to natural resources as embracing both living and non-living resources.[33]

The Appellate Body thus concluded on the scope of the concept of 'exhaustible natural resources':

> Given the recent acknowledgement by the international community of the importance of concerted bilateral or multilateral action to protect living natural resources, and recalling the explicit recognition by WTO Members of the objective of sustainable development in the preamble of the *WTO Agreement*, we believe it is too late in the day to suppose that Article XX(g) of the GATT 1994 may be read as referring only to the conservation of exhaustible mineral or other non-living natural resources. Moreover, two adopted GATT 1947 panel reports previously found fish to be an "exhaustible natural resource" within the meaning of Article XX(g). We hold that, in line with the principle of effectiveness in treaty interpretation, measures to conserve exhaustible natural resources, whether *living* or *non-living*, may fall within Article XX(g).[34]

With respect to the second element of the test under Article XX(g), namely, that the measure must be a measure 'relating to' the conservation of exhaustible natural resources, the GATT Panel in *Canada – Herring and Salmon* observed that:

> Article XX(g) does not state how the trade measures are to be related to the conservation ... This raises the question of whether *any* relationship with conservation ... [is] sufficient for a trade measure to fall under Article XX(g) or whether a *particular* relationship ... [is] required
>
> ... The Panel noted that some of the subparagraphs of Article XX state that the measure must be "necessary" or "essential" to the achievement of the policy purpose set out in the provision (cf. subparagraphs (a), (b), (d) and (j)) while subparagraph (g) refers only to measures "relating to" the conservation of exhaustible natural resources. This suggests that Article XX(g) does not only cover measures that are necessary or essential for the conservation of exhaustible natural resources but a wider range of measures. However, as the preamble of Article XX indicates, the purpose of including Article XX(g) in the General Agreement was not to widen the scope for measures

---

[33] Appellate Body Report, *US – Shrimp*, paras. 129 and 130.

[34] *Ibid.*, para. 131. In a footnote, the Appellate Body also noted that the drafting history does not demonstrate an intent on the part of the framers of the GATT 1947 *to exclude* 'living' natural resources from the scope of application of Article XX(g). The Appellate Body also noted that in the GATT 1947 panel reports in *US – Canadian Tuna*, para. 4.9, and in *Canada – Herring and Salmon*, para. 4.4, fish had previously been found to be an 'exhaustible' natural resource.

> serving trade policy purposes but merely to ensure that the commitments under the General Agreement do not hinder the pursuit of policies aimed at the conservation of exhaustible natural resources. The Panel concluded for these reasons that, while a trade measure did not have to be necessary or essential to the conservation of an exhaustible natural resource, it had to be primarily aimed at the conservation of an exhaustible natural resource to be considered as "relating to" conservation within the meaning of Article XX(g).[35]

In *US – Gasoline*, the Appellate Body accepted the *Canada – Herring and Salmon* interpretation of 'relating to ... conservation' as meaning 'primarily aimed at conservation'. The Appellate Body stated in *US – Gasoline*:

> All the participants and the third participants in this appeal accept the propriety and applicability of the view of the *Herring and Salmon* report and the Panel Report that a measure must be "primarily aimed at" the conservation of exhaustible natural resources in order to fall within the scope of Article XX(g). Accordingly, we see no need to examine this point further, save, perhaps, to note that the phrase "primarily aimed at" is not itself treaty language and was not designed as a simple litmus test for inclusion or exclusion from Article XX(g).[36]

Applying this test to the baseline establishment rules for the quality of gasoline, the measure at issue in *US – Gasoline*, the Appellate Body held that these rules were 'primarily aimed at' the conservation of clean air, an exhaustible natural resource. The Appellate Body considered that:

> the baseline establishment rules cannot be regarded as merely incidentally or inadvertently aimed at the conservation of clean air in the United States for the purposes of Article XX(g).[37]

According to the Appellate Body, a 'substantial relationship' existed between the baseline establishment rules and the policy objective of preventing further deterioration of the level of air pollution.

The Appellate Body further clarified its understanding of the concept of 'relating to' the conservation of exhaustible natural resources in *US – Shrimp*. In this case, the Appellate Body stated with regard to section 609 of Public Law 101–162 Relating to the Protection of Sea Turtles in Shrimp Trawl Fishing Operations, the measure in dispute:

> In its general design and structure ... Section 609 is not a simple, blanket prohibition of the importation of shrimp imposed without regard to the consequences (or lack thereof) of the mode of harvesting employed upon the incidental capture and mortality of sea turtles. Focusing on the design of the measure here at stake, it appears to us that Section 609, *cum* implementing guidelines, is not disproportionately wide in its scope and reach in relation to the policy objective of protection and conservation of sea turtle species. The means are, in principle, reasonably related to the ends. The means and ends relationship between Section 609 and the legitimate policy of conserving an exhaustible, and, in fact, endangered species, is observably a close and real one.[38]

---

[35] GATT Panel Report, *Canada – Herring and Salmon*, paras. 4.5–4.6.
[36] Appellate Body Report, *US – Gasoline*, 18–19. In a footnote, the Appellate Body noted that the same interpretation had been applied in two recent unadopted panel reports: GATT Panel Report, *US – Tuna (EEC)* and GATT Panel Report, *US – Taxes on Automobiles*.
[37] Appellate Body Report, *US – Gasoline*, 19.
[38] Appellate Body Report, *US – Shrimp*, para. 141.

Thus, according to the Appellate Body in *US – Shrimp*, Article XX(g) requires 'a close and real' relationship between the measure and the policy objective. The means employed, i.e. the measure, must be *reasonably* related to the end pursued, i.e. the conservation of an exhaustible natural resource. A measure may not be disproportionately wide in its scope or reach in relation to the policy objective pursued.

The third element of the test under Article XX(g), namely, that the measure at issue is 'made effective in conjunction with …', has been interpreted by the Appellate Body in *US – Gasoline* as follows:

> the ordinary or natural meaning of "made effective" when used in connection with a measure – a governmental act or regulation – may be seen to refer to such measure being "operative", as "in force", or as having "come into effect". Similarly, the phrase "in conjunction with" may be read quite plainly as "together with" or "jointly with". Taken together, the second clause of Article XX(g) appears to us to refer to governmental measures like the baseline establishment rules being promulgated or brought into effect together with restrictions on domestic production or consumption of natural resources. Put in a slightly different manner, we believe that the clause "if such measures are made effective in conjunction with restrictions on domestic product or consumption" is appropriately read as a requirement that the measures concerned impose restrictions, not just in respect of imported gasoline but also with respect to domestic gasoline. The clause is a requirement of *even-handedness* in the imposition of restrictions, in the name of conservation, upon the production or consumption of exhaustible natural resources.[39]

Basically, the third element of the Article XX(g) test is a requirement of 'even-handedness' in the imposition of restrictions on imported and domestic products. Article XX(g) does *not* require imported and domestic products to be treated equally: it merely requires that they are treated in an 'even-handed' manner. The Appellate Body in *US – Gasoline* stated in this respect:

> There is, of course, no textual basis for requiring identical treatment of domestic and imported products. Indeed, where there is identity of treatment – constituting real, not merely formal, equality of treatment – it is difficult to see how inconsistency with Article III:4 would have arisen in the first place.[40]

Note that, if the requirement of 'even-handedness' is not met, it is also doubtful whether the measure at issue meets the 'primarily aimed at …' requirement of the second element of the Article XX(g) test.[41] The Appellate Body observed in *US – Gasoline*:

> if *no* restrictions on domestically-produced like products are imposed at all, and all limitations are placed upon imported products *alone*, the measure cannot be accepted as primarily or even substantially designed for implementing conservationist goals. The measure would simply be naked discrimination for protecting locally-produced goods.[42]

Applying the 'even-handedness' test to the baseline establishment rules, the measure at issue in *US – Gasoline*, the Appellate Body held as follows:

> In the present appeal, the baseline establishment rules affect both domestic gasoline and imported gasoline, providing for – generally speaking – individual baselines for

---

[39] Appellate Body Report, *US – Gasoline*, 20–1.   [40] *Ibid.*, 21.
[41] See also GATT Panel Report, *Canada – Herring and Salmon*, para. 4.7.
[42] Appellate Body Report, *US – Gasoline*, 21.

domestic refiners and blenders and statutory baselines for importers. Thus, restrictions on the consumption or depletion of clean air by regulating the domestic production of "dirty" gasoline are established jointly with corresponding restrictions with respect to imported gasoline. That imported gasoline has been determined to have been accorded "less favourable treatment" than the domestic gasoline in terms of Article III:4, is not material for purposes of analysis under Article XX(g).[43]

In *US – Gasoline*, the Appellate Body also stated that it did not believe that the third element of Article XX(g) was intended to establish an empirical 'effects test' for the availability of the Article XX(g) exception. The Appellate Body reasoned as follows:

> In the first place, the problem of determining causation, well-known in both domestic and international law, is always a difficult one. In the second place, in the field of conservation of exhaustible natural resources, a substantial period of time, perhaps years, may have to elapse before the effects attributable to implementation of a given measure may be observable. The legal characterization of such a measure is not reasonably made contingent upon occurrence of subsequent events. We are not, however, suggesting that consideration of the predictable effects of a measure is never relevant. In a particular case, should it become clear that realistically, a specific measure cannot in any possible situation have any positive effect on conservation goals, it would very probably be because that measure was not designed as a conservation regulation to begin with. In other words, it would not have been "primarily aimed at" conservation of natural resources at all.[44]

In *US – Shrimp*, the Appellate Body confirmed its approach to the third element of the Article XX(g) test and stated as follows:

> We earlier noted that Section 609, enacted in 1989, addresses the mode of harvesting of imported shrimp only. However, two years earlier, in 1987, the United States issued regulations pursuant to the Endangered Species Act requiring all United States shrimp trawl vessels to use approved TEDs [turtle excluder devices], or to restrict the duration of tow-times, in specified areas where there was significant incidental mortality of sea turtles in shrimp trawls. These regulations became fully effective in 1990 and were later modified. They now require United States shrimp trawlers to use approved TEDs "in areas and at times when there is a likelihood of intercepting sea turtle", with certain limited exceptions. Penalties for violation of the Endangered Species Act, or the regulations issued thereunder, include civil and criminal sanctions. The United States government currently relies on monetary sanctions and civil penalties for enforcement. The government has the ability to seize shrimp catch from trawl vessels fishing in United States waters and has done so in cases of egregious violations. We believe that, in principle, Section 609 is an even-handed measure.[45]

Questions and Assignments 7.5

What are the constituent elements of the test under Article XX(g) of the GATT 1994? How has the Appellate Body interpreted the concept of 'exhaustible natural resources'? Pursuant to Article XX(g), what kind of relationship must exist between the measure at issue and the environmental conservation policy objective pursued? When does a Member meet the requirement of Article XX(g) that 'measures are made

[43] *Ibid.*   [44] *Ibid.*, 21–2.   [45] Appellate Body Report, *US – Shrimp*, para. 144.

effective in conjunction with restrictions on domestic production or consumption'? Must a Member impose identical conservation measures on imported and domestic products? What if a Member imposes restrictions on domestic production or consumption, but does not enforce these at all? Briefly describe the measures at issue in *US – Gasoline* and *US – Shrimp* and explain how the Appellate Body concluded that these measures were provisionally justified under Article XX(g).

7.2.3.4. *Other paragraphs of Article XX*

Among the other possible exceptions for measures protecting or promoting non-economic values provided for in Article XX, note in particular Article XX(a), which concerns measures necessary for the protection of public morals. Just as Members are free to determine, each for themselves, their appropriate level of protection of public health in the context of Article XX(b),[46] they should also be free to determine their public morals. Public morals will therefore differ from Member to Member; what is morally acceptable in one Member is not necessarily so in another. Arguably, public morals can be invoked as a ground for justification by a Member adopting or maintaining an import ban on products of child labour, on alcoholic beverages, on pornographic materials and on blood diamonds.[47] To be provisionally justified, the measure must be 'necessary' to protect the public morals of the Member taking the measure. The interpretation of the term 'necessary' within the meaning of Article XX(b) and (d), as discussed above, will undoubtedly be of relevance in the context of Article XX(a).[48]

Article XX(e) concerns measures 'relating to' the products of prison labour. On this basis, Members can, for example, ban the importation of goods that have been produced by prisoners.

Finally, Article XX(f) concerns measures 'imposed for' the protection of national treasures of artistic, historic or archaeological value. It allows Members to adopt or maintain trade-restrictive measures for the protection of national treasures. Note that Article XX(f) does not require that these measures are 'necessary' for the protection of national treasures.

7.2.4. **The chapeau of Article XX of the GATT 1994**

As discussed above, Article XX sets out a two-tier test for determining whether a measure, otherwise inconsistent with GATT obligations, can be justified. First, a measure must meet the requirements of one of the particular exceptions listed in the paragraphs of Article XX. Secondly, that measure must meet the requirements of the chapeau of Article XX.

---

[46] See above, pp. 605–6.
[47] 'Blood diamonds' are diamonds of which the sales revenue is used to finance civil war.
[48] See above, pp. 604–7, 609.

The legal requirements imposed by the chapeau of Article XX of the GATT 1994 have been highly relevant in dispute settlement practice. Several of the most controversial decisions by panels and the Appellate Body have turned on these standards. The chapeau of Article XX, with regard to measures provisionally justified under one of the paragraphs of Article XX, imposes:

> the requirement that such measures are not applied in a manner which would constitute a means of arbitrary or unjustifiable discrimination between countries where the same conditions prevail, or a disguised restriction on international trade.

7.2.4.1. Object and purpose of the chapeau of Article XX

With respect to the object and purpose of the chapeau of Article XX, the Appellate Body ruled in *US – Gasoline*:

> The chapeau by its express terms addresses, not so much the questioned measure or its specific contents as such, but rather the manner in which that measure is applied. It is, accordingly, important to underscore that the purpose and object of the introductory clauses of Article XX is generally the prevention of "abuse of the exceptions of [what was later to become] Article [XX]". This insight drawn from the drafting history of Article XX is a valuable one. The chapeau is animated by the principle that while the exceptions of Article XX may be invoked as a matter of legal right, they should not be so applied as to frustrate or defeat the legal obligations of the holder of the right under the substantive rule of the *General Agreement*. If those exceptions are not to be abused or misused, in other words, the measures falling within the particular exceptions must be applied reasonably, with due regard both to the legal duties of the party claiming the exception and the legal rights of the other parties concerned.[49]

In short, the object and purpose of the chapeau of Article XX is to avoid the possibility that the application of provisionally justified measures would constitute a misuse or abuse of the exceptions of Article XX.

Further, in *US – Shrimp*, the Appellate Body stated with regard to the chapeau:

> we consider that it embodies the recognition on the part of WTO Members of the need to maintain a balance of rights and obligations between the right of a Member to invoke one or another of the exceptions of Article XX, specified in paragraphs (a) to (j), on the one hand, and the substantive rights of the other Members under the GATT 1994, on the other hand. Exercise by one Member of its right to invoke an exception, such as Article XX(g), if abused or misused, will, to that extent, erode or render naught the substantive treaty rights in, for example, Article XI:1, of other Members. Similarly, because the GATT 1994 itself makes available the exceptions of Article XX, in recognition of the legitimate nature of the policies and interests there embodied, the right to invoke one of those exceptions is not to be rendered illusory.[50]

According to the Appellate Body, a balance must be struck between the *right* of a Member to invoke an exception under Article XX and the *duty* of that same Member to respect the treaty rights of the other Members. The chapeau

---

[49] Appellate Body Report, *US – Gasoline*, 22. In a footnote the Appellate Body referred to GATT Panel Report, *US – Spring Assemblies*, para. 56, and to EPCT/C. 11/50, 7.
[50] Appellate Body Report, *US – Shrimp*, 156. In a footnote to the following paragraph, the Appellate Body referred to GATT Panel Report, *US – Section 337*, para. 5.9.

was inserted at the head of the list of 'General Exceptions' in Article XX to ensure that this balance is struck and to prevent abuse. The Appellate Body held in *US – Shrimp*:

> In our view, the language of the chapeau makes clear that each of the exceptions in paragraphs (a) to (j) of Article XX is a *limited and conditional* exception from the substantive obligations contained in the other provisions of the GATT 1994, that is to say, the ultimate availability of the exception is subject to the compliance by the invoking Member with the requirements of the chapeau.[51]

According to the Appellate Body, the chapeau of Article XX is an expression of the principle of good faith, a general principle of law as well as a general principle of international law, which controls the exercise of rights by States. As the Appellate Body held:

> One application of this general principle, the application widely known as the doctrine of *abus de droit*, prohibits the abusive exercise of a State's rights and enjoins that, whenever the assertion of a right "impinges on the field covered by [a] treaty obligation, it must be exercised bona fide, that is to say, reasonably". An abusive exercise by a Member of its own treaty right thus results in a breach of the treaty rights of the other Members, and, as well, a violation of the treaty obligation of the Member so acting.[52]

In light of the above, the Appellate Body came to the following conclusion in *US – Shrimp* with respect to the interpretation and application of the chapeau:

> The task of interpreting and applying the chapeau is, hence, essentially the delicate one of locating and marking out a line of equilibrium between the right of a Member to invoke an exception under Article XX and the rights of the other Members under varying substantive provisions (e.g. Article XI) of the GATT 1994, so that neither of the competing rights will cancel out the other and thereby distort and nullify or impair the balance of rights and obligations constructed by the Members themselves in that Agreement. The location of the line of equilibrium, as expressed in the chapeau, is not fixed and unchanging; the line moves as the kind and the shape of the measures at stake vary and as the facts making up specific cases differ.[53]

In short, the interpretation and application of the chapeau in a particular case is a search for the appropriate *line of equilibrium* between the right of Members to adopt and maintain trade-restrictive legislation and measures that pursue certain legitimate societal values or interests *and* the right of other Members to trade. The search for this line of equilibrium is guided by the requirements set out in the chapeau that the application of the trade-restrictive measure may not constitute:

- either 'arbitrary or unjustifiable discrimination between countries where the same conditions prevail';
- or 'a disguised restriction on international trade'.

The following sections examine these requirements of the chapeau in more detail.

---

[51] Appellate Body Report, *US – Shrimp*, para. 157.   [52] *Ibid.*, para. 158.
[53] *Ibid.*, para. 159.

7.2.4.2. 'Arbitrary or unjustifiable discrimination between countries where the same conditions prevail'

For a measure to be justified under Article XX, the application of that measure, pursuant to the chapeau of Article XX, should *not* constitute 'arbitrary or unjustifiable discrimination between countries where the same conditions prevail'. In *US – Gasoline*, the Appellate Body found that the 'discrimination' at issue in the chapeau of Article XX must necessarily be different from the discrimination addressed in other provisions of the GATT 1994, such as Articles I and III. The Appellate Body stated:

> The enterprise of applying Article XX would clearly be an unprofitable one if it involved no more than applying the standard used in finding that the baseline establishment rules were inconsistent with Article III:4. That would also be true if the finding were one of inconsistency with some other substantive rule of the *General Agreement*. The provisions of the chapeau cannot logically refer to the same standard(s) by which a violation of a substantive rule has been determined to have occurred. To proceed down that path would be both to empty the chapeau of its contents and to deprive the exceptions in paragraphs (a) to (j) of meaning. Such recourse would also confuse the question of whether inconsistency with a substantive rule existed, with the further and separate question arising under the chapeau of Article XX as to whether that inconsistency was nevertheless justified.[54]

As the Appellate Body noted, the chapeau of Article XX does not prohibit discrimination *per se*, but rather, *arbitrary* and *unjustifiable* discrimination.

Furthermore, the Appellate Body, in *US – Gasoline*, addressed the meaning of the words 'discrimination *between countries* where the same conditions prevail'. The Appellate Body found that these words refer not only to discrimination *between exporting countries* where the same conditions prevail but also to discrimination *between an importing country and an exporting country* where the same conditions prevail.[55]

In *US – Gasoline* the Appellate Body concluded that the measure at issue constituted 'unjustifiable discrimination' for the following reasons:

> We have above located two omissions on the part of the United States: to explore adequately means, including in particular cooperation with the governments of Venezuela and Brazil, of mitigating the administrative problems relied on as justification by the United States for rejecting individual baselines for foreign refiners; and to count the costs for foreign refiners that would result from the imposition of statutory baselines. In our view, these two omissions go well beyond what was necessary for the Panel to determine that a violation of Article III:4 had occurred in the first place. The resulting discrimination must have been foreseen, and was not merely inadvertent or unavoidable. In the light of the foregoing, our conclusion is that the baseline establishment rules in the Gasoline Rule, in their application, constitute "unjustifiable discrimination".[56]

The Appellate Body therefore decided that the application of the measure at issue constituted unjustifiable discrimination because the discrimination resulting from the measure at issue 'must have been foreseen', i.e. it was

---

[54] Appellate Body Report, *US – Gasoline*, 23.   [55] *Ibid.*   [56] *Ibid.*, 28–9.

deliberate. The discrimination was 'unjustifiable' because it 'was not merely inadvertent or unavoidable'.

In *US – Shrimp*, the Appellate Body found that, in order for a measure to be applied in a manner which would constitute 'arbitrary or unjustifiable discrimination between countries where the same conditions prevail', three elements must exist:

> First, the application of the measure must result in *discrimination*. As we stated in *United States – Gasoline*, the nature and quality of this discrimination is different from the discrimination in the treatment of products which was already found to be inconsistent with one of the substantive obligations of the GATT 1994, such as Articles I, III or XI. Second, the discrimination must be *arbitrary* or *unjustifiable* in character … Third, this discrimination must occur *between countries where the same conditions prevail*. In *United States – Gasoline*, we accepted the assumption of the participants in that appeal that such discrimination could occur not only between different exporting Members, but also between exporting Members and the importing Member concerned.[57]

Applying and extending this test, the Appellate Body in *US – Shrimp* came to the following conclusions:

> It may be quite acceptable for a government, in adopting and implementing a domestic policy, to adopt a single standard applicable to all its citizens throughout that country. However, it is not acceptable, in international trade relations, for one WTO Member to use an economic embargo to *require* other Members to adopt essentially the same comprehensive regulatory program, to achieve a certain policy goal, as that in force within that Member's territory, *without* taking into consideration different conditions which may occur in the territories of those other Members.
>
> We believe that discrimination results not only when countries in which the same conditions prevail are differently treated, but also when the application of the measure at issue does not allow for any inquiry into the appropriateness of the regulatory program for the conditions prevailing in those exporting countries.
>
> Section 609, in its application, imposes a single, rigid and unbending requirement that countries applying for certification … adopt a comprehensive regulatory program that is essentially the same as the United States' program, without inquiring into the appropriateness of that program for the conditions prevailing in the exporting countries. Furthermore, there is little or no flexibility in how officials make the determination for certification pursuant to these provisions. In our view, this rigidity and inflexibility also constitute "arbitrary discrimination" within the meaning of the chapeau.[58]

The Appellate Body thus decided that discrimination may also result when the same measure is applied on countries where different conditions prevail. When a measure is applied without any regard for the difference in conditions between countries and this measure is applied in a rigid and inflexible manner, the discrimination may constitute 'arbitrary discrimination' within the meaning of the chapeau of Article XX.

To implement the recommendations and rulings in *US – Shrimp*, the United States modified the measure at issue in this case. Malaysia challenged the WTO consistency of the implementing measure before an Article 21.5 panel. This Panel in *US – Shrimp (Article 21.5 – Malaysia)* concluded that, unlike the

---

[57] Appellate Body Report, *US – Shrimp*, para. 150.   [58] *Ibid.*, paras. 164, 165 and 177.

original US measure, the implementing measure was justified under Article XX and thus WTO-consistent. In the appeal from this Panel report, the Appellate Body held:

> In our view, there is an important difference between conditioning market access on the adoption of essentially the same programme, and conditioning market access on the adoption of a programme *comparable in effectiveness*. Authorizing an importing Member to condition market access on exporting Members putting in place regulatory programmes *comparable in effectiveness* to that of the importing Member gives sufficient latitude to the exporting Member with respect to the programme it may adopt to achieve the level of effectiveness required. It allows the exporting Member to adopt a regulatory programme that is suitable to the specific conditions prevailing in its territory. As we see it, the Panel correctly reasoned and concluded that conditioning market access on the adoption of a programme *comparable in effectiveness*, allows for sufficient flexibility in the application of the measure so as to avoid "arbitrary or unjustifiable discrimination".[59]

The Appellate Body found in *US – Shrimp (Article 21.5 – Malaysia)* that the revised US measure at issue in the implementation dispute was sufficiently flexible to meet the standards of the chapeau.[60] The Appellate Body added:

> a measure should be designed in such a manner that there is sufficient flexibility to take into account the specific conditions prevailing in *any* exporting Member, including, of course, Malaysia. Yet this is not the same as saying that there must be specific provisions in the measure aimed at addressing specifically the particular conditions prevailing in *every individual* exporting Member. Article XX of the GATT 1994 does not require a Member to anticipate and provide explicitly for the specific conditions prevailing and evolving in *every individual* Member.[61]

The Appellate Body in *US – Shrimp* also addressed the question of whether the application of the measure at issue constituted an '*unjustifiable* discrimination' within the meaning of the chapeau. The Appellate Body noted the following:

> Another aspect of the application of Section 609 that bears heavily in any appraisal of justifiable or unjustifiable discrimination is the failure of the United States to engage the appellees, as well as other Members exporting shrimp to the United States, in serious, across-the-board negotiations with the objective of concluding bilateral or multilateral agreements for the protection and conservation of sea turtles, before enforcing the import prohibition against the shrimp exports of those other Members.[62]

The Appellate Body made three observations in this respect. First, the Congress of the United States expressly recognised in enacting Section 609 the importance of securing international agreements for the protection and conservation of the sea turtle species. Secondly, the protection and conservation of highly migratory species of sea turtle, i.e., the very policy objective of the measure, demands concerted and cooperative efforts on the part of the many countries whose waters are traversed in the course of recurrent sea turtle migrations. The need for, and the appropriateness of, such efforts have been

---

[59] Appellate Body Report, *US – Shrimp (Article 21.5 – Malaysia)*, para. 144.
[60] *Ibid.*, paras. 145–8.   [61] *Ibid.*, para. 149.
[62] Appellate Body Report, *US – Shrimp*, para. 166.

recognised in the WTO itself as well as in a significant number of other international instruments and declarations.[63] Thirdly, the United States negotiated and concluded *one* regional international agreement for the protection and conservation of sea turtles: the Inter-American Convention.[64] The existence of the Inter-American Convention provided convincing demonstration that an alternative course of action was reasonably open to the United States for securing the legitimate policy goal of its measure, a course of action other than the unilateral and non-consensual procedures of the import prohibition under Section 609. The record does not, however, show that serious efforts were made by the United States to negotiate similar agreements with any other country or group of countries. Finally, the record also does not show that the United States attempted to have recourse to such international mechanisms that exist to achieve cooperative efforts to protect and conserve sea turtles before imposing the import ban.[65] The Appellate Body therefore concluded:

> Clearly, the United States negotiated seriously with some, but not with other Members (including the appellees), that export shrimp to the United States. The effect is plainly discriminatory and, in our view, unjustifiable. The unjustifiable nature of this discrimination emerges clearly when we consider the cumulative effects of the failure of the United States to pursue negotiations for establishing consensual means of protection and conservation of the living marine resources here involved.[66]

As the Appellate Body noted, the principal consequence of the failure to pursue negotiations may be seen in the resulting unilateralism evident in the application of Section 609:

> As we have emphasized earlier, the policies relating to the necessity for use of particular kinds of TEDs in various maritime areas, and the operating details of these policies, are all shaped by the Department of State, without the participation of the exporting Members. The system and processes of certification are established and administered by the United States agencies alone. The decision-making involved in the grant, denial or withdrawal of certification to the exporting Members, is, accordingly, also unilateral. The unilateral character of the application of Section 609 heightens the disruptive and discriminatory influence of the import prohibition and underscores its unjustifiability.[67]

The extent to which a Member has to seek a multilateral solution to a problem before it may address the problem by unilateral measures was one of the main issues in *US – Shrimp (Article 21.5 – Malaysia)*. The Appellate Body made it clear that, in order to meet the requirement of the chapeau of Article XX, the Member needs to make serious efforts, in good faith, to negotiate a multilateral solution before resorting to unilateral measures.[68] Failure to do so may lead to the conclusion that the discrimination is 'unjustifiable'.

---

[63] The Appellate Body made reference to the Decision on Trade and Environment, the Rio Declaration on Environment and Development and Agenda 21, and the Convention on the Conservation of Migratory Species of Wild Animals.

[64] Appellate Body Report, *US – Shrimp*, para. 169.

[65] The United States, for example, did not make any attempt to raise the issue of sea turtle mortality due to shrimp trawling in the CITES Standing Committee as a subject requiring concerted action by States.

[66] Appellate Body Report, *US – Shrimp*, para. 172.   [67] *Ibid.*

[68] Appellate Body Report, *US – Shrimp (Article 21.5 – Malaysia)*, paras. 115–34.

Finally, the Appellate Body noted in *US – Shrimp* that the application of the US measures also resulted in other differential treatment among various countries desiring certification, for example, by granting different countries different phasing-in periods to comply with the US requirements.[69] The Appellate Body concluded:

> When the foregoing differences in the means of application of Section 609 to various shrimp exporting countries are considered in their cumulative effect, we find, and so hold, that those differences in treatment constitute "unjustifiable discrimination" between exporting countries desiring certification in order to gain access to the United States shrimp market within the meaning of the chapeau of Article XX.[70]

7.2.4.3. 'Disguised restriction on international trade'

With respect to the requirement that the application of the measure at issue does not constitute a 'disguised restriction on international trade', the Appellate Body stated in *US – Gasoline*:

> "Arbitrary discrimination", "unjustifiable discrimination" and "disguised restriction" on international trade may, accordingly, be read side-by-side; they impart meaning to one another. It is clear to us that "disguised restriction" includes disguised *discrimination* in international trade. It is equally clear that *concealed* or *unannounced* restriction or discrimination in international trade does *not* exhaust the meaning of "disguised restriction". We consider that "disguised restriction", whatever else it covers, may properly be read as embracing restrictions amounting to arbitrary or unjustifiable discrimination in international trade taken under the guise of a measure formally within the terms of an exception listed in Article XX.[71]

According to the Appellate Body in *US – Gasoline*:

> the kinds of considerations pertinent in deciding whether the application of a particular measure amounts to "arbitrary or unjustifiable discrimination", may also be taken into account in determining the presence of a "disguised restriction" on international trade. The fundamental theme is to be found in the purpose and object of avoiding abuse or illegitimate use of the exceptions to substantive rules available in Article XX.[72]

The Panel in *EC – Asbestos* further clarified the requirement of the chapeau that the application of the measure at issue does not constitute a 'disguised restriction on international trade' as follows:

> a restriction which formally meets the requirements of Article XX(b) will constitute an abuse if such compliance is in fact only a disguise to conceal the pursuit of trade-restrictive objectives. However, as the Appellate Body acknowledged in *Japan – Alcoholic Beverages*, the aim of a measure may not be easily ascertained. Nevertheless, we note that, in the same case, the Appellate Body suggested that the protective application of a measure can most often be discerned from its design, architecture and revealing structure.[73]

---

[69] Appellate Body Report, *US – Shrimp*, paras. 173–5.   [70] *Ibid.*, para. 176.
[71] Appellate Body Report, *US – Gasoline*, 25.   [72] *Ibid.*
[73] Panel Report, *EC – Asbestos*, para. 8.236. In a footnote, the Panel noted that '[a]lthough this approach was developed in relation to Article III:4 of the GATT 1994, we see no reason why it should not be applicable in other circumstances where it is necessary to determine whether a measure is being applied for protective purposes'.

The Panel in *US – Shrimp (Article 21.5 – Malaysia)* took the same approach.[74] In short, a measure which is provisionally justified under Article XX, will be considered to constitute 'a disguised restriction on international trade' if the design, architecture or structure of the measure at issue reveals that this measure does not pursue the legitimate policy objective on which the provisional justification was based but, in fact, pursues trade-restrictive, i.e. protectionist, objectives. Such a measure cannot be justified under Article XX.

Questions and Assignments 7.6

What is the object and purpose of the chapeau of Article XX? When is discrimination 'arbitrary or unjustifiable' within the meaning of Article XX? Which types of discrimination do the words 'discrimination *between countries* where the same conditions prevail' refer to? The Appellate Body in *US – Shrimp* observed that different conditions occurred in Members other than the US. Nevertheless it found unjustifiable and arbitrary discrimination. Can you explain this? What is 'a disguised restriction in international trade' within the meaning of the chapeau of Article XX? Briefly describe the measures at issue in *US – Gasoline* and *US – Shrimp* and discuss why the Appellate Body found that these measures did not meet the requirements of the chapeau of Article XX. How should the US redefine its measures condemned in *US – Gasoline* in order to comply with the requirements of the chapeau? According to the Appellate Body in *US – Shrimp (Article 21.5)*, what are 'serious, good faith efforts to negotiate a multilateral solution'?

7.2.5. Scope for Members to protect other societal values

In two prominent WTO disputes involving the protection of the environment, *US – Gasoline* and *US – Shrimp*, the measures at issue were found provisionally justified under Article XX(g) but the application of the measures failed to satisfy the requirements of the chapeau of Article XX. The public perception of the Appellate Body reports in these disputes has been negative and unsympathetic. In particular, there is a widely held view among environmental activists, that the WTO undermines necessary environmental legislation. It is noteworthy in this respect that the Appellate Body, with great foresight, but only with relative success, added a paragraph at the end of both its report in *US – Gasoline* and its report in *US – Shrimp*, explaining, in straightforward language, the scope for Members to enact environmental legislation and the limited nature of their rulings in both cases. In *US – Gasoline*, the Appellate Body concluded by stating:

> It is of some importance that the Appellate Body point out what this does *not* mean. It does not mean, or imply, that the ability of any WTO Member to take measures to control air pollution or, more generally, to protect the environment, is at issue. That would be to ignore the fact that Article XX of the *General Agreement* contains provisions

---

designed to permit important state interests – including the protection of human health, as well as the conservation of exhaustible natural resources – to find expression. The provisions of Article XX were not changed as a result of the Uruguay Round of Multilateral Trade Negotiations. Indeed, in the preamble to the *WTO Agreement* and in the *Decision on Trade and Environment*, there is specific acknowledgement to be found about the importance of coordinating policies on trade and the environment. WTO Members have a large measure of autonomy to determine their own policies on the environment (including its relationship with trade), their environmental objectives and the environmental legislation they enact and implement. So far as concerns the WTO, that autonomy is circumscribed only by the need to respect the requirements of the *General Agreement* and the other covered agreements.[75]

In *US – Shrimp*, the Appellate Body concluded with the following observation:

In reaching these conclusions, we wish to underscore what we have *not* decided in this appeal. We have *not* decided that the protection and preservation of the environment is of no significance to the Members of the WTO. Clearly, it is. We have *not* decided that the sovereign nations that are Members of the WTO cannot adopt effective measures to protect endangered species, such as sea turtles. Clearly, they can and should. And we have *not* decided that sovereign states should not act together bilaterally, plurilaterally or multilaterally, either within the WTO or in other international fora, to protect endangered species or to otherwise protect the environment. Clearly, they should and do.

What we *have* decided in this appeal is simply this: although the measure of the United States in dispute in this appeal serves an environmental objective that is recognized as legitimate under paragraph (g) of Article XX of the GATT 1994, this measure has been applied by the United States in a manner which constitutes arbitrary and unjustifiable discrimination between Members of the WTO, contrary to the requirements of the chapeau of Article XX. For all of the specific reasons outlined in this Report, this measure does not qualify for the exemption that Article XX of the GATT 1994 affords to measures which serve certain recognized, legitimate environmental purposes but which, at the same time, are not applied in a manner that constitutes a means of arbitrary or unjustifiable discrimination between countries where the same conditions prevail or a disguised restriction on international trade. As we emphasized in *United States – Gasoline*, WTO Members are free to adopt their own policies aimed at protecting the environment as long as, in so doing, they fulfill their obligations and respect the rights of other Members under the *WTO Agreement*.[76]

Questions and Assignments 7.7

How much freedom does the GATT 1994 leave WTO Members to define and pursue environmental policy objectives? Do you consider the environmentalist criticism of the decisions in *US – Gasoline* and *US – Shrimp* justified?

7.3. GENERAL EXCEPTIONS UNDER THE GATS

Like the GATT 1994, the GATS also provides for a 'general exceptions' provision allowing for Members to deviate, under certain conditions, from obligations

---

[75] Appellate Body Report, *US – Gasoline*, 29–30.
[76] Appellate Body Report, *US – Shrimp*, paras. 185 and 186.

and commitments under the GATS. Article XIV of the GATS provides, in relevant part:

> Subject to the requirement that such measures are not applied in a manner which would constitute a means of arbitrary or unjustifiable discrimination between countries where like conditions prevail, or a disguised restriction on trade in services, nothing in this Agreement shall be construed to prevent the adoption or enforcement by any Member of measures:
>
> a. necessary to protect public morals or to maintain public order;
> b. necessary to protect human, animal or plant life or health;
> c. necessary to secure compliance with laws or regulations which are not inconsistent with the provisions of this Agreement including those relating to:
>   i. the prevention of deceptive and fraudulent practices or to deal with the effects of a default on services contracts;
>   ii. the protection of the privacy of individuals in relation to the processing and dissemination of personal data and the protection of confidentiality of individual records and accounts;
>   iii. safety;
> d. inconsistent with Article XVII, provided that the difference in treatment is aimed at ensuring the equitable or effective imposition or collection of direct taxes in respect of services or service suppliers of other Members;
> e. inconsistent with Article II, provided that the difference in treatment is the result of an agreement on the avoidance of double taxation or provisions on the avoidance of double taxation in any other international agreement or arrangement by which the Member is bound.

The similarities between Article XX of the GATT 1994 and Article XIV of the GATS are striking. However, there are also differences. As with Article XX of the GATT 1994, Article XIV of the GATS sets out a two-tier test for determining whether a measure, otherwise inconsistent with GATS obligations and commitments, can be justified. To determine whether a measure can be justified under Article XIV of the GATS, it must be examined:

- first, whether this measure can provisionally be justified under one of the specific exceptions under the paragraphs (a) to (e) of Article XIV; and, if so
- secondly, whether the application of this measure meets the requirements of the chapeau of Article XIV.

This section therefore, first, discusses the specific exceptions provided for in Article XIV, and, secondly, analyses the requirements of the chapeau of Article XX.

7.3.1. Specific exceptions under Article XIV of the GATS

Article XIV of the GATS sets out, in paragraphs (a) to (e), specific grounds for justification for measures which are otherwise inconsistent with provisions of the GATS. These grounds of justification relate, *inter alia*, to:

- the protection of public morals;
- the maintenance of public order;
- the protection of human, animal or plant life or health;
- the prevention of deceptive and fraudulent practices;

- the protection of the privacy of individuals; and
- the equitable or effective imposition or collection of direct taxes.

Note that the 'protection of public order', the 'protection of the privacy of individuals' and the 'equitable or effective imposition or collection of direct taxes' are not, or at least not explicitly, mentioned as possible grounds of justification under Article XX of the GATT 1994. With regard to the 'protection of public order', footnote 5 to Article XIV(a) of the GATS states:

> The public order exception may be invoked only where a genuine and sufficiently serious threat is posed to one of the fundamental interests of society.

Note that the grounds for justification set out in paragraphs (d) and (e) of Article XIV of the GATS *only* justify inconsistency with the national treatment obligation (Article XVII) or the MFN treatment obligation (Article II) respectively. With regard to measures relating to direct taxation, Article XIV(d) of the GATS allows Members to adopt or enforce measures which are inconsistent with the national treatment obligation of Article XVII:

> provided that the difference in treatment is aimed at ensuring the equitable or effective imposition or collection of direct taxes in respect of services or service suppliers of other Members.[77]

Footnote 6 to Article XIV(d) contains a non-exhaustive list of measures that are aimed at ensuring the equitable or effective imposition or collection of direct taxes. This list includes, for example:

- measures taken by a Member under its taxation system which apply to non-residents in order to ensure the imposition or collection of taxes in the Member's territory; and
- measures taken by a Member under its taxation system which apply to non-residents or residents to prevent the avoidance or evasion of taxes, including compliance measures.

Article XIV(e) of the GATS allows a Member to adopt or enforce measures which are inconsistent with the MFN treatment obligation of Article II:

> provided that the difference in treatment is the result of an agreement on the avoidance of double taxation or provisions on the avoidance of double taxation in any other international agreement or arrangement by which the Member is bound.

To be provisionally justified under the exceptions listed in paragraphs (a), (b) and (c) of Article XIV, a measure must be *necessary* to achieve the policy objective pursued. No such requirement of necessity exists under paragraphs (d) and (e). To date, there has been no case law on the meaning of this requirement of necessity. However, it may be assumed that the extensive case law on the necessity requirement of Article XX(b) and (d) of the GATT 1994 – discussed at length above – is relevant to the interpretation of the necessity requirement

---

[77] Article XIV(d) of the GATS. Footnote 6 to Article XIV(d).

of Article XIV(a) to (c) of the GATS.[78] Recall that, in determining whether a measure is 'necessary', factors taken into consideration include:

- the importance of the common interests or values protected by the measure;
- the extent to which the measure contributes to the protection of the common interests or values at issue; and
- the impact of that measure on trade.[79]

Determining whether a measure is 'necessary' to protect the public policy objectives mentioned in paragraphs (a) to (c) requires a weighing and balancing of the evidence establishing a connection between the measure and the public policy objective it seeks to protect.[80]

Questions and Assignments 7.8

In what way do the exceptions of Article XIV of the GATS differ from the exceptions of Article XX of the GATT 1994? How does one determine whether a measure is 'necessary' within the meaning of Article XIV(a), (b) and (c) of the GATS? Discuss the measures relating to direct taxes, which Members are allowed to take under Article XIV of the GATS.

7.3.2. The chapeau of Article XIV of the GATS

As discussed above, Article XIV of the GATS sets out a two-tier test for determining whether a measure, otherwise inconsistent with GATS obligations, can be justified. Under this test, once it has been established that the measure at issue meets the requirements of one of the particular exceptions of paragraphs (a) to (e), it must be examined whether the measure meets the requirements of the chapeau of Article XIV. The chapeau of Article XIV requires that the *application* of the measure at issue does not constitute:

- either 'arbitrary or unjustifiable discrimination between countries where the same conditions prevail';
- or 'a disguised restriction on trade in services'.

To date, there has been no case law on the application of the chapeau of Article XIV. Note, however, that the language of the chapeau of Article XIV of the GATS is almost identical to that of the chapeau of Article XX of the GATT 1994. Therefore, many lessons can be drawn from the extensive case law on the application of the chapeau of Article XX, discussed in detail above.[81] On the basis of this Article XX case law, it can certainly be stated that the object and purpose of the chapeau of Article XIV of the GATS is to avoid the result that the application of the provisionally justified measures constitutes a misuse

---

[78] See above, pp. 604–7, 609.   [79] See above, p. 609.   [80] See above, pp. 604–7, 609.
[81] See above, pp. 615–23.

or abuse of the exceptions of Article XIV. A balance must be struck between the *right* of a Member to invoke an exception under Article XIV and the *duty* of that same Member to respect the treaty rights of the other Members. The chapeau was inserted at the head of the list of 'General Exceptions' in Article XIV to ensure that this balance is struck and to prevent abuse.[82]

Questions and Assignments 7.9

In what way does the chapeau of Article XIV of the GATS differ from the chapeau of Article XX of the GATT 1994? What is the object and purpose of the chapeau of Article XIV of the GATS?

7.4. SECURITY EXCEPTIONS

In addition to the 'general exceptions' contained in Article XX of the GATT 1994 and Article XIV of the GATS, WTO law also provides for exceptions relating to national and international security. This section discusses, first, the security exception of Article XXI of the GATT 1994 and, then, the security exception of Article XIV *bis* of the GATS.[83]

7.4.1. Article XXI of the GATT 1994

Article XXI of the GATT 1994, entitled 'Security Exceptions', states:

> Nothing in this Agreement shall be construed
>
> a. to require any [Member] to furnish any information the disclosure of which it considers contrary to its essential security interests; or
> b. to prevent any [Member] from taking any action which it considers necessary for the protection of its essential security interests
>   i. relating to fissionable materials or the materials from which they are derived;
>   ii. relating to the traffic in arms, ammunition and implements of war and to such traffic in other goods and materials as is carried on directly or indirectly for the purpose of supplying a military establishment;
>   iii. taken in time of war or other emergency in international relations; or
> c. to prevent any [Member] from taking any action in pursuance of its obligations under the United Nations Charter for the maintenance of international peace and security.

Unlike Article XX, Article XXI has not played a significant role in the practice of dispute settlement under the GATT 1947 or the WTO to date. Article XXI has been invoked in only a few disputes. Nevertheless, this provision is not without importance. WTO Members do, on occasion, take trade-restrictive measures, either unilaterally or multilaterally, against other Members as a means to achieve national or international security and peace. Members taking such

---

[82] See above, pp. 616–17.   [83] Note that the *TRIPS Agreement* contains a similar provision in Article 73.

measures will seek justification for these measures under Article XXI. As will be discussed, there is a significant structural and interpretative difference between Article XX and Article XXI.

7.4.1.1. Article XXI(a) and (b) of the GATT 1994: national security

Traditionally, in international relations, national security takes precedence over the benefits of trade. This may be the case in three types of situation. First, States may consider it necessary to restrict trade in order to protect strategic domestic production capabilities from import competition. The judgment as to which production capabilities deserve to be qualified as strategically important differs among countries and is, to a great extent, political. Defined broadly, all industries equipping the military, including for example boot manufacturers, could be viewed as being of strategic importance.

Secondly, States may wish to use trade sanctions, as an instrument of foreign policy, against other States who either violate international law or pursue policies considered to be unacceptable or undesirable.

Thirdly, States may want to prohibit the export of arms or other products of military use to countries with which they do not have friendly relations.

Article XXI of the GATT 1994 is not concerned with all of these situations. Note, for instance, that the *WTO Agreement* normally allows for sufficient leeway to preserve national industries of strategic importance. WTO Members can, subject to limitations, provide protection through import tariffs, production subsidies and government procurement. In some situations, however, Article XXI provides justification for otherwise GATT-inconsistent measures.

Article XXI(a) allows a Member to withhold information, that it would normally be required to supply, when 'it considers' disclosure of that information 'contrary to its essential security interests'. This provision has been interpreted broadly by some Members. In this regard, note the following statement by the United States:

> The United States does consider it contrary to its security interest – and to the security interest of other friendly countries – to reveal the names of the commodities that it considers to be most strategic.[84]

Article XXI(b) allows a Member to adopt or maintain:

- measures relating to fissionable materials,
- measures relating to trade in arms or in other materials, directly or indirectly, for military use, and
- measures taken in time of war or other emergency in international relations,

which 'it considers necessary for the protection of its essential security interests'. Unlike Article XX, Article XXI does not have a chapeau to prevent misuse or abuse of the exceptions in Article XXI.[85]

With respect to these exceptions and their requirements, a question that immediately arises is the question of their justiciability. As a matter of

---

[84] GATT/CP.3/38, 9.   [85] See above, pp. 615–23.

principle, Members must be able to seek judicial review of national measures taken by other Members pursuant to Article XXI. However, it is not clear how far this review can go. It remains to be seen whether a panel or the Appellate Body will define what an 'essential national security interest' is and what is 'necessary' to protect such an interest. The scope for judicial review seems to be limited by the language of Article XXI(b) itself. Article XXI(b) refers to what the *Member* concerned *considers* necessary for the protection of its essential security interests. However, it is imperative that a certain degree of judicial review be maintained; otherwise the provision would be prone to abuse without redress.[86] At a minimum, panels should have the authority to conduct an examination as to whether the explanation provided by the Member concerned is reasonable or whether the measure constitutes an apparent abuse.

Uncertainty regarding the justiciability of the exceptions of Article XXI, and their requirements, was apparent in the few cases in which Article XXI has been raised in the context of the GATT 1947. For instance, in the discussion on the complaint by Czechoslovakia against export restrictions imposed by the United States, it was stated that:

> every country must be the judge in the last resort on questions relating to its own security. On the other hand, every contracting party should be cautious not to take any step which might have the effect of undermining the General Agreement.[87]

In 1982, the Contracting Parties adopted the following *Decision Concerning Article XXI of the General Agreement*:

> *Considering* that the exceptions envisaged in Article XXI of the General Agreement constitute an important element for safeguarding the rights of contracting parties when they consider that reasons of security are involved; *Noting* that recourse to Article XXI could constitute, in certain circumstances, an element of disruption and uncertainty for international trade and affect benefits accruing to contracting parties under the General Agreement; *Recognizing* that in taking action in terms of the exceptions provided in Article XXI of the General Agreement, contracting parties should take into consideration the interests of third parties which may be affected; That until such time as the Contracting Parties may decide to make a formal interpretation of Article XXI it is appropriate to set procedural guidelines for its application;
>
> The Contracting Parties *decide* that:
>
> 1. Subject to the exception in Article XXI:a, contracting parties should be informed to the fullest extent possible of trade measures taken under Article XXI.
> 2. When action is taken under Article XXI, all contracting parties affected by such action retain their full rights under the General Agreement.
> 3. The Council may be requested to give further consideration to this matter in due course.[88]

Also in 1982, the European Economic Community and its Member States as well as Canada and Australia applied trade restrictions for non-economic

---

[86] See the GATT Panel's statement in *USA – Nicaragua*, in *GATT Activities 1986*, 58–9.
[87] GATT/CP.3/SR.22, Corr.1.   [88] L/5426, 29S/23.

reasons against imports from Argentina due to the armed conflict between the United Kingdom and Argentina over the Falkland Islands/Islas Malvinas. It is noted that in November 1982 the Contracting Parties adopted a Ministerial Declaration which stated:

> the contracting parties undertake, individually and jointly: ... to abstain from taking restrictive trade measures, for reasons of a non-economic character, *not consistent* with the General Agreement.[89]
>
> [Emphasis added]

In May 1985, the United States imposed a trade embargo on Nicaragua. The United States was strongly opposed to the communist Sandinistas who were in power in Nicaragua at that time. Nicaragua argued that the trade embargo imposed by the United States was inconsistent with Articles I, II, V, XI and XIII and Part IV of the GATT and could not be justified – as the United States argued – under Article XXI. Nicaragua requested the establishment of a panel. According to the United States, however, Article XXI left it to each Contracting Party to judge what action it considered necessary for the protection of its essential security interests.[90] A Panel was established in this case but the terms of reference of this Panel stated that the Panel could not examine or judge the validity or motivation for the invocation of Article XXI by the United States. In its report, the Panel therefore concluded that:

> as it was not authorized to examine the justification for the United States' invocation of [Article XXI], it could find the United States neither to be complying with its obligations under the General Agreement nor to be failing to carry out its obligations under that Agreement.[91]

Questions and Assignments 7.10

Which measures, otherwise GATT-inconsistent, can be justified under Article XXI(a) and (b) of the GATT 1994? Why is judicial review of the use of Article XXI(a) and (b) problematic? Is judicial review desirable and, if so, to what extent? Give an example of a trade measure of the European Communities or one of the Member States of the European Union justified under Article XXI(a) or (b) of the GATT 1994.

7.4.1.2. *Article XXI(c) of the GATT 1994: international peace and security*

Article XXI(c) of the GATT 1994 allows WTO Members to take actions required under the United Nations Charter. This means that Members may depart from their GATT obligations in order to implement economic sanctions imposed by the United Nations. Article 41 of the UN Charter empowers the Security Council to impose economic sanctions pursuant to Article 39 of the Charter,

---

[89] L/5424, adopted on 29 November 1982, 29S/9, 11.
[90] *GATT Analytical Index* (WTO, 1995), 601, 603 and 604.
[91] GATT Panel Report, *United States – Trade Measures Affecting Nicaragua*, L/6053, dated 13 October 1986, para. 5.3. This report was never adopted.

once it has determined the existence of any threat to the peace, breach of the peace, or act of aggression. Article 41 of the Charter provides:

> The Security Council may decide what measures not involving the use of armed force are to be employed to give effect to its decisions, and it may call upon the Members of the United Nations to apply such measures. These may include complete or partial interruption of economic relations and of rail, sea, air, postal, telegraphic, radio, and other means of communication, and the severance of diplomatic relations.

Such Security Council decisions to apply economic sanctions are binding on UN Members according to Article 25 of the Charter:

> The Members of the United Nations agree to accept and carry out the decisions of the Security Council in accordance with the present Charter.

Hence, Article XXI(c) enables WTO Members to honour their commitments under the UN Charter and gives effect to the rule of conflict contained in Article 103 of the Charter. Article 103 provides:

> In the event of a conflict between the obligations of the Members of the United Nations under the present Charter and their obligations under any other international agreement, their obligations under the present Charter shall prevail.

At first glance, the issue of justiciability appears to be less problematic for the exception provided in Article XXI(c), given that this provision does not refer to what the Member invoking the exception 'considers' to be necessary. The basis of the departure from GATT obligations must be an obligation under the UN Charter, and a panel can assess the question of whether there is such an obligation.

Questions and Assignments 7.11

Which measures, otherwise GATT-inconsistent, can be justified under Article XXI(c) of the GATT 1994? Would it have been possible, as a matter of international law, to take trade sanctions mandated by the UN Security Council, if there would not have been an Article XXI(c)? Can the use made of Article XXI(c) be subjected to judicial review? Give an example of a trade measure of the European Communities or one of the Member States of the European Union justified under Article XXI(c) of the GATT 1994.

7.4.2. Article XIV *bis* of the GATS

Article XIV *bis* of the GATS, entitled 'Security Exceptions', states, in its first paragraph:

> Nothing in this Agreement shall be construed:
>
> a. to require any Member to furnish any information, the disclosure of which it considers contrary to its essential security interests; or
> b. to prevent any Member from taking any action which it considers necessary for the protection of its essential security interests:

> i. relating to the supply of services as carried out directly or indirectly for the purpose of provisioning a military establishment;
> ii. relating to fissionable and fusionable materials or the materials from which they are derived;
> iii. taken in time of war or other emergency in international relations; or
> c. to prevent any Member from taking any action in pursuance of its obligations under the United Nations Charter for the maintenance of international peace and security.

Article XIV *bis* of the GATS thus allows Members to adopt and enforce measures, in the interest of national or international security, otherwise inconsistent with GATS obligations. The language of this provision is virtually identical to Article XXI of the GATT 1994. Like Article XXI of the GATT 1994, Article XIV *bis* of the GATS is not without importance. On occasion, WTO Members take unilateral or multilateral measures affecting trade in services against other Members, as a means to achieve national or international security and peace. Members taking such measures can seek justification for these measures under Article XIV *bis*.

Note that Article XIV *bis* of the GATS, unlike Article XXI of the GATT 1994, provides for a notification requirement. The second paragraph of Article XIV *bis* states:

> The Council for Trade in Services shall be informed to the fullest extent possible of measures taken under paragraphs 1(b) and (c) and of their termination.

Questions and Assignments 7.12

How does Article XIV *bis* of the GATS differ from Article XXI of the GATT 1994? Give an example of a trade measure of the European Communities or one of the Member States of the European Union justified under Article XIV *bis* of the GATS.

7.5. ECONOMIC EMERGENCY EXCEPTIONS

Apart from the 'general exceptions' and the 'security exceptions', discussed above, WTO law also provides for 'economic emergency exceptions'. These exceptions allow Members to adopt measures, otherwise WTO-inconsistent, in situations where a surge in imports causes, or threatens to cause, serious injury to the domestic industry. The possibility to restrict trade in such situations is a 'safety valve' which has always been, and still is, provided for in most trade agreements, including the *WTO Agreement*. It reflects the political reality that trade liberalisation may be difficult to sustain if and when it creates unexpected and severe economic hardship for certain sectors of a country's economy. The otherwise WTO-inconsistent measures taken in economic emergency situations are referred to as 'safeguard measures'. Safeguard measures temporarily restrict import competition to allow the domestic industry time to adjust to new economic realities. Its application does not depend upon 'unfair' trade actions, as is the case with anti-dumping or countervailing measures.[92] As safeguard measures are applied to 'fair trade', i.e. trade occurring under normal competitive conditions and in accordance with WTO law, the Appellate Body noted in *Argentina – Footwear (EC)*:

> Thus, the import restrictions that are imposed on products of exporting Members when a safeguard action is taken must be seen ... as *extraordinary*. And, when construing the prerequisites for taking such actions, their extraordinary nature must be taken into account.[93]
>
> [Emphasis added]

This section discusses the rules on safeguard measures with respect to trade in goods, provided for in Article XIX of the GATT 1994 and the *Agreement on Safeguards*. It examines the characteristics of safeguard measures, the conditions for the use of safeguard measures and the rules on the procedural requirements that Members must meet when imposing safeguard measures.

Note that WTO law also provides for *special* safeguard measures and *transitional* safeguard measures that may be applied on imports of agricultural products and textile products respectively.[94] Overall, the requirements for the use of these special or transitional safeguard measures are less stringent than those for the use of the normal safeguard measures. This section, however, does not discuss these special or transitional safeguard measures in detail. Recall that China's Accession Protocol provides for a specific *transitional* safeguard mechanism that other WTO Members can resort to in order to limit imports from China until December 2013.[95] Note also that the GATS does not currently provide for the possibility to take safeguard measures. Article X of the GATS, however, calls for multilateral negotiations on safeguard measures for trade in services.[96] Such negotiations are now conducted in the context of the Doha Development Round.[97]

Questions and Assignments 7.13

What is the political rationale behind the 'economic emergency exception'? In your opinion, are safeguard measures, justified under the 'economic emergency exception', applied to fair or unfair trade? According to the Appellate Body in *Argentina – Footwear (EC)*, how does the nature of the trade to which safeguard measures are applied affect the interpretation of the requirements for the application of safeguard measures?

---

[92] See above, pp. 512–95.   [93] Appellate Body Report, *Argentina – Footwear (EC)*, para. 94.

[94] For the special safeguard measures on imports of agricultural products, see Article 5 of the *Agreement on Agriculture*. On the transitional safeguard measures on imports of textile products, see Article 6 of the *Agreement on Textiles and Clothing*.

[95] On the accession of China to the WTO, see above, pp. 113–15.

[96] Pursuant to Article X of the GATS, the results of these negotiations should have entered into effect no later than 1 January 1998. However, this deadline of the negotiations has since repeatedly been extended.

[97] Ministerial Conference Ministerial Declaration, adopted on 14 November 2001, WT/MIN(01)/DEC/1, dated 20 November 2001, para. 15.

7.5.1. Article XIX of the GATT 1994 and the Agreement on Safeguards

Article XIX of the GATT 1994 and the provisions of the *Agreement on Safeguards* set out the rules according to which Members may take safeguard measures. Article XIX of the GATT 1994, entitled 'Emergency Action on Imports of Particular Products', provides, in paragraph 1(a):

> If, as a result of unforeseen developments and of the effect of the obligations incurred by a [Member] under this Agreement, including tariff concessions, any product is being imported in the territory of that [Member] in such increased quantities and under such conditions as to cause or threaten serious injury to domestic producers in that territory of like or directly competing products, the [Member] shall be free … to suspend the obligation in whole or in part or to withdraw or modify the concession.

Under Article XIX of the GATT 1947, which was, in all respects, identical to Article XIX of the GATT 1994, some 150 safeguard measures were officially notified to the Contracting Parties. However, Contracting Parties often resorted to measures other than safeguard measures, to address situations in which imports caused particular economic hardship. These other measures included voluntary export restraints (VERs), voluntary restraint arrangements (VRAs) and orderly marketing arrangements (OMAs), discussed above.[98] Unlike safeguard measures, these other measures did not require any compensation and could be applied selectively to the main exporting countries.[99] This explained the 'popularity' of VERs, VRAs and OMAs. The *Agreement on Safeguards* was negotiated during the Uruguay Round because of the need to clarify and reinforce the disciplines of Article XIX of the GATT, to re-establish multilateral control over safeguard measures and to eliminate measures that escaped such control.

The *Agreement on Safeguards*, which is part of Annex 1A to the *WTO Agreement*, confirms and clarifies the provisions of Article XIX of the GATT 1994 but also provides for new rules. The *Agreement on Safeguards* sets out:

- the characteristics of, and conditions relating to, the safeguard measures (Aricles 5 to 9);
- the substantive requirements that must be met in order to apply a safeguard measure (Articles 2 and 4); and
- the (national and international) procedural requirements that must be met by a Member applying a safeguard measure (Articles 3 and 12).

On the relationship between the provisions of the *Agreement on Safeguards* and Article XIX of the GATT 1994, the Appellate Body in *Korea – Dairy* ruled, on the basis of Articles 1 and 11.1(a) of the *Agreement on Safeguards*, that:

---

[98] See above, pp. 449–50.
[99] For a discussion on the requirement of compensation and the difficulty to apply safeguard measures selectively, see below, pp. 638–40.

> any safeguard measure imposed after the entry into force of the *WTO Agreement* must comply with the provisions of *both* the *Agreement on Safeguards* and Article XIX of the GATT 1994.[100]

As the Appellate Body noted in *Argentina – Footwear (EC)*, nothing in the *WTO Agreement* suggests the intention by the Uruguay Round negotiators to subsume the requirements of Article XIX of the GATT 1994 within the *Agreement on Safeguards* and thus render those requirements no longer applicable.[101] This is of particular importance for the requirement that the surge in imports be the result of 'unforeseen developments'. This requirement is included in Article XIX of the GATT 1994 but not in the more detailed *Agreement on Safeguards*. Nevertheless, this requirement is fully applicable. Article XIX of the GATT 1994 and the *Agreement on Safeguards* apply *cumulatively*.[102]

Questions and Assignments 7.14

Why was the *Agreement on Safeguards* negotiated in the context of the GATT Uruguay Round? Why did GATT Contracting Parties prefer voluntary export restraints (and other similar measures) over safeguard measures? How does the *Agreement on Safeguards* relate to Article XIX of the GATT 1994?

7.5.2. Characteristics of safeguard measures

Safeguard measures are measures, otherwise inconsistent with Articles II or XI of the GATT 1994, which are justified under the economic emergency exception provided for in Article XIX of the GATT 1994 and the *Agreement on Safeguards*.[103] The purpose of a safeguard measure is to give 'breathing space' to a domestic industry to adapt itself to the new market situation by temporarily restricting imports. Safeguard measures therefore typically take the form of:

* customs duties above the binding (inconsistent with Article II:1 of the GATT 1994); or
* quantitative restrictions (inconsistent with Article XI of the GATT 1994).[104]

Safeguard measures can also take other forms, because, unlike anti-dumping measures and countervailing measures, discussed above, safeguard measures are not limited to particular types of measures.[105] This does not mean,

---

[100] Appellate Body Report, *Korea – Dairy*, para. 77.
[101] See Appellate Body Report, *Argentina – Footwear (EC)*, para. 83. The Appellate Body therefore rejected the Panel's finding that those requirements of Article XIX of the GATT 1994 which are not reflected in the *Agreement on Safeguards* were superseded by the requirements of the latter.
[102] Note, however, that this does not prevent a panel or the Appellate Body from exercising judicial economy with respect to a claim of violation of Article XIX where it had found that the safeguard measure at issue is inconsistent with the *Agreement on Safeguards*. On the exercise of judicial economy, see above, pp. 240–1.
[103] This and the following sections concern 'definitive' safeguard measures. 'Provisional' safeguard measures are discussed below, pp. 640–1.
[104] On customs duties above the binding and on quantitative restrictions, see above, pp. 419–21 and pp. 441–6.
[105] See above, pp. 541–9 and pp. 574–83.

however, that safeguard measures are not subject to strict requirements. In general terms, Article 5.1 of the *Agreement on Safeguards* provides:

> A Member shall apply safeguard measures only to the extent necessary to prevent or remedy serious injury or to facilitate adjustment . . . Members should choose measures most suitable for the achievement of these objectives.

The *Agreement on Safeguards* sets out specific requirements with respect to:

- the duration of safeguard measures;
- the non-discriminatory application of safeguard measures;
- safeguard measures in the form of quantitative restrictions; and
- the compensation of affected exporting Members.

7.5.2.1. Duration of safeguard measures

Safeguard measures are, by nature, *temporary* measures. Article 7.1 of the *Agreement on Safeguards* provides that safeguard measures may only be applied:

> for such a period of time as may be necessary to prevent or remedy serious injury and to facilitate adjustment.

In fact, the initial period of application of a definitive safeguard measure must not exceed four years.[106] Furthermore, a safeguard measure exceeding one year must be progressively liberalised,[107] and, if the measure exceeds three years, the Member applying the measure must carry out a mid-term review to establish whether the measure still meets the requirements discussed below.[108] Extension of a safeguard measure beyond four years is possible but only if:

- the safeguard measure continues to be necessary to prevent or remedy serious injury to the domestic industry; and
- there is evidence that the domestic industry is adjusting.[109]

In no case, however, may the duration of a safeguard measure exceed eight years.[110] Once the import of a product was subjected to a safeguard measure, this product cannot be subjected to such a measure again for a period of time equal to the duration of the safeguard measure that had previously been applied.[111] In other words, if a Member applies a safeguard measure on imports of trucks for a period of eight years, it cannot apply any safeguard measure on imports of trucks during the eight years following the termination of the first

---

[106] See Article 7.1 of the *Agreement on Safeguards*. Pursuant to Article 6, the duration of a provisional safeguard measure, if applied, is included in this maximum period of four years.

[107] Article 7.4 of the *Agreement on Safeguards*.

[108] Article 7.3 of the *Agreement on Safeguards*. As a result of the review, the Member must, if appropriate, withdraw the safeguard measure or increase the rate of liberalisation of trade.

[109] Article 7.2 of the *Agreement on Safeguards*. A safeguard measure that is extended can never be more restrictive than it was at the end of the initial period.

[110] Article 7.3 of the *Agreement on Safeguards*.

[111] Article 7.5 of the *Agreement on Safeguards*. An exception to this rule, allowing for the application of safeguard measures of short duration (i.e. maximum 150 days), is provided for in Article 7.6 of the *Agreement on Safeguards*.

measure. In this way, the *Agreement on Safeguards* prevents a situation where the temporary character of safeguards is circumvented by the repeated application of safeguard measures on the imports of the same product.

Note that Article 9.2 of the *Agreement on Safeguards* allows developing-country Members to apply a safeguard measure for up to ten years, instead of eight. Developing-country Members may also apply a *new* safeguard measure on the same product sooner.[112]

Questions and Assignments 7.15

How long may a safeguard measure be applied? Can a safeguard measure be extended? What is the maximum duration of a safeguard measure? How does Article 7.5 of the *Agreement on Safeguards* ensure that the provision on the maximum duration of safeguard measures is not circumvented? In what way do the rules on the duration of safeguard measures applied by developing country Members differ from the rules on the duration of safeguard measures applied by other Members? Can a developing country Member impose a safeguard measure for six years?

7.5.2.2. Non-discriminatory application of safeguard measures

Article 2.2 of the *Agreement on Safeguards* provides:

> Safeguard measures shall be applied to a product being imported irrespective of its source.

Under the GATT 1947, there was much disagreement as to whether safeguard measures could be applied on a selective basis, i.e. only against certain supplying countries and not against others. The *Agreement on Safeguards* has put an end to that debate by clearly requiring that safeguard measures be applied on an MFN basis, i.e. without discrimination between supplying Members. If the computer industry of Member A suffers serious injury as a result of a sudden surge of imports of laptops from Member B, Member A may be entitled to take a safeguard measure, for example, in the form of a quota on laptops, but this measure will have to apply to the importation of all laptops, whether from Member B or from other exporting Members. The 'selective' application of safeguard measures is, in principle, prohibited.[113]

However, the *Agreement on Safeguards* provides for two exceptions to the prohibition of 'selective' application of safeguard measures. These exceptions are set out in Article 5.2(b) and Article 9.1 of the *Agreement on Safeguards*. Article

---

[112] Article 9.2 of the *Agreement on Safeguards*.

[113] The question has arisen whether a Member can exclude products from Members that are its partners in a free trade area or a customs union from the application of a safeguard measure. In *Argentina – Footwear (EC)*, the Appellate Body ruled that, if a WTO Member has imposed a measure after conducting an investigation on imports from *all* sources, it is also required under Article 2.2 of the *Agreement on Safeguards* to apply such a measure to all sources, including partners in a free trade area (see Appellate Body Report, *Argentina – Footwear (EC)*, para. 112). See also below, pp. 650–67.

5.2(b) allows the selective application of safeguard measures taken in the form of quotas allocated among supplying countries if, apart from other requirements:

> clear demonstration is provided to the Committee [on Safeguards] that ... imports from certain Members have increased in a disproportionate percentage in relation to the total increase of imports of the product.[114]

Article 9.1 of the *Agreement on Safeguards* provides for an exception to the prohibition of selective application for the benefit of developing country Members. Article 9.1 states:

> Safeguard measures shall not be applied against a product originating in a developing country Member as long as its share of imports of the product concerned in the importing Member does not exceed 3 per cent, provided that developing country Members with less than 3 per cent import share collectively account for not more than 9 per cent of total imports of the product concerned.[115]

Questions and Assignments 7.16

Member A imposes a safeguard measure on the importation of bicycles following a 200 per cent increase in imports from Member B. The safeguard measure takes the form of a quota to be allocated among the supplying Members. The shares of imports of bicycles are currently as follows: Member B, 70 per cent; Member C, 20 per cent; Member D, 7 per cent; and Members E and F each 1.5 per cent. Note that Members D, E and F are developing country Members. To which bicycles should the safeguard measure apply – bicycles originating in Member B, C, D, E and/or F? Is your answer different if Member A takes a safeguard measure in the form of an increased customs duty or a tariff quota on bicycles?

7.5.2.3. *Safeguard measures in the form of quantitative restrictions*

A safeguard measure in the form of a quantitative restriction may not reduce the quantity of imports below the average level of imports in the last three representative years. An exception to this rule can only be allowed when clear justification is given that a lower level is necessary to prevent or remedy serious injury.[116]

Furthermore, in cases in which the safeguard measure takes the form of a quota allocated among supplying countries, Article 5.2(a) of the *Agreement on Safeguards* provides for rules on the allocation of the share of the quota which are similar to the rules of Article XIII of the GATT 1994, discussed above.[117]

---

[114] For the other requirements, see Article 5.2(b) of the *Agreement on Safeguards*.
[115] On the application of Article 9.1 of the *Agreement on Safeguards*, see Appellate Body Report, *US – Line Pipe*, paras. 125–32.
[116] See Article 5.1 of the *Agreement on Safeguards*.
[117] See above, pp. 450–3. Note, however, that Members may deviate from these rules as provided in Article 5.2(b) of the *Agreement on Safeguards*, discussed above, pp. 638–9. Also note that, unlike Article XIII of the GATT 1994, Article 5.1, second sentence, and Article 5.2(a) do not apply to tariff quotas. See Panel Report, *US – Line Pipe*, para. 7.75.

7.5.2.4. Compensation of affected exporting Members

As discussed above, a safeguard measure is a measure that restricts *fair* trade from other Members.[118] A safeguard measure disturbs the balance of rights and obligations to the detriment of the affected exporting Members. Therefore, the *Agreement on Safeguards* requires that a Member taking a safeguard measure agree with the affected exporting Members on appropriate compensation so as to restore the balance of rights and obligations. Article 8.1 of the *Agreement on Safeguards* provides:

> A Member proposing to apply a safeguard measure or seeking an extension of a safeguard measure shall endeavour to maintain a substantially equivalent level of concessions and other obligations ... between it and the exporting Members which would be affected by such a measure ... To achieve this objective, the Members concerned may agree on any adequate means of trade compensation for the adverse effects of the measure on their trade.

If an agreement on compensation is not reached within thirty days, Article 8.2 of the *Agreement on Safeguards* provides that the affected exporting Members are free:

> to suspend ... the application of substantially equivalent concessions or other obligations under GATT 1994, to the trade of the Member applying the safeguard measure.[119]

However, affected exporting Members cannot always exercise this right of suspension. As set out in Article 8.3 of the *Agreement on Safeguards*, this right of suspension shall not be exercised for the first three years that a safeguard measure is in effect in cases where:

- the safeguard measure has been taken as a result of an absolute increase in imports; and
- the safeguard measure conforms to the provisions of the *Agreement on Safeguards*.

Questions and Assignments 7.17

Why must a Member applying a safeguard measure try to reach an agreement on compensation? Do exporting Members, adversely affected by a safeguard measure, have a right to suspend, in 'retaliation', equivalent concessions or other obligations? If so, are there any limitations to this right?

7.5.2.5. Provisional safeguard measures

Article 6 of the *Agreement on Safeguards* allows Members to take provisional safeguard measures in 'critical circumstances'. Critical circumstances are

---

[118] See above, pp. 633–4.
[119] The right of suspension of 'substantially equivalent concessions' is conditional upon the notification of the proposed suspension measure to the Council for Trade in Goods and the non-disapproval by this Council. As the Council for Trade in Goods takes decisions by consensus, disapproval is *de facto* excluded.

defined as circumstances 'where delay would cause damage which it would be difficult to repair'. In order to take provisional safeguard measures, the competent domestic authorities must make a preliminary determination that there is clear evidence that the increased imports have caused or are threatening to cause serious injury.

Provisional measures may only be applied for a maximum of 200 days and can only take the form of tariff increases.[120] If, after a fully fledged investigation, it is concluded that the conditions for imposing a safeguard measure are not fulfilled, the provisional measure shall lapse and duties collected must be refunded.[121]

Questions and Assignments 7.18

When can a Member take a provisional safeguard measure? Why does Article 6 of the *Agreement on Safeguards* provide that provisional safeguard measures can only take the form of tariff increases?

7.5.3. Requirements for the use of safeguard measures

Article 2.1 of the *Agreement on Safeguards* provides:

> A Member may apply a safeguard measure to a product only if that Member has determined, pursuant to the provisions set out below, that such product is being imported into its territory in such increased quantities, absolute or relative to domestic production, and under such conditions as to cause or threaten to cause serious injury to the domestic industry that produces like or directly competitive products.

Article XIX:1(a) of the GATT 1994, which – as explained above – applies together with the *Agreement on Safeguards*, provides for the same requirements for the application of safeguard measures as Article 2.1, but, in addition, requires that the increase in imports occurs:

> as a result of unforeseen developments and of the effect of the obligations incurred by a [Member] under this Agreement.

In short, Members may apply safeguard measures only when three requirements are met. These requirements are:

- the 'increased imports' requirement;
- the 'serious injury' requirement; and
- the causation requirement.

This section examines each of these requirements.

---

[120] Extension is not possible and the duration of the provisional safeguard measure will be counted for the purpose of calculating the duration of the definitive safeguard measure (see above, pp. 637–8).

[121] See Article 6 of the *Agreement on Safeguards*.

7.5.3.1. 'Increased imports' requirement

Article 2.1 of the *Agreement on Safeguards* explicitly states that the increase in imports can be:

- an *absolute* increase, i.e. an increase by tonnes or units of the imported products; *or*
- a *relative* increase, i.e. an increase in relation to domestic production.

This, however, leaves the question unanswered as to how much, and over what time span, imports must have increased. In *Argentina – Footwear (EC)*, the Appellate Body further clarified the 'increased imports' requirement for the application of safeguard measures by ruling that:

> the increase in imports must have been recent enough, sudden enough, sharp enough, and significant enough, both quantitatively and qualitatively, to cause or threaten to cause "serious injury".[122]

In *US – Steel Safeguards*, the Appellate Body reaffirmed this interpretation of the 'increased imports' requirement.[123]

Thus, the increase in imports must be:

- recent;
- sudden, i.e. over a relatively short period of time;
- sharp; and
- significant.

It is clear that, if the increase in imports is not recent, sudden and sharp, there can be no economic *emergency* situation justifying the application of a safeguard measure. Furthermore, the *rate* of the increase (e.g. an increase by 30 per cent) as well as the *amount* of the increase (e.g. an increase by 10,000 units) must be considered.[124] In addition, the import trends during the investigation period must be considered. It does not suffice to compare the level of imports at the start of the investigation period with the imports at the end to conclude that there is an increase in imports within the meaning of the *Agreement on Safeguards*.[125] The analysis of the import trends during the investigation period must also show an increase in imports. However, recall that the increase in imports must be sudden and recent.[126] Therefore, the investigation period should be the *recent past*. Thus, it is not appropriate to examine the import trends over an investigation period of, for example, five years.[127] Consider the examples in Figures 7.1 and 7.2 of imports of beer in Member A during the investigation period 2000–2. In both examples, there is an increase in imports

---

[122] Appellate Body Report, *Argentina – Footwear (EC)*, para. 131.
[123] Appellate Body Report, *US – Steel Safeguards*, para. 346. The Appellate Body upheld the Panel's ruling that 'a finding that imports have increased pursuant to Article 2.1 can be made when an increase evidences a certain degree of recentness, suddenness, sharpness and significance'. See Panel Report, *US – Steel Safeguards*, para. 10.167.
[124] Article 4.2 of the *Agreement on Safeguards*.
[125] See Appellate Body Report, *Argentina – Footwear (EC)*, para. 129.
[126] See above, p. 642.   [127] Appellate Body Report, *Argentina – Footwear (EC)*, para. 130.

Figure 7.1 'Increased imports' requirements: example 1

Figure 7.2 'Increased imports' requirements: example 2

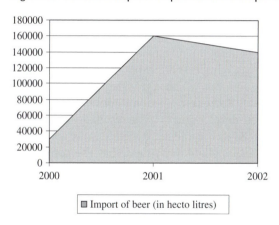

in the investigation period. The rate of increase as well as the amount of increase is quite significant. In both examples, imports increased from 30,000 hectolitres to 140,000 hectolitres, representing an increase of more than 460 per cent during the investigation period. However, if one also looks at the import trends, a different picture emerges. Example 1 is a clear case of a recent, sudden and sharp increase in imports within the meaning of the *Agreement on Safeguards*. It is doubtful whether that same conclusion can be reached with respect to example 2.[128]

Pursuant to Article XIX:1 of the GATT 1994, the increase in imports must occur as a result of an 'unforeseen development' and as a result of the effects of

---

[128] It may also be possible to conclude that there is an increase in imports in example 2, within the meaning of the *Agreement on Safeguards*, if it can be shown that the decline in 2002 was of a temporary and incidental nature.

obligations incurred under the GATT 1994. According to the Working Party in *US – Fur Felt Hats*, 'unforeseen developments' are:

> developments occurring after the negotiation of the relevant tariff concession which it would not be reasonable to expect that the negotiators of the country making the concession could and should have foreseen at the time when the concession was negotiated.[129]

In that case, in 1951, the Working Party held that the fact that hat styles had changed did not constitute an 'unforeseen development'. However, the degree to which the change in fashion affected the competitive situation could, according to the Working Party, not reasonably be expected to have been foreseen by the United States authorities in 1947.

In 2000, the Appellate Body ruled in *Korea – Dairy* that 'unforeseen developments' means unexpected developments.[130] Note that, before taking a safeguard measure, the Member concerned must demonstrate, as a matter of fact, that the increase in imports is indeed the result of unforeseen, i.e. unexpected, developments.[131]

In *US – Steel Safeguards*, the Appellate Body held that, when an importing Member wishes to apply safeguard measures on imports of several products, it is not sufficient for the competent authority merely to demonstrate that 'unforeseen developments' resulted in increased imports of a broad category of products which includes the specific products on which the safeguard measure is applied.[132] According to the Appellate Body, competent authorities are required to demonstrate that the unforeseen developments have resulted in increased imports for the specific products on which the safeguard measures are applied.[133]

Also in *US – Steel Safeguards*, the Appellate Body held that the competent authorities of the importing Member imposing a safeguard measure must demonstrate in its published report, *through a reasoned and adequate explanation*, that unforeseen developments and the effects of tariff concessions resulted in increased imports causing or threatening to cause serious injury to the relevant domestic producers.[134]

The Panel in *US – Steel Safeguards* ruled with respect to the determination of 'unforeseen circumstances':

> The nature of the facts, including their complexity, will dictate the extent to which the relationship between the unforeseen developments and increased imports causing injury needs to be explained. The timing of the explanation [relating to unforeseen developments], its extent and its quality are all factors that can affect whether [that] ... explanation is reasoned and adequate.[135]

---

[129] Working Party Report, *US – Fur Felt Hats*, para. 9.
[130] See Appellate Body Report, *Korea – Dairy*, para. 84.
[131] See *ibid.*, para. 85. See also Appellate Body Report *Argentina – Footwear (EC)*, para. 92.
[132] See Appellate Body Report, *US – Steel Safeguards*, para. 319.   [133] *Ibid.*
[134] Appellate Body Report, *US – Steel Safeguards*, paras. 289–91. See also para. 273.
[135] Panel Report, *US – Steel Safeguards*, para. 10.115.

On appeal from the United States, the Appellate Body upheld this finding.[136] The Appellate Body pointed out that, since a panel may not conduct a *de novo* review of the evidence before the competent authority, it is the *explanation* given by the competent authority for its determination alone that enables panels to determine whether there has been compliance with the substantive requirements for the imposition of a safeguard measure.[137]

Questions and Assignments 7.19

What constitutes 'increased imports' within the meaning of the *Agreement on Safeguards*? In your opinion, what could be 'unforeseen developments' within the meaning of Article XIX:1 of the GATT 1994?

7.5.3.2. *'Serious injury' requirement*

A second main substantive requirement for the application of a safeguard measure on the imports of a product is the existence of 'serious injury or threat thereof' to the domestic industry producing like or directly competitive products.

Article 4.1 of the *Agreement on Safeguards* defines 'serious injury' as 'a significant overall impairment in the position of a domestic industry'. A 'threat of serious injury' is defined as 'serious injury that is clearly imminent'.[138] The Appellate Body has recognised the standard of 'serious injury' to be very high and 'exacting'.[139] It is significantly stricter than the standard of 'material injury' of the *Anti-Dumping Agreement* and the *SCM Agreement*. Since safeguard measures, unlike anti-dumping and countervailing duties, are applied to 'fair' trade, it is not surprising that the threshold for applying these measures is higher.

Article 4.1(c) of the *Agreement on Safeguards* defines a 'domestic industry' as:

> the producers as a whole of the like or directly competitive products operating within the territory of a Member, or those whose collective output of the like or directly competitive products constitutes a major proportion of the total domestic production of those products.

Article 4.1(c) lays down two criteria to define the 'domestic industry' in a particular case. The first criterion relates to the products at issue; the second criterion relates to the number and the representative nature of the producers of these products.

As to the first criterion, note that the domestic industry consists of producers making products that are 'like or directly competitive' to the imported

---

[136] Appellate Body Report, *US – Steel Safeguards*, paras. 293–6.
[137] See *ibid.*, paras. 298–9 and paras. 301–3.
[138] Article 4.1(b) of the *Agreement on Safeguards*. The concept of 'clearly imminent' was clarified by the Appellate Body in *US – Lamb*, para. 125. 'Imminent' implies that the anticipated 'serious injury' must be on the verge of occurring; 'clearly' indicates that there must be a very high degree of likelihood that the threat will materialise in the very near future.
[139] Appellate Body Report, *US – Wheat Gluten*, para. 149.

products. Therefore, to determine what the 'domestic industry' is, in a particular case, one must first identify the domestic products which are 'like or directly competitive' to the imported products. The producers of those products will make up the 'domestic industry'. The concepts of 'like products' and 'directly competitive products' are not defined in the *Agreement on Safeguards* and there is little relevant case law, as yet, on the meaning of these concepts as used in the *Agreement on Safeguards*. However, there is a significant body of case law on the meaning of these concepts as used in the GATT 1994.[140] While the Appellate Body has ruled that the concept of 'like products' has different meanings in the different contexts in which it is used, this case law – discussed in detail above – is definitely of relevance here. It follows from this case law that the determination of whether products are 'like products' or 'directly competitive products' is, fundamentally, a determination about the nature and extent of the competitive relationship between these products. The factors that must be considered in determining 'likeness' or 'direct competitiveness' are, among other relevant factors:

- the physical characteristics of the products;
- their end use;
- consumer habits and preferences regarding the products; and
- the customs classification of the products.[141]

In *US – Lamb*, one of the very few safeguard cases in which the issue of 'like products' and 'directly competitive products' was addressed, the Appellate Body held that the fact that products are in a continuous line of production (for example, lambs and lamb meat), does not make these products 'like products'.[142] In general, production structures are – according to the Appellate Body – not relevant in determining whether products are 'like' or 'directly competitive'.[143]

As mentioned above, the second criterion to define the 'domestic industry' in a particular case relates to the number and the representative nature of the producers of the like or directly competitive products. The 'domestic industry' for the purposes of the *Agreement on Safeguards* is:

- the totality of the domestic producers; or
- at least a major proportion thereof.

There is no general explanation of what constitutes 'a major proportion' of the domestic producers. What is required to meet this condition will depend on the specific circumstances of a case and will most likely differ from case to case.[144]

Once the domestic industry has been identified, one can examine whether there has been serious injury or a threat thereof to this domestic industry. To

---

[140] See above, pp. 314–16, 334–8, 342–5, 354–60.   [141] See above, pp. 354–60.
[142] See Appellate Body Report, *US – Lamb*, para. 90.   [143] See *ibid.*, para. 94.
[144] This issue also arises in the context of anti-dumping measures and countervailing measures; see above, pp. 526–7 and p. 569.

this end, Article 4.2(a) of the *Agreement on Safeguards* requires an evaluation of 'all relevant factors of an objective and quantifiable nature having a bearing on the situation of that industry'. These so-called 'injury factors' include:

- the rate and amount of the increase in imports, of the product concerned, in absolute and relative terms;
- the share of the domestic market taken by increased imports; and
- changes in the level of sales, production, productivity, capacity utilisation, profits and losses, and employment.[145]

This list of injury factors is not exhaustive. *All* factors having a bearing on the situation of the domestic industry can and must be examined.[146] The examination of the factors expressly mentioned is, however, a minimum. Domestic authorities do not have an unlimited duty to investigate *all* other possible injury factors. However, if the domestic authority considers a factor, other than a factor raised by one of the interested parties, to be relevent, it must be investigated.[147]

It does not suffice for domestic authorities applying safeguard measures to examine all relevant injury factors. They must also give a reasoned and adequate explanation of how the facts support their conclusion that the domestic industry is suffering or is threatened with 'serious injury'.[148] To find 'serious injury', it is not necessary that all injury factors show that the domestic industry is under threat.[149] In a situation in which employment and capacity utilisation in an industry are declining but profitability remains positive, it may nevertheless be possible to conclude that 'serious injury' exists.

For the determination of a 'threat of serious injury', Article 4.1(b) of the *Agreement on Safeguards* requires, in addition, that this determination must 'be based on facts and not merely on allegation, conjecture or remote possibility'.[150]

Questions and Assignments 7.20

How does one define the 'domestic industry' in a particular case? Do producers of cars and producers of light trucks belong to the same 'domestic industry'? Do mills and bakeries belong to the same domestic industry? What is 'serious injury' to the domestic industry? What is a 'threat of serious injury'? How must domestic authorities determine whether there is serious injury or a threat thereof to the domestic industry?

---

[145] Article 4.2(a) of the *Agreement on Safeguards*.
[146] See Appellate Body Report, *Argentina – Footwear (EC)*, para. 136; Appellate Body Report, *US – Wheat Gluten*, para. 55; and Appellate Body Report, *US – Lamb*, para. 103. Failure to consider a relevant factor, in full or in part, amounts to a violation of Article 4.2(a) of the *Agreement on Safeguards*.
[147] See Appellate Body Report, *US – Wheat Gluten*, paras. 55–6.
[148] See Appellate Body Report, *US – Lamb*, para. 103. This is usually referred to as the *substantive* aspect of the examination of the injury factors.
[149] See *ibid.*, para. 144.
[150] As discussed above, the previous injury must be 'clearly imminent'. See above, footnote 138, p. 645.

7.5.3.3. 'Causation' requirement

The third and last main substantive requirement for the application of a safeguard measure to the imports of a product is the 'causation requirement'. Article 4.2(b) of the *Agreement on Safeguards* provides:

> The determination referred to in subparagraph (a) shall not be made unless this investigation demonstrates, on the basis of objective evidence, the existence of the causal link between increased imports of the product concerned and serious injury or a threat thereof. When factors other than increased imports are causing injury to the domestic industry at the same time, such injury shall not be attributed to increased imports.

The test for establishing causation is twofold:

- a demonstration of the causal link between the 'increased imports' and the 'serious injury or threat thereof' (the 'causal link' sub-requirement); and
- an identification of any injury caused by factors other than the increased imports and the non-attribution of this injury to these imports (the 'non-attribution' sub-requirement).[151]

With respect to the 'causal link' sub-requirement, the Appellate Body has ruled in *US – Wheat Gluten* that it is not necessary to show that increased imports *alone* must be capable of causing serious injury:

> the need to distinguish between the facts caused by increased imports and the facts caused by other factors does *not* necessarily imply ... that increased imports *on their own* must be capable of causing serious injury nor that injury caused by other factors must be *excluded* from the determination of serious injury.[152]

With respect to the 'non-attribution' sub-requirement, the Appellate Body ruled in *US – Lamb*:

> In a situation where *several factors* are causing injury "at the same time", a final determination about the injurious effects caused by *increased imports* can only be made if the injurious effects caused by all the different causal factors are distinguished and separated. Otherwise, any conclusion based exclusively on an assessment of only one of the causal factors – increased imports – rests on an uncertain foundation, because it *assumes* that the other causal factors are *not* causing the injury which has been ascribed to increased imports. The non-attribution language in Article 4.2(b) precludes such an assumption and, instead, requires that the competent authorities assess appropriately the injurious effects of the other factors, so that those effects may be disentangled from the injurious effects of the increased imports. In this way, the final determination rests, properly, on the genuine and substantial relationship of cause and effect between increased imports and serious injury.[153]

Domestic authorities therefore have to separate and distinguish the injurious effects of 'other factors' from the injurious effects of the increased imports. They have to give a reasoned and adequate explanation of the nature and the

---

[151] See e.g. Appellate Body Report, *US – Line Pipe*, para. 215.
[152] Appellate Body Report, *US – Wheat Gluten*, para. 70.
[153] Appellate Body Report, *US – Lamb*, para. 179.

extent of the injurious effects of the other factors, as distinguished from the injurious effects of the increased imports.[154]

Questions and Assignments 7.21

What does the 'causation requirement' of Article 4.2(b) of the *Agreement on Safeguards* entail? If a domestic industry suffers serious injury as a result of a mix of factors, including increased imports and changes in consumer preferences, can a domestic authority still conclude that the 'causation requirement' of Article 4.2(b) of the *Agreement on Safeguards* is met? How must domestic authorities determine whether the 'causation requirement' of Article 4.2(b) of the *Agreement on Safeguards* is met?

7.5.4. Domestic procedures

The *Agreement on Safeguards* also sets out procedural requirements which domestic authorities, wishing to impose safeguard measures, must meet.[155] Most importantly, Article 3 of the *Agreement on Safeguards* requires that a Member apply a safeguard measure only following an investigation by the competent authorities of that Member pursuant to procedures previously established and made public.[156] The competent domestic authorities must also publish a report setting forth their findings and reasoned conclusions reached on all pertinent issues of fact and law.[157] Failure to do so results in a formal defect of the safeguard measure. Moreover, if the report of the competent domestic authorities does not address the issues arising under Article 2 (increased imports) and/or Article 4 (serious injury), this failure amounts to a failure to show that the requirements of Articles 2 and 4 were met and results in a finding of violation of Articles 2 and/or 4.

Questions and Assignments 7.22

Discuss the main procedural requirements under the *Agreement on Safeguards* that a Member imposing a safeguard measure must meet.

---

[154] See Appellate Body Report, *US – Hot-Rolled Steel*, paras. 226 and 230. See also Appellate Body Report, *US – Line Pipe*, para. 213. The mere assertion that injury caused by other factors has not been attributed to increased imports is definitely not sufficient to meet the requirement of Article 4.2(b) of the *Agreement on Safeguards*.

[155] These procedural obligations are set out in Articles 3, 6 and 12 of the *Agreement on Safeguards*.

[156] Article 3.1 of the *Agreement on Safeguards*. Note that this investigation must include reasonable public notice to all interested parties and public hearings or other appropriate means by which importers, exporters and other interested parties could present evidence and their views, *inter alia*, as to whether or not the application of a safeguard measure would be in the public interest. These procedural 'due process rights' of the parties to a safeguard investigation are set out in Article 3.1 of the *Agreement on Safeguards*.

[157] Article 3.1 of the *Agreement on Safeguards*.

7.6. REGIONAL INTEGRATION EXCEPTIONS

In addition to the 'general exceptions', the 'security exceptions' and the 'economic emergency exceptions' discussed above, WTO law also provides for 'regional integration exceptions'. These exceptions allow Members to adopt measures, otherwise WTO – inconsistent, taken in the context of the pursuit of regional economic integration. The regional integration exceptions are set out in Article XXIV of the GATT 1994 and Article V of the GATS. The regional integration exception for trade in goods is elaborated on further in the *Understanding on the Interpretation of Article XXIV of the GATT 1994* (the *'Understanding on Article XXIV'*), which forms part of the GATT 1994.

Since the early 1990s, there has been a proliferation of regional trade agreements. Currently over 250 regional trade agreements are in force, and this number is likely to increase further in the near future.[158] Well-known examples of regional integration efforts are the European Communities, the North American Free Trade Agreement (NAFTA),[159] the ASEAN (Association of Southeast Asian Nations) Free Trade Area (AFTA), the Common Market of Eastern and Southern Africa (COMESA), the Common Market of the South (MERCOSUR),[160] the Common Market of the Carribean (CARICOM) and the Australia–New Zealand Closer Economic Relations Agreement. Thirty-four countries of North, Central and South America are currently negotiating the establishment of a Free Trade Area of the Americas (FTAA). In 2004, all but two WTO Members were party to one or more regional trade agreements.[161] A significant part of world trade takes place under the terms of regional trade agreements.

The key characteristic of regional trade agreements is that the parties to such agreements offer each other more favourable treatment in trade matters than they offer other trading partners. To the extent that these other trading partners are WTO Members, such discriminatory treatment is – as discussed in Chapter 4 – inconsistent with the MFN treatment obligation, one of the basic non-discrimination principles of WTO law. Yet, both the GATT 1994 and the GATS allow, under certain conditions, regional trade agreements establishing customs unions or free trade areas. As is stated in Article XXIV:4 of the GATT 1994:

> The [Members] recognize the desirability of increasing freedom of trade by the development, through voluntary agreements, of closer integration between the economies of the countries parties to such agreements.

WTO law recognises the advantages of economic integration and trade liberalisation even when these efforts involve only some of its Members. At a

---

[158] See www.wto.org, visited on 12 October 2003.
[159] A free trade agreement between Canada, Mexico and the United States.
[160] A customs union with Argentina, Brazil, Paraguay and Uruguay.
[161] Mongolia and Chinese Taipei were not party to any regional trade agreement. See http://www.wto.org/english/tratop_e/region_e/summary_e.xls, visited on 9 May 2004.

regional level, it may be possible to <u>achieve a degree</u> of trade liberalisation <u>which may be out of reach at the global level</u>. It is argued that trade liberalisation will occur more quickly if it is pursued within regional trading blocs. Also, regional trade liberalisation <u>may create</u> significant economic growth within the region concerned which can, in turn, generate more trade with the rest of the world. However, economic studies of customs unions and free trade areas have revealed that the trade-creation effects may often be smaller than the trade-diversion effects as trade between the participants replaces trade between the participants and non-participants. <u>It is not clear whether regional trade agreements *divert* rather than *create* trade.</u> Apart from economic reasons, countries may also have political reasons to pursue deeper economic integration and trade liberalisation with some other countries. The example *par excellence* here is the European Communities which through economic integration of, and trade liberalistion between, its members sought to create, and was successful in creating, 'an ever closer union' among the peoples of Europe to avoid the reoccurrence of war. The establishment of MERCOSUR, a customs union between Argentina, Brazil, Paraguay and Uruguay, was motivated by the wish to buttress democracy in these countries. WTO law should not stand in the way of such processes. However, a balance must be struck between the interests of countries pursuing closer economic integration among a select group of countries and the interests of countries excluded from that group. The *Understanding on Article XXIV* states in its preamble:

> the purpose of [regional trade] agreements should be to facilitate trade between the constituent territories and not to raise barriers to the trade of other Members with such territories; ... in their formation or enlargement the parties to them should to the greatest possible extent avoid creating adverse effects on the trade of other Members.

WTO rules should ensure that regional trade agreements create trade more than they divert it. In the context of the Doha Development Round, Members are negotiating with the aim of further clarifying and improving the current rules applying to regional trade agreements.[162]

While, in times of no or slow progress in multilateral trade liberalisation in the context of the WTO, regional trade liberalisation is often put forward as an alternative, note that such efforts may aggravate the lack of progress at the multilateral level and that they are likely to leave out many of the world's poorest countries. As Jagdish Bhagwati noted:

> Everyone loses out but the poor countries suffer the most because their companies are least prepared to deal with the confusion. In addition, where a significant power such as the US or the European Union is involved in an agreement, it almost always sneaks

---

[162] See Ministerial Conference *Ministerial Declaration*, adopted on 14 November 2001, WT/MIN(01)/DEC/1, dated 20 November 2001, para. 29. For an overview of the issues under negotiation, see *Compendium of Issues Related to Regional Trade Agreements*, Background Note by the Secretariat, TN/RL/W/8/Rev.1, dated 1 August 2002. Also noteworthy is the *Synopsis of 'Systemic' Issues Relating to Regional Trade Agreements*, Note by the Secretariat, WT/REG/W/37, dated 2 March 2000.

in reverse preferences – and trade-unrelated issues such as patent protection and labour standards – that exact a heavy cost on developing countries.[163]

This section will discuss first the regional integration exception and its limits under the GATT 1994. Then it will examine this exception under the GATS.

7.6.1. Article XXIV of the GATT 1994

The chapeau of Article XXIV:5 of the GATT 1994 provides, in relevant part:

> the provisions of this Agreement shall not prevent ... the formation of a customs union or of a free-trade area or the adoption of an interim agreement necessary for the formation of a customs union or of a free-trade area ...

In examining this provision in *Turkey – Textiles*, the Appellate Body noted:

> We read this to mean that the provisions of the GATT 1994 *shall not make impossible* the formation of a customs union. Thus, the chapeau makes it clear that Article XXIV may, under certain conditions, justify the adoption of a measure which is inconsistent with certain other GATT provisions, and may be invoked as a possible "defense" to a finding of inconsistency.[164]

There are two conditions under which Article XXIV may justify a measure otherwise GATT-inconsistent. As the Appellate Body stated in *Turkey – Textiles*:

> First, the party claiming the benefit of this defence must demonstrate that the measure at issue is introduced upon the formation of a customs union that fully meets the requirements of sub-paragraphs 8(a) and 5(a) of Article XXIV. And, second, that party must demonstrate that the formation of that customs union would be prevented if it were not allowed to introduce the measure at issue.[165]

There is therefore a two-tier test to determine whether a measure, otherwise inconsistent with the GATT 1994, is justified under Article XXIV. Such measure is justified:

- if the measure is introduced upon the formation of a customs union, a free trade area, or an interim agreement, that meet all the requirements set out in WTO law; and

---

[163] J. Bhagwati, 'A Costly Pursuit of Free Trade', *Financial Times*, 6 March 2001.
[164] Appellate Body Report, *Turkey – Textiles*, para. 45.
[165] *Ibid.*, para. 58. See also Appellate Body Report, *Argentina – Footwear (EC)*, para. 109.

- if the formation of the customs union or free trade area would be prevented, i.e. made impossible, if the introduction of the measure concerned were not allowed.

This section will discuss these conditions, first, with regard to a measure adopted in the context of a customs union, secondly, with regard to a measure adopted in the context of a free trade area, and, finally, with regard to a measure adopted under an interim agreement. This section also discusses, *in fine*, special rules for developing country Members' regional trade agreements as well as general procedural issues.

Questions and Assignments 7.24

In general terms, what is the test to determine whether a measure otherwise inconsistent with the GATT 1994 is justified under Article XXIV?

7.6.1.1. *Customs unions*

As noted above, a measure otherwise GATT-inconsistent is justified under Article XXIV of the GATT 1994:

- if that measure is introduced upon the formation of a customs union that meets the requirements of Article XXIV:8(a) and Article XXIV:5(a); and
- if the formation of that customs union would be made impossible if the introduction of the measure concerned were not allowed.

The Appellate Body noted in *Turkey – Textiles* that it is necessary to establish that both conditions are fulfilled and that it may not always be possible to determine whether the second condition is met 'without *first* determining whether there *is* a customs union'.[166]

A 'customs union' is defined in Article XXIV:8(a) of the GATT 1994 as follows:

> A customs union shall be understood to mean the substitution of a single customs territory for two or more customs territories so that
>
> i. duties and other restrictive regulations of commerce (except, where necessary, those permitted under Articles XI, XII, XIII, XIV, XV and XX) are eliminated with respect to *substantially all the trade* between the constituent territories of the union or at least with respect to substantially all the trade in products originating in such territories, and,
> ii. ... *substantially the same* duties and other regulations of commerce are applied by each of the members of the union to the trade of territories not included in the union.
>
> [Emphasis added]

---

[166] Appellate Body Report, *Turkey – Textiles*, para. 59. Emphasis on 'first' added.

To satisfy the definition of a 'customs union', Article XXIV:8(a) establishes

- a standard for the *internal trade* between constituent members (under (i)); and
- a standard for the trade of constituent members *with third countries* (under (ii)).

With respect to the first standard, i.e. the standard for the *internal trade* between the constituent members of a customs union, Article XXIV:8(a) requires that members of a customs union eliminate 'duties and other restrictive regulations of commerce' with respect to 'substantially all the trade' between them. As the Appellate Body noted in *Turkey – Textiles*, the WTO Members have never reached an agreement on the interpretation of the term 'substantially' in this provision.[167] According to the Appellate Body, it is clear that 'substantially all the trade' is not the same as *all* the trade, and also that 'substantially all the trade' is something considerably more than merely *some* of the trade.[168] It should also be noted that members of a customs union may maintain, where necessary, certain restrictive regulations of commerce in their internal trade that are permitted under Articles XI to XV and under Article XX of the GATT 1994.[169] The Appellate Body in *Turkey – Textiles* therefore agreed with the Panel in that case that Article XXIV:8(a)(i), which sets out the standard for the *internal trade*, offers 'some flexibility' to the constituent members of a customs union when liberalising their internal trade. However, the Appellate Body cautioned that the degree of 'flexibility' is limited by the requirement that 'duties and other restrictive regulations of commerce' be 'eliminated'.

In *Argentina – Footwear (EC)*, the question arose whether Article XXIV:8(a)(i) prohibited Argentina, as a member of MERCOSUR, from imposing safeguard measures on other MERCOSUR countries. The Appellate Body considered that Article XXIV:8(a)(i) did not prohibit the imposition of safeguard measures on other MERCOSUR countries. In the light of the specific circumstances of this case, the Appellate Body was even of the opinion that Argentina should have applied the safeguard measures also to other MERCOSUR countries. The Appellate Body ruled:

> we find that Argentina's investigation, which evaluated whether serious injury or the threat thereof was caused by imports from *all* sources, could only lead to the imposition of safeguard measures on imports from *all* sources. Therefore, we conclude that Argentina's investigation, in this case, cannot serve as a basis for excluding imports from other MERCOSUR member States from the application of the safeguard measures.[170]

As the Panel in *Argentina – Footwear (EC)* had already noted, there must be a 'parallelism between the scope of a safeguard *investigation* and the scope of the *application* of safeguard measures'.[171] The requirement of parallelism was reaffirmed by the Appellate Body in *US – Steel Safeguards*.[172] In that case, the

---

[167] *Ibid.*, para. 48.   [168] *Ibid.*
[169] See Article XXIV:8(a)(i) of the GATT 1994. For a discussion on Articles XI and XIII, see above, pp. 441–57; Article XII, see below, pp. 667–74; and Article XX, see above, pp. 598–624.
[170] Appellate Body Report, *Argentina – Footwear (EC)*, para. 113.
[171] Panel Report, *Argentina – Footwear*, para. 8.87.
[172] See Appellate Body Report, *US – Steel Safeguards*, paras. 440–4.

competent authority of the United States considered *all imports* in its injury investigation, but afterwards did not apply the safeguard measures to imports from Canada, Israel, Jordan and Mexico.

As to the question whether Article XXIV:8(a)(i) prohibits a member of a customs union from imposing a safeguard measure, or an anti-dumping measure or countervailing duty, on imports from other members of the customs union, note that, as discussed above, Article XXIV:8(a)(i) offers 'some flexibility' to the constituent members of a customs union when liberalising their internal trade.

With respect to the second standard, i.e., the standard for the trade of constituent members *with third countries*, Article XXIV:8(a)(ii) of the GATT 1994 requires that the constituent members of a customs union apply 'substantially the same' duties and other regulations of commerce to trade with third countries. The constituent members of a customs union are therefore required to apply a common external trade regime, relating to both duties and other regulations of commerce. As the Appellate Body noted in *Turkey – Textiles*, it is *not* required that each constituent member of a customs union applies the *same* duties and other regulations of commerce as other constituent members with respect to trade with third countries. Article XXIV:8(a)(ii) requires that *substantially the same* duties and other regulations of commerce shall be applied.[173] Also, the phrase 'substantially the same' offers a certain degree of 'flexibility' to the constituent members of a customs union in 'the creation of a common commercial policy'. However, as the Appellate Body cautioned again, this 'flexibility' is limited. Something closely approximating 'sameness' is definitely required.[174]

A customs union under Article XXIV must, however, not only meet the requirements of Article XXIV:8(a). It must also meet the requirement of Article XXIV:5(a). This provision states:

> with respect to a customs union ... the duties and other regulations of commerce imposed at the institution of any such union ... in respect of trade with [Members] not parties to such union ... shall not on the whole be higher or more restrictive than the general incidence of the duties and regulations of commerce applicable in the constituent territories prior to the formation of such union ... as the case may be.

The precise meaning of the requirement that the duties and other regulations of commerce, applicable after the formation of the customs union, are, *on the whole*, not higher or more restrictive than the *general incidence* of the duties and other regulations of commerce applicable prior to the formation of the customs union, has been controversial. Paragraph 2 of the *Understanding on Article XXIV* has sought to clarify this requirement. With respect to duties, paragraph 2

---

[173] Appellate Body Report, *Turkey – Textiles*, para. 49. The Appellate Body agreed with the Panel in *Turkey – Textiles* that the expression 'substantially the same duties and other regulations of commerce are applied by each of the Members of the [customs] union' would appear to encompass both quantitative and qualitative elements, the quantitative aspect being more emphasised in relation to duties (see Panel Report, *Turkey – Textiles*, para. 9.148).

[174] Appellate Body Report, *Turkey – Textiles*, para. 50.

requires that the evaluation under Article XXIV:5(a) of the *general incidence of the duties* applied before and after the formation of a customs union:

> shall ... be based upon an overall assessment of weighted average tariff rates and of customs duties collected.[175]

As noted by the Appellate Body in *Turkey – Textiles*, under the GATT 1947, there were different views among the GATT Contracting Parties as to whether one should consider, when applying the test of Article XXIV:5(a), the *bound* rates of duty or the *applied* rates of duty. This issue has been resolved by paragraph 2 of the *Understanding on Article XXIV*, which clearly states that the *applied* rate of duty must be used.[176]

With respect to 'other regulations of commerce', paragraph 2 of the *Understanding on Article XXIV* recognises that it may be difficult to evaluate whether the general incidence of the 'other regulations of commerce' after the formation of the customs union are more restrictive than before the formation. Paragraph 2 recognises, in particular, that the quantification and aggregation of regulations of commerce other than duties may be difficult. Therefore, paragraph 2 of the *Understanding on Article XXIV* provides:

> for the purpose of the overall assessment of the incidence of other regulations of commerce ... the examination of individual measures, regulations, products covered and trade flows affected may be required.

The test for assessing whether a specific customs union meets the requirements of Article XXIV:5(a) is, in essence, an *economic* test, i.e., a test of the extent of trade restriction before and after the formation of the customs union.[177]

If, in the formation of a customs union, a constituent member must increase a bound duty (because the duty of the customs union is higher than the bound duty applicable before the formation of the customs union), Article XXIV:6 of the GATT 1994 requires that the procedure for modification of schedules, set out in Article XXVIII of the GATT 1994, be applied.[178] This procedure for the withdrawal or modification of previously made tariff concessions must be entered into with a view to achieving mutually satisfactory compensatory adjustment.[179] Article XXIV:6 further stipulates, however, that:

> In providing for compensatory adjustment, due account shall be taken of the compensation already afforded by the reduction brought about in the corresponding duty of the other constituents of the union.

If the reduction in the corresponding duty of other constituent members of the customs union is not sufficient to provide the necessary compensatory

---

[175] This assessment shall be based on import statistics for a previous representative period to be supplied by the customs union, on a tariff-line basis and in values and quantities, broken down by WTO country of origin. The WTO Secretariat shall compute the weighted average tariff rates and customs duties collected in accordance with the methodology used in the assessment of tariff offers in the Uruguay Round. For this purpose, the duties and charges to be taken into consideration shall be the applied rates of duty. See para. 2 of the *Understanding on Article XXIV*.
[176] Appellate Body Report, *Turkey – Textiles*, para. 53.
[177] See Appellate Body Report, *Turkey – Textiles*, para. 55.   [178] See above, pp. 423–4.
[179] See *Understanding on Article XXIV*, para. 5.

adjustment, the customs union must offer compensation.[180] This compensation may take the form of reductions of duties on other tariff lines. If no agreement on compensatory adjustment can be reached, the customs union shall nevertheless be free to modify or withdraw the concessions at issue; and the affected WTO Members shall then be free to withdraw substantially equivalent concessions in accordance with Article XXVIII.[181]

As noted at the beginning of this section, a measure, otherwise GATT-inconsistent, is justified under Article XXIV of the GATT 1994 when two conditions are fulfilled. The first condition – the measure must be introduced upon the formation of a customs union that meets the requirements of Article XXIV:8(a) and Article XXIV:5(a) – is discussed in detail above. The second condition requires that, without the introduction of the measure concerned, the formation of a customs union would be impossible.

In *Turkey – Textiles*, the measures at issue were quantitative restrictions on textiles and clothing from India. Turkey did not deny that these quantitive restrictions were inconsistent with its obligations under Articles XI and XIII of the GATT 1994 and Article 2.4 of the *Agreement on Textiles and Clothing*. However, according to Turkey, these quantitative restrictions were justified under Article XXIV. Turkey argued that, unless it was allowed to introduce quantitative restrictions on textiles and clothing from India, it would be prevented from forming a customs union with the European Communities.[182] Turkey asserted that, had it not introduced the quantitative restrictions on textiles and clothing products from India that were at issue, the European Communities would have excluded these products from free trade within the EC–Turkey customs union. According to Turkey, the European Communities would have done so in order to prevent the circumvention of the EC's quantitative restrictions on textiles and clothing from India by importing them into the European Communities via Turkey. Turkey's exports of these products accounted for 40 per cent of Turkey's total exports to the European Communities. Therefore, Turkey expressed strong doubts as to whether the requirement of Article XXIV:8(a)(i) that duties and other restrictive regulations of commerce be eliminated with respect to 'substantially all trade' between Turkey and the European Communities could be met if 40 per cent of Turkey's total exports to the European Communities were excluded.[183] The Appellate Body rejected this argument. It ruled:

> We agree with the Panel that had Turkey not adopted the same quantitative restrictions that are applied by the European Communities, this would not have prevented Turkey and the European Communities from meeting the requirements of subparagraph 8(a)(i) of Article XXIV, and consequently from forming a customs union.

---

[180] Note that the GATT 1994 does not require a WTO Member, benefiting from a reduction of duties upon the formation of a customs union, to provide compensatory adjustment. See *Understanding on Article XXIV*, para. 6.

[181] See *Understanding on Article XXIV*, para. 5; and see above, p. 424.

[182] See Appellate Body Report, *Turkey – Textiles*, para. 61.

[183] For this summary of Turkey's argument, see *ibid.*, para. 61.

We recall our conclusion that the terms of sub-paragraph 8(a)(i) offer some – though limited – flexibility to the constituent members of a customs union when liberalizing their internal trade. As the Panel observed, there are other alternatives available to Turkey and the European Communities to prevent any possible diversion of trade, while at the same time meeting the requirements of sub-paragraph 8(a)(i). For example, Turkey could adopt rules of origin for textile and clothing products that would allow the European Communities to distinguish between those textile and clothing products originating in Turkey, which would enjoy free access to the European Communities under the terms of the customs union, *and* those textile and clothing products originating in third countries, including India.[184]

Questions and Assignments 7.25

What requirements must a 'customs union', within the meaning of Article XXIV of the GATT 1994, meet? What is the meaning of the concepts of 'substantially all trade' and 'substantially the same' in Article XXIV:8(a)? How does the *Understanding on Article XXIV* clarify the requirements that a 'customs union', within the meaning of Article XXIV, must meet? What did the Panel and the Appellate Body rule in *Turkey – Textiles* with respect to the question of whether the regional trade arrangement between Turkey and the European Communities is, in fact, a 'customs union' which meets the requirements of paragraphs 8(a) and 5(a) of Article XXIV? How did the Appellate Body come to the conclusion in *Turkey – Textiles* that the quantitative restriction at issue in that case could not be justified under Article XXIV of the GATT 1994?

7.6.1.2. Free trade areas

As noted above, a measure otherwise GATT-inconsistent is justified under Article XXIV of the GATT 1994:

- if that measure is introduced upon the formation of a free trade area that meets the requirements of Article XXIV:8(b) and Article XXIV:5(b); and
- if the formation of that free trade area would be made impossible if the introduction of the measure concerned were not allowed.

A 'free trade area' is defined in Article XXIV:8(b) of the GATT 1994 as follows:

A free-trade area shall be understood to mean a group of two or more customs territories in which the duties and other restrictive regulations of commerce (except, where necessary, those permitted under Articles XI, XII, XIII, XIV, XV and XX) are eliminated *on substantially all the trade* between the constituent territories in products originating in such territories.

[Emphasis added]

---

[184] *Ibid.*, para. 62. The Appellate Body also noted that Decision 1/95 of the EC–Turkey Association Council specifically provided for the possibility of applying a system of certificates of origin. Rather than making use of this possibility, Turkey had adopted quantitative restrictions on imports of textiles and clothing from India.

Unlike the definition of a 'customs union', discussed above, the definition of a 'free trade area' establishes only a standard for the *internal trade* between constituent members. There is no standard, i.e. there are no requirements, for the trade of constituent members *with third countries*.

The standard for the *internal trade* between constituent members of a free trade area – namely, the elimination of duties and other restrictive regulations of commerce on substantially all trade between constituent members – is identical to the standard for the internal trade between constituent members of a customs union. The case law discussed and observations made in the previous section on 'customs unions' are therefore also relevant for free trade areas.

A free trade area under Article XXIV, however, must not only meet the requirements of Article XXIV:8(b). It must also meet the requirement of Article XXIV:5(b). This provision states:

> with respect to a free-trade area … the duties and other regulations of commerce maintained in each of the constituent territories and applicable at the formation of such free-trade area … to the trade of [Members] not included in such area … shall not be higher or more restrictive than the corresponding duties and other regulations of commerce existing in the same constituent territories prior to the formation of the free-trade area.

Article XXIV:5(b) therefore requires that the duties and other regulations of commerce applied by a member of a free trade area to trade with third countries *after* the formation of the free trade area must *not be higher or more restrictive* than the duties and other regulations of commerce applied by that member *before* the formation of the free trade area. To establish that this is indeed the case is much less problematic than to establish whether the requirements of Article XXIV:5(a) with respect to customs unions are met.[185]

As noted at the beginning of this section, for a measure, otherwise GATT-inconsistent, to be justified under Article XXIV of the GATT 1994, that measure must be such that, if the introduction of the measure concerned were not allowed, the formation of a free trade area would be made impossible. There is no relevant WTO case law on this point yet.

Questions and Assignments 7.26

What requirements must a 'free-trade area' within the meaning of Article XXIV of the GATT 1994 meet? How does a 'free-trade area' differ from a 'customs union'?

---

[185] See above, pp. 653–8.

7.6.1.3. Interim agreements

Measures otherwise GATT-inconsistent may be justified under Article XXIV if taken in the context of interim agreements leading to the establishment of customs unions and free trade areas meeting the requirements discussed in the two previous sections.[186] This is a recognition of the fact that customs unions and free trade areas will not, and cannot, be established overnight. Nevertheless, although most customs unions and free trade areas have been – at least in part – implemented by stages, only a few have expressly been notified as 'interim agreements'.[187] The number of interim agreements is much lower than one would expect it to be.

Article XXIV:5(c) of the GATT 1994 requires with respect to interim agreements:

> any interim agreement ... shall include a plan and schedule for the formation of such a customs union or of such a free-trade area within a reasonable length of time.

Not surprisingly, the vague requirement that the customs union or free trade area be established 'within a reasonable length of time' was quite controversial under the GATT 1947. The *Understanding on Article XXIV* therefore provides that this reasonable period of time should not exceed ten years except in exceptional circumstances.[188] It remains to be seen whether and how this ten-year time limit will be applied.

Questions and Assignments 7.27

Why does Article XXIV provide rules for interim agreements leading to the formation of a customs union or free trade agreement? When may measures, otherwise GATT-inconsistent, be justified under Article XXIV as measures taken in the context of an interim agreement leading to the establishment of a customs union or a free trade area?

7.6.1.4. Regional trade agreements and developing country Members

The Decision of the GATT Contracting Parties of 28 November 1979 on *Differential and More Favourable Treatment, Reciprocity and Fuller Participation of Developing Countries*, commonly referred to as the 'Enabling Clause',[189] provides, in relevant part:

> 1. Notwithstanding the provisions of Article I of the General Agreement, [Members] may accord differential and more favourable treatment to developing countries, without according such treatment to other [Members].
> 2. The provisions of paragraph 1 apply to the following:
>
>   . . .

---

[186] See above, pp. 653–9.   [187] See WT/REG/W/37, para. 47.   [188] *Understanding on Article XXIV*, para. 3.
[189] On the Enabling Clause, see also above, pp. 393–4, and below, pp. 679–82.

> a. Regional or global arrangements entered into amongst less-developed [Members] for the mutual reduction or elimination of tariffs and, in accordance with criteria or conditions which may be prescribed by the [Ministerial Conference], for the mutual reduction or elimination of non-tariff measures, on products imported from one another.[190]

The Enabling Clause is now part of the GATT 1994, and is therefore still in force. It allows preferential arrangements among developing country Members in derogation from the MFN treatment obligation of Article I of the GATT 1994. The conditions that regional trade agreements under the Enabling Clause must meet are less demanding and less specific than those set out in Article XXIV of the GATT. In fact, paragraph 3 of the Enabling Clause 'merely' requires that:

> Any differential and more favourable treatment provided under this clause:
>
> a. shall be designed to facilitate and promote the trade of developing countries and not to raise barriers to or create undue difficulties for the trade of any other [Members].

The regional trade agreements under the Enabling Clause include:

- the Treaty Establishing the Common Market for Eastern and Southern Africa ('COMESA');
- the Treaty Establishing the Common Market of the South ('MERCOSUR'); and
- the Common Effective Preferential Tariffs Scheme for the ASEAN Free Trade Area ('AFTA').

Questions and Assignments 7.28

In your opinion, does Article XXIV of the GATT 1994 apply to regional trade agreements between developing country Members? What requirements apply to these agreements?

7.6.1.5. Procedural issues

Customs unions and free trade areas, as well as interim agreements leading to the formation of such a union or area, are reviewed by the WTO to determine their consistency with the GATT 1994. WTO Members deciding to enter into a customs union, free trade area or an interim agreement must notify this intention to the Council for Trade in Goods. Since 1996, such notifications are examined by the Committee on Regional Trade Agreements (CRTA).[191] The CRTA reports to the Council for Trade in Goods, which then makes a recommendation to the Members concerning the GATT-consistency.[192] The examination of the GATT-consistency is, as was stated by the Panel in

---

[190] BISD 26S/203.
[191] On the terms of reference of the CRTA, see WT/L/127. Note that the regional trade agreements falling under the Enabling Clause are examined by the Committee on Trade and Development.
[192] See *Understanding on Article XXIV*, para. 7. Note, however, the inability of the CRTA to finalise reports. See below, p. 662.

Turkey – Textiles, 'a very complex undertaking' requiring consideration by the CRTA 'from the economic, legal and political perspectives of different Members, of the numerous facets of a regional trade agreement'.[193] However, unable to reach consensus, the CRTA has thus far adopted only one report on the GATT-consistency of a customs union, free trade area or interim agreement.[194] Nevertheless, it has been suggested that in view of the existence of this political process of reviewing the GATT-consistency of customs unions, free trade areas and interim agreements, WTO dispute settlement panels (and the Appellate Body) would not have jurisdiction to decide on the GATT-consistency of such unions, areas or agreements. In *Turkey – Textiles*, the Appellate Body has effectively rejected this view.[195]

Customs unions and constituents of free trade areas must report periodically (i.e., every two years) to the Council for Trade in Goods.[196] Any significant changes to the agreements establishing customs unions or free-trade agreements should be reported as they occur.[197]

Questions and Assignments 7.29

Has the examination of the GATT-consistency of customs unions, free-trade areas and interim agreements by the CRTA been 'successful'? In your opinion, should panels have jurisdiction to assess the GATT-consistency of customs unions, free trade areas and interim agreements?

7.6.2. Article V of the GATS

Article V of the GATS, entitled 'Economic Integration', is the counterpart of Article XXIV of the GATT 1994 for trade in services. Article V:1 of the GATS provides:

> This Agreement shall not prevent any of its Members from being a party to or entering into an agreement liberalizing trade in services between or among the parties to such an agreement, provided that such an agreement:
>
> a. has substantial sectoral coverage,[198] and

---

[193] Panel Report, *Turkey – Textiles*, para. 9.52.

[194] Report on the Czech Republic–Slovak Republic Customs Union, see WT/REG/W/37, 10. Also, under the GATT 1947, the working groups examining the GATT-consistency of customs unions, free trade areas or interim agreements were unable, in all but a few cases, to come to a conclusion.

[195] Appellate Body Report, *Turkey – Textiles*, para. 60. Although the Appellate Body was not called upon to address this issue, it explicitly referred to its conclusions on a 'similar' issue in *India – Quantitative Restrictions*. See below, pp. 672–4. Furthermore, note para. 12 of the *Understanding on Article XXIV* which states: 'The provisions of Articles XXII and XXIII of GATT 1994 as elaborated and applied by the Dispute Settlement Understanding may be invoked with respect to any matters arising from the application of those provisions of Article XXIV relating to customs unions, free-trade areas or interim agreements leading to the formation of a customs union or free-trade area.'

[196] See *Understanding on Article XXIV*, para. 11.

[197] *Ibid*. These reporting requirements are not applicable to regional trade agreements among developing country Members.

[198] The original footnote 1 in the quote reads: 'This condition is understood in terms of number of sectors, volume of trade affected and modes of supply. In order to meet this condition, agreements should not provide for the *a priori* exclusion of any mode of supply.'

the 'substantial sectoral coverage' test. However, it is clear that the number of exclusions must be limited.

As the Panel in *Canada – Autos* stated:

> the purpose of Article V is to allow for ambitious liberalization to take place at a regional level, while at the same time guarding against undermining the MFN obligation by engaging in *minor preferential arrangements*.[201]
>
> [Emphasis added]

7.6.2.2. *'Substantially all discrimination' requirement*

Article V:1(b) of the GATS requires that an economic integration agreement should provide for 'the absence or elimination of substantially all discrimination'.[202] As Article V:1(b) does not require the absence or elimination of *all* discrimination, but rather the absence or elimination of *substantially all* discrimination, the question arises as to what extent discriminatory measures should be allowed to exist in an economic intergration agreement.[203] The scope of such permissible discriminatory measures is, of course, affected by the scope of the list of exceptions in Article V:1(b). This list explicitly includes exceptions permitted under Articles XI, XII, XIV and XIV *bis* of the GATS, but it is unclear whether this list is exhaustive. The scope of permissible discriminatory measures is also affected by the meaning given to the 'and/or' wording in Article V:1(b) linking provisions (i) and (ii). Some Members are of the opinion that the 'or' allows the parties to an economic integration agreement to choose between provisions (i) and (ii), that is, the elimination of existing discriminatory measures, or, alternatively, the use of a standstill. A party could therefore choose only to eliminate the possibility of adding new measures or of making existing measures more restrictive, rather than also having to eliminate existing measures. Other Members have rejected this interpretation. They argue that, considering that Article V:1(b) aims to deal with 'substantially all discrimination', it would be appropriate to interpret the 'and/or' wording in such a way that both (i) and (ii) are found to be applicable. Thus, it is argued that paragraphs (i) and (ii) are *options* to be judged as appropriate against the circumstances of the sector being considered, *not* as *alternatives* to be freely chosen by the parties to the economic integration agreement.[204]

The Panel in *Canada – Autos* noted with respect to the obligation under Article V:1(b):

---

[201] Panel Report, *Canada – Autos*, para. 10.271.

[202] Note that Article V:2 of the GATS states that the evaluation of an agreement's consistency with Article V:1(b) may also take into account its relationship with 'a wider process of economic integration or trade liberalization' among the parties to the agreement. A 'wider process of economic integration' refers to a process of economic integration involving the elimination of barriers to trade not only in services but also in goods.

[203] Note that Article V:6 of the GATS provides that a third-party service supplier, legally recognised as a juridical person by a party to an economic integration agreement, is entitled to equivalent treatment granted within the economic integration area, provided that it engages in 'substantive business operations' in the territory of the parties to that agreement.

[204] See Committee on Regional Trade Agreement, *Examination of the North American Free Trade Agreement*, Note on the Meeting of 24 February 1997, WT/REG4/M/4, dated 16 April 1997.

> Although the requirement of Article V:1(b) is to provide non-discrimination in the sense of Article XVII (National Treatment), we consider that once it is fulfilled it would also ensure non-discrimination between all service suppliers of other parties to the economic integration agreement. It is our view that the object and purpose of this provision is to eliminate all discrimination among services and service suppliers of parties to an economic integration agreement, including discrimination between the suppliers of other parties to an economic integration agreement.[205]

According to the Panel, it would be inconsistent with Article V:1(b) if a party to an economic integration agreement were to extend more favourable treatment to the service suppliers of one party than it does to the service suppliers of another party to that agreement.[206]

The concept of 'a reasonable timeframe' in Article V:1(b) is not defined or clarified in any way in the GATS. On the basis of Article XXIV:5(c) of the GATT 1994 and paragraph 3 of the *Understanding on Article XXIV* concerning the similar concept of 'a reasonable length of time', it would be reasonable to suppose that, in defining the 'reasonable timeframe' of Article V:1(b), a ten-year limit would be used as a general starting-point.

7.6.2.3. 'Barriers to trade' requirement

Article V:4 requires that an economic integration agreement must be designed to facilitate trade between the parties to the agreement and must *not*, in respect of any Member outside the agreement, *raise* the overall level of *barriers* to trade in services within the respective sectors or subsectors compared to the level applicable prior to such an agreement. The absence of detailed data on trade in services and differences in regulatory mechanisms between Members makes it difficult to evaluate the level of barriers in effect before the establishment of an economic integration agreement. A possible approach to the application of this 'barriers to trade' requirement would be to require that an economic integration agreement reduce neither the level, nor the growth, of trade in any sector or subsector below a historical trend.[207]

7.6.2.4. Economic integration agreements and developing-country Members

With regard to economic integration agreements to which developing countries are parties, Article V:3(a) of the GATS provides for flexibility regarding the conditions set out in Article V:1, quoted and discussed above. This flexibility is to be granted 'in accordance with the level of development of the countries concerned, both overall and in individual sectors and subsectors'.

Article V:3(b) of the GATS provides that, in the case of an economic integration agreement involving only developing countries, 'more favourable

---

[205] Panel Report, *Canada – Autos*, para. 10.270.   [206] *Ibid.*, para. 10.270.
[207] Changes in the volume of trade could be judged by data on domestic economic activities if data on trade in services is unavailable.

treatment may be granted to juridical persons owned or controlled by natural persons of the parties to such an agreement'.[208]

7.6.2.5. Procedural matters

Article V:7 requires WTO Members that are parties to an economic integration agreement promptly to notify such an agreement (and any enlargement or any significant modification of that agreement) to the Council for Trade in Services.[209] At the request of the Council for Trade in Services, the CRTA will examine such an agreement (or enlargement or modification of that agreement) and report back on its GATS-consistency.[210] The Council for Trade in Services may make such recommendations as it deems appropriate. The regional integration agreements referred to date to the CTRA for an examination of their GATS-consistency include:

- the Treaty of Accession of Austria, Finland and Sweden to the European Union;[211]
- the North American Free Trade Agreement;[212]
- the Australia–New Zealand Closer Economic Relations Trade Agreement;[213] and
- the Free Trade Agreement between Chile and Mexico.[214]

Article V:5 of the GATS requires a party to an economic integration agreement to provide at least ninety days advance notice of any modification or withdrawal of a specific commitment that was inconsistent with the terms and conditions set out in its Schedule. In such situations, that party must initiate the procedure for the modification of schedules and the compensatory adjustment set forth in Article XXI of the GATS.

7.6.2.6. Labour markets integration agreement

Article V bis, entitled 'Labour Markets Integration Agreements', deals with a specific form of economic integration agreement which establishes full integration of labour markets between or among the parties to such an agreement. Such agreements give the nationals of the parties free entry to each other's labour markets. Usually, these agreements also include provisions concerning conditions of pay, other conditions of employment and social benefits.

---

[208] Article V:3(b) applies notwithstanding Article V:6 of the GATS, referred to in footnote 203, p. 664 above.
[209] See Article V:7(a) of the GATS. Note that Members which are parties to an economic integration agreement which is implemented on the basis of a timeframe shall report periodically to the Council for Trade in Services on its implementation. See Article V:7(b) of the GATS.
[210] Recall that regional trade agreements under the Enabling Clause are examined by the Committee on Trade and Development. Regional trade agreements among developing-country Members will be examined by the CRTA.
[211] See S/C/M/2, paras. 9 and 10.   [212] See S/C/M/3, paras. 27 and 28.
[213] See S/C/M/14, Section E.   [214] See S/C/M/52, Section C.

Article V *bis* provides that the GATS shall not prevent any WTO Member from being a party to such agreement provided that the agreement:

- exempts citizens of parties to the agreement from requirements concerning residency and work permits; and
- is notified to the Council for Trade in Services.

Questions and Assignments 7.30

When is a measure, which is otherwise GATS-inconsistent, justified under Article V of the GATS? Give two examples of economic integration agreements not already mentioned above. When must a party to an economic integration agreement initiate the procedure for the modification of schedules and compensatory adjustment set forth in Article XXI of the GATS? What are labour markets integration agreements?

7.7. BALANCE-OF-PAYMENTS EXCEPTIONS

In addition to the 'general exceptions', the 'security exceptions', the 'economic emergency exceptions' and the 'regional integration exceptions' discussed above, WTO law also provides for 'balance-of-payments exceptions'. These exceptions allow Members to adopt measures, otherwise GATT- or GATS-inconsistent, taken to safeguard their external financial position and to protect their balance of payments. The outflow of money from a country can indeed be limited, in a fairly easy and effective manner, by imposing trade restrictive measures on imports into the country. In the past, the balance-of-payments exceptions have been quite important. In today's world of floating exchange rates, balance-of-payments problems may be resolved by other means than through trade restrictions. Nevertheless, the balance-of-payments exceptions are still of some importance: developing-country Members, in particular, continue to use these exceptions. In times of rapid economic development, countries often experience severe pressure on their monetary reserves.

The balance-of-payments exceptions are set out in Articles XII and XVIII:B of the GATT 1994 and Article XII of the GATS. The balance-of-payments exception for trade in goods is further elaborated in the *Understanding on Balance of Payments Provisions of the GATT 1994* (the *'Understanding on BoP Provisions'*), which is part of the GATT 1994.

7.7.1. Articles XII and XVIII:B of the GATT 1994

Article XII of the GATT 1994, entitled 'Restrictions to Safeguard the Balance of Payment', states, in its first paragraph:

> Notwithstanding the provisions of paragraph 1 of Article XI, any [Member], in order to safeguard its external financial position and its balance of payments, may restrict the quantity or value of merchandise permitted to be imported, subject to the provisions of the following paragraphs of this Article.

Article XVIII of the GATT 1994, entitled 'Governmental Assistance to Economic Development', provides in paragraph 4(a) as follows:

> a [Member], the economy of which can only support low standards of living and is in the early stages of development, shall be free to deviate temporarily from the provisions of the other Articles of this Agreement, as provided in Sections A, B and C of this Article.

Section B of Article XVIII, i.e. paragraphs 8 to 12 of Article XVIII, provides for a special balance-of-payments exception for developing-country Members. Article XVIII:9 states, in relevant part:

> In order to safeguard its external financial position and to ensure a level of reserves adequate for the implementation of its programme of economic development, a [Member] coming within the scope of paragraph 4 (*a*) of this Article may, subject to the provisions of paragraphs 10 to 12, control the general level of its imports by restricting the quantity or value of merchandise permitted to be imported; *Provided* that . . .

Under Article XII, the purpose of a Member's balance-of-payments (BoP) measure is 'to safeguard its external financial position and to protect its balance of payments'. Under Article XVIII:B, the purpose of a BoP measure taken by a developing-country Member is also 'to safeguard its external financial position' but, in addition, 'to ensure a level of reserves adequate for the implementation of its programme for economic development'.

This section of Chapter 7 examines:

- the nature of measures that may be taken for BoP purposes;
- the requirements for taking such measures; and
- procedural issues related to the taking of such measures.

7.7.1.1. *Nature of BoP measures*

Articles XII and XVIII:B of the GATT 1994 only allow quantitative restrictions to be used to address balance-of-payments problems. They do not allow for tariff measures.[215] However, it was common practice under the GATT 1947 for Contracting Parties to take balance-of-payments action in the form of tariff or tariff-like measures, such as import surcharges. In 1979 the use of such measures was formally authorised in the *Declaration on Trade Measures Taken for Balance of Payments Purposes* (the '*1979 Declaration*').[216] The 1994 *Understanding on BoP Provisions* goes much further and commits WTO Members to give preference to price-based BoP measures. Paragraph 2 of the *Understanding on BoP Provisions* states:

---

[215] Note that this rule is inconsistent with the general GATT preference for using tariffs instead of quantitative restrictions. See above, pp. 442–3.

[216] Adopted on 28 November 1979, BISD 26S/205–9. Note that this Declaration is still applicable law.

> Members confirm their commitment to give preference to those measures which have the least disruptive effect on trade. Such measures (referred to in this Understanding as "price-based measures") shall be understood to include import surcharges, import deposit requirements or other equivalent trade measures with an impact on the price of imported goods. It is understood that, notwithstanding the provisions of Article II, price-based measures taken for balance-of-payments purposes may be applied by a Member in excess of the duties inscribed in the Schedule of that Member . . .

If a Member decides to apply a price-based BoP measure, it must indicate the amount by which the price-based measure exceeds the bound duty clearly and separately.[217]

While under Article XII, quantitative restrictions were initially the only form of BoP measures allowed, paragraph 3 of the *Understanding on BoP Provisions* now provides:

> Members shall seek to avoid the imposition of new quantitative restrictions for balance-of-payments purposes unless, because of a critical balance-of-payments situation, price-based measures cannot arrest a sharp deterioration in the external payments position.

If a Member applies a quantitative restriction as a BoP measure, it must provide justification as to the reasons why price-based measures are not an adequate instrument to deal with the balance-of-payments situation.[218]

Pursuant to the *Understanding on BoP Provisions*, not more than one type of restrictive import measure, taken for balance-of-payments purposes, may be applied on the same product.[219] A combination of price-based measures and quantitative restrictions on the same product is therefore prohibited.

7.7.1.2. Requirements for the use of BoP measures

BoP measures, whether in the form of price-based measures or quantitative restrictions, are often inconsistent with the obligations under Articles II or XI of the GATT 1994. Therefore, they can only be applied when strict requirements are met.

First, BoP measures may not exceed what is necessary to address the balance-of-payments problem at hand. Article XII:2 of the GATT 1994 states that BoP measures adopted by Members:

> shall not exceed those necessary:
>
> i. to forestall the imminent threat of, or to stop, a serious decline in its monetary reserves, or
> ii. in the case of a [Member] with very low monetary reserves, to achieve a reasonable rate of increase in its reserves.

---

[217] See para. 2 of the *Understanding on BoP Provisions*. For this purpose, the notification procedure, discussed below, must be followed.

[218] See para. 3 of the *Understanding on BoP Provisions*. Note that Members applying quantitative restrictions as BoP measures must also indicate in successive consultations the progress made in significantly reducing the incidence and restrictive effect of such measures (*ibid.*).

[219] See para. 3 of the *Understanding on BoP Provisions*.

Article XVIII:9 of the GATT 1994 requires that BoP measures adopted by *developing-country* Members:

> shall not exceed those necessary:
>
> a. to forestall the threat of, or to stop, a serious decline in its monetary reserves, or
> b. in the case of a [Member] with inadequate monetary reserves, to achieve a reasonable rate of increase in its reserves.

Note that developing-country Members can adopt BoP measures to forestall a *threat* of a serious decline in monetary reserves, while other Members can only do so to forestall an *imminent threat* of such decline. Also, developing-country Members with *inadequate* monetary reserves may adopt BoP measures while other Members may do so only when they have *very low* monetary reserves. In *India – Quantitative Restrictions*, the Panel distinguished the requirements for taking BoP measures under Article XVIII from the requirements applicable under Article XII, and noted:

> These provisions reflect an acknowledgement of the specific needs of developing countries in relation to measures taken for balance-of-payments purposes.[220]

At its Doha Session in November 2001, the WTO Ministerial Conference explicitly affirmed that Article XVIII is a special and differential treatment provision for developing-country Members and that recourse to it should be *less onerous* than to Article XII.[221]

The determination of what constitutes a serious decline of monetary reserves or an (imminent) threat thereof, or the determination of what constitutes very low or inadequate monetary reserves, is primarily left to the IMF. The WTO consults the IMF on these matters, and Article XV:2 of the GATT 1994 states, in relevant part:

> The [WTO] in reaching [its] final decision in cases involving the criteria set forth in paragraph 2 (*a*) of Article XII or in paragraph 9 of Article XVIII, shall accept the determination of the [IMF] as to what constitutes a serious decline in the [Member's] monetary reserves, a very low level of its monetary reserves or a reasonable rate of increase in its monetary reserves, and as to the financial aspects of other matters covered in consultation in such cases.

Note that in *India – Quantitative Restricions* the IMF reported that India's reserves as of 21 November 1997 were US$25.1 billion and that an adequate level of reserves at that date would have been US$16 billion. The IMF had also reported that India did not face a serious decline of its monetary reserves or a threat thereof.[222] To a large extent, the Panel's conclusions in this case were based on these IMF findings.

Secondly, paragraph 4 of the *Understanding on BoP Provisions* provides that a BoP measure:

---

[220] Panel Report, *India – Quantitative Restrictions*, para. 5.155.
[221] Ministerial Conference, Ministerial Decision, adopted on 14 November 2001, WT/MIN(01)/17, dated 20 November 2001, para. 1.1.
[222] Panel Report, *India – Quantitative Restrictions*, paras. 5.174 and 5.177.

> may only be applied to control the general level of imports and may not exceed what is necessary to address the balance-of-payments situation.

BoP measures must avoid unnecessary damage to the commercial and economic interests of other Members.[223] BoP measures may be discriminatory with respect to products (i.e., apply to some products and not to others), but *not* with respect to countries (i.e., apply to some countries and not to others). Note, however, that the *Understanding on BoP Provisions* requires that Members administer BoP measures in a transparent manner. The authorities of the importing Member must therefore provide adequate justification as to the criteria used to determine which products are subject to the BoP measure.[224]

Thirdly, BoP measures are temporary measures. Members applying BoP measures must announce publicly, as soon as possible, time-schedules for the removal of these measures.[225] Referring to the conditions for their adoption (such as 'a serious decline in monetary reserves' or 'inadequate monetary reserves'), Article XII:2(b) of the GATT 1994 states:

> [Members] applying restrictions under sub-paragraph (*a*) of this paragraph shall progressively relax them as such conditions improve, maintaining them only to the extent that the conditions specified in that sub-paragraph still justify their application. They shall eliminate the restrictions when conditions would no longer justify their institution or maintenance under that sub-paragraph.

As the external financial situation improves, the BoP measures must be relaxed; when the external financial situation has returned to 'normal', the BoP measures must be eliminated.[226] Article XVIII:11 of the GATT 1994 provides for similar obligations with respect to the elimination or relaxation of BoP measures adopted by developing-country Members. However, Article XVIII:11 adds the proviso:

> ... that no [Member] shall be required to withdraw or modify restrictions on the ground that a change in its development policy would render unnecessary the restrictions which it is applying under this Section.

In *India – Quantitative Restrictions*, the Appellate Body upheld the Panel's finding that India could manage its balance-of-payments situation using macroeconomic policy instruments alone, without maintaining quantitative restrictions. India appealed this finding, arguing that the Panel required India to change its development policy. The Appellate Body, however, ruled:

---

[223] See Articles XII:3(c)(i) and XVIII:10 of the GATT 1994.

[224] In the case of certain 'essential products', Members may exclude or limit the application of surcharges applied across the board or other measures applied for balance-of-payments purposes. The concept of 'essential products' shall be understood to mean products which meet basic consumption needs or which contribute to the Member's effort to improve its balance-of-payments situation, such as capital goods or inputs needed for production. See Articles XII:3 and XVIII:10 of the GATT 1994; and para. 4 of the *Understanding on BoP Provisions*.

[225] See para. 1 of the *Understanding on BoP Provisions*.

[226] For BoP measures of developing-country Members, however, note that, if the elimination or relaxation of the BoP measures would produce immediately or very quickly the conditions justifying the adoption or intensification of BoP measures, the BoP measures 'may be maintained'. See Note *Ad* Article XVIII; and Appellate Body Report, *India – Quantitative Restrictions*, paras. 117–20.

> we are of the opinion that the use of macroeconomic policy instruments is not related to any particular development policy, but is resorted to by all Members regardless of the type of development policy they pursue.[227]

The Appellate Body clarified the meaning of the proviso of Article XVIII:11 by stating:

> We believe that structural measures are different from macroeconomic instruments with respect to their relationship to development policy. If India were asked to implement agricultural reform or to scale back reservations on certain products for small-scale units as indispensable policy changes in order to overcome its balance of payments difficulties, such a requirement would probably have involved a change in India's development policy.[228]

Questions and Assignments 7.31

When is a Member allowed to adopt a BoP measure? What form may such a measure take? With which obligations of the GATT 1994 may a BoP measure be inconsistent: the obligations under Article I, Article II or Article XI? When must a Member eliminate or relax the BoP measures it applies?

7.7.1.3. Procedural issues

BoP measures are reviewed by the WTO to determine their consistency with the GATT 1994. This review is conducted by the Committee on Balance-of-Payments Restrictions (the 'BoP Committee'). The procedures applicable to this review are set out in the *Understanding on BoP Provisions*.[229] A Member shall notify the introduction of or any changes in the application of a BoP measure to the General Council.[230] A Member applying new restrictions or raising the general level of its existing restrictions must enter into consultation with the BoP Committee within four months of the adoption of such measures.[231] If the Member concerned fails to request a consultation, the Chairman of the BoP Committee shall invite that Member to hold such a consultation. Any Member may request that notifications on BoP measures

---

[227] *Ibid.*, para. 126.   [228] *Ibid.*, para. 128.

[229] As para. 5 of the *Understanding on BoP Provisions* states, the BoP Committee shall follow the procedures for consultations on balance-of-payments restrictions approved on 28 April 1970 (BISD 18S/48–53) (the 'full consultation procedures'), subject to the provisions set out in the *Understanding*. Consultations may be held under the 'simplified consultation procedures' approved on 19 December 1972 (BISD 20S/47–9) in the case of least-developed-country Members or in the case of developing-country Members in certain situations. See para. 8 of the *Understanding on BoP Provisions*.

[230] See para. 9 of the *Understanding on BoP Provisions*. Every year, each Member shall make available to the WTO Secretariat a consolidated notification on all aspects of the BoP measures applied. *Ibid.*

[231] See para. 6 of the *Understanding on BoP Provisions*. Note that the Member adopting BoP measures may request that a consultation be held under Articles XII:4(a) or XVIII:12(a) of the GATT 1994 as appropriate. *Ibid.* On the course of the consultation process and the role of the WTO Secretariat, see paras. 11 and 12 of the *Understanding on BoP Provisions*.

are reviewed by the BoP Committee.[232] Furthermore, all BoP measures are subject to *periodic* review in the BoP Committee.[233]

The BoP Committee reports on its consultations to the General Council. Pursuant to paragraph 13 of the *Understanding on BoP Provisions*, the BoP Committee shall endeavour to include in its conclusions 'proposals for recommendations aimed at promoting the implementation of Articles XII and XVIII:B, the 1979 Declaration and this Understanding'. In those cases in which a time-schedule has been presented for the removal of BoP measures, the General Council may recommend that, in adhering to such a time-schedule, a Member shall be deemed to be in compliance with its GATT 1994 obligations. Whenever the General Council has made specific recommendations, the rights and obligations of Members shall be assessed in the light of such recommendations. In the absence of specific proposals for recommendations by the General Council, the Committee's conclusions should record the different views expressed in the Committee.[234]

Since its establishment in 1995, the BoP Committee has reviewed many BoP measures notified by Members. In most cases, the Members concerned made commitments to eliminate or relax the BoP measures under review and these commitments satisfied the BoP Committee. In other cases, Members were unable to agree within the BoP Committee on a timeframe for the relaxation and/or elimination of the BoP measures under review.

In *India – Quantitative Restrictions*, India argued that it had the right to maintain BoP measures until the BoP Committee or the General Council would have ordered it to eliminate or relax these measures. The Panel rejected this argument. It noted that the obligation of Article XVIII:11 to eliminate or relax BoP measures:

> is not conditioned on any BoP Committee or General Council decision. If we were to interpret Article XVIII:11 to be so conditioned, we would be adding terms to Article XVIII:11 that it does not contain.[235]

In *India – Quantitative Restrictions*, India also argued that WTO dispute settlement panels have no authority to examine Members' justifications of BoP measures. India based its position on the second sentence of footnote 1 to the *Understanding on BoP Provisions*, which reads:

> The provisions of Articles XXII and XXIII of GATT 1994 as elaborated and applied by the Dispute Settlement Understanding may be invoked with respect to any matters arising from the application of restrictive import measures taken for balance-of-payments purposes.

India interpreted this footnote to mean that the WTO dispute settlement system may be invoked in respect of matters relating to the specific use

---

[232] See para. 10 of the *Understanding on BoP Provisions*.

[233] See para. 7 of the *Understanding on BoP Provisions*, which refers in this respect to Articles XII:4(b) and XVIII:12(b) of the GATT 1994.

[234] Note also the powers given to the Ministerial Conference in Articles XII:4(c), (d) and (f) and XVIII:12(c), (d) and (f) of the GATT 1994. These powers have never been used.

[235] Panel Report, *India – Quantitative Restrictions*, para. 5.79.

or purpose of a BoP measure or to the manner in which a BoP measure is applied in a particular case, but not with respect to the question of the balance-of-payments *justification* of these measures. More generally, India argued the existence of a 'principle of institutional balance' that requires panels to refrain from reviewing the justification of balance-of-payments restrictions under Article XVIII:B. Such review was entrusted to the BoP Committee and the General Council. The Appellate Body rejected India's arguments and stated:

> Any doubts that may have existed in the past as to whether the dispute settlement procedures under Article XXIII were available for disputes relating to balance-of-payments restrictions have been removed by the second sentence of footnote 1 to the *BOP Understanding*...
>
> ...
>
> ... in light of footnote 1 to the *BOP Understanding*, a dispute relating to the justification of balance-of-payments restrictions is clearly within the scope of matters to which the dispute settlement provisions of Article XXIII of the GATT 1994, as elaborated and applied by the DSU, are applicable.[236]

The fact that panels are competent to review the justification of BoP measures does *not* make the competence of the BoP Committee and the General Council, discussed above, redundant. In *India – Quantitative Restrictions*, the Appellate Body ruled:

> We are cognisant of the competence of the BoP Committee and the General Council with respect to balance-of-payments restrictions under Article XVIII:12 of the GATT 1994 and the *BoP Understanding*. However, we see no conflict between that competence and the competence of panels. Moreover, we are convinced that, in considering the justification of balance-of-payments restrictions, panels should take into account the deliberations and conclusions of the BoP Committee, as did the panel in *Korea – Beef*.[237]

The Appellate Body agreed with the Panel that the BoP Committee and panels have different functions, and that the BoP Committee procedures and the dispute settlement procedures differ in nature, scope, timing and type of outcome.[238]

Questions and Assignments 7.32

What is the role of the BoP Committee? Find out whether India and Brazil still maintain BoP measures. Can a panel review the balance-of-payments justification of the BoP measure before or during the review of the GATT consistency of this measure by the BoP Committee?

7.7.2. Article XII of the GATS

Article XII of the GATS, entitled 'Restrictions to Safeguard the Balance of Payments', provides, in its first paragraph:

---

[236] Appellate Body Report, *India – Quantitative Restrictions*, paras. 87 and 95.
[237] *Ibid.*, para. 103.   [238] *Ibid.*, paras. 5.90 and 5.114.

> In the event of serious balance-of-payments and external financial difficulties or threat thereof, a Member may adopt or maintain restrictions on trade in services on which it has undertaken specific commitments, including on payments or transfers for transactions related to such commitments.

The GATS recognises that particular pressures on the balance of payments of a Member in the process of economic development or economic transition may necessitate the use of restrictions to ensure, *inter alia*, the maintenance of a level of financial reserves adequate for the implementation of its programme of economic development or economic transition.[239]

In situations of *serious* balance-of-payments and external financial difficulties or a threat thereof, Members may adopt or maintain BoP measures which restrict trade in services in a manner which is GATS-inconsistent. However, as is explicitly provided in Article XII:2 of the GATS, these BoP measures shall:

- not discriminate among Members;
- be consistent with the Articles of Agreement of the IMF;
- avoid unnecessary damage to the commercial, economic and financial interests of any other Member;
- not exceed those necessary to deal with the circumstances described in Article XII:1, quoted above; and
- be temporary and be phased out progressively as the situation specified in Article XII:1 improves.

Any BoP measure restricting trade in services, or any changes thereto, must be promptly notified to the General Council.[240] Members adopting or changing BoP measures must consult with the BoP Committee promptly.[241] As for BoP measures restricting trade in goods, BoP measures restricting trade in services are the subject of periodic consultations. The consultations with the BoP Committee shall address the compliance of BoP measures with the requirements of Article XII:2, in particular the progressive phase-out of restrictions.[242] The IMF also plays a central role with regard to BoP measures restricting trade in services in the consultations on the GATS-consistency of BoP measures.[243]

Questions and Assignments 7.33

When are measures which restrict trade in services, in a manner which is GATS-inconsistent, justified under Article XII of the GATS?

---

[239] See Article XII:1 of the GATS.   [240] See Article XII:4 of the GATS.
[241] See Article XII:5(c) of the GATS.   [242] See Article XII:5(d) of the GATS.
[243] See Article VII:5(e) of the GATS. All findings of statistical and other facts presented by the IMF relating to foreign exchange, monetary reserves and balance of payments, shall be accepted and conclusions of the BoP Committee shall be based on the assessment by the IMF of the balance of payments and the external financial situation of the consulting Member.

7.8. ECONOMIC DEVELOPMENT EXCEPTIONS

As explicitly stated in the Preamble to the *WTO Agreement*, there is:

> a need for positive efforts designed to ensure that developing countries ... secure a share in the growth in international trade commensurate with the needs of their economic development.

The 'positive efforts' in favour of developing countries currently undertaken by the WTO take many forms. Almost all WTO agreements provide for special and differential treatment provisions for developing-country Members to facilitate their integration into the world trading system and to promote their economic development. These provisions, also referred to as 'S&D treatment' provisions, can be subdivided into six categories:

- provisions aimed at increasing the trade opportunities of developing-country Members;
- provisions under which WTO Members should safeguard the interests of developing-country Members;
- flexibility of commitments, of action, and use of policy instruments;
- transitional time periods;
- technical assistance; and
- provisions relating to least-developed-country Members.[244]

Some of these provisions have been dealt with, or at least referred to, above. As discussed in Chapter 2, the *WTO Agreement* establishes a Committee on Trade and Development, and the WTO provides technical assistance to developing-country Members to allow these Members to exercise fully their rights and obligations under the *WTO Agreement* and to participate effectively in trade negotiations.[245] As discussed in Chapter 3, the Dispute Settlement Understanding contains special rules for developing-country Members in order to help those countries to overcome the problems they encounter as complainants or respondents in WTO dispute settlement proceedings.[246] As discussed in Chapter 5, Article XXXVI:8 of the GATT 1994 and the Enabling Clause provide that, in tariff negotiations with developed-country Members, developing-country Members are expected to 'reciprocate' only to the extent that is consistent with their development, financial and trade needs.[247] Article XXXVII:1 of the GATT 1994, on the other hand, calls upon developed-country

---

[244] See Committee on Trade and Development, *Implementation of Special and Differential Treatment Provisions in WTO Agreements and Decisions*, Note by the WTO Secretariat, WT/COMTD/W/77/Rev.1, dated 21 September 2001, para. 3. See also the addenda to this Note and, in particular, Addendum 4, WT/COMTD/W/77/Rev.1/Add.4, dated 7 February 2002.

[245] See above, pp. 128–9 and pp. 100–3.

[246] See above, pp. 226–8. These special DSU rules in favour of developing-country Members are found in Article 3.12 (regarding the application of the 1966 Decision), Article 4.10 (regarding consultations), Article 8.10 (regarding the composition of panels), Article 12.10 (regarding consultations and the time to prepare and present arguments), Article 12.11 (regarding the content of panel reports), Article 24 (regarding least-developed countries) and Article 27.2 (assistance from the WTO Secretariat).

[247] See above, pp. 393–4.

Members to give high priority to the reduction and elimination of existing market access barriers, and to refrain from introducing new barriers, on products currently or potentially of export interest to developing-country Members.[248] Chapter 6 discussed special rules that apply to developing countries applying anti-dumping duties or countervailing duties or that grant subsidies.[249] As discussed earlier in this chapter, special, more flexible rules exist for the benefit of developing-country Members taking safeguard measures, forming customs unions or free trade areas or taking BoP measures.[250]

In the last section of this chapter, the focus will be on two S&D treatment provisions that have not been discussed yet, namely:

• the infant-industry-protection exception under Article XVIII of the GATT 1994; and
• the Generalised System of Preferences (GSP) exception under the Enabling Clause.

These exceptions allow Members to adopt measures, otherwise WTO-inconsistent, to promote the economic development of developing-country Members.

7.8.1. Infant-industry-protection exception

As discussed in Chapter 1, one of the traditional arguments used to justify trade restrictions is the *infant-industry-protection* argument.[251] On the basis of this argument, during the nineteenth century, the infant manufacturing industries of the United States and Germany were protected against import competition. Today, this argument could be of relevance and importance for developing countries. While developing countries may have a potential comparative advantage in certain industries, their 'infant' producers are not yet in a position to compete with the already established producers in developed countries. By means of a customs duty or an import restriction, national producers can be affforded temporary protection, allowing them breathing space to become strong enough to compete with well-established producers.

Article XVIII of the GATT 1994 allows developing-country Members, under specific conditions, to take measures otherwise GATT-inconsistent to protect their infant industries against import competition. Article XVIII:2, entitled 'Governmental Assistance to Economic Development', states that, for Members 'the economies of which can only support low standards of living and are in the early stages of development',[252] i.e. developing-country Members:

---

[248] See above, p. 390.   [249] See above, pp. 549–51, 586–7.
[250] See above, pp. 638, 639, 660–1, 668, 670.
[251] See above, p. 26. Note that the argument for infant industry protection was already made by Alexander Hamilton in 1791.
[252] See Article XVIII:1 of the GATT 1994.

> it may be necessary ... in order to implement programmes and policies of economic development designed to raise the general standard of living of their people, to take protective or other measures affecting imports, and that such measures are justified in so far as they facilitate the attainment of the objectives of this Agreement.

Article XVIII:4 explicitly states that developing-country Members:

> shall be free to deviate temporarily from the provisions of the other Articles of this Agreement, as provided in Sections A, B and C of this Article.

Section A of Article XVIII, i.e. Article XVIII:7, of the GATT 1994 is of particular relevance to the infant-industry-protection exception.[253] Pursuant to this provision, if a developing-country Member considers it desirable, in order to promote the establishment of a particular industry, to modify or withdraw a tariff concession, it can do so. Article XVIII:7 therefore allows a developing-country Member to take a measure otherwise inconsistent with its obligations under Article II:1 of the GATT 1994. However, the developing-country Member concerned must enter into negotiations with the Members primarily affected by the modification or withdrawal of the tariff concession in order to come to an agreement on compensatory adjustment.[254] If no agreement is reached, it is for the General Council to decide whether the compensatory adjustment offered is adequate. Where the General Council considers the compensation to be adequate, the developing-country Member is then free to modify or withdraw the tariff concession provided that, at the same time, it gives effect to the compensatory adjustment. Should the General Council find the compensation offered to be inadequate, but also that every reasonable effort was made to offer adequate compensation, the developing-country Member may proceed with the modification or withdrawal of the tariff concession.[255] Any other Member affected by the modification or withdrawal is then free to modify or withdraw substantially equivalent concessions with regard to the developing-country Member concerned.[256] Under the GATT 1947, the GATT Council was generous in allowing developing-country Members to modify or withdraw tariff concessions without requiring any compensatory adjustment. As discussed in Chapter 1, the contribution of the exception under Article XVIII:7 to the economic development of developing countries has been limited.[257] In fact, the infant-industry-protection exception under Article XVIII:7 has not been invoked by any developing-country Member since the entry into force of the *WTO Agreement* in 1995.[258]

---

[253] Section B of Article XVIII, i.e. Article XVIII:7 to XVIII:12, of the GATT 1994 provides for a special balance-of-payments exception for developing-country Members, discussed in detail above, pp. 668, 670. Section C of Article XVIII, i.e. Articles XVIII:13 to XVIII:21, of the GATT 1994 allows developing-country Members to grant governmental assistance to 'promote the establishment of a particular industry'.
[254] Article XVIII:7(a) of the GATT 1994.   [255] Article XVIII:7(b) of the GATT 1994.
[256] *Ibid.*   [257] See above, p. 26.
[258] Committee on Trade and Development, *Implementation of Special and Differential Treatment Provisions in WTO Agreements and Decisions*, Note by the WTO Secretariat, Addendum 4, WT/COMTD/W/77/Rev.1/Add.4, dated 7 February 2002, 2.

7.8.2. Generalised System of Preferences exception

The 1979 GATT Decision on *Differential and More Favourable Treatment, Reciprocity, and Fuller Participation of Developing Countries*, which is commonly referred to as the 'Enabling Clause' and which is now an integral part of the GATT 1994,[259] states, in paragraph 1:

> Notwithstanding the provisions of Article I of the General Agreement, [Members] may accord differential and more favourable treatment to developing countries, without according such treatment to other [Members].[260]

7.8.2.1. *Preferential tariff treatment for developing countries under the Enabling Clause*

Paragraph 2(a) of the Enabling Clause provides that the differential and more favourable treatment referred to in paragraph 1 includes:

> Preferential tariff treatment accorded by [developed-country Members] to products originating in [developing-country Members] in accordance with the Generalized System of Preferences ...[261]

As the Appellate Body ruled in *EC – Tariff Preferences*, the Enabling Clause operates as an 'exception' to Article I:1 of the GATT 1994.[262] Paragraph 1 of the Enabling Clause explicitly exempts Members from complying with the obligation contained in Article I:1 for the purposes of providing differential and more favourable treatment to developing countries.[263] The Enabling Clause authorises developed-country Members to grant enhanced market access to products from developing countries extending beyond the access granted to like products from developed countries.[264] The Enabling Clause

---

[259] The Enabling Clause is one of the 'other decisions of the CONTRACTING PARTIES' within the meaning of para. 1(b)(iv) of Annex 1A incorporating the GATT 1994 into the *WTO Agreement*. See Appellate Body Report, *EC – Tariff Preferences*, para. 90 and footnote 192.

[260] GATT Document L/4903, dated 28 November 1979, BISD 26S/203. The Enabling Clause was adopted by the GATT CONTRACTING PARTIES in the context of the Tokyo Round of Multilateral Trade Negotiations. Note that the Enabling Clause replaced, and expanded, a 1971 Waiver Decision on the Generalised System of Preferences, GATT Document L/3545, dated 25 June 1971, BISD 18S/24. This Waiver Decision was in turn adopted to give effect to the Agreed Conclusions of the UNCTAD Special Committee on Preferences, adopted in 1970. These Agreed Conclusions recognised in para. I:2 that preferential tariff treatment accorded under a generalized scheme of preferences was key for developing countries "(a) to increase their export earnings; (b) to promote their industrialization; and (c) to accelerate their rates of economic growth".

[261] The footnote in the original reads: 'As described in the Decision of the CONTRACTING PARTIES of 25 June 1971, relating to the establishment of "generalized, non-reciprocal and non-discriminatory preferences beneficial to the developing countries" (BISD 18S/24).'

[262] See Appellate Body Report, *EC – Tariff Preferences*, para. 99. On this point, the Appellate Body upheld the finding of the Panel; see Panel Report, *EC – Tariff Preferences*, para. 7.53. The European Communities argued in *EC – Tariff Preferences* that the Enabling Clause, reflecting the fundamental objective of assisting developing-country Members, is not an exception to Article I:1 of the GATT 1994 but exists 'side-by-side and on an equal level' with Article I:1. The Appellate Body disagreed and ruled that: "characterising the Enabling Clause as an exception, in our view, does not undermine the importance of the Enabling Clause within the overall framework of the covered agreements and as a "positive effort" to enhance economic development of developing–country Members. Nor does it "discourag[e]" developed countries from adopting measures in favour of developing countries under the Enabling Clause." See Appellate Body Report, *EC – Tariff Preferences*, para. 95.

[263] See *ibid.*, para. 90.   [264] *Ibid.*, para. 106.

thus permits Members to provide 'differential and more favourable treatment' to developing countries 'in spite of' the MFN treatment obligation of Article I:1, which normally requires that such treatment be extended to all Members 'immediately and unconditionally'. What is more, WTO Members are *not merely allowed* to deviate from Article I:1 in the pursuit of 'differential and more favourable treatment' for developing countries; they are *encouraged* to do so.[265]

As discussed in Chapter 5, most developed-country Members grant preferential tariff treatment to imports from developing countries under their respective Generalised System of Preferences (GSP) schemes. The Enabling Clause thus plays a vital role in promoting trade as a means of stimulating economic growth and development.[266]

As with all of the other exceptions discussed in this chapter, before the Enabling Clause can successfully be invoked, certain conditions must be fulfilled. The deviation from the MFN obligation of Article I:1 is allowed only when, and to the extent that, the conditions set out in paragraphs 3 and 4 of the Enabling Clause are met. Paragraph 3 sets out the following substantive conditions:

> Any differential and more favourable treatment provided under this clause:
>
> a. shall be designed to facilitate and promote the trade of developing countries and not to raise barriers to or create undue difficulties for the trade of any other [Members];
> b. shall not constitute an impediment to the reduction or elimination of tariffs and other restrictions to trade on a most-favoured-nation basis;
> c. shall in the case of such treatment accorded by [developed-country Members] to developing countries be designed and, if necessary, modified, to respond positively to the development, financial and trade needs of developing countries.

Paragraph 4 sets out the procedural conditions for the introduction, modification and withdrawal of a preferential measure for developing countries. Pursuant to paragraph 4, Members granting preferential tariff treatment to developing countries must notify the WTO and afford adequate opportunity for prompt consultations at the request of any interested Member with respect to any difficulty or matter that may arise.

7.8.2.2. *Additional preferential tariff treatment under the Enabling Clause*

In *EC – Tariff Preferences*, the question arose as to whether the European Communities could grant *additional* preferential tariff treatment to certain developing countries to the exclusion of others. Council Regulation (EC) No. 2501/2001 of 10 December 2001, the EC's Generalised System of Preferences Regulation,[267] provides for five preferential tariff 'arrangements', namely:

• the 'General Arrangements';
• special incentive arrangements for the protection of labour rights;

---

[265] See Appellate Body Report, *EC – Tariff Preferences*, para. 111.
[266] *Ibid.*, para. 106.   [267] OJ 2001, L346, 1.

- special incentive arrangements for the protection of the environment;
- special arrangements for least-developed countries; and
- special arrangements to combat drug production and trafficking.

The General Arrangements, which provide for tariff preferences for all developing countries, and the special arrangements for least-developed countries, are not problematic. Both arrangements are justified under the Enabling Clause: the General Arrangements under paragraph 2(a), discussed above; and the special arrangements for least-developed countries under paragraph 2(d). The latter provision states that the Enabling Clause also covers:

> Special treatment of the least developed among the developing countries in the context of any general or specific measures in favour of developing countries.

However, questions as to GATT-consistency arise with regard to the other preferential arrangements, i.e. the special incentive arrangements for the protection of labour rights, the special incentive arrangements for the protection of the environment and the special arrangements to combat drug production and trafficking. Only some developing countries are beneficiaries of these special arrangements. For example, preferences under the special incentive arrangements for the protection of labour rights and the special incentive arrangements for the protection of the environment are restricted to those countries that 'are determined by the European Communities to comply with certain labour [or] environmental policy standards', respectively. Preferences under the special arrangements to combat drug production and trafficking (the 'Drugs Arrangements') are provided only to eleven Latin American countries and Pakistan.[268]

While India, the complainant in *EC – Tariff Preferences*, challenged, in its panel request, the WTO-consistency of the Drug Arrangements as well as the special incentive arrangements for the protection of labour rights and the environment, it later decided to limit its complaint to the Drug Arrangements. Accordingly, the *EC – Tariff Preferences* dispute, and the rulings in this case, only concerned the WTO-consistency of the Drug Arrangements. However, it is clear that the rulings in this case are also of relevance to other special arrangements.

The main substantive issue disputed between India and the European Communities in *EC – Tariff Preferences* was whether the Drug Arrangements are consistent with paragraph 2(a) of the Enabling Clause, and, in particular, the requirement of non-discrimination in footnote 3 thereto, quoted above.[269] On this issue, the Panel in *EC – Tariff Preferences* found that:

---

[268] See Appellate Body Report, *EC – Tariff Preferences*, para. 3. Preferences under the Drug Arrangements are provided to Bolivia, Colombia, Costa Rica, Ecuador, El Salvador, Guatemala, Honduras, Nicaragua, Pakistan, Panama, Peru and Venezuela.

[269] The requirement of non-discrimination is derived from the words 'non-discriminatory preferences' in footnote 3. See above, footnote 261, p. 679.

> the clear intention of the negotiators was to provide GSP equally to all developing countries and to eliminate all differentiation in preferential treatment to developing countries . . .[270]

As the Drugs Arrangements do not provide identical tariff preferences to *all* developing countries, the Panel concluded that the Drugs Arrangements are inconsistent with paragraph 2(a) of the Enabling Clause and, in particular, the requirement of non-discrimination in footnote 3 thereto.[271] According to the Panel, the term 'non-discriminatory' in footnote 3 requires that identical tariff preferences under GSP schemes be provided to all developing countries without differentiation.[272]

On appeal, the Appellate Body reversed this finding.[273] After a careful examination of the text and context of footnote 3 to paragraph 2(a) of the Enabling Clause, and the object and purpose of the *WTO Agreement* and the Enabling Clause, the Appellate Body came to the conclusion that:

> the term 'non-discriminatory' in footnote 3 does not prohibit developed-country Members from granting different tariffs to products originating in different GSP beneficiaries, provided that such differential tariff treatment meets the remaining conditions in the Enabling Clause. In granting such differential tariff treatment, however, preference-granting countries are required, by virtue of the term 'nondiscriminatory', to ensure that identical treatment is available to all similarly-situated GSP beneficiaries, that is, to all GSP beneficiaries that have the 'development, financial and trade needs' to which the treatment in question is intended to respond.[274]

In other words, a developed-country Member may grant additional preferential tariff treatment to some, and not to other, developing-country Members, as long as additional preferential tariff treatment is available to all *similarly situated* developing-country Members. *Similarly situated* developing-country Members are all those that have the development, financial and trade needs to which additional preferential tariff treatment is intended to respond.

The determination of whether developing-country Members are similarly situated must be based on objective criteria. With respect to the Drug Arrangements of the European Communities, however, the Appellate Body found in *EC – Tariff Preferences* that these arrangements provided for a *closed* list of twelve identified beneficiaries and contained no criteria or standards to provide a basis for distinguishing developing-country Members which are beneficiaries under the Drugs Arrangements from other developing-country Members.[275] The Appellate Body therefore upheld – albeit for different reasons – the Panel's conclusion that the European Communities 'failed to demonstrate that the Drug Arrangements are justified under paragraph 2(a) of the Enabling Clause'.[276]

---

[270] Panel Report, *EC – Tariff Preferences*, para. 7.144.   [271] *Ibid.*, para. 7.177.
[272] *Ibid.*, paras. 7.161 and 7.176.
[273] Appellate Body Report, *EC – Tariff Preferences*, para. 174.
[274] *Ibid.*, para. 173.   [275] *Ibid.*, paras. 187 and 188.   [276] *Ibid.*, para. 189.

Questions and Assignments 7.34

Give a brief overview of the different categories of S&D treatment provisions set out in the WTO agreements. Discuss the infant-industry-protection exception under Article XVIII:7 of the GATT 1994. What does the Generalised System of Preferences exception under the Enabling Clause allow Members to do that they would otherwise not be allowed to do? Where in the GATT 1994 can the Enabling Clause be found? Is it appropriate and correct to identify the Enabling Clause as an 'exception' to the basic MFN treatment obligation of the GATT 1994? Does the Enabling Clause allow developed-country Members to treat certain developing-country Members more favourably than others?

7.9. SUMMARY

Trade liberalisation and its principles of non-discrimination and rules on market access often conflict with other important societal values and interests, such as the promotion and protection of public health, consumer safety, the environment, employment, economic development and national security.

WTO law provides for rules to reconcile trade liberalisation with these other important societal values and interests. These rules take the form of wide-ranging *exceptions* to the basic WTO disciplines. There are six main categories of these exceptions:

- the 'general exceptions' of Article XX of the GATT 1994 and Article XIV of the GATS;
- the 'security exceptions' of Article XXI of the GATT 1994 and Article XIV *bis* of the GATS;
- the 'economic emergency exceptions' of Article XIX of the GATT 1994 and the *Agreement on Safeguards*;
- the 'regional integration exceptions' of Article XXIV of the GATT 1994 and Article V of the GATS;
- the 'balance of payments exceptions' of Articles XII and XVIII:B of the GATT 1994 and Article XII of the GATS; and
- the 'economic development exceptions'.

These exceptions allow Members, under specific conditions, to adopt and maintain legislation and measures that protect other important societal values and interests, even though this legislation or these measures are in conflict with substantive disciplines imposed by the GATT 1994 or the GATS. These exceptions clearly allow Members, under specific conditions, to give *priority* to certain societal values and interests *over* trade liberalisation.

The most important of these exceptions 'reconciling' trade liberalisation with other societal values and interests are the 'general exceptions' of Article XX of the GATT 1994 and Article XIV of the GATS.

In determining whether a measure otherwise GATT-inconsistent can be justified under Article XX of the GATT 1994, one must always examine:

- first, whether this measure can *provisionally* be justified under one of the specific exceptions under paragraphs (a) to (j) of Article XX; and, if so,
- secondly, whether the application of this measure meets the requirements of the chapeau of Article XX.

Article XX(b) concerns otherwise GATT-inconsistent measures allegedly adopted or maintained for the protection of public health or the environment. For such a measure to be provisionally justified under Article XX(b):

- the *policy objective* pursued by the measure must be the protection of the life or health of humans, animals or plants; and
- the measure must be *necessary* to fulfil that policy objective.

A measure is considered 'necessary' if no alternative measure exists that would achieve the same end and is less restrictive to trade than the measure at issue. In deciding whether a measure is necessary:

- the *importance* of the societal value pursued by the measure at issue,
- the *impact* of the measure at issue on trade, and
- the *extent* to which the alternative measure will contribute to the protection or promotion of that value, will be considered.

Article XX(d) concerns otherwise GATT-inconsistent measures allegedly adopted or maintained to secure compliance with national legislation. For such a measure to be provisionally justified under Article XX(d):

- the measure must be designed to *secure compliance* with national law, such as customs law or intellectual property law, which is in itself not GATT-inconsistent; and
- the measure must be *necessary* to ensure compliance.

The term 'necessary' in Article XX(d) is interpreted in the same way as is the term 'necessary' in Article XX(b).

Article XX(g) concerns otherwise GATT-inconsistent measures allegedly adopted or maintained for the conservation of exhaustible natural resources. For such a measure to be provisionally justified under Article XX(g):

- the measure must relate to the '*conservation of exhaustible natural resources*';
- the measure must '*relate to*' the conservation of exhaustible natural resources; and
- the measure must be made effective '*in conjunction with*' restrictions on domestic production or consumption.

The terms 'exhaustible natural resources' have been interpreted in a broad, evolutionary manner to include not only minerals and other non-living resources, but also living resources and, in particular, endangered species. A measure 'relates to' the conservation of exhaustible natural resources if the measure is 'primarily aimed' at the conservation of these resources. The relationship between the means, i.e. the measure, and the end, i.e. the conservation of exhaustible resources, must be a real and close relationship. Finally, the requirement that the measure must be 'made effective in conjunction with restrictions on domestic production or consumption' is, in essence, a requirement of 'even-handedness' in the imposition of restrictions on imported and domestic products.

Measures provisionally justified under one of the exceptions of Article XX(a) to (j) must subsequently meet the requirements of the chapeau of Article XX. The object and purpose of the chapeau is to avoid the possibility that the *application* of the measures provisionally justified could constitute a misuse or abuse of the exceptions of Article XX. The interpretation and application of the chapeau in a particular case is a search for the appropriate *line of equilibrium* between the right of Members to adopt and maintain trade-restrictive legislation and measures that pursue certain legitimate societal values *and* the right of other Members to trade. The search for this line of equilibrium is guided by the requirements set out in the chapeau that the *application* of the trade-restrictive measure may not constitute:

- an *arbitrary* or *unjustifiable discrimination* between countries where the same conditions prevail; or
- a *disguised restriction* on international trade.

Discrimination has been found to be 'unjustifiable discrimination' when the discrimination 'was not merely inadvertent or unavoidable'. Unjustifiable discrimination also exists when a Member fails to make serious, good faith efforts to negotiate a multilateral solution before resorting to the unilateral, discriminatory measure for which justification is sought. Discrimination has been found to be 'arbitrary' when a measure is applied without any regard for the difference in conditions between countries and this measure is applied in a rigid and inflexible manner. A measure which is provisionally justified under Article XX will be considered to constitute a 'disguised restriction on international trade' if the design, architecture or the structure of the measure at issue reveals that this measure does not in fact pursue the legitimate policy objectives on which the provisional justification was based but, in fact, pursues trade-restrictive, i.e. protectionist, objectives.

Although Article XX provides for exceptions to basic GATT rules and disciplines, the Appellate Body has not given a narrow interpretation to Article XX. Instead, it has insisted that a balance must be struck between trade liberalisation and the other societal values referred to in Article XX. The Appellate Body has repeatedly emphasised that WTO Members are free to adopt their own policies and measures aimed at protecting or promoting other societal values, such as public health or the environment, as long as, in so doing, they fulfil their obligations, and respect the rights of other Members, under the *WTO Agreement*. Note that, if the conditions discussed above are fulfilled, Article XX can justify inconsistencies with *any* of the GATT provisions.

As is the case for Article XX of the GATT 1994, Article XIV of the GATS sets out a *two-tier test* for determining whether a measure affecting trade in services, otherwise inconsistent with GATS obligations and commitments, can be justified under that provision. To determine whether a measure can be justified under Article XIV of the GATS, one must always examine:

- first, whether this measure can be provisionally justified under one of the specific exceptions under paragraphs (a) to (e) of Article XIV; and, if so,
- secondly, whether the application of this measure meets the requirements of the chapeau of Article XIV.

The similarities between Article XX of the GATT 1994 and Article XIV of the GATS are striking. However, there are also differences. The specific grounds of justification for measures which are otherwise inconsistent with provisions of the GATS set out in Article XIV(a) to (e) of the GATS include:

- the protection of public morals;
- the protection of public order;
- the protection of human, animal or plant life or health;
- the prevention of deceptive and fraudulent practices;
- the protection of the privacy of individuals; and
- the equitable or effective imposition or collection of direct taxes.

To be provisionally justified under the exceptions listed in paragraphs (a), (b) and (c) of Article XIV, a measure must be *necessary* to achieve the policy objective pursued. No such requirement of necessity exists under paragraphs (d) and (e). Just as with the chapeau of Article XX of the GATT 1994, the chapeau of Article XIV of the GATS requires that the *application* of the measure at issue does not constitute:

- *arbitrary or unjustifiable discrimination* between countries where the same conditions prevail; or
- a *disguised restriction* on trade in services.

In addition to the 'general exceptions' contained in Article XX of the GATT 1994 and Article XIV of the GATS, the GATT 1994 in Article XXI and the GATS in Article XIV *bis* also provide for exceptions relating to national and international security. WTO Members take, on occasion, either unilaterally or multilaterally, trade-restrictive measures against other Members as a means to achieve national or international security. Members taking such measures seek justification for these measures under Article XXI of the GATT 1994 or Article XIV *bis* of the GATS. Article XXI(b) allows a Member to adopt or maintain:

- measures relating to fissionable materials;
- measures relating to trade in arms or in other materials, directly or indirectly, for military use; and
- measures taken in time of war or other emergency in international relations,

if and when that Member considers such measures to be *necessary* for the protection of its essential security interests. Article XIV *bis*(b) of the GATS is virtually identical to Article XXI(b) of the GATT 1994. The justiciability of these exceptions is problematic. At a minimum, however, panels should have the authority to conduct an examination as to whether the explanation provided by the Member concerned is reasonable or whether the measure qualifies as apparent abuse. Article XXI(c) of the GATT 1994 and Article XIV *bis*(c) of the GATS are much less problematic in this respect as they allow WTO Members to take trade and economic sanctions imposed by the UN Security Council in the interest of international peace and security.

WTO law also provides for 'economic emergency exceptions'. These exceptions, set out primarily in Article XIX of the GATT 1994 and the *Agreement on Safeguards*, allow Members to adopt measures otherwise WTO-inconsistent in situations where a surge in imports causes, or threatens to cause, serious injury to the domestic industry. The otherwise WTO-inconsistent measures taken in economic emergency situations are referred to as *safeguard measures*. Safeguard measures temporarily restrict imports to allow the domestic industry concerned time for structural adjustment to new econonomic realities. Safeguard measures typically take the form of customs duties above the binding or quantitative restrictions. Safeguard measures must be limited in time and applied in a non-discriminatory manner. Moreover, a Member applying a safeguard measure must seek to compensate other Members affected by the measure. Safeguard measures may only be applied when three requirements are met:

- the 'increased imports' requirement;
- the 'serious injury or threat thereof' requirement; and
- the causation requirement.

The required 'increase in imports' must be recent, sudden, sharp and significant. The required 'serious injury' exists when there a significant overall impairment in the position of a domestic industry. A 'threat of serious injury' exists when serious injury is clearly imminent. The relevant domestic industry is the industry (i.e. all or most domestic companies) producing like or directly competitive products. To determine whether there is, in fact, serious injury or a threat thereof to a domestic industry, all relevant factors of an objective and quantifiable nature having a bearing on the situation of that industry must be considered. The test for establishing 'causation' is twofold:

- a demonstration of the causal link between the 'increased imports' and the 'serious injury or threat thereof' (the 'causal link' sub-requirement); and

- an identification of any injury caused by factors other than the increased imports and the non-attribution of this injury to these imports (the 'non-attribution' sub-requirement).

Besides the 'general exceptions', the 'security exceptions' and the 'economic emergency exceptions', WTO law also provides for 'regional integration exceptions'. These exceptions allow Members to adopt measures otherwise WTO-inconsistent taken in the context of the pursuit of regional economic integration. The regional integration exceptions are set out in Article XXIV of the GATT 1994 (elaborated in the *Understanding on Article XXIV*) and Article V of the GATS. WTO law recognises the advantages of economic integration and trade liberalisation even when these efforts involve only some of its Members. A measure otherwise inconsistent with the GATT 1994 is justified under Article XXIV of the GATT 1994:

- if the measure is introduced upon the formation of a customs union, a free trade area or an interim agreement that meets all the requirements set out in WTO law; and
- if the formation of the customs union or free trade area would be prevented, i.e. made impossible, if the introduction of the measure concerned were not allowed.

A measure otherwise GATS-inconsistent is justified under Article V of the GATS:

- if the measure is introduced as part of an agreement liberalising trade in services, that meets all the requirements set out Article V:1(a) (the 'substantial sectoral coverage' requirement), Article V:1(b) (the 'substantially all discrimination' requirement) and Article V:4 (the 'barriers to trade' requirement); and
- if WTO Members would be prevented from entering into such an agreement liberalising trade in services, if the measure concerned were not allowed.

WTO law also provides for 'balance-of-payments exceptions', set out in Articles XII and XVIII:B of the GATT 1994 (elaborated in the *Understanding on BoP Provisions*) and Article XII of the GATS. These exceptions allow Members to adopt measures, otherwise inconsistent with Article II and XI of the GATT, to safeguard their external financial position and to protect their balance of payments. BoP measures restricting trade in goods can take the form of quantitative restrictions *or* tariff-like, i.e. price-based, measures (such as import surcharges). The latter type of BoP measure is preferred. Generally speaking, BoP measures adopted by a Member must not exceed those necessary in view of the external financial situation of that Member (in terms of decline of its monetary reserves or the level of its monetary reserves). The requirements for BoP measures restricting trade in goods taken by developing-country Members (see Article XVIII:B) are less stringent than those for BoP measures taken by other Members (see Article XII).

Finally, WTO law provides for 'economic development exceptions' in favour of developing countries. Almost all WTO agreements provide for special and differential treatment provisions for developing-country Members to facilitate their integration in the world trading system and to promote their economic development. These provisions, also referred to as 'S&D treatment' provisions, can be subdivided into six categories:

- provisions aimed at increasing the trade opportunities of developing-country Members;
- provisions under which WTO Members should safeguard the interests of developing-country Members;
- flexibility of commitments, of action, and use of policy instruments;
- transitional time periods;
- technical assistance; and
- provisions relating to least-developed-country Members.

Of these S&D treatment provisions, the Generalised System of Preferences (GSP) exception under the Enabling Clause is of particular importance for developing-country Members. The Enabling Clause allows, under certain conditions, developed-country Members to grant preferential tariff treatment to imports from developing countries. This exception therefore allows Members to deviate from the basic MFN treatment obligation of Article I:1 of the GATT 1994 to promote the economic development of developing-country Members. Under specific conditions, the Enabling Clause also allows developing-country Members to grant preferential tariff treatment to some developing countries to the exclusion of others.

The 'general exceptions', 'security exceptions', 'economic emergency exceptions', 'regional integration exceptions', 'balance-of-payments exceptions' and the 'economic development exceptions' in the GATT 1994 and/or the GATS reconcile trade liberalisation with other important societal values and interests. These wide-ranging exceptions will often allow Members, promoting or protecting these other societal values or interests, to adopt otherwise GATT- or GATS-inconsistent measures. These exceptions demonstrate that WTO Members can, when necessary and under certain other conditions, give priority to societal values and interests other than trade liberalisation.

7.10. EXERCISE: GLASS BOTTLES AND TETRA-PACK CONTAINERS

Since 1997, Newland has prohibited the sale and importation of non-alcoholic beverages (such as milk and fruit juice) in tetra-pack containers. It only allows the sale and importation of non-alcoholic beverages in glass bottles. According to Newland, glass bottles can be recycled more easily and more efficiently than tetra-pack containers. Newland claims that glass bottles are almost 100 per cent recyclable while tetra-pack containers are only 70 per cent recyclable. Newland also claims that tetra-pack containers degrade with time and then contaminate any liquid they hold. Newland has some scientific studies in support of these contentions on the recyclabiltiy and the danger of contamination. Most scientific studies on the 'recyclability' of glass bottles and tetrapack containers conclude, however, that there is, in practice, little difference between the two types of container. Most scientific studies on the danger of contamination conclude that, if such danger exists, it arises only long after the due date of beverage held by tetra-pack containers.

Before 1997, Richland was the main exporter of non-alcoholic beverages in tetra-pack containers to Newland. It was, therefore, much affected by Newland's prohibition on the sale and importation of non-alcoholic beverages in tetra-pack containers. Ever since Newland became a WTO Member, Richland has been considering whether to challenge the import ban as inconsistent with WTO law. According to Richland, Newland sets an exaggeratedly high level of environmental and public health protection. Richland argues that there is no scientific basis for the import ban. In the alternative, Richland argues that Newland, rather than prohibiting the sale and importation of tetra-pack containers, could pursue its environmental policy objectives by discouraging the use of tetra-pack containers through the imposition of an environmental tax on tetra-pack containers. It should be noted that Newland does not prohibit the use of tetra-pack containers for alcoholic beverages such as wine. Moreover, Richland argues that Newland did not take into consideration that Richland, unlike Newland, has a long tradition of using tetra-pack containers for non-alcoholic beverages. Richland also notes that Newland rejected Richland's invitation to start multilateral negotiations on a gradual reduction of the use of tetra-pack containers for non-alcoholic beverages without much ado.

The prohibition of the sale and importation of non-alcoholic beverages in tetra-pack containers was adopted in 1997 under pressure from Newland's environmental NGOs and consumer organisations. However, behind the scenes, *TrueBleu* and *Verras*, Newland's manufacturers of glass bottles, had also lobbied hard for the prohibition on the sale and importation of non-alcoholic beverages in tetra-pack contrainers. While the prohibition initially benefited *TrueBleu* and *Verras*, both companies are now in dire straits. Over the last two years, they saw their combined share of the market in Newland for glass bottles drop from 60 per cent to 30 per cent and they had to lay off almost half of their workforce. Since 2001, the import of glass bottles into Newland has doubled every year. Most of these imports come from Richland, the home of the world's most efficient manufacturers of glass bottles. To prevent further job losses at *TrueBleu* and *Verras* and to give both companies some 'breathing space' to allow them to modernise their production, the Government of Newland decided last month to limit the import of glass bottles from Richland to 1999 levels. It should be noted that the problems of Newland's manufacturers of glass bottles are due not only to import competition but also to the fact that in recent times beer drinkers in Newland seem to prefer their beer in aluminium cans rather than glass bottles.

Richland has requested consultations with Newland on the import ban on non-alcoholic beverages in tetra-pack containers as well as on the import restriction of glass bottles.

Group A: You are the Legal Advisor to the Permanent Representative of Richland to the WTO. You have been instructed to prepare a legal brief in support of the position of Richland.

Group B: You are a lawyer with the Geneva-based Advisory Centre on WTO Law (ACWL). Newland, a member of the ACWL, has requested the ACWL to advise and assist the Ambassador of Newland to the WTO in the upcoming informal discussions. You have to write a legal brief in support of the position of Newland.

Please also note that the provisions of the *SPS Agreement* and the *TBT Agreement*, discussed in Chapter 5, may be of relevance.

8 Challenges for the future

8.1. INTRODUCTION

The challenges for the WTO in the years to come are multiple and daunting. First, there are the many challenges of further liberalisation of international trade. Most of these challenges are addressed in the ongoing Doha Development Round negotiations and have been discussed in this book. They include:

- the liberalisation of trade in agricultural products, in the form of increased market access for agricultural products and the reduction or elimination of agricultural export subsidies and domestic support measures;[1]

---

[1] Ministerial Conference, Doha Ministerial Declaration, WT/MIN(01)/DEC/1, dated 20 November 2001, paras. 13 and 14. See also above, pp. 447–8, 583–6.

- market access for non-agricultural products, including the further reduction or, where appropriate and possible, the elimination of customs duties as well as non-tariff barriers to trade;[2]
- the further liberalisation of trade in services, including mode 4 supply of services, which entails the free movement of natural persons;[3]
- the clarification and improvement of the WTO rules on dumping and sub-sidised trade;[4]
- the clarification and improvement of the WTO rules and procedures apply-ing to regional trade agreements;[5]
- the relationship between trade and the protection of the environment, and in particular the relationship between existing WTO rules and specific trade obligations set out in multilateral environmental agreements;[6] and
- the protection of intellectual property rights, and in particular the protec-tion of geographical indications.[7]

Negotiations on all these issues are currently ongoing.

Secondly, the challenges facing the WTO in the years to come include the institutional and procedural problems the WTO currently struggles with. To many, the WTO's negotiation and decision-making processes lack efficiency, legitimacy and transparency. As discussed in Chapter 2, since the Seattle Session of the Ministerial Conference in 1999, some improvements have been made.[8] However, as is apparent from the failure of the Cancún Session of the Ministerial Conference in 2003 and the slow progress made in the Doha Development Round negotiations, much more needs to be done to transform the WTO into an effective instrument of global economic governance. While not explicitly on the agenda of the Doha Development Round, significant institutional and pro-cedural reforms regarding, *inter alia*, internal as well as external transparency are necessary if the WTO is to remain the principal international body for negotiating rules on international trade. Furthermore, the WTO's dispute set-tlement system can and should be further improved. As discussed in Chapter 3, negotiations on the reform of the dispute settlement system are currently being conducted in the context of the Doha Development Round.[9]

The importance of these challenges for the future of the WTO and the multilateral trading system cannot be overstated. However, in addition to the further liberalisation of international trade and institutional and proce-dural problems of the WTO, other issues are also to be addressed. The most difficult or controversial among them are:

- the futher integration of developing countries into the WTO system; and
- the extension of the scope of WTO law in the fields of investment, competi-tion policy, government procurement and trade facilitation.

---

[2] *Ibid.*, para. 16. See also above, pp. 397–8.
[3] *Ibid.*, para. 15. See also above, pp. 486–7.   [4] *Ibid.*, para. 28. See also above, p. 515.
[5] *Ibid.*, para. 29. See also above, p. 651.   [6] *Ibid.*, paras. 31–3.
[7] *Ibid.*, paras. 17–19.   [8] See above, pp. 152–4, 159–62.   [9] See above, pp. 289–97.

This concluding chapter will focus on these two challenges for the future. Rather than giving an in-depth analysis, this chapter will refer to some recent developments which illustrate their importance, complexity and controversial nature.

Questions and Assignments 8.1

Briefly discuss the main challenges facing the WTO in the years to come.

8.2. INTEGRATION OF DEVELOPING COUNTRIES INTO THE WTO SYSTEM

Developing countries now participate in the WTO system much more than they did before 1995 in the multilateral trading system of the GATT 1947. Under the *WTO Agreement*, developing-country Members have undertaken far-reaching obligations regarding trade liberalisation. However, to many, the WTO has failed to deliver a fair share of the benefits of increased international trade to developing countries.[10] For the future of the WTO as well as for the economic development of developing countries, it is of the utmost importance that action be taken to 'rebalance' WTO rules in favour of developing-country Members and to ensure that developing-country Members do indeed benefit from the multi-lateral trading system. The WTO must respond fully to the needs and interests of all its Members, developed and developing-country Members alike. Therefore, in negotiating further trade liberalisation, as discussed above, Members have agreed in the Doha Development Declaration to take fully into account the special needs and interests of developing and least-developed countries.[11] Recall in this respect, for example, that Members promised at the Doha Session of the Ministerial Conference in November 2001, duty-free and quota-free market access for products from least-developed-country Members.[12]

Most importantly, in the effort to promote the integration of developing countries into the WTO system, Members agreed in Doha in November 2001:

- to address the specific problems that developing countries have in implementing the current WTO agreements;
- to strengthen the special and differential treatment provisions in the WTO agreements; and
- to increase, and better coordinate, trade-related technical assistance and capacity-building activities.

---

[10] See e.g. Action Aid International, *Beyond Cancún: Key Issues Facing the Multilateral Trading System*, December 2003, 8.

[11] See e.g. Ministerial Conference, Doha Ministerial Declaration, WT/MIN(01)/DEC/1, dated 20 November 2001, para. 16. See also above, p. 91.

[12] Several Members, including Canada, the European Communities, New Zealand, Norway and Switzerland, have given duty-free and quota-free market access for all or almost all exports from least-developed countries. See also above, p. 681.

As discussed below, the Doha Development Round negotiations have, to date, been unsuccessful in addressing these issues. However, in its Decision of 1 August 2004, the General Council:

> rededicates and recommits Members to fulfilling the development dimension of the Doha Development Agenda, which places the needs and interests of developing and least-developed countries at the heart of the Doha Work Programme.

The General Council stressed in its Decision of 1 August 2004 the important role that enhanced market access, balanced rules, and well-targeted financial and technical assistance and capacity-building can play in the economic development of developing countries.

This section looks at each of the three main efforts to promote the integration of developing and least-developed countries in the multilateral trading system.

Questions and Assignments 8.2

What action is currently being undertaken within the WTO to 'rebalance' WTO law in favour of developing-country Members and to promote their full integration in the multilateral trading system?

8.2.1. Problems in implementing current WTO agreements

Developing-country Members have considerable problems in implementing the current WTO agreements. These problems are commonly referred to as the 'implementation issues'. Implementation issues have been prominent on the agenda of the WTO since the failure of the Seattle Session of the Ministerial Conference in 1999.

Addressing these issues was an important element of the efforts to rebuild confidence in the WTO after the debacle in Seattle. As a result of these efforts, Members were able to adopt around fifty decisions, at the Doha Session of the Ministerial Conference in 2001, clarifying the obligations of developing-country Members under the WTO agreements. In the *Decision of the Ministerial Conference of 14 November 2001 on Implementation-Related Issues and Concerns* (the '*Doha Decision on Implementation Issues*'), the Members took concrete action to address the implementation issues raised by many developing-country Members with regard to:

- the GATT 1994;
- the *Agreement on Agriculture*;
- the *SPS Agreement*;
- the *Agreement on Textiles and Clothing*;
- the *TBT Agreement*;
- the *TRIMS Agreement*;
- the *Anti-Dumping Agreement*;
- the *Customs Valuation Agreement*;

- the *Agreement on Rules of Origin*;
- the *SCM Agreement*; and
- the *TRIPS Agreement*.[13]

The actions undertaken with regard to these implementation issues are now part of WTO law and have been sufficiently discussed in the previous chapters. While formally not adopted as authoritative interpretations within the meaning of Article IX:2 of the *WTO Agreement*, many of the decisions on implementation issues are, in fact, interpretations by the Ministerial Conference of existing provisions. In paragraph 1.1 of the *Doha Decision on Implementation Issues*, for example, the Ministerial Conference reaffirms that Article XVIII of the GATT 1994 is a special and differential treatment provision for developing countries and that recourse to it should be less onerous than recourse to Article XII of the GATT 1994.[14] Other decisions on implementation issues add to the rights, or diminish the obligations, of developing-country Members. For example, in paragraph 3.1 of the *Doha Decision on Implementation Issues*, the Ministerial Conference 'added' to Article 10.2 of the *SPS Agreement*, the Agreement's provision on S&D treatment, the following:

> Where the appropriate level of sanitary and phytosanitary protection allows scope for the phased introduction of new sanitary and phytosanitary measures, the phrase "longer time-frame for compliance" referred to in Article 10.2 of the Agreement on the Application of Sanitary and Phytosanitary Measures, shall be understood to mean normally a period of not less than 6 months.

While a significant number of implementation issues have been successfully addressed, many other implementation issues raised by developing-country Members have not yet been satisfactorily settled. With respect to these issues, Members agreed in Doha to a work programme.[15] For some of these unsettled issues, the Doha Ministerial Declaration provides for an explicit mandate for negotiations. These issues are therefore included in the agenda of the Doha Development Round negotiations.[16]

For other unresolved implementation issues, there is no mandate to negotiate, but Members agreed that these issues would be taken up as 'a matter of priority' by the relevant WTO bodies. Paragraph 1.2 of the *Doha Decision on Implementation Issues*, for example, states:

> Noting the issues raised in the report of the Chairperson of the Committee on Market Access (WT/GC/50) concerning the meaning to be given to the phrase "substantial interest" in paragraph 2(d) of Article XIII of the GATT 1994, the Market Access Committee is directed to give further consideration to the issue and make recommendations to the General Council as expeditiously as possible but in any event not later than the end of 2002.

---

[13] See Ministerial Conference, *Decision of 14 November 2001 on Implementation-Related Issues and Concerns*, WT/MIN(01)/17, dated 20 November 2001. See also Ministerial Conference, Doha Ministerial Declaration, WT/MIN(01)/DEC/1, dated 20 November 2001, para. 12.

[14] See above, p. 670.

[15] See also Ministerial Conference, Doha Ministerial Declaration, WT/MIN(01)/DEC/1, dated 20 November 2001, para. 12.

[16] See above, pp. 90–3.

As with most other deadlines in the *Doha Decision on Implementation Issues*, the deadline set out in paragraph 1.2, regarding recommendations on the interpretation of the concept of 'substantial interest' in Article XIII:2(d) of the GATT 1994, was not met.

In its Decision of 1 August 2004, the General Council reaffirmed the mandates the Ministerial Conference gave in the Doha Ministerial Declaration and in the Doha *Decision on Implementation Issues*, and renewed the Members' determination to find solutions to outstanding issues. The General Council instructed all competent WTO bodies to 'redouble their efforts to find appropriate solutions as a priority'. It required the WTO Director-General to continue with his consultations, and instructed him to report to the Trade Negotiations Committee and the General Council no later than May 2005, to allow the General Council to take appropriate action no later than July 2005.

Questions and Assignments 8.3

What has been done, and is being done, with respect to the problems encountered by developing-country Members with respect to the implementation of the WTO agreements? Give an example, other than those mentioned above. Search for the latest official report on the progress of the discussions and negotiations on the implementation issues.

8.2.2. Special and differential treatment

As discussed throughout this book, and in particular in Chapters 2 and 7, almost all WTO agreements include special and differential treatment provisions for developing-country Members to facilitate their integration into the world trading system and to promote their economic development.[17] As discussed in Chapter 7, these S&D treatment provisions can be divided into six categories:

- provisions aimed at increasing the trade opportunities of developing-country Members;
- provisions under which WTO Members should safeguard the interests of developing-country Members;
- provisions allowing for flexibility of commitments, of action, and use of policy instruments;
- transitional time periods;
- technical assistance; and
- provisions relating to least-developed-country Members.[18]

---

[17] See above, pp. 676–7.
[18] See Committee on Trade and Development, *Implementation of Special and Differential Treatment Provisions in WTO Agreements and Decisions*, Note by the WTO Secretariat, WT/COMTD/W/77/Rev.1, dated 21 September 2001, para. 3. See also the addenda to this Note and, in particular, Addendum 4, WT/COMTD/W/77/Rev.1/Add.4, dated 7 February 2002.

While significant in number, the effectiveness of many of the S&D treatment provisions is open to question. Therefore, the Ministerial Conference decided at its Doha Session in 2001 that:

> all special and differential treatment provisions shall be reviewed with a view to strengthening them and making them more precise, effective and operational.[19]

The Doha Ministerial Declaration, as well as the *Doha Decision on Implementation Issues*, mandate the WTO Committee on Trade and Development to identify which special and differential treatment provisions are mandatory, and to consider the legal and practical implications of turning those that are currently non-binding into mandatory obligations.[20] Furthermore, the Committee on Trade and Development is to examine additional ways in which S&D treatment provisions can be made more effective and to consider how developing-country Members, and, in particular, least-developed-country Members, may be helped to make the best use of S&D treatment.[21] The Committee must also examine, generally, how S&D treatment may be better incorporated into the architecture of WTO rules.[22]

The discussions in the Special Session of the Committee on Trade and Development on the strengthening of S&D treatment have been difficult and largely fruitless to date. Developing-country Members made a total of eighty-eight proposals for strengthening the S&D treatment provisions. Most of these proposals came from the African Group and the Group of Least-Developed Countries. Typically, the proposals suggest the introduction of new S&D treatment provisions or to strengthen existing ones. The *Doha Decision on Implementation Issues* originally foresaw that the Committee on Trade and Development would make its recommendations to the General Council by July 2002. At the request of the Committee, the General Council extended the deadline to 31 December 2002. By the end of 2002, however, Members could only agree on twelve of the eighty-eight proposals on the table. In early 2003, the Chairman of the Special Session of the Committee on Trade and Development reported to the General Council as follows:

> An important area of difference has been the interpretation of some aspects of the Doha mandate. While Members recognized the importance that Ministers attached to the S&D work programme, and accepted the need to review all S&D provisions "with a view to strengthening them and making them more precise, effective and operational", there were significant differences on how this could be achieved. Some Members considered that one way to make S&D provisions more precise, effective and operational, was to make them mandatory by changing the existing language of some of the 'best endeavour' provisions. Others did not wish to consider amending the text of the Agreements or otherwise altering what they considered to be the existing balance of rights and obligations.[23]

The Special Session of the Committee on Trade and Development could only recommend to the General Council:

---

[19] Ministerial Conference, Doha Ministerial Declaration, para. 44.
[20] See Ministerial Conference, *Doha Decision on Implementation Issues*, para. 21.1(i).
[21] See *ibid.*, para. 21.1(ii).   [22] See *ibid.*, para. 21.1(iii).
[23] See Committee on Trade and Development, *Report by the Chairman, Ambassador Ransford Smith (Jamaica), to the Trade Negotiations Committee*, TN/CTD/8, dated 4 March 2003, para. 3.

- to take note of the twelve proposals on which Members could agree in principle; and
- to provide clarification on the Doha mandate.

In April 2003, the Chair of the General Council subdivided the eighty-eight proposals for strengthening S&D treatment provisions into three distinct categories:

- the first category, with thirty-eight proposals, contains those proposals likely to be accepted with minor changes; this includes the twelve proposals on which Members agreed in February 2003;
- the second category contains thirty-eight proposals which, according to the Chair, would be discussed more effectively in the relevant WTO bodies; accordingly, he forwarded them to the relevant bodies; and
- the third category contains twelve proposals which would require major drafting in order to be agreed upon.[24]

Proposals in the first and third categories remain on the General Council's agenda. Over the past year, the Chairperson of the General Council has held several informal meetings with Members on these proposals.

In the run-up to the Cancún Session of the Ministerial Conference in September 2003, Members agreed to make recommendations for the possible adoption by Ministers of twenty-five proposals. These recommendations for adoption were contained in Annex C to the draft Cancún Ministerial Declaration.[25] At Cancún, agreement was reached on another three proposals. However, as the Cancún Session failed and the Cancún Ministerial Declaration was not adopted, Annex C was also not adopted. As a result, the package of twenty-eight proposals on which there is an in-principle agreement, are yet to be adopted.[26]

In its Decision of 1 August 2004, the General Council instructed the Special Session of the Committee on Trade and Development to complete expeditiously the review of all the outstanding 'Agreement-specific proposals'. The Special Session must report to the General Council, with clear recommendations for a decision, by July 2005.

Questions and Assignments 8.4

What has been done, and is being done, with respect to the mandate of the Doha Ministerial Declaration to review all S&D treatment provisions 'with a view to strengthening them and making them more precise, effective and operational'? Search for the latest official report on the progress of the discussions and negotiations on the review of the S&D treatment provisions.

---

[24] See *Special and Differential Treatment*, Cancún WTO Ministerial 2003 Briefing Notes, http://www.wto.org/english/thewto_e/minist_e/min03_e/brief_e/brief21_e.htm, visited on 12 February 2004.

[25] See Job(03)150/RW.1.

[26] Committee on Trade and Development Special Session, *Report by the Chairman, Mr Faizel Ismail (South Africa), to the Trade Negotiations Committee*, TN/CTD/9, dated 19 April 2004, para. 2.

8.2.3. Trade-related technical assistance and capacity-building

As WTO Members confirmed in the Doha Ministerial Declaration, technical assistance and capacity-building are core elements of the development dimension of the multilateral trading system.[27] The Members welcomed and endorsed the 'New Strategy for WTO Technical Cooperation for Capacity-building, Growth and Integration'.[28] If developing-country Members, and, in particular, least-developed-country Members, are to benefit from the rules of the WTO system, there is a considerable need for training and technical assistance. Throughout the Doha Ministerial Declaration, there are references to this need and specific commitments are included.[29] For example, paragraph 16 of the Doha Ministerial Declaration on market access for non-agricultural products states, in relevant part:

> The negotiations shall take fully into account the special needs and interests of developing and least-developed-country participants, including through less than full reciprocity in reduction commitments .... To this end, the modalities to be agreed will include appropriate studies and capacity-building measures to assist least-developed countries to participate effectively in the negotiations.

In paragraphs 38 to 40, the Doha Ministerial Declaration provided for a number of general commitments and directions regarding technical assistance and capacity-building.

First, the WTO Secretariat is instructed to support, in coordination and cooperation with other relevant agencies such as the IMF, the World Bank and UNCTAD, the domestic efforts of developing-country Members to mainstream trade into their national plans for economic development and strategies for poverty reduction.[30] The delivery of WTO technical assistance must be designed to assist developing-country Members to adjust to WTO rules and disciplines, to implement obligations and to exercise the rights of membership.[31]

Secondly, the Doha Ministerial Declaration underscored the urgent necessity for the effective coordinated delivery of technical assistance with bilateral donors, in the OECD Development Assistance Committee and relevant international and regional intergovernmental institutions.[32] Note, in this respect, the Doha Development Agenda Trade Capacity-building Database, established by the WTO and the OECD to provide information on, and allow for the better coordinaton of, trade-related technical assistance and capacity-building projects.[33] Members called for enhancing and rationalising the Integrated Framework for Trade-Related Technical Assistance to Least-Developed Countries (IF) and the Joint Integrated Technical Assistance Programme

---

[27] Ministerial Conference, Doha Ministerial Declaration, para. 38.
[28] *Ibid.* See also WT/COMTD/W/90, dated 21 September 2001.
[29] Para. 41 of the Doha Ministerial Declaration lists these commitments.
[30] Doha Ministerial Declaration, para. 38.   [31] *Ibid.*   [32] *Ibid.*, para. 39.
[33] See http://tcbdb.wto.org/index.asp?lang=ENG, visited on 1 May 2004.

(JITAP).[34] In technical assistance and capacity-building efforts, the WTO Secretariat and Members must give priority to least-developed-country Members.[35]

Thirdly, Members agreed that there is a need for technical assistance to benefit from secure and predictable funding.[36] As discussed above, the 2002 WTO budget provided for a very significant increase in technical assistance funding.[37] Moreover, in December 2001, the General Council established the Doha Development Agenda Global Trust Fund.[38] In response to the Doha Ministerial Declaration, most donors increased both the quantity and the value of their bilateral trade-related technical assistance and capacity-building activities, as well as their participation in multilateral trust funds and programmes such as the Global Trust Fund, the Integrated Framework and the JITAP.[39] In 2001 and 2002, there was an annual average of some 1,665 commitments, equivalent to US$719 million, to activities that cover all aspects of *trade policy and regulations* identified in the Doha Ministerial Declaration, and an average of a further 1,860 commitments, or US$1,408 million, to activities in *trade development*.[40] Commitments to trade-related technical assistance and capacity-building amounted to some 4.8 per cent of total aid commitments in 2001 and 2002. Over the past few years, donors have become much more active in trade-related technical assistance and capacity-building.

The Doha Ministerial Declaration instructed the WTO Director-General to report to the next session of the Ministerial Conference on the implementation and adequacy of the commitments with respect to trade-related technical assistance and capacity-building undertaken in Doha.[41] At the Cancún Session of the Ministerial Conference in September 2003, Dr Supachai Panitchpakdi presented a detailed report on the implementation and adequacy of the commitments undertaken.[42] In this report, the Director-General focused on the collective efforts of the WTO Secretariat in the delivery of training, technical cooperation and capacity-building. The Director-General mentioned, in particular, the strategic partnerships that have been built with other international organisations, as well as with regional development banks. These strategic partnerships have proven to be very beneficial in planning and executing technical assistance and training

---

[34] *Ibid.*, para. 39.   [35] *Ibid.*, para. 42.   [36] *Ibid.*, para. 40.

[37] See above, pp. 100–3.   [38] See above, p. 166.

[39] See Second Joint WTO/OECD Report on Trade-Related Technical Assistance and Capacity-Building (TRTA/CB), dated July 2003, 1, http://www.wto.org/english/tratop_e/devel_e/teccop_e/wto_oecd_report03_e.doc, visited on 1 May 2004.

[40] See *ibid.* Note that, in addition to these TRTA/CB activities, the average of US$8.1 billion committed to economic infrastructure in 2000 and 2001 (some 20 per cent of all aid) helps to build the transport, energy and communications networks essential for international trade. See also *ibid.*

[41] Ministerial Conference, Doha Ministerial Declaration, para. 41.

[42] *Report by the Director-General: Paragraph 41 of the Doha Ministerial Declaration*, WT/MIN(03)/3, dated 14 August 2003. An interim report was submitted to the General Council in December 2002, WT/GC/W/484, dated 2 December 2002. Note also that the WTO Secretariat provides quarterly status reports on the implementation of the Technical Assistance Plan. The first report, covering the first quarter of 2003, was presented to Members in Spring 2003 (WT/COMTD/W/112).

activities.[43] The Director-General also stressed the special efforts that have been made to assist least-developed countries in integrating into the multilateral trading system. In 2003, the number of technical assistance and training activities for least-developed countries had increased by almost 50 per cent over 2002.[44] Furthermore, the Director-General noted the establishment, within the WTO Secretariat, of the Institute for Training and Technical Cooperation (ITTC). As discussed above, the main purpose of the ITTC is to maximise synergies between training and technical cooperation, which essentially are 'two sides of the same coin and are geared towards enhancing institutional and human capacity in beneficiary countries to address trade policy issues'.[45] With regard to the funding for WTO technical assistance and training programmes, the Director-General stated:

> I am counting on Members' continuing support for the Global Trust Fund, which has significantly complemented the regular budget, to provide a stable and predictable source of funding for the Secretariat's training and technical assistance activities.[46]

Questions and Assignments 8.5

Discuss the WTO's current efforts to give trade-related technical assistance and capacity-building to developing-country Members and, in particular, to least-developed-country Members. Search for the most recent status report of the WTO Secretariat on the implementation of the current WTO Technical Assistance Plan.

8.3. EXTENDING THE SCOPE OF WTO LAW

The second challenge for the future of the WTO, discussed in this chapter, is the extension of the scope of WTO law. Important issues concerning the world economy, such as investment and competition policy, remain largely outside the scope of WTO law.[47] However, it is clear that there is a close relationship between trade and investment as well as between trade and competition policy. With respect to trade and investment, note that about one-third of

---

[43] Minsterial Conference, *Report by the Director-General: Paragraph 41 of the Doha Ministerial Declaration*, para. 1. To establish these strategic partnerships, the WTO signed memoranda of understanding with a number of international organisations and partners, including, most recently, UNCTAD. See also above, pp. 97–8.
[44] *Ibid.*, para. 2.   [45] *Ibid.*, para. 4. See also above, p. 139.   [46] *Ibid.*, para. 4.
[47] While investment and competition policy issues remain largely outside the scope of WTO law, it should be noted that WTO law already deals with specific aspects of these issues. As discussed in Chapters 4 and 5, the GATS provides for rules regarding the supply of services through commercial presence abroad, i.e. through foreign investment in the country where the services are supplied. Moreover, as mentioned in Chapter 1, the *Agreement on Trade-Related Investment Measures* (the '*TRIMS Agreement*') provides that Members' regulations dealing with foreign investments must respect the obligations in Article III (national treatment obligation) and Article XI (prohibition on quantitative restrictions) of the GATT 1994. Finally, both the GATT 1994 and the GATS provide for rules on monopolies and exclusive service suppliers, and both the GATS and the *TRIPS Agreement* allow governments to act against anti-competitive practices and recognise their rights to work together to limit these practices.

world trade in goods and services is trade within companies, i.e. trade between subsidiaries in different countries or between a subsidiary and its head parent.[48] With respect to trade and competition policy, note the rising concern that the gains from the reduction of the barriers to trade and foreign investment may be thwarted by private companies through anti-competitive practices such as price fixing or abuse of a dominant position.[49] Price fixing across borders by private companies is estimated to raise costs to consumers (including businesses) in the affected industries by 20 to 40 per cent.[50] The European Communities and some other developed-country Members have argued for years for WTO rules on investment and competition policy.

8.3.1. The 'Singapore issues' and the Doha Ministerial Declaration

At the Singapore Session of the Ministerial Conference in December 1996, the Members decided:

- to establish a working group to examine the relationship between trade and investment; and
- to establish a working group to study the interaction between trade and competition policy.[51]

However, as most developing-country Members strongly objected to negotiations on new WTO rules on trade and investment and competition policy, it was explictly agreed that the work of the newly established working groups would not prejudge whether negotiations would be initiated in the future.[52] The purpose of the working groups was to identify any areas that *may* merit further consideration in the WTO framework.

The WTO Members also decided in Singapore to set up a working group on transparency in government procurement and instructed the Council for Trade in Goods to examine possible ways of 'simplifying' customs procedures, an issue commonly referred to as 'trade facilitation'.[53] It is obvious that there is a close relationship between trade and these other two 'Singapore issues'. They are discussed in Chapter 5.[54] Most developing-country Members, however, also objected, albeit perhaps less strongly, to negotiations on new WTO rules on both transparency in government procurement and trade facilitation.

---

[48] See further WTO Secretariat, *Understanding the WTO: Cross-Cutting and New Issues*, http://www.wto.org/english/thewto_e/whatis_e/tif_e/bey3_e.htm, visited on 1 May 2004.
[49] See further WTO Secretariat, *Trade and Competition Policy: Dealing with Cartels and Other Anti-Competitive Practices*, Cancún WTO Ministerial 2003 Briefing Notes, http://www.wto.org/english/thewto_e/minist_e/min03_e/brief_e/brief08_e.htm, visited on 1 May 2004.
[50] See http://www.wto.org/english/thewto_e/minist_e/min03_e/brief_e/brief08_e.htm, visited on 1 May 2004. In the 1990s, international cartels were found to be operating in a large number of industries, including graphite electrodes, vitamins, citric acid, seamless steel tubes, lysine and bromine. See *ibid.*
[51] Ministerial Conference, Singapore Ministerial Declaration, adopted on 13 December 1996, WT/MIN(96)/DEC, dated 18 December 1996, para. 20.
[52] *Ibid.*   [53] *Ibid.*, para. 21.   [54] See above, pp. 474–6, 477–9.

As discussed above, the disagreement on whether to start negotiations on the Singapore issues could not be overcome at the Doha Session of the Ministerial Conference in 2001. The Doha Ministerial Declaration, in which Members agreed on the initiation of the Doha Development Round, included the four Singapore issues in the Doha Development Agenda. However, the Doha Ministerial Declaration provided that negotiations on these issues would only start *after* the next session of the Ministerial Conference, i.e. the Cancún Session in 2003, 'on the basis of a decision taken, by explicit consensus, at that Session on modalities of negotiation'.[55] In the meantime, the exploratory work in the working groups and the Council for Trade in Goods was to continue.[56]

Questions and Assignments 8.6

What are the 'Singapore issues' and how did they get that name? What did Members agree with respect to the Singapore issues at the Doha Session of the Ministerial Conference in November 2001?

8.3.2. Future negotiations on the Singapore issues?

The draft of the Cancún Ministerial Declaration, submitted to Members in August 2003 by the Chairperson of the General Council and the WTO Director-General, reflected the continued disagreement on each of the Singapore issues by including, in brackets, the two options available. For 'investment', for example, the draft Declaration stated:

> 13. [Taking note of the work done by the Working Group on the Relationship between Trade and Investment under the mandate in paragraphs 20–22 of the Doha Ministerial Declaration, we decide to commence negotiations on the basis of the modalities set out in Annex D of this document.]
>
> [We take note of the discussions that have taken place in the Working Group on the Relationship between Trade and Investment since the Fourth Ministerial Conference. The situation does not provide a basis for the commencement of negotiations in this area. Accordingly, we decide that further clarification of the issues be undertaken in the Working Group.][57]

In the revised draft Cancún Ministerial Declaration, submitted on the penultimate day of the Cancún Session by Luis Ernesto Derbez, the Chairperson of the Ministerial Conference and the Mexican Trade Minister, it was provided that discussions in the working groups, on investment and competition policy, would continue, while, on government procurement and trade facilitation, negotiations on new WTO rules would start immediately.

However, the divide in Cancún between developing-country Members *and* the European Communities and other developed countries was too big to

---

[55] Ministerial Conference, Doha Ministerial Declaration, adopted on 14 November 2001, WT/MIN(01)/DEC/1, dated 20 November 2001, paras. 20, 23, 26 and 27.
[56] *Ibid.*, paras. 22, 25, 26 and 27.   [57] Job(03)150/Rev. 1.

bridge. Members were unable to reach agreement on what to do with respect to the Singapore issues and this disagreement among Members was, in fact, a key contributing factor to the failure of the Cancún Session.

Developing-country Members oppose negotiations on WTO rules on the Singapore issues because they fear:

- the institutional burdens and financial burdens that new rules on these issues would impose on them; and
- the constraints on domestic social and economic development policies that would result from the new rules.

It is clear, for example, that new WTO rules on trade facilitation would have significant implications for developing-country Members. The cost of the work necessary to facilitate the entry of foreign products (such as the upgrading of ports, roads, computer systems, adminstrations, etc.) would inevitably divert resources away from basic needs such as health care and education.

Moreover, developing countries are unwilling to engage in complex negotiations that would add to the already overloaded agenda of the Doha Development Round. In view of their limited negotiating capacity, many developing-country Members would not be able to participate, fully and effectively, in any additional negotiations on the Singapore issues.

In its Decision of 1 August 2004 on the *Doha Work Programme*, the General Council finally took a decision on whether to include any of the Singapore issues on the agenda of the Doha Development Round. With regard to trade facilitation, the Decision states:

> taking note of the work done on trade facilitation by the Council for Trade in Goods under the mandate in paragraph 27 of the Doha Ministerial Declaration and the work carried out under the auspices of the General Council both prior to the Fifth Ministerial Conference and after its conclusion, the General Council decides by explicit consensus to commence negotiations on the basis of the modalities set out in Annex D to this document.[58]

Annex D to the Decision of 1 August 2004 states:

> Negotiations shall aim to clarify and improve relevant aspects of Articles V, VIII and X of the GATT 1994 with a view to further expediting the movement, release and clearance of goods, including goods in transit.[59]

To meet the concerns of developing-country Members with regard to negotiations on trade facilitation, Annex D explicitly provides that these negotiations will also 'aim at enhancing technical assistance and support for capacity-building in this area'.[60] Annex D calls on developed-country Members to give

---

[58] General Council, *Doha Work Programme*, Decision adopted on 1 August 2004, WT/L/579, dated 2 August 2004, para. 1(g).
[59] *Ibid.*, Annex D, para. 1. Note that footnote 1 to this sentence reads: 'It is understood that this is without prejudice to the possible format of the final result of the negotiations and would allow consideration of various forms of outcomes.'
[60] *Ibid.*

technical assistance and support for capacity-building to enable developing-country Members to fully participate in the negotiations and to enable them to implement the commitments resulting from the negotiations.[61] Annex D also deals with the consequences which a lack of support and assistance from developed-country Members may have. Annex D states in relevant part:

> it is recognized that negotiations could lead to certain commitments whose implementation would require support for infrastructure development on the part of some Members. In these limited cases, developed-country Members will make every effort to ensure support and assistance directly related to the nature and scope of the commitments in order to allow implementation. It is understood, however, that, *in cases where required support and assistance for such infrastructure is not forthcoming*, and where a developing or least-developed Member continues to lack the necessary capacity, *implementation will not be required.*[62]

This is a remarkable provision, which may prove difficult to apply but definitely sends a clear political signal.

With respect to the other three Singapore issues, i.e. investment, competition policy and transparency in government procurement, the General Council decided on 1 August 2004:

> that these issues, mentioned in the Doha Ministerial Declaration in paragraphs 20–22, 23–25 and 26 respectively, will not form part of the Work Programme set out in that Declaration and therefore no work towards negotiations on any of these issues will take place within the WTO during the Doha Round.[63]

In the next few years, negotiations on these issues will therefore not take place in the multilateral context of the WTO. However, it is to be expected that negotiations on these issues will continue to take place in a bilateral or regional context. The results of these negotiations, and the experience acquired, may in time form a solid basis for a renewed effort to agree upon multilateral rules.

Questions and Assignments 8.7

Why are developing-country Members opposed to negotiations on new WTO rules on the Singapore issues? What are the latest developments regarding the Singapore issues?

8.4. CONCLUSION

In the introduction to Chapter 1, reference is made to the United Nations Millennium Declaration and the objective of the international community to

---

[61] *Ibid.*, paras. 5 and 6.
[62] *Ibid.*, para. 6. Note that Annex D further states that: 'While every effort will be made to ensure the necessary support and assistance, it is understood that the commitments by developed countries to provide such support are not open-ended.' *Ibid.*
[63] *Ibid.*, para. 1(g).

halve the number of people living in absolute poverty by 2015. There is a broad consensus in the international community that economic globalisation in general and international trade in particular offer an unprecedented *opportunity* to eradicate poverty and hunger worldwide. However, to ensure that this opportunity is realised, economic globalisation and international trade have to be *managed* and *regulated* at the international level. In its Millennium Declaration, the UN General Assembly therefore stressed

> We are committed to an open, equitable, rule-based, predictable and non-discriminatory multilateral trading ... system.[64]

In the absence of such a system, economic globalisation and international trade is likely to be a curse, rather than a blessing, to humankind, aggravating economic inequality, social injustice, environmental degradation and cultural dispossession. The law of the WTO, as discussed in Chapters 2 to 7, is currently the most ambitious effort to provide the international community with an open, equitable, rule-based, predictable and non-discriminatory trading system. The ongoing Doha Development Round offers hope for a further improvement of this system.

---

[64] United Nations General Assembly, *UN Millennium Declaration*, Resolution adopted on 8 September 2000, para. 13.

> b. provides for the absence or elimination of substantially all discrimination, in the sense of Article XVII, between or among the parties, in the sectors covered under subparagraph (a), through:
>   i. elimination of existing discriminatory measures, and/or
>   ii. prohibition of new or more discriminatory measures, either at the entry into force of that agreement or on the basis of a reasonable time-frame, except for measures permitted under Articles XI, XII, XIV and XIV *bis*.

The Panel in *Canada – Autos* noted that:

> Article V provides legal coverage for measures taken pursuant to economic integration agreements, which would otherwise be inconsistent with the MFN obligation in Article II.[199]

It follows from Article V:1 that a measure otherwise GATS-inconsistent is justified under Article V:

- if the measure is introduced as part of an agreement liberalising trade in services, that meets all the requirements set out in Article V:1(a) (the 'substantial sectoral coverage' requirement), Article V:1(b) (the 'substantially all discrimination' requirement) and Article V:4 (the 'barriers to trade' requirement); and
- if WTO Members would be prevented from entering into such an agreement liberalising trade in services, if the measure concerned were not allowed (see the chapeau of Article V:1).

This section will, further, discuss primarily the requirements that an economic integration agreement pursuant to Articles V:1(a), V:1(b) and V:4 of the GATS must meet.

7.6.2.1. *'Substantial sectoral coverage' requirement*

Pursuant to Article V:1(a) of the GATS, an economic integration agreement must have 'substantial sectoral coverage' of the trade in services among the parties to the agreement. The footnote to the provision states that 'substantial sectoral coverage' should be 'understood in terms of the number of sectors, volume of trade affected and modes of supply'.[200] The footnote also provides that an economic integration agreement may not *a priori* exclude any of the four modes of supply. In particular, no economic integration agreement should *a priori* exclude investment or labour mobility in the sense of modes 3 and 4. Members disagree on whether one or more service sectors can be excluded from an economic integration agreement but the use of the wording 'number of sectors' in the footnote to paragraph 1(a) seems to indicate that not all sectors must be covered under an economic integration agreement to meet

---

[199] Panel Report, *Canada – Autos*, para. 10.271.
[200] It is not clear whether the parameters to be examined in order to determine conformity between an economic integration agreement and Article V of the GATS are limited to the parameters listed in the footnote, or whether there are other considerations.